www.wileyplus.com

WileyPLUS is a research-based online environment for effective teaching and learning.

WileyPLUS builds students' confidence because it takes the guesswork out of studying by providing students with a clear roadmap:

- what to do
- how to do it
- if they did it right

It offers interactive resources along with a complete digital textbook that help students learn more. With *WileyPLUS*, students take more initiative so you'll have greater impact on their achievement in the classroom and beyond.

Psychology
inAction

TENTH EDITION

Karen Huffman
Palomar College

John Wiley & Sons, Inc.

VP & PUBLISHER	Jay O'Callaghan
ASSOCIATE PUBLISHER & EDITOR	Christopher Johnson
ASSOCIATE EDITOR	Eileen McKeever
SENIOR MARKETING MANAGER	Danielle Torio Hagey
PRODUCTION MANAGER	Dorothy Sinclair
PRODUCTION EDITOR	Sandra Dumas
SENIOR ILLUSTRATION EDITOR	Anna Melhorn
SENIOR DESIGNER	Maureen Eide
EXECUTIVE MEDIA EDITOR	Thomas Kulesa
MEDIA EDITOR	Lynn Pearlman
PHOTO DEPARTMENT MANAGER	Hilary Newman
SENIOR PHOTO EDITOR	Jennifer MacMillan
PRODUCTION MANAGEMENT SERVICES	Furino Production
PHOTO RESEARCHER	Sara Wright

This book was typeset in 10/13 Janson Text at MPS Limited, a MacMillan Company, Chennai, India and printed and bound by R. R. Donnelley/Jefferson City. The cover was printed by R. R. Donnelley/Jefferson City.

Founded in 1807, John Wiley & Sons, Inc. has been a valued source of knowledge and understanding for more than 200 years, helping people around the world meet their needs and fulfill their aspirations. Our company is built on a foundation of principles that include responsibility to the communities we serve and where we live and work. In 2008, we launched a Corporate Citizenship Initiative, a global effort to address the environmental, social, economic, and ethical challenges we face in our business. Among the issues we are addressing are carbon impact, paper specifications and procurement, ethical conduct within our business and among our vendors, and community and charitable support. For more information, please visit our website: www.wiley.com/go/citizenship.

The paper in this book was manufactured by a mill whose forest management programs include sustained yield harvesting of its timberlands. Sustained yield harvesting principles ensure that the number of trees cut each year does not exceed the amount of new growth.

This book is printed on acid-free paper. @

978-1-1118-01908-5 (Main Book)
978-1-1118-12913-5 (Binder Ready Version)

Printed in the United States of America.
10 9 8 7 6 5 4 3 2 1

BriefContents

Contents

ChapterFourteen
Psychological Disorders 491

ChapterFifteen
Therapy 531

ChapterSixteen
Social Psychology 567

Preface

Engaging and Inspiring Today's Students!

Did you notice the beautiful and inspiring art and photos on the cover of this book? Have you ever wondered why authors, editors, or publishers choose certain paintings or photos for their books? In our case, we wanted to capture the theme or essence of this text: *Engaging and Inspiring Today's Students*.

How can a textbook engage and inspire today's students? Most would agree that good teaching largely depends on the commitment and excitement of the teacher, and I believe the same can be said about a textbook and its author. As you'll see in the next section, we've done everything we can in this Tenth Edition to engage and inspire the reader, and psychology has always been a deep passion and love for me. I truly believe it can enrich and improve virtually every aspect of our lives—work, play, home, college, national and international affairs, as well as our everyday interactions with others. My non-psychologist friends and family often tease me about how often I bring the latest psychological research into our discussions, and I frequently tell anyone who will listen that teaching psychology and writing this text are the two best jobs in the world! I actually get paid to research and prepare lectures and chapters on extremely interesting and exciting topics. Then I get to present and discuss this material with the best and the brightest of people—my students and readers!

Unfortunately, studies find that this first class in introductory or general psychology is the only formal course in psychology that most students will ever encounter, and our field is so large and complex that it's a constant juggling act to try to cover all our major concepts and theories. How can one text and one course capture all the essential content, while still engaging and inspiring today's students who are truly different from those in the past? These so-called "Millenials" experience all the pressures and challenges of previous generations, yet they also face unique and enormous challenges from our fast-paced technology and economically and politically troubled world.

How can we engage and inspire today's students? For me this is an intimidating, but provocative challenge. To meet it, I try to be a "master choreographer." I must lead my readers and students step-by-step through the basic foundations of psychology. At the same time, I need to provide time and space for application and hands-on active learning to keep them engaged and inspired. How do I do this within the limited number of pages in this text? I begin with concise, straight-forward concepts, key terms, and theories, followed by quick activities (self-tests, Check & Reviews), examples (analogies, case studies/personal stories), and demonstrations (Try This Yourself, Psychology at Work). Beginning with the first edition in 1987, this text has always emphasized active learning—hence the title "Psychology in *Action*." Each edition has continued and improved upon this foundation, and this latest edition of *Psychology in Action* takes active learning to an even higher level—*engagement* and *inspiration*.

What's New in the Tenth Edition?

Focus on Student Engagement

Student engagement is much more than the latest educational buzz term. Like active learning, the underlying principle of student engagement is active involvement and connection with the material. When thinking of ways to engage my readers (and students), I find it helpful to identify all the generally agreed upon components of student engagement and organize them into an easily remembered ABC pattern (see Figure 1).

Figure 1 Students are engaged when they are *Affectively, Behaviorally,* and *Cognitively* invested in their own learning.

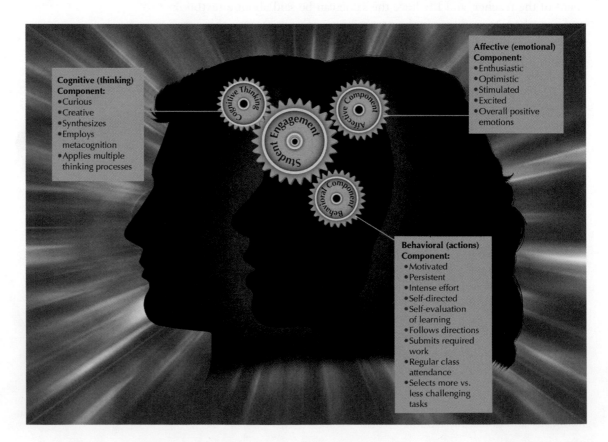

Cognitive (thinking) Component:
• Curious
• Creative
• Synthesizes
• Employs metacognition
• Applies multiple thinking processes

Affective (emotional) Component:
• Enthusiastic
• Optimistic
• Stimulated
• Excited
• Overall positive emotions

Behavioral (actions) Component:
• Motivated
• Persistent
• Intense effort
• Self-directed
• Self-evaluation of learning
• Follows directions
• Submits required work
• Regular class attendance
• Selects more vs. less challenging tasks

Here is a sample of the Tenth Edition's special features specifically designed to increase student engagement:

1. **NEW** Over 100 **Myth Busters**. Why focus on myths? No one wants to be embarrassed by misinformation, and this natural desire to avoid being wrong not only increases student engagement, but it also has a significant educational side benefit. While studying the myths of psychology, students automatically and easily learn some of the most important terms and concepts—along with improving their critical thinking skills!

PSYCHOLOGY ENGAGES

MYTH BUSTERS

SAMPLE

How Well Do You Know Psychology?

True or false?

___1. Your first hunch on a multiple-choice test is your best guess (Chapter 1).

___2. Most of us use only 10 percent of our brains (Chapter 2).

___3. Advertisers and politicians often use subliminal persuasion to influence our behavior (Chapter 4).

___4. Most brain activity stops during sleep (Chapter 5).

___5. The best way to learn and remember information is to "cram," or study it intensively during one concentrated period (Chapter 7).

___6. Most middle-aged people experience a midlife crisis (Chapter 10).

___7. Polygraph ("lie detector") tests can accurately and reliably reveal whether or not a person is lying (Chapter 12).

___8. People who threaten suicide seldom follow through with it (Chapter 14).

___9. People with schizophrenia have multiple personalities (Chapter 14).

___10. Modern electroconvulsive ("shock") therapy is a physically dangerous and ineffective therapy (Chapter 15).

___11. Similarity is one of the best predictors of long-term relationships (Chapter 16).

___12. In an emergency, as the number of bystanders increases, your chance of getting help decreases (Chapter 16).

Answers: 1–10 are false, 11 and 12 are true. (Details provided in designated chapters.)

---

2. **Increased Emphasis on Assessment.** Why focus on assessment? Higher education faces growing pressure to show "results," and today's students are more concerned than ever about their grades and getting their degrees ASAP. Recognizing this understandable desire as a key to student engagement, we've added several new features and upgraded others to provide students with a wide assortment of self-assessment tools.

   • **NEW** Interactive **Research Challenges** for each chapter. Given that the scientific method and its various components is one of the most common learning objectives in psychology, we decided students needed more practice and exposure than just the basic introduction traditionally provided in Chapter 1. For each chapter of the Tenth Edition, we've added an expanded discussion of the latest research on various "Hot Topics" (e.g., problems with multitasking, embodied cognition, sex addiction), followed by a special "Student Engagement Exercise," which asks students to identify the research method, IV, DV, etc. (See the sample on the next page.) These interactive, self-testing exercises help reinforce a core learning objective, while also building student appreciation and engagement with the latest research.

   • **NEW Test Yourself** exercises. People naturally habituate to unchanging stimuli. To offset this habituation and increase student engagement, we've included a

SAMPLE

Student Engagement Exercise

Given the admittedly limited information in the Stanford University study (Ophir, Nass, & Wagner, 2009) described above, what is the most likely:

1. *Research method* (experimental, descriptive, correlational, or biological)?

2. If you chose the:

   - *Experimental method*—label the IV, DV, experimental group, and control group.

   - *Descriptive method*—identify whether this is a naturalistic observation, survey, or case study.

   - *Correlational method*—label whether this is a positive, negative, or zero correlation.

   - *Biological method*—identify the specific research tool (e.g., brain dissection, CT scan, etc.).

wide variety of testing exercises that assess their understanding in unique ways. [This new "Test Yourself" feature focuses on self-assessment, and differs from our well-known "Try This Yourself" enrichment exercises that involve hands-on activities (see comparative samples below).]

- **UPGRADED Check & Reviews.** To increase student engagement, we've upgraded this self-assessment feature by:

  - Adding a **NEW** "Retrieval Practice" section that reflects the latest research on the most effective technique for learning and retention. (See the sample on the next page.)

  - Increasing the previous number of multiple-choice and fill-in questions.

  - Streamlining and moving the previous learning objectives and answers to the new narrative summary at the end of each chapter.

SAMPLE

TEST YOURSELF

Can you explain why the hands and the face on this drawing are so large? Or why these same proportions may be different in nonhuman animals?

Answer: The larger size of the hands and face reflects the larger cortical area necessary for the precise motor control and greater sensitivity humans need in our hands and faces (see also Concept Diagram 2.1). Other nonhuman animals have different needs, and the proportions are different. Spider monkeys, for example, have large areas of their motor and somatosensory cortices devoted to their tails, which they use like another arm and hand.

TRY THIS YOURSELF

Are You a Good Multitasker?

GREEN	RED	BROWN	RED
BROWN	GREEN	GREEN	BLUE
GREEN	BROWN	RED	BLUE

(a) Using a stopwatch, test to see how fast you can name the color of each rectangular box.

(b) Now, time yourself to see how fast you can state the color of ink used to print each word, ignoring what each word says.

Most people find it takes more time and that they make more errors on (b) than on (a). Your tendency to read the words in (b), instead of saying the color of ink as instructed, is known as the *Stroop effect*, after the psychologist who discovered it.

Versions of this test have been used to detect subtle problems in brain function due to lack of sleep, fatigue, brain injuries, brain disease, and even the effects of high altitudes on mountain climbers. We include it here to demonstrate how difficult it is to override highly practiced skills (reading words), in favor of new material or tasks (naming the color of ink in the word). Just as the distraction of a trying to ignore the words in (b) greatly increased your time and errors, trying to ignore or answer a cell-phone call, while listening to a lecture or driving a car can lead to increased errors on exams and increased odds of a serious traffic accident. In short, it's difficult and sometimes dangerous to do two things at once—especially when one task is more highly practiced.

SAMPLE

CHECK & REVIEW

STOP *Before going on, be sure to complete this Check & Review. It is an invaluable study tool!*

Neural Bases of Behavior

Part A: Retrieval Practice

1. Without looking at the book, spend 10 minutes writing a free-form essay recalling all you can remember from the previous section.

2. Now, reread the previous section, and once again spend 10 minutes writing a free-form essay on the SAME material.

   (Although time consuming, this exercise has been shown to be the single best way to improve your test scores! For more information, check out www.sciencemag .org/content/early/2011/01/19/science .1199327.abstract)

Part B: Practice Quiz

1. Identify the five key parts of a neuron.

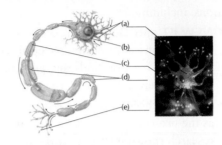

2. An impulse travels through the structures of the neuron in the following order: (a) cell body, axon, dendrites; (b) cell body, dendrites, axon; (c) dendrites, cell body, axon; (d) axon, cell body, dendrites

3. Chemical messengers that are released by axons and stimulate dendrites are called ___. (a) chemical messengers; (b) neurotransmitters; (c) synaptic transmitters; (d) neuromessengers

4. Briefly explain how neurotransmitters carry messages throughout the body.

Check your answers in Appendix B.

---

3. **New Topics and Significant Updates.** In addition to the normal revision practice of updating, streamlining, and refining what worked well in the previous edition, *Psychology in Action* (10e) includes numerous sections devoted to STUDENT ENGAGEMENT. Here's a small sample:

   - **NEW A crash course in multitasking (pp. 35–36)**
   - **NEW Nicotine addiction (pp. 198–199)**
   - **NEW Language, the brain, and bilingualism (pp. 295–297)**
   - **NEW IQ and genius (pp. 313–314)**
   - **NEW Overcoming egocentric thinking (p. 351)**
   - **NEW Embodied morality (pp. 378–379)**
   - **NEW The Scarlet Letter (pp. 413–414)**
   - **NEW Sex addiction and cybersex (pp. 414–415)**
   - **NEW The new psychology of success (p. 449)**
   - **NEW Self-esteem (pp. 483–484)**
   - **NEW Maslow revisited (p. 485)**
   - **NEW Black Swan on the couch (pp. 521–522)**
   - **NEW Pill-popping preschoolers (pp. 557–558)**
   - **NEW To Kill a Mockingbird (pp. 599–600)**
   - **NEW Empathy (pp. 600–601)**

Focus on Student Inspiration

If you look back at Figure 1 (p. xiv), you'll note that student engagement relies on qualities within the learner—the student must make a psychological investment in his or her own learning. So how can a textbook *inspire* students to be *persistent, enthusiastic, motivated*, and to *exert intense effort*? Here's a description of our strategy and a sample of our efforts:

1. **Inspiration** through **Psychological Science**. Today's students are justifiably worried about their futures. How are they going to succeed in our rapidly changing global economy? Psychological science has produced a wealth of research showing that the keys to success aren't necessarily high IQs and "who you know." Instead, the time tested and previously described student engagement qualities of *persistence*, *motivation*, and *intense effort* are all important. To clarify what science has to say on these topics (and hopefully inspire the reader), we've included several **NEW** sections, including:

   • **NEW IQ and Genius** (pp. 313–314). Modern observers suggest Mozart's early compositions were nothing special. So how do we explain his success? Research cited in this section finds that personal attributes, like self-discipline, motivation, and persistence, are far more important than S. A. T. or IQ scores.

   • **NEW Psychology of Success** (pp. 448–449). Students often cite Michael Jordan as the prototype of excellence in sports, and this section discusses Carol Dweck's research showing that success like his depends on a growth mindset founded on hard work and determination.

   • **NEW Self Esteem** (pp. 483–484). Many have blamed the so-called "self-esteem movement" for creating a generation of overly-entitled, unrealistic people who are ill-suited for today's economy. This section clarifies the difference between narcissistic, fragile self-esteem and healthy self-esteem, which is based on responsibility and the recognition that we must work hard to earn the high opinion of others.

2. **Inspiration** through **Set** and **Setting**. Henry David Thoreau was right when he said, "We must learn to awaken and keep ourselves awake, not by mechanical aid, but by an infinite expectation of the dawn." Nothing works quite as well as personal expectation to create true inspiration. How can a textbook inspire the reader? We believe the following features will increase student expectations (set) and provide an uplifting, inspiring backdrop (setting):

   • **NEW Design.** Beauty is a well-known source of inspiration, and we believe that an attractively designed text filled with carefully chosen photos and professional line art will similarly inspire the reader. Each page of each chapter in this Tenth Edition has been carefully designed to maximize its visual appeal and educational value.

   • **NEW Chapter Openers.** Each photo was painstakingly debated by a committee dedicated to finding only the most uplifting and beautiful shots that also captured the essence of each chapter (e.g., Ch. 1, p. 2; Ch. 2, p. 50).

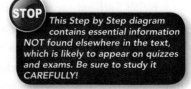

STOP *This Step by Step diagram contains essential information NOT found elsewhere in the text, which is likely to appear on quizzes and exams. Be sure to study it CAREFULLY!*

   • **NEW** and **Revised Step-by-Step Diagrams** and **Concept Organizers.** Known for their visual appeal and educational foundation, each of these diagrams and organizers has been significantly revised (e.g., Ch. 2, pp. 54–55, 57). Please Note: To increase student retention, we also included a **NEW** small, STOP sign icon with a reminder to readers to carefully study the material in these diagrams!

Participant	SAMPLE	Experimenter
	Single-blind procedure Only the experimenter knows who is in the experimental group versus the control groups.	
	Double-blind procedure Neither the experimenter nor the participants know who is in which group.	

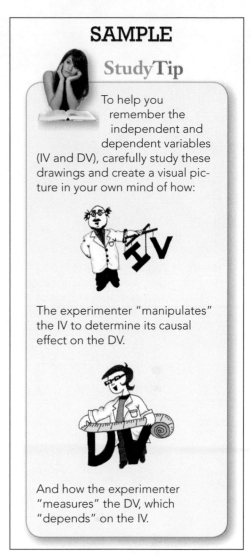

SAMPLE

StudyTip

To help you remember the independent and dependent variables (IV and DV), carefully study these drawings and create a visual picture in your own mind of how:

The experimenter "manipulates" the IV to determine its causal effect on the DV.

And how the experimenter "measures" the DV, which "depends" on the IV.

- **NEW line art.** All figures and tables have been professionally rendered and educationally designed to artfully depict complex topics. (See samples above and to the right.)
- **NEW Psychology Engages sections.** To streamline the design, all CORE material is presented first in each chapter, followed by a special "Psychology Engages" section that includes all enrichment material (e.g., Research Challenges, Critical Thinking exercises, Gender and Cultural Diversity sections, etc.). This "meat and potatoes followed by dessert" approach not only increases the flow of the most essential material, it also preserves the highly engaging, supplemental material that enriches and maximizes student learning.
- **NEW Narrative end-of-chapter summaries** followed by **UPGRADED Visual Summaries.** In response to reviewers who prefer a "cumulative, narrative summary" at the end of the chapter, we now gather the learning objectives distributed throughout the chapter, along with sample answers, into a two-page spread at the end of each chapter. The addition of this new narrative summary also allowed us to redesign the Visual Summary—to make it less textual and even more visually appealing!

Continuing Features

Focus on Application

In response to reviewers, teachers, and students, *Psychology in Action* (10e) continues its well-known focus on applications. Given the current problems with the national and world economy, today's students are concerned more than ever with how their college classes relate to the "real world" and how their college degrees might help them find employment. This edition includes a large number of new and upgraded applications to work, college, relationships, and virtually all other aspects of everyday life (see Table 1).

Table 1 SAMPLE APPLICATION HIGHLIGHTS FROM *PSYCHOLOGY IN ACTION* (10E)

(in addition to the shorter discussions and examples throughout the text)

- Careers in the Field (pp. 7–10)
- Becoming a Better Consumer of Scientific Research (p. 32)
- Tools for Student Success (pp. 39–45)
- How Neurotransmitters Affect Us (pp. 56–57)
- Overcoming Genetic Misconceptions (p. 82)
- Is My Job Too Stressful? (pp. 104–105)
- Would You Like to Be a Health Psychologist? (pp. 111–112)
- Why You Shouldn't Procrastinate (p. 118)
- Problems with Believing in Extrasensory Perception (pp. 158–159)
- Self-Help for Sleep Problems (p. 182)
- Club Drug Alert! (pp. 191–192)
- Classical Conditioning (pp. 233–236)
- Operant Conditioning (pp. 236–238)
- Cognitive-Social Learning (p. 238)
- Improving Long-Term Memory (pp. 256–259)
- Overcoming Problems with Forgetting (pp. 260–266)
- Recognizing Barriers to Problem Solving (pp. 288–290)
- Are Your Relationship Expectations Unrealistic? (pp. 367–368)
- Dealing with Your Own Death Anxiety (pp. 377–378)
- Overcoming Test Anxiety (pp. 404–405)
- Protection Against STIs (p. 409)
- Self-actualization (p. 485)
- Careers in Mental Health (pp. 553–554)
- What's Wrong with Movie Portrayals of Therapy? (p. 560)
- The Art and Science of Flirting (pp. 575–576)
- *Optional Chapter 17 Job Satisfaction and Psychotherapy (pp. 629–630).*
- *Optional Chapter 18 Improving Communication (pp. 638–650), Improving Powers of Persuasion (pp. 650–658), Conflict Resolution (pp. 659–671).*

Focus on the Latest in Psychological Science

To keep pace with the rapid progress in our field, I've added over 1000 new references from 2010 to 2012, and Table 2 presents a brief overview of the current topics most directly related to psychological science.

Table 2 SAMPLES OF PSYCHOLOGICAL SCIENCE

(in addition to the shorter discussions and examples throughout the text)

Research Challenges

- **NEW** A crash course in multitasking (pp. 35–36)
- Video games and spatial skills (p. 84)
- Does stress cause gastric ulcers? (pp. 110–111)
- Is there scientific evidence for ESP (pp. 157–158)
- **NEW** Nicotine addiction (pp. 198–199)
- Mirror neurons (p. 231)
- How quickly we forget (p. 260)
- **NEW** IQ and Genius (pp. 313–314)
- Scientific research with infants (pp. 350–351)
- **NEW** Embodied morality (pp. 378–379)
- **NEW** Sex addiction and cybersex (pp. 414–415)
- Love at first fright (p. 449)
- **NEW** Self-esteem (pp. 483–484)
- **NEW** Black Swan on the couch (pp. 521–522)
- **NEW** Pill-popping preschoolers (pp. 557–558)
- Implicit bias (p. 596)

Research Methods

- Basic versus applied research (p. 17)
- The scientific method (pp. 17–19)
- Ethical guidelines for research with human and nonhuman animals (pp. 19–20)
- Experimental, descriptive, correlational, and biological research (pp. 21–35)
- Split-brain research (pp. 79–82)
- Methods for studying behavioral genetics (pp. 80–81)
- Is there scientific evidence for subliminal perception and ESP? (pp. 157–158)
- How scientists study sleep (pp. 173–177)
- Discovering classical conditioning (pp. 206–209)
- Studying language development in human and nonhuman animals (pp. 295–296)
- Language and the brain (pp. 295–297)
- Scientific measures of intelligence (pp. 302–307)
- Research methods for life span development (pp. 326–327)
- Scientific research with infants (pp. 350–351)
- Studying human sexuality (pp. 388–389)
- Scientific measures of personality (pp. 478–481)

Neuroscience

- Biological methods of research (pp. 33–34)
- How neurons communicate (pp. 53–55)
- How neurotransmitters affect us (pp. 56–57)
- Neuroplasticity, neurogenesis, and stem cell research (pp. 59–60)
- SAM system and HPA axis (pp. 100–103)
- Psychoneuroimmunology (p. 103)
- Biology of sleep and dreams (pp. 178–179)
- Biology and psychoactive drugs (pp. 186–192)
- Neuroscience and learning (pp. 230–233)
- Neuronal and synaptic changes in memory (pp. 267–268)
- Hormonal changes and memory (p. 268)
- Where are memories stored? (pp. 268–269)
- Biology and memory loss (pp. 269–271)
- **NEW** Language, brain, and bilingualism (pp. 295–297)
- Biological influences on intelligence, including brain size, speed, and efficiency (pp. 307–309)
- Brain changes during development (pp. 331–337)
- Brain's role in gender differences and sexual behavior (pp. 396–398, 401–402)
- Biological processes and motivation (pp. 423–426)
- Brain and emotion (pp. 435–437)
- Biological aspects of personality (pp. 475–476)
- Biological contributors to mental disorders (pp. 503, 508, 513–514)
- Biomedical psychotherapy (pp. 548–552)
- Biology of aggression (p. 590)

Behavioral Genetics

- Basic principles and recent research (pp. 78–84)
- Methods for studying (pp. 80–81)

- Genetic influences on intelligence and the Bell Curve debate (pp. 306–311)
- Nature versus nurture controversy (p. 325)
- Genetics and aging (p. 334–337)
- Attachment and imprinting (pp. 346–347)
- Genetics and sexual orientation (p. 401)
- Genetic influences on eating disorders (p. 431)
- Genetic contributions to personality (pp. 476)
- The role of genetics in mental disorders (pp. 503, 508, 514)
- Genetic contributors to aggression (p. 590)

Cognitive Psychology

- Cognitive appraisal and coping (pp. 112–113)
- Bottom-up and top-down processing (pp. 126–127)
- Controlled versus automatic processing (pp. 168–169)
- Cognitive view of dreams (pp. 179–180)
- Cognitive-social learning (pp. 228–230)
- Memory processes and problems (pp. 247–276)
- Thinking, creativity, language, and intelligence (pp. 283–316)
- Cognitive development over the life span (pp. 338–345)
- Cognitive theories of motivation and emotion (pp. 426, 430, 436–437, 440–441)
- Social-cognitive approaches to personality (pp. 473–474)
- Cognitive processes in mental disorders (pp. 502–503, 508–509, 515)
- Cognitive therapy (pp. 536–539)
- Cognitive processes in attitudes and prejudice (pp. 568–575)

Cultural Psychology

- Psychology from a global perspective (pp. 38–39)
- Evolution of sexual selection and gender differences (pp. 85–86)
- "Karoshi"—Can job stress be fatal? (pp. 118–119)
- Are the Gestalt laws universally true? (pp. 159–160)
- How do gender and culture affect dreams? (pp. 196–197)
- **NEW** Avatar—a modern fable (pp. 239–240)
- Cultural differences in memory and forgetting (pp. 275–276)
- Unspoken accents (p. 315)
- Cultural psychology's research guidelines (pp. 352–353)
- Cultural influences on development (pp. 380–382)
- Sexuality across cultures (pp. 410–411)
- Culture, evolution, and emotion (pp. 450–451)
- How gender and culture affect abnormal behavior (pp. 523–525)
- Cultural similarities and differences in therapy (pp. 557–560)
- Is beauty in the eye of the beholder? (p. 599)

Evolutionary Psychology

- Genetics and evolution (pp. 78–84)
- Basic principles such as natural selection (p. 83)
- Evolution of sex differences (pp. 85–86)
- Evolutionary/circadian theory of sleep (p. 171)
- Evolution and learning (pp. 233)
- Classical conditioning, taste aversions, and biological preparedness (pp. 232–233)
- Operant conditioning and instinctive drift (pp. 232–233)
- Evolution and language development (pp. 295–298)

Table 2 SAMPLES OF PSYCHOLOGICAL SCIENCE (CONT.)

Evolutionary Psychology (Cont.)

- Genetic effects on intelligence (pp. 306–311)
- Instincts and motivation (pp. 423–424)
- Evolution and emotions (pp. 450–452)
- Evolution and personality (pp. 476)
- Evolution and aggression (pp. 590)
- Evolution and altruism (pp. 591–593)

Positive Psychology

- Dealing with pseudopsychology (pp. 5–6)
- Ethical research (pp. 19–20)
- **NEW** A crash course in multitasking (pp. 35–36)
- Better living through neuroscience (pp. 59–60)
- Overcoming genetic misconceptions (pp. 82–83)
- Wellness (pp. 93–120)
- Job satisfaction (pp. 104–105)
- Hardiness and positive psychology (pp. 108–109)
- Coping with crisis (p. 110)
- Health and stress management (pp. 111–116)
- Resources for healthy living (pp. 113–115)
- Coping with techno stress (pp. 116–117)
- Perils of procrastination (p. 118)
- Preventing hearing loss (pp. 140–141)
- Understanding and overcoming sleep disorders (pp. 185–188)
- Attaining the benefits of meditation (pp. 193–194)
- Healthier routes to alternate states (pp. 193–195)

- Therapeutic uses of hypnosis (p. 195)
- Successful use of reinforcement and punishment (pp. 223–224)
- Overcoming prejudice and discrimination (pp. 234)
- Understanding and overcoming superstition (pp. 236–237)
- Improving and understanding memory (pp. 247–276)
- Improved problem-solving (pp. 286–290)
- Creativity and multiple intelligences (pp. 297–299, 300–302)
- **NEW** IQ and genius (pp. 313–314)
- Promoting secure attachment and positive parenting (pp. 346–350)
- Romantic love and attachment (p. 348)
- Marriage and family health and improvement (pp. 366–371)
- Positive careers and retirement (pp. 371–374)
- Positive aspects of aging and dying (pp. 374–378)
- Benefits of androgyny (pp. 392–393)
- Overcoming test anxiety (pp. 424–425)
- High achievers (pp. 432–434)
- Emotional intelligence (pp. 443–447)
- Increasing motivation (p. 446)
- Psychology of success (pp. 448–449)
- **NEW** Self-esteem (pp. 483–484)
- Suicide and its prevention (pp. 506–507)
- How your thoughts can make you depressed (p. 522–523)
- Love and interpersonal attraction (pp. 575–581)
- Aggression understanding and reducing (pp. 590–591)
- Altruism and helping behaviors (pp. 591–593)
- Reducing prejudice and discrimination (pp. 594–596)
- Reducing destructive obedience (pp. 596–597)

Focus on Visual Learning

As most instructors and students know, well-designed visuals greatly improve the efficiency with which information in processed. *Psychology in Action* (10e) incorporates the best of visual learning with ongoing Try This Yourself exercises, the latest line art (figures, tables) and end-of–chapter Visual Summaries. This edition also includes a special focus on Step-by-Step Diagrams and Concept Organizers that have earned rave reviews from students and teachers alike (Table 3).

Table 3 VISUAL LEARNING

Chapters	Step-by-Step Diagrams	Concept Organizers
Chapter 1	**1.1** Scientific Method (p. 18) **1.2** Key Features of an Experiment (pp. 23–24) **1.3** Using the SQ4R Method (p. 42)	**1.1** Understanding Correlations (p. 30)
Chapter 2	**2.1** How Neurons Communicate (pp. 54–55) **NEW 2.2** How the Spinal Reflex Operates (p. 61)	**NEW 2.1** How Poisons and Drugs Affect Our Brain (p. 57) **2.2** Visualizing Your Motor Cortex and Somatosensory Cortex (p. 74) **2.3** Explaining Split-Brain Research (p. 76) **2.4** Four Methods of Behavioral Genetics (p. 81)

Chapters	Step-by-Step Diagrams	Concept Organizers
Chapter 3	**3.1** The General Adaptation Syndrome (GAS) (p. 101) **3.2** The Biology of Stress (p. 102) **3.3** Cognitive Appraisal and Coping (p. 113)	**NEW 3.1** Three Types of Conflict (p. 98) **NEW 3.2** Resources for Healthy Living (pp. 114–115)
Chapter 4	**4.1** How the Eye Sees (p. 135) **4.2** How the Ear Hears (p. 139) **4.3** How the Nose Smells (p. 142)	**4.1** Measuring the Senses (p. 129) **NEW 4.2** Optical Illusions (p. 147) **4.3** Four Perceptual Constancies (p. 152) **4.4** Binocular Cues (p. 154) **4.5** Monocular Cues (p. 155)
Chapter 5	**5.1** Understanding Consciousness (p. 169) **5.2** How Drugs Work (p. 184)	**5.1** Scientific Study of Sleep and Dreaming (p. 175) **5.2** Meditation and the Brain (p. 194)
Chapter 6	**6.1** Pavlov's Classical Conditioning (p. 207) **6.2** Prejudice and Classical Conditioning (p. 235)	**NEW 6.1** Six Principles of Classical Conditioning (p. 210) **6.2** Higher-Order Conditioning (p. 214) **6.3** Four Key Factors in Observational Learning (p. 229)
Chapter 7	**7.1** Why We forget (p. 261)	**NEW 7.1** Improving Long-Term Memory (LTM) (p. 257) **7.2** The Brain and Memory (p. 269) **7.3** Mnemonic Devices (p. 274)
Chapter 8	**8.1** Building Blocks of Language (p. 294) **8.2** Language Acquisition (p. 296)	**NEW 8.1** Three Steps to the Goal (p. 287) **NEW 8.2** Language and the Brain (p. 297) **8.3** Stereotype Threat (p. 312)
Chapter 9	**9.1** Prenatal Development (p. 329) **NEW 9.2** Changes in Brain Development (p. 332) **NEW 9.3** Motor Development (p. 333) **9.4** Piaget's Four Stages of Cognitive Development (p. 340)	**9.1** Attachment (p. 347)
Chapter 10	**10.1** Kohlberg's Moral Development (p. 362) **10.2** Erikson's Eight Stages of Psychosocial Development (p. 365)	
Chapter 11	**11.1** Masters and Johnson's Sexual Response Cycle (p. 400)	**NEW 11.1** Major Male and Female Sexual Dysfunctions (p. 403)
Chapter 12	**12.1** Four Theories of Emotion (p. 439) **NEW 12.2** Two-Factor Theory (p. 441)	**NEW 12.1** Key Mechanisms in Hunger Regulation (p. 431) **12.2** Extrinsic vs. Intrinsic Motivation (p. 444) **12.3** Polygraph Testing (p. 445)
Chapter 13	**13.1** Freud's Five Psychosexual Stages of Development (p. 467)	**13.1** Projective Tests (p. 481)
Chapter 14	**14.1** Four Criteria and a Continuum of Abnormal Behavior (p. 493) **14.2** Biopsychosocial Model and Schizophrenia (p. 516)	**14.1** Seven Psychological Perspectives on Abnormal Behavior (p. 495)
Chapter 15	**15.1** Ellis's A-B-C-D Approach (p. 538) **15.2** Overcoming Maladaptive Behaviors (p. 546)	**15.1** Drug Treatments for Psychological Disorders (p. 550) **15.2** Five Most Common Goals of Therapy (p. 553)
Chapter 16	**NEW 16.1** Cognitive Dissonance (p. 572) **16.2** Groupthink (p. 589)	**16.1** What Influences Obedience? (p. 584) **16.2** Helping (p. 592)

Table 4 APA UNDERGRADUATE LEARNING GOALS AND OUTCOMES

Goal 1: Knowledge Base of Psychology

Demonstrate familiarity with the major concepts, theoretical perspectives, empirical findings, and historical trends in psychology.

1.1 Characterize the nature of psychology as a discipline.

1.2 Demonstrate knowledge and understanding representing appropriate breadth and depth in selected content areas of psychology (e.g., theory and research, history of psychology, relevant levels of analysis, overarching themes, and relevant ethical issues).

1.3 Use the concepts, language, and major theories of the discipline to account for psychological phenomena.

1.4 Explain major perspectives of psychology (e.g., behavioral, biological, cognitive, evolutionary, humanistic, psychodynamic, and sociocultural).

Huffman Learning Objectives *Psychology in Action* (10e)	
Ch. 1	1.1–1.5
Ch. 2	2.1–2.21
Ch. 3	3.1–3.2, 3.5–3.18
Ch. 4	4.1–4.27
Ch. 5	5.1–5.2, 5.3–5.10, 5–12–5.16
Ch. 6	6.1–6.15, 6.17–6.19
Ch. 7	7.1–7.8, 7.10–7.13
Ch. 8	8.1–8.7, 8.9–8.20
Ch. 9	9.1–9.3, 9.5–9.15
Ch. 10	10.1–10.6, 10.8–10.12, 10.14
Ch. 11	11.1–11.6, 11.8–11.14
Ch. 12	12.1–12.3, 12.5–12.13
Ch. 13	13.1–13.2, 13.4–13.16
Ch. 14	14.2, 14.4–14.8, 14.10, 14.13–14.15, 14.17–14.19
Ch. 15	15.1–15.19, 15.24–15.25
Ch. 16	16.1–16.2, 16.4–16.8, 16.11–16.20
*Ch. 17	17.1–17.11, 17.13–17.19
*Ch. 18	18.1–18.3, 18.5–18.8, 18.10–18.13

Knowledge base also emphasized in Student Study and Review Guide, Instructor's Resource Guide, WileyPlus, Wiley web site assets www.wiley.com/college/huffman, etc.

*Optional Chapters 17 and 18

Focus on APA Learning Objectives

Given increasing calls for national and state mandated learning outcomes (SLOs), which are directly tied to accreditation, *Psychology in Action* (10e) and its ancillaries are all directly linked to the American Psychological Association (APA) task force's 10 learning goals for undergraduate psychology (http://www.apa.org/ed/psymajor_guideline .pdf). A sample of how this edition is tied to the first APA learning goal is included in Table 4. For a complete listing of all our objectives and their direct connection to the APA goals, please visit the instructor website at www.wiley.com/college/huffman.

Focus on Gender and Cultural Diversity and Critical Thinking

Numerous integrated cross cultural examples are found throughout the text, along with extended discussion sections generally placed in the "Psychology Engages" section of each chapter.

Table 5 CRITICAL THINKING EXERCISES

- Applying critical thinking to psychological science (p. 37).
- Biology and critical thinking (pp. 83–84)
- **NEW** Perils of Procrastination (p. 118)
- Why do so many people believe in ESP? (pp. 158–159)
- Interpreting your dreams (pp. 197–198)
- Using learning principles to succeed in college (p. 238)
- Memory and metacognition (p. 276)
- Solving problems in college life (p. 314)
- **NEW** Overcoming egocentric thinking (p. 351)
- Morality and academic cheating (p. 379)
- **NEW** The Scarlet Letter (pp. 413–414)
- **NEW** The new psychology of success (pp. 448–449)
- **NEW** Maslow revisited (p. 485)
- How your thoughts can make you depressed (pp. 522–523)
- Hunting for good therapy films (pp. 560–561)
- **NEW** To kill a Mockingbird (pp. 599–600)
- **NEW** Empathy (pp. 600–601)

A great friend and colleague who specializes in critical thinking, Tom Frangicetto at Northampton Community College, authored or co-authored the Critical Thinking Prologue to this text (see pp. xxxiii–xliii) as well as numerous critical thinking exercises (see Table 5).

Supplements

Psychology in Action (10e) is accompanied by a host of ancillary materials designed to facilitate the mastery of psychology. Additional ordering information and policies may be obtained by contacting your local Wiley sales representative.

Teaching and Learning Program: Learn more at www.wileyplus.com

WileyPLUS is an online teaching and learning environment that builds students' confidence because it takes the guesswork out of studying by providing a clear roadmap: What to do, how to do it, if they did it right." Powered by proven technology and built on a foundation of cognitive research, *WileyPLUS* has enriched the education of millions of students in over 20 countries around the world.

What do instructors receive with *WileyPLUS*?

WileyPLUS provides reliable, customizable resources that reinforce course goals inside and outside of the classroom as well as instructor visibility into individual student progress.
Powerful Multimedia Resources for Classroom Presentations:
- **90+ Wiley Psychology Videos** represent a collection of brief video clips, applying psychology concepts and themes to issues in the news.
- **20+ Wiley Psychology Animations** have been developed around key concepts and themes in psychology. The animations go beyond what is presented in the book, providing additional visual examples and descriptive narration.

- New to this edition, **50 Tutorial Videos** featuring author Karen Huffman and Katherine Dowdell of Des Moines Area Community College, provide your students with explanations and examples of some of the most challenging concepts in psychology. These 3–5 minute videos reflect the richness and diversity of psychology, from the steps of the experimental method to the interaction of genes and our environment, to the sources of stress.
- New to this edition, **20 Virtual Field Trips,** allow your students to view psychology concepts in the real world as they've never seen them before. These 5 to 10 minute virtual field trips include visits to places such as a neuroimaging center, a film studio where 3-D movies are created, and a sleep laboratory, to name only a few.
- New to this edition, the **Psychology in Action Blog,** authored by Thomas Frangicetto of Northampton Community College, provides instructors with timely and exciting activities to share in the classroom. Updated weekly, this blog will relate current topics in the news to the chapters in Psychology in Action, as well as provide psychology videos of the week, and a wealth of activities to engage your students in the classroom. Contact your local Wiley representative to sign up.

Pre-created teaching materials and assessments help instructors optimize their time:

- The **Instructor's Manual,** prepared by Danielle Sprague of Hocking College, is carefully crafted to help instructors maximize student learning. It provides teaching suggestions for each chapter of the text, including lecture starters, lecture extensions, classroom discussions and activities, out of the classroom assignments, internet and print resources, and more!
- Every chapter contains a **Lecture PowerPoint Presentation,** prepared by Katie Townsend-Merino of Palomar College, with a combination of key concepts, figures and tables, and examples from the textbook.
- **Media Enriched PowerPoint™ presentations,** also prepared by Katie Townsend-Merino, are only available in WileyPLUS, contain up-to-date, exciting embedded links to multimedia sources, both video and animation and can be easily modified according to your needs.
- **The Test Bank,** prepared by Becky Howell of Forsythe Technical Community College, is available in a word document format or through Respondus. The questions are available to instructors to create and print multiple versions of the same test by quickly and easily scrambling the order of all questions found in the Word version of the test bank. This allows users to customize exams by altering or adding new problems. The test bank has over 2,000 multiple choice questions, including approximately 10 essay questions for each chapter (with suggested answers). Each multiple-choice question has been linked to a specific, student learning outcome, coded as "Factual" or "Applied" and the correct answer provided with section references to its source in the text.

Assignable Course Plans: WileyPLUS comes with pre-created Course Plans designed by a subject matter expert uniquely for this course. A simple drag-and-drop tool makes it easier than ever before to assign readings in psychology to your students.

Gradebook: WileyPLUS provides instant access to reports on trends in class performance, student use of course materials, and progress toward learning objectives, helping inform decisions and drive classroom discussions.

What do students receive with *WileyPLUS?*

WileyPLUS builds students' confidence because it takes the guesswork out of studying by providing a clear roadmap; what to do, how to do it, if they did it right. With

WileyPLUS, psychology students take more initiative outside of the classroom, so you'll have a greater impact with them in the classroom.

- The dynamic and visual course calendar contained within *WileyPLUS* shows students their reading assignments that include thoughtful questions, video clips and animations within the context of what they are learning in your classroom.
- Students' completed assignments feed directly in their *WileyPLUS* gradebook allowing students to immediately track their progress.
- *WileyPLUS* includes a Progress Check enabling students to identify concepts and topics of weakness. Accompanied by automatically generated self-quizzes, the Progress Check offers a personalized plan to help students succeed in your course.

A Research-Based Design. WileyPLUS provides an online environment that integrates relevant resources, including the entire digital textbook, in an easy-to-navigate framework that helps students study more effectively. WileyPLUS also adds structure by organizing textbook content into smaller, more manageable "chunks."

- Related media, examples, and sample practice items reinforce the learning objectives.
- Innovative features such as calendars, visual progress tracking, and self-evaluation tools improve time management and strengthen areas of weakness.

One-on-One Engagement. With *WileyPLUS* for *Psychology in Action*, students receive 24/7 access to resources that promote positive learning outcomes. Students engage with related examples (in various media) and sample practice items.

Measurable Outcomes. Throughout each study session, students can assess their progress and gain immediate feedback. *WileyPLUS* provides precise reporting of strengths and weaknesses, as well as individualized quizzes, so that students are confident they are spending their time on the right things. With *WileyPLUS*, students always know the exact outcome of their efforts.

WileyPLUS Student Resources

- **A digital version of the complete textbook** with integrated videos, animations, and quizzes
- **Chapter exams** prepared by Kay Fernandes at Trident Technical College, give students a way to test themselves on course material before exams. Each chapter exam contains page referenced fill-in-the-blank, application, and multiple-choice questions, which provide immediate feedback with the correct answer. Each question also is linked to a specific learning objective within the book to aid a student's concept mastery.
- **Flashcards** This interactive module gives students the opportunity to easily test their knowledge of vocabulary terms.
- **Handbook for Non-Native Speakers** This handbook clarifies idioms, special phrases, and difficulty vocabulary to help students that do not use English as their first language.
- **Web Resources** Annotated web links put useful electronic resources for psychology into the context of your Introduction to Psychology course.

Other Resources

Available for student purchase is the *Student Study and Review Guide* for Psychology in Action:
Prepared by Karen Huffman and Richard Hosey, this valuable resource offers you, as a student, an easy way to review the text and ensure that you know the material before

your in-class quizzes and exams. For each textbook chapter, the study guide offers numerous tools designed to save you time, while also helping you master the core information. These tools include chapter outlines, core learning outcomes, key terms, key term crossword puzzles, matching exercises, fill-in exercises, an active learning exercise, and two sample tests (20 items each) with text-referenced correct answers. Each chapter of the *Student Study and Review Guide* also includes copies of the Step-by-Step Diagrams and Concept Organizers, as well as a copy of the *Visual Summaries* that appear at the end of each chapter in the text. Students in the past have copied these summaries to use during class lecture or text reading, so we've made your studying easier by including them in this study guide.

Acknowledgments

The writing of this text has been a group effort involving the input and support of my family, friends, and colleagues. To each person I offer my sincere thanks. A special note of appreciation goes to Jay Alperson, Bill Barnard, Dan Bellack, Siri Carpenter, Haydn Davis, Katherine Dowdell, Tom Frangicetto, Denise Frank, Ann Haney, Herb Harari, Sandy Harvey, Richard Hosey, Terry Humphrey, Teresa Jacob, Rita Jeffries, Kandis Mutter, Tyler Mutter, Roger Morrissette, Nancy Simpson, Emma Townsend-Merino, Katie Townsend-Merino, Fred Rose, Sabine Schoen, Judy Wilson, and Kathy Young.

To the reviewers, focus group, and telesession participants who gave their time and constructive criticism, I also offer my sincere appreciation. I am deeply indebted to the following individuals and trust that they will recognize their contributions throughout the text.

Student Feedback

To help us verify that our book successfully addressed the needs of today's college students, we asked current introductory psychology students to provide feedback about each chapter of the text. Their reactions confirmed our belief that the book is an effective (and some even said "entertaining") learning tool. We are particularly grateful to the following students who took extra time to share their honest opinions with us: Erin Decker, *San Diego State University*; Laura Decker, *University of California at Davis*; Amanda Nichols, *Palomar College*; Idalia S. Carrillo, *University of Texas at San Antonio*; Sarah Dedford, *Delta College (Michigan)*; Laural Didham, *Cleveland State University*; Danyce French, *Northampton Community College (Pennsylvania)*; Tyler Mutter, *University of Redlands*, Stephanie Renae Reid, *Purdue University-Calumet*; Betsy Schoenbeck, *University of Missouri at Columbia*; and Sabrina Walkup, *Trident Technical College (South Carolina)*.

Professional Feedback

The following professionals have helped us test and refine the pedagogy that is found in this book: Thomas Alley, *Clemson University*; David R. Barkmeier, *Northeastern University*; Steven Barnhart, *Rutgers University*; Dan Bellack, *Trident Technical College*; JoAnn Brannock, *Fullerton College*; Michael Caruso, *University of Toledo*; Nicole Judice Campbell, *University of Oklahoma*; Sandy Deabler, *North Harris College*; Diane K. Feibel, *Raymond Walters College*; Thomas Frangicetto, *Northampton Community College*, Richard Griggs, *University of Florida*; Richard Harris, *Kansas State University*; John Haworth, *Florida Community College at Jacksonville*; Guadalupe King, *Milwaukee Area*

Technical College; Roger Morrissette, *Palomar College*; Barbara Nash, *Bentley College*; Maureen O'Brien, *Bentley College*; Jan Pascal, *DeVry University*; John Pennachio, *Adirondack Community College*; Gary E. Rolikowki, *SUNY, Geneseo*; Ronnie Rothschild, *Broward Community College*; Ludo Scheffer, *Drexel University*; Kathy Sexton-Radek, *Elmhurst College*; Matthew Sharps, *California State University-Fresno*; Richard Topolski, *Augusta State University*; Katie Townsend-Merino, *Palomar College*; Elizabeth Young, *Bentley College*.

Focus Group and Telesession Participants

Brian Bate, *Cuyahoga Community College*; Hugh Bateman, *Jones Junior College*; Ronald Boykin, *Salisbury State University*; Jack Brennecke, *Mount San Antonio College*; Ethel Canty, *University of Texas-Brownsville*; Joseph Ferrari, *Cazenovia College*; Allan Fin-garet, *Rhode Island College*; Richard Fry, *Youngstown State University*; Roger Harnish, *Rochester Institute of Technology*; Richard Harris, *Kansas State University*; Tracy B. Henley, *Mississippi State University*; Roger Hock, *New England College*; Melvyn King, *State University of New York at Cortland*; Jack Kirschenbaum, *Fullerton College*; Cynthia McDaniel, *Northern Kentucky University*; Deborah McDonald, *New Mexico State University*; Henry Morlock, *State University of New York at Plattsburgh*; Kenneth Murdoff, *Lane Community College*; William Overman, *University of North Carolina at Wilmington*; Steve Platt, *Northern Michigan University*; Janet Proctor, *Purdue University*; Dean Schroeder, *Laramie Community College*; Michael Schuller, *Fresno City College*; Alan Schultz, *Prince George Community College*; Peggy Skinner, *South Plains College*; Charles Slem, *California Polytechnic State University-San Luis Obispo*; Eugene Smith, *Western Illinois University*; David Thomas, *Oklahoma State University*; Cynthia Viera, *Phoenix College*; and Matthew Westra, *Longview Community College*.

Additional Reviewers

L. Joseph Achor, *Baylor University*; M. June Allard, *Worcester State College*; Joyce Allen, *Lakeland College*; Worthon Allen, *Utah State University*; Jeffrey S. Anastasi, *Francis Marion University*; Susan Anderson, *University of South Alabama*; Emir Andrews, *Memorial University of Newfoundland*; Marilyn Andrews, *Hartnell College*; Richard Anglin, *Oklahoma City Community College*; Susan Anzivino, *University of Maine at Farmington*; Peter Bankart, *Wabash College*; Susan Barnett, *Northwestern State University (Louisiana)*; Patricia Barker, *Schenectady County Community College*; Daniel Bellack, *College of Charleston*; Daniel Bitran, *College of Holy Cross*; Terry Blu-menthal, *Wake Forest University*; Theodore N. Bosack, *Providence College*; Linda Bosmajian, *Hood College*; John Bouseman, *Hillsborough Community College*; John P. Broida, *University of Southern Maine*; Lawrence Burns, *Grand Valley State University*; Bernado J. Carducci, *Indiana University Southeast*; Charles S. Carver, *University of Miami*; Marion Cheney, *Brevard Community College*; Meg Clark, *California State Polytechnic University-Pomona*; Dennis Cogan, *Texas Tech University*; David Cohen, *California State University, Bakersfield*; Anne E. Cook, *University of Massachessetts*; Kathryn Jennings Cooper, *Salt Lake Community College*; Steve S. Cooper, *Glendale Community College*; Amy Cota-McKinley, *The University of Tennessee, Knoxville*; Mark Covey, *University of Idaho*; Robert E. DeLong, *Liberty University*; Linda Scott DeRosier, *Rocky Mountain College*; Grace Dyrud, *Augsburg College*; Thomas Eckle, *Modesto Junior College*; Tami Eggleston, *McKendree College*; James A. Eison, *Southeast Missouri State University*; A. Jeanette Engles, *Southeastern Oklahoma State University*; Eric Fiazi, *Los Angeles City College*; Sandra Fiske, *Onondaga Community College*; Kathleen A. Flannery, *Saint Anselm College*; Pamela Flynn, *Community College of Philadelphia*; William F. Ford, *Bucks City Community College*; Harris Friedman, *Edison Community College*; Paul Fuller,

Muskegon Community College; Frederick Gault, *Western Michigan University;* Russell G. Geen, *University of Missouri, Columbia;* Joseph Giacobbe, *Adirondack Community College;* Robert Glassman, *Lake Forest College;* Patricia Marks Greenfield, *University of California-Los Angeles;* David A. Griese, *SUNY Farmingdale;* Sam Hagan, *Edison County Community College;* Sylvia Haith, *Forsyth Technical College;* Frederick Halper, *Essex County Community College;* George Hampton, *University of Houston-Downtown;* Joseph Hardy, *Harrisburg Area Community College;* Algea Harrison, *Oakland University;* Mike Hawkins, *Louisiana State University;* Linda Heath, *Loyola University of Chicago;* Sidney Hochman, *Nassau Community College;* Richard D. Honey, *Transylvania University;* John J. Hummel, *Valdosta State University;* Nancy Jackson, *Johnson & Wales University;* Kathryn Jennings, *College of the Redwoods;* Charles Johnston, *William Rainey Harper College;* Dennis Jowaisis, *Oklahoma City Community College;* Seth Kalichman, *University of South Carolina;* Paul Kaplan, *Suffolk County Community College;* Bruno Kappes, *University of Alaska;* Kevin Keating, *Broward Community College;* Guadalupe Vasquez King, *Milwaukee Area Technical College;* Norman E. Kinney, *Southeast Missouri State University;* Richard A. Lambe, *Providence College;* Sherri B. Lantinga, *Dordt College;* Marsha Laswell, *California State Polytechnic University-Pomona;* Elise Lindenmuth, *York College;* Allan A. Lippert, *Manatee Community College;* Thomas Linton, *Coppin State College;* Virginia Otis Locke, *University of Idaho;* Maria Lopez-Trevino, *Mount San Jacinto College;* Tom Marsh, *Pitt Community College;* Edward McCrary III, *El Camino Community College;* David G. McDonald, *University of Missouri, Columbia;* Yancy McDougal, *University of South Carolina-Spartanburg;* Nancy Meck, *University of Kansas Medical Center;* Juan S. Mercado, *McLennan Community College;* Michelle Merwin, *University of Tennessee, Martin;* Mitchell Metzger, *Penn State University;* David Miller, *Daytona Beach Community College;* Michael Miller, *College of St. Scholastica;* Phil Mohan, *University of Idaho;* Ron Mossler, *LA Valley College;* Kathleen Navarre, *Delta College;* John Near, *Elgin Community College;* Steve Neighbors, *Santa Barbara City College;* Leslie Neumann, *Forsyth Technical Community College;* Susan Nolan, *Seton Hall University;* Sarah O'Dowd, *Community College of Rhode Island;* Joseph J. Palladino, *University of Southern Indiana;* Linda Palm, *Edison Community College;* Richard S. Perroto, *Queensborough Community College;* Larry Pervin, *Rutgers University, New Brunswick;* Valerie Pinhas, *Nassau Community College;* Leslee Pollina, *Southeast Missouri State University;* Howard R. Pollio, *University of Tennessee-Knoxville;* Christopher Potter, *Harrisburg Community College;* Derrick Proctor, *Andrews University;* Antonio Puete, *University of North Carolina-Wilmington;* Joan S. Rabin, *Towson State University;* Lillian Range, *University of Southern Mississippi;* George A. Raymond, *Providence College;* Celia Reaves, *Monroe Community College;* Michael J. Reich, *University of Wisconsin-River Falls;* Edward Rinalducci, *University of Central Florida;* Kathleen R. Rogers, *Purdue University North Central;* Leonard S. Romney, *Rockland Community College;* Thomas E. Rudy, *University of Pittsburgh;* Carol D. Ryff, *University of Wisconsin-Madison;* Neil Salkind, *University of Kansas-Lawrence;* Richard J. Sanders, *University of North Carolina-Wilmington;* Harvey Richard Schiffman, *Rutgers University;* Steve Schneider, *Pima College;* Michael Scozzaro, *State University of New York at Buffalo;* Tizrah Schutzengel, *Bergen Community College;* Lawrence Scott, *Bunker Hill Community College;* Michael B. Sewall, *Mohawk Valley Community College;* Fred Shima, *California State University-Dominquez Hills;* Royce Simpson, *Campbellsville University;* Art Skibbe, *Appalachian State University;* Larry Smith, *Daytona Beach Junior College;* Emily G. Soltano, *Worcester State College;* Debra Steckler, *Mary Washington College;* Michael J. Strube, *Washington University;* Kevin Sumrall, *Montgomery College;* Ronald Testa, *Plymouth State College;* Cynthia Viera, *Phoenix College;* John T. Vogel,

Baldwin Wallace College; Benjamin Wallace, *Cleveland State University*; Mary Wellman, *Rhode Island College*; Paul J. Wellman, *Texas A & M University*; I. Eugene White, *Salisbury State College*; Delos D. Wickens, *Colorado State University-Fort Collins*; Fred Whitford, *Montana State University*; Charles Wiechert, *San Antonio College*; Jeff Walper, *Delaware Technical and Community College*; Bonnie S. Wright, *St. Olaf College*; Brian T. Yates, *American University*; Todd Zakrajsek, *Southern Oregon University*; and Mary Lou Zanich, *Indiana University of Pennsylvania*.

Special Thanks

- I am deeply indebted to the superb editorial and production teams at John Wiley and Sons. This project benefited from the infinite patience, wisdom, and insight of Katherine Dowdell, Sandra Dumas, Anna Melhorn, Jennifer MacMillan, Sara Wright, and many others. Like any cooperative effort, writing a book requires an incredible support team, and I am deeply grateful to this remarkable group of people.

- *Psychology in Action* (10e) could not exist without a great ancillary author team. I gratefully acknowledge the expertise and talents of our Video Tutorials director, Katherine Dowdell, and her teammates, Test Bank author, Becky Howell, Instructor's Resource Guide author, Danielle Sprague, Psychology Blog author, Thomas Frang icetto, Power Point presentations author, Katie Townsend-Merino, and a host of others. I realize how indebted I am to each of these individuals for their high-quality work, attention to detail, and loving friendship. Thank you for "having my back."

- I would like to express my deepest gratitude to Chris Johnson, Executive Editor. Chris came aboard during the production of the 8th edition and has stuck with me through the 9th and 10th editions. I am continually impressed and eternally grateful for his invaluable feedback and suggestions. He's also a fun guy who's a delightful work partner!

- The success of this book is directly related to the amazing efforts of Danielle Hagey, Marketing Manager. Her unflagging energy, eternal optimism, and constant encouragement inspired and sustained me throughout the entire process. Lynn Pearlman, Media Editor, Eileen McKeever, Assistant Editor, Carrie Tupa, Marketing Assistant, and a host of others also helped enormously in the initial launch and ongoing production. Without them, this book and its wide assortment of ancillaries would not have been possible.

- My sincerest thanks also go to the team at *Furino Production*. Their careful and professional approach was critical to the successful production of this book. I especially thank Jeanine Furino, for her gracious handholding and personal support throughout the inevitable ups and downs of "bookmaking." She is a gifted manager with a kindred, "obsessive" desire for perfection. She's my PPJ (Perfectionist Pal Jeanine)!

- These individuals deserve special recognition: Siri Carpenter, Tom Frangicetto, Denise Frank, Rita Jeffries, Sandy Harvey, Michelle Hernandez, Jordan Hertzog-Merino, Richard Hosey, Teresa Jacob, Jim Matiya, Christine McLean, Kandis Mutter, Tyler Mutter, Maria Pok, Emma Townsend-Merino and Katie Townsend-Merino. They provided careful editing of this text, library research, and a unique sense of what should and should not go into an introduction to psychology text.

- Last, and definitely *not least*, I dedicate this book to my beloved husband, Bill Barnard, who has provided countless hours of careful editing, advice, and unwavering support for all 10 editions of this book!
- Finally, my students deserve a large degree of credit and appreciation for their contributions. They taught me what students want to know and inspired me to share my love of psychology. I enjoy hearing from you, my readers and instructors. Your input is invaluable so please email me to share your feedback.

Karen R. Huffman

KAREN HUFFMAN
Palomar College
San Marcos, CA
khuffman@palomar.edu

Prologue

Student Engagement Through Critical Thinking

Co-authored with Thomas Frangicetto (and personal contributions from his students at Northampton Community College, Bethlehem, PA)

Critical thinking has many meanings, and some books dedicate entire chapters to defining the term. As previous users of this text know, we have been defining **critical thinking** as *thinking about and evaluating thoughts, feelings, and behavior so that we can clarify and improve them* (adapted from Chaffee, 1988, p. 29). This basic definition still works for us, and will be expanded over the next few pages with specific critical thinking components that have practical application value in the real world. Unlike the common use of "critical," as a negative type of criticism and faultfinding, critical thinking is a positive, life-enhancing process.

In addition to critical thinking, another major teaching and learning tool has emerged in higher education that seems to have tremendous potential for enhancing your overall learning experience, *student engagement*, which is much more than the latest educational buzz term. We intend to demonstrate just how useful it can be.

Student engagement can be defined as *an approach to education characterized by intense student involvement in the quality of their learning that results from the interaction between **motivation** and **active learning*** (adapted from Barkley, 2009). This means student engagement is both a learning *process* that students are involved in and a *product*, that is, the amount of actual learning that takes place.

One of the most important factors in student engagement is your own level of **motivation**, defined in Chapter 12 as *a set of factors that activate, direct, and maintain behavior, usually—ideally—toward some goal*. More than anything else your level of motivation will determine how well you do in this course—as well as in all other parts of your life.

Finally, student engagement requires you to be an *active learner*, which involves being a dynamic participant in your own learning by reflecting on and monitoring

Many people think they are thinking when they are merely rearranging their prejudices.

WILLIAM JAMES

xxxiii

both the way you learn and the results of your learning (Barkley, 2009). Using the SQ4R study method explained in the Tools for Success section at the end of Chapter 1 is a good example of active learning.

As you discovered in the Preface, the overarching goal for this edition of Psychology in Action is student engagement through critical thinking, motivation, and active learning. At the end of this Prologue, you will find a short interview with a former psychology student who exemplifies the three "gears" in Figure 2.

Figure 2 Critical Thinking + Motivation + Active Learning = Student Engagement

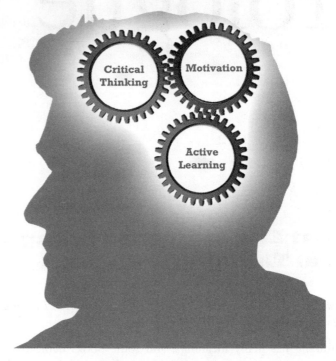

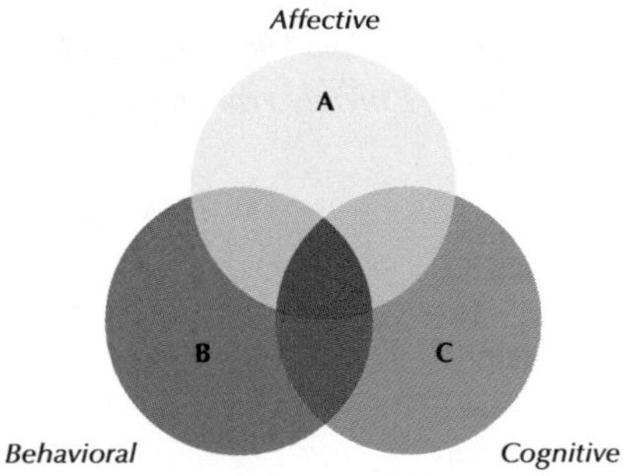

How can you develop the first element of student engagement--your critical thinking skills? Each chapter of *Psychology in Action* (10e) includes a specific *Critical Thinking Exercise* devoted to improving one or more of the 21 Critical Thinking Components (CTCs), which are divided into three ABC domains: *Affective* (emotional), *Behavioral* (action), and *Cognitive* (thinking) (see Figure 3). In the next few pages, we'll present a brief description of each component with several specific examples supplied from students at Northampton Community College.

Figure 3 ABCs of Critical Thinking

21 Critical Thinking Components (CTCs)

Affective Components (*Emotional* foundation for critical thinking)

1. **Valuing Truth Above Self-Interest**: Critical thinkers hold themselves and those they agree with to the same intellectual standards to which they hold their opponents. This is one of the most difficult components to employ on a regular basis. Almost everyone has a tendency to cater to their own needs (see "self-serving bias" p. 569) and to ignore information that appears to conflict with our desires. Critical

thinkers recognize that, even when it appears otherwise, the "truth" is always in our self-interest.

Psychic John Edward makes a lot of money off his supposed power to communicate with people's dead relatives . . . his "customers" should value the truth over self-interest. *This means accepting the truth, even when it is not what they want to believe. We learned from the text that one reason people believe in psychics like Edward is because they "want to"--they willingly suspend disbelief" and put their self-interest above the truth.*

LISA SHANK

2. **Recognizing Personal Biases:** This involves using your highest intellectual skills to detect personal biases and self-deceptive reasoning so you can design realistic plans for self-correction. Being an effective critical thinker does not mean the total absence of bias, but rather the willingness to admit, recognize, and correct it.

Because America is such a huge country of immigrants, many people—including me as a foreigner from Japan—become sensitive about discrimination and prejudice. I have had some difficult times. Once one of my American friends described some Asian people as "foxes," because of the way they look. She was joking, but I was not laughing. I felt very sad because she didn't even notice that I felt disrespected. She definitely needs to begin recognizing personal biases if she wants to have friends from different cultures.

SAEMI SUZUKI

3. **Empathizing:** Critical thinkers appreciate and try to understand others' thoughts, feelings, and behaviors. Noncritical thinkers view everything and everyone in relation to themselves, which is known as "egocentrism." The ability to consider the perspective of another person—to empathize with them—is the most effective antidote to egocentric thinking. (See Final Take Home Message, pp. 600–601.)

I think that one thing that everyone should do when they've lost a loved one is empathizing. Empathy is a great way to help each other in a time of need. Many times there is someone who just needs to talk and express his or her feelings. Being able to listen and understand what they are going through, helps make your response to them more effective and helpful.

CHRISTOPHER FEGLEY

4. **Welcoming Divergent Views:** Critical thinkers value examining issues from every angle and know that it is especially important to explore and understand positions with which they disagree. This quality would be especially valuable to groups in the process of decision-making. Welcoming divergent views would effectively inoculate the decision making process from "groupthink"—faulty decision making that occurs when a highly cohesive group strives for agreement and avoids inconsistent information.

Most Americans don't even try to understand the sociocultural influences that affect suicide bombers . . . but this issue has influenced me to welcome divergent views and try to understand that people in different cultures have different beliefs. Most Americans believe that martyrs are crazy, while Palestinians believe that martyrdom is something to be idolized. My decision to believe that martyrdom is a form of self-expression may clash with the views of many Americans but I grew up in a country where I have the right to believe what I want.

SOPHIA BLANCHET

5. **Tolerating Ambiguity:** Although formal education often trains us to look for a single "right" answer (aka "convergent thinking"), critical thinkers recognize that many issues are complex and subtle, and that complicated issues may not have just one "right" answer. They recognize and value qualifiers such as "probably," "highly likely," and "not very likely." Creative artists, in particular, must be willing to deal with uncertainty and be willing to consider many possible solutions, also known as *divergent thinking* (see CTC *Being Eclectic*, #17, and Chapter 8, p. 291).

One big difference between high school and college level thinking is "tolerating ambiguity." In high school we were often taught there was one right answer. That such and such happened at this time and this is why. In college we learn that things are more complex than just "this is the answer because it is." We also learn that some questions do not even have an "answer," or that some questions have multiple answers depending on the circumstances involved. College level thinking involves learning new ways to solve problems by trying different solutions. Being able to tolerate ambiguity is the key.

CHEREEN NAWROCKI

6. **Accepting Change:** Critical thinkers remain open to the need for adjustment and adaptation throughout the life cycle. Resisting change is one of the most common characteristics that human beings share, and the notion that many of us are "threatened by change" is a widely held belief. Because critical thinkers fully trust the processes of reasoned inquiry, they are willing to use these skills to examine even their most deeply held values and beliefs, and to modify these beliefs when evidence and experience contradict them.

I believe that accepting change is a crucial skill that an abused woman must possess in order to leave the situation. It is so much easier to tell another woman that she should get out of a bad relationship because she does not deserve to be abused—it is much harder to do when you are the one in the damaging relationship because along with the depression that you may be suffering, there is also the need to "resist change" because of the fear of the unknown. It is important for the abused woman to stop trying to "change" the man, thinking the situation will get better. It is vital not to be stuck in such a toxic situation and accepting change is the first step to begin the process of leaving.

KATRINA KELLY

Behavioral Components (*Actions* necessary for critical thinking)

7. **Employing Precise Terms:** Precise terms help critical thinkers identify issues clearly and concretely so that they

can be objectively defined and empirically tested. In the everyday realm, when two people argue about an issue they are often defining it differently without even knowing it. For example, in a romantic relationship two individuals can have very different definitions of words such as "love" and "commitment." Open communication that explores and identifies these precise shades of meaning is an important key to successful relationships—and critical thinking!

Relationships are very hard, but I believe that even people from different cultures can get along and solve their differences by employing precise terms. As the text says, "open communication that identifies the precise shades of meaning is a key to successful relationships." I have experience with this by having a Japanese girlfriend for the last year and a half. Our cultures are very different and at times we do not understand each other. But, if we remain open, and help each other understand what words like "love" and "commitment" mean to us, we learn how to understand each other better. Love can be explained in various ways, but when we think critically the relationship gets easier.

ANAR AKHUNDOV

8. **Gathering Information and Delaying Judgment until Adequate Data is Available:** Impulsivity is one of the surest obstacles to good critical thinking. Rash judgments about others, impulse purchases of a new car or home, uninformed choices for political candidates, or "falling in love at first sight" can all be costly mistakes that we may regret for many years. A critical thinker does not make snap judgments. Instead, he or she collects up-to-date, relevant information on all sides of an issue and delays decisions or judgment until adequate information is available.

When it comes to debating the Iraqi war people are often misinformed and I believe it is my responsibility to inform them of the truth since I am in the U.S. Army Reserves. At first I did not agree with the war, but as a soldier I am supposed to do what I am told. I have worked with people who were part of the unit responsible for the Abu Ghraib prison scandal, and I have friends who are over in Iraq, some who support the war and others who do not . . . (but) some people judge the situation before they get all the information they need. This is why I try to convince them to delay judgment until adequate data is available.

LONGSU CHENG

9. **Listening Actively:** Critical thinkers fully engage their thinking skills when listening to another person. This may sound like the easiest or most obvious of all components, but more likely it is one of the most difficult. Test this yourself the next time you are in a conversation with someone. After you've talked for a while ask the other person to summarize what you were saying. Or monitor your own listening prowess when the other person is speaking.

How often does your attention wander? Critical thinkers "actively" engage in the conversation by "encouraging critical dialogue." They ask questions, nonverbally affirm what they hear, and request clarification or elaboration.

10. **Encouraging Critical Dialogue:** Critical thinkers are active questioners who challenge existing facts and opinions and welcome questions in return. Socratic questioning is an important type of critical dialogue in which the questioner deeply probes the meaning, justification, or logical strength of a claim, position, or line of reasoning. In everyday communication it is often easier to avoid the type of dialogue that would help solve problems and strengthen relationships, but it is an essential part of living an emotionally healthy life.

My mother has been calling me for the last year and I know she is only talking to me because she is dying. It has taken me a long time to warm up to her because of the past . . . I currently find myself encouraging critical dialogue with her . . . after many years we have finally started to express our feelings with each other. This dialogue has been most gratifying because now we have learned to become friends and enjoy each other's company. My hope is that when the end comes we will know that despite our faults we really loved each other.

TIM WALKER

11. **Distinguishing Fact from Opinion:** Facts are statements that can be proven true. Opinions are statements that express how a person feels about an issue or what someone *believes* to be true. It is easy to have an uninformed opinion about any subject, critical thinkers seek out facts before forming their opinions.

At the beginning of the semester, I held the opinion that I hated Introduction to Music with a burning passion. My friend told me that I had to give the class a fair chance and that it was fun and interesting. I refused to believe her, I believed I was wasting my time and just procrastinated about everything related to that course. With my friend's insistence, I began paying more attention and found that I my opinion was wrong. I learned was that there was a lot for me to learn and enjoy in that class, but initially I was too stubborn to let myself fully experience it.

YARILIZ CASTILLO

12. **Employing a Variety of Thinking Processes:** Critical thinkers are not bound to one way of thinking. Instead they employ numerous approaches, including (a) *inductive logic*—moving from the specific to the general, (b) *deductive logic*—moving from the general to the specific, (c) *dialogical thinking*—an extended verbal exchange between differing points of view or frames of reference, and (d) *dialectical thinking*—tests of the strengths and weaknesses of opposing points of view.

13. **Modifying Judgments in Light of New Information:** Critical thinkers are willing to abandon or modify their judgments if compelling evidence or experience contradicts them. Noncritical thinkers stubbornly stick to their beliefs and often "value self-interest above the truth." The ability to say "I read the information you sent me on the topic and I'm rethinking my opinion" reflects the necessary flexibility of a good critical thinker.

For much of my high school years, I procrastinated on almost every assignment. The process of change has been a slow one . . . however, I procrastinate less now that I am in college. In addition to prioritizing my work, and finishing the more important assignments sooner . . . I have modified my judgment in light of new information. I know now that these assignments are primarily for my own benefit and that a certain level of self-motivation is required in order to succeed in life. I also realized that I am paying for my education so I may as well get as much out of it as I can.

TOM SHIMER

14. **Applying Knowledge to New Situations:** When critical thinkers master a new skill or experience an insight, they transfer this information to new contexts. Noncritical thinkers can often provide correct answers, repeat definitions, and carry out calculations, yet be unable to transfer their knowledge to new situations because of a basic lack of understanding or an inability to "synthesize" seemingly unrelated content.

History has taught us that war has rarely completely put an end to a conflict. The American experience in the recent war with Iraq argues that military action against Iran means inviting more trouble. Iran would undoubtedly retaliate inviting a tit-for-tat escalation in a wider war putting American interest in great danger. This is a situation where we should "apply knowledge of history to all new situations" with other countries. At present, polls indicate that the vast majority of Americans say no to another unnecessary war and the waste of their tax money. Most Democrats and increasing numbers of Republicans agree that a strong case can be made for trying diplomatic options.

NIVEDITA "MINU" MAHATO

Cognitive Components (*Thought processes* required for critical thinking)

15. **Defining Problems Accurately:** To the extent possible, a critical thinker identifies the issues in clear and concrete terms in order to prevent confusion and lay the foundation for gathering relevant information. At first glance, this component appears to contradict "tolerating ambiguity," but that is not so. Critical thinkers are able to tolerate ambiguity until it is possible to "define problems accurately."

The character Claire (Molly Ringwold) in the movie "The Breakfast Club" is able to "define problems accurately." In her answer to Brian's inquiry "Will we still be friends on Monday?" she says "no" and explains "why?" Basically she says "because her friends won't allow it." She hates following the "groupthink" but at the same time feels compelled to do so. Even though she seems confused as to why she goes along with the group, she understands the problem with her behavioral choices. I really think this inability to "think independently" is one of the major dilemmas faced by adolescents within a group. It is the cause for so much confusion, anxiety, and drama.

MIKE DE ROSA

16. **Analyzing Data for Value and Content:** By carefully evaluating the nature of evidence and the credibility of the source, critical thinkers recognize illegitimate appeals to emotion, unsupported assumptions, and faulty logic. This enables them to discount sources of information that lack a record of honesty, contradict themselves on key questions, or have a vested interest in selling product, idea, or viewpoint that are only partially accurate (a "half truth").

17. **Being Eclectic:** Critical thinkers select what appears to be the best or most useful option when faced with competing ideas, approaches, and beliefs. For example, a psychotherapist might have training in a particular theoretical perspective, such as cognitive or behavioral, but also use techniques from other perspectives when deemed to be more appropriate for the unique problems presented by any individual they try to help. This component is more than just a matter of *welcoming divergent views*, it also involves *analyzing* all potential sources for *value and content*.

18. **Resisting Overgeneralization:** Overgeneralization is the temptation to apply a fact or experience to situations that are only superficially similar—for example, having a bad experience with and forming a negative judgment of a person from a particular ethnic heritage and then applying that same judgment to all members of the same ethnic group. The failure to resist overgeneralization is often at the core of "prejudice." This can also be defined as avoiding "tunnel vision"—failing to see the bigger picture because your focus is on just a small sample of the whole.

19. **Synthesizing.** After taking an "eclectic" approach to a situation and selecting the best options available, critical thinkers are able to combine the various elements into a meaningful and useful composite. For example, blending the affective, cognitive, and behavioral components

of critical thinking into a deeper understanding of your world involves synthesizing. Consider a real world situation: Feeling depressed because "nobody likes you" might lead to asking other people for feedback (*welcoming divergent views*), their views might help you realize that you do have good qualities that people like and that it isn't as bad as you thought (*resisting overgeneralization*), which could inspire you to try new behaviors (*applying knowledge to new situations*).

Understanding a suicidal person is the key to saving them. By synthesizing, critical thinkers' "recognize that comprehension and understanding result from combining various elements into meaningful patterns." By seeing patterns of various "warning signs"—such as different symptoms of depression and changes in attitude or behavior—you can recognize that a person is suicidal. One sad truth about the Virginia Tech tragedy is that many individuals had information about the "shooter," but there was no way to "synthesize" all of it. It is clear that not only can synthesizing save one life, it can save many.

MICELLE PASCOE

20. **Thinking Independently:** Critical thinking is independent thinking. Critical thinkers do not passively accept the beliefs of others and are not easily manipulated. They maintain a healthy amount of skepticism, especially about unusual or remarkable claims or reports. They also are able to differentiate being "skeptical" from just being stubborn and unyielding. They are, for example, willing to welcome divergent views (CTC #4), weigh the substance of those views (CTC #12), and adjust their own thinking if warranted (CTCs #6, #13, #14).

"Thinking independently" means discovering things yourself without letting other people's ideas or opinions influence you. For example, in order for people to have any kind of religious beliefs, they need to decide for themselves what seems right for them. People with different religions are going to believe different things about death and the afterlife, but every person needs to decide these issues independent of what others think.

JONATHAN SNYDER

21. **Employing Metacognition.** Also known as reflective or recursive thinking, it involves reviewing and analyzing your mental processes—thinking about your own thinking. Critical thinkers who are motivated to trace the origin of their beliefs put their thinking under intense scrutiny and can often be heard saying things like "What was I thinking?" or "I don't know why I believe that, I'll have to think about it."

My dad and I had a torn relationship following my parents' divorce. At one point I couldn't live with my mother anymore so

I thought about living with my dad, but I had a lot of things to consider before I made the decision. I began employing metacognition about my thoughts and feelings toward my dad. I wanted to really understand what had happened to cause my anger toward my dad so I could release it and rebuild our relationship. I did a lot of thinking and realized I wasted years being angry, and that when we fought we were just releasing frustration. We were all living in a difficult situation. As a result, I decided to move in with my dad and I'm happy to say my relationship has changed dramatically for the better. Using critical thinking made a huge difference.

LAURA MARKLEY

A Student Engaged: The Perfect Storm

The following interview with a former psychology student, Neal Amundsen, is a case study of student engagement in action.

Psychology in Action (PIA): Neal, we would like to explore your performance in Introduction to Psychology. At the midsemester break, after two exams, you were averaging a mid-C. Then something changed. You averaged a 96 on the third exam and final and also received a 50/50 on the Critical Thinking Journal. You also began participating more in class at a high level. Can you tell us what happened?

Neal: It was a combination of topics I learned in psychology, mainly about motivation, emotions, and classical conditioning, as well as my personal desire to fulfill life goals that came together to brew the perfect storm.

PIA: Can you be more specific?

Neal: In a nutshell, it was a matter of planning long, medium, and short-term goals. Then, utilizing conditioning techniques to change my unhelpful behaviors into productive ones. For example, a typical day would begin with me reading through the chapter and writing notes on all key terms and summarizing paragraphs, then after completing a chapter I'd reward myself with something simple. I made sure, however, that in the first few days I'd study for the same lengths of time, at the same times of day. Later on, I built a tolerance for studying and was able to work from 10 minutes a day to 8 hours a day. There was times when I'd want to take breaks from studying, so if I was ahead of schedule I'd allow myself free time for relaxation on the weekends.

PIA: Did this approach work immediately?

Neal: No. At first, I looked at studying as if it were a form of torture. I'd skim over the material superficially and get as far away from it as possible. But after spinning my wheels a good bit of the time and getting nowhere,

I realized that studying requires a student to immerse themselves completely in the material. Simply reading a book wouldn't help, I had to actively engage myself with the material.

PIA: We call that "student engagement."

Neal: And it really works. Before class, I'd summarize each paragraph, create self-test quizzes, in addition to what the book provided, and write out all the key terms. I also finally started to use the text online study guide as was suggested in the first week. When I came into class I would not have to take rushed notes, but instead I paid attention to the subjects that were brought up. I was able to apply what I learned, before class and lay a solid foundation of knowledge for future chapters to base themselves upon.

PIA: Could you comment on how going from a C to an A student made you feel, in other words, to what extent was the improvement some sort of emotional affirmation or "reinforcement" for you as well—did it boost your "self-esteem" or "locus of control"?

Neal: No question. I felt pride in the fruits of my labor. My grades improved throughout all subjects, but, more importantly, the grades were only a small step along a much larger path. Knowing I was one step closer to my dreams was all the reinforcement I needed to continue my disciplined study behavior. My self-esteem and locus of control grew tremendously.

PIA: Are you confident that you can continue this academic success?

Neal: Absolutely. I didn't just improve in psychology. I took what I learned in psychology and applied it to all my courses, all of which I was muddling through at around a C average. I received only one grade below an A for that semester, but I evaluated and strengthened my weaknesses and now face summer courses with unrelenting vigor. On top of my excellent grades, my healthy self-esteem and high locus of control contributed to my promotion to head lifeguard at a local YMCA. My overall health improved and everyday I awake full of energy, ready to learn and overcome my past weaknesses.

PIA: The biopsychosocial model in action, huh?

Neal: Exactly.

PIA: Any regrets about not adopting this approach sooner?

Neal: Not really. Better late than not at all, right? When I look at my high-school grades I know I could have done better, but I lacked the motivation and discipline recently extracted from my psychology course to succeed. I no longer hide from the future responsibilities of adulthood. I embrace them.

Psychology in Action

TENTH EDITION

ChapterOne

Introduction to Psychology and Its Research Methods

Welcome to the exciting world of *Psychology in Action*. As the cover of this text and its name imply, psychology is a *living*, dynamic field that affects every part of our lives—our relationships at home, college, and work, as well as politics, television, movies, newspapers, radio, and the Internet.

When I took my first general psychology course, I didn't realize or fully appreciate its invaluable personal applications and incredible range of topics. Like you, perhaps, I thought all psychologists were therapists, and I expected to study mostly abnormal behavior.

Today, as a college psychology professor, I find that most of my students share many of my original expectations—and misconceptions. Although psychologists do study and treat abnormal behavior, we also study sleep, dreaming, stress, health, drugs, personality, sexuality, motivation, emotion, learning, memory, childhood, aging, death, love, conformity, intelligence, creativity, and so much more.

My goal as your textbook author is to serve as your personal "tour guide" to all these fascinating topics. And my goal, "Dear Reader," is to take you on a fast-paced journey through all the major fields of psychology, along with exciting forays into little-known or previously uncharted territories filled with intriguing discoveries into yourself and the world around you. Be sure to pack your bags with an ample supply of curiosity, enthusiasm, and an open-minded spirit of adventure. That's all the supplies you'll need for what promises to be the most exciting and unforgettable trip of your academic lifetime!

Fondly,

Karen R. Huffman

KAREN HUFFMAN

ChapterOutline

3

WHY STUDY PSYCHOLOGY

Chapter 1 (and all other chapters in this text) will:

- **Increase your understanding of your-self and others.** The Greek philosopher Socrates admonished long ago, "Know thyself." Studying psychology will greatly contribute to your understanding (and appreciation) of yourself and others.

- **Better your social relations and enhance your career.** Thanks to years of scientific research and application, psychology has developed numerous guidelines and techniques that will improve your relationships with friends, family, and coworkers, while also improving your professional life.

- **Broaden your general education.** Psychology is an integral part of today's political, social, and economic world. Understanding its principles and concepts is essential to becoming an educated, well-informed person.

- **Improve your critical thinking.** Would you like to become a more independent thinker, a better decision maker, and a more effective problem solver? These are only a few of the many critical thinking skills that are enhanced through a study of psychology.

StudyTip

Learning Objectives

Each section of every chapter contains numbered learning objectives, which you should attempt to answer as you read that section. These objectives are later repeated and summarized in the end-of-chapter summary.

Psychology Scientific study of behavior and mental processes

Introducing Psychology

What Is Psychology? Scientific Methods and Scientific Thinking

Objective 1.1: Define psychology.

The term *psychology* derives from the roots *psyche*, meaning "mind," and *logos*, meaning "word." Early psychologists focused primarily on the study of mind and mental life. By the 1920s, however, many psychologists believed the mind was not a suitable subject for objective *scientific* study. They initiated a movement to restrict psychology to observable behavior alone. Today we recognize the importance of both areas. Accordingly, **psychology** is now defined as the *scientific study of behavior and mental processes*. Note the three key concepts in this definition—*scientific*, *behavior*, and *mental processes* (Figure 1.1).

Scientific is a key part of the definition of psychology. Psychological science collects and evaluates information using systematic observations and measurements.

Behavior is anything we do that can be directly observed and recorded—talking, sleeping, text messaging, etc.

Mental processes are our private, internal experiences—thoughts, perceptions, feelings, memories—that cannot be observed directly.

Figure 1.1 Defining psychology

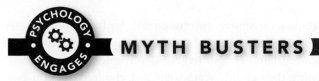

MYTH BUSTERS

How Well Do You Know Psychology?

True or false?

___1. Your first hunch on a multiple-choice test is your best guess (Chapter 1).

___2. Most of us use only 10 percent of our brains (Chapter 2).

___3. Advertisers and politicians often use subliminal persuasion to influence our behavior (Chapter 4).

___4. Most brain activity stops during sleep (Chapter 5).

___5. The best way to learn and remember information is to "cram," or study it intensively during one concentrated period (Chapter 7).

___6. Most middle-aged people experience a midlife crisis (Chapter 10).

___7. Polygraph ("lie detector") tests can accurately and reliably reveal whether or not a person is lying (Chapter 12).

___8. People who threaten suicide seldom follow through with it (Chapter 14).

___9. People with schizophrenia have multiple personalities (Chapter 14).

___10. Modern electroconvulsive ("shock") therapy is a physically dangerous and ineffective therapy (Chapter 15).

___11. Similarity is one of the best predictors of long-term relationships (Chapter 16).

___12. In an emergency, as the number of bystanders increases, your chance of getting help decreases (Chapter 16).

Answers: 1–10 are false, 11 and 12 are true. (Details provided in designated chapters.)

As part of this scientific emphasis, psychologists place particular value on empirical evidence that can be objectively tested and evaluated. We also emphasize **critical thinking**, the *process of objectively evaluating, comparing, analyzing,* and *synthesizing information*. If you would like to exercise your critical thinking skills and test how much you already know about psychology, complete the above "Myth Busters" exercise.

My students often miss several questions on this same quiz because they rely on common sense, personal experience, or media reports of "pop psychology." Mistakes also are made when they confuse scientific psychology with *pseudopsychologies,* which give the appearance of science but are actually false (*Pseudo* means "false.") Pseudopsychologies include:

- *Psychics* supposedly sensitive to supernatural forces.

- *Mediums* claiming to be channels of communication between the earthly and spiritual worlds.

- *Palmists* reportedly able to predict a person's future or character from the lines on the palms.

- *Astrologers* claiming the positions of the stars and planets influence our personalities and future events.

Critical Thinking Process of objectively evaluating, comparing, analyzing, and synthesizing information

"The Amazing Randi" Magician James Randi has dedicated his life to educating the public about fraudulent pseudopsychologists. Along with the prestigious MacArthur Foundation, Randi has offered $1 million to "anyone who proves a genuine psychic power under proper observing conditions." After many years, the money has never been collected. If you would like more information, visit Randi's website at www.randi.org. (*About James Randi,* 2002; Randi, 1997; The amazing meeting, 2011).

For some, horoscopes or palmists are simple entertainment. Unfortunately, some true believers seek guidance and waste large sums of money on charlatans purporting to know the future. Broken-hearted families also have lost valuable time and emotional energy on psychics claiming they could locate their lost children. As you can see, distinguishing scientific psychology from pseudopsychology is vitally important (Lilienfeld et al., 2010; Loftus, 2010; Smith, 2010).

Psychology's Goals: Describe, Explain, Predict, and Change

Objective 1.2: What are psychology's four main goals?

In contrast to pseudopsychologies, which rely on personal testimonials and opinions, psychology bases its findings on rigorous, scientific methods. When conducting their research, psychologists have four basic goals: to *describe*, *explain*, *predict*, and *change* behavior and mental processes.

1. **Description** Description tells "what" occurred. In some studies, psychologists attempt to *describe*, or name and classify, particular behaviors by making careful scientific observations. Description is usually the first step in understanding behavior. For example, if someone says, "Boys are more aggressive than girls," what does that mean? The speaker's definition of aggression may differ from yours. Science requires specificity.

2. **Explanation** An explanation tells "why" a behavior or mental process occurred. In other words, *explaining* a behavior or mental process depends on discovering and understanding its causes. One of the most enduring debates in science has been the **nature–nurture controversy** (Tyson & Jones, 2011). Are we controlled by biological and genetic factors (the nature side)? Or by environment and learning (the nurture side)? As you will see throughout the text, psychology (like all sciences) generally avoids "either-or" positions and focuses instead on *interactions*. Today, almost all scientists agree that most psychological, and even physical traits, reflect an interaction between nature and nurture. For example, research indicates that there are numerous interacting causes or explanations for aggression, including culture, learning, genes, brain damage, and high levels of testosterone (e.g., Bhanoo, 2011; Kelly et al., 2008; Pournaghash-Tehrani, 2011).

3. **Prediction** Psychologists generally begin with description and explanation (answering the "whats" and "whys"). Then they move on to the higher-level goal of *prediction*, identifying the conditions under which a future behavior or mental process is likely to occur. For instance, knowing that alcohol leads to increased aggression (Ferguson, 2010; Mihic et al., 2009), we can predict that more fights will erupt in places where alcohol is consumed than in those where alcohol isn't consumed.

4. **Change** For some people, "change" as a goal of psychology brings to mind evil politicians or cult leaders "brainwashing" unknowing victims. However, to psychologists, *change* means applying psychological knowledge to prevent unwanted outcomes or bring about desired goals. In almost all cases, change as a goal of psychology is positive. Psychologists help people improve their work environment, stop addictive behaviors, become less depressed, improve their family relationships, and so on. Furthermore, as you know from personal experience, it is very difficult (if not impossible) to change someone against her or his will. (*Joke question:* Do you know how many psychologists it takes to change a light bulb? *Answer:* None. The light bulb has to want to change itself!)

Nature–Nurture Controversy
Ongoing dispute over the relative contributions of nature (heredity) and nurture (environment)

Study Tip

Key Terms and Running Glossary

Pay close attention to all key terms and concepts, which are boldfaced in the text, and then defined again in the margin. Key terms from all chapters also appear in a cumulative glossary at the end of this text.

In Sum, psychology's four goals are to answer four basic questions about behavior and mental processes:

1. *What* is their nature? (Description)

2. *Why* do they occur? (Explanation)

3. *When* will they occur? (Prediction)

4. How can we *change* them? (Change)

StudyTip

Check & Review

Each major topic concludes with self-test questions that allow you to stop and check your understanding of the important concepts just discussed. Answers appear in Appendix B at the back of the text.

Psychology at Work

Careers in the Field

Objective 1.3: Summarize psychology's major career specialties.

Knowing what psychology is, and understanding its four major goals, would you consider a career in the field? Many students think of psychologists only as therapists. However, many psychologists work as researchers, teachers, and consultants in academic, business, industry, and government settings (Table 1.1). Many psychologists also work in a combination of settings. Your college psychology instructor may be an experimental psychologist who teaches, conducts research, and works as a paid business or government consultant—all at the same time. Similarly, a clinical psychologist might be a full-time therapist, while also teaching college courses.

What is the difference between a psychiatrist and a clinical or counseling psychologist? The joke answer would be "about $100 an hour." The serious answer is that psychiatrists are medical doctors. They have M.D. degrees with a specialization in psychiatry and a license to prescribe medications and drugs. In contrast, most counseling and clinical psychologists have advanced degrees in human behavior and methods of therapy (e.g., Ph.D. or Psy.D.). Many clinical and counseling psychologists also work as a team with psychiatrists.

Table 1.1 SAMPLE CAREERS AND SPECIALTIES IN PSYCHOLOGY

Biopsychology/neuroscience Candace Pert (and others) identified the body's natural painkillers called endorphins.

Biopsychology/ neuroscience	Investigates the relationship between biology, behavior, and mental processes, including how physical and chemical processes affect the structure and function of the brain and nervous system
Clinical psychology	Specializes in the evaluation, diagnosis, and treatment of psychological disorders
Cognitive psychology	Examines "higher" mental processes, including thought, memory, intelligence, creativity, and language
Comparative psychology	Studies the behavior and mental processes of nonhuman animals; emphasizes evolution and cross-species comparisons

(continued)

Table 1.1 *(Continued)*

Clinical and counseling psychology For most people, this is the role they most commonly associate with psychology.

Experimental psychology Louis Herman's research with dolphins has provided important insight into human and nonhuman behavior and mental process.

Psychologists often wear many hats Dan Bellack teaches full-time at Trident Technical College, serves as Department Chair, and also works with faculty on teaching improvement.

Counseling psychology	Overlaps with clinical psychology, but generally works with less seriously disturbed individuals and focuses more on social, educational and career adjustment
Cross-cultural psychology	Studies similarities and differences in and across various cultures and ethnic groups
Developmental psychology	Studies the course of human growth and development from conception to death
Educational and school psychology	Studies the process of education and works to promote the intellectual, social, and emotional development of children in the school environment
Environmental psychology	Investigates how people affect and are affected by the physical environment
Experimental psychology	Examines processes such as learning, conditioning, motivation, emotion, sensation, and perception in humans and other animals (Note that psychologists working in almost all areas of specialization also conduct experiments)
Forensic psychology	Applies principles of psychology to the legal system, including jury selection, psychological profiling, assessment, and treatment of offenders
Gender and/or cultural psychology	Investigates how men and women and different cultures differ from one another and how they are similar
Health psychology	Studies how biological, psychological, and social factors affect health and illness
Industrial/organizational psychology	Applies principles of psychology to the workplace, including personnel selection and evaluation, leadership, job satisfaction, employee motivation, and group processes within the organization
Personality psychology	Studies the unique and relatively stable patterns in a person's thoughts, feelings, and actions
Positive Psychology	Examines factors related to optimal human functioning
School psychology	Collaborates with teachers, parents, and students within the educational system to help children with academic, social, and disability needs; also provides evaluation and assessment of a student's functioning and eligibility for special services
Social psychology	Investigates the role of social forces in interpersonal behavior, including aggression, prejudice, love, helping, conformity, and attitudes
Sports psychology	Applies principles of psychology to enhance physical performance

To get an idea of the relative number of psychologists working in different fields of psychology, see Figure 1.2. If you are considering a career in psychology, you also may be wondering what you can do with a bachelors degree (see Figure 1.3). In addition, this text also will present a rich variety of career options that may interest you. For example, Chapter 2 looks at the world of neuroscience. After studying it, you may decide you would like a career as a neuroscientist/biopsychologist. Chapter 3 explores

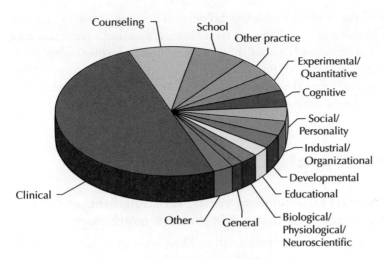

Counseling
School
Other practice
Experimental/Quantitative
Cognitive
Social/Personality
Industrial/Organizational
Developmental
Educational
Biological/Physiological/Neuroscientific
General
Other
Clinical

Figure 1.2 Percentage of psychology advanced degrees awarded by subfield This is a small sampling of the numerous specialty areas in psychology, and the percentages shown here are based on data from the American Psychological Association (APA), the largest professional psychological organization. The other major organization is the American Psychological Society (APS). Source: American Psychological Association, 2007.

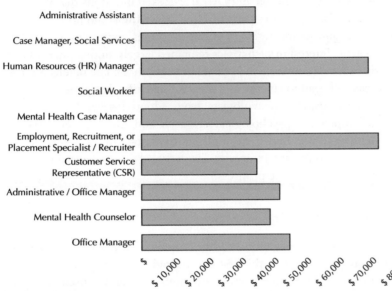

Administrative Assistant
Case Manager, Social Services
Human Resources (HR) Manager
Social Worker
Mental Health Case Manager
Employment, Recruitment, or Placement Specialist / Recruiter
Customer Service Representative (CSR)
Administrative / Office Manager
Mental Health Counselor
Office Manager

$ | $10,000 | $20,000 | $30,000 | $40,000 | $50,000 | $60,000 | $70,000 | $80,000

Figure 1.3 Ten most popular jobs for psychology majors This is a recent listing of the approximate pay for Bachelor's degree graduates without higher degrees. (Check out the complete methodology: www.payscale.com/best-colleges/salary -report.asp)

 **CHECK & REVIEW** STOP *Before going on, be sure to complete this Check & Review. It is an invaluable study tool!*

Introducing Psychology

Part A: Retrieval Practice

1. Without looking at the book, spend 10 minutes writing a free-form essay recalling all you can remember from the previous section.

2. Now, reread the previous section, and once again spend 10 minutes writing a free-form essay on the SAME material.

(Although time consuming, this exercise has been shown to be the single best way to improve your test scores! For more information, check out www.sciencemag.org/content/early/2011/01/19/science.1199327.abstract)

Part B: Practice Quiz

1. Identify the three key concepts in the definition of psychology.

2. Define critical thinking.

3. _____ rely on nonscientific or deliberately fraudulent methods to explain personality.
   a. Pseudopsychologies
   b. Sociologists
   c. Astronomers
   d. Counselors

4. Briefly explain the four goals of psychology.

5. You dread going to the grocery store because you got lost there when you were a child. This illustrates psychology's goal of _____ behavior.

6. The goal of _____ is to tell "what" occurred, whereas the goal of _____ is to tell "when."
   a. health psychologists; biological psychologists
   b. description; prediction
   c. psychologists; psychiatrists
   d. pseudopsychologists; clinical psychologists

7. Which of the specialties in Table 1.1 would you possibly choose for a career?

Check your answers in Appendix B.

health psychology and the work of health psychologists. Chapters 4 and 15 examine problems in mental health and how therapists treat them. If you find a particular area of interest, ask your instructor and campus career counselors for further career guidance. It's also a good idea to check out the American Psychological Association's (APA) home page (www.apa.org/) and the Association for Psychological Science's (APS) website (www.psychologicalscience.org).

Origins of Psychology

Objective 1.4: Contrast structuralism versus functionalism, and list the seven major perspectives that guide modern psychology.

Humans have always been interested in human nature. Most of the great historical scholars, from Socrates and Aristotle to Bacon and Descartes, asked questions that we would today call psychological. What motivates people? How do we think and problem solve? Where do our emotions and reason reside? Do our emotions control us, or are they something we can control? Interest in such topics remained largely among philosophers, theologians, and writers for several thousand years. However, in the late nineteenth century, psychological science began to emerge as a separate scientific discipline.

Throughout its short history, psychologists have adopted several perspectives on the "appropriate" topics for psychological research and the "proper" research methods. As a student, you may find these multiple (and sometimes contradictory) approaches frustrating and confusing. However, diversity and debate have always been the life blood of science and scientific progress.

Psychology's Past: A Brief History

Psychology's history as a science began in 1879 in Leipzig, Germany when Wilhelm Wundt (Vill-helm Voont) established the first psychological laboratory. Wundt and his followers were primarily interested in studying mental life and conscious experience—how we form sensations, images, and feelings. One of their earliest research methods was termed *introspection*, which means "looking inward" to monitor and report on the contents of consciousness (Baker, 2012; Goodwin, 2012). If you were one of Wundt's participants trained in introspection, you might be presented with the sound of a clicking metronome. You would be told to focus solely on the clicks and report only your immediate reactions to them—your basic sensations and feelings.

Structuralism

Edward Titchener, a student of Wundt's, brought his ideas to the United States and established a psychological laboratory at Cornell University. Titchener was a type of mental chemist who sought to identify the basic building blocks, or *structures*, of the mind. Titchener's approach later came to be known as *structuralism*, which dealt with the *structure* of mental life. Just as the elements hydrogen and oxygen combine to form the compound water, it was believed the "elements" of conscious experience combined to form the "compounds" of the mind. Structuralists sought to identify the elements of thought through introspection and then to determine how these elements combined to form the whole of experience.

Unfortunately, it soon became clear that structuralism was doomed to failure. When different observers introspected and then disagreed on their experiences, no scientific way existed to settle the dispute. Furthermore, introspection could not be used to study nonhuman animals, children, or complex topics like mental disorders or personality. Though short-lived, structuralism established a model for studying mental processes scientifically.

Functionalism

Structuralism's intellectual successor, *functionalism*, studied how the mind *functions* to adapt human and nonhuman animals to their environment. Earlier structuralists might have studied "anger" by asking people to introspect and report on their individual experiences. In comparison, functionalists would have asked, "Why do we have the emotion of anger? What function does it serve? How does it help us adapt to our environment?" As you can see, functionalism was strongly influenced by Darwin's *theory of evolution* and his emphasis on *natural selection* (Green, 2009).

William James, an American scholar, was a leading force in the functionalist school. He also broadened psychology to include nonhuman animal behavior, various biological processes, and behaviors. In the late 1870s, James established the first psychology laboratory in the United States, at Harvard University.

Like structuralism, functionalism eventually declined. But it expanded the scope of psychology to include research on emotions and observable behaviors, initiated the psychological testing movement, and changed the course of modern education and industry.

Psychoanalytic Approach

During the late 1800s and early 1900s, while functionalism was prominent in the United States, the **psychoanalytic approach** was forming in Europe. Its founder, Austrian physician Sigmund Freud, believed that a part of the human mind, the *unconscious*, contains thoughts, memories, and desires that lie outside of personal awareness, yet still exert great influence. According to Freud, a man who is cheating on his wife might slip up and say, "I wish you were her," when he consciously planned to say, "I wish you were here." These seemingly meaningless, so-called Freudian slips supposedly revealed a person's true, unconscious desires and conflicts. He also believed many psychological problems are caused by conflicts between "acceptable" behavior and "unacceptable," unconscious sexual or aggressive motives (Chapter 13). To deal with these unconscious conflicts, Freud developed a form of psychotherapy, or "talk therapy," called *psychoanalysis* (Chapter 14).

Modern Psychology: Seven Major Perspectives

As summarized in Table 1.2, contemporary psychology reflects seven major perspectives: *psychodynamic*, *behavioral*, *humanistic*, *cognitive*, *biological*, *evolutionary*, and *sociocultural*.

Although there are numerous differences between the seven modern perspectives in psychology, keep in mind that most psychologists recognize the value of each orientation and agree that no one view has all the answers.

Psychodynamic

Freud's nonscientific approach and emphasis on sexual and aggressive impulses have long been controversial, and today there are few strictly Freudian psychoanalysts left. But the broad features of his theory remain in the modern **psychodynamic perspective**.

Although psychodynamic psychologists are making increasing use of experimental methods, their primary method is the analysis of case studies. Their general goal is to explore unconscious *dynamics*, internal motives, conflicts, and childhood experiences.

William James (1842–1910) James, an influential American scholar and leader of the functionalist school, wrote, *Principles of Psychology*, which became a leading text that took 12 years to write and was over 1300 pages in length!

Psychoanalytic Approach Focuses on unconscious processes and unresolved conflicts

Sigmund Freud (1856–1939) Freud founded the psychoanalytic perspective, an influential theory of personality, and a type of therapy known as psychoanalysis.

Psychodynamic Perspective Focuses on unconscious dynamics, internal motives, conflicts, and childhood experiences

StudyTip

Illustrations

Do not skip over photos, figures, and tables. They visually reinforce important concepts and often contain material that may appear on exams.

Table 1.2 MODERN PSYCHOLOGY'S SEVEN MAJOR PERSPECTIVES

	Perspectives	Major Emphases
	Psychodynamic	Unconscious drives, motives, conflicts, and childhood experiences
	Behavioral	Objective, observable, environmental influences on overt behavior
	Humanistic	Free will, self-actualization, and human nature as naturally positive and growth-seeking
	Cognitive	Thinking, perceiving, problem solving, memory, language, and information processing
	Biological	Genetics and biological processes in the brain and other parts of the nervous system
	Evolutionary	Natural selection, adaptation, and evolution of behavior and mental processes
	Sociocultural	Social interaction and the cultural determinants of behavior and mental processes

TEST YOURSELF

Research has shown that some nonhuman animals, such as newly hatched ducks or geese, follow and become attached to (or imprinted on) the first large moving object they see or hear. Konrad Lorenz, an influential figure in early psychology, hatched these geese in an incubator. Because he was the first large moving object they saw at birth, they now closely follow him everywhere—as if he were their mother. When Lorenz was asleep on the ground with his mouth open, a goose even tried to feed him a live worm.

Using the information in Table 1.2, can you identify which perspective of psychology would most likely study and explain these behaviors?

Answer: Evolutionary

Behavioral

Behavioral Perspective Emphasizes objective, observable environmental influences on overt behavior

In the early 1900s, another major school of thought appeared that dramatically shaped the course of psychology. Unlike earlier approaches, the **behavioral perspective** emphasizes objective, observable environmental influences on overt behavior.

John B. Watson (1913), the acknowledged founder of behaviorism, rejected the earlier emphasis on introspection and the influence of unconscious forces. He believed these practices and topics were unscientific and too obscure to be studied empirically. Watson adopted Russian physiologist Ivan Pavlov's concept of conditioning to explain how behavior results from observable *stimuli* (in the environment) and observable *responses* (behavioral actions). In Pavlov's famous experiment teaching a dog to salivate in response to the sound of a bell, the bell is the stimulus and the salivation is the response (Chapter 6).

Because nonhuman animals are ideal subjects for studying objective, overt behaviors, the majority of early behavior research was done with dogs, rats, pigeons, and other nonhuman animals. However, one of the most well-known behaviorists, B. F. Skinner, was convinced that we could (and should) use behavior approaches to actually "shape" human behavior. This shaping could thereby change the present negative course (as he perceived it) of humankind. Modern behaviorists have been most successful in treating people with overt (observable, behavioral) problems, such as phobias (irrational fears) and alcoholism (Chapters 14 and 15) (Miltenberger, 2011; Watson & Tharp, 2007).

Humanistic

In sharp contrast to psychoanalysts and behaviorists who saw human behavior as shaped and determined by external causes beyond personal control, the **humanistic perspective** stresses *free will*, self-actualization, and human nature as naturally positive and growth seeking. According to Carl Rogers and Abraham Maslow, two central figures in the development of humanism, all individuals naturally strive to grow, develop, and move toward *self-actualization* (a state of self-fulfillment in which we realize our highest potential). They are called "humanistic" because unlike other animals we create personal belief systems about ourselves and our world, and then govern our lives in accordance with these stories.

Many psychologists have criticized the humanistic approach for its lack of rigorous experimental methods and consider it more of a philosophy of life than a major perspective in scientific psychology. However, humanism, like psychoanalysis and behaviorism, has had an important influence on personality theories and psychotherapy (see Chapters 13 and 15).

In addition, the humanistic approach provides the foundation for a contemporary research specialty known as **positive psychology**—the scientific study of optimal human functioning (Cornum, Matthews, & Seligman, 2011; Diener, 2008; Seligman, 2003, 2007, 2011; Taylor & Sherman, 2008). For many years, psychology *understandably* focused on negative states, such as aggression, depression, and prejudice. In recent years, leaders in the positive psychology movement, such as Ed Diener, Martin Seligman, and Shelly Taylor, have pushed for a broader study of human experiences, with an emphasis on: (1) *positive emotions* (like hope, love, and happiness), (2) *positive traits* (such as altruism, courage, and compassion), and (3) *positive institutions* that help promote better lives (such as improved schools and healthier families) (Seligman, 2003). Thanks to its scientific methodology and broader focus on optimal functioning, *positive psychology* has provided a wealth of new research found throughout this text.

Cognitive

One of the most influential modern approaches, the **cognitive perspective**, recalls psychology's earliest days in that it emphasizes thinking, perceiving, and information processing (Kellogg, 2011; Sternberg, 2012).

B. F. Skinner (1904–1990) Skinner developed the so-called "Skinner box" to investigate behavior. Here he uses the box to train a rat to press a lever for a reward.

Humanistic Perspective Emphasizes free will, self-actualization, and human nature as naturally positive and growth-seeking

Positive Psychology Scientific study of optimal human functioning, emphasizing positive emotions, positive traits, and positive institutions

Cognitive Perspective Focuses on thinking, perceiving, and information processing

StudyTip

Throughout this text, you will see citations (authors' names and publication dates) at the end of many sentences, such as (Goodwin, 2012). Most instructors rarely expect you to memorize the names and dates in parentheses. They are provided as a starting point for research projects, for additional information on a topic of interest, and to double-check the research sources. Complete publication information (title of article or chapter, author, journal name or book title, date, and page numbers) is provided in the References section at the back of this book.

Biological Perspective Emphasizes genetics and biological processes in the brain and other parts of the nervous system

Evolutionary Perspective Focuses on natural selection, adaptation, and evolution of behavior and mental processes

Psychology in a global economy
Technological advances allow instant communication for people who not long ago were isolated from events in the rest of the world. How do you think these changes affect these men from Enaotai Island in West Papua New Guinea?

Sociocultural Perspective Emphasizes social interaction and cultural determinants of behavior and mental processes

Modern-day cognitive psychologists, however, study how we gather, encode, and store information from our environment using a vast array of mental processes. These processes include thinking, perception, memory, language, and problem solving. If you were listening to a friend describe her whitewater rafting trip, a cognitive psychologist would be interested in how you decipher the meaning of her words, how you form mental images of the turbulent water, how you incorporate your impressions of her experience into your previous concepts and experience of rafting, and so on.

Many cognitive psychologists also use an *information-processing* approach, likening the mind to a computer that sequentially takes in information, processes it, and then produces a response.

Biological

During the last few decades, scientists have explored the role of biological factors in almost every area of psychology, including sensation, perception, learning, memory, language, sexuality, and abnormal behavior. This exploration has given rise to an increasingly important trend in psychology, known as the **biological perspective**.

As you will see in the upcoming discussion of psychological research in this chapter, biopsychologists have developed sophisticated "tools" and technologies to conduct their research. They use these tools to study the structure and function of individual nerve cells, the roles of various parts of the brain, and how genetics and other biological processes contribute to our behavior and mental processes.

Evolutionary

The **evolutionary perspective** derives from a focus on natural selection, adaptation, and evolution of behavior and mental processes (Buss, 2011; Confer, 2010; Swami, 2011). Its proponents argue that natural selection favors inherited traits that contribute to reproduction and survival. That is, human and nonhuman animals possessing genetic traits that contribute to reproduction or survival will pass them on through their genes to the next generation.

Consider aggression. Behaviorists would argue that we learn aggressiveness at an early age. "Hitting another child stops him or her from taking your toys." Cognitive psychologists would emphasize how thoughts contribute to aggression. "He intended to hurt me. Therefore, I should hit him back!" Biopsychologists might say aggressiveness results primarily from neurotransmitters, hormones, and structures in the brain. In comparison, evolutionary psychologists would argue that human and nonhuman animals behave aggressively because aggression conveys a survival or reproductive advantage. They believe aggression evolved over many generations because it successfully met the adaptive pressures faced by our ancestors.

Sociocultural

The **sociocultural perspective** emphasizes social interactions and cultural determinants of behavior and mental processes. Sociocultural psychologists have shown how factors such as ethnicity, religion, occupation, and socioeconomic class all have an enormous psychological impact (Berry et al., 2011; Gergen, 2010).

Unless someone points it out, however, few of us recognize the importance of these factors. As Segall and his colleagues (1990) suggest, when you go to school, you probably walk into a classroom at the same time on the same days, sit in the same chair, and either listen to a trained teacher or participate in an activity designed and directed by that teacher. This is because it is the schooling system of your social world and culture. In another society or culture, such as a remote region of East Africa, you and your friends might gather informally around a respected elder, some of you sitting and others standing, all of you listening to the elder tell stories of the history of the tribe.

As they say, "a fish doesn't know it is in water," and, similarly, most of us are unaware of the social and cultural forces that shape our lives. This is one of many reasons why we include such heavy coverage of sociocultural psychology throughout this text.

Women and Minorities

During the late 1800s and early 1900s, most colleges and universities provided little opportunity for women and minorities, as either students or faculty. Despite these early limitations, both women and minorities made important contributions to psychology.

For example, Mary Calkins conducted valuable research on memory, and in 1905 served as the first female president of the American Psychological Association (APA). Her achievements are particularly noteworthy, considering the significant discrimination against women in those times. Even after completing all the requirements for a Ph.D. at Harvard, and being described by William James as his brightest student, the university refused to grant the degree to a woman. The first woman to receive a Ph.D. in psychology was Margaret Floy Washburn (in 1894), who wrote several influential books and served as the second female president of APA.

Francis Cecil Sumner, without benefit of a formal high school education, became the first African American to earn a Ph.D. in psychology from Clark University in 1920. He also translated over 3000 articles from German, French, and Spanish and founded one of the country's leading psychology departments at Howard University. In 1971, one of Sumner's students, Kenneth B. Clark, became the first African American to be elected APA president. Clark's research with his wife, Mamie Clark, documented the harmful effects of prejudice and directly influenced the Supreme Court's ultimate ruling against racial segregation in schools.

Today, minorities and women are more actively encouraged to pursue graduate degrees in psychology. But as you can see in Figure 1.4, white (non-Hispanic) people still make up the majority of new doctorate recipients in psychology.

Biopsychosocial Model

Objective 1.5: Describe the biopsychosocial model.

One of the most widely accepted, and unifying, themes of modern psychology is the **biopsychosocial model**. This approach views *biological* processes (genetics, brain functions, neurotransmitters, evolution), *psychological* factors (learning, thinking, emotion, personality, motivation), and *social forces* (family, culture, ethnicity, social class, politics) as interrelated influences that interact with the previously described seven major perspectives (Figure 1.5).

This new, integrative model proposes that all three forces *affect* and *are affected by* one another. They are inseparable. For example, feelings of depression are often influenced by genetics and neurotransmitters (biology). They are also affected by our learned responses and patterns of thinking (psychology) and by our socioeconomic status and cultural views of emotion (social).

Biopsychosocial Model Unifying theme of modern psychology that incorporates biological, psychological, and social processes

Kenneth Clark (1914–2005) and Mamie Clark (1917–1985) Kenneth Clark was the first African American president of the American Psychological Association. He and his wife, Mamie, also conducted research on prejudice that was cited in 1964 by the U.S. Supreme Court.

African American 4%

Asian and Pacific Islander 4%

American Indian 1%

Hispanic (Latino) 6%

White (non-Hispanic) 85%

Figure 1.4 Ethnicities of doctorate recipients in psychology

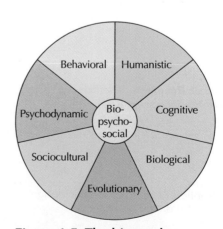

Behavioral
Humanistic
Psychodynamic
Bio-psycho-social
Cognitive
Sociocultural
Biological
Evolutionary

Figure 1.5 The biopsychosocial model combines and interacts with the seven major perspectives

TRY THIS YOURSELF

Why do we need multiple and competing perspectives?

What do you see in the drawing to the right? Do you see two profiles facing each other or a white vase? Your ability to see both figures is similar to a psychologist's ability to study behavior and mental processes from a number of different perspectives.

CHECK & REVIEW

STOP *Before going on, be sure to complete this Check & Review. It is an invaluable study tool!*

Origins of Psychology

Part A: Retrieval Practice

1. Without looking at the book, spend 10 minutes writing a free-form essay recalling all you can remember from the previous section.

2. Now, reread the previous section, and once again spend 10 minutes writing a free-form essay on the SAME material.

Part B: Practice Quiz

1. The _____ school of psychology sought to identify the basic building blocks of the mind.

2. _____ investigated the function of mental processes in adapting to the environment.

3. Why are Freudian slips considered important to psychoanalysts?

4. Which of the following terms do not belong together? (a) structuralism, observable behavior; (b) behaviorism, stimulus-response; (c) psychoanalytic, unconscious conflict; (d) humanism, free will.

5. What is the biopsychosocial model?

Check your answers in Appendix B

Science of Psychology

Objective 1.6: Differentiate between basic and applied research, and list the six steps of the scientific method.

Basic Research Research conducted to advance scientific knowledge

Applied Research Research designed to solve practical problems

In science, research strategies are generally categorized as either *basic* or *applied*. **Basic research** is typically conducted in universities or research laboratories by researchers interested in advancing general scientific understanding—knowledge for its own sake without known real-world uses. Discoveries linking aggression to testosterone, genes, learning, and other factors came primarily from basic research. Basic research meets the first three goals of psychology (*description*, *explanation*, and *prediction*).

In contrast, **applied research** is generally conducted outside the laboratory, and it meets the fourth goal of psychology—to *change* existing real-world problems. Applied research has designed programs for conflict resolution and counseling for perpetrators and victims of violence. It also has generated important safety and design improvements in automobiles, airplanes, stovetop burner arrangements, and even cell phones and computer key pads (Figure 1.6).

(a) Spatial correspondence Controls for stovetops should be arranged in a pattern that corresponds to the placement of the burners.

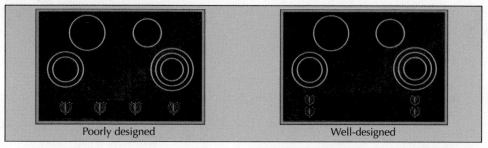

Poorly designed   Well-designed

(b) Visibility Automobile gauges for fuel, temperature, and speed should be easily visible to the driver.

(c) Arrangement of numbers A top-down arrangement of numbers on a cell phone is more efficient than the bottom-up arrangement on a computer's key board.

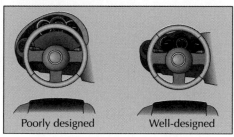

Poorly designed   Well-designed

Figure 1.6 Applied research in psychology Note how psychological research has helped design safer and more reliable appliances, machinery, and instrument controls (*Psychology Matters*, 2006).

Replication Repeating a research study, using different procedures or participants in varied settings, to check the confidence in prior findings

Meta-Analysis Statistical procedure for combining and analyzing data from many studies

Theory Systematic, interrelated set of concepts that explain a body of data

Basic and applied research also frequently interact—one leading to or building on the other. For example, after basic research documented a strong relationship between alcohol consumption and increased aggression, applied research led some sports stadium operators to limit the sale of alcohol during the final quarter of football games and the last two innings of baseball games.

Now that you understand the distinction between basic and applied research, we can explore two core topics in psychological research: the scientific method and research ethics.

Scientific Method: A Way of Discovering

Like scientists in any other scientific field, psychologists follow strict, standardized scientific procedures so that others can understand, interpret, and repeat or test their findings. Most scientific investigations generally involve six basic steps (Step-by-Step Diagram 1.1). As you can see in this diagram, the *scientific method* is cyclical and cumulative, and scientific progress comes from repeatedly challenging and revising existing theories and building new ones. If numerous scientists, using different procedures or participants in varied settings, can repeat, or **replicate**, a study's findings, there is increased scientific confidence in the results. However, if the findings cannot be replicated, researchers look for other explanations and conduct further studies. When different studies report contradictory findings, researchers may average or combine the results of all such studies and reach conclusions about the overall weight of the evidence. This popular statistical technique is known as **meta-analysis.**

One additional important point. Many people misuse the term "theory" to suggest it's only a "mere hunch" or someone's personal opinion. In science, **theory** is based on a systematic, interrelated set of concepts that explain a body of data. Although all scientific theories are tentative and subject to continual revision, they are far more than casual everyday hunches. They are the heart of the scientific method and virtually all scientific advances.

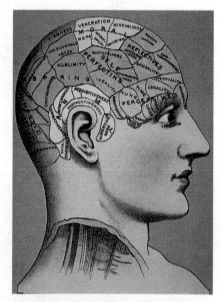

Theories gone wild! In the 1800s, many believed in *phrenology*, a theory that personality could be "read" from bumps on the skull. Thanks to the self-correcting nature of scientific research, this theory was later discredited.

Step-by-StepDiagram1.1

Scientific Method

Cycle begins

Cycle continues

Step 1
Question and literature review
After identifying a question of interest, the psychological scientist conducts a *literature review*, reading what has been previously published in major professional, scientific journals.

Step 2
Testable hypothesis
The scientist develops a *testable hypothesis*, or a specific prediction about how one factor, or *variable*, is related to another. To be scientifically testable, the variables must be **operationally defined**—that is, stated precisely and in *measurable* terms.

Step 3
Research design
To test the hypothesis the scientist then chooses the best research design (e.g., experimental descriptive correlational, or biological).

Step 4
Data collection and analysis
The data are collected and *statistical analyses* are performed to determine whether or not the findings are **statistically significant**, and if the original hypothesis should be supported or rejected.

Step 5
Publication
The scientist writes up the study and its results and submits it to a *peer-reviewed scientific journal*, which asks other scientists to critically evaluate the research. On the basis of these peer reviews, the study may then be accepted for publication.

Step 6
Theory development
After publication of one or more studies on a topic, researchers may propose a new *theory* or a revision of an existing *theory* to explain the results. This information then leads to new (possibly different) hypotheses and additional methods of inquiry.

StudyTip

The ongoing, circular nature of theory building often frustrates students. In most chapters you will encounter numerous and sometimes conflicting scientific theories, and you'll be tempted to ask.: Which theory is right?" But, like most aspects of behavior, the "correct" answer is usually an interaction. In most cases, multiple theories contribute to the full understanding of complex concepts.

StudyTip

Statistics play a vital role in the scientific method. (see Appendix A at the back of this book).

Authors   Year study published   Title of study

Cehajic, S., Brown, R., & Castano, E. (2008). Forgive and forget? Antecedents and consequences of intergroup forgiveness in Bosnia and Herzegovina. *Political Psychology, 29*, 351–367.

Title of journal   Volume number   Page numbers

Checking references As a critical thinker, do you wonder where psychologists and other scientists publish their findings? Do you question the information found in this and your other college texts? If so, go to the References section at the back of this book and you'll find specific, detailed accounting for each citation throughout this text.

Hypothesis Specific, testable prediction about how one factor, or variable, is related to another

Operational Definition Precise description of how the variables in a study will be observed and measured (For example, drug abuse might be operationally defined as "the number of missed work days due to excessive use of an addictive substance.")

Statistical Significance Statistical statement of how likely it is that a study's result occurred merely by chance

Ethical Guidelines: Protecting the Rights of Others

Objective 1.7: What are the three key areas of ethical concern in psychological research and therapy?

The two largest professional organizations of psychologists, the Association for Psychological Science (APS) and the American Psychological Association (APA), both recognize the importance of maintaining high ethical standards in research, therapy, and all other areas of professional psychology. The preamble and amendments to the APA's publication *Ethical Principles of Psychologists and Code of Conduct* (2002, 2010) admonishes psychologists to respect and promote civil and human rights. It also requires them to maintain their competence and to preserve the dignity and best interests of their clients, colleagues, students, research participants, and society. In this section, we will explore three important areas of ethical concern: human participants, nonhuman animal rights, and clients in therapy.

Respecting the Rights of Human Participants

The APA has developed rigorous guidelines regulating research with human participants, including:

- *Informed consent* One of the first research principles is obtaining an **informed consent** from all participants before initiating an experiment. Participants should be aware of the nature of the study and significant factors that might influence their willingness to participate. This includes all physical risks, discomfort, or unpleasant emotional experiences.

- *Voluntary participation* Participants should be told they are free to decline to participate or to withdraw from the research at any time.

- *Restricted use of deception and debriefing* If participants know the true purpose behind certain studies, they may not respond naturally. Therefore, researchers sometimes need to *deceive* participants as to the actual design and reason for the research. But when deception is used, important guidelines and restrictions apply, including debriefing participants at the end of the experiment. **Debriefing** involves explaining the reasons for conducting the research and clearing up any participant's misconceptions, questions, or concerns.

- *Confidentiality* All information acquired about people during a study must be kept private and not published in such a way that individual rights to privacy are compromised.

- *Alternative activities* If research participation is a course requirement or an opportunity for extra credit for college students, all students must be given the choice of an alternative activity of equal value.

Informed Consent Participant's agreement to take part in a study after being told what to expect

Debriefing Upon completion of the research, participants are informed of the study's design and purpose, and explanations are provided for any possible deception

Respecting the Rights of Nonhuman Animal Participants

Research in psychology usually involves human participants. Only about 7 to 8 percent of research is done on nonhuman animals, and 90 percent of that is done with rodents and birds (mostly rats and mice). Only 5 percent are monkeys and primates (APA, 2009; ILAR, 2009; MORI, 2005, 1999).

There are important reasons for using nonhuman animals in psychological research. For example, the field of *comparative psychology* is dedicated to the study of behavior of different species. In other cases, nonhuman animals are used because researchers need to study participants continuously over months or years (longer than people are willing to participate). Occasionally, they also want to control aspects of life that people will not let them control and that would be unethical to control (such as who mates

Is nonhuman animal research ethical?
Opinions are sharply divided on this question, but ethical guidelines help offset the criticism, and the findings can yield significant benefits for both human and nonhuman animals.

with whom or the effects of serious food restrictions). The relative simplicity of some nonhuman animals' nervous systems also provides important advantages for research.

Most psychologists recognize the tremendous scientific contributions that laboratory nonhuman animals have made—and continue to make. Without nonhuman animals in *medical research*, how would we test new drugs, surgical procedures, and methods for relieving pain? *Psychological research* with nonhuman animals has led to significant advances in virtually every area of psychology, including the brain and nervous system, health and stress, sensation and perception, sleep, learning, memory, stress, emotion, and so on.

Nonhuman animal research also has produced significant gains for animals themselves. Effective training techniques and natural environments have been created for pets and wild animals in captivity. Also, successful breeding techniques have been developed for endangered species. Despite the advantages, using nonhuman animals in psychological research remains controversial (Guidelines for Ethical Conduct, 2008).

While debate continues over ethical questions surrounding such research, psychologists take great care in the handling of nonhuman research animals. They also actively search for new and better ways to protect them (Appiah, 2008; Guidelines for Ethical Conduct, 2008). In all institutions where nonhuman animal research is conducted, animal care committees are established to ensure proper treatment of research animals, to review projects, and to set guidelines that are in accordance with the APA standards for the care and treatment of nonhuman (and human) research animals.

Respecting the Rights of Psychotherapy Clients

Like psychological scientists, therapists must maintain the highest of ethical standards. They also must uphold their clients' trust. All personal information and therapy records must be kept confidential, with records being available only to authorized persons and with the client's permission. However, the public's right to safety ethically outweighs the client's right to privacy. Therapists are legally required to break confidentiality if a client threatens violence to him- or herself or to others. This breaking of confidentiality also applies if a client is suspected of abusing a child or an elderly person, and in other limited situations. In general, however, a counselor's primary obligation is to protect client disclosures (Campbell et al., 2010; Tyson & Jones, 2011).

Any member of the APA who disregards the association's principles for the ethical treatment of humans or nonhuman research participants or therapy clients may be censured or expelled from the organization. Clinicians who violate the ethical guidelines for working with clients risk severe sanctions and can permanently lose their licenses to practice. In addition, both researchers and clinicians are held professionally and legally responsible by their institutions as well as by local and state agencies.

A Final Note on Ethical Issues

What about ethics and beginning psychology students? Once friends and acquaintances know you're taking a course in psychology, they may ask you to interpret their dreams, help them discipline their children, or even ask your opinion on whether they should end their relationships. Although you will learn a great deal about psychological functioning in this text and in your psychology class, take care that you do not overestimate your expertise. Remember that the theories and findings of psychological science are circular and cumulative—and continually being revised.

David L. Cole (1982), a recipient of the APA Distinguished Teaching in Psychology Award, reminds us that "Undergraduate psychology can, and I believe should, seek to

CHECK & REVIEW

STOP *Before going on, be sure to complete this Check & Review. It is an invaluable study tool!*

Science of Psychology

Part A: Retrieval Practice

1. Without looking at the book, spend 10 minutes writing a free-form essay recalling all you can remember from the previous section.

2. Now, reread the previous section, and once again spend 10 minutes writing a free-form essay on the SAME material.

Part B: Practice Quiz

1. If you conducted a study on areas of the brain most affected by drinking alcohol, it would be called _____ research. (a) unethical; (b) experimental; (c) basic; (d) applied

2. A cardinal rule of a scientific _____ is that it must make testable predictions about observable behavior.

3. A precise definition of how the variables in a study will be observed and measured is called _____. (a) a meta-analysis; (b) a theory; (c) an independent observation; (d) an operational definition

4. A participant's agreement to take part in a study after being told what to expect is known as _____.

5. Briefly explain the importance of informed consent, deception, and debriefing in scientific research.

6. Label the six steps in the scientific method.

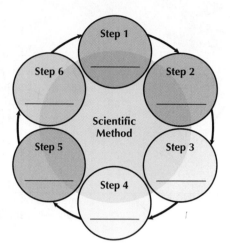

Check your answers in Appendix B.

---

liberate the student from ignorance, but also the arrogance of believing we know more about ourselves and others than we really do."

At the same time, psychological findings and ideas developed through careful research and study can make important contributions to our lives. As Albert Einstein once said, "One thing I have learned in a long life: that all our science, measured against reality, is primitive and childlike—and yet, it is the most precious thing we have."

Research Methods

What is research, but a blind date with knowledge.
WILLIAM HENRY

Now that you have a good basic understanding of the scientific method, we can examine four major types of psychological research—*experimental, descriptive, correlational,* and *biological*. As Table 1.3 shows, all four research methods have advantages and disadvantages, and most psychologists use several methods to study a single problem. In fact, when multiple methods are used and lead to similar conclusions, scientists have an especially strong foundation for concluding that one variable does affect another in a particular way.

Experimental Research: A Search for Cause and Effect

Objective 1.8: Explain how experiments help researchers determine cause and effect.

Experimental research is the most powerful research method because it allows experimenters to manipulate, isolate, and control chosen variables, and thereby determine *cause and effect*. Only through an experiment can researchers isolate a single factor and examine the effect of that factor alone on a particular behavior. For example, in studying for an

Experimental Research Carefully controlled scientific procedure that involves manipulation of variables to determine cause and effect

Table 1.3 COMPARING THE FOUR MAJOR RESEARCH METHODS*

	Method	Purpose	Advantages	Disadvantages
	Experimental (manipulation and control of variables)	Identify cause and effect (meets psychology's goal of *explanation*)	Allows researchers precise control over variables, helps identify cause and effect	Ethical concerns, practical limitations, artificiality of lab conditions, uncontrolled variables may confound results, researcher and participant biases
	Descriptive (naturalistic observation, surveys, case studies)	Observe, collect, and record data (meets psychology's goal of *description*)	Minimizes artificiality, easier data collection, and allows description of behavior and mental processes as they occur	Little or no control over variables, researcher and participant biases, and cannot identify cause and effect
	Correlational (statistical analyses of relationships between variables)	Identify relationships and assess how well one variable predicts another (meets psychology's goal of *prediction*)	Helps clarify relationships between variables, which cannot be examined by other methods, and allows prediction	No control over variables, cannot identify cause and effect
	Biological (studies the brain and other parts of the nervous system)	Identify contributing biological factors (meets one or more of psychology's goals)	Shares many or all of the advantages of experimental, descriptive, and correlational research	Shares many or all of the disadvantage of experimental, descriptive, and correlational research

*Note that the four methods are not mutually exclusive. Researchers may use two or more methods to explore the same topic.

upcoming test, you probably use several methods—reading lecture notes, rereading highlighted sections of your textbook, and repeating key terms with their definitions. Using multiple methods, however, makes it impossible to determine which study methods are effective or ineffective. The only way to discover which method is most effective is to isolate each one in an *experiment*. In fact, several experiments have been conducted to determine effective learning and study techniques (Rohrer & Pashler, 2010; Son & Metcalfe, 2000). If you are interested in the results of this research or want to develop better study habits, you can jump ahead to the "Tools for Student Success" at the end of this chapter. Valuable "Study Tips" also are identified throughout the text with this icon 🐧 StudyTip

Key Features of an Experiment

An experiment has several key components: *experimental* versus *control groups* and *independent* versus *dependent variables* (see Step-by-Step Diagram 1.2).

Experimental Safeguards

Objective 1.9: Compare and contrast experimental versus control groups and independent variables (IVs) versus dependent variables (DVs).

Every experiment is designed to answer essentially the same question: Does the independent variable (IV) *cause* the predicted change in the dependent variable (DV)?

Step-by-StepDiagram1.2

STOP *This Step by Step diagram contains essential information NOT found elsewhere in the text, which is likely to appear on quizzes and exams. Be sure to study it CAREFULLY!*

Key Features of an Experiment

Imagine yourself as a psychologist interested in determining how watching violence on television affects aggressiveness in viewers. After reviewing the literature and developing your hypothesis (Steps 1 and 2 of the scientific method), you decide to use an experiment for your research design (Step 3). (See Step-by-Step 1.1, p. 18, for a full review of the scientific method.)

Experimental Versus Control Groups

Using a very simple experiment, you begin by *randomly* assigning research participants to one of two groups: the **experimental group**, who watch a prearranged number of violent television programs, and the **control group**, who watch the same amount of television, except the programs they watch are neutral. (Having at least two groups allows the performance of one group to be compared with that of another.)

Independent and Dependent Variables

Next, you arrange the factors, or *variables*, you will control and

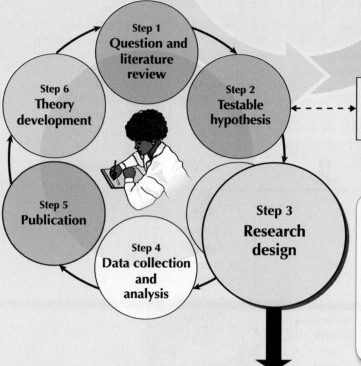

Step 1
Question and literature review

Step 2
Testable hypothesis

Step 6
Theory development

Step 5
Publication

Step 4
Data collection and analysis

Step 3
Research design

Hypothesis
"Watching violence on TV increases aggression."

StudyTip

If this were a real experiment, we would operationally define the type and amount of violent TV and what is meant by "aggression." In this example, aggression is the number of times the child hits the "Bobo" doll.

manipulate, which are called **independent variables (IV),** as well as the variables you plan to measure and examine for possible change, known as **dependent variables (DV)**. [Note: The goal of any experiment is to learn how the dependent variable is *affected by* (depends on) the independent variable.]

Then, the experimenter (you) would randomly assign children to watch either violent or neutral TV programs—the *independent variable (IV)*.

Note also that in experiments, all extraneous variables (such as time of day, lighting conditions, and participants' age and sex) must be held constant across experimental and control groups so that they are exactly the same between the two groups. This ensures these **confounding variables** do not affect the groups' results.

StudyTip

Because the IV is independent and freely selected and varied by the experimenter, it is called independent. The DV is called dependent because the behavior (or outcome) exhibited by the participants is assumed to depend, on manipulations of the IV.

Experimental Group Group that receives a treatment in an experiment

Control Group Group that receives no treatment in an experiment

Independent Variable (IV) Variable that is manipulated to determine its causal effect on the dependent variable

Dependent Variable (DV) Variable that is measured; it is affected by (or dependent on) the independent variable

Confounding Variables Nuisance variables that may affect the outcome of the study and lead to erroneous conclusions

Step-by-StepDiagram1.2

STOP This Step by Step diagram contains essential information NOT found elsewhere in the text, which is likely to appear on quizzes and exams. Be sure to study it CAREFULLY!

(continued)

After all children watch either violent or neutral programs, you then place a large plastic, "Bobo," doll in front of each child and record for one hour the number of times the child hits, kicks, or punches the plastic doll—the *dependent variable* (DV).

[Note: Experiments also can have different *levels* of an independent variable (IV). In the TV violence example, two experimental groups could be created, with one group watching three hours of violent TV programs and the other watching six hours. The control group would watch only neutral programs. Then a researcher could relate differences in aggressive behavior (DV) to the *amount* (or level) of violent programming viewed (IV).]

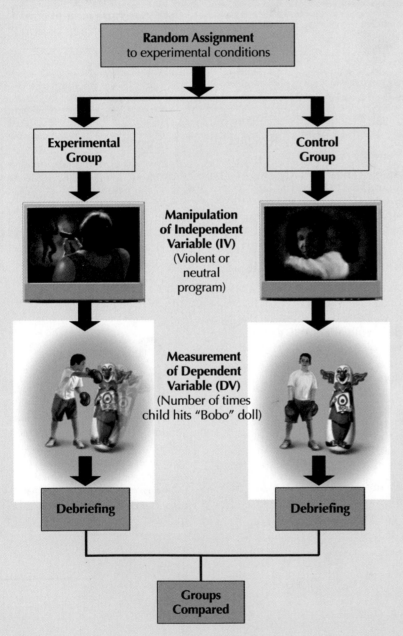

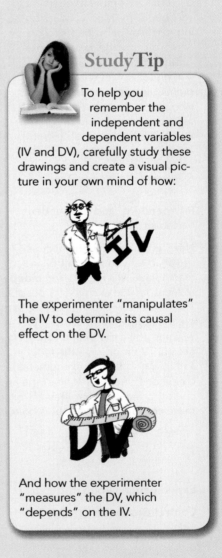

StudyTip

To help you remember the independent and dependent variables (IV and DV), carefully study these drawings and create a visual picture in your own mind of how:

The experimenter "manipulates" the IV to determine its causal effect on the DV.

And how the experimenter "measures" the DV, which "depends" on the IV.

To answer this question, the experimenter must establish several safeguards. In addition to the previously mentioned controls within the experiment itself (e.g., operational definitions, a control group, and holding extraneous variables constant), a good scientific experiment also protects against potential sources of error from both the researcher and the participant. As we discuss these potential problems (and their possible solutions), you may want to refer several times to the summary in Figure 1.7.

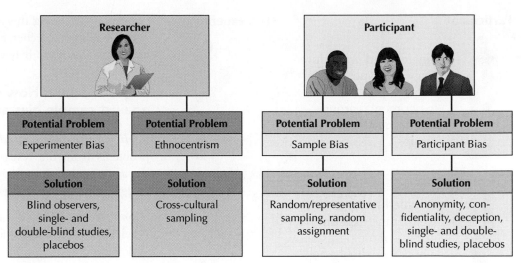

Researcher		**Participant**	
Potential Problem Experimenter Bias	**Potential Problem** Ethnocentrism	**Potential Problem** Sample Bias	**Potential Problem** Participant Bias
Solution Blind observers, single- and double-blind studies, placebos	**Solution** Cross-cultural sampling	**Solution** Random/representative sampling, random assignment	**Solution** Anonymity, confidentiality, deception, single- and double-blind studies, placebos

Figure 1.7 Potential research problems and solutions

Researcher Problems and Solutions

Objective 1.10: How do researchers guard against experimenter bias and ethnocentrism?

Researchers must guard against two particular problems—*experimenter bias* and *ethnocentrism*.

- *Experimenter bias* Experimenters, like everyone else, have their own personal beliefs and expectations. The danger in research, however, is that **experimenter bias** may produce flawed results.

Consider the case of Clever Hans, the famous mathematical "wonder horse" (Rosenthal, 1965) (Figure 1.8). When asked to multiply 6 times 8, minus 42, Hans would tap his hoof 6 times. Or if asked to divide 48 by 12, add 6, and take away 6, he would tap 4 times. Even when Hans's owner was out of the room and others asked the question, he was still able to answer correctly. How did he do it? Researchers eventually discovered that all questioners naturally lowered their heads to look at Hans's hoof at the end of their question. And Hans had learned that this was a signal to start tapping. When the correct answer was approaching, the questioners also naturally looked up, which in turn signaled Hans to stop.

Just as Hans's questioners unintentionally signaled the correct answer by lowering or raising their heads, an experimenter might breathe a sigh of relief when a participant gives a response that supports the researcher's hypothesis.

You can see how experimenter bias might destroy the validity of the participant's response. But how can we prevent it? One technique is to set up objective methods for collecting and recording data, such as audiotape recordings to present the stimuli and computers to record the responses. Another option is to use "blind observers" (neutral people other than the researcher) to collect and record the data without knowing what the researcher has predicted. In addition, researchers can arrange a **single-blind study**, in which the researcher knows who is in the experimental and the control groups, but the participants do not. They also can set up a **double-blind study**, in which *neither* the observer nor the participant knows which group received the experimental treatment (Figure 1.9).

- *Ethnocentrism* When we assume that behaviors typical in our culture are typical in all cultures, we are committing a bias known as **ethnocentrism**. (*Ethno* refers to *ethnicity*, and *centrism* comes from *center*.) One way to avoid this problem is to have two researchers, one from one culture and one from another, conduct the same research study two times, once in their own culture and once in at least one other

Figure 1.8 Can a horse add, multiply, and divide? Clever Hans and his owner, Mr. Von Osten, convinced many people that this was indeed the case. Can you see how this provided an early example of experimenter bias? See the text for an explanation.

Experimenter Bias Occurs when researcher influences research results in the expected direction

Single-Blind Study Only the researcher, and not the participants, knows who is in either the experimental or control group

Double-Blind Study Both the researcher and the participants are unaware (blind) of who is in the experimental or control group

Ethnocentrism Believing one's culture is typical of all cultures; also, viewing one's own ethnic group (or culture) as central and "correct" and judging others according to this standard

Participant

Single-blind procedure
Only the experimenter knows who is in the experimental group versus the control groups.

Double-blind procedure
Neither the experimenter nor the participants know who is in which group.

Figure 1.9 A double-blind experimental design In a double-blind experiment to test a new drug, both the experimenters administering the drug and the participants are unaware (or "blind") as to who is receiving a **placebo** (a fake pill or injection) and who is receiving the drug itself. Researchers use placebos (thus treating experimental and control group participants exactly the same) because they know that the mere act of taking a pill or receiving an injection can change a participant's condition or responses (Barbui et al., 2011; Price, Finniss, & Benedetti, 2008).

Placebo (pluh-SEE-boh) Inactive substance or fake treatment used as a control technique, usually in drug research, or given by a medical practitioner to a patient

Sample Bias Occurs when research participants are not representative of the larger population

Random Assignment Using chance methods to assign participants to experimental or control conditions, thus minimizing the possibility of biases or preexisting differences in the groups

Participant Bias Occurs when experimental conditions influence the participant's behavior or mental processes

Experimenter

culture. When using this kind of *cross-cultural sampling*, differences due to researcher ethnocentrism can be isolated from actual differences in behavior between the two cultures.

Objective 1.11: How do researchers safeguard against sample bias and participant bias?

Participant Problems and Solutions In addition to potential problems from the researcher, several possibilities for error are associated with participants. These errors can be grouped under the larger categories of *sample bias* and *participant bias*.

- *Sample bias* A *sample* is a group of research participants selected to represent a larger group, or *population*. When we do research, we obviously cannot measure the entire population, so we select and test a limited sample. However, using such a small group requires that the sample be reasonably similar to the composition of the population at large. If **sample bias**—systematic differences among the groups being studied—exists, experimental results may not truly reflect the influence of the independent variable.

For example, much research has been done on the increased safety of having air bags in automobiles. Unfortunately, however, the research has been conducted almost exclusively with men. When car manufacturers apply findings from this research, with no regard for the sample bias, they create air bags sized for men. Tragically, these male-sized bags may seriously damage (or even decapitate) small adults (mostly women) and kids. Because the purpose of conducting experiments is to apply, or generalize, the results to a wide population, it is extremely important that the sample represent the general population.

To safeguard against sample bias, research psychologists generally use random/representative sampling and random assignment:

- *Random/representative sampling* Obviously, psychologists want their research findings to be applicable to more people than just those who took part in the study. For instance, critics have suggested that much psychological literature is biased because it is based primarily on white participants (see Robert Guthrie's 2004 book, *Even the Rat Was White*). One way to ensure less bias and more relevance is to select participants who constitute a representative sample of the entire population of interest. Proper *random sampling* will likely produce a representative, unbiased sample.

- *Random assignment* To ensure the validity of the results, participants must also be assigned to experimental groups using a chance, or random, system, such as tossing a coin or drawing numbers out of a hat. This procedure of **random assignment** ensures that each participant is equally likely to be assigned to any particular group and that differences among the participants will be spread out across all experimental conditions.

- *Participant bias* In addition to problems with sample bias, **participant bias** can occur when experimental conditions influence participants' behavior or mental processes. For example, participants may try to present themselves in a good light (the *social desirability response*) or may deliberately attempt to mislead the researcher. They also may be less than truthful when asked embarrassing questions or placed in awkward experimental conditions.

Researchers attempt to control for this type of participant bias by offering anonymous participation and other guarantees for privacy and confidentiality. Also, as mentioned earlier, single- and double-blind studies and placebos offer additional safeguards.

If participants do not know whether they are receiving the real drug or the "fake one," they will not try to overly please or deliberately mislead the experimenter.

Finally, one of the most effective, but controversial, ways to prevent participant bias is *deception*. Just like unsuspecting subjects on popular TV programs, like the old *Candid Camera* show or the newer *Punk'd* program, research participants will behave more naturally when they do not know they are part of a research project. However, many researchers consider the use of deception unethical—as we discussed in the previous section.

 **TRY THIS YOURSELF**

Want to participate in psychological research?

The Association for Psychological Science (APS) has a website with links to ongoing studies that need participants. A recent visit to this site revealed several exciting studies, including:

- What Should Be Done with Child Abusers?
- Leadership Styles and Emotional Intelligence

- Bem Sex Role Inventory
- Internet Usage, Personality, and Behavior
- Adult Attention Deficit Hyperactivity Disorder (ADHD/ADD)
- Sensation and Perception Laboratory
- Web of Loneliness
- Sexual Behavior and Alcohol Consumption

- Marriage Inventory
- Are You a Logical Thinker?
- Web Experimental Psychology Lab

If you'd like to participate, go to http://psych.hanover.edu/research/exponnet.html.

 **CHECK & REVIEW** STOP *Before going on, be sure to complete this Check & Review. It is an invaluable study tool!*

Experimental Research

Part A: Retrieval Practice

1. Without looking at the book, spend 10 minutes writing a free-form essay recalling all you can remember from the previous section.

2. Now, reread the previous section, and once again spend 10 minutes writing a free-form essay on the SAME material.

Part B: Practice Quiz

1. Why is an experiment the only way we can determine the cause of behavior?

2. In experiments, researchers measure the _____ variables. (a) independent; (b) feature; (c) extraneous; (d) dependent

3. If researchers gave participants varying amounts of a new "memory" drug and then gave them a story to read and measured their scores on a quiz, the _____ would be the IV, and the _____ would be the DV. (a) response to the drug, amount of the drug; (b) experimental group, control group; (c) amount of the drug, quiz scores;

(d) researcher variables, extraneous variables

4. What are the two primary sources of problems for both researchers and participants? What are the solutions?

Check your answers in Appendix B.

Descriptive Research: Naturalistic Observation, Surveys, and Case Studies

Objective 1.12: Explain descriptive research and its three key methods—naturalistic observation, surveys, and case studies.

We all watch others, think about their behavior, and try to explain and understand what we see. However, when conducting **descriptive research**, psychologists do it systematically and scientifically. In this section, we will examine three key types of descriptive research: *naturalistic observation*, *surveys*, and *case studies*. Most of the

Descriptive Research Research methods that observe and record behavior and mental processes without producing causal explanations

problems and safeguards discussed with the experimental method also apply to these nonexperimental methods.

Naturalistic Observation

Naturalistic Observation
Observation and recording behavior and mental processes in the participant's natural state or habitat

When conducting **naturalistic observation**, researchers systematically measure and record the observable behavior of participants as it occurs in the real world, without interfering. The purpose of most naturalistic observation is to gather descriptive information. Because of the popularity of researchers like Jane Goodall, who studied chimpanzees in the jungle, most people picture naturalistic observation occurring in wild, remote areas. But supermarkets, libraries, subways, airports, museums, classrooms, assembly lines, and other settings also lend themselves to naturalistic observation.

The chief advantage of naturalistic observation is that researchers can obtain data about natural behavior, rather than about behavior that is a reaction to an artificial experimental situation. But, naturalistic observation can be difficult and time consuming, and the lack of control by the researcher makes it difficult to conduct observations of behavior that occurs infrequently.

If a researcher wants to observe behavior in a more controlled setting, *laboratory observation* has many of the advantages of naturalistic observation, but with greater control over the variables (Figure 1.10).

Surveys

Survey Research technique that questions a large sample of people to assess their behaviors and attitudes

Most of us are familiar with Gallup and Harris Polls, which sample voting preferences before important state or national elections. Psychologists use similar polls (or **surveys**) and interviews to measure a wide variety of psychological behaviors and attitudes (Dillman, Smith, & Christian, 2009; Rosnow & Rosenthal, 2008). (The psychological survey technique also includes tests, questionnaires, and interviews.)

One key advantage of surveys is that they can gather data from a much larger sample of people than is possible with other research methods. Unfortunately, most surveys rely on self-reported data, and not all participants are completely honest. In addition, survey techniques cannot, of course, be used to explain *causes* of behavior.

Case Studies

Case Study In-depth study of a single research participant

What if a researcher wants to investigate *photophobia*—fear of light? Because most people are not afraid of light, it would be difficult to find enough participants to conduct an experiment or to use surveys or naturalistic observation. In the case of such rare disorders, researchers try to find someone who has the problem and study him or her intensively. Such an in-depth study of a single research participant is called a **case study** (Kazdin, 2011).

Throughout this text, we will present numerous case studies, which add a "human interest" touch and help you remember core concepts. Keep in mind, however, that case studies have their own research limits, including possible lack of generalizability and inaccurate or biased recall among participants.

Figure 1.10 Laboratory observation In this type of observation, the researcher brings participants into a specially prepared room in the laboratory, and while hidden from view, observes the participants. Why would researchers try to hide? Have you ever been driving down the street, singing along with the radio, and quickly stopped when you noticed the person in the next car was watching you? Similar reactions occur when participants in scientific studies realize they are being observed.

Correlational Research: Looking for Relationships

Objective 1.13: Differentiate between correlational research and correlation coefficients.

We all know that certain things go together—for example, hot weather and fewer clothes; higher annual income and more vacations; and height and weight. Researchers can formally observe and measure these types of relationships by using a nonexperimental technique called **correlational research**. Correlational research determines what the degree of relationship (or *correlation*) is between two variables. As the name implies, when any two variables are *correlated*, a change in one variable is accompanied by a change in the other. Concept Organizer 1.1 provides a visual depiction and additional examples of correlations. Study it carefully!

Correlational Research Research method in which variables are observed or measured (without directly manipulating) to identify relationships between them

Value of Correlations

Correlational research is an important research method for psychologists and understanding correlations may help us live a safer and more productive lives. For example, correlational studies have repeatedly found high correlation coefficients between birth defects and a pregnant mother's use of tobacco, alcohol, and other drugs (e.g., Singer & Richardson, 2011). This information enables us to make predictions about relative risks and fosters more informed decisions. If you would like additional information about correlations, see Appendix A at the back of this text.

Problems with Correlations

Before we leave this topic, it's important to note that *correlation does not imply causation* (Figure 1.11). What if I said there was a high correlation between the size of a young child's feet and how fast he or she reads? Would this mean that having small feet *causes* a child to be a slow reader? Obviously not! Nor do increases in reading speed cause increases in foot size. Instead, both are caused by a third variable—an increase in children's age. Although we can safely *predict* that as a child's foot size increases, his or her reading speed will also increase, this *correlation does not imply causation*. Keep in mind that correlational studies *do* sometimes point to possible causes. But only the experimental method manipulates the independent variable (IV) under controlled conditions, and therefore, can support conclusions about cause and effect.

I use this extreme example to make an important point about an all too common public reaction to research findings. People read media reports about *relationships* between stress and cancer or between family dynamics and homosexuality. They then jump to the conclusion that "stress causes cancer" or that "withdrawn fathers and overly protective mothers cause their sons' homosexuality." Unfortunately, they fail to realize that a third factor, perhaps genetics, may cause greater susceptibility to both cancer and increased rates of homosexuality.

Once again, as Figure 1.12 shows, a correlation between two variables does not mean that one variable *causes* another. Correlational studies do sometimes point to *possible* causes, like the correlation between alcohol and birth defects. However, only the experimental method manipulates the IV under controlled conditions and therefore allows one to

Figure 1.11 Correlation is NOT causation Correlational, nonexperimental, studies are important because they reveal associations between variables. But causality (what causes what) is much more difficult to prove. For example, ice cream consumption and drowning are highly correlated. Does this mean that eating ice cream causes people to drown? Of course not! A third factor, such as time of year, affects both ice cream consumption and swimming and other summertime activities.

ConceptOrganizer1.1

Understanding Correlations

Using the *correlational method*, researchers first measure participants' responses or behaviors on variables of interest. Next, researchers analyze these results using a statistical formula that gives a **correlation coefficient**, a numerical value that provides two pieces of information: the *strength* and *direction* of the relationship between the two variables.

1. **Strength of the correlation** Correlation coefficients are calculated by a formula (described in Appendix A) that produces a number ranging from −1.00 to +1.00, which indicates the strength of the relationship. Note that both +1.00 and a −1.00 are the strongest possible relationship. As the number decreases and gets closer to 0.00, the relationship weakens. Thus, if you had a correlation of +.92 or −.92, you would have a *strong correlation*. By the same token, a correlation of +.15 or −.15 would represent a *weak correlation*. Correlations close to zero are often interpreted as representing no relationship between the variables— as is the relationship between broken mirrors and years of bad luck.

2. **Direction of the correlation** The sign (+ or −) indicates the *direction* of the correlation, positive (+) or negative (−).

   • A *positive correlation* is one in which the two variables move (or vary) in the same direction—the two factors increase or decrease together. As you know, for most students a positive correlation exists between hours of study and scores on exams. When studying *increases*, exam scores *increase*. Conversely, when studying *decreases*, exam scores also *decrease*. Can you see why both examples are positive correlations? The factors vary in the same direction—upward or downward.

   • A *negative correlation* exists when two factors vary in opposite directions. As one factor *increases*, the other factor *decreases*—the more hours you work (or party) outside of college, the lower your exam scores. Working and partying both vary in opposite directions to exam scores.

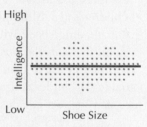

Pregnancy and smoking Research shows that cigarette smoking is highly correlated with serious fetal damage. The more the mother smokes the more the fetus is damaged. Is this a positive or negative correlation?

Three types of correlation

Each dot on these graphs (called *scatterplots*) represents one participant's score on two factors, or variables. (Note: For simplicity, we have not included values on the graph axes).

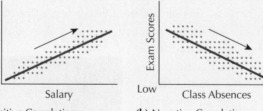
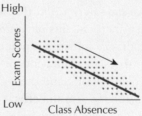

(a) Positive Correlation

In a positive correlation, the two factors move (or vary) in the same direction.

(b) Negative Correlation

In a negative correlation, the two factors vary in opposite directions—that is, as one factor increases, the other factor decreases.

(c) Zero, or no Correlation

Sometimes no relationship exists between two variables—a zero correlation.

PSYCHOLOGY ENGAGES

▶ TEST YOURSELF ▶

Can you spot the positive, negative, and zero correlations?

1. Health and exercise.
2. Hours of TV viewing and student grades.
3. Level of happiness and level of helpfulness.
4. Age of driver and weight of car.
5. Resale value and age of car.

Answers: positive, negative, positive, zero, negative)

Correlation Coefficient Number indicating strength and direction of the relationship between two variables (from −1.00 to +1.00)

draw conclusions about cause and effect. If you compared psychological research to a criminal investigation, finding a correlation is like finding a person at the scene of the crime. In contrast, results from an experiment are more like the "smoking gun."

Before going on, it's important to recognize that although the experimental method is considered the "gold standard" in research, the other methods offer their own unique and significant value. For example, are you concerned about the increasing research on the dangers of cell phone use (e.g., Davis & Balzano, 2011; Park, 2011; Volkow et al., 2011)? If so, can you see how it might be impossible (and unethical) to do long-term experiments on humans? Instead, we may have to rely on the accumulating weight of the evidence from surveys, correlational studies, and nonhuman animal research. In the meantime, we can play it safe by investing in an expensive ear piece (Parks, 2011).

Biological Research: Tools for Exploring the Nervous System

Objective 1.14: Describe biological research and its major tools for discovery.

In the previous section, we explored traditional research methods in psychology—experimental, descriptive, and correlational. But how do we study the living human brain and other parts of the nervous system? This is the province of **biological research**, which has developed and employed remarkable scientific tools and research methods (Table 1.4).

For most of history, examination of the human brain was possible only after an individual died. The earliest explorers dissected the brains of deceased humans and conducted experiments on nonhuman animals using *lesioning techniques*. (Lesioning in brain research involves systematically destroying brain tissue to study the effects on behavior and mental processes.) By the mid-1800s, this early research had produced a basic map of the nervous system, including some areas of the brain. Early researchers also relied on clinical observations and case studies of living people who had injuries, diseases, and disorders that affected brain functioning.

Modern researchers still use *dissection, ablation/lesioning, observation/case studies*, and the other methods in Table 1.4 (pp. 33–34). However, they also employ other techniques, such as electrical recordings of the brain's activity. To make these electrical recordings, scientists paste *electrodes* (tiny electricity-conducting disks or wires) to the skin of the skull. These electrodes collect electrical energy from the brain (brain waves), and the equipment to which they are attached depict the information as wavy lines. The recording of these brain waves is called an *electroencephalogram (EEG)*. (*Electro* means "electrical," *encephalon* means "brain," and *gram* means "record.") The instrument itself, called an *electroencephalograph*, is a major research tool for studying changes in brain waves during sleep and dreaming (Chapter 5).

In addition to electrical recordings, researchers also use *electrical stimulation of the brain (ESB)*. In this case, electrodes are inserted directly into the brain to stimulate certain areas with weak electrical currents.

Other new windows into the brain include several *brain-imaging scans* (see Table 1.4). Most of these methods are relatively *noninvasive*. That is, they are performed without breaking the skin or entering the body. They can be used in clinical settings to examine suspected brain damage and disease. They are also used in laboratory settings to study brain function during ordinary activities like sleeping, eating, reading, and speaking.

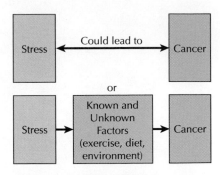

Figure 1.12 Correlation versus causation Research has found a strong correlation between stress and cancer (Chapter 3). However, this correlation does not tell us whether stress causes cancer, cancer causes stress, or whether other known and unknown factors, such as eating, drinking, and smoking, could contribute to both stress and cancer. Can you think of a way to study the effects of stress on cancer that is not correlational?

Biological Research Scientific studies of the brain and other parts of the nervous system

A Cautionary Note—fMRI Overselling!

Like the experimental, descriptive, and correlational methods of scientific research, each of the biological methods also has its own unique advantages and disadvantages. Before moving on, one particular problem with fMRI brain scans deserves special attention.

As mentioned in Table 1.4, fMRI scans measure brain activity by monitoring blood flow to specific areas, and scientific journals turn out hundreds of brain-imaging articles each month. However, brain activity and blood flow within the brain can reflect and be altered by a large range of different biological processes. Scientist Nikos Logothetis warns us that conclusions drawn from fMRI scans "often ignore the actual limitations of the methodology" (Logothetis, 2008). Ignoring these limitations, journalists, the public, and some scientists have leapt to unwarranted (and potentially dangerous) conclusions (Lavazza & De Caro, 2010; Weisberg et al., 2008). For example, newspapers and other media sources eagerly cover research alledgedly documenting how Democrat and Republican brains are different, how different parts of your brain "light up" when you're having religious experiences, watching Super Bowl ads, or eating chocolate, and supposedly even when you're telling a lie versus the truth (Carlat, 2008; Hutson, 2007; Vaughan, 2008). Even more shocking, a court in India sentenced a woman to death because a brain scan supposedly indicated she knew details only the murderer could (Begley, 2009)!

As you'll discover in Chapter 2, and throughout this text, behavior and mental processes are incredibly complex, and our scientific understanding evolves over time. While fMRI brain scans have provided unprecedented insights and invaluable aid to scientists and people around the world, they've also been oversold and overinterpreted. This is just a brief caution to not be seduced by the "pretty pictures." Brain scans, like all scientific tools, have their limits.

TEST YOURSELF

Becoming a Better Consumer of Scientific Research

The news media, advertisers, politicians, teachers, close friends, and other individuals frequently use research findings in their attempts to change your attitudes and behavior. How can you tell whether their information is accurate and worthwhile? The previous discussion of psychological research methods will help you identify the primary problem with each of the following sample research reports:

- CC = Report is misleading because correlation data are used to suggest causation.
- CG = Report is inconclusive because there was no control group.
- EB = Results of the research were unfairly influenced by experimenter bias.
- SB = Results of the research are questionable because of sample bias.

____1. A clinical psychologist strongly believes that touching is an important adjunct to successful therapy. For two months, he touches half his patients (group A) and refrains from touching the other half (group B). He then reports a noticeable improvement in group A.

____2. A newspaper reports that violent crime corresponds to phases of the moon. The reporter concludes that the gravitational pull of the moon controls human behavior.

____3. A researcher interested in women's attitudes toward premarital sex sends out a lengthy survey to subscribers of *Vogue* and *Cosmopolitan* magazines.

____4. An experimenter is interested in studying the effects of alcohol on driving ability. Before being tested on an experimental driving course, group A consumes 2 ounces of alcohol, group B consumes 4 ounces of alcohol, and group C consumes 6 ounces of alcohol. After the test drive, the researcher reports that alcohol consumption adversely affects driving ability.

____5. After reading a scientific journal that reports higher divorce rates among couples living together before marriage, a college student decides to move out of the apartment she shares with her boyfriend.

____6. A theater owner reports increased beverage sales following the brief flashing of a subliminal message to "Drink Coca-Cola" during the film showing.

Answers: 1. EB; 2. CC; 3. SB; 4. CG; 5. CC; 6. CG 7. EB

Table 1.4 TOOLS FOR BIOLOGICAL RESEARCH

	Method	Description	Purpose
	Brain dissection Photo of a deceased person's brain that has been vertically sliced in half to reveal inner structures.	Careful cutting and study of a cadaver's brain and other anatomical structures reveals structural details.	Brain dissections of Alzheimer's disease victims often show identifiable changes in various parts of the brain (Chapter 7).
	Ablation/lesions This stereotaxic instrument is used in small animal studies to provide accurate placement of lesions in anaesthesized animals.	Surgically removing parts of the brain (ablation), or destroying specific areas of the brain (lesioning), is followed by observation of changes in behavior or mental processes.	Lesioning specific parts of the rat's hypothalamus greatly affects its eating behavior (Chapter 12).
	Observation/case studies	Observing and recording changes in personality, behavior, or sensory capacity is sometimes associated with brain disease or injuries.	Damage to one side of the brain often causes numbness or paralysis on the body's opposite side.
	Electrical recordings Electrical activity throughout the brain sweeps in regular waves across its surface, and the electroencephalogram (EEG) is a readout of this activity.	Using electrodes attached to the skin or scalp, brain activity is detected and recorded on an electroencephalogram (EEG). To explore deep brain activity, a thin wire probe is inserted inside the brain in or near a neuron (see "Other Methods" p. 34).	Reveals areas of the brain most active during particular tasks or mental states, like reading or sleeping; also traces abnormal brain waves caused by brain malfunctions, like epilepsy or tumors. Intrabrain wire probes allow scientists to "see" individual neuron activity.
	Electrical stimulation of the brain (ESB)	Using an electrode, a weak electric current stimulates specific areas or structures of the brain.	Penfield (1947) mapped the surface of the brain and found that different areas have different functions.
	TMS (transcranial magnetic stimulation)	Method of brain stimulation that exposes the brain to powerful magnetic fields via a wire coil held near the skull. The magnetic field changes neural activity in the brain.	Can be used to elicit a motor response or to temporarily inactivate an area for observation of the effects; used to treat depression (Chapter 15).

(continued)

Table 1.4 *(Continued)*

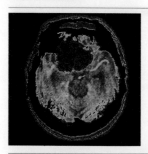

CT (computed tomography) scan
This CT scan used X-rays to locate a brain tumor, which is the deep purple mass at the top left.

Computer-created cross sectional X-rays of the brain or other parts of the body, which produce 3-D images. Least expensive type of imaging and is widely used in research.

Reveals the effects of strokes, injuries, tumors, and other brain disorders.

PET (positron emission tomography) scan
The left PET scan shows brain activity when the eyes are open, whereas the one on the right is with the eyes closed. Note the increased activity, red and yellow, in the left photo when the eyes are open.

Radioactive form of glucose injected into the blood-stream; scanner records amount of glucose used in particularly active areas of the brain producing a computer-constructed picture of the brain.

Originally designed to detect abnormalities, now used to identify brain areas active during ordinary activities (reading, singing, etc.).

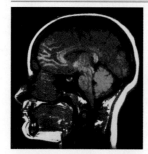

MRI (magnetic resonance imaging)
Note the fissures and internal structures of the brain. The throat, nasal airways, and fluid surrounding the brain are dark.

Powerful electro magnets produce high-frequency magnetic field that is passed through the brain.

Produces high-resolution three-dimensional pictures of the brain useful for identifying abnormalities and mapping brain structures and function.

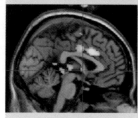

fMRI (functional magnetic resonance imaging)

Newer, faster version of the MRI that detects blood flow by picking up magnetic signals from blood, which has given up its oxygen to activate brain cells.

Measures blood flow, which indicates areas of the brain that are active or inactive during ordinary activities or responses (like reading or talking); also shows changes associated with various disorders.

Other Methods:
(a) **Cell body or tract (myelin) staining**
(b) **Microinjections**
(c) **Intrabrain electrical recordings**

(a) Colors/stains selected neurons or nerve fibers.
(b) Injects chemicals into specific areas of the brain.
(c) Records activity of one or a group of neurons inside the brain.

Increases overall information of structure and function through direct observation and measurement.

StudyTip

One way to remember the difference between these four brain scans is to keep in mind that CT and MRI scans produce static visual slices of the brain (like a photo). PET and fMRI create ongoing images (like a video).

CHECK & REVIEW

STOP *Before going on, be sure to complete this Check & Review. It is an invaluable study tool!*

Descriptive, Correlational, and Biological Research

Part A: Retrieval Practice

1. Without looking at the book, spend 10 minutes writing a free-form essay recalling all you can remember from the previous section.

2. Now, reread the previous section, and once again spend 10 minutes writing a free-form essay on the SAME material.

Part B: Practice Quiz

1. _____ research observes and records behavior without producing causal explanations.

2. Tatiana is thinking of running for student body president. She wonders whether her campaign should emphasize campus security, improved parking facilities, or increased health services. Which scientific method of research would you recommend? (a) a case study; (b) naturalistic observation; (c) an experiment; (d) a survey

3. Which of the following correlation coefficients indicates the strongest relationship? (a) +.43; (b) −.64; (c) −.72; (d) 0.00

4. The four major techniques used for scanning the brain are the _____, _____, _____, and _____.

Check your answers in Appendix B.

Psychology Engages

RESEARCH CHALLENGE

A Crash Course in Multitasking

By Thomas Frangicetto (Northampton Community College, Bethlehem, PA)

Objective 1.15: What are the two key multitasking myths?

Eighteen-year-old Amy's cell phone's ringtone blared as she climbed into her trusty Pathfinder. She took the call, buckled her seatbelt, and slipped in a Radiohead CD. A few blocks later, Amy heard another ring, but when she clicked to TALK, her left hand slipped just a bit. The Pathfinder slid off the road, bounced down a hill, and crashed into the side of a brick house. As fumes were leaking from a cracked gas line, Amy, bleeding and too stunned to move, was pulled to safety by onlookers.

- Have you ever, like Amy, driven a car, while also handling a cell phone, iPod, or a hot cup of Starbuck's?

- Do you text your friends, or listen to your iPOD, while simultaneously trying to follow a class lecture?

Obviously, there is a huge difference between driving two tons of steel, while answering a cell phone, and text messaging during a class lecture. Yet both can be hazardous to your health, and we need to explore some of the myths and misconceptions related to multitasking. Before we begin, complete the Try This Yourself exercise on page 36.

Myth #1: Multitasking increases overall output and efficiency

Many people believe that they're much more efficient and productive when they multitask. However, as you've just seen with the Try This Yourself Stroop test, multitasking often leads to more errors and more time. This was further documented by a recent Stanford University study, which investigated so-called "high-tech jugglers"— people who are consistently exposed to

The high price of multitasking As the text and research describe, errors and inefficiency increase whenever we multitask, so while it may be "safe" to listen to your IPOD while doing your homework, the potential errors while driving can be fatal!

several sources of electronic information at the same time. Using 100 college students as their population, the researchers ran a series of three tests on attention to detail, memory, and ability to switch from one task to another. In each test, the subjects were divided into two groups, those who regularly multitask and those who don't. The outcomes for all three tests were consistent: The heavy multitaskers were outperformed by the nonmultitaskers. To watch a short demonstration of this study, visit www.youtube.com/watch?v=2zuDXzVYZ68.

In sum, the researchers found that the self-described multitaskers paid less attention to detail, displayed poorer memory, and had more trouble switching from one task to another compared to subjects who preferred doing only one task at a time (Ophir, Nass, & Wagner, 2009). According to one of the researchers, "We kept looking for what they're better at, and we didn't find it. The high multitaskers couldn't help thinking about the task they weren't doing. They are always drawing from all the information in front of them. They can't keep things separate in their minds" (Gorlick, 2009). Like the Stroop test, they failed to selectively attend to what was relevant versus irrelevant.

Myth #2: Young people are best at technology multitasking

There is little doubt that young people are the most "tech-fluent" members of our "lightning-paced, many-threaded digital world." Yet, the current research overwhelmingly shows that for all their technical savvy, young people show less patience, persistence, and overall skill than adults in navigating the Web. To make matters worse, they also consistently overrate

their abilities (Jackson & McKibben, 2009). So not only do they not multitask very well, they're convinced they are better at it than they actually are.

Are you still under the delusion that multitasking is a good thing? If so, listen to researcher David Meyer: "When people try to perform two or more related tasks either at the same time or alternating rapidly between them, errors go way up" (Wallis, 2006). Stating the issue in starker terms, Meyer points out that a half second of time lost in switching tasks can be the difference between life and death for a driver using a cell phone, because in the fleeting moment when the car is not under control, it can travel just enough to crash into an otherwise avoidable obstacle (APA Press Release, 2001).

This brings us back to our lucky young friend Amy, who learned the multitasking lesson the hard way. Sadly, the lesson was too late for David Meyer's 17-year-old son, Timothy, who was killed by a distracted driver running a red light in 1995 (Jackson & McKibben, 2009). Like other researchers on this topic, Meyer has spent much of his considerable research talent and time trying to spread the warning about multitasking. He wants everyone to know that it's better—and safer—to do one thing at a time, and

to do it well (Austin, 2009; Clay, 2009; Meyer & Kieras, 1999, 2004; Rubinstein, Meyer, & Evans, 2001).

Student Engagement Exercise

Given the admittedly limited information in the Stanford University study (Ophir, Nass, & Wagner, 2009) described above, what is the most likely:

1. *Research method* (experimental, descriptive, correlational, or biological)?

2. If you chose the:

  - *Experimental method*—label the IV, DV, experimental group, and control group.

  - *Descriptive method*—identify whether this is a naturalistic observation, survey, or case study.

  - *Correlational method*—label whether this is a positive, negative, or zero correlation.

  - *Biological method*—identify the specific research tool (e.g., brain dissection, CT scan, etc.).

(Answers appear in Appendix B.)

 **TRY THIS YOURSELF**

Are You a Good Multitasker?

(a) Using a stopwatch, test to see how fast you can name the color of each rectangular box.

GREEN	RED	BROWN	RED
BROWN	GREEN	GREEN	BLUE
GREEN	BROWN	RED	BLUE

(b) Now, time yourself to see how fast you can state the color of ink used to print each word, ignoring what each word says.

altitudes on mountain climbers. We include it here to demonstrate how difficult it is to override highly practiced skills (reading words), in favor of new material or tasks (naming the color of ink in the word). Just as the distraction of a trying to ignore the words in (b) greatly increased your time and errors, trying to ignore or answer a cell-phone call, while listening to a lecture or driving a car can lead to increased errors on exams and increased odds of a serious traffic accident. In short, it's difficult and sometimes dangerous to do two things at once—especially when one task is more highly practiced.

Most people find it takes more time and that they make more errors on (b) than on (a). Your tendency to read the words in (b), instead of saying the color of ink as instructed, is known as the *Stroop effect*, after the psychologist who discovered it. Versions of this test have been used to detect subtle problems in brain function due to lack of sleep, fatigue, brain injuries, brain disease, and even the effects of high

CRITICAL THINKING

Applying Critical Thinking to Psychological Science

By Thomas Frangicetto (Northampton Community College, Bethlehem, PA)

Scientists in all fields must be good critical thinkers, and students of psychology are no exception. This first critical thinking exercise will help you in many ways, including:

- Insight into the interconnectivity of critical thinking and psychological science.

- Practice applying numerous critical thinking components.

- Review of important text content your professor may include on exams.

In the space beside each "Text Key Concept," enter the number of the appropriate "Suggested Critical Thinking Component."

Expanded discussions of each component can be found in the Prologue of this text. Although you may find several possible matches, list only your top one or two choices. For example, for the first item, "Literature Review," if you decide that "Gathering Data" is the best critical thinking component, enter the number "16" in the blank space.

Text Key Concepts	Suggested Critical Thinking Components
Scientific Method	• Valuing truth above self-interest (#1)
_____ Literature review	• Welcoming divergent views (#4)
_____ Testable hypothesis, operationally defined	• Tolerating ambiguity (#5)
	• Recognizing personal biases (#6)
_____ Research design	• Empathizing (#7)
_____ Statistical analysis	• Thinking independently (#7)
_____ Peer-reviewed scientific journal	• Defining problems accurately (#8)
	• Analyzing data for value and content (#9)
_____ Theory	• Synthesizing (#11)
	• Resisting overgeneralization (#12)
	• Delaying judgment until adequate data are available (#14)
Research Problems	
_____ Experimenter bias	• Employing precise terms (#15)
_____ Ethnocentrism	• Gathering data (#16)
_____ Sample bias	• Distinguishing fact from opinion (#17)
_____ Participant bias	• Modifying judgments in light of new information (#20)
	• Applying knowledge to new situations (#21)

StudyTip

GENDER AND CULTURAL DIVERSITY

Gender & Cultural Diversity

These sections embedded in the narrative are identified with a separate heading and a special icon, as seen here. To succeed in today's world, it is important to be aware of other cultures and important gender issues.

Psychology from a Global Perspective
Objective 1.16: Are there cultural universals?

Psychology is a broad field with numerous subdisciplines and professions. Until recently, most psychologists worked and conducted research primarily in Europe and North America. Given this "one-sided" research, psychology's findings may not apply equally to people in other countries—or to minorities and women in Europe and North America, for that matter (Berry et al., 2011; Matsumoto & Juang, 2008). However, modern psychology, in particular *cultural psychology*, is working to correct this imbalance. Key research from cross-cultural and multiethnic studies is integrated throughout this text. Each chapter also includes an expanded "Gender & Cultural Diversity" section with a special icon like this:

In this first gender and cultural diversity discussion, we explore a central question in cultural psychology: Are there *cultural universals*? That is, are there aspects of human behavior and mental processes that are true and *pancultural* or *universal* for all people of all cultures?

For many "universalists," emotions and facial recognition of emotions provide the clearest examples of possible cultural universals. Numerous studies conducted over many years with people from very different cultures suggest that everyone can easily identify facial expressions for at least six basic emotions: happiness, surprise, anger, sadness, fear, and disgust. All humans supposedly have this capacity whether they are shown the face of a child or an adult, a Western or non-Western person (Anguas-Wong & Matsumoto, 2007; Ekman, 1980, 1993, 2003, 2004; Swami, 2011). Moreover, nonhuman primates and congenitally blind infants also display similarly recognizable facial signals. In other words, across cultures (and some species), a frown is recognized as a sign of displeasure, and a smile, as a sign of pleasure (Figure 1.13). Although facial expressions of basic emotions appear to be universal, how, when, and where they are expressed varies according to cultural standards called *display rules* (Fok et al., 2008).

Critics suggest the universalist position overlooks the importance of learning and cultural factors (Dailey et al., 2010; Ko et al., 2011). For example, how do you label and study the emotion described by Japanese as *hagaii* (feeling helpless anguish mixed with frustration). How can Western psychologists study a culturally specific emotion like *hagaii* if they have no experience with these emotions and no equivalent English words? Other critics argue that *if* cultural universals exist, it is because they are biological and innate—and they should be labeled as such. However, equating biology with universality has its own problem. Behaviors or mental processes that are universal may be so because of culture-constant learning rather than biological destiny (Matsumoto & Juang, 2008). For example, *if* we found that certain gender roles were expressed the same way in all cultures, it might reflect shared cultural training beginning at birth, not an "anatomy is destiny" position.

As you'll discover throughout this text, psychological scientists avoid the tendency to compartmentalize behaviors into either/or categories. Like the nature–nurture controversy, the answer once again is an *interaction*. Certain behaviors, like emotions and their recognition, may be both biological and culturally universal. As a beginning student in psychology, you will encounter numerous areas of conflict, with well-respected arguments and opponents on each side. Your job is to adopt an open-minded, critically thinking approach to each of these debates.

Figure 1.13 Do you recognize this emotions? The recognition and display of basic facial expressions may be true "cultural universals."

In addition to building your critical thinking skills, hearing arguments from both sides also will develop your understanding of and appreciation for diversity, both intellectual and cultural. It might even improve your personal and business interactions. Richard Brislin (1997) told the story of a Japanese executive who gave a speech to a *Fortune* 500 company in New York. He was aware that Americans typically begin speeches by telling an amusing story or a couple of jokes. However, Japanese typically begin speeches by apologizing for the "inadequate" talk they are about to give.

This savvy executive began his speech: "I realize that Americans often begin by making a joke. In Japan, we frequently begin with an apology. I'll compromise by apologizing for not having a joke" (p. 9). By appreciating cultural diversity, we can, like the Japanese executive, learn to interact successfully in other cultures.

Tools for Student Success

Objective 1.17: List the psychological and pedagogical tools for studying and learning psychology.

Congratulations! At this very moment, you are demonstrating one of the most important traits of a critical thinker and successful college student—your willingness to accept *suggestions for improvement*. Many students think they already know how to be a student, but would they similarly assume they could become top-notch musicians, athletes, or plumbers without mastering the tools of those trades? Trying to compete in a college environment with minimal, or even average, study skills is like trying to ride a bicycle on a high-speed freeway. *All students* (even those who seem to get A's without much effort) can improve their "student tools."

In this section, you will find several important tools—specific, well-documented study tips and techniques—guaranteed to make you a more efficient and successful college student (Figure 1.14).

Figure 1.14 Tools for student success

Personal Control

Do you recall the joke at the start of this chapter that asked how many psychologists it takes to change a light bulb (p. 6)? The punch line, "None. The light bulb has to want to change itself," reflects an underlying truth about psychology and our shared human nature. As mentioned earlier, we're all heavily influenced by interacting biological, psychological, and social forces (the *biopsyhosocial model*). However, if you want to change things like your current study habits and become a highly successful student, psychological forces is the one area where you have the greatest control. You have the power to decide that you can, and will, improve your academic skills!

This explains why *personal control* is listed as the first step in Figure 1.14. To succeed at virtually anything, you need to focus on your ABCs: A = Affect (feelings), B = Behavior (actions), and C = Cognitions (thoughts, beliefs, values). For example, to control your affect and cognitions, instead of saying things, like "I have to study" or "Going to class feels like a waste of time," try counter statements, such as "I'm going to learn how to study and make better use of my class time." Similarly, to change your behavior, rather than thinking and saying "I never do well on tests," you can take college success and/or test preparation courses at your college. In the meantime, the following pages also provide a brief, overview of the key Tools for Student Success. Be sure to study them carefully, and remember that you already have the #1 principle for success—*personal control*!

Active Reading

How to Study (and Master) This Text

Have you ever read several pages of a text only to later find that you could not recall a single detail? Or have you read the chapters (possibly many times) and still performed poorly on an exam? If so, stop and complete the "Try this Yourself" exercise on the next page. Most Americans cannot select a real penny among fake pennies even after years of using them to make purchases. Similarly, students can read and reread chapters yet still fail to recognize the correct answers on a test. To learn and remember, you must make a conscious effort. You must "intend to learn."

Admittedly, some learning (like remembering the lyrics to your favorite song) occurs somewhat automatically and effortlessly. However, most complex information (like textbook reading) requires effort and deliberate attention. There are a number of ways to *actively read*, remember, and master a college text.

STEP ONE: Familiarizing Yourself with the General Text

Your textbook is the major tool for success in any course. Most instructors rely on it to present basic course material, reserving class time for clarifying and elaborating on important topics. How can you become a more successful student (and test taker) and take full advantage of all the special features in this text? Consider the following:

- *Preface* If you have not already read the Preface, do it now. It provides an invaluable "road map" for the rest of the text.

- *Table of contents* Scan the table of contents for a bird's-eye view of what you will study in this course. Get the big picture from the chapter titles and the major topics within each chapter.

- *Individual chapters* Each chapter of *Psychology in Action* contains numerous learning aids to help you master the material. There are chapter outlines, learning outcomes,

StudyTip

Tools for Student Success

This special feature in Chapter 1 includes tips for success in this and all your other college courses. In addition, watch for these "study tip" boxes throughout this text.

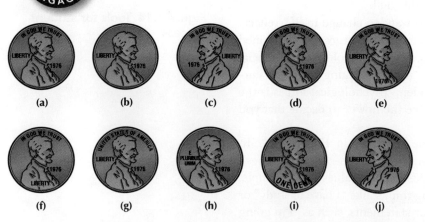

TRY THIS YOURSELF

(a) (b) (c) (d) (e)

(f) (g) (h) (i) (j)

Which one of these 10 pennies is an exact duplicate of a real U.S. penny?

The correct answer is (a). But unless you are a coin collector, you probably can't easily choose the correct one without comparing it to a real coin—despite having seen it thousands of times. Why? As you will discover later in the text (Chapter 7), you must encode (or process) the information in some way before it will be successfully stored in your long-term memory.

running glossaries, "Check & Review" (summaries and self-test questions), "Visual Summaries," and more. These learning aids are highlighted and explained in the margin of this first chapter.

- *Appendixes* Appendix A (Statistics) and Appendix B (Answers to Check & Review Questions and Activities) present important information. The statistics appendix further discusses some of the concepts introduced in Chapter 1. It also explains how to read and interpret the graphs and tables found throughout the text. Appendix B contains answers to the "Check & Review" questions, "Try This Yourself" activities, and other exercises found in the chapters.

- *Glossary* This text presents two glossaries. A running glossary appears in the margins of each chapter alongside key terms and concepts. A cumulative glossary, which gathers all key terms from each chapter, appears at the end of this text. Use this end-of-book glossary to review terms from other chapters.

- *References* As you read each chapter, you will see references cited in parentheses, not in footnotes, as is common in other disciplines. For example, (Venter et al., 2001) refers to an article written by Craig Venter and his colleagues announcing the first successful mapping of the full human genome, which was published in 2001. All the references cited in the text are listed in alphabetical order (by the author's last name) in the References section at the back of the book.

- *Name index and subject index* If you are interested in learning more about a particular individual, look for his or her name in the Name Index. The page numbers refer you to every place in the text where the individual is mentioned. If you are interested in a specific subject (e.g., anorexia nervosa or stress), check the Subject Index for page references.

STEP TWO: How to Read a Chapter

Once you have a sense of the book as a whole, your next step to success is improving your general reading skills. The most important tool for college success is the ability to read and master the assigned class text. Many colleges offer instruction in reading efficiency, and I highly recommend that you take the course. All students can become faster and more efficient readers, and this section can offer only the highlights of a full-length course.

One of the best ways to read *actively* is to use the SQ4R method, developed by Francis Robinson (1970). The initials stand for six steps in effective reading: *Survey, Question, Read, Recite, Review, and wRite.* Robinson's technique helps you better understand and remember what you read. As you might have guessed, *Psychology in Action* was designed to incorporate each of these six steps (Step-by-Step Diagram 1.3).

Time Management
How to Succeed in College and Still Have a Life

Time management is not only desirable; it is also essential to college success. If you answer yes to each of the following, congratulate yourself and move on to the next section.

1. I have a good balance among work, college, and social activities.

2. I complete my assignments and papers on time and seldom stay up late to cram the night before an exam.

3. I am generally on time for classes, appointments, and work.

4. I prioritize my responsibilities and assign time accordingly.

5. I arrange my life to avoid unnecessary interruptions (visitors, meetings, telephone calls during study hours).

Step-by-StepDiagram1.3

STOP This Step by Step diagram contains essential information NOT found elsewhere in the text, which is likely to appear on quizzes and exams. Be sure to study it CAREFULLY!

Using the SQ4R Method

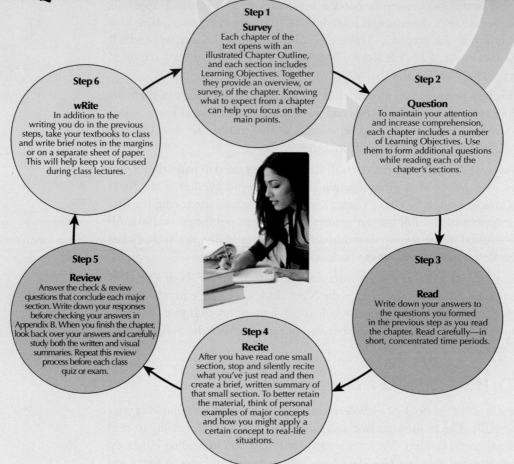

Step 1
Survey
Each chapter of the text opens with an illustrated Chapter Outline, and each section includes Learning Objectives. Together they provide an overview, or survey, of the chapter. Knowing what to expect from a chapter can help you focus on the main points.

Step 2
Question
To maintain your attention and increase comprehension, each chapter includes a number of Learning Objectives. Use them to form additional questions while reading each of the chapter's sections.

Step 3
Read
Write down your answers to the questions you formed in the previous step as you read the chapter. Read carefully—in short, concentrated time periods.

Step 4
Recite
After you have read one small section, stop and silently recite what you've just read and then create a brief, written summary of that small section. To better retain the material, think of personal examples of major concepts and how you might apply a certain concept to real-life situations.

Step 5
Review
Answer the check & review questions that conclude each major section. Write down your responses before checking your answers in Appendix B. When you finish the chapter, look back over your answers and carefully study both the written and visual summaries. Repeat this review process before each class quiz or exam.

Step 6
wRite
In addition to the writing you do in the previous steps, take your textbooks to class and write brief notes in the margins or on a separate sheet of paper. This will help keep you focused during class lectures.

If you cannot answer yes to each of these statements and need help with time management, here are four basic strategies:

1. *Establish a baseline* To break any bad habit (poor time management, excessive TV watching, overeating), you must first establish a *baseline*—a characteristic level of performance for assessing changes in behavior. Before attempting any changes, simply record your day-to-day activities for one to two weeks (see the sample in Figure 1.15). Like most dieters who are shocked at their daily eating habits, most students are unpleasantly surprised when they recognize how poorly they manage their time.

2. *Set up a realistic activity schedule* Start by making a daily and weekly "to do" list. Include all required activities (class attendance, study time, work, etc.), as well as basic maintenance tasks like laundry, cooking, cleaning, and eating. Using this list, create a daily schedule of activities with realistic time allotments for required activities, as well as for "downtime," including leisure and social activities with friends and family.

   Keep in mind that permanent time management changes require bahavior shaping (see Chapter 6). That is, start small and build. For example, schedule 15 minutes increased study time for the first few days, then move to 30 minutes, 60 minutes, and so on.

3. *Reward yourself for good behavior* The most efficient way to maintain good behavior is to reward it—the sooner, the better (Chapter 6). Unfortunately, the rewards of

	Sunday	Monday	Tuesday	Wednesday	Thursday	Friday	Saturday
7:00		Breakfast		Breakfast		Breakfast	
8:00		History	Breakfast	History	Breakfast	History	
9:00		Psychology	Statistics	Psychology	Statistics	Psychology	
10:00		Review History & Psychology	Campus Job	Review History & Psychology	Statistics Lab	Review History & Psychology	
11:00		Biology		Biology		Biology	
12:00		Lunch / Study		Exercise	Lunch	Exercise	
1:00		Bio Lab	Lunch	Lunch	Study	Lunch	
2:00			Study	Study			

Figure 1.15 Sample record of daily activities To help manage your time, draw a grid similar to this and record your daily activities in appropriate boxes. Then fill in other necessities, such as daily mainte-nance tasks and "downtime."

college (a degree and/or job advancement) are generally years away. Therefore, give yourself *immediate*, tangible rewards for sticking with your daily schedule. Allow yourself a guilt-free call to a friend, for example, or time for a favorite TV program after studying for your set period.

4. *Maximize your time* Many students believe they are studying all the time. Ironically, they may be confusing "fret time" (worrying and complaining) and useless prep time (fiddling around getting ready to study) with real, *concentrated* study time.

Time experts also point out that people often overlook important *time opportunities*. When you use public transportation, use travel time to review notes or read a textbook. While waiting for doctor or dental appointments or to pick up your kids after school, take out your text and study for 10 to 20 minutes. Hidden moments count!

Strategies For Grade Improvement

Note Taking, Study Habits, and General Test-Taking Tips

- **Note taking** Effective note taking depends on *active listening*. Find a seat in the front of the class and focus your attention on what is being said by the instructor. Ask yourself, "What is the main idea?" Write down key ideas and supporting details and examples, including important names, dates, and new terms. Do not try to write down everything word for word. This is passive, rote copying—not active listening. Also, be sure to take extra notes if your professor says, "This is an important con-cept," or if he or she writes notes on the board. Finally, arrive in class on time and do not leave early—you may miss important notes and assignments.

- **Distributed study time** Although it does help to intensively review before a quiz or exam, if this is your major method of studying, you are not likely to do well in any college course. One of the clearest findings in psychology is that spaced practice is a much more efficient way to study and learn than massed practice (Chapter 7). Just as you would not wait until the night before a big basketball game to begin practicing your free throws, you should not wait until the night before an exam to begin studying.

- **Overlearn** Many students study just to the point where they can recite the imme-diate information. For best results, you should fully master the material, and be able to apply key terms and concepts to examples other than the ones in the text. You also should repeatedly review the material (using visualization and rehearsal) until it is firmly locked in place. This type of *overlearning* is particularly important if you suffer from test anxiety. For additional help on test anxiety and improving memory in general, see Chapter 7.

- **Understand your professor** Pay close attention to the lecture time spent on various topics. This is generally a good indication of what your instructor considers important (and what may appear on exams). Also, try to understand the perspective (and personality) of your instructor. Most professors went into education because they love the academic life. They probably enjoyed lectures during college and were trained under this system. Never say, "I missed last week's classes. Did I miss anything important?" This is guaranteed to upset the most even-tempered instructor!

- **General test taking** To improve your performance on multiple-choice exams:

  1. *Take your time* Carefully read each question and each of the alternative answers. Do not choose the first answer that looks correct. There may be a better alternative.

  2. *Be test smart* If you are unsure of an answer, begin by eliminating any answer that you know is incorrect. If two answers both seem reasonable, try to recall specific information from the text or professor's lecture. Be sure to choose "all of the above" if you know that at least two of the options are correct. Similarly, if you are confident that one of the options is incorrect, *never* choose "all of the above."

  3. *Review test answers* After you finish a test, always go back and check your answers. Make sure you have responded to all the questions and recorded your answers correctly. Also, bear in mind that information relevant to one question is often found in another test question. Do not hesitate to change an answer if you get more information—or even if you simply have a better guess about an answer. Contrary to the popular myth widely held by many students (and faculty) that "your first hunch is your best guess," research suggests this is NOT the case. (Benjamin, Cavell, & Shallenberger, 1984; Lilienfeld et al., 2010). Changing answers is far more likely to result in a higher score (Figure 1.16).

  4. *Practice test taking* Complete the "Check & Review" sections found throughout each chapter and then check your answers in Appendix B. Make up questions from your lectures and text notes. Also, try the interactive quizzes on our website http://www.wiley.com/college/huffman. Each chapter of the text has numerous quizzes, most with individualized feedback. If you answer a question incorrectly, you also get immediate feedback and further explanations that help you master the material.

MYTH BUSTERS

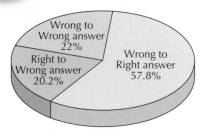

Figure 1.16 Should you change your answers? Yes! Research clearly shows that, answer changes that go from a wrong to a right answer (57.8 percent) greatly outnumber those that go from a right to a wrong answer (20.2 percent). *Source:* Benjamin, Cavell, & Shallenberger (1984).

Additional Resources

Frequently Overlooked Helpers

1. *Instructors* Your instructors can provide useful tips for succeeding in their course. However, it is up to you to discover their office hours and office location. If you can't meet during their office hours, ask for an alternative appointment, try to stop by right before or after class, or e-mail them.

2. *College courses All students* can improve their reading speed and comprehension, and their study skills, by taking additional college courses designed to develop these specific abilities.

3. *Friends and family* After completing your daily activity schedule (page 43), set up weekly (or biweekly) appointments with a friend or family member to check your progress and act as your "conscience." Encourage your conscience/coach to ask pointed questions about your actual study time versus your *fretting* and *prepping* time.

4. *Roommates and classmates* Ask your classmates and roommates for study tips, such as how to take tests or what tricks/techniques they use to maintain attention and interest during lectures or while reading texts.

If you'd like more information on student success skills, consult the *Psychology in Action* website www.wiley.com/college/huffman. In addition to the interactive tutorials and quizzes mentioned earlier, we also offer numerous Internet links for student success and time management.

A Final Word

Your Attitude

Imagine for a moment that the toilet in your bathroom is overflowing and creating a horrible, smelly mess. Whom should you reward? The plumber who quickly and efficiently solves the problem? Or someone who "tries very hard"?

Some students may believe they can pass college courses by simply attending class and doing the assignments. This may have worked for *some* students in *some* classes in high school. But most college professors seldom assign homework and may not notice if you skip class. They assume students are independent, self-motivated adult learners, and that grades should generally reflect knowledge and performance—not effort. Although hard work and perseverance are the true keys to college and life success (Chapter 10), you'll ultimately be rewarded for your final output. Did you fix the toilet or not?

CHECK & REVIEW

STOP *Before going on, be sure to complete this Check & Review. It is an invaluable study tool!*

Psychology Engages

Part A: Retrieval Practice

1. Without looking at the book, spend 10 minutes writing a free-form essay recalling all you can remember from the previous section.

2. Now, reread the previous section, and once again spend 10 minutes writing a free-form essay on the SAME material.

Part B: Practice Quiz

1. Imagine your friend is text messaging while driving a car. Using information from the research challenge, how would you convince him/her of the problems with texting while driving.

2. According to "universalists," _____ and _____ provide the clearest examples of possible cultural universals?

3. List the six steps in the SQ4R method.

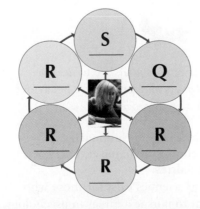

4. According to the text, _____ might be the single most important key to improved grades.

Check your answers in Appendix B.

WileyPLUS presents an on-line version of this textbook along with a wealth of study resources including quizzes, practice tests, flash cards, videos, animations and other activities designed to improve your mastery of the content. Working in conjunction with these study tools, the *Psychology in Action* WileyPLUS course features Professor Karen Huffman, author of this textbook, explaining and expanding upon some of the most challenging concepts in psychology. Here is a sample of the tutorial videos available for this chapter:

- The value of the scientific method and critical thinking, featuring Professor Huffman's "magic trick"
- Four basic research methods (experimental, descriptive, correlational, biological)
- Experimental method, emphasizing independent and dependent variables
- Interactive animation of correlations and what they mean
- Virtual Field Trip to a neuroimaging center to see the brain in action, using fMRI, PET and other brain imaging technology

Key Terms

StudyTip

Key Terms

To increase your mastery of the most important concepts, recite aloud and/or write a brief definition for each key term. Then, return to the relevant pages in the chapter and check your understanding.

To assess your understanding of the **Key Terms** in Chapter 1, write a definition for each (in your own words), and then compare your definitions with those in the text.

Introducing Psychology
psychology (p. 4)
critical thinking (p. 5)
nature–nurture controversy (p. 6)

Origins of Psychology
psychoanalytic approach (p. 11)
psychodynamic perspective (p. 11)
behavioral perspective (p. 12)
humanistic perspective (p. 13)
positive psychology (p. 13)
cognitive perspective (p. 13)
biological perspective (p. 14)
evolutionary perspective (p. 14)
sociocultural perspective (p. 14)
biopsychosocial model (p. 15)

Science of Psychology
basic research (p. 16)
applied research (p. 16)

replication (p. 17)
meta-analysis (p. 17)
theory (p. 17)
hypothesis (p. 18)
operational definition (p. 18)
statistical significance (p. 18)
informed consent (p. 19)
debriefing (p. 19)

Research Methods
experimental research (p. 21)
experimental group (p. 23)
control group (p. 23)
independent variable (IV) (p. 23)
dependent variable (DV) (p. 23)
confounding variables (p. 23)
experimenter bias (p. 25)
single-blind study (p. 25)
double-blind study (p. 25)
ethnocentrism (p. 25)

placebo (pluh-SEE-bo) (p. 26)
sample bias (p. 26)
random assignment (p. 26)
participant bias (p. 26)
descriptive research (p. 27)
naturalistic observation (p. 28)
survey (p. 28)
case study (p. 28)
correlational research (p. 29)
correlation coefficient (p. 30)
biological research (p. 31)

Chapter Summary

Introducing Psychology

Objective 1.1: Define psychology.
Psychology is the scientific study of behavior and mental processes. It emphasizes the empirical approach and the value of **critical thinking**. Psychology is not the same as common sense, "pop psychology," or pseudopsychology.

Objective 1.2: What are psychology's four main goals?

Psychology's goals are to *describe*, *explain*, *predict*, and *change* behavior and mental processes.

Objective 1.3: Summarize psychology's major career specialties.
Many avenues exist for those who want to pursue a career in psychology. These include biopsychology/ neuroscience, experimental, cognitive, developmental, clinical, counseling,

industrial/organizational, educational/ school, social, health, and so on.

Origins of Psychology

Objective 1.4: Contrast structuralism versus functionalism, and list the seven major perspectives that guide modern psychology.
Among the early contributors to psychology, the *structuralists* sought to identify elements of consciousness and how those elements formed the

structure of the mind. *Functionalists* studied how mental processes help individuals adapt to the environment. The **psychodynamic, behavioral, humanistic, cognitive, biological, evolutionary,** and **sociocultural** perspectives are the seven key approaches in contemporary psychology.

Objective 1.5: Describe the biopsychosocial model.
The **biopsychosocial model** complements all seven modern perspectives and emphasizes the interrelated biological, psychological, and social processes.

Science of Psychology

Objective 1.6: Differentiate between basic and applied research, and list the six steps of the scientific method.
Basic research studies theoretical issues. **Applied research** seeks to solve specific problems. The scientific method consists of six carefully planned steps: (1) question and literature review, (2) testable **hypothesis**, (3) research design, (4) data collection and analysis, (5) publication, and (6) **theory** development.

Objective 1.7: What are the three key areas of ethical concern in psychological research and therapy?
Psychologists must maintain high standards in their relations with human and nonhuman research participants, as well as in their therapeutic relationships with clients. The APA has published specific guidelines detailing these ethical standards.

Experimental Research

Objective 1.8: Explain how experiments help researchers determine cause and effect.
By manipulating and carefully controlling variables, **experimental research** is the only research method that can be used to identify cause-and-effect relationships.

Objective 1.9: Compare and contrast experimental versus control groups and independent variables (IVs) versus dependent variables (DVs).
Experimental groups receive treatment, whereas **control groups** receive no treatment. **Independent variables (IVs)** are the factors the experimenter manipulates,

and **dependent variables (DVs)** are measurable behaviors of the participants.

Objective 1.10: How do researchers guard against experimenter bias and ethnocentrism?
To safeguard against the researcher problem of **experimenter bias**, researchers employ blind observers, **single-** and **double-blind studies**, and **placebos.** To control for **ethnocentrism**, they use cross-cultural sampling.

Objective 1.11: How do researchers safeguard against sample bias and participant bias?
To offset participant problems with **sample bias**, researchers use random/representative sampling and **random assignment.** To control for **participant bias**, they rely on many of the same controls in place to prevent experimenter bias, such as **double-blind studies.** They also attempt to ensure anonymity and confidentiality and sometimes use deception.

Descriptive, Correlational, and Biological Research

Objective 1.12: Explain descriptive research and its three key methods—naturalistic observation, surveys, and case studies.
Descriptive research observes and describes, but it cannot determine the causes of behavior and mental processes. **Naturalistic observation** is used to study and describe behavior in its natural habitat without altering it. **Surveys** use interviews or questionnaires to obtain information on a sample of participants. Individual **case studies** are in-depth studies of a participant.

Objective 1.13: Differentiate between correlational research and correlation coefficients.
Correlational research examines how one naturally occurring trait or behavior accompanies another, and how well one variable predicts the other. **Correlation coefficients** are numerical values from correlational research that indicate the degree and direction of the relationship between two variables. (Correlation coefficients range from 0 to +1.00 or 0 to −1.00, and the plus and minus signs

indicate whether the relationships are positively or negatively correlated.) Both correlational studies and correlational coefficients provide important research findings and valuable predictions. However, it is important to remember that *correlation does not imply causation.*

Objective 1.14: Describe biological research and its major tools for discovery.
Biological research studies the brain and other parts of the nervous system through dissection of brains of cadavers, ablation/lesion techniques, observation or case studies, electrical recordings, and electrical stimulation of the brain (ESB). Computed tomography (CT), positron emission tomography (PET), magnetic resonance imaging (MRI), functional magnetic resonance imaging (fMRI), and transcranial magnetic stimulation (TMS) are noninvasive techniques that provide important information on intact, living brains.

Psychology Engages

Objective 1.15: What are the two key multitasking myths?
Young people are best at technology multitasking. Multitasking increases overall efficiency.

Objective 1.16: Are there cultural universals?
Some cultural psychologists do believe certain aspects of human behavior and mental processes are true and universal for all cultures, and they suggest that emotions and facial recognition of emotions are prime examples. Critics say that Western psychologists have little experience with culturally specific emotions, and that if cultural universals exist they are innate and biological. The answer appears to be that certain behaviors are both biological and culturally universal.

Objective 1.17: List the psychological and pedagogical tools for studying and learning psychology.
There are several important psychological and pedagogical techniques, including *personal control, active reading, time management, strategies for grade improvement,* and *additional resources.*

ChapterOne VISUAL SUMMARY

Introducing Psychology

What Is Psychology?
Scientific study of behavior and mental processes

Psychology's Goals
Describe, explain, predict, change

Origins of Psychology

Psychology's Past

Modern Psychology
7 major perspectives & a new biopsychosocial model

Behavioral · Humanistic · Cognitive · Biological · Evolutionary · Sociocultural · Psychodynamic · Bio-psycho-social

Science of Psychology

Scientific Method

Step 1 Question and literature review
Step 2 Testable hypothesis
Step 3 Research design
Step 4 Data collection and analysis
Step 5 Publication
Step 6 Theory development

Ethical Guidelines
Human Participants
Nonhuman Participants
Psychotherapy Clients

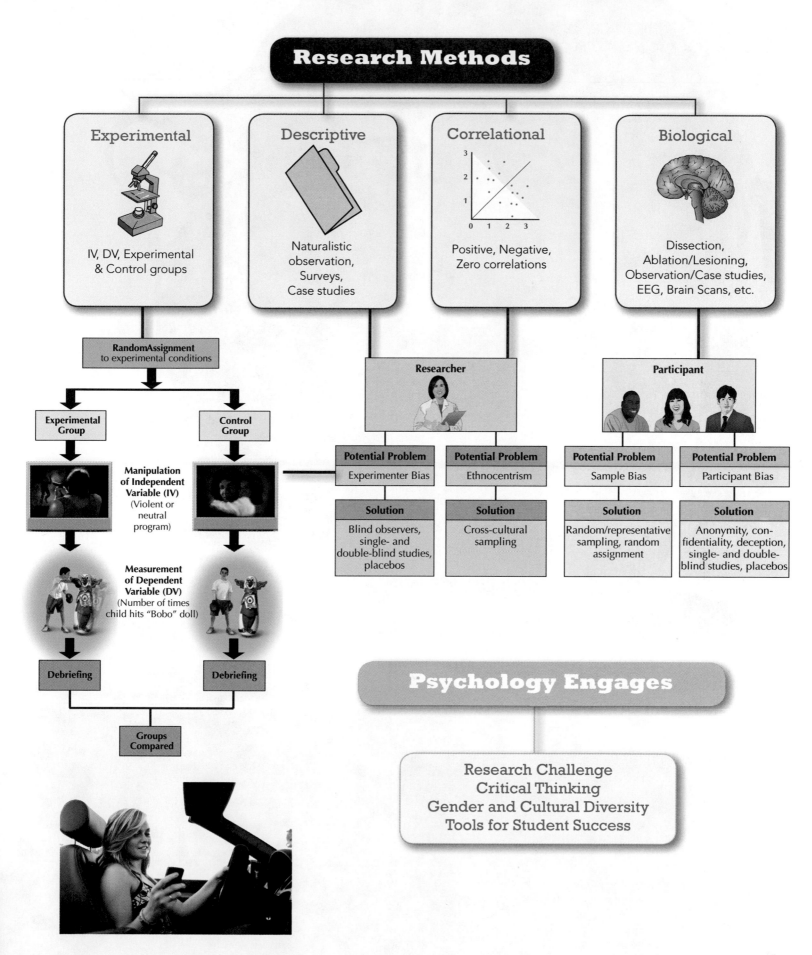

Research Methods

Experimental
IV, DV, Experimental & Control groups

Descriptive
Naturalistic observation, Surveys, Case studies

Correlational
Positive, Negative, Zero correlations

Biological
Dissection, Ablation/Lesioning, Observation/Case studies, EEG, Brain Scans, etc.

RandomAssignment to experimental conditions

Experimental Group

Control Group

Manipulation of Independent Variable (IV) (Violent or neutral program)

Measurement of Dependent Variable (DV) (Number of times child hits "Bobo" doll)

Debriefing

Debriefing

Groups Compared

Researcher

Potential Problem
Experimenter Bias

Solution
Blind observers, single- and double-blind studies, placebos

Potential Problem
Ethnocentrism

Solution
Cross-cultural sampling

Participant

Potential Problem
Sample Bias

Solution
Random/representative sampling, random assignment

Potential Problem
Participant Bias

Solution
Anonymity, confidentiality, deception, single- and double-blind studies, placebos

Psychology Engages

Research Challenge
Critical Thinking
Gender and Cultural Diversity
Tools for Student Success

Chapter Two

Neuroscience and Biological Foundations

What are you doing at this very moment? Obviously, you're reading, which means that you're busily translating squiggly little black symbols called "letters" into meaningful patterns called "words." But what part of your body does the translation? If you put this book down and walk away to get a snack or talk to a friend, what moves your legs and enables you to speak? You've heard the saying, "I think; therefore I am." What if you were no longer capable of thought or feeling? Would "you" still exist?

Ancient cultures, including the Egyptian, Indian, and Chinese, believed the heart was the center of all thoughts and emotions. Today we know that the brain and the rest of the nervous system are the power behind our psychological life and much of our physical being. This chapter introduces you to the important and exciting field of **neuroscience** and *biopsychology*, the scientific study of the *biology* of behavior and mental processes. It also provides a foundation for understanding several fascinating discoveries and facts, as well as important biological processes discussed throughout the text.

> *The brain is the last and grandest biological frontier, the most complex thing we have yet discovered in our universe. It contains hundreds of billions of cells interlinked through trillions of connections. The brain boggles the mind.*
>
> JAMES WATSON
> (Nobel Prize Winner)

> *We sit on the threshold of important new advances in neuroscience that will yield increased understanding of how the brain functions and of more effective treatments to heal brain disorders and diseases. How the brain behaves in health and disease may well be the most important question in our lifetime.*
>
> RICHARD D. BROADWELL
> (from *Neuroscience, Memory and the Brain*, 1995)

Neuroscience Interdisciplinary field studying how biological processes relate to behavior and mental processes

ChapterOutline

WHY STUDY PSYCHOLOGY

Did you know...

- The venom of a black widow spider is one of the most potent of all biologic toxins? Its bite releases a neurotransmitter, called *acetylcholine* (ACH), which causes severe muscle pain and hypertension. Thankfully, it can only inject a small amount each time it bites.

- All your thoughts, feelings, and actions result from neurotransmitter messages flashing between billions of tiny nerve cells? Or that organisms from lizards to elephants all depend on much the same neurotransmitters that our own brains use?

- Scientists have established a link between sports-related repeated concussions and permanent and possibly fatal brain damage?

- The reappearance of certain infant reflexes in adults may be a sign of serious brain damage?

- A physician can declare you legally dead if your brain stops functioning—even though your heart and lungs are still working?

- Strong emotions, such as fear or anger, can stop digestion and sexual arousal?

- Cells in our brains die and regenerate throughout our lifetime? . . . They are also physically shaped and changed by learning and from experiences we have with our environment?

- Scientists have created human embryos through cloning? Or that extracted stem cells from embryos are also used for research and possible treatment for

diseases like cancer, Parkinson's disease, and diabetes?

Sources: Abbott, 2004; Anderson et al., 2011; Banich & Compton, 2011; Carlson, 2011; Hampton, 2007; Lee et al., 2011; Plomin, 1999; Romero et al., 2008; Slobounov, 2008).

Neural Bases of Behavior

What Is a Neuron? Psychology at the Micro Level

Objective 2.1: What are the key parts and functions of the neuron?

Have you heard the expression "Information is power?" Nowhere is this truer than in our human body. Without information, we could not survive. Cells within our nervous system must take in sensory information from the outside world through our eyes, ears, and other sensory receptors, and then decide what to do with it. Just as the circulatory system handles *blood*, which conveys chemicals and oxygen, our nervous system uses chemicals and electrical processes that convey *information*.

Your brain and the rest of your nervous system essentially consist of **neurons**, cells of the nervous system that communicate electrochemical information throughout the brain and the rest of the body. Each neuron is a tiny information-processing system with thousands of connections for receiving and sending signals to other neurons. Although no one knows for sure, one well-educated guess is that each human body has as many as 100 *billion* neurons, about the same number as there are stars in the galaxy.

These neurons are held in place and supported by **glial cells** (from the Greek word for "glue"), which make up about 90 percent of the brain's cells. Glial cells surround and hold neurons in place. They also supply nutrients and oxygen, perform cleanup tasks, and insulate one neuron from another so that their neural messages are not scrambled. Research also shows that glial cells play a direct role in nervous system communication (Perea & Arague, 2010; Sills & Garman, 2011). However, the "star" of the communication show, at least for now, is still the neuron.

Basic Parts of a Neuron

Just as no two people are alike, no two neurons are the same. However, most neurons do share three basic features: dendrites, cell body, and axon (Figure 2.1). **Dendrites** look like leafless branches of a tree. In fact, the word *dendrite* means "little tree" in

Neuron Nerve cell that processes and transmits information; basic building block of the nervous system responsible for receiving and transmitting electrochemical information

Glial Cells Cells that provide structural, nutritional, and other support for the neurons, as well as communication within the nervous system; also called glia or neuroglia

Dendrites Branching neuron structures that receive neural impulses from other neurons and convey impulses toward the cell body

StudyTip

Be careful not to confuse the term *neuron* with the term *nerve*. Nerves are large bundles of axons that carry impulses to and from the brain and spinal cord.

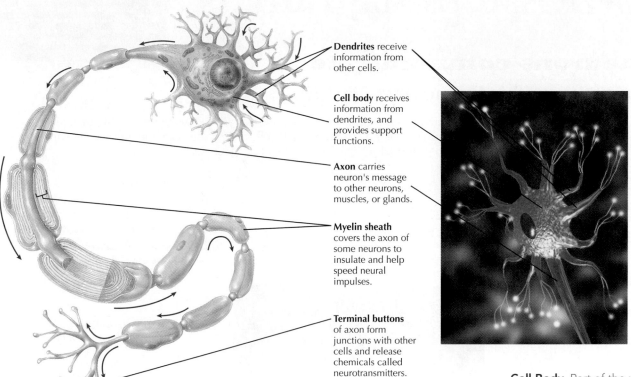

Dendrites receive information from other cells.

Cell body receives information from dendrites, and provides support functions.

Axon carries neuron's message to other neurons, muscles, or glands.

Myelin sheath covers the axon of some neurons to insulate and help speed neural impulses.

Terminal buttons of axon form junctions with other cells and release chemicals called neurotransmitters.

Figure 2.1 The structure of a motor neuron

Greek. Dendrites act like antennas, receiving electrochemical information from other neurons and transmitting it to the cell body. Each neuron may have hundreds or thousands of dendrites and their branches. From the many dendrites, information flows into the **cell body**, or soma (Greek for "body"), which accepts the incoming messages. If the cell body receives enough stimulation from its dendrites, it will pass the message on to the **axon** (from the Greek word for "axle"). Like a miniature cable, this long, tubelike structure then carries information away from the cell body.

The **myelin sheath**, a white, fatty coating around the axons of some neurons, is not considered one of the three key features of a neuron, but it does insulate and speed neural impulses. Its importance becomes readily apparent in certain diseases, such as multiple sclerosis, in which the myelin progressively deteriorates and the person gradually loses muscular coordination. Thankfully, the disease often goes into remission, but it can be fatal if it strikes the neurons that control basic life-support processes, such as breathing or heartbeat.

Near each axon's end, the axon branches out, and at the tip of each branch are *terminal buttons*, which release chemicals (called *neurotransmitters*). These chemicals move the message from the end of the sending neuron to the dendrites or cell body of the next receiving neuron, and the message continues. How neurons communicate via neurotransmitters will be studied in depth in the upcoming section.

How Do Neurons Communicate? An Electrical and Chemical Language

Objective 2.2: Describe how communication occurs within the neuron (the action potential) and between neurons.

A neuron's basic function is to transmit information throughout the nervous system. Neurons "speak" to each other or, in some cases, to muscles or glands, in a type of electrical and chemical language (Step-by-Step Diagram 2.1a,b).

Cell Body Part of the neuron containing the cell nucleus, as well as other structures that help the neuron carry out its functions; also known as the soma

Axon Long, tubelike structure that conveys impulses away from the neuron's cell body toward other neurons or to muscles or glands

Myelin [My-uh-lin] Sheath Layer of fatty insulation wrapped around the axon of some neurons, which increases the rate at which nerve impulses travel along the axon

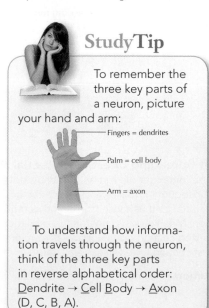

Study Tip

To remember the three key parts of a neuron, picture your hand and arm:

Fingers = dendrites

Palm = cell body

Arm = axon

To understand how information travels through the neuron, think of the three key parts in reverse alphabetical order: <u>D</u>endrite → <u>C</u>ell <u>B</u>ody → <u>A</u>xon (D, C, B, A).

Step-by-StepDiagram2.1

STOP This Step by Step diagram contains essential information NOT found elsewhere in the text, which is likely to appear on quizzes and exams. Be sure to study it CAREFULLY!

How neurons communicate

Communication *within* the neuron (Part A)

The process of neural communications begins within the neuron itself when the dendrites and cell body receive information and conduct it toward the axon. From there, the information travels down the entire length of the axon via a brief traveling electrical charge (like fans doing the "wave") called an **action potential**, which can be described in four steps:

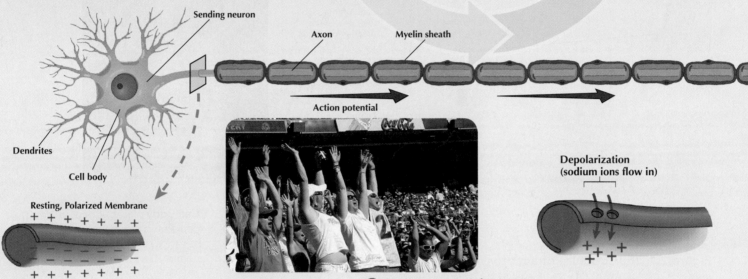

Sending neuron
Axon
Myelin sheath
Action potential
Dendrites
Cell body
Resting, Polarized Membrane

Depolarization (sodium ions flow in)

❶ Resting potential

When an axon is not stimulated, it is in a polarized state, called the *resting potential.* "At rest," the fluid inside the axon has more negatively charged ions than the fluid outside. This results from the selective permeability of the axon membrane and a series of mechanisms, called *sodium-potassium pumps,* which pull potassium ions in and pump sodium ions out of the axon. The inside of the axon has a charge of about −70 millivolts relative to the outside.

❷ Action potential initiation

When an "at rest" axon membrane is stimulated by a sufficiently strong signal, it produces an *action potential* (or depolarization). This action potential begins when the first part of the axon opens its "gates" and positively charged sodium ions rush through. The additional sodium ions change the previously negative charge inside the axon to a positive charge—thus depolarizing the axon.

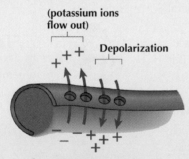

(potassium ions flow out)
Depolarization

Flow of depolarization
Action potential
Action potential
Action potential

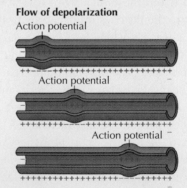

❸ Spreading of action potential and repolarization

The initial depolarization (or action potential) of Step 2 produces a subsequent imbalance of ions in the adjacent axon membrane. This imbalance thus causes the action potential to spread to the next section. Meanwhile, "gates" in the axon membrane of the initially depolarized section open and potassium ions flow out, thus allowing the first section to repolarize and return to its resting potential.

❹ Overall summary

As you can see in the figure above, this sequential process of depolarization, followed by repolarization, transmits the action potential along the entire length of the axon from the cell body to the terminal buttons. This is similar to an audience at an athletic event doing "the wave." One section of fans initially stands up for a brief time (action potential). This section then sits down (resting potential), and the "wave" then spreads to adjacent sections.

Action Potential Neural impulse, or brief electrical charge, that carries information along the axon of a neuron. The action potential is generated when positively charged ions move in and out through channels in the axon's membrane

Step-by-Step Diagram 2.1
(continued)

STOP *This Step by Step diagram contains essential information NOT found elsewhere in the text, which is likely to appear on quizzes and exams. Be sure to study it CAREFULLY!*

Communication *between* neurons (Part B)

Communication *within* the neuron (Part A) is not the same as communication *between* neurons (Part B). Within the neuron, messages travel electrically. Between neurons, messages are transmitted chemically. Steps 5, 6, and 7 summarize this chemical transmission.

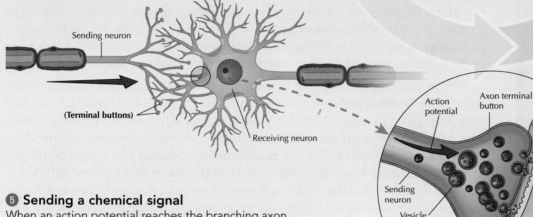

Sending neuron

(Terminal buttons)

Receiving neuron

Action potential

Axon terminal button

Sending neuron

Vesicle containing neurotransmitters

Synaptic gap

Neurotransmitter

Receptor sites on receiving neuron

Receiving neuron

❺ Sending a chemical signal

When an action potential reaches the branching axon terminals it triggers the terminal buttons at the axon's end to open and release thousands of **neurotransmitters** into the **synapse**, the tiny opening between the sending and receiving neuron. These chemicals then move across the synaptic gap and attach to the membranes of the receiving neuron. In this way, they carry the message from the sending neuron to the receiving neuron.

❻ Receiving a chemical signal

After a chemical message flows across the synaptic gap, it attaches to the receiving neuron. It's important to know that each receiving neuron gets multiple neurotransmitter messages. As you can see in this close-up photo, the axon terminals from thousands of other nearby neurons almost completely cover the cell body of the receiving neuron. It's also important to understand that neurotransmitters deliver either *excitatory* or *inhibitory* messages, and that the receiving neuron will only produce an action potential and pass along the message if the number of excitatory messages outweigh the inhibitory messages.

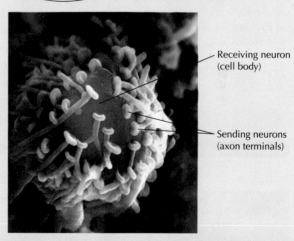

Receiving neuron (cell body)

Sending neurons (axon terminals)

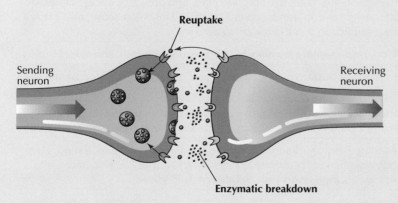

Reuptake

Sending neuron

Receiving neuron

Enzymatic breakdown

❼ Dealing with leftovers

Given that some neurons have thousands of receptors, which are only responsive to specific neurotransmitters, what happens to excess neurotransmitters or to those that do not "fit" into the adjacent receptor sites? The sending neuron normally reabsorbs the excess (called "reuptake"), or they are broken down by special enzymes.

Neurotransmitters Chemicals released by neurons that travel across the synaptic gap and allow neurons to communicate with one another

Synapse [SIN-aps] Gap between the axon tip of the sending neuron and the dendrite or cell body of the receiving neuron. During an action potential, chemicals called neurotransmitters are released and flow across the synaptic gap

55

How Do Neurotransmitters Affect Us? Disease, Endorphins, Poisons, and Drugs

Objective 2.3: How do neurotransmitters affect our everyday life?

After studying the admittedly complex processes of neural communication in the Step-by-Step Diagram 2.1, are you wondering what all of this has to do with you and your everyday life? If so, you'll be excited by the following details.

Researchers have discovered hundreds of substances known (or suspected) to function as neurotransmitters. Some of the neurotransmitters' functions are to regulate the actions of glands and muscles, and to promote sleep, mental and physical alertness, learning and memory, motivation, and emotions. They also influence, or may cause, psychological disorders, including schizophrenia and depression. Table 2.1 lists a few of the better-understood neurotransmitters and their known or suspected effects.

Disease Studying the brain and its neurotransmitters also increases our understanding of various medical problems and their treatment. For example, Michael J. Fox retired from his popular TV sitcom, *Spin City* because of muscle tremors and movement problems related to *Parkinson's disease (PD)*. As Table 2.1 shows, the neurotransmitter *dopamine* is a suspected factor in PD, and its symptoms are reduced with L-dopa (levodopa), a drug that increases dopamine levels in the brain (Friedman, 2010; Stoessl, 2011).

Interestingly, when some Parkinson's patients are adjusting to L-dopa and higher levels of dopamine, they may experience symptoms that mimic schizophrenia, a serious psychological disorder that disrupts thought processes and produces delusions and hallucinations. As you will see in Chapter 14, excessively high levels of *dopamine* are a suspected contributor to some forms of *schizophrenia*. When patients with schizophrenia take antipsychotic drugs that suppress dopamine, their psychotic symptoms are often reduced or eliminated (Iversen & Iversen, 2007). However, the drugs may also create symptoms of Parkinson's. Why is this so? *Decreased* levels of dopamine are associated with Parkinson's disease, whereas *increased* levels are related to some forms of schizophrenia.

Another neurotransmitter, *serotonin* (Table 2.1), may contribute to the depression that often accompanies Parkinson's disease. Although some researchers believe Parkinson's patients become depressed in reaction to the motor disabilities of the disorder, others think the depression is directly related to lower levels of serotonin. As Chapter 14 discusses, antidepressant drugs, like *Prozac* and *Zoloft*, work by boosting levels of available serotonin.

Why study neurotransmitters? Actor Michael J. Fox has been diagnosed with Parkinson's disease, which involves a decrease in cells that produce dopamine. In this photo, he is testifying before a U.S. congressional subcommittee to urge increased funding for research on Parkinson's and other medical conditions. For more information on his foundation for Parkinson's research, see www.michaeljfox.org.

Summary Table 2.1 HOW NEUROTRANSMITTERS AFFECT US

Neurotransmitter	Known or Suspected Effects
Acetylcholine (ACh)	Muscle action, learning, memory, REM (rapid-eye-movement) sleep, emotion; decreased ACh plays a suspected role in Alzheimer's disease
Dopamine (DA)	Movement, attention, memory, learning, and emotion; excess DA associated with schizophrenia, too little with Parkinson's disease; also plays a role in addiction and the reward system
Endorphins	Mood, pain, memory, learning, blood pressure, appetite, and sexual activity
Epinephrine (or adrenaline)	Emotional arousal, memory storage, and metabolism of glucose necessary for energy release
GABA (gamma aminobutyric acid)	Neural inhibition in the central nervous system; tranquilizing drugs, like Valium, increase GABA's inhibitory effects and thereby decrease anxiety
Norepinephrine (NE) (or noradrenaline)	Learning, memory, dreaming, emotion, waking from sleep, eating, alertness, wakefulness, reactions to stress; low levels of NE associated with depression, high levels with agitated, manic states
Serotonin	Mood, sleep, appetite, sensory perception, arousal, temperature regulation, pain suppression, and impulsivity; low levels associated with depression

Which neurotransmitters best explain this professional tennis player's exceptional skills?

ConceptOrganizer2.1

How Poisons and Drugs Affect our Brain

Foreign chemicals, like poisons and drugs, can mimic or block ongoing actions of neurotransmitters, thus interfering with normal functions.

Normal neurotransmission

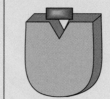

Postsynaptic receptor site

Nerve impulse

Somewhat like a key fitting into a lock, receptor sites on receiving neurons' dendrites recognize neurotransmitters by their particular shape.
When the shape of the neurotransmitter matches the shape of the receptor site a message is sent.

Neurotransmitters without the correct shape won't fit the receptors, so they cannot stimulate the dendrite, and that neurotransmitter's message is blocked.

(a) Normal neurotransmitter activation

(b) Blocked neurotransmitter activation

How poisons and drugs affect neurotransmission

Some *agonist drugs*, like the poison in the black widow spider or the nicotine in cigarettes, are similar enough in structure to a specific neurotransmitter (in this case, acetylcholine) that they mimic its effects on the receiving neuron, and a message is sent.

Some *antagonist drugs* block neurotransmitters like acetylcholine, which is vital in muscle action. Blocking it paralyzes muscles, including those involved in breathing, which can be fatal.

(c) Agonist drug "mimics" neurotransmitter

(d) Antagonist drug fills receptor space and blocks neurotransmitter

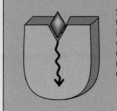

Most snake venom and some poisons, like *botulinum* toxin (Botox®), seriously affect normal muscle contraction. Ironically, these same poisons are sometimes used to treat certain medical conditions involving abnormal muscle contraction—as well as for some cosmetic purposes.

Endorphins Perhaps the best-known neurotransmitters are the *endogenous opioid peptides*, commonly known as **endorphins**. These chemicals mimic the effects of opium-based drugs such as morphine—they elevate mood and reduce pain.

Endorphins were discovered in the early 1970s, when Candace Pert and Solomon Snyder (1973) were doing research on morphine, a pain-relieving and mood-elevating opiate derived from opium, which is made from poppies. They found that the morphine was taken up by specialized receptors in areas of the brain linked with mood and pain sensations.

Why would our brains have special receptors for morphine—a powerfully addictive drug? Pert and Snyder reasoned that the brain must have its own internally produced, or *endogenous*, morphine-like chemicals. They later confirmed that such chemicals do exist and named them *endorphins* (a contraction of *endogenous* ["self-produced"] and *morphine*). The brain evidently produces its own naturally occurring chemical messengers that elevate mood and reduce pain, as well as affect memory, learning, blood pressure, appetite, and sexual activity (Chapters 3, 4, and 11). Endorphins also help explain why soldiers and athletes continue to fight or play the game despite horrific injuries.

Poisons and Mind-Altering Drugs The study of neurotransmitters helps explain the origin of certain diseases, and the psychological effects of our body's naturally produced neurotransmitters, such as endorphins. It also helps us understand how poisons from the bites of black widow spiders and snakes, and mind-altering drugs, like nicotine, alcohol, caffeine, and cocaine, affect the brain (see Concept Organizer 2.1 and Chapter 5).

Most poisons and drugs act at the synapse by replacing, decreasing, or enhancing the amount of neurotransmitter. Given that transmission of messages *between* neurons is chemical, it is not surprising that many chemicals we ingest from drugs and other sources can significantly affect neurotransmission.

Endorphins [en-DOR-fins] Chemical substances in the nervous system that are similar in structure and action to opiates; involved in pain control, pleasure, and memory

CHECK & REVIEW

Before going on, be sure to complete this Check & Review. It is an invaluable study tool!

Neural Bases of Behavior

Part A: Retrieval Practice

1. Without looking at the book, spend 10 minutes writing a free-form essay recalling all you can remember from the previous section.

2. Now, reread the previous section, and once again spend 10 minutes writing a free-form essay on the SAME material.

   (Although time consuming, this exercise has been shown to be the single best way to improve your test scores! For more information, check out www.sciencemag .org/content/early/2011/01/19/science .1199327.abstract)

Part B: Practice Quiz

1. Identify the five key parts of a neuron.

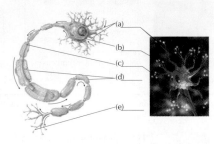

2. An impulse travels through the structures of the neuron in the following order: (a) cell body, axon, dendrites;

(b) cell body, dendrites, axon; (c) dendrites, cell body, axon; (d) axon, cell body, dendrites

3. Chemical messengers that are released by axons and stimulate dendrites are called ___. (a) chemical messengers; (b) neurotransmitters; (c) synaptic transmitters; (d) neuromessengers

4. Briefly explain how neurotransmitters carry messages throughout the body.

Check your answers in Appendix B.

Nervous System Organization

Objective 2.4: Describe the nervous system's two major divisions, and explain their respective functions.

To fully comprehend the complex intricacies of the nervous system, it helps to start with an overall map or "big picture." Look at Figure 2.2. Note the organization of the nervous system as a whole, and how it is divided and subdivided into several branches. Now, look at the drawing of the body in the middle of Figure 2.2, and imagine it as your own. Visualize your entire nervous system as two separate, but interrelated, parts—the **central nervous system (CNS)** and the **peripheral nervous system (PNS)**. The first part, the CNS, consists of your brain and a bundle of nerves (your spinal cord) that runs through your spinal column. Because it is located in the *center* of your body (within your skull and spine), it is called the *central* nervous system (CNS). Your CNS is primarily responsible for processing and organizing information.

Now, picture the many nerves that lie outside your skull and spine. This is the second major part of your nervous system—the PNS. Because it carries messages (action potentials) between the central nervous system and the *periphery* of the body, it is known as the *peripheral* nervous system (PNS). Your PNS links your CNS to your body's sense receptors (skin, eyes, ears, etc.), muscles, and glands.

Having completed our quick overview of the complete nervous system, we can go inside each of these two divisions for a closer look. Let's begin with the central nervous system (CNS).

Central Nervous System (CNS): Brain and Spinal Cord

Although we seldom think about it, our central nervous system (CNS) is what makes us unique and special. Most other animals can smell, run, see, and hear far

Central Nervous System (CNS) Brain and spinal cord

Peripheral Nervous System (PNS) All nerves and neurons connecting the central nervous system to the rest of the body

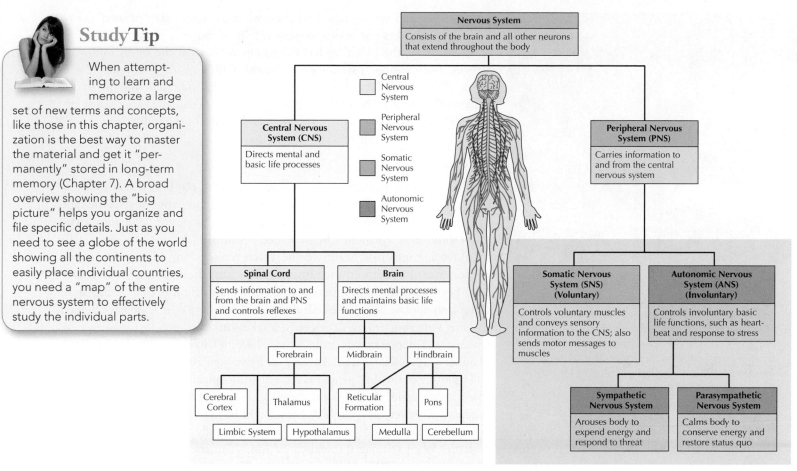

Figure 2.2 Organizational and functional divisions of the nervous system Note how the nervous system is divided and subdivided into various subsystems according to their differing functions in this figure. It will help orient you as you study upcoming sections.

better than we can. But thanks to our CNS, we can process information and adapt to our environment in ways that no other animal can. Unfortunately, our CNS is also incredibly fragile. Unlike neurons in the PNS, which require less protection because they can regenerate, damage to neurons in the CNS is usually serious, permanent, and sometimes fatal. However, the brain may not be as "hard wired" as we once believed.

Scientists long believed that after the first two or three years of life, humans and nonhuman animals are unable to repair or replace damaged neurons in the brain or spinal cord. We now know that the brain is capable of lifelong *neuroplasticity* and *neurogenesis*.

Objective 2.5: Discuss neuroplasticity, neurogenesis, and stem cells.

Neuroplasticity

Rather than being a fixed, solid organ, our brains are flexible and capable of changing their structure and function as a result of usage and experience (Park & Bischof, 2011; Romero et al., 2008; Rossignol et al., 2008). The basic brain organization (cortex, cerebellum, etc.) is irreversibly established before birth, but thanks to **neuroplasticity** some neural tissue can reorganize and change its structure and function throughout the life span. As we're learning a new sport or foreign language, for example, our brains change and "rewire." New synapses form and others disappear. Some dendrites

Neuroplasticity Brain's ability to reorganize and change its structure and function throughout the life span

Figure 2.3 A breakthrough in neuroscience
By immobilizing the unaffected arm or leg and requiring rigorous and repetitive exercise of the affected limb, psychologist Edward Taub and colleagues "recruit" stroke patients' intact brain cells to take over for damaged cells. The therapy has restored function in some patients as long as 21 years after their strokes.

Neurogenesis [nue-roe-JEN-uh-sis] Process by which new neurons are generated

Stem Cell Immature (uncommitted) cells that have the potential to develop into almost any type of cell depending on the chemical signals they receive

Reflex Innate, automatic response to a stimulus (e.g., knee-jerk reflex)

grow longer and sprout new branches, whereas others are "pruned" away. This is what makes our brains so wonderfully adaptive.

Remarkably, this rewiring has even helped remodel the brain following strokes. For example, psychologist Edward Taub and his colleagues (2002, 2004, 2007, 2010) have had unusual success restoring function in stroke patients (Figure 2.3). Note that recovery from brain damage varies considerably, depending in large part on the age and health of the individual, as well as the extent of the damage.

Neurogenesis

In addition to the amazing process of *neuroplasticity*, our brains also continually replace lost cells with new cells, a process called **neurogenesis**. One type of neurogenesis involves the transplantation of immature, "uncommitted" **stem cells** into a patient's brain. Once inside the brain, these stem cells then develop into new healthy cells, which replace those that have died or degenerated. In addition, to transplantation into the brain, stem cells also have been used for bone marrow transplants, and clinical trials using stem cells to repopulate or replace cells devastated by injury or disease have helped patients suffering from Alzheimer's, Parkinson's, diabetes, epilepsy, stress, strokes, and depression (Chang et al., 2005; Fleischmann & Welz, 2008; Hampton, 2006, 2007; Leri, Anversa, & Frishman, 2007).

Does this mean that people paralyzed from spinal cord injuries might be able to walk again? At this point, neurogenesis in the brain and spinal cord is minimal. However, one possible bridge might be to transplant stem cells in the damaged area of the spinal cord. Researchers have successfully transplanted nonhuman embryonic stem cells into damaged spinal cords (Jones, Anderson, & Galvin, 2003; Lee et al., 2011; Sieber-Blum, 2010). When the damaged spinal cords were viewed several weeks later, the implanted cells had survived and spread throughout the injured spinal cord area. More important, the transplant animals also showed some movement in previously paralyzed parts of their bodies. Medical researchers have also begun human trials using nerve grafts to repair damaged spinal cords (Lopez, 2002; Saltus, 2000, Tewarie et al., 2010).

Spinal Cord

Objective 2.6: What are the major functions of the spinal cord?

Now that we have discussed the remarkable adaptability of the central nervous system (CNS), let's take an even closer look at its components—the brain and spinal cord. Because of its central importance for psychology, we'll discuss the brain in detail in the next major section. The spinal cord also is very important. It is a great highway of information into and out of the brain. But it is much more than a simple set of cables relaying messages. Your spinal cord is involved in all voluntary movements and can even initiate some automatic behaviors on its own. These involuntary, automatic behaviors are called **reflexes**, or *reflex arcs*. The response to the incoming stimuli is "reflected" back—automatically (Step-by-Step Diagram 2.2).

We're all born with numerous reflexes (see Figure 2.4), many of which fade over time. But even as adults, we still blink in response to a puff of air in our eyes, gag when the back of our throat is stimulated, and urinate and defecate in response to pressure in the bladder and rectum. Reflexes also influence our sexual responses. Just as a puff of air produces an automatic closing of the eyes, certain stimuli, such as the stroking of the genitals, can lead to arousal and the reflexive muscle contractions of orgasm in both men and women. However, in order to have the passion, thoughts, and emotion we normally associate with sex, the sensory information from the stroking or orgasm must be carried to the brain.

Step-by-StepDiagram2.2

STOP *This Step by Step diagram contains essential information NOT found elsewhere in the text, which is likely to appear on quizzes and exams. Be sure to study it CAREFULLY!*

How the spinal reflex operates

In a simple reflex arc, a sensory receptor responds to stimulation and initiates a neural impulse that travels to the spinal cord. This signal then travels back to the appropriate muscle, which then contracts. The response is automatic and immediate in a reflex because the signal only travels as far as the spinal cord before action is initiated, not all the way to the brain. The brain is later "notified" of the action when the spinal cord sends along the message.

What might be the evolutionary advantages of the reflex arc?

① In a simple reflex circuit, skin receptors in the fingertips detect heat from the sauce pan, and then send neural messages to sensory neurons.

② Sensory neurons carry messages to the spinal cord.

③ Interneurons in the spinal cord relay messages to motor neurons.

④ Motor neurons send messages to hand muscles, causing a withdrawal reflex. (This occurs before the brain perceives the actual sensation of pain.)

⑤ While the spinal reflex occurs, sensory neurons also send messages up the spinal cord to the brain.

⑥ A small structure in the brain, the thalamus, relays incoming sensory information to the higher, cortical areas of the brain.

⑦ An area of the brain, known as the somatosensory cortex, receives the message from the thalamus and interprets it as PAIN!

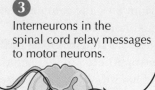
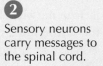

Spinal cord (cross section)

Answer: If messages had to travel all the way to the brain before they could be acted upon, the animal (human and nonhuman) might be fatally wounded.

PSYCHOLOGY ENGAGES

TRY THIS YOURSELF

If you have a newborn or young infant in your home, you can easily (and safely) test for these simple reflexes. (Note: Most infant reflexes disappear within the first year of life. If they reappear in later life, it generally indicates damage to the central nervous system.)

(a) **Rooting reflex** Lightly stroke the cheek or side of the mouth, and the infant will automatically (reflexively) turn toward the stimulation and attempt to suck.

(b) **Grasping reflex** Place your finger in the infant's palm and note the automatic grasp.

(c) **Babinski reflex** Lightly stroke the sole of the infant's foot, and the toes will fan out and the foot will twist inward.

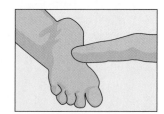

Figure 2.4 Infant reflexes

Peripheral Nervous System (PNS): Connecting the CNS to the Rest of the Body

Objective 2.7: What are the subdivisions of the peripheral nervous system, and what are their functions?

The *peripheral nervous system (PNS)* is just what it sounds like—the part that involves nerves *peripheral* to (or outside of) the brain and spinal cord. The chief function of the peripheral nervous system is to carry information to and from the central nervous system. It links the brain and spinal cord to the body's sense receptors, muscles, and glands.

Scientists further divide the PNS into the somatic nervous system and the autonomic nervous system. The **somatic nervous system (SNS)** (also called the *skeletal nervous system*) consists of all the nerves that connect to sensory receptors and skeletal muscles. The name comes from the term *soma*, which means "body," and the somatic nervous system plays a key role in communication throughout the entire *body*. In a kind of "two-way street," the SNS first carries sensory information to the CNS and then carries messages from the CNS to skeletal muscles (Figure 2.5).

The other subdivision of the PNS, the **autonomic nervous system (ANS)**, is responsible for *involuntary* tasks, such as heart rate, digestion, pupil dilation, and breathing. Like an automatic pilot, the ANS can sometimes be consciously overridden. But as its name implies, the autonomic system normally operates independently (*autonomic* means "autonomous").

The autonomic nervous system is itself further divided into two branches, the **sympathetic** and **parasympathetic**, to regulate the functioning of target organs like the heart, intestines, and lungs (Figure 2.6). These two subsystems tend to work in opposition to each other. A convenient, if somewhat oversimplified, distinction is that the *sympathetic branch* of the autonomic nervous system arouses the body and mobilizes it for action—the "fight-or-flight" response. In contrast, the *parasympathetic branch* calms the body and conserves energy—the relaxation response. Keep in mind that

Somatic Nervous System (SNS) Subdivision of the peripheral nervous system (PNS) that connects to sensory receptors and controls skeletal muscles

Autonomic Nervous System (ANS) Subdivision of the peripheral nervous system (PNS) that controls involuntary functions, such as heart rate and digestion. It is further subdivided into the sympathetic nervous system, which arouses, and the parasympathetic nervous system, which calms

Sympathetic Nervous System Subdivision of the autonomic nervous system (ANS) responsible for arousing the body and mobilizing its energy during times of stress; also called the "fight-or-flight" system

Parasympathetic Nervous System Subdivision of the autonomic nervous system (ANS) responsible for calming the body and conserving energy

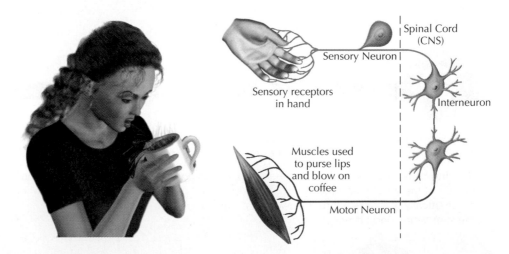

Figure 2.5 Sensory and motor neurons In order for you to be able to function, your brain and body must communicate with one another. This is the job of the *somatic nervous system* (SNS), which receives sensory information, sends it to the brain, and allows the brain to direct the body to act. Messages (action potentials) within the nervous system can cross the synapse in only one direction. *Sensory neurons* carry messages inward from other body areas *to* the CNS. In contrast, *motor neurons* carry messages *away* from the CNS. *Interneurons* internally communicate and intervene between the sensory inputs and the motor outputs. Most of the neurons in the brain are interneurons.

Stress, high activity, fight-or-flight

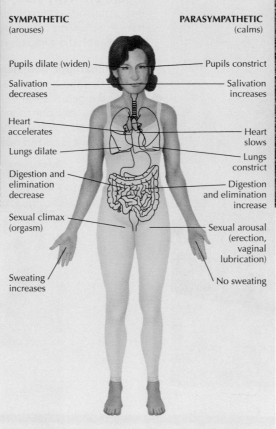

SYMPATHETIC
(arouses)

PARASYMPATHETIC
(calms)

Pupils dilate (widen) — Pupils constrict

Salivation decreases — Salivation increases

Heart accelerates — Heart slows

Lungs dilate — Lungs constrict

Digestion and elimination decrease — Digestion and elimination increase

Sexual climax (orgasm) — Sexual arousal (erection, vaginal lubrication)

Sweating increases — No sweating

Relaxation, low stress, rest-and-digest

Figure 2.6 Actions of the autonomic nervous system (ANS) The ANS is responsible for a variety of independent (autonomous) activities, such as salivation and digestion. It exercises this control through its two divisions—the *sympathetic* and *parasympathetic* branches.

StudyTip

One way to differentiate the two subdivisions of the ANS is to imagine skydiving out of an airplane. When you initially jump, your sympathetic nervous system has "sympathy" for your stressful situation. It alerts and prepares you for immediate action. Once your "para" chute opens, your "para" sympathetic nervous system takes over, and you can relax as you float safely to earth.

these two systems are not an "on/off" or either/or arrangement. Like two children on a playground teeter-totter, one will be up while the other is down. But they essentially balance each other out. In everyday situations, the sympathetic and parasympathetic nervous systems work together to maintain a steady, balanced, internal state.

When you hear a question from your instructor and want to raise your hand, your *somatic nervous system* will report to your brain the current state of your skeletal muscles. It then carries instructions back to your muscles, allowing you to lift your arm and hand. But the somatic nervous system does not make your pupils dilate or your heartbeat quicken if a dangerous snake comes sliding into the classroom. For this, you need your *sympathetic nervous system*. It would simultaneously shut down your digestive processes and cause hormones, such as *cortisol*, to be released into the bloodstream. The net result of sympathetic activation is to get more oxygenated blood and energy to the skeletal muscles, thus allowing us to "fight or flee."

In contrast to the sympathetic nervous system, which arouses the body, the *parasympathetic nervous system* calms and returns your body to its normal functioning. It slows your heart rate, lowers your blood pressure, and increases your digestive and eliminative processes. Now, we understand why arguments during meals often cause stomachaches! Strong emotions, like anger, fear, or even joy, put the sympathetic system in dominance and prevent digestion and elimination. Strong emotions and sympathetic dominance also explain many sexual problems (Figure 2.7).

It is important to remember, however, that the sympathetic nervous system does provide adaptive, evolutionary advantages. At the beginning of human evolution, when we faced a dangerous bear or aggressive human intruder, there were only two reasonable responses—fight or flight. This automatic mobilization of bodily resources

Figure 2.7 Why study psychology? The complexities of sexual interaction—and in particular, the difficulties that couples sometimes have in achieving sexual arousal or orgasm—illustrate the balancing act between the sympathetic and parasympathetic nervous systems.

Parasympathetic dominance Sexual arousal and excitement require that the body be relaxed enough to allow increased blood flow to the genitals—in other words, the nervous system must be in *parasympathetic dominance.* Parasympathetic nerves carry messages from the central nervous system directly to the sexual organs, allowing for a localized response (increased blood flow and genital arousal).

Sympathetic dominance During strong emotions, such as anger, anxiety, or fear, the body shifts to *sympathetic dominance,* and blood flow to the genitals and other organs decreases as the body readies for a "fight or flight." As a result, the person is unable (or less likely) to become sexually aroused. Any number of circumstances—for example, performance anxiety, fear of unwanted pregnancy or disease, or tensions between partners—can trigger sympathetic dominance.

still has significant survival value in our modern life. But today our sympathetic nervous system is often activated by less life-threatening events. Instead of bears and intruders, we have chronic stressors like full-time college classes mixed with part- or full-time jobs, dual-career marriages, daily traffic jams, and rude drivers on high-speed freeways—not to mention terrorist attacks and global pollution. Unfortunately, our body responds to these sources of stress with sympathetic arousal. And, as you will see in Chapter 3, chronic arousal to stress can be very detrimental to our health.

Endocrine System

Endocrine [EN-doh-krin] system Collection of glands located throughout the body that manufacture and secrete hormones into the bloodstream

Hormones Chemicals manufactured by endocrine glands and circulated in the bloodstream to produce bodily changes or maintain normal bodily functions

Objective 2.8: Briefly discuss the importance of hormones and the endocrine system.

We've just seen how the nervous system is organized into the CNS and PNS, and earlier how it uses neurons and neurotransmitters to transmit messages throughout the body. A second type of communication system also exists, which is made up of a network of glands, called the **endocrine system** (Figure 2.8). Rather than neurotransmitters, the endocrine system uses **hormones** (from the Greek *horman*, meaning to "stimulate" or "excite") to carry its messages (Figure 2.9).

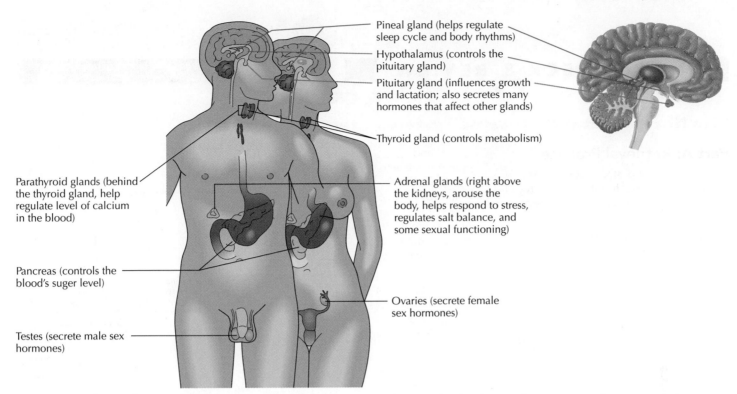

Pineal gland (helps regulate sleep cycle and body rhythms)

Hypothalamus (controls the pituitary gland)

Pituitary gland (influences growth and lactation; also secretes many hormones that affect other glands)

Thyroid gland (controls metabolism)

Parathyroid glands (behind the thyroid gland, help regulate level of calcium in the blood)

Adrenal glands (right above the kidneys, arouse the body, helps respond to stress, regulates salt balance, and some sexual functioning)

Pancreas (controls the blood's suger level)

Ovaries (secrete female sex hormones)

Testes (secrete male sex hormones)

Figure 2.8 The endocrine system This figure shows the major endocrine glands, along with some internal organs to help you locate the glands. Hormones secreted by the endocrine system are as essential as neurotransmitters to the regulation of our bodily functions.

Why is the endocrine system important? Without the hypothalamus and pituitary, the testes in men would not produce *testosterone* and the ovaries in women would not produce *estrogen*. As you may know, these hormones are of critical importance to sexual behavior and reproduction. In addition, the pituitary produces its own hormone that controls body growth. Too much of this hormone results in *gigantism*; too little will make a person far smaller than average, a *hypopituitary dwarf*.

Other hormones released by the endocrine system play important roles in maintaining your body's normal functioning. For example, hormones released by the kidneys help regulate blood pressure. The pancreatic hormone (insulin) allows cells to use sugar from the blood. Stomach and intestinal hormones help control digestion and elimination.

An additional function of the endocrine system is its control of our body's response to emergencies. In times of crisis, the hypothalamus sends messages through two pathways—the neural system and endocrine system (primarily the pituitary). The pituitary sends hormonal messages to the adrenal glands (located right above the kidneys). The adrenal glands then release *cortisol*, a "stress hormone" that boosts energy and blood sugar levels, *epinephrine* (commonly called adrenaline), and *norepinephrine* (or noradrenaline). (Remember from Table 2.1 that these same chemicals also serve as neurotransmitters when released by neurons.)

Neurotransmitters send individual messages

Hormones send global messages

Figure 2.9 Why do we need two communication systems? Just as some e-mail messages are only sent to certain people, neurotransmitters only deliver messages to specific receptors, which other neurons nearby probably don't "overhear." Hormones, in contrast, are like a global e-mail message that you send to everyone in your address book. Endocrine glands release these hormones directly into the bloodstream, which then travel throughout the body, carrying messages to any cell that will listen. Hormones also function like your global e-mail recipients forwarding your message to yet more people. For example, a small part of the brain called the hypothalamus releases hormones that signal the pituitary (another small brain structure), which stimulates or inhibits the release of other hormones.

CHECK & REVIEW

STOP *Before going on, be sure to complete this Check & Review. It is an invaluable study tool!*

The Nervous and Endocrine Systems

Part A: Retrieval Practice

1. Without looking at the book, spend 10 minutes writing a free-form essay recalling all you can remember from the previous section.

2. Now, reread the previous section, and once again spend 10 minutes writing a free-form essay on the SAME material.

Part B: Practice Quiz

1. The nervous system is separated into two major divisions: the _____ nervous system, which consists of the brain and spinal cord, and the _____ nervous system, which consists of all the nerves going to and from the brain and spinal cord.

2. The autonomic nervous system is subdivided into two branches called the _____ and _____ systems. (a) automatic, semiautomatic; (b) somatic, peripheral; (c) afferent, efferent; (d) sympathetic, parasympathetic

3. If you are startled by the sound of a loud explosion, the _____ nervous system will become dominant.

4. What is the major difference between the sympathetic and parasympathetic nervous systems?

5. Fill in the blank lines.

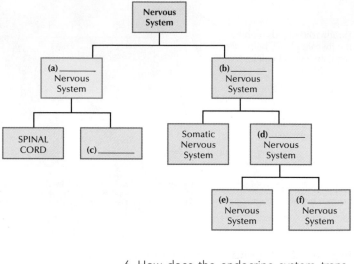

6. How does the endocrine system transmit its messages?.

Check your answers in Appendix B.

A Tour through the Brain

Brainstem Area of the brain that houses parts of the hindbrain, midbrain, and forebrain, and helps regulate reflex activities critical for survival (such as heartbeat and respiration)

As you can see in Figure 2.10, brain size and complexity vary significantly among species. We begin our exploration of the *human* brain at the lower end, where the spinal cord joins the base of the brain, and then continue upward toward the skull. Note that as we move from bottom to top, "lower," basic processes like breathing generally give way to "higher," more complex mental processes.

The brain can be divided into three major sections: the *hindbrain*, *midbrain*, and *forebrain* (Figure 2.11). Also note the large section labeled as the **brainstem**, which includes parts of all three of these sections and helps regulate reflex activities important to survival (such as heartbeat and respiration). The distinctive shape of the brainstem provides a handy geographical landmark to keep us oriented.

Lower-Level Brain Structures: Hindbrain, Midbrain, and Parts of the Forebrain

Objective 2.9: Identify the three major sections of the brain.

Throughout our tour of the brain, note that certain brain structures are specialized to perform certain tasks, a process known as *localization of function*.

Figure 2.10 Brain Comparisons In general, lower species (such as fish and reptiles) have smaller, less complex brains. The most complex brains belong to dolphins, whales, and higher primates (such as gorillas, chimps, and humans).

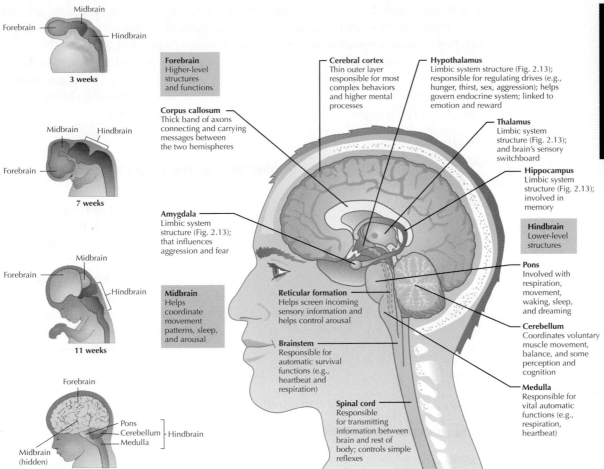

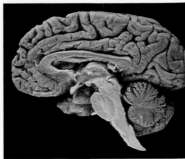

Actual photo of human brain This deceased human's brain is sliced down the center, splitting it into right and left halves. The right half is shown in this photo.

Forebrain Higher-level structures and functions

Corpus callosum Thick band of axons connecting and carrying messages between the two hemispheres

Amygdala Limbic system structure (Fig. 2.13); that influences aggression and fear

Midbrain Helps coordinate movement patterns, sleep, and arousal

Cerebral cortex Thin outer layer responsible for most complex behaviors and higher mental processes

Hypothalamus Limbic system structure (Fig. 2.13); responsible for regulating drives (e.g., hunger, thirst, sex, aggression); helps govern endocrine system; linked to emotion and reward

Thalamus Limbic system structure (Fig. 2.13); and brain's sensory switchboard

Hippocampus Limbic system structure (Fig. 2.13); involved in memory

Hindbrain Lower-level structures

Pons Involved with respiration, movement, waking, sleep, and dreaming

Reticular formation Helps screen incoming sensory information and helps control arousal

Brainstem Responsible for automatic survival functions (e.g., heartbeat and respiration)

Spinal cord Responsible for transmitting information between brain and rest of body; controls simple reflexes

Cerebellum Coordinates voluntary muscle movement, balance, and some perception and cognition

Medulla Responsible for vital automatic functions (e.g., respiration, heartbeat)

3 weeks

7 weeks

11 weeks

At birth

Figure 2.11 The human brain (a) Note how the forebrain, midbrain, and hindbrain radically change in their size and placement during prenatal development. (b) The profile drawing above highlights key structures and functions of the right half of the brain. As you read about each of these structures, keep this drawing in mind and refer back to it as necessary. (The diagram shows the brain structures as if the brain were split vertically down the center and the left hemisphere were removed.)

But keep in mind that most parts of both the human and nonhuman brain are not so specialized—they perform integrating, overlapping functions.

Hindbrain

Objective 2.10: What are the three key components of the hindbrain, and what are their functions?

Have you ever wondered what allows you to automatically breathe and your heart to keep pumping despite your being sound asleep? Automatic behaviors and survival responses like these are either controlled by or influenced by parts of your **hindbrain**, which includes the *medulla*, *pons*, and *cerebellum*.

The **medulla** is essentially an extension of the spinal cord, with many nerve fibers passing through it carrying information to and from the brain. It also controls many essential automatic bodily functions, such as respiration and heartbeat.

The **pons**, located above the cerebellum, is involved in respiration, movement, sleep, waking, and dreaming (among other things). It also contains many axons that cross from one side of the brain to the other (*pons* is Latin for "bridge").

The cauliflower-shaped **cerebellum** ("little brain" in Latin) is, evolutionarily, a very old structure. It coordinates fine muscle movement and balance. Although the

Hindbrain Collection of brain structures including the medulla, pons, and cerebellum

Medulla [muh-DUL-uh] Hindbrain structure responsible for vital, automatic functions, such as respiration and heartbeat

Pons Hindbrain structure involved in respiration, movement, waking, sleep, and dreaming

Cerebellum [sehr-uh-BELL-um] Hindbrain structure responsible for coordinating fine muscle movement, balance, and some perception and cognition

actual commands for movement come from higher brain centers in the cortex, the cerebellum coordinates the muscles so that movement is smooth and precise. The cerebellum is also critical to our sense of equilibrium or physical balance.

Researchers using functional magnetic resonance imaging (fMRI) have also shown that parts of the cerebellum are important for some memory, sensory, perceptual, cognitive, and language tasks, as well as some learning and conditioning (Bellabaum & Daum, 2011; Thompson, 2005; Woodruff-Pak & Disterhoft, 2008).

Midbrain

Objective 2.11: Describe the functions of the midbrain and the reticular formation.

The **midbrain** helps orient our eye and body movements to visual and auditory stimuli, and works with the pons to help control sleep and level of arousal. It also contains a small structure involved with the neurotransmitter dopamine, which deteriorates in Parkinson's disease.

Running through the core of the hindbrain, midbrain, and brainstem is the **reticular** (netlike) **formation (RF)**. This diffuse, finger-shaped network of neurons helps screen incoming sensory information and alerts the higher brain centers to important events. Without your RF, you would not be alert or perhaps even conscious. In fact, some general anesthics target the RF so pain sensations never register in the brain (Simon, 2007).

Forebrain

Objective 2.12: Identify the major structures of the forebrain, and describe their functions.

The **forebrain** is the largest and most prominent part of the human brain. It includes the *thalamus, hypothalamus, limbic system*, and *cerebral cortex* (Figure 2.12). The first three structures are located near the top of the brainstem. Wrapped above and around them is the cerebral cortex. (*Cerebrum* is Latin for "brain," and *cortex* is Latin for "covering" or "bark.") In this section, we will discuss only the first three structures. Because of its vital role in all complex mental activities, the cerebral cortex will have its own separate discussion following this one.

Thalamus Resembling two little footballs joined side by side, the **thalamus** serves as the major sensory relay center for the brain. Like an air traffic control center that receives information from all aircraft and then directs them to the appropriate landing or takeoff areas, the thalamus receives input from nearly all the sensory systems, except smell, and then directs this information to the appropriate cortical areas. For example, while you're reading this page, your thalamus sends incoming visual signals to the visual area of your cortex. While listening to music, the information is transferred to the auditory (or hearing) area of your cortex. The thalamus also transmits some higher brain information to the cerebellum and medulla.

In addition to relaying sensory information to the cortex, the thalamus also integrates information from various senses and may be involved in learning and memory (Bailey & Mair, 2005; Ridley et al., 2005). Injury to the thalamus can cause deafness, blindness, or loss of any other sense (except smell). This suggests that some analysis of sensory messages may occur here. Because the thalamus is the major sensory relay area to the cerebral cortex, damage or abnormalities also might cause the cortex to misinterpret or not receive vital sensory information. Interestingly, brain-imaging research links thalamus abnormalities to *schizophrenia*, a serious psychological disorder involving problems with sensory filtering and perception (Bor et al., 2011; De Witte et al., 2011; Preuss et al., 2005).

Midbrain Collection of brain structures in the middle of the brain responsible for coordinating movement patterns, sleep, and arousal

Reticular Formation (RF) Diffuse set of neurons that helps screen incoming information and controls arousal

Forebrain Collection of upper level brain structures including the thalamus, hypothalamus, limbic system, and cerebral cortex

Thalamus [THAL-uh-muss] Forebrain structure at the top of the brainstem; serves as the brain's switchboard relaying sensory messages to the cerebral cortex

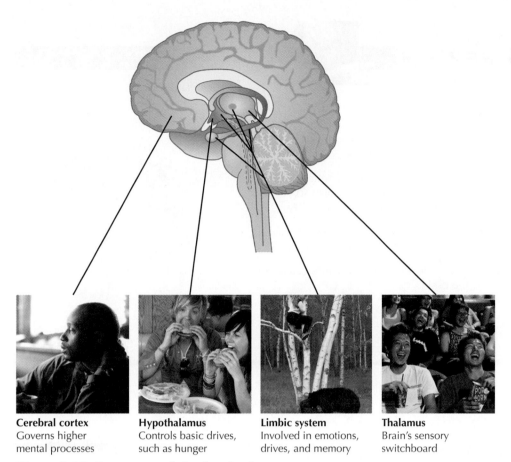

Cerebral cortex	Hypothalamus	Limbic system	Thalamus
Governs higher mental processes	Controls basic drives, such as hunger	Involved in emotions, drives, and memory	Brain's sensory switchboard

Figure 2.12 Structures of the forebrain

Hypothalamus Beneath the thalamus lies the **hypothalamus** (*hypo-* means "under"). Although no larger than a kidney bean, it has been called the "master control center" for basic drives such as hunger, thirst, sex, and aggression (Banich & Compton, 2011; Hull, 2011; Lenz & McCarthy, 2010). It also helps govern hormonal processes by regulating the endocrine system. Hanging down from the hypothalamus, the *pituitary gland* is usually considered a key endocrine gland because it releases hormones that activate the other endocrine glands. The hypothalamus influences the pituitary through direct neural connections and by releasing its own hormones into the blood supply of the pituitary.

Limbic System An interconnected group of forebrain structures, known as the **limbic system**, is located roughly along the border between the cerebral cortex and the lower-level brain structures (hence the term *limbic*, which means "edge" or "border"). Scientists disagree about which structures should be included in the limbic system, but most include the *hippocampus, amygdala, thalamus,* and *hypothalamus* (Figure 2.13).

The limbic system is generally responsible for emotions, drives, and memory. As we'll see in Chapter 7, the **hippocampus** is involved in forming and retrieving memories. However, the major focus of interest in the limbic system, and particularly the **amygdala**, has been its production and regulation of emotions (e.g., aggression and fear) (LeDoux, 1998, 2002, 2007; Pessoa, 2010; Ritchey, LaBar, & Cabeza, 2011).

Another well-known function of the limbic system is its role in pleasure or reward. James Olds and Peter Milner (1954) were the first to note that electrically stimulating certain areas of the limbic system caused a "pleasure" response in rats. The feeling was apparently so rewarding that the rats would cross electrified grids, swim through water (which they normally avoid), and press a lever thousands of times until they collapsed

Why do police officers ask drivers to "walk the line"?

Answer: The cerebellum is responsible for smooth and precise movement, and it is also one of the first areas of the brain affected by alcohol. Asking drivers to perform tasks like walking the white line is a quick and easy measure of potential drunk driving.

Hypothalamus [hi-poh-THAL-uh-muss] Small brain structure beneath the thalamus that helps govern drives (hunger, thirst, sex, and aggression) and hormones

Limbic System Interconnected group of forebrain structures involved with emotions, drives, and memory

Hippocampus Part of the limbic system involved in forming and retrieving memories

Amygdala Limbic system structure linked to the production and regulation of emotions (e.g., aggression and fear)

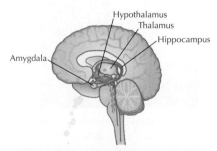

Figure 2.13 Major brain structures commonly associated with the limbic system

PSYCHOLOGY ENGAGES

CHECK & REVIEW

STOP *Before going on, be sure to complete this Check & Review. It is an invaluable study tool!*

Lower-Level Brain Structures

Part A: Retrieval Practice

1. Without looking at the book, spend 10 minutes writing a free-form essay recalling all you can remember from the previous section.

2. Now, reread the previous section, and once again spend 10 minutes writing a free-form essay on the SAME material.

Part B: Practice Quiz

1. What are the three major structures within the hindbrain?

2. Roadside tests for drunk driving primarily test responses of the _____.

3. What is the major sensory relay area for the brain? (a) hypothalamus; (b) thalamus; (c) cortex; (d) hindbrain?

4. Why is the amygdala a major focus of interest for researchers?

5. Label the following structures/areas of the brain.

   a. brainstem   b. cerebellum
   c. corpus callosum   d. thalamus
   e. amygdala   f. cerebral cortex

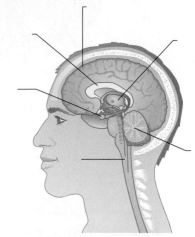

Check your answers in Appendix B.

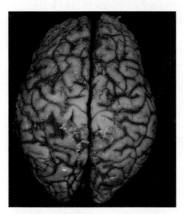

(a) Looking at this photo of the top side of a human brain, all you can see is its outer, wrinkled surface, known as the cerebral cortex.

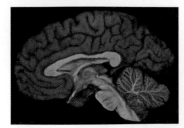

(b) If you made a vertical cut along the center crevice of the brain, you would have this inside view of the right hemisphere. Note how the many wrinkles, or folds, allow this large mass of tissue to fit inside your skull.

Figure 2.14 The cerebral cortex

from exhaustion—just to have this area of their brains stimulated. Follow-up studies found somewhat similar responses in other animals and even among human volunteers (e.g., Bühler et al., 2010; Dackis & O'Brien, 2001). Modern research suggests that brain stimulation may activate neurotransmitters rather than discrete "pleasure centers."

Keep in mind that even though limbic system structures and neurotransmitters are instrumental in emotional behavior, emotion in humans is also tempered by higher brain centers in the cerebral cortex. Damage to the front part of the cortex, which connects to the amygdala and other parts of the limbic system, can permanently impair social and emotional behavior. This is yet another example of the inseparable interconnectivity of the entire brain.

Cerebral Cortex: The Center of "Higher" Processing

Objective 2.13: What is the cerebral cortex, and what is its major function?

The gray, wrinkled **cerebral cortex** is responsible for most complex behaviors and higher mental processes (Figure 2.14). It plays such a vital role in human life that many consider it the essence of life. Without a functioning cortex, we would be almost completely unaware of ourselves and our surroundings.

Although the cerebral cortex is only about one-quarter of an inch thick, it is made up of approximately 30 billion neurons and nine times as many supporting glial cells. When spread out, the cortex would cover an area almost the size of a standard newspaper page. How does your cortex, along with all your other brain structures, fit inside your skull? Imagine crumpling and rolling the newspaper sheet into a ball. You would retain the same surface area but in a much smaller space. The cortex contains numerous "wrinkles" (called *convolutions*), allowing it to hold billions of neurons in the restricted space of the skull.

Cerebral Cortex Thin surface layer on the cerebral hemispheres that regulates most complex behavior, including sensations, motor control, and higher mental processes

Have you watched brain surgeries in movies or on television? After the skull is opened, you'll first see a gray, wrinkled, cerebral cortex that closely resembles an over-sized walnut. Also like a walnut, the cortex has a similar division (or fissure) down the center, which marks the *left* and *right hemispheres* of the brain. The two hemispheres make up about 80 percent of the brain's weight and they are mostly filled with axon connections between the cortex and other brain structures. Each hemisphere controls the opposite side of the body (Figure 2.15).

The two cerebral hemispheres are divided into eight distinct areas, or *lobes*—four in each hemisphere (Figure 2.16). Like the lower-level brain structures, each lobe specializes in somewhat different tasks—another example of *localization of function*. However, some functions overlap between lobes.

Figure 2.15 Information crossover The right hemisphere of your brain controls the left side of your body, whereas the left hemisphere controls the right side.

Frontal Lobes

Objective 2.14: Describe the major functions of the lobes of the cerebral cortex.

By far the largest of the cortical lobes, the two **frontal lobes** are located at the top front portion of the two brain hemispheres—right behind your forehead. The frontal

Frontal Lobes Two lobes at the front of the brain governing motor control, speech production, and higher functions, such as thinking, personality, emotion, and memory

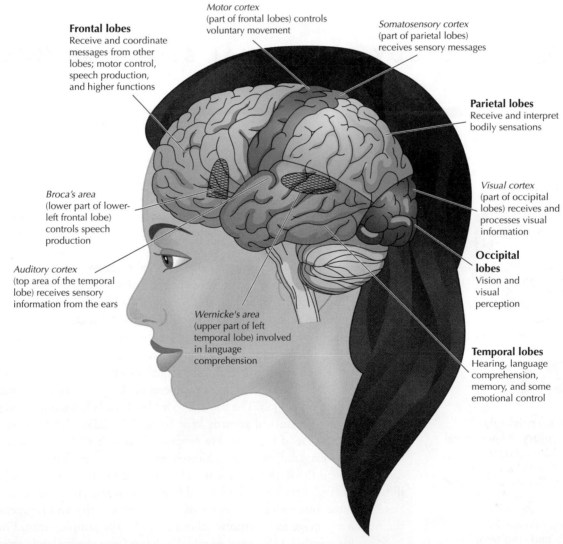

Motor cortex (part of frontal lobes) controls voluntary movement

Somatosensory cortex (part of parietal lobes) receives sensory messages

Frontal lobes Receive and coordinate messages from other lobes; motor control, speech production, and higher functions

Parietal lobes Receive and interpret bodily sensations

Broca's area (lower part of lower-left frontal lobe) controls speech production

Visual cortex (part of occipital lobes) receives and processes visual information

Auditory cortex (top area of the temporal lobe) receives sensory information from the ears

Occipital lobes Vision and visual perception

Wernicke's area (upper part of left temporal lobe) involved in language comprehension

Temporal lobes Hearing, language comprehension, memory, and some emotional control

Figure 2.16 Lobes of the brain This is a view of the brain's left hemisphere showing its four lobes—*frontal, parietal, temporal,* and *occipital*. The right hemisphere has the same four lobes. Divisions between the lobes are marked by visibly prominent folds. Keep in mind that Broca's and Wernicke's areas are only in the left hemisphere.

lobes receive and coordinate messages from all other lobes of the cortex, while also being responsible for at least three additional functions:

1. *Motor control* At the very back of the frontal lobes lies the *motor cortex*, which sends messages to the various muscles that instigate voluntary movement (Figure 2.16). When you want to call your friend on your cell phone, the motor control area of your frontal lobes guides your fingers to press the desired sequence of numbers.

2. *Speech production* In the *left* frontal lobe, on the surface of the cortex near the bottom of the motor control area, lies *Broca's area*, which is known to play a crucial role in speech production. In 1865, French physician Paul Broca discovered that damage to this area causes difficulty in speech, but not language comprehension. This type of impaired language ability is known as *Broca's aphasia*.

3. *Higher functions* Most functions that distinguish humans from other animals, such as thinking, personality, emotion, and memory, are controlled primarily by the frontal lobes. Damage to the frontal lobe affects motivation, drives, creativity, self-awareness, initiative, reasoning, and emotional behavior. Abnormalities in the frontal lobes are often observed in patients with schizophrenia (Chapter 14).

CASE STUDY / PERSONAL STORY

Phineas Gage

Objective 2.15: Why is the case study of Phineas Gage important?

In 1848, a railroad accident sent a metal rod (13 pounds, 1¼ inches in diameter, and 3½ feet long) through the foreman's face and brain (Figure 2.17). Amazingly, the blow was not fatal. The victim, Phineas Gage, was stunned and his extremities shook convulsively. But in just a few minutes, he was able to talk to his men, and he even walked with little or no assistance up a flight of stairs before receiving medical treatment 1½ hours later.

Although Gage did survive physically, he did not fare well psychologically. A serious personality transformation had occurred because of the accident. Before the explosion, Gage was "a most efficient and capable foreman," "a shrewd, smart businessman," and very energetic and persistent in executing all his plans. After the accident, he "frequently changed what he proposed doing, and was, among other things, fitful, capricious, impatient of advice, obstinate, and lacking in deference to his fellows" (Macmillan, 2000, p. 13). In the words of his friends and acquaintances, "Gage was no longer Gage" (Harlow, 1868). Following months of recuperation, Gage attempted to return to work but was refused his old job. The damage to his brain had changed him too profoundly.

According to historical records kept by his physician, Gage never again held a job equal to that of foreman. He supported himself with odd jobs and traveled around New England, exhibiting himself and the tamping iron, and for a time he did the same at the Barnum Museum. He even lived in Chile for seven years before ill health forced a return to the United States. Near the end of his life, Gage experienced numerous epileptic seizures of increasing severity and frequency. Despite the massive damage to his frontal lobes caused by the tamping iron, Phineas Gage lived on for another 11½ years, eventually dying from the epileptic seizures.

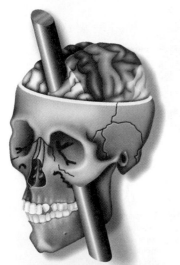

Figure 2.17 A surprisingly nonfatal brain injury An accidental explosion sent a 13-pound tamping iron through the brain of a young railroad supervisor, Phineas Gage. The careful record keeping and in-depth reporting of his behavior after the accident provided valuable information on the short- and long-term effects of damage to the frontal lobes.

How did Gage physically survive? What accounts for his radical change in personality? If the tamping iron had traveled through the brain at a slightly different angle, Gage would have died immediately. But as you can see in Figure 2.17, the rod entered and exited the front part of the brain, a section unnecessary for physical survival. Gage's personality changes resulted from damage to his frontal lobes. As this case study and other research show, the frontal lobes are intimately involved in motivation, emotion, and a host of other cognitive activities (Banich & Compton, 2011; Besnard et al., 2010; Werner et al., 2007).

Music and your brain Have you ever wondered if great musicians' brains are different from yours and mine? The answer is yes! Our brains are physically shaped and changed by learning and from experiences we have with our environment (e.g., Romero et al., 2008; Rossignol et al., 2008). These musicians, from the Circa Survive band have trained (and shaped) the auditory cortex in their temporal lobes to detect even the smallest gradations of sound.

Parietal Lobes

At the top of the brain, just behind the frontal lobes, are the two **parietal lobes**. They contain the *somatosensory cortex*, which receive and interpret bodily sensations including pressure, pain, touch, temperature, and location of body parts. When you step on a sharp nail, you quickly (and reflexively) withdraw your foot because the messages travel directly to and from your spinal cord. However, you do not experience "pain" until the neural messages reach the parietal lobes of the brain. Concept Organizer 2.2 shows how different parts of the body are represented on the motor cortex and somatosensory cortex.

Temporal Lobes

The two **temporal lobes** (Latin for "pertaining to the temples") are responsible for audition (hearing), language comprehension, memory, and some emotional control. The *auditory cortex* (which processes sound) is located at the top front of each temporal lobe. This area processes incoming sensory information from the ears and sends it to the parietal lobes, where it is combined with visual and other sensory information.

A section of the *left* temporal lobe, *Wernicke's area*, is involved in language comprehension. About a decade after Broca's discovery, German neurologist Carl Wernicke noted that patients with damage in this area could not understand what they read or heard, but they could speak quickly and easily. Unfortunately, their speech was often unintelligible. It contained made-up words, like *chipecke*, sound substitutions (*girl* became *curl*), and word substitutions (*bread* became *cake*). This syndrome is now referred to as *Wernicke's aphasia*.

Occipital Lobes

As the name implies, the two **occipital lobes** (Latin *ob*, "in back of," and *caput*, "head") are located at the lower back of the brain. Among other things, the occipital lobes are responsible for vision and visual perception. Damage to the occipital lobe can produce blindness, even though the eyes and their neural connection to the brain are perfectly healthy. The occipital lobes are also involved in shape, color, and motion perception.

Association Areas

Thus far, we have focused on relatively small areas of the eight lobes that have specific functions. If a surgeon electrically stimulated the parietal lobes, you would most likely report physical sensations, such as feeling touch, pressure, and so on. On the other hand, if the surgeon stimulated your occipital lobe, you would see flashes of light or color.

Surprisingly, most areas of your cortex, if stimulated, produce nothing at all. These so-called quiet sections are not dormant, however. They are clearly involved in interpreting, integrating, and acting on information processed by other parts of the brain. Thus, these collective "quiet areas" are aptly called **association areas** because they *associate* various areas and functions of the brain. The association areas in the frontal lobe, for example, help in decision making and planning. Similarly, the association area right in front of the motor cortex is involved in the planning of voluntary movement.

Parietal [puh-RYE-uh-tul] lobes Two lobes at the top of the brain where bodily sensations are received and interpreted

Temporal Lobes Two lobes on each side of the brain above the ears involved in audition (hearing), language comprehension, memory, and some emotional control

Occipital [ahk-SIP-ih-tul] Lobes Two lobes at the back of the brain responsible for vision and visual perception

Study Tip

Remember that Broca's area in the left frontal lobes is responsible for speech production. Wernicke's area in the left temporal lobe is involved in language comprehension.

Association Areas So-called quiet areas in the cerebral cortex involved in interpreting, integrating, and acting on information processed by other parts of the brain

ConceptOrganizer2.2

STOP *This Concept Organizer contains essential information NOT found elsewhere in the text, which is likely to appear on quizzes and exams. Be sure to study it CAREFULLY!*

Visualizing Your Motor Cortex and Somatosensory Cortex

This drawing represents a vertical cross section taken from the left hemisphere's *motor cortex* and right hemisphere's *somatosensory cortex*. If body areas were truly proportional to the amount of tissue in the motor and somatosenory cortices, your body would look like the oddly shaped figures draped around the outer edges.

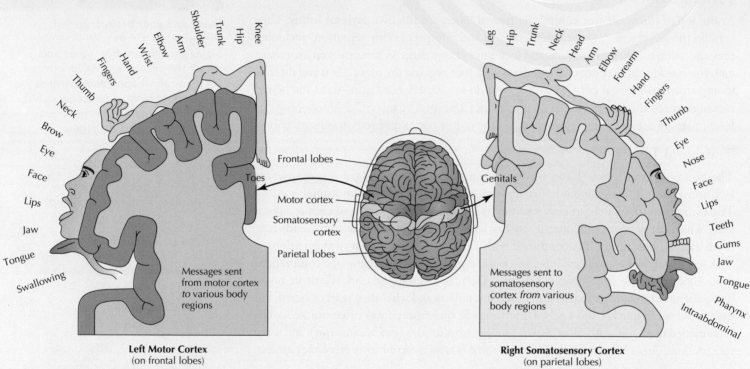

Left Motor Cortex
(on frontal lobes)

(a) Note how larger areas of the *motor cortex* are devoted to body parts that need to be controlled with great precision, such as the hands, face, and tongue.

Right Somatosensory Cortex
(on parietal lobes)

(b) Similar areas of the *somatosensory cortex* are also disproportionately large because these body parts contain a high number of sensory receptors, which makes them particularly sensitive.

 **TRY THIS YOURSELF**

Would you like a quick way to understand your motor cortex and somatosensory cortex?

1. **Motor cortex** Try wiggling each of your fingers one at a time. Now try wiggling each of your toes. Note on this figure how the area of your motor cortex is much larger for your fingers than for your toes, thus explaining the greater control in your fingers.

2. **Somatosensory cortex** Ask a friend to close his or her eyes. Using a random number of fingers (one to four), press down on the skin of your friend's back for one or two seconds. Then ask, "How many fingers am I using?"

Repeat the same procedure on the palm or back of the hand. Note the increased accuracy of reporting after pressing on the hand, which explains why the area of the somatosensory cortex is much larger for the hands than for the back, as well as the greater sensitivity in our hands versus our backs.

As you recall from Chapter 1, one of the most popular myths in psychology is that we use only 10 percent of our brain. This myth might have begun with early research on association areas of the brain. Given that approximately three-fourths of the cortex is "uncommitted" (with no precise, specific function responsive to electrical brain stimulation), researchers might have mistakenly assumed that these areas were nonfunctional.

Two Brains in One? A House Divided

Objective 2.16: Explain why the corpus callosum and split-brain research are important.

We mentioned earlier that the brain's left and right hemispheres control opposite sides of the body. Each hemisphere also has separate areas of specialization. (This is another example of *localization of function*, yet it is technically referred to as *lateralization*.)

Early researchers believed that the right hemisphere was "subordinate" or "nondominant" compared to the left, and that it had few functions or abilities. In the 1960s, landmark research with **split-brain surgery** began to change this view.

Split-Brain Research

The primary connection between the left and right hemispheres is a thick, ribbonlike band of nerve fibers under the cortex called the **corpus callosum** (Figure 2.18). In some rare cases of *severe* epilepsy, when other forms of treatment have failed, surgeons cut the corpus callosum to stop the spread of epileptic seizures from one hemisphere to the other. Because this operation cuts only the direct communication link between the two hemispheres, it reveals what each half of the brain can do in isolation from the other. The resulting research has profoundly improved our understanding of how the two halves of the brain function.

Although, most patients generally show very few outward changes in their behavior, other than fewer epileptic seizures, the surgery does create a few unusual responses. For example, one split-brain patient reported that when he dressed himself, he sometimes pulled his pants down with his left hand and up with his right (Gazzaniga, 2009). The subtle changes associated with split-brain surgery normally appear only with specialized testing (Concept Organizer 2.3).

Split-Brain Surgery Cutting of the corpus callosum to separate the brain's two hemispheres. When used medically to treat severe epilepsy, split-brain patients provide data on the functions of the two hemispheres

Corpus Callosum [CORE-pus] [cah-LOH-suhm] Bundle of nerve fibers connecting the brain's left and right hemispheres

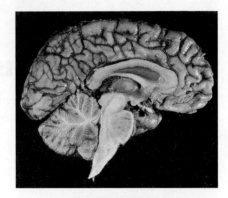

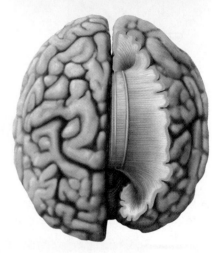

Figure 2.18 Views of the corpus callosum In the left photo, a human brain was sliced vertically from the top to the bottom to expose the corpus callosum, which conveys information between the two hemispheres of the cerebral cortex. In the photo on the right, a deceased person's brain was cut horizontally, which shows how fibers, or *axons*, of the corpus callosum link to both the right and left hemispheres.

TEST YOURSELF

Can you explain why the hands and the face on this drawing are so large? Or why these same proportions may be different in nonhuman animals?

Answer: The larger size of the hands and face reflects the larger cortical area necessary for the precise motor control and greater sensitivity humans need in our hands and faces (see also Concept Diagram 2.1). Other nonhuman animals have different needs, and the proportions are different. Spider monkeys, for example, have large areas of their motor and somatosensory cortices devoted to their tails, which they use like another arm and hand.

ConceptOrganizer2.3

Explaining Split-Brain Research

Experiments on split-brain patients often present visual information to only the patient's left or right hemisphere, which leads to some intriguing results. For example,

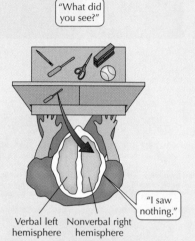

"What did you see?"

"I saw nothing."

Verbal left hemisphere   Nonverbal right hemisphere

(a) When a split-brain patient is asked to stare straight ahead while a photo of a screwdriver is flashed only to the right hemisphere, he will report that he "saw nothing."

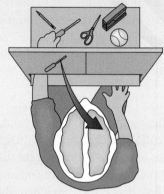

"With your left hand, pick up what you saw"

(b) However, when asked to pick up with his left hand what he saw, he can reach through and touch the items hidden behind the screen and easily pick up the screwdriver.

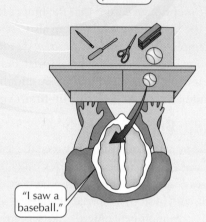

"What did you see?"

"I saw a baseball."

(c) When the left hemisphere receives an image of a baseball, the split-brain patient can easily name it.

Assuming you have an intact, nonsevered corpus callosum, if the same experimental photos were presented to you in the same way, you could easily name both the screwdriver and the baseball. Can you explain why? The answers lie in our somewhat confusing visual wiring system:

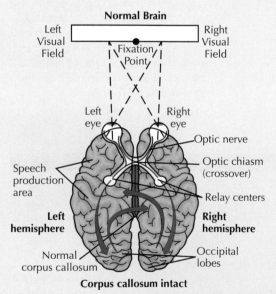

Normal Brain

Left Visual Field   Right Visual Field
Fixation Point

Left eye   Right eye
Optic nerve
Optic chiasm (crossover)
Speech production area
Relay centers
Left hemisphere   **Right hemisphere**
Normal corpus callosum   Occipital lobes

Corpus callosum intact

As you can see, our eyes connect to our brains in such a way that, when we look straight ahead, information from the left visual field (the blue line) travels to our right hemisphere, and information from the right visual field (the red line) travels to our left hemisphere. The messages received by either hemisphere are then quickly sent to the other across the corpus callosum.

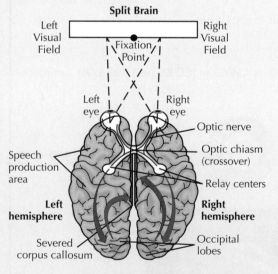

Split Brain

Left Visual Field   Right Visual Field
Fixation Point

Left eye   Right eye
Optic nerve
Optic chiasm (crossover)
Speech production area
Relay centers
Left hemisphere   **Right hemisphere**
Severed corpus callosum   Occipital lobes

Corpus callosum severed

When the corpus callosum is severed, and information is presented only to the right hemisphere, a split-brain patient cannot verbalize what he or she sees because the information cannot travel to the opposite (verbal) hemisphere.

Hemispheric Specialization

Most complex activities involve both hemispheres, however, specialization of function occurs in some areas (Figure 2.19). In general, for most adults the left hemisphere is specialized not only for language functions (speaking, reading, writing, and understanding language) but also for analytical functions, such as mathematics. In contrast, the right hemisphere is specialized primarily for nonverbal abilities. This includes art and musical abilities and perceptual and spatiomanipulative skills, such as maneuvering through space, drawing or building geometric designs, working jigsaw puzzles, building model cars, painting pictures, and recognizing faces and facial expressions (e.g., Bethmann et al., 2007; Bjornaes et al., 2005; Gazzaniga, 1970, 1995, 2009; Maillard et al., 2011; Pinel & Dehaene, 2010). In addition, the right hemisphere also contributes to complex word and language comprehension (Diaz, Barrett, & Hogstrom, 2011; Maillard et al., 2011; Rapp & Lipka, 2011).

Is this left- and right-brain specialization reversed in left-handed people? About 68 percent of left-handers (people who use their left hands to write, hammer a nail, and throw a ball) and 97 percent of right-handers have their major language areas on the left hemisphere. This suggests that even though the right side of the brain is dominant for movement in left-handers, other types of skills are often localized in the same brain areas as for right-handers.

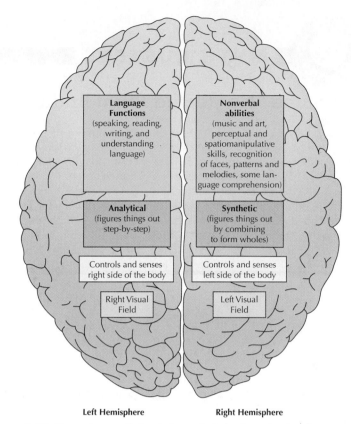

Figure 2.19 Functions of the left and right hemispheres In general, the left hemisphere specializes in verbal and analytical functions. The right hemisphere focuses on nonverbal abilities, such as spatiomanipulative skills (the ability to locate and manipulate objects in three-dimensional space), art and visual recognition tasks. Keep in mind that both hemispheres are activated when we perform almost any task or respond to any stimuli.

TRY THIS YOURSELF

Would you like a demonstration of the specialized functions of your own two hemispheres?

Some research suggests that the eyes tend to move to the right when a mental task involves the left hemisphere and to the left when the task involves the right hemisphere (see Kinsbourne, 1972). Read the following questions to a friend and record whether his or her eyes move to the right or to the left as he or she ponders the answers. Try to keep the monitoring of your friend's eye movements as natural as possible.

1. Define the word "heredity."
2. What is a function of punctuation marks?
3. Which arm is raised on the Statue of Liberty?
4. On a keyboard, where is the "enter" key.

The first two questions involve language skills and the left hemisphere. Answering them should produce more eye movement to the right. Questions 3 and 4 require spatial reasoning and the right hemisphere, which should elicit more eye movement to the left.

Try the same test on at least four other friends or family members. You will note two major points: (1) Cerebral lateralization is a matter of degree—not all or nothing, and (2) individual differences do exist, especially among left-handers.

Myth of the "Neglected Right Brain"

Courses and books directed at "right-brain thinking" and "drawing on the right side of the brain" often promise to increase your intuition, creativity, and artistic abilities by waking up your neglected and underused right brain. Contrary to this myth, research has clearly shown that the two hemispheres work together in a coordinated, integrated way, with each making important contributions. If you are a married student with small children, you can easily understand this principle. Just as you and your partner often "specialize" in different jobs (one giving the kids their baths, the other washing the dinner dishes), the hemispheres also divide their workload. However, both parents and both hemispheres are generally aware of what the other "half" is doing.

In our tour of the nervous system, the principles of *localization of function, lateralization,* and *specialization* are common—dendrites receive information, the occipital lobe specializes in vision, and so on. Keep in mind, however, that all parts of the brain and nervous system play *overlapping and synchronized* roles.

STOP *Before going on, be sure to complete this Check & Review. It is an invaluable study tool!*

Cerebral Cortex and Two Brains in One

Part A: Retrieval Practice

1. Without looking at the book, spend 10 minutes writing a free-form essay recalling all you can remember from the previous section.

2. Now, reread the previous section, and once again spend 10 minutes writing a free-form essay on the SAME material.

Part B: Practice Quiz

1. The bumpy, convoluted area making up the outside surface of the brain is the _____.

2. You are giving a speech. Name the cortical lobes involved in the following behaviors:

   a. Seeing faces in the audience

   b. Hearing questions from the audience

   c. Remembering where your car is parked when you are ready to go home

   d. Noticing that your new shoes are too tight and hurting your feet

3. The _____ lobes regulate our personality and are largely responsible for much of what makes us uniquely human. (a) frontal; (b) temporal; (c) parietal; (d) occipital

4. Label the four lobes of the brain:

5. Although the left and right hemispheres of the brain are specialized, they are

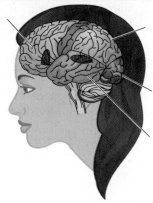

normally in close communication thanks to the _____.

Check your answers in Appendix B.

Our Genetic Inheritance

Objective 2.17: What is behavioral genetics, and what are the two keys to heredity?

Some of what we are today results from evolutionary forces at play thousands of years before you or I were even on this planet. During that time, our ancestors foraged for food, fought for survival, and passed on traits that were selected and transmitted down through the generations. How do these transmitted traits affect us today? For answers, psychologists often turn to **behavioral genetics**, how heredity and environment affect us, and **evolutionary psychology**, how the natural process of adapting to our environment affects us.

Behavioral Genetics: Is It Nature or Nurture?

> With a good heredity, nature deals you a fine hand at cards; and with a good environment, you learn to play the hand well.
>
> WALTER C. ALVAREZ

In earlier times, people thought inherited characteristics were passed along through the blood—"He's got his family's bad blood." We now know it's a lot more complicated than that. Let's start at the beginning.

At the moment of your conception, your mother and father each contributed 23 **chromosomes** to you, and thousands of **genes** are found on each chromosome (Figure 2.20). For some of your traits, such as blood type, a single pair of genes (one from each parent) determines what characteristics you will possess. But most traits, including aggressiveness, sociability, and even height are determined by a combination of many genes.

Dominant and Recessive Traits

When the two genes for a given trait conflict, the outcome depends on whether the gene is *dominant* or *recessive*. A dominant gene normally reveals its trait whenever

Behavioral Genetics Study of the relative effects of heredity and the environment on behavior and mental processes

Evolutionary Psychology Branch of psychology that studies how evolutionary processes, like natural selection and genetic mutations, affect behavior and mental processes

Chromosome Threadlike molecule of DNA (deoxyribonucleic acid) that carries genetic information

Gene Segment of DNA (deoxyribonucleic acid) that occupies a specific place on a particular chromosome and carries the code for hereditary transmission

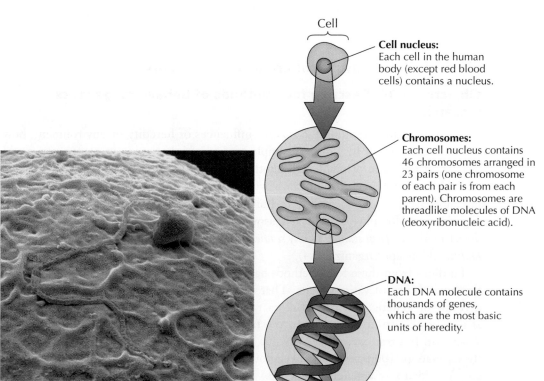

Cell

Cell nucleus: Each cell in the human body (except red blood cells) contains a nucleus.

Chromosomes: Each cell nucleus contains 46 chromosomes arranged in 23 pairs (one chromosome of each pair is from each parent). Chromosomes are threadlike molecules of DNA (deoxyribonucleic acid).

DNA: Each DNA molecule contains thousands of genes, which are the most basic units of heredity.

Figure 2.20 Hereditary codes? (a) An actual photo of the moment of conception when sperm meets egg. (b) The nucleus of every cell in our body contains chromosomes, DNA, and genes—the essence of our heredity.

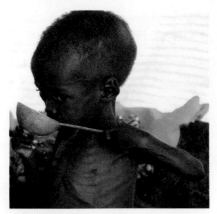

Figure 2.22 Gene–environment interaction Children who are malnourished may not reach their full potential genetic height or maximum intelligence. Can you see how environment factors like nutrition interact with genetic factors to influence development?

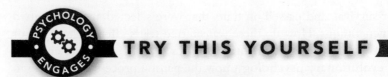

TRY THIS YOURSELF

Can you curl your tongue lengthwise?

Figure 2.21 Tongue curling is a dominant gene

Tongue curling is one of the few traits that depends on only one dominant gene. If you can curl your tongue, either both or at least one of your biological parents can also curl his or her tongue. However, if both of your parents are "noncurlers," you are also a "noncurler."

the gene is present. In contrast, the gene for a recessive trait will normally be expressed only if the other gene in the pair is also recessive (Figure 2.21).

It was once assumed that characteristics such as eye color, hair color, or height were the result of either one dominant gene or two paired recessive genes. But modern geneticists have found that each of these particular characteristics is *polygenic*, meaning they are controlled by multiple genes. Many polygenic traits like height or intelligence also are affected by environmental and social factors (Figure 2.22). Fortunately, most serious genetic disorders are not transmitted through a dominant gene. Can you understand why?

Methods for Studying Inheritance in Humans

Objective 2.18: Describe four methods of behavioral genetics research.

If you wanted to determine the relative influences of heredity or environment, how would you go about it? For very simple studies of inheritance in plants, you could just breed one type of plant with another to see what your desired trait would be like in the next generation. But how would you conduct research on complex traits like aggressiveness or sociability in humans? Scientists can't use selective breeding experiments—for obvious ethical reasons. Instead, they generally rely on four less direct methods: *twin studies*, *family studies*, *adoption studies*, and studies of *genetic abnormalities* (Concept Organizer 2.4).

Findings from these four methods have allowed behavioral geneticists to estimate the **heritability** of various traits. That is, to what degree are individual differences a result of genetic, inherited factors rather than differences in the environment? If genetics contributed *nothing* to the trait, it would have a heritability estimate of 0 percent. If a trait were *completely* due to genetics, we would say it had a heritability estimate of 100 percent. (Correlations of .70 and above are generally accepted as strong evidence of a genetic influence.)

Heritability Measure of the degree to which a characteristic is related to genetic, inherited factors versus the environment

ConceptOrganizer2.4

STOP *This Concept Organizer contains essential information NOT found elsewhere in the text, which is likely to appear on quizzes and exams. Be sure to study it CAREFULLY!*

Four Methods of Behavioral Genetics Research

1. **Twin studies** *Identical (monozygotic—one egg)* twins share 100 percent of the same genes, whereas *fraternal (dizygotic—two egg)* twins share, on average, 50 percent of their genes, just like any other pair of siblings. As you can see in the figure to the right, identical twins develop from a single egg fertilized by a single sperm. They share the same placenta and have the same sex and same genetic makeup. Fraternal twins are formed when two separate sperm fertilize two separate eggs. They are genetically no more alike than brothers and sisters born at different times. Fraternal twins are simply nine-month "womb mates."

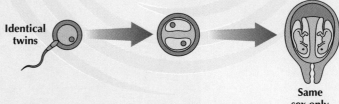

Identical twins → Same sex only

Fraternal twins → Same or opposite sex

Because both identical and fraternal twins share the same parents and develop in relatively the same environment, they provide a valuable type of "natural experiment." If heredity influences a trait or behavior to some degree, identical twins should be more alike than fraternal twins. Furthermore, if researchers find that identical twins who were reared apart are more like their biological families than their adoptive families, this provides even stronger evidence for a genetic influence.

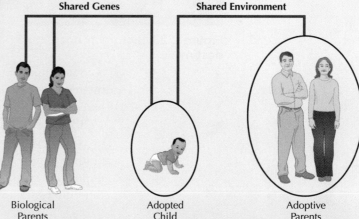

Shared Genes — Shared Environment

Biological Parents — Adopted Child — Adoptive Parents

2. **Family studies** If a specific trait is inherited, blood relatives should show increased trait similarity, compared with unrelated people. Also, closer relatives, like siblings, should be more similar than distant relatives. Family studies have shown that many traits and mental disorders, such as intelligence, sociability, and depression, do run in families.

3. **Adoption studies** If adopted children are more like their biological family in some trait, then genetic factors probably had the greater influence. Conversely, if adopted children resemble their adopted family, even though they do not share similar genes, then environmental factors may predominate.

4. **Genetic abnormalities** Behavioral genetics research explores disorders and diseases that result when genes malfunction. For example, an extra twenty-first chromosome fragment almost always causes a condition called *Down syndrome*. Abnormalities in several genes or chromosomes also are suspected in *Alzheimer's disease*, which involves serious brain deterioration and memory loss, and *schizophrenia*, a severe mental disorder characterized by loss of contact with reality.

Psychology at Work

Overcoming Genetic Misconceptions

Objective 2.19: Identify three key genetic misconceptions.

Behavioral genetics and heritability are hot topics in the general press—and in modern psychology. Each day we are bombarded with new discoveries regarding genes and the supposed heritability of intelligence, sexual orientation, and athletic abilities. But press reports are often misleading and invite misunderstanding. As you hear estimates of heritability, keep these cautions in mind:

1. *Genetic traits are not fixed or inflexible.* After listening to the latest research, some people become unreasonably discouraged. They fear they are destined

for heart disease, obesity, breast cancer, depression, alcoholism, or other problems because of their particular biological inheritance. Genes do have a strong influence on diseases and behaviors. However, these genetic studies do not reflect how an environmental intervention might change the outcome. If you inherited a possible genetic predisposition for some undesirable trait, you can often improve your odds by adopting lifestyle changes, such as improved diet and frequent exercise. (Also, remember that nothing in life is 100 percent inherited—except sex. If your parents did not have it, it is 100 percent sure that you won't.)

Figure 2.23 Biology is not destiny

2. *Heritability estimates do not apply to individuals.* When you hear media reports that intelligence or athletic talents are 30 to 50 percent inherited, do you assume this applies to you as an individual? Do you believe that if intelligence is 50 percent inherited, then 50 percent is due to your parents and 50 percent to your environment? This is a common misconception. Heritability statistics are mathematical computations of the proportion of total variance in a trait that is explained by genetic variation within a group—not *individuals*. Height, for example, has one of the highest heritability estimates—around 90 percent (Plomin, 1990). However, your own personal height may be very different from that of your parents or other blood relatives (Figure 2.23). We each inherit a unique combination of genes (unless we are identical twins). Therefore, it is impossible to predict your individual height from a heritability estimate. You can only estimate for the group as a whole.

Figure 2.24 Similar ingredients— different outcomes

3. *Genes and the environment are inseparable.* As first discussed in Chapter 1, biological, psychological, and social forces all influence one another and are inseparable—the *biopsychosocial model*. Imagine your inherited genes as analogous to water, sugar, salt, flour, eggs, baking powder, and oil (Figure 2.24). When you mix these ingredients and pour them on a hot griddle (one environment), you get pancakes. Add more oil (a different combination of genes) and a waffle iron (a different environment), and you get waffles. With another set of ingredients and environments (different pans and an oven), you can have crepes, muffins, or cakes. How can you separate the effects of ingredients and cooking methods?

Evolutionary Psychology: Darwin Explains Behavior and Mental Processes

Objective 2.20: What is evolutionary psychology, and how does it affect behavior and mental processes?

As we have seen, behavioral genetics studies help explain the role of heredity (nature) and the environment (nurture) in our individual behavior. To increase our understanding of genetic predispositions, we also need to look at universal behaviors transmitted from our evolutionary past.

Evolutionary psychology is the branch of psychology that studies how evolutionary processes affect behavior and mental processes (Buss, 2011; Confer et al., 2010). It suggests that many behavioral commonalities, from eating to fighting with our enemies, emerged and remain in human populations because they helped our ancestors (and ourselves) survive. This perspective is based on the writings of Charles Darwin (1859), who suggested that natural forces select traits that are adaptive to the organism's survival. This process of **natural selection** occurs when one particular genetic trait gives a person a reproductive advantage over others. Some people mistakenly believe that natural selection means "survival of the fittest." What really matters is *reproduction*—the survival of the genome. Because of natural selection, the fastest or otherwise most fit organisms will be most likely to live long enough to pass on their genes to the next generation.

Genetic mutations also help explain behavior. Everyone carries at least one gene that has *mutated*, or changed from the original. But, only very rarely, a mutated gene will be significant enough to change an individual's behavior. It might cause someone to be more social, more risk taking, or more careful. If the gene then gives the person reproductive advantage, he or she will be more likely to pass on the gene to future generations. However, this mutation does not guarantee long-term survival. A well-adapted population can perish if its environment changes.

Natural Selection Driving mechanism behind evolution that allows individuals with genetically influenced traits that are adaptive in a particular environment to stay alive and produce offspring

Psychology Engages

CRITICAL THINKING

Biology and Critical Thinking

By Thomas Frangicetto (Northampton Community College, Bethlehem, PA)

Many students find this chapter difficult because of the large number of unfamiliar terms and concepts. This exercise will help you:

- Review key biological terms that may appear on exams.
- Apply these terms to critical thinking components.
  (Be sure to check your answers in Appendix B.)

Part I: Match each term from Chapter 2 with the correct abbreviated description.

1. _____Amygdala   a. arousal
2. _____Corpus Callosum   b. language/analytical
3. _____Dopamine   c. mood, impulsivity, depression
4. _____Frontal Lobes   d. vision/visual perception
5. _____Hypothalamus   e. hearing/language
6. _____Left Hemisphere   f. coordination
7. _____Cerebellum   g. internal environment
8. _____Occipital Lobes   h. calming
9. _____ Parasympathetic i. connects two hemispheres
         Nervous System   j. bodily sensations
10. _____Parietal Lobes   k. emotion

11. _____Right Hemisphere   l. motor, speech, and higher functions
12. _____Serotonin   m. nonverbal abilities
13. _____Sympathetic Nervous System   n. movement, attention, schizophrenia
14. _____Temporal Lobes

Part II: As mentioned earlier, your brain and nervous system control everything you do, feel, see, or think. They also control your critical thinking. For each of situations below, first identify which critical thinking component (CTC) from the Prologue is being described. Then decide which area of the brain or nervous system listed in Part I would most likely be involved in the application of this CTC. (*Tip:* If you need help, review the related text content for each term, not just the abbreviated description in Part I.)

1. Tamara wrote several children's storybooks and attempted to do the illustrations herself. After many failed attempts, she accepted her limitations and hired a professional artist.
   CTC: _____ Biological Area (s): _____

2. Samantha was falling behind in her college courses primarily because she was not paying close attention during class lectures. She decided to listen carefully and to take detailed notes, and her grades improved dramatically.
   CTC: _____ Biological Area (s): _____

3. After two weeks on a new job, Alex was so stressed and overwhelmed he planned to quit, but his boss persuaded him to stay on. Once Alex accepted his boss's reassurance that uncertainty and mistakes are a normal part of getting adjusted to a new job, his symptoms of stress (shortness of breath and increased blood pressure) soon disappeared.
   CTC: _____ Biological Area (s): _____

RESEARCH CHALLENGE

Video Games and Spatial Skills

By Siri Carpenter (Science Writer, Madison, WI)

Objective 2.21: How do video games affect gender differences in spatial skills?

Playing an action-packed video game nearly wipes out traditional gender differences in a basic spatial thinking task, research reveals. In a study of college students, men were better than women at rapidly switching their attention among stimuli displayed on a computer screen, a common test of spatial ability (Feng, Spence, & Pratt, 2007). But after both sexes played the role of a World War II soldier in a video game for 10 hours over several weeks, women caught up to men on the spatial-attention task, as well as on an object-rotation test of more advanced spatial ability. Although both men and women action video game players showed significant gains compared to men and women who played a non-action game, the women benefitted more. And, the women's gains persisted when the volunteers were retested an average of five months later.

The study's lead author, University of Toronto psychologist Ian Spence, speculates that the video game practice may have caused "massive overexercising" of the brain's attentional system or even switched on previously inactive genes that underlie spatial cognition. Either way, he says, the results hold tantalizing potential for designing action-intensive video games that appeal to girls and women, perhaps eventually boosting women's participation in fields such as mathematics and engineering, which demand good spatial ability.

(*Source:* Originally published in *Scientific American Mind*, December 2007/January 2008, p. 10. Adapted and reprinted with permission of author, Siri Carpenter.)

Student Engagement Exercise

Given the admittedly limited information in the video game portion of the spatial skills study described above, what is the most likely:

1. *Research method* (experimental, descriptive, correlational, or biological)?

2. If you chose the:

   • *Experimental method*—label the IV, DV, experimental group, and control group.

   • *Descriptive method*—identify whether this is a naturalistic observation, survey, or case study.

   • *Correlational method*—label whether this is a positive, negative, or zero correlation.

   • *Biological method*—identify the specific research tool (e.g., brain dissection, CT scan, etc.).

(Answers appear in Appendix B.)

GENDER AND CULTURAL DIVERSITY

Evolution of Sexual Selection and Gender Differences

Co-authored with Thomas Frangicetto (Northampton Community College, Bethlehem, PA)

Objective 2.22: How does evolutionary theory explain current sex differences?

FEEDING TIME AT THE NATURAL SELECTION ZOO

Why do we find some people more attractive than others? Can evolution help explain our choice is sexual partners? The answers to these questions are linked in part to the central issue in evolutionary psychology—*natural selection* and *reproduction* (Gallup & Frederick, 2010).

Consider the issue of facial attractiveness and its relationship to reproduction or the "survival of the genome." Researchers have found interesting links between perceived attractiveness and sperm count and sperm vitality. For example, when female college students were asked to rate the attractiveness of facial photos of fellow male students, the sperm of the attractively rated men tended to be of considerably higher quality and fertility (Soler et al, 2003). How does this relate to evolution? According to Gallup and Frederick (2010), "Attractive men may garner more interest from women, which may boost their testosterone and sperm production, or men who are generally more robust and healthy overall may have more attractive faces and enhanced ability to produce sperm."

What about the widely publicized differences between the sexes, such as those in language and math skills? Are they also shaped by evolution?

Research using brain scans, autopsies, and volumetric measurements of brain parts have found several sex differences in the brains of men and women (Figure 2.25). For example, after allowing for the natural differences in overall brain volume which exist between the brains of men and women, two areas in the frontal and temporal lobes (*Broca* and *Wernicke*), found to be associated with language skills, are larger in women (Harasty et al., 1997; Schlaepfer et al., 1995). In contrast, a region in the parietal lobes (just above the ears), which is correlated with manipulating spatial relationships and mathematical abilities, is larger in men than in women (Frederikse et al., 1999). Table 2.2 illustrates the tasks researchers have used to demonstrate these and other sex differences.

How do we explain this? Evolutionary psychologists often suggest that gender differences like these may be the product of gradual genetic adaptations (Buss, 2011; Swami, 2011). If ancient societies assigned men the task of "hunters" and "gatherers," the male's superiority on many spatial tasks and target-directed motor skills may have evolved from the adaptive demands of hunting. Similarly, activities such as food gathering, child-rearing, and domestic tool construction and manipulation may have contributed to the woman's language superiority and fine motor coordination.

Some critics, however, suggest that evolution progresses much too slowly to account for this type of behavioral adaptation. Furthermore, there is wide cross-cultural variability in gender differences, and evolutionary explanations of sex differences are highly speculative and obviously difficult to test scientifically (Gallup & Frederick, 2010; Geary, 2010; Hyde, 2007; Newcombe, 2010). And, as we just discovered in the previous Research Challenge, simply having both women and men play action-packed video games for a few short weeks almost completely removes the previously reported gender role differences in some spatial tasks (Feng, Spence, & Pratt, 2007).

In sum, evolutionary psychology suggests that heredity and other evolutionary processes help explain gender differences in some cognitive processes. However, it is dangerous to assume that these biological differences are innate or "hardwired," given what we learned earlier about the plasticity, or malleability, of the brain (p. 79). Furthermore, all currently known variations *between* the two sexes are much smaller than differences *within* each sex, and almost all reported gender differences are *correlational*. This means that the exact mechanisms that *cause* certain human behaviors have yet to be determined. To repeat a theme discussed throughout this text, it is extremely difficult to separate the various effects of biological, psychological, and social forces—the *biopsychosocial model*.

For further information on interpersonal attractiveness and research-supported sex and gender differences, see Chapters 11 and 16.

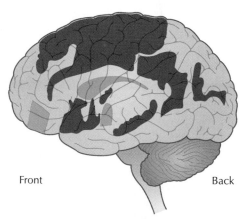

Front   Back

Figure 2.25 Brain sex differences Note that the areas in purple are, on the average, larger in women, whereas the areas in green are on the average, larger in men. Keep in mind that men on average have overall larger brains than women, even if we take into account differences in height. However, a bigger brain doesn't necessarily mean greater intelligence (see Chapter 8 pp. 307–308).

Table 2.2 PROBLEM-SOLVING TASKS FAVORING WOMEN AND MEN

Problem-Solving Tasks Favoring Women		Problem-Solving Tasks Favoring Men	
Perceptual speed: As quickly as possible identify matching items.		**Spatial tasks:** Mentally rotate the 3-d object to identify its match.	
Displaced objects: After looking at the middle picture, tell which item is missing from the the picture on the right.		Mentally manipulate the folded paper to tell where the holes will fall when it is unfolded.	
Verbal fluency: List words that begin with the same letter. (Women also tend to perform better in ideational fluency tests, for example, listing objects that are the same color.)	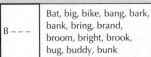 B – – – Bat, big, bike, bang, bark, bank, bring, brand, broom, bright, brook, bug, buddy, bunk	**Target-directed motor skills:** Hit the bull's eye.	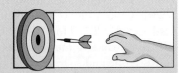
Precision manual tasks: Place the pegs in the holes as quickly as possible.		**Disembedding tests:** Find the simple shape on the left in the more complex figures.	 
Mathematical calculation: Compute the answer.	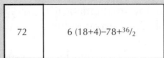 72 6 (18+4)−78+^{36}/$_2$	**Mathematical reasoning:** What is the answer?	5 $^1/_2$ If you bicycle 24 miles a day, how many days will it take to travel 132 miles?

MYTH BUSTERS

True or False?

1. Our brains are hard-wired and can't be "rewired."
2. Most people are either left-brained or right-brained.
3. When we learn something new, our brains become more wrinkled.
4. We generally use only 10% of our brains.
5. Brain damage is always permanent.
6. The human brain is the largest in the animal kingdom.
7. People remain conscious for several minutes after decapitation.
8. You can get holes in your brain from drug use.
9. Alcohol kills brain cells.
10. If a trait is heritable, that means it can't be changed.

Answers: All of these statements are false. Details were provided in this chapter, and/or in the following sources: Lilienfeld, 2010; http://www.smithsonianmag.com/science-nature/Top-Ten-Myths-About-the-Brain.html; http://health.howstuffworks.com/human-body/systems/nervous-system/10-brain-myths1.htm

CHECK & REVIEW

STOP *Before going on, be sure to complete this Check & Review. It is an invaluable study tool!*

Our Genetic Inheritance and Psychology Engages

Part A: Retrieval Practice

1. Without looking at the book, spend 10 minutes writing a free-form essay recalling all you can remember from the previous section.

2. Now, reread the previous section, and once again spend 10 minutes writing a free-form essay on the SAME material.

Part B: Practice Quiz

1. Threadlike molecules of DNA that carry genetic information are known as _____. (a) stem cells; (b) genes; (c) neurons; (d) chromosomes

2. What are the four chief methods used to study behavioral genetics?

3. Briefly explain how playing video games in an experimental setting affects gender differences in spatial skills.

4. Evolutionary psychology is the branch of psychology that looks at _____. (a) how fossil discoveries affect behavior; (b) the relationship between genes and the environment; (c) how evolutionary processes affect behavior and mental processes. (d) the effect of culture change on behavior

5. From an evolutionary perspective, can you explain why people are more likely to help family members than strangers?

Check your answers in Appendix B.

www.wileyplus.com

WileyPLUS presents an on-line version of this textbook along with a wealth of study resources including quizzes, practice tests, flash cards, videos, animations and other activities designed to improve your mastery of the content. Working in conjunction with these study tools, the *Psychology in Action* WileyPLUS course features Professor Karen Huffman, author of this textbook, explaining and expanding upon some of the most challenging concepts in psychology. Here is a sample of the tutorial videos available for this chapter:

- Interactive animation depicting how neurons communicate
- Professor Huffman's classroom demonstration using profile drawings and Play Doh to "build a brain"
- Interactive animation identifying major parts of the brain and their primary functions
- Virtual Field Trip to a genetic testing center to discover the secrets hidden in our DNA
- Virtual Field Trip to GiGi's Playhouse for an inspiring look into the world of individuals with Down syndrome

Key Terms

To assess your understanding of the **Key Terms** in Chapter 2, write a definition for each (in your own words), and then compare your definitions with those in the text.

neuroscience (p. 51)

Neural Bases of Behavior
neuron (p. 52)
glial cells (p. 52)
dendrites (p. 52)
cell body (p. 53)
axon (p. 53)
myelin [MY-uh-lin] sheath (p. 53)
action potential (p. 54)
neurotransmitters (p. 55)
synapse [SIN-aps] (p. 55)
endorphins [en-DOR-fins] (p. 57)

Nervous System Organization
central nervous system (CNS) (p. 58)
peripheral nervous system (PNS) (p. 58)
neuroplasticity (p. 59)
neurogenesis [nue-roe-JEN-uh-sis] (p. 60)
stem cell (p. 60)
reflex (p. 60)

somatic nervous system (SNS) (p. 62)
autonomic nervous system (ANS) (p. 62)
sympathetic nervous system (p. 62)
parasympathetic nervous system (p. 62)

Endocrine System
endocrine [EN-doh-krin] system (p. 64)
hormones (p. 64)

A Tour through the Brain
brainstem (p. 66)
hindbrain (p. 67)
medulla [muh-DUL-uh] (p. 67)
pons (p. 67)
cerebellum [sehr-uh-BELL-um] (p. 67)
midbrain (p. 68)
reticular formation (RF) (p. 68)
forebrain (p. 68)
thalamus [THAL-uh-muss] (p. 68)
hypothalamus [hi-poh-THAL-uh-muss] (p. 69)

limbic system (p. 69)
hippocampus (p. 69)
amygdala (p. 69)
cerebral cortex (p. 70)
frontal lobes (p. 71)
parietal [puh-RYE-uh-tul] lobes (p. 73)
temporal lobes (p. 73)
occipital [ahk-SIP-ih-tul] lobes (p. 73)
association areas (p. 73)
split-brain surgery (p. 75)
corpus callosum [CORE-pus] [cah-LOH-suhm] (p. 75)

Our Genetic Inheritance
behavioral genetics (p. 79)
evolutionary psychology (p. 79)
chromosome (p. 79)
gene (p. 79)
heritability (p. 80)
natural selection (p. 83)

Chapter Summary

Neural Bases of Behavior

Objective 2.1: What are the key parts and functions of the neuron?

Neurons are cells that transmit information throughout the body. They have three main parts: **dendrites**, which receive information from other neurons; the **cell body**, which provides nourishment and "decides" whether the axon should fire; and the **axon**, which sends along the neural information. **Glial cells** support and provide nutrients for neurons in the central nervous system (CNS).

Objective 2.2: Describe how communication occurs within the neuron (the action potential) and between neurons.

The process of neural communication begins *within* the neuron when the dendrites and cell body receive information and transmit it to the axon.

The axon is specialized for transmitting neural impulses, or **action potentials**. During times when no action potential is moving down the axon, the axon is at rest. The neuron is activated, and an **action potential** occurs when positively charged ions move in and out through channels in the axon's membrane. Action potentials travel more quickly down myelinated axons because the **myelin sheath** serves as insulation.

Information is transferred from one neuron to another at **synapses** by chemicals called **neurotransmitters**. Neurotransmitters bind to receptor sites much as a key fits into a lock, and their effects can be excitatory or inhibitory.

Objective 2.3: How do neurotransmitters affect our everyday life?

Neurotransmitters regulate glands and muscles, sleep, alertness, learning, memory, motivation, emotion, psychological disorders, etc. They also play a role in diseases and help explain how poisons and drugs affect us.

The Nervous and Endocrine Systems

Objective 2.4: Describe the nervous system's two major divisions, and explain their respective functions.

The nervous system is divided into two major divisions: the **central nervous system (CNS)**, composed of the brain and spinal cord, and the **peripheral nervous system (PNS)**, including all nerves connecting the CNS to the rest of the body. The CNS processes and organizes information, whereas the PNS carries information to and from the CNS.

Objective 2.5: Discuss neuroplasticity, neurogenesis, and stem cells.

Neuroplasticity is the brain's ability to reorganize and change its structure and function throughout the life span. **Neurogenesis** is the process by which new neurons are generated. **Stem cells** are immature (uncommitted) cells that have the potential to develop into almost any type of cell depending on the chemical signals they receive.

Objective 2.6: What are the major functions of the spinal cord?

The spinal cord is the communications link between the brain and the rest of the body, and it is involved in all voluntary and **reflex** responses.

Objective 2.7: What are the subdivisions of the peripheral nervous system, and what are their functions?

The two major subdivisions of the PNS are the **somatic nervous** system and the autonomic nervous system.

The **somatic nervous** system includes all nerves carrying incoming sensory information and outgoing motor information to and from the sense organs and skeletal muscles. The **autonomic nervous system** includes the nerves outside the brain and spinal cord that maintain normal functioning of glands, heart muscle, and the smooth muscle of blood vessels and internal organs.

The autonomic nervous system is further divided into two branches, the *parasympathetic* and the *sympathetic*, which tend to work in opposition to one another. The **parasympathetic nervous system** normally dominates when a person is relaxed. The **sympathetic nervous system** dominates when a person is under physical or mental stress. It mobilizes the body for fight or flight by increasing heart rate and blood pressure and slowing digestive processes.

Objective 2.8: Briefly discuss the importance of hormones and the endocrine system.

Hormones are released from glands in the **endocrine system** directly into the bloodstream. They act at a distance on other glands, on muscles, and in the brain. The major functions of the endocrine system, including the hypothalamus, pituitary, thyroid, adrenals, testes, ovaries, and pancreas, are to help with regulation of long-term bodily processes (such as growth and sex characteristics), maintain ongoing bodily processes, and assist in regulating the emergency response to crises.

Lower-Level Brain Structures

Objective 2.9: Identify the three major sections of the brain.

The brain is generally divided into three major sections: the hindbrain, midbrain, and forebrain.

Objective 2.10: What are the three key components of the hindbrain and what are their functions?
Parts of the **hindbrain**, the **pons** and **medulla**, are involved in sleeping, waking, dreaming, and control of automatic bodily functions; another part, the **cerebellum**, coordinates fine muscle movement, balance, and some perception and cognition.

Objective 2.11: Describe the functions of the midbrain and the reticular formation.
The **midbrain** helps coordinate movement patterns, sleep, and arousal. The **reticular formation** runs through the midbrain, hindbrain, and brainstem, and is responsible for arousal and screening incoming information.

Objective 2.12: Identify the major structures of the forebrain, and describe their functions.
The **forebrain** includes several structures, including the thalamus, hypothalamus, limbic system, and cerebral cortex. The **thalamus** relays sensory messages to the cerebral cortex. The **hypothalamus** helps govern basic drives and hormones. The **limbic system** is a group of forebrain structures (including the **hippocampus** and **amygdala**) involved with emotions and memory. Because the cerebral cortex controls most complex mental activities, it is discussed separately in the next section.

Cerebral Cortex and Two Brains in One

Objective 2.13: What is the cerebral cortex, and what is its major function?
The **cerebral cortex**, the thin surface layer on the cerebral hemispheres, regulates most complex behaviors and higher mental processes.

Objective 2.14: Describe the major functions of the lobes of the cerebral cortex.

The two **frontal lobes** are responsible for motor control, speech production, and higher functions, such as thinking. The two **parietal lobes** are the receiving and interpretation area for sensory information. The two **temporal lobes** are concerned with hearing, language, memory, and some emotional control. The two **occipital lobes** are dedicated to vision and visual information processing.

Objective 2.15: Why is the case study of Phineas Gage important?
Phineas Gage experienced a horrific blow to his frontal lobes when a metal rod pierced his face and brain. Historical records of changes in his behavior and mental processes following the accident provide invaluable clues to the important role of the frontal lobe in motivation, emotion, and other cognitive activities.

Objective 2.16: Explain why the corpus callosum and split-brain research are important.
The two hemispheres are linked by the **corpus callosum**, through which they communicate and coordinate behavior and mental processes. **Split-brain** research shows that each hemisphere performs somewhat separate functions. In most people, the left hemisphere is dominant in verbal skills, such as speaking and writing, and analytical tasks. The right hemisphere appears to excel at nonverbal tasks, such as spatio-manipulative skills, art and music, and visual recognition.

Our Genetic Inheritance

Objective 2.17: What is behavioral genetics, and what are the two keys to heredity?
Behavioral genetics studies the relative effects of heredity and the environment on behavior and mental processes. Two important keys to heredity are genes and chromosomes. **Genes** hold the code for certain traits that are passed on from parent to child,

and they can be dominant or recessive. Each of the 46 human **chromosomes** contains many genes, which are found in DNA molecules.

Objective 2.18: Describe four methods of behavioral genetics research.
Behavioral geneticists use twin studies, family studies, adoption studies, and genetic abnormalities to explore genetic contributions to behavior and make estimates of **heritability**.

Objective 2.19: Identify three key genetic misconceptions.
The three key misconceptions are: Genetic traits are not fixed or inflexible, heritability estimates do not apply to individuals, and genes and the environment are inseparable.

Objective 2.20: What is evolutionary psychology, and how does it affect behavior and mental processes?
Evolutionary psychology is the branch of psychology that looks at evolutionary changes related to behavior and mental processes. Several different evolutionary processes, including **natural selection** and genetic mutations can affect behavior and mental processes.

Psychology Engages

Objective 2.21: How do video games affect gender differences in spatial skills?
Playing action-packed video games nearly wipes out traditional gender differences reported in earlier studies.

Objective 2.22: How does evolutionary theory explain current sex differences?
According to evolutionary theory, modern sex differences (like the male's superior spatial and motor skills and the female's superior verbal fluency and fine motor coordination) are the product of gradual genetic adaptations. They helped our ancestors adapt and survive in their environment.

Chapter Two VISUAL SUMMARY

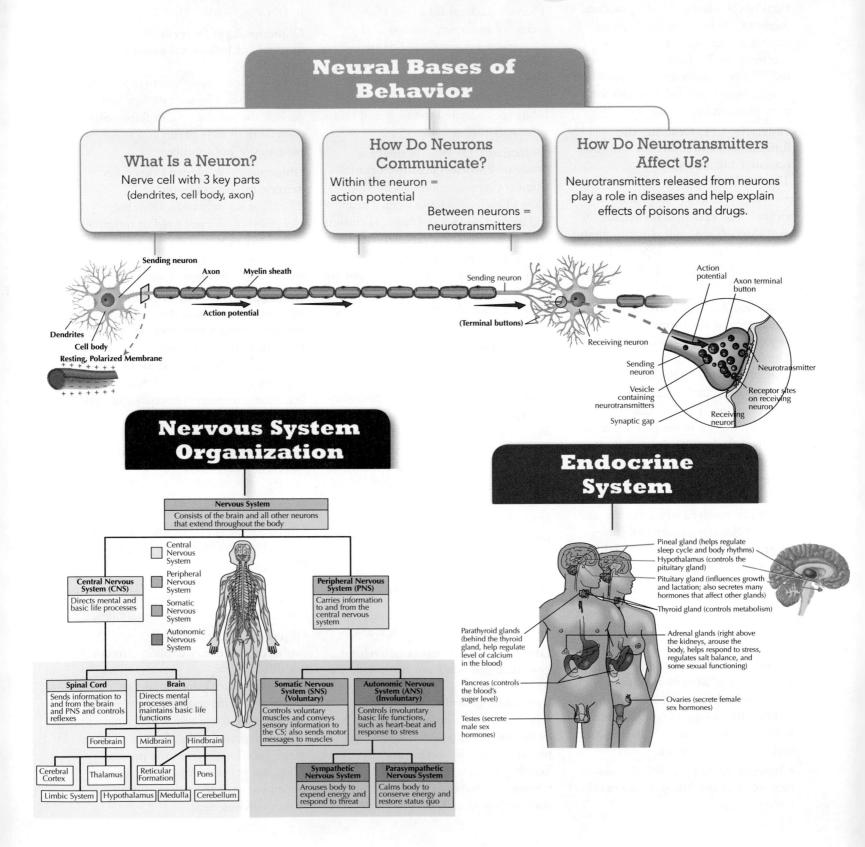

Neural Bases of Behavior

What Is a Neuron?
Nerve cell with 3 key parts (dendrites, cell body, axon)

How Do Neurons Communicate?
Within the neuron = action potential

Between neurons = neurotransmitters

How Do Neurotransmitters Affect Us?
Neurotransmitters released from neurons play a role in diseases and help explain effects of poisons and drugs.

Sending neuron

Axon   Myelin sheath

Action potential

Dendrites

Cell body

Resting, Polarized Membrane

Sending neuron

(Terminal buttons)

Receiving neuron

Action potential

Axon terminal button

Sending neuron

Neurotransmitter

Vesicle containing neurotransmitters

Receptor sites on receiving neuron

Synaptic gap

Receiving neuron

Nervous System Organization

Nervous System
Consists of the brain and all other neurons that extend throughout the body

- Central Nervous System
- Peripheral Nervous System
- Somatic Nervous System
- Autonomic Nervous System

Central Nervous System (CNS)
Directs mental and basic life processes

Peripheral Nervous System (PNS)
Carries information to and from the central nervous system

Spinal Cord
Sends information to and from the brain and PNS and controls reflexes

Brain
Directs mental processes and maintains basic life functions

Somatic Nervous System (SNS) (Voluntary)
Controls voluntary muscles and conveys sensory information to the CS; also sends motor messages to muscles

Autonomic Nervous System (ANS) (Involuntary)
Controls involuntary basic life functions, such as heart-beat and response to stress

Forebrain   Midbrain   Hindbrain

Cerebral Cortex   Thalamus   Reticular Formation   Pons

Limbic System   Hypothalamus   Medulla   Cerebellum

Sympathetic Nervous System
Arouses body to expend energy and respond to threat

Parasympathetic Nervous System
Calms body to conserve energy and restore status quo

Endocrine System

Pineal gland (helps regulate sleep cycle and body rhythms)

Hypothalamus (controls the pituitary gland)

Pituitary gland (influences growth and lactation; also secretes many hormones that affect other glands)

Thyroid gland (controls metabolism)

Parathyroid glands (behind the thyroid gland, help regulate level of calcium in the blood)

Adrenal glands (right above the kidneys, arouse the body, helps respond to stress, regulates salt balance, and some sexual functioning)

Pancreas (controls the blood's suger level)

Ovaries (secrete female sex hormones)

Testes (secrete male sex hormones)

A Tour through the Brain

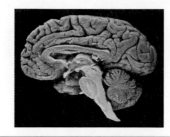

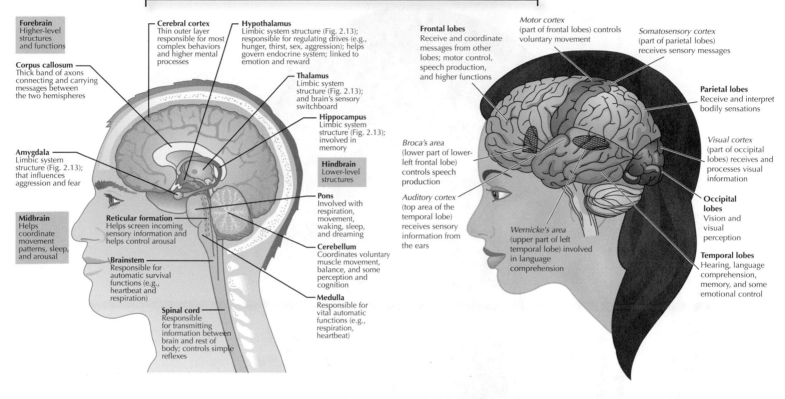

Forebrain
Higher-level structures and functions

Corpus callosum
Thick band of axons connecting and carrying messages between the two hemispheres

Amygdala
Limbic system structure (Fig. 2.13); that influences aggression and fear

Midbrain
Helps coordinate movement patterns, sleep, and arousal

Cerebral cortex
Thin outer layer responsible for most complex behaviors and higher mental processes

Hypothalamus
Limbic system structure (Fig. 2.13); responsible for regulating drives (e.g., hunger, thirst, sex, aggression); helps govern endocrine system; linked to emotion and reward

Thalamus
Limbic system structure (Fig. 2.13); and brain's sensory switchboard

Hippocampus
Limbic system structure (Fig. 2.13); involved in memory

Hindbrain
Lower-level structures

Pons
Involved with respiration, movement, waking, sleep, and dreaming

Cerebellum
Coordinates voluntary muscle movement, balance, and some perception and cognition

Medulla
Responsible for vital automatic functions (e.g., respiration, heartbeat)

Reticular formation
Helps screen incoming sensory information and helps control arousal

Brainstem
Responsible for automatic survival functions (e.g., heartbeat and respiration)

Spinal cord
Responsible for transmitting information between brain and rest of body; controls simple reflexes

Frontal lobes
Receive and coordinate messages from other lobes; motor control, speech production, and higher functions

Motor cortex
(part of frontal lobes) controls voluntary movement

Somatosensory cortex
(part of parietal lobes) receives sensory messages

Parietal lobes
Receive and interpret bodily sensations

Visual cortex
(part of occipital lobes) receives and processes visual information

Occipital lobes
Vision and visual perception

Temporal lobes
Hearing, language comprehension, memory, and some emotional control

Broca's area
(lower part of lower-left frontal lobe) controls speech production

Auditory cortex
(top area of the temporal lobe) receives sensory information from the ears

Wernicke's area
(upper part of left temporal lobe) involved in language comprehension

Our Genetic Inheritance

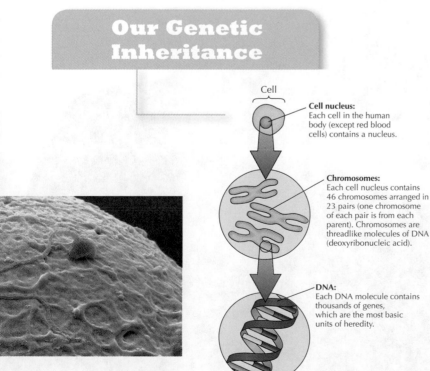

Cell

Cell nucleus:
Each cell in the human body (except red blood cells) contains a nucleus.

Chromosomes:
Each cell nucleus contains 46 chromosomes arranged in 23 pairs (one chromosome of each pair is from each parent). Chromosomes are threadlike molecules of DNA (deoxyribonucleic acid).

DNA:
Each DNA molecule contains thousands of genes, which are the most basic units of heredity.

Psychology Engages

Critical Thinking
Research Challenge, Gender and Cultural Diversity

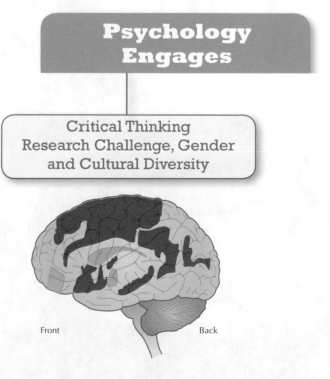

Front   Back

Chapter Three

Stress and Health Psychology

Stress is all around us. In addition to clear-and-present dangers from hurricanes, tsunamis, and earthquakes, we also live in a time of unusually high unemployment and a shaky economy. In addition, as a student you experience chronically high levels of tension over the rising costs of tuition and fees combined with internal and external pressures to do well on all exams and assignments.

How do you manage these and other stressors? What do you do to protect your health? Psychologists and other scientists have identified several clear and compelling ways to help on both fronts, but few people take advantage of this research. For example, most people don't know that the top five causes of death in the world are coronary heart disease, strokes, lower respiratory infections, COPD (chronic obstructive pulmonary disease), and diarrhea. Even fewer know that more than half the mortality from these five sources results from behaviors which are largely under our control, such as cigarette smoking, lack of exercise, ignoring doctor's orders, and poor nutrition.

Ironically, instead of focusing on logical lifestyle changes, our attention is too-often misdirected toward mythical health crises that are either completely unfounded or have received an unwarranted amount of media coverage, such as killer bees, sharks, autism-causing vaccines, flouridated drinking water, and anthrax (Frieden, 2011)!

The good news is that in this chapter we'll explore the latest information on how biological, psychological, and social factors (the *biopsychosocial model*) affect illness as well as health and well being. You'll also discover ways to protect your health, how to manage your stress, and how to change your risky behaviors. Welcome to the practical and exciting world of *Stress and Health Psychology!*

ChapterOutline

MYTH BUSTERS

True or False?

1. Even positive events, like graduating from college and getting married, are major sources of stress.

2. Small, everyday hassles can impair your immune system functioning.

3. Police officers, nurses, doctors, social workers, and teachers are particularly prone to "burnout".

4. Stress causes cancer.

5. Having a positive attitude helps fight off cancer.

6. Hardy personality types may cope better with stress.

7. Having a cynical, hostile Type A personality contributes to heart disease.

8. Ulcers are caused primarily or entirely by stress.

9. Procrastinating on homework can be harmful to your health as well as to your grades.

10. Friends are one of your best health resources.

11. Prolonged stress can lead to death.

12. You can control, or minimize, most of the negative effects of stress.

Answers: Three out of the 12 questions are false. *After reading this chapter, check your answers in Appendix B.*

Understanding Stress

Objective 3.1: Define stress, stressor, eustress, and distress.

Stress Nonspecific response of the body to any demand made upon it; the arousal, both physical and mental, to situations or events that we perceive as threatening or challenging

Stressor Trigger or stimulus that prompts a stressful reaction

Eustress Pleasant, desirable stress

Distress Unpleasant, threatening stress

Hans Selye (SELL-yay), a Canadian physician renowned for his research and writing in the area of stress since the 1930s, defined **stress** as the nonspecific response of the body to any demand made upon it. The trigger that prompts the stressful reaction is called a **stressor.** When you play two nonstop tennis matches in the middle of a heat wave, your body responds with a fast heartbeat, rapid breathing, and an outpouring of perspiration. When you suddenly remember that the term paper you just started is due today rather than next Friday, your body has the same physiological stress response to a very different stressor. Stress reactions can result from either internal, cognitive stimuli or external, environmental stimuli (Marks et al., 2011; Straub, 2011).

Our bodies are nearly always in some state of stress, whether pleasant or unpleasant, mild or severe. *Anything* placing a demand on the body can cause stress. A total absence of stress would mean a total absence of stimulation, which would eventually lead to death. When stress is short-lived or perceived as a challenge, it can be beneficial. As seen in athletes, business tycoons, entertainers, or great leaders, this type of pleasant stress, called **eustress**, helps arouse and motivate us toward great accomplishments. Stress that is unpleasant and threatening is called **distress** (Selye, 1974). Because health psychology has been chiefly concerned with the negative effects of stress, we will adhere to convention and use the word *stress* to refer primarily to harmful or unpleasant stress.

Sources of Stress: Seven Major Stressors

Objective 3.2: Describe the seven major sources of stress.

Although stress is pervasive in our lives, some things cause more stress than others. The seven major sources of stress are life changes, chronic stressors, job stressors, hassles, frustration, conflict, and cataclysmic events (Figure 3.1).

Sources of Stress

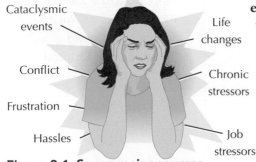

Cataclysmic events

Life changes

Conflict

Chronic stressors

Frustration

Hassles

Job stressors

Figure 3.1 Seven major sources of stress

Life Changes

Early stress researchers Thomas Holmes and Richard Rahe (1967) believed that change of any kind that required some adjustment in behavior or lifestyle could cause some degree of stress (Figure 3.2). They also believed that exposure to numerous stressful events within a short period could have a direct detrimental effect on health.

To investigate the relationship between change and stress, Holmes and Rahe created a Social Readjustment Rating Scale (SRRS) that asked people to check off all the life events they had experienced in the last year (Table 3.1).

The SRRS scale is an easy and popular way to measure stress, and cross-cultural studies have shown that most people rank the magnitude of stressful events in similar ways (De Coteau, Hope, & Anderson, 2003; Sandoval & Acuna, 2008; Thoits, 2010). However, the SRRS is not foolproof. For example, it only shows a _correlation_ between stress and illness. It does not prove that stress actually causes illnesses.

Chronic Stressors

Not all stressful situations are single, life-changing events, like the death of a spouse or a divorce. Ongoing, unrelenting stressors, such as war, a bad marriage, poverty, ill health, or an intolerable political climate, also contribute to stress. Interestingly, these

Figure 3.2 Life changes—stressful ordeal or exciting opportunity? Different people may perceive any given event differently, depending on how they interpret and appraise the event (Holt & Dunn, 2004). Also, some people are better able to deal with change than others, perhaps because of good coping skills, general physical health, healthier lifestyles, or even genetic predisposition.

Table 3.1 MEASURING LIFE CHANGES

Social Readjustment Rating Scale (SRRS)

To score yourself on this scale, add up the "life change units" for all life events you have experienced during the last year. Now compare your total score with the following standards: 0–49 = No significant problems; 150–199 = Mild life crisis (33 percent chance of illness); 200–299 = Moderate life crisis (50 percent chance of illness); 300 and above = Major life crisis (80 percent chance of illness).

Life Events	Life Change Units	Life Events	Life Change Units	Life Events	Life Change Units
Death of spouse	100	Change to different line of work	36	Change in work hours or conditions	20
Divorce	73	Change in number of arguments with spouse	35	Change in residence	20
Marital separation	65			Change in schools	20
Jail term	63	Mortgage or loan for major purchase	31	Change in recreation	19
Death of a close family member	63			Change in church activities	19
Personal injury or illness	53	Foreclosure on mortgage or loan	30	Change in social activities	18
Marriage	50			Mortgage or loan for lesser purchase (car, major appliance)	17
Fired at work	47	Change in responsibilities at work	29		
Marital reconciliation	45	Son or daughter leaving home	29		
Retirement	45	Trouble with in-laws	29	Change in sleeping habits	16
Change in health of family member	44	Outstanding personal achievement	28	Change in number of family get-togethers	15
Pregnancy	40	Spouse begins or stops work	26	Change in eating habits	15
Sex difficulties	39	Begin or end school	26	Vacation	13
Gain of a new family member	39	Change in living conditions	25	Christmas	12
Business readjustment	39	Revision of personal habits	24	Minor violations of the law	11
Change in financial state	38	Trouble with boss	23		
Death of a close friend	37				

Source: Reprinted from _Journal of Psychosomatic Research,_ Vol. III; Holmes and Rahe: "The Social Readjustment Rating Scale," 213–218, 1967, with permission from Elsevier.

Chronic Stressors State of ongoing arousal in which the parasympathetic system cannot activate the relaxation response

types of **chronic stressors**, a state of ongoing physiological arousal, may be some of the most damaging of all stressors (Enoch, 2011; Torpy, Lynm, & Glass, 2007). As you'll see in the upcoming section on the effects of stress, our bodies were designed to handle acute, short-acting stress, not chronic stress.

Recall from Chapter 2 that when we see a bear, our *sympathetic system* automatically kicks into "fight or flight." Once the threat passes, the *parasympathetic system* takes over and relaxes us. But our modern-day stressors are much more complex and ongoing, and our parasympathetic system rarely has the chance to activate the relaxation response. How do soldiers cope with the day-to-day fear of attacks, the ever-changing military demands, and the decreased time for "R and R" (rest and relaxation)? How do college students manage the ongoing threats of increasing tuition, quizzes, exams, and term papers, while also holding down part- or full-time jobs? Being in a constant state of perceived threat, without the required relaxation time, can wear down our bodies—both physically and psychologically. That's why it's so important to practice the stress management techniques discussed at the end of this chapter.

Job Stressors

Job Stressors Work-related stress, including unemployment, role conflict, and burnout

For many workers, the largest source of stress are **job stressors** resulting from unemployment, keeping or changing jobs, job performance, lack of control, and the like (Hoppe, 2011; O'Neill & Davis, 2011). However, the most stressful jobs are those that make great demands on performance and concentration, but allow little control, creativity, or opportunity for advancement (Smith et al., 2008; Straub, 2011). Assembly-line work ranks very high in this category.

Job strain is a direct contributor to both initial and recurrent heart attacks, while also causing serious problems at home, not only for the worker but for other family members as well (Aboa-Éboulé, 2008; Aboa-Éboulé et al., 2007; Rosenström et al., 2011).

Role Conflict Forced choice between two or more different and incompatible role demands

Another common source of job stress comes from **role conflict**, which occurs when one is forced to take on two or more different and incompatible roles at the same time (Andreassi & Thompson, 2007; Ergeneli, Ilsev, & Karapinar, 2010; Huffman et al., 2008; Rantenen et al., 2011). Being a student and a worker is a prime example of a role conflict. Stress is inescapable when your professor schedules an exam on the same day that your employer requires you to work overtime.

Burnout State of psychological and physical exhaustion resulting from chronic exposure to high levels of stress and little personal control

Chronic exposure to high levels of job stress and little personal control can also lead to a state of psychological and physical exhaustion known as **burnout**. Although the term has become an overused buzzword, health psychologists use it to describe a specific syndrome that develops most commonly in idealistic people who are involved in chronically stressful and emotionally draining professions (Gray-Stanley & Muramatsu, 2011; Hamaideh, 2011; Shirom, 2011).

A cautionary note: A spokesman for the American Heart Association (AHA), Philip Greenland, is concerned that some might conclude that all one has to do to avoid heart disease is to deal with one's job stress. He warns us that the top three factors for heart disease are still "smoking, high blood pressure, and high cholesterol" (cited in "Job Stress Can Kill," 2002).

Hassles

Hassles Small problems of daily living that accumulate and sometimes become a major source of stress

In addition to life changes, chronic stress, and job stress, we also experience a great deal of daily stress from **hassles**—little problems of daily living that are not significant in themselves but that pile up to become a major source of stress. We all share many

TEST YOURSELF

What Are Your Major Hassles?

List the top 10 hassles you most commonly experience, then compare your answers to the following:

The 10 Most Common Hassles for College Students

	Percentage of Times Checked
1. Troubling thoughts about the future	76.6
2. Not getting enough sleep	72.5
3. Wasting time	71.1
4. Inconsiderate smokers	70.7
5. Physical appearance	69.9
6. Too many things to do	69.2
7. Misplacing or losing things	67.0
8. Not enough time to do the things you need to do	66.3
9. Concerns about meeting high standards	64.0
10. Being lonely	60.8

Source: Kanner, A. D., Coyne, J. C., Schaefer, C., & Lazarus, R. S. (1981). Comparison of two modes of stress measurement: Daily hassles and uplifts versus major life events. *Journal of Behavioral Medicine*, 4, 1–39.

hassles, such as time pressures and financial concerns, but our reactions to hassles may vary. Some authorities believe hassles often are more significant than major life events in creating stress (Cheng & Li, 2010; Kubiak et al., 2008; Pettit et al., 2010). For example, divorce is extremely stressful, but it may be so because of the increased number of hassles—a change in finances, child-care arrangements, longer working hours, and so on.

Can you explain this man's approach–avoidance conflict?

Frustration

Frustration is a negative emotional state generally associated with a blocked goal, such as not being accepted for admission to your first-choice college. The more motivated we are, the more frustration we experience when our goals are blocked. After getting stuck in traffic and missing an important job interview, we may become very frustrated. However, if the same traffic jam causes us to be five minutes late getting home, we may experience little or no frustration.

Conflict

Another source of stress is **conflict,** which arises when we are forced to make a choice between at least two incompatible alternatives. There are three basic types of conflict: *approach–approach, avoidance–avoidance,* and *approach–avoidance* (see Concept Organizer 3.1).

Frustration Unpleasant tension, anxiety, and heightened sympathetic activity resulting from a blocked goal

Conflict Forced choice between two or more incompatible goals or impulses

ConceptOrganizer3.1

Three Types of Conflict

Conflict	Description/Resolution	Example/Resolution	
Approach–Approach ➕ ➕	Forced choice between two options both of which have equally desirable characteristics	Two equally desirable job offers, but you must choose one of them because you're broke.	
	Generally easiest and least stressful conflict to resolve	You make a pro/con list and/or "flip a coin."	
Avoidance–Avoidance ➖ ➖	Forced choice between two options both of which have equally undesirable characteristics	Two equally undesirable job offers, but you must choose one of them because you're broke.	
	Difficult, stressful conflict, generally resolved with delay and denial as long as possible	You make a pro/con list and/or "flip a coin," and then delay decision hoping for additional job offers.	
Approach–Avoidance ➕ ➖	Forced choice within one option, which has equally desirable and undesirable characteristics	One high salary job offer requiring you to relocate to an undesirable location leaving all your friends and family.	
	Difficult, stressful conflict, generally resolved with delay and/or partial approach	You make a pro/con list and/or "flip a coin;" delay the decision until you get a better job offer (partial approach).	

In the book (and film) Sophie's Choice, Sophie (played by Meryl Streep) and her two children are sent to a German concentration camp. A soldier orders Sophie to choose either her son or her daughter, or else both children will be killed. Obviously, both alternatives will have tragic results. What kind of conflict does this example illustrate?

Approach–Approach Conflict Forced choice between two options both of which have equally desirable characteristics

Avoidance–Avoidance Conflict Forced choice between two options both of which have equally undesirable characteristics

Approach–Avoidance Conflict Forced choice within one option, which has equally desirable and undesirable characteristics

Generally, approach–approach conflicts are the easiest to resolve and produce the least stress. Avoidance–avoidance conflicts, on the other hand, are usually the most difficult because all choices lead to unpleasant results. Keep in mind that in addition to the stress of a forced choice, the longer any conflict exists, or the more important the decision, the more stress we will experience.

Cataclysmic Events

The 2001 terrorist attacks in America, the Indian Ocean earthquake and tsunami waves in 2004, Hurricane Katrina in 2005, the Gulf oil spill in 2010, and the earthquake, tsunami, and nuclear accident in Japan in 2011 are what stress researchers call **cataclysmic events**. They occur suddenly and generally affect many people simultaneously. Politicians and the public often imagine that such catastrophes inevitably create huge numbers of seriously depressed and permanently scarred survivors. Relief agencies typically send large numbers of counselors to help with the psychological aftermath. Ironically, researchers have found that because the catastrophe is shared by so many others, there is a great deal of mutual social support from those with firsthand experience with the same disaster, which may help people cope (Collocan, Tuma, & Fleischman, 2004; Ginzburg & Bateman, 2008). On the other hand, these cataclysmic events are clearly devastating to all parts of the victims' lives (Alvarez, 2011; Belson, 2011; Dean-Borenstein, 2007; Lindal & Stefánsson, 2011). And some survivors may develop a prolonged and severe stress reaction, known as *posttraumatic stress disorder* (*PTSD*), which we discuss later in this chapter.

Effects of Stress: How the Body Responds

Have you ever experienced a near accident or some other sudden, frightening event? If so, you may have noticed how stress increased your heart rate, blood pressure, respiration, and muscle tension, while simultaneously decreasing your digestion and constricting your blood vessels. As you recall from Chapter 2, under stressful conditions, the *sympathetic* part of the autonomic nervous system is dominant, and your reactions to the stressor are part of the general "fight-or-flight" syndrome.

Once the danger passes, a longer sequence of important health-related reactions occurs. Selye's *general adaptation syndrome* and the SAM-HPA axis (discussed next) control the most significant of these changes.

Cataclysmic Event Stressful occurrences that occur suddenly and generally affect many people simultaneously

Stress and cataclysmic events The 2011 ▲ Japanese earthquake and tsunami provide recent examples of what most people would consider extremely stressful events. But it may not be as stressful as you imagine (see text for an explanation).

CHECK & REVIEW

STOP *Before going on, be sure to complete this Check & Review. It is an invaluable study tool!*

Understanding Stress and Sources of Stress

Part A: Retrieval Practice

1. Without looking at the book, spend 10 minutes writing a free-form essay recalling all you can remember from the previous section.

2. Now, reread the previous section, and once again spend 10 minutes writing a free-form essay on the SAME material.

   (Although time consuming, this exercise has been shown to be the single best way to improve your test scores! For more information, check out www.sciencemag.org/content/early/2011/01/19/science.1199327.abstract)

Part B: Practice Quiz

1. John was planning to ask Susan to marry him. When he saw Susan kissing another man at a party, he was quite upset. In this situation, John's seeing Susan kissing another man is _____, and it illustrates _____. (a) a stressor, distress; (b) eustress, a stressor; (c) distress, a stressor; (d) a stressor, eustress

2. The Social Readjustment Rating Scale (SRRS) constructed by Holmes and Rahe measures the stress situation in a person's life based on _____.

3. Frustration is a negative emotional state that is generally associated with _____, whereas _____ is a negative emotional state caused by difficulty in choosing between two or more incompatible goals or impulses.

4. List everyday examples for each of the three types of conflict: approach–approach, approach–avoidance, and avoidance–avoidance.

5. Of the seven major stressors, which do you find most stressful in your own life?

Check your answers in Appendix B.

Selye's General Adaptation Syndrome (GAS)

Objective 3.3: What is the generalized adaptation syndrome (GAS)?

General Adaptation Syndrome (GAS) Selye's three-stage (alarm, resistance, exhaustion) reaction to chronic stress

Stress clearly causes destructive biological changes that can be detrimental to health. Hans Selye (1936), mentioned earlier in our definition of *stress*, described a generalized physiological reaction to severe stressors that he called the **general adaptation syndrome (GAS)**. The GAS occurs in three phases—*alarm*, *resistance*, and *exhaustion*—activated by efforts to adapt to any stressor, whether physical or psychological (carefully study the Step-by-Step Diagram 3.1 on the next page for important details.)

Modern Approaches Over the years, most of Selye's ideas about the GAS pattern of stress response have proven to be correct. However, he also believed that all stressors had similar effects, and we now know that different stressors evoke different responses. In addition, people vary widely in their reactions. Our learning histories, genetic predispositions, personalities, and preexisting medical conditions all affect how well or how poorly we respond to stress.

One of the most interesting ways that people differ in their stress response has to do with gender. Men more often "fight or flight," whereas women "*tend and befriend*." They take care of themselves and their children (tending), and form strong social bonds with others (befriending) (Taylor, 2008, 2011). Some researchers believe these differences are hormonal in nature. Although oxytocin is released during stress in both men and women, the female's higher level of estrogen tends to enhance oxytocin, which results in more calming and nurturing feelings. In contrast, the hormone testosterone, which men produce in high levels during stress, reduces the effects of oxytocin.

What is Selye's most important take-home message? *Our bodies are relatively well designed for temporary stress, but poorly equipped for prolonged stress.* The same biological processes that are adaptive in the short run, such as the fight-or-flight response, can become hazardous in the long run. A look at modern research findings on the SAM and HPA axis will help you understand exactly how this happens.

Visible effects of stress Would you like to be President of the United States? Note how the stress of the office has aged President Barack Obama in just two short years!

The SAM System and HPA Axis

Objective 3.4: Describe the SAM system and the HPA axis.

SAM System Body's initial, rapid-acting stress response, involving the sympathetic nervous system and the adrenal medulla; also called the sympatho-adreno-medullary (SAM) system

Current research has shown that we have two major brain–body pathways for dealing with stress (shown in the Step-by-Step Diagram 3.2, p. 102). The first *alarm reaction* is controlled by the **sympatho-adreno-medullary (SAM) system.** As shown on the left side of the figure, page 101, stressors trigger a cascade of effects that begin when the brain's hypothalamus activates the sympathetic nervous system, which stimulates the medulla (inner part) of the adrenal glands. The adrenals, in turn, secrete *catecholamines* (kat-uh-KOH-luh-meens), especially norepinephrine and epinephrine), which activate bodily changes necessary for "fight or flight."

HPA Axis Body's delayed stress response, involving the hypothalamus, pituitary, and adrenal cortex; also called the hypothalamic-pituitary-adrenocortical (HPA) system

The second pathway, the **hypothalamic-pituitary-adrenocortical (HPA) axis,** involves more direct communication between the brain and the endocrine system. As

Step-by-StepDiagram3.1

General Adaptation Syndrome (GAS)

Note how the three stages of this syndrome (*alarm*, *resistance*, and *exhaustion*) focus on the biological response to stress—particularly the "wear and tear" on the body with prolonged stress.

1 Alarm Reaction
When surprised or threatened, your body enters an alarm phase during which your resistance to stress is temporarily suppressed, while your arousal is high (e.g., increased heart rate and blood pressure) and blood is diverted to your skeletal muscles to prepare for "fight-or-flight" (Chapter 2).

2 Stage of Resistance
If the stress continues, your body rebounds to a phase of increased resistance. Physiological arousal remains higher than normal, and there is an outpouring of stress hormones. During this resistance stage, people use a variety of coping methods. For example, if your job is threatened, you may work longer hours and give up your vacation days

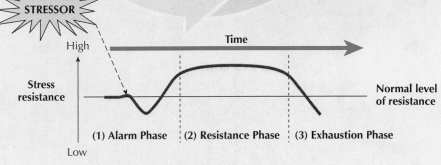

STRESSOR

High

Time

Stress resistance

Normal level of resistance

Low

(1) Alarm Phase | (2) Resistance Phase | (3) Exhaustion Phase

3 Stage of Exhaustion
Your body's resistance to stress can only last so long before exhaustion sets in. During this final stage, you become more susceptible to serious illnesses, and possibly irreversible damage to your body. Selye maintained that one outcome of this stage for some people is the development of *diseases of adaption*, including asthma, ulcers, and high blood pressure.Unless a way of relieving stress is found, the eventual result may be complete collapse and death.

◀ **Stress in ancient times** As shown in these ancient cave drawings, the automatic fight-or-flight response was adaptive and necessary for early human survival. However, in modern society it occurs as a response to ongoing situations where we often cannot fight or flee. This repeated arousal can be detrimental to our health.

shown in the right side of the figure, page 102, the hypothalamus sends signals to the pituitary gland, which stimulates the cortex (outer surface) of the adrenal glands to secrete *corticosteroids*. These hormones, especially cortisol, activate the body's energy supplies and help fight inflammation.

Once the cortisol levels reach a certain level, parts of the brain, particularly the *hippocampus*, tell the hypothalamus to turn off the stress response. This is the proper feedback loop that "turns on and off" a healthy, appropriate response to stress. In sum, a combination of the SAM system and HPA axis allows us to effectively cope with life-threatening stressors.

So why do we hear so much about the dangers of stress? Researchers regard cortisol as the key "stress hormone" because it plays such a critical role in both adaptive and maladaptive responses to stress, and the level of circulating cortisol is the most common physiological measure of stress. In the short run, cortisol helps reduce inflammation and promotes healing in case of injury. It also helps mobilize the body's

Step-by-StepDiagram3.2

The Biology of Stress

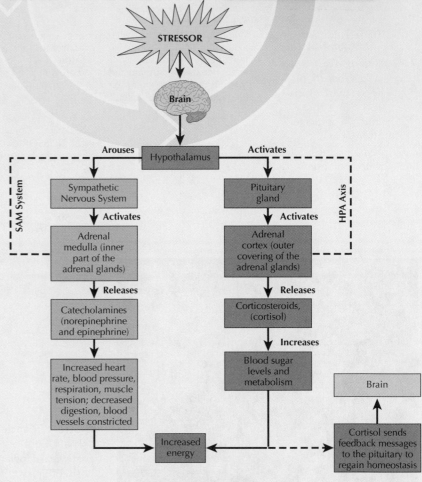

STRESSOR

Brain

Arouses Hypothalamus **Activates**

SAM System | HPA Axis

Sympathetic Nervous System → **Activates**

Pituitary gland → **Activates**

Adrenal medulla (inner part of the adrenal glands) → **Releases**

Adrenal cortex (outer covering of the adrenal glands) → **Releases**

Catecholamines (norepinephrine and epinephrine)

Corticosteroids, (cortisol) → **Increases**

Increased heart rate, blood pressure, respiration, muscle tension; decreased digestion, blood vessels constricted

Blood sugar levels and metabolism

Brain

Increased energy

Cortisol sends feedback messages to the pituitary to regain homeostasis

TEST YOURSELF

Reviewing the SAM and HPA Axis

Arrange the following 10 key terms in their proper order and place, and then compare your answers with those in Appendix B.

Key terms: *corticosteroids, adrenal cortex, catecholamines, fight-or-flight, adrenal medulla, endocrine system, cortisol, norepinephrine, epinephrine, pituitary*

SAM System	HPA Axis
_____	_____
_____	_____
_____	_____
_____	_____
_____	_____

1. The **SAM system** (short for Sympatho-Adreno-Medullary) provides an initial, rapid-acting stress response thanks to cooperation between the sympathetic nervous system and the adrenal medulla.

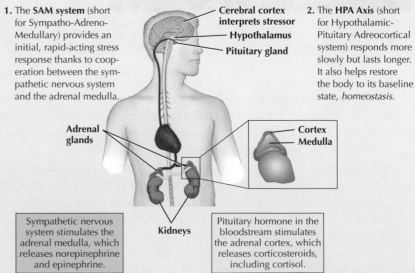

Cerebral cortex interprets stressor

Hypothalamus

Pituitary gland

2. The **HPA Axis** (short for Hypothalamic-Pituitary Adreocortical system) responds more slowly but lasts longer. It also helps restore the body to its baseline state, *homeostasis.*

Adrenal glands

Cortex
Medulla

Kidneys

Sympathetic nervous system stimulates the adrenal medulla, which releases norepinephrine and epinephrine.

Pituitary hormone in the bloodstream stimulates the adrenal cortex, which releases corticosteroids, including cortisol.

energy resources. After the stress threat has passed, the body normally regains equilibrium, or **homeostasis**.

Unfortunately for some people, however, homeostasis is not restored. The stress response becomes stuck in an under- or overaroused state leading to dangerously low or high levels of cortisol. In the underaroused state, the adrenal glands become exhausted from the demands of chronic stress, which leads to chronically low levels of cortisol (*hypocortisolism*). Hypocortisolism is associated with several disorders, including asthma, rheumatoid arthritis, and fibromyalgia (Marks et al., 2011; Straub, 2011).

In contrast to this underarousal and low levels of cortisol, some individuals are chronically overaroused by stress, leading to a prolonged elevation of cortisol (*hypercortisolism*). Hypercortisolism not only depletes the normal supply of cortisol, but it can also permanently disrupt the feedback system that normally shuts off the stress response. Prolonged elevation of cortisol also has serious physical and psychological consequences, including hypertension, depression, posttraumatic stress disorder (PTSD), drug and alohol abuse, and even low-birth-weight infants (Bagley, Weaver, & Buchanan, 2011; Johnson, Delahanty, & Pinna, 2008; Stalder et al., 2010; Straub, 2011). As if this long list of ill-effects weren't enough, severe or prolonged stress can also produce overall physical deterioration, premature aging, and even death.

In sum, the SAM system and HPA axis are designed to increase our energy for dealing with emergencies. However, continued arousal and chemical onslaught may deplete our body's energy reserves, and thereby contribute to various stress-related health problems (Lundberg, 2011; Pace & Heim, 2011). For example, increased cortisol levels initially help us fight stressors, but if these levels stay high, the body's disease-fighting immune system is suppressed—our next topic for discussion.

Homeostasis Body's tendency to maintain a relatively balanced and stable internal state, such as a constant internal temperature

Stress and the Immune System

Objective 3.5: How does stress affect our immune system?

Now that you've studied Selye's *general adaptation syndrome*, the SAM system, and the HPA axis, we can explore why the discovery of the relationship between stress and the immune system is so very important. When our immune system is impaired, we are at greatly increased risk of suffering from a number of diseases, including cancer, bursitis, colitis, Alzheimer's disease, rheumatoid arthritis, periodontal disease, and even the common cold (Carroll et al., 2011; Cohen et al., 2002; Cohen & Lemay, 2007; Dantzer et al., 2008; Gasser & Raulet, 2006; Segerstrom & Miller, 2004).

Knowledge that psychological factors have considerable control over infectious diseases has upset long-held assumptions in biology and medicine that these diseases are "strictly physical." The clinical and theoretical implications are so important that a new field of biopsychology has emerged, **psychoneuroimmunology**, which studies the interactions of psychological factors ("psycho"), the nervous and endocrine systems ("neuro"), and the immune system ("immunology") (Ayers et al., 2007; Kemeny, 2007).

Psychoneuroimmunology [sye-koh-NEW-roh-IM-you-NOLL-oh-gee] Interdisciplinary field that studies the effects of psychological and other factors on the immune system

Stress and Cognitive Functioning

Objective 3.6: How does stress affect cognitive functioning?

Having discovered the overall general effects of stress on the body are you wondering what happens to your brain and information processing during both acute and chronic stress? Have you noticed that you sometimes forget important information

low stakes testing

Figure 3.3 Stress and the brain—a *vicious cycle*

Damage to Hippocampus

Increased Cortisol

Increased Cortisol

Hippocampus

Increased Damage to Hippocampus

during a stressful exam? What about people who "freeze" during a crisis and fail to run for cover?

As you know, cortisol helps us deal with immediate dangers by increasing our immunity and mobilizing our energy resources. However, it also can prevent the retrieval of existing memories, as well as the laying down of new memories and general information processing (Almela et al., 2011; Hurlemann et al., 2007; Mahoney et al., 2007; Pechtel & Pizzagalli, 2011). This interference with immediate cognitive functioning helps explain why people sometimes become dangerously confused and can't find the fire exit during a fire and later may not remember much of what happened during a traumatic event. The good news is that once the cortisol "washes out," memory performance generally returns to normal levels.

In addition to the problems with cognitive functioning during acute stress, Robert Sapolsky (1992, 2003) has shown that prolonged stress can permanently damage the hippocampus, a key part of the brain involved in memory (Chapter 7). Furthermore, once the hippocampus is damaged, it cannot provide proper feedback to the hypothalamus, so cortisol continues to be secreted and a vicious cycle can develop (Figure 3.3).

Psychology at Work

Is My Job Too Stressful?

Objective 3.7: Identify four factors important to job satisfaction.

In addition to "burnout," researchers have identified several additional factors in job-related stress. Their findings suggest that one way to prevent these stresses is to gather lots of information before making a career decision.

If you would like to apply this to your own career plans, start by identifying what you like and don't like about your current (and past) jobs. With this information in hand, you'll be prepared to find jobs that will better suit your interests, needs, and abilities, which will likely reduce your stress. To start your analysis, answer yes or no to these questions:

1. Is there a sufficient amount of laughter and sociability in my workplace?
2. Does my boss notice and appreciate my work?
3. Is my boss understanding and friendly?
4. Am I embarrassed by the physical conditions of my workplace?
5. Do I feel safe and comfortable in my place of work?
6. Do I like the location of my job?
7. If I won the lottery and were guaranteed a lifetime income, would I feel truly sad if I also had to quit my job?
8. Do I watch the clock, daydream, take long lunches, and leave work as soon as possible?
9. Do I frequently feel stressed and overwhelmed by the demands of my job?
10. Compared to others with my qualifications, am I being paid what I am worth?
11. Are promotions made in a fair and just manner where I work?
12. Given the demands of my job, am I fairly compensated for my work?

Is nursing a stressful career? Over time, some people in chronically stressful professions who think of their job as a "calling" become emotionally drained and disillusioned—they "burn out." Burnout can cause more work absences, less productivity, and increased risk for physical problems. What other occupations might pose an especially high risk for burnout?

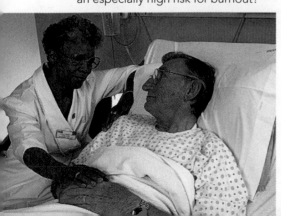

Now score your answers. Give yourself one point for each answer that matches the following: 1. No; 2. No; 3. No; 4. Yes; 5. No; 6. No; 7. No; 8. Yes; 9. Yes; 10. No; 11. No; 12. No.

The questions you just answered are based on four factors that research shows are conducive to increased job satisfaction and reduced stress: supportive colleagues, supportive working conditions, mentally challenging work, and equitable rewards (Robbins, 1996). Your total score reveals your overall level of dissatisfaction. A look at specific questions can help identify which of these four factors is most important to your job satisfaction—and most lacking in your current job.

Supportive colleagues (items 1, 2, 3): For most people, work fills important social needs. Therefore, having friendly and supportive colleagues and superiors leads to increased satisfaction.

Supportive working conditions (items 4, 5, 6): Not surprisingly, most employees prefer working in safe, clean, and relatively modern facilities. They also prefer jobs close to home.

Mentally challenging work (items 7, 8, 9): Jobs with too little challenge create boredom and apathy, whereas too much challenge creates frustration and feelings of failure.

Equitable rewards (items 10, 11, 12): Employees want pay and promotions based on job demands, individual skill levels, and community pay standards.

CHECK & REVIEW

STOP *Before going on, be sure to complete this Check & Review. It is an invaluable study tool!*

Effects of Stress

Part A: Retrieval Practice

1. Without looking at the book, spend 10 minutes writing a free-form essay recalling all you can remember from the previous section.

2. Now, reread the previous section, and once again spend 10 minutes writing a free-form essay on the SAME material.

Part B: Practice Quiz

1. The GAS consists of three phases: the _____ reaction, the _____ phase, and the _____ phase.

2. As Michael watches his instructor pass out papers, he suddenly realizes this is the first major exam, and he is unprepared. Which phase of the GAS is he most likely experiencing? (a) resistance; (b) alarm; (c) exhaustion; (d) phase out.

3. How does the SAM system help us respond to stress?

4. How does the HPA axis help us respond to stress?

5. Label the three major structures in the figure to your right.

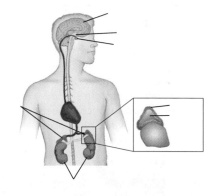

Check your answers in Appendix B

Stress and Illness

As we have just seen, stress has dramatic effects on our bodies. This section explores how stress is related to four serious illnesses—*cancer, coronary heart disease, posttraumatic stress disorder (PTSD),* and *gastric ulcers.*

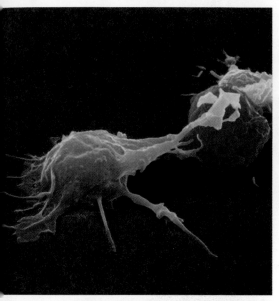

Figure 3.4 The immune system in action Stress can compromise the immune system, and the actions of a healthy immune system are shown here. The round red structures are leukemia cells. Note how the yellow killer cells are attacking and destroying the cancer cells.

Controllable risk factors for premature death Heart disease and cancer are the leading causes of death for Americans, but among young adults, suicide and accidents are the biggest killers. Why do you think there are these types of age-related differences? In what ways might suicide and accidents, such as those caused by texting while driving, be considered somewhat controllable?

Cancer: A Variety of Causes—Including Stress?

Objective 3.8: Is stress related to cancer?

Cancer is among the leading causes of death for adults in the United States. It occurs when a cell begins rapidly dividing and then forms a tumor that invades healthy tissue. In a healthy person, whenever cancer cells start to multiply, the immune system checks the uncontrolled growth by attacking the abnormal cells (Figure 3.4). Unless destroyed or removed, the tumor eventually damages organs and causes death. More than 100 types of cancer have been identified. They appear to be caused by an interaction between environmental factors (such as diet, smoking, pollutants) and inherited predispositions. It's important to note that research does *not* support the popular myths that stress *causes* cancer or that positive attitudes can fight off cancer (Coyne & Tennen, 2010; Lilienfeld et al., 2010; Surtees et al., 2009).

However, this is not to say that developing a positive attitude and reducing our stress levels aren't worthy health goals (Dempster et al., 2011; O'Brien & Moorey, 2010). As you read earlier, stress causes the adrenal glands to release hormones that suppress the immune system, and a compromised immune system is less able to resist infection (Ben-Eliyahu, Page, & Schleifer, 2007; Bernabé et al., 2011; Kemeny, 2007; Krukowski et al., 2011). For example, when researchers interrupted the sleep of 23 men and then measured their *natural killer cells* (a type of immune system cell), they found the number of killer cells was 28 percent below average (Irwin et al., 1994). Can you see how staying up late studying for an exam (or partying) can decrease the effectiveness of your immune system? Fortunately, these researchers found that a normal night's sleep after the deprivation returned the killer cells to their normal levels.

Cardiovascular Disorders: The Leading Cause of Death in the United States

Objective 3.9: Describe the links between stress and heart disease.

Cardiovascular disorders cause over half of all deaths in the United States (American Heart Association, 2008). Understandably, health psychologists are concerned because unlike the myth that stress causes cancer, researchers find that stress is a major contributor to heart disease deaths (Aboa-Éboulé et al., 2007; Landsbergis et al., 2011; Montoro-Garcia, Shantsila, & Lip, 2011; Phillips & Hughes, 2011). *Heart disease* is a general term for all disorders that eventually affect the heart muscle and lead to heart failure. *Coronary heart disease* results from *arteriosclerosis*, a thickening and hardening of the walls of the coronary arteries that reduces or blocks the blood supply to the heart. Arteriosclerosis causes *angina* (chest pain due to insufficient blood supply to the heart) or *heart attack* (death of heart muscle tissue). Controllable factors that contribute to heart disease include stress, smoking, certain personality characteristics, obesity, a high-fat diet, and lack of exercise (Aboa-Éboulé, 2008; Ayers et al., 2007; Straub, 2011).

How does stress contribute to heart disease? Recall that one of the major brain and nervous system "fight-or-flight" reactions is the release of epinephrine (adrenaline) and cortisol into the bloodstream. These hormones increase heart rate and release fat and glucose from the body's stores to give muscles a quickly available source of energy. *autonomic activatn*

If no physical "fight-or-flight" action is taken (as often happens in our modern lives), the fat that was released into the bloodstream is not burned as fuel. Instead, it may adhere to the walls of blood vessels (Figure 3.5). These deposits are a major cause of blood supply blockage that causes heart attacks.

Personality Types

The effects of stress on heart disease may be amplified if an individual tends to be hard-driving, competitive, ambitious, impatient, and hostile. People with such **Type A personalities** are chronically on edge, feel intense time urgency, and are preoccupied with responsibilities. The antithesis of the Type A personality is the **Type B personality**, having a laid-back, calm, relaxed attitude toward life.

Two cardiologists, Meyer Friedman and Ray Rosenman (1959), were the first to identify and describe the Type A personality. The story goes that in the mid-1950s, an upholsterer who was re-covering the waiting room chairs in Friedman's office noticed an odd wear pattern. He mentioned to Friedman that the chairs looked like new except for the front edges, which were badly worn, as if all the patients sat only on the edges of the chairs. Initially, this did not seem too important to Friedman. However, he later came to believe that this chronic sense of time urgency, being literally "on the edge of your seat," was a possible contributing factor to heart disease and the hallmark of the Type A personality.

Initial research into Type A behavior suggested that Friedman and Rosenman were right. But when later researchers examined the relationship between characteristics of the Type A behavior pattern and heart disease, they found that _hostility_ was the _strongest predictor of heart_ disease (Bunde & Suls, 2006; Elovainio et al., 2011; Mittag & Maurischat, 2004) (Figure 3.6).

Actually, _cynical_ hostility appears to be the most important factor in the Type A relationship to heart disease. Constantly being "on watch" for problems translates physiologically into higher blood pressure and heart rate, and production of stress-related hormones. In addition, people who are hostile, suspicious, argumentative, and competitive tend to have more frequent interpersonal conflicts. This can heighten autonomic activation, leading to increased risk of cardiovascular disease (Boyle et al., 2004; Bunde & Suls, 2006; Eaker et al., 2007; Williams, 2010).

Can people with a Type A personality change their behavior? Health psychologists have developed two types of behavior modification for people with Type A personality—the _shotgun approach_ and the _target behavior approach_. The _shotgun approach_ aims to change all the behaviors that relate to the Type A personality. Friedman and his colleagues (1986) use the shotgun approach in their Recurrent Coronary Prevention Program. The program provides individual counseling, dietary advice, exercise, drugs, and group therapy to eliminate or modify Type A behaviors. Type A's are specifically encouraged to slow down and perform tasks incompatible with their personalities. For example, they might try to listen to other people without interrupting, or they could deliberately choose the longest supermarket line. The major criticism of the shotgun approach is that it may decrease _desirable_ Type A traits, such as ambition, as well as _undesirable_

Type A Personality Behavior characteristics including intense ambition, competition, exaggerated time urgency, and a cynical, hostile outlook

Type B Personality Behavior characteristics consistent with a calm, patient, relaxed attitude

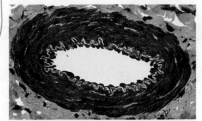
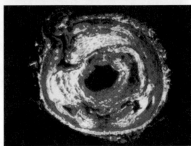

Figure 3.5 Fatty deposits in arteries One major cause of heart disease is the blockage of arteries that supply blood to the heart. The artery at the top is normal; the one on the bottom is almost completely blocked. Reducing stress, exercising, and eating a low-fat diet can help prevent the buildup of fatty deposits in the arteries.

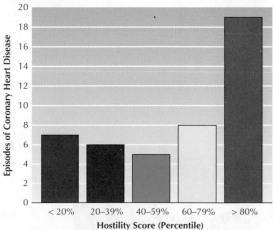

Figure 3.6 Type A personality, hostility and heart disease
Source: Niaura et al., _Health Psychology_, 2002.

(TEST YOURSELF)

Are You a Type A?

Answer "yes" or "no" to the following:

___ 1. Do you find it difficult to restrain yourself from hurrying others' speech (finishing their sentences for them)?

___ 2. Do you often try to do more than one thing at a time (such as eat and read simultaneously)?

___ 3. Do you often feel guilty if you use extra time to relax?

___ 4. Do you tend to get involved in a great number of projects at once?

___ 5. Do you find yourself racing through yellow lights when you drive?

___ 6. Do you need to win in order to derive enjoyment from games and sports?

___ 7. Do you generally move, walk, and eat rapidly?

___ 8. Do you agree to take on too many responsibilities?

___ 9. Do you detest waiting in lines?

___ 10. Do you have an intense desire to better your position in life and impress others?

If you answered yes to most of these items, you may be a Type A, but short quizzes like these provide only a brief snapshot of your full personality.

Source: Adapted from Friedman and Rosenman (1974).

---

traits, like cynicism and hostility. The alternative therapy, the *target behavior approach*, focuses on only those Type A behaviors that are likely to cause heart disease—namely, cynical hostility.

Hardiness and Positive Psychology

Hardiness Resilient personality with a strong commitment to personal goals, control over life, and viewing change as a challenge rather than a threat

We cannot wait for the storm to blow over. We must learn to work in the rain
JENNIFER GRANHOLM

In addition to Type A and Type B personalities, other personality patterns may affect the way we respond to stress. Have you ever wondered how some people survive in the face of great tragedy and stress? Suzanne Kobasa was among the first to study this question, but was soon joined by others (Eschleman, Bowling, & Alarcon, 2010; Kobasa, 1979; Maddi et al., 2006; Vogt et al., 2008). Examining male executives with high levels of stress, she found that some people are more resistant to stress than others because of a personality factor called **hardiness**, a resilient type of optimism that comes from three distinctive attitudes:

1. *Commitment* Hardy people feel a strong sense of commitment to both their work and their personal life. They also make intentional commitments to purposeful activity and problem solving.

2. *Control* Hardy people see themselves as being in control of their lives rather than as victims of their circumstances.

3. *Challenge* Finally, hardy people look at change as an opportunity for growth and improvement—not as a threat. They look at setbacks as challenges (Maddi et al., 2006).

The important lesson from this research is that hardiness is a *learned behavior*—not something based on luck or genetics. If you are not one of the *hardy* souls, you can develop the trait. The next time you face a bad stressor, such as four exams in one week, try using the 3 C's: "I am fully *committed* to my college education." "I can *control* the number of tests by taking one or two of them earlier than scheduled, or I can rearrange my work schedule." "I welcome this *challenge* as a final motivation to enroll in those reading improvement and college success courses I've always planned to take."

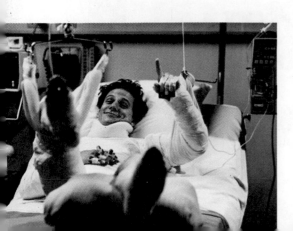

Before we go on, it is also important to note that Type A personality and lack of hardiness are not the only controllable risk factors associated with heart disease. Smoking, obesity, diet, and lack of exercise are very important factors. Smoking restricts blood circulation, and obesity stresses the heart by causing it to pump more blood to the excess body tissue. A high-fat diet, especially one high in cholesterol, contributes to the fatty deposits that clog blood vessels. Lack of exercise contributes to weight gain. It also prevents the body from obtaining important exercise benefits, including strengthened heart muscle, increased heart efficiency, and the release of neurotransmitters such as serotonin that alleviate stress and promote well-being.

Posttraumatic Stress Disorder (PTSD): A Disease of Modern Times?

Objective 3.10: How is stress connected to PTSD and ulcers?

One of the most powerful examples of the effects of severe stress is **posttraumatic stress disorder (PTSD)** (Baker, Nievergelt, & O'Connor, 2011; Pace & Heim, 2011; Ruzek et al., 2011). Children, as well as adults, can experience PTSD after exposure to a traumatic life event. Specifically, a person may have been involved in, was a witness to, or had even heard of an extreme traumatic stressor. The essential feature of PTSD is *severe anxiety* (a state of constant or recurring alarm and fearfulness). The anxiety develops after experiencing a traumatic event (such as rape, natural disaster, or war), learning about a violent or an unexpected death of a family member, or even being a witness or bystander to violence (American Psychiatric Association, 2002). The individual's reaction to the trauma tends to be one of helplessness and fear, with persistent reexperiencing of the event through dreams and daily thoughts (flashbacks), unsuccessful attempts to consciously try to avoid reminders of the event, a pattern of avoidance and emotional numbness, and fairly constant hyperarousal (easily startled, hypervigilant of their surroundings). These symptoms may continue for months or years after the event itself. To reduce the stress, some victims of PTSD turn to alcohol and other drugs, which often compound the problem (Cougle et al., 2011; Kaysen et al., 2008; Mc Cart et al., 2011; Sullivan & Holt, 2008).

During the Industrial Revolution, workers who survived horrific railroad accidents sometimes developed a condition very similar to PTSD. It was called "railway spine" because experts thought the problem resulted from a twisting or concussion of the spine. In later times, PTSD was primarily associated with military combat. Doctors called it "shell shock" because they believed it was a response to the physical concussion caused by exploding artillery. PTSD did not become a formal category of mental disorders until 1980, and today it is officially diagnosed when the symptoms last for more than a month after the event and significantly impact occupational and social functioning (APA, 1994, 2000). In cases, where individuals' symptoms have been present for less than 1 month, a more appropriate diagnosis may be *Acute Stress Disorder* (ASD).

According to the American Psychological Association (2011) website (www.apa.org/helpcenter/traumatic-stress.aspx), about 70 percent of U.S. adults have experienced a severe traumatic event, and one out of five go on to develop symptoms of PTSD. The primary symptoms of PTSD are summarized in Table 3.2. The table also includes five important tips for coping with traumatic events.

Posttraumatic Stress Disorder (PTSD) Anxiety disorder following exposure to a life-threatening or other extreme event that evoked great horror or helplessness; characterized by flashbacks, nightmares, and impaired functioning

Table 3.2 IDENTIFYING PTSD AND COPING WITH CRISIS

Primary Symptoms of Posttraumatic Stress Disorder (PTSD)

- Reexperiencing the event through vivid memories or flashbacks
- Reduced awareness; feeling "emotionally numb"
- Feeling overwhelmed by what would normally be considered everyday situations
- Showing diminished interest in performing normal tasks or pursuing usual interests
- Crying uncontrollably
- Isolating oneself from family and friends and avoiding social situations
- Relying increasingly on alcohol or drugs to get through the day
- Feeling extremely moody, irritable, angry, suspicious, or frightened
- Having difficulty falling or staying asleep, sleeping too much, and experiencing nightmares
- Feeling guilty about surviving the event or being unable to solve the problem, change the event, or prevent the disaster
- Experiencing fear, helplessness, hopelessness

Five Important Tips for Coping with Crisis

1. Recognize your feelings about the situation and talk to others about your fears. Know that these feelings are a normal response to an abnormal situation.

2. Be willing to listen to family and friends who have been affected and encourage them to seek counseling if necessary.

3. Be patient with people. Tempers are short in times of crisis, and others may be feeling as much stress as you.

4. Recognize normal crisis reactions, such as sleep disturbances and nightmares, withdrawal, reverting to childhood behaviors, and trouble focusing on work or school.

5. Take time with your children, spouse, life partner, friends, and coworkers to do something you enjoy.

Source: American Psychological Association (2011); American Counseling Association (2006), Pomponio (2002)

 RESEARCH CHALLENGE

Does Stress Cause Gastric Ulcers?

Do you have gastric ulcers or know someone who does? If so, you know that these lesions to the lining of the stomach (and duodenum—the upper section of the small intestine) can be quite painful. In extreme cases, they may even be life threatening.

Did you answer true to the Myth Buster question in the chapter opener suggesting ulcers are caused primarily or entirely by stress? Would you like to know what modern science believes?

Beginning in the 1950s, psychologists reported strong evidence that stress can lead to ulcers. Studies found that people who live in stressful situations have a higher incidence of ulcers than people who don't. And numerous experiments with laboratory animals have shown that stressors, such as shock or confinement to a very small space

for a few hours, can produce ulcers in some laboratory animals (Andrade & Graeff, 2001; Bhattacharya & Muruganandam, 2003; Gabry et al., 2002; Landeira-Fernandez, 2004).

The relationship between stress and ulcers seemed well established until researchers reported a bacterium (*Helicobacter pylori* or *H. pylori*) that appears to be associated with ulcers. Because many people prefer medical explanations, like bacteria or viruses, to psychological or *psychosomatic* ones, the idea of stress as a cause of ulcers was later largely abandoned by many people.

Is this warranted? Let's take a closer look at the research. First, most ulcer patients do have the *H. pylori* bacterium in their stomachs, and it clearly damages the stomach wall. In addition, antibiotic treatment does help

 Study Tip

Psychosomatic illness is not the same as an imagined, hypochondriacal, illness. Psychosomatic (*psyche* means "mind" and *soma* means "body") refers to symptoms or illnesses that are caused or aggravated by psychological factors, especially stress (Lipowski, 1986). Most researchers and health practitioners believe that almost all illnesses are partly psychosomatic in this sense.

many patients. However, approximately 75 percent of normal control subjects' stomachs also have the bacterium. This suggests that the bacterium may cause the ulcer, but only in people who are compromised by stress. Furthermore, behavior modification and other psychological treatments, used alongside antibiotics, can help ease ulcers. Finally, studies of the hypothalamus and amygdala (parts of the brain involved in emotional response) show that they also play a role in gastric ulcer formation (Aou, 2006; Tanaka et al., 1998).

Apparently, stressful situations cause an increase in stress hormones and hydrochloric acid and a decrease in blood flow in the stomach walls. This combination leaves the stomach more vulnerable to attack by the *H. pylori* bacteria.

In sum, it appears that *H. pylori*, increased hydrochloric acid, stress hormones, and decreased blood flow all lead to the formation of gastric ulcers. Although the verdict is still out on the precise role of stress in the development of ulcers, in all likelihood biological, psychological, and social forces interact with one another (the biopsychosocial model) to create conditions ripe for the growth of H. pylori. In other words, the myth that stress *by itself* causes ulcers is clearly wrong (Lilienfeld et al., 2010). And, for now, the psychosomatic explanation for ulcers is back in business.

Student Engagement Exercise

Given the admittedly limited information in the studies of people who live in stress-

ful situations described above, what is the most likely:

1. Research method (experimental, descriptive, correlational, or biological)?
2. If you chose the:
   - *Experimental method*—label the IV, DV, experimental group, and control group.
   - *Descriptive method*—is this a naturalistic observation, survey, or case study?
   - *Correlational method*—is this a positive, negative, or zero correlation?
   - *Biological method*—identify the specific research tool (e.g., brain dissection, CT scan, etc.)

(Answers appear in Appendix B.)

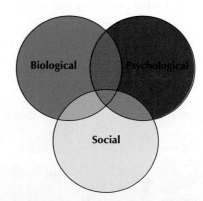

CHECK & REVIEW   STOP   *Before going on, be sure to complete this Check & Review. It is an invaluable study tool!*

Stress and Illness

Part A: Retrieval Practice

1. Without looking at the book, spend 10 minutes writing a free-form essay recalling all you can remember from the previous section.
2. Now, reread the previous section, and once again spend 10 minutes writing a free-form essay on the SAME material.

Part B: Practice Quiz

1. Stress may contribute to heart disease by releasing _____ and _____, which increase the level of fat in the blood.
2. Which of the following is not among the characteristics associated with Type A personality? (a) time urgency; (b) patience; (c) competitiveness; (d) hostility

3. Explain how the three characteristics of the hardy personality help reduce stress.
4. What is the essential feature of PTSD?
5. How has stress contributed to your own illnesses?

Check your answers in Appendix B.

Health Psychology and Stress Management

Objective 3.11: What is health psychology?

Health psychology, the study of how biological, psychological, and social factors affect health and illness, is a growing field in psychology (Figure 3.7). In this section, we will first discuss the work of health psychologists and then explore how we cognitively appraise potential stressors, cope with perceived threats, and make use of eight resources for stress management.

Psychology at Work

Would You Like to Be a Health Psychologist?

Health psychologists study how people's lifestyles and activities, emotional reactions, ways of interpreting events, and personality characteristics influence their physical health and well-being.

As researchers, health psychologists are particularly interested in how changes in behavior can improve health outcomes (Suls, Davidson, & Kaplan, 2010). They also

Health Psychology Studies how biological, psychological, and social factors interact in health and illness

Figure 3.7 Health psychology in action Note how all three factors in the *biopsychosocial model* interact in health and illness.

Figure 3.8 Using health psychology to prevent smoking For adolescents, the long-term health disadvantages of smoking seem irrelevant compared with its short-term social rewards and the addictive, reinforcing properties of the nicotine. Therefore, as shown in this photo, many smoking prevention programs focus on more immediate problems with smoking. Films and discussion groups try to educate teens about peer pressure and the media's influence on smoking, as well as to help them hone their decision-making and coping skills. Unfortunately, the effect of such psychosocial programs is small (Hatsukami, 2008; Villanti et al., 2010). To have even a modest effect, these programs must begin early and continue for many years. To reduce the health risk and help fight peer pressure, many schools ban smoking in college and university buildings. The rising cost of cigarettes—now averaging $10 per pack in most states when taxes are included—may also deter teen smoking. The annual cost for smoking just 10 cigarettes a day is more than $1,800!

emphasize the relationship between stress and the immune system. As we discovered earlier, a normally functioning immune system helps defend against disease. And a suppressed immune system leaves the body susceptible to a number of diseases.

As practitioners, health psychologists can work as independent clinicians or as consultants alongside physicians, physical and occupational therapists, and other health care workers. The goal of health psychologists is to reduce psychological distress or unhealthy behaviors. They also help patients and families make critical decisions and prepare psychologically for surgery or other treatment. Health psychologists have become so involved with health and illness that medical centers are one of their major employers (Considering a Career, 2011).

Health psychologists also educate the public about health *maintenance* (Figure 3.8). They provide information about the effects of stress, smoking, alcohol, lack of exercise, and other health issues. In addition, health psychologists help people cope with conditions such as chronic pain, diabetes, and high blood pressure, as well as unhealthful behaviors such as anger expression and lack of assertiveness. Due to space limitations, only a brief overview of the wide variety of work activities and interests of health psychologists can be provided here. If you are seriously interested in pursuing a career in this field, you may want to check with the counseling or career center on your campus. Also try exploring the career website included at wiley.com/college/huffman.

Cognitive Appraisal and Coping

Objective 3.12: How do we cognitively appraise and cope with stress?

Simply defined, *coping* is an attempt to manage stress in some effective way. It is not one single act but a process that allows us to deal with various stressors. However, it often seems like stress is an environmental thing that just happens to us and that we're helpless to control. But as we've seen before, stress is most often in the "eye of the beholder" (Figure 3.9). According to psychologist Richard Lazarus (1993, 2000), *cognitive appraisal, or how we interpret events,* is perhaps the most important determinant of how we cope with stress.

As you can see in the Step-by-Step Diagram 3.3, in Lazarus's view, we appraise events in two steps: **primary appraisal** (deciding if a situation is harmful, threatening, or challenging) and **secondary appraisal** (assessing our resources and choosing a coping method). Most people then tend to choose either *emotion- or problem-focused methods of coping*.

In **emotion-focused coping**, we attempt to manage our emotional reactions. Suppose you are turned down for a highly desirable job or rejected by a long-term friend or partner. You could deal with your disappointment by rationalizing that you did not get the job because you didn't have the right "connections," or by telling yourself that the friend you lost wasn't really that important after all. Although this approach may make you feel better temporarily, failing to realistically evaluate the situation might block you from valuable knowledge important to future jobs and relationships.

A healthier form of emotion-focused coping is *distraction*, such as reading a book, exercising, or calling a friend. This approach helps us cope with initially overwhelming emotions, and research has shown that bereaved people who directed their attention away from their negative emotions had fewer health problems and were seen as

Primary Appraisal Deciding if a situation is harmful, threatening, or challenging

Secondary Appraisal Assessing one's resources and choosing a coping method

Emotion-Focused Coping Managing one's emotional reactions to a stressful situation

Figure 3.9 Extreme stress or exhilaration? Traveling to India might be extremely stressful for some Americans because of overcrowding and the fact that no one lines up in the railway stations. However, as cross-cultural psychologist Pittu Luangani (2007) says: "One individual's trauma might be another individual's thrill."

Step-by-StepDiagram3.3

STOP This Step by Step diagram contains essential information NOT found elsewhere in the text, which is likely to appear on quizzes and exams. Be sure to study it CAREFULLY!

Cognitive Appraisal and Coping

Research suggests that our emotional response to an event depends largely on how we interpret the event.

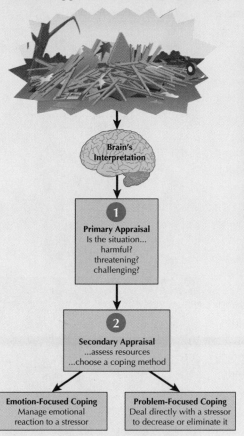

Brain's Interpretation

1

Primary Appraisal
Is the situation...
harmful?
threatening?
challenging?

2

Secondary Appraisal
...assess resources
...choose a coping method

| **Emotion-Focused Coping** Manage emotional reaction to a stressor | **Problem-Focused Coping** Deal directly with a stressor to decrease or eliminate it |

People often combine *emotion-focused* and *problem-focused* coping strategies to resolve complex stressors or to respond to a stressful situation that is in flux. In some situations, an emotion-focused strategy can allow people to step back from an especially overwhelming problem. Then they can reappraise the situation and use the problem-solving approach to look for solutions. Can you see how each form of coping is represented in these two photos?

better adjusted by their friends than bereaved individuals who did not use this approach (Coifman et al., 2007; Keefe, Shelby, & Somers, 2010). (Keep in mind, it's also normal and okay to give in to your emotions for a period of time—to cry, feel sad, and grieve your loss.)

As you can see, emotion-focused coping may reduce or postpone our stress and help us "make it through the night." Many times, however, it is necessary and more effective to use **problem-solving coping**, which deals directly with the stressor to decrease or eliminate it (Bond & Bunce, 2000; Jopp & Schmitt, 2010; Lever, 2008). As you'll discover in Chapter 8, good problem solving includes identifying the stressful problem, generating possible solutions, selecting the appropriate solution, and applying the solution to the problem.

Problem-Solving Coping Dealing directly with a stressor to decrease or eliminate it

Resources for Healthy Living: From Good Health to Money

Objective 3.13: What are the best resources for stress management?

As noted at the beginning of this chapter, stress is a normal, and necessary, part of our life. Therefore, stress *management* is the goal—not stress elimination. Although our initial, bodily responses to stress are largely controlled by nonconscious, autonomic processes, our higher brain functions can help us avoid the serious damage of chronic overarousal. The key is to consciously recognize when we are overstressed and then to choose resources that activate our parasympathetic, relaxation response. Researchers have identified at least eight important resources for healthy living and stress management, see Concept Organizer 3.2 (Archer, 2011; Chou, Chiao, & Fu, 2011; Krypel & Henderson-King, 2010; Marks et al., 2011; McLoyd, 2011; Veselka et al., 2010).

ConceptOrganizer3.2

Resources for Healthy Living

STOP *This Concept Organizer contains essential information NOT found elsewhere in the text, which is likely to appear on quizzes and exams. Be sure to study it CAREFULLY!*

Health and exercise	Exercising and keeping fit helps minimize anxiety, depression, and tension, which are associated with stress. Exercise also helps relieve muscle tension; improves cardiovascular efficiency; and increases strength, flexibility, and stamina. 
Positive beliefs	A positive self-image and attitude can be especially significant coping resources. Even temporarily raising self-esteem reduces the amount of anxiety caused by stressful events. Also, hope can sustain a person in the face of severe odds, as is often documented in news reports of people who have triumphed over seemingly unbeatable circumstances. 
Social skills	People who acquire social skills (such as knowing appropriate behaviors for certain situations, having conversation starters up their sleeves, and expressing themselves well) suffer less anxiety than people who do not. In fact, people who lack social skills are more at risk for developing illness than those who have them. Social skills not only help us interact with others but also communicate our needs and desires, enlist help when we need it, and decrease hostility in tense situations.
Social support	Having the support of others helps offset the stressful effects of divorce, the loss of a loved one, chronic illness, pregnancy, physical abuse, job loss, and work overload. When we are faced with stressful circumstances, our friends and family often help us take care of our health, listen, hold our hands, make us feel important, and provide stability to offset the changes in our lives. 
Control	Believing that you are the "master of your own destiny" is an important resource for effective coping. People with an **external locus of control** feel powerless to change their circumstances and are less likely to make healthy changes, follow treatment programs, or positively cope with a situation. Conversely, people with an **internal locus of control** believe that they are in charge of their own destinies and are therefore able to adopt more positive coping strategies. 

External Locus of Control Believing that chance or outside forces beyond one's control determine one's fate
Internal Locus of Control Believing that one controls one's own fate

ConceptOrganizer3.2
(continued)

Material resources	Money increases the number of options available for eliminating sources of stress or reducing the effects of stress. When faced with the minor hassles of everyday living, or when faced with chronic stressors or major catastrophes, people with money and the skills to effectively use it generally fare better and experience less stress than people without money. 
Sense of humor	Research shows that humor is one of the best ways to reduce stress. The ability to laugh at oneself, and at life's inevitable ups and downs, allows us to relax and gain a broader perspective. In short: "Don't sweat the small stuff." 
Relaxation	There are a variety of relaxation techniques. Biofeedback is often used in the treatment of chronic pain, but it is also useful in teaching people to relax and manage their stress. **Progressive relaxation** helps reduce or relieve the muscular tension commonly associated with stress. Using this technique, patients first tense and then relax specific muscles, such as those in the neck, shoulders, and arms. This technique teaches people to recognize the difference between tense and relaxed muscles. 

 **TRY THIS YOURSELF**

Progressive Relaxation

You can use progressive relaxation techniques anytime and anywhere you feel stressed, such as before or during an exam. Here's how:

1. Sit in a comfortable position, with your head supported.

2. Start breathing slowly and deeply.

3. Let your entire body relax. Release all tension. Try to visualize your body getting progressively more relaxed with each breath.

4. Systematically tense and release each part of your body, beginning with your toes. Curl them tightly while counting to 10. Now, release them. Note the difference between the tense and relaxed state. Next, tense your feet to the count of 10. Then relax them and feel the difference. Continue upward with your calves, thighs, buttocks, abdomen, back muscles, shoulders, upper arms, forearms, hands and fingers, neck, jaw, facial muscles, and forehead.

Try practicing progressive relaxation twice a day for about 15 minutes. You will be surprised at how quickly you can learn to relax—even in the most stressful situations.

TEST YOURSELF

Applying Key Terms

By Thomas Frangicetto (Northampton Community College, Bethlehem, PA)

According to cognitive therapist Albert Ellis, "If people look at what they are telling themselves, look at their thinking, at their irrational beliefs and self-defeating attitudes . . . they can then experience *healthy stressful reactions*" (Palmer & Ellis, 1995). In addition to other useful coping resources described in this chapter, this exercise will help you

- Understand the link between how we cognitively interpret a stressor and the amount and type of stress we actually experience.
- Review important text content your professor may include on exams.

Fill in the letter from the list of key terms and concepts that best applies to each of the 8 stressful situations.

Text Key Terms and Concepts

a. Approach–Avoidance Conflict

b. Avoidance–Avoidance Conflict

c. Burnout

d. Chronic Stress

e. External Locus of Control

f. Frustration

g. Posttraumatic Stress Disorder

h. Type A Personality

Stressful Situation

____1. Wendy is *forced to choose* between the *undesirable alternative* of studying boring subjects AND the *undesirable alternative* of poor grades.

____2. John is a soldier who has returned home after serving three tours of duty in Iraq. He's now working at a stressful job, is deep in debt, and his wife is threatening divorce.

____3. Marci was fortunate to escape the terrorist attack on September 11, 2001. But ever since that *life-threatening day*, her functioning has been impaired by *flashbacks, nightmares*, and an overwhelming sense of *anxiety, helplessness, and emotional numbing*.

____4. Rodney is a high-powered executive whose *intense ambition* and *competitiveness* seem to have paid off. However, his wife complains about his *exaggerated sense of time urgency* and his *persistent cynicism and hostility*.

____5. Juanita is trapped in a traffic jam on her way to an important exam. She feels *tension and anxiety* building because she is being *blocked from achieving her goal*.

____6. Jennifer's job is *emotionally demanding* and she feels *physically, emotionally*, and *mentally exhausted*.

____7. Selena believes that all of the bad things that happen to her are the result of *bad luck or fate*, and she feels *powerless to change* her situation.

____8. James is a high-achieving college student, but he recently met a wonderful person and his grades are falling. He feels *forced to choose* between dating and high grades.

Check your answers in Appendix B.

Psychology Engages

Psychology at Work

Coping with TechnoStress

Are you hassled and stressed by the ever-changing technology at your workplace? Do the expensive machines your employers install to "aid productivity" create stress-related problems instead? Are you on the verge of burning all "operating" manuals, and are you secretly planning to "shave Michael Dell and Bill Gates with a broken beer bottle"? (Hurt, 2008).

Clinical psychologists Michelle Weil and Larry Rosen (1997) warn that our entire society is being profoundly affected and stressed by our modern "cyberculture." In their book, *TechnoStress: Coping with technology @work @home @play*, Weil and Rosen explore the problems and solutions with the new technology, and they begin by identifying three Techno-Types—*eager adopter, hesitant*, and *resister*. Which one are you?

1. Your boss just bought everyone in your department a new, advanced cell phone, and directs that all future communication be done through text messages, instant messages, and e-mail. You've never owned an e-mail-enabled cell phone before. How would you feel opening the package?

   a. Thrilled, excited, and eager—can't wait to give it a try.

   b. Hesitant and wondering if you really need it. Your current system works just fine. Maybe you'll just put it away for now.

   c. Upset, worried, or nervous. Unsure of your ability to use it correctly.

2. You are looking for a new job, and a potential employer invites you to interview via a web-based teleconference. You know nothing about this technology. What would you do?

   a. Immediately go on the Internet and learn everything you can about web-based teleconferencing and then eagerly set up a practice conference session with an expert in the field.

   b. Call your best friend who's participated in this type of interview and grill him or her for information to see if it is worth your time.

   c. Decide this isn't the job you wanted after all and decline the invitation.

3. When you want to record a television show that airs while you are at work, what do you do?

   a. Quickly, confidently, and easily program the VCR or DVR to record the show.

   b. Ask your roommate, teenage child, or spouse to set the VCR or DVR, or find the manual and try to figure out how to do it. You know it's possible but are unsure that you'll be able to make it work.

   c. Squelch the thought, unless there is someone you know who will do it for you.

4. Your coworker calls and tells you that she just bought a new state-of-the-art, souped-up multimedia computer system and wants you to come and see it. How do you respond?

   a. Drop all your plans for the weekend, run right over, and play with the new toy for eight hours.

   b. Murmur words of congratulations and promise to get over to see it as soon as your schedule clears.

   c. Pretend to listen, adding appropriately placed "oh's" and "uh huh's" while clearly evading the request. (Not your idea of fun!)

   - If you answered (a) to three or four of the questions, chances are that you are an *Eager Adopter*.

   - If you mostly answered (b) you, like most people, are most probably a *Hesitant* "Prove It."

   - If you felt that (c) was most often the answer for you, you are a *Resister*.

In general, *Eager Adopters* love technology. Although they make up only 10 to 15 percent of the population, eager adopters consider technology fun and are the first to upgrade their equipment. The *Hesitant* "Prove Its" account for half to two-thirds of the population. They take a wait-and-see attitude, but once they are convinced that a new technology will make their lives easier, they try to adopt it. Finally, the *Resisters* avoid—or even fear—new technology. They feel insecure around new technology and actively oppose any new purchases or upgrades.

If you are an *Eager Adopter*, you are probably not stressed by technology. But what do you do if you are one of the other types? How do you control TechnoStress? First, evaluate each new technology on its usefulness for you and your lifestyle. It isn't a black or white, "technophobe" or "technophile" choice. If something works for you, invest the energy to adopt it. Second, establish clear boundaries. Technology came into the world with an implied promise of a better and more productive life. But, for many, the servant has become the master. We've all watched harried executives frantically checking their e-mail while on vacation and families eating dinners at restaurants with their preschoolers playing video games, teenagers text messaging, and parents loudly talking on separate cell phones. We can (and must) control technology and its impact on our lives. Finally, relax and slow down. "Rethink how you react to the new wizardry," says Larry Rosen. "Just because technology works at lightning speed does not mean you should."

CRITICAL THINKING

Perils of Procrastination (Attention Procrastinators—Don't Skip this Section!)

Co-Authored with Thomas Frangicetto (Northampton Community College, Bethlehem, PA)

"Procrastination is a very hard thing for me not to do. Almost all my life, when it came to school work that needed to be done, I always put it off until the last possible minute, and I know it affected my grades."

Gina Smereczynsky,
College Student

Estimates are that 90 percent of college students procrastinate and 25 percent of these students are chronic procrastinators, many of whom end up dropping out of college (Knaus, 2010). Studies also find that procrastination negatively affects not only your academic potential, but also your career success, relationship happiness, mental and physical health, and overall well-being (Burka & Yuen, 2008; Marano, 2003; Sirois, 2003).

In one classic study, Diane Tice and Roy Baumeister (1997) assigned a term paper in their health psychology class at the beginning of the semester. Throughout the semester, they carefully monitored the stress, health, and procrastination levels of 44 student volunteers from the class. After the term papers were submitted at the end of the course, researchers found that procrastinators were more likely to turn in their papers late and earn lower grades on those papers. They also suffered significantly higher levels of stress and developed more health problems than nonprocrastinators.

We all occasionally put things off, and some forms of procrastination are actually helpful, such as "intentional delay," which is necessary for careful preparation (Novotney,

2010). The problem comes with chronic, destructive procrastination, which is irrational, self-defeating, and self-sabotaging (Pychyl, 2010; Steel, 2010).

Why is destructive procrastination so common? Some research suggests it reflects a lack of self-regulatory ability, which involves low persistence in seeing something through to completion, as well as being easily distracted (Pychyl, 2010). Other possible personality factors include self-doubt, performance worries, fear of failure, indecisiveness, negative thinking, anger turned into passive-aggressiveness, and perfectionism (Frost, 2008; Pychyl, 2010).

Psychologists also believe procrastination is *a learned* behavior (Marano, 2010). Have you ever sat down at your computer determined to begin a research paper that you've been putting off for months and suddenly had an overwhelming urge to check your Facebook page? Your e-mail? Text messages? All it takes is one click of the mouse and the tension or boredom are gone . . . CLICK!

→Can you see how procrastination offers an immediate payoff and reward, while the punishment of lower grades and increased stress is delayed?

How can you combat destructive procrastination?

Part I

Start by employing solid critical thinking. By resisting *overgeneralization* (see Prologue at front of book), you can recognize destructive procrastination versus times when

delaying action is the prudent thing to do and not counterproductive (Knaus, 2010).

Next, recognize the potential danger of a self-fulfilling prophecy. When you call yourself a "procrastinator," as many students do, "you risk linking your worth to the label . . . you've fallen into an identity trap and overgeneralization is the trigger" (Knaus, 2010).

Part II

Carefully read the material and complete the self-test provided on this website: www.mindtools.com/pages/article/newHTE_96.htm

Do you agree with these results? Why or why not? Identify one specific example of personal procrastination that you would like to improve (e.g., school work, returning phone calls, disagreeable tasks assigned by your boss, etc.).

Now list TWO specific things you plan to do to help you overcome your tendency to procrastinate.

Want more help with procrastination? Check out the following:

http://http-server.carleton.ca/~tpychyl/

www.psychologytoday.com/blog/dont-delay

www.apa.org/gradpsych/2010/01/rationalizations.aspx

In sum, the message from research and our personal experience is clear: *Procrastination may be hazardous to your health—and to your grades!*

GENDER AND CULTURAL DIVERSITY

"Karoshi"—Can Job Stress Be Fatal?

Objective 3.14: Discuss how karoshi is related to stress.

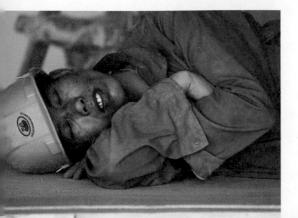

Have you ever dragged yourself home from work so tired you feared you couldn't make it to your bed? Do you think your job may be killing you? You may be right! Some research suggests that job stress and overwork can greatly increase your risk of dying from heart disease and stroke (Landsbergis et al., 2011; Nakao, 2010). And the Japanese even have a specific word for it, "karoshi" [KAH-roe-she], which is translated literally as "death from overwork."

Starting in the late 1970s, Japanese health officials began to notice serious, and potentially lethal, effects of working 10 or 12 hours a day six and seven days a week, year after year) (Kanai, 2009; Kondo & Oh, 2010; Nakashima et al., 2011). Some research suggests that more than 10,000 workers die from work-related cardiovascular diseases in Japan each year, but few victims of karoshi are compensated under the Japanese workers' compensation system (Hsiu-Hui, 2007). Intense job stressors reportedly not only increase the risk for karoshi, but they also leave some workers disoriented and suffering from serious stress even when they're not working. Sadly, working and living conditions in Japan are much worse today, after the catastrophic earthquake, tsunami, and nuclear accidents in 2011.

Interestingly, the average number of work hours per week in the United States is among the highest in the developed world (Brown, 2011). Unfortunately, in our global economy, pressures to reduce costs and to increase productivity will undoubtedly continue, and job stress may prove to be a serious and growing health risk.

 **CHECK & REVIEW**  STOP *Before going on, be sure to complete this Check & Review. It is an invaluable study tool!*

Health Psychology, Stress Management, Psychology Engages

Part A: Retrieval Practice

1. Without looking at the book, spend 10 minutes writing a free-form essay recalling all you can remember from the previous section.

2. Now, reread the previous section, and once again spend 10 minutes writing a free-form essay on the SAME material.

Part B: Practice Quiz

1. Describe a personal stressor and how you used both primary and secondary appraisal.

2. Imagine that you forgot your best friend's birthday. Now, identify the form of coping you would be using in each of the following reactions.

   (a) "I can't be expected to remember everyone's birthday"; (b) "I'd better put Cindy's birthday on my calendar so this won't happen again."

3. People with a(n) _____ locus of control are better able to cope with stress.

4. What are the eight major resources for healthy living and stress management? Which resource is most helpful for you? Least helpful?

Check your answers in Appendix B.

→ Key Terms

To assess your understanding of the **Key Terms** in Chapter 3, write a definition for each (in your own words), and then compare your definitions with those in the text.

Understanding Stress
stress (p. 94)
stressor (p. 94)
eustress (p. 94)
distress (p. 94)
chronic stressors (p. 96)
job stressors (p. 96)
role conflict (p. 96)
burnout (p. 96)
hassles (p. 96)
frustration (p. 97)
conflict (p. 97)
approach–approach conflict (p. 98)
approach–avoidance conflict (p. 98)

avoidance–avoidance conflict (p. 98)
cataclysmic event (p. 99)
general adaptation syndrome (GAS) (p. 100)
SAM system (p. 100)
HPA axis (p. 100)
homeostasis (p. 103)
psychoneuroimmunology [sye-koh-NEW-roh-IM-you-NOLL-oh-gee] (p. 103)

Stress and Illness
Type A personality (p. 107)
Type B personality (p. 107)

hardiness (p. 108)
posttraumatic stress disorder (PTSD) (p. 109)

Health Psychology and Stress Management
health psychology (p. 111)
primary appraisal (p. 112)
secondary appraisal (p. 112)
emotion-focused coping (p. 112)
problem-solving coping (p. 113)
external locus of control (p. 114)
internal locus of control (p. 114)

www.wileyplus.com

WileyPLUS presents an on-line version of this textbook along with a wealth of study resources including quizzes, practice tests, flash cards, videos, animations and other activities designed to improve your mastery of the content. Working in conjunction with these study tools, the *Psychology in Action* WileyPLUS course features Professor Karen Huffman, author of this textbook, explaining and expanding upon some of the most challenging concepts in psychology. Here is a sample of the tutorial videos available for this chapter:

- Interactive animation depicting how stress affects our body and everyday functioning
- Sources of stress, featuring Professor Huffman's classroom demonstration to identify students' personal stressors
- Coping with stress, continuing Professor Huffman's classroom demonstration to identify resources for coping
- Positive psychology helps us thrive rather than just survive, featuring tools for self assessment
- Virtual Field Trip to a biofeedback center, where clients learn techniques to manage physical and psychological challenges

TRY THIS YOURSELF

Reacting to and Dealing With Stress

In this video lab exercise, provided to WileyPlus subscribers, your involvement with stress will be "virtual," allowing you just enough psychological space to observe your reactions and coping mechanisms at the same time that you are experiencing stress.

While doing all this, you'll compare your reactions and coping mechanisms to those of other people and categorize them using the terms laid out in the chapter. Along the way, you'll learn a lot about your personal ways of feeling and coping with stress, and the merits or drawbacks of your approach.

As you are working on this on-line exercise, consider the following:

- What kind of stressors do people confront and what are the components of stress?
- Why do certain situations feel more stressful than others, and why do some people feel more stressed than others by a given situation?
- What's going on in the brain and body as we confront stressors?
- What are the various ways in which people try to manage, reduce, or tolerate stress? Do those approaches work?

Chapter Summary

Understanding Stress

Objective 3.1: Define stress, stressor, eustress, and distress.
Stress is the body's arousal, both physical and mental, to situations or events that we perceive as threatening or challenging, whereas a **stressor** is the trigger for a stressful reaction. **Eustress** is pleasurable, desirable stress, whereas **distress** is unpleasant, threatening stress.

Objective 3.2: Describe the seven major sources of stress.
The seven major sources of stress are life changes, chronic stressors, job stressors, hassles, frustration, conflict, and cataclysmic events. *Life changes* require adjustment in our behaviors which cause stress. **Chronic stressors** produce a state of ongoing physiological arousal, in which our parasympathetic system cannot activate the relaxation response. Work related

job stressors include **role conflict** and **burnout**. **Hassles** are little everyday life problems that pile up to cause major stress. **Frustration** refers to blocked goals, whereas **conflict** involves two or more competing goals. Conflicts can be classified as **approach-approach, avoidance-avoidance**, or **approach-avoidance. Cataclysmic events** are disasters that occur suddenly and generally affect many people simultaneously.

Objective 3.3: What is the generalized adaptation syndrome (GAS)?
Hans Selye described a generalized physiological reaction to severe stressors, which he called the **general adaptation syndrome (GAS)**. It has three phases: the *alarm reaction*, the *resistance phase*, and the *exhaustion phase*.

Objective 3.4: Describe the SAM system and the HPA axis.
When stressed, our bodies undergo significant biological changes due primarily to the SAM system and the HPA axis. The **SAM system** (short for *Sympatho-Adreno-Medullary*) provides an initial, rapid-acting stress response from an interaction between the sympathetic nervous system and the adrenal medulla.

The **HPA axis** (short for the *Hypothalamic-Pituitary-Adrenocortical (HPA) system*) allows for a delayed stress response, involving the hypothalamus, pituitary, and adrenal cortex. One of the main stress hormones released by the HPA axis, cortisol, helps combat inflammation and mobilize energy resources. It also sends feedback messages to the brain and pituitary to regain **homeostasis**.

Objective 3.5: How does stress affect our immune system?
Prolonged stress suppresses the immune system, which increases the risk for many diseases (e.g., colds, colitis, cancer). The new field of **psychoneuroimmunology** studies the effects of stress and other factors on the immune system.

Objective 3.6: How does stress affect cognitive functioning?
During acute stress, cortisol can prevent the retrieval of existing memories, as well as the laying down of new memories and general information processing. Under prolonged stress, cortisol can permanently damage the hippocampus, a key part of the brain involved in memory.

Objective 3.7: Identify four factors important to job satisfaction.
Supportive colleagues, supportive working conditions, mentally challenging work, and *equitable rewards* are all very important to our job satisfaction.

Stress and Illness

Objective 3.8: Is stress related to cancer?
Cancer appears to result from an interaction of heredity, environmental insults (such as smoking), and immune system deficiency. Although stress is linked to a decreased immunity, research does *not* show that it *causes* cancer, or that a positive attitude will stave it off.

Objective 3.9: Describe the links between stress and heart disease.
The leading cause of death in the United States is heart disease. Risk factors include smoking, stress, obesity, a high-fat diet, lack of exercise, and **Type A personality** (if it includes *cynical hostility*). The two main approaches to modifying Type A behavior are the *shotgun approach* and the *target behavior approach*. People with psychological **hardiness** are less vulnerable to stress because of three distinctive personality characteristics—*commitment, control,* and *challenge*.

Objective 3.10: How is stress connected to PTSD and ulcers?
Exposure to extraordinary stress (like war or rape) may lead to **posttraumatic stress disorder (PTSD)**. Contrary to the myth that stress by itself causes ulcers, as well as current opinion that gastric ulcers are caused only by the *H. pylori* bacterium, psychological research shows that biopsychosocial factors interact to increase vulnerability to the bacterium.

Health Psychology and Stress Management

Objective 3.11: What is health psychology?
Health psychology, the study of how biological, psychological, and social factors affect health and illness, is a growing field in psychology.

Objective 3.12: How do we cognitively appraise and cope with stress?
When facing a stressor, we first evaluate it in two steps: **primary appraisal** (deciding if a situation is harmful, threatening, or challenging) and **secondary appraisal** (assessing our resources and choosing a coping method). We then tend to choose either **emotion-focused coping** (managing emotional reactions to a stressor) or **problem-solving coping** (dealing directly with the stressor to decrease or eliminate it).

Objective 3.13: What are the best resources for stress management?
Researchers have indentified at least eight important resources: health and exercise, positive beliefs, social skills, social support, control, material resources, sense of humor, and relaxation.

Psychology Engages

Objective 3.14: Discuss how karoshi is related to stress.
Job stress and overwork can greatly increase your risk of dying from heart disease and stroke, and the Japanese have a specific word, "Karoshi," which means "death from overwork."

Understanding Stress

Sources of Stress

Effects of Stress
General adaptation syndrome (GAS) SAM system and HPA Axis Cognitive functioning Immune system

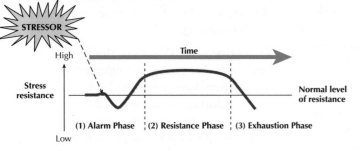

Sources of Stress

Cataclysmic events — Life changes

Conflict — Chronic stressors

Frustration

Hassles — Job stressors

❶ Alarm Reaction
When surprised or threatened, your body enters an alarm phase during which your resistance to stress is temporarily suppressed, while your arousal is high (e.g., increased heart rate and blood pressure) and blood is diverted to your skeletal muscles to prepare for "fight-or-flight" (Chapter 2).

❷ Stage of Resistance
If the stress continues, your body rebounds to a phase of increased resistance. Physiological arousal remains higher than normal, and there is an outpouring of stress hormones. During this resistance stage, people use a variety of coping methods. For example, if your job is threatened, you may work longer hours and give up your vacation days

STRESSOR

High

Time

Stress resistance

Normal level of resistance

(1) Alarm Phase (2) Resistance Phase (3) Exhaustion Phase

Low

❸ Stage of Exhaustion
Your body's resistance to stress can only last so long before exhaustion sets in. During this final stage, you become more susceptible to serious illnesses, and possibly irreversible damage to your body. Selye maintained that one outcome of this stage for some people is the development of *diseases of adaption*, including asthma, ulcers, and high blood pressure. Unless a way of relieving stress is found, the eventual result may be complete collapse and death.

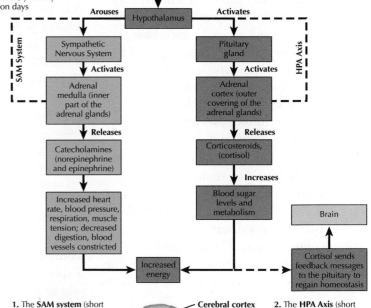

STRESSOR

Brain

Arouses — **Hypothalamus** — Activates

SAM System | HPA Axis

Sympathetic Nervous System — **Activates** — Pituitary gland — **Activates**

Adrenal medulla (inner part of the adrenal glands) — **Releases** — Adrenal cortex (outer covering of the adrenal glands) — **Releases**

Catecholamines (norepinephrine and epinephrine) — Corticosteroids, (cortisol)

Increases

Increased heart rate, blood pressure, respiration, muscle tension; decreased digestion, blood vessels constricted — Blood sugar levels and metabolism — Brain

Increased energy — Cortisol sends feedback messages to the pituitary to regain homeostasis

1. The **SAM system** (short for Sympatho-Adreno-Medullary) provides an initial, rapid-acting stress response thanks to cooperation between the sympathetic nervous system and the adrenal medulla.

Cerebral cortex interprets stressor

Hypothalamus

Pituitary gland

2. The **HPA Axis** (short for Hypothalamic-Pituitary Adreocortical system) responds more slowly but lasts longer. It also helps restore the body to its baseline state, *homeostasis*.

Adrenal glands

Cortex
Medulla

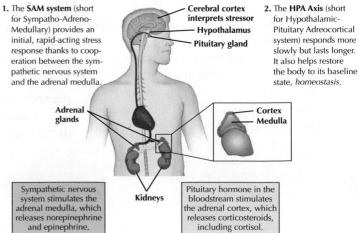

Sympathetic nervous system stimulates the adrenal medulla, which releases norepinephrine and epinephrine.

Kidneys

Pituitary hormone in the bloodstream stimulates the adrenal cortex, which releases corticosteroids, including cortisol.

Stress and Illness

Cancer
Caused by hereditary dispositions and environmental factors that lead to changes in body chemistry and the immune system.

Cardiovascular Disorders
Contributing factors:
- Behaviors such as smoking, obesity, lack of exercise
- Stress hormones
- **Type A personality**
- Lack of hardiness

Posttraumatic Stress Disorder (PTSD) and Ulcers
Exposure to extraordinary stress may lead to PTSD, and chronic stress may increase vulnerability to the *H. pylori* bacterium, which causes gastric ulcers.

Health Psychology and Stress Management

Cognitive Appraisal and Coping

Brain's Interpretation

1

Primary Appraisal
Is the situation...
harmful?
threatening?
challenging?

2

Secondary Appraisal
...assess resources
...choose a coping method

Emotion-Focused Coping	**Problem-Focused Coping**
Manage emotional reaction to a stressor	Deal directly with a stressor to decrease or eliminate it

Resources for Healthy Living

Health and exercise

Positive beliefs

Control

Material resources

Social skills

Social support

Relaxation

Sense of humor

Psychology Engages

Psychology at Work
Critical Thinking
Gender & Cultural Diversity

ChapterFour

Sensation and Perception

The senses collect the surface facts of matter
It was sensation, when memory came
It was knowledge, when mind acted on it
As knowledge it was thought

RALPH WALDO EMERSON

All our knowledge has its origins in our perceptions.

LEONARDO DA VINCI

Imagine that your visual field is suddenly inverted and reversed. Things you normally expect to be on your right are now on your left. Things you expect to be above your head are now below your head. How would you ride a bike, read a book, or even walk through your home? Do you think you could ever adapt to this upside-down world?

To answer that question, psychologist George Stratton (1896) invented, and for eight days wore, special goggles that flipped up to down and right to left. For the first few days, Stratton had a great deal of difficulty navigating in this environment and coping with everyday tasks. But by the third day, he noted:

> *Walking through the narrow spaces between pieces of furniture required much less care than hitherto. I could watch my hands as they wrote, without hesitating or becoming embarrassed thereby.*

By the fifth day, Stratton had almost completely adjusted to his strange perceptual environment, and when he later removed the headgear, he quickly readapted.

What does this experiment have to do with everyday life? At this very moment, our bodies are being bombarded with stimuli from the outside world—light, sound, heat, pressure, texture, and so on—while our brains are floating in complete silence and utter darkness. Stratton's experiment shows us that sensing the world is not enough. Our brains must receive, convert, and constantly adapt the information from our sense organs into useful mental representations of the world. How we get the outside world inside to our brains, and what our brains do with this information, are the key topics of this chapter.

MYTH BUSTERS

True or False?

1. Subliminal advertising is very effective.

2. Humans have one blind spot in each eye.

3. Most color-blind people can only see the world in black and white.

4. Loud music can lead to permanent hearing loss.

5. There are discrete spots on our tongues for specific tastes.

6. Humans have only five senses.

7. Illusions are not the same as hallucinations.

8. People tend to see what they expect to see.

9. There is strong scientific evidence for ESP.

10. We generally remember our "hits" and forget our "misses."

(*Answers:* 1. False, 2. True, 3. False, 4. True, 5. False, 6. False, 7. True, 8. True, 9. False, 10. True. Detailed answers appear in this chapter.)

Sensation Process of detecting, converting, and transmitting raw sensory information from the external and internal environments to the brain

Perception Process of selecting, organizing, and interpreting sensory information into meaningful patterns

Bottom-Up Processing Information processing beginning "at the bottom," with raw sensory data that are sent "up" to the brain for higher-level analysis; data-driven processing that moves from the parts to the whole

Top-Down Processing Information processing starting "at the top," with higher-level cognitive processes (such as, expectations and knowledge), and then working down; conceptually driven processing that moves from the whole to the parts

Understanding Sensation

Objective 4.1: Define sensation and perception.

Psychologists are keenly interested in our senses—*sensation* is the mind's window to the outside world. We're equally interested in *perception*—how the brain gives meaning to sensory information. **Sensation** begins with specialized receptor cells located in our sense organs (eyes, ears, nose, tongue, skin, and internal body tissues) (Figure 4.1). When sense organs detect an appropriate stimulus (light, mechanical pressure, chemical molecules), they convert it into neural impulses (action potentials) that are transmitted to our brain. The brain then selects, organizes, and interprets the coded neural messages into meaningful patterns—a process called **perception**.

Processing: Getting the Outside Inside

Objective 4.2: Compare bottom-up processing with top-down processing.

Ordinarily, sensation and perception blend into one continuous process, but to understand them we need to break them into two sections. In this chapter, we start with sensation, the sensory receptors (eyes, ears, and other senses), and then work up to perception. Psychologists sometimes refer to the flow of information from the sensory receptors to the brain as **bottom-up processing** (Mulckhuyse et al., 2008; Prouix, 2007). Imagine yourself as an engineer who has received an urgent package filled with wires, gauges, and an assortment of metal pieces. There are no directions or pictures in the package, and you're asked to assemble everything into a functional object. This assignment would require *bottom-up processing*.

Perception and **top-down processing** begin at the "top" with higher-level cognitive processes, such as knowledge, experience, and expectations, and then works down

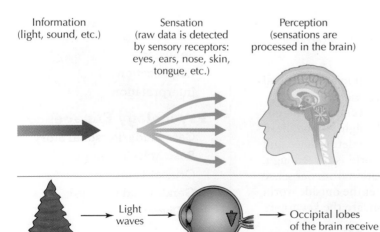

Information (light, sound, etc.)

Sensation (raw data is detected by sensory receptors: eyes, ears, nose, skin, tongue, etc.)

Perception (sensations are processed in the brain)

Light waves → Occipital lobes of the brain receive sensory information from the eye and process it as a "tree."

Figure 4.1 Sensation and perception *Sensation* involves the detection, conversion, and transmission of raw data provided by our sensory receptors. But to make sense of these sensations, we also need our brains to select, organize, and interpret the sensory information—a process called *perception*.

 **TRY THIS YOURSELF**

Sensation or Perception?

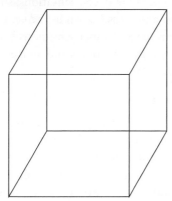

(a) When you stare at this drawing, which area is the top, front, and back of the cube? Does it "flip" after you stare at it for a few seconds?

(b) Do you see a young woman looking back over her shoulder, or an older woman with her chin buried in the fur of her jacket?

While initially looking at these two drawings, you are engaged in the process of *sensation*. Your visual sensory system receives an assortment of light waves, and then this sensory data is converted and transmitted to your brain. In contrast, during *perception* your brain *interprets* the sensory information into lines and patterns.

Interestingly, if you stare at either the cube (a) or the woman (b) long enough, your perception/interpretation will inevitably change. Although basic sensory input stays the same, your brain's attempt to interpret ambiguous stimuli creates a type of perceptual "dance," shifting from one interpretation to another (Gaetz, Rzempoluck, & Jantzen, 1998).

---

to the sensory level (Freeman & Ambady, 2011; Latinus, VanRullen, & Taylor, 2010; Schuett et al., 2008; Zhaoping & Guyader, 2007). If you, the engineer, were given the same package, along with a picture and diagram, and then asked to assemble a specific object, you would be using top-down, or *conceptually driven* processing.

In short, bottom-up processing is a type of *data-driven* processing that moves from the parts to the whole, whereas top-down processing is *conceptually* driven and moves from the whole to the parts. Both bottom-up and top-down processing are important components of sensation and perception, as well as other parts of everyday life (Figure 4.2).

Converting Raw Sensory Data

Objective 4.3: Explain how raw sensory data are turned into signals the brain can understand.

How do we turn light and sound waves from the environment into something our brain can comprehend? To do this, we first must have a means of detecting stimuli and of converting them into a language the brain can understand.

Let's start with *sensory detection*. Our eyes, ears, skin, and other sense organs all contain special cells called *receptors*, which detect and process sensory information from the environment. For each sense, these specialized cells respond to a distinct stimulus, such as light or sound waves or chemical molecules (see Figure 4.3).

Figure 4.2 Bottom-up or top-down processing? When learning to read, you initially used bottom-up processing. You first learned that certain arrangements of lines and squiggles represented specific letters. Later on, you recognized that these letters combine in memorable chunks to make up words.

Now, yuor aiblity to raed uisng top-dwon prcessoing mkaes it psosible to unedrstnad thsi sntenece desipte its mnay mssipl-lengis.

Figure 4.3 Sample sensory receptor cells Each sensory system contains specialized cells that are activated by particular physical stimuli.

Smell   Taste   Touch   Hearing   (rods) (cones) Vision

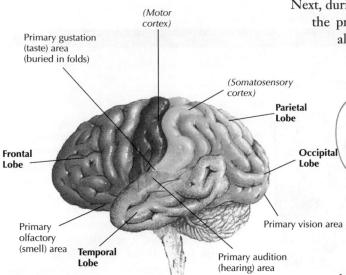

(Motor cortex)

Primary gustation (taste) area (buried in folds)

(Somatosensory cortex)

Parietal Lobe

Frontal Lobe

Occipital Lobe

Primary olfactory (smell) area

Temporal Lobe

Primary vision area

Primary audition (hearing) area

Figure 4.4 Sensory processing within the brain Shown here are the primary locations in the cerebral cortex for vision, hearing, taste, smell, and somatosensation (which includes touch, pain, and temperature sensitivity). Regardless of where they come from (eyes, ears, nose, skin, and other sense organs), neural messages from the various sense organs must travel to the brain in order for us to actually "see," "hear," and so on. Interestingly, if we could somehow rewire these connections, sending messages from the eyes to the auditory brain areas and vice versa, we would hear light and see sound!

Psychophysics Studies the link between the physical characteristics of stimuli and the sensory experience of them

Reducing sensations By adding a sleeping mask and special noise eliminating headphones, this traveler obtains welcome relief from unwanted sensations. The headphones work by creating opposing sound waves that cancel sounds from the environment.

Next, during the process of *transduction*, the receptors convert energy from the previously detected stimuli into neural impulses, which are sent along to the brain. In hearing, for example, tiny receptor cells in the inner ear convert mechanical vibrations (from sound waves) into electrochemical signals. These messages are then carried by neurons to the brain for higher-level interpretation and analysis.

How does our brain differentiate between sensations, such as sights and sounds? Thanks to a process known as *coding*, different physical stimuli are interpreted as distinct sensations because their neural impulses travel by different routes and arrive at different parts of the brain (Figure 4.4).

Reducing Sensory Input

Interestingly, during *transduction* and *coding*, there are processes that purposely reduce the amount of stimuli we receive. Why would we want to reduce sensory information? Can you imagine what would happen if you did not have some natural filtering of stimuli? You would constantly hear blood rushing through your veins and continually feel your clothes brushing against your skin. Some level of filtering is needed so that the brain is not overwhelmed with unnecessary information.

In the process of *sensory reduction*, we not only filter incoming sensations, we also analyze the sensations sent through before a neural impulse is finally sent to the cortex of the brain. For example, sudden loud noises will generally awaken sleeping animals (both human and nonhuman). This is because cells in the *reticular formation* (Chapter 2) send messages via the thalamus to alert the cortex. However, these reticular formation cells can learn to screen out certain messages, while allowing others to go on to higher brain centers. This explains why parents of a newborn can sleep through passing sirens and blaring stereos, yet still awaken to the slightest whimper of their baby.

Measuring the Senses: Psychophysics and Thresholds

Objective 4.4: Define psychophysics, and differentiate between absolute and difference thresholds.

All species have evolved selective receptors that suppress or amplify information to allow survival. For example, hawks have an acute sense of vision but a poor sense of smell. Similarly, we humans possess several remarkable sensory abilities. But we cannot sense many stimuli, such as ultraviolet light, microwaves, the ultrasonic sound of a dog whistle, or infrared heat patterns from warm-blooded animals (which rattlesnakes can).

How do we know this? How can scientists measure the exact amount of stimulus energy it takes to trigger a conscious experience? The answers come from the field of **psychophysics,** which studies and measures the link between the physical characteristics of stimuli and the sensory experience of them (see Concept Organizer 4.1).

Psychology at Work

Do Subliminal Messages Improve Sales?

Objective 4.5: What are the effects of subliminal stimuli?

Now that we've discussed the concept of *absolute thresholds* in Concept Organizer 4.1, we can tackle an interesting and ongoing controversy. Are we affected by sensations at levels below our absolute threshold, even when we're not aware

ConceptOrganizer4.1

Measuring the Senses

To measure our senses, a series of signals that vary in intensity are presented, and people are asked to report those signals they can detect. Imagine yourself as a patient undergoing a hearing test:

- When testing for hearing loss, a hearing specialist commonly uses a tone generator to produce sounds of differing pitches and intensities.

- You listen with earphones and indicate the earliest point at which you hear a tone. This is your **absolute threshold**, or the smallest amount of a stimulus that an observer can reliably detect.

- To test your **difference threshold**, or *just noticeable difference* (JND), the examiner gradually changes the volume and asks you to respond when you notice a change.

- The examiner then compares your thresholds with those of people with normal hearing to determine whether you have a hearing loss and, if so, the extent of the loss.

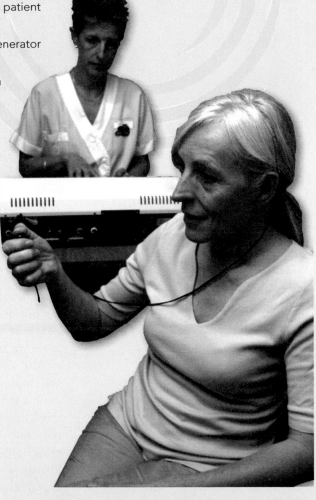

ABSOLUTE THRESHOLDS FOR VARIOUS SENSES

Sense	Stimulus	Receptors	Absolute Threshold
Vision	Light waves	Light-sensitive rods and cones in eye's retina	A candle flame seen from 30 miles away on a clear, dark night
Audition (hearing)	Sound waves	Pressure-sensitive hair cells in ear's cochlea	The tick of a watch at 20 feet
Olfaction (smell)	Molecules dissolved on nose's mucous membranes	Neurons in the nose's olfactory epithelium	One drop of perfume spread throughout a six-room apartment
Gustation (taste)	Molecules dissolved on tongue	Taste buds on tongue's surface	One teaspoon of sugar in two gallons of water
Body Senses	Variety of stimuli	Variety of receptors	A bee's wing falling on your check from a height of about half an inch

Psychophysics at work—amazing animal senses A dog's *absolute* and *difference thresholds* for smell are far more sensitive than those of a human. For this reason, specially trained dogs provide invaluable help in sniffing out dangerous plants, drugs, and explosives, tracking criminals, and assisting in search-and-rescue operations. Some researchers believe dogs can even detect chemical signs of certain illnesses, such as diabetes or cancer (Akers & Denbow, 2008). ▶

Absolute Threshold Minimum amount of a stimulus that an observer can reliably detect

Difference Threshold Minimal difference needed to notice a stimulus change; also called the "just noticeable difference" (JND)

Subliminal Pertaining to stimuli presented below conscious awareness

of them? Years ago many people believed movie theaters were manipulating consumers by subliminally presenting messages like "Eat popcorn" and "Drink Coca-Cola." Similarly, record companies were supposedly embedding **subliminal** messages in rock music that encouraged violence and sex. The words on the movie screen and the messages in the music were allegedly presented so quickly that they were below the threshold for awareness. Most people were both fascinated and outraged. Politicians rushed to pass laws against the "invisible sell" and the "moral corruption" of our youth. Were they right to be concerned? Is there even such a thing as subliminal messages?

Two major questions surround *subliminal perception*. First, is it possible to perceive something without conscious awareness? The answer is clearly yes. Scientific research on subliminal (literally, "below the threshold") stimuli demonstrates that information processing does occur even when we are not aware of it (Aarts, 2007; Bermeitinger et al., 2009; Boccato et al., 2008; Cleeremans & Sarrazin, 2007; Martens, Ansorge, & Kiefer, 2011).

Experimental studies commonly use an instrument called a *tachistoscope* to flash images too quickly for conscious recognition, but slowly enough to be registered. For example, in one study the experimenter flashed one of two pictures subliminally (either a happy or an angry face) followed by a neutral face. They found this subliminal presentation evoked matching unconscious facial expressions in the participant's own facial muscles (Dimberg, Thunberg, & Elmehed, 2000). As you will discover in Chapter 12, the fact that participants were unaware of the subliminal stimuli, as well as their own matching facial response, also raises questions regarding our own emotional states (Yang & Tong, 2010). Do we unconsciously become a little happier when we're exposed to good-natured, pleasant people? And upset when we are around those who are angry?

Although this research shows that subliminal perception *does* occur, the second—and more important—question is, "Does it lead to *subliminal persuasion?*" The answer to this question is less clear. Subliminal stimuli are basically *weak* stimuli. At most, they have a modest effect on consumer behavior, and absolutely *no effect* on the minds of youth listening to rock music or citizens' voting behavior (Bermeitinger et al., 2009; Dijksterhuis, Aarts, & Smith, 2005; Fennis & Stroebe, 2010; Karremans, Stroebe, & Claus, 2006). If you're wondering about buying subliminal tapes promising to help you lose weight or relieve stress, save your money. Blank "placebo" tapes appear to be just as "effective" as subliminal tapes.

In sum, evidence exists that subliminal perception occurs, but the effect on subliminal persuasion is uncertain. When it comes to commercials and self-help tapes, advertisers are better off using above-threshold messages—the loudest, clearest, and most attention-getting stimuli possible. And for weight loss, the money and time are better spent on the old-fashioned methods of exercise and diet.

Sensory Adaptation: Weakening the Response

Objective 4.6: Define sensory adaptation and explain why it is helpful.

Imagine that friends have invited you to come visit their beautiful new baby. As they greet you at the door, you are overwhelmed by the odor of a wet diaper. Why don't they do something about the smell? The answer lies in the previously mentioned *sensory reduction* and **sensory adaptation**. When a constant stimulus is presented for a length of time, sensation often fades or disappears. In *sensory adaptation*, receptors within our sensory system get "tired" and actually fire less frequently.

Sensory adaptation makes sense from an evolutionary perspective. To survive, we can't afford to waste attention and time on unchanging, normally unimportant stimuli. "Turning down the volume" on repetitive information helps the brain cope with an overwhelming amount of sensory stimuli and allows time to pay attention to change. Sometimes, however, adaptation can be dangerous, as when people stop paying attention to a gas leak in the kitchen.

Some senses like smell and touch adapt quickly. Interestingly, we never completely adapt to visual stimuli because our eyes are constantly moving. They quiver just enough to guarantee constantly changing sensory information. Otherwise, if we stared long enough at an object, it would vanish from sight! We also don't adapt to extremely intense stimuli, such as the heat of the desert sun or the pain of a cut hand. Again, from an evolutionary perspective, these limitations on sensory adaptation aid survival. They remind us to avoid intense heat and to do something about the damaged tissue on that cut hand.

If we don't adapt to pain, how do athletes keep playing despite painful injuries? In certain situations the body releases natural painkillers called *endorphins* (see Chapter 2). Endorphins are neurotransmitters that act in the same way as morphine. They relieve pain by inhibiting pain perception. Pleasant stimuli, like the "runner's high," as well as unpleasant stimuli, such as injuries, can cause a release of endorphins. Pain relief through endorphins may also be the secret behind *acupuncture*, the ancient Chinese technique of gently twisting thin needles placed in the skin (Agrò et al., 2005; Cabyóglu, Ergene, & Tan, 2006).

Objective 4.7: Explain the gate-control theory of pain perception.

In addition to endorphin release, another explanation for pain relief is provided by the **gate-control theory**, first proposed by Ronald Melzack and Patrick Wall (1965). According to this theory, the experience of pain depends partly on whether the neural message gets past a "gate-keeper" in the spinal cord. Normally, the gate is kept shut by impulses coming down from the brain, or by messages coming from large-diameter nerve fibers that conduct most sensory signals, such as touch and pressure. However, when body tissue is damaged, impulses from smaller pain fibers open the gate.

According to the gate-control theory, massaging an injury or scratching an itch can temporarily relieve discomfort because pressure on large-diameter neurons interferes with pain signals. Messages from the brain can also control the pain gate, explaining how athletes and soldiers can carry on despite excruciating pain. When we are soothed by endorphins or distracted by competition or fear, our experience of pain can be greatly diminished.

Sensory Adaptation Sensory system's reduced responsiveness to unchanging stimuli

Gate-Control Theory Theory that pain sensations are processed and altered by mechanisms within the spinal cord

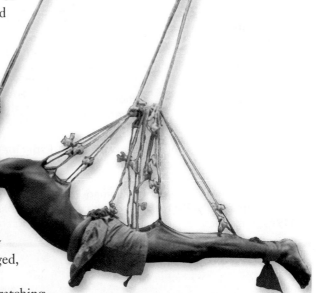

How does he do it? The fact that this man willingly endures such normally excruciating pain illustrates the complex mixture of psychological and biological factors in the experience of pain.

Ironically, when we get anxious or dwell on our pain, we can intensify it (Roth et al., 2007; Sullivan, 2008; Sullivan, Tripp, & Santor, 1998). Therefore, well-meaning friends who ask chronic pain sufferers about their pain may unintentionally reinforce and increase it (Jolliffe & Nicholas, 2004).

Research also suggests that the pain gate may be chemically opened by a neurotransmitter called *substance P*, while endorphins close it (Bianchi et al., 2008; Cesaro & Ollat, 1997; Papathanassoglou et al., 2010). Other research finds that the brain not only responds to incoming signals from sensory nerves but also is capable of *generating* pain (and other sensations) entirely on its own (Melzack, 1999; Snijders et al., 2010; Vertosick, 2000). Have you heard of *tinnitus*, the ringing-in-the-ears sensation that sometimes accompanies hearing loss? In the absence of normal sensory input, nerve cells send conflicting messages ("static") to the brain, and in this case the brain interprets the static as "ringing." A similar process happens with the strange phenomenon of *phantom pain*, in which people continue to feel pain (and itching or tickling) long after a limb is amputated. The brain interprets the static as pain because it arises in the area of the spinal cord responsible for pain signaling. Interestingly, when amputees are fitted with prosthetic limbs and begin using them, phantom pain often disappears (Crawford, 2008; Gracely, Farrell, & Grant, 2002).

Each of the sensory principles we've discussed thus far—transduction, reduction, coding, thresholds, and adaptation—applies to all the senses. Yet the way in which each sense is processed is uniquely different, as we will see in the remainder of the chapter.

CHECK & REVIEW

STOP *Before going on, be sure to complete this Check & Review. It is an invaluable study tool!*

Understanding Sensation

Part A: Retrieval Practice

1. Without looking at the book, spend 10 minutes writing a free-form essay recalling all you can remember from the previous section.

2. Now, reread the previous section, and once again spend 10 minutes writing a free-form essay on the SAME material.

   (Although time consuming, this exercise has been shown to be the single best way to improve your test scores! For more nformation, check out www.sciencemag.org/content/early/2011/01/19/science.1199327.abstract)

Part B: Practice Quiz

1. The key functions of sensation and perception are, respectively, _____.

2. If a researcher were testing to determine the dimmest light a person could perceive, the researcher would be measuring the _____.

3. Experiments on subliminal perception have _____. (a) supported the existence of the phenomenon, but it has little or no effect on persuasion; (b) shown that subliminal perception occurs only among children and some adolescents; (c) shown that subliminal messages affect only people who are highly suggestible; (d) failed to support the phenomenon

4. Why can't you smell your own perfume or aftershave after a few minutes?

5. The _____ theory of pain helps explain why it sometimes helps to rub or massage an injured thumb. (a) sensory adaptation; (b) gate-control; (c) just noticeable difference; (d) Lamaze

Check your answers in Appendix B.

How We See and Hear

Pictures, propagated by motion along the fibers of the optic nerves in the brain, are the cause of vision.

ISAAC NEWTON

Many people mistakenly believe that what they see and hear is a copy of the outside world. They are not. Vision and hearing are the result of what our brains create in response to light and sound waves. Three physical properties of light and sound (*wavelength*, *complexity*, and *amplitude*) help determine our sensory experience of them (Figure 4.5).

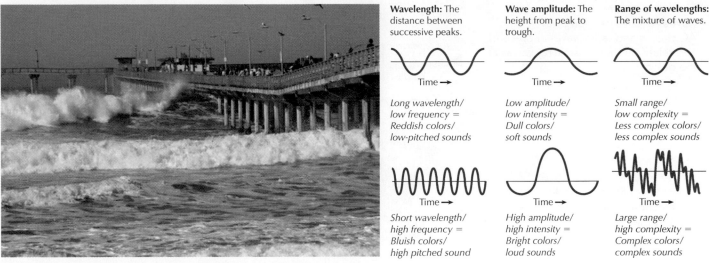

Wavelength: The distance between successive peaks.

*Long wavelength/
low frequency =
Reddish colors/
low-pitched sounds*

*Short wavelength/
high frequency =
Bluish colors/
high pitched sound*

Wave amplitude: The height from peak to trough.

*Low amplitude/
low intensity =
Dull colors/
soft sounds*

*High amplitude/
high intensity =
Bright colors/
loud sounds*

Range of wavelengths: The mixture of waves.

*Small range/
low complexity =
Less complex colors/
less complex sounds*

*Large range/
high complexity =
Complex colors/
complex sounds*

Figure 4.5 The physical properties of light and sound waves Both vision and hearing are based on wave phenomena, similar to ocean waves. Standing on a pier you see that waves have a certain distance between them (the *wavelength*), and that they pass by you at intervals. If you counted the number of passing waves in a set amount of time (e.g., 5 waves in 60 seconds), you could calculate the *frequency* (the number of complete wavelengths that pass a point in a given time). Larger wavelength means smaller frequency, and vice versa. Waves also have the characteristic of height (technically called *amplitude*)—some large (an exciting surf ride), and others small. Finally, some waves have a very simple, uniform shape, which would be good for surfing. Others are a combination of waves of different wavelengths and heights, resulting in a wave too irregular for surfing.

Vision: The Eyes Have It

Did you know major league batters can hit a 90-mile-per-hour fastball four-tenths of a second after it leaves the pitcher's hand? How can the human eye receive and process information that quickly? To fully appreciate the marvels of sight, we first need to examine the properties of light waves. We will then examine the structure and function of the eye and, finally, the way in which visual input is processed.

Waves of Light

Objective 4.8: What is light?

Let's consider how the wave characteristics we discussed with regard to ocean waves (Figure 4.3) apply to light waves. The *wavelength* determines the hue (color) we see. (We could also say the *frequency* determines the color, since they are inversely related. But by convention, we use wavelength when talking about light waves.) The *amplitude* (height) of the light waves determines the intensity or brightness of the light we see. And the complexity or mix of light waves determines whether we see a pure color or one that is a mix of different colors.

Vision is based on light waves, which have the same characteristics as ocean waves, although they are very much smaller and faster moving. Technically, light is waves of electromagnetic energy in a certain range of wavelengths. As you can see in Figure 4.6, there are many different types of electromagnetic waves. Together they form what is known as the *electromagnetic spectrum*. Keep in mind that most wavelengths are invisible to the human eye. Only a small part of the spectrum, known as the *visible spectrum*, can be detected by our eye's visual receptors.

Eye Anatomy and Function

Objective 4.9: Identify the key structures and functions of the eye.

Several structures in the eye are involved in capturing and focusing light and converting it into neural signals to be sent along to the brain. As you study the

(a) The full spectrum of electromagnetic waves contains very long wavelength AC circuits and radio waves at one end, and relatively short cosmic ray waves at the other.

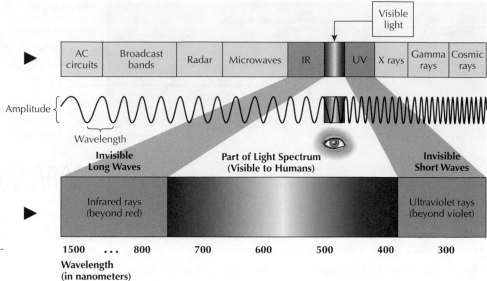

(b) Only the light waves, in the middle of the electromagnetic spectrum can be seen by the human eye. Note how the longer visible wavelengths are the light waves that we see as red, and the shortest are those we perceive as blue. In between are the rest of the colors.

Figure 4.6 The electromagnetic spectrum

Accommodation Automatic adjustment of the eye, which occurs when muscles change the shape of the lens so that it focuses light on the retina from objects at different distances

Retina Light-sensitive inner surface of the back of the eye, which contains the receptor cells for vision (rods and cones)

Rods Visual receptor cells in the retina that detect shades of gray and are responsible for peripheral vision; most important in dim light and at night

Cones Visual receptor cells, concentrated near the center of the retina, responsible for color vision and fine detail; most sensitive in brightly lit conditions

Fovea Tiny pit in the center of the retina filled with cones; responsible for sharp vision

Blind Spot Point at which the optic nerve leaves the eye; contains no receptor cells for vision—thus creating a "blind spot"

Step-by-Step Diagram 4.1, carefully note how light waves travel from the outside world and first enter the eye at the *cornea*, which protects the eye and bends the incoming light waves to provide focus. Directly behind the cornea is the *iris*, which provides the color (usually brown or blue) of the eye. Muscles in the iris allow the *pupil* (or opening) to dilate or constrict in response to light intensity or even to inner emotions. (Recall from Chapter 2 that our pupils dilate when we're in sympathetic arousal and constrict when we're in parasympathetic dominance.) Behind the iris and pupil is the *lens*, which focuses the incoming light rays onto receptor cells in the back surface of the eyeball. The lens does this by changing its shape through a process known as **accommodation**.

After light waves enter the eye through the cornea and pass through the pupil and lens, they ultimately end up on the **retina**, an area at the back of the eye that contains special light-sensitive cells called **rods** and **cones**, so named for their distinctive shapes. Rods cannot distinguish between wavelengths of light so they only detect white, black, and gray, but they do enable us to see in dim light and at night. Because rods are concentrated at the outer edges of the retina, they're also responsible for peripheral vision. In contrast to the rods, cones function in daylight or well-lit conditions and allow us to see color. Cones are concentrated near the center of the retina around an area called the **fovea**, a tiny pit responsible for our sharpest vision because it's filled entirely with cones. Ironically, near the fovea lies an area that has no visual receptors at all and absolutely no vision. This aptly named **blind spot** is where blood vessels and the optic nerve enter and exit the eyeball. Normally, we are unaware of this blind spot because our eyes are always moving. We fill in the information missing from the blind spot with information from adjacent areas on the retina or with images from the other eye.

There are two final steps in the visual process. After the rods and cones receive the light energy, they convert it into neural signals, which travel along the optic nerve to the brain. When the visual cortex receives and interprets these neural messages, we see!

Problems with Vision
Objective 4.10: Identify common problems with vision.

Thoroughly understanding how the eye normally sees also gives us clues for understanding common visual problems, such as *nearsightedness* (*myopia*) and *farsightedness*

Step-by-Step Diagram 4.1

How the Eye Sees

3 Behind the iris and pupil, the muscularly controlled lens focuses incoming light into an image on the light sensitive *retina*, located on the back surface of the fluid-filled eyeball. Note how the lens reverses the image from the right to left and top to bottom when it is projected on to the retina. The brain later reverses the visual input into the final "right-side up" image that we perceive.

4 In the **retina**, light waves are detected and transduced into neural signals by vision receptor cells (rods and cones). **Rods** are visual receptors that detect white, black, and gray and are responsible for peripheral vision. They are most important in dim light and at night. **Cones** are visual receptors adapted for color, daytime, and detailed vision. They are sensitive to many wavelengths, but each is maximally sensitive to red, green, or blue. Note that the **fovea**, a tiny pit filled with cones, is responsible for our sharpest vision.

5 Rods and cones project backwards to interneurons which communicate with ganglion cells in the retina. Ganglion cells then send visual input from the retina to the brain via the optic nerve.

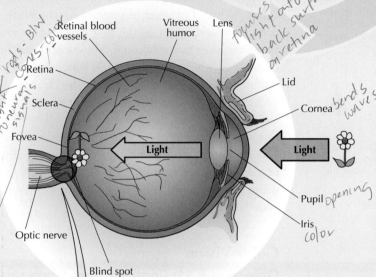

Handwritten notes: focuses light onto back surface on retina; convert light to neurons — rods - B/w signals, cones - color; Cornea bends waves; Pupil opening; Iris color; sent to optic nerve, to brain's visual cortex

2 The light then passes through the *pupil*, a small adjustable opening. Muscles in the *iris* allow the *pupil* to dilate or constrict in response to light intensity or emotional factors.

1 Light first enters through the *cornea*, which helps focus incoming light rays.

Labels: Retinal blood vessels, Vitreous humor, Lens, Retina, Lid, Sclera, Cornea, Fovea, Light, Light, Optic nerve, Pupil, Iris, Blind spot

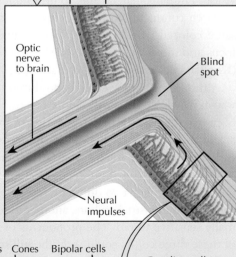

Labels: Receptor cells, Optic nerve to brain, Blind spot, Neural impulses

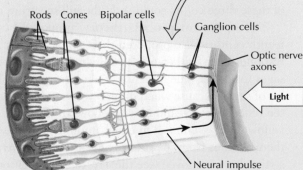

Labels: Rods, Cones, Bipolar cells, Ganglion cells, Optic nerve axons, Light, Neural impulse

Do you have a blind spot?
At the back of the retina lies an area that has no visual receptors at all and absolutely no vision. This **blind spot** is where blood vessels and nerves enter and exit the eyeball. To find yours, hold this book about one foot in front of you, close your right eye, and stare at the X with your left eye. Very slowly, move the book closely to you. You should see the worm disappear and the apple become whole.

135

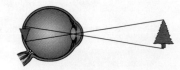

Normal vision The image is focused on the retina.

Nearsightedness (myopia) The eyeball is too long and incoming light waves focus in *front* of the retina, which blurs the images for distant objects.

Farsightedness (hyperopia) The eyeball is too short and incoming light waves focus *behind* the retina, blurring the image for nearby objects.

Figure 4.7 Common visual problems

Trichromatic Theory Theory stating that color perception results from three types of cones in the retina, each most sensitive to either red, green or blue. Other colors result from a mixture of these three

Opponent-Process Theory Hering's theory that color perception is based on three systems of color opposites—blue–yellow, red–green, and black–white

Figure 4.8 Primary colors
Trichromatic theory found that the three primary colors (red, green, and blue) can be combined to form all colors. For example, a combination of green and red creates yellow.

(*hyperopia*), which can occur at any age (Figure 4.7). Around middle age, most people also begin having trouble reading and focusing on nearby objects because the lens becomes less flexible (*presbyopia*). The good news is that these three common visual problems are generally corrected with glasses, contact lens, and, in some cases, with surgery (LASIK), which reshapes the cornea.

In addition to *myopia*, *hyperopia*, and *presbyopia*, which have to do with the shape of the eyeball or the elasticity of the *lens*, we also commonly experience visual peculiarities related to the eye's *rods* and *cones*. If you are walking outside on a sunny day and then enter a dark house, you will at first be momentarily blinded. A few minutes later, you'll see well enough to make your way around, but it takes 20 to 30 minutes to fully adjust. Why? The *cones* in your eyes, which are responsible for color, daytime, and detailed vision, adapt in the first couple of minutes after you enter the dark house. However, they never become fully functioning because the light intensity is too low. In contrast, the *rods* in your eyes, which are responsible for peripheral and nighttime vision, take longer to adapt, but they're far more sensitive to faint light than the cones.

This process of gradual adjustment is called *dark adaptation*, which involves physical and chemical changes in our eyes that allow us to see well in the dark. The fact that this adaptation is relatively slow-acting is important to keep in mind—especially when you are stepping out of a brightly lit building at night or driving a car from a brightly lit garage into a dark street. However, *light adaptation*, the adjustment that takes place when you go from darkness to a bright setting, happens relatively quickly—thanks to your faster-adapting cones.

Color Vision

Objective 4.11: Contrast the trichromatic, opponent-process, and dual process theories of color vision.

Now that we understand how the eye functions we can describe the mysteries of color vision. Humans may be able to discriminate among seven million different hues, and research conducted in many cultures suggests that we all seem to see essentially the same colored world (Davies, 1998). Furthermore, studies of infants old enough to focus and move their eyes show that they are able to see color nearly as well as adults (Knoblauch, Vital-Durand, & Barbur, 2000; Werner & Wooten, 1979).

Although we know color is produced by different wavelengths of light, the actual way in which we perceive color is a matter of scientific debate. Traditionally, there have been two theories of color vision, the *trichromatic* (three-color) theory and the *opponent-process* theory. The **trichromatic theory** was first proposed by Thomas Young in the early nineteenth century. It was later refined by Hermann von Helmholtz and others. Apparently, we have three types of color receptors (cone cells in the retina) that are particularly sensitive to different, but overlapping, ranges of wavelengths. One system is maximally sensitive to blue, another maximally sensitive to green, and another maximally sensitive to red. The proponents of this theory demonstrated that mixing lights of these three colors could yield the full spectrum of colors we perceive (Figure 4.8).

The **opponent-process theory**, proposed by Ewald Hering later in the nineteenth century, also proposed three color systems. But he suggested that each system responds in an "either-or" fashion. In other words, our visual system can produce messages for either blue or yellow, red or green, and black-or-white. This theory makes a lot of sense because when different-colored lights are combined, people are unable to see reddish greens and bluish yellows. In fact, when red and green lights or blue and yellow lights are mixed in equal amounts, we see white. Further support for Hering's theory comes from the studies of *negative color afterimages*, sensations that remain after a stimulus is removed (see the Try This Yourself on p. 137).

TRY THIS YOURSELF

Testing the Power of Negative Afterimages

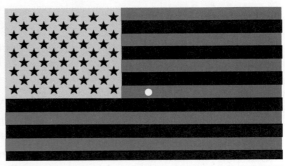

Try staring at the dot in the middle of this color-distorted United States flag for 60 seconds. Then stare at a plain sheet of white paper. You should get interesting color aftereffects—red in place of green, blue in place of yellow, and white in place of black. You perceive a "genuine" red, white, and blue U.S. flag. (If you have trouble seeing it, blink, and try again.)

What happened? This is a good example of the *opponent-process theory*. As you stared at the green, black, and yellow colors, the neural systems that process those colors became fatigued. Then when you looked at the plain white paper, which reflects all wavelengths, a reverse *opponent process* occurred. Each fatigued receptor responded with its opposing red, white, and blue colors!

Two Correct Theories

Judging from the discussion so far, it would seem the opponent-process theory is the correct one. Actually, however, both theories are correct (Valberg, 2006). In 1964, George Wald demonstrated that there are indeed three different types of cones in the retina, each with its own type of photopigment. One type of pigment is sensitive to blue light, one is sensitive to green light, and the third is sensitive to red light.

At nearly the same time that Wald was doing his research on cones, R. L. DeValois (1965) was studying electrophysiological recording of cells in the optic nerve and optic pathways to the brain. DeValois discovered cells that respond to color in an opponent fashion in the thalamus. Thus, it appears that both theories have been correct all along. According to the modern *dual-process theory*, color is processed in a *trichromatic* fashion at the level of the retina (in the cones) and in an *opponent* fashion at the level of the optic nerve and the thalamus (in the brain).

Color-Deficient Vision

Complete color blindness is rare. Most "color blind" people can see some colors but not others. People with normal color vision perceive three different colors—red, green, and blue—and are called *trichromats*. However, a small percentage of the population (mostly men) has a genetic deficiency in either the red–green system, the blue–yellow system, or both. Those who perceive only two colors are called *dichromats*. People who are sensitive to only the black–white system are called *monochromats*, and they are totally color blind. If you'd like to test yourself for red–green color blindness, see the following Try This Yourself.

TRY THIS YOURSELF

Color-Deficient Vision

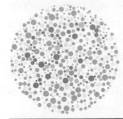

The left circle tests for blue–yellow color blindness, whereas the one on the right tests for red–green deficiency. Do you have trouble perceiving the numbers within these two designs? Although we commonly use the term *color blindness*, most problems involve color confusion rather than color blindness. Furthermore, most people who have some color blindness are not even aware of it. A complete color blind assessment would involve the use of 15 stimuli like these two.

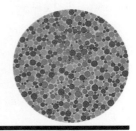

CHECK & REVIEW

STOP *Before going on, be sure to complete this Check & Review. It is an invaluable study tool!*

How we See

Part A: Retrieval Practice

1. Without looking at the book, spend 10 minutes writing a free-form essay recalling all you can remember from the previous section.

2. Now, reread the previous section, and once again spend 10 minutes writing a free-form essay on the SAME material.

Part B: Practice Quiz

1. Identify the parts of the eye, placing the appropriate letter on the figure:

(a) cornea   (d) lens   (g) optic nerve
(b) iris   (e) retina (h) fovea
(c) pupil   (f) sclera (i) blind spot

2. Describe the normal path of light waves through the eye.

3. Explain how the modern dual-process theory explains color vision.

4. Which theory of color vision best explains the negative color afterimage?
   (a) trichromatic theory;
   (b) opponent-process theory;
   (c) both of these theories;
   (d) neither of these theories.

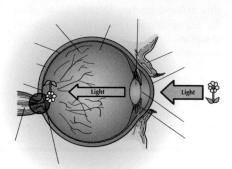

Check your answers in Appendix B.

Hearing: A Sound Sensation

Objective 4.12: Define audition and identify the three key sections of the ear.

Audition Sense or act of hearing

The sense or act of hearing, officially known as **audition**, has a number of important functions, ranging from alerting us to dangers to helping us communicate with others. In this section we talk first about the ear's anatomy and function, then about waves of sound, and, finally, about problems with hearing.

Ear Anatomy and Function

Outer Ear Pinna, auditory canal, and eardrum, which funnel sound waves to the middle ear

Middle Ear Hammer, anvil, and stirrup, which concentrate eardrum vibrations onto the cochlea's oval window

Inner Ear Cochlea, semicircular canals, and vestibular sacs, which generate neural signals sent to the brain

Cochlea [KOK-lee-uh] Three-chambered, snail-shaped structure in the inner ear containing the receptors for hearing

The ear has three major sections that function as shown in the Step-by-Step Diagram 4.2. The **outer ear** (pinna, auditory canal, and eardrum) funnels sound waves to the middle ear. In turn, the three tiny bones of the **middle ear** (hammer, anvil, and stirrup) amplify and send along the eardrum's vibrations to the cochlea's oval window, which is part of the **inner ear** (cochlea, semicircular canals and vestibular sacs). Vibrations from the oval window cause ripples in the fluid-filled **cochlea**, which then cause bending of the hair cells in the cochlea's basilar membrane. The bending hair cells then trigger neural messages that are sent to the brain via the auditory nerve. Finally, when the brain's temporal lobe receives and interprets the neural messages, we hear! Be sure to carefully study the Step-by-Step Diagram 4.2 before going on.

Waves of Sound

Objective 4.13: Briefly explain the physical properties of sound waves.

Have you heard the philosophical question, "If a tree falls in the forest, and there is no one to hear it, does it make a sound?" The answer depends on whether you define *sound* as a sensation (which requires a receptor such as a person's ear) or as a physical stimulus. As a physical phenomenon, sound is based on pressure waves in air or other mediums. These pressure variations can result from an impact, such as a tree hitting the ground, or from a vibrating object, like a guitar string. Sound waves (like light waves) have the characteristics of *wavelength* (or frequency), *amplitude* (intensity or height), and *complexity* (mix).

Step-by-StepDiagram4.2

STOP This Step by Step diagram contains essential information NOT found elsewhere in the text, which is likely to appear on quizzes and exams. Be sure to study it CAREFULLY!

How the Ear Hears

Step 1 Sound waves enter ear canal, which focuses the sound and deflects the tympanic membrane.

Step 2 Vibrations of the tympanic membrane strike the ossicles (hammer, anvil, and stirrup). The stirrup then hits the oval window.

Step 3 Vibrations of the oval window create waves in the fluid-filled cochlea, which deflects the basilar membrane. *hairs*

Step 4 Movement of hair cells on the basilar membrane creates neural messages carried by the auditory nerve to the brain.

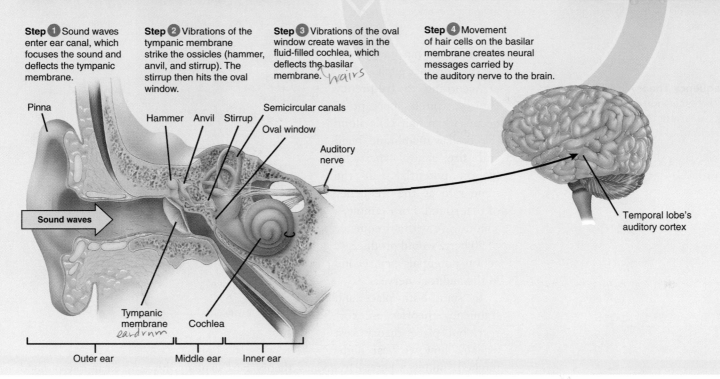

Pinna

Hammer Anvil Stirrup

Semicircular canals

Oval window

Auditory nerve

Sound waves

Tympanic membrane *eardrum*

Cochlea

Temporal lobe's auditory cortex

Outer ear Middle ear Inner ear

When talking about sound waves, we generally use the term *frequency* rather than wavelength. The *frequency* of the sound wave determines the *pitch* of the sound we hear. High-frequency waves produce high notes, and low-frequency waves produce the bass tones. The *amplitude* determines the *loudness* of the sound we hear. And the *complexity* determines what is called *timbre*. A sound could be a pure tone of a single frequency (we seldom hear pure tones, except during a hearing test). Sound can also be a complex mix of frequencies and amplitudes. In this latter case, the timbre is what allows us to distinguish whether a C note is played on a piano or on a trumpet. Timbre is also what allows us to distinguish all the many human voices we hear.

Why are some sounds louder than others? It depends on the intensity of the sound waves. Waves with high peaks and low valleys produce loud sounds. Those that are relatively small produce soft sounds. The relative loudness or softness of sounds is measured on a scale of decibels (Figure 4.9).

Objective 4.14: Describe the place and frequency theories related to hearing.

The mechanisms determining how we distinguish among sounds of different pitches (low to high) differ depending on the frequency of the sound waves (Table 4.1). According to **place theory**, pitch perception corresponds to the particular spot (or place) on the *basilar membrane* that is most stimulated. When we hear a particular sound, it causes the eardrum, the ossicles, and the oval window to vibrate. This vibration produces a "traveling wave" through the fluid in the cochlea. This wave causes some bending of hair cells all along the basilar membrane. But there is a single point where the

Place Theory Explains that pitch perception is linked to the particular spot on the cochlea's basilar membrane that is most stimulated

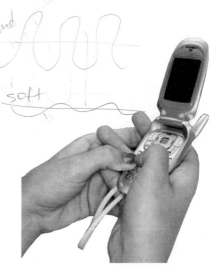

For whom the bell tolls Stealthy teenagers now have a biological advantage over their teachers; a cell phone ringtone that sounds at 17 kilohertz—too high for adult ears to detect. The ringtone is an ironic offshoot of another device using the same sound frequency. That invention, dubbed the Mosquito, was designed to help shopkeepers annoy and discourage loitering teens.

Figure 4.9 How loud is too loud? The loudness of a sound is measured in *decibels*. The higher a sound's decibel reading, the more damaging it is to the ear. Chronic exposure to loud noise, such as loud music or heavy traffic—or brief exposure to really loud sounds, such as a stereo at full blast, a jackhammer, or a jet engine—can cause permanent nerve deafness. Disease and biological changes associated with aging can also cause nerve deafness. ▶

Frequency Theory Explains that pitch perception occurs when nerve impulses sent to the brain match the frequency of the sound wave

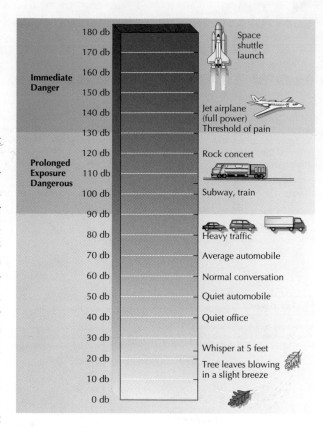

	180 db — Space shuttle launch
	170 db
	160 db
Immediate Danger	150 db
	140 db — Jet airplane (full power) / Threshold of pain
	130 db
	120 db — Rock concert
Prolonged Exposure Dangerous	110 db
	100 db — Subway, train
	90 db
	80 db — Heavy traffic
	70 db — Average automobile
	60 db — Normal conversation
	50 db — Quiet automobile
	40 db — Quiet office
	30 db
	20 db — Whisper at 5 feet / Tree leaves blowing in a slight breeze
	10 db
	0 db

hair cells are maximally bent for each distinct pitch.

According to **frequency theory**, pitch perception occurs when hair cells along the basilar membrane bend and fire neural messages (action potentials) at the same rate as the frequency of that sound. For example, a sound wave with a frequency of 90 hertz would produce 90 action potentials per second in the auditory nerve.

In sum, both place and frequency theories are correct, but place theory best explains how we hear high-pitched sounds, whereas frequency theory best explains how we hear low-pitched sounds.

Problems with Hearing

Objective 4.15: Differentiate between conduction and nerve deafness.

Conduction Deafness Middle-ear deafness resulting from problems with transferring sound waves to the inner ear

Nerve Deafness Inner-ear deafness resulting from damage to the cochlea, hair cells, or auditory nerve

There are two major causes of hearing loss. **Conduction deafness**, or middle-ear deafness, results from problems with the mechanical system that conducts sound waves to the cochlea. **Nerve deafness**, or inner-ear deafness, involves damage to the inner ear or auditory nerve. Disease and biological changes associated with aging can cause nerve deafness. But the most common (and preventable) cause of nerve deafness is continuous exposure to loud noise, which can damage hair cells and lead to permanent hearing loss. Even brief exposure to really loud sounds, like a stereo or headphones at full blast, a jackhammer, or a jet airplane engine, can cause permanent nerve deafness (see again Figure 4.9).

The best way to prevent hearing loss is to avoid exceptionally loud noises (rock concerts, jackhammer, stereo headphones at full blast), and to wear earplugs when such

Table 4.1   HOW THE EAR DISTINGUISHES AMONG SOUNDS OF DIFFERENT PITCHES

Theory	Frequency	Pitch	Example
Place theory Hair cells are stimulated at different locations on basilar membrane.	High frequency	High-pitched sounds	A squeal or a child's voice
Frequency theory Hair cells fire at the same rate as the frequency for the sound.	Low frequency	Low-pitched sounds	A growl or a man's voice

situations cannot be avoided. In addition, we need to pay attention to bodily warnings, including changes in our normal hearing threshold and *tinnitus*, a whistling or ringing sensation in our ears. These are often the first signs of hearing loss. Although normal hearing generally returns after exposure to a loud concert, keep in mind that the risk of permanent damage increases with repeated exposure.

Loud noise and nerve deafness
The rock band The Who held the Guinness World Record in 1976 for the loudest rock concert ever with a documented loudness of 126 dB measured at 32 meters from the speakers. Roger Daltry, and his fellow band member, PeteTownshend, now have significant nerve damage hearing loss caused by their prolonged exposure to this noise level. Incidentally, Guinness World Records no longer includes this category as it does not want to promote activities that cause hearing loss.

Other Important Senses

One of the most common myths about sensation is that we have only five senses, when in fact we have numerous senses—sight, hearing, smell, taste, the so-called skin senses (touch, temperature, pain), balance, bodily posture, and orientation.

Vision and audition may be the most prominent of our senses, but the others—taste, smell, and the body senses—are also important for gathering information about our environment. The enjoyment of a summer's day comes not only from the visual and auditory beauty of the world but also from the taste of a fresh garden tomato, the smell of honeysuckle, and the feel of a warm gentle breeze.

Smell and Taste: Sensing Chemicals

Objective 4.16: Briefly explain the processes of olfaction and gustation.

Smell and taste are sometimes referred to as the *chemical senses* because they involve *chemoreceptors* that are sensitive to certain chemical molecules. Have you noticed how food seems bland when your nose is blocked by a cold and you cannot smell your food? Smell and taste receptors are located near each other and often interact so closely that we have difficulty separating the sensations.

Olfaction

Our sense of smell, or **olfaction**, is remarkably useful and sensitive, but biologically complex (see Step-by-Step Diagram 4.3). We possess about 1,000 different types of

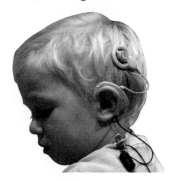

A treatment for nerve damage
Because damage to the nerve or receptor cells is almost always irreversible, the only current treatment for nerve deafness is a small electronic device called a *cochlear implant*. If the auditory nerve is intact, the implant bypasses hair cells and directly stimulates the nerve. At present, a cochlear implant produces only a crude approximation of hearing, but the technology is improving.

Olfaction Sense of smell

CHECK & REVIEW  STOP *Before going on, be sure to complete this Check & Review. It is an invaluable study tool!*

How we Hear

Part A: Retrieval Practice

1. Without looking at the book, spend 10 minutes writing a free-form essay recalling all you can remember from the previous section.

2. Now, reread the previous section, and once again spend 10 minutes writing a free-form essay on the SAME material.

Part B: Practice Quiz

1. Identify the parts of the ear, placing the appropriate letter on the figure at right.

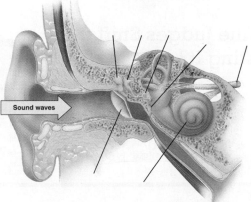

Sound waves

(a) auditory nerve   (d) hammer
(b) tympanic   (e) stirrup
    membrane   (f) oval window
(c) anvil   (g) cochlea

2. Describe the path of sound waves through the ear.

3. Explain how place theory differs from frequency theory.

4. Repeated exposure to loud noise may cause _____ deafness.

Check your answers in Appendix B.

Step-by-StepDiagram4.3

STOP *This Step by Step diagram contains essential information NOT found elsewhere in the text, which is likely to appear on quizzes and exams. Be sure to study it CAREFULLY!*

How the Nose Smells

Sense stimulation

Olfactory bulb

2 The stimulation of the odor molecules then initiates a neural impulse that travels to the *olfactory bulb,* where most olfactory information is processed before being sent to other parts of the brain.

3 Each odorous chemical appears to excite a specific portion of the olfactory bulb and is coded according to the stimulated area (Dalton, 2002).

Olfactory tract

Olfactory bulb

Bone

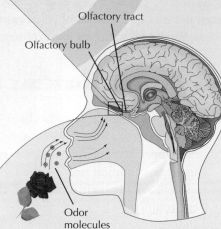

Olfactory epithelium

1 Odor molecules stimulate the dendrites of receptors embedded in the *olfactory epithelium,* a mucus-coated membrane in the nasal cavity.

Odor molecules

4 From the olfactory bulb, messages then travel to other areas of the brain, including the *temporal lobe* and *limbic system.* The temporal lobe is responsible for our conscious recognition of smells; the limbic system is involved in emotion and memory, which explains why smells often elicit emotion-laden memories.

Olfactory receptor cell

olfactory receptors, and we can detect over 10,000 distinct smells (floral, musky, rotten, and so on). The nose is more sensitive to smoke than any electronic detector, and—through practice—blind people can quickly recognize others by their unique odors.

Does smell affect sexual attraction? Some research on **pheromones**—compounds found in natural body scents that may affect various behaviors—supports the idea that these chemical odors increase sexual behaviors in humans (Marazziti et al., 2010; Savic, Berglund, & Lindström, 2007; Thornhill et al., 2003). Other findings question the results, suggesting that human sexuality is far more complex than that of other animals—and more so than perfume advertisements would have us believe.

Pheromones [FARE-oh-mones]
Airborne chemicals that affect behavior, including recognition of family members, aggression, territorial marking, and sexual mating

TRY THIS YOURSELF

Why Do Professional Wine Judges Sniff the Wine Instead of Just Tasting It?

Answer: Sniffing draws more smell molecules into the nose and helps speed their circulation. Professional wine judges also know that the mouth is important because smells reach the nasal cavity by wafting up the throat like smoke in a chimney. Furthermore, most of what we perceive as taste or flavor is a combination of both smell and taste, which explains why this wine-tasting judge will use both his nose and his mouth.

MYTH BUSTERS

Scientists once believed there were specific areas of the tongue dedicated to detecting bitter, sweet, salty, and other tastes. However, we now know that taste receptors, like smell receptors, respond differently to the varying shapes of food and liquid molecules. The major taste receptors (or taste buds) are clustered on our tongues within little bumps called papillae (Figure 4.10). A small number of taste receptors are also found in the palate and the back of our mouths. Thus, even people without a tongue experience some taste sensations.

Figure 4.10 Taste sensation When we eat and drink, liquids and dissolved foods flow over bumps on our tongue called *papillae* (the lavender circular areas) and into their pores to the taste buds, which contain the receptors for taste.

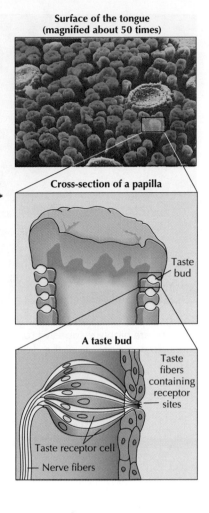

Surface of the tongue
(magnified about 50 times)

Cross-section of a papilla

Taste bud

A taste bud

Taste fibers containing receptor sites

Taste receptor cell

Nerve fibers

Gustation

Today, the sense of taste, **gustation**, may be the least critical of our senses. In the past, however, it probably contributed more directly to our survival. The major function of taste, aided by smell, is to help us avoid eating or drinking harmful substances. Humans have five major taste sensations—sweet, sour, salty, bitter, and *umami*. You are undoubtedly familiar with the first four. But *umami* (which means "delicious" or "savory") has only recently been added to the list. Umami is a separate taste and type of taste receptor that is sensitive to *glutamate* (the taste of protein) (Chandrashekar et al., 2006; Jinap & Hajeb, 2010; McCabe & Rolls, 2007). Glutamate is found in meats, meat broths, and monosodium glutamate (MSG).

Why are children so picky about food? In young people, taste buds die and are replaced about every seven days. As we age, however, the buds are replaced more slowly, so taste diminishes. Thus, children, who have abundant taste buds, often dislike foods with strong or unusual tastes (such as liver and spinach). But as they grow older and lose taste buds, they often come to like these foods.

Some pickiness is also related to learning. Many food and taste preferences result from childhood experiences and cultural influences. Many Japanese children eat raw fish, and some Chinese children eat chicken feet as part of their normal diet. American children might consider these foods "yucky." However, most American children love cheese, which children in many other cultures find repulsive.

Similar cultural and learning experiences also help explain why adults being told a bottle of wine is $90 versus its real $10 price makes it taste better. Ironically, these false expectations actually trigger more brain activity in areas that respond to pleasant experiences (Plassmann et al., 2008). Pickiness also relates to the fact that the sense of taste normally enables human and nonhuman animals to discriminate between foods that are safe to eat and foods that are poisonous (Figure 4.11).

Gustation Sense of taste

Figure 4.11 Is this emotional response to bitterness hard-wired? Infants and newborn babies show the same facial response as an adult to a bitter taste. This shared avoidance response suggests an evolutionary function because many plants that taste bitter contain toxic chemicals, and animals are more likely to survive if they avoid bitter-tasting plants (Cooper et al., 2002; Kardong, 2008; Skelhorn et al., 2008). Humans and other animals also have a preference for sweet foods that are generally nonpoisonous and good sources of energy. Unfortunately, this evolutionary preference for sweet foods now contributes to obesity problems in affluent countries where such high-calorie foods are easily available.

The power of the skin senses
Humans are highly responsive to touch, in part because of the density of our skin receptors.

Body Senses: More Than Just Touch

Objective 4.17: What are the body senses, and how do they work?

Imagine for a moment that you are an Olympic downhill skier, eagerly awaiting the starting signal that will begin your once-in-a-lifetime race for the gold medal. What senses will you need to manage the subtle and ever-changing balance adjustments required for Olympic-level skiing? How will you make your skis carve the cleanest, shortest, fastest line from start to finish? What will enable your arms, legs, and trunk to work in perfect harmony so that you can record the shortest time and win the gold? The senses that will allow you to do all this, and much more, are the *body senses*. They tell the brain how the body is oriented, where and how the body is moving, the things it touches or is touched by, and so on. These senses include the *skin senses*, the *vestibular sense*, and *kinesthesis*.

Skin Senses

The skin senses are vital. Skin not only protects the internal organs but also provides the brain with basic survival information. With nerve endings in the various layers of skin, our skin senses tell us when we are touching something (or being touched), when a pot is dangerously hot, when the weather is freezing cold, and when we have been hurt (Figure 4.12). Researchers have "mapped" the skin by applying probes to all areas of the body. Mapping shows there are three basic skin sensations: *touch* (or pressure), *temperature*, and *pain*. Receptors for these sensations occur in various concentrations and depths in the skin. For example, touch (pressure) receptors are maximally concentrated on the face and fingers and minimally in the back and legs. As your hands move over objects, pressure receptors register the indentations created in the skin, allowing perception of texture. For people who are blind, this is the principle underlying their ability to learn to read the raised dots that constitute Braille.

The relationship between the types of sensory receptors and the different sensations is not clear. It used to be thought that each receptor responded to only one type of stimulation. But we now know that some receptors respond to more than one. For example, because sound waves are a type of air pressure, our skin's pressure receptors also respond to certain sounds. And itching, tickling, and vibrating sensations seem to be produced by light stimulation of both pressure and pain receptors.

In conducting studies on temperature receptors, researchers have found that the average square centimeter of skin contains about six cold spots where cold can be

How does he do it? This surfer's finely tuned vestibular and kinesthetic senses allow him to ride his board in perfect balance, constantly compensating for the changing shape of the wave.

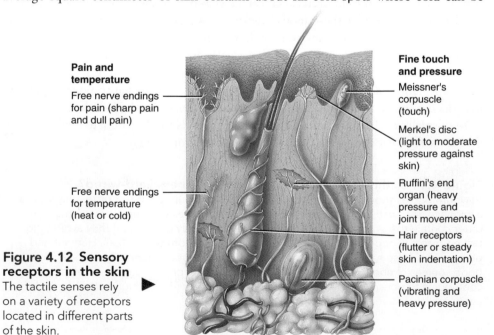

Figure 4.12 Sensory receptors in the skin
The tactile senses rely on a variety of receptors located in different parts of the skin.

Pain and temperature

Free nerve endings for pain (sharp pain and dull pain)

Free nerve endings for temperature (heat or cold)

Fine touch and pressure

Meissner's corpuscle (touch)

Merkel's disc (light to moderate pressure against skin)

Ruffini's end organ (heavy pressure and joint movements)

Hair receptors (flutter or steady skin indentation)

Pacinian corpuscle (vibrating and heavy pressure)

sensed, and one or two warm spots where warmth can be felt. Interestingly, we don't seem to have separate "hot" receptors (Craig & Bushnell, 1994). See Figure 4.13.

Vestibular Sense

The **vestibular sense** (also called the *sense of balance*) provides information on body movement and position. Even the most routine activities—riding a bike, walking, or even sitting up—would be impossible without this sense (Baizer, Paolone, & Witelson, 2011; Lackner & Di Zio, 2005). Located in the inner ear, the vestibular sense is composed of the vestibular sacs and the semicircular canals. The *semicircular canals* provide the brain with balance information, particularly information about rotation of the head. As the head moves, liquid in the canals moves and bends hair cell receptors. At the end of the semicircular canals are the *vestibular sacs*, which contain hair cells sensitive to the specific angle of the head—straight up and down or tilted. Information from the semicircular canals and the vestibular sacs is converted to neural impulses, which are then carried to the appropriate section of the brain.

What causes motion sickness? Information from the vestibular sense is used by the eye muscles to maintain visual fixation and, sometimes, by the body to change body orientation. If the vestibular sense gets overloaded or becomes confused by boat, airplane, or automobile motion, the result is often dizziness and nausea. Random versus expected movements also are more likely to produce motion sickness. Thus, automobile drivers are better prepared than passengers for upcoming movement and are less likely to feel sick. Motion sickness also seems to vary with age. Infants are generally immune, children between ages 2 and 12 years have the highest susceptibility, and the incidence declines in adulthood.

Kinesthesis

Kinesthesis (kin-ehs-THEE-sehs), a companion to the vestibular sense, provides information about bodily posture and orientation, as well as movement of individual body parts. Unlike receptors for sight, hearing, smell, taste, and balance, which are clumped together in one organ or area, kinesthetic receptors are found throughout the muscles, joints, and tendons of the body. As we sit, walk, bend, lift, turn, and so on, our kinesthetic receptors respond by sending messages to the brain. They tell which muscles are being contracted and which relaxed, how our body weight is distributed, and where our arms and legs are in relation to the rest of our body. Without these sensations, we would literally have to watch every step or movement we make.

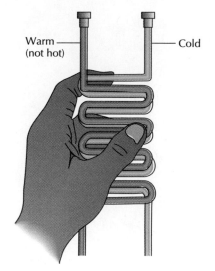

Figure 4.13 The thermal grill illusion Researchers use an instrument called a "heat grill"—two pipes twisted together, one containing warm water and the other cold. If you grasp both pipes, you experience intense heat because both warm and cold receptors are activated simultaneously (Boettger, Schwier, & Bär, 2011).

Vestibular Sense Sense of body movement and position, also called the sense of balance

Kinesthesis Sensory system for detecting body posture, orientation, and movement of individual body parts

CHECK & REVIEW   STOP   *Before going on, be sure to complete this Check & Review. It is an invaluable study tool!*

Other Important Senses

Part A: Retrieval Practice
1. Without looking at the book, spend 10 minutes writing a free-form essay recalling all you can remember from the previous section.
2. Now, reread the previous section, and once again spend 10 minutes writing a free-form essay on the SAME material.

Part B: Practice Quiz
1. Human and nonhuman animals may be affected by chemical scents found in natural body odors, which are called _____.
2. The skin senses include _____. (a) pressure; (b) pain; (c) warmth and cold; (d) all of these

3. The weightlessness experienced by space travelers from zero gravity has its greatest effect on the _____ senses. (a) visceral; (b) reticular; (c) somasthetic; (d) vestibular
4. Receptors located in the muscles, joints, and tendons of the body provide _____ information to maintain bodily posture, orientation, and movement.

Check your answers in Appendix B.

Understanding Perception

Objective 4.18: What are illusions and why are they important?

We are ready to move from *sensation* and the major senses to *perception*, the process of selecting, organizing, and interpreting incoming sensations into useful mental representations of the world.

Illusion False or misleading perception

Normally, our perceptions agree with our sensations. When they do not, the result is an **illusion**, a false or misleading perception (Reddy et al., 2011; Skewes, Roepstorff, & Frith, 2011). See the Concept Organizer 4.2 for more information about how illusions provide psychologists with a tool for studying the normal process of perception.

Selection: Extracting Important Messages

Objective 4.19: Describe the selection process and its three key factors—selective attention, feature detectors, and habituation.

The first step in perception is *selection*—choosing where to direct our attention. Three major factors are involved in the act of paying attention to some stimuli in our environment and not to others: *selective attention*, *feature detectors*, and *habituation*.

Selective Attention

In almost every situation, there is an excess of sensory information, but the brain manages to sort out the important messages and discard the rest (Arieh & Marks, 2008; Haab et al., 2011; Prado, Carp, & Weissman, 2011). As you sit reading this chapter, you may be ignoring sounds from another room or the discomfort of the chair you're sitting on. This process is known as **selective attention** (Figure 4.14).

Selective Attention Filtering out and attending only to important sensory messages

Feature Detectors

Feature Detectors Specialized neurons that respond only to certain sensory information

The second major factor in selection is the presence of specialized neurons in the brain called **feature detectors** (or *feature analyzers*) that respond only to certain sensory information. In 1959, researchers discovered specialized neurons in the optic nerve of a frog. They called these receptors "bug detectors" because they respond only to moving bugs (Lettvin et al., 1959). Later researchers found feature detectors in cats that respond to specific lines and angles (Hubel & Wiesel, 1965, 1979).

Similar studies with humans have found feature detectors in the temporal and occipital lobes that respond maximally to faces. Problems in these areas can produce a condition called *prosopagnosia* (*prosopon* means "face" and *agnosia* means "failure to know") (Barton, 2008; Palermo et al., 2011; Stollhoff et al., 2011). Interestingly, people with prosopagnosia can recognize that they are looking at a face. But they cannot say whose face is reflected in a mirror, even if it is their own or that of a friend or relative.

Certain basic mechanisms for perceptual selection are thus built into the brain. However, a certain amount of interaction with the environment is apparently necessary for feature detector cells to develop normally. One well-known study demonstrated that kittens raised in a cylinder with only vertically or horizontally striped

◀ **Figure 4.14 Selective attention** When you are in a group of people, surrounded by various conversations, you can still select and attend to the voices of people you find interesting. Another example of selective attention occurs with the well-known "cocktail party phenomenon." Have you noticed how you can suddenly pick up on a nearby group's conversation if someone in that group mentions your name?

ConceptOrganizer4.2

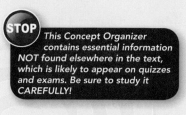

Optical Illusions

Objective 4.18: What are illusions and why are they important?

An *illusion* is a false or misleading impression produced by errors in the perceptual process or by actual physical distortions, as in desert mirages. As you may have noticed, this text highlights numerous popular *myths* about psychology because it's important to understand and correct our misperceptions. For similar reasons, you need to know how illusions mislead our normal information processing and recognize that "seeing is believing, but seeing isn't always believing correctly" (Lilienfeld et al., 2010, p. 7).

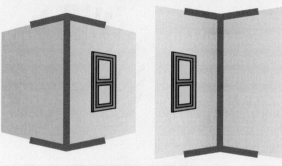

(a) Müller-Lyer illusion

The two vertical lines are the same length, but psychologists have learned that people who live in urban environments normally see the one on the right as longer. This is because they have learned to make size and distance judgments from perspective cues created by right angles and horizontal and vertical lines of buildings and streets.

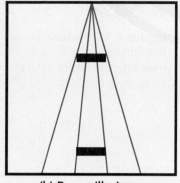

(b) Ponzo illusion

Do you perceive the top black line as being much larger than the one on the bottom? Both lines are the exact same size, but the converging lines provide depth cues telling you that the top dark, horizontal, line is farther away than the bottom line and therefore much larger.

(c) The horizontal-vertical illusion

Which is longer, the horizontal (flat) or the vertical (standing) line? People living in areas where they regularly see long straight lines, such as roads and train tracks, perceive the horizontal line as shorter because of their environmental experiences.

StudyTip

Be careful not to confuse *illusion* with *hallucination* or *delusion* [Chapters 5 and 14]. Hallucinations are false sensory experiences that occur without an external stimulus, such as hearing voices during a psychotic episode or seeing "pulsating flowers" after using LSD [lysergic acid diethylamide] and other hallucinogenic drugs. Delusions refer to false beliefs, often of persecution or grandeur, which may accompany drug or psychotic experiences.

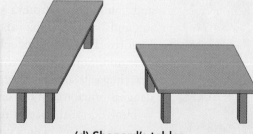

(d) Shepard's tables

Do these two table tops have the same dimensions? Get a ruler and check it for yourself.

(e) Illusions, delusions, and hallucinations

If you watched the 2011 movie, *Black Swan*, you may remember scenes showing Nina (Natalie Portman) bending her legs like a swan's, having webbed feet, and growing black feathers. Were these *illusions*, *delusions*, or *hallucinations*? Check the study tip to the left for clarification.

walls developed severe behavioral and neurological impairments (Blakemore & Cooper, 1970) (Figure 4.15). When "horizontal cats"—those raised with only horizontal lines in their environment—were removed from the cylinder and allowed to roam, they could easily jump onto horizontal surfaces. But they had great difficulty negotiating objects with vertical lines, such as chair legs. The reverse was true for the "vertical cats." They could easily avoid table and chair legs but never attempted to jump onto horizontal structures. Examination of the visual cortex of these cats showed they had failed to develop their potential feature detectors for either vertical or horizontal lines.

TEST YOURSELF

Figure 4.15 Nature versus nurture Studies show that kittens reared in a vertical world failed to develop their innate ability to detect horizontal lines or objects. In contrast, kittens restricted to only horizontal lines cannot detect vertical lines. Can you explain why?

Answer: Without appropriate stimulation, brain cells sensitive to vertical or horizontal lines deteriorate during a critical (and irreversible) period in visual development.

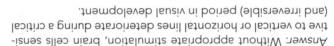

Habituation

Habituation The brain's reduced responsiveness to unchanging stimuli

Another physiological factor important in selecting only certain sensory data is **habituation**. The brain seems "prewired" to pay more attention to changes in the environment than to stimuli that remain constant. We quickly **habituate** (or respond less) to predictable and unchanging stimuli. For example, when you buy a new CD, you initially listen carefully to all the songs. Over time, your attention declines and you can play the entire CD and not really notice it. This may not matter with CDs—we can always replace them when we become bored. But this same habituation phenomenon also applies to your friends and love life. And people aren't as easily replaced. Have you noticed how attention and compliments from a stranger are almost always more exciting and "valuable" than those from long-time friends and lovers? Unfortunately, some people misinterpret and overvalue this new attention. Some may even leave good relationships, not realizing that they will soon *habituate* to the new person. (Understanding the dangers of habituation is another payoff for studying psychology!)

Habituation Thanks to habituation, these three girls may "choose to ignore" their initially painful braces. (Sensory adaptation may have also occurred. Over time pressure sensors send fewer messages to the brain.)

How does habituation differ from sensory adaptation, which we discussed earlier? Habituation is a perceptual process that occurs in the brain, and it involves a reduced responsiveness to unchanging (boring) stimuli. In contrast, sensory adaptation occurs within the sensory receptors. The receptor cells in our eyes, ears, skin, and so on actually slow down their rate of firing if a stimulus doesn't change much. A smoky bar might smell very smoky when you first arrive, but you hardly notice it after a few minutes.

To combat both habituation and sensory adaptation, parents and teachers often select stimuli that are *intense*, *novel*, and *contrasting*. But advertisers and politicians have spent millions of dollars developing these same attention-getting principles into a fine art. The next time you're watching TV, note the commercial and political ads. Are they flashier or brighter than the regular program (intensity)? Do they use talking cows to promote California cheese (novelty)? Is the promoted product or candidate set in *favorable* contrast to the competition?

Organization: Form, Constancy, and Depth

Objective 4.20: Describe the Gestalt laws of perceptual organization.

Having selected incoming information (our previous section), we must organize it into patterns and principles that will help us understand the world. Raw sensory data are like the parts of a watch. They must be assembled in a meaningful way before they are useful. We organize and perceive sensory data in terms of *form*, *constancy*, and *depth*.

Form Perception

Look at the first drawing in Figure 4.16a. What do you see? Can you draw a similar object on a piece of paper? This is known as an "impossible figure." Now look at Figure 14.6b, which shows a painting by M. C. Escher, a Dutch painter who created striking examples of perceptual distortion. Although drawn to represent three-dimensional objects or situations, the parts don't assemble into logical wholes. Like the illusions studied earlier, impossible figures and distorted painting help us understand perceptual principles—in this case, the principle of *form organization*.

Why Study "Impossible Figures"?

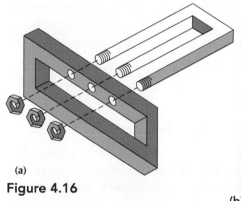

(a)

Figure 4.16

(b)

Answer: When you first glance at figure (a) and the famous painting by M. C. Escher in (b), you detect specific features of the stimuli and judge them as sensible figures. But as you try to sort and organize the different elements into a stable, well-organized whole, you realize they don't add up—they're illogical or "impossible." The point of the illustration is that there is no one-to-one correspondence between your actual sensory input and your final perception. The same stimuli looked at from another perspective can lead to very different perceptions.

Gestalt psychologists were among the first to study how the brain organizes sensory impressions into a whole. (The German word *gestalt* means "whole" or "pattern.") Rather than perceiving its discrete parts as separate entities, the Gestaltists emphasized the importance of organization and patterning in enabling us to perceive the whole stimulus. The Gestaltists proposed several laws of organization

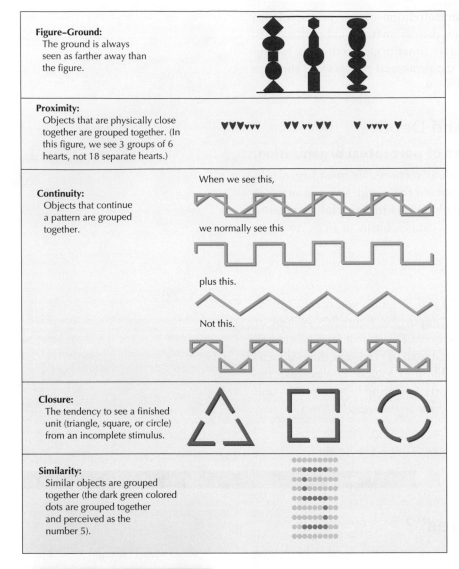

Figure–Ground:
The ground is always seen as farther away than the figure.

Proximity:
Objects that are physically close together are grouped together. (In this figure, we see 3 groups of 6 hearts, not 18 separate hearts.)

Continuity:
Objects that continue a pattern are grouped together.

When we see this,

we normally see this

plus this.

Not this.

Closure:
The tendency to see a finished unit (triangle, square, or circle) from an incomplete stimulus.

Similarity:
Similar objects are grouped together (the dark green colored dots are grouped together and perceived as the number 5).

◀ **Figure 4.17 Gestalt principles of organization** Gestalt principles are based on the notion that we all share a natural tendency to force patterns onto whatever we see. Although the examples of the Gestalt principles in this figure are all visual, each principle applies to other modes of perception as well. For example, the Gestalt principle of *contiguity* cannot be shown because it involves nearness in time, not visual nearness. You also may have experienced *aural figure and ground effects* at a movie or a concert when there was a conversation going on close by and you couldn't sort out what sounds were the background and what you wanted to be your focus.

Another good example of a Gestalt principle not shown in this figure is *visual closure*, which happens every time you watch television. The picture on the TV screen appears to be a solid image, but it's really a very fast stream of small dots being illuminated one by one, "painting" tiny horizontal lines down the screen one line at a time. Your brain closes the momentary blank gaps on the screen.

that specify how people perceive form (Figure 4.17). The most fundamental Gestalt principle of organization is our tendency to distinguish between *figure* and *ground*. For example, while reading this sentence, your eyes receive only sensations of black lines and white paper. Your brain then organizes these sensations into letters and words perceived against a backdrop of white pages. The letters constitute the *figure*, and the pages are the *ground*. Interestingly, the boundary between figure and ground is sometimes so vague that we have difficulty perceiving which is which. This is known as a *reversible figure* (see Figure 4.18).

Perceptual Constancies

Objective 4.21: What are perceptual constancies, and why are they important?

Now that we have seen how *form perception* contributes to organization, we will examine **perceptual constancies**. As noted earlier with sensory adaptation and habituation, we are particularly alert to change. However, we also manage to perceive a great deal of consistency in the environment. Without perceptual constancy, our world would be totally chaotic. Things would seem to grow as we got closer to them, to change shape as our viewing angle changed, and to change color as light levels changed. The four best-known constancies are *size*, *shape*, *color*, and *brightness* (Concept Organizer 4.3).

Perceptual Constancy Tendency for the environment to be perceived as remaining the same even with changes in sensory input

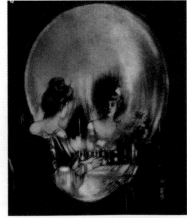

Figure 4.18 Reversible figure
This so-called reversible figure demonstrates alternating figure–ground relations. It can be seen as a woman looking in a mirror or as a skull, depending on what you see as figure or ground.

ConceptOrganizer4.3

Four Perceptual Constancies

1. **Size Constancy** Our retinal image of the person in the foreground is much larger than the trees and mountains behind her. Thanks to size constancy, however, we readily perceive her as a person of normal size. Interestingly, size constancy, like all constancies, appears to develop from learning and experience. Studies of people who have been blind since birth, and then have their sight restored, find they have little or no size constancy (Sacks, 1995).

2. **Shape Constancy** As the coin is rotated, it changes shape, but we still perceive it as the same coin because of shape constancy.

Want another example of size and shape constancy? In this drawing, the young boy on the right appears to be much larger than the woman on the left. The illusion is so strong that when a person walks from the left corner to the right, the observer perceives the person to be "growing," even though that is not possible. How can this be?

This so-called Ames room illusion is based on the unusual construction of the room, and our perceptual constancies have falsely filled in the wrong details. To the viewer, peering through the peephole, the Ames room appears to be a normal cubic-shaped room. But the true shape is trapezoidal. In addition, the walls are slanted and the floor and ceiling are at an incline. Because our brains mistakenly assume the two people are the same distance away, we compensate for the apparent size difference by making the person on the left appear much smaller.

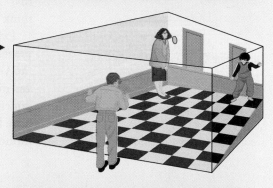

Several Ames room sets were used in *The Lord of the Rings* film series to make the heights of the hobbits appear correct when standing next to Gandalf.

3. **Color Constancy** and 4. **Brightness Constancy** We perceive the dog's fur in this photo as having a relatively constant hue (or color) and brightness despite the fact that the wavelength of light reaching our retinas may vary as the light changes.

BIZARRO

I HAVE NO SENSE OF DEPTH PERCEPTION. COULD YOU TELL ME—IS THAT SOMEONE STANDING WAY UP THERE ON THE CORNER, OR IS THERE A LITTLE MAN IN YOUR HAIR?

Depth Perception The ability to perceive three-dimensional space and to accurately judge distance

Binocular Cues Visual input from two eyes that allows perception of depth or distance

Monocular Cues Visual input from a single eye alone that contributes to perception of depth or distance

Depth Perception

Objective 4.22: How do we perceive depth, and why are binocular and monocular cues important?

As we've just seen in the examples of form and constancies, experience and learning are vital to organizing perceptions. This is also true in depth perception. **Depth perception** allows us to accurately estimate the distance of perceived objects and thereby perceive the world in three dimensions. It is possible to judge the distance of objects with nearly all senses. If a person enters a dark room and walks toward you, his or her voice and footsteps get louder, body smells grow stronger, and you may even be able to feel the slight movement of air from his or her approaching movement. In most cases, however, we rely most heavily on vision to perceive distance. When you add the ability to accurately perceive distance to the ability to judge the height and width of an object, you are able to perceive the world in three dimensions. But no matter which sense you use to perceive our three-dimensional world, perception of depth is primarily learned.

Take the classic example of a patient known as S.B. Blind since the age of 10 months, his sight was restored at age 52. Following the operation that removed cataracts from both eyes, S.B. had great difficulty learning to use his newly acquired vision for judging distance and depth. On one occasion, he even tried to crawl out of the window of his hospital room. He thought he would be able to lower himself by his hands to the ground below, even though the window was on the fourth floor.

Didn't S.B. have some inborn depth and distance perception? As you recall from Chapter 1, one of the most enduring debates in psychology (and other sciences) is the question of "nature versus nurture," inborn versus learned. In this case, naturists argue that depth perception is inborn. Nurturists insist it is learned. Today, most scientists think there is some truth in both viewpoints.

Evidence for the innate (inborn) position comes from a set of interesting experiments with an apparatus called the *visual cliff* (Figure 4.19).

We all recognize that in our three-dimensional world, the ability to perceive depth and distance is essential. But how do we perceive a three-dimensional world with a two-dimensional receptor system? One mechanism is the interaction of both eyes to produce **binocular cues** (Concept Organizer 4.4, p. 153). The other mechanism involves **monocular cues**, which work with each eye separately (Concept Organizer 4.5, p. 154).

Figure 4.19 Visual cliff Crawling infants hesitate or refuse to move to the "deep end" of the visual cliff (Gibson & Walk, 1960; Witherington et al., 2005). indicating that they perceive the difference in depth. (The same is true for baby animals that walk almost immediately birth.) Even 2-month-old infants show a change in heart rate when placed on the deep versus shallow side of the visual cliff (Banks & Salapatek, 1983).

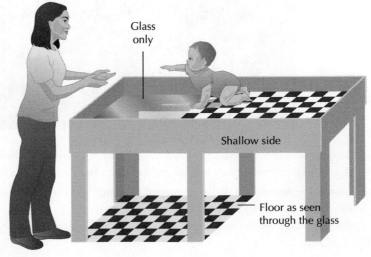

Glass only

Shallow side

Floor as seen through the glass

ConceptOrganizer4.4

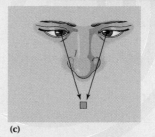

Binocular Depth Cues

One of the most important cues for depth perception comes from **retinal disparity**. Because our eyes are about 2½ inches apart, the retina of each eye receives a slightly different view of the world. Such *stereoscopic vision* provides important cues to depth. You can demonstrate this for yourself by trying the following exercise:

(a)

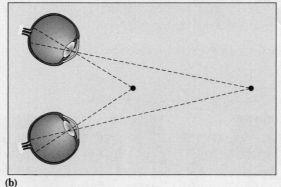

(b)

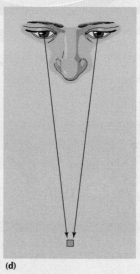

(c)

(d)

Stare at your two index fingers a few inches in front of your eyes with their tips half an inch apart. Do you see the "floating finger"? Move it farther away and the "finger" will shrink. Move it closer and it will enlarge.

Because of retinal disparity, objects at different distances (such as the "floating finger") project their images on different parts of the retina. Far objects project on the retinal area near the nose, whereas near objects project farther out, closer to the ears.

As we move closer and closer to an object, a second binocular (and neuromuscular) cue, **convergence**, helps us judge depth (c) and (d). The closer the object, the more our eyes are turned inward toward our noses. Hold your index finger at arm's length in front of you and watch it as you bring it closer and closer until it is right in front of your nose. The amount of strain in your eye muscles created by the *convergence*, or turning inward of the eyes, is used as a cue by your brain to interpret distance.

Why are coaches always reminding players to "keep their eyes on the ball"? Convergence and depth perception are better when you are looking directly at an object, rather than out of the corner of your eye. Thus, if you turn your body or your head so that you look straight at your tennis opponent or the pitcher, you will more accurately judge the distance of the ball and thereby be more likely to swing at the right time.

Retinal Disparity Binocular cue to distance in which the separation of the eyes causes different images to fall on each retina

Convergence Binocular depth cue in which the closer the object, the more the eyes converge, or turn inward

ConceptOrganizer4.5

Monocular Depth Cues

The binocular (two eyes) cues of retinal disparity and convergence are inadequate in judging distances longer than the length of a football field. Luckily, we have several monocular (one eye) cues available separately to each eye. Imagine yourself as an artist and see if you can identify each of these cues in this fascinating sidewalk painting by artist Julian Beever.

Monocular Depth Cues

Linear perspective Parallel lines converge, or angle toward one another, as they recede into the distance.

Interposition Objects that obscure or overlap other objects are perceived as closer.

Relative size Close objects cast a larger retinal image than distant objects.

Texture gradient Nearby objects have a coarser and more distinct texture than distant ones.

Aerial perspective Distant objects appear hazy and blurred compared to close objects because of intervening atmospheric dust or haze.

Light and shadow Brighter objects are perceived as being closer than darker objects.

Relative height Objects positioned higher in our field of vision are perceived as farther away.

Two additional monocular cues for depth perception, *accommodation* of the lens of the eye and *motion parallax*, cannot be used by artists. In *accommodation*, muscles that adjust the shape of the lens as it focuses on an object send neural messages to the brain, which interprets the signal to perceive distance. For near objects, the lens bulges; for far objects, it flattens.

Motion parallax (also known as *relative motion*) refers to the fact that when we are moving, close objects appear to whiz by, whereas farther objects seem to move more slowly or remain stationary. This effect can easily be seen when traveling by car or train.

CHECK & REVIEW

STOP Before going on, be sure to complete this Check & Review. It is an invaluable study tool!

Selection and Organization

Part A: Retrieval Practice

1. Without looking at the book, spend 10 minutes writing a free-form essay recalling all you can remember from the previous section.

2. Now, reread the previous section, and once again spend 10 minutes writing a free-form essay on the SAME material.

Part B: Practice Quiz

1. Explain how illusions differ from delusions and hallucinations.

2. Specialized cells in the brain called _____ respond only to certain types of sensory information.

3. Explain why "horizontal cats" can jump only onto horizontal surfaces.

4. You write a reminder of an appointment on a Post-it and stick it on the door, where you see it every day. A month later, you forget your appointment because of your brain's tendency to ignore constant stimuli. This is known as _____. (a) sensory adaptation; (b) selective perception; (c) habituation; (d) selective attention.

5. The principle of _____ is at work when, as your brother walks away from you, you don't perceive him to be shrinking.

6. The visual cliff is an apparatus designed to study _____ in young children and animals. (a) color discrimination; (b) shape constancy; (c) depth perception; (d) monocular vision

7. Since Jolly Roger, the pirate, lost one eye in a fight, he can no longer use _____ as a cue for the perception of depth and distance.

Check your answers in Appendix B.

Interpretation: Explaining Our Perceptions

Objective 4.23: What factors influence how we interpret sensations?

After selectively sorting through incoming sensory information and organizing it into patterns, the brain uses this information to explain and make judgments about the external world. This final stage of perception—*interpretation*—is influenced by several factors, including *perceptual adaptation*, *perceptual set*, and *frame of reference*.

1. *Perceptual adaptation* Do you recall the discussion about George Stratton's experiment in the chapter opener? Stratton's research illustrates the critical role that *perceptual adaptation* plays in how we interpret the information that our brains gather. Without his brain's ability to "rewire" itself and adapt his perceptions to a skewed environment, Stratton would not have been able to function. However, thanks to perceptual adaptation, he was able to create coherence out of what would otherwise have been chaos.

2. *Perceptual set (or expectancies)* Our previous experiences, assumptions, and expectations also affect how we interpret and perceive the world. If a car backfires, runners at a track meet may jump the gun. People who believe that extraterrestrials occasionally visit the earth may interpret a weather balloon or an odd-shaped cloud as a spaceship. These mental predispositions, or **perceptual sets**, prepare us in a certain way and greatly influence our perception. In other words, we largely see what we expect to see.

    For example, studies using the famous reversible figure of the young/old woman that you saw on page 127, found that when people are led to expect either a young woman or an old woman, they generally saw "what they expected to see." Another study recruited participants from a Jewish organization and briefly flashed pictures on a screen (Erdelyi & Applebaum, 1973). When the center symbol was a swastika, the Jewish participants were less likely to recognize and remember the symbols around the edges (Figure 4.20). Can you see how the life experiences of the Jewish subjects led them to create a perceptual set for the swastika? Can you also see how expressions like "stingy jew," "lazy mexican," "crazy schizo," "dirty fag," or even "nerd" can lead to painful and dangerous forms of prejudice and discrimination (Chapters 12, 14, 16)?

3. *Frame of reference* Our perceptions of people, objects, or situations are also affected by their frame of reference, or context. An elephant is perceived as much larger when it is next to a mouse than when it stands next to a giraffe.

Perceptual Set Readiness to perceive in a particular manner based on expectations

Figure 4.20 Perceptual set and life experiences Can you see why members of a Jewish organization would be less likely to pay attention to (and remember) the other stimuli in this photo when the center item is a swastika?

Perceptual set: Is it a log on the water or the Loch Ness Monster? Imagine yourself driving along the road beside Loch Ness in the Scottish Highlands at dusk. This large, very deep freshwater lake near Inverness is most famous for the alleged sightings of the Loch Ness Monster or "Nessie." How might your perceptual system interpret this image if you saw it out of your car window as you drove by? Is it a tree branch sticking up out of the water or is it the legendary monster? How you perceive it depends in part on your previous assumptions and expectations about the existence of the monster. If you believe in Nessie, then that is what you probably will think you have seen.

 **TEST YOURSELF**

Perceptual Set

Do you notice anything unusual in this photo? What happens when you turn the book upside down? Despite the extreme distortion, most people see the upside-down photo as normal. Can you explain why?

Answer: Because of perceptual set, we expect both photos to be the same.

Psychology Engages

  CASE STUDY / PERSONAL STORY

Helen Keller greets Eleanor Roosevelt (1955)

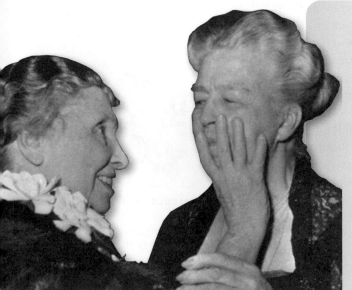

Helen Keller's Triumph and Advice

Objective 4.24: What can Helen Keller teach us about sensation and perception?

Helen Keller recognized how crucial vision and hearing are to our lives. She learned to "see" and "hear" with her sense of touch and often recognized visitors by their smell or by vibrations from their walk. Helen Keller wasn't born deaf and blind. When she was 19 months old, she suffered a fever that left her without sight or hearing and thus virtually isolated from the world. Keller's parents realized they had to find help for their daughter. After diligently searching, they found Anne Sullivan, a young teacher who was able to break through Keller's barrier of isolation by taking advantage of her sense of touch. One day, Sullivan took Keller to the pumphouse and, as Sullivan (1902) wrote:

> I made Helen hold her mug under the spout while I pumped. As the cold water gushed forth, filling the mug, I spelled "w-a-t-e-r" in Helen's free hand. The word coming so close upon the sensation of cold water rushing over her hand seemed to startle her. She dropped the mug and stood as one transfixed. A new light came into her face. (p. 257)

That one moment, brought on by the sensation of cold water on her hand, was the impetus for a lifetime of learning about, understanding, and appreciating the world through her remaining senses. In 1904, Helen Keller graduated cum laude from Radcliffe College and went on to become a famous author and lecturer, inspiring physically limited people throughout the world.

Despite her incredible accomplishments, Keller often expressed a lifelong yearning to experience a normal sensory world. She offered important advice to all whose senses are "normal":

> *I who am blind can give one hint to those who see: use your eyes as if tomorrow you would be stricken blind. And the same method can be applied to the other senses. Hear the music of voices, the song of a bird, the mighty strains of an orchestra as if you would be stricken deaf tomorrow. Touch each object as if tomorrow your tactile sense would fail. Smell the perfume of flowers, taste with relish each morsel as if tomorrow you could never smell and taste again. Make the most of every sense; glory in all the facets of pleasure and beauty that the world reveals to you through the several means of contact which nature provides. (Keller, 1962, p. 23)*

RESEARCH CHALLENGE

Is There Scientific Evidence for ESP?

Co-authored with Thomas Frangicetto (Northampton Community College, Bethlehem, PA)

Objective 4.25: What is ESP and why is it so controversial?

Psychic John Edward: *"This is very strong energy coming through. Your father wants you to know that he 'found the ring.' Does this make sense to you?"*

   Subject: *"Yes, when my father died I put my ring in the coffin with him. I don't think anyone else knew that I did that."*

Claims such as Edward's so-called ability to "cross over" and speak to the dead invoke the controversial "sixth sense" known as **extrasensory perception** or **ESP**, which purportedly involves "energy" that goes beyond the detection range of the five known sensory receptors covered earlier in this chapter. Psychics claim to have extraordinary abilities in many realms— to be able to read other people's minds (*telepathy*), perceive objects or events that are inaccessible to the normal senses (*clairvoyance*), predict the future (*precognition*), or move objects without touching them

(*psychokinesis*). Can Sylvia Browne predict the future? Has Allison Dubois—the inspiration for *Medium*—really used psychic abilities to help law enforcement officials solve crimes?

As we discussed in Chapter 1, all of these claims fall under the name "parapsychology," and the claims of psychics such as these have been successfully debunked (Irwin, 2008; Lancaster, 2007; Nickell, 2001; Shaffer & Jadwiszczok, 2010). The motto "extraordinary claims require extraordinary evidence" is central to the skeptic's code (Gracely, 1998; Sagan, 1980), and professional skeptics have held psychics and ESP researchers to extremely high standards.

But there is an important distinction to be made here. There are "entertainer"-type practitioners of ESP, such as psychics or mediums, whom skeptics believe take advantage of people who are emotionally vulnerable by charging them exorbitant rates for their "readings," seminars, books, and DVDs. There are also scientific

researchers with university training and research affiliations who investigate ESP in their university laboratories. One such researcher is Daryl Bem.

In 2011, Dr. Bem, a Cornell University researcher with a "stellar reputation as a rigorous experimentalist" (Shermer, 2003) and a 20-year interest in paranormal investigation, published an article in the highly prestigious *Journal of Personality and Social Psychology* that offered scientific evidence for the existence of ESP—what parapsychologists call *psi*. Bem's research focused on two types of *psi*, precognition (conscious cognitive awareness) and premonition (affective apprehension) of a future event that "could not otherwise be anticipated through any known inferential process" (Bem, 2011).

Bem reported on nine separate studies involving more than 1,000 participants, and "all but one of the experiments yielded statistically significant results" (Bem, 2011). For example, in one study volunteers looking at a computer monitor with two curtains were

Extrasensory Perception (ESP) Perceptual, or "psychic," abilities that supposedly go beyond the known senses (e.g., telepathy, clairvoyance, precognition, and psychokinesis)

Zener cards and ESP research In the early 1900s, Joseph B. Rhine, a respected researcher, began experiments using Zener cards, a procedure spoofed in the popular 1984 movie, *Ghostbusters*. This deck of 25 cards included five different symbols, depicted above. "Senders" were asked to concentrate on the card, while "receivers" tried to "read the mind" of the sender. Although Rhine found a few people who scored somewhat better than chance, his methodology was severely criticized and his findings were discredited. The road to respectability and credibility has been a difficult one for parapsychological researchers ever since.

told to guess which curtain had an erotic photo behind it. Both sides were actually blank and the computer randomly placed a picture behind either side *after* the guess. Bem also ran control sessions "in which the computer again randomly selected word practice sets" that were not actually administered—so the computer was the "control group" (Bem, 2011). Bem reported that 53 percent of the subjects picked the curtain where the computer subsequently placed the photo. Bem believes their "guess" was informed by an event that had not yet occurred. "Fifty-three percent may sound small when fifty percent is chance," Bem told an ABC reporter, "but in a political election fifty-three percent is sometimes called a landslide" (Potter, 2011).

Whereas comparing people guessing where photos will appear on a screen with voters enacting a predetermined choice of candidates may be specious reasoning, Bem's claim of "statistical significance" (see Appendix A at back of book) was verified by one team of independent reviewers (Wagensmakers et al., 2011). Bem interpreted his overall results as confirmation of the hypothesis that people "use psi information implicitly and nonconsciously to enhance their performance in a wide variety of everyday tasks" (precognition) (Wagensmakers et al., 2011).That same group of reviewers concluded, however, that Bem's "p-values"—the probability that a finding will occur by chance (see Appendix A at back of book)—"do not

indicate evidence in favor of precognition; instead they indicate that experimental psychologists need to change the way they conduct their experiments and analyze their data" (Wagensmakers et al., 2011).

This reaction accurately reflects the deep skepticism that the field of psychology holds for the "pseudopsychologies" (refer back to Ch. 1, pp. 5–6). Indeed, the publication of Bem's research raised many doubts and concerns (Alcock, 2011; Hawes, 2010; Krueger, 2010; Wagensmakers et al., 2011). For example, one noted critic accused Bem of *experimenter bias* (see p. 2) and flawed data, and seriously questioned the decision "by the editors of an esteemed psychology journal to publish this badly flawed research article" (Alcock, 2011, Krueger, 2010; Wagensmakers et al., 2011). Bem responded to this criticism by pointing out that the reviewers for the journal apparently understood his analytical procedures better than his critics (Bem, 2011).

Perhaps the most serious weakness of parapsychology is the failure of replication by rivals in independent laboratories (Hyman, 1996; Nisbet, 2000). (Recall from Ch. 1, p. 17, that replicability is a core requirement for scientific acceptance.) Furthermore, findings in ESP are notoriously "fragile" in that they do not hold up to intense scrutiny (Alcock, 2011; Hyman, 1996; Nisbet, 2000).

Where does this leave us? Does the acceptance of Bem's research in a respected psychology journal prove that ESP exists? As physicist Lawrence M. Krauss

(2011) said: "The proof of the pudding is not publication, but rather if the idea catches the interest of others, who then do more research to test it and push it forward . . . the good research survives, and the bad research gets happily buried in the dustbin of history, which is what I expect will happen in this case."

Student Engagement Exercise

Carefully read the article and watch the two-minute video embedded in the link below. (Note: It may take up to 20 seconds to load.) http://abcnews.go.com/Technology/extrasensory-perception-scientific-journal-esp-paper-published-cornell/story?id=12556754

Now, identify each of the following research components from the Bem study described above and portrayed in the video:

1. *Research method* (experimental, descriptive, correlational, or biological)?

2. If you chose the:
   - *Experimental method*—label the IV, DV, experimental group, and control group.
   - *Descriptive method*—is this a naturalistic observation, survey, or case study?
   - *Correlational method*—is this a positive, negative, or zero correlation?
   - *Biological method*—identify the specific research tool (e.g., brain dissection, CT scan, etc.

(Answers appear in Appendix B.)

 CRITICAL THINKING

Why Do So Many People Believe in ESP?

Objective 4.27: Identify four forms of faulty reasoning behind ESP.

The subject of *extrasensory perception* (ESP) often generates not only great interest but also strong emotional responses. Unfortunately, when we feel strongly about

an issue, we often fail to recognize the faulty reasoning underlying our beliefs. Belief in ESP is particularly associated with illogical, noncritical thinking.

To test your critical thinking skills as they apply to ESP, study the following four types of faulty reasoning:

1. **Confirmation bias**—*noting and remembering events that confirm personal expectations and beliefs (the "hits") and ignoring nonsupportive evidence (the "misses").*

   Can celebrated psychic John Edward, mentioned in the previous

Research Challenge, really communicate with the dead? According to psychic debunker and skeptic James Randi, Edward uses a technique known as "cold reading," in which the "psychic" makes guesses, puts out suggestions, and watches the recipient's reactions (Randi, 2006).

Even what seems like an impressive "hit"—*a dead father finding the ring his son placed in his coffin*—can be explained as a high probability guess, as many funerals involve jewelry such as rings, bracelets, and watches (Nickell, 2001). If Edward had been wrong about the ring—a "miss"—he would have simply moved on to another guess or question until he got a *hit*.

In our everyday life, most Internet search engines track our searches and then tailor all our later searches to present what they think we want to see. Can you see how this might create a confirmation bias? Do we end up seeing only things that confirm our prior beliefs?

2. **Innumeracy**—*failing to recognize chance occurrences for what they are owing to a lack of training in statistics and probabilities.*

Unusual events are misperceived as statistically impossible (such as predicting a president's illness). And extraordinary explanations, such as ESP, are seen as the logical alternative.

3. **Willingness to suspend disbelief**—*refusing to engage one's normal critical thinking skills because of wishful thinking or a personal need for power and control.*

Most of us find it hard to accept our human limits, and ESP satisfies some of our deepest fantasies. Also, given today's fast-paced technological world and scientific progress, it's tempting to believe that virtually anything is possible.

4. **The "vividness" problem**—*remembering and preferring vivid, dramatic information.*

Human information processing and memory storage and retrieval are often based on the initial "vividness" of the information. Sincere personal testimonials, theatrical demonstrations, and detailed anecdotes easily capture our attention and tend to be remembered better than rational, scientific descriptions of events. This is the heart of most stories about extraterrestrial visitations.

Now, using these four types of faulty reasoning, decide which one BEST applies to each of the following cases. Then compare your answers with those of your classmates and friends.

_____ John hasn't thought of Paula, his old high school sweetheart, for years. This morning he woke up from a dream about her—wondering what she looked like and if she were married. Suddenly the phone rang. For some strange reason, he felt sure the call was from Paula. He was right. John now believes this is evidence for the existence of ESP.

_____ A psychic visits a college class and predicts that out of this class of 23 students, two individuals will have birthdays on the same day. When a tally of birthdays is taken, his prediction is supported. Many students leave class believing that the psychic has demonstrated true ESP.

_____ A National League baseball player dreams of hitting a bases-loaded triple. Two months later, during the final game of the World Series, he gets this exact triple and wins the game. He informs the media of his earlier dream and of his personal experience with ESP.

_____ Alone in her office at work, a mother suddenly sees a vivid image of her home on fire. She calls home and awakens the sitter. The sitter then notices smoke coming under the door and quickly extinguishes the fire. The media attribute the mother's visual images to ESP.

"What do you mean you didn't know that we were having a pop quiz today?"

GENDER AND CULTURAL DIVERSITY

Are the Gestalt Laws Universally True?

Objective 4.27: Do the Gestalt laws apply cross-culturally?

Gestalt psychologists conducted most of their work with formally educated people from urban European cultures. A.R. Luria (1976) was one of the first to question whether their laws held true for all participants, regardless of their education and cultural setting. Luria recruited a wide range of participants living in what was then the USSR. He included Ichkeri women from remote villages (with no formal education), collective farm activists (who were semiliterate), and female students in a teachers' school (with years of formal education).

Luria found that when presented with the stimuli shown in Figure 4.19, the formally trained female students were the only ones who identified the first three shapes

Figure 4.21 Luria's stimuli When you see these shapes, you readily identify them as circles, triangles, and other geometric forms. According to cross-cultural research, this is due to your formal educational training. If you were from a culture without formal education, you might identify them instead as familiar objects in your environment—"the circle is like the moon."

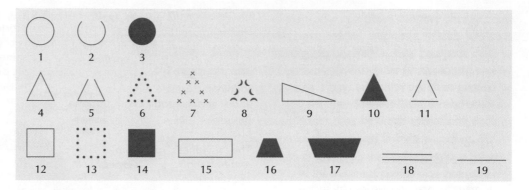

by their categorical name of "circle." Whether circles were made of solid lines, incomplete lines, or solid colors, they called them all circles. However, participants with no formal education named the shapes according to the objects they resembled. They called a circle a watch, plate, or moon, and referred to the square as a mirror, house, or apricot-drying board. When asked if items 12 and 13 from Figure 4.21 were alike, one woman answered, "No, they're not alike. This one's not like a watch, but that one's a watch because there are dots."

Apparently, the Gestalt laws of perceptual organization are valid only for people who have been schooled in geometrical concepts. But an alternative explanation for Luria's findings has also been suggested. Luria's study, as well as most research on visual perception and optical illusions, relies on two-dimensional presentations—either on a piece of paper or projected on a screen. It may be that experience with pictures and photographs (not formal education in geometrical concepts) is necessary for learning to interpret two-dimensional figures as portraying three-dimensional forms. Westerners who have had years of practice learning to interpret two-dimensional drawings of three-dimensional objects may not remember how much practice it took to learn the cultural conventions about judging the size and shape of objects drawn on paper (Berry et al., 2011; Keith, 2010).

CHECK & REVIEW   **STOP** *Before going on, be sure to complete this Check & Review. It is an invaluable study tool!*

Interpretation and Psychology Engages

Part A: Retrieval Practice

1. Without looking at the book, spend 10 minutes writing a free-form essay recalling all you can remember from the previous section.

2. Now, reread the previous section, and once again spend 10 minutes writing a free-form essay on the SAME material.

Part B: Practice Quiz

1. George Stratton was able to cope with an upside-down world thanks to _____.

2. When we tend to "see what we expect to see, this would be an example of _____.

3. The supposed ability to read other people's minds is called _____, perceiving objects or events that are inaccessible to the normal senses is known as _____, predicting the future is called _____, and moving or affecting objects without touching them is known as _____.

4. A major criticism of studies that indicate the existence of ESP is that they _____.

Check your answers in Appendix B.

www.wileyplus.com

WileyPLUS presents an on-line version of this textbook along with a wealth of study resources including quizzes, practice tests, flash cards, videos, animations and other activities designed to improve your mastery of the content. Working in conjunction with these study tools, the *Psychology in Action* WileyPLUS course features Professor Karen Huffman, author of this textbook, explaining and expanding upon some of the most challenging concepts in psychology. Here is a sample of the tutorial videos available for this chapter:

• Interactive animation illustrating the anatomy and functions of the eye and ear
• Anatomy of the eye and ear, featuring classroom demonstrations of peripheral vision and hearing loss
• Understanding vision, featuring Professor Huffman's classroom demonstration of Stratton's inversion goggles
• Interactive animation illustrating perception
• Virtual Field Trip inside the world of 3-D media to learn how binocular and monocular cues bring movies to life.

Key Terms

To assess your understanding of the **Key Terms** in Chapter 4, write a definition for each (in your own words), and then compare your definitions with those in the text.

Understanding Sensation
sensation (p. 126)
perception (p. 126)
bottom-up processing (p. 126)
top-down processing (p. 126)
psychophysics (p. 128)
absolute threshold (p. 129)
difference threshold (p. 129)
subliminal (p. 130)
sensory adaptation (p. 131)
gate-control theory (p. 131)

How We See and Hear
accommodation (p. 134)
retina (p. 134)
rods (p. 134)
cones (p. 134)

fovea (p. 134)
blind spot (p. 134)
trichromatic theory (p. 136)
opponent-process theory (p. 136)
audition (p. 138)
outer ear (p. 138)
middle ear (p. 138)
inner ear (p. 138)
cochlea [KOK-lee-uh] (p. 138)
place theory (p. 139)
frequency theory (p. 140)
conduction deafness (p. 140)
nerve deafness (p. 140)

Other Important Senses
olfaction (p. 141)
pheromones [FARE-oh-mones] (p. 142)
gustation (p. 143)

vestibular sense (p. 145)
kinesthesis (p. 145)

Understanding Perception
illusion (p. 146)
selective attention (p. 146)
feature detectors (p. 146)
habituation (p. 148)
perceptual constancy (p. 150)
depth perception (p. 152)
binocular cues (p. 152)
monocular cues (p. 152)
retinal disparity (p. 153)
convergence (p. 153)
perceptual set (p. 155)

Psychology Engages
extrasensory perception (ESP) (p. 157)

Chapter Summary

Understanding Sensation

Objective 4.1: Define sensation and perception.
Sensation refers to the process of detecting, converting, and transmitting sensory information from the external and internal environments to the

brain. In contrast, **perception** is the process of selecting, organizing, and interpreting sensory information into meaningful patterns.

Objective 4.2: Compare bottom-up processing with top-down processing.

Bottom-up processing refers to information processing that begins "at the bottom" with raw sensory data that are sent "up" to the brain for higher-level analysis. **Top-down processing** starts "at the top," with higher-level cognitive processes (such as, expectations and knowledge), and then works down.

Objective 4.3: Explain how raw sensory data are turned into signals the brain can understand.
First, our eyes and other sense organs contain specific cells, *receptors*, which detect and process the environmental stimuli. Next, information from these receptors is converted (transduced) into neural messages that are sent to the brain. These messages are then further converted (*coded*) into specific sensations (e.g., sight vs. sound).

Objective 4.4: Define psychophysics, and differentiate between absolute and difference thresholds.
Psychophysics studies the link between the physical characteristics of stimuli and our sensory experience of them. The **absolute threshold** is the minimum amount of a stimulus we can reliably detect, whereas the **difference threshold** is the minimal difference needed to notice a stimulus change.

Objective 4.5: What are the effects of subliminal stimuli?
Research shows that we can perceive **subliminal** stimuli that are presented below our conscious awareness. However, they are weak stimuli that have little or no persuasive effect.

Objective 4.6: Define sensory adaptation and explain why it is helpful.
Sensory adaptation is a sensory system's reduced responsiveness to unchanging stimuli. It offers important survival benefits because we can't afford to waste time paying attention to unchanging stimuli.

Objective 4.7: Explain the gate-control theory of pain perception.
Our experience of pain depends in part on a "gate" in the spinal cord that either blocks or allows pain signals to pass on to the brain.

How We See

Objective 4.8: What is light?
Light is composed of waves of electromagnetic energy of a certain wavelength. The *wavelength* of a light determines its *hue* (color); how often a light or sound wave cycles is known as the *frequency*; and the *amplitude* (height) of a light wave determines its intensity.

Objective 4.9: Identify the key structures and functions of the eye.
The function of the eye is to capture light and focus it on visual receptors that convert light energy to neural impulses. Light first enters through the pupil and lens, and then travels through to the retina. Neural impulses generated by the retina are then carried by the optic nerve to the brain. Receptor cells in the **retina** called **rods** are specialized for night vision, whereas **cones** are specialized for color and fine detail.

Objective 4.10: Identify common problems with vision.
Nearsightedness (myopia) and *farsightedness (hyperopia)* result from problems with the lens and cornea focusing the image in front or behind the retina. *Presbyopia* occurs when the lens becomes less flexible. *Light adaptation* and *dark adaptation* result from visual peculiarities related to the rods and cones. *Dichromats* and *monochromats* are terms related to problems with color perception.

Objective 4.11: Contrast the trichromatic, opponent-process, and dual-process theories of color vision.
The **trichromatic theory** proposes three color systems in the retina, each of which is maximally sensitive to blue, green, or red. The **opponent-process theory** also proposes three color systems but holds that each responds in an "either-or" fashion—blue or yellow, red or green, and black or white. According to the modern *dual-process theory*, both theories are correct.

The trichromatic system operates at the level of the retina, whereas the opponent-process system occurs in the brain.

How We Hear

Objective 4.12: Define audition and identify the three key sections of the ear.
The sense of hearing is known as **audition**. The ear has three parts: The **outer ear** conducts sound waves to the **middle ear**, which in turn conducts vibrations to the **inner ear**. Hair cells in the inner ear are bent by a traveling wave in the fluid of the **cochlea** and transduced into neural impulses. The neural message is then carried along the auditory nerve to the brain.

Objective 4.13: Briefly explain the physical properties of sound waves.
We hear sounds via *sound waves*, which result from rapid changes in air pressure caused by vibrating objects. The *wavelength* of these sound waves is sensed as the pitch of the sound. The *amplitude* of the waves is perceived as loudness. And the *complexity*, or mix of sound waves, is sensed as timbre, the purity or complexity of the tone.

Objective 4.14: Describe the place and frequency theories related to hearing.
Place theory proposes that pitch perception corresponds to the particular spot (or place) on the cochlea's basilar membrane that is most stimulated. **Frequency theory** suggests that pitch perception occurs when nerve impulses sent to the brain match the frequency of the sound waves. Both place and frequency theories are correct, but place theory best explains how we hear high-pitched sounds, whereas frequency theory best explains how we hear low-pitched sounds.

Objective 4.15: Differentiate between conduction and nerve deafness.
Conduction deafness results from problems with conducting sound waves to the cochlea, whereas **nerve deafness** involves damage to the inner ear or auditory nerve.

Other Important Senses

Objective 4.16: Briefly explain the processes of olfaction and gustation.
The sense of smell (**olfaction**) and the sense of taste (**gustation**) are called the chemical senses and are closely interrelated. The receptors for olfaction are at the top of the nasal cavity. The receptors for gustation are located primarily on the tongue and are sensitive to five basic tastes: salty, sweet, sour, bitter, and umami.

Objective 4.17: What are the body senses and how do they work?
The body senses include the skin senses, the **vestibular sense**, and **kinesthesis**. The skin senses detect touch or pressure, temperature, and pain. The vestibular apparatus is located in the inner ear and supplies balance information. The kinesthetic sense provides the brain with information about body posture and orientation, as well as body movement. The kinesthetic receptors are spread throughout the body in muscles, joints, and tendons.

Selection

Objective 4.18: What are illusions and why are they important?
Illusions are false or misleading perceptions that can be produced by actual physical distortions, as in desert mirages, or by errors in perception. These errors allow psychologists insight into normal perceptual processes.

Objective 4.19: Describe the selection process and its three key factors—selective attention, feature detectors, and habituation.
The selection process allows us to choose which of the billions of separate sensory messages will eventually be processed. **Selective attention** refers to the process of filtering out and attending only to important sensory messages. **Feature detectors** are specialized brain cells that distinguish between different sensory inputs. We **habituate** to unchanging stimuli and only pay attention when stimuli change in intensity, novelty, and contrast.

Organization

Objective 4.20: Describe the Gestalt laws of perceptual organization.
The Gestalt psychologists set forth laws explaining how people perceive form. The most fundamental principle is the distinction between figure and ground. Other visual laws include proximity, continuity, closure, and similarity.

Objective 4.21: What are perceptual constancies, and why are they important?
Through the **perceptual constancies** of *size, shape, color,* and *brightness,* we are able to perceive a stable environment, even though the actual sensory information we receive may be constantly changing. These constancies develop from prior experiences and learning.

Objective 4.22: How do we perceive depth and why are binocular and monocular cues important?
Depth perception allows us to accurately estimate the distance of perceived objects and thereby perceive the world in three dimensions. But how do we perceive a three-dimensional world with two-dimensional receptors called eyes? There are two major types of cues: **binocular cues,** which require two eyes, and **monocular cues,** which require only one eye. Two binocular cues are **retinal disparity** and **convergence.** Monocular cues include *linear perspective, interposition, relative size, texture gradient, aerial perspective, light and shadow, accommodation,* and *motion parallax.*

Interpretation and Psychology Engages

Objective 4.23: What factors influence how we interpret sensations?
Interpretation, the final stage of perception, can be influenced by *perceptual adaptation,* **perceptual set,** and *frame of reference.*

Objective 4.24: What can Helen Keller teach us about sensation and perception?
Although blind and deaf from an early age. Helen Keller used her remaining senses to achieve greatness, and reminded everyone to fully appreciate all our senses.

Objective 4.25: What is ESP and why is it so controversial?
Extrasensory perception (ESP) is the supposed ability to perceive things that go beyond the normal senses. ESP research has produced "fragile" results, and critics condemn its lack of experimental control and replicability.

Objective 4.26: Identify four forms of faulty reasoning behind ESP.
Belief in ESP may reflect the *confirmation bias, innumeracy, willingness to suspend disbelief,* and the "vividness" problem.

Objective 4.27: Do the Gestalt laws apply cross-culturally?
Some believe they only apply to cultures formally educated in geometrical concepts, while others say the laws reflect experience with two-dimensional figures portraying three-dimensional forms.

Understanding Sensation

Processing
- Bottom-up vs. top-down
- Converting the senses
- Reducing sensory input

Measuring the Senses
Psychophysics
(absolute and difference thresholds)

Sensory Adaptation
Sensory Adaptation
(little adaptation to pain)

How We See and Hear

❸ Behind the iris and pupil, the muscularly controlled lens focuses incoming light into an image on the light sensitive *retina*, located on the back surface of the fluid-filled eyeball. Note how the lens reverses the image from the right to left and top to bottom when it is projected on to the retina. The brain later reverses the visual input into the final "right-side up" image that we perceive.

❹ In the **retina**, light waves are detected and transduced into neural signals by vision receptor cells (rods and cones). **Rods** are visual receptors that detect white, black, and gray and are responsible for peripheral vision. They are most important in dim light and at night. **Cones** are visual receptors adapted for color, daytime, and detailed vision. They are sensitive to many wavelengths, but each is maximally sensitive to red, green, or blue. Note that the **fovea**, a tiny pit filled with cones, is responsible for our sharpest vision.

❺ Rods and cones project backwards to interneurons which communicate with ganglion cells in the retina. Ganglion cells then send visual input from the retina to the brain via the optic nerve.

❷ The light then passes through the *pupil*, a small adjustable opening. Muscles in the *iris* allow the *pupil* to dilate or constrict in response to light intensity or emotional factors.

❶ Light first enters through the *cornea*, which helps focus incoming light rays.

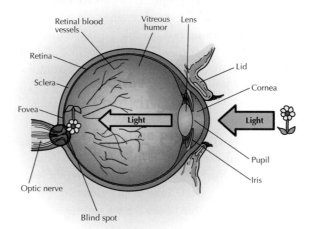

Step ❶ Sound waves enter ear canal, which focuses the sound and deflects the tympanic membrane.

Step ❷ Vibrations of the tympanic membrane strike the ossicles (hammer, anvil, and stirrup). The stirrup then hits the oval window.

Step ❸ Vibrations of the oval window create waves in the fluid-filled cochlea, which deflects the basilar membrane.

Step ❹ Movement of hair cells on the basilar membrane creates neural messages carried by the auditory nerve to the brain.

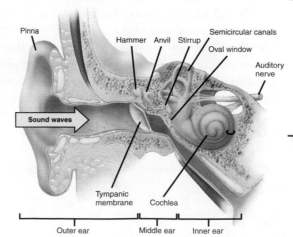

Other Important Senses

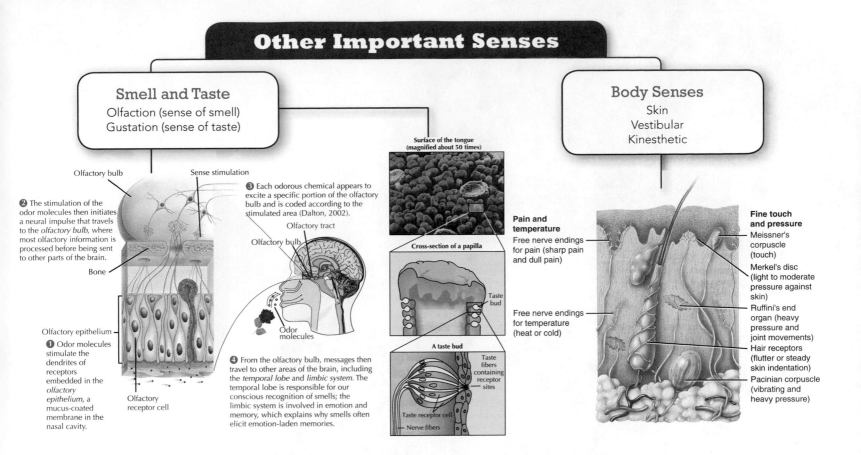

Smell and Taste
Olfaction (sense of smell)
Gustation (sense of taste)

Olfactory bulb   Sense stimulation

❷ The stimulation of the odor molecules then initiates a neural impulse that travels to the *olfactory bulb*, where most olfactory information is processed before being sent to other parts of the brain.

Bone

Olfactory epithelium

❶ Odor molecules stimulate the dendrites of receptors embedded in the *olfactory epithelium*, a mucus-coated membrane in the nasal cavity.

Olfactory receptor cell

❸ Each odorous chemical appears to excite a specific portion of the olfactory bulb and is coded according to the stimulated area (Dalton, 2002).

Olfactory tract

Olfactory bulb

Odor molecules

❹ From the olfactory bulb, messages then travel to other areas of the brain, including the *temporal lobe* and *limbic system*. The temporal lobe is responsible for our conscious recognition of smells; the limbic system is involved in emotion and memory, which explains why smells often elicit emotion-laden memories.

Surface of the tongue (magnified about 50 times)

Cross-section of a papilla

Taste bud

A taste bud

Taste fibers containing receptor sites

Taste receptor cell

Nerve fibers

Body Senses
Skin
Vestibular
Kinesthetic

Pain and temperature
Free nerve endings for pain (sharp pain and dull pain)

Free nerve endings for temperature (heat or cold)

Fine touch and pressure
Meissner's corpuscle (touch)

Merkel's disc (light to moderate pressure against skin)

Ruffini's end organ (heavy pressure and joint movements)

Hair receptors (flutter or steady skin indentation)

Pacinian corpuscle (vibrating and heavy pressure)

Understanding Perception

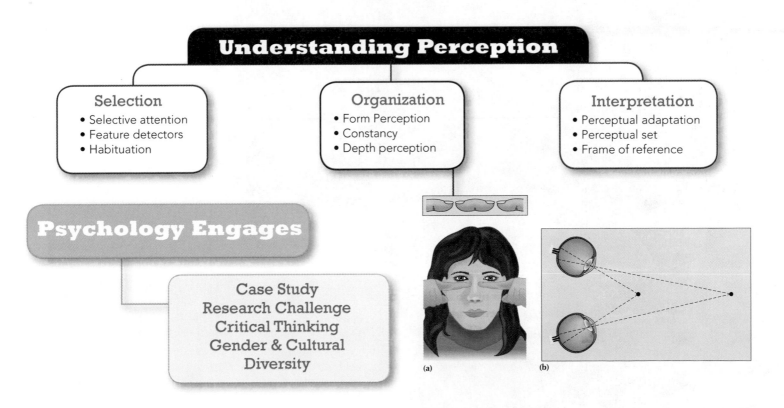

Selection
- Selective attention
- Feature detectors
- Habituation

Organization
- Form Perception
- Constancy
- Depth perception

Interpretation
- Perceptual adaptation
- Perceptual set
- Frame of reference

Psychology Engages

Case Study
Research Challenge
Critical Thinking
Gender & Cultural
Diversity

(a)   (b)

Chapter Five

States of Consciousness

On November 5, 1999, 16-year-old Erik Ramsey was a passenger in his friend's Camaro when it collided with a minivan. Erik sustained significant injuries but worst among them was the head injury that led to the formation of a blood clot in his brain, which caused an extremely rare and permanent condition known as *locked-in syndrome*.

Erik's consciousness, memory, emotions, and reason were all intact, and he could see, hear, and feel. But he could not move or speak. The only muscles that remained under Erik's voluntary command were the ones that controlled the up and down movement of his eyes. Soon after the accident a speech therapist suggested to Erik that since he could look up and down he could use this eye movement to say yes or no—up for *yes* and down for *no*.

"Erik, are you deaf?" was the first question the therapist asked. Erik looked down. "So you must be tired of people yelling at you?" Erik looked up opening his eyes emphatically (Foer, 2008). What if Erik had not been able to move his eyes? If he couldn't communicate at all, would he still be "conscious"?

People commonly use the term *consciousness*, but what exactly does it mean? Is it simple awareness? What would it be like to be unaware? How can we study the contents of our consciousness when the only tool of discovery is the object itself?

In this chapter, we begin with a general overview of consciousness, and then go on to see how consciousness changes with circadian rhythms, sleep, and dreams. We also look at psychoactive drugs and their effects on consciousness. Finally, we explore alternative routes to altered consciousness through meditation and hypnosis.

No problem can be solved from the same level of consciousness that created it.

ALBERT EINSTEIN

The woods are lovely, dark and deep. But I have promises to keep, and miles to go before I sleep.

ROBERT FROST

I don't do drugs, my dreams are frightening enough.

M.C. ESCHER

Meditation is the dissolution of thoughts in eternal awareness or pure consciousness without objectification, knowing without thinking, merging finitude in infinity.

VOLTAIRE

Chapter Outline

167

MYTH BUSTERS

True or False?

1. Our brains "turn off" when we sleep.

2. Some people never dream.

3. Approximately two-thirds of all American adults suffer from sleep problems.

4. Sleep deprivation and shift work are key contributors to industrial and automobile accidents.

5. People who suffer from narcolepsy may fall instantly asleep while walking, talking, or driving a car.

6. Since the beginning of civilization, people of all cultures have used and abused psychoactive drugs.

7. Even small initial doses of cocaine can be fatal because they interfere with the electrical signals of the heart.

8. An amount of LSD the size of an aspirin tablet is enough to produce psychoactive effects in over 3000 people.

9. People can be hypnotized against their will.

10. Hypnotized people can perform acts of superhuman strength.

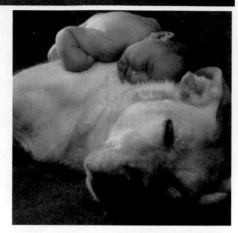

Answers: 1. F, 2. F, 3. T, 4. T, 5. T, 6. T, 7. T, 8. T, 9. F, 10. F. Detailed answers found in this chapter.

Understanding Consciousness

Objective 5.1: Define and describe consciousness and alternate states of consciousness (ASCs).

Consciousness Organism's awareness of its own self and surroundings (Damasio, 1999)

What is **consciousness**? One common definition is fairly simple: *an organism's awareness of its own self and surroundings* (Damasio, 1999). William James, the first American psychologist, likened consciousness to a stream that's constantly changing, yet always the same. It meanders and flows, sometimes where the person wills and sometimes not. However, through the process of *selective attention* (Chapter 4), we can control our consciousness by deliberate concentration and full attention. For example, at the present moment you are (I hope) fully awake and concentrating on the words on this page. At times, however, your control may weaken, and your stream of consciousness may drift to thoughts of a computer you want to buy, your job, or an attractive classmate.

The centermost processes of the brain with which consciousness is presumably associated are simply not understood. They are so far beyond our comprehension that no one I know of has been able to imagine their nature.

Roger W. Sperry

Levels of Awareness: A Continuum

In addition to meandering and flowing, your "stream of consciousness" also varies in depth. Your level of consciousness is not an all-or-nothing phenomenon—conscious or unconscious. Instead, it exists along a continuum. As you can see in the Step-by-Step Diagram 5.1, this continuum goes from high awareness and sharp, focused alertness at one extreme, to middle levels of awareness such as daydreaming, to nonconsciousness and coma at the other extreme. Other than being awake, two of the more common states of consciousness are sleep and dreaming. You may think of yourself as being unconscious while you sleep, but that's not the case. Rather, you are in an **alternate state of consciousness (ASC)**.

Alternate States of Consciousness (ASCs) Mental states, other than ordinary waking consciousness, found during sleep, dreaming, psychoactive drug use, hypnosis, and so on

Controlled versus Automatic Processes

Objective 5.2: Contrast controlled versus automatic processing.

Consciousness exists on a continuum, and it also involves both *controlled* and *automatic* processes. When you're working at a demanding task or learning something new, such as how to drive a car, your consciousness is at the high end of the continuum. These

Step-by-StepDiagram5.1

Understanding Consciousness

One of the oldest philosophical debates is the *mind–body problem*. Is the "mind" (consciousness and other mental functions) fundamentally different from matter (the body)? How can a supposedly nonmaterial mind influence a physical body and vice versa? Most neuropsychologists today believe the mind *is* the brain and *consciousness* involves an activation and integration of several parts of the brain. However, awareness is generally limited to the *cerebral cortex*, particularly the frontal lobes. And arousal generally results from *brain-stem activation* (Banich & Compton, 2011; Carlson, 2011; Zillmer, Spiers, & Culbertson, 2011).

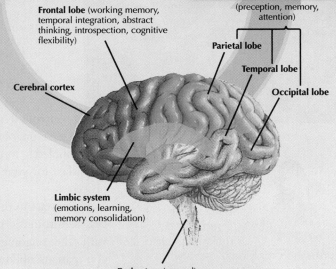

Frontal lobe (working memory, temporal integration, abstract thinking, introspection, cognitive flexibility)

(preception, memory, attention)

Parietal lobe

Temporal lobe

Occipital lobe

Cerebral cortex

Limbic system (emotions, learning, memory consolidation)

Brain stem (arousal)

Levels of Awareness

CONTROLLED PROCESSES
Require focused, maximum attention (e.g., studying for an exam, learning to drive a car)

High Awareness

AUTOMATIC PROCESSES
Require minimal attention (e.g., walking to class while talking on a cell phone, listening to your boss while daydreaming)

Middle Awareness

SUBCONSCIOUS
Below conscious awareness (e.g., subliminal perception, sleeping, dreaming)

NO AWARENESS
Biologically based lowest level of awareness (e.g., head injuries, anesthesia, coma); also the *unconscious mind* (a Freudian concept discussed in Chapter 13) reportedly consisting of unacceptable thoughts and feelings too painful to be admitted to consciousness)

Low Awareness

Alternate States of Consciousness (ASCs): Can exist on many levels of awareness, from high awareness to no awareness (e.g., drugs, sensory deprivation, sleep, dreaming, etc.)

Problems with automatic processing? Automatic processes are generally helpful. However, there are times when we are wrestling with our inner robots and operating on "automatic pilot" and don't want to be. Consider the problems of novelist Colin Wilson (1967): "When I first learned to type, I had to do it painfully and with much nervous wear and tear. But at a certain stage a miracle occurred, and this complicated operation was learned by a useful robot that I conceal in my subconscious mind. Now I only have to think about what I want to say; my robot secretary does the typing. He is really very useful. He also drives the car for me, speaks French (not very well), and occasionally gives lectures at American universities. [My robot] is most annoying when I am tired, because then he tends to take over most of my functions without even asking me. I have even caught him making love to my wife" (p. 98).

controlled processes demand focused attention and generally interfere with other ongoing activities. Have you ever been so absorbed during an exam that you completely forgot your surroundings until the instructor announced, "Time is up," and asked for your paper? This type of focused attention is the hallmark of controlled processes.

In contrast to the high awareness and focused attention required for controlled processes, **automatic processes** require minimal attention and generally do not interfere with other ongoing activities. Think back to your childhood when you first marveled at your parents' ability to drive a car. Are you surprised that you can now effortlessly steer a car, work the brakes, and change gears all at one time with little or no focused attention? Learning a new task requires complete concentration and *controlled processing*. Once that task is well learned, you can switch to *automatic processing* (DeKleine & Van der Lubbe, 2011; Scheel, 2010).

Controlled Processes Mental activities requiring focused attention that generally interfere with other ongoing activities

Automatic Processes Mental activities requiring minimal attention and having little impact on other activities

StudyTip

Keep in mind that you need to use controlled processing when studying this or any material you want to learn and remember. Although reading is a well-learned automatic process for most college students, you can't casually (automatically) read complex, new material (like this text) if you want to do well on upcoming quizzes and exams.

 **CHECK & REVIEW**  **STOP** *Before going on, be sure to complete this Check & Review. It is an invaluable study tool!*

Understanding Consciousness

Part A: Retrieval Practice

1. Without looking at the book, spend 10 minutes writing a free-form essay recalling all you can remember from the previous section.

2. Now, reread the previous section, and once again spend 10 minutes writing a free-form essay on the SAME material.

   (Although time consuming, this exercise has been shown to be the single best way to improve your test scores!

For more information, check out //www.sciencemag.org/content/early/2011/01/19/science.1199327.abstract)

Part B: Practice Quiz

1. _____ is (are) best defined as an organism's awareness of its own self and surroundings. (a) Alternate states of consciousness (ASCs); (b) Consciousness; (c) States of consciousness; (d) Selective attention

2. What are alternate states of consciousness (ASCs)?

3. Controlled processes require _____ attention, whereas automatic processes need _____ attention.

4. As you read this text, you should _____. (a) be in an alternate state of consciousness; (b) employ automatic processing; (c) let your stream of consciousness take charge; (d) employ controlled processing

Check your answers in Appendix B.

Sleep and Dreams

Having explored the definition and description of everyday, waking consciousness, we now turn to two of our most common alternate states of consciousness (ASCs)—sleep and dreaming. These ASCs are fascinating to both scientists and the general public. Why are we born with a mechanism that forces us to sleep and dream for approximately a third of our lives? How can an ASC that requires reduced awareness and responsiveness to our environment be healthy? What are the functions and causes of sleep and dreams?

Circadian Rhythms: Sleep and the 24-Hour Cycle

Objective 5.3: What are circadian rhythms and how do they affect our lives?

To understand sleep and dreaming, we need to first explore the topic of **circadian rhythms**. Most animals have adapted to our planet's cycle of days and nights by developing a pattern of bodily functions that wax and wane over each 24-hour period. Our sleep–wake cycle, alertness, moods, learning efficiency, blood pressure, metabolism, pulse rate, and other responses all follow circadian rhythms (Daan, 2011; Karatsoreos et al., 2011; Kyriacou & Hastings, 2010; Sack et al., 2007). Usually, these activities reach their peak during the day and their low point at night. What controls our circadian rhythms? (See Figure 5.1 below.)

Circadian [sir-KADE-ee-un] Rhythms Biological changes that occur on a 24-hour cycle (circa = "about" and dies = "day")

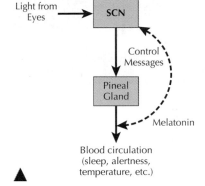

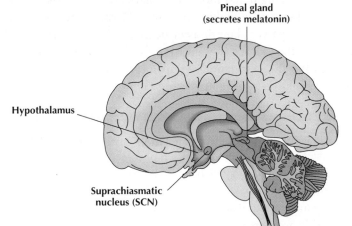

(a) Circadian rhythms are regulated by a part of the hypothalamus, the *suprachiasmatic nucleus* (SCN), and the pineal gland.

(b) The SCN receives information about light and darkness from the eyes and then sends control messages to the *pineal gland*, which releases *melatonin*—a hormone thought to influence sleep, alertness, and body temperature. Like other feedback loops in the body, the level of melatonin in the blood is sensed by the SCN, which then can modify the output of the pineal to maintain the optimal level.

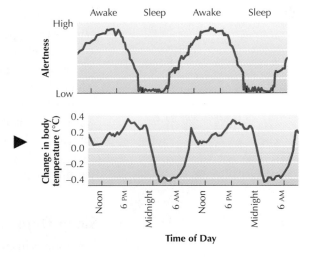

(c) and (d) Note how our degree of alertness and core body temperature rise and fall in similar ways.

Figure 5.1 Understanding circadian rhythms

Psychology at Work

Dangers of Sleeping on the Job!

Disruptions in circadian rhythms lead to increased fatigue, decreased concentration, sleep disorders, depression, and other health problems (Daan, 2011; Karatsoreos

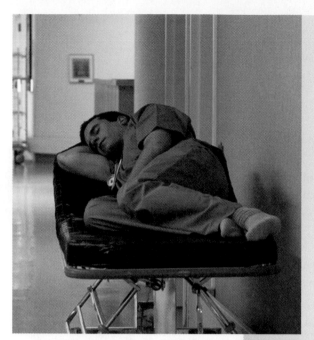

et al., 2011; Kyriacou & Hastings, 2010; Salvatore et al., 2008). As a student, you may find it comforting to know that your late-night study sessions and full- or part-time night jobs help explain your fatigue and other complaints. Less reassuring is the knowledge that a large percentage of employees in the United States (primarily in the fields of health care, data processing, and transportation) have rotating work schedules that create many of the same problems. Although many physicians, nurses, police, and others who have rotating work schedules manage to function well, studies do find that shift work and sleep deprivation lead to decreased concentration and productivity—and increased accidents (Dawson et al., 2011; Dorrian et al., 2011; Pruchnicki, Wu, & Belenky, 2011; Williamson et al., 2011).

For example, in February, 2011, an air-traffic controller in Knoxville, Tennessee fell asleep on the job for five hours. A month later a second controller at Washington's Reagan national airport fell asleep for at least 24 minutes. Both incidents occurred during the midnight shift. Similarly, in a major review of Japanese near-collision train incidents, 82 percent took place between midnight and morning (Charland, 1992). Also, some of the worst recent disasters, including the Union Carbide chemical accident in Bhopal, India, the nuclear power plant disaster in Chernobyl, the Alaskan oil spill from the *Exxon Valdez*, and the Gulf of Mexico BP oil spill in 2010 all occurred during the night shift. And official investigations of airline crashes often cite pilot shift work and sleep deprivation as possible contributing factors.

Although catastrophic accidents can sometimes be traced to simple, but unusual, coincidences, we need to recognize that shift workers may be fighting a dangerous battle with their own circadian rhythms. What can be done to help? Some research shows that workers find it easier to adjust when their schedules are shifted from days to evenings to nights (8–4, 4–12, 12–8). This may be because it's easier to go to sleep later than normal rather than earlier. Also, when shifts are rotated every three weeks, rather than every week, productivity increases and accidents decrease. Finally, some research suggests that brief naps for shift workers (or anyone) can help increase performance and learning potential (Faraut et al., 2011; Ficca et al., 2010; Roach et al., 2011).

Not only can rotating work schedules disrupt circadian cycles, but so can flying across several time zones. Have you ever taken a long airline flight and felt fatigued, sluggish, and irritable for the first few days after arriving? If so, you experienced symptoms of *jet lag*. Like rotating shift work, jet lag correlates with decreased alertness, decreased mental agility, exacerbation of psychiatric disorders, and overall reduced efficiency (Leglise, 2008; Paul et al., 2011; Sack, 2010). Jet lag also tends to be worse when we fly eastward rather than westward. This is because our bodies adjust more readily to going to sleep later, rather than earlier.

Sleep Deprivation

Disruptions in circadian cycles due to shift work and jet lag can have serious effects. But what about long-term sleep deprivation? History tells us that during Roman times and in the Middle Ages, sleep deprivation was a form of torture. Today, the armed forces of the United States and other countries sometimes use loud, blaring music and noise to disrupt their enemy's sleep.

Scientifically exploring the effects of severe sleep loss is limited by obvious ethical concerns. Research is also hampered by practical considerations. For example, after about 72 hours without sleep, research participants unwillingly slip into brief, repeated periods of "microsleep" lasting a few seconds at a time. To complicate things further, sleep deprivation increases stress, making it difficult to separate the effects of sleep deprivation from those of stress.

Despite these problems, sleep researchers have documented several hazards related to sleep deprivation that coincide with the previously mentioned effects of disrupted circadian cycles. Sleep deprivation is correlated with significant mood alterations, decreased self-esteem, reduced concentration and motivation, increased irritability, lapses in attention, reduced motor skills, and increased cortisol levels (a sign of stress) (Doane et al., 2010; Martella, Casagrande, & Lupiáñez, 2011; Orzel-Gryglewska, 2010). Severe sleep deprivation in rats results in even more serious, and sometimes fatal, side effects (Buysse et al., 2008; Cirelli et al., 1999; Siegel, 2008; Süer et al., 2011; Zhao et al., 2010). In addition, lapses in attention among sleep-deprived pilots, physicians, truck drivers, and other workers can also cause serious accidents and cost thousands of lives (Dorrian, Sweeney, & Dawson, 2011; Williamson et al., 2011; Yegneswaran & Shapiro, 2007).

Interestingly, however, many physiological functions are not significantly disrupted by periods of sleep deprivation. In fact, in 1965, a 17-year-old student named Randy Gardner, who wanted to earn a place in the *Guinness Book of World Records*, stayed awake for 264 consecutive hours. He did become irritable and had to remain active to stay awake. But he did not become incoherent or psychotic (Coren, 1996; Sleep Education Blog, 2010; Spinweber, 1993). After his marathon sleep deprivation, Randy slept a mere 14 hours and then returned to his usual 8-hour sleep cycle (Dement, 1992).

 TRY THIS YOURSELF

Are You Sleep Deprived?

Part 1 Set up a small mirror next to the text and see if you can copy the star using your nondominant hand while watching your hand in the mirror. The task is difficult, and sleep-deprived people typically make more errors than those who are not sleep deprived.

Part 2 Now give yourself one point each time you answer yes to the following questions:

Do you often fall asleep . . .
watching TV?
during boring meetings or lectures or in warm rooms?
after heavy meals or after a small amount of alcohol?
while relaxing after dinner?
within five minutes of getting into bed?

In the morning, do you generally . . .
need an alarm clock to wake up at the right time?
struggle to get out of bed?
hit the snooze bar several times to get more sleep?

During the day, do you . . .
feel tired, irritable, and stressed out?
have trouble concentrating and remembering?
feel slow when it comes to critical thinking, problem solving, and being creative?
feel drowsy while driving?
need a nap to get through the day?
have dark circles around your eyes?

Sleep deprivation Insufficient sleep can seriously affect your college grades, as well as your physical health, motor skills, and overall mood.

If you answered yes to three or more items, you are probably sleep deprived.

Source: Quiz adapted and reprinted from Maas, 1999, with permission.

Stages of Sleep: How Scientists Study Sleep

Objective 5.4: List the phases of sleep and describe a typical night's sleep.

Sleep is an important component of our circadian rhythms. Each night, we normally go through five phases of sleep: Stages 1, 2, 3, 4 and REM (rapid eye movement). And each phase has its own rhythm and corresponding changes in brain activity and behavior. How do we know this? How can scientists study private mental events like sleep?

Surveys and interviews can provide some information about the nature of sleep. But researchers in sleep laboratories use a number of sophisticated instruments to study physiological changes during sleep.

Imagine that you are a participant in a sleep experiment. When you arrive at the sleep lab, you are assigned one of several bedrooms. The researcher hooks you up to various physiological recording devices (Concept Organizer 5.1a). You'll probably need a night or two to adapt to all this equipment before the researchers can begin to monitor your typical night's sleep.

Sleep-Assisted Learning

Myth: It is easy to learn complicated things, like a foreign language, while asleep. Although some learning can occur during the lighter stages (1 and 2) of sleep, the processing and retention of this material is minimal (Lilienfeld, 2010; Ogilvie, Wilkinson, & Allison, 1989). Wakeful learning is much more effective and efficient.

Early Stages of Sleep

Once adapted, you are ready for the researchers to monitor your typical night's sleep. As your eyes close and you begin to relax, the researcher in the next room notices that your EEG recordings have moved from the wave pattern associated with normal wakefulness, *beta waves*, to the slower *alpha waves*, which indicate drowsy relaxation (Concept Organizer 5.1b).

As you continue relaxing, your brain's electrical activity slows even further. You are now in *Stage 1* sleep. During this stage, your breathing becomes more regular, your heart rate slows, and your blood pressure decreases. But you could still be readily awakened. During this relaxed "presleep" period, you may experience strange images and unusual bodily sensations resembling *hallucinations*. This aptly-named *hypnagogic state* is characterized by feelings of floating, weightlessness, visual images (such as flashing lights or colors), or swift, jerky movements and a corresponding feeling of slipping or falling. Hypnagogic experiences are sometimes incorporated into fragmented dreams and remembered in the morning. They also may explain reported accounts of alien abduction, which typically occur while the victim is falling asleep, and many abductees report "strange flashes of light" and "floating off the bed."

If you are not awakened during Stage 1 sleep, you will relax more deeply and slide gently into *Stage 2* sleep. This stage is noted on your electroencephalograph by occasional short bursts of rapid, high-amplitude brain waves known as *sleep spindles*. During Stage 2 sleep, you become progressively more relaxed and less responsive to the external environment.

Even deeper levels of sleep are found in *Stages 3* and *4*, which are marked by the appearance of slow, high-amplitude *delta* waves. It is very hard to awaken you in Stages 3 and 4, even by shouting and shaking. Stage 4 sleep also is the time when children are most likely to wet the bed and when most sleepwalking occurs.

REM and NREM Sleep

Concept Organizer 5.1c also shows an interesting phenomenon that occurs at the end of the downward part of the first sleep cycle. You reverse back through Stage 3, and then to Stage 2. But instead of reentering the calm, relaxed Stage 1, something totally different happens. Quite abruptly, your scalp recordings display a pattern of small-amplitude, fast-wave activity, similar in many ways to an awake, vigilant person's brain waves. Your breathing and pulse rates become fast and irregular. And your genitals very likely show signs of arousal (an erection or vaginal lubrication).

Interestingly, although your brain and body are giving many signs of active arousal, your musculature is deeply relaxed and unresponsive. The sleeper is in some ways experiencing the deepest stage of sleep. Yet, in other ways the lightest. Because of these

ConceptOrganizer5.1

Scientific Study of Sleep and Dreaming

(a) Participants in sleep research labs wear electrodes on their heads and bodies to measure brain and bodily responses during the sleep cycle. An **electroencephalograph (EEG)** detects and records brain-wave changes by means of small electrodes on the scalp. Other electrodes measure muscle activity and eye movements.

Awake
Low-voltage, high-frequency beta waves

Drowsy
Alpha waves prominent

Stage 1 sleep
Theta waves prominent

Stage 2 sleep
Sleep spindles and mixed EEG activity

Slow-wave sleep (stage 3 and stage 4 sleep)
Progressively more delta waves (stage 4 shown)

REM sleep
Low-voltage, high-frequency waves

Note how REM sleep lengthens over time

Awake

Stages of sleep

Hours of sleep

(b) The stages of sleep, defined by telltale changes in brain waves, are indicated by the jagged lines. The compact brain waves of alertness gradually lengthen as we drift into Stages 1–4. By the end of Stage 4, a change in body position generally occurs and heart rate, blood pressure, and respiratory rates all decrease. The sleeper then reverses through Stages 3 and 2 before entering the first REM period of the night. Although the brain and body are giving many signs of active arousal during REM sleep, the musculature is deeply relaxed and unresponsive. Sleepers awakened from REM sleep often report vivid, bizarre dreams. Those awakened from Stages 1–4 sleep often have more peaceful thoughts.

(c) Your first sleep cycle generally lasts about 90 minutes (from awake and alert, downward through Stages 1-4, and then back up through Stages 3, 2, and REM. If you sleep 8 hours, you'll typically go through approximately four or 5 sleep cycles (as shown by the vertical dotted lines). Note, however, that each stage is a bit different with the overall amount of REM sleep increasing as the night progresses, while the amout of deep sleep (Stages 3 and 4) decreases. By early morning, you'll spend nearly all your sleep time in Stages 1, 2. and REM.

contradictory qualities, this stage is sometimes referred to as "paradoxical sleep." The term *paradoxical* means "apparently self-contradictory." (As a critical thinker, can you see how the muscle "paralysis" of paradoxical sleep may serve an important adaptive function? Think about the problems and dangers that would ensue if we were able to move around and act out our dreams while we were sleeping.)

During this stage of "paradoxical sleep," rapid eye movements occur under your closed eyelids. When researchers discovered that these eye movements are a clear, biological signal that the sleeper is dreaming, they labeled this stage **rapid-eye-movement sleep (REM)**. Although some people believe they do not dream, when sleepers are awakened during REM sleep they almost always report dreaming. Because

Rapid-Eye-Movement (REM) Sleep Stage of sleep marked by rapid eye movements, high-frequency brain waves, paralysis of large muscles, and dreaming

Non–Rapid-Eye-Movement (NREM) Sleep Stages 1 to 4 of sleep with Stage 1 as the lightest level and Stage 4 as the deepest level

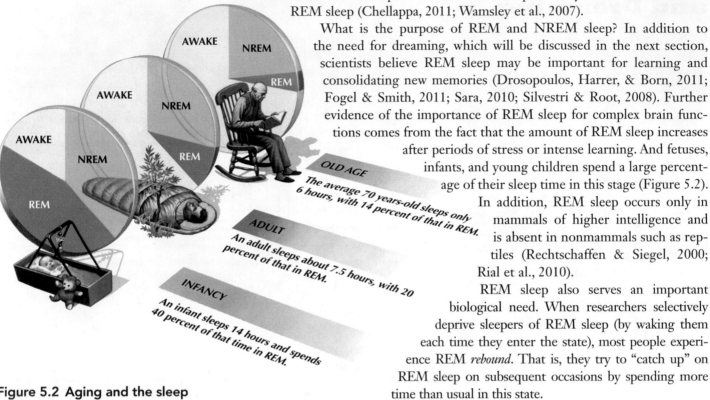

Figure 5.2 Aging and the sleep cycle Our biological need for sleep changes throughout our life span. The pie charts in this figure show the relative amounts of REM sleep (dark blue), non-REM sleep (medium blue), and awake time (light blue) that the average person experiences as an infant, an adult, and an elderly person.

OLD AGE
The average 70 years-old sleeps only 6 hours, with 14 percent of that in REM.

ADULT
An adult sleeps about 7.5 hours, with 20 percent of that in REM.

INFANCY
An infant sleeps 14 hours and spends 40 percent of that time in REM.

of the importance of dreaming and the fact that REM sleep is so different from the other periods of sleep, Stages 1 to 4 are often collectively called **NREM (or non–rapid-eye-movement) sleep**. Keep in mind that dreaming does occur during NREM sleep, but less frequently. Contrary to popular misconceptions, recent research also shows that dream reports from NREM sleep are very similar to those from REM sleep (Chellappa, 2011; Wamsley et al., 2007).

What is the purpose of REM and NREM sleep? In addition to the need for dreaming, which will be discussed in the next section, scientists believe REM sleep may be important for learning and consolidating new memories (Drosopoulos, Harrer, & Born, 2011; Fogel & Smith, 2011; Sara, 2010; Silvestri & Root, 2008). Further evidence of the importance of REM sleep for complex brain functions comes from the fact that the amount of REM sleep increases after periods of stress or intense learning. And fetuses, infants, and young children spend a large percentage of their sleep time in this stage (Figure 5.2).

In addition, REM sleep occurs only in mammals of higher intelligence and is absent in nonmammals such as reptiles (Rechtschaffen & Siegel, 2000; Rial et al., 2010).

REM sleep also serves an important biological need. When researchers selectively deprive sleepers of REM sleep (by waking them each time they enter the state), most people experience REM *rebound*. That is, they try to "catch up" on REM sleep on subsequent occasions by spending more time than usual in this state.

NREM sleep may be even more important to our biological functioning than REM sleep. When people are deprived of *total* sleep, they spend more time in NREM sleep during their first uninterrupted night (Borbely, 1982). Apparently, it is only after our need for NREM sleep has been satisfied each night that we begin to devote more time to REM sleep. Furthermore, studies show that adults who are "short sleepers" (5 or fewer hours each night) spend less time in REM sleep than do "long sleepers" (9 or more hours each night). Similarly, infants get more sleep and have a higher percentage of REM sleep than do adults (see again Figure 5.2). Apparently, the greater the total amount of sleep, the greater the percentage of REM sleep.

 **TEST YOURSELF**

The Sleep Cycle in Cats

During NREM (non–rapid-eye-movement) sleep, cats often sleep in an upright position. With the onset of REM sleep, cats normally lie down. Can you explain why?

Answer: During REM sleep, large muscles are temporarily paralyzed, which causes the cat to lose motor control and lie down.

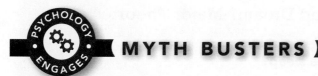

MYTH BUSTERS

Common Myths about Sleep and Dreams

Objective 5.5: List six common myths about sleep.

Before reading on, test your personal knowledge of sleep and dreaming by reviewing these common myths.

- *Myth: Everyone needs 8 hours of sleep a night to maintain sound mental and physical health.* Although most of us average 7.6 hours of sleep a night, some people get by on an incredible 15 to 30 minutes. Others may need as much as 11 hours (Colrain, 2011; Daan, 2011; Doghramji, 2000; Maas et al., 1999).

- *Myth: Dreams have special or symbolic meaning.* Many people mistakenly believe dreams can foretell the future, reflect unconscious desires, have secret meaning, can reveal the truth, or contain special messages, but scientific research finds little or no support for these beliefs (Blum, 2011; Carey, 2009; Domhoff, 2010; Hobson et al., 2011; Lilienfeld et al., 2010; Morewedge & Norton, 2009).

- *Myth: Some people never dream.* In rare cases, adults with certain brain injuries or disorders do not dream (Solms, 1997). But otherwise, virtually all adults regularly dream. Even people who firmly believe they never dream report dreams if they are repeatedly awakened during an overnight study in a sleep laboratory. Children also dream regularly. For example, between ages 3 and 8, they dream during approximately 20 to 28 percent of their sleep time (Foulkes, 1993, 1999). Apparently, almost everyone dreams, but some people don't remember their dreams.

- *Myth: Dreams last only a few seconds and only occur in REM sleep.* Research shows that some dreams seem to occur in "real time." For example, a dream that seemed to last 20 minutes probably did last approximately 20 minutes (Dement & Wolpert, 1958). Dreams also occur in NREM sleep.

- *Myth: When genital arousal occurs during sleep, it means the sleeper is having a sexual dream.* When sleepers are awakened during this time, they are no more likely to report sexual dreams than at other times.

- *Myth: Most people only dream in black and white, and blind people don't dream.* People frequently report seeing color in their dreams. Those who are blind do dream, but only report visual images if they lost their sight after age seven (Lilienfeld et al., 2010).

- *Myth: Dreaming of dying can be fatal.* This is a good opportunity to exercise your critical thinking skills. Where did this myth come from? Although many people have personally experienced and recounted a fatal dream, how would we scientifically prove or disprove this belief?

 # CHECK & REVIEW

STOP *Before going on, be sure to complete this Check & Review. It is an invaluable study tool!*

Circadian Rhythms and Stages of Sleep

Part A: Retrieval Practice

1. Without looking at the book, spend 10 minutes writing a free-form essay recalling all you can remember from the previous section.

2. Now, reread the previous section, and once again spend 10 minutes writing a free-form essay on the SAME material.

Part B: Practice Quiz

1. Biological rhythms that occur on a daily basis are called _____ rhythms.

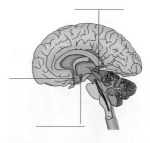

2. Identify the three main areas of the brain involved in the operation of circadian rhythms in the figure above.

3. Jet lag primarily results from _____. (a) sleep deprivation; (b) disruption of the circadian rhythms; (c) the effect of light on the pineal gland; (d) disruption of brain-wave patterns that occurs at high altitudes.

4. The machine that measures the voltage (or brain waves) that the brain produces is _____.

5. Just before sleep onset, brain waves move from _____ waves, indicating normal wakefulness, to _____ waves associated with drowsy relaxation. (a) beta, alpha; (b) theta, delta; (c) alpha, beta; (d) sigma, chi

6. Which of the six common myths about sleep did you previously believe to be factual?

Check your answers in Appendix B.

Why do we sleep? According to the *evolutionary/circadian theory*, a major function of sleep is to keep humans and other animals still and quiet during the time their most dangerous predators are active. In contrast, repair/restoration theory suggests we need sleep to rest and recuperate.

Evolutionary/Circadian Theory Sleep evolved to conserve energy and as protection from predators; also serves as part of the circadian cycle

Repair/Restoration Theory Sleep serves a recuperative function, allowing organisms to repair or replenish key factors

Why Do We Sleep and Dream? Major Theories and Recent Findings

Objective 5.6: Why do we sleep?

In addition to the growing body of facts that we now know about sleep and dreaming, scientists also have developed several important, overarching theories, which we'll explore in this section.

Two Major Theories of Sleep

Why do we need to sleep? No one knows precisely all the functions sleep serves, but there are two prominent theories. The **evolutionary/circadian theory** emphasizes the relationship of sleep to basic circadian rhythms. According to this view, sleep evolved so that human and nonhuman animals could conserve energy when they were not foraging for food or seeking mates. Sleep also serves to keep them still at times when predators are active (Acerbi & Nunn, 2011; Capellini et al., 2010; Siegel, 2008; Swami, 2011). In addition, the evolutionary/ circadian theory helps explain differences in sleep patterns across species (Figure 5.3). Opossums sleep many hours each day because they are relatively safe in their environment and are able to easily find food and shelter. In comparison, sheep and horses sleep very little because their diets require constant foraging for food. In addition, their only defense against predators is vigilance and running away.

In contrast, the **repair/restoration theory** suggests that sleep helps us recuperate from depleting daily activities. Essential factors in our brain or body are apparently repaired or replenished while we sleep. We recover not only from physical fatigue but also from emotional and intellectual demands (Colrain, 2011).

Which theory is correct? Both theories have merit. Obviously, we need to repair and restore ourselves after a busy day. But bears don't hibernate all winter simply to recover from a busy summer. Like humans and other animals, they also need to conserve energy when the environment is hostile. It may be that sleep initially served to conserve energy and keep us out of trouble, and that, over time, it has evolved to allow for repair and restoration.

PSYCHOLOGY ENGAGES **TEST YOURSELF**

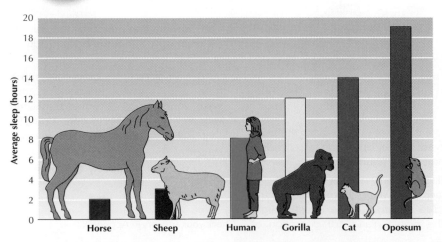

Figure 5.3 Average daily hours of sleep for different mammals How does the fact that an opossum spends almost 20 hours a day sleeping, yet a horse spends only 2 hours support the evolutionary/circadian theory?

Answer: According to the evolutionary/circadian theory of sleep, animals that sleep the longest are least threatened by the environment and can easily find food and shelter. Note how the opossum and cat spend longer hours in sleep than the horse and sheep, presumably because of differences in diet and the number of predators.

Three Major Theories of Dreams

Objective 5.7: Why do we dream?

Is there special meaning and information in our dreams? Why do we have bad dreams? Why do we dream at all? These questions have long fascinated writers and poets, as well as psychologists.

Psychoanalytic View One of the oldest and most scientifically controversial explanations for why we dream comes from the founder of psychoanalysis, Sigmund Freud (1900/1953), who believed dreams were the "royal road to the unconscious" because they reveal a dreamer's unconscious thoughts, feelings, and motivations. And one of the main purposes of dreaming is supposedly *wish fulfillment*, the gratification of unconscious desires and needs (e.g., a lonely person's dream about romance, or a child's dream of revenge against a class bully).

According to Freud, dreams have both a **manifest content** (the "surface" story that the dreamer reports) and a **latent content** (the unconscious, hidden meaning). Because this latent content contains threatening unconscious wishes and drives, it must be transformed into acceptable *symbols* within the dream's story line or manifest content. Thus, a dream about being with an attractive stranger on a train going through a tunnel (*manifest content*) might represent a hidden desire for forbidden sex (*latent content*). By disguising the threatening, personally unacceptable desires as symbols, the dreamer avoids anxiety and remains asleep.

What is the scientific evidence for Freud's theory of dreams? Most modern research finds little or no scientific support for Freud's view (Domhoff, 2004; Dufresne, 2007; Siegel, 2010). Critics also say that Freud's theory is highly subjective. The symbols can be interpreted according to the particular analyst's view or training. After being confronted about the symbolic nature of his beloved cigars, even Freud supposedly remarked, "Sometimes a cigar is just a cigar."

Biological View

In contrast to the Freudian perspective, the **activation–synthesis hypothesis** suggests dreams are a by-product of random stimulation of brain cells during REM sleep (Hobson, 1988, 2005; Wamsley & Stickgold, 2010). Alan Hobson and Robert McCarley (1977) proposed that specific neurons in the brain stem are "turned on" (*activated*) during REM sleep. The cortex then struggles to *synthesize* or make sense out of this random stimulation by manufacturing dreams.

Have you ever dreamed that you were trying to run away from a frightening situation but found that you could not move? The activation–synthesis hypothesis might explain this dream as random stimulation of the amygdala. As you recall from Chapter 2, the amygdala is a specific brain area linked to strong emotions, especially fear. If your amygdala is randomly stimulated and you feel afraid, you may try to run. But you can't move because your major muscles are temporarily paralyzed during REM sleep. To make sense of this conflict, you might create a dream about a fearful situation in which you were trapped in heavy sand or someone was holding on to your arms and legs.

This is *not* to say that Hobson believes dreams are totally meaningless. He suggests that even if dreams begin with essentially random brain activity, your individual personality, motivations, memories, and life experiences guide how your brain constructs the dream (Hobson, 1999, 2005).

Cognitive View

Finally, some researchers suport the cognitive view that dreams are simply another type of *information processing*. That is, our dreams help us sift, sort, and process our everyday experiences and thoughts. And the brain periodically shuts out sensory input so that it can process, assimilate, and update information.

Manifest Content According to Freud, a dream's "surface" remembered story line, which contains dream symbols that disguise the hidden, latent content of the dream

Latent Content According to Freud, a dream's unconscious, hidden meaning, which is transformed into symbols within the story line or manifest content of the dream

Activation–Synthesis Hypothesis Hobson's theory that dreams are by-products of random stimulation of brain cells; the brain attempts to combine (or synthesize) this spontaneous activity into coherent patterns, known as dreams

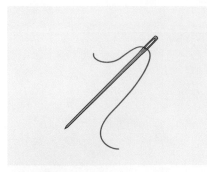

(a) In the early 1800s, clothing was all made by hand using the standard hand-held needle with the threading hole at the top and the sharp end at the bottom.

(b) In 1846, American inventor Elias Howe allegedly had a dream of being chased by men carrying spears with a hole in the tip.

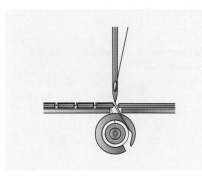

(c) When Howe awoke, he realized his dream offered a key solution to problems with existing machine-operated sewing machines. Like the spear tips, the threading hole needed to be at the sharp end of the needle!

Figure 5.4 Creative dreaming
Which of the three major theories of dreaming best explains Elias Howe's dream?

The cognitive view of dreaming is supported by the fact that REM sleep increases following stress and intense learning periods. Furthermore, other research reports strong similarities between dream content and waking thoughts, fears, and concerns (Domhoff, 2005, 2007, 2010; Erlacher & Schredl, 2004). For example, college students often report "examination-anxiety" dreams. You can't find your classroom, you're running out of time, your pen or pencil won't work, or you've completely forgotten a scheduled exam and show up totally unprepared. (Sound familiar?)

In Sum

The psychoanalytic/psychodynamic, biological, and cognitive views of dreaming offer three widely divergent perspectives. And numerous questions remain. How would the psychoanalytic/psychodynamic theory explain why human fetuses show REM patterns? On the other hand, how would the activation–synthesis hypothesis explain complicated, storylike dreams or recurrent dreams? Finally, according to the information-processing approach, how can we explain dreams that lie outside our everyday experiences? And how is it that the same dream can often be explained by many theories (see Figure 5.4)?

Sleep Disorders: When Sleep Becomes a Problem

Objective 5.8: Describe the major sleep disorders.

Are you one of the lucky people who takes sleep for granted? If so, you may be surprised to discover the following facts (Lader, Cardinali, & Pandi-Perumal, 2006; National Sleep Foundation, 2007; Trew et al., 2011; Wilson & Nutt, 2008).

- An estimated two-thirds of American adults suffer from sleep problems, and about 25 percent of children under age 5 have a sleep disturbance.
- One in five adults is so sleepy during the day that sleepiness interferes with their daily activities. Each year Americans spend more than $98 million on over-the-counter sleep aids and another $50 million on coffee to keep them awake during the day.
- Twenty percent of all automobile drivers have fallen asleep for a few seconds (microsleep) at the wheel.
- 49.5 percent of the health professionals who operate the heart lung machine during cardiac surgery have reported microsleep incidents at the time of the surgery.

The costs of sleep disorders are enormous, not only for the individual but also for the public. Psychologists and other mental health professionals divide sleep disorders into two major diagnostic categories: (1) *dyssomnias*, which involve problems in the amount, timing, and quality of sleep, and (2) *parasomnias*, which include abnormal disturbances occurring during sleep (Table 5.1).

Table 5.1 SUMMARIZING SLEEP DISORDERS

Sleep Disorders	Characteristics
Dyssomnias	
Insomnia	Persistent difficulty falling asleep or staying asleep, or waking up too early
Narcolepsy	Sudden, irresistible onsets of sleep during waking hours, characterized by sudden sleep attacks while standing, talking, or even driving
Sleep apnea	Repeated interruption of breathing while asleep, causing loud snoring or poor-quality sleep
Parasomnias	
Nightmares	Bad dreams during REM sleep, which significantly disrupts sleep
Night terrors	Abrupt awakenings with feelings of panic during NREM sleep, which significantly disrupt sleep

Dyssomnias

There are at least three prominent examples of dyssomnias:

1. *Insomnia* The term *insomnia* literally means "lack of sleep." People with **insomnia** have persistent difficulty falling asleep or staying asleep, or they wake up too early. Many people think they have insomnia if they cannot sleep before an exciting event, which is normal. They also wrongly assume that everyone must sleep 8 hours a night. Sometimes, too, people think they are not sleeping when they really are.

   However, a significant percentage of the population (as much as 10 percent) genuinely suffers from insomnia, and nearly everyone occasionally experiences unwanted sleeplessness (Bastien, 2011; Colrain, 2011; Wilson & Nutt, 2008). A telltale complaint of insomnia is that the person feels poorly rested the next day. Most people with serious insomnia have other medical or psychological disorders as well, such as alcohol and other drug abuse, anxiety disorders, and depression.

   Unfortunately, the most popular treatment for insomnia is drugs—either over-the-counter pills, such as Sominex, or prescription tranquilizers and barbiturates. The problem with nonprescription pills is that they generally don't work. Prescription pills, on the other hand, do help you sleep. But they decrease Stage 4 and REM sleep, thereby seriously affecting the quality of sleep. Frequently prescribed drugs like Ambien, Lunesta, Xanax, and Halcion may be helpful in treating sleeping problems related to anxiety and specific stressful situations, such as losing a loved one. However, chronic users run the risk of psychological and physical drug dependence. In sum, sleeping pills may be useful for occasional, short-term (two to three nights) use, but they may create more problems than they solve.

2. *Narcolepsy* A serious sleep disorder that is somewhat the opposite of insomnia is **narcolepsy**—sudden, irresistible onsets of sleep during normal waking hours which afflicts about one person in 2000 and generally runs in families (Billiard, 2007; Majid & Hirshkowitz, 2010; Pedrazzoli et al., 2007; Raggi et al., 2011). During an attack, REM-like sleep suddenly intrudes into the waking state of consciousness. Victims may experience sudden attacks of muscle weakness or paralysis (known as *cataplexy*). Such people may fall asleep while standing, talking, or driving a car. Long daily naps and stimulant or antidepressant drugs may help reduce the frequency of narcoleptic attacks. But the causes and cure of narcolepsy are still unknown (Figure 5.5).

3. *Sleep apnea* A third major dyssomnia, closely related to insomnia, is **sleep apnea**. (*Apnea* literally means "no breathing.") Many people have either irregular breathing or occasional periods of 10 seconds or less without breathing during their sleep. People with sleep apnea, however, may fail to breathe for a minute or longer and then wake up gasping for breath. When they do breathe during their sleep, they often snore. Repeated awakenings result in insomnia and leave the person feeling tired and sleepy during the day. Unfortunately, people are often unaware of these frequent awakenings and may fail to recognize the reason for their daytime fatigue.

   Sleep apnea seems to result from blocked upper airway passages or from the brain ceasing to send signals to the diaphragm, thus causing breathing to stop. If you snore loudly or have repeated awakenings followed by gasps for breath, you may be suffering from sleep apnea and should seek medical attention. Recent research shows that sleep apnea may kill neurons in your brain that are critical for learning and memory. It also can lead to high blood pressure, stroke, heart attack, and accidents (Bourke et al., 2011; Billiard, 2007; Furukawa et al., 2011; Nikolaou, 2011).

   Treatment for sleep apnea depends partly on its severity. If the problem occurs only when you're sleeping on your back, sewing tennis balls on the back of your

Insomnia Persistent problems in falling asleep, staying asleep, or awakening too early

Narcolepsy [NAR-co-lep-see] Sudden and irresistible onsets of sleep during normal waking hours. (narco = "numbness" and lepsy = "seizure")

Sleep Apnea Repeated interruption of breathing while asleep because air passages to the lungs are physically blocked or the brain stops activating the diaphragm

Figure 5.5 Narcolepsy William Dement and his colleagues at Stanford University's Sleep Disorders Center have bred a group of narcoleptic dogs, which has increased our understanding of the genetics of this disorder. Research on these specially bred dogs has found degenerated neurons in certain areas of the brain (Siegel, 2000). Whether human narcolepsy results from similar degeneration is a question for future research. (Note how these hungry puppies have lapsed suddenly from alert wakefulness to deep sleep even when offered their preferred food.)

▲ **Figure 5.6 Nightmare or night terror?** Nightmares, or bad dreams, occur toward the end of the sleep cycle, during REM sleep. Less common but more frightening are night terrors, which occur early in the cycle, during Stage 3 or Stage 4 of NREM sleep. Like the child in this photo, the sleeper may sit bolt upright, screaming and sweating, walk around, and talk incoherently, and the person may be almost impossible to awaken.

pajama top may help remind you to sleep on your side. Obstruction of the breathing passages is also related to obesity and heavy alcohol use, so dieting and alcohol restriction are often recommended. For others, surgery, dental appliances that reposition the tongue, or ventilating machines may be the answer.

For many years, researchers assumed that snoring (without the accompanying stoppages of breathing in sleep apnea) was a minor problem—except for bed partners. Recent findings, however, suggest that even this "simple snoring" can also lead to heart disease and possible death (Stone & Redline, 2006). Although occasional mild snoring may be normal, chronic snoring is a possible "warning sign that should prompt people to seek help" (Christensen, 2000).

Parasomnias

The second major category of sleep disorders, *parasomnias*, includes abnormal sleep disturbances such as **nightmares** and **night terrors** (Figure 5.6).

Sleepwalking, which tends to accompany night terrors, also occurs during NREM sleep. (Recall that large muscles are "paralyzed" during REM sleep, which explains why sleepwalking normally occurs during NREM sleep.) *Sleeptalking*, on the other hand, occurs with about equal probability in REM and NREM sleep. It can include single, indistinct words or long, articulate sentences. It is even possible to engage some sleeptalkers in a limited conversation.

Nightmares, night terrors, sleepwalking, and sleeptalking are all more common among young children. But they can also occur in adults, usually during times of stress or major life events (Billiard, 2007; Hobson & Silvestri, 1999). Patience and soothing reassurance at the time of the sleep disruption are usually the only treatment recommended for both children and adults.

Nightmares Anxiety-arousing dreams generally occurring near the end of the sleep cycle, during REM sleep

Night Terrors Abrupt awakenings from NREM (non–rapid-eye-movement) sleep accompanied by intense physiological arousal and feelings of panic

 **TRY THIS YOURSELF**

Self-Help for Sleep Problems

Are you wondering what is recommended for sleep problems other than drugs? Research finds consistent benefits from behavior therapy (Constantino et al., 2007; Smith et al., 2005). You can use these same techniques in your own life. For example, when you're having a hard time going to sleep, don't keep checking the clock and worrying about your loss of sleep. Instead, remove all TVs, stereos, and books, and limit the use of the bedroom to sleep (and sex). If you need additional help, try some of the relaxation techniques suggested by the Better Sleep Council, a nonprofit education organization in Burtonsville, Maryland.

During the day

Exercise. Daily physical activity works away tension. But don't exercise vigorously late in the day, or you'll get fired up instead. Keep regular hours. An erratic schedule can disrupt biological rhythms. Get up at the same time each day.

Avoid stimulants. Coffee, tea, soft drinks, chocolate, and some medications contain caffeine. Nicotine may be an even more potent sleep disrupter.

Avoid late meals and heavy drinking. Overindulgence can interfere with your normal sleep pattern.

Stop worrying. Focus on your problems at a set time earlier in the day.

Use presleep rituals. Follow the same routine every evening: listen to music, write in a diary, meditate.

In bed

Use progressive muscle relaxation. Alternately tense and relax various muscle groups.

Apply yoga. These gentle exercises help you relax.

Use fantasies. Imagine yourself in a tranquil setting. Feel yourself relax.

Use deep breathing. Take deep breaths, telling yourself you're falling asleep.

Try a warm bath. This can induce drowsiness because it sends blood away from the brain to the skin surface.

For more information, check these websites:

• www.sleepfoundation.org

• www.stanford.edu/~dement

Why Do We Sleep and Dream and Sleep Disorders

Part A: Retrieval Practice

1. Without looking at the book, spend 10 minutes writing a free-form essay recalling all you can remember from the previous section.

2. Now, reread the previous section, and once again spend 10 minutes writing a free-form essay on the SAME material.

Part B: Practice Quiz

1. How does the repair/restoration theory of sleep differ from the evolutionary/circadian theory?

2. Freud believed that dreams were the "royal road to the _____." (a) therapeutic alliance; (b) psyche; (c) latent content; (d) unconscious

3. _____ theory states that dreams are by-products of random stimulation of brain cells. In contrast, the _____ view suggests dreams serve an information-processing function and help us sift and sort our everyday experiences and thoughts. (a) Biological, learning; (b) Cognitive, wish-fulfillment; (c) Activation–synthesis, cognitive; (d) Psychodynamic, infodynamic

4. After periods of stress and intense learning, _____ sleep increases.

5. Following are four descriptions of people suffering from sleep disorders. Label each type.

(a) George awakens many times each night and feels fatigued and poorly rested the next day.

(b) While sleeping, Joan often snores loudly and frequently stops breathing temporarily.

(c) Xavier complains to his physician about sudden and irresistible onsets of sleep during his normal work day.

(d) Tyler is a young child who often wakes up terrified and cannot describe what has happened. These episodes occur primarily during NREM sleep.

Check your answers in Appendix B.

Psychoactive Drugs

Objective 5.9: Define psychoactive drugs and explain how they work.

Since the beginning of civilization, people of all cultures have used—and abused—psychoactive drugs (Abadinsky, 2011; Levinthal, 2011; Saniotis, 2010). **Psychoactive drugs** are generally defined as chemicals that change conscious awareness, mood, and/or perception. Do you (or does someone you know) use caffeine (in coffee, tea, chocolate, or cola) or nicotine (in cigarettes) as a pick-me-up? How about alcohol (in beer, wine, and cocktails) as a way to relax and lessen inhibitions? All three—caffeine, nicotine, and alcohol—are psychoactive drugs. How use differs from abuse, and how chemical alterations in consciousness affect a person, psychologically and physically, are important topics in psychology. In this section, we begin by clarifying how psychoactive drugs work and differences in terminology. We then go on to look at the four major categories of psychoactive drugs and "club drugs" like MDMA, or ecstasy.

Psychoactive Drugs Chemicals that change conscious awareness, mood, and/or perception

Understanding Psychoactive Drugs: Clarifying the Mechanics and Terminology

How Drugs Work

Psychoactive drugs influence the nervous system (and our thoughts, feelings, and behaviors) in a variety of ways. Alcohol, for example, has a diffuse effect on neural membranes throughout the nervous system. Most psychoactive drugs, however, act in a more specific way. They either enhance a particular neurotransmitter's effect (an **agonistic drug** *action*) or they inhibit it (an **antagonistic drug** action) (see the Step-by-Step Diagram 5.2).

Agonist Drug Mimics and enhances a neurotransmitter's effect

Antagonist Drug Blocks normal neurotransmitter functioning

Step-by-StepDiagram5.2

STOP This Step by Step diagram contains essential information NOT found elsewhere in the text, which is likely to appear on quizzes and exams. Be sure to study it CAREFULLY!

How Drugs Work

Most psychoactive drugs produce their mood-, energy-, and perception-altering effects by changing the body's supply of neurotransmitters. They can alter *synthesis, storage,* and *release of neurotransmitters* (Step 1), and change the *binding* effect of neurotransmitters on the receiving site of the receptor neuron (Step 2). After neurotransmitters carry their messages across the synapse, the sending neuron normally *deactivates* the excess, or leftover, neurotransmitter (Step 3). However, when *agonistic* drugs block this process, excess neutrotransmitter remains in the synapse, which prolongs the psychoactive drug's effect.

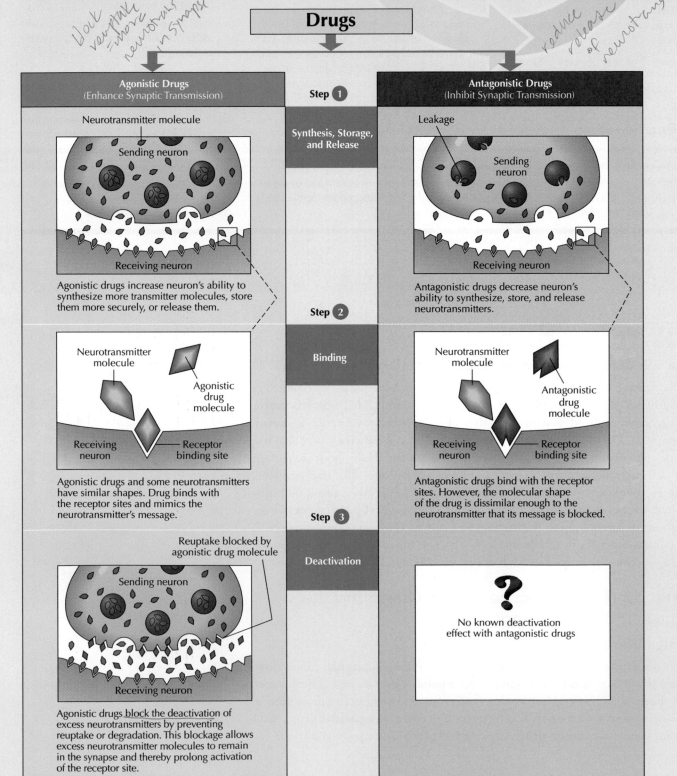

Drugs

(handwritten note, left) block reuptake → more neurotrans in synapse

(handwritten note, right) reduce release of neurotrans

Agonistic Drugs (Enhance Synaptic Transmission)

Step 1 — Synthesis, Storage, and Release

Neurotransmitter molecule
Sending neuron
Receiving neuron

Agonistic drugs increase neuron's ability to synthesize more transmitter molecules, store them more securely, or release them.

Step 2 — Binding

Neurotransmitter molecule
Agonistic drug molecule
Receiving neuron — Receptor binding site

Agonistic drugs and some neurotransmitters have similar shapes. Drug binds with the receptor sites and mimics the neurotransmitter's message.

Step 3 — Deactivation

Reuptake blocked by agonistic drug molecule
Sending neuron
Receiving neuron

Agonistic drugs block the deactivation of excess neurotransmitters by preventing reuptake or degradation. This blockage allows excess neurotransmitter molecules to remain in the synapse and thereby prolong activation of the receptor site.

Antagonistic Drugs (Inhibit Synaptic Transmission)

Leakage
Sending neuron
Receiving neuron

Antagonistic drugs decrease neuron's ability to synthesize, store, and release neurotransmitters.

Neurotransmitter molecule
Antagonistic drug molecule
Receiving neuron — Receptor binding site

Antagonistic drugs bind with the receptor sites. However, the molecular shape of the drug is dissimilar enough to the neurotransmitter that its message is blocked.

?

No known deactivation effect with antagonistic drugs

History of psychoactive drugs
Before the Food and Drug Administration (FDA) regulated the sale of such drugs as heroin, opium, and cocaine, they were commonly found in over-the-counter, nonprescription drugs.

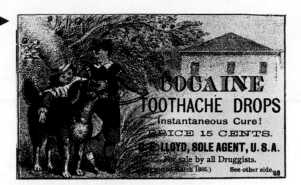

▲ **Early abuse of drugs** William Hogarth's eighteenth-century engraving shows the social chaos caused by the "gin epidemic." Infant mortality was so high that only one of four babies survived to the age of 5. In one section of London, one out of five houses was a gin shop (cited in Levinthal, 2011, p. 85).

Misconceptions and Confusing Terminology

Objective 5.10: Clarify the major misconceptions and confusing terminology related to psychoactive drugs.

Is drug abuse the same as drug addiction? The term **drug abuse** generally refers to drug taking that causes emotional or physical harm to the individual or others. The drug consumption is also typically compulsive, frequent, and intense. **Addiction** is a broad term referring to a condition in which a person feels compelled to use a specific drug. People now use the term to describe almost any type of compulsive activity from working to surfing the Internet (Padwa & Cunningham, 2010; Ross et al., 2010). In fact, research has shown that risky trading in financial markets can create a high that is indistinguishable from the highs experienced by drug addicts (Zweig, 2007).

Because of problems associated with the terms *addiction* and *drug abuse*, many drug researchers now use **psychological dependence** to refer to the mental desire or craving to achieve a drug's effects. They use the term **physical dependence** to refer to changes in bodily processes that make a drug necessary for minimum daily functioning. Physical dependence is shown most clearly when the drug is withheld and the user undergoes painful **withdrawal** reactions, including physical pain and intense cravings.

After repeated use of a drug, many of the body's physiological processes adjust to higher and higher levels of the drug, producing a decreased sensitivity called **tolerance**. Tolerance leads many users to escalate their drug use and to experiment with other drugs in an attempt to re-create the original pleasurable altered state. Sometimes, using one drug increases tolerance for another. This is known as *cross-tolerance*. Despite the benign sound of the words *tolerance* and *cross-tolerance*, it's important to remember that the brain, heart, liver, and other body organs can be seriously damaged.

Psychological dependence is often no less dangerous than physical dependence. The craving in psychological dependence can be strong enough to keep the user in a constant drug-induced state—and to lure an "addict" back to a drug habit long after he or she has overcome physical dependence.

Drug Abuse Drug taking that causes emotional or physical harm to the drug user or others

Addiction Broad term describing a compulsion to use a specific drug or engage in a certain activity

Psychological Dependence Desire or craving to achieve a drug's effect

Physical Dependence Changes in bodily processes that make a drug necessary for minimal functioning

Withdrawal Discomfort and distress, including physical pain and intense cravings, experienced after stopping the use of addictive drugs

Tolerance Bodily adjustment to higher and higher levels of a drug, which leads to decreased sensitivity

TRY THIS YOURSELF

Are You Physically or Psychologically Dependent on Alcohol or Other Drugs?

Before we go on, you may want to take the following test.

1. Have you gotten into financial difficulties due to drinking or using other drugs?

2. Has drinking alcohol or using other drugs ever been behind your losing a job?

3. Has your efficiency or ambition decreased due to drinking and using other drugs?

4. Is your drinking and drug use jeopardizing your academic performance?

5. Does drinking or using other drugs cause you to have difficulty sleeping?

6. Have you ever felt remorse after drinking and using other drugs?

7. Do you crave a drink or other drug at a definite time daily, or do you want a drink or other drug the next morning?

8. Have you ever had a complete or partial loss of memory because of drinking or using other drugs?

9. Have you ever been to a hospital or institution because of drinking or other drug use?

If you answered yes to these questions, you are more likely to be a substance abuser than someone who answered no.

Source: Bennett et al., "Identifying Young Adult Substance Abusers: The Rutgers Collegiate Substance

Abuse Screening Test." *Journal of Studies on Alcohol* 54: 522–527. Copyright 1993 Alcohol Research Documentation, Inc., Piscataway, NJ. Reprinted by permission. The RCSAST is to be used only as part of a complete assessment battery because more research needs to be done with this instrument.

Psychology at Work

Addictive Drugs as the Brain's "Evil Tutor"

Objective 5.11: Why do addicts abuse drugs?

Why do alcoholics and other addicts continue to take drugs that are clearly destroying their lives? One explanation may be that the brain "learns" to be addicted. Scientists have long known that various neurotransmitters are key to all forms of normal learning. Now evidence suggests that addictive drugs (acting on certain neurotransmitters) "teach" the brain to want more and more of the destructive substances—whatever the cost. Drugs become the brain's "evil tutor" (Wickelgren, 1998, p. 2045).

How does this happen? The neurotransmitter dopamine has been a primary focus of drug abuse research because of its well-known effect on a part of the brain's reward system known as the nucleus accumbens (Carr, 2011; Mark et al., 2011). Nicotine and amphetamines, for example, stimulate the release of dopamine, and cocaine blocks its reuptake. Drugs that increase dopamine activity are most likely to result in physical dependence.

Recently, however, evidence points to the importance of another neurotransmitter, glutamate. Although surges in dopamine caused by drug use appear to activate the brain's reward system, glutamate may explain compulsive drug taking. Even after the initial effects of a drug disappear, glutamate-induced learning encourages the addict to want more and more of the drug and directs the body to get it. Glutamate apparently creates lasting memories of drug use by changing the nature of "conversations" between neurons. Changes in neuronal connections result whenever we learn something and store it in memory. But in this case, glutamate "teaches" the brain to be addicted.

Glutamate's lesson is rarely forgotten. Even when users are highly motivated to end the vicious cycle of drug abuse, glutamate-related changes in the brain keep them "hooked." In addition to the well-known intense cravings and pain of withdrawal, the addicted brain also creates cravings at the mere sight of drug-related items. When 13 cocaine addicts and 5 controls watched films of people using both neutral objects and drug-associated items (such as glass pipes and razor blades), the addicts reported significant cravings. During this same time, positron emission tomography (PET) scans of the addicts' brains showed significant neural activity in brain regions known to release glutamate (Grant et al., 1996). Apparently, activating the glutamate system—through drug use or some reminder of the drug—creates strong cravings, which helps explain the common problem of drug relapse.

As a critical thinker, are you wondering how this new research might help with drug abuse and relapse? Recalling earlier information about *agonists* and *antagonists*, what about developing and trying a glutamate antagonist? When shown drug-related objects, long-term drug addicts who received a glutamate antagonist reported a significant reduction in cravings and less drug-seeking behavior (Herman & O'Brien, 1997). Drugs that interfere with glutamate transmission are also being tested for the treatment of general drug abuse (Wickelgren, 1998).

"That is not one of the seven habits of highly effective people."

Categorizing Psychoactive Drugs: Depressants, Stimulants, Opiates, and Hallucinogens

Objective 5.12: List the four main categories of psychoactive drugs and explain how they work.

For convenience, psychologists divide psychoactive drugs into four broad categories: depressants, stimulants, opiates, and hallucinogens (Summary Table 5.2). In this section, we also explore a modern concern with "club drugs" like ecstasy.

Summary Table 5.2 EFFECTS OF THE MAJOR PSYCHOACTIVE DRUGS

	Category	Desired Effects	Undesirable Effects
	Depressants (Sedatives)		
	Alcohol, barbiturates, anxiolytics, also known as antianxiety drugs or tranquilizers (Xanax), Rohypnol (roofies), Ketamine (Special K), GHB	Tension reduction, euphoria, disinhibition, drowsiness, muscle relaxation	Anxiety, nausea, disorientation, impaired reflexes and motor functioning, amnesia, loss of consciousness, shallow respiration, convulsions, coma, death
	Stimulants		
	Cocaine, amphetamine, methamphetamine (crystal meth), MDMA (Ectasy)	Exhilaration, euphoria, high physical and mental energy, reduced appetite, perceptions of power, sociability	Irritability, anxiety, sleeplessness, paranoia, hallucinations, psychosis, elevated blood pressure and body temperature, convulsions, death
	Caffeine	Increased alertness	Insomnia, restlessness, increased pulse rate, mild delirium, ringing in the ears, rapid heartbeat
	Nicotine	Relaxation, increased alertness, sociability	Irritability, raised blood pressure, stomach pains, vomiting, dizziness, cancer, heart disease, emphysema
	Opiates (Narcotics)		
	Morphine, heroin, codeine, OxyContin	Euphoria, "rush" of pleasure, pain relief, sleep, prevention of withdrawal discomfort	Nausea, vomiting, constipation, painful withdrawal, shallow respiration, convulsions, coma, death
	Hallucinogens (Psychedelics)		
	LSD (lysergic acid diethylamide), mescaline (extract from the peyote cactus), psilocybin (magic mushrooms), *Salvia divinorum**	Heightened aesthetic responses, euphoria, mild delusions, hallucinations, distorted perceptions and sensations	Panic, nausea, headaches, longer and more extreme delusions, hallucinations, perceptual distortions ("bad trips"), psychosis **Long-term effects of excessive Salvia currently unknown*
	Marijuana	Relaxation, mild euphoria, increased appetite	Perceptual and sensory distortions, hallucinations, fatigue, lack of motivation, paranoia

Depressants Drugs that act on the brain and other parts of the nervous system to decrease bodily processes and overall responsiveness

Drunk driving As in this fatal car accident in Austin, Texas, drunk drivers are responsible for almost half of all highway-related deaths in America.

Stimulants Drugs that act on the brain and other parts of the nervous system to increase overall activity and general responsiveness

Depressants

Depressants (sometimes called *downers*) act on the central nervous system (CNS), causing relaxation, sedation, loss of consciousness, and even death. This category includes ethyl alcohol, barbiturates like Seconal, and antianxiety drugs like Valium. Because tolerance and dependence (both physical and psychological) are rapidly acquired with these drugs, there is strong potential for abuse.

It's often said that alcohol is a *stimulant* at low doses, which accounts for its reputation as a "party drug," and a *depressant* at higher doses. The truth is that alcohol is always a depressant. People become less self-conscious, less inhibited, more relaxed, and more in the mood to "party," even after just one or two drinks, because the alcohol has depressed neural activity in their brain and other parts of their nervous system. As drinking increases, so too do relaxation, disinhibition, poor judgment, and lessened emotional and behavioral control—all of which lead to serious personal and social problems. In very large doses, alcohol can be lethal (Table 5.3).

Finally, alcohol should not be combined with *any* other drug. But combining alcohol and barbiturates—both depressants—is particularly dangerous. Together, they can relax the diaphragm muscles to such a degree that the person literally suffocates.

Stimulants

Depressants suppress central nervous system (CNS) activity, whereas **stimulants** increase its overall activity and responsiveness. Stimulant drugs (such as caffeine, nicotine, amphetamine, methamphetamine, and cocaine) produce alertness, excitement, elevated mood, decreased fatigue, and sometimes increased motor activity. They also may lead to serious problems. Let's look more closely at nicotine and cocaine.

MYTH BUSTERS

PSYCHOLOGY ENGAGES

What's Your Alcohol IQ?

True or False?

1. Alcohol increases sexual desire.
2. Alcohol helps you sleep.
3. Alcohol kills brain cells
4. It's easier to get drunk at high altitudes.
5. Switching among different types of alcohol is more likely to lead to drunkenness.
6. Drinking coffee or taking a cold shower are great ways to sober up after heavy drinking.
7. Alcohol warms the body.
8. You can't become an alcoholic if you only drink beer.
9. Alcohol's primary effect is as a stimulant.
10. People only experience impaired judgment after drinking if they show obvious signs of intoxication.

Answer: All of these are false. Detailed answers are provided in this chapter and in Lilienfeld et al., 2010.

Table 5.3 ALCOHOL'S EFFECTS ON THE BODY AND BEHAVIOR

Number of drinks in two hours (a)	Blood Alcohol Content (%) (b)	Effect
(2)	0.05	Relaxed state; increased sociability
(3)	0.08	Everyday stress lessened
(4)	0.10	Movements and speech become clumsy
(7)	0.20	Very drunk; loud and difficult to understand; emotions unstable
(12)	0.40	Difficult to wake up; incapable of voluntary action
(15)	0.50	Irregular heartbeats, convulsions, coma, and/or death

(a) *A drink refers to one 12-ounce beer, a 4-ounce glass of wine, or a 1.25-ounce shot of hard liquor.*

(b) *In America, the legal blood alcohol level for "drunk driving" varies from 0.05 to 0.12.*

Alcohol's effects are determined primarily by the amount that reaches the brain. Because the liver breaks down alcohol at the rate of about 1 ounce per hour, the number of drinks and the speed of consumption are both very important. People can die after drinking large amounts of alcohol in a short period of time. In addition, men's bodies are more efficient than women's at breaking down alcohol. Even after accounting for differences in size and muscle-to-fat ratio, women have a higher blood alcohol level than do men following equal consumption.

Nicotine Like caffeine, nicotine is a widely used legal stimulant. But unlike caffeine, it kills many of its users. A sad, ironic example of the dangers of nicotine addiction is Wayne McLaren, the rugged Marlboro Man in cigarette ads, who died of lung cancer at age 51. But McLaren was only one of 400,000 who die from smoking-related illnesses each year in the United States. Tobacco kills more than AIDS, legal drugs, illegal drugs, road accidents, murder, and suicide combined (CDC, 2008).

When smoking doesn't kill, it can result in chronic bronchitis, emphysema, and heart disease (CDC, 2011). Countless others are affected by secondhand smoke, by smoking-related fires, and by prenatal exposure to nicotine (Chapters 3 and 9). The U.S. Public Health Service considers cigarette smoking the single most preventable cause of death and disease in the United States.

As scientific evidence of the dangers of smoking accumulates, and as social pressure from nonsmokers increases, many smokers are trying to kick the habit. Although some succeed, others find it extremely difficult to quit smoking. Researchers have found that nicotine use is linked to usage of other addictive drugs, and that nicotine activates the same brain areas (nucleus accumbens) as cocaine—a drug well known for its addictive potential (Dandekar et al., 2011; Kuhn & Gallinat, 2011; Tronci & Balfour, 2011; Zanetti, Picciotto, & Zoli, 2007). The reported pleasures of smoking (relaxation, increased alertness, diminished pain and appetite) are so powerfully reinforcing that some smokers continue to smoke even after having a cancerous lung removed.

Cocaine Cocaine is a powerful central nervous system stimulant extracted from the leaves of the coca plant. It can be sniffed as a white powder, injected intravenously, or smoked in the form of crack. It produces feelings of alertness, euphoria, well-being, power, energy, and pleasure. But it also acts as an *agonist drug* to block the reuptake of our body's natural neurotransmitters that produce these same effects (Figure 5.7). P18A

Although cocaine was once considered a relatively harmless "recreational drug," its potential for physical damage and severe psychological dependence is now recognized. Sigmund Freud often is cited as a supporter of cocaine use. But few people know that in his later writings Freud called cocaine the "third scourge" of humanity, after alcohol and heroin. Even small initial doses can be fatal because cocaine interferes with the electrical system of the heart, causing irregular heartbeats and, in some cases, heart failure. It also can produce heart attacks and strokes by temporarily constricting blood vessels (Abadinsky, 2011; NIDA, 2010; Westover, McBride, & Haley, 2007). The most dangerous form of cocaine is the smokeable, concentrated version known as crack or rock. Its lower price makes it affordable and attractive to a large audience. But its greater potency also makes it more quickly addictive and dangerous.

Opiates

Opiates (or narcotics), which include morphine and heroin, numb the senses and thus are used medically to relieve pain (Maisto, Galizio, & Connors, 2011). The classification term *opiates* is used because the drugs are derived from (or are similar to those derived from) the opium poppy. They are attractive to people seeking an alternate state of consciousness because they produce feelings of relaxation and euphoria. They produce their effect by mimicking the brain's own natural chemicals for pain control and mood elevation, called *endorphins*. (Recall from Chapter 2 that the word *endorphin* was derived from "endogenous morphine.")

This mimicking of the body's natural endorphins creates a dangerous pathway to drug abuse. After repeated flooding with artificial opiates, the brain eventually reduces or stops the production of its own opiates. If the user later attempts to stop, the brain lacks both the artificial and normal level of painkilling chemicals. And withdrawal becomes excruciatingly painful (Figure 5.8).

The euphoria, pain relief, and avoidance of withdrawal all contribute to make opiates, like heroin, extremely addictive. Interestingly, when opiates are used medically

Figure 5.7 Cocaine: an agonist drug in action

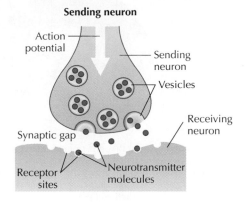

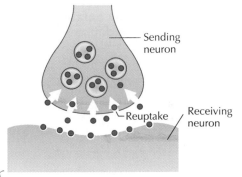

▲ (a) The two figures above depict how after releasing neurotransmitter into the synapse, the sending neuron normally reabsorbs (or reuptakes) excess neurotransmitter back into the terminal buttons.

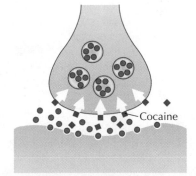

▲ (b) This figure shows that when cocaine is present in the synapse, it will block the reuptake of dopamine, serotonin, and norepinephrine, and levels of these substances will increase. The result is overstimulation and a brief euphoric high. When the drug wears off, the depletion of neurotransmitters may cause the drug user to "crash."

Opiates Drugs derived from opium that numb the senses and relieve pain (The word *opium* comes from the Greek word meaning "juice.")

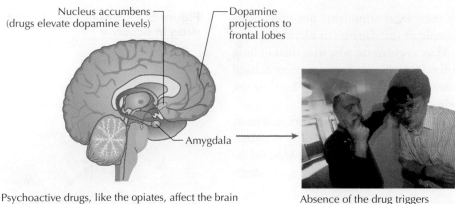

Nucleus accumbens
(drugs elevate dopamine levels)

Dopamine
projections to
frontal lobes

Amygdala

Psychoactive drugs, like the opiates, affect the brain and body in a variety of ways. Most researchers believe that increased dopamine activity in this so-called *reward pathway of the brain* accounts for the reinforcing effects of most addictive drugs.

Absence of the drug triggers withdrawal symptoms (e.g., intense pain and cravings).

Figure 5.8 How opiates create physical dependence

Hallucinogens [hal-LOO-sin-oh-jenz]
Drugs that produce sensory or perceptual distortions called hallucinations

Vision from an LSD trip?

to relieve intense pain, they are very seldom habit-forming. However, when taken recreationally, they are strongly addictive (Dacher & Nugent, 2011; Levinthal, 2011).

Hallucinogens

One of the most intriguing alterations of consciousness comes from **hallucinogens**. These drugs produce sensory or perceptual distortions, including visual, auditory, or kinesthetic hallucinations. According to some reports, colors are brighter and more luminous, patterns seem to pulsate and rotate, and senses may seem to fuse—that is, colors are "heard" or sounds "tasted."

Some cultures have used hallucinogens for religious purposes, as a way to experience "other realities" or to communicate with the supernatural. In Western societies, most people use hallucinogens for their reported "mind-expanding" potential. For example, some artists highly value hallucinogens as a way of increasing creativity. But the experience is not always positive. Terror-filled "bad trips" can occur. Also, dangerous flashbacks may unpredictably recur long after the initial ingestion. The flashback experience may be brought on by stress, fatigue, marijuana use, illness, emerging from a dark room, and occasionally by the individual's intentional effort (Baggott et al., 2011; Iaria et al., 2010; Levinthal, 2011).

Hallucinogens are also commonly referred to as *psychedelics* (Greek for "mind manifesting"). They include mescaline (derived from the peyote cactus), psilocybin (from mushrooms), phencyclidine (chemically derived), and LSD (lysergic acid diethylamide, derived from ergot, a rye mold). We will focus on LSD and marijuana in our discussion because they are the most widely used hallucinogens.

Lysergic acid diethylamide (LSD) LSD, or "acid," is a synthethic substance that produces dramatic alterations in sensation and perception. This odorless, tasteless, and colorless substance is also one of the most potent drugs known. As little as 10 micrograms of LSD can produce a measurable psychoactive effect in one individual. An amount the size of an aspirin is enough to produce effects in 3,000 people. In 1943 Albert Hofman, the Swiss chemist who first synthesized LSD in a laboratory, accidentally licked some of the drug off his finger and later recorded this in his journal:

> *Last Friday, April 16, 1943, I was forced to stop my work in the laboratory in the middle of the afternoon and to go home, as I was seized by a peculiar restlessness associated with a feeling of mild dizziness. Having reached home, I lay down and sank in a kind of drunkenness which was not unpleasant and which was characterized by extreme activity of imagination. As I lay in a dazed condition with my eyes closed (I experienced daylight as disagreeably bright) there surged upon me an uninterrupted stream of fantastic images of extraordinary plasticity and vividness and accompanied by an intense, kaleidoscope-like play of colors. This condition gradually passed after about two hours. (Hofman, 1968, pp. 184–185)*

Perhaps because the LSD experience is so powerful, few people actually "drop acid" on a regular basis. This may account for its relatively low reported abuse rate. However, LSD can be a dangerous drug. Bad LSD trips can be terrifying and may lead to accidents, death, or suicide (Levinthal, 2011; Maisto, Galizio, & Connors, 2011).

Marijuana Marijuana is also generally classified as a hallucinogen, even though it has some properties of a depressant (including drowsiness and lethargy) and a narcotic (acting as a weak painkiller). In low doses, it also produces mild euphoria. Moderate doses lead to an intensification of sensory experiences and the illusion that time is passing very slowly. At the highest doses, marijuana may produce hallucinations, delusions, and distortions of body image (Köfalvi, 2008; Ksir, Hart, & Ray, 2008). Regardless of its classification, it is one of the most popular of all illegal consciousness-altering drugs in the Western world.

The active ingredient in marijuana (cannabis) is THC, or tetrahydracannabinol, which attaches to receptors that are abundant throughout the brain. The presence of these receptors implies that the brain produces some THC-like chemicals of its own. In fact, researchers have discovered a brain chemical (called anandamide) that binds to the same receptors that THC was previously found to use. In 1997, a second THC-like chemical (2-AG) was also discovered (Stella, Schweitzer, & Piomelli, 1997). At this point, no one knows the function of anandamide or 2-AG or why the brain has its own marijuana-like receptors.

Culture and marijuana Can you see how culture might affect attitudes toward terms like drug abuse and addiction?

With the exception of alcohol during the time of Prohibition, there has never been a drug more hotly debated than marijuana. On the positive side, some research has found marijuana helps with glaucoma (an eye disease), increasing appetite and alleviating the nausea and vomiting associated with chemotherapy, and with the treatment of asthma, seizures, epilepsy, and anxiety (Darmani & Crim, 2005; Fogarty et al., 2007; Green & De-Vries, 2010; Köfalvi, 2008).

But researchers also report impaired memory, attention, and learning with marijuana. In addition, it may be related to an increased risk of developing psychotic symptoms, and birth defects, as well as lower IQ in children (Carter & Wang, 2007; Goldschmidt et al., 2008; Medina et al., 2007). Chronic marijuana use also can lead to throat and respiratory disorders, impaired lung functioning, decreased immune response, declines in testosterone levels, reduced sperm count, and disruption of the menstrual cycle and ovulation (Hall & Degenhardt, 2010; Levinthal, 2011; Skinner et al., 2011).

Some research supports the popular belief that marijuana serves as a "gateway" to other illegal drugs, however, other studies find little or no connection (Jacquette, 2010; Ksir, Hart, & Ray, 2008; Sabet, 2007; Tarter et al., 2006). Finally, marijuana can be habit-forming, but few users experience the intense cravings associated with cocaine or opiates. Withdrawal symptoms are mild because the drug dissolves in the body's fat and leaves the body very slowly, which explains why a marijuana user can test positive for days or weeks after the last use.

Psychology at Work

Club Drug Alert!

Objective 5.13: Discuss issues and concerns related to "club drugs."

As you may know from television or newspapers, psychoactive drugs like Rohypnol (the date rape drug) and MDMA (ecstasy) are fast becoming some of our nation's most popular drugs of abuse—especially at "raves" and other all-night dance parties. Other "club drugs," like GHB (gamma-hydroxybutyrate), ketamine (Special K), methamphetamine (crystal meth), and LSD, also are gaining in popularity (Abadinsky, 2011; Hopfer, 2011; Weaver & Schnoll, 2008) (Figure 5.9).

Although these drugs can produce desirable effects (e.g., ecstasy's feeling of great empathy and connectedness with others), it's important to note that almost all psychoactive drugs may cause serious health problems and, in some cases, even death.

High doses of MDMA, for example, can cause dangerous increases in body temperature and blood pressure that may lead to seizures, heart attacks, and strokes (Chamberlin & Saper, 2009; Jaehne et al., 2011; Rodsiri et al., 2011). In addition,

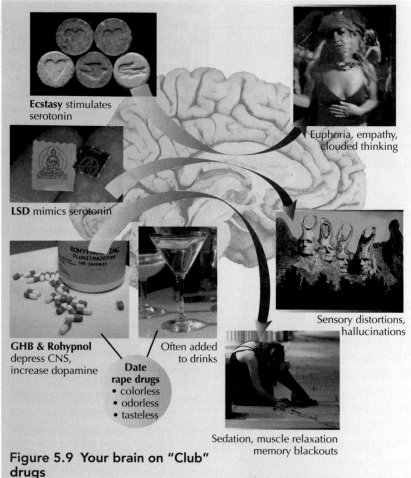

Ecstasy stimulates serotonin

Euphoria, empathy, clouded thinking

LSD mimics serotonin

GHB & Rohypnol depress CNS, increase dopamine

Often added to drinks

Date rape drugs
• colorless
• odorless
• tasteless

Sensory distortions, hallucinations

Sedation, muscle relaxation memory blackouts

Figure 5.9 Your brain on "Club" drugs

research shows that chronic use of MDMA may increase depression because it affects neurons that release the neurotransmitter serotonin (Frick, Wang, & Carlson, 2008; Gudelsky & Yamamoto, 2008). As you recall from Chapter 2, serotonin is critical to emotional regulation, learning, memory, and other cognitive functions.

One of the most threatening recent trends in "club drugs" is the swallowing or snorting of synthetic stimulants, usually mephedrone, which are currently legally sold in small packets labeled as "bath salts." Although marked "not for human ingestion," they are increasingly popular among those associated with the dance music scene. Widely available on the Internet and marketed with enticing names such as "White Lightning" or "Lovey Dovey," the bath salts produce cocaine or ecstasy-like effects. But they're far more toxic. Following reports of cases like Neil Brown, who slit his face and stomach repeatedly with a skinning knife, and numerous overdoses or deaths, several states now ban its sale (Oz, 2011; Sinclair, 2011).

Club drugs, like all illicit drugs, are particularly dangerous because there are no truth-in-packaging laws to protect buyers from unscrupulous practices. Sellers often substitute unknown cheaper, and possibly even more dangerous, substances for the ones they claim to be selling. Also, club drugs (like most psychoactive drugs) affect the motor coordination, perceptual skills, and reaction time necessary for safe driving.

Impaired decision making is a serious problem as well. Just as "drinking and driving don't mix," club drug use may lead to risky sexual behaviors and increased risk of AIDS (acquired immunodeficiency syndrome) and other sexually transmitted infections (see Chapter 11). Add in the fact that some drugs, like Rohypnol, are odorless, colorless, tasteless, and can easily be added to beverages by individuals who want to intoxicate or sedate others, and you can see that the dangers of club drug use go far beyond the drug itself. If you would like more information on the specific dangers and effects of these club drugs, check www.drugabuse.gov/clubalert/clubdrugalert.html.

CHECK & REVIEW

STOP *Before going on, be sure to complete this Check & Review. It is an invaluable study tool!*

Psychoactive Drugs

Part A: Retrieval Practice

1. Without looking at the book, spend 10 minutes writing a free-form essay recalling all you can remember from the previous section.

2. Now, reread the previous section, and once again spend 10 minutes writing a free-form essay on the SAME material.

Part B: Practice Quiz

1. _____ drugs change conscious awareness, mood, and/or perception.

2. _____ drugs inhibit normal synaptic transmission, whereas _____ drugs enhance synaptic transmission.

3. Drug taking that causes emotional or physical harm to the drug user or others is known as _____. (a) addiction; (b) physical dependence; (c) psychological dependence; (d) drug abuse

4. How does physical dependence differ from psychological dependence?

5. Identify the four major categories of psychoactive drugs.

Check your answers in Appendix B.

Healthier Ways to Alter Consciousness

Objective 5.14: Define meditation and discuss its effects.

As we have just seen, alternate states of consciousness (ASCs) may be reached through everyday activities such as sleep and dreaming or psychoactive drugs. But there are also less common, and perhaps healthier, routes to alternate states. In this section, we will explore the fascinating world of meditation and hypnosis.

Getting "High" on Meditation: A Positive Route to Altered Consciousness?

> Suddenly, with a roar like that of a waterfall, I felt a stream of liquid light entering my brain through the spinal cord. The illumination grew brighter and brighter, the roaring louder. I experienced a rocking sensation and then felt myself slipping out of my body, entirely enveloped in a halo of light. I felt the point of consciousness that was myself growing wider, surrounded by waves of light. (Krishna, 1999, pp. 4–5)

This is how spiritual leader Gopi Khrishna describes his experience with meditation. Does it sound attractive? Most people in the beginning stages of meditation report a simpler, mellow type of relaxation, followed by a mild euphoria. With long practice some advanced meditators experience feelings of profound rapture and joy or strong hallucinations (Cvetkovic & Cosic, 2011; Harrison, 2005).

What is **meditation**? The term is generally used to refer to a group of techniques designed to focus attention, block out all distractions, and produce an alternate state of consciousness (ASC) (Concept Organizer 5.2). Success in meditation requires controlling the mind's natural tendency to wander.

Meditation Group of techniques designed to focus attention, block out all distractions, and produce an alternate state of consciousness (ASC)

TRY THIS YOURSELF

Want the Benefits of Meditation?

Try this relaxation technique developed by Herbert Benson (1977):

1. Pick a focus word or short phrase that is calming and rooted in your personal value system (such as love, peace, one, shalom).

2. Sit quietly in a comfortable position, close your eyes, and relax your muscles.

3. Focusing on your breathing, breathe through your nose, and as you breathe out, say your focus word or phrase silently to yourself. Continue for 10 to 20 minutes. You may open your eyes to check the time, but do not use an alarm. When you have finished, sit quietly for several minutes, first with closed eyes and later with opened eyes.

4. Maintain a passive attitude throughout the exercise—permit relaxation to occur at its own pace. When distracting thoughts occur, ignore them and gently return to your repetition.

5. Practice the technique once or twice daily, but not within two hours after a meal—the digestive processes seem to interfere with a successful relaxation response.

The Mystery of Hypnosis: Recreational and Therapeutic Uses

Objective 5.15: Define hypnosis, and describe its myths and potential benefits.

> Relax . . . your body is so tired . . . your eyelids are so very heavy . . . your muscles are becoming more and more relaxed . . . your breathing is becoming deeper and deeper . . . relax . . . your eyes are closing and your whole body feels like lead . . . let go . . . relax.

These are the types of suggestions most hypnotists use to begin hypnosis. Once hypnotized, some people can be convinced they are standing at the edge of the ocean listening to

ConceptOrganizer5.2

STOP *This Concept Organizer contains essential information NOT found elsewhere in the text, which is likely to appear on quizzes and exams. Be sure to study it CAREFULLY!*

Meditation and the Brain

Some meditation techniques, such as t'ai chi and hatha yoga, involve body movements and postures, while in other techniques the meditator remains motionless, chanting or focusing on a single point, like a candle flame.

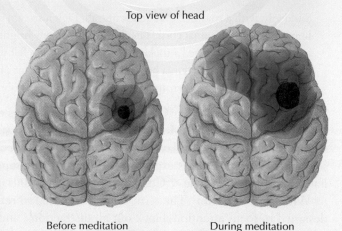

Top view of head

Before meditation   During meditation

An extensive body of research has established that mindfulness-based stress reduction (MBSR) meditation leads to improvements in psychological health and well-being (Kilpatrick et al., 2011; Rosenzweig et al., 2010). But did you know that it's also a great "mind expander"? Recent research using MRI brain scans found that an 8-week program of MBSR significantly altered gray matter in several areas of the brain involved in learning and memory processes, emotion regulation, self-referential processing, and perspective taking (Hölzel et al., 2011). In short, the brain literally *expands*! How does this happen? Recall that our adult brains have a lifelong capacity for plasticity (Chapter 2, p. 59), and studies have found that increased gray matter results from repeated activation of a brain region (Ilg et al., 2008; May et al., 2007).

▲ Researchers also have found that a wider area of the brain responds to sensory stimuli during meditation, suggesting that meditation enhances the coordination between the brain hemispheres (see graphic, above) (Kilpatrick et al., 2011; Lyubimov, 1992).

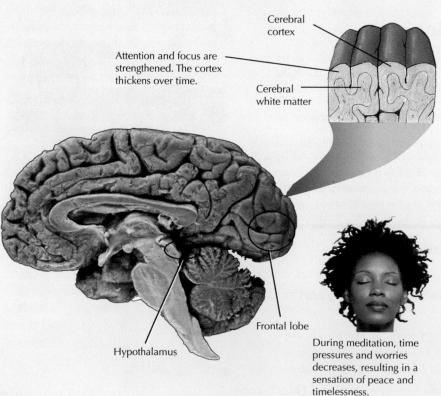

Cerebral cortex

Attention and focus are strengthened. The cortex thickens over time.

Cerebral white matter

Frontal lobe

Hypothalamus

During meditation, time pressures and worries decreases, resulting in a sensation of peace and timelessness.

Finally, research has verified that meditation can produce dramatic changes in basic physiological processes, including heart rate, oygen consumption, sweat gland activity, and brain activity. Meditation has also been somewhat successful in reducing pain, anxiety and stress, lowering blood pressure, and improving negative moods (Evans et al., 2008; Grant, Courtemanche, & Rainville, 2011; Yu et al., 2011). Studies have even implied that meditation can change the body's parasympathetic response (Sathyaprabha et al., 2008; Young & Taylor, 1998) and increase structural support for the sensory, decision-making, and attention-processing centers of the brain (Lazar et al., 2005). It seems that during meditation, the part of the brain that is responsible for both sympathetic and parasympathetic responses, the *hypothalamus*, diminishes the sympathetic response and increases the parasympathetic response. Shutting down the so-called fight-or-flight response in this way allows for deep rest, slower respiration, and increased and more coordinated use of the brain's two hemispheres. At the same time, meditation engages the part of the brain that is responsible for decision making and reasoning, the *frontal lobe*.

the sound of waves and feeling the ocean mist on their faces. Invited to eat a delicious apple that is actually an onion, the hypnotized person may relish the flavor. Told they are watching a very funny or sad movie, they may begin to laugh or cry at their self-created visions.

What is hypnosis? Scientific research has removed much of the mystery surrounding **hypnosis**. It is defined as a trancelike state of heightened suggestibility, deep relaxation, and intense focus. It is characterized by one or more of the following:

Hypnosis Trancelike state of heightened suggestibility, deep relaxation, and intense focus

- Narrowed, highly focused attention (the participant is able to "tune out" competing sensory stimuli)
- Increased use of imagination and hallucinations (in the case of visual hallucinations, a person may see things that aren't there or not see things that are)
- Passive and receptive attitude
- Decreased responsiveness to pain
- Heightened suggestibility (a willingness to respond to proposed changes in perception—"this onion is an apple") (Jamieson & Hasegawa, 2007; Jensen et al., 2008; Nash & Barnier, 2008).

Therapeutic Uses

From the 1700s to modern times, hypnosis has been used (and abused) by entertainers and quacks (see the Myth Buster box, p. 196). At the same time, it also has been employed as a respected clinical tool by physicians, dentists, and therapists. This curious dual existence began with Franz Anton Mesmer (1734–1815). Mesmer believed that all living bodies were filled with magnetic energy, and he claimed to use this "knowledge" to cure diseases. After lulling his patients into a deep state of relaxation and making them believe completely in his curative powers, Mesmer passed magnets over their bodies and told them their problems would go away. For some people, it worked—hence the term *mesmerized*.

Mesmer's theories were eventually discredited. But James Braid, a Scottish physician, later put people in this same trancelike state for surgery. Around the same time, however, powerful and reliable anesthetic drugs were discovered, and interest in Braid's technique dwindled. It was Braid who coined the term *hypnosis* in 1843, from the Greek word for "sleep."

Today, even with available anesthetics, hypnosis is occasionally used in surgery and for the treatment of chronic pain and severe burns (Jensen et al., 2008, 2011; Nash & Barnier, 2008; Nusbaum et al., 2011; Smith, 2011). Hypnosis has found its best use, however, in medical areas in which patients have a high degree of anxiety, fear, and misinformation, such as dentistry and childbirth. Because pain is strongly affected by tension and anxiety, any technique that helps the patient relax is medically useful.

In psychotherapy, hypnosis can help patients relax, remember painful memories, and reduce anxiety. It has been used with modest success in the treatment of phobias and in efforts to lose weight, stop smoking, and improve study habits (Amundson & Nuttgens, 2008; Golden, 2006; Manning, 2007; Smith, 2011).

Many athletes use self-hypnosis techniques (mental imagery and focused attention) to improve performance. Long-distance runner Steve Ortiz, for example, mentally relives all his best races before a big meet. He says that by the time the race actually begins, "I'm almost in a state of self-hypnosis. I'm just floating along" (cited in Kiester, 1984, p. 23).

 **TRY THIS YOURSELF**

Hypnosis or Simple Trick?

You can re-create a favorite trick that stage hypnotists promote as evidence of superhuman strength under hypnosis. Simply arrange two chairs as shown in the picture. You will see that hypnosis is not necessary—all that is needed is a highly motivated volunteer willing to stiffen his or her body.

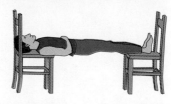

MYTH BUSTERS

Hypnosis Myths and Facts

Myth	Fact
1. **Forced hypnosis:** People can be involuntarily hypnotized or hypnotically "brainwashed."	Hypnosis requires a willing, conscious choice to relinquish control of one's consciousness to someone else. The best potential subjects are those who are able to focus attention, are open to new experiences, and are capable of imaginative involvement or fantasy (Carvalho et al., 2008; Green & Lynn, 2011; Lynn Rhue, & Kirsch, 2010; Terhune, Cardena, & Lindgren, 2011; Wickramasekera, 2008).
2. **Unethical behavior:** Hypnosis can make people behave immorally or take dangerous risks against their will.	Hypnotized people retain awareness and control of their behavior, and they can refuse to comply with the hypnotist's suggestions (Kirsch, Mazzoni, & Montgomery, 2006; Lynn, Rhue, & Kirsch, 2010).
3. **Faking:** Hypnosis participants are "faking it," playing along with the hypnotist.	There are conflicting research positions about hypnosis. Although most participants are not consciously faking hypnosis, some researchers believe the effects result from a blend of conformity, relaxation, obedience, suggestion, and role playing (Lynn, Rhue, & Kirsch, 2010; Orne, 2006). Other theorists believe that hypnotic effects result from a special altered state of consciousness (Bob, 2008; Naish, 2006; Bowers & Woody, 1996; Hilgard, 1978, 1992). A group of "unified" theorists suggests that hypnosis is a combination of both relaxation/role playing and a unique alternate state or consciousness.
4. **Superhuman strength:** Hypnotized people can perform acts of special, superhuman strength.	When nonhypnotized people are simply asked to try their hardest on tests of physical strength, they generally can do anything that a hypnotized person can (Orne, 2006).
5. **Exceptional memory:** Under hypnosis, people can recall things they otherwise could not. 	Although the heightened relaxation and focus that hypnosis engenders improves recall for some information, it adds little if anything to regular memory and hypnotized people also are more willing to guess (Erdelyi, 2010; Lynn, Rhue, & Kirsch, 2010; Wagstaff et al., 2007; Wickramasekera, 2008). Because memory is normally filled with fabrication and distortion (Chapter 7), hypnosis generally increases the potential for error. 

Psychology Engages

GENDER AND CULTURAL DIVERSITY

Dream Variations and Similarities

Objective 5.16: How do gender and culture affect dreams?

A quick glance at the list of common dream themes in Table 5.4 shows that most people, at least in the Western world, dream a lot about being chased, sex, and misfortune. But do men and women dream about different things? Are there differences between cultures in dream content? In reference to gender, research shows that men and women tend to share many common dream themes. But women are more likely to dream of children, family and familiar people, household objects, and indoor events. Men, on the other hand, more often dream about strangers, violence, weapons, sexual activity, achievement, and outdoor events (Blume-Marcovici, 2010; Domhoff, 2003, 2007, 2010; Schredl et al., 2004). Interestingly, other evidence suggests gender differences in dream recall and dream content may result from sex role orientation, whereas others propose that as gender differences and stereotypes lessen, segregation of dream content by gender becomes less distinct (Hobson, 2002; Schredl, et al., 2010).

Likewise, researchers have found both similarities and differences in dream content across cultures. Dreams involving basic human needs and fears (like sex, aggression, and death) seem to be found in all cultures. And children around the world often dream about large, threatening wild animals. People of all ages and cultures dream of falling, being chased, and being unable to do something they need to do. In addition, dreams around the world typically include more misfortune than good fortune, and the dreamer is more often the victim of aggression than the cause of it (Domhoff, 2003, 2007, 2010; Domhoff & Schneider, 2008; Hall & Van de Castle, 1996).

Yet there are some cultural differences. The Yir Yoront, an Australian hunting-and-gathering group, generally prefer marriage between a man and his mother's brother's daughter (Schneider & Sharp, 1969).

Table 5.4 COMMON DREAM THEMES

Rank	Dream content	Total prevalance
1	Chased or pursued, not physically injured	81.5
2	Sexual experiences	76.5
3	Falling	73.8
4	School, teachers, studying	67.1
5	Arriving too late, e.g., missing a train	59.5
6	Being on the verge of falling	57.7
7	Trying again and again to do something	53.5
8	A person now alive as dead	54.1
9	Flying or soaring through the air	48.3
10	Vividly sensing . . . a presence in the room	48.3
11	Failing an examination	45.0
12	Physically attacked (beaten, stabbed, raped)	42.4

This list shows the 12 dreams most frequently reported by the students. Total prevalence refers to the percentage of students reporting each dream. The data shown here are from a study of 1,181 college students in Canada (Nielsen et al., 2003) Source: Nielsen, T. A., Zadra, A. L., Simard, V., Saucier, S., Stenstrom, P., Smith, C., & Kuiken, D. (2003). The typical dreams of Canadian university students. *Dreaming, 13,* 211–235. Copyright © 2003 Association for the Study of Dreams. [from Table 1, p. 217]

Therefore, it is not uncommon (or surprising) that young, single men in the group often report recurrent dreams of aggression from their mother's brother (their future father-in-law). Similarly, Americans often report embarrassing dreams of being naked in public. Such dreams are rare in cultures where few clothes are worn.

How people interpret and value their dreams also varies across cultures (Berry et al., 2011; Laungani, 2007; Triandis, 2007). The Iroquois of North America believe that one's spirit uses dreams to communicate unconscious wishes to the conscious mind (Wallace, 1958). They often share their dreams with religious leaders, who help them interpret and cope with their underlying psychic needs to prevent illness and even death. On the other hand, the Maya of Central America share their dreams and interpretations at communal gatherings as an important means of teaching cultural folk wisdom (Tedlock, 1992). (As a critical thinker, do you notice the close similarity between Freudian theory and the Iroquois concept of dreaming? Some historians believe that Freud borrowed many concepts from the Iroquois—without giving appropriate credit.)

CRITICAL THINKING

Interpreting Your Dreams

By Thomas Frangicetto (Northampton Community College, Bethlehem, PA)

> "Dreams feel real while we're in them. It's only when we wake up that we realize something was actually strange."
>
> Dom Cobb (Leonardo DiCaprio) in the popular 2010 film *Inception*

Television, movies, and other popular media often portray dreams as highly significant, yet easily interpreted. That is, until *Inception*, the popular and critically acclaimed 2010 movie, took the use of dreams in cinema to a new level. Writer/director Christopher Nolan posed an intriguing challenge to his audience—what part of the movie's storyline was a *dream* versus what was *real*?

Throughout history, people have always been intrigued by dreams, but, as you've seen in this chapter, scientists are deeply divided about the meaning of dreams and their relative importance. Fortunately, these differences in scientific opinion provide an excellent opportunity to practice the critical thinking components (CTCs) of *tolerating ambiguity* and *welcoming divergent views*. In addition, employing the CTC of *being eclectic* (using whatever works best from each theory) also helps in dream interpretation. As you'll see throughout this text, psychological science often prefers this "pick and choose," eclectic approach.

Critical Thinking Application

Begin by studying the following dream.

> I had this dream—I'd call it a nightmare—about 10 years ago when I was 14. I was standing outside of my house, much higher in the dream than in real life, when bricks began falling, then shutters, shingles, and windows. There was screaming. I couldn't move. I started running around picking up pieces of the house, trying to put them back in place, crying throughout. Exhausted, I fell to the ground in tears, and then I actually woke up crying. It wasn't until I talked to a school counselor about the dream that I began to understand its meaning.

SARAH, A NORTHAMPTON COLLEGE
PSYCHOLOGY STUDENT

Part A *Analyze Sarah's dreams from the following perspectives:*

- **Psychoanalytic/psychodynamic:** According to this view, what might be the dreamer's thoughts, feelings, and motivations? Can you identify the *manifest content* (storyline) and *latent content* (true meaning)? What are the most obvious symbols, and what do they supposedly represent?

- **Biological:** Hobson and McCarley's *activation–synthesis hypothesis* claims that dreams are mainly a biological process. But even if dreams begin with more or less random activity in various brain areas, the dreamer's interpretations of this activity depend on his or her personality, motivations, memories, and life experiences. Can you imagine possible life experiences or specific thoughts that might have triggered this particular dream for Sarah?

- **Cognitive:** Psychologists from this perspective believe dreams provide important information, which may suggest solutions to real-life problems. For example, one cognitive theorist, Calvin Hall, believed that dreams provide "maps" that the dreamer can use to anticipate problems and conflicts—sort of a GPS system of the mind—in order to find the best route to a solution (Hall, 1953). Does Sarah's dream provide a possible solution to her life problems?

(*Note*: An important clue and possible interpretation of Sarah's dream is provided in Appendix B. But please do not check them until you've fully explored your own interpretations.)

Part B *Apply both your critical thinking and new knowledge from this chapter to your own dream:*

1. Write down a dream you vividly recall, ideally one that you're uncertain about. Record every detail, no matter how irrelevant it may seem.

2. Repeating the same three theories in Part A, examine all possible meanings and interpretations of your dream—no matter how bizarre.

   - *Psychoanalytic/psychodynamic:* Identify the likely manifest and latent content. What are the main symbols, and what do the represent?

   - *Biological:* Was there a particular experience or thought that might have stimulated your dream?

   - *Cognitive:* What possible life problem did your dream highlight? Did it provide possible solutions?

So what do you think? Are dreams just the reflection of random firing of brain activity, do they offer valuable insight into our lives, or do you agree with Freud that many dreams reflect hidden desires and *wish fulfillment*, as seen in this exchange from the movie *Inception*:

Ariadne: Why is it so important to dream?

Cobb: Because, in my dreams we are together

RESEARCH CHALLENGE

Nicotine Addiction: It Takes More Than an Iron Will . . . to Quit Smoking!

By Thomas Frangicetto (Northampton Community College, Bethlehem, PA)

Iron Man couldn't defeat it. Sherlock Holmes couldn't solve the mystery of it. Robert Downey Jr., the resurgent actor who has played both the super hero and super sleuth, admitted on the Jay Leno Show that he had started smoking again. It would not have been a big deal for most stars, but Downey's infamous addiction to both alcohol and drugs had put him in prison and nearly destroyed his career.

Why did he begin smoking again? "Because I get really stressed," he explained, "and I despise myself." When Leno pushed him on the need to quit, Downey became defensive. "Leave me alone about it," he said, "I'm doing the best I can."

Did Downey see his nicotine addiction as the lesser of the addiction evils? While it could be safer for his acting career, it certainly isn't safer for his health, as no addiction is associated with more disease, disability, and death than smoking (NIDA, 2011; Peele, 2010).

Just how serious is nicotine addiction? According to the National Institute on Drug Abuse (NIDA, 2011), one out of five adults—roughly 46 million people in all—still smoke, despite all of the warnings of its deadly effects. Three out of four smokers who try to stop smoking relapse within six months, and many attempts are often necessary to quit permanently (Superville,

2011). When asked if he would quit smoking again, Iron Man Downey laughed: "Of course I will, it's easy. I've done it *hundreds* of times."

There was some laughter from the audience, but probably less than he was anticipating. Was the audience sensing an undercurrent of seriousness to Downey's joke? This was, after all, a notorious addict making light of a fiercely lethal habit that in all likelihood would end his life prematurely.

Consider that tobacco smoking leads to more than 5 million deaths each year and is responsible for nearly 90 percent of all deaths linked to lung cancer (Fowler et al., 2011). And what is the principal reinforcing agent in tobacco smoke that causes addiction? Simple: *nicotine*.

The National Institute on Drug Abuse (NIDA, 2008) cites research showing that nicotine affects the same areas of the brain as other frequently abused drugs—the so-called reward system. Nicotine, like marijuana, cocaine, and heroin, increases levels of the neurotransmitter dopamine in the reward system, resulting in durable changes in brain cells, changes that can lead to addiction (NIDA, 2008).

So, is there hope for someone like Robert Downey, Jr. and so many others who seem hopelessly addicted to nicotine? The good news is yes, scientists have been relentlessly investigating the link between nicotine and addiction, and there have

been numerous findings that give hope to smokers who seem permanently hooked.

A recent example came from a team of scientists at the Florida Scripps Research Institute who identified a pathway in the brain called the habenulo-interpenduncular tract (near the thalamus, see p. 68), which is linked to a susceptibility to nicotine addiction. Using animal models, the researchers studied the effects of a "nicotinic acetylcholine receptor" that responds to the presence of nicotine in the brain. They found that when a genetic mutation was induced that inhibited the receptor, the desire for nicotine increased. However, when the effects on the receptor were reversed, the desire for nicotine returned to normal (Fowler et al., 2011).

"The habenula and brain structures into which it projects, play such a profound role in controlling the desire to consume nicotine," Christine Fowler, the first author of the study, explained. "The habenula appears to be activated by nicotine when consumption of the drug has reached an adverse level. But it the pathway isn't functioning properly, you simply take more" (Science Daily, 2011).

In sum, when an individual's nicotine receptors do not function properly, the habenula is not as responsive to nicotine, so much more of the drug will be consumed (Fowler et al., 2011). These findings provide a new framework for comprehending the "motivational drives in nicotine

consumption," and also the brain pathways involved in the vulnerability for tobacco addiction (Science Daily, 2011).

Looking ahead, the study's lead researcher believes the new data "point the way to a promising target for the development of potential anti-smoking therapies."

For Iron Man, Robert Downey, Jr. and others like him, these new treatments can't come soon enough.

Student Engagement Exercise

Given the admittedly limited information in the Scripps Research Institute study described above, what is the most likely:

1. *Research method* (experimental, descriptive, correlational, or biological)?

2. If you chose the:

- *Experimental method*—label the IV, DV, experimental group, and control group.

- *Descriptive method*—is this a naturalistic observation, survey, or case study?

- *Correlational method*—is this a positive, negative, or zero correlation?

- *Biological method*—identify the specific research tool (e.g., brain dissection, CT scan, etc.)

(Answers appear in Appendix B.)

CHECK & REVIEW

STOP *Before going on, be sure to complete this Check & Review. It is an invaluable study tool!*

Healthier Ways to Alter Consciousness and Psychology Engages

Part A: Retrieval Practice

1. Without looking at the book, spend 10 minutes writing a free-form essay recalling all you can remember from the previous section.

2. Now, reread the previous section, and once again spend 10 minutes writing a free-form essay on the SAME material.

Part B: Practice Quiz

1. _____ is a group of techniques designed to focus attention, block out all distractions, and produce an alternate state of consciousness (ASC). (a) Hypnosis; (b) Scientology; (c) Parapsychology; (d) Meditation

2. List the five major characteristics of hypnosis.

3. Why is it almost impossible to hypnotize an unwilling participant?

4. List the five myths of hypnosis.

5. Which of the common dream themes are closest to your own experience?

Check your answers in Appendix B.

WileyPLUS presents an on-line version of this textbook along with a wealth of study resources including quizzes, practice tests, flash cards, videos, animations and other activities designed to improve your mastery of the content. Working in conjunction with these study tools, the *Psychology in Action* WileyPLUS course features Professor Karen Huffman, author of this textbook, explaining and expanding upon some of the most challenging concepts in psychology. Here is a sample of the tutorial videos available for this chapter:

- Interactive animation depicting various stages of a normal sleep cycle
- Debunking popular myths about sleep, dreams, drugs, and hypnosis
- Interactive animation depicting how drugs affect neurons and the brain
- Conscious vs. unconscious processing, featuring Professor Huffman's classroom demonstrations of the Stroop Effect and the dangers of multitasking
- Virtual Field Trip to a sleep laboratory to learn how sleep disorders are diagnosed and treated
- Virtual Field Trip to a drug treatment center to learn about different approaches to this challenging problem.

Key Terms

To assess your understanding of the **Key Terms** in Chapter 5, write a definition for each (in your own words), and then compare your definitions with those in the text.

Understanding Consciousness
consciousness (p. 168)
alternate states of consciousness (ASCs) (p. 168)
controlled processes (p. 170)
automatic processes (p. 170)

Sleep and Dreams
circadian [sir-KADE-ee-un] rhythms (p. 171)
rapid-eye-movement (REM) sleep (p. 175)
non-rapid-eye-movement (NREM) sleep (p. 176)
evolutionary/circadian theory (p. 178)

repair/restoration theory (p. 178)
manifest content (p. 179)
latent content (p. 179)
activation–synthesis hypothesis (p. 179)
insomnia (p. 181)
narcolepsy [NAR co-lep-see] (p. 181)
sleep apnea (p. 181)
nightmares (p. 182)
night terrors (p. 182)

Psychoactive Drugs
psychoactive drugs (p. 183)
agonist drug (p. 183)
antagonist drug (p. 183)
drug abuse (p. 185)

addiction (p. 185)
psychological dependence (p. 185)
physical dependence (p. 185)
withdrawal (p. 185)
tolerance (p. 185)
depressants (p. 188)
stimulants (p. 188)
opiates (p. 189)
hallucinogens [hal LOO-sin-o-jenz] (p. 190)

Healthier Ways to Alter Consciousness
meditation (p. 193)
hypnosis (p. 195)

Chapter Summary

Understanding Consciousness

Objective 5.1: Define and describe consciousness and alternate states of consciousness (ASCs).
Consciousness can be defined as an organism's awareness of its own self and surroundings.

Most of our lives are spent in normal, waking **consciousness**, an organism's awareness of its own self and surroundings. However, we also spend considerable time in various **alternate states of**

consciousness (ASCs), such as sleep and dreaming, daydreams, and states induced by psychoactive drugs, hypnosis, and meditation.

Objective 5.2: Contrast controlled versus automatic processing.
Controlled processes, which require focused attention, are at the highest level of the continuum of awareness. **Automatic processes**, which require minimal attention, are found in the middle. Unconsciousness and coma are at the lowest level.

Circadian Rhythms and Stages of Sleep

Objective 5.3: What are circadian rhythms and how do they affect our lives?
Circadian rhythms are biological changes that occur on a 24-hour cycle. Our sleep–wake cycle, alertness, moods, learning, blood pressure, and the like all follow circadian rhythms. Disruptions to circadian rhythms due to shift work, jet lag, and sleep

deprivation can cause accidents and other serious problems.

Objective 5.4: List the phases of sleep and describe a typical night's sleep.
A typical night's sleep consists of four to five 90-minute cycles. The cycle begins in Stage 1 and then moves through Stages 2, 3, and 4. After reaching the deepest level of sleep, the cycle reverses up to **REM (rapid-eye-movement) sleep**, in which the person often is dreaming. Sleep stages 1, 2, 3, 4 are called **NREM (non-rapid-eye-movement) sleep**.

Objective 5.5: List six common myths about sleep.
Six of the most common myths include: Everyone needs 8 hours of sleep. It's easy to learn complicated things while asleep. Some people never dream. Dreams only last a few seconds. Genital arousal means the sleeper is having a sexual dream. And, dreaming of dying can be fatal.

Theories of Sleep and Dreams

Objective 5.6: Why do we sleep?
The exact function of sleep is unknown. But according to the **evolutionary/circadian theory**, sleep evolved to conserve energy and protect us from predators. According to **repair/restoration theory**, sleep is thought to be necessary for its restorative value, both physically and psychologically.

Objective 5.7: Why do we dream?
Three major theories attempt to explain why we dream. According to the *psychoanalytic/psychodynamic view*, dreams are disguised symbols of repressed desires, conflicts, and anxieties. The *biological perspective* (**activation–synthesis hypothesis**) proposes that dreams are simple by-products of random stimulation of brain cells. The *cognitive view* suggests that dreams are an important type of information processing of everyday experiences.

Sleep Disorders

Objective 5.8: Describe the major sleep disorders.
Sleep disorders fall into two major diagnostic categories—*dyssomnias* (including insomnia, narcolepsy, and sleep apnea) and *parasomnias* (such as nightmares and night terrors).

People who have repeated difficulty falling or staying asleep, or awakening too early, experience **insomnia**. **Narcolepsy** is excessive daytime sleepiness characterized by sudden sleep attacks. A person with **sleep apnea** temporarily stops breathing during sleep, causing loud snoring or poor-quality sleep. **Nightmares** are bad dreams that occur during REM (rapid-eye-movement) sleep. **Night terrors** are abrupt awakenings with feelings of panic that occur during NREM sleep.

Psychoactive Drugs

Objective 5.9: Define psychoactive drugs and explain how they work.
Psychoactive drugs are chemicals that change conscious awareness, mood, and/or perception. These drugs work primarily by changing the amount and effect of neurotransmitters in the synapse. Some drugs act as *agonists* that mimic a neurotransmitter's effects, whereas other drugs act as *antagonists* and block normal neurotransmitter functioning.

Objective 5.10: Clarify the major misconceptions and confusing terminology related to psychoactive drugs.
Drug abuse refers to drug taking that causes emotional or physical harm to the individual or others. **Addiction** is a broad term referring to a person's feeling of compulsion to use a specific drug or to engage in certain activities.

Psychoactive drug use can lead to psychological dependence or physical dependence or both. **Psychological dependence** is a desire or craving to achieve the effects produced by a drug. **Physical dependence** is a change in bodily processes due to continued drug use that results in **withdrawal** symptoms when the drug is withheld. **Tolerance** is a decreased sensitivity to a drug brought about by its continuous use.

Objective 5.11: Why do addicts abuse drugs?
Research shows that their brains "learn" to be addicted. Neurotransmitters, like dopamine and glutamate, activate the brain's reward system and create lasting cravings and memories of the drug use.

Objective 5.12: List the four main categories of psychoactive drugs and explain how they work.
The major categories of psychoactive drugs are **depressants, stimulants, opiates**, and **hallucinogens**. Depressant drugs slow the central nervous system, whereas stimulants increase its activity. Opiates numb the senses and relieve pain. And hallucinogens produce sensory or perceptual distortions called hallucinations.

Objective 5.13: Discuss issues and concerns related to "club drugs."
Club drugs can produce desirable effects, but they also can cause serious health problems and impair good decision making.

Healthier Ways to Alter Consciousness and Psychology Engages

Objective 5.14: Define meditation and discuss its effects.
Meditation is a group of techniques designed to focus attention, block out all distractions, and produce an alternate state of consciousness. It can produce dramatic changes in physiological processes, including brain changes, heart rate, and respiration.

Objective 5.15: Define hypnosis, and describe its myths and potential benefits.
Hypnosis is an alternate state of heightened suggestibility characterized by deep relaxation and intense focus. Hypnosis is the subject of many myths, such as "forced hypnosis." But it also has been used successfully to reduce pain, to increase concentration, and as an adjunct to psychotherapy.

Objective 5.16: How do gender and culture affect dreams?
Researchers have found many similarities and differences in dream content between men and women and across cultures. How people interpret and value their dreams also varies across cultures.

ChapterFive VISUAL SUMMARY

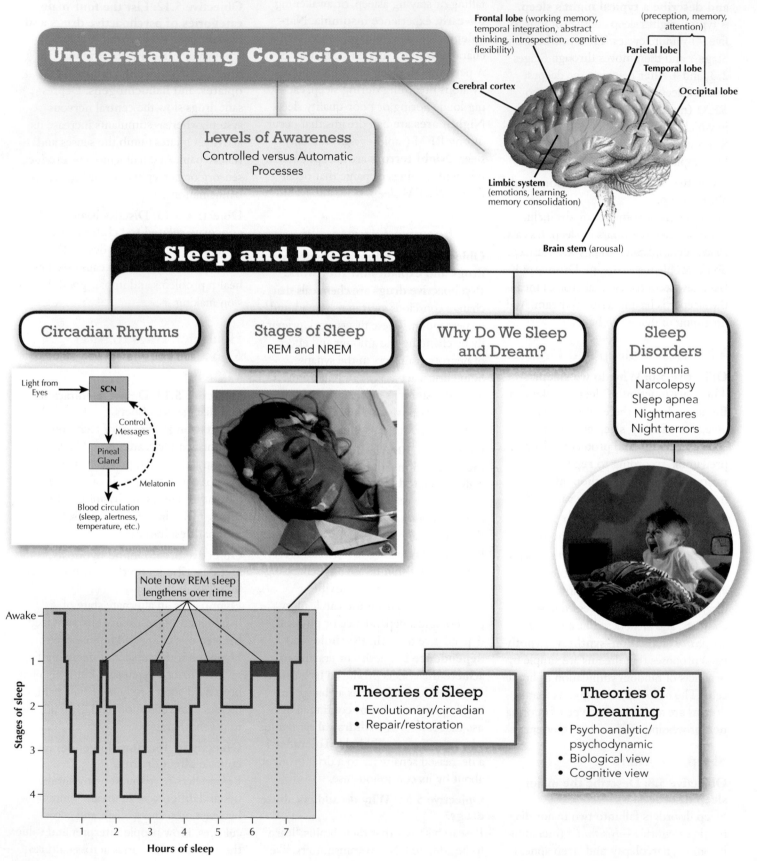

Understanding Consciousness

Frontal lobe (working memory, temporal integration, abstract thinking, introspection, cognitive flexibility)

(preception, memory, attention)

Parietal lobe

Temporal lobe

Occipital lobe

Cerebral cortex

Limbic system (emotions, learning, memory consolidation)

Brain stem (arousal)

Levels of Awareness
Controlled versus Automatic Processes

Sleep and Dreams

Circadian Rhythms

Light from Eyes → SCN

Control Messages

Pineal Gland

Melatonin

Blood circulation (sleep, alertness, temperature, etc.)

Stages of Sleep
REM and NREM

Note how REM sleep lengthens over time

Awake

Stages of sleep

1

2

3

4

1 2 3 4 5 6 7

Hours of sleep

Why Do We Sleep and Dream?

Sleep Disorders
Insomnia
Narcolepsy
Sleep apnea
Nightmares
Night terrors

Theories of Sleep
• Evolutionary/circadian
• Repair/restoration

Theories of Dreaming
• Psychoanalytic/ psychodynamic
• Biological view
• Cognitive view

Psychoactive Drugs

Understanding Psychoactive Drugs
- How Drugs Work (agonist versus antagonist)
- Terminology (e.g., addiction)

Categorizing Psychoactive Drugs
- Depressants (e.g., alcohol)
- Stimulants (e.g., cocaine)
- Opiates (e.g., morphine)
- Hallucinogens (e.g., LSD)

Sending neuron

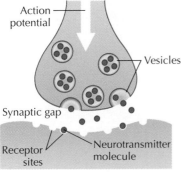

Action potential

Vesicles

Synaptic gap

Receptor sites

Neurotransmitter molecule

Receiving neuron

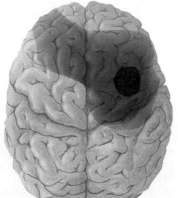

Nucleus accumbens (drugs elevate dopamine levels)

Dopamine projections to frontal lobes

Amygdala

Absence of the drug triggers withdrawal symptoms (e.g., intense pain and cravings).

Psychoactive drugs, like the opiates, affect the brain and body in a variety of ways. Most researchers believe that increased dopamine activity in this so-called *reward pathway of the brain* accounts for the reinforcing effects of most addictive drugs.

Healthier Ways to Alter Consciousness

Top view of head

Meditation
Group of techniques designed to focus attention and block out distractions

Hypnosis
Trancelike state of heightened suggestibility, deep relaxation, and intense focus

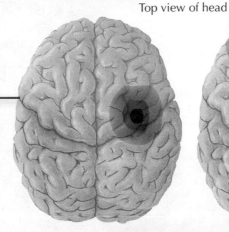

Before meditation

During meditation

Psychology Engages

Gender & Cultural Diversity
Critical Thinking
Research Challenge

ChapterSix

Learning

Animals (both human and nonhuman) are born with a complex set of genetic instructions that will govern numerous aspects of their entire lives. However, most of what we do we *learn* from experience. Picture yourself in these imaginary situations:

On your way to campus, you note a traffic jam up ahead and quickly decide to try a new shortcut someone mentioned several weeks ago. Later, in your general psychology class, you watch a video on service dogs for the blind, and are amazed by these dogs opening and closing doors, helping their owners dress and undress, carrying items in a backpack, and even differentiating between classrooms, bathrooms, escalators, and elevators. How did you successfully navigate a new route to campus? How did these guide dogs perform such amazing acts?

While leaving campus, you stop by to watch your college's baseball game. You note that the pitcher has a wad of gum stuck on his hat and engages in several strange, ritualistic behaviors. Before each pitch, he kicks the dirt twice with each foot, spits in his glove, and then taps the top of his ball cap three times. What explains this type of superstitious behavior?

When you arrive at your nighttime job, you observe your manager destroying several birds' nests within the store. Your coworker explains that barn swallows in Minnesota have been building nests inside stores to protect their babies from predators and the winter weather. The problem is that these birds also have discovered how to open and close the doors—they flutter their wings around the motion sensors!

Objective 6.1: Compare learning and conditioning.

These examples of human and nonhuman animal behaviors are clearly not genetic and present at the moment of birth. They all result from *learning*. We usually think of learning as classroom activities, such as math and reading, or as motor skills, like riding a bike or playing the piano. However, psychologists define **learning** more broadly, as a *relatively permanent change in behavior and mental processes due to experience.* This relative permanence applies not only to useful and admirable behaviors, such as finding a new route to campus or serving as guide dog, but also to less adaptive behaviors, like superstitious acts and building nests inside commercial buildings. The good news is: What is learned can be unlearned—through retraining, counseling, and perseverance.

Learning Relatively permanent change in behavior or mental processes due to experience

Did you know that this chapter can . . .

- *Enhance your enjoyment of life?* Unfortunately, many people (who haven't taken introductory psychology) choose marital partners hoping to change or "rescue" them. Or they pursue jobs they hate because they want to "make a lot of money." If you carefully study and actively apply the information in this chapter, you can avoid these mistakes and thereby greatly enrich your life.

- *Expand your understanding and control of behavior?* A core research finding from learning theory is that people (and nonhuman animals) *do not persist in behaviors that are not reinforced.* Using this information, we can remove reinforcers of destructive or undesirable behaviors and recognize that bad habits will continue until we change the reinforcers. Keep in mind that behavior is not random! There's a reason for everything we do.

- *Improve the predictability of your life?* Another key finding from research in learning is that the *best predictor of future behavior is past behavior.* People can (and do) change, and all learned behavior can be unlearned. However, the statistical odds are still high that old patterns of behavior will persist in the future. If you want to predict whether the person you're dating is good marriage material, look to his or her past.

- *Help you change the world?* Reinforcement also motivates greedy business practices, unethical political and environmental decisions, prejudice, and war.

Knowing this, if we all work together to remove the inappropriate reinforcers, we can truly change the world. Admittedly, this sounds grandiose and simplistic. But I sincerely believe in the power of education and the usefulness of the material in this chapter. Your life and the world around you can be significantly improved with a "simple" application of learning principles.

Conditioning Process of learning associations between stimuli and behavioral responses

In this chapter, we discuss classical and operant **conditioning**, the two most basic forms of learning. Then we look at cognitive-social learning and biological factors in learning. Finally, we explore how learning theories and concepts touch on everyday life.

Classical Conditioning

Objective 6.2: Define classical conditioning, and describe Pavlov's and Watson's contributions.

Have you noticed that when you're hungry and see a large slice of chocolate cake or a juicy steak, your mouth starts to water? It seems natural that your mouth should water once you put food into it. But why do you salivate at just the sight of the food?

Pavlov and Watson's Contributions: The Beginnings of Classical Conditioning

The answer to this question was accidentally discovered in the laboratory of Russian physiologist Ivan Pavlov (1849–1936). Pavlov's work focused on the role of saliva in digestion, and one of his experiments involved measuring salivary responses in dogs, using a tube attached to the dog's salivary glands (Step-by-Step Diagram 6.1).

Pavlov's (Accidental) Discovery

One of Pavlov's students noticed that many dogs began salivating at the mere sight of the food or the food dish, the smell of the food, or even the sight of the person who delivered the food long *before* receiving the actual food. This "unscheduled" salivation was

Step-by-StepDiagram6.1

Pavlov's Classical Conditioning

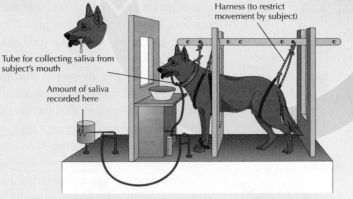

Harness (to restrict movement by subject)

Tube for collecting saliva from subject's mouth

Amount of saliva recorded here

Pavlov Example   **Modern-day Example**

Step 1
Before conditioning
Neutral stimulus (NS) produces no relevant response; unconditioned (unlearned) *stimulus* (UCS) elicits the unconditioned *response* (UCR)

NS (Tone) → No relevant response   NS (Cardboard box) → No relevant response

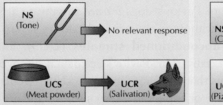

UCS (Meat powder) → UCR (Salivation)   UCS (Pizza) → UCR (Salivation)

Step 2
During conditioning
Neutral stimulus (NS) is repeatedly paired with the unconditioned (unlearned) *stimulus* (UCS) to produce the unconditioned *response* (UCR)

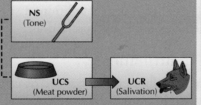

NS (Tone)   NS (Cardboard box)

UCS (Meat powder) → UCR (Salivation)   UCS (Pizza) → UCR (Salivation)

Step 3
After conditioning
Neutral stimulus (NS) becomes a conditioned (learned) stimulus (CS); CS produces a conditioned (learned) *response* (CR), which is usually similar to the previously unconditioned (unlearned) response (UCR)

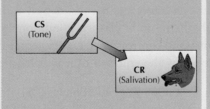
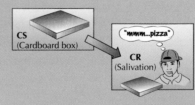

CS (Tone) → CR (Salivation)   CS (Cardboard box) → "mmm...pizza" CR (Salivation)

Summary
Originally neutral stimulus (NS) becomes a conditioned stimulus (CS), which elicits a conditioned response (CR)

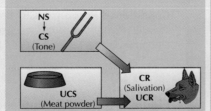

NS → CS (Tone)   NS → CS (Cardboard box)

UCS (Meat powder) → CR (Salivation) UCR   UCS (Pizza) → CR (Salivation) UCR

StudyTip

Use this figure to help you visualize and organize the three major stages of classical conditioning and their associated key terms. Also, remember conditioning is essentially the same as learning. In addition, when thinking of a UCS or UCR, picture how a newborn baby, with little or no previous learning, would respond. The baby's innate, unlearned response to the UCS would be the UCR.

"PERHAPS, DR. PAVLOV, HE COULD BE TAUGHT TO SEAL ENVELOPES."

Classical Conditioning Learning through involuntarily paired associations; it occurs when a previously neutral stimulus (NS) is paired (associated) with an unconditioned stimulus (UCS) to elicit a conditioned response (CR)

Unconditioned Stimulus (UCS) Stimulus that elicits an unconditioned response (UCR) without previous conditioning

Unconditioned Response (UCR) Unlearned reaction to an unconditioned stimulus (UCS) that occurs without previous conditioning

Neutral Stimulus (NS) Stimulus that, before conditioning, does not naturally bring about the response of interest

intriguing. Pavlov recognized that an involuntary reflex (salivation) that occurred *before* the appropriate stimulus (food) was presented could not be inborn and biological. It had to have been acquired through experience—through *learning*.

Excited by this accidental discovery, Pavlov and his students conducted several experiments. Their most basic method involved sounding a tone on a tuning fork just before food was placed in the dog's mouth. After several pairings of tone and food, the dogs would salivate on hearing the tone alone. Pavlov and others went on to show that all sorts of things can be conditioned stimuli for salivation if they are paired with food—the ticking of a metronome, a bell, a buzzer, a light, and even the sight of a circle or triangle drawn on a card.

The type of learning that Pavlov discovered came to be known as **classical conditioning**, *learning through involuntarily paired associations. It occurs when a neutral stimulus (NS) becomes paired (associated) with an unconditioned stimulus (UCS) to elicit a conditioned response (CR)*.

To understand classical conditioning, you first need to realize that *conditioning* is technically just another word for learning. You also need to know that some responses are inborn and don't need conditioning or learning.

Before Pavlov's dogs *learned* to salivate at something extraneous like the sight of the experimenter, the original salivary reflex was *inborn* and biological. It consisted of an **unconditioned stimulus (UCS)**, food, and an **unconditioned response (UCR)**, salivation. Pavlov's accidental discovery (and great contribution to psychology) was that learning can occur when a **neutral stimulus (NS)** (a stimulus that does not evoke or bring out a response) is regularly paired with an unconditioned stimulus (UCS). The originally neutral stimulus (the tone or the cardboard box in Step-by-Step Diagram 6.1) then becomes a **conditioned stimulus (CS)**, which elicits or produces a **conditioned response (CR)** (salivation).

Watson's Contribution

What does a dog salivating to the sound of a tone have to do with your life? Classical conditioning is the most basic and fundamental way that all animals, including humans, learn most new responses, emotions, and attitudes. Your fears, likes, dislikes, and love for your family and friends, as well as drooling at the sight of chocolate cake are all largely the result of classical conditioning.

In a famous (and controversial) experiment, John Watson and Rosalie Rayner (1920) demonstrated how the emotion of fear could be classically conditioned (Figure 6.1).

Conditioned Stimulus (CS) Previously neutral stimulus that, through repeated pairings with an unconditioned stimulus (UCS), now elicits a conditioned response (CR)

Conditioned Response (CR) Learned reaction to a conditioned stimulus (CS) that occurs because of previous repeated pairings with an unconditioned stimulus (UCS)

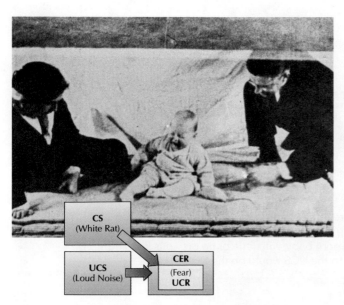

Figure 6.1 Conditioning and the case of Little Albert In the famous "Little Albert" study, a healthy 11-month-old child was first allowed to play with a white laboratory rat. Like most infants, Albert was curious and reached for the rat, showing no fear. Using the fact that infants are naturally frightened (UCR) by loud noises (UCS), Watson stood behind Albert and again put the rat (NS) near him. When the infant reached for the rat, Watson banged a steel bar with a hammer. The loud noise frightened Albert and made him cry. The white rat (NS) was paired with the loud noise (UCS) only seven times before the white rat alone produced a *conditioned emotional response* (CER) in Albert, fear of the rat.

Although this study remains a classic in psychology, the research procedures used by Watson and Rayner violated several ethical guidelines for scientific research (Chapter 1). Watson and Rayner not only deliberately created a serious fear in a child, but they also ended their experiment without *extinguishing* (removing) it. In addition, the researchers have been criticized because they did not measure Albert's fear objectively. Their subjective evaluation raises doubt about the degree of fear conditioned.

Despite such criticisms, John B. Watson made important and lasting contributions to psychology. At the time he was conducting research, psychology's early founders were defining the field as the *scientific study of the mind* (Chapter 1). Watson criticized this focus on internal mental activities, insisting that they were impossible to study objectively. Instead, he emphasized strictly *observable* behaviors. Watson is also credited with founding the new approach known as *behaviorism*, which explains behavior as a result of observable *stimuli* (in the environment) and observable *responses* (behavioral actions). In addition, Watson's study of Little Albert showed us that many of our likes, dislikes, prejudices, and fears are **conditioned emotional responses (CER)**. In Chapter 15, you will also see how Watson's research in *producing* Little Albert's fears later led to powerful clinical tools for *eliminating* extreme, irrational fears known as *phobias*.

Historical note: Shortly after the Little Albert experiment, Watson was fired from his academic position. And no other university would hire him, despite his international fame and scientific reputation. His firing resulted from his scandalous and highly publicized affair with his graduate student Rosalie Rayner and subsequent divorce. Watson later married Rayner and became an influential advertising executive. He is credited with many successful ad campaigns based on classical conditioning, including those for Johnson & Johnson baby powder, Maxwell House coffee, and Lucky Strike cigarettes (Schultz & Schultz, 2012; Hunt, 1993).

Conditioned Emotional Response (CER) Classically conditioned emotional response to a previously neutral stimulus (NS)

CHECK & REVIEW

STOP *Before going on, be sure to complete this Check & Review. It is an invaluable study tool!*

Pavlov and Watson's Contributions

Part A: Retrieval Practice

1. Without looking at the book, spend 10 minutes writing a free-form essay recalling all you can remember from the previous section.

2. Now, reread the previous section, and once again spend 10 minutes writing a free-form essay on the SAME material.

   (Although time consuming, this exercise has been shown to be the single best way to improve your test scores! For more information, check out http://www.sciencemag.org/content/early/2011/01/19/science.1199327.abstract)

Part B: Practice Quiz

1. Based on the humor in this cartoon, the sound of the doorbell would be a(n) _____, and the dogs inside Pavlov's laboratory would begin salivating, which would be a(n) _____. (a) unconditioned

stimulus (UCS), conditioned response (CR); (b) conditioned stimulus (CS), conditioned response (CR); (c) neutral stimulus (NS), unconditioned response (UCR); (d) none of these options

2. Eli's grandma gives him a Tootsie Roll every time she visits. When Eli sees his grandma arriving, his mouth begins to

water. In this example the conditioned stimulus (CS) is _____.

3. After conditioning, the _____ elicits the _____.

4. In John Watson's demonstration of classical conditioning with Little Albert, the unconditioned stimulus was _____. (a) symptoms of fear; (b) a rat; (c) a bath towel; (d) a loud noise

5. After pairing the rat with a loud noise, Little Albert demonstrated an intense emotional reaction to the sight of the rat. His emotional response is an example of a(n) _____. (a) CS; (b) UCS; (c) CER; (d) UCR

6. Describe a personal CER that presents problems in your own life.

Check your answers in Appendix B.

Acquisition Basic classical conditioning when a neutral stimulus (NS) is consistently paired with an unconditioned stimulus (UCS) so that the NS comes to elicit a conditioned response (CR)

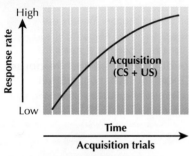

Figure 6.2 The process of acquisition During the initial, *acquisition*, phase of classical conditioning, a neutral stimulus (NS) that is consistently followed by an unconditioned stimulus (UCS) will become a conditioned stimulus (CS), which elicits a conditioned response (CR).

Stimulus Generalization Stimuli similar to the original conditioned stimulus (CS) elicit a conditioned response (CR)

Basic Principles: Understanding Classical Conditioning

Objective 6.3: Describe the six principles of classical conditioning.

Now that you understand the major key terms in classical conditioning and how they explain CERs, we can build on this foundation. In this section, we will discuss six important principles of classical conditioning: *acquisition, stimulus generalization, stimulus discrimination, extinction, spontaneous recovery,* and *higher-order conditioning* (Concept Organizer 6.1).

Acquisition

After Pavlov's original (accidental) discovery of classical conditioning, he and his associates were interested in expanding their understanding of the basic experiment we've just described. They wanted to go beyond the basic **acquisition** phase, a term describing general classical conditioning when a neutral stimulus (NS) is consistently paired with an unconditioned stimulus (UCS) so that the NS comes to elicit a conditioned response (CR) (Figure 6.2).

What is the optimal amount of time for presenting the neutral stimulus (NS), and what is the best order of presentation? Should the neutral stimulus (NS) always come first? Researchers have investigated four different ways to pair stimuli (Table 6.1), and they found that both the timing and the order in which the NS is presented are very important (Chang, Stout, & Miller, 2004; Griffin & Galef, 2005; Harris, 2011; LeFrancois, 2012). For example, *delayed conditioning*, in which the NS is presented before the UCS and remains until the UCR begins, generally yields the fastest learning. On the other hand, *backward conditioning*, in which the UCS is presented before the NS, is the least effective.

Generalization and Discrimination

In addition to the basic *acquisition phase* of classical conditioning, Pavlov and his associates also discovered that other stimuli similar to the neutral stimuli often produced a similar conditioned response (CR), a phenomenon known as **stimulus generalization**.

Table 6.1 ACQUISITION AND CONDITIONING SEQUENCES*

Delayed conditioning (most effective)	NS presented before UCS and remains until UCR begins	Tone presented before food
Simultaneous conditioning	NS presented at the same time as UCS	Tone and food presented simultaneously
Trace conditioning	NS presented and then taken away, or ends before UCS presented	Tone sounds, but food presented only once the sound stops
Backward conditioning (least effective)	UCS presented before NS	Food presented before the tone

*NS = neutral stimulus; UCR = unconditioned response; UCS = unconditioned stimulus.

ConceptOrganizer6.1

Six Principles of Classical Conditioning

Process	Description	Example
Acquisition	Neutral stimulus (NS) and unconditioned stimulus (UCS) are paired; neutral stimulus (NS) becomes a conditioned stimulus (CS), eliciting a conditioned response (CR)	You learn to fear (CR) a dentist's office (CS) by associating it with a reflexive response to a painful tooth extraction (UCS).
Stimulus generalization	Conditioned response (CR) is elicited not only by the conditioned stimulus (CS) but also by stimuli similar to the conditioned stimulus (CS)	You learn to fear most dentists' offices and other places that smell like them.
Stimulus discrimination	Certain stimuli similar to the conditioned stimulus (CS) do not elicit the conditioned response (CR)	You learn that your physician's office is not associated with the painful tooth extraction (UCS).
Extinction	Conditioned stimulus (CS) is presented alone, without the unconditioned stimulus (UCS). Eventually the conditioned stimulus (CS) no longer elicits the conditioned response (CR)	You return to your dentist's office for routine check-ups, with no extractions, and your fear (CR) gradually disappears.
Spontaneous recovery	Sudden reappearance of a previously extinguished conditioned response (CR)	While watching a movie depicting oral surgery, your previous fear (CR) suddenly and temporarily returns.
Higher-order conditioning	Neutral stimulus (NS) becomes a conditioned stimulus (CS) through repeated pairings with a previously conditioned stimulus (CS)	The sign outside your dentist's office, an originally neutral stimulus (NS), becomes a conditioned stimulus (CS), associated with the previous conditioned stimulus (CS) of the dentist's office, and you experience fear whenever you see just the sign.

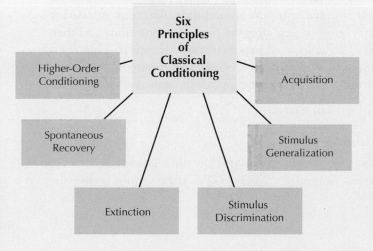

Six Principles of Classical Conditioning
- Higher-Order Conditioning
- Spontaneous Recovery
- Extinction
- Stimulus Discrimination
- Stimulus Generalization
- Acquisition

PSYCHOLOGY ENGAGES — **TEST YOURSELF**

Identifying Classical Conditioning

True or False

_____ 1. The mere smell of coffee helps wake me up in the morning.

_____ 2. The sound of a dentist's drill makes me cringe.

_____ 3. The sight of a squeezed lemon makes my mouth pucker.

_____ 4. Pictures of chocolate cake make my mouth water.

*Adding additional examples from your personal life will further help you understand, appreciate, and master the important principles of classical conditioning.

For example, after first conditioning dogs to salivate at the sound of low-pitched tones, Pavlov later demonstrated that the dogs would also salivate in response to high-pitched tones. Similarly, after conditioning, the infant in Watson and Rayner's experiment ("Little Albert") feared not only rats, but also a rabbit, a dog, and a bearded Santa Claus mask.

Would little Albert still be afraid of a Santa Claus mask as an adult? As a child in the United States, he undoubtedly had numerous encounters with Santa Claus masks and would have learned to recognize differences between rats and other stimuli. This process of learning responses to a specific stimulus, but not to other similar stimuli, is called **stimulus discrimination**.

Although stimulus generalization seems to follow naturally from initial classical conditioning, organisms only learn to distinguish (or *discriminate*) between an original conditioned stimulus (CS) and similar stimuli if they have enough experience with both. Just as you learn to discriminate between the sound of your cellular phone and the ringing of others, when Pavlov repeatedly presented food following a high-pitched tone, but not with a low-pitched tone, the dogs gradually learned to distinguish between the two tones. Thus, both Little Albert and Pavlov's dogs produced conditioned responses only to specific stimuli—*stimulus discrimination*.

Extinction and Spontaneous Recovery

Classical conditioning, like all learning, is only *relatively* permanent. Most responses that are learned through classical conditioning can be weakened or suppressed through *extinction*. **Extinction** *is the gradual disappearance of a conditioned response (CR)*. It occurs when the unconditioned stimulus (UCS) is repeatedly withheld whenever the conditioned stimulus (CS) is presented, which gradually weakens the conditioned response (CR). When Pavlov sounded the tone again and again without presenting food, the dogs' salivation gradually declined. Similarly, if you have a classically conditioned fear of the sound of a dentist's drill and later start to work as a dental assistant, your fear will gradually diminish. Can you see the usefulness of this information if you're trying to get over a destructive love relationship? Rather than thinking, "I'll always be in love with this person," remind yourself that given time and repeated contact in a nonloving situation, your feelings will gradually lessen.

Keep in mind, extinction is not *unlearning* (Bouton, 1994). A behavior becomes *extinct* when the response rate decreases and the person or animal no longer responds to the stimulus. It does not mean the person or animal has "erased" the previous learned connection between the stimulus and the response. In fact, if the stimulus is reintroduced, the conditioning is much faster the second time. Furthermore, Pavlov found that if he allowed several hours to pass after the extinction procedure and then presented the tone again, the salivation would spontaneously reappear. This reappearance of a conditioned response after extinction is called **spontaneous recovery**. For a visual summary comparing acquisition extinction, an spontaneous recovery, see Figure 6.3.

Higher-Order Conditioning

Children are not born salivating at the sign of McDonald's golden arches. So why do they beg their parents to stop at "Mickey D's" after simply seeing the

Stimulus Discrimination Only the conditioned stimulus (CS) elicits the conditioned response (CR)

Extinction Gradual disappearance of a conditioned response (CR); occurs when unconditioned stimulus (UCS) is withheld whenever the conditioned stimulus (CS) is presented

Spontaneous Recovery Sudden, temporary reappearance of a previously extinguished conditioned response (CR)

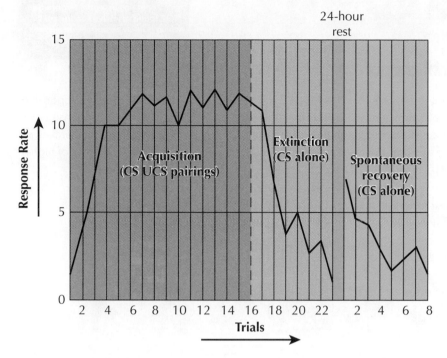

24-hour rest

Figure 6.3 Acquisition, extinction, and spontaneous recovery During acquisition, the strength of the conditioned response (CR) rapidly increases and then levels off near its maximum. During extinction, the CR declines erratically until its extinguished. After a "rest" period in which the organism is not exposed to the conditioned stimulus (CS), spontaneous recovery occurs, and the CS once again elicits a (weakened) CR. Note that during both extinction and spontaneous recovery the CR diminishes back to extinction levels. This is because the CS is "alone"—meaning the unconditioned stimulus is NOT presented.

 **TRY THIS YOURSELF**

The Power of Spontaneous Recovery

Why do people sometimes feel suddenly very excited at the sight of a high school sweetheart they haven't seen for many years—and extinction has presumably occurred?

Answer: People (who haven't read this book and taken psychology) might mislabel this renewed excitement as "lasting love." You, on the other hand, would recognize it as simple *spontaneous recovery*. This phenomenon also explains why couples who've broken up sometimes misinterpret and overvalue a similar sudden flare-up of feelings. They may even return to destructive and doomed relationships, only to later break up again when the spontaneous recovery subsides.

golden arches on a passing billboard? It is because of **higher-order conditioning**, which occurs when a neutral stimulus (NS) becomes a conditioned stimulus (CS) through repeated pairings with a previously conditioned stimulus (CS) (Concept Organizer 6.2).

Higher-Order Conditioning Neutral stimulus (NS) becomes a conditioned stimulus (CS) through repeated pairings with a previously conditioned stimulus (CS)

ConceptOrganizer6.2

Higher-Order Conditioning

If you wanted to demonstrate higher-order conditioning in Pavlov's dogs, you would first condition the dogs to salivate in response to the sound of the tone (a). Then you would pair a flash of light with the tone (b). Eventually, the dogs would salivate in response to the flash of light alone (c). Similarly, children first learn to pair McDonald's restaurants with food and later learn that two golden arches are a symbol for McDonald's. Their salivation and begging to eat at the restaurant upon seeing the arches are classic examples of higher-order conditioning (and successful advertising).

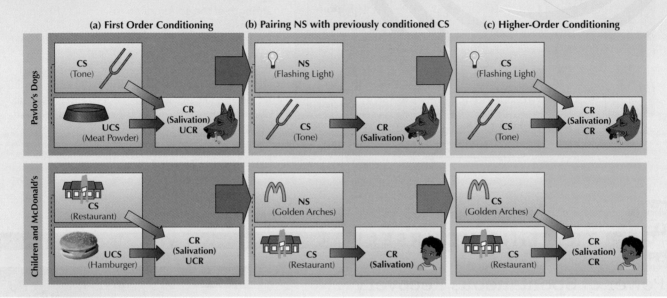

(a) First Order Conditioning | **(b) Pairing NS with previously conditioned CS** | **(c) Higher-Order Conditioning**

Pavlov's Dogs
- CS (Tone), UCS (Meat Powder) → CR (Salivation) UCR
- NS (Flashing Light), CS (Tone) → CR (Salivation)
- CS (Flashing Light), CS (Tone) → CR (Salivation) CR

Children and McDonald's
- CS (Restaurant), UCS (Hamburger) → CR (Salivation) UCR
- NS (Golden Arches), CS (Restaurant) → CR (Salivation)
- CS (Golden Arches), CS (Restaurant) → CR (Salivation) CR

PSYCHOLOGY ENGAGES

CHECK & REVIEW

Basic Principles

Part A: Retrieval Practice

1. Without looking at the book, spend 10 minutes writing a free-form essay recalling all you can remember from the previous section.

2. Now, reread the previous section, and once again spend 10 minutes writing a free-form essay on the SAME material.

Part B: Practice Quiz

1. List the six principles of classical conditioning

2. A baby is bitten by a dog and then is afraid of all small animals. This is an example of _____. (a) stimulus discrimination; (b) extinction; (c) reinforcement; (d) stimulus generalization

3. When a conditioned stimulus is used to reinforce the learning of a second conditioned stimulus, _____ has occurred.

4. If you wanted to use higher-order conditioning to get Little Albert to fear Barbie dolls, you would present a Barbie doll with _____. (a) the loud noise; (b) the original unconditioned response; (c) the white rat; (d) the original conditioned response

5. Like most of us, your heart rate and blood pressure greatly increase when the fire alarm sounds. If the fire alarm system was malfunctioning and rang every half hour, by the end of the day, your heart rate and blood pressure would no longer increase. Using classical conditioning terms, explain this change in your response.

6. Which of the six basic principles of classical conditioning best explain(s) this cartoon? _____

S.Gross

"I don't care if she is a tape dispenser. I love her."

Check your answers in Appendix B.

MYTH BUSTERS

True or False?

1. The best way to maintain a desired behavior is to reward every response.
2. Punishment is a very effective way to change long-term behavior.
3. Negative reinforcement is another type of punishment.
4. Prejudiced and superstitious people are born that way.
5. B. F. Skinner raised his daughter in cage-like "Skinner box," which led to her adult mental illness.

Answer: All of these are false. Detailed answers are provided in this chapter and in Lilienfeld et al. (2010).

Operant Conditioning

Objective 6.4: Define operant conditioning, reinforcement, and punishment.

As we've just seen, classical conditioning is based on what happens *before* we *involuntarily* respond—something happens to us and we learn a new response. In contrast, **operant conditioning** is based on what happens *after* we *voluntarily* perform a behavior—we do something and learn from the consequences (see Figure 6.4).

Note that consequences are the heart of *operant conditioning*. In classical conditioning, consequences are irrelevant—Pavlov's dogs still got the meat powder whether or not they salivated. But in operant conditioning, the organism performs a voluntary behavior (an *operant*) that produces either *reinforcement* or *punishment*, which influence whether the response will occur again in the future. **Reinforcement** strengthens the response and makes it more likely to recur. **Punishment** weakens the response and makes it less likely to recur.

In the sections that follow, we'll first examine the historical contributions of Thorndike and Skinner, followed by the basic principles of operant conditioning—reinforcement and punishment. Note that the chapter closes with several interesting applications of operant conditioning to everyday life.

Operant Conditioning Learning through voluntary behavior and its subsequent consequences; reinforcement increases behavioral tendencies, whereas punishment decreases them

Reinforcement Strengthens a response and makes it more likely to recur

Punishment Weakens a response and makes it less likely to recur

Involuntary Behavior

Subject is *passive*
(Something happens *to* you, and you learn a new response due to pairing of CS with UCS.)

Classical Conditioning

Stimulus — CS
UCS — Response: CR UCR

Voluntary Behavior

Subject is *active*
(*You* do something, you "operate" on the environment; then your behavioral tendencies increase or decrease as a result of consequences — either reinforcement or punishment.)

Operant Conditioning

Behavior → Reinforcement → Behavioral tendencies *increase*
Behavior → Punishment → Behavioral tendencies *decrease*

Figure 6.4 Visually summarizing classical versus operant conditioning

Thorndike and Skinner's Contributions: The Beginnings of Operant Conditioning

Objective 6.5: Describe Thorndike and Skinner's contributions.

Edward Thorndike (1874–1949), a pioneer of operant conditioning, was among the first to examine how voluntary behaviors are influenced by their consequences (Figure 6.5). According to Thorndike's **law of effect**, the probability of an action being repeated is *strengthened* if it is followed by a pleasant or satisfying consequence. In short, rewarded behavior is more likely to recur (Thorndike, 1911). Thorndike's law of effect was a first step in understanding how active *voluntary* behaviors can be modified by their consequences.

B. F. Skinner (1904–1990) extended Thorndike's law of effect to more complex behaviors. (The general behavioral perspective was discussed in Chapter 1, pp. 12–13). As a strict behaviorist, however, Skinner avoided terms like *pleasant*, *desired*, and *voluntary* because they make unfounded assumptions about what an organism feels and wants. The terms also imply that behavior is due to conscious choice or intention. Skinner believed that to understand behavior, we should consider only observable, external, or environmental stimuli and responses. We must look outside the learner, not inside.

In keeping with his focus on external, observable behavior, Skinner emphasized that reinforcement (which increases the likelihood of a response) and punishment (which decreases it) are always defined *after the fact*. This emphasis on only reinforcing or punishing *after* the behavior is important. Suppose you ask to borrow the family car on Friday night, but your parents say you have to wash the car first. If they let you put off washing the car until the weekend, what is the likelihood that you will do it? From their own "trial-and-error" experiences, most parents have learned to make sure the payoff comes *after* the car washing is completed—not before!

In addition to warning that both reinforcement and punishment must come after the response, Skinner also cautions us to check the respondent's behavior to see if it increases or decreases. Sometimes we *think* we're reinforcing or punishing when we're doing the opposite. For example, a professor may think she is encouraging shy students to talk by repeatedly praising them each time they speak up in class. But what if shy students are embarrassed by this attention? If so, they actually may decrease the number of times they talk in class. Similarly, men may buy women candy and flowers because they *know* all women like these things. However, some women hate candy (imagine that!) or may be allergic to flowers. In this case, the man's attempt at reinforcement becomes a punishment!

It's important to note, what is reinforcing or punishing for one person may *not* be so for another. Skinner suggests we should watch our target's *actual* responses—not what we *think* the other person *should* like or do.

To effectively use operant conditioning in your life, you need to understand several important principles. We'll focus first on factors that *strengthen* or *weaken* a response: Reinforcement or punishment (Figure 6.6). Then we'll look at the pros and cons of punishment, and how to use operant conditioning in the workplace. We conclude with a brief overview and comparison of classical versus operant conditioning.

Reinforcement: Consequences that Strengthen a Response

Objective 6.6: Explain how primary and secondary reinforcers and positive and negative reinforcement strengthen behavior.

Earlier, we said that Skinner was a strict behaviorist who insisted that scientific observation be limited to that which can be observed. Therefore, instead of using words

Law of Effect Thorndike's rule that the probability of an action being repeated is strengthened when it is followed by a pleasant or satisfying consequence

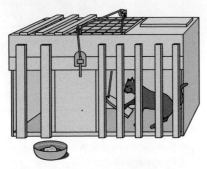

Figure 6.5 Thorndike box To investigate animal learning, Thorndike put a cat inside a specially built puzzle box. When the cat stepped on a pedal inside the box (at first, through trial and error), the door opened and the cat could get out to eat. With each additional success, the cat's actions became more purposeful, and it soon learned to open the door immediately (from Thorndike, 1898).

Figure 6.6 Consequences are the key to operant conditioning If consequences control behavior, why don't students with poor grades simply study more? The answers are complex. Pay careful attention to the upcoming material!

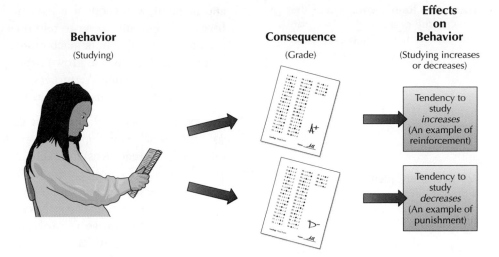

like *good*, *bad*, or *rewards* (which focus on feelings), Skinner talked about reinforcers and reinforcement in terms of "strengthening the response." If a toddler whines for candy and the parent gives in, the child's whining will likely increase. But what if the parent yelled at the child for whining, yet still gave him or her the lollipop? The child might feel both happy to get the candy and sad because the parent is upset.

Because we can't know the full extent of the child's internal, mixed feelings, it's cleaner (and more scientific) to limit our focus to observable behaviors and consequences. If the child's whining for lollipops increases, we can say that whining was reinforced.

As you can see in Table 6.2, reinforcers are grouped into two types, *primary* or *secondary*, which function as either *positive* or *negative* reinforcement.

1. *Primary and secondary reinforcers* One of the chief methods for strengthening a response is with primary and secondary reinforcers. Reinforcers such as food, water, and sex are called **primary reinforcers** because they normally satisfy an unlearned biological need. In contrast, reinforcers such as money, praise, attention,

Primary Reinforcers Stimuli that increase the probability of a response because they satisfy an unlearned, biological need (e.g., food, water, and sex)

Table 6.2 HOW REINFORCEMENT STRENGTHENS AND INCREASES BEHAVIORS

	Positive reinforcement Adds stimulus (+) and strengthens behavior	**Negative reinforcement** Takes stimulus away (−) and strengthens behavior
Primary reinforcers Satisfy *biological* needs	You hug your baby and he smiles at you. The "addition" of his smile strengthens the likelihood that you will hug him again.	You baby is crying, so you hug him and he stops crying. The "removal" of crying strengthens the likelihood that you will hug him again when he cries.
	You do a favor for a friend and she buys you lunch in return.	You take an aspirin for your headache, which takes away the pain.
Secondary reinforcers Satisfy *learned* needs	You increase profits and receive $200 as a bonus.	After high sales, your boss says you won't have to work on weekends.
	You study hard and receive a good grade on your psychology exam.	You're allowed to skip the final exam because you did so well on your unit exams.

Secondary Reinforcers Stimuli that increase the probability of a response because of their learned value (e.g., money and material possessions)

Positive Reinforcement Adding (or presenting) a stimulus, thereby strengthening a response and making it more likely to recur

Negative Reinforcement Taking away (or removing) a stimulus, thereby strengthening a response and making it more likely to recur

[handwritten: both strengthen response]

Reinforcement in action Is this father's attention a primary or secondary reinforcer?

Premack Principle Using a naturally occurring high-frequency response to reinforce and increase low-frequency responses

and material possessions that have no intrinsic value are called **secondary reinforcers**. Their only power to reinforce behavior results from learning. A baby, for example, would find milk much more reinforcing than a $100 bill. Needless to say, by the time this baby has grown to adolescence, he or she will have learned to prefer the money. Among Westerners, money may be the most widely used secondary reinforcer because of its learned association with desirable commodities.

2. *Positive and negative reinforcement* Adding or taking away certain stimuli also strengthens behavior. Suppose you tickle your baby and he smiles at you. His smile increases (or strengthens) the likelihood that you will tickle him again in the future. The smile itself is a *positive reinforcer* for you. This is called **positive reinforcement**. On the other hand, suppose your baby is upset and crying, so you pick him up and he stops crying. The removal of crying is a *negative reinforcer* for you. The *process* is called **negative reinforcement** because picking him up takes away, or removes, the crying, which also increases (or strengthens) the likelihood that you will pick him up again in the future when he cries.

(As a critical thinker, are you worried about what's happening for the baby in these examples? While you, the parent, were being both *positively* and *negatively reinforced*, your baby was only *positively reinforced*. He learned that his smile led to more tickling and that his crying caused you to pick him up. If you're concerned that reinforcing the crying will create lasting problems, you can relax. Your baby soon will learn to talk and develop "better" ways to communicate.)

Why Negative Reinforcement Is NOT Punishment
Objective 6.7: Explain why negative reinforcement is not punishment.

Many people hear the term *negative reinforcement* and automatically think of punishment. But it's important to remember that these two terms are completely opposite procedures. Reinforcement (either positive or negative) *strengthens a behavior*. And, as we will see in the next section, punishment *weakens a behavior*.

My students find it easier if they think of positive and negative reinforcement in the *mathematical* sense (see again Table 6.2, p. 217) rather than as personal values of positive as "good" or negative as "bad." Think of positive reinforcement as something being added (+) that increases the likelihood that the behavior will increase. Conversely, think of negative reinforcement as something being taken away (−) that also increases the likelihood that the behavior will continue. For example, if your boss compliments you on a job well done, the compliment is added (+) as a consequence of your behavior. And, therefore, your hard work is likely to increase (*positive reinforcement*). Similarly, if your boss tells you that you no longer have to do a boring part of your job because of your excellent work, the taking away (−) of the boring task is a *negative reinforcement*. And your hard work is also likely to increase.

Can you see how making yourself study before going to the movies is also a form of *positive reinforcement*? Because you *add* "going to the movies" only *after* you study, this should increase (positively reinforce) your studying behaviors.

In this same example, you're also using the **Premack principle** (Lefrancois, 2012; Poling, 2010). Psychologist David Premack believes any naturally occurring, high-frequency response can be used to reinforce and increase low-frequency responses. Recognizing that you love to go to movies, you intuitively tied your less desirable low-frequency activity (studying) to your high-frequency or highly desirable behavior (going to the movies). You also can use the Premack principle in other aspects of your college life, such as making yourself write 4 pages on your term paper or read 20 pages before you allow yourself to call a friend or have a snack.

Schedules of Reinforcement

Objective 6.8: Contrast continuous and partial (intermittent) reinforcement, and identify the four schedules of partial reinforcement.

What are the best circumstances for using reinforcement? It depends on the desired outcome. To make this decision, you need to understand various *schedules of reinforcement*, which refer to the rate or interval at which responses are reinforced. Although there are numerous schedules of reinforcement, the most important distinction is whether they are *continuous* or *partial*.

When Skinner was training his animals, he found that learning was most rapid if the response was reinforced each time it occurred—a procedure called **continuous reinforcement**. As you have probably noticed, real life seldom provides continuous reinforcement. You do not get an A each time you write a paper or a date each time you ask. Yet your behavior persists because your efforts are occasionally rewarded. Most everyday behavior is similarly rewarded on a **partial** (or **intermittent**) schedule of **reinforcement**, which involves reinforcing only some responses, not all (Miltenberger, 2011).

Although a continuous schedule of reinforcement leads to faster initial learning, it is *not* an efficient system for maintaining long-term behaviors. It is therefore important to move to a partial schedule of reinforcement once a task is well learned. Why? Because under partial schedules, behavior is more resistant to extinction. Have you noticed that people spend long hours pushing buttons and pulling levers on slot machines in hopes of winning the jackpot? This high response rate and the compulsion to keep gambling in spite of significant losses are evidence of the strong resistance to extinction with partial schedules of reinforcement. This type of partial, intermittent reinforcement also helps parents maintain behaviors like tooth brushing and bed making. After the child has initially learned these behaviors with continuous reinforcement, you should move on to occasional, partial reinforcement.

Four Partial (Intermittent) Schedules of Reinforcement

There are four partial schedules of reinforcement: **fixed ratio (FR)**, **variable ratio (VR)**, **fixed interval (FI)**, and **variable interval (VI)**. Table 6.3 defines these terms and provides examples.

How do we know which schedule to choose? The type of partial schedule selected depends on the type of behavior being studied and on the speed of learning desired (Borrero et al., 2011; Dack, Reed, & McHugh, 2010; Rothstein, Jensen, & Neuringer, 2008). For example, suppose you want to teach your dog to sit. First, you could reinforce your dog with a cookie every time he sits (continuous reinforcement). To make his training more resistant to extinction, you then could switch to a partial reinforcement schedule. Using the *fixed ratio* schedule, you would offer a cookie only after your dog sits a certain number of times. As you can see in Figure 6.7, a fixed ratio leads to the highest overall response rate. But each of the four types of partial schedules has different advantages and disadvantages (see again Table 6.3).

Shaping

Objective 6.9: Define shaping and tell why it's important.

Each of the four schedules of partial reinforcement is important for maintaining behavior. But how do you teach new or complex behaviors like playing the piano or speaking a foreign language? For new and complex behaviors

Continuous Reinforcement Every correct response is reinforced

Partial (Intermittent) Reinforcement Some, but not all, correct responses are reinforced

Fixed Ratio (FR) Schedule Reinforcement occurs after a predetermined set of responses; the ratio (number or amount) is fixed

Variable Ratio (VR) Schedule Reinforcement occurs unpredictably; the ratio (number or amount) varies

Fixed Interval (FI) Schedule Reinforcement occurs after a predetermined time has elapsed; the interval (time) is fixed

Variable Interval (VI) Schedule Reinforcement occurs unpredictably; the interval (time) varies

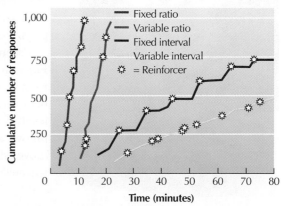

Figure 6.7 Which schedule is best? Each of the different schedules of *reinforcement* produces its own unique pattern of response. The best schedule depends on the specific task—see Table 6.3. (The "stars" on the lines represent the delivery of a reinforcer.) (Adapted from Skinner, 1961.)

Table 6.3   FOUR PARTIAL (INTERMITTENT) SCHEDULES OF REINFORCEMENT

		Definitions	Response Rates	Examples
Ratio Schedules (response based)	**Fixed ratio (FR)**	Reinforcement occurs after a predetermined set of responses; the ratio (number or amount) is fixed	Produces a high rate of response, but a brief drop-off just after reinforcement	Car wash employee receives $10 for every 3 cars washed. In a laboratory, a rat receives a food pellet every time it presses the bar 7 times.
	Variable ratio (VR)	Reinforcement occurs unpredictably; the ratio (number or amount) varies	High response rates, no pause after reinforcement, and very resistant to extinction	Slot machines are designed to pay out after an average number of responses (maybe every 10 times), but any one machine may pay out on the first response, then seventh, then the twentieth.
Interval Schedules (time based)	**Fixed interval (FI)**	Reinforcement occurs after a predetermined time has elapsed; the interval (time) is fixed	Responses tend to increased as the time for the next reinforcer is near, but drop off after reinforcement and during interval	You receive a monthly paycheck. In a laboratory, a rat's behavior is reinforced with a food pellet when (or if) it presses a bar after 20 seconds have elapsed.
	Variable interval (VI)	Reinforcement occurs unpredictably; the interval (time) varies	Relatively low, but steady, response rates because respondents cannot predict when reward will come	Rat's behavior is reinforced with food pellet after a response and a variable, unpredictable interval of time has elapsed. In a class with pop quizzes, you study at a slow, but steady, rate because you can't anticipate the next quiz.

Study Tip

Remember that interval is *time* based, whereas ratio is *response* based.

Shaping in action

such as these, which aren't likely to occur naturally, **shaping** is a particularly valuable tool. Shaping teaches a desired response by reinforcing a series of successively improving steps leading to the final goal response. Skinner believed that shaping explains a wide variety of skills and abilities that each of us possesses, from eating with a fork, to playing a musical instrument, to driving a car (Chance, 2009; Lefrancois, 2012).

Parents, athletic coaches, teachers, and animal trainers all use shaping techniques. For example, if you want to shape a child to make his bed, you could begin by reinforcing when he first gets the sheets and pillows in the right general area on the bed—even if it's sloppily done. Over time, you would stop reinforcing that beginning level of behavior. You would only reinforce when he got the sheets, bedspread, and pillows all in the right place, with most of the wrinkles removed. Each step in shaping moves slightly beyond the previously learned behavior. This allows the person to link the new step to the behavior previously learned.

Shaping Reinforcement delivered for successive approximations of the desired response

Punishment: Consequences that Weaken a Response

Objective 6.10: Explain how positive and negative punishment weaken behavior.

Unlike reinforcement, punishment *decreases* the strength of the response—that is, the likelihood that a behavior will be repeated again is weakened. When your dog begs for food off your plate, and you loudly (and *consistently*) say "No," the begging will likely decrease.

Just as with reinforcement, there are two kinds of punishment, *positive* and *negative* (Miltenberger, 2011; Skinner, 1953). Also, as with reinforcement, remember to think in mathematical terms of adding and taking away, rather than good and bad (Table 6.4). **Positive punishment** is the addition (+) of a stimulus that decreases (or weakens) the likelihood of the response occurring again. If a parent adds new chores each time the child is late getting home, the parent is applying positive punishment. **Negative punishment** is the taking away (−) of a stimulus that decreases (or weakens) the likelihood of the response occurring again. Parents use negative punishment when they take the car keys away from a teen who doesn't come home on time. Notice that in *both* positive and negative punishment, the behavior has been punished and the behavioral tendencies have been weakened.

> **Positive Punishment** Adding (or presenting) a stimulus, thereby weakening a response and making it less likely to recur
>
> **Negative Punishment** Taking away (or removing) a stimulus, thereby weakening a response and making it less likely to recur

The Tricky Business of Punishment

Objective 6.11: Why is punishment "tricky," and what are its serious side effects?

First, it's important to acknowledge that punishment plays a significant and unavoidable role in our social world. In his book *Walden Two* (1948), Skinner described a utopian (ideal) world where reinforcers almost completely replaced punishment. Unfortunately, in our real world, reinforcement is not enough. Dangerous criminals must be stopped and, possibly, removed from society. Parents must stop their children from running into the street and their teenagers from drinking and driving. Teachers must stop disruptive students in the classroom and bullies on the playground. There is an obvious need for punishment. But it can be confusing and problematic (Borrego et al., 2007; Leary et al., 2008; Loxton et al., 2008).

When we hear the word *punishment*, most people think of disciplinary procedures used by parents, teachers, and other authority figures. But punishment is much more than parents giving a child a time-out for misbehaving or teachers giving demerits. Any process that adds or takes away something and causes the behavior to decrease is *punishment*. By this definition, if parents ignore all the A's on their child's report card and ask repeated questions about the B's and C's, they may unintentionally punish

Table 6.4 HOW PUNISHMENT WEAKENS AND DECREASES BEHAVIORS

Positive punishment Adds stimulus (+) and weakens behavior	Negative punishment Takes stimulus away (−) and weakens behavior
You must run four extra laps in your gym class because you were late.	You're excluded from gym class because you were late.
A parent adds extra chores following a child's misbehavior.	A parent takes away a teen's cell phone following a poor report card.
Your boss complains about your performance.	Your boss reduces your expense account after a poor performance.

Is this positive or negative punishment?

and weaken the likelihood of future A's. Dog owners who yell at or spank their dogs for finally coming to them after being called several times are actually punishing the desired behavior—coming when called. Similarly, college administrators who take away "leftover" money from a department's budget because it wasn't spent by the end of the year are punishing desired behavior—saving money. (Yes, I did add this last example as a subtle message to our college administrators!)

As you can see, punishment is a tricky business. We often unintentionally punish the very behaviors we're trying to encourage. Furthermore, to be effective, punishment should be immediate and consistent. However, in the real world, this is extremely hard to do. Police officers cannot immediately stop every driver every time he or she speeds.

To make matters worse, when punishment is not immediate and consistent, during the delay the undesirable behavior is likely to be reinforced. This delay and intermittent reinforcement puts the undesirable behavior on a *partial schedule of reinforcement*. And as you learned earlier, this makes the undesirable behavior even more resistant to extinction. Think about gambling. For almost everyone, it should be a *punishing* situation. On most occasions, you lose far more money than you win! However, the fact that you occasionally win keeps you "hanging in there."

Perhaps, most important, even if punishment immediately follows the misbehavior, the recipient may learn what *not* to do but not learn what he or she *should* do. Imagine trying to teach a child the word *dog* by only saying "No!" each time she said *dog* when it was inappropriate. The child (and you) would soon become very frustrated. It's much more efficient to teach someone by giving him or her clear examples of correct behavior, such as showing a child pictures of dogs and saying *dog* after each photo. Punishment has several other serious side effects, as Table 6.5 shows.

Summary Table 6.5   **SIDE EFFECTS OF PUNISHMENT**

1. **Passive aggressiveness** For the recipient, punishment often leads to frustration, anger, and an urge to fight back. But most of us have learned from experience that retaliatory aggression toward a punisher (especially one who is bigger and more powerful) is usually followed by more punishment. We therefore tend to control our impulse toward open aggression and instead resort to more subtle techniques, such as showing up late or "forgetting" to do chores. This is a form of *passive aggressiveness* (Girardi et al., 2007; Johnson, 2008).

2. **Avoidance** No one likes to be punished, so we naturally try to avoid the punisher. If every time you come home a parent or spouse starts yelling at you, you will delay coming home or find another place to go.

3. **Inappropriate modeling** Have you ever seen a parent spank or hit a child for hitting another child? If so, the parent may unintentionally serve as a "model" for the same behavior he or she is attempting to stop.

4. **Temporary suppression versus elimination** Punishment generally suppresses the behavior only temporarily, while the punisher is nearby. For example, have you noticed how drivers immediately slow down when they see a nearby police car? And how quickly they later resume their previous speed once the police officer is out of sight?

5. **Learned helplessness** Why do some people stay in abusive relationships? Research shows that if you repeatedly fail in your attempts to escape or control your environment, you acquire a general sense of powerlessness or *learned helplessness*, and you may become depressed and make no further attempts to escape (Bargai, Ben-Shakhar, & Shalev, 2007; Diaz-Berciano et al., 2008; Kim, 2008).

6. **Increased aggression** Because punishment often produces a decrease in undesired behavior, at least for the moment, the punisher is in effect rewarded for applying punishment. Thus, a vicious circle may be established in which both the punisher and recipient are reinforced for inappropriate behavior—the punisher for punishing and the recipient for being fearful and submissive. This side effect partially explains the escalation of violence in family abuse and bullying (Anderson, Buckley, & Carnagey, 2008; Fang & Corso, 2007; Huesman, Dubow, & Boxer, 2011). In addition to fear and submissiveness, the recipient also might become depressed and/or respond with his or her own form of aggression.

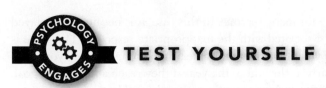

TEST YOURSELF

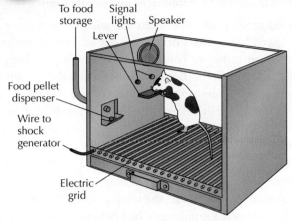

To food storage — Signal lights — Speaker — Lever — Food pellet dispenser — Wire to shock generator — Electric grid

Using the terms, *positive reinforcement*, *negative reinforcement*, *positive punishment*, or *negative punishment*, fill in the name of the appropriate learning principle in the spaces provided in each box.

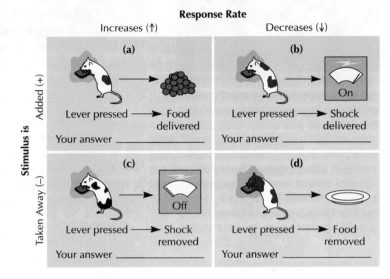

Response Rate

Increases (↑)   Decreases (↓)

Stimulus is

Added (+)

(a) Lever pressed → Food delivered   Your answer _____

(b) Lever pressed → Shock delivered   Your answer _____

Taken Away (−)

(c) Lever pressed → Shock removed   Your answer _____

(d) Lever pressed → Food removed   Your answer _____

Answers: (a) positive reinforcement, (b) positive punishment, (c) negative reinforcement, (d) negative punishment.

The Skinner Box Application

To test his behavioral theories, Skinner used an animal, usually a pigeon or a rat, and an apparatus that has come to be called a *Skinner Box*. In Skinner's basic experimental design, an animal such as a rat received a food pellet each time it pushed a lever, and the number of responses was recorded. Note in this drawing that an electric grid on the cage floor could be used to deliver small electric shocks.

Psychology at Work

Why Can't We Get Anything Done Around Here?

Objective 6.12: How can we effectively use reinforcement and punishment?

Imagine yourself as a midlevel manager for a big company. Your bonuses (and job) depend on your ability to motivate your employees and increase production. How could you use reinforcement and punishment to meet your goals?

1. **Provide clear directions and feedback.** Have you noticed how frustrating it is when a boss (or an instructor) asks you to do something, but doesn't give you clear directions or helpful feedback on your work? When using either reinforcement or punishment, be sure to offer specific, frequent, and clear directions and feedback to the employee whose behavior you want to encourage or change. When using punishment, it is particularly important to clearly explain and perhaps demonstrate the desired response because punishment is merely an indication that the current response is undesirable. Like all of us, employees need to know precisely what to do, as well as what NOT to do.

expectations

2. **Use appropriate timing.** Reinforcers and punishers should be presented as close in time to the response as possible. The old policy of "wait till the boss gets here"

Have you noticed how the TV star of *The Nanny* uses some or all of these five principles?

is obviously inappropriate for many reasons. In this case, it is because the delayed punishment is no longer associated with the inappropriate response. The same is true for reinforcement. If you're trying to increase production, don't tell your staff that you'll have a large party at the end of the year if they reach a significant goal. Instead, reward them with immediate compliments and small bonuses.

3. **Be consistent.** To be effective, both reinforcement and punishment must be consistent. Have you noticed how some workers get out of difficult assignments and gain special favors because they're constantly complaining or begging? A manager often responds by saying "No." But sometimes when the employee persists, gets loud, or throws an adult temper tantrum, his or her employer gives in. Although the manager is momentarily relieved (negatively reinforced) when the complaining and begging stop, can you see how this inconsistency creates larger and longer-lasting problems?

   First, the employee is being *positively reinforced* for complaining, begging, and throwing a tantrum, which almost guarantees that these inappropriate behaviors are likely to increase. To make matters worse, the manager's inconsistency (saying "No" and then giving in) places the employee's bad behavior on a *partial schedule of reinforcement*—and, therefore, highly resistant to extinction. Like a toddler screaming for, a lollipop, or the gambler continuing to play despite the odds, the employee will continue the begging, screaming, and temper tantrums in hopes of the occasional payoff.

   Because effective punishment requires constant surveillance and consistent responses, it's almost impossible to be a "perfect punisher." It's best (and easiest) to use consistent reinforcement for good behavior and extinction for bad behavior. Praise the employee for productive and cooperative behavior in the workplace, and extinguish the begging, complaining, and tantrums by consistently refusing the request and ignoring the bad behavior.

4. **Follow correct order of presentation.** As a teenager, did you ever ask for an extra few dollars as an advance on your allowance and promise to mow the grass before the end of the week? Did you later conveniently "forget" your promise? As an employer, have you ever refused an employee's request to telecommute (or work from home) because you believe "all employees slough off if they're not being watched"? Can you see why advances on allowance or refusals that come before the negligent behavior may create frustration and resentment? Both reinforcement and punishment should come after the behavior, never before.

5. **Combine key learning principles.** The overall best method seems to be a combination of the major principles: Reinforce appropriate behavior, extinguish inappropriate behavior, and save punishment for the most extreme cases (such as an employee caught lying or cheating).

Comparing Classical and Operant Conditioning: Similarities and Differences

Objective 6.13: Briefly summarize the similarities and differences between classical and operant conditioning.

Are you feeling overwhelmed with all the important (and seemingly overlapping) terms and concepts for both classical and operant conditioning? This is a good time to stop and carefully review Table 6.6, which summarizes all the key terms and compares the two major types of conditioning. Keep in mind that while it's convenient

Summary Table 6.6 COMPARING CLASSICAL AND OPERANT CONDITIONING

	Classical Conditioning	Operant Conditioning
Example	Cringing at the sound of a dentist's drill	A baby cries and you pick it up
Pioneers	Ivan Pavlov John B. Watson	Edward Thorndike B. F. Skinner
Key Terms	Neutral stimulus (NS) Unconditioned stimulus (UCS) Conditioned stimulus (CS) Unconditioned response (UCR) Conditioned response (CR) Conditioned emotional response (CER)	Reinforcers (primary and secondary) Reinforcement (positive and negative) Punishment (positive and negative) Shaping Reinforcement schedules (continues and partial) Superstitions
Major Similarities	Acquisition Generalization Discrimination Extinction Spontaneous recovery Higher-Order Conditioning	Acquisition (Shaping) Generalization Discrimination Extinction Spontaneous recovery Higher-Order Conditioning (discriminative stimulus)
Major Differences	Learning based on paired associations Involuntary (subject is passive) Order of effects (NS generally comes *before* the UCS)	Learning based on consequences Voluntary (subject is active and "operators" on the environment) Order of effects (reinforcement or punishment generally come *after* the behavior)

to divide classical and operant conditioning into separate categories, almost all behaviors result from a combination of both forms of conditioning (Watson & Tharp, 2007).

As you can see, there are several similarities and differences in classical and operant conditioning.

Let's first explore the *similarities*:

- **Acquisition** During classical conditioning, new responses are *acquired* through paired associations of an unconditioned stimulus (UCS) with a conditioned stimulus (CS). In operant conditioning, new behaviors are *acquired* through reinforcement and shaping.

- **Generalization and Discrimination** A small child might acquire a classically conditioned fear of a small dog, then begin to fear all small dogs (generalization), and later learn not to fear large dogs (discrimination). Similarly, under operant conditioning, a child who was bitten after petting a small dog might learn to avoid all small dogs (generalization) because of the punishing consequences, and later learn to approach larger dogs (*discrimination*) if the large dog happily licked his or her face after the petting.

- **Extinction** In both classical and operant conditioning, *extinction* occurs when the original source of the learning is withheld or removed. Just as Pavlov's classically conditioned dogs learned *not* to salivate (UCR) when the tone (CS) was *not* presented, the rat's operantly conditioned behavior (bar pressing) will gradually decline if the reinforcement (food) is withheld.

- **Spontaneous Recovery** Following extinction in classical or operant conditioning, the fear of rats or the bar pressing may *spontaneously reoccur*.

Figure 6.8 Discriminative stimuli in everyday life An English-speaking traveler in Japan, quickly learns that this red triangle is the discriminative stimulus for "stop," whereas the arrow sign below it is internationally recognized as a signal for a left turn. Similarly, we learn to answer our doorbells only when they ring, and we use either a woman or man sign on the bathroom door to know which room to enter.

Discriminative Stimulus Cue signaling when a specific response will lead to the expected reinforcement

- **Higher-Order Conditioning** During classical conditioning, the pairing of the McDonald's golden arches sign (NS) with a previously conditioned stimulus (CS) (the McDonald's restaurant) led to a conditioned response (CR) (salivation) at the mere sight of the golden arches. Similarly, during operant conditioning, a rat will learn to only bar press when a light is flashing if that is the only time food is presented. In this case, the flashing light has become a **discriminative stimulus**, which signals whether or not an operant response will pay off. Learning discriminative stimuli is also helpful for the human animal (Figure 6. 8).

Now, we'll discuss the three major *differences*:

- **Paired associations versus Consequences** During classical conditioning, learning occurs when an organism *pairs* and *associates* the unconditioned stimulus (UCS) with the neutral stimulus (NS) to create a conditioned stimulus (CS). Under operant conditioning, learning results from the *consequences*—behavior followed by reinforcement increases, whereas behavior followed by punishment decreases.

- **Involuntary versus Voluntary Responses** Subjects in classical conditioning are *passive*—something *involuntarily* happens "to" them. In contrast, subjects in operant conditioning are *active*—they *voluntarily* "do" something and then learn from the consequences.

- **Order of Effects** For the fastest and most efficient learning during classical conditioning, the neutral stimulus (NS) comes *before* the UCS. In contrast, under operant conditioning, the consequences (reinforcement and punishment) come *after* the behavior.

It's important to note that these distinctions between classical and operant conditioning are *generally* true-but not *always* true. For example, classical conditioning does sometimes influence voluntary behavior, and operant conditioning can influence involuntary, reflexive behavior. Furthermore, both forms of conditioning often interact to produce and maintain behavior. But for most purposes, the distinctions hold.

CHECK & REVIEW   **STOP** *Before going on, be sure to complete this Check & Review. It is an invaluable study tool!*

Operant Conditioning

Part A: Retrieval Practice

1. Without looking at the book, spend 10 minutes writing a free-form essay recalling all you can remember from the previous section.

2. Now, reread the previous section, and once again spend 10 minutes writing a free-form essay on the SAME material.

Part B: Practice Quiz

1. Define operant conditioning.

2. For both the mother and baby in this photo, touch appears to be _____.

(a) negative reinforcement; (b) a secondary reinforcer; (c) continuous reinforcement; (d) positive reinforcement

3. Negative punishment _____ and negative reinforcement _____ the likelihood the response will continue.

4. Partial reinforcement schedules make responses more _____ to extinction.

5. Andriana is very disruptive in class, and her teacher uses various forms of punishment hoping to decrease her misbehavior. List five potential problems with this approach.

6. Describe how operant conditioning differs from classical conditioning

Check your answers in Appendix B.

Cognitive-Social Learning

Objective 6.14: Define cognitive-social theory, and describe Köhler and Tolman's contributions.

So far, we have examined learning processes that involve associations between a stimulus and an observable behavior. Some behaviorists believe that almost all learning can be explained in such stimulus–response terms. Other psychologists feel there is more to learning than can be explained solely by operant and classical conditioning. **Cognitive-social theory** (also called *cognitive-social learning* or *cognitive-behavioral theory*) incorporates the general concepts of conditioning. But rather than a simple S–R (stimulus and response), this theory emphasizes the interpretation or thinking that occurs within the organism—S–O–R (stimulus–organism–response). According to this view, people (as well as rats, pigeons, and other nonhuman animals) have attitudes, beliefs, expectations, motivations, and emotions that affect learning. Furthermore, both human and nonhuman animals are social creatures capable of learning new behaviors through observation and imitation of others. We begin with a look at the *cognitive* part of cognitive-social theory, followed by an examination of the *social* aspects of learning.

Insight and Latent Learning: Where Are the Reinforcers?

As you'll discover throughout this text, cognitive factors play a large role in human behavior and mental processes. Given that these factors are covered in several other chapters (such as those on memory and thinking/language/intelligence), our discussion here is limited to the classic research of Wolfgang Köhler and Edward Tolman and their studies of *insight* and *latent learning*.

Köhler's Study of Insight

Early behaviorists likened the mind to a "black box," whose workings could not be observed directly. German psychologist Wolfgang Köhler wanted to look inside the box. He believed there was more to learning—especially learning to solve a complex problem—than responding to stimuli in a trial-and-error fashion. In one series of experiments, Köhler placed a banana just outside the reach of a caged chimpanzee. To reach the banana, the chimp would have to use a stick placed near the cage to extend its reach. The chimp did not solve this problem in the random trial-and-error fashion of Thorndike's cats or Skinner's rats and pigeons. Köhler noticed that he seemed to sit and think about the situation for a while. Then, in a flash of **insight** (a sudden understanding), the chimp picked up the stick and maneuvered the banana within its grasp (Köhler, 1925).

Another one of Köhler's chimps, an intelligent fellow named Sultan, was put in a similar situation. This time two sticks were made available to him and the banana was placed even farther away, too far to reach with a single stick. Sultan seemingly lost interest in the banana, but he continued to play with the sticks. When he later discovered that the two sticks could be interlocked, he instantly used the now-longer stick to pull the banana within reach. Köhler designated this type of learning *insight learning*. Some internal mental event that we can only describe as "insight" went on between the presentation of the banana and the use of the stick to retrieve it. (See Figure 6.9 for a second example of how another Köhler chimp used insight.)

Tolman's Study of Latent Learning

Like Köhler, Edward C. Tolman (1898–1956) believed that previous researchers underestimated animals' cognitive processes and cognitive learning. He noted that when allowed to roam aimlessly in a maze with no food reward at the end, rats seemed to develop a **cognitive map**, or mental representation, of the maze.

Cognitive-Social Theory Emphasizes the roles of thinking and social learning in behavior

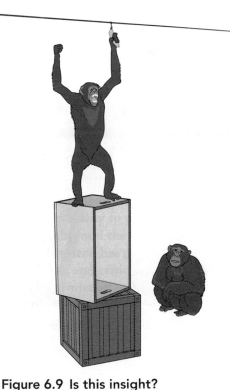

Figure 6.9 Is this insight? Grande, one of Wolfgang Köhler's chimps, has stacked boxes to solve the problem of how to get the banana. (Also, the chimp in the background is engaged in observational learning—our next topic.)

Insight Sudden understanding of a problem that implies the solution

Cognitive Map Mental image of a three-dimensional space that an organism has navigated

To test the idea of cognitive learning, Tolman allowed one group of rats to explore a maze in an aimless fashion with no reinforcement. A second group was always reinforced with food whenever they reached the end of the maze. The third group was not rewarded during the first 10 days of the trial, but starting on day 11 they found food at the end of the maze. As expected from simple operant conditioning, the first and third groups were slow to learn the maze. The second group, which had reinforcement, showed fast, steady improvement. However, when the third group started receiving reinforcement (on the 11th day), their learning of the maze quickly caught up to the group that had been reinforced every time (Tolman & Honzik, 1930). For Tolman, this was significant. It proved that the nonreinforced rats had been thinking and building cognitive maps of the area during their aimless wandering. Their hidden **latent learning** only showed up when there was a reason to display it (the food reward).

Cognitive maps and latent learning are not limited to rats. If a new log is placed in its territory, a chipmunk will explore it for a time, but will soon move on if no food is found. When a predator comes into the same territory, however, the chipmunk heads directly for and hides beneath the log. Similarly, as a child you may have casually ridden a bike around your neighborhood with no particular reason or destination in mind. You only demonstrated your hidden knowledge of the area when your dad was later searching for the closest mailbox. The fact that Tolman's nonreinforced rats quickly caught up to the reinforced ones, that the chipmunk knew about the hiding place under the log, that you knew the location of the mailbox, and recent experimental evidence all provide clear evidence of latent learning and the existence of internal cognitive maps (Gómez-Laplaza & Gerlai, 2010; Lahav & Mioduser, 2008; Lew, 2011).

Latent Learning Hidden learning that exists without behavioral signs

Observational Learning Learning new behaviors or information by watching and imitating others (also known as social learning or modeling)

Observational Learning: What We See Is What We Do

Objective 6.15: What is observational learning, and what are the four factors needed for learning by observation?

After watching her first presidential debate, my friend's 5-year-old daughter asked, "Do we like him, Mommy?" What form of learning is this? In addition to classical and operant conditioning and cognitive processes (such as insight and latent learning), this child's question shows that we also learn many things through **observational learning**. From birth to death, observational learning is very important to our biological, psychological, and social survival (the *biopsychosocial* model). Watching others helps us avoid dangerous stimuli in our environment, teaches us how to think and feel, and shows us how to act and interact socially (Chance, 2009).

Some of the most compelling examples of observational learning come from the work of Albert Bandura and his colleagues (Bandura, 2003, 2006; Bandura, Ross, & Ross, 1961; Huesmann & Kirwil, 2007). Wanting to know whether children learn to be aggressive by watching others be aggressive, Bandura and his colleagues set up several experiments. They allowed children to watch a live or televised adult model kick, punch, and shout at a large inflated Bobo doll. Later, the children were allowed to play in the same room with the same toys (Figure 6.10). As Bandura hypothesized, children who had seen the live or televised aggressive model were much more aggressive with

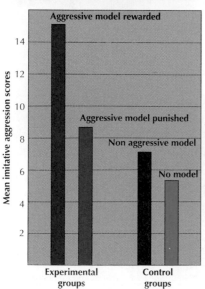

◀ **Figure 6.10 Bandura's classic Bobo doll studies** Bandura's "Bobo doll" study is considered a classic in psychology. It demonstrated how children will imitate models they observe. As you can see in the figure to the left, children who saw the aggressive model rewarded later initiated this behavior and delivered the most aggressive acts when allowed to play with the Bobo doll. In contrast, children who saw the aggressive model punished still learned something—they showed more aggression than those who watched a nonaggressive model or no model.

ConceptOrganizer6.3

Four Key Factors in Observational Learning

STOP *This Concept Organizer contains essential information NOT found elsewhere in the text, which is likely to appear on quizzes and exams. Be sure to study it CAREFULLY!*

1. ATTENTION

Observational learning requires attention. This is why teachers insist on having students watch their demonstrations.

2. RETENTION

To learn new behaviors, we need to carefully note and remember the model's directions and demonstrations.

3. REPRODUCTION

Observational learning cannot occur if we lack the motivation or motor skills necessary to imitate the model.

4. REINFORCEMENT

We are more likely to repeat a modeled behavior if the model is reinforced for the behavior.

the Bobo doll than children who had not seen the modeled aggression. In other words, "Monkey see, monkey do."

We obviously don't copy or model everything we see, however. According to Bandura, learning by observation requires at least four separate processes: *attention*, *retention*, *reproduction*, and *reinforcement* (Concept Organizer 6.3).

Psychology in action Does the sight of this litter upset you? Some stores are now banning plastic bags or charging extra for their use. Is this the best way to reduce litter? Can you explain how littering (and its solution) could involve a combination of all four factors of observational learning—attention, retention, reproduction, and reinforcement? ▶

CHECK & REVIEW

STOP *Before going on, be sure to complete this Check & Review. It is an invaluable study tool!*

Cognitive-Social Learning

Part A: Retrieval Practice

1. Without looking at the book, spend 10 minutes writing a free-form essay recalling all you can remember from the previous section.

2. Now, reread the previous section, and once again spend 10 minutes writing a free-form essay on the SAME material.

Part B: Practice Quiz

1. _____ were influential in early studies of cognitive learning.

2. The chimpanzee in Köhler's insight experiment _____
   a. used trial-and-error to reach a banana placed just out of reach
   b. turned its back on the banana out of frustration
   c. sat for a while, then used a stick to bring the banana within reach
   d. didn't like bananas

3. Learning that occurs in the absence of a reward and remains hidden until some future time when it can be retrieved is called _____.

4. Mental images of an area that an organism has navigated are known as _____.

5. Bandura's observational learning studies focused on how _____. (a) rats learn cognitive maps through exploration; (b) children learn aggressive behaviors by observing aggressive models; (c) cats learn problem solving through trial and error; (d) chimpanzees learn problem solving through reasoning

Check your answers in Appendix B.

Biology of Learning

As you recall, learning is defined as a *relatively permanent change in behavior and mental processes due to experience*. For this change in behavior to persist over time, lasting biological changes must occur within the organism. In this section, we will examine neurological and evolutionary influences on learning.

Neuroscience and Learning: The Adaptive Brain

Objective 6.16: How does learning affect the brain?

Each time we learn something, either consciously or unconsciously, that experience changes our brains. We create new synaptic connections and alterations in a wide network of brain structures, including the cortex, cerebellum, hypothalamus, thalamus, and amygdala (Fu & Zuo, 2011; Lozano, 2011; Mohler et al., 2008; Romero, 2008).

Evidence that experience changes brain structure first emerged in the 1960s from studies of animals raised in *enriched* versus *deprived environments*. Research on this topic generally involves raising one group of rats in large cages with other rats and many objects to explore. This rat "Disneyland" is colorfully decorated, and each cage has ladders, platforms, and cubbyholes to investigate. In contrast, rats in the second group are raised in stimulus-poor, deprived environments. They live alone and have no objects to explore except food and water dispensers. After weeks in these environments, the brains of these two groups of rats are significantly different. Rats and mice in the enriched environment typically develop a thicker cortex, increased nerve growth factor (NGF), more fully developed synapses, more dendritic branching, and improved performance on many tests of learning and memory (Diniz et al., 2010; Harati et al., 2011; Lores-Arnaiz et al., 2007; Pham et al., 2002; Rosenzweig & Bennett, 1996; Shoji & Mizoguchi, 2011).

Admittedly, it is a big leap from rats to humans. But research suggests that the human brain also responds to environmental conditions (Figure 6.11). For example, older adults exposed to stimulating environments generally perform better on intellectual and perceptual tasks than those who are in restricted environments (Daffner, 2010; Merrill & Small, 2011; Schaie, 1994, 2008).

Recent research has identified another neurological influence on learning processes particularly observation and imitation (see the Research Challenge, p. 231).

Figure 6.11 Environmental enrichment For human and nonhuman animals alike, environmental conditions play an important role in enabling learning. How might a classroom rich with stimulating toys, games, and books foster intellectual development in young children?

RESEARCH CHALLENGE

Mirror Neurons—"I Share Your pain!"

Objective 6.17: Discuss how mirror neurons reflect both biology and observational learning.

Why do we often suffer and cry when we watch our loved ones in pain—or even while simply observing actors in a sad movie?

Using electrical recordings, fMRIs, and other brain-imaging techniques, researchers have identified specific **mirror neurons** believed to be responsible for human empathy and imitation (Ahlsén, 2008; Baird, Scheffer, & Wilson, 2011; Caggiano et al., 2011; Carlson, 2011; Fogassi et al., 2005; Hurley, 2008; Jacob, 2008). These neurons are found in several key areas of the brain, and they help us identify with what others are feeling and to imitate their actions. When we see another person in pain, one reason we empathize and "share their pain" is that our mirror neurons are firing. Similarly, if we watch others smile, our mirror neurons make it harder for us to frown.

Mirror neurons were first discovered by neuroscientists who implanted wire probes into the brains of monkeys to record and monitor areas involved in planning and carrying out movement (Ferrari,

Rozzi, & Fogassi, 2005; Rizzolatti et al., 2002, 2006). When these monkeys moved and grasped an object, specific neurons fired, but they also fired when the monkeys simply observed another monkey performing the same or similar tasks.

Mirror neurons in humans also fire when we perform a movement or watch someone else perform. Have you noticed how spectators at an athletic event sometimes slightly move their arms or legs in synchrony with the athletes? Also, you'll discover in Chapter 9 that newborns tend to automatically imitate adult facial expressions. Mirror neurons may be the underlying biological mechanism for this imitation, as well as for the infants copying of lip and tongue movements necessary for speech. They also might help explain the emotional deficits of children and adults with autism or schizophrenia who often misunderstand the verbal and nonverbal cues of others (Arbib & Mundhenk, 2005; Kana, Wadsworth, & Travers, 2011; Mitrani, 2010).

Although scientists are excited about the promising links between mirror neurons and human emotions, imitation, language, learning, and mental disorders, we do not yet know

how they develop. Are we born with mirror neurons, or do they develop in response to our interactions with others? Stay tuned.

Student Engagement Exercise

Given the admittedly limited information on the group of studies described above, which initially studied mirror neurons (e.g., Ferrari, Rozzi, & Fogassi, 2005; Rizzolatti et al., 2002, 2006), what was their most likely:

1. *Research method* (experimental, descriptive, correlational, or biological)?

2. If you chose the:
   - *Experimental method*—label the IV, DV, experimental group, and control group.
   - *Descriptive method*—is this a naturalistic observation, survey, or case study?
   - *Correlational method*—is this a positive, negative, or zero correlation?
   - *Biological method*—identify the specific research tool (e.g., brain dissection, CT scan, etc.)

(Answers appear in Appendix B.)

Mirror Neurons Brain cells that fire both when performing specific actions and when observing specific actions or emotions of another. This "mirroring" may explain empathy, imitation, language, and the emotional deficits of some mental disorders.

Figure 6.12 Taste aversion in the wild In applied research, Garcia and his colleagues used classical conditioning to teach coyotes not to eat sheep (Gustavson & Garcia, 1974). The researchers began by lacing freshly killed sheep with a chemical that caused extreme nausea and vomiting in the coyotes that ate the tainted meat. The conditioning worked so well that the coyotes would run away from the mere sight and smell of sheep. This taste aversion developed involuntarily, but the research has since been successfully applied many times and with many animals in the wild and in the laboratory (Aubert & Dantzer, 2005; Domjan, 2005; Workman & Reader, 2008).

Taste Aversion Classically conditioned negative reaction to a particular taste that has been associated with nausea or other illness

Biological Preparedness Built-in (innate) readiness to form associations between certain stimuli and responses

Evolution and Learning: Biological Preparedness and Biological Constraints

Objective 6.18: What role does evolution play in learning?

So far, we have emphasized the learned aspects of behavior. But humans and other nonhuman animals are born with other innate, biological tendencies that help ensure their survival. When your fingers touch a hot object, you immediately pull your hand away. When a foreign object approaches your eye, you automatically blink. Although these inborn, innate abilities are important to our evolutionary survival, they are inherently inflexible. Only through learning are we are able to react to important environmental cues—such as spoken words and written symbols. From an evolutionary perspective, *learning* is an adaptation that enables organisms to survive and prosper in a constantly changing world. In this section, we will explore how our biological heritage helps us learn some associations more easily than others *(biological preparedness)*, while also restricting us from learning in other situations *(biological constraints)*.

Taste Aversions—Biological Preparedness

Years ago, Rebecca (a student in my psychology class) unsuspectingly bit into a Butterfinger candy bar filled with small, wiggling bugs. Horrified, she ran gagging and screaming to the bathroom. Many years later, Rebecca still feels nauseated when she sees a Butterfinger candy bar.

Rebecca's graphic (and true!) story illustrates an important evolutionary process. When a food or drink is associated with nausea or vomiting, that particular food or drink can become a conditioned stimulus (CS) that triggers a conditioned **taste aversion**. Like other classically conditioned responses, taste aversions develop involuntarily (Figure 6.12).

Can you see why this automatic response would be adaptive? If our cave-dwelling ancestors became ill after eating a new plant, it would increase their chances for survival if they immediately developed an aversion to that plant—but not to other family members who might have been present at the time. Similarly, people tend to develop phobias to snakes, darkness, spiders, and heights more easily than to guns, knives, and electric outlets. We apparently inherit a built-in (innate) readiness to form associations between certain stimuli and responses, known as **biological preparedness**.

Laboratory experiments have provided general support for both taste aversion and biological preparedness. For example, Garcia and his colleagues (1966) produced taste aversion in lab rats by pairing flavored water (NS) and a drug (UCS) that produced gastrointestinal distress (UCR). After being conditioned and recovering from the illness, the rats refused to drink the flavored water (CS) because of the conditioned taste aversion. Remarkably, however, Garcia discovered that only certain neutral stimuli could produce the nausea. Pairings of a noise (NS) or a shock (NS) with the nausea-producing drug (UCS) produced no taste aversion. Garcia suggested that when we are sick to our stomachs, we have a natural, evolutionary tendency to attribute it to food or drink. Being *biologically prepared* to quickly associate nausea with food or drink is adaptive. It helps us avoid that or similar food or drink in the future (Domjan, 2005; Garcia, 2003; Kardong, 2008; Swami, 2011).

Instinctive Drift—Biological Constraint

Just as Garcia couldn't produce noise–nausea associations, other researchers have found that an animal's natural behavior pattern can sometimes place limits, or *biological constraints*, on learning. For example, the Brelands (1961) tried to teach a chicken to play baseball. Through shaping and reinforcement, the chicken first learned to pull a loop that activated a swinging bat. It later learned to actually hit the ball. But instead of running to first base, it would chase the ball as though it were food. Regardless of the lack of reinforcement for chasing the ball, the chicken's natural behavior took precedence. This biological constraint is known as **instinctive drift**, when an animal's conditioned responses tend to shift (or *drift*) back toward innate response patterns.

Human and nonhuman animals can be operantly conditioned to perform a variety of novel behaviors (like jumping through hoops, turning in circles, and even water skiing). However, reinforcement alone does not determine behavior. There is a biological tendency to favor natural inborn actions. In addition, learning theorists initially believed that the fundamental laws of conditioning would apply to almost all species and all behaviors. However, later researchers have identified several constraints (such as biological preparedness and instinctive drift) that limit the generality of conditioning principles. As you discovered in Chapter 1, scientific inquiry is a constantly changing and evolving process.

Instinctive Drift Conditioned responses shift (or drift) back toward innate response patterns

CHECK & REVIEW

STOP *Before going on, be sure to complete this Check & Review. It is an invaluable study tool!*

Biology of Learning

Part A: Retrieval Practice

1. Without looking at the book, spend 10 minutes writing a free-form essay recalling all you can remember from the previous section.

2. Now, reread the previous section, and once again spend 10 minutes writing a free-form essay on the SAME material.

Part B: Practice Quiz

1. _____ neurons may be responsible for human empathy and imitation.

2. From a(n) _____ perspective, learning is an adaptation that enables organisms to survive and prosper in a constantly changing world.

3. How did Garcia condition a taste aversion in coyotes?

4. What is biological preparedness?

5. _____ occurs when an animal's learned responses tend to shift backward toward innate response patterns.

Check your answers in Appendix B.

Psychology Engages

Do you remember what I promised in the "Why Study Psychology" box at the start of this chapter? I claimed that studying this chapter would *expand your understanding and control of behavior, improve the predictability of your life, enhance your enjoyment of life,* and even *help you change the world!* I sincerely believe each of these claims. Unfortunately, many introductory psychology students focus only on studying all the terms and concepts. They fail to see "the forest for the trees." I don't want this to happen to you. To help you understand and appreciate the profound (and practical) benefits of this material, let's examine several applications for classical conditioning, operant conditioning, and cognitive-social learning.

Applying Classical Conditioning: From Marketing to Medical Treatments

Objective 6.19: How can classical conditioning be applied to everyday life?

Advertisers, politicians, film producers, music artists, and others routinely and deliberately use classical conditioning to market their products and manipulate our

Classical conditioning in action Have you every wondered why politicians kiss babies? Or why beautiful women are so often used to promote products?

Figure 6.13 Conditioned race prejudice

(a) The Clarks' research with the black and white dolls played a pivotal role in the famous *Brown v. Board of Education of Topeka* decision in 1954, which ruled that segregation of public facilities was unconstitutional.

(b) Kenneth Clark (1914–2005), pictured here with his co-author, researcher, and wife, Mamie, was also elected the first African American president of the American Psychological Association.

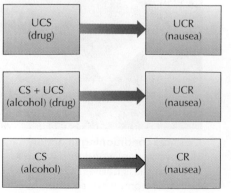

purchases, votes, emotions, and motivation. In addition to marketing and manipulation, classical conditioning also helps explain how (and why) we learn to be prejudiced and experience problems with phobias and certain medical procedures.

Marketing Beginning with John B. Watson's academic firing and subsequent career in advertising in the 1920s, marketers have employed numerous classical conditioning principles to promote their products. For example, TV commercials, magazine ads, and business promotions often pair their products or company logo (the neutral stimulus/ NS) with pleasant images, such as attractive models and celebrities (the conditioned stimulus/CS). Through higher-order conditioning, these attractive models then trigger favorable responses (the conditioned response/CR). Advertisers know that after repeated viewings, the previously neutral stimulus (their products or logo) will become a conditioned stimulus that elicits favorable responses (CR)—purchasing their products (Fennis & Stroebe, 2010; Lefrancois, 2012; Sweldens, Van Osselaer, & Janiszewski, 2010). Psychologists caution that these ads also help produce visual stimuli that trigger conditioned responses such as urges to smoke, overeat, and drink alcohol (Goodall & Slater, 2010; Hofmann, 2010; Tirodkar & Jain, 2003; Wakfield et al., 2003).

Prejudice Are children born with prejudice? Or are they the victims of classical conditioning? In a classic study in the 1930s, Kenneth Clark and Mamie P. Clark (1939) found that given a choice, both black and white children preferred white dolls to black dolls. When asked which doll was good and which was bad, both groups of children also responded that the white doll was good and nice. The black doll was seen as bad, dirty, and ugly.

The Clarks reasoned that the children had *learned* to associate inferior qualities with darker skin and positive qualities with light skin. If you're thinking this 1930 study no longer applies, follow-up research in the late 1980s found that 65 percent of the African-American children and 74 percent of the white children still preferred the white doll (Powell-Hopson & Hopson, 1988).

The Clark study not only led to important civil rights legislation (Figure 6.13), but it also provided important insights into the negative effects of prejudice on the victims—African American children. But what about the white children who also strongly preferred the white doll? Prejudice of many types (racism, ageism, sexism, homophobia, and religious intolerance) can be classically conditioned (Jackson, 2011; Tropp & Mallett, 2011) (Step-by-Step Diagram 6.2).

Medical Treatments Examples of classical conditioning are also found in the medical field. For example, a program conducted by several hospitals in California gives an *emetic* (a nausea-producing drug) to their alcohol-addicted patients (Figure 6.14).

Nausea is deliberately produced in this treatment for alcoholism. Unfortunately, it is an unintended side effect of many cancer treatments. The nausea and vomiting produced by chemotherapy increase the patient's discomfort and often generalize to other environmental cues, such as the hospital room color or odor. Using their knowledge of classical conditioning to change associations, therapists can help cancer patients control their nausea and vomiting response.

UCS (drug)	→	UCR (nausea)
CS + UCS (alcohol) (drug)	→	UCR (nausea)
CS (alcohol)	→	CR (nausea)

Figure 6.14 A treatment for alcoholism Before the nausea begins, the patient gargles with his or her preferred alcoholic beverage to maximize the taste and odor cues paired with nausea. As a form of classical conditioning, the smell and taste of various alcoholic drinks (neutral stimulus/NS) are paired with the nausea-producing drug (the unconditioned stimulus/UCS). The drug then makes the patient vomit or feel sick (the unconditioned response/UCR). Afterward, just the smell or taste of alcohol (the conditioned stimulus/CS) makes the person sick (the conditioned response/CR). Some patients have found this treatment successful, but not all (see Chapter 15).

Step-by-StepDiagram6.2

STOP *This Step by Step diagram contains essential information NOT found elsewhere in the text, which is likely to appear on quizzes and exams. Be sure to study it CAREFULLY!*

Prejudice and Classical Conditioning

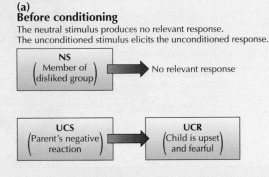

(a) Before conditioning
The neutral stimulus produces no relevant response.
The unconditioned stimulus elicits the unconditioned response.

NS (Member of disliked group) → No relevant response

UCS (Parent's negative reaction) → UCR (Child is upset and fearful)

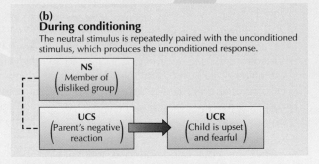

(b) During conditioning
The neutral stimulus is repeatedly paired with the unconditioned stimulus, which produces the unconditioned response.

NS (Member of disliked group)

UCS (Parent's negative reaction) → UCR (Child is upset and fearful)

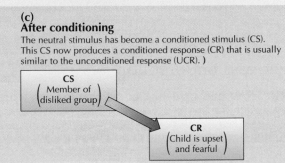

(c) After conditioning
The neutral stimulus has become a conditioned stimulus (CS). This CS now produces a conditioned response (CR) that is usually similar to the unconditioned response (UCR).)

CS (Member of disliked group) → CR (Child is upset and fearful)

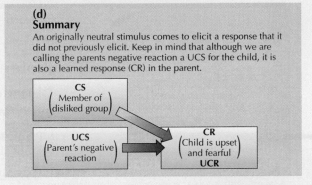

(d) Summary
An originally neutral stimulus comes to elicit a response that it did not previously elicit. Keep in mind that although we are calling the parents negative reaction a UCS for the child, it is also a learned response (CR) in the parent.

CS (Member of disliked group)

UCS (Parent's negative reaction) → CR (Child is upset and fearful) UCR

◄ How did this child's prejudice develop? (a) Before children are conditioned to be prejudiced, they show no response to a member of a different group. (b) Given that children are naturally upset and fearful when they see their parents upset, they can learn to be upset and fearful (UCR) if they see their parents respond negatively (UCS) to a member of a disliked group (NS). (c) After several pairings of the person from this group with their parents' negative reactions, the sight of the other person becomes a conditioned stimulus (CS). Being upset and fearful becomes the conditioned response (CR). (d) A previously unbiased child has now learned to be prejudiced.

Phobias Do you know someone who "freaks out" at the sight of a cockroach (Figure 6.15)? Researchers have found that most everyday fears are classically conditioned emotional responses. As you'll see in Chapter 15, classical conditioning also produces most *phobias*, exaggerated and irrational fears of a specific object or situation (Cal et al., 2006; Field, 2006; Schachtman & Reilly, 2011; Schweckendiek et al., 2011). The good news is that extreme fear of cockroaches, hypodermic needles, spiders, closets, and even snakes can be effectively treated with *behavior modification* (Chapter 15).

Figure 6.15 Cockroach phobia? If just looking at this phobia leads to unreasonable, irrational fears, you may have learned to associate the NS (cockroach) with a UCS (perhaps hearing a parent scream at the sight of a cockroach) until a CR (fear at the sight of a cockroach) was conditioned.

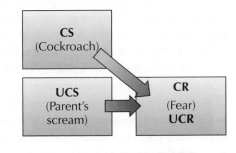

CS (Cockroach)

UCS (Parent's scream) → CR (Fear) UCR

TRY THIS YOURSELF

Discovering Classical Conditioning in Your Own Life

To appreciate the influences of classical conditioning on your own life, try this:

1. Look through a popular magazine and examine several advertisements. What images are used as the unconditioned stimulus (UCS) or conditioned stimulus (CS)? Note how you react to these images.

2. While watching a movie or a favorite TV show, identify what sounds and images are serving as conditioned stimuli (CS). What are your conditioned emotional responses (CERs)?

(*Hint*: Differing types of music are used to set the stage for happy stories, sad events, and fearful situations.)

3. Read the words below and pay attention to your emotional response. Your reactions—positive, negative, or neutral—are a result of your own personal classical conditioning history. Can you trace back to the UCS for each of these stimuli?

father	final exams	spinach
Santa Claus	beer	mother

Applying Operant Conditioning: Prejudice, Biofeedback, and Superstition

Objective 6.20: How can operant conditioning be applied to everyday life?

Operant conditioning has numerous and important applications in everyday life. Here we talk about *prejudice*, *biofeedback*, and *superstitious behavior*.

Prejudice Just as people can learn prejudice through classical conditioning, they also can learn prejudice through operant conditioning. Demeaning others is sadly reinforcing because it sometimes gains attention and sometimes approval from others, as well as increasing one's self-esteem (at the victim's expense) (Fein & Spencer, 1997; Jackson, 2011). People also may have a single negative experience with a specific member of a group, which they then generalize and apply to all members of that group. Can you see how this is another example of *stimulus generalization*?

Given that most people disapprove of prejudice, why do we still hear so many racist jokes and racial slurs? Punishment does weaken and suppress behavior. But, as mentioned earlier, to be effective it must be consistent and immediate. Unfortunately, this seldom happens. Even worse, when people laugh at these jokes or slurs, the racist behaviour is reinforced and put on a *partial (intermittent) schedule of reinforcement*. Thus it is more likely to be repeated and to become more resistant to *extinction*.

Biofeedback Involuntary bodily process (such as blood pressure or heart rate) is recorded, and the information is fed back to an organism to increase voluntary control over that bodily function

Biofeedback Sit quietly for a moment and try to determine your blood pressure. Is it high or low? Is it different from what it was a few minutes ago? You can't tell, can you? For most people, it is impossible to learn to control blood pressure consciously. But if you were hooked up to a monitor that recorded, amplified, and displayed this information to you by visual or auditory means, you could learn to control it (Figure 6.16). In this type of **biofeedback** (short for *biological feedback* and sometimes called *neurofeedback*), information about some biological function, such as heart rate, is conveyed to the individual through some type of signal.

Researchers have successfully used biofeedback to treat hypertension and anxiety by lowering blood pressure and muscle tension. It's also used to treat epilepsy by changing brain-wave patterns; urinary incontinence by gaining better pelvic muscle control; and cognitive functioning, chronic pain, low heart rate variability, and headache by redirecting blood flow (Andrasik, 2006; Bohm-Starke et al., 2007; Hammond, 2005; Kazdin, 2008; Moss, 2004; Stokes & Lappin, 2010; Wheat & Larkin, 2010).

Biofeedback involves several operant conditioning principles. Something is added (feedback) that increases the likelihood that the behavior will be repeated—*positive reinforcement*. The biofeedback itself is a *secondary reinforcer* because of the learned value of the relief from pain or other aversive stimuli (*primary reinforcer*). Finally, biofeedback involves *shaping*. The person watches a monitor screen (or other instrument) that provides graphs or numbers indicating his or her blood pressure (or other bodily states). Like a mirror, the biofeedback reflects back the results of the various strategies the participant uses to gain control. Through trial and error, the participant gets progressively better at lowering heart rate (or making other desired changes). Biofeedback techniques are limited, however. They are most successful when used in conjunction with other techniques, such as behavior modification (Chapter 15).

Figure 6.16 Biofeedback In biofeedback training, internal bodily processes (like blood pressure or muscle tension) are electrically recorded. The information is then amplified and reported back to the patient through headphones, signal lights, and other means. This information helps the person learn to control bodily processes not normally under voluntary control.

Accidental Reinforcement and Superstitious Behavior B. F. Skinner (1948, 1992) conducted a fascinating experiment to show how accidental reinforcement could lead to *superstitious behaviors*. He set the feeding mechanism in the cages of eight pigeons to release food once every 15 seconds. No matter what the birds did, they were reinforced at 15-second intervals. Interestingly, six of the pigeons acquired behaviors that they repeated over and over, even though the behaviors were not necessary to receive the food. For example, one pigeon kept turning in counterclockwise circles, and another kept making jerking movements with its head.

Why did the pigeons engage in such repetitive and unnecessary behavior? Recall that a *reinforcer* increases the probability that a response just performed will be repeated. Skinner was not using the food to reinforce any particular behavior. However, the pigeons associated the food with whatever behavior they were engaged in when the food was randomly dropped into the cage. Thus, if the bird was circling counterclockwise when the food was presented, it would repeat that motion to receive more food.

Like Skinner's pigeons, we humans also believe in many superstitions that may have developed from accidental reinforcement. In addition to the superstitions shown by the baseball player mentioned in the chapter opener, and those in Table 6.7,

Table 6.7 **COMMON WESTERN SUPERSTITIONS**

	Behavior	Superstition
	Wedding plans: *Why do brides wear something old and something borrowed?*	The something old is usually clothing that belongs to an older woman who is happily married. Thus, the bride will supposedly transfer that good fortune to herself. Something borrowed is often a relative's jewelry. This item should be golden, because gold represents the sun, which was once thought to be the source of life.
	Spilling salt: *Why do some people throw a pinch of salt over their left shoulder?*	Years ago, people believed good spirits lived on the right side of the body and bad spirits on the left. When a man spilled salt, he believed his guardian spirit had caused the accident to warn him of evil nearby. At the time, salt was scarce and precious. Therefore, to bribe the spirits who were planning to harm him, he would quickly throw a pinch of salt over his left shoulder.
	Knocking on wood: *Why do some people knock on wood when they're speaking of good fortune or making predictions?*	Down through the ages, people have believed that trees were homes of gods, who were kind and generous if approached in the right way. A person who wanted to ask a favor of the tree god would touch the bark. After the favor was granted, the person would return to knock on the tree as a sign of thanks.

professional and Olympic-level athletes sometimes carry lucky charms or perform a particular ritual before every competition. Phil Esposito, a hockey player with the Boston Bruins and the New York Rangers for 18 years, always wore the same black turtleneck and drove through the same tollbooth on his way to a game. In the locker room, he put on all his clothes in the same order and laid out his equipment in exactly the same way he had for every other game. All this because once when he had behaved that way years before, he had been the team's high scorer. Alas, the power of accidental reinforcement.

Applying Cognitive-Social Learning: We See, We Do?

Objective 6.21: How can cognitive-social learning be applied to everyday life?

We use cognitive-social learning in many ways in our everyday lives, yet one of the most powerful examples is frequently overlooked—*media influences*. Experimental and correlational research clearly show that when we watch television, go to movies, and read books and magazines that portray minorities, women, and other groups in demeaning and stereotypical roles, we often learn to expect these behaviors and to accept them as "natural." Exposure of this kind initiates and reinforces the learning of prejudice (Dill & Thill, 2007; Jackson, 2011; Neto & Furnham, 2005).

In addition to prejudice, the media also can teach us what to eat, what toys to buy, what homes and clothes are most fashionable, and what constitutes "the good life." When a TV commercial shows children enjoying a particular cereal and beaming at their Mom in gratitude (and Mom is smiling back), both children and parents in the audience are participating in a form of observational learning. They learn that they, too, will be rewarded for buying the advertised brand (with happy children) or punished (with unhappy children who won't eat) for buying a competitor's product.

Unfortunately, observational learning also encourages destructive, aggressive behaviors. Correlational evidence from more than 50 studies indicates that observing violent behavior is related to later desensitization and increased aggression (Azar, 2010; Kalnin et al., 2011; Krahe, et al., 2011; Mitchell et al., 2011). As a critical thinker, you may be automatically noting that correlation is not causation. However, over 100 *experimental* studies have shown a causal link between observing violence and later performing it.

 **CRITICAL THINKING**

Using Learning Principles to Succeed in College

Psychological theory and research have taught us that an active approach to learning is rewarded by better grades. Active learning means using the SQ4R (Survey, Question, Read, Recite, Review, and Write) study techniques discussed in the "Tools for Student Success" (pp. 41–42). An active learner also rises above old, easy patterns of behavior and applies new knowledge to everyday situations. When you transfer ideas or concepts you learn from class to your personal life, your insight grows.

Now that you have studied the principles of learning, use the following activity to help you apply your new knowledge to achieve your education goals and have an enjoyable college experience:

1. List three ways you can positively reinforce yourself for studying, completing assignments, and attending class.

2. Discuss with friends how participating in club and campus activities can reinforce your commitment to education.

3. Examine the time and energy you spend studying for an exam in a course you like with your study effort in a course you don't like. How could you apply the Premack principle to your advantage in this situation?

4. When you take exams, are you anxious? How might this be a classically conditioned response? Describe how you could use the principle of extinction to weaken this response.

GENDER AND CULTURAL DIVERSITY

Avatar: A Modern Fable

By Thomas Frangicetto (Northampton Community College, Bethlehem, PA)

"This film should be seen by every man, woman and child."

DR. JEFFREY FINE, PSYCHOLOGIST (2010)

What do you think? Was *Avatar* the best movie ever made? Should everyone see it? It was reportedly the most expensive movie ever made, as well as the most financially successful. It also was wildly popular—receiving a positive, "thumbs-up" rating from 83% of reviewers and 92% of the general audience (Rotten Tomatoes, 2011).

But what can *Avatar* teach us about learning and gender and cultural diversity? In the unlikely event that you did not see the movie, or simply need a review, let's begin with a brief summary. *Avatar* is set in the year 2154 and earthlings have traveled to the distant planet of Pandora to mine a rare mineral. In an attempt to maintain good relations with the indigenous people, corporate leaders hire Jake Sully, a paraplegic ex-veteran Marine, to infiltrate the Na'vi who are increasingly agitated with the humans' encroachment on their sacred lands.

Given that the Na'vi are nine feet tall and blue-skinned, Jake must be transformed into an organic avatar, modeled on Na'vi DNA but controlled by human consciousness. Jake's job is to learn the ways of the Na'vi, gain their trust, and convince them to move from their land so it can be mined for its precious mineral—Unobtainium.

Right off, Jake's out-of-body, soul-changing learning experience is fraught with danger, and his life is saved by Neytiri, a female Na'vi warrior. She is then given the "job" of teaching Avatar-Jake the ways of the Na'vi. In true Hollywood fashion, Jake quickly discovers that this is a race of people of profound spiritual depth and wisdom about the interconnectedness of all living things. Intrigued by their wisdom and harmony with nature, Jake wishes to become one of them, and, against all odds, Jake and Neytiri fall in love. The film ends with a vicious battle waged by the imperialistic humans, but it's the Na'vi who triumph.

Avatar compellingly dramatizes the issues of gender and diversity. Some critics lament that in its depiction of the Na'vi, *Avatar* "seemed to get stuck in traditional views of women and gender" (Plaufcan, 2010). While some stereotypes do prevail—man as tribal leader, woman as spiritual leader, Neytiri is a complex and dynamic combination of courage, intelligence, passion, sensitivity, and spirituality, along with a repertoire of fighting skills as prodigious as any of the male warriors. It also should be noted that the spiritual realm is the lifeblood of the Na'vi. And it's Neytiri, magnificent in battle, who ends up saving Jake's "soul."

In contrast to the claim of traditional stereotypes, reviewer Jessica Burstrem (2010) emphasizes Avatar's notable absence of gender role differentiation. The head scientist is female, as well as members of the security force, and both male and female Na'vi engage in warfare. "There are no sexist jokes," Burstrem writes, and "there are no remarks about "a woman's place." The underlying message is that earth is no longer a sexist place in 2154 . . . and neither is Pandora.

Perhaps the greatest value of *Avatar* is its challenge to *ethnocentrism*, believing that one's culture is "correct" or superior, and judging others according to this standard. In an ugly show of ethnocentrism, the executive head of the mining company, and commander of the mercenary force, refer to the Na'vi as lesser life forms, calling them "savages," "hostiles," and, during the horrific military assault on them, as "roaches." Avatar's rejection of this view is skillfully depicted by the subtle unfolding of the Na'vi as much more than Hollywood's typical portrayal of the "noble savage" (Goldberg, 2009).

Dr. Grace Augustine (Sigourney Weaver), the lead scientist, and defender of the Na'vi, says it best when she offers the head of the mining company the key to diversity training:

"You need to wake up, Parker. The wealth of this world isn't in the ground—it's all around us. The Na'vi know that, and they're fighting to defend it. If you want to share this world with them, *you* need to understand *them*."

TEST YOURSELF

Can you use Avatar-related examples to improve your mastery of Chapter 6 key terms? Filling-in the open areas (?) in Table 6.8 requires at least two key study aids—*deeper levels of processing* and *elaborative rehearsal*. (Chapter 7, p. 250) (Check your answers in Appendix B.)

Table 6.8   APPLYING AVATAR TO KEY LEARNING PRINCIPLES

Example	Learning Principle	Explanation
Jake is a paraplegic. The head of security, asks Avatar-Jake to cooperate and get information from the Na'vi, which will help defeat them. He tells Jake: "Get me what I need and I'll get you your legs back."	?	*Stimulus* (offer of new legs) is *added. Response* (Jake's cooperation) is *strengthened,* and thus more likely to recur.
When Jake is chased by a ferocious Thanator, he runs away and escapes by jumping from a high cliff into a waterfall.	Negative Reinforcement	?
Jake innocently thanks Neytiri for killing the viperwolves who attacked him. She smacks her bow across his face, and yells: "Don't thank! You don't thank for this! This is sad."	?	*Stimuli* (Neytiri's hitting and yelling) are *added. Response* (Jake saying "Thanks") is *weakened,* and thus less likely to recur.
After Jake reveals his real purpose for wanting to learn the ways of the Na'vi, he is immediately shunned by Neytiri and her people	Negative Punishment	?
After Neytiri strikes Jake with her bow, he winces in anticipation whenever he sees her holding it.		Previous NS (bow) became a CS when Jake paired it with the UCS (pain). Previous UCR (fear) became a CR (fear). [The CR is also a CER (fear) because it involved an emotion.]
Jake watches Neytiri mount and ride her flying banshee. He then copies her behavior, clumsily at first, but soon gets the hang of it.	Observational Learning	?

CHECK & REVIEW

STOP *Before going on, be sure to complete this Check & Review. It is an invaluable study tool!*

Psychology Engages

Part A: Retrieval Practice

1. Without looking at the book, spend 10 minutes writing a free-form essay recalling all you can remember from the previous section.

2. Now, reread the previous section, and once again spend 10 minutes writing a free-form essay on the SAME material.

Part B: Practice Quiz

1. Politicians often depict their opponent as immoral and irresponsible because they know it helps create a ___ toward their rival. (a) classically conditioned phobia; (b) negative social-learning cue; (c) conditioned aversive response; (d) negative conditioned emotional response (CER)

2. Biofeedback reinforces desired physiological changes that have beneficial results. This makes it a(n) ___. (a) operant conditioner; (b) primary reinforcer; (c) secondary reinforcer; (d) biological marker

3. You insist on wearing a red sweater each time you take an exam because you believe it helps you get higher scores. This is an example of ___. (a) classical conditioning; (b) secondary reinforcement; (c) superstition; (d) redophilia reinforcement

4. If you saw the movie *Avatar*, list three additional examples of learning principles other than those in Table 6.8 (p. 240)

Check your answers in Appendix B.

www.wileyplus.com

WileyPLUS presents an on-line version of this textbook along with a wealth of study resources including quizzes, practice tests, flash cards, videos, animations and other activities designed to improve your mastery of the content. Working in conjunction with these study tools, the *Psychology in Action* WileyPLUS course features Professor Karen Huffman, author of this textbook, explaining and expanding upon some of the most challenging concepts in psychology. Here is a sample of the tutorial videos available for this chapter:

* Animated interactive exploration of classical conditioning
* Watch Karen Huffman explain classical conditioning while secretly being conditioned herself
* Classroom discussion of positive and negative reinforcement versus positive and negative punishment
* Virtual Field Trip to see how operant conditioning is used to train animals to entertain us, assist the disabled and save lives.

→ Key Terms

To assess your understanding of the **Key Terms** in Chapter 6, write a definition for each (in your own words), and then compare your definitions with those in the text.

learning (p. 205)
conditioning (p. 206)

Classical Conditioning
classical conditioning (p. 208)
unconditioned stimulus (UCS) (p. 208)
unconditioned response (UCR) (p. 208)
neutral stimulus (NS) (p. 208)
conditioned stimulus (CS) (p. 208)
conditioned response (CR) (p. 208)
conditioned emotional response (CER) (p. 209)
acquisition (p. 210)

stimulus generalization (p. 210)
stimulus discrimination (p. 212)
extinction (p. 212)
spontaneous recovery (p. 212)
higher-order conditioning (p. 213)

Operant Conditioning
operant conditioning (p. 215)
reinforcement (p. 215)
punishment (p. 215)
law of effect (p. 216)
primary reinforcers (p. 217)
secondary reinforcers (p. 218)

positive reinforcement (p. 218)
negative reinforcement (p. 218)
Premack principle (p. 218)
continuous reinforcement (p. 219)
partial (intermittent) reinforcement (p. 219)
fixed ratio (FR) schedule (p. 219)
variable ratio (VR) schedule (p. 219)
fixed interval (FI) schedule (p. 219)
variable interval (VI) schedule (p. 219)
shaping (p. 220)

Chapter Summary

Classical Conditioning

Objective 6.1: Compare learning and conditioning.

Learning is a general term referring to a relatively permanent change in behavior and mental processes due to experience. **Conditioning** is a specific type of learning of associations between environmental stimuli and behavioral responses.

Objective 6.2: Define classical conditioning, and describe Pavlov and Watson's contributions.

In **classical conditioning**, the type of learning investigated by Pavlov and Watson, an originally **neutral stimulus (NS)** is paired with an **unconditioned stimulus (UCS)** that causes an **unconditioned response (UCR)**. After several pairings, the neutral stimulus becomes a **conditioned stimulus (CS)**, which alone will produce a **conditioned response (CR)** or **conditioned emotional response (CER)** similar to the original reflex response.

Pavlov's work laid a foundation for Watson's later insistence that psychology must be an objective science, studying only overt behavior without considering internal mental activity. Watson called this position *behaviorism*. His controversial "Little Albert" study demonstrated how simple emotions, like fear, could be classically conditioned to become a **conditioned emotional response (CER)**.

Basic Principles of Classical Conditioning

Objective 6.3: Describe the six principles of classical conditioning.

Acquisition, the first of the six components, is a term describing basic classical conditioning when a neutral stimulus (NS) is consistently paired with an unconditioned stimulus (UCS) so that the NS comes to elicit a conditioned response (CR).

Stimulus generalization occurs when stimuli similar to the original conditioned stimulus (CS) elicit the conditioned response (CR). **Stimulus discrimination** takes place when only the CS elicits the CR. **Extinction** occurs when the CS is repeatedly presented without the UCS, which gradually weakens the CR. **Spontaneous recovery** occurs when a CR that had been extinguished suddenly reappears. In **higher- order conditioning**, a NS becomes a CS through repeated pairings with a previously conditioned stimulus (CS).

Operant Conditioning

Objective 6.4: Define operant conditioning, reinforcement, and punishment.

Operant conditioning occurs when humans and nonhuman animals learn by the consequences of their voluntary behaviors. Behavior is strengthened if followed by reinforcement and weakened if followed by punishment. **Reinforcement** is any procedure that strengthens or increases a response. **Punishment** is any procedure that weakens or decreases behavior.

Objective 6.5: Describe Thorndike and Skinner's contributions.

Thorndike and Skinner are the two major contributors to operant conditioning. Thorndike's **law of**

effect states that rewarded behavior is more likely to recur. Skinner extended Thorndike's work to more complex behaviors, with a special emphasis on external, observable behaviors.

Objective 6.6: Explain how primary and secondary reinforcers and positive and negative reinforcement strengthen behavior.

Primary reinforcers, which satisfy an unlearned biological need (e.g., hunger, thirst), and **secondary reinforcers**, which have learned value (e.g., money), both strengthen a response. **Positive reinforcement** (adds something) and **negative reinforcement** (takes something away) both strengthen a response and increase the likelihood it will occur again.

Objective 6.7: Explain why negative reinforcement is not punishment.

Reinforcement (either positive or negative) always strengthens a behavior, whereas punishment always weakens behavior and makes it less likely to recur.

Objective 6.8: Contrast continuous and partial (intermittent) reinforcement, and identify the four schedules of partial reinforcement.

Continuous reinforcement rewards each correct response. A **partial (intermittent)** schedule reinforces some, but not all correct responses. The four partial reinforcement schedules are **variable ratio (VR)**, **variable interval (VI)**, **fixed ratio (FR)**, and **fixed interval (FI)**.

Objective 6.9: Define shaping and tell why it's important.

Shaping is reinforcement that is delivered for successive approximations of the desired response. It is particularly important for new and complex behaviors that are unlikely to occur naturally.

Objective 6.10: Explain how positive and negative punishment weaken behavior.

Both **positive punishment** (adding something) and **negative punishment** (taking something away) decrease the likelihood the response will occur again.

Objective 6.11: Why is punishment "tricky," and what are its serious side effects?

Punishment plays an important role, but it is tricky because we often unintentionally punish the very behaviors we're trying to increase. Also, to be effective, punishment must be immediate and consistent. When it's delayed and/ or inconsistent, the undesirable behavior can be unintentionally reinforced. This reinforcement then places the undesirable behavior on a *partial schedule of reinforcement*—thus making it even more resistant to extinction. Furthermore, punishment only teaches what not to do—not what should be done.

Punishment also has several undesirable side effects: increased aggression, passive aggressiveness, avoidance, inappropriate modeling, temporary suppression versus elimination, and learned helplessness.

Objective 6.12: How can we effectively use reinforcement and punishment?

To be effective, reinforcement and punishment require *clear directions and feedback, appropriate timing, consistency, a correct order of presentation*, and a *combination of key learning principles.*

Objective 6.13: Briefly summarize the similarities and differences between classical and operant conditioning.

Classical conditioning is learning through involuntary paired associations, whereas operant conditioning is learning through voluntary behavior and its subsequent consequences.

Both classical and operant conditioning share terms, such as acquisition, generalization, discrimination, extinction, spontaneous recovery, and higher-order conditioning. The three major differences are paired associations versus consequences, involuntary versus voluntary responses, and order of effects. Almost all behaviors result from a combination of both classical and operant conditioning.

Cognitive-Social Learning

Objective 6.14: Define cognitive-social theory, and describe Köhler and Tolman's contributions.

Cognitive-social theory emphasizes thought processes, or cognitions, and social learning.

Wolfgang Köhler showed that learning could occur with a sudden flash of **insight**. Tolman demonstrated that **latent learning** takes place in the absence of reward and remains hidden until some future time when it can be retrieved as needed. A **cognitive map** is a mental image of an area that a person or nonhuman animal has navigated.

Objective 6.15: What is observational learning, and what are the four factors needed for learning by observation?

According to Albert Bandura, **observational learning** is the process of learning by watching and imitating others. It requires at least four processes. We must pay attention, retain the information, be able to reproduce the behavior, and be motivated by some reinforcement.

The Biology of Learning

Objective 6.16: How does learning affect the brain?

Learning and conditioning produce relatively permanent changes in biochemistry and various parts of the brain.

Objective 6.17: Discuss how mirror neurons reflect both biology and observational learning.

Mirror neurons fire both when performing specific actions and when simply observing the actions or emotions of others. This "mirroring" involves a combination of both biology and observational learning, and it may explain infant imitation of adults, as well as the emotional deficits of some mental disorders.

Objective 6.18: What role does evolution play in learning?

At least some behavior is innate, or inborn, in the form of either reflexes or instincts. Learning and conditioning are further adaptations that have evolutionary survival benefits.

Through **biological preparedness** an organism is innately predisposed to form associations between certain stimuli and responses. **Taste aversions** are conditioned associations of food to illness that are rapidly learned, often in a single pairing. These aversions offer a protective survival mechanism. Findings on **instinctive drift** show there are also biological constraints on learning.

Psychology Engages

Objective 6.19: How can classical conditioning be applied to everyday life?

Classical conditioning explains how people market their products, how we sometimes learn negative attitudes toward groups of people (prejudice), and how we sometimes have problems with certain medical treatments and phobias.

Objective 6.20: How can operant conditioning be applied to everyday life?

Operant conditioning helps explain how we learn prejudice through positive reinforcement and stimulus generalization. **Biofeedback**, another application, is the feeding back of biological information, such as heart rate or blood pressure, which a person uses to control normally automatic functions of the body. Operant conditioning also helps explain many superstitions, which involve accidentally reinforced behaviors that are continually repeated because they are believed to cause desired effects.

Objective 6.21: How can cognitive-social learning be applied to everyday life?

Cognitive-social theory helps to further explain prejudice and media influences. People often learn their prejudices by observing and imitating what they've seen modeled by friends, family, and the media. The media affect our purchasing behaviors, as well as our aggressive tendencies.

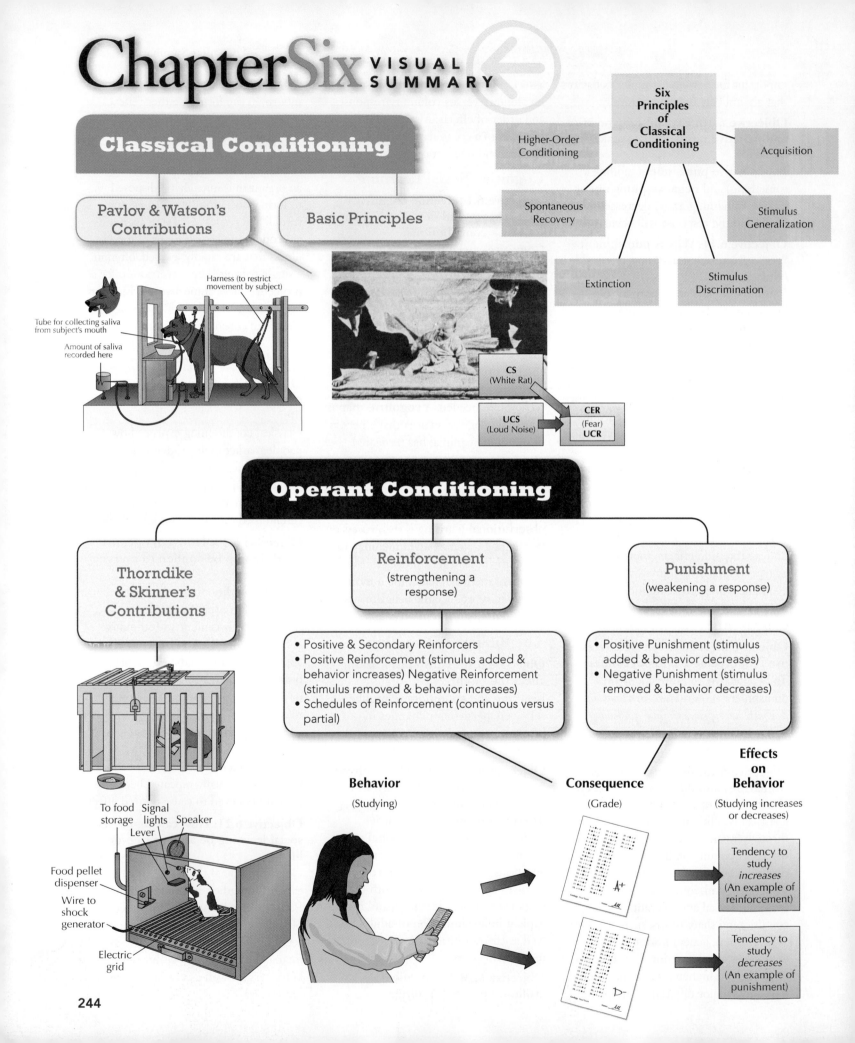

Classical Conditioning

Six Principles of Classical Conditioning

- Higher-Order Conditioning
- Acquisition
- Spontaneous Recovery
- Stimulus Generalization
- Extinction
- Stimulus Discrimination

Pavlov & Watson's Contributions

Basic Principles

Harness (to restrict movement by subject)

Tube for collecting saliva from subject's mouth

Amount of saliva recorded here

CS (White Rat)

UCS (Loud Noise) → CER (Fear) UCR

Operant Conditioning

Thorndike & Skinner's Contributions

Reinforcement (strengthening a response)

- Positive & Secondary Reinforcers
- Positive Reinforcement (stimulus added & behavior increases) Negative Reinforcement (stimulus removed & behavior increases)
- Schedules of Reinforcement (continuous versus partial)

Punishment (weakening a response)

- Positive Punishment (stimulus added & behavior decreases)
- Negative Punishment (stimulus removed & behavior decreases)

To food storage Signal lights Speaker
Lever

Food pellet dispenser

Wire to shock generator

Electric grid

Behavior
(Studying)

Consequence
(Grade)

Effects on Behavior
(Studying increases or decreases)

Tendency to study *increases* (An example of reinforcement)

Tendency to study *decreases* (An example of punishment)

Cognitive-Social Learning

Insight & Latent Learning

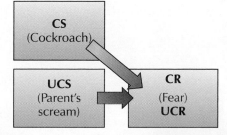

Observational Learning

1. ATTENTION

Observational learning requires attention. This is why teachers insist on having students watch their demonstrations.

2. RETENTION

To learn new behaviors, we need to carefully note and remember the model's directions and demonstrations.

3. REPRODUCTION

Observational learning cannot occur if we lack the motivation or motor skills necessary to imitate the model.

4. REINFORCEMENT

We are more likely to repeat a modeled behavior if the model is reinforced for the behavior.

Biology of Learning

Neuroscience & Learning

Evolution & Learning

Psychology Engages

Applying Classical Conditioning
Applying Operant Conditioning
Applying Cognitive-Social Learning
Critical Thinking
Gender & Cultural Diversity

CS
(Cockroach)

UCS
(Parent's scream)

CR
(Fear)
UCR

ChapterSeven

Memory

When Elizabeth was 14 years old, her mother drowned in their pool. As she grew older, the details surrounding her mother's death became increasingly vague. Decades later, a relative told Elizabeth that she had been the one to find her mother's body. Despite her initial shock, memories slowly started coming back.

> *I could see myself, a thin, dark-haired girl, looking into the flickering blue-and-white pool. My mother, dressed in her nightgown, is floating face down. I start screaming. I remember the police cars, their lights flashing, and the stretcher with the clean, white blanket tucked in around the edges of the body. The memory had been there all along, but I just couldn't reach it.*
>
> (LOFTUS & KETCHAM, 1994, P. 45)

This is the true story of Elizabeth Loftus. Today she is a well-known psychologist specializing in the study of memory. Compare her life story with this one:

When H.M. was 27, he underwent brain surgery to correct his severe epileptic seizures. Although the surgery improved his medical problem, now something was clearly wrong with H.M.'s long-term memory. When his uncle died, he grieved in a normal way. But soon after, he began to ask why his uncle never visited him. H.M. had to be repeatedly reminded of his uncle's death, and each reminder would begin a new mourning process.

H.M. lived another 55 years not recognizing the people who cared for him daily. Each time he met his caregivers, read a book, or ate a meal, it was as if for the first time (Barbeau, Puel, & Pariente, 2010; Carey, 2008; Corkin, 2002). Sadly, H.M. died in 2008—never having regained his long-term memory.

What should we make of these two stories? How could a child forget finding her mother's body? What would it be like to be H.M.—existing only in the present moment, unable to learn and form new memories? How can we remember our second-grade teacher's name, but forget the name of someone we just met? In this chapter, you'll discover answers to these and other fascinating questions about memory.

ChapterOutline

Nature of Memory
Memory Models
Sensory Memory
Short-Term Memory (STM)
Long-Term Memory (LTM)
Improving Long-Term
  Memory (LTM)

Forgetting
Why Do We Forget?
Research Challenge
Key Factors in Forgetting
Memory and the Criminal
  Justice System

Biological Bases of Memory
How Are Memories Formed?
Where Are Memories
  Located?
Biological Causes of
  Memory Loss

Psychology Engages
Overall Memory
  Improvement
Gender and Cultural
  Diversity
Critical Thinking

WHY STUDY PSYCHOLOGY?

Did you know . . .

- Long-lasting "flashbulb" memories for intense emotional events, like the birth of your first child, or the 9/11 terrorist attack on the United States, may be influenced by "fight-or-flight" hormones?

- Without memory, you would be unable to recognize movie stars or politicians, or even family members?

- Long-term memory is like a magical credit card with unlimited cash and no known expiration date?

- Eyewitness testimony is common in many legal cases, but research shows it to be highly unreliable?

- People can be led to create false memories they later believe to be true?

- Memory tricks and techniques (e.g., mnemonics) can help improve your memory?

The charm, one might say the genius, of memory is that it is choosy, chancy, and temperamental.

ELIZABETH BOWEN
(AUTHOR, 1899–1973)

Memory Internal record or representation of some prior event or experience

Constructive Process Organizing and shaping of information during processing, storage, and retrieval of memories

Nature of Memory

Objective 7.1: Define memory and explain how it is a constructive process.

Memory is most often defined as an internal record or representation of some prior event or experience. It allows us to learn from our experiences and adapt to ever-changing environments. Without memory, we would have no past or future. We could not dress or feed ourselves, communicate, or even recognize ourselves in a mirror.

However, as we've seen with the opening stories of Elizabeth Loftus and H.M., our memories also are highly fallible. Although some people think of memory as a gigantic library or an automatic tape recorder, our memories are *not* exact recordings of events. Instead, memory is a **constructive process**. We actively organize and shape information as it is being processed, stored, and retrieved. As you might expect, this construction often leads to serious errors and biases, which we'll discuss throughout this chapter.

TRY THIS YOURSELF

A Memory Test

Carefully read through all the words in the following list.

Bed	Awake	Tired	Dream
Wake	Snooze	Snore	Rest
Blanket	Doze	Slumber	Nap
Peace	Yawn	Drowsy	Nurse
Sick	Lawyer	Medicine	Health
Hospital	Dentist	Physician	Patient
Stethoscope	Curse	Clinic	Surgeon

Now cover the list and write down all the words you remember.

Number of correctly recalled words:
21 to 28 words = excellent memory

16 to 20 words = better than most
12 to 15 words = average
8 to 11 words = below average
7 or fewer = you might need a nap

How did you do? Do you have a good or an excellent memory? Did you recall seeing the words *sleep* and *doctor*? Look back over the list. These words are not there. However, over 65 percent of students commonly report seeing these words. Why? Memory is not a faithful recording or duplicate of an event. It is a *constructive process*. We actively shape and build on information as it is *encoded* and *retrieved*, terms you'll discover later in this chapter.

Memory Models: An Overview

Objective 7.2: Briefly summarize the four models of memory.

To understand memory (and its constructive nature), you first need a model of how it operates. Over the years, psychologists have developed numerous models, and we begin with a brief overview of the major approaches (Table 7.1) and then explore the traditional, *three-stage*, model in some depth.

Encoding, Storage, Retrieval (ESR)

According to the **encoding, storage, retrieval (ESR) model,** information goes through three basic operations—*encoding, storage,* and *retrieval.* Each of these three processes represents a different function closely analogous to the parts and functions of a computer (Figure 7.1).

To input data into a computer, you begin by typing letters and numbers on the keyboard. The computer then translates these key strokes into its own electronic language. In a roughly similar fashion, your brain **encodes** sensory information (sound, visual images, and other senses) into a neural code (language) it can understand and use.

Once computer or human information is *encoded,* it must be **stored.** Computer information is stored on a flash or hard drive. Human memories are stored in the brain. Finally, memories must be **retrieved,** or taken out of storage. To do well on your quizzes and exams in psychology, or any other course, you must successfully encode, store and retrieve a large amount of facts and concepts. Later in this chapter (pp. 256–259), we'll discuss ways to improve your memory during each of these processes.

Levels of Processing

Fegus Craik and Robert Lockhart's (1972) **levels of processing model** suggests that memory relies on how *deeply* we process and store information. During shallow processing, we're only somewhat aware of incoming information. Little or no memory is

Encoding, Storage, Retrieval (ESR) Model   Memory is formed through three processess: *encoding* (getting information in), *storage* (retaining information for future use), and *retrieval* (recovering information)

Encoding   Processing information into the memory system

Storage   Retaining information for future use

Retrieval   Recovering information from memory storage

Levels of Processing Model   Degree or depth of mental processing occurring when material is initially encountered; determines how well material is later remembered

---

Table 7.1   COMPARING MEMORY MODELS

Encoding, Storage, Retrieval (ESR)

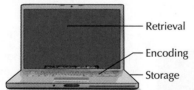
Retrieval
Encoding
Storage

◀ Memory is *a process,* roughly analogous to a computer, where information goes through three basic processes—*encoding, storage,* and *retrieval.*

The more deeply material is processed, the better we are at remembering it. ▶

Levels of Processing

Memory Bits

Shallow = poor memory

Deeper = better memory

Parallel Distributed Processing (PDP)

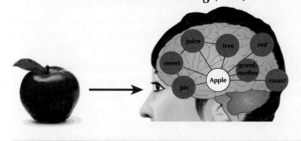
juice   tree   red
sweet   grand-mother
pie   Apple   round

◀ Memory is distributed across a wide network of interconnected neurons located throughout the brain. When activated, this network works simultaneously (in a *parallel* fashion) to process information.

Memory requires three different storage boxes or stages to hold and process ▶ information for various lengths of time.

Three-Stage Memory

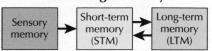
Sensory memory → Short-term memory (STM) ⇄ Long-term memory (LTM)

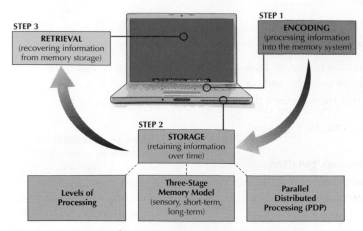

STEP 3
RETRIEVAL
(recovering information from memory storage)

STEP 1
ENCODING
(processing information into the memory system)

STEP 2
STORAGE
(retaining information over time)

| Levels of Processing | Three-Stage Memory Model (sensory, short-term, long-term) | Parallel Distributed Processing (PDP) |

Figure 7.1 Encoding, Storage, Retrieval (ESR) model Memory processes have been likened to a computer's information-processing system. Data are entered on a keyboard and *encoded* in a way that the computer can understand and use. Information is then *stored* on a flash or hard drive, and later *retrieved* and brought to the computer screen for viewing. (Note how the other three memory models are connected to the storage of information, which is central to the memory process.)

Maintenance Rehearsal Repeating information over and over to maintain it in short-term memory (STM)

Elaborative Rehearsal Linking new information to previously stored material (also known as deeper levels of processing)

formed. However, when we do something more with the information, such as adding meaning, developing organizations and associations, or relating it to things we already know, the information is more deeply processed and can be stored for a lifetime.

For example, what if you were asked to remember a phone number? You could do a type of juggling act called **maintenance rehearsal**, which involves simply repeating the information over and over until you make the phone call. However, this type of *shallow processing* only works for information that you need for a short period of time. What if you needed to remember important information for hours, months, or years? In this case you need *deeper levels of processing*, and a technique called **elaborative rehearsal** (Moulin, 2011). When we *elaborate*, we expand. We think *deeply* about new information and tie it into previously stored memories. If you're casually reading this text and giving the words little thought (shallow processing), you will retain the information only for the briefest period of time—and you'll remember little or nothing on exams or quizzes! But if you stop and think deeply about the meaning of the words and relate them to your own experiences (an example of elaborative rehearsal), you'll greatly increase your learning and memory of the material.

For example, if you want to master and retain the distinction between maintenance and elaborative rehearsal, think about a new music student trying to understand that the five lines of printed music of the treble clef are called E-G-B-D-F. The student will process it at a deeper level if he or she ties those letters to the sentence "*Every Good Boy Does Fine.*" By *elaborating* and noting that the first letter of each word in the sentence is the same as one of the lines of printed music, the new music student will create deeper and more lasting memories. (See the Try This Yourself exercise below for further tips.)

 **TRY THIS YOURSELF**

Improving Elaborative Rehearsal

Think about the other students in your college classes. Have you noticed that older students often tend to get better grades? This is because they've lived longer and can tap into a greater wealth of previously stored material. If you're a younger student (or an older student just returning to college), you can learn to process information at a deeper level and build your elaborative rehearsal skills by:

• *Expanding (or elaborating on) the information* The more you elaborate or try to understand something, the more likely you are to remember it. To store the term *long-term memory*, think about what it would be like if you only had STM and could store information for only 30 seconds. Picture the life of H.M. (the man introduced at the beginning of the chapter).

If you can't easily tag information to what you already know, create a new link or "tag." For instance, to encode and store the term *echoic memory*, look

for examples of this in other people or in yourself. Make a mental note when you find an example and store it with the term *echoic memory*.

• *Actively exploring and questioning new information* Think about the term *iconic memory*. Ask yourself, "Why did they use this term?" Look up the term *icon* in the dictionary. You'll learn that it comes from the Greek word for "image" or "likeness."

• *Finding meaningfulness* When you meet people at a party, don't just maintenance-rehearse their name. Ask about their favorite TV shows, their career plans, political beliefs, or anything else that requires deeper analysis. You'll be much more likely to remember their names.

Parallel Distributed Processing (PDP)

A third way of thinking about memory is the **parallel distributed processing (PDP)**, or *connectionist*, model of memory (Levy & Krebs, 2006; McClelland, 1995, 2011). As the name implies, instead of recognizing patterns as a sequence of facts and information bits to be stored and later retrieved later one at a time, our brain and memory processes perform multiple *parallel* operations all at one time. These facts are combined with what we already know. In addition, memory is spread out, or *distributed*, throughout our brains in a weblike network of processing units.

For example, if you're swimming in the ocean and see a large fin nearby, your brain does not conduct a complete search of all fish with fins before urging you to begin a rush to the beach. Instead, you conduct a mental *parallel* search. You note the color of the fish, the fin, and the potential danger all at the same time. Because the processes are parallel, you can quickly process the information—and possibly avoid being eaten by the shark!

The PDP model seems consistent with neurological information of brain activity (Chapter 2). Thanks to our richly interconnected synapses, activation of one neuron can influence many other neurons. This model also has been useful in explaining perception (Chapter 4), language (Chapter 8), and decision making (Chapter 8). Perhaps most importantly, it allows a faster response time to sharks and other threats to our survival.

Traditional Three-Stage Memory Model

Since the late 1960s, one of the most widely used information-processing models in memory research has been the **three-stage memory model** or the *three-box model* (Atkinson & Shiffrin, 1968; Moulin, 2011). According to this approach, memory requires three different storage "boxes," or memory stages (*sensory, short-term,* and *long-term*), to hold and process information. Because information must pass through each of these stages to get to the next, they are often depicted as three boxes with directional arrows indicating the flow of information (Figure 7.2). Note how each of the three stages has a somewhat different purpose, duration, and capacity.

Modern research has added new findings and complexities to this model (Jonides et al., 2008), and it remains the leading paradigm. Therefore we need to explore each of the three stages in more detail.

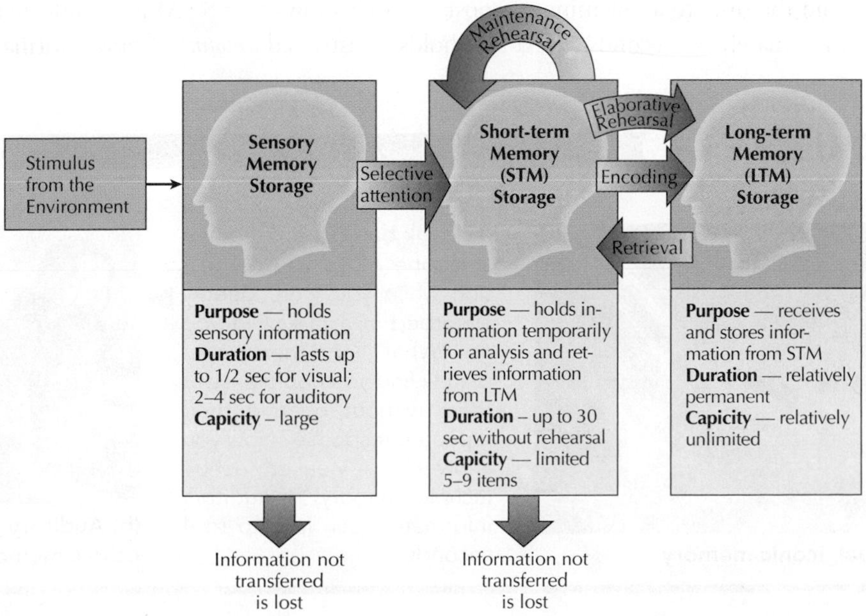

Parallel Distributed Processing (PDP) Model Memory results from weblike connections among interacting processing units operating simultaneously, rather than sequentially (also known as the connectionist model)

Three-Stage Memory Model Memory storage requires passage of information through three stages (sensory, short-term, and long-term)

Stimulus from the Environment → **Sensory Memory Storage** —Selective attention→ **Short-term Memory (STM) Storage** —Encoding→ **Long-term Memory (LTM) Storage**

Maintenance Rehearsal · *Elaborative Rehearsal* · *Retrieval*

Sensory Memory Storage
Purpose—holds sensory information
Duration—lasts up to 1/2 sec for visual; 2–4 sec for auditory
Capicity – large

Information not transferred is lost

Short-term Memory (STM) Storage
Purpose—holds information temporarily for analysis and retrieves information from LTM
Duration–up to 30 sec without rehearsal
Capicity—limited 5–9 items

Information not transferred is lost

Long-term Memory (LTM) Storage
Purpose—receives and stores information from STM
Duration—relatively permanent
Capicity—relatively unlimited

Figure 7.2 Traditional three-stage memory model Each "box" represents a separate memory system that differs in purpose, duration, and capacity. When information is not transferred from sensory memory or short-term memory, it is assumed to be lost. Information stored in long-term memory can be retrieved and sent back to short-term memory for use.

K	Z	R	A
Q	B	T	P
S	G	N	Y

Figure 7.3 How do researchers test sensory iconic memory? In an early study of iconic memory, George Sperling (1960) flashed an arrangement of letters like these for 1/20 of a second. Most people, he found, could recall only 4 or 5 letters. But when instructed to report just the top, middle, or bottom row, depending on whether they heard a high, medium, or low tone, they reported almost all the letters correctly. Apparently, all 12 letters are held in sensory memory right after they are viewed, but only those that are immediately attended to are noted and processed.

Sensory Memory First memory stage that holds sensory information; relatively large capacity, but duration is only a few seconds

Short-Term Memory (STM) Second memory stage that temporarily stores sensory information and decides whether to send it on to long-term memory (LTM); capacity is limited to five to nine items and duration is about 30 seconds

Sensory Memory: First Impressions

Objective 7.3: What is sensory memory?

Everything we see, hear, touch, taste, and smell must first enter our **sensory memory**. Information remains in sensory memory just long enough to locate relevant bits of information and transfer them to the next stage of memory. For visual information, known as *iconic memory*, the visual icon (or image) lasts about one-half of a second (Figure 7.3). Auditory information (what we hear) is held in sensory memory about the same length of time as visual information, one-quarter to one-half of a second. However, a weaker "echo," or *echoic memory*, of this auditory information can last up to four seconds (Inui et al., 2010; Lu, Williamson, & Kaufman, 1992; Neisser, 1967; Radvansky, 2011).

Early researchers believed sensory memory had an unlimited capacity. However, later research suggests that sensory memory does have limits and that stored memories are fuzzier than once thought (Goldstein, 2010; Grondin, Ouellet, & Roussel, 2004; Moulin, 2011).

Short-Term Memory (STM): Memory's Second Stage

Objective 7.4: Describe short-term memory (STM), and explain why its often called "working memory."

The second stage of memory processing, **short-term memory (STM)**, temporarily stores and processes information from sensory memory until the brain "decides" whether or not to send it along to long-term memory (LTM). STM also retrieves stored memories from LTM.

Unlike sensory memory, STM does not store exact *duplicates* of information but rather a mixture of perceptual analyses. For example, when your sensory memory registers the sound of your professor's voice, it holds the actual auditory information for a few seconds. If the information requires further processing, it moves on to STM. While being transferred from sensory memory, the sound of your professor's words is converted into a larger, more inclusive type of message capable of being analyzed and interpreted during short-term memory. If the information is important (or may be on a test), STM organizes and sends this information along to relatively permanent storage, called long-term memory (LTM).

Both the *duration* and *capacity* of STM are relatively limited. Although some researchers extend the time to a few minutes, most research shows that STM holds information for approximately 30 seconds. STM also holds a restricted *amount* of new information,

 TRY THIS YOURSELF

Demonstrating Iconic and Echoic Memory

To demonstrate the duration of visual, or *iconic memory*, swing a flashlight in a dark room. Because the image, or icon, lingers for a fraction of a second after the flashlight is moved, you see the light as a continuous stream, as in this photo, rather than as a succession of individual points.

(a) Visual, iconic memory

Think back to times when someone asked you a question while you were deeply absorbed in a task. Did you ask "What?" and then immediately find you could answer them without hearing their repeated response? Now you know why. A weaker "echo" (echoic memory) of auditory information can last up to 4 seconds.

(b) Auditory, echoic memory

Figure 7.4 Chunking in chess To the inexpert eye, a chess game in progress looks like little more than a random assembly of black and white game pieces. Accordingly, novice chess players can remember the positions of only a few pieces when a chess game is under way. But expert players generally remember all the positions. To the experts, the scattered pieces form meaningful patterns—classic arrangements that recur often. Just as you group the letters of this sentence into meaningful words and remember them long enough to understand the meaning of the sentence, expert chess players group the chess pieces into easily recalled patterns (or chunks) (Huffman, Matthews, & Gagne, 2001; Waters & Gobet, 2008).

five to nine items (Bankó & Vidnyánszky, 2010; Goldstein, 2010; Kareev, 2000; Moulin, 2011). As with sensory memory, information in STM either is transferred quickly into the next stage (LTM) or it decays and is lost.

How can we increase the duration and capacity of our STM? Look back to the memory model in Figure 7.2. Note the looping arrow at the top labeled "maintenance rehearsal." You can extend the *duration* of your STM almost indefinitely if you consciously and continuously repeat the information over and over again. This is what we earlier discussed as *maintenance rehearsal*, when you look up a phone number and repeat it over and over until you dial the number.

Unfortunately, this technique requires constant vigilance. If you stop repeating the phone number it's quickly lost. Like juggling a set of plates, the plates stay in perfect shape only as long as you keep juggling them. Once you stop, the plates fall and are destroyed. (In the case of memory, the memory is lost.) As you recall, when you want to ensure that important information is properly encoded and sent along to long-term memory (LTM), you should use *elaborative rehearsal*, a deeper level of processing.

Chunking Grouping separate pieces of information into a single unit (or chunk)

To extend the *capacity* of STM, you can use **chunking**—grouping separate pieces of information into a single unit (or *chunk*) (Glicksohn & Cohen, 2011; Miller, 1956; Perlman et al., 2010) (Figure 7.4). Have you noticed that numbers on credit cards, your Social Security identification, and telephone number are all grouped into three or four units separated by hyphens? This is because most people find it easier to remember numbers in chunks like *(760) 744–1129* rather than as a string of single digits. Similarly, in reading-improvement courses, students are taught to chunk groups of words into phrases. This allows fewer eye movements, and the brain can process the phrases as units rather than as individual words.

Given that we have room for five to nine units or chunks, why doesn't chunking help us remember even three or four names during introductions? The limited capacity and brief duration of STM both work against us in this situation. Instead of concentrating on the name of someone you meet for the first time, you sometimes use all your short-term memory capacity wondering how you look and thinking about what to say. You might even fill STM space worrying about your memory (Figure 7.5).

Figure 7.5 Problems with short-term memory? People who are good at remembering names repeat the name of each person out loud or silently to keep it entered in STM (maintenance rehearsal). Keep in mind, however, that maintenance rehearsal saves the name only while you're actively rehearsing. If you want to really learn that name, you will need to transfer it into long-term memory.

Short-Term Memory as a "Working Memory"

Does it sound as if short-term memory (STM) is just a *passive*, temporary "holding area?" Most current researchers (Baddeley, 1992, 2007; Berti, 2010; Buchsbaum,

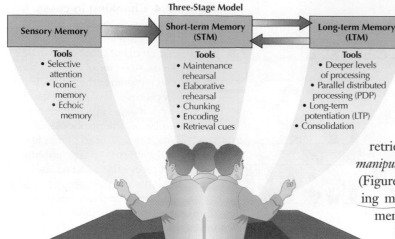

Three-Stage Model

Sensory Memory	Short-term Memory (STM)	Long-term Memory (LTM)
Tools • Selective attention • Iconic memory • Echoic memory	**Tools** • Maintenance rehearsal • Elaborative rehearsal • Chunking • Encoding • Retrieval cues	**Tools** • Deeper levels of processing • Parallel distributed processing (PDP) • Long-term potentiation (LTP) • Consolidation

Figure 7.6 How working memory might "work" Although no one is certain exactly how working memory operates, there is general agreement that it is not a passive storehouse with shelves to store information until it moves along to long-term memory (LTM). Instead, it involves active processing of incoming information, followed by active encoding and retrieval of information from LTM. Note the "tools" the "worker" uses during this processing.

Working Memory Alternate term for short-term memory (STM), which emphasizes the active processing of information

Long-Term Memory (LTM) Third stage of memory that stores information for long periods of time; its capacity is virtually limitless, and its duration is relatively permanent

Explicit (Declarative) Memory Subsystem within long-term memory that consciously stores facts, information, and personal life experiences

Padmanabhan, & Berman, 2011; Camos & Barrouillet, 2011) emphasize that *active* processing of information also occurs in STM.

Because short-term memory (STM) is active, or *working*, some researchers prefer the term **working memory**. It helps to visually picture STM as a "workbench," with a "worker" at the bench who selectively attends to certain sensory information, and also sends and retrieves it from long-term memory (LTM). The worker also *manipulates* the incoming, transferred, and retrieved information (Figure 7.6). All our conscious thinking occurs in this "working memory," and the manipulation helps explain some of our memory errors and false constructions described in this chapter.

Long-Term Memory (LTM): The Third Stage of Memory

Objective 7.5: Summarize long-term memory (LTM), and how it's divided into several subsystems.

Think back to the opening story of H.M. If you had met him, you might not have recognized his problem. But if you walked away and then ran into one another again 10 minutes later, H.M. would not remember having ever met you. His surgery was successful in stopping the severe epileptic seizures. Unfortunately, it also apparently destroyed the mechanism that transfers information from short-term to long-term memory.

What would it be like to live eternally in just the present—without your long-term memory? The *purpose* of the third stage, **long-term memory (LTM)**, is to serve as a storehouse for information that must be kept for long periods of time. Once information is transferred from STM, it is organized and integrated with other information in LTM. It remains there until we need to retrieve it. Then it is sent back to STM for our use.

Compared to sensory memory and short-term memory, long-term memory has relatively unlimited *capacity* and *duration*. It's like a magical credit card that lets you spend an unlimited amount of money for an unlimited time. In fact, the more you learn, or the more money you spend, the better it is!

Why does it feel like the more we learn, the harder it is to find things? During the transfer of information from STM to LTM, incoming information is "tagged" or filed, hopefully in the appropriate place. If information is improperly stored, it creates major delays and problems during retrieval. The better we label and arrange things (whether it's our CD collection, bills, or computer files), the more likely they'll be accurately stored and readily available for retrieval.

Types of Long-Term Memory

Given that LTM is believed to be generally unlimited in duration and capacity, we obviously collect a vast amount of information over a lifetime. How do we store it? As you can see in Figure 7.7, several types of LTM exist.

1. **Explicit (declarative) memory** *Explicit memory* refers to intentional learning or conscious knowledge. It is *memory with awareness*. If asked to remember your phone number or the name of your first-grade teacher you can state (*declare*) the answers directly (*explicitly*). When people think of memory, they often are referring to this type of explicit (declarative) memory.

Figure 7.7 Systems and subsystems of long-term memory (LTM) Note how LTM is divided and subdivided into various types of memory. Taking time to study and visualize these separate systems and subsystems will improve your understanding and mastery of this material because it involves a deeper level of processing.

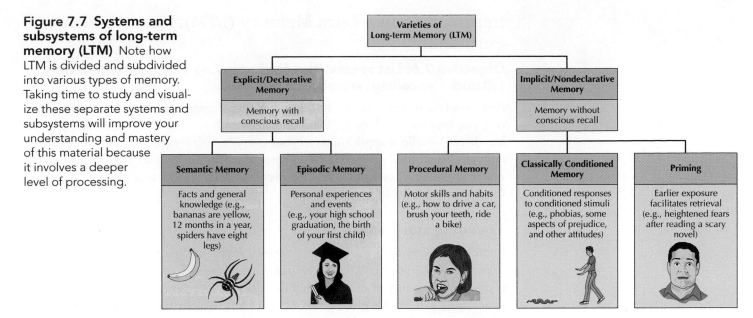

Explicit (declarative) memory has two subsystems—*semantic memory* and *episodic memory*. **Semantic memory** is memory for facts and general knowledge (e.g., names of objects, days of the week). It is our internal mental dictionary or encyclopedia of stored knowledge. If you read and remember terms like *semantic, episodic, explicit (declarative)*, and *implicit (nondeclarative)*, it is because you have stored them in your semantic memory.

In contrast, **episodic memory** is the explicit memory of our own past experiences—our personal mental diary. It records the major events (or *episodes*) that happen to us or take place in our presence. Some of our episodic memories are short-lived (what you ate for breakfast today). Others can last a lifetime (your first romantic kiss, your high school graduation, the birth of your first child).

Have you ever wondered why toddlers are quite capable of remembering events they experienced in previous months, yet most of us as adults can recall almost nothing of those years before the age of 3? Why don't we remember our birth, our second birthday, or our family's big move to a new city? These were major events at that point in our life. Research suggests that a concept of "self," sufficient knowledge of our emotions and language development, and growth of the frontal lobes of the cortex (along with other structures) may be necessary before these early events (or episodes) can be encoded and retrieved many years later (Bauer & Lukowski, 2010; Morris, 2007; Prigatano & Gray, 2008; Rose et al., 2011).

2. **Implicit (nondeclarative) memory** Unlike explicit memory, *implicit memory* refers to unintentional learning or unconscious knowledge. It is memory *without awareness*. Can you describe how you skateboard or even tie your shoelaces without demonstrating the actual behavior? Because your memory of this skill is unconscious and hard to describe in words (to "declare"), implicit memory is also referred to as *nondeclarative*.

Implicit (nondeclarative) memory consists of *procedural* motor skills like tying your shoes, riding a bike, and brushing your teeth. It also includes simple, classically conditioned responses, such as fears or taste aversions. As you recall from Chapter 6, my student who ate the Butterfinger candy bar filled with bugs has a conditioned emotional response (or *implicit memory*). This memory makes her immediately and (unconsciously) nauseated whenever she sees or thinks about this particular candy.

Semantic Memory Subsystem of explicit/declarative memory that stores general knowledge; a mental encyclopedia or dictionary

Episodic Memory Subsystem of explicit/declarative memory that stores memories of personally experienced events; a mental diary of a person's life

Implicit (Nondeclarative) Memory Subsystem within long-term memory consisting of unconscious procedural skills and simple classically conditioned responses

Improving Long-Term Memory (LTM): Practice Makes Permanent

Objective 7.6: List several/tips for improving LTM, and where they fall under encoding, storage, or retrieval.

After reading through all the terms and concepts associated with long-term memory, you may be wondering, "Why do I need to know this?" Understanding LTM has direct beneficial applications to your everyday life—particularly to college success. In this section, we will focus on numerous tips for improving LTM, which fall under the general categories of improved *encoding*, *storage*, and *retrieval* (Concept Organizer 7.1).

Encoding and LTM

Successful encoding involves several factors, including *selective vs. divided attention*, (Chapter 4, p. 146) *automatic vs. controlled processing* (Chapter 5, p. 168), and *levels of processing*. It's easy to understand how selective attention and effortful (*controlled*) processing will improve your encoding, which in turn will enhance your LTM. However, the concept and importance of a *deeper level of processing* warrants further discussion.

Have you ever studied very hard and even read the chapters several times, yet still did poorly on exams? Can you see how this may reflect that you're "simply" using *shallow processing*? Look back at Figure 7.1, p. 250, and note how you first must get sensory information into your short-term memory (STM). To do this, you must sharply focus and *selectively attend* to what your instructor says during lectures and while reading the text.

Second, you need to carefully *encode* all the important information that you want to send on for storage in your long-term memory (LTM). In addition to effortful, *controlled processing*, you need to employ elaborative rehearsal, which requires *deeper levels of processing*. My students often forget that maintenance rehearsal, just repeating it over and over, only works for STM. It is NOT a good technique for information you want to store and retrieve for more than a few seconds.

Storage and LTM

To successfully *store* information in LTM, we need to *organize* the material into *hierarchies*. Like Concept Organizer 7.1, this strategy involves arranging a number of related items into broad categories that are further divided and subdivided. (This organization strategy for LTM is similar to the strategy of *chunking* material in STM, which we discussed earlier.) By grouping small subsets of ideas together (as subheadings under larger, main headings, and within diagrams, tables, and so on), I hope to make the material in this book more understandable and memorable.

Admittedly, organization and hierarchies take time and work, so you'll be happy to know that some memory organization and other tasks are done automatically while you sleep (Fogel & Smith, 2011; Mograss, Guillem, & Godbout, 2008; Sara, 2010; Verleger et al., 2011). (Unfortunately, as you recall from Chapter 5, research shows that we can't recruit our sleeping hours to memorize new material, such as a foreign language.)

Retrieval and LTM

Finally, effective *retrieval* is critical to LTM, and it involves several factors, including the *serial-position effect* and *retrieval cues*.

ConceptOrganizer7.1

Improving Long-Term Memory

Strategies for improving LTM Just as the diagram of the nervous system in Chapter 2 (p. 59) helped organize complex material, this diagram on improving LTM memory helps you order and master the various terms in this chapter. Encoding, storage, and retrieval in LTM are all improved through the use of hierarchies. This also is why this text contains so many tables, figures, Step-by-Step Diagrams, Concept Organizers, and end-of-chapter Visual Summaries.

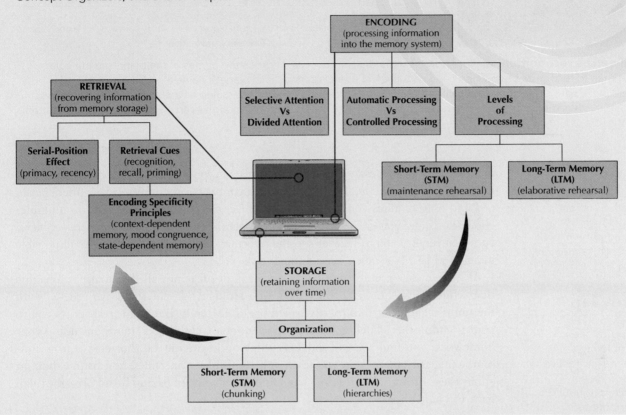

According to the **serial-position effect**, when study participants are given lists of words to learn and are allowed to recall them in any order they choose, they remember the words at the beginning (*primacy effect*) and the end of the list (*recency effect*) better than those in the middle (Azizian & Polich, 2007; Bonk & Healy, 2010; Overstreet & Healy, 2011) (Figure 7.8). The reasons for this effect are complex, but it does help explain why material at the beginning and end of a chapter is better remembered than that in the middle. It also helps clarify why you remember the first and last people you meet at a party better than those you meet in-between.

Three of the most important **retrieval cues** are *recall*, *recognition*, and *priming*. **Recall** is a

Serial-Position Effect Information at the beginning and end of a list is remembered better than material in the middle

Retrieval Cue Clue or prompt that helps stimulate recall or retrieval of a stored piece of information from long-term memory

Recall Retrieving a memory using a general cue

StudyTip

Don't hesitate to ask questions of your professor during exams. Most professors allow questions, and their answers often provide valuable *retrieval cues.*

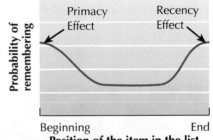

Figure 7.8 The serial-position effect If you try to recall a list of similar items, you'll tend to remember the first and last items best. Can you see how you can use this information to improve your chances for employment success? If a potential employer calls to set up an interview, you can increase their memory of you (and your application) by asking to be either the first or last candidate.

(a)

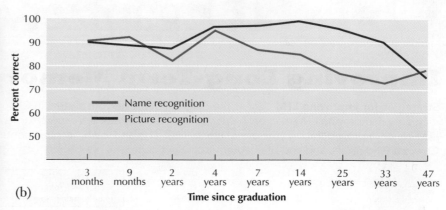

(b)

Figure 7.9 Recall versus recognition (a) Note how it's more difficult to *recall*, in order, the names of the planets in our solar system (general cue) than to *recognize* them when cued with the first three letters of each planet's name (specific retrieval cue): Mer-, Ven-, Ear-, Mar-, Jup-, Sat-, Ura-, Nep-, Plu-. (Note that in 2006, Pluto was officially declassified as a planet, but this finding is still being debated.) (b) Both name and picture *recognition* for high school classmates remain high even many years after graduation, whereas *recall* memory drops significantly over time.

Recognition Retrieving a memory using a specific cue

Priming Prior exposure to a stimulus (or prime) facilitates or inhibits the processing of new information, even when one has no conscious memory of the initial learning and storage

StudyTip

If you've been completing the "Retrieval Practice" Part I of the Check & Review sections sprinkled throughout this text, you've undoubtedly noticed a sharp increase on your exam scores. Can you see how this activity helps improve recall, recognition, and priming?

memory task, like an essay exam, that requires you to retrieve previously learned information with only *general*, nonspecific *cues*. In contrast, a **recognition** task offers *specific cues* and only requires you to identify (*recognize*) the correct response, as on multiple-choice tests. As you can see in Figure 7.9, recall tests have vague, general retrieval cues that require you to recover specific information by searching through all possible matches in LTM—a much more difficult task.

Whether cues require recall or only recognition is not all that matters. Imagine that while house hunting, you walk into a stranger's kitchen and are greeted with the unmistakable smell of freshly baked bread. Instantly, the aroma transports you to your grandmother's kitchen, where you spent many childhood afternoons doing your homework. You find yourself suddenly thinking of the mental shortcuts your grandmother taught you to help you learn your multiplication tables. You hadn't thought about these little tricks for years, but somehow a whiff of baking bread brought them back to you. Why?

In this imagined episode, you have stumbled upon the third retrieval cue, known as **priming**. This form of memory occurs when a prior exposure to a stimulus (or *prime*) facilitates or inhibits the processing of new information (Diamond, Mayes, & Meudell, 2011; Gagnepain et al., 2011; Woollams et al., 2008). Such priming effects may occur even when we do not consciously remember being exposed to the *prime* (Figure 7.10).

Finally, do you want to improve your retrieval cues? According to the **encoding specificity principle**

Encoding Specificity Principle Retrieval of information is improved when conditions of recovery are similar to the conditions when information was encoded

Figure 7.10 The power of priming Have you noticed how your fears are heightened during and after watching a horror film? This is because your previous experiences *prime* you to more easily notice and recall related instances. (It also suggests a practical way to improve your love life—go to romantic movies!)

(Tulving & Thompson, 1973), memory retrieval is increased when we have *matching* context, moods, and states:

- *Context-dependent memory* In most cases, we're able to remember better when we attempt to recall information in the *same* context in which it was learned. Have you noticed that you tend to do better on exams when you take them in the same seat and classroom in which you originally studied the material? This happens because the matching location acts as a retrieval cue for the information (Figure 7.11).

- *Mood congruence* People also remember information better if their moods during learning and retrieval match (Kenealy, 1997; Robinson & Rollings, 2011). This phenomenon, called *mood congruence*, occurs because a given mood tends to evoke memories that are consistent with that mood. When you're sad (or happy or angry), you're more likely to remember events and circumstances from other times when you were sad (or happy or angry).

  If you suffer from test anxiety, you might try re-creating the relaxed mood you had while studying. Take deep breaths and reassure yourself during exams. To further match your study and test-taking moods, try to deliberately increase your anxiety level while studying. Consciously remind yourself of the importance of good grades and your long-range career plans. By lowering your test anxiety and upping your study anxiety, you create a better balance or match between your exam and study moods. This should improve your retrieval.

- *State-dependent memory* As generations of coffee-guzzling college students have discovered, if you learn something while under the influence of a drug, such as caffeine, you will remember it more easily when you take that drug again than at other times (Nasehi et al., 2010; Patti et al., 2010; Rezayat et al., 2010). This is called *state-dependent retrieval*.

Figure 7.11 Context-dependent memory One important contextual cue for retrieval is location. In a clever study, Godden and Baddeley (1975) had underwater divers learn a list of 40 words either on land or underwater. The divers had better recall for lists that they had encoded underwater if they were also underwater at the time of retrieval; similarly, lists that were encoded above water were better recalled above water.

CHECK & REVIEW

STOP *Before going on, be sure to complete this Check & Review. It is an invaluable study tool!*

Nature of Memory

Part A: Retrieval Practice

1. Without looking at the book, spend 10 minutes writing a free-form essay recalling all you can remember from the previous section.

2. Now, reread the previous section, and once again spend 10 minutes writing a free-form essay on the SAME material.

   (Although time consuming, this exercise has been shown to be the single best way to improve your test scores! For more information, check out www.sciencemag.org/content/early/2011/01/19/science.1199327.abstract)

Part B: Practice Quiz

1. Our brains organize and shape information during processing, storage, and retrieval of memories. This is known as _____.

2. Label the following *terms* on the figure above:

3. How do the levels of processing and PDP models differ in their explanations of memory processing?

4. Label the three-stage memory model on the figure below:

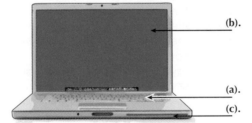

5. Multiple-choice questions require _____, whereas essay questions require _____.

6. Give personal examples of context-dependent memory, mood congruence, and state-dependent memory.

Check your answers in Appendix B.

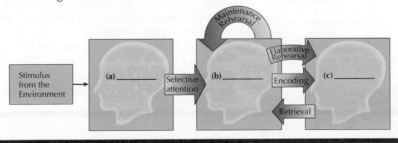

Forgetting

Think about what your life would be like if you couldn't forget. Your LTM would be filled with meaningless data, such as what you ate for breakfast every morning of your life. Similarly, think of the incredible pain and sorrow you would continuously endure if you couldn't distance yourself from tragedy through forgetting. The ability to forget is essential to the proper functioning of memory. But what about those times when forgetting is an inconvenience or even dangerous?

Why Do We Forget? Five Key Theories

DIMER "dimmer"

Objective 7.8: What are the five major theories of forgetting?

Five major theories have been offered to explain why forgetting occurs: *decay, interference, motivated forgetting, encoding failure,* and *retrieval failure*. Each theory focuses on a different stage of the memory process or on a particular type of problem in processing information (Step-by-Step Diagram 7.1).

RESEARCH CHALLENGE

How Quickly We Forget

Objective 7.7: Describe Ebbinghaus's contributions to memory research.

Hermann Ebbinghaus first introduced the official study of learning and forgetting in 1885. Using himself as a subject, he calculated how long it took to learn a list of three-letter *nonsense syllables* such as *SIB* and *RAL*. He found that one hour after he knew a list perfectly, he remembered only 44 percent of the syllables. A day later, he recalled 35 percent, and a week later, only 21 percent. Figure 7.12 shows his famous "forgetting curve."

Depressing as these findings may seem, keep in mind that meaningful material is much more memorable than nonsense syllables. Even so, we all forget some of what we have learned.

On a cheerier note, after some time passed and he had forgotten the list,

Ebbinghaus found that **relearning** the list took less time than the initial learning did. This research suggests that we often retain some memory for things that we have learned, even when we seem to have forgotten them completely.

More recent research based on Ebbinghaus's discoveries has found that there is an ideal time to practice something you have learned. Practicing too soon is a waste of time, and if you practice too late you will already have forgotten what you learned. The ideal time to practice is when you are about to forget.

Polish psychologist Piotr Wozniak used this insight to create a software program called SuperMemo. The program can be used to predict the future state of an individual's memory and help the person schedule reviews of learned information at the optimal time. So far the program has been applied mainly to language learning, helping users retain huge amounts of vocabulary. But Wozniak hopes that someday programs like SuperMemo will tell people when to wake and when to exercise, help them remember what they have read and whom they have met, and remind them of their goals (Wolf, 2008).

As a critical thinker, can you explain how Ebbinghaus's findings might be

applied to learning to play a musical instrument? Can you think of any disadvantages of depending on a program like SuperMemo?

Student Engagement Exercise

Given the admittedly limited information about the Ebbinghaus study described above, what is the most likely:

1 *Research method* (experimental, descriptive, correlational, or biological)?

2 If you chose the:
  - *Experimental method*—label the IV, DV, experimental group, and control group.
  - *Descriptive method*—is this a naturalistic observation, survey, or case study?
  - *Correlational method*—is this a positive, negative, or zero correlation?
  - *Biological method*—identify the specific research tool (e.g., brain dissection, CT scan, etc.)

(Answers appear in Appendix B.)

Relearning Learning material a second time, which usually takes less time than original learning (also called the savings method)

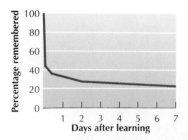

Figure 7.12 Ebbinghaus's forgetting curve Note how rapidly nonsense syllables are forgotten, especially in the first few hours after learning.

Step-by-Step Diagram 7.1

Why We Forget: Five Key Theories

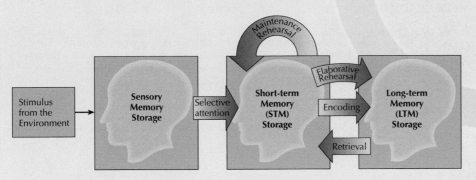

Study Tip

If you want to remember the five theories, think of how forgetting involves memories that grow "dimmer." Note that the first letter of each theory has almost the same spelling—D-I-M-E-R.

Decay Theory (Memory deteriorates over time)

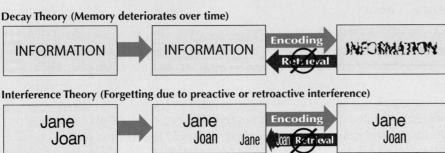

Interference Theory (Forgetting due to proactive or retroactive interference)

Motivated Forgetting Theory (Painful memories forgotten)

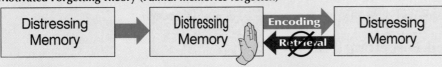

Encoding Failure Theory (Material from STM to LTM never encoded)

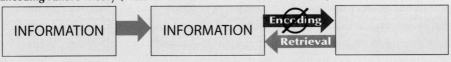

Retrieval Failure Theory (Information cannot be retrieved)

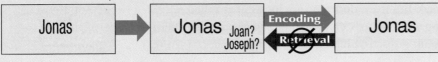

PSYCHOLOGY ENGAGES **TEST YOURSELF**

Which of the five theories of forgetting best applies to this cartoon?

"I forget to drink."

Answers will vary even among memory researchers.

Decay Theory

Decay theory is based on the commonsense assumption that memory, like all biological processes, degrades with time. Because memory is processed and stored in a physical form—for example, in a network of neurons—the relevant connections between neurons could be expected to decrease over time. It is well documented that skills and memory degrade if they go unused (Rosenzweig, Barnes, & McNaughton, 2002; Villarreal, Do, Haddad, & Derrick, 2002). In other words, "use it or lose it." However, conclusive experimental support for decay theory is difficult to obtain. How can you prove that a previously stored memory does *not* exist?

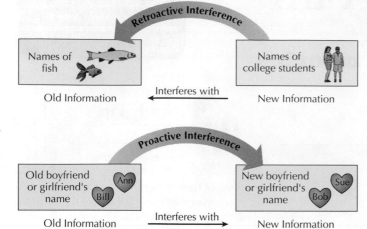

(a) **Retroactive** (backward-acting) **interference** occurs when new information interferes with old information. This example comes from a story about an absent-minded icthyology professor (fish specialist) who refused to learn the name of his college students. Asked why, he said, "Every time I learn a student's name, I forget the name of a fish!"

(b) **Proactive** (forward-acting) **interference** occurs when old information interferes with new information. Have you ever been in trouble because you used an old partner's name to refer to your new partner? You now have a guilt-free explanation—proactive interference.

Figure 7.13 Two types of interference

Retroactive Interference New information interferes with remembering old information; backward-acting interference

Proactive Interference Old information interferes with remembering new information; forward-acting interference

Interference Theory

Interference theory suggests that forgetting is caused by competing memories (Anderson, Bjork, & Bjork, 1994; Conway & Pleydell-Pearce, 2000; Wixted, 2004). Interference is particularly strong among memories with similar qualities. At least two types of interference exist: *retroactive* and *proactive* (Figure 7.13). When new information leads to forgetting old material, it is called **retroactive interference** (acting backward in time). Learning your new phone number often causes forgetting of your old phone number (old, "retro" information is forgotten). Conversely, when old information leads to forgetting of new information, it is called **proactive interference** (acting forward in time). Old information (like the Spanish you learned in high school) may interfere with your ability to learn and remember your new college course in French.

Motivated Forgetting Theory

According to the *motivated forgetting theory*, we forget some information—such as a dental appointment or an embarrassing remark we once made—for a reason. We inhibit the retrieval! However, Sigmund Freud (Chapter 13) claimed we are motivated to forget unpleasant or painful memories to minimize anxiety and protect our self-image. When we make a conscious decision to forget, such as telling ourselves not to worry about an upcoming medical exam, it would be an act of *suppression* (we deliberately push the memory away). But if we do it unconsciously, it is called *repression* (we're not aware of the forgetting). The controversy surrounding so-called *repressed memories* of child abuse or sexual assault is discussed later in this chapter (pp. 265–266).

Encoding Failure Theory

Whose head is on a U.S. penny? What is written at the top of a penny? Despite having seen a real penny thousands of times in our lives, most of us have difficulty recognizing the details (Figure 7.14). The U.S. penny has eight easily distinguishing characteristics (Lincoln's head, the date it was minted, which way Lincoln is facing, and so on). However, the average person can only remember three (Nickerson & Adams, 1979). This is a great example of *encoding failure*. Unless we are coin collectors, we have little motivation to properly encode the details of a penny. Our sensory memory certainly received the information and passed it along (encoded it) to STM. But during STM, we probably decided there was no need to remember the precise details of the penny. Because we can easily recognize pennies by their size and color, we don't encode the fine details and pass them on for storage in LTM.

Figure 7.14 Can you spot the real penny? If not, can you see how this may be an example of encoding failure? (See text for explanation)

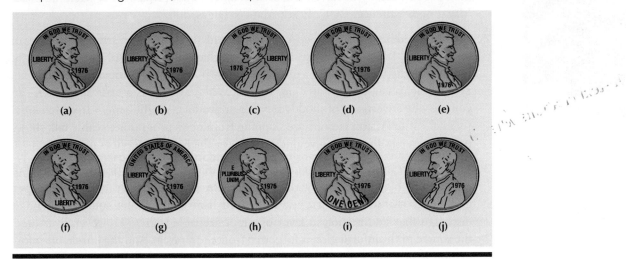

Retrieval Failure Theory

If you've ever "blanked out" during an exam or in a conversation and remembered the "forgotten" information later, you've had firsthand experience with the *retrieval failure* (or *cue-dependent*) *theory of forgetting*. According to this theory, memories stored in LTM aren't forgotten. They're just momentarily inaccessible as a result of such things as interference, faulty cues, or emotional states.

One of the most common experiences of *retrieval failure* is the **tip-of-the-tongue (TOT) phenomenon**. Have you ever felt that at any second, a word or event you are trying to remember will pop out from the "tip of your tongue" (Abrams, White, & Eitel, 2003; Brown & McNeill, 1966; Gollan & Acenas, 2004)? Even though you can't say the word, you can often tell how many syllables it has, the beginning and ending letters, or what it rhymes with.

Tip-of-the-Tongue (TOT) Phenomenon Feeling that specific information is stored in long-term memory but being temporarily unable to retrieve it

Key Factors in Forgetting

Objective 7.9: Describe four factors key to forgetting.

Scientists have discovered numerous factors that contribute to legitimate forgetting. Four of the most important are the *misinformation effect*, *source amnesia*, the *sleeper effect*, and *information overload*.

1. *Misinformation effect* Many people (who haven't studied this chapter or taken a psychology class) believe that when they're recalling an event, they're remembering it as if it were an "instant replay." However, as you know, our memories are highly fallible and filled with personal "constructions" that we create during encoding and storage. Research on the **misinformation effect** shows that information that occurs *after* an event may further alter and revise these constructions. For example, later in this chapter we describe a study in which subjects watched a film of a car driving through the countryside, and were then asked to estimate how fast the car was going when it passed the barn. Although there was no actual barn in the film, subjects were six times more likely to report having seen one than those who were not asked about a barn (Loftus, 1982).

Misinformation Effect Memory distortion resulting from misleading post-event information

Capitalizing on the sleeper effect and source amnesia The sleeper effect and source amnesia can be significant problems when reliable and unreliable information are intermixed—for example, when advertising or PR are disguised to look like more objective reports. Can you see how, after a time, we may forget the source and no longer discount the information in the ad?

Source Amnesia Forgetting the true source of a memory (also called source confusion or source misattribution)

Sleeper Effect Information from an unreliable source, which was initially discounted, later gains credibility because the source is forgotten

Figure 7.15 Dangers of eyewitness testimony Seven eyewitnesses identified the man in the far left photo (Father Pagano) as the "Gentleman Bandit" accused of several armed robberies. However, the man in the right photo (Robert Clouser) later confessed and was convicted of the crimes.

Other experiments have created false memories by showing subjects doctored photos of themselves taking a completely fictitious hot-air balloon ride, or by asking subjects to simply imagine an event, such as having a nurse remove a skin sample from their finger. In these and similar cases, a large number of subjects later believed that misleading information was correct and that fictitious or imagined events actually occurred (Allan & Gabbert, 2008; Mazzoni & Memon, 2003; Mazzoni & Vannucci, 2007; Pérez-Mata & Diges, 2007).

2. *Source amnesia* Each day we read, hear, and process an enormous amount of information. It's easy to confuse "who said what to whom" and in what context. Forgetting the true source of a memory is known as **source amnesia** (Kleider et al., 2008; Leichtman, 2006; Paterson, Kemp, & Ng, 2011). As a critical thinker, can you see why advertisers of shoddy services or products might benefit from "channel surfing"? If television viewers are skipping from news programs to cable talk shows to infomercials, they may give undue credit to the inferior services or products.

3. *Sleeper effect* In addition to source amnesia, with the passage of time we also tend to confuse reliable information with unreliable. Research on this aptly named **sleeper effect** finds that when we first hear something from an unreliable source, we tend to disregard that information in favor of a more reliable source. However, over time, the source of the information is forgotten (source amnesia). And the unreliable information is no longer discounted (the sleeper effect) (Appel & Richter, 2007; Ecker, Lewandowsky, & Apai, 2011; Nabi, Moyer-Gusé, & Byrne, 2007). This sleeper effect can be a significant problem when reliable and unreliable information are intermixed.

4. *Information overload* Do you attempt to memorize too much at one time by "cramming" the night before an exam? As the "Tools for Student Success" section in Chapter 1 emphasized, the single most important key to improving grades may be *distributed study*. **Distributed practice** refers to spacing your learning periods, with rest periods between sessions. Cramming is called **massed practice** because the time spent learning is *massed* into long, unbroken intervals.

Memory and the Criminal Justice System: When Memory Goes Wrong

When our memory errors interact with the criminal justice system, they may lead to wrongful judgments of guilt or innocence and even life-or-death decisions. Let's explore two of the most well-known problems—*eyewitness testimony* and *repressed memories*.

Eyewitness Testimony
Objective 7.10: What's wrong with eyewitness testimony?

Misremembering the name of your new friend or forgetting where you left your car keys may be relatively harmless memory problems. But what if police mistakenly arrest and convict an innocent man because of your erroneous eyewitness testimony (Figure 7.15)?

In the past, one of the best forms of trial evidence a lawyer could have was an eyewitness. "I was there. I saw it with my own eyes." Unfortunately for lawyers, numerous research studies have identified several problems with eyewitness testimony (Loftus, 2000, 2001, 2007, 2011; Paterson, Kemp, & Ng, 2011; Rubinstein, 2008).

Distributed Practice Practice (or study) sessions are interspersed with rest periods

Massed Practice Time spent learning is grouped (or massed) into long, unbroken intervals (also known as cramming)

"Thank you, gentlemen—you may all leave except for No. 3."

Figure 7.16 How often are eyewitnesses mistaken? In one experiment, participants watched people committing a staged crime. Only an hour later, 20 percent of the eyewitnesses identified innocent people from mug shots, and a week later, 8 percent identified innocent people in a lineup (Brown, Deffenbacher, & Sturgill, 1977). What memory processes might have contributed to the eyewitnesses' errors? What can we do to help prevent future mistakes? Officials now recommend that suspects should never "stand out" from the others in a lineup. Witnesses also are cautioned to not assume that the real criminal is in the lineup, and they should never "guess" when asked to make an identification.

In one classic study, participants watched a film of a car driving through the countryside. Later, those who were asked to estimate how fast the car was going when it passed the barn (actually nonexistent) were six times more likely to report that they had seen a barn in the film than participants who hadn't been asked about a barn (Loftus, 1982).

Seeing nonexistent barns and other related problems are so well established and important that judges now allow expert testimony on the unreliability of eyewitness testimony. They also routinely instruct jurors on its limits (Benton et al., 2007; Rubinstein, 2008). If you serve as a member of a jury or listen to accounts of crimes in the news, remind yourself of these problems. Also, keep in mind that research participants in eyewitness studies generally report their inaccurate memories with great self-assurance and strong conviction. Eyewitnesses to actual crimes may similarly identify—with equally high confidence—an innocent person as the perpetrator (Figure 7.16).

False Versus Repressed Memories

Objective 7.11: What do psychologists believe about repressed memories?

Is it impossible to forget painful memories? Or can we erase what is unnecessary? The topic of false versus repressed memories is one of the hottest debates in memory research. Do you recall the opening story of Elizabeth, who suddenly remembered finding her mother's drowned body decades after it had happened? Elizabeth's recovery of these gruesome childhood memories, though painful, initially brought great relief. "I started putting everything into place. Maybe that's why I'm such a workaholic." It also seemed to explain why she had always been fascinated by the topic of memory and had spent so many years on its research.

After all this relief and resolution, however, her brother called to say there had been a mistake! The relative who told Elizabeth that she had been the one to discover her mother's body later remembered—and other relatives confirmed—that it had actually been Aunt Pearl, not Elizabeth Loftus. Like the eyewitnesses who erroneously recalled seeing a nonexistent barn, Loftus, an expert on memory distortions, had unknowingly created her own *false memory*.

As we've seen throughout this chapter, our memories are frequently faulty, and researchers have demonstrated that it is relatively easy to create false

Nothing fixes a thing so intensely in the memory as the wish to forget it.
MICHEL DE MONTAIGNE
(1533–1592)

Memory is the greatest of artists, and erases from your mind what is unnecessary.
MAURICE BARING (1874–1945)

Elizabeth Loftus

memories (Eslick et al., 2011; Frenda, Nichols, & Loftus, 2011; Loftus & Cahill, 2007; Strange et al., 2011; Zaragoza et al., 2011).

What about repressed memories? Are they true childhood memories? *Repression*, which was mentioned earlier as a potential factor in motivated forgetting, is the supposed unconscious coping mechanism that prevents anxiety-provoking thoughts from reaching consciousness (see Chapter 13).

This is a complex and controversial topic in psychology. No one doubts that some memories are forgotten and later recovered. What is questioned is the concept of repressed memories of painful experiences (especially childhood sexual abuse) and their storage in the unconscious mind (Goodman et al., 2003; Kihlstrom, 2004; Loftus, 2007; Loftus & Cahill, 2007).

Critics suggest that most people who have witnessed or experienced a violent crime, or are adult survivors of childhood sexual abuse, have intense, persistent memories. They have trouble forgetting, not remembering. Some critics also wonder whether therapists sometimes inadvertently create false memories in their clients during therapy. Some worry that if a clinician even suggests the possibility of abuse, the client's own constructive processes may lead him or her to create a false memory. The client might start to incorporate portrayals of abuse from movies and books into his or her own memory, forgetting their original sources and eventually coming to see them as reliable.

This is not to say that all psychotherapy clients who recover memories of sexual abuse (or other painful incidents) have invented those memories. Indeed, the repressed memory debate has grown increasingly bitter, and research on both sides is hotly contested. The stakes are high because some lawsuits and criminal prosecutions of sexual abuse are sometimes based on recovered memories of childhood sexual abuse. As researchers continue exploring the mechanisms underlying delayed remembering, we must be careful not to ridicule or condemn people who recover true memories of abuse. In the same spirit, we must protect the innocent from wrongful accusations that come from false memories. We look forward to a time when we can justly balance the interests of the victim with those of the accused.

(For more information about this continuing controversy, call or write the American Psychological Association in Washington, D.C. Ask for the pamphlet "Questions and Answers about Memories of Childhood Abuse." Also check the *Psychology in Action* website.)

A Final Word

As we have seen throughout this chapter, our memories are remarkable—yet highly fickle. Recognizing these limits will make us better jurors in the courtroom. It will also make us better consumers of daily news reports when we assess accounts of "eyewitness testimony" and "repressed memories." Knowing the frailties of memory might similarly improve our skills as students, teachers, and friends.

Unfortunately, sometimes our memories are better than we would like. Traumatic and extremely emotional memories can persist even when we would very much like to forget. Though painful, these memories can sometimes provide important insights. As Elizabeth Loftus suggests in a recent letter to her deceased mother:

> I thought then [as a 14-year-old] that eventually I would get over your death. I know today that I won't. But I've decided to accept that truth. What does it matter if I don't get over you? Who says I have to? David and Robert still tease me: "Don't say the M word or Beth will cry." So what if the word mother affects me this way? Who says I have to fix this? Besides, I'm too busy (Loftus, 2002, p. 70).

Memory problems Unfortunately, some memories persevere even when they cause tremendous pain and suffering.

CHECK & REVIEW

STOP *Before going on, be sure to complete this Check & Review. It is an invaluable study tool!*

Forgetting, Memory and the Criminal Justice System

Part A: Retrieval Practice

1. Without looking at the book, spend 10 minutes writing a free-form essay recalling all you can remember from the previous section.

2. Now, reread the previous section, and once again spend 10 minutes writing a free-form essay on the SAME material.

Part B: Practice Quiz

1. Which theory of forgetting is being described in each of the following examples?

   a. You are very nervous about having to introduce all the people at a party, and you forget a good friend's name.

   b. You meet someone you haven't seen for 25 years and you cannot remember his name.

   c. You seriously mistreated a good friend in high school, and now you can't remember her name.

2. Briefly describe a personal example of source amnesia and the sleeper effect from your own life.

3. How would you study for a test using distributed practice? Using massed practice?

4. According to research, eyewitnesses generally report _____ confidence in the accuracy of their inaccurate memories. (a) very little; (b) little; (c) moderate; (d) high

5. _____ memories are related to anxiety-provoking thoughts or events that are supposedly prevented from reaching consciousness. (a) Flashbulb; (b) Flashback; (c) Motivated; (d) Repressed

6. Researchers have found that it is relatively _____ to create false memories.

7. Explain the difference between false memories and repressed memories.

Check your answers in Appendix B.

Biological Bases of Memory

Objective 7.12: How do we form memories, and where do we store them?

The previous sections have emphasized the theories and models of memory and forgetting. Now we focus on the biological aspects of memory. We first explore how memories are formed and where they are located in the brain. Then we examine memory problems related to biological factors.

How Are Memories Formed? The Biological Perspective

It is obvious that something physical must happen in the brain and nervous system when we learn something new. (How else could we later recall and use this information?)

Neuronal and Synaptic Changes

We know that learning modifies the brain's neural networks (Chapters 2 and 6). As you learn to play tennis, for example, repeated practice builds neural "pathways" that make it easier and easier for you to get the ball over the net. This prolonged strengthening of neural firing, called **long-term potentiation (LTP)**, happens in at least two ways:

1. *Repeated stimulation of a synapse can strengthen the synapse by causing the dendrites to grow more spines.* As seen in Chapter 6, rats raised in "enriched" environments grew more sprouts on their dendrites compared to rats raised in "deprived" environments.

2. *The ability of a particular neuron to release or accept neurotransmitters can be increased or decreased.* This is shown in research with sea slugs (Figure 7.17) and "smart" mice (Figure 7.18). Although it is difficult to generalize from sea slugs and mice, research on long-term potentiation (LTP) in humans has been widely supportive (Berger et al., 2008; Kullmann & Lamsa, 2011; Shin et al., 2010).

Long-Term Potentiation (LTP)
Long-lasting increase in neural excitability, which may be a biological mechanism for learning and memory

Figure 7.17 How does a sea slug learn and remember? After repeated squirting with water, followed by a mild shock, the sea slug, *Aplysia*, releases more neurotransmitters at certain synapses. These synapses then become more efficient at transmitting signals that allow the slug to withdraw its gills when squirted. As a critical thinker, can you explain why this ability might provide an evolutionary advantage?

Figure 7.18 Creating "smart mice" through genetic engineering Further evidence for biological effects on learning and memory comes from studies with genetically engineered "smart mice," which have extra receptors for a neurotransmitter called NMDA (N-methyl-d-aspartate). These mice performed significantly better on memory tasks than did normal mice (Tang et al., 2001; Tsien, 2000).

Figure 7.19 The ultimate flashbulb memory Due to the extraordinary level of emotionality that most Americans experienced after the terrorist attacks on 9/11/2001, we tend to have detailed, longlasting memories of our whereabouts and actions during this stressful, cataclysmic event.

Emotional Arousal

When stressed or excited, we naturally produce "fight-or-flight" neurotransmitters and hormones that arouse the body, such as epinephrine and cortisol (see Chapter 3). These chemicals in turn affect the amygdala (a brain structure involved in emotion), which then stimulates the hippocampus and cerebral cortex (other parts of the brain important for memory storage). Research has shown that direct injections of epinephrine or cortisol, or electrical stimulation of the amygdala, will increase the encoding and storage of new information (Hamilton & Gotlib, 2008; Jurado-Berbel et al., 2010; van Stegeren, 2008). However, prolonged or extreme stress (and increased levels of cortisol) can *interfere* with memory (see Chapter 3).

Can you see why heightened (but not excessive) arousal might enhance memory? To survive, human or nonhuman animals must remember exactly how they got into a dangerous situation and how they got out of it. The naturally produced surge of hormones apparently alerts our brains to "pay attention and remember!" It also is important to note the problems with "hormonally induced memory." Have you ever become so anxious that you "blanked out" during an exam or while giving a speech? If so, you understand how extreme arousal and stress hormones can interfere with both the formation and retrieval of memories.

Flashbulb Memory The powerful effect of emotions on memory also can be seen in what are known as *flashbulb memories*—vivid images of circumstances associated with surprising or strongly emotional events (Brown & Kulik, 1977). Do you remember the moment you learned about the September 11, 2001 terrorist attacks on the World Trade Center and the Pentagon (Figure 7.19). Is this memory so clear that it seems like a flashbulb went off, capturing every detail of the event in your memory? Assassinations (John Kennedy, Robert Kennedy, Martin Luther King Jr.), important personal events (graduation, illnesses, birth of a child), and, of course, horrific terrorist attacks have lasting effects on memory. We secrete fight-or-flight chemicals when we initially hear of the event. We later replay these events in our minds again and again, which further strengthens our memories.

Despite their intensity, flashbulb memories are not as accurate as you might think (Kvavilashvili et al., 2010; Lanciano, Curei, & Semin, 2010; Talarico & Rubin, 2007). When asked how he heard the news of the September 11 attacks, President George W. Bush's answers contained numerous inconsistencies (Greenberg, 2004). Thus, not even flashbulb memories are immune to alteration.

Where Are Memories Located? Tracking Down Memory Traces

So far, our discussion of the biological bases of memory has focused on the formation of memories as a result of neural changes or emotional influences. But where is memory stored? What parts of the brain are involved?

Early memory researchers believed that memory was *localized* and stored in a particular brain area. Instead, as we discovered earlier with the *parallel distributed-processing model* (PDP), memories are stored in a vast network of associations located throughout our brains.

Today, research techniques are so advanced that we can experimentally induce and measure memory-related brain changes as they occur—on-the-spot reporting! For example, James Brewer and his colleagues (1998) used functional magnetic resonance imaging (fMRI) to locate areas of the brain responsible for encoding memories of pictures. They showed 96 pictures of indoor and outdoor scenes to participants while scanning their brains, and then later tested them on their ability to recall those pictures. Brewer and his colleagues identified the *right prefrontal cortex* and the *parahippocampal cortex* as the most active regions of the brain during the encoding of the pictures. As you can see in Concept Organizer 7.2, these are only two of several brain regions involved in memory storage.

ConceptOrganizer7.2

STOP *This Concept Organizer contains essential information NOT found elsewhere in the text, which is likely to appear on quizzes and exams. Be sure to study it CAREFULLY!*

The Brain and Memory

Damage to any one of these areas can affect encoding, storage, and retrieval of memories. For example, what effect might damage to your amygdala have on your relationships with others? How might damage to your thalamus affect your day-to-day functioning?

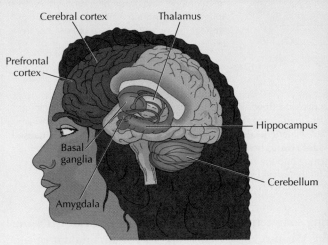

Amygdala	Emotional memory (Gerber et al., 2008; Hamilton & Gotlib, 2008; Murty et al., 2011)
Basal ganglia and Cerebellum	Creation and storage of the basic memory trace and implicit (nondeclarative) memories (such a skills, habits, and simple classical conditions responses) (Chiricozzi et al., 2008; Gluck, 2008; Thompson, 2005)
Hippocampal formation (hippocampus and surrounding area)	Memory recognition; implicit, explicit, spatial, episodic memory; declarative long-term memory; sequences of events (Gimbel & Brewer, 2011; Murty et al., 2011)
Thalamus	Formation of new memories and spatial and working memory (Hart & Kraut, 2007; Hofer et al., 2007; Ponzi, 2008)
Cortex	Encoding of explicit (declarative) memories; storage of episodic and semantic memories; skill learning; printing; working memory (Davidson et al., 2008; Dougal et al., 2007; Thompson, 2005)

Biological Causes of Memory Loss: Injury and Disease

Imagine a total loss of memory. With no memories of the past and no way to make new memories, there would be no way to use our previous skills or to learn new ones. We wouldn't know each other, nor would we know ourselves. In fact, our very survival would be in question.

Some memory problems are the result of injury and disease (organic pathology). When people are in serious accidents, suffer strokes, or encounter other events that cause trauma to the brain, memory loss or deterioration can occur. Disease also can alter the physiology of the brain and nervous system and thereby affect memory processes. This section focuses on two of the most common causes of biological memory failure: *brain injury* and *Alzheimer's disease*.

The Injured Brain
Objective 7.13: What are the major biological causes of memory loss?

The leading cause of neurological disorders—including memory loss—among Americans between the ages of 15 and 25 is traumatic brain injury (TBI). These injuries most commonly result from car accidents, falls, blows, and gunshot wounds.

As we discussed in Chapter 2, *traumatic brain injury* (*TBI*) occurs when the skull has a sudden collision with another object. The compression, twisting, and distortion of the brain inside the skull all cause serious and sometimes permanent damage to the brain. The frontal and temporal lobes often take the heaviest hit because they directly impact against the bony ridges inside the skull.

Loss of memory as a result of brain injury or trauma is called *amnesia*, and there are two major types—*retrograde* and *anterograde* (Figure 7.19). In **retrograde amnesia** (acting backward in time), the person loses memory (is amnesic) for events that occurred *before* the brain injury. However, the same person has no trouble remembering things that happened after the injury. As the name implies, only the old, "retro" memories are lost.

What causes retrograde amnesia? In cases where the individual is only amnesic for the events right before the brain injury, the cause may be a failure of consolidation.

Retrograde Amnesia Loss of memory for events before a brain injury; backward-acting amnesia

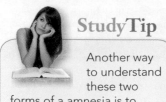

StudyTip

Another way to understand these two forms of a amnesia is to compare them to a computer. *Retrograde amnesia* would be like having your latest stored data (memories) on your hard drive erased. In contrast, *anterograde amnesia* would be similar to disconnecting your keyboard from the hard drive—no new data (memories) could be entered or stored.

Retrograde Amnesia — Old memories are lost | New memories OK

Accident occurs that causes amnesia

Anterograde Amnesia — Old memories OK | Can't form new memories

(a) In *retrograde amnesia*, the person loses memories of events that occured *before* the accident, yet has no trouble remembering things that happened afterward. Old, "retro" memories are lost.

(b) In *anterograde amnesia*, the person cannot form new memories for events that occur *after* the accident (new, "antero" memories are lost). Anterograde amnesia also may result from a surgical injury (as in the case of H.M.) or from diseases, such as chronic alcoholism.

Bodyguard Trevor Rees-Jones, the sole survivor of the car accident that killed Diana, Princess of Wales, Dodi Al-Fayed, and Henri Paul, experienced both anterograde and retrograde amnesia caused by his serious head injuries. He reports having no memory after getting into the black Mercedes and no memory of the accident or what happened soon after.

Figure 7.20 Two types of amnesia

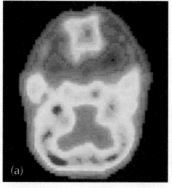

(a)

Note the large amount of red and yellow color (signs of brain activity) in the positron emission tomography scans of the normal brain.

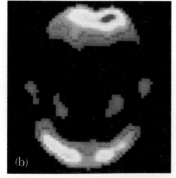

(b)

Now compare the reduced activity in the brain of the Alzheimer's disease patient. The loss is most significant in the temporal and parietal lobes, which indicates that these areas are particularly important for storing memories.

Figure 7.21 The effect of Alzheimer's disease on the brain

We learned earlier that during long-term potentiation (LTP) our neurons change to accommodate new learning. We also know that it takes a certain amount of time for these neural changes to become fixed and stable in long-term memory, a process known as **consolidation**. Like heavy rain on wet cement, the brain injury "wipes away" unstable memories because the cement has not had time to harden (*retrograde amnesia*).

In contrast to retrograde amnesia, in which people lose memories for events *before* a brain injury, some people lose memory for events that occur *after* a brain injury, which is called **anterograde amnesia** (acting forward in time). This type of amnesia generally results from a surgical injury or from diseases such as chronic alcoholism. Continuing our analogy with wet cement, anterograde amnesia would be like having permanently hardened cement. You can't lay down new long-term memories because the cement is hardened.

Are you confused about these two similar sounding forms of amnesia? If so, consider the Study Tip on Figure 7.20. Also think back to the story of H.M. (the man introduced at the start of this chapter) who suffered from both forms of amnesia. He had a mild memory loss for events in his life that happened the year or two *before* the operation (*retrograde amnesia*). Because his surgery destroyed the mechanism that transfers information from short-term memory to long-term memory, he also could not form new lasting memories for events after the operation (*anterograde amnesia*) (Barbeau, Puel, & Pariente, 2010; Bohbot & Corkin, 2007; Corkin, 2002). In most cases, retrograde amnesia is temporary and patients generally recover slowly over time. Unfortunately, anterograde amnesia is usually permanent. But patients also show surprising abilities to learn and remember implicit/nondeclarative tasks (such as procedural motor skills).

Alzheimer's Disease (AD)

Like traumatic brain injuries, disease can alter the physiology of the brain and nervous system, affecting memory processes. For example, **Alzheimer's disease** (**AD**) is a progressive mental deterioration that occurs most commonly in later life (Figure 7.21).

Consolidation Process by which neural changes associated with recent learning become durable and stable

Anterograde Amnesia Inability to form new memories after a brain injury; forward-acting amnesia

Alzheimer's [ALTS-high-merz] Disease (AD) Progressive mental deterioration characterized by severe memory loss

The most noticeable early symptoms are disturbances in memory, beginning with typical incidents of forgetfulness that everyone experiences from time to time. With Alzheimer's, however, the forgetfulness progresses. In the final stages, the person fails to recognize loved ones, needs total nursing care, and ultimately dies.

AD does not attack all types of memory equally. A hallmark of the disease is the extreme decrease in *explicit/declarative memory* (Irish et al., 2011; Libon et al., 2007; Satler et al., 2007). AD patients fail to recall facts, information, and personal life experiences. However, they still retain some *implicit/nondeclarative memories*, such as simple classically conditioned responses and procedural tasks, like brushing their teeth.

What causes this disease? Autopsies of the brains of people with Alzheimer's disease (AD) show unusual *tangles* (structures formed from degenerating cell bodies) and *plaques* (structures formed from degenerating axons and dendrites). Hereditary AD generally strikes its victims between the ages of 45 and 55. Some experts believe the cause of Alzheimer's is primarily genetic. But others think genetic makeup may make some people more susceptible to environmental triggers (Bekris et al., 2010; Ertekin-Taner, 2007; Persson et al., 2008; Sillén et al., 2011).

CHECK & REVIEW   STOP   Before going on, be sure to complete this Check & Review. It is an invaluable study tool!

Biological Bases of Memory

Part A: Retrieval Practice

1. Without looking at the book, spend 10 minutes writing a free-form essay recalling all you can remember from the previous section.

2. Now, reread the previous section, and once again spend 10 minutes writing a free-form essay on the SAME material.

Part B: Practice Quiz

1. Describe the two processes involved in LTP.

2. Your vivid memory of what you were doing when you learned about the attack on the World Trade Center is an example of _____. (a) the encoding specificity principle; (b) long-term potentiation; (c) latent learning; (d) a flashbulb memory

3. Forgetting that results from brain damage or trauma is called _____.

4. Ralph can't remember anything that happened to him before he fell through the floor of his tree house. His lack of memory for events before his fall is called _____ amnesia. (a) retroactive; (b) proactive; (c) anterograde; (d) retrograde

5. Label the two types of amnesia on the figure below:

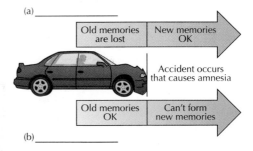

(a) _____

Old memories are lost   New memories OK

Accident occurs that causes amnesia

Old memories OK   Can't form new memories

(b) _____

Check your answers in Appendix B.

Psychology Engages

Overall Memory Improvement: Memory Distortions and Tips for Improvement

One of my first memories would date, if it were true, from my second year. I can still see, most clearly, the following scene, in which I believed until I was about fifteen. I was sitting in my pram, which my nurse was pushing in the Champs-Élysées, when a man tried to kidnap me. I was held in by the strap fastened round me while my nurse bravely tried to stand between the thief and me. She received various scratches, and I can still vaguely see the scratches on her face. Then a crowd gathered, a policeman with a short cloak and a white baton came up, and the man took to his heels. I can still see the whole scene, and can even place it near the tube station. When I was about fifteen, my parents received a letter from my former nurse saying that she had been converted to the Salvation Army. She wanted to confess her past faults, and in particular to return the watch she had been given as a reward on this occasion. She had made up the whole story, faking the scratches. I, therefore, must have heard, as a child, the account of this story, which my parents believed, and projected it into the past in the form of a visual memory, which was a memory of a memory, but false. (Piaget, 1962, pp. 187–188)

This is the self-reported childhood memory of Jean Piaget, a brilliant and world-famous cognitive and developmental psychologist (Chapter 9). Why did Piaget create such a strange and elaborate memory for something that never happened?

Understanding Memory Distortions
Objective 7.14: Why do we distort our memories?

There are several reasons why we shape, rearrange, and distort our memories. One of the most common is our need for *logic* and *consistency*. When we're initially forming new memories or sorting through old ones, we fill in missing pieces, make "corrections," and rearrange information to make it logical and consistent with our previous experiences. If Piaget's beloved nurse said someone attempted to kidnap him, it was only logical for the boy to "remember" the event.

We also shape and construct our memories for the sake of efficiency. Think about a recent, important lecture from your psychology instructor that you (hopefully) encoded for storage in LTM. You obviously did not record a word-for-word copy of the lecture. You summarized, augmented, and tied it in with related memories you have in LTM. Similarly, when you need to retrieve the stored lecture from your LTM, you recover only the general ideas or facts that were said.

Despite all their problems and biases, our memories are normally quite efficient and serve us well in most situations. Our memories have evolved to encode, store, and retrieve information vital to our survival. Even while sleeping, we process and store important memories. However, when faced with tasks like remembering precise details in a college lecture, this textbook, the faces and names of potential clients, or where you left your house keys, your brain is simply not as well equipped.

Eight Tips for Memory Improvement
Objective 7.15: How can we improve our memory?

The beauty of the human brain is that we can recognize the limits and problems of memory and then develop appropriate coping mechanisms. Just as our ancestors domesticated wild horses and cattle to overcome the physical limits of the human body, we can develop similar approaches to improve our mental limits for fine detail.

The following eight tips are particularly helpful for college success.

- *Pay attention and reduce interference*. If you really want to remember something, you must pay attention to it. When you're in class, focus on the instructor and sit away from people who might distract you. When you study, choose a place with minimal interferences.

- *Use rehearsal techniques*. Remember that the duration of STM is about 30 seconds. To lengthen this time, use *maintenance rehearsal*. To effectively encode memory into LTM, use *elaborative* rehearsal, which involves thinking about the material and relating it to other information that has already been stored. Hopefully, you've noticed that I formally define each key term immediately in the text, in the margin, and in the glossary at the back of the book. I also give a brief explanation and one or two examples for each of these terms. While studying this text, use these tools to help your elaborative rehearsal. Also try making up your own examples. The more elaborate the encoding of information, the more memorable it will be.

- *Use the encoding specificity principle*. When we form memories, we store them with links to the way we thought about them at the time. Therefore, the closer the retrieval cues are to the original encoding situation, the better the retrieval. Because you encode a lot of material during class time, avoid "early takes" or makeup exams, which are generally scheduled in other classrooms. The *context* will be different and your retrieval may suffer. Similarly, when you take a test, try to remain calm and reinstate the same psychological and physiological state that you were in when you originally learned the material. According to the *mood congruence* effect, you will recall more if the mood of your test taking matches the mood of the original learning. Also, according to the *state-dependent memory* research, if you normally drink a cup of coffee while studying, you might want to have a cup of coffee before your exam.

- *Improve your organization*. This may be the most important key to a good memory. Although the capacity of STM is only around five to nine items, you can expand the capacity of STM by *chunking* (organizing) information into a few groups. To improve your LTM, create *hierarchies* that organize the material in meaningful patterns. The tables in this book and the Visual Summaries at the end of each chapter are examples of hierarchies that help you organize chapter material. Be sure to study them carefully—and make up your own whenever possible.

- *Counteract the serial-position effect*. Because we tend to remember information that occurs at the beginning or end of a sequence, spend extra time with the information in the middle. When reading or reviewing the text, start at different places—sometimes at the second section, sometimes at the fourth.

- *Manage your time*. Study on a regular basis and avoid cramming. *Distributed* (spaced) learning sessions are more efficient than *massed* practice (cramming). In other words, five separate half-hour sessions tend to produce better encoding and storage than one session of 2½ hours. When you learn something new, take the time to associate it with what you already know. By doing this, you'll be organizing the new information so that you can easily retrieve it later on. Also, get plenty of sleep, for two reasons: (1) We don't remember information acquired when we're drowsy as well as that gained when we're alert, and (2) during REM sleep we process and store most of the new information we acquired when awake.

- *Employ self-monitoring and overlearning*. When studying a text, you should periodically stop and test your understanding of the material. This is why we include numerous "Check & Review" sections throughout each chapter. Stopping to read these reviews and completing the short quiz section will provide personal feedback on your mastery of the material. Even when you are studying a single sentence, you need to monitor your understanding. Poor readers tend to read at the same speed for both easy and difficult material. Good readers tend to recognize when they are having difficulty. They slow down or repeat difficult sentences.

  When you finish reading a chapter, wait a few minutes and then do an additional monitoring of your understanding. If you evaluate your learning only while you're actively reading the material, you may overestimate your understanding (because the information is still in STM). However, if you delay making your judgment (for at least a few minutes), your evaluation will be more accurate. The best way to ensure your full understanding of material (and success on an exam) is through *overlearning*—studying information even after you think you already know it. Don't just study until you *think* you know it. Work hard until you *know* you know it!

- *Use mnemonics*. **Mnemonic devices** (derived from the Greek word for "memory") are memory aids (or tricks) based on encoding items in a special way (Concept Organizer 7.3).

[handwritten margin note: metacognition]

Mnemonic [nih-MON-ik] Device Memory-improvement technique based on encoding items in a special way

ConceptOrganizer7.3

Mnemonic Devices

As you review the key points from this chapter, think about how you might exploit basic principles of memory, using them to your own advantage. One additional "trick" for giving your memory a boost is to use the following *mnemonic devices* to encode items in a special way. (But be warned—you may get more "bang for your buck" using the well-researched principles discussed throughout this chapter.)

(a) **Method of loci** Greek and Roman orators developed the *method of loci* to keep track of the many parts of their long speeches. Orators would imagine the parts of their speeches attached to places in a courtyard. For example, if an opening point in a speech was the concept of *justice*, they might visualize a courtroom placed in the first corner of their garden. As they mentally walked around their garden during their speech, they would encounter, in order, each of the points to be made.

(a) Method of loci

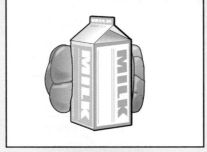

Grocery list

One is a bun

Two is a shoe

Three is a tree

(b) **Peg words** To use the *peg-word* mnemonic, you first need to memorize a set of 10 images that you can use as "pegs" on which to hang ideas. For example, if you learn 10 items that rhyme with the numbers they stand for, you can then use the images as pegs to hold the items of any list. Try it with items you might want to buy on your next trip to the grocery store: milk, eggs, and bread.

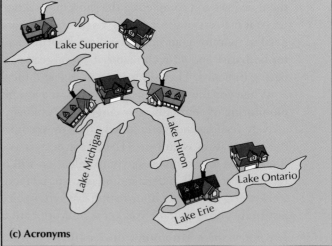

(c) Acronyms

(c) **Acronyms** To use the acronym method, create a new code word from the first letters of the items you want to remember. For example, to recall the names of the Great Lakes, think of *HOMES* on a great lake (*H*uron, *O*ntario, *M*ichigan, *E*rie, *S*uperior). Visualizing homes on each lake also helps you remember your code word "homes."

GENDER AND CULTURAL DIVERSITY

Cultural Differences in Memory and Forgetting

Objective 7.16: How does culture affect memory?

How do you remember the dates for all your quizzes, exams, and assignments in college? What memory aids do you use if you need to buy 15 items at the supermarket? Most people from industrialized societies rely on written shopping lists, calendars, books, notepads, or computers to store information and prevent forgetting. Can you imagine living in a culture without these aids? What would it be like if you had to rely solely on your memory to store and retrieve all your learned information? Do people raised in preliterate societies with rich oral traditions develop better memory skills than do people raised in literate societies?

Ross and Millson (1970) designed a cross-cultural study to explore these questions. They compared American and Ghanaian college students' abilities to remember stories that were read aloud. Students listened to the stories without taking notes and without being told they would be tested. Two weeks later, all students were asked to write down as much as they could remember. As you might expect, the Ghanaian students had better recall than the Americans. Their superior performance was attributed to their culture's long oral tradition, which requires developing greater skill in encoding oral information.

Does this mean that people from cultures with an oral tradition simply have better memories? Recall from Chapter 1 that a core requirement for scientific research is *replication* and the generation of related hypotheses and studies. In this case, when other researchers orally presented nonliterate African participants with lists of words instead of stories, they did *not* perform better (Cole et al., 1971). However, when both educated Africans and uneducated Africans were compared for memory of lists of words, the educated Africans performed very well (Scribner, 1977). This suggests that formal schooling helps develop memory strategies for things like lists of words. Preliterate participants may see such lists as unrelated and meaningless (Berry et al., 2011).

Wagner (1982) conducted a study with Moroccan and Mexican urban and rural children that helps explain the effect of formal schooling. Participants were presented with seven cards that were placed facedown in front of them, one at a time. They were then shown a card and asked to point out which of the seven cards was its duplicate. Everyone, regardless of culture or amount of schooling, was able to recall the latest cards presented (the *recency effect*). However, the amount of schooling significantly affected overall recall and the ability to recall the earliest cards presented (*primacy effect*).

Wagner suggests that the primacy effect depends on *rehearsal*—the silent repetition of things you're trying to remember—and that this strategy is strongly related to schooling. As a child in a typical classroom, you were expected to memorize letters, numbers, multiplication tables, and a host of other basic facts. This type of formal schooling provides years of practice in memorization and in applying these skills in test situations. According to Wagner, memory has a "hardware" section that does not change across culture. It also contains a "software" part that develops particular strategies for remembering, which are learned.

In summary, research indicates that the "software" part of memory is affected by culture. In cultures in which communication relies on oral tradition, people develop

Culture and memory In many societies, tribal leaders pass down vital information through stories related orally. Because of this rich oral tradition, children living in these cultures have better memories for information related through stories than do other children.

good strategies for remembering orally presented stories. In cultures in which formal schooling is the rule, people learn memory strategies that help them remember lists of items. From these studies, we can conclude that, across cultures, people tend to remember information that matters to them. They develop memory skills to match the demands of their environment.

 CRITICAL THINKING

Memory and Metacognition

Metacognition is the ability to review and analyze your own mental processes—to "think about your thinking." It is also a vital part of critical thinking because it helps you objectively examine your thoughts and cognitive strategies and then to evaluate their appropriateness and accuracy. In the context of this chapter, you can use metacognition to examine and successfully employ the memory improvement tips we have just discussed.

Start by placing a "+" mark by those skills and strategies that you are currently using and a "−" by those that you avoid or that cause you problems. Now carefully review those items you've identified with a "−" mark. Why are you avoiding or not employing these particular skills? Are your reasons rational? Can you think of areas of your life where these skills might be useful? If so, go back and place a mark by those items you want to develop. Use these checkmarks as the starting point for your personal memory improvement plan.

_____ Pay attention and reduce interference.

_____ Use rehearsal techniques.

_____ Improve your organization.

_____ Counteract the serial-position effect.

_____ Manage your time.

_____ Use the encoding specificity principle.

_____ Employ self-monitoring and overlearning.

_____ Use mnemonic devices.

 **CHECK & REVIEW**  **STOP** *Before going on, be sure to complete this Check & Review. It is an invaluable study tool!*

Psychology Engages

Part A: Retrieval Practice

1. Without looking at the book, spend 10 minutes writing a free-form essay recalling all you can remember from the previous section.

2. Now, reread the previous section, and once again spend 10 minutes writing a free-form essay on the SAME material.

Part B: Practice Quiz

1. How can maintenance rehearsal and elaborative rehearsal improve your memory?

2. Explain how you can overcome the serial-position effect while studying.

3. The best way to ensure your full understanding of material (and success on an exam) is through_____.

4. Which mnemonic device is being described in each of the following situations?
   a. You remember items to bring to a meeting by visualizing them in association with a previously learned sequence.

   b. You remember a speech for your communications class by forming visual images of the parts of your speech and associating them with areas in the classroom.

   c. You remember the five key theories of forgetting by creating a new word "DIMER" and then visualize forgetting as your memory getting "dimmer."

Check your answers in Appendix B.

WileyPLUS presents an on-line version of this textbook along with a wealth of study resources including quizzes, practice tests, flash cards, videos, animations and other activities designed to improve your mastery of the content. Working in conjunction with these study tools, the *Psychology in Action* WileyPLUS course features Professor Karen Huffman, author of this textbook, explaining and expanding upon some of the most challenging concepts in psychology. Here is a sample of the tutorial videos available for this chapter:

www.wileyplus.com

- The nature of memory, featuring classroom demonstration of the constructivist model of memory and its implications
- Classroom demonstration of various types of long-term memory (explicit vs. implicit, semantic vs. procedural)
- Ways to enhance your memory, featuring Professor Huffman's classroom demonstration of various helpful techniques
- An interactive, animated look at memory improvement
- Virtual Field Trip to the USA Memory Championships, where Mental Athletes test their ability to recall everything from ransom numbers to poetry
- Virtual Field Trip to an Alzheimer's Treatment Center, where patients learn to cope with this degenerative memory disorder.

Key Terms

To assess your understanding of the **Key Terms** in Chapter 7, write a definition for each (in your own words), and then compare your definitions with those in the text.

Nature of Memory
memory (p. 248)
constructive process (p. 248)
encoding, storage, retrieval (ESR) model (p. 249)
encoding (p. 249)
storage (p. 249)
retrieval (p. 249)
levels of processing model (p. 249)
maintenance rehearsal (p. 250)
elaborative rehearsal (p. 250)
parallel distributed processing (PDP) model (p. 251)
three-stage memory model (p. 251)
sensory memory (p. 252)
short-term memory (STM) (p. 252)
chunking (p. 253)
working memory (p. 254)

long-term memory (LTM) (p. 254)
explicit (declarative) memory (p. 254)
semantic memory (p. 255)
episodic memory (p. 255)
implicit (nondeclarative) memory (p. 255)
serial-position effect (p. 257)
retrieval cue (p. 257)
recall (p. 257)
recognition (p. 258)
priming (p. 258)
encoding specificity principle (p. 258)

Forgetting
relearning (p. 260)
retroactive interference (p. 262)
proactive interference (p. 262)
tip-of-the-tongue (TOT) phenomenon (p. 263)

misinformation effect (p. 263)
source amnesia (p. 264)
sleeper effect (p. 264)
distributed practice (p. 264)
massed practice (p. 264)

Biological Bases of Memory
long-term potentiation (LTP) (p. 267)
retrograde amnesia (p. 269)
consolidation (p. 270)
anterograde amnesia (p. 270)
Alzheimer's [ALTS-high-merz] disease (AD) (p. 270)

Psychology Engages
mnemonic [nih-MON-ik] device (p. 273)

Chapter Summary

Nature of Memory

Objective 7.1: Define memory and explain how it is a constructive process.

Memory is an internal record or representation of some prior event or experience. It is not an exact recording of events. Instead it is a

constructive process, in which we actively organize and shape information as it is being processed, stored, and retrieved.

Objective 7.2: Briefly summarize the four models of memory.

The **encoding, storage, retrieval (ESR) model** draws analogies between human memory and a computer. Like typing on a keyboard, **encoding** translates information into neural codes that match the brain's language. **Storage** retains neural coded information over time, like saving material on the computer's hard drive or a disk. **Retrieval** gets information out of LTM storage and sends it to STM to be used, whereas the computer retrieves information and displays it on the monitor.

According to the **levels of processing** model, the degree or depth of mental processing that occurs when material is initially encountered determines how well it is later remembered. The **parallel distributed processing (PDP) model** suggests that the contents of our memory exist as a vast number of interconnected units distributed throughout a huge network, all operating simultaneously in parallel.

The **three-stage memory model**, proposes that information must pass through each of three stages before being stored—*sensory memory, short-term memory (STM),* and *long-term memory (LTM)*.

Objective 7.3: What is sensory memory?

Sensory memory preserves a brief replica of sensory information. It has a large capacity, and information lasts from a fraction of a second to four seconds. Selected information is sent to short-term memory (STM).

Objective 7.4: Describe short-term memory (STM) and explain why it's often called "working memory."

Short-term memory (STM) involves memory for current thoughts, and it can hold five to nine items for about 30 seconds before they are lost. The capacity of STM can be increased with **chunking,** whereas information can be stored longer in STM through **maintenance rehearsal.**

STM is often called **working memory** not only because it actively receives information from sensory memory and transfers it to and from LTM, but it also actively manipulates the incoming, transferred, and retrieved information.

Objective 7.5: Summarize long-term memory (LTM), and how it's divided into several subsystems.

Long-term memory (LTM) is a relatively permanent storage system, with an apparently unlimited capacity. It is divided into **implicit (nondeclarative) memory**, and also into **explicit (declarative)** memory, which is subdivided into **semantic** and **episodic memory.**

Objective 7.6: List several tips for improving LTM, and where they fall under encoding, storage, or retrieval.

Under the category of encoding, we can improve LTM by using *selective vs. divided attention, controlled vs. automatic processing,* and *deeper levels of processing.* When storing information, LTM is improved if we first use *chunking* during STM, and then use *organization* and *hierarchies* during LTM. During retrieval, we should be aware of the **serial-position effect** (primacy and recency) and **retrieval cues** (**recall, recognition,** and **priming**). Finally, to improve our use of retrieval cues, we also should be aware of the **encoding specificity principle**, which involves *context-dependent memory, mood congruence,* and *state-dependent memory.*

Forgetting

Objective 7.7: Describe Ebbinghaus's contribution to memory research.

Ebbinghaus's famous "curve of forgetting" shows that it occurs most rapidly immediately after learning. However, Ebbinghaus also showed that **relearning** usually takes less time than original learning.

Objective 7.8: What are the five major theories of forgetting?

The *decay theory* of forgetting simply states that memory, like all biological processes, deteriorates as time passes. The *interference theory* of forgetting suggests that memories are forgotten because of either retroactive or proactive interference. **Retroactive interference** occurs when new information interferes with previously learned information. **Proactive interference** occurs when old information interferes with newly learned information. The *motivated forgetting theory* states that people forget things that are painful, threatening, or embarrassing. According to *encoding failure theory*, some material is forgotten because it was never encoded from short-term memory to long-term memory (LTM). *Retrieval failure theory* suggests information stored in LTM is not forgotten, but may at times be inaccessible.

Objective 7.9: Describe four factors key to forgetting.

To prevent problems with forgetting, you should be aware of four important factors: the **misinformation effect** (distorting memory with misleading post event information); **source amnesia** (forgetting the true source of a memory); the **sleeper effect** (initially discounting information from an unreliable source, but later judging it as reliable because the source is forgotten); and *information overload* (in which **distributed practice** is found to be superior to **massed practice**).

Memory and the Criminal Justice System

Objective 7.10: What's wrong with eyewitness testimony?

Memories are not exact duplicates. We actively shape and *construct* information as it is encoded, stored, and retrieved. Eyewitness accounts are highly persuasive in the courtroom. But they're subject to potential errors.

Objective 7.11: What do psychologists believe about repressed memories?

Psychologists continue to debate whether recovered memories are accurate recollections or false memories. Concern about the reliability of recovered memories has led many experts to encourage a cautious approach.

Biological Bases of Memory

Objective 7.12: How do we form memories, and where do we store them?

Memories are formed in at least two ways: (1) through changes in neurons, called **long-term potentiation (LTP)** or (2) through emotional arousal.

Memory storage tends to be both localized and distributed throughout the brain.

Objective 7.13: What are the major biological causes of memory loss?

Some memory problems are the result of injury and disease (organic pathology). Problems that result from serious brain injuries or trauma are called *amnesia*. In **retrograde amnesia**, memory for events that occurred before an accident is lost. In **anterograde amnesia**, memory for events that occur after an accident is lost.

Alzheimer's disease (AD) is a progressive mental deterioration and severe memory loss occurring most commonly in later life.

Psychology Engages

Objective 7.14: Why do we distort our memories?

Memory distortions tend to arise from our human need for logic and consistency, as well as because it's sometimes more efficient to do so.

Objective 7.15: How can we improve our memory?

This section offers eight concrete strategies for improving memory. These strategies include paying attention and reducing interference, using rehearsal techniques (both maintenance and elaborative rehearsal), using the encoding specificity principle, improving your organization (by chunking and creating hierarchies), counteracting the serial position effect, better time management, employing self-monitoring and overlearning, and using **mnemonic devices**.

Objective 7.16: How does culture affect memory?

Across cultures, people remember information that matters to them, and we develop memory skills to match our differing environments.

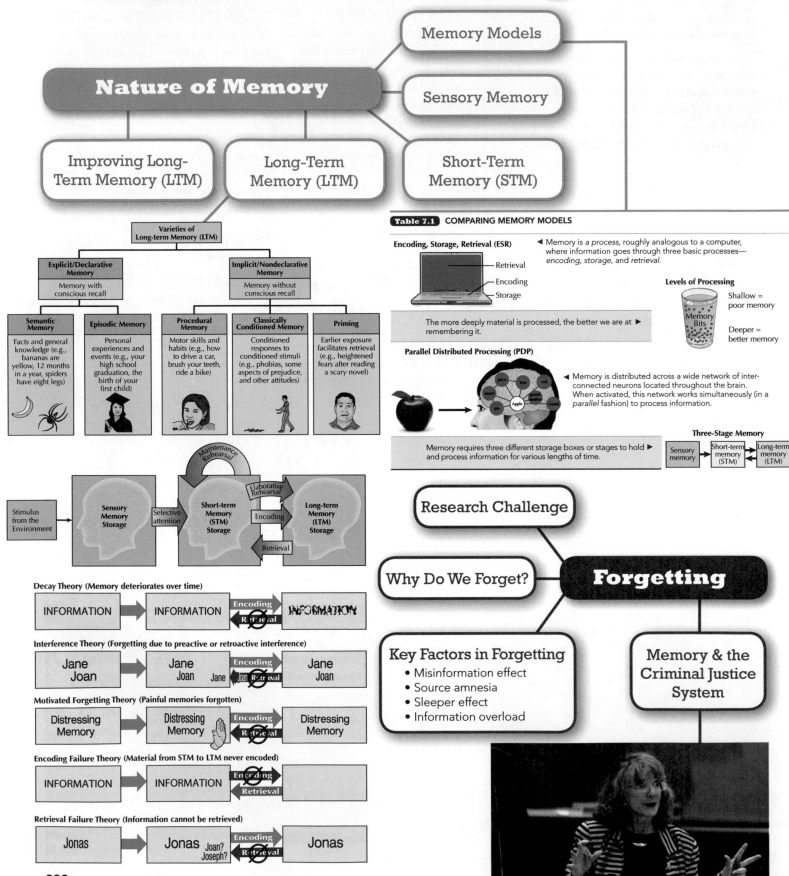

Nature of Memory

- Memory Models
- Sensory Memory
- Improving Long-Term Memory (LTM)
- Long-Term Memory (LTM)
- Short-Term Memory (STM)

Varieties of Long-term Memory (LTM)

Explicit/Declarative Memory — Memory with conscious recall

- **Semantic Memory** — Facts and general knowledge (e.g., bananas are yellow, 12 months in a year, spiders have eight legs)
- **Episodic Memory** — Personal experiences and events (e.g., your high school graduation, the birth of your first child)

Implicit/Nondeclarative Memory — Memory without conscious recall

- **Procedural Memory** — Motor skills and habits (e.g., how to drive a car, brush your teeth, ride a bike)
- **Classically Conditioned Memory** — Conditioned responses to conditioned stimuli (e.g., phobias, some aspects of prejudice, and other attitudes)
- **Priming** — Earlier exposure facilitates retrieval (e.g., heightened fears after reading a scary novel)

Table 7.1 COMPARING MEMORY MODELS

Encoding, Storage, Retrieval (ESR) — Retrieval, Encoding, Storage

◄ Memory is *a process*, roughly analogous to a computer, where information goes through three basic processes— *encoding, storage, and retrieval.*

Levels of Processing — Memory Bits — Shallow = poor memory; Deeper = better memory

The more deeply material is processed, the better we are at ► remembering it.

Parallel Distributed Processing (PDP)

◄ Memory is distributed across a wide network of inter-connected neurons located throughout the brain. When activated, this network works simultaneously (in a *parallel* fashion) to process information.

Three-Stage Memory

Memory requires three different storage boxes or stages to hold ► and process information for various lengths of time.

Sensory memory → Short-term memory (STM) → Long-term memory (LTM)

Stimulus from the Environment → Sensory Memory Storage → (Selective attention) → Short-term Memory (STM) Storage → (Encoding) → Long-term Memory (LTM) Storage; Maintenance Rehearsal; Elaborative Rehearsal; Retrieval

Research Challenge

Why Do We Forget?

Forgetting

Key Factors in Forgetting
- Misinformation effect
- Source amnesia
- Sleeper effect
- Information overload

Memory & the Criminal Justice System

Decay Theory (Memory deteriorates over time)
INFORMATION → INFORMATION → (Encoding / Retrieval) → INFORMATION

Interference Theory (Forgetting due to proactive or retroactive interference)
Jane Joan → Jane Joan Jane → (Encoding / Joan Retrieval) → Jane Joan

Motivated Forgetting Theory (Painful memories forgotten)
Distressing Memory → Distressing Memory → (Encoding / Retrieval) → Distressing Memory

Encoding Failure Theory (Material from STM to LTM never encoded)
INFORMATION → INFORMATION → (Encoding / Retrieval) →

Retrieval Failure Theory (Information cannot be retrieved)
Jonas → Jonas Joan? Joseph? → (Encoding / Retrieval) → Jonas

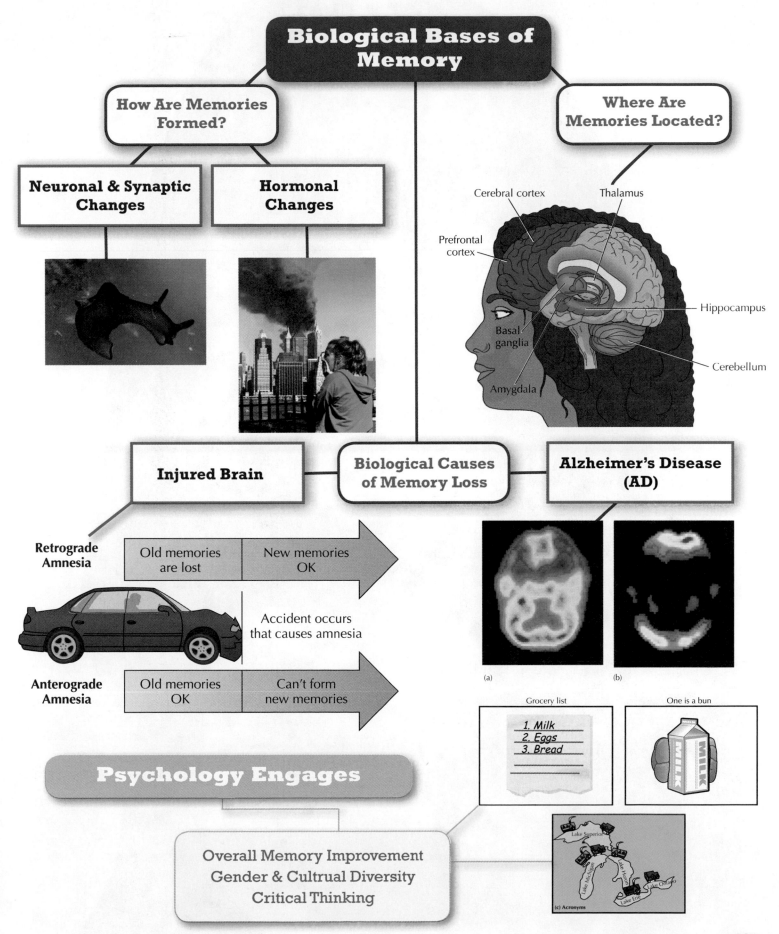

Biological Bases of Memory

How Are Memories Formed?

Neuronal & Synaptic Changes

Hormonal Changes

Where Are Memories Located?

Cerebral cortex

Thalamus

Prefrontal cortex

Hippocampus

Basal ganglia

Cerebellum

Amygdala

Biological Causes of Memory Loss

Injured Brain

Retrograde Amnesia

Old memories are lost | New memories OK

Accident occurs that causes amnesia

Anterograde Amnesia

Old memories OK | Can't form new memories

Alzheimer's Disease (AD)

(a)   (b)

Grocery list

1. Milk
2. Eggs
3. Bread

One is a bun

MILK

Lake Superior

Lake Michigan

Lake Huron

Lake Ontario

Lake Erie

(c) Acronyms

Psychology Engages

Overall Memory Improvement
Gender & Cultrual Diversity
Critical Thinking

ChapterEight

Thinking, Language, and Intelligence

Have you heard about the famous "wild child" Genie? From the age of 20 months until authorities rescued her at the age of 13, Genie lived in a tiny, windowless room in solitary confinement. By day, she sat naked and tied to a chair with nothing to do and no one to talk to. At night, she was put in a kind of straitjacket and caged in a covered crib. Genie's abusive father forbade anyone to speak to her for the entire time, and if Genie made any noise, her father would beat her, while he barked and growled like a dog.

After she was discovered at age 13, linguists and psychologists worked with her intensively for many years. Sadly, Genie never progressed much beyond sentences like "Genie go" (Curtiss, 1977; LaPointe, 2005; Rymer, 1993; Saxton, 2010). With her limited language skills, would you say Genie is intelligent?

What about Thomas Edison, the famous inventor of the lightbulb? Despite having attended school for only three months and suffering progressive deafness throughout his life, Edison patented over 1,000 inventions—more than any other single individual in history. Being the "greatest inventor in American history" obviously requires a large repertoire of thinking processes and intellectual agility. Would you consider Thomas Edison intelligent?

To be intelligent, you must be able to think, and the three topics of this chapter—"Thinking," "Language," and "Intelligence"—obviously overlap, which explains why they're combined into this one chapter. However, if you go on to major in psychology, you'll discover that researchers often group these same topics under the larger umbrella of **cognition**, *the mental activities of acquiring, storing, retrieving, and using knowledge*. In a real sense, we discuss cognition throughout the text (e.g., chapters on sensation and perception, consciousness, learning, and memory).

ChapterOutline

Cognition Mental activities involved in acquiring, storing, retrieving, and using knowledge

WHY STUDY PSYCHOLOGY

Did you know...

- Chimps and dolphins can use nonvocal language to make simple sentences and communicate with human trainers?

- Thomas Edison patented over 1,000 inventions, yet some believe he added little to scientific knowledge?

- Shortly after the 9/11 terrorist attack on the World Trade Center, surveys found many Americans believed they had a 20 percent chance of being hurt in a terrorist attack within the next year?

- Children all over the world go through similar stages in language development at about the same age, and their babbling is the same in all languages?

- Many cultures have no language equivalent for our notion of intelligence?

Thinking

Objective 8.1: What is thinking and where is it located?

Every time you use information and mentally act on it you are thinking. Like learning and memory, our thought processes are distributed throughout our brains in networks of neurons. However, they're also localized. For example, during problem solving or decision making, our brains are active in the *prefrontal cortex*. This region associates complex ideas, makes plans, forms, initiates, and allocates attention, and supports multitasking. The prefrontal cortex also links to other areas of the brain, such as the *limbic system* (Chapter 2), to synthesize information from several senses (Anderson et al., 2011; Banich & Compton, 2011; Heyder, Suchan, & Daum, 2004; Sacchetti, Sacco, & Strata, 2007).

Mental Image Mental representation of a previously stored sensory experience, including visual, auditory, olfactory, tactile, motor, or gustatory imagery (e.g., visualizing a train and hearing its horn)

Cognitive Building Blocks: Foundation of Thought

Objective 8.2: How are mental images and concepts involved in thinking.

Now that we have a general understanding of thinking, and how and where it's occurring in our brains, we need to understand its three basic components—*mental images*, *concepts*, and *language*. We'll study the first two in this section, and then explore language in depth later in the chapter.

Mental Images

Imagine yourself lying relaxed in the warm sand on an ocean beach. Do you see tall palms swaying in the wind? Can you smell the salty ocean water and taste the dried salt on your lips? Can you hear children playing in the surf? What you've just created is a **mental image**, a mental representation of a previously stored sensory experience, which includes visual, auditory, olfactory, tactile, motor, and gustatory imagery.

We all have a mental space where we visualize and manipulate our sensory images (Borst et al., 2011; Moulton & Kosslyn, 2011; Schifferstein & Hilscher, 2010) (Figure 8.1). Interestingly, using mental imagery activates many of the same brain regions that are used for the actual experience itself. For example, visualizing an event or scene activates the occipital lobes, whereas thinking about a fearful event arouses the amygdala (Bensafi, Sobel, & Khan, 2007; Shin et al., 2010).

Figure 8.1 Mental imagery
Some of our most creative and inspired moments come when we're forming and manipulating mental images. This ballet dancer is probably mentally visualizing her next move, and her ability to do so is critical to her success.

TRY THIS YOURSELF

Manipulating Mental Images

How are the top two yellow figures the same, whereas the bottom two blue figures are different? Solving this problem requires mental imagery and manipulation. Those of you who are familiar with the computer game Tetris might find this puzzle rather simple. Others might want to turn to Appendix B for an explanation.

Concepts

Objective 8.3: How do we learn concepts?

In addition to mental images, our thinking involves **concepts**—mental representations of a group or category that share similar characteristics. Concepts can be concrete (*car, classroom*) or abstract (*intelligence, pornography*), but they are essential to thinking and communication because they simplify and organize information.

Imagine being Genie, the "wild child" described at the beginning of the chapter. If you had been confined to a small, windowless room your entire life, how would you think and process the world around you without concepts? Normally, when you see a new object or encounter a new situation, you relate it to your existing conceptual structure and categorize it according to where it fits. If you see a metal box with four wheels driving on the highway, you know it's a car, even if you've never seen that particular model before. But if you were Genie, how would you identify a car, a telephone, or even a bathroom, having never seen them and compared them to other cars, telephones, and rooms?

How do we learn concepts? They develop through our environmental interactions and a combination of three major building blocks:

1. ***Artificial concepts*** Some of our concepts are created from logical rules or definitions. Consider the definition of *triangle:* "a geometric figure with three sides and three angles." Any geometric form that contains these features would be included in the concept triangle, and if any feature were missing, it would not qualify as a triangle. Such concepts are called *artificial* (or *formal*) because the rules for inclusion are sharply defined. As you've seen in this and other college texts, artificial concepts are a core part of the sciences and other academic disciplines.

2. ***Natural concepts/prototypes*** In everyday life, we seldom use artificial definitions. When we see birds, we do not think "warm-blooded animals that fly, have wings, and lay eggs"—an *artificial concept*. Instead, we use *natural concepts*, called **prototypes**, which are based on a personal "best example" or a typical representative of that concept (Rosch, 1973; Petrov, 2011) (Figure 8.2).

3. ***Hierarchies*** Some of our concepts also develop when we create *hierarchies*, that is, grouping specific concepts as subcategories within broader concepts. Note in the hierarchy depicted in Figure 8.3 how the top (superordinate) category of *animals* is very broad and includes lots of members. The midlevel categories of *bird* and *dog* are more specific but still rather general. And the lowest (subordinate) categories of *parakeet* and *poodle* are the most specific.

Concept Mental representation of a group or category that shares similar characteristics (e.g., the concept of a river groups together the Nile, the Amazon, and the Mississippi because they share the common characteristic of being a large stream of water that empties into an ocean or lake)

Prototype Representation of the "best" or most typical example of a category (e.g., baseball is a prototype of the concept of sports)

(a) Most people have a *prototype* bird that captures the essence of "birdness" and allows us to quickly classify flying animals correctly.

(b) When we encounter an example that doesn't quite fit our prototype, we need time to review our artificial concept. Because the penguin doesn't fly, it's harder to classify than a robin.

Figure 8.2 Some birds are "birdier" than others

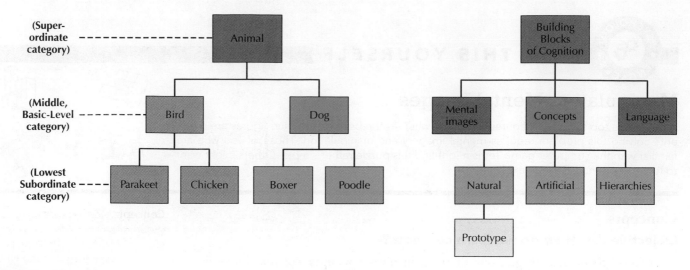

StudyTip

Recall from Chapter 7 that organization and hierarchies are essential to efficient encoding and storage in long-term memory (LTM), which is why we include so many tables and figures throughout this text and create "Visual Summaries" at the end of each chapter. Built-in hierarchies like these will help you master the material. However, it is even better if you develop your own.

(a) When we think, we naturally organize concepts according to superordinate and subordinate classes. We place concepts, like *animals* or *birds*, at the top and the most specific examples at the bottom. Interestingly, when we first *learn* something, we begin with the middle categories, which are called basic-level concepts (Rosch, 1978). Thus, children tend to learn *bird* before they learn higher, superordinate concepts like animal or lower, subordinate concepts like *parakeet*. Even as adults, when shown a picture of a parakeet, we classify it as a *bird* first.

Figure 8.3 Using hierarchies to improve your thinking

(b) Hierarchies can be generated from almost any set of interrelated facts. For example, instead of attempting to memorize the key terms *concept, mental image,* and *prototype,* you could create a hierarchy of how these terms are interrelated. Although they may look complicated, hierarchies significantly reduce the time and effort necessary for learning. Once you have this "big picture," it speeds up your mastery of the material, which translates into better exam scores.

Problem Solving: Three Steps to the Goal

Several years ago in Los Angeles, a 12-foot-high tractor-trailer got stuck under a bridge that was 6 inches too low. After hours of towing, tugging, and pushing, the police and transportation workers were stumped. Then a young boy happened by and asked, "Why don't you let some air out of the tires?" It was a simple, creative suggestion—and it worked.

Our lives are filled with problems, some simple, some difficult. For example, figuring out a way to make coffee without a filter is much easier than rescuing a large corporation on the brink of bankruptcy. However, most problem solving generally requires moving from a *given state* (the problem) to a *goal state* (the solution) (Bourne, Dominowski, & Loftus, 1979). (See Concept Organizer 8.1.)

Psychology at Work

Heuristics and Your Career

Considering your long-term career and relationship plans, you obviously can't try all possible options (an algorithm) to solve these problems. However, the three heuristics presented in Table 8.1 may help you narrow your desired alternatives.

ConceptOrganizer8.1

Three Steps to the Goal

Objective 8.4: Describe the three stages of problem solving.

STEP 1: PREPARATION
(Clarifying the problem)

Define Ultimate Goal
Are you looking for love and a satisfying career? If so, how are you planning to get them? (Note: This 3-step process of problem-solving also works well for "lesser," ultimate goals like finding a new apartment, getting an A in your psychology class, etc.)

Once the possible solutions are tested, they must be evaluated to see if they meet the criteria in all three parts of Step 1. If so, problem solved—you know what you want in a career or partner and the best route to finding them. If not, return to the preparation and/or production stages.

Looking for love in all the wrong places Are singles' bars a good place to find lasting love? Why or why not?

Identify Available Options
Start by outlining your limits and/or desires: Do you have the abilities or assets for your desired job or career? Will you move to another city or country for a career or a partner? What if your parents disapproved of your choice in a career or a partner?

STEP 3: EVALUATION
(Problem solved?)

Employ Heuristics
A **heuristic** is a simple rule or strategy for problem solving that provides shortcuts but does not guarantee a solution. It works most of the time, but not always. When seeking a serious love partner, family and friends often offer practical advice (or *heuristics*) such as, "Do what you naturally love to do (dancing, skiing, movies) and you'll find someone with similar interests." Your goal of finding a satisfying career may be helped by the heuristics in Table 8.1 (p. 288).

Use Algorithms
An **algorithm** is a step–by–step procedure that, if followed correctly, will always produce the solution. An algorithm for solving the problem 10×2 is $2 + 2 + 2 + 2 + 2 + 2 + 2 + 2 + 2 + 2$. Algorithms will eventually lead to the correct answer. But they may take a long time—especially for complex problems.

You're unlikely to use algorithms in your career or partner goals. but they're very useful in balancing your checkbook or computing your grade point average.

Separate the Negotiable from Non-Negotiable
Decide which factors are negotiable (irrelevant and easily compromised) versus non-negotiable (critical to your life happiness and long-term plans). For example, how important are shared values, money, or religion in your career or partner choices?

STEP 2: PRODUCTION
(Testing possible paths and solutions)

Algorithm Logical, step-by-step procedure that, if followed correctly, will eventually solve the problem

Heuristic Simple rule or shortcut for problem solving that does not guarantee a solution but does narrow the alternatives

Summary Table 8.1   THREE PROBLEM-SOLVING HEURISTICS AND YOUR CAREER

Problem-solving Heuristics	Description	Example	
Working backward	Starts with the solution, a known condition, and works backward through the problem. Once the search has revealed the steps to be taken, the problem is solved.	Deciding you want to be an experimental psychologist, you ask your psychology professor to recommend graduate colleges and universities. Then you contact these institutions for information on their admission policies. Next, you adapt your current college courses and work hard to meet your goal to become an experimental psychologist.	**Problem Solving in action** Graduating from college requires many skills. Try these problem-solving heuristics.
Means–end analysis	Problem solver determines what measures would reduce the difference between the given state and the end goal. Once the means to reach the goal are determined, the problem is solved.	Knowing you need a high GPA to get into a good graduate school for experimental psychology, you ask your professors for study suggestions, interview several A students to compare and contrast their study habits, assess your own study habits, and then determine the specific means (the number of hours and specific study techniques) required to meet your end goal of high GPA.	
Creating subgoals	Large, complex problems are broken down into a series of small subgoals. These subgoals then serve as a series of stepping-stones, which can be taken one at a time to reach the end goal.	Getting a good grade in many college courses requires specific subgoals like writing a successful term paper. To do this, you first choose a topic, go to the library and Internet to locate information related to the topic. Once you have the information, you organize it, create an outline, write the paper, review the paper, rewrite, rewrite again, and then submit the final paper on or before the due date.	

TRY THIS YOURSELF

Problem Solving Heuristics

In this classic thinking problem (Bartlett, 1958), your task is to determine the numerals 0 through 9 that are represented by letters, with each letter representing a separate, distinct number. Here's a hint to get you started: $D = 5$.

```
  D O N A L D
+ G E R A L D
-----------
  R O B E R T
```

Given there are 362,880 possible combinations of letters and numbers, *algorithms* obviously won't work. At the rate of 1 combination per minute, 8 hours per day, 5 days a week, 52 weeks a year, it would take nearly 3 years to try all the possible combinations.

Here's a second hint using the *creating subgoals* heuristic in Table 8.1. Start by determining what number T represents (if $D = 5$, then $D + D = 10$, so $T = 0$, with a carryover of 1 into the tens column).

Solution is found in the next Check & Review.

Barriers to Problem Solving
Objective 8.5: Identify five common barriers to problem solving.

Everyone frequently encounters barriers that prevent effective problem solving. The most common barriers are:

Mental Set Persisting in using problem-solving strategies that have worked in the past rather than trying new ones

1. ***Mental sets*** Like the police and transportation workers who were trying to pull or shove the truck that was stuck under the bridge, we often stick to problem-solving strategies (**mental sets**) that worked in the past, rather than trying new, possibly

more effective ones. The habit (or *mental set*) of working arithmetic problems from the right column to the left explains why most people fail to see the solution to the DONALD + GERALD problem. In the same way, looking for love only by going to singles' bars can be a barrier to finding a lasting love partner. To practice overcoming mental sets, try the nine-dot problem in Figure 8.4.

2. *Functional fixedness* The tendency to view objects as functioning only in the usual or customary way is known as **functional fixedness**. When a child uses sofa cushions to build a fort, or you use a table knife instead of a screwdriver to tighten a screw, you both have successfully avoided functional fixedness. Similarly, the individual who discovered a way to retrofit diesel engines to allow them to use discarded restaurant oil as fuel has overcome functional fixedness—and may become a very rich man! See Figure 8.5 for practice with functional fixedness.

3. *Confirmation bias* Do you pay greater attention to common sayings that support your personal biases (e.g., "opposites attract") and overlook contradictory findings (e.g., "similarity is the best predictor of long-term relationships")? As we first discovered in Chapter 4, this inclination to seek confirmation for our preexisting beliefs and to overlook contradictory evidence is known as the **confirmation bias** (Christandl, Fetchenhauer, & Hoelzl, 2011; Kerschreiter et al., 2008; Nickerson, 1998).

   British researcher Peter Wason (1968) first demonstrated the confirmation bias. He asked participants to generate a list of numbers that conformed to the same rule that applied to this set of numbers: 2   4   6

   Hypothesizing that the rule was "numbers increasing by two," most participants generated sets such as (4, 6, 8) or (1, 3, 5). Each time, Wason assured them that their sets of numbers conformed to the rule but that the rule "numbers increasing by two" was incorrect. The problem was that the participants were searching only for information that confirmed their hypothesis. Proposing a series such as (1, 3, 4) would have led them to reject their initial hypothesis and discover the correct rule: "numbers in increasing order of magnitude."

4. *Availability heuristic* Cognitive psychologists Amos Tversky and Daniel Kahneman found that heuristics, as handy as they can be, can lead us to ignore relevant information (De Neys & Vanderputte, 2011; Kahneman, 2003; Kliger & Kudryavtsev, 2010; Tversky & Kahneman, 1974, 1993). When we use the **availability heuristic**, we judge the likelihood of an event based on how easily recalled (available) other instances of the event are (Buontempo & Brockner, 2008; Caruso, 2008; Oppenheimer, 2004). Shortly after the September 11, 2001, terrorist attacks, one study found that the average American believed that he or she had a 20.5 percent chance of being hurt in a terrorist attack within a year (Lerner et al., 2003). Can you see how intense media coverage of the attacks created this erroneously high perception of risk?

5. *Representativeness heuristic* Tversky and Kahneman also demonstrated how the **representativeness heuristic** sometimes hinders problem solving. Using this heuristic, we estimate the probability of something based on how well the circumstances match (or *represent*) our *prototype* (Fisk, Burg, & Holden, 2006; Greene &

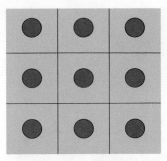

Figure 8.4 The nine-dot problem Without lifting your pencil, draw no more than four lines to connect all the dots. Then compare your response to the solution on p. 290.

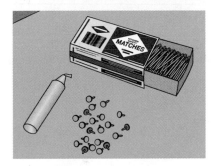

Figure 8.5 Overcoming functional fixedness Can you use these supplies to mount the candle on a wall so that it can be lit in a normal way—without toppling over? See the Check & Review, p. 290, for the solution.

StudyTip

Are mental sets blocking you from trying newer and more efficient study techniques, like those described in the "Tools for Student Success" at the end of Chapter 1? If so, remember that our brains are "plastic" and bad habits can be overcome with hard work and new experiences (see Chapters 2 and 6).

Functional Fixedness Tendency to think of an object functioning only in its usual or customary way

Confirmation Bias Preferring information that confirms preexisting positions or beliefs, while ignoring or discounting contradictory evidence

Availability Heuristic Judging the likelihood or probability of an event based on how readily available other instances of the event are in memory

Representativeness Heuristic Estimating the probability of something based on how well the circumstances match (or represent) our previous prototype

Ellis, 2008; Read & Grushka-Cockayne, 2011). (Remember: A prototype is a most common or representative example.) For instance, if John is 6 feet, 5 inches tall, we may erroneously conclude that he is an NBA basketball player rather than, say, a bank president. But in this case, the representative heuristic ignores *base-rate information*—the probability of a characteristic occurring in the general population. In the United States, bank presidents outnumber NBA players by about 50 to 1. So despite his height, John is statistically much more likely to be a bank president.

As you can see, this heuristic can lead to cognitive errors, but it also has more common practical applications (Figure 8.6).

Figure 8.6 Psychology at work—Fast food and representative heuristics McDonald's, Dunkin' Donuts, and other fast-food franchise restaurants have found that using the same ingredients and methods at every location helps increase their sales. But do they know why? It's primarily because this repetition creates a representative heuristic for their specific restaurant. For example, after a few experiences with different McDonald's in various locations, you create a prototype that guides your expectations about how long it will take to get your food and what it will taste like. When traveling and looking for a quick "bite to eat," your "McDonald's representative heuristic" makes it easier for you to choose their restaurant over the competition.

CHECK & REVIEW

STOP *Before going on, be sure to complete this Check & Review. It is an invaluable study tool!*

Cognitive Building Blocks and Problem Solving

Part A: Retrieval Practice

1. Without looking at the book, spend 10 minutes writing a free-form essay recalling all you can remember from the previous section.

2. Now, reread the previous section, and once again spend 10 minutes writing a free-form essay on the SAME material.

   (This activity is admittedly time consuming but it has been shown to be the single best way to improve your test scores: http://www.sciencemag.org/content/early/2011/01/19/science.1199327.abstract)

Part B: Practice Quiz

1. Compare and contrast mental images and concepts.

2. All of the following are examples of concepts except _____. (a) trees; (b) tools; (c) blue; (d) umbrellas

3. How do we learn concepts?

4. When asked to describe the shape and color of an apple, you probably rely on a _____.

5. For most psychologists, consciousness is a(n) _____ concept, whereas for the layperson it is a(n) _____ concept. (a) automatic, health; (b) artificial, natural;

(c) mental image, natural; (d) superordinate, basic-level

6. List and describe the three stages of problem solving.

7. Rosa is shopping in a new supermarket and wants to find a specific type of mustard. Which problem-solving strategy would be most efficient? (a) algorithm; (b) heuristic; (c) instinct; (d) mental set

8. Which of the three stages of problem solving is demonstrated in the figure below.

Problem = Finding a New Apartment

Solution to the DONALD + GERALD = ROBERT problem:

```
  5 2 6 4 8 5
+ 1 9 7 4 8 5
  7 2 3 9 7 0
```

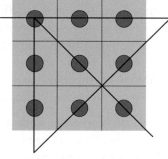

Solution to the nine-dot problem. Most people find this puzzle difficult because they see the arrangement of dots as a square, and "naturally" assume they can't go out of the boundaries of the square. Can you see how this mental set limits their ability to solve the problem?

Solution to the candle problem. Use the tacks to mount the matchbox tray to the wall. Light the candle and use some melted wax to mount the candle to the matchbox.

Check your answers in Appendix B.

Table 8.2 THREE ELEMENTS OF CREATIVE THINKING

	Explanations	Thomas Edison Examples
Originality	Seeing unique or different solutions to a problem	After noting that electricity passing through a conductor produces a glowing red or white heat, Edison imagined using this light for practical uses.
Fluency	Generating a large number of possible solutions	Edison tried literally hundreds of different materials to find one that would heat to the point of glowing white heat without burning up.
Flexibility	Shifting with ease from one type of problem-solving strategy to another	When he couldn't find a long-lasting material Edison tried heating it in a vacuum—thereby creating the first lightbulb.

Creativity: Finding Unique Solutions

Objective 8.6: What is creativity, and what are its three major characteristics?

Are you a creative person? Like many students, you may think of painters, dancers, and composers as creative and fail to recognize examples of your own creativity. Definitions of *creativity* vary among psychologists and among cultures. But it is generally agreed that **creativity** is the *ability to produce valued outcomes in a novel way*. In general, creativity possesses three characteristics: *originality*, *fluency*, and *flexibility*. As you can see in Table 8.2, Thomas Edison's invention of the lightbulb offers a prime example of each of these characteristics.

Creativity Ability to produce valued outcomes in a novel way

Measuring Creativity

Objective 8.7: How do we measure creativity?

Most tests of creativity focus on **divergent thinking**, a type of thinking in which many possibilities are developed from a single starting point.

In the divergent thinking *Unusual Uses Test*, you would be asked to think of as many uses as possible for an object (such as "How many ways can you use a brick?"). In the *Anagrams Test*, you would need to reorder the letters in a word to make as many new words as possible. Try rearranging the letters in these words to make new words. Then decide what they share in common. (Answers appear in the "Check & Review" on p. 292.)

Divergent Thinking Thinking that produces many alternatives from a single starting point; a major element of creativity (e.g., finding as many uses as possible for a paper clip)

1. grevenidt _____
2. neleecitlgni _____
3. ytliibxilef _____
4. ptoyropet_____
5. yvitcearti_____

 TRY THIS YOURSELF

Everyday Creativity

(a)   (b)

(a) Noticing the filmsy handles that used to be on paper cups, and how people commonly grabbed paper napkins as a wrapper to protect their hand from the hot liquid inside, one creative individual came up with a clever solution (b), and became a rich man.

To test your own creativity:
- Arrange ten coins in the configuration shown here. By moving only two coins, form two rows that each contain 6 coins (see page 000 for the solution).
- See how many words you can make using the letters in the word *hippopotamus*.
- List all the things you can do with a paper clip.

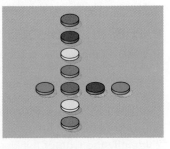

Table 8.3 RESOURCES OF CREATIVE PEOPLE

Intellectual Ability	Knowledge	Thinking Style	Personality	Motivation	Environment
Enough intelligence to see problems in a new light	Sufficient basic knowledge of the problem to effectively evaluate possible solutions	Novel ideas and ability to distinguish between the worthy and worthless	Willingness to grow and change, take risks, and work to overcome obstacles	Sufficient motivation to accomplish the task and more internal than external motivation	An environment that supports creativity

▲ Which resources best explain Lady Gaga's phenomenal success?

Convergent Thinking Narrowing down alternatives to converge on a single correct answer (e.g., standard academic tests generally require convergent thinking)

The opposite of divergent thinking is **convergent thinking**, or *conventional thinking*. In this case, lines of thinking *converge* (come together) on one correct answer. You used convergent thinking in the DONALD + GERALD problem p. 288 to find the one correct number represented by each letter.

Researching Creativity

Objective 8.8: How do creative people differ from others?

Some researchers view creativity as a special talent or ability and look for common personality traits among people they define as creative. Other researchers believe creative and noncreative people differ in how they encode information, how they store it, and what information they generate to solve problems (Abraham & Windman, 2007; Bink & Marsh, 2000; Fink et al., 2010; Shamay-Tsoory et al., 2011; Thagard & Stewart, 2011).

For example, according to Sternberg and Lubart's *investment theory* (1992, 1996), creative people are willing to "buy low and sell high" in the realm of ideas, championing ideas that others dismiss. Once their creative ideas are supported and highly valued, they "sell high" and move on to another unpopular but promising idea.

Investment theory further suggests that creativity requires the coming together of six interrelated resources (Kaufman, 2002; Mieg, 2011; Sternberg, 2010; Sternberg & Lubart, 1996). These resources are summarized in Table 8.3. One way to improve your personal creativity may be to study this list and then strengthen yourself in those areas that you see need improvement.

CHECK & REVIEW

STOP *Before going on, be sure to complete this Check & Review. It is an invaluable study tool!*

Creativity

Part A: Retrieval Practice

1. Without looking at the book, spend 10 minutes writing a free-form essay recalling all you can remember from the previous section.

2. Now, reread the previous section, and once again spend 10 minutes writing a free-form essay on the SAME material.

Part B: Practice Quiz

1. Which of the following items would most likely appear on a test measuring creativity? (a) How long is the Ohio River? (b) What are the primary colors? (c) List all the uses of a pot. (d) Who was the first governor of New York?

2. Identify the type of thinking for each of these examples.

a. You create numerous excuses ("reasons") for not studying.
b. On a test, you must select one correct answer for each question.
c. You make a list of ways to save money.

3. List the six resources of creative people.

4. Considering the six resources of creative people (Table 8.3), which resource(s) do you possess? How could you develop the resource(s) you lack?

Solutions to the Anagrams Test

1. divergent
2. intelligence
3. flexibility
4. prototype
5. creativity

Note that the answers are also key terms found in this chapter

Coin Problem Solution

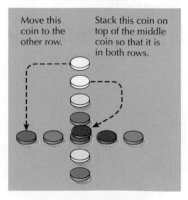

Move this coin to the other row.

Stack this coin on top of the middle coin so that it is in both rows.

Check your answers in Appendix B.

Language

Characteristics of Language: Structure and Production

Objective 8.9: What is language, and what are its basic building blocks?

Have you heard about Koko, the gorilla who reportedly uses more than 1,000 words in American Sign Language (ASL)? According to her teacher, Penny Patterson, Koko has used ASL to converse with others, talk to herself, rhyme, joke, and even lie (Kaufman et al., 2010; Linden, 1993; Patterson, 2002). Koko also uses signs to communicate her personal preferences, including a strong attraction to cats. Do you think Koko is using true language? Do beavers slapping their tails, birds singing their songs, and ants laying their trails use language? As noted earlier, scientists develop precise definitions and restrictions for certain *artificial concepts*, like **language.** Therefore, psychologists, linguists, and other scientists define it as a form of communication using sounds and symbols combined according to specified rules.

Language Form of communication using sounds and symbols combined according to specified rules

Building Blocks of Language

Language enables us to mentally manipulate symbols, thereby expanding our thinking. Whether it's spoken, written, or signed, language also allows us to communicate our thoughts, ideas, and feelings. To produce language, we first build words using *phonemes* and *morphemes*. Then we string words into sentences using rules of *grammar* (*syntax* and *semantics*) (Step-by-Step Diagram 8.1).

Language and Thought: A Complex Interaction

Objective 8.10: How is language related to thought?

Does the fact that you speak English instead of Spanish—or Chinese instead of Swahili—determine how you reason, think, and perceive the world? Linguist Benjamin Whorf (1956) believed so. As evidence for his *linguistic relativity hypothesis*, Whorf offered a now classic example: Because Inuits (previously known as Eskimos) have many words for snow (*apikak* for "first snow falling," *pukak* for "snow for drinking water"), they supposedly perceive and think about snow differently from English speakers, who have only one word—*snow*.

Though intriguing, Whorf's hypothesis has not fared well. He apparently exaggerated the number of Inuit words for snow (Pullum, 1991), and he ignored the fact that English speakers have a number of terms to describe various forms of snow, such as *slush*, *sleet*, *hard pack*, and *powder*. Other research has directly contradicted Whorf's theory. Eleanor Rosch (1973) found that although people of the Dani tribe in New Guinea possess only two color names—one indicating cool, dark colors, and the other describing warm, bright colors—they discriminate among multiple hues as well as English speakers do.

Whorf apparently was mistaken in his belief that language *determines* thought, but there is no doubt that it *influences* thinking (Deutscher, 2010; Jarvis 2011; Malt & Wolff, 2010; Walther et al., 2011). For example, people who speak both Chinese and English report that the language they're currently using affects their sense of self (Berry et al., 2011; Matsumoto, 2010). When using Chinese, they tend to conform to Chinese cultural norms; when speaking English, they tend to adopt Western norms.

Our words also influence the thinking of those who hear them. That's why companies avoid *firing* employees. Instead, employees are *laid off* or *nonrenewed*. Similarly, the military uses terms like *preemptive strike* to cover the fact that they attacked first and

Step-by-StepDiagram8.1

STOP This Step by Step diagram contains essential information NOT found elsewhere in the text, which is likely to appear on quizzes and exams. Be sure to study it CAREFULLY!

Building Blocks of Language

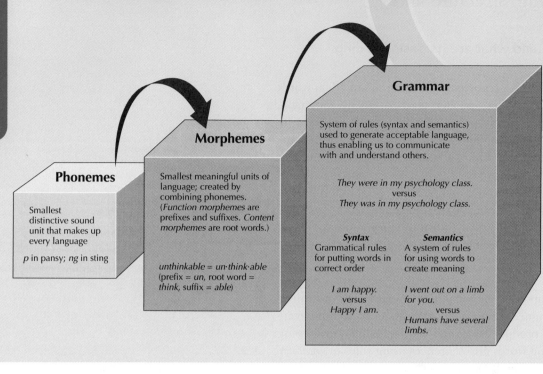

Phonemes

Smallest distinctive sound unit that makes up every language

p in pansy; *ng* in sting

Morphemes

Smallest meaningful units of language; created by combining phonemes. (*Function morphemes* are prefixes and suffixes. *Content morphemes* are root words.)

unthinkable = *un·think·able*
(prefix = *un*, root word = *think*, suffix = *able*)

Grammar

System of rules (syntax and semantics) used to generate acceptable language, thus enabling us to communicate with and understand others.

They were in my psychology class.
versus
They was in my psychology class.

Syntax
Grammatical rules for putting words in correct order

I am happy.
versus
Happy I am.

Semantics
A system of rules for using words to create meaning

I went out on a limb for you.
versus
Humans have several limbs.

"GOT IDEA. TALK BETTER. COMBINE WORDS. MAKE SENTENCES."

Phoneme [FOE-neem] Smallest basic unit of speech or sound

Morpheme [MOR-feem] Smallest meaningful unit of language, formed from a combination of phonemes

Grammar System of rules (syntax and semantics) used to create language and communication

Syntax Grammatical rules that specify how words and phrases should be arranged in a sentence to convey meaning

Semantics Set of rules for using words to create meaning; or the study of meaning

---

tactical redeployment to refer to a retreat. Interestingly, research has even shown that consumers who receive a "rebate" are less likely to spend the money than those who receive a "bonus" (Epley, 2008).

Word choice also has had embarrassing and financial consequences for North American businesses. When Pepsi-Cola used its "Come alive with Pepsi" slogan in Japan, they learned that it translated as "Pepsi brings your dead ancestors back from the grave." Similarly, Chevrolet Motor Company had great difficulty marketing its small Nova car in Mexico because *No va* means "doesn't go" in Spanish. Words evoke different images and value judgments. Our words, therefore, *influence* not only our own thinking but also the thinking of those who hear them.

Language Development: From Crying to Talking

Objective 8.11: Describe the two major stages in language development.

From birth, a child communicates through facial expressions, eye contact, and body gestures. Babies only hours old begin to "teach" their caregivers when and how they want to be held, fed, and played with. As early as the late 1800s, Charles Darwin proposed that most emotional expressions, such as smiles, frowns, and looks of disgust, are universal and innate (Figure 8.7). Darwin's contention is supported by the fact that children who are born blind and deaf exhibit the same facial expressions for emotions as sighted and hearing children.

Stages of Language Development

In addition to nonverbal communication, children also communicate verbally, progressing through several distinct stages of language acquisition (Step-by-Step Diagram 8.2). By age 5, most children have mastered basic grammar and typically use about 2,000 words (a level of mastery considered adequate for getting by in any given culture). Past this point, vocabulary and grammar gradually improve throughout life (Owens, 2011; Rowe & Levine, 2011).

Theories of Language Development
Objective 8.12: Contrast the "nativist" versus "nurturist" views of language development.

What motivates children to develop language? Some theorists believe that language capability is innate, being primarily a matter of maturation. Noam Chomsky (1968, 1980) suggests that children are "prewired" with a neurological ability known as a **language acquisition device (LAD)** that enables a child to analyze language and to extract the basic rules of grammar. This mechanism needs only minimal exposure to adult speech to unlock its potential. As evidence for this nativist position, Chomsky observes that children everywhere progress through the same stages of language development at about the same ages. He also notes that babbling is the same in all languages and that deaf babies babble just like hearing babies.

"Nurturists" argue that the nativist position doesn't fully explain individual differences in language development. They hold that children learn language through a complex system of rewards, punishments, and imitation. For example, parents smile and encourage any vocalizations from a very young infant. Later, they respond even more enthusiastically when the infant babbles "mama" or "dada." In this way, parents unknowingly use *reinforcement* and *shaping* (Chapter 6) to help babies learn language (Figure 8.8).

Language, the Brain, and Bilingualism

What happens in our brains when we produce and comprehend language? As you may recall from Chapter 2 (p. 72), for most of us our language centers are located in the left frontal lobe, with *Broca's area* linked to speech production and *Wernicke's area* being important for language comprehension (Concept Organizer 8.2). Keep in mind, however, that in our everyday conversations both areas are active at the same time, along with other parts of the brain.

As we've seen in the previous section of this chapter, language development occurs in a rather predictable sequence for almost all humans. But, there are individual differences, such as the rate at which language is acquired, the quality and size of vocabulary, and overall verbal skills. Chapters 2 and 11 also discuss ways that men and women may differ in their language abilities.

One important area we haven't discussed is the number of languages we acquire. A *bilingual speaker* is someone who speaks two languages, and some people are fluent in three or more. These lucky individuals enjoy several advantages. In addition to the obvious advantages in your career and travel, being bilingual also is linked to more creative problem-solving (Cushen & Wiley, 2011), more efficient task switching and cognitive flexibility (Prior & MacWhinney, 2011; Vega, 2010), and enhanced attention in early adulthood (Stafford, 2011). There's even evidence that bilingualism promotes greater "cognitive reserves," which significantly delays the onset of Alzheimer's disease (AD) (Chapter 7) (Craik, Bialystok, & Freedman, 2010).

Before going on, it's important to dispel some long-held myths about bilingualism. Over the years, people have wrongly touted several "harms" supposedly associated with

Figure 8.7 Can you identify this emotion? Infants as young as 2.5 months can nonverbally express emotions, such as joy, surprise, or anger.

Language Acquisition Device (LAD) According to Chomsky, an innate mechanism that enables a child to analyze language and extract the basic rules of grammar

Figure 8.8 Nature or nurture? Both sides of the nature-versus-nurture debate have staunch supporters. However, most psychologists believe that language acquisition is a combination of both biology (nature) and environment (nurture) (Hoff, 2009; Plomin, DeFries, & Fulker, 2007).

Step-by-StepDiagram8.2

STOP *This Step by Step diagram contains essential information NOT found elsewhere in the text, which is likely to appear on quizzes and exams. Be sure to study it CAREFULLY!*

Language Acquisition

Developmental Stage and Language Features	Examples
Prelinguistic stage Birth to 12 months	
Crying (reflexive in newborns) becomes more purposeful	hunger cry anger cry pain cry
Cooing (vowel-like sounds) (2–3 months)	"ooooh," "aaaah"
Babbling (consonants added) (4–6 months)	"bahbahbah," "dahdahdah"
Linguistic stage 12 months to 5 years	
Babbling resembles language of the environment, and child understands sounds relate to meaning	
Speech consists of one-word utterances	"Mama," "juice," "Daddy," "up"
Expressive ability more than doubles once child joins words into short phrases	"Daddy milk," "no night-night!"
Overextension (using words to include objects that do not fit the word's meaning)	all men = "Daddy" all furry animals = doggy
Telegraphic speech (like telegrams, omits nonessential connecting words)	"Me want cookie" "Grandma go bye-bye?"
Vocabulary increases at a phenomenal rate	
Child acquires wide variety of grammar rules	adding -ed for past tense adding s to form plurals
Overgeneralization (applying basic rules of grammar even to cases that are exceptions to the rule)	"I goed to the zoo" "Two mans"

Cooing Vowel-like sounds infants produce beginning around 2 to 3 months of age

Babbling Vowel/consonant combinations that infants begin to produce at about 4 to 6 months of age

Overextension Overly broad use of a word to include objects that do not fit the word's meaning (e.g., calling all men "Daddy")

Telegraphic Speech Two- or three-word sentences of young children that contain only the most necessary words

Overgeneralization Applying the basic rules of grammar even to cases that are exceptions to the rule (e.g., saying "mans" instead of "men")

Baby signs Have you heard that babies and toddlers—beginning as young as 9 months of age—can learn to communicate by using a modified form of sign language, sometimes called "Baby Sign"? Advocates suggest that teaching symbolic gestures for basic ideas, such as "more," "milk," or "love," enhances parents' and caregivers' interactions with children who cannot yet talk. They report that signing with infants or toddlers gives them a fascinating "window" into the baby's mind—and eliminates a lot of frustration for both signer and baby! Some researchers also believe that teaching babies to sign helps foster better language comprehension and can speed up the process of language acquisition.

StudyTip

Are you having difficulty differentiating between overextension and overgeneralization? Remember the g in overgeneralize as a cue that this term applies to problems with grammar.

ConceptOrganizer8.2

Language and the Brain

The (a) and (b) scans below illustrate the major areas of the brain active during language expression and comprehension. Interestingly, the amygdala (shown in the diagram on the right) also is active when we engage in a special type of language—cursing or swearing. Why? Recall from Chapter 2, that the amygdala is linked to emotions, especially fear and rage. So it's logical that the brain regions activated by swearing or hearing swear words would be the same as those for fear and aggression.

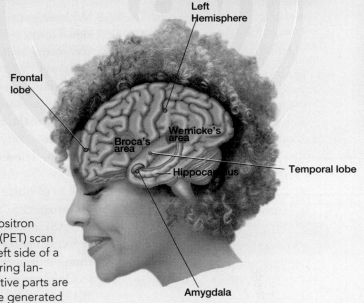

Labels: Left Hemisphere, Frontal lobe, Broca's area, Wernicke's area, Temporal lobe, Hippocampus, Amygdala

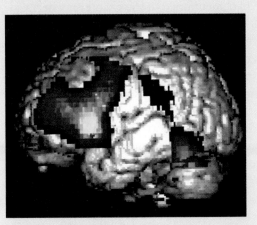

(a) This is a colored positron emission tomography (PET) scan showing areas of the left side of a human brain active during language generation. (Active parts are red/orange.) Language generated in the frontal lobe (center left) has its cognition checked in the temporal lobe (lower right). Brain activity was detected by injecting the radioactive isotope oxygen-15 into the bloodstream to allow areas of the brain with high metabolic activity to be seen.

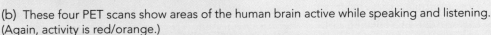

(b) These four PET scans show areas of the human brain active while speaking and listening. (Again, activity is red/orange.)
- *Top left*, the person is monitoring imagined speech. Note how areas in the temporal lobe light up.
- *Top right*, working out the meaning of heard words activates other areas of the temporal lobe.
- *Lower left*, note how repeating words increases activity in the region responsible for speech generation (Broca's area, center left), the region for language comprehension (Wernicke's area, center right), as well as a motor region responsible for pronouncing words (reddish area above Broca's and Wernicke's).
- *Lower right*, note the relatively large areas activated when a person is listening and monitoring speech.

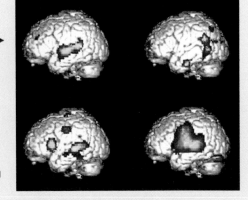

speaking more than one language, including "cerebral confusion" and "split personality." Some children have even been beaten or had their mouths washed out with soap and water for speaking in their native languages (Chipongian, 2000). Although early studies did find some disadvantages to bilingualism, the research was so flawed that it has been widely dismissed, and modern research continues to find significant advantages.

What's the important take home message? Push yourself to study and become fluent in as many languages as possible, and if you're a parent be sure to introduce other languages as soon as possible. There is strong agreement in the scientific community that it's much easier to acquire multiple languages in early childhood. If you wait until adulthood, you'll generally speak other languages with the accent of your first.

Animals and Language: Can Humans Talk to Nonhuman Animals?

Objective 8.13: Describe the language research conducted with nonhuman animals.

Without question, nonhuman animals communicate. They commonly send warnings, signal sexual interest, share locations of food sources, and so on. But can they master the complexity of human language? Since the 1930s, many language studies have attempted to answer this question by probing the language abilities of chimpanzees, gorillas, and other animals (e.g., Barner et al., 2008; Berwick et al., 2011; Call, 2011; Lyn, Greenfield, & Savage-Rumbaugh, 2011).

One of the most successful early studies was conducted by Beatrice and Allen Gardner (1969), who recognized chimpanzees' manual dexterity and ability to imitate gestures. The Gardners used American Sign Language (ASL) with a chimp named Washoe. By the time Washoe was 4 years old, she had learned 132 signs and was able to combine them into simple sentences such as "Hurry, gimme toothbrush" and "Please tickle more." The famous gorilla Koko, mentioned in the chapter opener, also uses ASL to communicate. In another well-known study, a chimp named Lana learned to use symbols on a computer to get things she wanted, such as food, a drink, a tickle from her trainers, and having her curtains opened (Rumbaugh et al., 1974).

Dolphins are also the subject of interesting language research (e.g., May-Collado, 2010). Communication with dolphins is done by means of hand signals or audible commands transmitted through an underwater speaker system (Figure 8.9). In one typical study, trainers gave dolphins commands made up of two- to five-word sentences, such as "Big ball—square—return," which meant that they should go get the big ball, put it in the floating square, and return to the trainer (Herman, Richards, & Woltz, 1984). By varying the syntax (for example, the order of the words) and specific content of the commands, the researchers showed that dolphins are sensitive to these aspects of language.

Evaluating Animal Language Studies

Psychologists disagree about how to interpret these findings on apes and dolphins. Most psychologists believe that nonhuman animals communicate but that their ideas are severely limited. Critics

Figure 8.9 Communicating through art? Dolphins have learned to respond to complicated hand signals and vocal commands from their trainers. They've even learned to "express themselves" throught art. But is this simple communication, operant conditioning, or true language?

claim that apes and dolphins are unable to convey subtle meanings, use language creatively, or communicate at an abstract level (Jackendoff, 2003; Siegala & Varley, 2008).

Other critics claim that these animals do not truly understand language but are simply operantly conditioned (Chapter 6) to imitate symbols to receive rewards. Finally, other critics suggest that data regarding animal language has not always been scientifically well documented (Font & Carazo, 2010; Lieberman, 1998; Willingham, 2001; Wynne, 2007).

Proponents of animal language respond that apes can use language creatively and have even coined some words of their own. For example, Koko reportedly signed "finger bracelet" to describe a ring and "eye hat" to describe a mask (Patterson & Linden, 1981).

"ALTHOUGH HUMANS MAKE SOUNDS WITH THEIR MOUTHS AND OCCASIONALLY LOOK AT EACH OTHER, THERE IS NO SOLID EVIDENCE THAT THEY ACTUALLY COMMUNICATE WITH EACH OTHER."

Proponents also argue that, as demonstrated by the dolphin studies, animals can be taught to understand basic rules of sentence structure.

Still, the gap between human and nonhuman animals' language is considerable. Current evidence suggests that, at best, nonhuman animal language is less complex, less creative, and has fewer rules than any language used by humans. (As a critical thinker, have you ever thought about an opposite approach to this type of language research? Why don't humans learn nonhuman animal language? Could humans be taught to comprehend and use chimpanzee, whale, or elephant communication systems, for example?)

CHECK & REVIEW

STOP *Before going on, be sure to complete this Check & Review. It is an invaluable study tool!*

Language

Part A: Retrieval Practice

1. Without looking at the book, spend 10 minutes writing a free-form essay recalling all you can remember from the previous section.

2. Now, reread the previous section, and once again spend 10 minutes writing a free-form essay on the SAME material.

Part B: Practice Quiz

1. Label the three building blocks of language on the following figure:

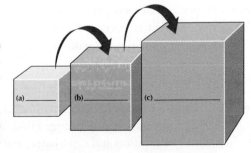

2. The basic speech sounds /ch/ and /v/ are known as _____. The smallest meaningful units of language, such as *book, pre-,* and *-ing,* are known as _____.

3. A child says "I hurt my foots." This is an example of _____.

4. Chomsky believes we possess an inborn ability to learn language known as a _____. (a) telegraphic understanding device (TUD); (b) language acquisition device (LAD); (c) language and grammar translator (LGT); (d) overgeneralized neural net (ONN)

5. Human language differs from the communication of nonhuman animals in that it is _____. (a) used more creatively to express thoughts and ideas; (b) the expression of an innate capability; (c) essential for thought; (d) composed of sounds

Check your answers in Appendix B.

StudyTip

Intelligence is not a *thing*. It has no mass. It occupies no space. There are no specific sites within the brain where intelligence resides. When people talk about intelligence as though it were a concrete, tangible object, they commit an error in reasoning, known as reification. Like the concepts of consciousness and memory, intelligence is a hypothetical, abstract construct.

Intelligence Global capacity to think rationally, act purposefully, and deal effectively with the environment

Fluid Intelligence Aspects of innate intelligence, including reasoning abilities, memory, and speed of information processing, that are relatively independent of education and tend to decline as people age

Crystallized Intelligence Knowledge and skills gained through experience and education that tend to increase over the life span

Intelligence

Are Koko, Genie, and Thomas Edison intelligent? What exactly is intelligence? Many people equate intelligence with "book smarts," which explains the common jokes and stereotypes about "absentminded professors" and geniuses with no common or practical sense. For others, what is intelligent depends on the characteristics and skills valued in a particular social group or culture (Berry et al., 2011; Hunt, 2011; Sternberg, Jarvin, & Grigorenko, 2011). For example, did you know that many languages have no word that corresponds to our Western notion of intelligence? The closest Mandarin word is a Chinese character meaning "good brain and talented." Interestingly, this Chinese word is commonly associated with traits like imitation, effort, and social responsibility.

What Is Intelligence? Do We Have One or Many Intelligences?

Objective 8.14: What is intelligence, and is it one or many abilities?

Even among Western psychologists there is debate over the definition of *intelligence*. In this discussion, we rely on a formal definition developed by psychologist David Wechsler (WEX-ler) (1944, 1977). Wechsler defined **intelligence** as *the global capacity to think rationally, act purposefully, and deal effectively with the environment*. In other words, intelligence is your ability to effectively use your thinking processes to cope with the world. An advantage of this definition is that it incorporates most modern viewpoints as well as most cultural and social influences.

For many Western psychologists, one of the prime areas of research and debate is whether intelligence is a single ability or a collection of many specific abilities.

In the 1920s, British psychologist Charles Spearman first observed that high scores on separate tests of mental abilities tend to correlate with each other. Spearman (1923) thus proposed that intelligence is a single factor, which he termed *general intelligence* (*g*). He believed that *g* underlies all intellectual behavior, including reasoning, solving problems, and performing well in all areas of cognition. Spearman's work laid the foundations for today's standardized intelligence tests (Goldstein, 2010; Johnson et al., 2004).

About a decade later, L. L. Thurstone (1938) proposed seven primary mental abilities: verbal comprehension, word fluency, numerical fluency, spatial visualization, associative memory, perceptual speed, and reasoning. J. P. Guilford (1967) later expanded this number, proposing that as many as 120 factors were involved in the structure of intelligence.

Around the same time, Raymond Cattell (1963, 1971) reanalyzed Thurstone's data and argued against the idea of multiple intelligences. He believed that two subtypes of *g* exist:

- **Fluid intelligence (*gf*)** refers to innate, inherited reasoning abilities, memory, and speed of information processing. Fluid intelligence is supposedly relatively independent of education and experience, and like other biological capacities it declines with age (Jost et al., 2011; Murray et al., 2011; Rozencwajg et al., 2005). However, other research has shown that physical exercise and cognitively stimulating activity in older adults can increase fluid intelligence (Archer, 2011; Hertzog & Jopp, 2010; Tranter & Koutstaal, 2008).

- **Crystallized intelligence (*gc*)** refers to the store of knowledge and skills gained through experience and education (Hunt, 2011; Sternberg & Kaufman, 2012). Crystallized intelligence tends to increase over the life span.

Today the concept of *g* as a measure of "academic smarts" has considerable support. However, many contemporary cognitive theorists believe that intelligence is not a single general factor but a collection of many separate specific abilities.

Modern Theories–Gardner vs. Sternberg

Objective 8.15: Contrast Gardner's and Sternberg's theories of intelligence.

According to Howard Gardner's (1983, 1999, 2008, 2011) *theory of multiple intelligences*, people have different profiles of intelligence because they are stronger in some areas than in others (Figure 8.10). They also use their intelligences differently to learn new material, perform tasks, and solve problems.

Robert Sternberg's *triarchic theory of successful intelligence* also involves multiple abilities. As shown in Table 8.4, Sternberg proposed three separate, learned aspects of intelligence: (1) *analytic*, (2) *creative*, and (3) *practical* (Sternberg, 1985, 2007, 2008, 2009, 2012). He emphasizes the process underlying thinking rather than just the product, along with the importance of measuring mental abilities in real-world situations rather than testing mental abilities in isolation. He also introduced the term *successful intelligence* to describe the ability to adapt to, shape, and select environments in order to accomplish personal and societal goals.

As you can see, psychologists have struggled for years with competing definitions and differing components of intelligence, and a similar struggle continues within the field of intelligence assessment–the topic of our next section. It's important to note that these struggles have culminated in the most comprehensive and best supported modern theory of intelligence, the *Cattell-Horn-Carroll (CHC) theory*. This CHC theory combines Cattell's *fluid intelligence (gf)* and *crystallized intelligence (gc)*, along with eight other intelligences, into 10 broad categories that are further subdivided into 70 narrower cognitive and academic abilities (Cattell, 1941; Carroll, 1993; Gregory, 2011; Horn, 1965; Keith & Reynolds, 2010).

Although this admittedly complex theory is highly valued by researchers and psychometrists (psychologists who measure intelligence), it offers less value to your everyday life. Therefore, at this time it's best to focus on Gardner's and Sternberg's theories of multiple intelligences, which offer more direct and practical applications (e.g., your career search, p. 302).

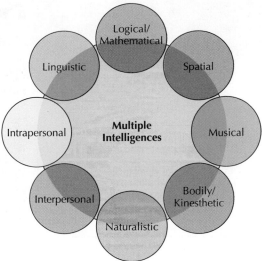

Figure 8.10 Gardner's theory of multiple intelligences Howard Gardner believes that there are numerous forms of intelligence and that the value of these intelligences may change according to culture. He also proposed a possible ninth intelligence, spiritual/existential, shown in Table 8.5.

Table 8.4 STERNBERG'S TRIARCHIC THEORY OF SUCCESSFUL INTELLIGENCE

	Analytical Intelligence	**Creative Intelligence**	**Practical Intelligence**
Sample Skills	Good at analysis, evaluation, judgement, and comparison skills	Good at invention, coping with novelty, and imagination skills	Good at application, implementation, execution, and utilization skills
Sample Methods of Assessment	Intelligence tests assess the meaning of words based on context, and how to solve number-series problems	Open-ended tasks, writing a short story, drawing a piece of art, solving a scientific problem requiring insight	Solutions to practical, personal problems

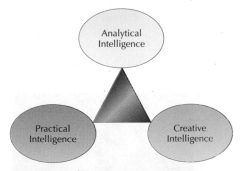

Sternberg's triarchic (three-part) theory of successful intelligence Robert Sternberg suggests there are three separate and different aspects of intelligence and each of these components is learned, not the result of genetics. Therefore, each can be strengthened or improved.

Psychology at Work

Multiple Intelligences and Your Career

Have you heard from others that you're naturally good at something like writing, math, or spatial skills? Gardner's research shows that most people possess one or more natural intelligences important to success in various occupations. Carefully consider each of the multiple intelligences in Table 8.5 and how they might help guide you toward a satisfying career.

How Do We Measure Intelligence? IQ Tests and Scientific Standards

Objective 8.16: Describe how psychologists measure intelligence.

As you've just seen, intelligence is difficult to define. And the scientific community remains divided over whether it is one or multiple abilities. Despite this uncertainty, most college admissions officers and scholarship committees, as well as many employers, commonly use scores from intelligence tests as a significant part of their selection criteria. How well do these tests predict student and employee success? Different IQ tests approach the measurement of intelligence from different perspectives. However, most are designed to predict grades in school. Let's look at the most commonly used IQ tests.

Table 8.5 GARDNER'S MULTIPLE INTELLIGENCES AND POSSIBLE CAREERS

Linguistic: language, such as speaking, reading a book, writing a story	Spatial: mental maps, such as mentally rear-ranging furniture or drawing blueprints	Bodily/ Kinesthetic: body move-ment, such as dancing or skate boarding	Intrapersonal: understand-ing oneself, such as setting achievable goals	Logical/ Mathematical: problem solv-ing or scien-tific analysis, such as solving budget or research problems	Musical: musical skills, such as singing or playing a musical instrument	Interpersonal: social skills, such as man-aging diverse groups of people	Naturalistic: being attuned to nature, such as noting seasonal changes or environmen-tal problems	(Possible) Spiritual/ Existential: attunement to meaning of life and death and other condi-tions of life
Careers: novelist, journalist, teacher	Careers: engineer, architect, pilot	Careers: athlete, dancer, ski instructor	Careers: increased suc-cess in almost all careers	Careers: mathemati-cian, scientist, engineer	Careers: singer, musician, composer	Careers: salesperson manager, therapist, teacher	Careers: biologist, naturalist	Careers: philosopher, theologian

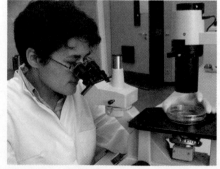

Source: Adapted from Gardner, 1983, 1999, 2008, 2011.

Stanford-Binet

The *Stanford-Binet Intelligence Scale* is loosely based on the first IQ tests developed in France around the turn of the last century by Alfred Binet [bih-NAY]. In the United States, Lewis Terman (1916) developed the Stanford-Binet (at Stanford University) to test the intellectual ability of U.S.-born children ages 3 to 16. The test is revised periodically, and the current test measures individuals from the age of 2 through adulthood. It includes both verbal and nonverbal tasks, such as copying geometric designs, identifying similarities, and repeating number sequences.

In the original version of the Stanford-Binet, results were expressed in terms of a mental age. For example, if a 7-year-old's score equaled that of an average 8-year-old, the child was considered to have a mental age of 8. To determine the child's *intelligence quotient* (*IQ*), mental age was divided by the child's chronological age (actual age in years) and multiplied by 100 ($IQ = MA/CA \times 100$). Using this example, of the 7-year-old's score, the formula would look like this:

$$IQ = \frac{MA}{CA} \times 100 = \frac{8}{7} \times 100 = 1.14 \times 100 = 114$$

Thus, a 7-year-old with a mental age of 8 would have an IQ of 114. A "normal" child would have a mental age equal to his or her chronological age. (*Normal* in this case refers to the norms or statistics used to standardize the test.)

Today, most intelligence tests, including the Stanford-Binet, no longer compute an IQ. Instead, the test scores are expressed as a comparison of a single person's score to a national sample of similar-aged people. These deviation IQs are based on how far the person's score on the test deviates from the national average (Figure 8.11). Note how this figure also shows how the distribution of IQ scores follows a bell-shaped curve. The majority of individuals (68 percent) who take the test score within the normal range—85 to 115. Even though the actual IQ is no longer calculated, the term *IQ* remains as a shorthand expression for intelligence test scores.

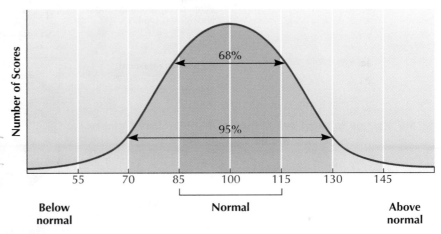

Figure 8.11 The distribution of scores on the Stanford-Binet intelligence test Sixty-eight percent of children score within one standard deviation (16 points) above or below the national average, which is 100 points. About 16 percent score above 116, and about 16 percent score below 84.

Wechsler Tests

David Wechsler developed the most widely used intelligence test, the *Wechsler Adult Intelligence Scale* (WAIS), now in a fourth edition (WAIS IV). He also created a similar test for school-age children, the *Wechsler Intelligence Scale for Children* (WISC-IV; Table 8.6), and one for preschool children, the *Wechsler Preschool and Primary Scale of Intelligence* (WPPSI), now revised as WPPSI-III.

Like the Stanford-Binet, the Wechsler tests yield a final intelligence score. But they have separate *verbal* (vocabulary, comprehension, knowledge of general information) and *performance* scores (arranging pictures to tell a story, arranging blocks to match a given pattern). Wechsler's approach has three advantages: (1) The WAIS, WISC, and WPPSI were specifically designed for different age groups. (2) Different abilities can be evaluated either separately or together. (3) People who are unable to speak or understand English can still be tested. The verbal portion of the test doesn't have to be administered because each subtest yields its own score.

Table 8.6 SUBTESTS OF THE WISC-IV

	Example*
Verbal Subtests	
Information	How many senators are elected from each state?
Similarities	How are computers and books alike?
Arithmetic	If one baseball card costs three cents, how much will five baseball cards cost?
Vocabulary	Define *lamp*.
Comprehension	What should you do if you accidentally break a friend's toy?

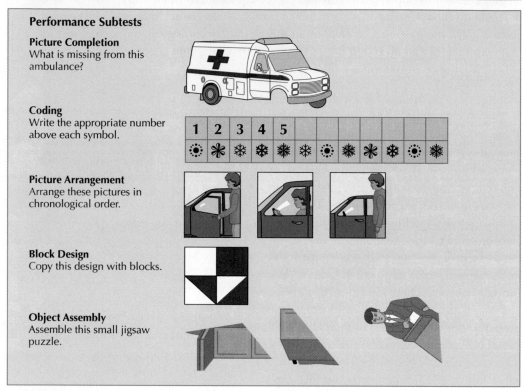

Performance Subtests

Picture Completion
What is missing from this ambulance?

Coding
Write the appropriate number above each symbol.

Picture Arrangement
Arrange these pictures in chronological order.

Block Design
Copy this design with blocks.

Object Assembly
Assemble this small jigsaw puzzle.

*These examples are similar to but not the same as those used on the actual test.

Scientific Standards for Psychological Tests

Objective 8.17: What are the three key requirements for a scientifically useful test?

What makes a good test? How are the tests developed by Binet and Wechsler any better than those published in popular magazines and presented on television? To be scientifically acceptable, all psychological tests must fulfill three basic requirements:

- *Standardization* Intelligence tests (as well as personality, aptitude, and most other tests) must exhibit **standardization** in two senses (Gregory, Beins, 2010; Gregory, 2011). First, every test must have *norms*, or average scores, developed by giving the test to a representative sample of people (a diverse group of people who resemble those for whom the test is intended). Second, testing procedures must be uniform. All test takers must be given the same instructions, questions, and time limits, and all test administrators must follow the same objective score standards.

Standardization Establishment of the norms and uniform procedures for giving and scoring a test

- *Reliability* To be trustworthy, test scores must be consistent and reproducible. **Reliability** is usually determined by retesting subjects to see whether their test scores change significantly (Gregory, 2011). Retesting can be done via the *test-retest method*, in which participants' scores on two separate administrations of the same test are compared, or via the *split-half method*, which involves splitting a test into two equivalent parts (e.g., odd and even questions) and determining the degree of similarity between the two halves.

Reliability Measure of the consistency and reproducibility of test scores when the test is readministered

- *Validity* How do we know if a test is valid and actually measures what it was designed to measure? The most common measure of **validity** is *criterion-related validity*, or the accuracy with which test scores can be used to predict another variable of interest (known as the criterion). Criterion-related validity is expressed as the *correlation* (Chapter 1) between the test score and the criterion. If two variables are highly correlated, then one variable can be used to predict the other. Thus, if a test is valid, its scores will be useful in predicting people's behavior in some other specified situation. One example of this is using intelligence test scores to predict grades in college.

Validity Ability of a test to measure what it was designed to measure

Can you see why a test that is standardized and reliable—but not valid—is worthless? A test for skin sensitivity may be easy to standardize (the instructions specify exactly how to apply the test agent), and it may be reliable (similar results are obtained on each retest), but it certainly would not be valid for predicting college grades.

 CHECK & REVIEW  STOP *Before going on, be sure to complete this Check & Review. It is an invaluable study tool!*

Intelligence

Part A: Retrieval Practice

1. Without looking at the book, spend 10 minutes writing a free-form essay recalling all you can remember from the previous section.

2. Now, reread the previous section, and once again spend 10 minutes writing a free-form essay on the SAME material.

Part B: Practice Quiz

1. The *g* factor, originally proposed by Spearman, is best defined as _____.

2. What is the difference between fluid and crystallized intelligences?

3. _____ suggested that people differ in their "profiles of intelligence" and that each person shows a unique pattern of strengths and weaknesses. (a) Spearman; (b) Binet; (c) Wechsler; (d) Gardner

4. Explain Sternberg's triarchic theory of successful intelligence.

5. What is the major difference between the Stanford-Binet and the Wechsler Intelligence Scales?

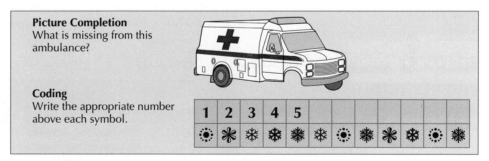

Picture Completion
What is missing from this ambulance?

Coding
Write the appropriate number above each symbol.

| 1 | 2 | 3 | 4 | 5 | | | | | | | |

6. If a 10-year-old's score on an original version of the Stanford-Binet test was the same as that of an average 9-year-old, the child would have an IQ of _____.

7. The IQ test sample in the figure above is from the _____, the most widely used intelligence test.

8. Identify which testing principle—standardization, reliability, or validity—is being described in each of the following statements:

   a. _____ ensures that if a person takes the same test two weeks after taking it the first time, his or her score will not significantly change.

   b. _____ ensures that a test or other measurement instrument actually measures what it purports to measure.

   c. _____ ensures that the test has been given to large numbers of people to determine which scores are average, above average, and below average—in short, which scores are representative of the general population.

Check your answers in Appendix B.

Intelligence Controversy

As noted earlier, intelligence is extremely difficult to define. Psychologists also differ on whether it is composed of a single factor (*g*) or multiple abilities. Therefore, how valid is it to develop tests that measure intelligence? Furthermore, is intelligence inherited, or is it a result of environment? Are IQ tests culturally biased against certain ethnic groups? Intelligence testing has long been the subject of intense interest and great debate. In this section, we explore the use of intelligence tests for measuring extremes in intelligence (mental retardation and giftedness). Then we examine three possible explanations for overall differences in intelligence (the brain, genetics, and the environment). We close with a look at *supposed* ethnic differences in intelligence.

Extremes in Intelligence: Intellectual Disability and Giftedness

If you want to judge the validity of any test (academic, intelligence, personality, etc.), one of the best methods is to compare people who score at the extremes. Students who get an A on a major exam should clearly know more than those who fail. As you will see, the validity of IQ tests is somewhat supported by the fact that individuals who score at the lowest level on standard IQ tests *do* have clear differences in intellectual abilities compared to those who score at the top. Intelligence tests provide one of the major criteria for diagnosing *intellectual disability* and *giftedness*.

Intellectual Disability

Objective 8.18: How do studies of extremes in intelligence help validate intelligence tests?

Savant Syndrome Condition in which a person with limited mental abilities exhibits exceptional skill or brilliance in some limited field

According to clinical standards, the clinical label *intellectually disabled* (previously referred to as *mentally retarded*) is applied when someone is significantly below average in general intellectual functioning (IQ less than 70) and has significant deficits in adaptive functioning (such as communicating with others, living independently, social or occupational functioning, and maintaining safety and health) (American Psychiatric Association, 2000).

As you can see in Table 8.7, fewer than 3 percent of people are classified as having an intellectual disability. Of this group, 85 percent have only mild disability and many become self-supporting, integrated members of society. Furthermore, people can score low on some measures of intelligence and still be average or even gifted in others. The most dramatic examples are people with **savant syndrome** (Figure 8.12).

Some forms of intellectual disability stem from genetic abnormalities, such as Down syndrome, fragile-X syndrome, and phenylketonuria (PKU). Other causes are environmental,

Table 8.7 DEGREES OF INTELLECTUAL DISABILITY

Level of Disability	IQ Scores	Characteristics
Mild (85%)	50–70	Usually able to become self-sufficient: may marry, have families, and secure full-time jobs in unskilled occupations
Moderate (10%)	35–49	Able to perform simple unskilled tasks; may contribute to a certain extent to their livelihood
Severe (3–4%)	20–34	Able to follow daily routines, but with continual supervision; with training, may learn basic communication skills
Profound (1–2%)	below 20	Able to perform only the most rudimentary behaviors, such as walking, feeding themselves, and saying a few phrases

including prenatal exposure to alcohol and other drugs, extreme deprivation or neglect in early life, and brain damage from accidents. However, in many cases, there is no known cause of the intellectual disability.

Mental Giftedness

At the other end of the intelligence spectrum, we have people who are "gifted" and have especially high IQs (typically defined as 135 and above or being in the top 1 or 2 percent). Have you ever wondered what happens to people with such superior intellectual abilities?

In 1921, Lewis Terman used teacher recommendations and IQ tests to identify 1,500 gifted children with IQs of 140 or higher. He then tracked their progress through adulthood. His study of these gifted children—affectionately nicknamed the "Termites"—destroyed many myths and stereotypes about gifted people. As children, these Termites not only received excellent grades but were also found to be socially well adjusted. In addition, they were taller and stronger than their peers of average IQ. By the age of 40, the number of individuals who became research scientists, engineers, physicians, lawyers, or college teachers, or who were highly successful in business and other fields, was many times the number a random group would have provided (Campbell & Feng, 2011; Leslie, 2000; Terman, 1954).

Although Terman's research found high intelligence to be correlated with higher academic and occupational success, as well as with better athletic ability, not every Termite was successful. There were some notable failures. The members who were the most successful tended to have extraordinary motivation and someone at home or school who was especially encouraging. However, some in this gifted group were like others their age of average intelligence. They became alcoholics, got divorced, and committed suicide at close to the national rate (Leslie, 2000). A high IQ is therefore no guarantee for success in every endeavor. It only offers more intellectual opportunities.

Figure 8.12 An unusual form of intelligence People with *savant syndrome* generally score very low on IQ tests (usually between 40 and 70), yet they demonstrate exceptional skills or brilliance in specific areas, such as rapid calculation, art, memory, or musical ability (Meyer, 2011; Olson, 2010; Pring et al., 2008). Seventeen-year-old Brittany Maier, pictured here, is an autistic *savant*, a highly knowledgeable person with autism. She also is a gifted composer and pianist who performs publicly and has recorded a CD. Her musical repertoire includes more than 15,000 songs.

Explaining Differences in IQ: Why Do We Differ?

Objective 8.19: Describe how research on the brain, genetics, and the environment helps explain differences in IQ.

Some people are mentally gifted, some are intellectually disabled, and most are somewhere in between. To explain these differences, we need to look at the brain, genetics, and the environment.

The Brain's Influence on Intelligence

A basic tenet of neuroscience is that all mental activity (including intelligence) results from neural activity in the brain. Three major questions have guided neuroscience research on intelligence:

1. **Does a bigger brain mean greater intelligence?** It makes logical sense. After all, humans have relatively large brains. And, as a species, we are more intelligent than dogs, which have smaller brains. Some nonhuman animals, such as whales and dolphins, do have larger brains than humans. But the brains of humans are larger in relation to the size of their bodies. Since the early 1800s, researchers have asked whether "bigger is better," and some modern studies using magnetic resonance imaging (MRI) have found a correlation between brain size (adjusted for body size) and intelligence (Christensen et al., 2008; Deary et al., 2007; Lee, 2007; Ivanovic et al., 2004; Stelmack, Knott, & Beauchamp, 2003).

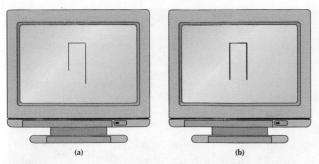

(a)   **(b)**

Figure 8.13 A test for intelligence? Which "leg" of the drawing in (a) is longer, the right or the left? Although the answer seems simple, researchers have found that when images like these are flashed for a few milliseconds on a computer screen, the amount of time people need to make correct judgments may reveal something about their intelligence. The second figure (b) is shown immediately after figure (a) to block, or "mask," the lingering afterimage.

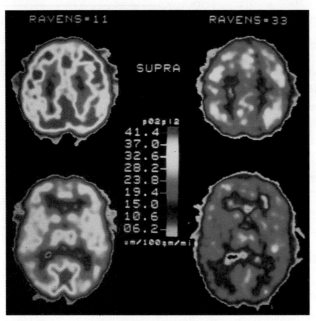

Figure 8.14 Do intelligent brains work harder? The PET scans in the left column are from a person with a tested low IQ. The scans on the right are from someone with a high IQ. Note that when solving problems, the brain on the left is more active. (Red and yellow indicate more brain activity.) Contrary to popular opinion, this research suggests that lower-IQ brains actually work harder, but less efficiently, than higher IQ brains.

On the other hand, other studies have failed to fully support this possible correlation between brain size and mental functioning (Gignac & Vernon, 2003; Wickett, Vernon, & Lee, 2000). Furthermore, anatomical studies of Einstein's brain found that it was not heavier or larger than normal (Witelson, Kigar, & Harvey, 1999). Some areas were, in fact, smaller than average. However, the area of the brain responsible for processing mathematical and spatial information (the lower region of the parietal lobe) was 15 percent larger. Also, we cannot know if Einstein was born with this difference, or if his brain changed due to his intellectual pursuits. Rather than focusing on brain size, therefore, most of the recent research on the biology of intelligence has focused on brain functioning.

2. **Is a faster brain more intelligent?** The public seems to think so, and neuroscientists have found that a faster response time is indeed related to higher intelligence (e.g., Sheppard & Vernon, 2008, Sternberg, Jarvin, & Grigorenko, 2011). A standard experiment flashes simple images like the one in Figure 8.13, and participants must inspect them quickly and make an accurate decision. As simple as it may seem, those participants who respond most quickly also tend to score highest on intelligence tests.

3. **Does a smart brain work harder?** As you read in Chapter 1, PET scans measure brain activity by recording the amount of radioactive glucose used in different parts of the brain. (A more active area of the brain uses more glucose than a less active area.) Surprisingly, as can be seen in Figure 8.14, researchers have found that areas of the brain involved in problem solving show less activity in people of high intelligence than in people of lower intelligence when they are given the same problem-solving tasks (Jung & Haier, 2007; Neubauer et al., 2004; Posthuma et al., 2001). Apparently, intelligent brains work smarter, or more efficiently, than less intelligent brains.

Genetic and Environmental Influences on Intelligence

The central tenet of neuroscience is that all mental activity is linked to the brain and other parts of the nervous system. A similar, repeated theme of this text (and most areas of psychology) is that nature and nurture play interacting, *inseparable* roles. In the case of intelligence, any similarities between family members are due to *heredity* (family members share similar genetic material) combined with *inseparable environmental* factors (family members share similar living arrangements).

Researchers interested in the role of heredity in intelligence often focus on *twin studies*. Recall from Chapter 2 that one of the most popular ways to study the relative effects of genetics versus the environment is to use monozygotic (identical, one-egg) twins. Such studies have found significant hereditary influences for intelligence (Figure 8.15), personality, and psychopathology (Blonigen et al., 2008; Johnson et al., 2007; Plomin, DeFries, & Fulkner, 2007; Sternberg, 2008, 2012; Sternberg & Kaufman, 2012).

Perhaps the most important and most extensive of all twin studies is the Minnesota Study of Twins. Beginning in 1979 and continuing for more than two decades, researchers from the University of Minnesota have been studying identical twins who grew up in different homes (Bouchard, 1994, 1999; Bouchard et al., 1998; Johnson et al., 2007). Each of these "reared-apart" twins was separated from his or her sibling and adopted by a different family early in life. They were reunited only as adults.

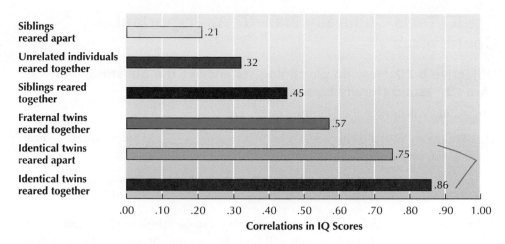

Siblings reared apart .21
Unrelated individuals reared together .32
Siblings reared together .45
Fraternal twins reared together .57
Identical twins reared apart .75
Identical twins reared together .86

.00 .10 .20 .30 .40 .50 .60 .70 .80 .90 1.00
Correlations in IQ Scores

Figure 8.15 Genetic and environmental influences Note the higher correlations between identical twins' IQ test scores compared to correlations between all other pairs. Genes no doubt play a significant role in intelligence, but these effects are difficult to separate from environmental influences. (Based on Bouchard & McGue, 1981; Bouchard et al., 1998; McGue et al., 1993.)

Because each twin has identical genetic material but was raised in a different family, researchers have a unique natural experiment that can be used to distinguish the effects of genetics from the effects of the environment. When the IQ data were collected and the statistics computed, researchers found that genetic factors appear to play a surprisingly large role in the IQ score of monozygotic (identical) twins reared apart.

How would you critique these findings? First, adoption agencies tend to look for similar criteria in their choice of adoptive parents. Therefore, the homes of these reared-apart twins could have been quite similar. In addition, these twins also shared the same 9-month prenatal environment, which might have influenced their brain development and intelligence. Furthermore, some of the separated twins in this study had been together for many months before their adoption, and some had been reunited (for months and even years) before testing.

What about the famous reunited "Jim twins" who had the same name and almost the same personality? This is one of the most widely publicized cases of the entire Minnesota study. These two children were separated 37 days after their birth and reared with no contact until 38 years later. Despite this lifelong separation, James Lewis and James Springer both had divorced and remarried women named Betty, had undergone police training, loved carpentry, vacationed at the same beach each summer, and had named their firstborn sons James Allan and James Alan (Holden, 1980). This is only a short list of their incredible similarities.

Heredity undoubtedly plays an important role, but can you think of other explanations? One study of *unrelated* pairs of students of the same age and gender also found a striking number of similarities. People of the same age apparently share a common historical time that influences large aspects of their personality. In addition, do you recall our earlier discussion of the *confirmation bias* (the tendency to seek out and pay attention to information that confirms our existing positions or beliefs, while ignoring contradictory data)? Imagine suddenly finding your long-lost identical twin. Wouldn't you be highly excited and thrilled with all your similarities and disinclined to note the differences?

As you can see, the research is inconclusive. Although heredity equips each of us with innate intellectual capacities, the environment significantly influences whether a person will reach his or her full intellectual potential. For example, early malnutrition can cause retarded brain development, which in turn affects the child's curiosity, responsiveness to the environment, and motivation for learning—all of which can lower the child's IQ. We are reminded once again that nature and nurture are inseparable.

Identical twins reared apart Jerry Levy and Mark Newman, twins separated at birth, first met each other as adults at a firefighters' annual convention.

Are IQ Tests Culturally Biased? An Important Controversy

Objective 8.20: How do psychologists answer the question, "Are IQ tests culturally biased"?

How would you answer the following questions?

1. A symphony is to a composer as a book is to a(n) _____. (a) musician; (b) editor; (c) novel; (d) author

2. If you throw dice and they land with a 7 on top, what is on the bottom? (a) snake eyes; (b) box cars; (c) little Joes; (d) eleven

Can you see how the content and answers to these questions might reflect *cultural bias*? People from some backgrounds will find the first question easier. Other groups will more easily answer the second. Which of these two questions do you think is most likely to appear on standard IQ tests?

One of the most hotly debated and controversial issues in psychology involves group differences in intelligence test scores and what they really mean. In 1969, Arthur Jensen sparked a heated debate when he argued that genetic factors are "strongly implicated" as the cause of ethnic differences in intelligence. A book by Richard J. Herrnstein and Charles Murray titled *The Bell Curve: Intelligence and Class Structure in American Life* reignited this debate in 1994 when the authors claimed that African Americans score below average in IQ because of their "genetic heritage."

Psychologists have responded to these inflammatory claims with several points:

"You can't build a hut, you don't know how to find edible roots and you know nothing about predicting the weather. In other words, you do terribly on our I.Q. test."

- **IQ tests may be culturally biased, making them an inaccurate measure of true capability.** African Americans and other minorities are often unfairly disadvantaged because they are underrepresented in standardization samples and IQ test items often are loaded toward white, middle-class culture. Minorities also are overrepresented in lower-paying jobs, which limit access to better schools and avenues for academic success. Moreover, traditional IQ tests do not measure many of our multiple intelligences (Gardner, 2002, 2011; Manly et al., 2004; Naglieri & Ronning, 2000; Rutter, 2007; Sternberg, 2007, 2012; Sternberg & Grigorenko, 2008).

- **Race, like intelligence itself, is almost impossible to define.** Depending on the definition that you use, there are between 3 and 300 races, and scientists have discovered that no single gene, trait, or characteristic distinguishes one "race" from another. Famous people of mixed race, like President Barack Obama, Tiger Woods, and Mariah Carey, demonstrate the limits of these outdated categories. In short, the concept of race has no meaning. It is *a social construct* (Fujimura et al., 2010; Navarro, 2008; Sternberg & Grigorenko, 2008).

- **Intelligence (as measured by IQ tests) is not a fixed trait.** Around the world, IQ scores have increased over the last half century, and this well-established phenomenon is known as the *Flynn effect* in honor of New Zealand researcher James Flynn. Because these increases have occurred in a relatively short period of time, the cause or causes can not be due to genetics or heredity. Other possible factors include improved nutrition, better public education, more proficient test-taking skills, and rising levels of education for a greater percentage of the world's population (Flynn, 1987, 2006, 2007; Huang & Hauser, 1998; Mingroni, 2004; Pietschnig, Voracek, & Formann, 2011). Further evidence for the lack of stability in IQ scores comes from even more recent international research. In the last decade this rise in scores

Figure 8.16 If plants could talk! Note that even when you begin with the exact same package of seeds (genetic inheritance), the average height of corn plants in the fertile soil will be greater than those in the poor soil (environmental influences). The same may be true for intelligence. Therefore, no conclusions can be drawn about possible genetic contributions to the differences between groups.

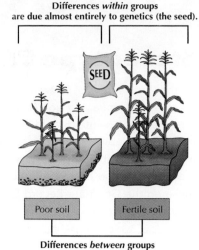

Differences *within* groups are due almost entirely to genetics (the seed).

Poor soil   Fertile soil

Differences *between* groups are due almost *entirely* to environment (the soil).

has reversed itself, and several countries are now reporting a *decline* in IQ scores (Ang, Rodgers, & Wänström, 2010; Lynn & Harvey, 2008; Teasdale & Owen, 2008). Possible causes for this so-called *negative Flynn effect* are poorly understood. But whether IQ scores rise or fall, the important point is that *intelligence is not a fixed trait*.

- **Environmental factors play a significant role in IQ scores.** Minority children more often grow up in lower socioeconomic conditions with inadequate schools, fewer academic role models, lack of funds and resources, and less parental and community support. In some ethnic groups, a child who excels in school is ridiculed for trying to be different from his or her classmates. Moreover, if children's own language and dialect do not match their education system or the IQ tests they take, they are obviously at a disadvantage (Cathers-Shiffman & Thompson, 2007; García & Náñez, 2011; Johnson, Brett, & Deary, 2010; Sidhu, Malhi, & Jerath, 2010; Sternberg & Grigorenko, 2008). No matter what the cause, the findings suggest that the environment is a significant contributor to group differences in intelligence (Figure 8.16).

- **Different groups' distribution of IQ scores overlap considerably.** IQ scores and intelligence have their greatest relevance in terms of individuals, not groups; many individual African Americans receive higher IQ scores than many individual white Americans (Garcia & Stafford, 2000; Myerson et al., 1998; Reifman, 2000).

- **Negative stereotypes about minorities can cause some members to doubt their abilities, which may, in turn, significantly reduce their IQ test scores** (Keller & Bless, 2008; Owens & Massey, 2011; Shapiro, 2011). (Concept Organizer 8.3).

The ongoing debate over the nature of intelligence and its measurement highlights the complexities of studying *cognition*. In this chapter, we've explored three cognitive processes: *thinking*, *language*, and *intelligence*. As you've seen, all three processes are greatly affected by numerous interacting factors.

A Final Word

Think back to the questions we asked at the very beginning of our discussion of intelligence: Are Genie and Thomas Edison intelligent? How would you answer these questions now? Hopefully, you now understand that all three cognitive processes discussed in this chapter (thinking, language, and intelligence) are complex phenomena, which are greatly affected by numerous interacting factors. As evidence, let's update our story of Genie. Her life, as you might have guessed, does not have a happy Hollywood ending. Genie's tale is a heartbreaking account of the lasting scars from a disastrous childhood. At the time of her rescue, at age 13, Genie's intellectual performance was at the level of a normal 1-year-old. Over the years, she was given thousands of hours of special training and rehabilitation, so that by the age of 19 she could use public transportation and was adapting well to her foster home and special classes at school (Rymer, 1993).

ConceptOrganizer8.3

Stereotype Threat

In the first study of **stereotype threat**, Claude Steele and Joshua Aronson (1995) recruited African American and white Stanford University students (with similar ability levels) to complete a "performance exam" that supposedly measured intellectual abilities. The exam's questions were similar to those on the Graduate Record Exam (GRE). Results showed that African American students performed far below white students. In contrast, when the researchers told students it was a "laboratory task," there was no difference between African American and white scores.

As you can see in Figure 8.17, subsequent work showed that stereotype threat occurs because members of stereotyped groups begin to doubt themselves and fear they will fulfill their group's negative stereotype. This anxiety in turn hinders their performance on tests. Some people cope with stereotype threat by *disidentifying*, telling themselves they don't care about the test scores (Major et al., 1998). Unfortunately, this attitude lessens motivation, decreasing performance.

Stereotype threat affects many social groups, including African Americans, women, Native Americans, Latinos, low-income people, elderly

Obama's election as President vs. stereotype threat Preliminary research has found a so-called "Obama effect," which may offset problems related to the stereotype threat. (Dillon, 2009).

people, and white male athletes (e.g., Bates, 2007; Keller & Bless, 2008; Owens & Massey, 2011; Shapiro, 2011). This research helps explain some group differences in intelligence and achievement tests. As such, it underscores why relying solely on such tests to make critical decisions affecting individual lives—for example, in hiring, college admissions, or clinical application—is unwarranted and possibly even unethical.

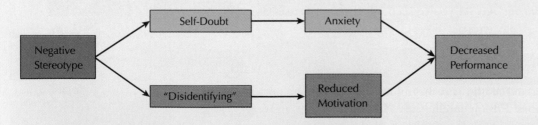

Figure 8.17 The process of stereotype threat

Stereotype Threat Negative stereotypes about minority groups cause some members to doubt their abilities

Genie was far from normal, however. Her intelligence scores were still close to the cutoff for intellectual disability. And, as noted earlier, her language skills were similar to those of a 2- or 3-year-old. To make matters worse, she was also subjected to a series of foster home placements—one of which was abusive. At last report, Genie was living in a home for the intellectually disabled (Rymer, 1993; LaPointe, 2005).

Psychology Engages

RESEARCH CHALLENGE

IQ and Genius: Are They the Secret to Success?

By Rita Jeffries (School Psychologist, San Diego, CA)

Objective 8.21: What are the key factors in success?

In our culture, high IQ and genius status are idolized. Einstein and Mozart are revered icons. Movies such as *Good Will Hunting* glorify an impoverished, emotionally troubled young man whose brilliance allowed him to solve graduate-level math problems on a whim. *The Social Network* portrayed Mark Zuckerberg (creator of Facebook) as having such innate, blazing intelligence that he could easily break in and control several Harvard University computer networks in one night.

Are these cultural icons successful because they inherited superior cognitive abilities or some divine spark? Modern research suggests that success is not the result of inherited, fixed traits. Instead, it is highly malleable and the result of numerous personality, social, and biological factors.

Personality Factors

Modern observers suggest that Mozart's early compositions were nothing special and that he would not stand out among today's top child-performers (Brooks, 2009). So how do we explain his genius-level musical achievements? Several studies have found that personal attributes such as *self-discipline* (Duckworth & Seligman, 2005), *motivation* (Steinmayr & Spinath, 2009), and *positive beliefs about one's intelligence* (Cho & Lin, 2011) are often stronger predictors of achievement than S.A.T. or IQ scores.

Perhaps even more interesting, *perseverance* (the willingness to practice for extended periods of time) and a *determination to succeed* can be just as important as the amount of talent a person possesses (Haynes Stewart et al., 2011; Pekun, Goetz, & Barchfeld, 2011). For example, much has been made of Mozart's childhood compositions and flashes of boyhood brilliance, while the amount of time he spent practicing, learning, and working on musical compositions is rarely reported. Research has shown that internationally recognized experts in a variety of fields (e.g., athletes, musicians, scientists, authors, chess grandmasters, etc.) require approximately 10 years of intensive training before reaching their level of success (Ericsson, 1993, 2006; Ericsson, Krampe, & Tesch-Roemer, 1993).

Others suggest that it's not just the amount of practice, or factors such as intelligence, visual-spatial reasoning, or motor reflexes that matter. Instead, they believe the one factor most predictive of expertise is the number of hours spent in what they call "deliberate practice." Highly competent professionals not only practice more, they practice better. When they train, experts constantly evaluate their own performance and then concentrate more time in areas where they are weak (Colvin, 2008; Coyle, 2009; Ericsson, Krampe, & Tesch-Roemer, 1993).

Albert Einstein (1879–1955) Noted as one of the most prolific intellects in human history.

Picture someone who plays in a recreational tennis group versus someone who uses "deliberate practice." If both individuals have difficulties serving, but limited practice opportunities, the recreational player will likely spend his or her time practicing a wide range of skills. In contrast, the "deliberate practice" player will focus only on perfecting his or her serves—over and over again, trying different techniques to improve, until he or she has fully mastered this particular skill (Hunt, 2011).

In a less conscious and conscientious way, other high achievers also spent years in "deliberate practice." Quentin Tarantino (director of the *Kill Bill* series, *Pulp Fiction*, and *Inglorious Bastards*) began watching movies—and a wide selection of them—from a young age. For hours at a time, he used his G.I. Joes (action figure dolls) to reenact the plots from movies and make up stories of his own. As a young adult, he also worked for 5 years in a video store where he spent a great deal of time discussing movies he knew, watching movies he'd never heard of, and arguing the merits of movies with coworkers and customers (Rose, 1994).

Through hours of informal practice and intense experiences, Tarantino absorbed the insights and background necessary for his genius-level achievements in the film industry. When people ask if he went to film school, he is quoted as saying, "No, I went to films" (Faces of the Week, 2008).

Social Factors

Social factors also influence genius and intelligence (Ford, 2011; Nisbett, 2009). What Mozart (and Tiger Woods) had was not just the ability to focus and practice for long periods of time; they also had fathers intent on improving their sons' skills (Brooks, 2009). Research shows that families and cultures that place high value on literacy and education tend to have children who are more likely to develop their genetic abilities to their highest potential. Also, when a culture, community, and family assume that hard work is more important than innate abilities, that education and learning should be a joy, and that a child's accomplishments reflect on the family and the community, a child is more likely to internalize the same values and attempt to achieve maximum success (Cho & Lin, 2011).

One study followed Chinese American students from elementary school until high school. At first, the IQ tests did not show an advantage of Asian Americans over other Americans. However, over time their academic abilities flourished in comparison to their peers. By high school, their grades were significantly higher than their peers with similar IQ scores (Flynn, 1991). Researchers conclude that cultural beliefs about education and hard work played a dominant role in their accomplishments.

Biological Factors

What biological factors do athletes like Tiger Woods have that we don't? Years ago, researchers presumed athletes were born with faster reflexes, larger hearts, superior lung capacity, more muscle tissue, and so on. This is not necessarily the case. Most athletes develop these characteristics thanks to years of intensive training. In fact, when they abruptly stop training, these physical attributes decline—in some cases quite rapidly (Ericsson & Charness, 1994).

In sum, whether it's great athletic, musical, or intellectual achievement, the media and public seem most interested in the innate genetics and "hard wiring" supposedly underlying great success. However, as you've discovered throughout this text, our brains are remarkably "plastic," and the latest research combining personality, social, and biological factors reinforces once again the importance of the biopsychosocial model.

It's also important to note that we all inherit a genetic "rubber band," but what we achieve in life depends on a host of factors. The most important way to "stretch" our individual rubber bands is through hard work!

[On a personal note, I (Rita Jeffries) wondered how expertise and deliberate practice applied to my own life, particularly as a guest author of this Research challenge. I've concluded that the three best rules for writing are—rewrite, rewrite, rewrite—which may be another example of deliberate practice on the way to developing expertise.]

Student Engagement Exercise

Given the admittedly limited information in the social factors study cited by Flynn (1991) described above, what is the most likely:

1. *Research method* (experimental, descriptive, correlational, or biological)?

2. If you chose the:

   - *Experimental method*—label the IV, DV, experimental group, and control group.

   - *Descriptive method*—is this a naturalistic observation, survey, or case study?

   - *Correlational method*—is this a positive, negative, or zero correlation?

   - *Biological method*—identify the specific research tool (e.g., brain dissection, CT scan, etc.)

Answers appear in Appendix B.)

CRITICAL THINKING

Solving Problems in College Life

Critical thinking requires adaptive, flexible approaches to thinking and problem solving. The following exercise offers practice in critical thinking, new insights into common college-related problems, and a quick review of terms and concepts discussed in this section.

Be sure to use the major problem-solving approaches we have discussed—algorithms (step-by-step procedures that guarantee solutions) and heuristics (shortcuts to possible solutions based on previous knowledge and experience). See Table 8.1 for three specific heuristics: working backward, means–end analysis, and creating subgoals.

Problem 1 It is the end of the semester and you have a term paper due Friday. Thursday night you try to print your previously prepared paper, and you can't find the file on your computer.

Problem 2 The financial aid office has denied your student loan until you verify your income and expenses from last year. You need to find all your pay stubs and receipts.

For each problem, answer the following:

1. What was your first step in approaching the problem?

2. Which problem-solving approach did you select and why?

3. Did you experience mental sets, functional fixedness, confirmation bias, the availability heuristic, and the representativeness heuristic during the problem-solving process?

GENDER AND CULTURAL DIVERSITY

Unspoken Accents—Nonverbal Language Reveals Your Roots

By Siri Carpenter (Science Writer, Madison, WI)

Objective 8.22: How does nonverbal language reveal cultural origins?

Just as an Irish brogue or a Minnesota lilt betrays one's background, facial expressions and body language can also reveal our cultural origins. According to new research, such "nonverbal accents" also provoke stereotyped perceptions of others' personalities. Many researchers regard nonverbal behavior to be a universal language—wherever you go, a smile looks like a smile. But a growing body of research suggests that where we hang our hats shapes both how we display emotion and how we perceive it in others. In a recent study, psychologists found that American volunteers could distinguish American from Australian faces when the faces were photographed smiling but not when they were photographed with neutral expressions (Marsh, Elfenbein, & Ambady, 2007). In addition, the way Americans and Australians walked or waved in greeting not only telegraphed their nationality but also triggered prevailing stereotypes about the two groups: Americans were judged more dominant (think, "Carry a big stick") and Australians more likable (think, "G'day, mate!").

A different study, led by psychologist Masaki Yuki of Hokkaido University in Japan (Yuki, Maddux, & Masuda, 2007), suggests that people from different cultures are attuned to different nonverbal cues. The study found that Americans, who tend to express emotion overtly, look to the mouth to interpret others' true feelings. Japanese, who tend to be more emotionally guarded, give greater weight to the eyes, which are less easily controlled.

"These studies show both that people can be sensitive to cultural cues that they are barely aware of, and also that their own cultural norms can lead them astray," comments Judith Hall, who studies nonverbal communication at Northeastern University. For example, "Americans who think the Japanese are unexpressive mistake subtlety for lack of expression. These Americans would misjudge facial cues that Japanese might be very successful at interpreting."

Such misjudgments can have unintended consequences, Marsh argues. "Everyone knows how spoken communication breakdowns can lead to cross-cultural misunderstandings," she says. "These studies highlight the importance of nonverbal communication as well. Improving awareness of these differences might go a long way toward improving cross-cultural interactions."

(*Source*: Originally published in *Scientific American Mind*, August/September 2007, p. 13. Reprinted with permission of author, Siri Carpenter)

CHECK & REVIEW

STOP *Before going on, be sure to complete this Check & Review. It is an invaluable study tool!*

Intelligence Controversy and Psychology Engages

Part A: Retrieval Practice

1. Without looking at the book, spend 10 minutes writing a free-form essay recalling all you can remember from the previous section.

2. Now, reread the previous section, and once again spend 10 minutes writing a free-form essay on the SAME material.

Part B: Practice Quiz

1. People with _____ are often categorized as intellectually disabled, but they also possess incredible abilities in specific areas, such as musical memory or math calculations. (a) IQ scores below 70; (b) phenylketonuria (PKU); (c) fragile-X syndrome; (d) savant syndrome

2. A longitudinal study of the "Termites" found that high intelligence is correlated with _____. (a) higher academic success; (b) better athletic ability; (c) higher occupational achievement; (d) all of the above

3. The more efficient brain uses fewer _____ to solve problems than a less efficient brain. (a) parts of the brain; (b) neurotransmitters; (c) synapses, (d) energy resources

4. In your own opinion, what is more important in determining intelligence—heredity or environment

5. Which of the personality, social, and biological factors do you believe are the true secrets to success?

Check your answers in Appendix B.

www.wileyplus.com

WileyPLUS presents an on-line version of this textbook along with a wealth of study resources including quizzes, practice tests, flash cards, videos, animations and other activities designed to improve your mastery of the content. Working in conjunction with these study tools, the *Psychology in Action* WileyPLUS course features Professor Karen Huffman, author of this textbook, explaining and expanding upon some of the most challenging concepts in psychology. Here is a sample of the tutorial videos available for this chapter:

- An animated, interactive exploration of problem solving
- Classroom demonstration of barriers to problem solving
- Standards for psychological tests, emphasizing standardization, reliability and validity
- Understanding IQ tests: What does that number mean anyway?
- Virtual Field Trip to learn how sign language gives voice to those who are unable to speak

Key Terms

To assess your understanding of the **Key Terms** in Chapter 8, write a definition for each (in your own words), and then compare your definitions with those in the text.

cognition (p. 283)

Thinking

mental image (p. 284)
concept (p. 285)
prototype (p. 285)
algorithm (p. 287)
heuristic (p. 287)

mental set (p. 288)
functional fixedness (p. 289)
confirmation bias (p. 289)
availability heuristic (p. 289)
representativeness heuristic (p. 289)
creativity (p. 291)

divergent thinking (p. 291)
convergent thinking (p. 292)

Language

language (p. 293)
phoneme [FOE-neem] (p. 294)
morpheme [MOR-feem] (p. 294)
grammar (p. 294)

TRY THIS YOURSELF

General Intelligence versus Specific Intelligence

After reading this chapter, you can appreciate that defining and measuring intelligence is one of psychology's most controversial, complex, and challenging tasks. Where do you stand on the issue of intelligence? On what basis do you conclude that someone is intelligent? And how do your notions of intelligence compare to those proposed by the various theorists and researchers in this chapter?

In this video lab exercise, available to WileyPlus subscribers, you'll be looking at several people and deciding if they are intelligent, how they are intelligent, and why you believe they are intelligent. Over the course of your work, you'll come to appreciate even more the difficulties—some would say the misguidedness—at work in the field

of intelligence and intelligence testing. In addition, along the way, this lab exercise will help you to appreciate the power, impact, and dangers of intelligence labels.

As you are working on this on-line exercise, consider the following:

- How do your assessments of intelligence compare to each of the leading theories on intelligence?
- Are cognitive, emotional, and creative intelligence related?
- Does intelligence increase over the course of a person's life? Can it increase once a person reaches adulthood?
- Is intelligence related to wisdom? conscientiousness? achievement? likeability? social perceptions and expectations?

Chapter Summary

Thinking

Objective 8.1: What is thinking and where is it located?
Thinking involves using and mentally acting on information.

Thought processes are distributed throughout the brain in neural networks. However, they are also localized in the *prefrontal cortex*, which links to other areas of the brain, such as the *limbic system*.

Objective 8.2: How are mental images and concepts involved in thinking.
Mental images are mental representations of a sensory experience, including visual, auditory, olfactory, tactile, motor, and gustatory imagery.
Concepts are mental representations of members of a group or category that that share similar characteristics.

Objective 8.3: How do we learn concepts?
We develop concepts using three key strategies: (1) *Artificial concepts* are formed by logical, specific rules or characteristics. (2) *Natural concepts* are formed by experience in everyday life. When we are confronted with a new item, we compare it with a **prototype** (most typical example) of a concept. (3) Concepts are generally organized

into *hierarchies*. We most frequently use the middle, basic-level category of a hierarchy when first learning material.

Objective 8.4: Describe the three stages of problem solving.
Problem solving entails three stages: *preparation*, *production*, and *evaluation*. During the preparation stage, we identify given facts, separate relevant from irrelevant facts, and define the ultimate goal.

During the production stage, we generate possible solutions, called hypotheses. We typically generate hypotheses by using *algorithms* and *heuristics*. **Algorithms**, as problem-solving strategies, are guaranteed to lead to an eventual solution. But they are not practical in many situations. **Heuristics**, or simplified rules based on experience, are much faster but do not guarantee a solution. Three common heuristics are *working backward*, *means-end analysis*, and *creating subgoals*.

The evaluation stage in problem solving involves judging the hypotheses generated during the production stage against the criteria established in the preparation stage.

Objective 8.5: Identity five common barriers to problem solving.
Five major barriers to successful problem solving are **mental sets**, **functional fixedness**, **confirmation bias**, the **availability heuristic**, and the **representativeness heuristic**.

Objective 8.6: What is creativity, and what are its three major characteristics?
Creativity is the ability to produce valued outcomes in a novel way. Creative thinking involves *originality*, *fluency*, and *flexibility*.

Objective 8.7: How do we measure creativity?
Most tests of creativity focus on **divergent thinking**, which involves generating as many alternatives or ideas

as possible. In contrast, **convergent thinking**—or conventional thinking—works toward a single correct answer.

Objective 8.8: How do creative people differ from others?
Creative people may have a special talent or differing cognitive processes. The *investment theory of creativity* proposes that creative people "buy low" by pursuing promising but unpopular ideas. They then "sell high" when these ideas are widely accepted. The theory also proposes that creativity depends on six specific resources: *intellectual ability*, *knowledge*, *thinking style*, *personality*, *motivation*, and *environment*.

Language

Objective 8.9: What is language, and what are its basic building blocks?
Human **language** is a form of communication using sounds and symbols combined according to a set of specified rules. **Phonemes** are the smallest distinctive sound units. They are combined to form **morphemes**, the smallest meaningful units of language. Phonemes, morphemes, words, and phrases are put together by rules of **grammar** (syntax and semantics). **Syntax** refers to the grammatical rules for ordering words in sentences. **Semantics** refers to rules for deriving meaning in language.

Objective 8.10: How is language related to thought?
According to Benjamin Whorf's *linguistic relativity hypothesis*, language shapes thought. Generally, Whorf's hypothesis is not supported. However, our choice of vocabulary can influence our mental imagery and social perceptions.

Objective 8.11: Describe the two major stages in language development.
Children go through two stages in their acquisition of language: *prelingustic* (crying, **cooing**, **babbling**) and

linguistic (single utterances, **telegraphic speech**, and the acquisition of rules of grammar).

Objective 8.12: Contrast the "nativist" versus and "nurturist" views of language development.
Nativists believe that language is an inborn capacity and develops primarily by maturation. Chomsky suggests that human brains possess a **language acquisition device (LAD)** that needs only minimal environmental input. Nurturists emphasize the role of the environment and suggest that language development results from rewards, punishments, and imitation of models.

Objective 8.13: Describe the language research conducted with nonhuman animals.
The most successful nonhuman animal language studies have been done with apes using American Sign Language and computer symbols. Dolphins also have been taught to comprehend sentences that vary in syntax and meaning. Some psychologists believe that nonhuman animals can truly learn human language. Others suggest that nonhuman animals are merely responding to rewards.

Intelligence

Objective 8.14: What is intelligence, and is it one or many abilities?
Today, **intelligence** is commonly defined as the global capacity to think rationally, act purposefully, and deal effectively with the environment. Several theorists have debated whether intelligence is one or many abilities. Spearman viewed intelligence as one factor, called *g*, for general intelligence. Thurstone saw it as seven distinct mental abilities. Guilford believed it was composed of 120 or more separate abilities. And Cattell viewed it as two types of general intelligence (*g*), which he called **fluid intelligence** and **crystallized intelligence**.

Objective 8.15: Contrast Gardner's and Sternberg's theories of intelligence.

Both Gardner and Sternberg believe intelligence is a collection of multiple abilities. Gardner's theory of multiple intelligences identifies eight (and possibly nine) types of intelligence. He believes that both teaching and assessing should take into account people's learning styles and cognitive strengths. Sternberg's triarchic theory of intelligence (*analytical, creative*, and *practical*) proposed that each of these components is learned, rather than the result of genetics.

Objective 8.16: Describe how psychologists measure intelligence.

Although there are many tests for intelligence, the Stanford-Binet and Wechsler are the most widely used. Both tests compute an *intelligence quotient (IQ)* by comparing a person's test score to the norm for that person's age group.

Objective 8.17: What are the three key requirements for a scientifically useful test?

For any test to be useful, it must be standardized, reliable, and valid. **Standardization** refers to (a) giving a test to a large number of people in order to determine norms and (b) using identical procedures in administering a test so that everyone takes the test under exactly the same testing conditions. **Reliability** refers to the stability and reproducibility of test scores over time. **Validity** refers to how well the test measures what it is intended to measure.

Intelligence Controversy and Psychology Engages

Objective 8.18: How do studies of extremes in intelligence help validate intelligence tests?

Intelligence testing has long been the subject of great debate. To determine whether these tests are valid, you can examine people who fall at the extremes of intelligence. People with IQs of 70 and below (referred to intellectually disabled) and those with IQs of 135 and above (identified as gifted) do differ in their respective intellectual abilities.

Objective 8.19: Describe how research on the brain, genetics, and the environment helps explain differences in IQ.

Research on the brain's role in intelligence has focused on three major questions: (1) Does a bigger brain mean greater intelligence? (Answer: "Not necessarily.") (2) Is a faster brain more intelligent? (Answer: "A qualified yes.") And (3) Does a smart brain work harder? (Answer: "No, the smarter brain is more efficient.")

Another topic of debate is whether intelligence is inherited or due to the environment. According to the Minnesota Study of Twins Reared Apart (1979 to present), heredity and environment are important, inseparable factors in intellectual development. Heredity equips each of us with innate capacities. The environment significantly influences whether an individual will reach full potential.

Objective 8.20: How do psychologists answer the question, "Are IQ tests culturally biased"?

Perhaps the most hotly debated topic is whether ethnic differences on IQ tests are primarily "genetic in origin." Research has shown IQ tests may be culturally biased. And environmental factors, including the *Flynn effect*, cultural exposure, socioeconomic differences, language, and **stereotype threat**, have all been found to be contributing factors in score differences.

Objective 8.21: What are the key factors in success?

Research shows that success depends on a combination of personality, social, and biological factors, including self-discipline, motivation, positive beliefs, determination, perseverance, deliberate practice, family and cultural values, and so on.

Objective 8.22: How does nonverbal language reveal cultural origins?

Nonverbal emotions are somewhat universal, but there are slight differences between cultures in how we display and perceive emotions. These subtle differences also can lead to problems in communication.

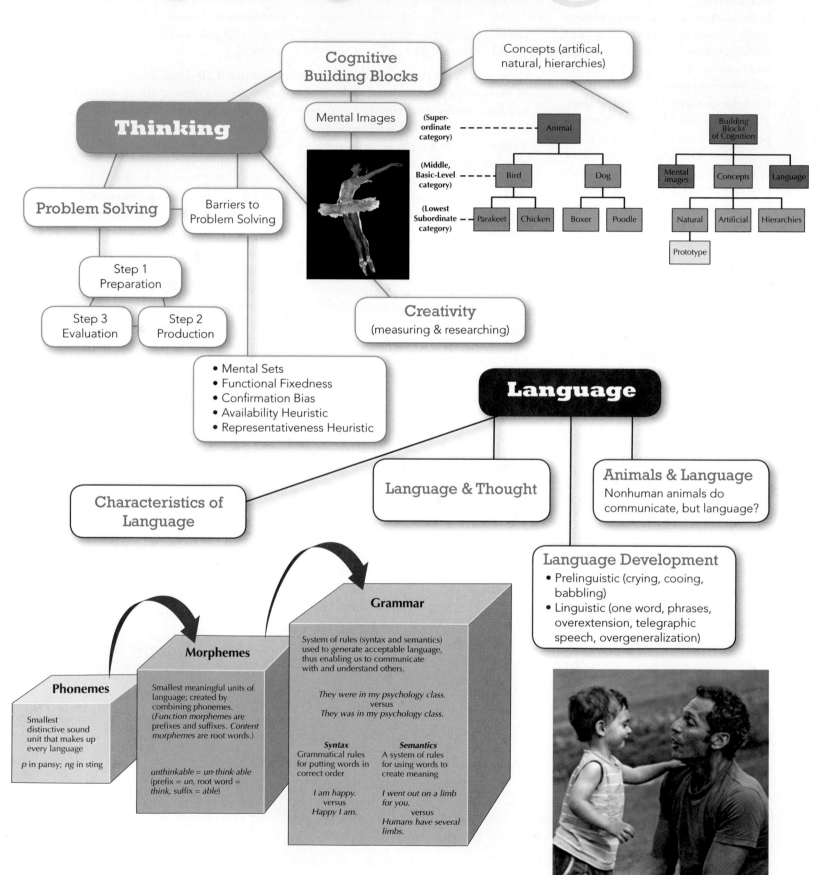

Cognitive Building Blocks

Concepts (artifical, natural, hierarchies)

Mental Images

Thinking

Problem Solving

Barriers to Problem Solving

Step 1 Preparation

Step 3 Evaluation

Step 2 Production

- Mental Sets
- Functional Fixedness
- Confirmation Bias
- Availability Heuristic
- Representativeness Heuristic

Creativity (measuring & researching)

(Super-ordinate category) --- Animal

(Middle, Basic-Level category) --- Bird | Dog

(Lowest Subordinate category) --- Parakeet | Chicken | Boxer | Poodle

Building Blocks of Cognition

Mental images | Concepts | Language

Natural | Artificial | Hierarchies

Prototype

Language

Characteristics of Language

Language & Thought

Animals & Language
Nonhuman animals do communicate, but language?

Language Development
- Prelinguistic (crying, cooing, babbling)
- Linguistic (one word, phrases, overextension, telegraphic speech, overgeneralization)

Grammar

System of rules (syntax and semantics) used to generate acceptable language, thus enabling us to communicate with and understand others.

They were in my psychology class.
versus
They was in my psychology class.

Syntax
Grammatical rules for putting words in correct order

I am happy.
versus
Happy I am.

Semantics
A system of rules for using words to create meaning

I went out on a limb for you.
versus
Humans have several limbs.

Morphemes

Smallest meaningful units of language; created by combining phonemes. (*Function morphemes* are prefixes and suffixes. *Content morphemes* are root words.)

unthinkable = un·think·able
(prefix = *un*, root word = *think*, suffix = *able*)

Phonemes

Smallest distinctive sound unit that makes up every language

p in pansy; *ng* in sting

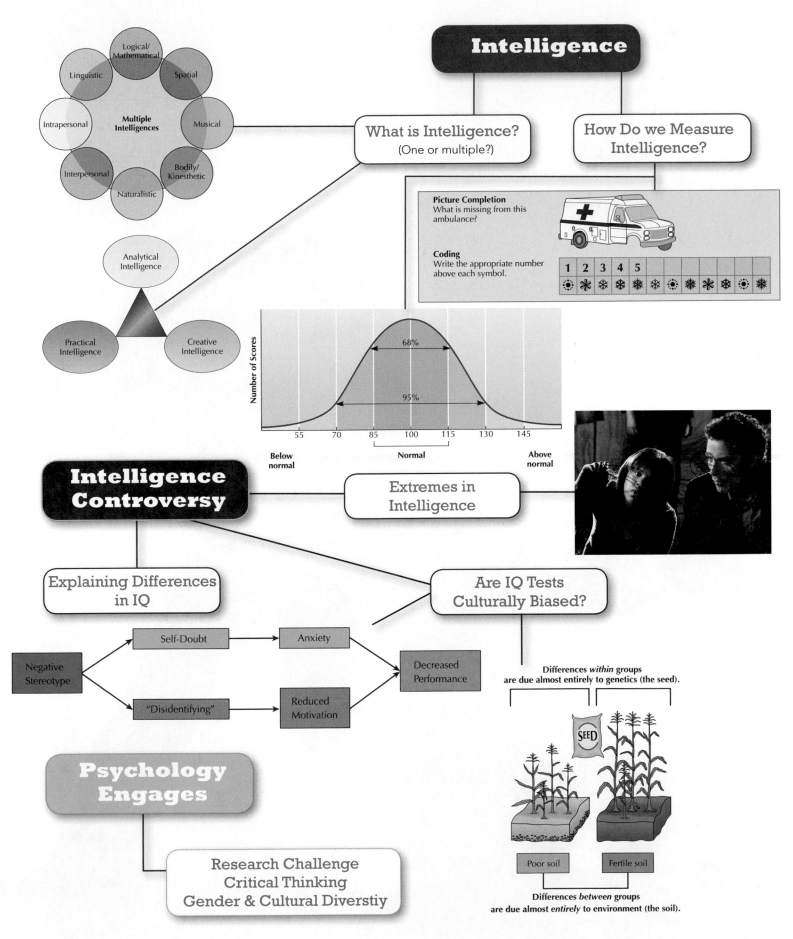

Intelligence

What is Intelligence?
(One or multiple?)

Multiple Intelligences
- Logical/Mathematical
- Spatial
- Linguistic
- Musical
- Intrapersonal
- Bodily/Kinesthetic
- Interpersonal
- Naturalistic

- Analytical Intelligence
- Practical Intelligence
- Creative Intelligence

How Do we Measure Intelligence?

Picture Completion
What is missing from this ambulance?

Coding
Write the appropriate number above each symbol.

| 1 | 2 | 3 | 4 | 5 | | | | | | | |

Number of Scores

68%
95%

55   70   85   100   115   130   145

Below normal   Normal   Above normal

Intelligence Controversy

Extremes in Intelligence

Explaining Differences in IQ

Are IQ Tests Culturally Biased?

Negative Stereotype → Self-Doubt → Anxiety → Decreased Performance

Negative Stereotype → "Disidentifying" → Reduced Motivation → Decreased Performance

Differences *within* groups are due almost entirely to genetics (the seed).

SEED

Poor soil   Fertile soil

Differences *between* groups are due almost *entirely* to environment (the soil).

Psychology Engages

Research Challenge
Critical Thinking
Gender & Cultural Diverstiy

321

ChapterNine

Life Span Development I

Imagine for a moment that you could go back to the moment right before your conception—when your father's sperm met your mother's egg—and could change certain things. Would you still be "you" if you had a different father or mother? What if you chose another hometown or added or subtracted siblings? How might these changes affect who you are today?

As you can see from this brief fantasy, what you are now is a reflection of thousands of contributors from the past, and what you will be tomorrow is still unwritten. Life doesn't stand still. You and I (and every other human on this planet) will be many people in our lifetime—infant, child, teenager, adult, and senior citizen.

Infancy. . .

What is learned in the cradle, lasts to the grave.

FRENCH PROVERB

Childhood. . .

Childhood has its own way of seeing, thinking, and feeling. And there is nothing more foolish than the attempt to put ours in its place.

JEAN-JACQUES ROUSSEAU

Adolescence. . .

Adolescents are not monsters. They are just people trying to learn how to make it among the adults in the world, who are probably not so sure themselves.

VIRGINIA SATIR

Parenthood. . .

At last I feel the equal of my parents. Knowing you are going to have a child is like extending yourself in the world, setting up a tent and saying "Here I am, I am important." Now that I'm going to have a child it's like the balance is even. My hand is as rich as theirs, maybe for the first time. I am no longer just a child.

ANONYMOUS FATHER

There are only two lasting bequests we can hope to give our children. One of these is roots; the other wings.

HODDING CARTER

ChapterOutline

WHY STUDY PSYCHOLOGY

Did you know...

- At the moment of conception, you were smaller than the period at the end of this sentence?

- During the last few months of pregnancy, you (as a fetus) could hear sounds outside your mother's womb?

- At birth, your head was approximately one-fourth of your total body size, but as an adult it's only one-eighth?

- Within the first few days of life, breast-fed newborns can recognize and show preference for the odor and taste of their own mother's milk over another mother's?

- Children in many cultures sleep alongside their parents for several years—not in a separate bed or room?

- Human brains aren't fully developed until the mid-twenties?

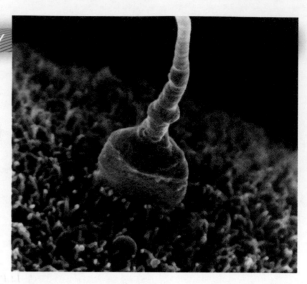

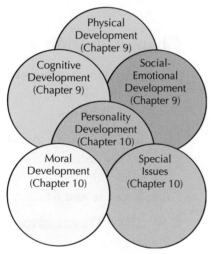

Figure 9.1 Developmental changes result from numerous overlapping processes

Physical Development (Chapter 9)

Cognitive Development (Chapter 9)

Social-Emotional Development (Chapter 9)

Personality Development (Chapter 10)

Moral Development (Chapter 10)

Special Issues (Chapter 10)

Objective 9.1: Define developmental psychology.

Would you like to know more about yourself at each of these stages? There is an entire field of knowledge, called **developmental psychology**, which *studies age-related changes in behavior and mental processes from conception to death* (Table 9.1). To emphasize that development is an ongoing, lifelong *process*, throughout this chapter we will take a *topical* approach (as opposed to a *chronological* approach, which arbitrarily divides the field into two periods—childhood–adolescence and adulthood). Thus, in this chapter, we will trace physical, cognitive, and social-emotional development—one at a time—from conception to death. Then, in Chapter 10, we will explore moral development, personality development, and special issues related to grief and death—again, one topic at a time. This topical approach will allow us to see how development affects an individual over the entire life span. Keep in mind that each of these topics is intricately interwoven (Figure 9.1).

Developmental Psychology Study of age-related changes in behavior and mental processes from conception to death

---

THE FOUR AGES OF MAN

INFANCY   CHILDHOOD   YOUTH   MATURITY

Table 9.1	LIFE SPAN DEVELOPMENT
Stage	**Approximate Age**
Prenatal	Conception to birth
Infancy	Birth to 18 months
Early childhood	18 months to 6 years
Middle childhood	6–12 years
Adolescence	12–20 years
Young adulthood	20–45 years
Middle adulthood	45–60 years
Later adulthood	60 years to death

Studying Development

In this section, we first explore three theoretical issues in developmental psychology, and then we'll examine how developmental psychologists conduct their research.

Theoretical Issues: Ongoing Debates

Objective 9.2: Identify the three major issues in developmental psychology.

In all fields of psychology, certain theoretical issues guide the basic direction of research. These are the three most important debates or questions in human development:

1. *Nature versus nurture* The issue of *nature versus nurture* has been with us since the beginning of psychology. Even the ancient Greeks had the same debate—Plato argued that humans are born with innate knowledge and abilities, whereas Aristotle held that learning occurs through the five senses. Some early philosophers also proposed that at birth our minds are a *tabula rasa* (or blank slate) and that the environment determines what messages are written on the slate.

    According to the modern *nature position*, human behavior and development are governed by automatic, genetically predetermined signals in a process known as **maturation**. Just as a flower unfolds in accord with its genetic blueprint, we humans crawl before we walk and walk before we run. Furthermore, there is an optimal period shortly after birth, one of several **critical periods** during our lifetime, when we are particularly sensitive to certain experiences that shape the capacity for future development.

    On the other side of the debate, those who hold an extreme *nurturist position* would argue that development occurs by learning through personal experience and observation of others.

2. *Continuity versus stages* Continuity theorists maintain that development is *continuous*, with new abilities, skills, and knowledge gradually added at a relatively uniform pace. Therefore, adult thinking and intelligence differ quantitatively from a child's. Stage theorists, on the other hand, believe development occurs at different rates, alternating between periods of little change and periods of abrupt, rapid change. In this chapter, we discuss stages in physical development and Piaget's stage theory of cognitive development. In Chapter 10, we discuss two other stage theories—Erikson's psychosocial theory of personality development and Kohlberg's theory of moral development.

3. *Stability versus change* Have you generally maintained your personal characteristics as you matured from infant to adult (stability)? Or does your current personality bear little resemblance to the personality you displayed during infancy (change)? Psychologists who emphasize stability in development believe measurements of personality taken during childhood are important predictors of adult personality. Of course, psychologists who emphasize change disagree.

Which of these positions is most correct? Most psychologists do not take a hard line either way. Rather, they prefer an *interactionist perspective* and/or the *biopsychosocial model*. For example, in the *nature-versus-nurture* debate, psychologists generally agree that development emerges from unique genetic predispositions *and* from experiences in the environment (Hartwell, 2008; Hudziak, 2008; Rutter, 2007).

Maturation Development governed by automatic, genetically predetermined signals

Critical Period A time of special sensitivity to specific types of learning, which shapes the capacity for future development

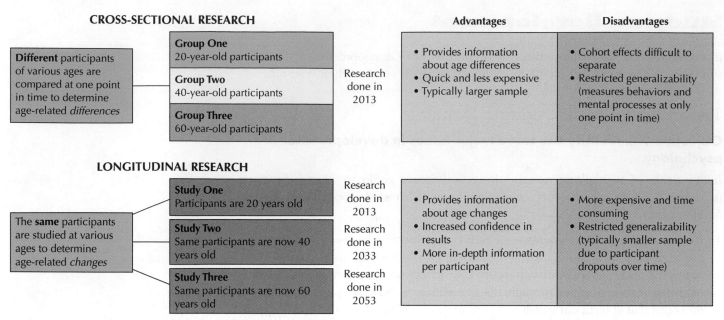

CROSS-SECTIONAL RESEARCH

| Different participants of various ages are compared at one point in time to determine age-related *differences* | Group One 20-year-old participants | Research done in 2013 |

Group Two 40-year-old participants

Group Three 60-year-old participants

Advantages	Disadvantages
• Provides information about age differences • Quick and less expensive • Typically larger sample	• Cohort effects difficult to separate • Restricted generalizability (measures behaviors and mental processes at only one point in time)

LONGITUDINAL RESEARCH

| The **same** participants are studied at various ages to determine age-related *changes* | Study One Participants are 20 years old | Research done in 2013 |

Study Two Same participants are now 40 years old — Research done in 2033

Study Three Same participants are now 60 years old — Research done in 2053

Advantages	Disadvantages
• Provides information about age changes • Increased confidence in results • More in-depth information per participant	• More expensive and time consuming • Restricted generalizability (typically smaller sample due to participant dropouts over time)

Figure 9.2 Cross-sectional versus longitudinal research

Research Methods: Two Basic Approaches

Objective 9.3: What are the two most common research methods in developmental psychology?

Cross-Sectional Method Measures individuals of various ages at one point in time and gives information about age differences

Longitudinal Method Measures a single individual or group of individuals over an extended period and gives information about age changes

To study development, psychologists often use either a *cross-sectional* or *longitudinal* method. The **cross-sectional method** examines individuals of various ages (e.g., 20, 40, 60, and 80 years) at one point in time and gives information about *age differences*. The **longitudinal method** follows a single individual or group of same-aged individuals over an extended period and gives information about *age changes* (Figure 9.2).

Imagine you are a developmental psychologist interested in studying intelligence in adults. Which method would you choose—cross-sectional or longitudinal? Before you decide, note the different research results shown in Figure 9.3.

TEST YOURSELF

Why do these two methods of research show such different results?

Answer: Cross-sectional studies show that reasoning and intelligence reach their peak in early adulthood and then gradually decline. But these results may reflect a problem with the research method, which is picking up on different educational experiences for the various age groups versus a true effect of aging. In contrast, longitudinal studies have found that a marked decline does not begin until about age 60 (Schaie, 1994). But these longitudinal studies have also been questioned because they generally begin with a smaller sample, and people often drop out along the way. This means that the final results may only apply to a small group of people. (Adapted from Schaie, 1994, with permission.)

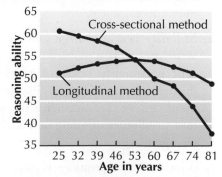

Figure 9.3 Reasoning ability and cross-sectional versus longitudinal research

Why do the two methods show such different results? Researchers suggest that the different results may reflect a central problem with cross-sectional studies. These studies often confuse genuine age differences with *cohort effects*—differences that result from specific histories of the age group studied. As Figure 9.3 shows, the 81-year-olds measured by the cross-sectional method have dramatically lower scores than the 25-year-olds. But is this due to aging or possibly to broad environmental differences, such as less formal education or poorer nutrition? Because the different age groups, called *cohorts*, grew up in different historical periods, the results may not apply to people growing up at other times. With the cross-sectional method, age effects and cohort effects are sometimes hopelessly tangled.

In contrast, a key advantage of longitudinal research is that researchers can be reasonably confident that any observed changes are the result of time and developmental experiences. However, these studies also have their limits. Given the need to follow participants over many years, longitudinal studies are very expensive in terms of time and money.

One disadvantage shared by both cross-sectional and longitudinal research is the problem of *generalizability*—how well the results from a study conducted on a sample population can be applied ("generalized") to the population at large. Cross-sectional studies only measure behaviors and mental processes at one point in time, which doesn't identify how or when age-related changes may have occurred. For example, if older participants show memory declines, cross-sectional studies can't answer whether those declines appeared suddenly in their 60s, if they accumulated gradually over several years. Longitudinal research has its own problems with generalizability due to a restricted, self-selected sample. Participants often drop out, lose interest, move away, or even die during extended testing periods.

As you can see in the right hand side of Figure 9.2, each method of research has its own comparative strengths and weaknesses. Keep these differences in mind when you read the findings of developmental research in this chapter and in the popular press.

CHECK & REVIEW

STOP *Before going on, be sure to complete this Check & Review. It is an invaluable study tool!*

Studying Development

Part A: Retrieval Practice

1. Without looking at the book, spend 10 minutes writing a free-form essay recalling all you can remember from the previous section.

2. Now, reread the previous section, and once again spend 10 minutes writing a free-form essay on the SAME material.

   (Although time consuming, this exercise has been shown to be the single best way to improve your test scores! For more information, check out http://

www.sciencemag.org/content/early/2011/01/19/science.1199327.abstract)

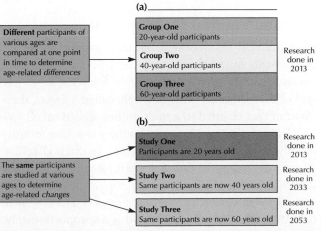

(a)_____

Different participants of various ages are compared at one point in time to determine age-related *differences*

| Group One |
| 20-year-old participants |

| Group Two |
| 40-year-old participants |

| Group Three |
| 60-year-old participants |

Research done in 2013

(b)_____

The **same** participants are studied at various ages to determine age-related *changes*

| Study One |
| Participants are 20 years old |
Research done in 2013

| Study Two |
| Same participants are now 40 years old |
Research done in 2033

| Study Three |
| Same participants are now 60 years old |
Research done in 2053

Part B: Practice Quiz

1. What three major questions are studied in developmental psychology?

2. Label the two basic types of research studies in the figure to the left:

3. Differences in age groups that reflect factors unique to a specific age group are called _____ effects. (a) generational; (b) social-environmental; (c) operational; (d) cohort

4. _____ studies are the most time-efficient method, whereas _____ studies provide the most in-depth information per participant.

Check your answers in Appendix B.

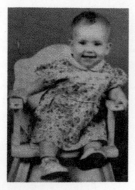

Figure 9.4 Changes in physical development As these photos of this text's author at ages 1, 4, 10, 30, and 55 show, physical changes are the most obvious signs of aging and development. However, our cognitive, social, moral, and personality processes and traits also change across our life span.

Physical Development

After studying my photos in Figure 9.4, or looking at your own child and adult photos, you may be amused and surprised by the dramatic changes in physical appearance. But have you stopped to appreciate the incredible underlying process that transformed all of us from birth to our current adult bodies? In this section, we will explore the fascinating world of physical development. We begin with the prenatal period and early childhood, followed by adolescence and adulthood.

Prenatal Period and Early Childhood: A Time of Rapid Change

Objective 9.4: Identify the three major stages of prenatal development.

Do you remember being a young child and feeling like it would "take forever to grow up"? Contrary to a child's sense of interminable, unchanging time, the early years of development are characterized by rapid and unparalleled change. In fact, if you continued to develop at the same rapid rate that marked your first two years of life, you would weigh over a thousand pounds and be over 12 feet tall as an adult! Thankfully, physical development slows, yet it is important to note that change continues until the very moment of death. Let's look at some of the major physical changes occurring throughout the life span.

Figure 9.5 The moment of conception (a) Note the large number of sperm surrounding the ovum. (b) Although a "joint effort" is required to break through the outer coating, only one sperm will actually fertilize the egg.

Prenatal Physical Development

Your prenatal development began at *conception*, when your mother's egg, or *ovum*, united with your father's *sperm* cell (Figure 9.5). At that time, you were a single cell barely *1/175* of an inch in diameter—smaller, as we have said, than the period at the end of this sentence. This new cell, called a *zygote*, then began a process of rapid cell division that resulted in a multimillion-celled infant (you) some nine months later.

The vast changes that occur during the nine months of a full-term pregnancy are usually divided into three stages (Step-by-Step Diagram 9.1). Prenatal growth, as well as growth during the first few years after birth, is *proximodistal* (near to far), with the innermost parts of the body developing before the outermost parts. Thus, a fetus's arms develop before its hands and fingers. Development also proceeds *cephalocaudally* (head to tail). Thus, a fetus's head is disproportionately large compared to the lower part of its body.

Step-by-StepDiagram9.1

Prenatal Development

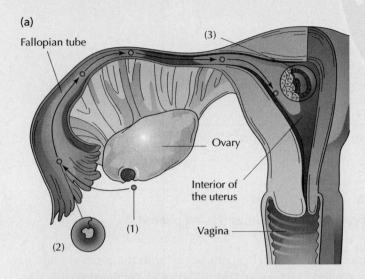

(a) Fallopian tube — (3) — Ovary — Interior of the uterus — (1) — (2) — Vagina

◀ **Germinal period: From ovulation and conception to implantation** After discharge from either the left or right ovary (a), the ovum travels to the opening of the fallopian tube.

If fertilization occurs (2), it normally takes place in the first third of the fallopian tube. The fertilized ovum is referred to as a zygote.

When the zygote reaches the uterus, it implants itself in the wall of the uterus (3) and begins to grow tendril-like structures that intertwine with the rich supply of blood vessels located there. After implantation, the organism is known as an embryo.

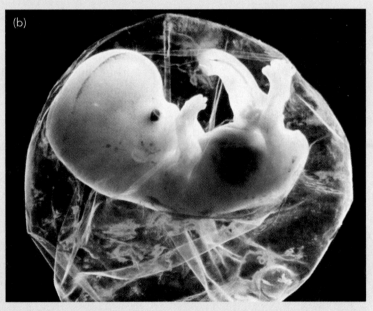

(b)

▲ **Embryonic period** This stage lasts from implantation to eight weeks. At eight weeks, the major organ systems have become well differentiated. Note that at this stage, the head grows at a faster rate than other parts of the body.

(c)

▲ **Fetal period** This is the period from the end of the second month to birth. At four months, all the actual body parts and organs are established. The fetal stage is primarily a time for increased growth and "fine detailing."

Germinal Period First stage of prenatal development, which begins with ovulation, conception, and implantation in the uterus (the first two weeks)

Embryonic Period Second stage of prenatal development, which begins after uterine implantation and lasts through the eighth week

Fetal Period Third, and final, stage of prenatal development (eight weeks to birth), which is characterized by rapid weight gain in the fetus and the fine detailing of bodily organs and systems

Summary Table 9.2 THREATS TO PRENATAL DEVELOPMENT

Maternal and Environmental Factors	Possible Effects on Embryo, Fetus, Newborn, or Young Child
Malnutrition	Low birth weight, malformations, less developed brain, greater vulnerability to disease
Stress exposure	Low birth weight, hyperactivity, irritability, feeding difficulties
Exposure to X-rays	Malformations, cancer
Legal and illegal drugs	Inhibition of bone growth, hearing loss, low birth weight, fetal alcohol syndrome, mental retardation, attention deficits in childhood, and death.
Diseases German measles (rubella), herpes, AIDS, and toxoplasmosis	Blindness, deafness, mental retardation, heart and other malformations, brain infection, spontaneous abortion, premature birth, low birth weight, and death

Sources: Abadinsky, 2011; Howell, Coles, & Kable, 2008; Levinthal, 2011; Maisto, Galizio, & Connors, 2011; Whitbourne, 2011.

StudyTip

Are you confused by the term "epigenetics"? If so, think of *genetics* as this book and *epigenetics* as you the reader. Like traditional genetic inheritance, once this text is printed, the information is somewhat "hard wired" and will be passed along to all readers in the same fashion. But how this information is later interpreted will vary depending on you and all other readers—the epigenetic factors.

Teratogen [Tuh-RAT-uh-jen]
Environmental agent that causes damage during prenatal development; the term comes from the Greek word *teras*, meaning "malformation"

Fetal Alcohol Syndrome (FAS)
Combination of birth defects, including organ deformities and mental, motor, and/or growth retardation, that results from maternal alcohol abuse

Hazards to Prenatal Development
Objective 9.5: What are the major hazards to prenatal development?

As you recall from Chapter 2, human development begins with the genes we inherit from our parents. However, extrinsic, environmental factors (*epigenetics*) also dramatically affect how these inherited genes are expressed at each prenatal stage and throughout our lives ("epi" literally means "above" (Coila, 2009; Jeltsch & Fischle, 2011; Meaney, 2010). For example, during pregnancy, the *placenta* (the vascular organ that unites the fetus to the mother's uterus) serves as the link for food and excretion of wastes. It also screens out some, but not all, harmful substances. Environmental hazards such as X-rays or toxic waste, drugs, and diseases such as rubella (German measles) can cross the *placental barrier* (Table 9.2). These influences generally have their most devastating effect during the first three months of pregnancy—making this a *critical period* in development.

Perhaps the most important, and generally avoidable, danger to the fetus comes from drugs—both legal and illegal. Nicotine and alcohol are two of the most important **teratogens**, environmental agents that cause damage during prenatal development. Mothers who drink alcohol or use tobacco during pregnancy have significantly higher rates of spontaneous abortions, premature births, low-birth-weight infants, and fetal deaths. Their children also show increased behavioral abnormalities and cognitive problems (Coles et al., 2011; Espy et al., 2011; Larkby et al., 2011). In short, when a pregnant woman takes drugs, her unborn child does too.

The pregnant mother obviously plays a primary role in prenatal development because her nutrition and health directly influence the child she is carrying. Almost everything she ingests can cross the placental barrier (a better term might be *placental sieve*). However, the father also plays a role—other than just fertilization. Environmentally, the father's smoking may pollute the air the mother breathes, and genetically, he may transmit heritable diseases. In addition, research suggests that alcohol, opiates, cocaine, various gases, lead, pesticides, and industrial chemicals all can damage sperm (Baker & Nieuwenhuijsen, 2008; Ferreti, et al., 2006; Levy et al., 2011).

Alcohol readily crosses the placenta, affects fetal development, and can result in a neurotoxic syndrome called **fetal alcohol syndrome (FAS)** (Figure 9.6). About one in a hundred babies in the United States is born with FAS or other birth defects resulting from the mother's alcohol use during pregnancy (National Organization on Fetal Alcohol Syndrome, 2008; Popova et al., 2011).

Early Childhood Physical Development

Objective 9.6: Summarize early childhood physical development.

Although Shakespeare described newborns as capable of only "mewling and puking in the nurse's arms," they are actually capable of much more. Let's explore three key areas of change in early childhood: *brain, motor,* and *sensory/perceptual development.*

Brain Development As you recall from Chapter 2, the human brain is divided into three major sections—the *hindbrain, midbrain,* and *forebrain.* Note in Step-by-Step Diagram 9.2a how the prenatal brain begins as a fluid-filled neural tube and then rapidly progresses.

Rapid brain growth during infancy and early childhood slows down in later childhood. Further brain development and learning occur primarily because neurons grow in size and because the number of axons and dendrites, as well as the extent of their connections, increases (Step-by-Step Diagram 9.2b).

Figure 9.6 Fetal alcohol syndrome Prenatal exposure to alcohol may also cause facial abnormalities and stunted growth. But the most disabling features of FAS are neurobehavioral problems, ranging from hyperactivity and learning disabilities to mental retardation, depression, and psychoses. *Source:* Pellegrino & Pellegrino, 2008; Sowell et al., 2008; Wass, 2008.

The brain and other parts of the nervous system grow faster than any other part of the body during both prenatal development and the first two years of life. At birth, a healthy newborn's brain is one-fourth its full adult size, and it will grow to about 75 percent of its adult weight and size by the age of two. The brain and the head develop ahead of the body. In the newborn, the head is much larger in proportion to the body than in the adult (See Step-by-Step Diagram 9.2c).

Motor Development Compared to the hidden, internal changes in brain development, the orderly emergence of active movement skills, known as *motor development,* is easily observed and measured. The newborn's first motor abilities are limited to *reflexes*—involuntary responses to stimulation. For example, the rooting reflex occurs when something touches a baby's cheek, and the infant automatically turns its head, opens its mouth, and roots for a nipple.

In addition to simple reflexes, the infant soon begins to show voluntary control over the movement of various body parts. As shown in the Step-by-Step Diagram 9.3, a helpless newborn who cannot even lift her head is soon transformed into an active toddler capable of crawling, walking, and climbing. Keep in mind that motor development is largely due to natural maturation, but it can also be affected by environmental influences like disease and neglect, as well as by cultural factors. Recent research has shifted from describing the age at which motor skills develop to *how* they develop (Adolph et al., 2011; Newell et al., 2010).

Sensory and Perceptual Development At birth, a newborn can smell most odors and distinguish between sweet, salty, and bitter tastes. Breast-fed newborns also recognize, show preference for, and are calmed by the odor and taste of their mother's milk over another mother's milk or other substances (Allam et al., 2010; DiPietro, 2000; Rattaz et al., 2005). In addition, the newborn's sense of touch and pain is highly developed, as evidenced by reactions to circumcision and heel pricks for blood testing.

Step-by-StepDiagram9.2

STOP *This Step by Step diagram contains essential information NOT found elsewhere in the text, which is likely to appear on quizzes and exams. Be sure to study it CAREFULLY!*

Changes in Brain Development

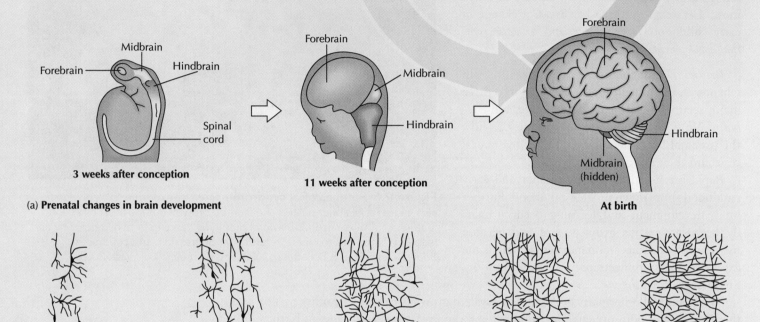

(a) **Prenatal changes in brain development**

3 weeks after conception

11 weeks after conception

At birth

At birth

1 month

3 months

15 months

24 months

(b) **Brain growth in the first two years** As infants learn and develop, synaptic connections between active neurons strengthen, and dendritic connections become more eleborate. *Synaptic pruning* (reduction of unused synapses) helps support this process. *Myelination*, the accumulation of fatty tissue coating the axons of nerve cells, continues until early adulthood. Myelin increases the speed of neural impulses, and the speed of information processing shows a corresponding increase (Chapter 2). In addition, synaptic connections in the frontal lobes and other parts of the brain continue growing and changing throughout the entire life span (Chapters 2 and 6).

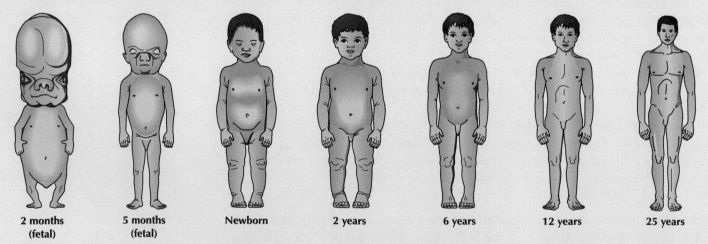

2 months (fetal)

5 months (fetal)

Newborn

2 years

6 years

12 years

25 years

(c) **Brain and body changes over the life span** As mentioned earlier, a large part of human development results from an orderly sequence of genetically designed biological processes we call *maturation*. Note the dramatic changes in our brain and body proportions as we grow older.

Step-by-StepDiagram9.3

Motor Development

Chin up
2.2 mo.

Rolls over
2.8 mo.

Sits with support
2.9 mo.

Sits alone
5.5 mo.

Stands holding furniture

5.8 mo.

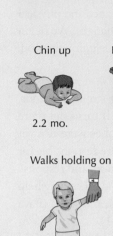
Walks holding on
9.2 mo.

Stands alone
11.5 mo.

Walks alone
12.1 mo.

Walks up steps
17.1 mo.

(a) **A Milestones in motor development** In the typical progression of motor abilities, "chin up" occurs at 2.2 months. However, no two children are exactly alike; all follow their own individual timetables for physical development. (Adapted from Frankenburg et al., 1992, with permission.)

(b) **Maturation and motor development** Although there are large individual differences in the ages at which each ability appears, infants around the world develop according to the same maturational sequence, despite wide variations in cultural beliefs and practices. For example, some Hopi Indian infants spend a great portion of their first year of life being carried in a cradleboard, rather than crawling and walking freely on the ground. Yet by age 1, their motor skills are very similar to those of infants who have not been restrained in this fashion (Dennis & Dennis, 1940).

The sense of vision, however, is poorly developed. At birth, a newborn is estimated to have vision between 20/200 and 20/600. Imagine what an infant's visual life is like. The level of detail you see at 200–600 feet (if you have 20/20 vision) is what they see at 20 feet! Within the first few months, vision quickly improves, and by 6 months, it is 20/100 or better. At 2 years, visual acuity reaches a near-adult level of 20/20 (Courage & Adams, 1990).

One of the most interesting findings in infant sensory and perceptual research concerns hearing. Not only can the newborn hear quite well at birth, but also, during the last few months in the womb, the fetus can hear sounds outside the mother's body. This raises the interesting possibility of fetal learning, and some have advocated special stimulation for the fetus as a way of increasing intelligence, creativity, and general alertness (e.g., Van de Carr & Lehrer, 1997).

Studies on possible fetal learning have found that newborn infants easily recognize their own mother's voice over that of a stranger (Kisilevsky et al., 2003). They also show preferences for children's stories (such as *The Cat in the Hat* or *The King, the Mice, and the Cheese*) that were read to them while they were still in the womb (DeCasper & Fifer, 1980; Music, 2011). On the other hand, some experts caution that too much or the wrong kind of stimulation before birth can be stressful for both the mother and fetus. They suggest that the fetus gets what it needs without special stimulation.

How can scientists measure perceptual abilities and preferences in such young babies? Newborns and infants obviously cannot talk or follow directions, so researchers have had to create ingenious experiments to evaluate their perceptual skill (see the Research Challenge p. 350).

Adolescence and Adulthood: A Time of Both Dramatic and Gradual Change

Objective 9.7: Describe the major physical changes associated with adolescence and adulthood.

Whereas the adolescent years are marked by dramatic changes in appearance and physical capacity, middle age and later adulthood are times of gradual physical changes. We begin with adolescence and a look at important changes in the brain during this unique period.

Adolescence

Think back for a moment to your teen years. Do you remember making stupid decisions, feeling overly emotional, and taking risks you wouldn't dream of today? It turns out there may have been a very good reason for these behaviors—your frontal lobes were not yet fully mature (Figure 9.7). Recall from Chapter 2 that your frontal lobes are responsible for high-level cognitive functions, such as planning ahead, emotional regulation, and response inhibition, and theorists suggest the immaturity of the adolescent's frontal lobes may help explain examples of their poor decisions, reckless behavior, mood swings, and so on (Bava & Tapert, 2010; Christankou, Brammer, & Rubia, 2011; Moshman, 2011).

What about the physical changes you were going through as an adolescent? Did you worry about how you differed from your classmates? Changes in height and weight, breast development and menstruation for girls, and a deepening voice and beard growth for boys are important milestones for adolescents. **Puberty**, the period

Puberty Biological changes during adolescence that lead to an adult-sized body and sexual maturity

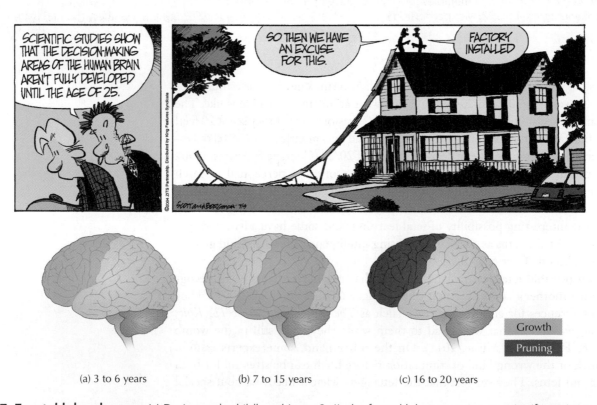

(a) 3 to 6 years   (b) 7 to 15 years   (c) 16 to 20 years

Figure 9.7 Frontal lobe changes (a) During early childhood (ages 3–6), the frontal lobes experience a significant increase in the connections between neurons, which helps explain a child's rapid cognitive growth—especially the ability to think symbolically. (b) This rapid synaptic growth shifts to the temporal and parietal lobes during the ages of 7 to 15, which corresponds to their significant increases in language. (c) During the teen years (ages 16–20), *synaptic pruning* is widespread in the frontal lobes. In contrast to the rapid synaptic *growth* experienced in the earlier years, the adolescent's brain actively destroys (prunes) unneeded connections. Although it may seem counterintuitive, this pruning actually improves brain functioning by making the remaining neurons more efficient. Full maturity of the frontal lobes occurs around the mid-twenties.

Figure 9.8 Ready for responsibility? Adolescence is not a universal concept. Unlike in the United States and other Western nations, some nonindustrialized countries have no need for a slow transition from childhood to adulthood; children simply assume adult responsibilities as soon as possible.

in adolescence when a person becomes capable of reproduction, is a major physical milestone for everyone. It is a clear biological signal of the end of childhood.

Although commonly associated with puberty, *adolescence* is the loosely defined psychological period of development between childhood and adulthood. In the United States, it roughly corresponds to the teenage years. The concept of adolescence and its meaning vary greatly across cultures (Figure 9.8).

The clearest and most dramatic physical sign of puberty is the *growth spurt*, characterized by rapid increases in height, weight, and skeletal growth (Figure 9.9), and by significant changes in reproductive structures and sexual characteristics. Maturation and hormone secretion cause rapid development of the ovaries, uterus, and vagina and the onset of menstruation *(menarche)* in the adolescent female. In the adolescent male, the testes, scrotum, and penis develop, and he undergoes *spermarche* (the first ejaculation). The ovaries and testes in turn produce hormones that lead to the development of *secondary sex characteristics*, such as the growth of pubic hair, deepening of the voice, growth of facial hair, growth of breasts, and so on (Figure 9.10).

Once the large and obvious pubertal changes have occurred, further age-related physical changes are less dramatic. Other than some modest increase in height and muscular development during the late teens and early twenties, most individuals experience only minor physical changes until middle age.

Middle Age

For women, *menopause*, the cessation of the menstrual cycle, which occurs somewhere between ages 45 and 55, is the second most important life milestone in physical development. The decreased production of estrogen (the dominant female hormone) produces certain physical changes. However, the popular belief that menopause (or "the change of life") causes serious psychological mood swings, loss of sexual interest, and major depression is *not* supported by current research (Matlin, 2012; Moilanen et al., 2010). In fact, most studies find that postmenopausal women report relief, increased

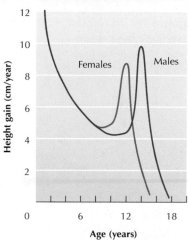

Figure 9.9 Adolescent growth spurt Note the gender differences in height gain during puberty. Most girls are about two years ahead of boys in their growth spurt and therefore are taller than most boys between the ages of 10 and 14.

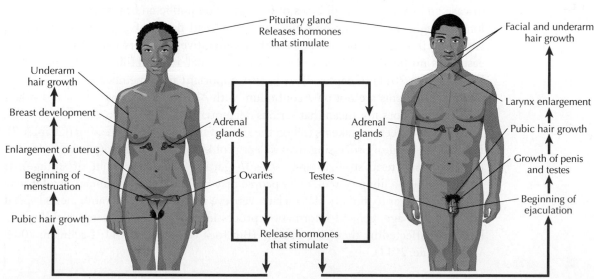

Figure 9.10 Secondary sex characteristics Complex physical changes in puberty primarily result from hormones secreted from the ovaries and testes, the pituitary gland in the brain, and adrenal glands near the kidneys.

"As I get older, I find I rely more and more on these sticky notes to remind me."

Ageism Prejudice or discrimination based on physical age

Figure 9.11 Use it or lose it?
Recent research shows that cognitive functioning in older adults can be greatly enhanced with simple aerobic training (Berchtold, 2008; Hillier & Barrow, 2011).

libido, and other positive reactions to the end of their menstrual cycles (Chrisler, 2008; Strauss, 2010). When psychological problems exist, they may reflect the social devaluation of aging women, not the physiological process of menopause itself. Given our Western society in which women are highly valued for their youth and beauty, can you understand why such a biological landmark of aging may be difficult for some women?

For men, youthfulness is less important, and the physical changes of middle age are less obvious. Beginning in middle adulthood, men experience a gradual decline in the production of sperm and testosterone (the dominant male hormone), although they may remain capable of reproduction into their eighties or nineties. Physical changes such as unexpected weight gain, decline in sexual responsiveness, loss of muscle strength, and graying or loss of hair may lead some men (and women as well) to feel depressed and to question their life progress. They often see these alterations as a biological signal of aging and mortality. Such physical and psychological changes in men are known as the *male climacteric*.

Late Adulthood

Objective 9.8: Define ageism, and explain what causes us to age and die?

After middle age, most physical changes in development are gradual and occur in the heart, arteries, and sensory receptors. For example, cardiac output (the volume of blood pumped by the heart each minute) decreases, whereas blood pressure increases due to the thickening and stiffening of arterial walls. Visual acuity and depth perception decline, hearing acuity lessens, especially for high-frequency sounds, and smell and taste sensitivity decreases (Baldwin & Ash, 2011; Heinrich & Schneider, 2011; Morgan & Murphy, 2010; Snyder & Alain, 2007; Whitbourne, 2011).

In addition to these physical losses, television, magazines, movies, and advertisements generally portray aging as a time of balding and graying hair, sagging parts, poor vision, hearing loss, and, of course, no sex life. Such negative portrayals contribute to our society's widespread **ageism**, prejudice or discrimination based on physical age. However, as advertising companies pursue revenues from the huge aging babyboomer population, there has been a recent shift toward a more accurate portrayal of aging also as a time of vigor, interest, and productivity (Figures 9.11 and 9.12).

What about memory problems and inherited genetic tendencies toward Alzheimer's disease and other serious diseases of old age? The public and most researchers have long thought aging is accompanied by widespread death of neurons in the brain. Although this decline does happen with degenerative disorders like Alzheimer's disease, it is no longer believed to be a part of normal aging (Hillier & Barrow, 2011; Whitbourne, 2011) (Chapter 2). It is also important to remember that age-related memory problems are not on a continuum with Alzheimer's disease. That is, normal forgetfulness does not mean that serious dementia is around the corner.

Aging does seem to take its toll on the *speed* of information processing (Chapter 7). Decreased speed of processing may reflect problems with *encoding* (putting information into long-term storage) and *retrieval* (getting information out of storage). If memory is like a filing system, older people may have more filing cabinets, and it may take them longer to initially file and later retrieve information. Although mental speed declines with age, general information processing and much of memory ability are largely unaffected by the aging process (Binstock & George, 2011; Lachman, 2004; Whitbourne, 2011).

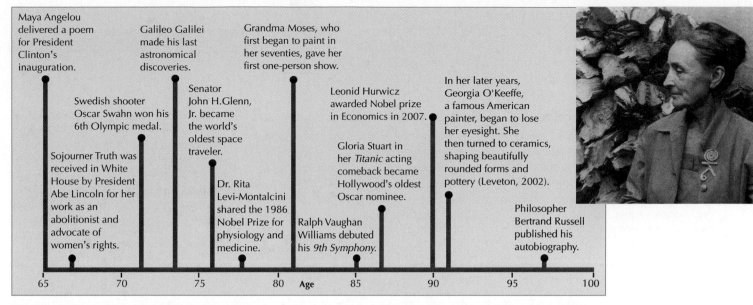

Figure 9.12 Achievement in later years Note the high level of productivity among some of the world's most famous elder figures.

Despite their concerns about "keeping up with 18-year-olds," older returning students often do as well or better than their younger counterparts in college classes.

This superior performance by older adult students is due in part to their generally greater academic motivation, but it also reflects the importance of prior knowledge. Cognitive psychologists have demonstrated that the more people know, the easier it is for them to lay down new memories (Goldstein, 2011; Matlin, 2012). Older students, for instance, generally find this chapter on development easier to master than younger students. Their interactions with children and greater knowledge about life changes create a framework on which to hang new information.

In summary, the more you know, the more you can learn. Thus, having a college degree and a stimulating occupation may help you stay mentally sharp in your later years.

What causes us to age and die? If we set aside aging and deaths resulting from disease, abuse, or neglect, which is known as *secondary aging*, we are left to consider *primary aging* (gradual, inevitable age-related changes in physical and mental processes). There are two main theories explaining primary aging and death—programmed theory and damage theory.

According to *programmed theory*, aging is genetically controlled. Once the ovum is fertilized, the program for aging and death is set and begins to run. Researcher Leonard Hayflick (1977, 1996) found that human cells seem to have a built-in life span. After about 50 doublings of laboratory-cultured cells, they cease to divide—they have reached the *Hayflick limit*. The other explanation of primary aging is *damage theory*, which proposes that an accumulation of damage to cells and organs over the years ultimately causes death.

Whether aging is genetically controlled or caused by accumulated damage over the years, scientists generally agree that humans appear to have a maximum life span of about 110 to 120 years. Although we can try to control secondary aging in an attempt to reach that maximum, so far we have no means to postpone primary aging.

CHECK & REVIEW

STOP *Before going on, be sure to complete this Check & Review. It is an invaluable study tool!*

Physical Development

Part A: Retrieval Practice

1. Without looking at the book, spend 10 minutes writing a free-form essay recalling all you can remember from the previous section.

2. Now, reread the previous section, and once again spend 10 minutes writing a free-form essay on the SAME material.

Part B: Practice Quiz

1. What are the three stages of prenatal development?

2. Teratogens are _____ that can cause birth defects.

3. The _____ grow faster than any other part of the body during prenatal development and the first two years of life.

4. The period of life when an individual first becomes capable of reproduction is known as _____. (a) the age of fertility; (b) adolescence; (c) puberty; (d) the adolescent climacteric

5. Gradual, inevitable age-related changes in physical and mental processes are called _____.

Check your answers in Appendix B.

Cognitive Development

Objective 9.9: Describe Piaget's theory of cognitive development, and compare schema, assimilation, and accommodation.

The following fan letter was written to Shari Lewis (1963), a children's television performer, about her puppet Lamb Chop:

> *Dear Shari:*
>
> *All my friends say Lamb Chop isn't really a little girl that talks. She is just a puppet you made out of a sock. I don't care even if it's true. I like the way Lamb Chop talks. If I send you one of my socks will you teach it how to talk and send it back?*
>
> RANDI

Randi's understanding of fantasy and reality is certainly different from an adult's. Just as a child's body and physical abilities change, his or her way of knowing and perceiving the world also grows and changes. This seems intuitively obvious. But early psychologists—with one exception—focused on physical, emotional, language, and personality development. The one major exception was Jean Piaget (Pee-ah-ZHAY).

TRY THIS YOURSELF

Testing Your Artistic Schemas

Study the "impossible figure" to the right, and then try drawing this same figure without tracing it. Students with artistic training generally find it relatively easy to reproduce, whereas the rest of us find it "impossible." This is because we lack the necessary artistic schema and cannot assimilate what we see. With practice and training, we could accommodate the new information and easily draw the figure.

Piaget's Theory: Children Are Not Miniature Adults

Piaget demonstrated that a child's intellect is fundamentally different from an adult's. He showed that an infant begins at a cognitively "primitive" level and that intellectual growth progresses in distinct stages, motivated by an innate need to know. Piaget's theory, developed in the 1920s and 1930s, has proven so comprehensive and insightful that it remains the major force in the cognitive area of developmental psychology today.

To appreciate Piaget's contributions, we need to consider three major concepts: schemas, assimilation, and accommodation. **Schemas** are the most basic units of intellect. They act as patterns that organize our interactions with the environment, like architect's drawings or builder's blueprints.

Figure 9.13 Accommodation in action An infant's first attempt to eat solid food with a spoon is a good example of accommodation. When the spoon first enters her mouth, the child attempts to assimilate it by using the previously successful sucking schema—shaping lips and tongue around the spoon as around a nipple. After repeated trials, she accommodates by adjusting her lips and tongue in a way that moves the food off the spoon and into her mouth.

In the first few weeks of life, for example, the infant apparently has several schemas based on the innate reflexes of sucking, grasping, and so on. These schemas are primarily motor skills and may be little more than stimulus-and-response mechanisms—the nipple is presented and the baby sucks. Soon, however, other schemas emerge. The infant develops a more detailed schema for eating solid food, a different schema for the concepts of *mother* and *father*, and so on. It is important to recognize that schemas, our tools for learning about the world, are enlarged and changed throughout our lives. For example, older music lovers previously accustomed to LP records have had to develop different schemas for playing CDs and MP3s.

Assimilation and accommodation are the two major processes by which schemas grow and change over time. **Assimilation** is using existing mental patterns (schemas) in new situations. For instance, infants use their sucking schema not only in sucking nipples but also in sucking blankets or fingers.

In **accommodation**, existing ideas are modified to fit new information. It generally occurs when new information or stimuli cannot be assimilated. New schemas must be developed, or old schemas must be changed to better fit with the new information. Just as a baby must learn to accommodate to a spoon versus a nipple (Figure 9.13), if you meet someone through an online chat room and are later surprised when you talk face to face, it is because of the unexamined schemas you constructed. The awkwardness and discomfort you now feel are due, in part, to the work involved in readjusting, or accommodating, your earlier schemas to match the new reality.

Schema Cognitive structures or "blueprints" of organized ideas that grow and differentiate with experience

Assimilation In Piaget's theory, applying existing mental patterns (schemas) to new information; new information is incorporated (assimilated) into existing schemas

Accommodation In Piaget's theory, adjusting existing mental patterns (schemas), or developing new ones, to better fit with new information; mental schemas are changed to accommodate new information

Stages of Cognitive Development: Birth to Adolescence

Objective 9.10: Compare how children's cognitive development changes during Piaget's four stages.

According to Piaget, all children go through approximately the same four stages of cognitive development, regardless of the culture in which they live (Step-by-Step Diagram 9.4). Stages cannot be skipped because skills acquired at earlier stages are essential to mastery at later stages. Let's take a closer look at these four stages: sensorimotor, preoperational, concrete operational, and formal operational.

Sensorimotor Stage

During the **sensorimotor stage**, lasting from birth until "significant" language acquisition (about age 2), children explore the world and develop their schemas primarily through their senses and motor activities—hence the term *sensorimotor*.

Sensorimotor Stage Piaget's first stage of cognitive development (birth to approximately age 2), in which schemas are developed through sensory and motor activities

Step-by-StepDiagram9.4

Piaget's Four Stages of Cognitive Development

Birth to 2

Sensorimotor

Abilities:
- Uses senses and motor skills to explore and develop cognitively

Limits:
- Beginning of stage lacks object *permanence* (understanding things continue to exist even when not seen, heard, or felt)

What's happening in these photos? The child in these two photos seems to believe the toy no longer exists once it is blocked from sight. Can you explain why?

Answer: According to Piaget, young infants lack object permanence—an understanding that objects continue to exist even when they cannot be seen, heard, or touched.

Ages 2–7

Preoperational

Abilities:
- Has significant language and thinks symbolically

Limits:
- Preoperational thinking (lacks reversibility and very intuitive)
- *Egocentrism* (inability to consider another's point of view)
- *Animistic thinking* (believing all things are living)

THE FAMILY CIRCUS. By Bil Keane

"Look what I can do, Grandma!"

Applying Piaget Can you identify this child's Piagetian stage of cognitive development? Why does he think his Grandma can see him?

Answer: The child is in the preoperational stage, and his egocentrism prevents him from recognizing that Grandma does not see everything he sees.

Ages 7–11

Concrete Operational

Abilities:
- Less egocentric and capable of true logical thinking
- Understands *conservation* (*realizing changes in shape or appearance can be reversed*)

Limits:
- Thinking tied to *concrete*, tangible objects and events
- Cannot think abstractly and hypothetically.

 (a)  (b)  (c)

Test for conservation (a) In the classic conservation of liquids test, the child is first shown two identical glasses with liquid at the same level. (b) The liquid is poured from one of the short, wide glasses into the tall, thin one. (c) When asked whether the two glasses have the same amount or if one has more, the preoperational child replies that the tall, thin glass has more. This demonstrates a failure to conserve volume.

Ages 11 and up

GO GREEN

Formal Operational

Abilities:
- Can think abstractly and hypothetically

Limits:
- *Adolescent egocentrism* at the beginning of this stage, with related problems of the personal fable and *imaginary audience*

Self-consciousness What developmental phenomenon might explain why adolescents sometimes display what seems like extreme forms of self-consciousness and concern for physical appearance?

One important concept acquired during this stage is **object permanence**. At birth and for the next three or four months, children lack object permanence. They seem to have no schemas for objects they cannot see, hear, or touch—out of sight is apparently out of mind.

Preoperational Stage

During the **preoperational stage** (roughly age 2 to 7), language advances significantly, and the child begins to think *symbolically*—using symbols, such as words, to represent concepts. Three other qualities characterize problems or limits during this stage:

1. *Preoperational thinking* Piaget labeled this period "preoperational" because the child lacks *operations*, *reversible* mental processes. For instance, if a preoperational boy who has a brother is asked, "Do you have a brother?" he will easily respond, "Yes." However, when asked, "Does your brother have a brother?" he will answer, "No!" To understand that his brother has a brother, he must be able to *reverse* the concept of "having a brother." In addition, thinking is still very *intuitive*—with little use of reasoning and logic (e.g., believing the sun follows them while they're taking a walk).

2. *Egocentrism* Children at this stage are **egocentric**, which refers to the preoperational child's limited ability to distinguish between his or her own perspective and someone else's.

Egocentrism is not the same as "selfishness." Preschoolers who move in front of you to get a better view of the TV or repeatedly ask questions while you are talking on the telephone are not being selfish. They are demonstrating their natural limits and egocentric thought processes. Children in this stage naively assume that others see, hear, feel, and think exactly as they do. Consider the following telephone conversation between a 3-year-old, who is at home, and her mother, who is at work:

MOTHER: Emma, is that you?

EMMA: (Nods silently.)

MOTHER: Emma, is Daddy there? May I speak to him?

EMMA: (Twice nods silently.)

Egocentric preoperational children fail to understand that the phone caller cannot see their nodding head. Charming as this is, preoperational children's egocentrism also sometimes leads them to believe their "bad thoughts" caused their sibling or parent to get sick or that their misbehavior caused their parents' marital problems. Because they think the world centers on them, they often cannot separate reality from what goes on inside their own head.

3. *Animistic thinking* Believing objects such as the sun, trees, clouds, and bars of soap have motives, feelings, and intentions (for example, "dark clouds are angry" and "soap sinks to the bottom of the bathtub because it is tired"). *Animism* refers to the belief that all things are living (or animated). Our earlier example of Randi's letter asking puppeteer Shari Lewis to teach her sock to talk like Lamb Chop is an example of animistic thinking.

Can preoperational children be taught how to use operations and to avoid egocentric and animistic thinking? Although some researchers have reported success in accelerating the preoperational stage, Piaget did not believe in pushing children ahead of their own developmental schedule. He believed children should be allowed to grow at their own pace, with minimal adult interference (Elkind, 1981, 2000). Piaget

Object Permanence Piagetian term for an infant's understanding that objects (or people) continue to exist even when they cannot be seen, heard, or touched directly

Early experimentation Piaget believed children are natural experimenters biologically driven to explore their environment.

Preoperational Stage Piaget's second stage of cognitive development (roughly age 2 to 7), characterized by the ability to employ significant language and to think symbolically, but the child lacks operations (reversible mental processes), and thinking is egocentric and animistic

Egocentrism Inability to consider another's point of view, which Piaget considered a hallmark of the preoperational stage

Concrete Operational Stage
Piaget's third stage of cognitive development (roughly age 7 to 11); child can perform mental operations on concrete objects and understand reversibility and conservation, but thinking is tied to concrete, tangible objects and events

Conservation Understanding that certain physical characteristics (such as volume) remain unchanged, even when their outward appearance changes

Formal Operational Stage
Piaget's fourth stage of cognitive development (around age 11 and beyond), characterized by abstract and hypothetical thinking

Personal fable in action? Can you see how this type of risk-taking behavior may reflect the personal fable—the adolescents' tendency to believe they are unique and special and that dangers don't apply to them?

thought Americans were particularly guilty of pushing children, calling American childhood the "Great American Kid Race."

Concrete Operational Stage

Between the approximate ages of 7 and 11, children are in the **concrete operational stage**. During this stage many important thinking skills emerge. Children in this stage are less egocentric in their thinking and become capable of true logical thought. As most parents know, this is the age when children stop believing in Santa Claus because they logically conclude that one man can not deliver presents to everyone in one night.

Because they understand the concept of *reversibility*, concrete operational children can now successfully perform "operations." They recognize that certain physical attributes (such as volume) remain unchanged, although the outward appearance is altered, a process known as **conservation**. These children also are less egocentric and more logical. However, as the name implies, their thinking tends to be limited to *concrete*, tangible objects and events.

Formal Operational Stage

The final period in Piaget's theory is the **formal operational stage**, which typically begins around age 11. In this stage, children begin to apply their operations to abstract concepts in addition to concrete objects. Children now find it much easier to master the abstract thinking required for geometry and algebra. For example, $(a + b)^2 = a^2 + 2ab + b^2$. They also become capable of hypothetical thinking ("What if?"), which allows systematic formulation and testing of concepts.

Adolescents considering part-time jobs, for example, may think about possible conflicts with school and friends, the number of hours they want to work, and the kind of work for which they are qualified before they start filling out applications. Formal operational thinking also allows the adolescent to construct a well-reasoned argument based on hypothetical concepts and logical processes. Consider the following argument:

1. If you hit a glass with a feather, the glass will break.
2. You hit the glass with a feather.

What is the logical conclusion? The correct answer, "The glass will break," is contrary to fact and direct experience. Therefore, the child in the concrete operational stage would have difficulty with this task, whereas the formal operational thinker understands that this problem is about abstractions that need not correspond to the real world.

Problems with Early Formal Operational Thinking

Along with the benefits of this cognitive style come several problems. Adolescents in the early stages of the formal operational period demonstrate a type of *egocentrism* different from that of the preoperational child. Although adolescents do recognize that others have unique thoughts and perspectives, they often fail to differentiate between what others are thinking and their own thoughts. This *adolescent egocentrism* has two characteristics that may affect social interactions as well as problem solving:

1. *Personal fable* Given their unique form of egocentrism, adolescents may conclude that they alone are having certain insights or difficulties and that no one else could understand or sympathize. David Elkind (1967, 2000, 2007) described this as the formation of a *personal fable*, an intense investment in their own thoughts and feelings, and a belief that these thoughts are unique. One student in my class remembered being very upset in junior high when her mother tried to comfort her over the loss of an important relationship. "I felt like she couldn't possibly know how it felt—no one could. I couldn't believe that anyone had ever suffered like this or that things would ever get better."

Several forms of risk taking, such as engaging in sexual intercourse without contraception, driving dangerously, and experimenting with drugs, also seem to arise from the personal fable (Alberts, Elkind, & Ginsberg, 2007; Flavell, Miller, & Miller, 2002; Hill & Lapsley, 2011; Moshman, 2011). Although adolescents will acknowledge the risks of these activities, they don't feel personally endangered because they feel uniquely invulnerable and immortal.

As you read earlier, recent scientific studies have shown that the prefrontal cortex of the adolescent's brain is one of the later areas to develop, which may provide a possible biological basis for risk taking and other cognitive limits during adolescence.

2. *Imaginary audience* Adolescents also tend to believe they are the center of others' thoughts and attentions, instead of considering that everyone is equally wrapped up in his or her own concerns and plans. Elkind referred to this as the *imaginary audience*. This new form of egocentrism may explain what seems like extreme forms of self-consciousness and concern for physical appearance ("Everyone knows I don't know the answer"; or "They're noticing how fat I am and this awful haircut").

If the imaginary audience results from an inability to differentiate the self from others, the personal fable is a product of differentiating too much. Thankfully, these two forms of adolescent egocentrism tend to decrease during later stages of the formal operational period.

Assessing Piaget's Theory: Criticisms and Contributions

Objective 9.11: Identify the major criticisms and contributions of Piaget's theories.

As influential as Piaget's account of cognitive development has been, it has received significant criticisms. Let's look briefly at two major areas of concern: *underestimated abilities* and *underestimated genetic* and *cultural influences*.

Underestimated Abilities

Research shows that Piaget may have underestimated young children's cognitive development (Figure 9.14). For example, researchers report that very young infants have a basic concept of how objects move, are aware that objects continue to exist even when screened from view, and can recognize speech sounds (Baillargeon, 2000, 2008; Madole, Oaks, & Rakison, 2011).

Nonegocentric responses also appear in the earliest days of life. For example, newborn babies tend to cry in response to the cry of another baby (Diego & Jones, 2007; Geangu et al., 2010). And preschoolers will adapt their speech by using shorter, simpler expressions when talking to 2-year-olds rather than to adults (Figure 9.15).

Underestimated Genetic and Cultural Influences

Piaget's model, like other stage theories, has also been criticized for not sufficiently taking into account genetic and cultural differences (Cole & Gajdamaschko, 2007; Shweder, 2011; Zelazo, Chandler, & Crone, 2010). During Piaget's time, the genetic influences on cognitive abilities were poorly understood, but as you know there has been a rapid explosion of information in this field in the last few years. In addition, formal education and specific cultural experiences can significantly affect cognitive

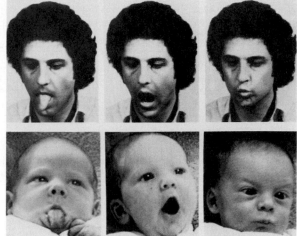

Figure 9.14 Infant imitation In a series of well-known studies, Andrew Meltzoff and M. Keith Moore (1977, 1985, 1994) found that newborns could imitate such facial movements as tongue protrusion, mouth opening, and lip pursing. At 9 months, infants will imitate facial actions a full day after seeing them (Heimann & Meltzoff, 1996). Can you see how this early infant facial expression raises questions about Piaget's estimates of early infant abilities? When an adult models a facial expression, even very young infants will respond with a similar expression. Is this true imitation or a simple stimulus-response reflex?

Figure 9.15 Are preoperational children always egocentric? Contrary to Piaget's beliefs, children at this age often do take the perspective of another.

TRY THIS YOURSELF

Putting Piaget to the Test

This is a sample of experiments used to test Piaget's different types of conservation. If you have access to children in the pre-operational or concrete operational stages, you may enjoy testing their grasp of conservation by trying some of these experiments. The equipment is easily obtained, and you will find their responses fascinating. Keep in mind that this should be done as a game. The child should not feel that he or she is failing a test or making a mistake.

Type of Conservation Task (Average age at which concept is grasped)	Your task as experimenter...	Child is asked...
Length (ages 6–7)	**Step 1** Center two sticks of equal length. (Child agrees that they are of equal length.) **Step 2** Move one stick	**Step 3** *"Which stick is longer?"* Preoperational child will say that one of the sticks is longer. Child in concrete stage will say that they are both the same length.
Substance amount (ages 6–7)	**Step 1** Center two identical clay balls. (Child acknowledges that the two have equal amounts of clay.) **Step 2** Flatten one of the balls.	**Step 3** *"Do the two pieces have the same amount of clay?"* Preoperational child will say that the flat piece has more clay. Child in concrete stage will say that the two pieces have the same amount of clay.
Area (ages 8–10)	**Step 1** Center two identical Sheets of cardboard with wooden blocks placed on them in identical positions. (Child acknowledges that the same amount of space is left open on each piece of cardboard.) **Step 2** Scatter the blocks on one piece of the cardboard.	**Step 3** *"Do the two pieces of cardboard have the same amount of open space?"* Preoperational child will say that the cardboard with scattered blocks has less open space. Child in concrete stage will say that both pieces have the same amount of open space.

development. In contrast to Piaget's belief that the most important source of cognition is the child itself, Lev Vygotsky, a famous Russian psychologist, proposed that our social and cultural environments play a more influential role (Ferrari, Robinson & Yasnitsky, 2010; Trawick-Smith & Dziurgot, 2011). Consider the following example from a researcher attempting to test the formal operational skills of a farmer in Liberia (Scribner, 1977):

RESEARCHER: All Kpelle men are rice farmers. Mr. Smith is not a rice farmer. Is he a Kpelle man?

KPELLE FARMER: I don't know the man. I have not laid eyes on the man myself.

Instead of reasoning in the "logical" way of Piaget's formal operational stage, the Kpelle farmer reasoned according to his specific cultural and educational training, which apparently emphasized personal knowledge. Not knowing Mr. Smith, the Kpelle farmer did not feel qualified to comment on him. Thus, Piaget's theory may have underestimated the effect of culture on a person's cognitive functioning.

Despite criticisms, Piaget's contributions to psychology are enormous. As one scholar put it, "assessing the impact of Piaget on developmental psychology is like assessing the impact of Shakespeare on English literature or Aristotle on philosophy—impossible" (Beilin, 1992, p. 191).

CHECK & REVIEW

STOP *Before going on, be sure to complete this Check & Review. It is an invaluable study tool!*

Cognitive Development

Part A: Retrieval Practice

1. Without looking at the book, spend 10 minutes writing a free-form essay recalling all you can remember from the previous section.

2. Now, reread the previous section, and once again spend 10 minutes writing a free-form essay on the SAME material.

Part B: Practice Quiz

1. _____ was one of the first scientists to prove that a child's cognitive processes are fundamentally different from an adult's.

2. Match the following list of key terms with the correct Piagetian stage:
   ___1. Egocentrism, animism
   ___2. Object permanence
   ___3. Abstract and hypothetical thinking
   ___4. Conservation, reversibility
   ___5. Personal fable, imaginary audience
   a. Sensorimotor
   b. Preoperational
   c. Concrete operational
   d. Formal operational

3. A child's belief that the moon follows him as he travels in a car is an example of _____.

4. Briefly summarize the major contributions and criticisms of Jean Piaget.

Check your answers in Appendix B.

Social-Emotional Development

Objective 9.12: Define *attachment*, and discuss its contributions across the life span.

The poet John Donne wrote, "No man is an island, entire of itself." In addition to physical and cognitive development, developmental psychologists are very interested in social-emotional development. That is, they study how our social relations and emotions grow and change over the life span. Two of the most important topics are *attachment* and *parenting styles*.

Attachment: The Importance of Bonding

Attachment Strong emotional bond with special others that endures over time

An infant arrives in the world with a multitude of behaviors that encourage a strong and lasting emotional bond of **attachment** with primary caregivers. Most research has focused on the attachment between mother and child. However, infants also form attachment bonds with fathers, grandparents, and other caregivers.

In studying attachment behavior, researchers are often divided along the lines of the now familiar nature-versus-nurture debate. Those who advocate the nurture position suggest attachment results from a child's interactions and experiences with his or her environment. In contrast, the nativist, or innate, position cites John Bowlby's work (1969, 1989, 2000). He proposed that newborn infants are biologically equipped with verbal and nonverbal behaviors (such as crying, clinging, smiling) and with "following" behaviors (such as crawling and walking after the caregiver) that elicit instinctive nurturing responses from the caregiver. Konrad Lorenz's (1937) early studies of **imprinting** further support the biological argument for attachment (Figure 9.16). Attachment is discussed in more detail in Concept Organizer 9.1.

Imprinting Innate form of learning within a critical period that involves attachment to the first large moving object seen

What if a child doesn't form an attachment? Researchers have investigated this question in two ways: They have looked at children and adults who spent their early years in institutions without the stimulation and love of a regular caregiver or those who lived at home but were physically isolated under abusive conditions.

Infants raised in impersonal or abusive surroundings suffer from a number of problems. They seldom cry, coo, or babble; they become rigid when picked up; and they have few language skills. As for their social-emotional development, they tend to form shallow or anxious relationships. Some appear forlorn, withdrawn, and uninterested in their caretakers, whereas others seem insatiable in their need for affection. They also tend to show intellectual, physical, and perceptual retardation, along with increased susceptibility to infection, and neurotic "rocking" and isolation behaviors. In some cases, these infants are so deprived they die from lack of attachment (Bowlby, 1973, 1982, 2000; Duniec & Raz, 2011; Gunnar, 2010; Spitz & Wolf, 1946; Zeanah, 2000).

Most children, of course, are never exposed to such extreme institutional conditions. However, Mary Ainsworth (1967; Ainsworth et al., 1978), a world-renowned developmental psychologist who was educated at the University of Toronto, found significant differences in the typical levels of attachment between infants and their mothers. In additional, level of attachment affects long-term behaviours. Using a method called the *strange situation procedure*, in which she observed how infants responded to the presence or absence of their mother and a stranger, Ainsworth found that children could be divided into three groups: *Secure, anxious/avoidant,* and *anxious/ambivalent.* A later psychologist, Mary Main, added a fourth category, *disorganized/disoriented* (Main & Solomon, 1986, 1990) (Figure 9.17).

Researchers found that infants with a secure attachment style had caregivers who were sensitive and responsive to their signals of distress, happiness, and fatigue (Ainsworth, 1967; Ainsworth et al., 1978; Gini et al., 2007; Higley, 2008; Völker, 2007). Avoidant infants had caregivers who were aloof and distant, and anxious/ambivalent infants and inconsistent caregivers who alternated between strong affection and indifference. Follow-up studies found that, over time, securely attached children were the most sociable, emotionally aware, enthusiastic, cooperative, persistent, curious, and competent (Bar-Haim et al., 2007; Brown & Whiteside, 2008; Johnson, Dweck, & Chen, 2007).

Figure 9.16 Imprinting Lorenz's studies on imprinting demonstrated that baby geese attach to, and then follow, the first large moving object they see during a certain critical period in their development.

ConceptOrganizer9.1

STOP *This Concept Organizer contains essential information NOT found elsewhere in the text, which is likely to appear on quizzes and exams. Be sure to study it CAREFULLY!*

Attachment: The Power of Touch

(a) In a classic experiment involving infant rhesus monkeys, Harry Harlow and Robert Zimmerman (1959) investigated the variables that might affect attachment. They created two types of wire-framed surrogate (substitute) "mother" monkeys: one covered by soft terry cloth and one left uncovered.

The infant monkeys were fed by either the cloth or the wire mother, but they otherwise had access to both mothers. The researchers found that monkeys "reared" by a cloth mother clung frequently to the soft material of their surrogate mother, and developed greater emotional security and curiosity than did monkeys assigned to the wire mother.

In later research (Harlow & Harlow, 1966), monkey babies were exposed to rejection. Some of the "mothers" contained metal spikes that would suddenly protrude from the cloth covering and push the babies away; others had air jets that would sometimes blow the babies away. Nevertheless, the infant monkeys waited until the rejection was over and then clung to the cloth mothers as tightly as before. From these and related findings, Harlow concluded that **contact comfort**, the pleasurable tactile sensations provided by a soft and cuddly "parent," is a powerful contributor to attachment.

(b) Several studies suggest that contact comfort between human infants and mothers is similarly important. For example, touching and massaging premature infants produce significant physical, emotional, and even mental benefits (Feldman, 2007; Field, 1998, 2007; Field, Diego, Hernandez-Reif, 2007; Guzzetta et al., 2009; McGrath, 2009; Procianov, Mendes, & Silveira, 2009). Mothers around the world tend to kiss, nuzzle, nurse, comfort, clean, and respond to their children with lots of physical contact.

(c) Although almost all research on attachment and contact comfort has focused on mothers and infants, recent research shows that the same results also apply to fathers and other caregivers (Diener et al., 2008; Grossmann et al., 2002, Lindberg, Axelsson & Öhrling, 2008; Martinelli, 2006).

Figure 9.17 Degrees of Attachment
Research identified four different types of attachment.

- *Secure (60 percent)* When exposed to the stranger, the infant seeks closeness and contact with the mother, (a) uses the mother as a safe base from which to explore, (b) shows moderate distress on separation from the mother, and is happy when the mother returns.

- *Anxious/ambivalent (10 percent)* Infant becomes very upset when the mother leaves the room. When she returns, the infant seeks close contact and then squirms angrily to get away.

(a) (b)

60% Secure attachment

15% Disorganized/disoriented attachment

15% Anxious/avoidant attachment

10% Anxious/ambivalent attachment

- *Anxious/Avoidant (15 percent)* Infant does not seek closeness or contact with the mother; treats the mother much like a stranger, and shows little emotion when the mother departs or returns.

- *Disorganized/disoriented (15 percent)* Infant shows a mixture of avoidant and ambivalent behaviors, often seeming either confused or apprehensive in the presence of the mother.

The importance of attachment
Researchers have found that the degree and quality of attachments you formed as an infant are correlated with your adult romantic relationships.

Psychology at Work

Romantic Love and Attachment

Objective 9.13: Discuss how infant attachment may be related to romantic love.

If you've been around young children, you've probably noticed how often they share toys and discoveries with a parent and how they seem much happier when a parent is nearby. You may also have thought how cute and sweet it is when infants and parents coo and share baby talk with each other. But have you noticed that these very same behaviors often occur between adults in romantic relationships?

Intrigued by these parallels, several researchers have studied the relationship between an infant's attachment to a parent figure and an adult's love for a romantic partner (Clulow, 2007; Feeney, 2008; Lele, 2008). In one study, Cindy Hazan and Phillip Shaver (1987, 1994) discovered that adults who had an anxious/avoidant pattern in infancy find it hard to trust others and to self-disclose, and they rarely report finding "true love." In short, they block intimacy by being emotionally aloof and distant.

In contrast, anxious/ambivalent infants tend to be obsessed with their romantic partners as adults, fearing that their intense love will not be reciprocated. As a result, they tend to smother intimacy by being possessive and emotionally demanding.

Happily, individuals who are securely attached as infants easily become close to others, expect intimate relationships to endure, and perceive others as generally trustworthy. As you may expect, the securely attached lover has intimacy patterns that foster long-term relationships and is the most desired partner by the majority of adults, regardless of their own attachment styles (Lele, 2008; Mikulincer & Goodman, 2006; Vorria et al., 2007).

As you consider these correlations between infant attachment and adult romantic love styles, remember that it is always risky to infer causation from correlation. Accordingly, the relationship between romantic love style and early infant attachment is subject to several alternative explanations. Also, be aware that early attachment experiences may predict the future, but they do not determine it. Throughout life, we can learn new social skills and different attitudes toward relationships.

(TRY THIS YOURSELF)

What's Your Romantic Attachment Style?

Thinking of your current and past romantic relationships, place a check next to those statements that best describe your feelings.

1. *I find it relatively easy to get close to others and am comfortable depending on them and having them depend on me. I don't often worry about being abandoned or about someone getting too close.*

2. *I am somewhat uncomfortable being close. I find it difficult to trust partners* *completely or to allow myself to depend on them. I am nervous when anyone gets close, and love partners often want me to be more intimate than is comfortable for me.*

3. *I find that others are reluctant to get as close as I would like. I often worry that my partner doesn't really love me or won't stay with me. I want to merge completely with another person, and this desire sometimes scares people away.*

According to research, 55 percent of adults agree with item 1 (secure attachment), 25 percent choose number 2 (avoidant attachment), and 20 percent choose item 3 (anxious/ambivalent attachment) (adapted from Fraley & Shaver, 1997; Hazan & Shaver, 1987). Note that the percentages for these adult attachment styles are roughly equivalent to the percentages for infant–parent attachment.

Do your responses match your attachment experiences as a child? Does this affect your present relationship?

Parenting Styles: Their Effect on Development

Objective 9.14: Discuss the three key parenting styles.

How much of our personality comes from the way our parents treat us as we're growing up? Researchers since the 1920s have studied the effects of different methods of child rearing on children's behavior, development, and mental health. Studies done by Diana Baumrind (1980, 1991, 1995) found that parenting styles could be reliably divided into three broad patterns, *permissive*, *authoritarian*, and *authoritative*, which could be identified by their degree of *control/demandingness* (C) and *warmth/responsiveness* (W) (Table 9.3).

Evaluating Baumrind's Research

Before you conclude that the authoritative pattern is the only way to raise successful children, you should know that many children raised in the other styles also become caring, cooperative adults. Criticism of Baumrind's findings generally falls into three areas:

- *Child temperament* Results may reflect the child's unique temperament and reactions to parental efforts rather than the parenting style per se (Bradley & Corwyn, 2008; Miller, Tserakhava, & Miller, 2011; Rhoades et al., 2011). That is, the parents of mature and competent children may have developed the authoritative style because of the child's behavior rather than vice versa.

Table 9.3   PARENTING STYLES

Parenting Style	Description	Example	Possible Effects on Children
Permissive-neglectful (permissive-indifferent) (low control, low warmth)	Parents make few demands, with little structure or monitoring, and show little interest or emotional support; may be actively rejecting.	"I don't care about you—or what you do."	Children tend to have poor social skills and little self-control (being overly demanding and disobedient).
Permissive-indulgent (low control, high warmth)	Parents set few limits or demands but are highly involved and emotionally connected.	"I care about you—and you're free to do what you like!"	Children often fail to learn respect for others and tend to be impulsive, immature, and out of control.
Authoritarian (high control, low warmth)	Parents are rigid and punitive while also being low on warmth and responsiveness.	"I don't care what you want. Just do it my way, or else!"	Children tend to be easily upset, moody, aggressive, and often fail to learn good communication skills.
Authoritative (high control, high warmth)	Parents generally set and enforce firm limits while also being highly involved, tender, and emotionally supportive.	"I really care about you, but there are rules and you need to be responsible."	Children become self-reliant, self-controlled, high achieving, and emotionally well-adjusted; also seem more content, goal oriented, friendly, and socially competent.

> **StudyTip**
>
> These last two terms (authoritarian and authoritative) are very similar. An easy way to remember is to notice the two Rs in authoRitaRian, and imagine a Rigid Ruler. Then note the last two Ts in authoriTaTive, and picture a Tender Teacher.

Sources: Areepattamannil, 2010; Celada, 2011; Driscoll, Russell, & Crockett, 2008; Martin & Fabes, 2009; McKinney, Donnelly, & Renk, 2008; Topham et al., 2011.

• ***Child expectations*** Cultural research suggests that a child's expectations of how parents should behave also play an important role in parenting styles (Laungani, 2007; Zhang et al., 2011). As you'll discover on p. 352, adolescents in Korea expect strong parental control and interpret it as a sign of love and deep concern. Adolescents in North America, however, might interpret the same behavior as a sign of parental hostility and rejection.

• ***Parental warmth*** Cross-cultural studies suggest that the most important variable in parenting styles and child development might be the degree of warmth versus rejection parents feel toward their children. Analyses of over 100 societies have shown that parental rejection adversely affects children of all cultures (Kakihara et al., 2010; Lundy & Skeel, 2010; Parmar, Ibrahim, & Rohner, 2008; Rohner, 1986, 2008; Wu & Chao, 2011). The neglect and indifference shown by rejecting parents tend to be correlated with hostile, aggressive children who have a difficult time establishing and maintaining close relationships. These children also are more likely to develop psychological problems that require professional intervention.

Do fathers differ from mothers in their parenting style? Until recently, the father's role in discipline and child care was largely ignored. But as more fathers have begun to take an active role in child-rearing, there has been a corresponding increase in research. From these studies, we now know that children do best with authoritative dads, and with fathers who are equally absorbed with, excited about, and responsive to their newborns. Researchers also find few differences in the way children form attachments to either parent (Diener et al., 2002; Lopez & Hsu, 2002; Talitwala, 2007). After infancy, the father becomes increasingly involved with his children, yet he still spends less overall time in direct child care than the mother does. In general, fathers are just as responsive, nurturing, and competent as mothers when they assume child-care responsibilities.

Psychology Engages

RESEARCH CHALLENGE

Scientific Research with Infants

How can psychological scientists conduct research with nonverbal infants? One of the earliest experimenters, Robert Fantz (1956, 1963), designed a "looking chamber" to find out what infants can see and what holds their attention. Babies are placed on their backs inside the chamber facing the lighted, "testing" area above.

Fantz and his colleagues used this type of apparatus to measure how long infants stared at various stimuli, and found that infants prefer complex rather than simple patterns and pictures of faces rather than nonfaces (Figure 9.18).

Other researchers use newborns' heart rates and innate abilities, such as the sucking reflex, to study learning and perceptual development (Bendersky & Sullivan, 2007).

To study the sense of smell, researchers measure changes in the newborns' heart rates when odors are presented.

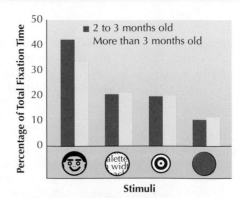

Figure 9.18 Infant visual preferences

Presumably, if they can smell one odor but not another, their heart rates will change in the presence of the first but not the second. As you may recall from Chapter 4, what all of these researchers are measuring is *habituation*—a decreased responsiveness after repeated stimulation.

Brain scans, such as fMRI, MRI, and CTs, also help developmental scientists detect changes in the infant's brain.

Student Engagement Exercise

Given the admittedly limited information in Fantz's "looking chamber" study described above, what is the most likely:

1. *Research method* (experimental, descriptive, correlational, or biological)?
2. If you chose the:
   - *Experimental method*—label the IV, DV, experimental group, and control group.

- *Descriptive method*—is this a naturalistic observation, survey, or case study?
- *Correlational method*—is this a positive, negative, or zero correlation?
- *Biological method*—identify the specific research tool (e.g., brain dissection, CT scan, etc.)

(Answers appear in Appendix B.)

CRITICAL THINKING

Overcoming Egocentric Thinking

By Thomas Frangicetto (Northampton Community College, Bethlehem, PA)

> *Egocentric thinking results from the unfortunate fact that humans do not naturally consider the rights, needs, or point of view of others.*
>
> Paul and Elder,
> *The Miniature Guide to Critical Thinking*

When a 6-year-old boy won't share his toys or is unwilling to take turns, he is demonstrating *childhood egocentrism*. When a 14-year-old girl refuses to go to school because she is convinced everyone will make fun of the huge zit on her chin, she is exhibiting *adolescent egocentrism*. In both cases, the egocentrism can be seen as a part of normal development.

But what about when adults display egocentric behavior? When we see things mainly through our own perspective, care mainly about our view of things, and relentlessly value self-interest above the truth. . . or anything else? Have you ever been called *selfish* or *self-centered? Arrogant? Stubborn? Difficult to get along with*? According to Paul and Elder (2009), egocentric thinkers use the five basic illogical standards listed below—standards any of us might use. Here's a chance to take a personal inventory of your own egocentric tendencies.

Part A: Provide a brief personal example (or from family, friends, or the media) for each of the following:

1. *It's true because I believe it.*

   Innate egocentrism—assuming personal beliefs are true without examining the basis for those beliefs. Example: *"I am special and I will never be one of you and you will never be able to process who I am, so go back to sleep and don't even try."* Charlie Sheen

2. *It's true because WE believe it.*

   Innate sociocentrism—assuming dominant beliefs within personal groups are correct without questioning their underlying basis. Example: *"We're not saying there's anything wrong with the other sororities. We just know ours is the best!"* Anonymous

3. *It's true because I want to believe it.*

   Innate wish-fulfillment—believing whatever puts one in a positive light, whatever "feels good" or supports other beliefs, and whatever does not require individual to change his or her thinking or admit the possibility of errors. Example: *"I get everything my way, and not just because I'm a huge celebrity, which I totally am. But because I believe I deserve it. And that's why I have Comcast."* Jane Lynch in Xfinity commercial

4. *It's true because I have always believed it.*

   Innate self-validation—strong desire to maintain long-held beliefs without examination of the justification of those beliefs. Example: *"I don't care what the skeptics say, I believe in John Edward [the psedo-psychologist discussed in Chapter 4, p. 157] because he told me things that no one else knew."* Pam F.

5. *It's true because it's in my selfish interest to believe it.*

   Innate selfishness—clinging to beliefs that justify additional power, money, or personal advantage even though these beliefs are not grounded in sound reasoning or evidence. Example: *"It never was enough, they don't want to own one home, they want to own five homes, and they want to have an expensive penthouse on Park Avenue and they want to have their own private jet."* Quote from the film, *Inside Job*

Part B
- For each example listed in Part A, identify at least one Critical Thinking Component (CTC) from the Prologue that you believe can combat that tendency. Explain your choice.
- How can critical thinking help keep our egocentric tendencies in check? Which three critical thinking components (CTCs) do you believe are most important in your own life?

GENDER AND CULTURAL DIVERSITY

Cultural Psychology's Research Guidelines·

Objective 9.15: Describe cultural psychology's four guidelines for understanding development.

How would you answer the following question: "If you wanted to predict how a human child anywhere in the world was going to grow up, what his or her behavior was going to be like as an adult, and you could have only one fact about that child, what fact would you choose to have?"

According to cultural psychologists, the answer to this question should be "culture." Developmental psychology has traditionally studied people (children, adolescents, and adults) with little attention to the sociocultural context. In recent times, however, psychologists are paying increasing attention to the following points:

- *Culture may be the most important determinant of development* If a child grows up in an individualistic/independent culture (such as North America or most of western Europe), we can predict that this child will probably be competitive and question authority as an adult. Were this same child reared in a collectivist/interdependent culture (common in Africa, Asia, and Latin America), she or he would most likely grow up to be cooperative and respectful of elders (Berry et al., 2011; Manago & Greenfield, 2011).

- *Human development, like most areas of psychology, cannot be studied outside its sociocultural context* In parts of Korea, most teenagers see a strict, authoritarian style of parenting as a sign of love and concern (Kim & Choi, 1995). Korean American and Korean Canadian teenagers, however, see the same behavior as a sign of rejection. Thus, rather than studying specific behaviors, such as "authoritarian parenting styles," discussed earlier, researchers in child development suggest that children should be studied only within their *developmental niche* (Fuller & García Coll, 2010; Worthman, 2010; Yamagishi, 2011). A developmental niche has three components: the physical and social contexts in which the child lives, the culturally determined rearing and educational practices, and the psychological characteristics of the parents (Bugental & Johnston, 2000; Harkness et al., 2007).

- *Each culture's ethnotheories are important determinants of behavior* Within every culture, people have a prevailing set of ideas and beliefs that attempt to explain the world around them (an *ethnotheory*) (Lau, 2010; Tucker, 2007). In the area of child development, for example, cultures have specific ethnotheories about

Cultural influences on development How might these two groups differ in their physical, social-emotional, cognitive, and personality development?

how children should be trained. As a critical thinker, you can anticipate that differing ethnotheories can lead to problems between cultures. In fact, even the very idea of "critical thinking" is part of our North American ethnotheory regarding education. And it, too, can produce culture clashes.

Concha Delgado-Gaitan (1994) found that Mexican immigrants from a rural background have a difficult time adjusting to North American schools, which teach children to question authority and think for themselves. In their culture of origin, these children are trained to respect their elders, be good listeners, and participate in conversation only when their opinion is solicited. Children who argue with adults are reminded not to be *malcriados* (naughty or disrespectful).

• ***Culture is largely invisible to its participants*** Culture consists of ideals, values, and assumptions that are widely shared among a given group and that guide specific behaviors (Matsumoto & Kitayama, 2010; Ratner, 2011). Precisely because these ideals and values are widely shared, they are seldom discussed or directly examined. Just as a "fish doesn't know it's in water," we take our culture for granted, operating within it, though being almost unaware of it.

TRY THIS YOURSELF

Culture Invisibility

If you would like a personal demonstration of the invisibility of culture, try this simple experiment: The next time you walk into an elevator, don't turn around. Remain facing the rear wall. Watch how others respond when you don't turn around or stand right next to them rather than going to the other side of the elevator. Our North American culture has rules that prescribe the "proper" way to ride in an elevator, and people become very uncomfortable when these rules are violated.

CHECK & REVIEW

STOP *Before going on, be sure to complete this Check & Review. It is an invaluable study tool!*

Social-Emotional Development and Psychology Engages

Part A: Retrieval Practice

1. Without looking at the book, spend 10 minutes writing a free-form essay recalling all you can remember from the previous section.

2. Now, reread the previous section, and once again spend 10 minutes writing a free-form essay on the SAME material.

Part B: Practice Quiz

1. According to Harlow and Zimmerman's research with cloth and wire surrogate mothers, _____ is the most important variable for attachment.

2. List the four types of attachment reported by Ainsworth.

3. Using Hazan and Shaver's research on adult attachment styles, match the following adults with their probable type of infant attachment:

___ Mary is nervous around attractive partners and complains that lovers often want her to be more intimate than she finds comfortable.

___ Bob complains that lovers are often reluctant to get as close as he would like.

___ Rashelle finds it relatively easy to get close to others and seldom worries about being abandoned.

4. Briefly explain Baumrind's three parenting styles.

Check your answers in Appendix B.

WileyPLUS presents an on-line version of this textbook along with a wealth of study resources including quizzes, practice tests, flash cards, videos, animations and other activities designed to improve your mastery of the content. Working in conjunction with these study tools, the *Psychology in Action* WileyPLUS course features Professor Karen Huffman, author of this textbook, explaining and expanding upon some of the most challenging concepts in psychology. Here is a sample of the tutorial videos available for this chapter:

- Understanding development in a cultural context
- An animated, interactive exploration of Piaget's stages of cognitive development
- Exploring the role of attachment in life span development, featuring an animated Strange Situation procedure
- Professor Huffman's classroom demonstration of the relationship between infant attachment and adult romantic love.
- Virtual Field Trip to a parenting class, where theory and practice come together to provide the owner's manual that didn't come with your baby

Key Terms

To assess your understanding of the **Key Terms** in Chapter 9, write a definition for each (in your own words), and then compare your definitions with those in the text.

developmental psychology (p. 324)

Studying Development
maturation (p. 325)
critical period (p. 325)
cross-sectional method (p. 326)
longitudinal method (p. 326)

Physical Development
germinal period (p. 329)
embryonic period (p. 329)

fetal period (p. 329)
teratogen [Tuh-RAT-uh-jen] (p. 330)
fetal alcohol syndrome (FAS) (p. 330)
puberty (p. 334)
ageism (p. 336)

Cognitive Development
schema (p. 339)
assimilation (p. 339)
accommodation (p. 339)
sensorimotor stage (p. 339)

object permanence (p. 341)
preoperational stage (p. 341)
egocentrism (p. 341)
concrete operational stage (p. 342)
conservation (p. 342)
formal operational stage (p. 342)

Social-Emotional Development
attachment (p. 346)
imprinting (p. 346)

 TRY THIS YOURSELF

School Days, "Cool" Days

During schoolyard recess, children's conversations, physical activities, and mental processes generally follow the principles, milestones, and even rules cited in developmental stage theories. While the children play, your job is to identify and explain the stages of physical, cognitive, and social-emotional development reflected by their recess activities.

Fast forward to adolescence and to a teenage party. Are individuals finally doing their own thing? Once again, the answer is no. And once again, your job is to detect the developmental stages and principles that their "cool" behaviors, talk, and posturing reflect.

As you are working on this online exercise, which is available to WileyPLUS subscribers, consider the following:

- What does this lab exercise say about the nature-versus-nurture debate in developmental psychology?
- Do the behaviors and interactions on display in the lab exercise indicate that stage differences are *qualitative* or *quantitative*?
- What events and steps have helped transform the enthusiastic (but awkward) elementary school kids of one video into the "cool" (though still awkward) high school kids of the second video?
- Stages or no stages, the children and teenagers in the lab exercise also show many individual differences. How did that happen?

Chapter Summary

Studying Development

Objective 9.1: Define developmental psychology.
Developmental psychology studies age-related changes in behavior and mental processes from conception to death.

Objective 9.2: Identify the three major issues in developmental psychology.
Three important research issues are *nature versus nurture*, *continuity versus stages*, and *stability versus change*.

Objective 9.3: What are the two most common research methods in developmental psychology?
Researchers in developmental psychology generally use **cross-sectional** (different participants of various ages at one point in time) or **longitudinal** (same participants over an extended period) **methods**. Each has advantages and disadvantages.

Physical Development

Objective 9.4: Identify the three major stages of prenatal development.
The prenatal period of development consists of three major stages: the **germinal**, (ovulation to implantation), **embryonic**, (implantation to eight weeks), and **fetal** (eight weeks to birth).

Objective 9.5: What are the major hazards to prenatal development?
Doctors advise pregnant women to avoid all unnecessary drugs, especially nicotine and alcohol. Both legal and illegal drugs are potentially **teratogenic** (capable of producing birth defects).

Objective 9.6: Summarize early childhood physical development.
During the prenatal period and the first two years of life, the brain and nervous system grow faster than any other part of the body. Early motor development (crawling, standing, and walking) is largely the result of maturation, not experience. Except for vision, the sensory and perceptual abilities of newborns are relatively well developed.

Objective 9.7: Describe the major physical changes associated with adolescence and adulthood.
At **puberty**, the individual becomes capable of reproduction and experiences a sharp increase in height, weight, and skeletal growth, called the *pubertal growth spurt*. Both men and women experience *significant* bodily changes in middle age.

Objective 9.8: Define ageism, and explain what causes us to age and die.
Ageism is prejudice or discrimination based on physical age.

Although many of the changes associated with physical aging (such as decreases in cardiac output and visual acuity) are the result of *primary aging*, others are the result of disease, abuse, or neglect. Physical aging may be genetically built in from the moment of conception (programmed theory), or it may result from the body's inability to repair damage (damage theory).

Cognitive Development

Objective 9.9: Describe Piaget's theory of cognitive development, and compare schema, assimilation, and accommodation.
Piaget believed an infant's intellectual growth progresses in distinct stages, motivated by an innate need to know. He also proposed three major concepts: *schemas*, patterns that organize our interactions with the environment; *assimilation*, absorbing new information "as is" into existing schemas; and *accommodation*, adjusting old schemas or developing new ones to fit with new information.

Objective 9.10: Compare how children's cognitive development changes during Piaget's four stages.
According to Piaget, cognitive development occurs in an invariant sequence of four stages: **sensorimotor** (birth to age 2), **preoperational** (ages 2–7), **concrete operational** (ages 7–11), and **formal operational** (ages 11–up).

In the sensorimotor stage, children acquire **object permanence**. During the preoperational stage, children are better equipped to use symbols. But their language and thinking are limited by their lack of operations, **egocentrism**, and animism.

In the concrete operational stage, children learn to perform operations (to think about concrete things while not actually doing them). They understand the principles of **conservation** and reversibility. During the formal operational stage, the adolescent is able to think abstractly and deal with hypothetical situations but again is prone to a type of adolescent egocentrism.

Objective 9.11: Identify the major criticisms and contributions of Piaget's theories.

Although Piaget has been criticized for underestimating abilities and genetic and cultural influences, he remains one of the most respected psychologists in modern times.

Social-Emotional Development

Objective 9.12: Define *attachment*, and discuss its contributions across the life span.
Attachment is a strong affectional bond with special others that endures over time.

Nativists believe it is innate. Nurturists believe it is learned. The Harlow and Zimmerman experiments with monkeys raised by cloth or wire surrogate mothers found that contact comfort might be the most important factor in attachment.

Infants who fail to form attachments may suffer serious effects. When attachments are formed, they may differ in level or degree.

Objective 9.13: Discuss how infant attachment may be related to romantic love.
Research that identified *securely attached*, *avoidant*, and *anxious/ambivalent* infants found that their early behavioral differences may persist into romantic relationships in adulthood.

Objective 9.14: Discuss the three key parenting styles.
Parenting styles fall into three major categories: permissive, authoritarian, and authoritative. Researchers suggest that a child's unique temperament, his or her expectations of parents, and the degree of warmth versus rejection from parents may be the three most important variables in parenting styles.

Objective 9.15: Describe cultural psychology's four guidelines for understanding development.
Cultural psychologists suggest that developmental researchers keep the following points in mind:

- Culture may be the most important determinant of development.
- Human development cannot be studied outside its sociocultural context.
- Each culture's ethnotheories are important determinants of behavior.
- Culture is largely invisible to its participants.

Studying Development

Theoretical Issues

- Nature versus nurture
- Continuity versus stages
- Stability versus change

Research Methods

- Cross-sectional
- Longitudinal

CROSS-SECTIONAL RESEARCH

Different participants of various ages are compared at one point in time to determine age-related *differences*

Group One 20-year-old participants	
Group Two 40-year-old participants	Research done in 2013
Group Three 60-year-old participants	

Advantages	Disadvantages
• Provides information about age differences • Quick and less expensive • Typically larger sample	• Cohort effects difficult to separate • Restricted generalizability (measures behaviors and mental processes at only one point in time)

LONGITUDINAL RESEARCH

The **same** participants are studied at various ages to determine age-related *changes*

Study One Participants are 20 years old	Research done in 2013
Study Two Same participants are now 40 years old	Research done in 2033
Study Three Same participants are now 60 years old	Research done in 2053

Advantages	Disadvantages
• Provides information about age changes • Increased confidence in results • More in-depth information per participant	• More expensive and time consuming • Restricted generalizability (typically smaller sample due to participant dropouts over time)

Physical Development

Prenatal and Early Childhood

Adolescence and Adulthood

- Adolescence: Psychological period between childhood and adulthood
- Puberty: When sex organs become capable of reproduction
- Menopause: Cessation of menstruation
- Male climacteric: Physical and psychological changes in midlife
- Primary aging: Inevitable, biological changes with age
- Explanations of primary aging: *Programmed theory* (genetically built-in) and *damage theory* (body's inability to repair damage)

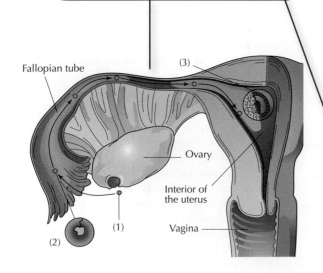

Fallopian tube

(3)

Ovary

Interior of the uterus

(1)

(2)

Vagina

Chin up
2.2 mo.

Rolls over
2.8 mo.

Sits with support
2.9 mo.

Sits alone
5.5 mo.

Stands holding furniture

5.8 mo.

Walks holding on
9.2 mo.

Stands alone

11.5 mo.

Walks alone
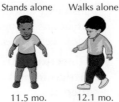
12.1 mo.

Walks up steps

17.1 mo.

Cognitive Development

Piaget's Theory
- Schema
- Assimilation
- Accommodation

Stages of Cognitive Development

Assessing Piaget's Theory
- Underestimated abilities
- Underestimated genetic and cultural influences
- Contributions enormous

	Four Stages	Abilities	Limits
	Sensorimotor (Birth to 2)	Uses senses and motor skills to explore and develop cognitively	At beginning of stage, infant lacks **object permanence** (understanding things continue to exist even when not seen, heard, or felt)
	Preoperational (Age 2 to 7)	Has significant language and thinks symbolically	• Preoperational thinking (lacks reversibility and very intuitive) • **Egocentric** thinking (inability to consider another's point of view). Animistic thinking (believing all things are living)
	Concrete Operational (Age 7 to 11)	• Less egocentric and capable of true logical thinking • Understands **conservation** (realizes changes in shape or appearance can be reversed)	• Thinking tied to concrete tangible objects and events • Cannot think abstractly and hypothetically
	Formal Operational (11 and up)	Can think abstractly and hypothetically.	Adolescent egocentrism at the beginning of this stage, with related problems of the *personal fable* and *imaginary audience*.

Social-Emotional Development

Attachment
- Imprinting
- Harlow: contact comfort
- Ainsworth's three types: secure, avoidant, anxioius/ambivalent

Parenting Styles
Baumrind's three styles: permissive, authoritarian, and authoritative

Psychology Engages

Research Challenge
Critical Thinking
Gender & Cultural Diversity

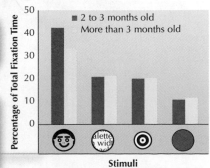

ChapterTen

Life Span Development II

Imagine that you are standing on a bridge over a railroad track when you see that a runaway train is about to kill five people. Coincidentally, you are standing next to a switching mechanism, and you realize that by simply throwing a switch, you can divert the train onto a spur, allowing the five to survive. But here is the catch: diverting the train will condemn *one* person, who is standing on the spur, to death (Appiah, 2008, 2010). What would you do? Would you allow one person to die in order to save five others? Would your answer be different if that person were your mother, father, or some other much-loved person? What might lead different people to make different decisions?

It's unlikely that you will ever have to make such a gruesome choice. Yet everyone encounters moral dilemmas from time to time. (Should you remind the cable company that they forgot to disconnect the cable after you discontinued the service? Should you give spare change to a friendly panhandler in your neighborhood?) Likewise, everyone has personal relationships and particular character traits that color our decisions. How we approach moral dilemmas—as well as many other events and circumstances throughout our lives—reflects several key facets of our life span development. Chapter 9 explored life span changes in physical development, cognitive development, and social-emotional development. In this chapter, we'll look at moral development, personality development, special challenges of adulthood, and grief and death.

Morality is the basis of things and truth is the substance of all morality.
MOHANDAS GANDHI

When morality comes up against profit, it is seldom that profit loses.
SHIRLEY CHISHOLM

Quien teme la muerte no goza la vida. (He who fears death cannot enjoy life.)
SPANISH PROVERB

Let us endeavor so to live that when we come to die even the undertaker will be sorry.
SAMUEL CLEMENS (MARK TWAIN)

ChapterOutline

359

Did you know...

- A 5-year-old typically believes that *accidentally* breaking 15 cups is "badder" and more deserving of punishment than *intentionally* breaking 1 cup?

- Juvenile chimpanzees will soothe a frightened or injured peer, and adult female chimps will "adopt" a motherless baby?

- Erikson believed that adolescents who fail to resolve their "identity crises" may later have difficulty in maintaining close personal relationships and be more prone to delinquency?

- Parents typically experience their highest levels of marital satisfaction before children are born and after they leave home?

- Kübler-Ross believed that most people go through five predictable psychological stages when facing death?

Moral Development

Objective 10.1: What is the biological perspective on morality?

In Chapter 9, we noted that newborns cry when they hear another baby cry. But did you know that by age 2, most children use words like *good* or *bad* to evaluate actions that are aggressive or that might endanger their own or another's welfare? Or that juvenile chimpanzees will soothe a frightened or injured peer, and adult female chimps will "adopt" a motherless baby (Hoffman, 2007; Goodall, 1990; Malti, 2007)? How can we explain such early emergence and cross-species evidence of *morality*—the ability to take the perspective of, or empathize with, others and distinguish between right and wrong?

From a biological perspective, some researchers suggest that morality may be prewired and evolutionarily based (Brosnan, 2011; Churchland, 2011; Gorelik, Shackelford, & Salmon, 2010; Krebs & Hemingway, 2008). Behaviors like infant empathic crying and adoption of motherless chimp babies help the species survive. Therefore, evolution may have provided us with biologically based provisions for moral acts. But as with most human behaviors, biology is only one part of the *biopsychosocial model*. In this section, we will focus our attention on the psychological and social factors that explain how moral thoughts, feelings, and actions change over the life span.

Kohlberg's Research: What Is Right?

Developing a sense of right and wrong, or *morality*, is a part of psychological development. Consider the following situation in terms of what you would do.

In Europe, a woman was near death from a special kind of cancer. There was one drug that doctors thought might save her. It was a form of radium that a druggist in the same town had recently discovered. The drug was expensive to make, but the druggist was charging 10 times what the drug cost him. He paid $200 for the radium and charged $2000 for a small dose of the drug. The sick woman's husband, Heinz, went to everyone he knew to borrow the money, but he could gather together only about $1000, half of what it cost. He told the druggist that his wife was dying and asked him to sell it cheaper or let him pay later. But the druggist said, "No, I discovered the drug, and I'm going to make money from it." So Heinz got desperate and broke into the man's store to steal the drug for his wife. (Kohlberg, 1964, pp. 18–19)

Was Heinz right to steal the drug? What do you consider moral behavior? Is morality "in the eye of the beholder," or are there universal truths and principles? Whatever your answer, your ability to think, reason, and respond to Heinz's dilemma demonstrates another type of development that is very important to psychology—*morality*.

One of the most influential researchers in moral development was Lawrence Kohlberg (1927–1987). He presented what he called "moral stories" like this Heinz dilemma to people of all ages. On the basis of his findings, he developed a highly influential model of moral development (1964, 1984).

What is the right answer to Heinz's dilemma? Kohlberg was interested not in whether participants judged Heinz right or wrong but in the reasons they gave for their decision. On the basis of participants' responses, Kohlberg proposed three broad levels in the evolution of moral reasoning, each composed of two distinct stages (Step-by-Step Diagram 10.1). Individuals at each stage and level may or may not support Heinz's stealing of the drug, but their reasoning changes from level to level.

Kohlberg believed that, like Piaget's stages of cognitive development (Chapter 9), his stages of moral development are *universal* and *invariant*. That is, they supposedly exist in all cultures, and everyone goes through each of the stages in a predictable fashion.

Assessing Kohlberg's Theory: Three Major Criticisms

Objective 10.3: What are the three major criticisms of Kohlberg's theory?

Kohlberg has been credited with enormous insights and contributions about how we think about moral issues (Appiah, 2008; Krebs, 2007; Lapsley, 2006). But his theories have also been the focus of three major areas of criticism.

1. ***Moral reasoning versus behavior*** Are people who achieve higher stages on Kohlberg's scale really more moral than others? Or do they just "talk a good game"? Some studies show a positive correlation between higher stages of reasoning and higher levels of moral behavior (Gasser & Malti, 2011; Gini, Pozzoli, & Hauser, 2011; Langdon, Clare, & Murphy, 2011). But others have found that situational factors are better predictors of moral behavior (Bandura, 1986, 1991, 2008; Kaplan, 2006; Satcher, 2007; Slováčková & Slováček, 2007) (Figure 10.1). For example, research participants are more likely to steal when they are told the money comes from a large company rather than from individuals (Greenberg, 2002). And both men and women will tell more sexual lies during casual relationships than during close relationships (Williams, 2001).

2. ***Cultural differences*** Cross-cultural studies report that children from a variety of cultures generally follow Kohlberg's model and progress sequentially from his first level, the *preconventional*, to his second, the *conventional* (Rest et al., 1999; Snarey, 1995).

   Other studies find differences among cultures (Jensen, 2011; LePage et al., 2011; Rai & Fiske, 2011). For example, cross-cultural comparisons of responses to Heinz's moral dilemma show that Europeans and Americans tend to consider whether they like or identify with the victim in questions of morality. In contrast, Hindu Indians consider social responsibility and personal concerns two separate issues (Miller & Bersoff, 1998). Researchers suggest that the difference reflects the Indians' broader sense of social responsibility.

GREGORY

▲ *"I swear I wasn't looking at smut—I was just stealing music."*

Figure 10.1 Morality gap? What makes people who normally behave ethically willing to steal intellectual property such as music or software?

Step-by-StepDiagram10.1

Kohlberg's Stages of Moral Development

Objective 10.2: Describe Kohlberg's three levels and six stages of moral development.

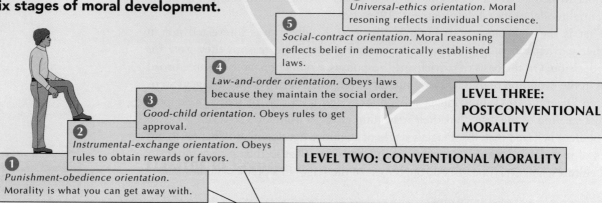

⑥ *Universal-ethics orientation.* Moral resoning reflects individual conscience.

⑤ *Social-contract orientation.* Moral reasoning reflects belief in democratically established laws.

④ *Law-and-order orientation.* Obeys laws because they maintain the social order.

③ *Good-child orientation.* Obeys rules to get approval.

② *Instrumental-exchange orientation.* Obeys rules to obtain rewards or favors.

① *Punishment-obedience orientation.* Morality is what you can get away with.

LEVEL THREE: POSTCONVENTIONAL MORALITY

LEVEL TWO: CONVENTIONAL MORALITY

LEVEL ONE: PRECONVENTIONAL MORALITY

---

*PRECONVENTIONAL LEVEL (Stages 1 and 2— birth to adolescence) Moral judgment is *self-centered.* What is right is what one can get away with, or what is personally satisfying. Moral understanding is based on rewards, punishments, and the exchange of favors.

Punishment-obedience orientation:

Focus is on self-interest—obedience to authority and avoidance of punishment. Because children at this stage have difficulty considering another's point of view, they also ignore people's intentions.

Instrumental-exchange orientation:

Children become aware of others' perspectives, but their morality is based on reciprocity—an equal exchange of favors.

CONVENTIONAL LEVEL (Stages 3 and 4— adolescence and young adulthood) Moral reasoning is *other-centered.* Conventional societal rules are accepted because they help ensure the social order.

Good-child orientation:

Primary moral concern is being nice and gaining approval, and judges others by their intentions—"His heart was in the right place."

Law-and-order orientation:

Morality based on a larger perspective—societal laws. Understanding that if everyone violated laws, even with good intentions, there would be chaos.

POSTCONVENTIONAL LEVEL (Stages 5 and 6— adulthood) Moral judgments based *on personal standards for right and wrong.* Morality also defined in terms of abstract principles and values that apply to all situations and societies.

Social contact orientation:

Appreciation for the underlying purposes served by laws. Societal laws are obeyed because of the "social contract," but they can be morally disobeyed if they fail to express the will of the majority or fail to maximize social welfare.

Universal-ethics orientation:

"Right" is determined by universal ethical principles (e.g., nonviolence, human dignity, freedom) that *all* religions or moral authorities might view as compelling or fair. These principles apply whether or not they conform to existing laws.

---

*(This level is called "preconventional" because children have not yet internalized society's "conventional" rules.)

Preconventional Level Kohlberg's first level of moral development, in which morality is based on rewards, punishment, and exchange of favors

Conventional Level Kohlberg's second level of moral development, in which moral judgments are based on compliance with the rules and values of society

Postconventional Level Kohlberg's highest level of moral development, in which individuals develop personal standards for right and wrong and define morality in terms of abstract principles and values that apply to all situations and societies

In India, Papua New Guinea, and China, as well as in Israeli kibbutzim, people don't choose between the rights of the individual and the rights of society (as the top levels of Kohlberg's model require). Instead, most people seek a compromise solution that accommodates both interests (Killen & Hart, 1999; Miller & Bersoff, 1998). Thus, Kohlberg's standard for judging the highest level of morality (the postconventional) may be more applicable to cultures that value individualism over community and interpersonal relationships.

3. ***Possible gender bias*** Researcher Carol Gilligan criticized Kohlberg's model because on his scale women often tend to be classified at a lower level of moral reasoning than men (Figure 10.2). Gilligan suggested that this difference occurred because Kohlberg's theory emphasizes values more often held by men, such as rationality and independence, while deemphasizing common female values, such as concern for others and belonging (Gilligan, 1977, 1990, 1993; Kracher & Marble, 2008).

Although some studies have found gender differences in overall moral reasoning (Bateman & Valentine, 2010; Fumagalli et al., 2010; Mercadillo et al., 2011), most follow-up studies of Gilligan's specific theory, have found few, if any, gender differences (Hoffman, 2000; Hyde, 2007; Pratt, Skoe, & Arnold, 2004; Smith, 2007).

▲ **Figure 10.2 Gilligan versus Kohlberg** According to Carol Gilligan, women score "lower" on Lawrence Kohlberg's stages of moral development because they are socialized to assume more responsibility for the care of others. What do you think?

  **CHECK & REVIEW** STOP *Before going on, be sure to complete this Check & Review. It is an invaluable study tool!*

Moral Development

Part A: Retrieval Practice

1. Without looking at the book, spend 10 minutes writing a free-form essay recalling all you can remember from the previous section.

2. Now, reread the previous section, and once again spend 10 minutes writing a free-form essay on the SAME material.

   (Although time consuming, this exercise has been shown to be the single best way to improve your test scores! For more information, check out http://www .sciencemag.org/content/early/ 2011/01/19/science.1199327.abstract)

Part B: Practice Quiz

1. According to Kohlberg's theory of morality, self-interest and avoiding punishment are characteristic of the _____ level, personal standards or universal principles characterize the _____ level, and gaining approval or following the rules describes the _____ level.

2. Calvin would like to wear baggy, torn jeans and a nose ring, but he is concerned that others will disapprove. Calvin is at Kohlberg's _____ level of morality. (a) conformity; (b) approval seeking; (c) conventional; (d) preconventional

3. Five-year-old Tyler believes "bad things are what you get punished for." Tyler is at Kohlberg's _____ level of morality.

4. Explain the possible cultural and gender bias in Kohlberg's theory.

Check your answers in Appendix B.

Personality Development

Thomas and Chess's Temperament Theory: Biology and Personality Development

Objective 10.4: Describe Thomas and Chess's temperament theory.

As an infant, did you lie quietly and seem oblivious to loud noises? Or did you tend to kick and scream and respond immediately to every sound? Did you respond warmly to people, or did you fuss, fret, and withdraw? Your answers to these questions help determine what developmental psychologists call your **temperament**, an individual's disposition or innate, biological behavioral style and characteristic emotional response.

Temperament An individual's innate disposition or behavioral style and characteristic emotional response

One of the earliest and most influential theories regarding temperament came from the work of psychiatrists Alexander Thomas and Stella Chess (Thomas & Chess, 1977, 1987, 1991). Thomas and Chess found that approximately 65 percent of the babies they observed could be reliably separated into three categories:

1. *Easy children* These infants were happy most of the time, relaxed and agreeable, and adjusted easily to new situations (approximately 40 percent).

2. *Difficult children* Infants in this group were moody, easily frustrated, tense, and overreactive to most situations (approximately 10 percent).

3. *Slow-to-warm-up children* These infants showed mild responses, were somewhat shy and withdrawn, and needed time to adjust to new experiences or people (approximately 15 percent).

Follow-up studies have found that certain aspects of these temperament styles tend to be consistent and enduring throughout childhood and even adulthood (Buss, 2011; Canals et al., 2011; Kagan, 2005; McCrae, 2004). That is not to say every shy, cautious infant ends up a shy adult. Many events take place between infancy and adulthood that shape an individual's development.

One of the most influential factors in early personality development is *goodness of fit* between a child's nature, parental behaviors, and the social and environmental setting (Lanfranchi, 2010; Mahoney, 2011; Salekin & Averett, 2008). For example, a slow-to-warm-up child does best if allowed time to adjust to new situations. Similarly, a difficult child thrives in a structured, understanding environment but not in an inconsistent, intolerant home. Alexander Thomas, the pioneer of temperament research, thinks parents should work with their child's temperament rather than trying to change it. Can you see how this idea of goodness of fit is yet another example of how nature and nurture interact?

Erikson's Psychosocial Theory: Eight Stages of Life

Objective 10.5: Describe Erikson's eight psychosocial stages.

Like Piaget and Kohlberg, Erik Erikson developed a stage theory of development. He identified eight **psychosocial stages** of social development, each stage marked by a "psychosocial" crisis or conflict related to a specific developmental task (Step-by-Step Diagram 10.2).

The name for each psychosocial stage reflects the specific crisis encountered at that stage and two possible outcomes. For example, the crisis or task of most young adults is *intimacy versus isolation*. This age group's developmental task is developing deep, meaningful relations with others. Those who don't meet this developmental challenge risk social isolation. Erikson believed that the more successfully we overcome each psychosocial crisis, the better chance we have to develop in a healthy manner (Erikson, 1950).

Evaluating Erikson's Theory: What Do the Critics Say?

Objective 10.6: What are the major criticisms of Erikson's stages?

Many psychologists agree with Erikson's general idea that psychosocial crises, which are based on interpersonal and environmental interactions, do contribute to personality development (Conzen, 2010; Fukase & Okamoto, 2010; Markstrom & Marshall, 2007; Zhang & He, 2011). However, Erikson also has his critics (Beyers & Seiffge-Krenke, 2010; Spano et al., 2010). First, Erikson's psychosocial stages are difficult to test scientifically. Second, the labels Erikson used to describe the eight stages may not be

Psychosocial Stages Erikson's theory that individuals pass through eight developmental stages, each involving a crisis that must be successfully resolved

Step-by-StepDiagram10.2

STOP This Step by Step diagram contains essential information NOT found elsewhere in the text, which is likely to appear on quizzes and exams. Be sure to study it CAREFULLY!

Erikson's Eight Stages of Psychosocial Development

Stage 1
Trust versus mistrust (birth–age 1)

Infants learn to *trust* or *mistrust* their caregivers and the world based on whether or not their needs—such as food, affection, safety—are met.

Stage 2
Autonomy versus shame and doubt (ages 1–3)

Toddlers start to assert their sense of independence (*autonomy*). If caregivers encourage this self-sufficiency, the toddler will learn to be independent versus feelings of *shame* and *doubt*.

Stage 3
Initiative versus guilt (ages 3–6)

Preschoolers learn to *initiate* activities and develop self-confidence and a sense of social responsibility. If not, they feel irresponsible, anxious, and *guilty*.

Stage 4
Industry versus inferiority (ages 6–12)

Elementary school-aged children who succeed in learning new, productive life skills develop a sense of pride and competence (industry). Those who fail to develop these skills feel inadequate and unproductive (*inferior*).

Stage 5
Identity versus role confusion (ages 12–20)

Adolescents develop a coherent and stable self-definition (identity) by exploring many roles and deciding who or what they want to be in terms of career, attitudes, etc. Failure to resolve this **identity crisis** may lead to apathy, withdrawal and/or *role confusion*.

Stage 6
Intimacy versus isolation (early adulthood)

Young adults form lasting, meaningful relationships, which help them develop a sense of connectedness and *intimacy* with others. If not, they become psychologically *isolated*.

Stage 7
Generativity versus stagnation (middle adulthood)

The challenge for middle-aged adults is to be nurturant of the younger generation. Failing to meet this challenge leads to self-indulgence and a sense of *stagnation*.

Stage 8
Ego integrity versus despair (late adulthood)

During this stage, older adults reflect on their past. If this reflection reveals a life well-spent, the person experiences self-acceptance and satisfaction (*ego integrity*). If not, he or she experiences regret and deep dissatisfaction (*despair*).

entirely appropriate cross-culturally. For example, in individualistic cultures, *autonomy* is highly preferable to *shame and doubt*. But in collectivist cultures, the preferred resolution might be *dependence* or *merging relations* (Berry et al., 2011).

Despite their limits, Erikson's stages have greatly contributed to the study of North American and European psychosocial development. By suggesting that development continues past adolescence, Erikson's theory has encouraged ongoing research and theory development.

CHECK & REVIEW

STOP *Before going on, be sure to complete this Check & Review. It is an invaluable study tool!*

Personality Development

Part A: Retrieval Practice

1. Without looking at the book, spend 10 minutes writing a free-form essay recalling all you can remember from the previous section.

2. Now, reread the previous section, and once again spend 10 minutes writing a free-form essay on the SAME material.

Part B: Practice Quiz

1. An infant's inborn disposition is known as _____. (a) personality; (b) reflexes; (c) temperament; (d) traits

2. Briefly describe Thomas and Chess's temperament theory.

3. Erikson suggested that problems in adulthood are sometimes related to unsuccessful resolution of one of his eight stages. For each of the following individuals, identify the most likely "problem" stage:

a. Marcos has trouble keeping friends and jobs because he continually asks for guarantees and reassurance of his worth.

b. Ann has attended several colleges without picking a major, has taken several vocational training programs, and has had numerous jobs over the last 10 years.

c. Teresa is reluctant to apply for a promotion even though her coworkers have encouraged her to do so. She worries that she will be taking a job from someone else and questions her worth.

d. George continually obsesses over the value of his life. He regrets that he left his wife and children for a job in another country and failed to maintain contact.

4. According to Erikson, humans progress through eight stages of psychosocial development. Label the two Eriksonian stages depicted in the photos below.

Stage 2_____   Stage 8_____

Check your answers in Appendix B.

Meeting the Challenges of Adulthood

Having completed our whirlwind trip through the major theories and concepts explaining moral and personality development across the life span, you may be wondering how this information can be helpful in your current adult life. In this section, we will explore three of the most important developmental tasks we all face as adults: developing a long-term, committed relationship with another person, coping with the challenges of family life, and finding rewarding work and retirement.

Committed Relationships: Overcoming Unrealistic Expectations

Objective 10.7: Discuss the major problems with long-term relationships.

One of the most important tasks faced during adulthood is that of establishing some kind of continuing, loving, sexual relationship with another person. Yet navigating such partnerships is often very challenging. For example, research shows that marriage is associated with improved overall health outcomes, greater life satisfaction, lower stress, less depression, and lower waking blood pressure (Ali & Ajilore, 2011; Osler et al., 2008; Rendell et al., 2011; Trombello, Schoebi, & Bradbury, 2011). Unfortunately, nearly half of all marriages in the United States end in divorce, with serious implications for both adult and child development (Barczak et al., 2010; Hakvoort et al., 2011; Li, 2008; Osler et al., 2008; Steiner et al., 2011). For the adults, both spouses generally experience emotional as well as practical difficulties and are at high risk for depression and physical health problems. However, many problems assumed to be due to divorce are actually present before marital disruption, and, for some, divorce can be life enhancing. In a "healthy" divorce, ex-spouses must accomplish three tasks: *let go*, *develop new social ties*, and, when children are involved, *redefine parental roles* (Everett & Everett, 1994).

In addition to stresses on the divorcing couple, some research shows that children also suffer both short-term and long-lasting effects. Compared with children in continuously intact two-parent families, children of divorce reportedly exhibit more behavioral problems, poorer self-concepts, more psychological problems, lower academic achievement, and more substance abuse and social difficulties (D'Onofrio et al., 2007; Hetherington, 2006; Kim, 2011). On the other hand, other research finds little or no effect on children's social and behavioral problems, and that previously reported negative effects may reflect the child's level of attachment, the child's unique personality, and/or the warmth and personality traits of the parents (Amato, 2006; Brown et al., 2007; Rhoades et al., 2011; Sentse et al., 2011). Other researchers have suggested that both parents and children may also do better without the constant tension and fighting of an intact, but unhappy, home (Bernet & Ash, 2007; Hakvoort et al., 2011).

Whether children become "winners" or "losers" in a divorce depends on the (1) individual attributes of the child, (2) qualities of the custodial family, (3) continued involvement with noncustodial parents, and (4) resources and support systems available to the child and parents (Hetherington, 2006; Johnson, 2011; Vélez et al., 2011). If you or your parents are currently considering or going through a divorce, you may want to keep these four factors in mind when making legal and other decisions about children.

Psychology at Work

Potential Pitfalls of Relationship Expectations

Do you want to have a successful relationship and avoid a breakup and/or divorce? One of the first steps is to examine your personal dreams and expectations for long-term relationships. Where did they come from? Are they realistic? Marriage therapists and researchers consistently find that realistic expectations are a key ingredient in successful relationships (Beachkofsky, 2010; Cheever, 2010; Gottman & Levenson, 2002; Hall & Adams, 2011).

TRY THIS YOURSELF

Are Your Relationship Expectations Realistic?

To evaluate your own expectations, answer the following questions about traits and factors common to happy marriages and committed long-term relationships (Beachkofsky, 2010; Gonzaga, Carter, Buckwalter, 2010; Gottman & Levenson, 2002; Gottman & Notarius, 2000; Marks et al., 2008; Rauer, 2007):

1. **Established "love maps"**
   Do you believe that emotional closeness "naturally" develops when two people have the right chemistry?

   Yes—   No—

   In successful relationships, both partners are willing to share their feelings and life goals. This sharing leads to detailed "love maps" of each other's inner emotional life and the creation of shared meaning in the relationship.

2. **Shared power and mutual support**

   Have you unconsciously accepted the imbalance of power promoted by many TV sitcoms, or are you willing to fully share power and to respect your partner's point of view, even if you disagree?

   Yes— No—

   The common portrayal of husbands as "head of household" and wives as the "little women" who secretly wield the true power may help create unrealistic expectations for marriage.

3. **Conflict management**

   Do you expect to "change" your partner or to be able to resolve all your problems?

   Yes— No—

   Successful couples work hard (through negotiation and accommodation) to solve their solvable conflicts, to accept their unsolvable ones, and to know the difference.

4. **Similarity**

   Do you believe that "opposites attract?"

   Yes— No—

Although we all know couples who are very different but are still happy, similarity (in values, beliefs, religion, and so on) is one of the best predictors of longlasting relationships (Chapter 15).

5. **Supportive social environment**

   Do you believe that "love conquers all"?

   Yes— No—

   Unfortunately, several environmental factors can overpower or slowly erode even the strongest love. These include age (younger couples have higher divorce rates), money and employment (divorce is higher among the poor and unemployed), parents' marriages (divorce is higher for children of divorced parents), length of courtship (longer is better), and premarital pregnancy (no pregnancy is better, and waiting a while after marriage is even better).

6. **Positive emphasis**

   Do you believe that an intimate relationship is a place where you can indulge your bad moods and openly criticize one another?

   Yes— No—

   Think again. Positive emotions, positive mood, and positive behavior toward

one's partner are vitally important to a lasting, happy relationship.

If you'd like a quick personal demonstration of the power of a positive emphasis, pick two or three of your most "troublesome" friends, family members, or coworkers, and try giving them four positive comments before allowing yourself to say anything even remotely negative. Note how their attitudes and behaviors quickly change. More important, pay attention to the corresponding change in your own feelings and responses toward this troublesome person when you apply this positive emphasis. Can you see how this type of positivism can dramatically improve marital satisfaction?

Families: Their Effect on Development

As we saw in the discussions of attachment and parenting styles in the last chapter, our families exert an enormous influence on our development. But it is not always for the best. Family violence, as well as teen pregnancy and teen parenthood, can have significant effects on development.

Family Violence

Families can be warm and loving. They also can be cruel and abusive. Maltreatment and abuse are more widely recognized than in the past, however it is difficult to measure family violence because it usually occurs in private and victims are reluctant to report it out of shame, powerlessness, or fear of reprisal. Nevertheless, every year millions of cases of domestic violence, child abuse, and elder abuse occur, but many more are not reported to police and social service agencies (Buzawa, Buzawa, & Stark, 2012; Fife & Schrager, 2011; Lewin & Herron, 2007; McGuinness & Schneider, 2007).

What causes family violence? Violence occurs more often in families experiencing marital conflict, substance abuse, mental disorders, and economic stress (Abadinsky, 2011; Koss, White, & Kazdin, 2011; Raphel, 2008; Siever, 2008). It is important to remember that abuse and violence occur at all socioeconomic levels. However, abuse and violence do occur more frequently in families disrupted by unemployment or other financial distress.

In addition to having financial problems, many abusive parents are also socially isolated and lack good communication and parenting skills. Their anxiety and frustration may explode into spouse, child, and elder abuse. In fact, one of the clearest identifiers of abuse potential is *impulsivity*. People who abuse their children, their spouses, or their elderly parents seem to lack impulse control, especially when stressed. They also respond to stress with more intense emotions and greater arousal (Gansler et al., 2011; Venables et al., 2011). This impulsivity is related not only to psychosocial factors like economic stress and social isolation (with no one to turn to for help or feedback) but also to possible biological influences.

Biologically, three regions of the brain are closely related to the expression and control of aggression: the amygdala, the prefrontal cortex, and the hypothalamus (see Chapter 2 to review these regions). Interestingly, head injuries, strokes, dementia, schizophrenia, alcoholism, and abuse of stimulant drugs have all been linked to these three areas and to aggressive outbursts. Research also suggests that low levels of the neurotransmitters serotonin and GABA (gamma-aminobutyric acid) are associated with irritability, hypersensitivity to provocation, and impulsive rage (Lee, Chong, & Coccaro, 2011; Levinthal, 2011; Livingston, 2011; Takahashi et al., 2011).

How can we reduce this type of aggression? Treatment with antianxiety and serotonin-enhancing drugs like fluoxetine (Prozac) may lower the risk of some forms of impulsive violence.

However, treating only biological factors that may contribute to a perpetrator's aggression detracts from the serious and potentially fatal consequences for the victim, as well as all members of the family (Christensen, 2011; Lepistö, Luukkaala, & Paavilainen, 2011; van Marle, 2010). It's also important to note that the primary goal of most abusers is the ultimate power and control over their victims and the relationship.

When people hear about domestic violence, they often wonder why the victim doesn't immediately report the abuse to authorities and/or simply leave. Like most social problems, the causes of family violence are complex and the solutions are far from simple. First, abuse is almost never a single, isolated explosion. Instead, it generally involves numerous events that follow a cyclical and escalating pattern. In the beginning, perpetrators can be devoted and caring partners or parents, but when disagreements happen the abuser responds with increasing levels of intimidation, bullying, and violence, while the victim learns that the only way to calm the situation is to respond with their own increasing levels of compliance and subservience. Second, abuse occurs in many forms (physical, verbal, and emotional), which makes it harder to identify and report. Finally, domestic violence is much more difficult to report and prosecute than attacks by strangers. Child abuse may be dismissed as a parent's right to discipline, and spousal assault is often ignored with a "slap on the wrist."

Despite these obstacles, there is help if you or someone you know is involved in family violence. Trained counselors are available 24 hours a day anywhere in North America by calling 1-800-799-SAFE, and on the Internet at www.ndvh.org, or internationally at ndvh@ndvh.org.

Teen Pregnancy and Parenthood

Another factor that may affect development is becoming a parent and starting a family at too early an age. Pregnancy during adolescence also carries with it considerable health risk for both the mother and child (Chapter 9) and lower educational achievement. Pregnancy, in fact, is the most common reason for girls dropping out of high school. In view of these facts, is it any wonder that teen mothers also report one of the highest levels of depression (Figure 10.3)?

What can be done to reduce the number of teen pregnancies? *Comprehensive education and health-oriented services* seem to be the most promising avenue for decreasing the rate of pregnancy among high-risk teenagers (Goldberg et al., 2011; Sieving et al., 2011).

Juno—an Oscar-nominated film Does "Juno" glorify teen pregnancy—or show strength? What do you think?

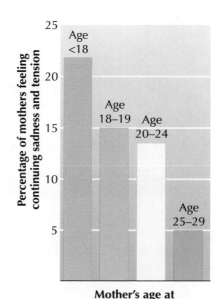

Figure 10.3 Maternal age and satisfaction Note how the age of the mother relates to the percentage of reported feelings of sadness and tension.

The Johns Hopkins Pregnancy Prevention Program, for example, provides complete medical care, contraceptive services, social services (such as counseling), and parenting education. This approach postponed the age of onset of sexual activity, increased contraception use, reduced the frequency of sex, and decreased the actual pregnancy rate in the experimental group by 30 percent. During the same period, pregnancy rates in a comparison school rose by 58 percent (Hardy & Zabin, 1991).

A number of other outreach programs are also working to enhance social development among adolescents through structured volunteer community service and classroom discussions of life choices, careers, and relationships. Research shows that while some teen pregnancies are planned and actually increase teenagers' motivation to stay in school, many teen pregnancies are due to poverty and the perception that life options and choices are limited (Goldstein, 2011; McNeill, 2011; Schultz, 2008; SmithBattle & Leonard, 2006).

Most research and social programs (like the two described here) focus on economics: how money (or the lack of it) affects teen pregnancies. But researchers Rebekah Coley and Lindsay Chase-Lansdale (1998) suggest we also should be exploring the *psychological* consequences of early parenting. If adolescence is a time for solidifying identity and developing autonomy from parents, what happens with teen parents? What are the effects on a teen mother if she lives with her mother? What happens to the life span development of the "early" grandparents? What about the teen father? How does early fatherhood affect his course of development? And what about the child who is being raised by a teen mother or teen father or grandparent? How does this affect his or her development? Answers to these questions rest with the next generation of researchers (perhaps some of you who are reading this text).

Psychology at Work

Resilience—children Who Survive Despite the Odds

Resiliency Ability to adapt effectively in the face of threats

Children fortunate enough to grow up with days filled with play and discovery, nights that provide rest and security, and dedicated, loving parents usually turn out fine. But what about those who are raised in violent, impoverished, or neglectful situations? As we saw in the previous discussions of family violence, divorce, and teen pregnancy and parenting, a troubled childhood creates significantly higher risk of serious physical, emotional, and behavioral problems. There are exceptions to this rule. Some offspring of wonderful, loving parents have serious problems. And some children growing up amid major stressors are remarkably well adjusted.

What is it about children living in harsh circumstances that helps them survive and prosper—despite the odds? The answer holds great interest for both parents and society. Such resilient children can teach us better ways to reduce risk, promote competence, and shift the course of development in more positive directions. **Resiliency** refers to the ability to adapt effectively in the face of threats.

Resilience has been studied throughout the world in a variety of situations, including poverty, natural disasters, war, and family violence (e.g., Burt & Masten, 2010; Easterbrooks et al., 2011; Masten & Wright, 2010; Schmitt-Rodermund & Silbereisen, 2008). Two researchers—Ann Masten at the University of Minnesota and Douglas Coatsworth at the University of Miami (1998)—identified several traits of the resilient child and the environmental circumstances that might account for the resilient child's success.

Most children who do well have (1) good intellectual functioning; (2) relationships with caring adults; and, as they grow older, (3) the ability to regulate their attention, emotions, and behavior. These traits obviously overlap. Good intellectual functioning, for example, may help resilient children solve problems or protect themselves from adverse conditions. Their intelligence may also attract the interest of teachers who serve as nurturing adults. These greater intellectual skills may also help resilient children learn from their experiences and from the caring adults, so in later life they have better self-regulation skills.

In times of growing concern about homelessness, poverty, abuse, teen pregnancy, violence, and divorce, studies of successful children can be very important. On the other hand, there is no such thing as an invulnerable child. Masten and Coatsworth (1998) remind us that "if we allow the prevalence of known risk factors for development to rise, while resources for children fall, we can expect the competence of individual children and the human capital of the nation to suffer" (p. 216).

TRY THIS YOURSELF

Are You Resilient?

Did you grow up in a "high-risk" environment? Are you a resilient child? A 30-year longitudinal study of resilience (Werner, 1989, 2006) identified several environmental factors of high-risk children. Place a check mark by each risk factor that applies to your childhood:

___ Born into chronic poverty

___ Stressful fetal or birth conditions (e.g., prenatal hazards, low birth weight)
___ Chronic discord in the family environment
___ Parents divorced
___ Mental illness in one or both parents

Two-thirds of the high-risk children who had experienced four or more of these factors by

age 2 developed serious adjustment problems in later years. Although the other one-third of the children also experienced four or more such risk factors, they were resilient, and developed into competent, confident, and caring adults.

Work and Retirement: How They Affect Us

Objective 10.8: Describe how work and retirement affect development.

Positive Careers

Throughout most of our adult lives, work defines us in fundamental ways. It affects our health, our friendships, where we live, and even our leisure activities. Too often, however, career choices are driven by dreams of high income. Nearly 74 percent of college freshmen surveyed by the Higher Education Research Institute said that being "very well off financially" was "very important" or "essential." Seventy-one percent felt the same way about raising a family ("This Year's Freshmen," 1995).

In sharp contrast to this 1995 study, a similar survey in 2005 found that two out of three (66.3 percent) entering college freshmen believed it was "essential" or "very important" to help others, which is the highest this figure has been in the past 25 years (Engle, 2006). What explains this change? John Pryor, director of the 2005 survey, suggests that the Indian Ocean tsunami and Hurricane Katrina occurred during an "impressionable time of their lives," which might explain why this cohort will likely have a special commitment to social and civic responsibility.

Unfortunately, many college students from the original 1995 survey who dreamed of high incomes may have ended up in unsatisfying, "dead-end" jobs, or working long hours and weekends at high-paying jobs with little or no time for their families. Likewise, the idealistic 2005 students seeking to help others may have entered service professions, which are at a much higher risk for "burnout" (see Chapter 3).

How can we find personally satisfying and long-lasting careers? Choosing an occupation is one of the most important decisions in our lives, and the task is becoming ever more difficult and complex as career options rapidly change due to increasing specialization, job fluctuations, and the global economy. The *Dictionary of Occupational Titles*, a government publication, currently lists more than 200,000 job categories. One way to learn more about these job categories and potential careers is to visit your college career center. These centers typically offer an abundance of books and pamphlets as well as interesting and helpful vocational interest tests.

In addition to researching a variety of career options, psychologist John Holland's *personality–job fit theory* suggests a match (or "good fit") between our individual personalities and our career choices, is a major factor in determining jobs success and satisfaction. Holland's *Self-Directed Search* questionnaire scores each person on six personality types and then matches their individual interests and abilities to the job demands of various occupations (Holland, 1985, 1994; see also Borchers, 2007; Donohue, 2006; Gottfredson & Duffy, 2008; Kieffer, Schinka, & Curtiss, 2004) (Table 10.1).

Enjoying Retirement

Objective 10.9: What are the three major theories of aging?

Work is a big part of adult life and self-identity. But the large majority of men and women in the United States choose to retire sometime in their sixties. Fortunately, the loss of self-esteem and depression that are commonly assumed to accompany retirement may be largely a myth. Life satisfaction after retirement appears to be most strongly related to good health, control over one's life, social support, adequate income, and participation in community services and social activities (Burr, Santo, &

Table 10.1   ARE YOU IN THE RIGHT JOB?

Personality characteristics	Holland personality type	Matching/congruent occupations
Shy, genuine, persistent, stable, conforming, practical	1. *Realistic*: Prefers physical activities that require skill, strength, and coordination	Mechanic, drill press operator, assembly-line worker, farmer
Analytical, original, curious, independent	2. *Investigative*: Prefers activities that involve thinking, organizing, and understanding	Biologist, economist, mathematician, news reporter
Sociable, friendly, cooperative, understanding	3. *Social*: Prefers activities that involve helping and developing others	Social worker, counselor, teacher, clinical psychologist
Conforming, efficient, practical, unimaginative, inflexible	4. *Conventional*: Prefers rule-regulated, orderly, and unambiguous activities	Accountant, bank teller, file clerk, corporate manager
Imaginative, disorderly, idealistic, emotional, impractical	5. *Artistic*: Prefers ambiguous and unsystematic activities that allow creative expression	Painter, musician, writer, interior decorator
Self-confident, ambitious, energetic, domineering	6. *Enterprising*: Prefers verbal activities with opportunities to influence others and attain power	Lawyer, real estate agent, public relations specialist, small business manager

Pushkar, 2011; Fernández-Ballesteros et al., 2011; Kubicek et al., 2011; Reynolds, 2008). This type of active involvement is the key ingredient to a fulfilling old age, according to the **activity theory of aging**. In contrast, other theorists believe that successful aging is a natural and graceful withdrawal from life, the **disengagement theory** (Achenbaum & Bengtson, 1994; Cummings & Henry, 1961; Feldman & Beehr, 2011; Marshall & Bengtson, 2011; Neugarten, Havighurst, & Tobin, 1968; Sanchez, 2006) (Figure 10.4).

For obvious reasons, the disengagement theory has been seriously questioned and largely abandoned. Successful aging does *not* require withdrawal from society. I mention this theory because of its historical relevance, and also because of its connection to an influential modern perspective, **socioemotional selectivity theory**. This latest model helps explain the predictable decline in social contact that almost everyone experiences as they move into their older years (Carstensen et al., 2011; Charles & Carstensen, 2007; Yeung, Wong, & Lok, 2011). According to socioemotional selectivity theory, we don't naturally withdraw from society in our later years—we just become more *selective* with our time. We deliberately choose to decrease our total number of social contacts in favor of familiar people who provide emotionally meaningful interactions (Figure 10.5).

▲ **Figure 10.4 Disengagement versus activity** The disengagement theory of aging suggests that older people naturally disengage and withdraw from life. However, judging by the people in this photo, activity theory may be a better theory of aging because it suggests that everyone should remain active and involved throughout the entire life span.

TEST YOURSELF

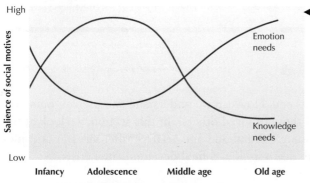

◀ **Figure 10.5 Socioemotional selectivity** Note how our emotional needs appear to change over our life span. Can you explain why?

Answer: During infancy, emotional connection is essential to our survival. During childhood, adolescence, and early adulthood, information gathering is critical, and the need for emotional connection declines. During late adulthood, emotional satisfaction is again more important—we tend to invest our time in those who can be counted on in times of need.

Activity Theory of Aging Successful aging is fostered by a full and active commitment to life

Disengagement Theory of Aging Successful aging is characterized by mutual withdrawal between the elderly and society

Socioemotional Selectivity Theory of Aging A natural decline in social contact occurs as older adults become more selective with their time

MYTH BUSTERS

Myths of Development

A number of popular beliefs about age-related crises are not supported by research. The popular idea of a *midlife crisis* began largely as a result of Gail Sheehy's national best-seller *Passages* (1976). Sheehy drew on the theories of Daniel Levinson (1977, 1996) and psychiatrist Roger Gould (1975), as well as her own interviews. She popularized the idea that almost everyone experiences a "predictable crisis" at about age 35 for women and 40 for men. Middle age often *is* a time of reexamining one's values and lifetime goals. However, Sheehy's book led many people to automatically expect a midlife crisis with drastic changes in personality and behavior. Research suggests that a severe reaction or crisis may be quite rare and unlike what most people experience during middle age (Freund & Ritter, 2009; Whitbourne & Mathews, 2009).

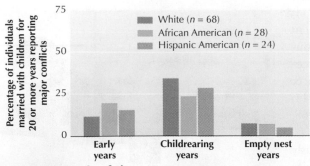

Figure 10.6 **Myth of the empty nest**

Many people also believe that when the last child leaves home, most parents experience an *empty-nest syndrome*—a painful separation and time of depression for the mother, the father, or both parents. Again, research suggests that the empty-nest syndrome may be an exaggeration of the pain experienced by a few individuals and an effort to downplay positive reactions (Clay, 2003; Mitchell & Lovegreen, 2009). For example, one major benefit of the empty nest is a decrease in conflicts and an increase in marital satisfaction (Figure 10.6). Moreover, parent–child relationships do continue once the child leaves home. As one mother said, "The empty nest is surrounded by telephone wires" (Troll, Miller, & Atchley, 1979).

CHECK & REVIEW

STOP *Before going on, be sure to complete this Check & Review. It is an invaluable study tool!*

Meeting the Challenges of Adulthood

Part A: Retrieval Practice

1. Without looking at the book, spend 10 minutes writing a free-form essay recalling all you can remember from the previous section.

2. Now, reread the previous section, and once again spend 10 minutes writing a free-form essay on the SAME material.

Part B: Practice Quiz

1. What do you think should be done to reduce family violence and teenage pregnancy?

2. Identify the three traits of resilient children.

3. The _____ theory of aging suggests that you should remain active and involved until death, whereas the _____ theory suggests that you should naturally and gracefully withdraw from life.

4. Briefly explain the socioemotional selectivity theory of aging.

5. Explain the myths of the midlife crisis and the empty-nest syndrome.

Check your answers in Appendix B.

Grief and Death

One unavoidable part of life is its end. How can we understand and prepare ourselves for the loss of our own life and those of loved others? In this section, we look at the four stages of grief. We then study cultural and age-related differences in attitudes toward death. We conclude with death itself as a final developmental crisis.

Grief: Lessons in Survival

Objective 10.10: Describe grief and list its four stages.

What do I do now that you're gone? Well, when there's nothing else going on, which is quite often, I sit in a corner and I cry until I am too numbed to feel. Paralyzed motionless for a while, nothing moving inside or out. Then I think how much I miss you. Then I feel fear, pain, loneliness, desolation. Then I cry until I am too numbed to feel. Interesting pastime.

PETER MCWILLIAMS, *HOW TO SURVIVE THE LOSS OF A LOVE*, P. 18

Have you ever felt like this? If so, you are not alone. Loss and grief are an inevitable part of all our lives. Feelings of desolation, loneliness, and heartache, accompanied by painful memories, are common reactions to loss, disaster, or misfortune. Ironically, such painful emotions may serve a useful function. Evolutionary psychologists suggest that bereavement and grief may be adaptive mechanisms for both human and nonhuman animals. The pain may motivate parents and children or mates to search for one another. Obvious signs of distress also may be adaptive because they bring the group to the aid of the bereaved individual.

What does it mean if someone seems emotionless after an important loss? Grieving is a complicated and personal process. Just as there is no right way to die, there is no right way to grieve. People who restrain their grief may be following the rules for emotional display that prevail in their cultural group. Moreover, outward signs of strong emotion may be the most obvious expression of grief. But this is only one of four stages in the "normal" grieving process (Houck, 2007; Koppel, 2000; Parkes, 1972, 1991).

In the initial phase of grief, *numbness*, bereaved individuals often seem dazed and may feel little emotion other than numbness or emptiness. They also may deny the death, insisting that a mistake has been made.

In the second stage of grief, individuals enter a stage of *yearning*, intense longing for the loved one, and pangs of guilt, anger, and resentment. The bereaved may also experience illusions. They "see" the deceased person in his or her favorite chair or in the face of a stranger, they have vivid dreams in which the deceased is still alive, or they feel the "presence" of the dead person. They also experience strong guilt feelings ("If only I had gotten her to a doctor sooner" "I should have been more loving") and anger or resentment ("Why wasn't he more careful?" "It isn't fair that I'm the one left behind").

Once the powerful feelings of yearning subside, the individual enters the third *disorganization/despair* phase. Life seems to lose its meaning. The mourner feels listless, apathetic, and submissive. As time goes by, however, the survivor gradually begins to accept the loss both intellectually (the loss makes sense) and emotionally (memories are pleasurable as well as painful). This acceptance, combined with building a new self-identity ("I am a single mother" "We are no longer a couple"), characterizes the fourth and final stage of grief—the *resolution/reorganization stage*.

Grief is obviously not the same for everyone. People vary in they way they grieve, the stages of grief that they experience, and the length of time needed for "recovery" (Corr, Nabe & Corr, 2009; Doka & Martin, 2010; Howarth, 2011; Leaming & Dickinson, 2011; Potter, 2012). You can help people who are grieving by accepting these individual differences and recognizing that there is no perfect response. Simply say, "I'm sorry." And then let the person talk if he or she wishes. Your quiet presence and caring are generally the best type of support.

When it comes to dealing with your own losses and grief, psychologists offer several techniques that you may find helpful (Balk, 2008; Corr & Corr, 2007; Kauffman, 2008; Riebschleger & Cross, 2011; Strada, 2011).

1. *Recognize the loss and allow yourself to grieve.* Despite feelings of acute loneliness, remember that loss is a part of everyone's life and accept comfort from others. Take care of yourself by avoiding unnecessary stress, getting plenty of rest, and giving yourself permission to enjoy life whenever possible.

2. *Set up a daily activity schedule.* One of the best ways to offset the lethargy and depression of grief is to force yourself to fill your time with useful activities (studying, washing your car, doing the laundry, and so on).

3. *Seek help.* Having the support of loving friends and family helps offset the loneliness and stress of grief. Recognize, however, that professional counseling may be necessary in cases of extreme or prolonged numbness, anger, guilt, or depression. (You will learn more about depression and its treatment in Chapters 14 and 15.)

Attitudes Toward Death and Dying: Cultural and Age Variations

Objective 10.11: Discuss cultural and age variations in attitudes toward death and dying.

Cultures around the world interpret and respond to death in widely different ways: "Funerals are the occasion for avoiding people or holding parties, for fighting or

▲ **Grieving** Individuals vary in their emotional reactions to loss. There is no right or wrong way to grieve.

Figure 10.7 Culture influences our response to death In October 2006, a dairy truck driver took over a one-room Amish schoolhouse in Pennsylvania, killed and gravely injured several young girls, then shot himself. Instead of responding in rage, his Amish neighbors attended his funeral. Amish leaders urged forgiveness for the killer and called for a fund to aid his wife and three children. Rather than creating an on-site memorial, the schoolhouse was razed, to be replaced by pasture. What do you think of this response? The fact that many Americans were offended, shocked, or simply surprised by the Amish reaction illustrates how strongly culture affects our emotion, beliefs, and values.

Figure 10.8 How do children understand death? Preschoolers seem to accept the fact that the dead person cannot get up again, perhaps because of their experiences with dead butterflies and beetles found while playing outside (Furman, 1990). Later, they begin to understand all that death entails and that they, too, will someday die.

having sexual orgies, for weeping or laughing, in a thousand combinations" (Metcalf & Huntington, 1991, p. 62).

Similarly, subcultures within the United States also have different responses to death (Figure 10.7). Irish Americans are likely to believe the dead deserve a good send-off—a wake with food, drink, and jokes. African Americans traditionally regard funerals as a time for serious grief, demonstrated in some congregations by wailing and singing spirituals. And most Japanese Americans try to restrain their grief and smile so as not to burden others with their pain. They also want to avoid the shame associated with losing emotional control (Corr, Nabe, & Corr, 2009; Kastenbaum, 2007; Schim et al., 2007).

Attitudes toward death and dying vary among cultures and subcultures, as well as with age. As adults, we understand death in terms of three basic concepts: (1) *permanence*—once a living thing dies, it cannot be brought back to life; (2) *universality*—all living things eventually die; and (3) *nonfunctionality*—all living functions, including thought, movement, and vital signs, end at death.

Research shows that permanence, the notion that death cannot be reversed, is the first and most easily understood concept (Figure 10.8). Understanding of universality comes slightly later. By about the age of 7, most children have mastered nonfunctionality and have an adultlike understanding of death. Adults may fear that discussing death with children and adolescents will make them unduly anxious. But those who are offered open, honest discussions of death have an easier time accepting it (Buckle & Fleming, 2011; Corr, Nabe, & Corr, 2009; Kastenbaum, 2007; Talwar, Harris, & Schleifer, 2011).

The Death Experience: Our Final Developmental Task

Objective 10.12: What are Kübler-Ross's five stages of dying, are they a myth, and what is thanatology?

Have you thought about your own death? Would you like to die suddenly and alone? Or would you prefer to know ahead of time so you could plan your funeral and spend time saying good-bye to your family and friends? If you find thinking about these questions uncomfortable, it may be because most people in Western societies deny death. Unfortunately, avoiding thoughts and discussion of death and associating aging with death contribute to *ageism*. Moreover, the better we understand death, and the more wisely we approach it, the more fully we can live until it comes.

During the Middle Ages (from about the fifth until the sixteenth century), people were expected to recognize when death was approaching so they could say their farewells and die with dignity, surrounded by loved ones. In recent times, Western societies have moved death out of the home and put it into the hospital and funeral parlor. Rather than personally caring for our dying family and friends, we have shifted responsibility to "experts"—physicians and morticians. We have made death a medical failure rather than a natural part of the life cycle.

This avoidance of death and dying may be changing, however. Since the late 1990s, right-to-die and death-with-dignity advocates have been working to bring death out in the open. And mental health professionals have suggested that understanding the psychological processes of death and dying may play a significant role in good adjustment (Leaming & Dickinson, 2011).

Confronting our own death is the last major crisis we face in life. What is it like? Is there a "best" way to prepare to die? Is there such a thing as a "good death"? After spending hundreds of hours at the bedsides of the terminally ill, Elisabeth Kübler-Ross developed a highly controversial stage theory of the psychological processes surrounding death (1983, 1997, 1999).

Based on interviews with dying patients, Kübler-Ross proposed that most people go through five sequential stages when facing death:

- *Denial* of the terminal condition ("This can't be true; it's a mistake!")

- *Anger* ("Why me? It isn't fair!")

- *Bargaining* ("God, if you let me live, I'll dedicate my life to you!")
- *Depression* ("I'm losing everyone and everything I hold dear")
- *Acceptance* ("I know that death is inevitable and my time is near").

Evaluating Kübler-Ross's Theory—A National Myth

Critics of the stage theory of dying stress that the five-stage sequence has not been scientifically validated and that each person's bereavement or death is a unique experience (Christianson, 2010; Kastenbaum, 2007; Konisberg, 2011; O'Rourke, 2010). Emotions and reactions depend on the individual's personality, life situation, age, and so on. Others worry that popularizing such a stage theory will cause further avoidance and stereotyping of those who are grieving or dying ("He's just in the anger stage right now"), and grieving or dying people may feel pressured to conform to the stages Kübler-Ross described (Friedman & James, 2008; Lilienfeld et al., 2010).

In spite of its lack of empirical support and potential abuses, Kübler-Ross's theory has encouraged research into a long-neglected topic. **Thanatology**, the study of death and dying, has become a major topic in human development. Thanks in part to thanatology research, the dying are being helped to die with dignity by the *hospice* movement. This organization has trained staff and volunteers to provide loving support for the terminally ill and

their families in special facilities, hospitals, or the patient's own home (Casarett, 2011; Claxton-Oldfield et al., 2011; DeSpelder & Strickland, 2007; Kumar, Markert, & Patel, 2011).

One important contribution by Kübler-Ross (1975) may have been her suggestion that:

It is the denial of death that is partially responsible for [people] living empty, purposeless lives; for when you live as if you'll live forever, it becomes too easy to postpone the things you know you must do. In contrast, when you fully understand that each day you awaken could be the last you have, you take the time that day to grow, to become more of whom you really are, to reach out to other human beings. (p. 164)

Thanatology [than-uh-TAHL-uh-gee] The study of death and dying; the term comes from thanatus, the Greek name for a mythical personification of death, and was borrowed by Freud to represent the death instinct

Psychology at Work

Dealing with Your Own Death Anxiety

Woody Allen once said, "It's not that I'm afraid to die. I just don't want to be there when it happens." Although some people who are very old and in poor health may welcome death, most of us have difficulty facing it. One of the most important elements of critical thinking is *self-knowledge*, which includes the ability to critically evaluate our deepest and most private fears.

Death Anxiety Questionnaire

To test your own level of death anxiety, indicate your response according to the following scale:

0	1	2
not at all	somewhat	very much

_____1. Do you worry about dying?

_____2. Does it bother you that you may die before you have done everything you wanted to do?

_____3. Do you worry that you may be very ill for a long time before you die?

_____4. Does it upset you to think that others may see you suffering before you die?

_____5. Do you worry that dying may be very painful?

_____6. Do you worry that the persons closest to you won't be with you when you are dying?

_____7. Do you worry that you may be alone when you are dying?

_____8. Are you bothered by the thought that you might lose control of your mind before death?

_____9. Do you worry that expenses connected with your death will be a burden to other people?

_____10. Does it worry you that your will or instructions about your belongings may not be carried out after you die?

_____11. Are you afraid that you may be buried before you are really dead?

_____12. Does the thought of leaving loved ones behind when you die disturb you?

_____13. Do you worry that those you care about may not remember you after your death?

_____14. Are you worried by the thought that with death you will be gone forever?

_____15. Are you worried about not knowing what to expect after death?

How does your total score compare to the national average of 8.5? When this same test was given to nursing-home residents, senior citizens, and college students, researchers found no significant differences, despite the fact that those tested ranged in age from 30 to 80.

Source: H. R. Conte, M. B. Weiner, & R. Plutchik (1982). Measuring death anxiety: Conceptual, psychometric, and factor-analytic aspects. *Journal of Personality and Social Psychology*, 43, 775–785. Reprinted with permission.

Psychology Engages

RESEARCH CHALLENGE

Embodied Morality: Clean Hands, Pure Heart

By Siri Carpenter (Science Writer, Madison, WI)

Have you heard about **embodied cognition,** a current hot topic in psychology, philosophy, and artificial life (e.g., robotics)? It refers to a research program in cognitive science emphasizing the formative role of the environment in the development of cognitive processes. In other words, our cognitions (thoughts, perceptions, attitudes, beliefs) are shaped ("grounded") by our interactions with the environment.

For example, studies have shown that holding a hot cup of coffee, or being in a comfortably heated room warms a person's feelings toward strangers (Carpenter, 2011; Williams & Bargh, 2008; Zhong & Leonardelli, 2008). Furthermore, when people have difficulty with visuo-spatial tasks, they spontaneously produce gestures to help them, and these gestures do in fact improve their performance (Chu & Kita, 2011).

How does this apply to developmental psychology? As you recall from Chapter 9 (p. 339), Piaget believed that cognitive development begins with the sensorimotor stage (birth to age 2). Before we can advance to the adult level of abstract thinking, he believed we must first lay down layers of schemas (cognitive structures or "blueprints") from our interactions (play) with the environment. A child learns to reach for a ball through a series of complex trial and error responses (sensorimotor processes), which are only one of innumerable schemas needed for later cognitive processes. Developmental psychologist Esther Thelen suggests that saying "cognition is embodied means that it arises from bodily interactions with the world" (p. 3) (Thelan et al., 2001).

Our bodies also play an important role in moral reasoning—and maybe even our moral behavior. Consider, for example, the link between physical cleanliness and moral purity—the relation that Shakespeare's Lady Macbeth felt so desperately as she tried to scrub away her sins.

A modern, scientific study of physical cleansing and morality asked participants to recall doing ethical or unethical deeds, and then gave them an ostensibly unrelated word-completion task (Zhong & Liljenquist, 2006). Interestingly, those who had remembered unethical behavior were more likely than those who had summoned up ethical behavior to generate cleansing-related words such as "wash" and "soap," rather than words such as "wish" and "step." In a follow-up experiment, 75 percent of people who had recalled unethical deeds later selected an antiseptic wipe (rather than a pencil) as a parting gift, compared with only 37.5 percent of people who had brought to mind ethical deeds.

The presence of a mental connection between physical cleanliness and moral

Embodied Cognition A cognitive science research program emphasizing the environment's formative role in the development of cognitive processes; cognitions (thoughts, perceptions, attitudes, beliefs) are shaped ("grounded") by interactions with the environment

purity is obvious in the language we use to describe moral violations—we speak of keeping dirty secrets and yearning for a clean conscience. Our language further suggests that moral cognition is tightly bound to the specific body parts responsible for ethical transgression—say, the mouth for swearing or the hands for groping.

The specificity of such sayings led researchers to wonder whether people actually project immoral behavior onto specific body parts (Lee & Schwarz, 2010). They first asked research participants to role-play a scenario that required them to tell a malevolent lie using either voicemail or e-mail, and then rate the desirability of several consumer products. Lee and

Schwarz found that people rated hand sanitizer more highly after lying via e-mail rather than voicemail. They also rated mouthwash more highly after lying via voicemail rather than e-mail. Thus, people did seem to make a subconscious, nonverbal connection between a part of their body and the specific type of unsavory deed.

Student Engagement Exercise

Given the admittedly limited information in the Lee & Schwarz 2010 study described above, what is the most likely:

1. *Research method* (experimental, descriptive, correlational, or biological)?

2. If you chose the:
   - *Experimental method*—label the IV, DV, experimental group, and control group.
   - *Descriptive method*—is this a naturalistic observation, survey, or case study?
   - *Correlational method*—is this a positive, negative, or zero correlation?
   - *Biological method*—identify the specific research tool (e.g., brain dissection, CT scan, etc.)

(Answers appear in Appendix B.)

(*Source*: Originally published in *Scientific American Mind*, January/February 2011, pp. 38–45. Adapted and reprinted with permission of author, Siri Carpenter.)

CRITICAL THINKING

Morality and Academic Cheating

By Thomas Frangicetto (Northampton Community College, Bethlehem, PA)

P. xxxiv

Recent research from The Center for Academic Integrity on cheating among American high school students found that: (1) cheating is widespread, (2) students have little difficulty rationalizing cheating, (3) the Internet is causing new concerns, and (4) students cheat for a variety of reasons. Do you think academic cheating is a moral issue? Consider the following moral dilemma:

It is close to final exam time in your psychology course, and you are on the border between a C or B grade. You go to your professor's office to see what you can do to make sure you get the B grade. But there's a note on the open door, "I'll be right back. Please wait." You notice the stack of exams for your upcoming final, and you could easily take one and leave without being seen.

Part A Describe what you would do in this situation, and briefly explain your reasons.

Now review Kohlberg's six stages of moral development (Step-by-Step Diagram 10.1), and label your level and stage of moral development based on your responses to this student's moral dilemma–level _____ stage _____.

Part B To further develop your critical thinking (and help prepare you for exams on this material), read and label the following responses to the same situation.

Student A: "I wouldn't take the exam because it would be wrong. What if

everybody cheated every chance they got? What kind of credibility would grades have? It would cheapen the value of education and the whole system would be worthless." Stage # _____.

Student B: "I would take the exam because I really need the B in this course. Psychology is not my major, and I have to keep my scholarship. Otherwise, I will not be able to stay in school and my children will suffer." Stage # _____.

Student C: "I wouldn't take it because I would be too afraid of getting caught. With my luck, the teacher would return early and catch me in the act." Stage # _____.

Student D: "I wouldn't take the exam because I wouldn't be able to live with myself. I believe that cheating is the same as stealing and is therefore a crime. My own opinion of myself as an honest person of high integrity would be permanently damaged." Stage # _____.

Student E: "I wouldn't take it because if I got caught and my parents found out they would be devastated. I care too much about what they think of me to risk that. Stage # _____.

Student F: "I wouldn't do it because it wouldn't be fair to other students who have to take the exam without any advantages. The system is designed to work fairly for everyone and cheating definitely violates that ideal." Stage # _____.

Part C Critical Thinking Application

Review the 21 critical thinking components (CTCs) from the Prologue at the front of this text. Below are a few student comments quoted in the report of The Center for Academic Integrity. Apply at least one CTC to each.

"I think that cheating has become so common that it's starting to become 'normal' in some cases." CTC: _____

"There is no way of stopping it. Only the students themselves have the power to do so. Restrictions aren't the problem, but the morals of students sure are." CTC: _____

"Cheating will always exist as long as parents place the emphasis on grades rather than learning. The parent–student relation adds greatly to the dumbing down of America." CTC: _____

"Unless someone makes teachers care about cheating, it won't be stopped. It is unfair that teachers don't take it seriously because then the honest students get the bad end of the deal." CTC: _____

GENDER AND CULTURAL DIVERSITY

Cultural Influences on Development

What is the self?

Objective 10.13: How do individualistic versus collectivistic cultures affect personality development?

As we've just seen in our discussion of Erikson and Kohlberg, and other theorists in Chapter 9, developmental psychology's theories are largely rooted in the concept of *self*—how we define and understand ourselves. Yet the very concept of self reflects our culture. In **individualistic cultures**, the needs and goals of the individual are emphasized over the needs and goals of the group. When asked to complete the statement "I am . . .," people from individualistic cultures tend to respond with personality traits ("I am shy"; "I am outgoing") or their occupation ("I am a teacher"; "I am a student").

In **collectivistic cultures**, however, the opposite is true. The person is defined and understood primarily by looking at his or her place in the social unit (Berry et al., 2011; Dierdorff, Bell, & Belohlav, 2011; McCrae, 2004). Relatedness, connectedness, and interdependence are valued, as opposed to separateness, independence, and individualism. When asked to complete the statement "I am . . .," people from collectivistic cultures tend to mention their families or nationality ("I am a daughter"; "I am Chinese").

If you are North American or western European, you are more likely to be individualistic than collectivistic (Table 10.2). And you may find the concept of a self defined in terms of others almost contradictory. A core selfhood probably seems intuitively obvious to you. Recognizing that over 70 percent of the world's population lives in collectivistic cultures, however, may improve your cultural sensitivity and prevent misunderstandings. For example, North Americans generally define *sincerity* as behaving in accordance with one's inner feelings, whereas Japanese see it as behavior that conforms to a person's role expectations (carrying out one's duties) (Yamada, 1997). Can you see how Japanese behavior might appear insincere to a North American and vice versa?

Individualistic Cultures Needs and goals of the individual are emphasized over the needs and goals of the group

Collectivistic Cultures Needs and goals of the group are emphasized over the needs and goals of the individual

 TRY THIS YOURSELF

Cultural Effects on Personality development

If asked to draw a circle with yourself in the center, and the people in your life as separate circles surrounding you, which of the two diagrams comes closest to your personal view?

If you chose (a), you probably have an *individualistic* orientation, seeing yourself as an independent, separate self. However, if you chose (b), you're more closely aligned with a *collectivist* culture, seeing yourself as interdependent and interconnected with others (Berry et al., 2011; Kitayama & Cohen, 2007; Markus & Kitayama, 2010).

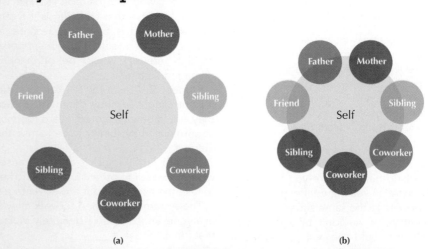

(a)   (b)

Table 10.2 WORLDWIDE RANKING OF CULTURES

Individualistic	Intermediate	Collectivistic
United States	Israel	Hong Kong
Australia	Spain	Chile
Great Britain	India	Singapore
Canada	Argentina	Thailand
Netherlands	Japan	West Africa region
New Zealand	Iran	El Salvador
Italy	Jamaica	Taiwan
Belgium	Arab region	South Korea
Denmark	Brazil	Peru
France	Turkey	Costa Rica
Sweden	Uruguay	Indonesia
Ireland	Greece	Pakistan
Norway	Philippines	Colombia
Switzerland	Mexico	Venezuela

▲ How might these two groups differ in their physical, socioemotional, cognitive, moral, and personality development?

Cultural Differences in Ageism
Objective 10.14: Discuss the major cultural differences in ageism.

In addition to cultural differences in identifying the "self," there are also differences in the losses and stress associated with the aging process—although much less than most people think. Perhaps the greatest challenge for the elderly, at least in the United States, is the *ageism* they encounter. In societies that value older people as wise elders or keepers of valued traditions, the stress of aging is much less than in societies that view them as mentally slow and socially useless. In cultures like that in the United States in which youth, speed, and progress are strongly emphasized, a loss or decline in any of these qualities is deeply feared and denied.

Aren't there also cultures that honor their elderly? In Japan, China, and the United States among African Americans and most tribes of Native Americans, the elderly generally are more revered. Aging parents are typically more respected for their wisdom and experience, deferred to in family matters, and expected to live with their children until they die (Berry et al., 2011; Chan & Chui, 2011; Miller et al., 2006). However, as these cultures become more urbanized and Westernized, there is often a corresponding decline in respect for the elderly. In Japan, for example, over 80 percent of the elderly lived with their adult children in 1957. This percentage declined to only 55 percent in 1994. But Japan still has one of the highest rates of adult children caring for elderly relatives (Koropeckyj-Cox & Call, 2007).

Ageism, Gender, and Ethnicity in the United States There also is considerable difference in the status and treatment of different subgroups of the elderly. In the United States, for example, studies show that older men have more social status, income, and sexual partners than do older women. Elderly women, on the other hand, have more friends and are more involved in family relationships. But they have lower status and income. Contrary to the popular stereotype of the "rich old woman," elderly females represent one of the lowest income levels in North America.

Ethnicity also plays a role in aging in the United States. Ethnic minority elderly, especially African Americans and Latinos, face problems related to both ageism and racism. They are more likely to become ill but less likely to receive treatment. And they are overrepresented among the elderly poor living below the poverty line (Flores, 2008; Hillier & Barrow, 2011; McNamara, 2007; Miller et al., 2006).

▲ **Elder respect** Native Americans generally revere and respect the elder members of their tribe. How would the aging experience be different if being old was an honor and blessing versus a dreaded curse?

Other research, however, reports that African Americans are more likely than Anglo Americans to regard elderly persons with respect (Mui, 1992). Also, compared with whites, other ethnic groups often have a greater sense of community and may have stronger bonds of attachment, owing to their shared traits and experiences with prejudice. Ethnicity itself may therefore provide some benefits. "In addition to shielding them from majority attitudes, ethnicity provides the ethnic elderly with a source of esteem" (Fry, 1985, p. 233).

CHECK & REVIEW

STOP *Before going on, be sure to complete this Check & Review. It is an invaluable study tool!*

Grief and Death and Psychology Engages

Part A: Retrieval Practice

1. Without looking at the book, spend 10 minutes writing a free-form essay recalling all you can remember from the previous section.

2. Now, reread the previous section, and once again spend 10 minutes writing a free-form essay on the SAME material.

Part B: Practice Quiz

1. List the four stages of grief.
2. Describe how preschoolers view death.

3. Match the following statements with Elisabeth Kübler-Ross's supposed five-stage theory of death and dying:

___a. "I understand that I'm dying, but if I could just have a little more time . . ."

___b. "I refuse to believe the doctors. I want a fourth opinion."

___c. "I know my time is near. I'd better make plans for my spouse and children."

___d. "Why me? I've been a good person. I don't deserve this."

___e. "I'm losing everything. I'll never see my children again. Life is so hard."

4. Describe the major criticisms of Kübler-Ross's theory of death and dying.

5. The study of death and dying is known as _____.

6. Explain how ethnicity may help the elderly overcome some problems with aging.

Check your answers in Appendix B.

WileyPLUS presents an on-line version of this textbook along with a wealth of study resources including quizzes, practice tests, flash cards, videos, animations and other activities designed to improve your mastery of the content. Working in conjunction with these study tools, the *Psychology in Action* WileyPLUS course features Professor Karen Huffman, author of this textbook, explaining and expanding upon some of the most challenging concepts in psychology. Here is a sample of the tutorial videos available for this chapter:

www.wileyplus.com

• An animated, interactive look at Kohlberg's stages of moral development
• Animated overview of Erikson's psychosocial theory
• Professor Huffman's classroom demonstration of factors in marital satisfaction
• Explorations of attitudes towards aging
• Virtual Field Trip to learn how hospice care provides for the unique needs of individuals in their final days.

Key Terms

To assess your understanding of the **Key Terms** in Chapter 10, write a definition for each (in your own words), and then compare your definitions with those in the text.

Moral Development
preconventional level (p. 362)
conventional level (p. 362)
postconventional level (p. 362)

Personality Development
temperament (p. 363)
psychosocial stages (p. 364)

Meeting the Challenges of Adulthood
resiliency (p. 370)
activity theory of aging (p. 373)
disengagement theory of aging (p. 373)
socioemotional selectivity
    theory of aging (p. 373)

Grief and Death
thanatology [than-uh-TAHL-uh-gee]
    (p. 377)

Psychology Engages
embodied cognition (p. 378)
individualistic cultures (p. 380)
collectivistic cultures (p. 380)

Chapter Summary

Moral Development

Objective 10.1: What is the biological perspective on morality?

From a biological perspective, morality may be prewired and evolutionarily based (e.g., adoption of motherless chimp babies by other chimps promotes species survival).

Objective 10.2: Describe Kohlberg's three levels and six stages of moral development.

According to Kohlberg, morality progresses through three levels. Each level consists of two stages. At the **preconventional level**, morality is self-centered. What is right is what one can get away with (Stage 1) or what is personally satisfying (Stage 2). **Conventional level** morality is based on a need for approval (Stage 3) and obedience to laws because they maintain the social order (Stage 4). **Postconventional level** morality comes from adhering to the social contract (Stage 5) and the individual's own principles and universal values (Stage 6).

Objective 10.3: What are the three major criticisms of Kohlberg's theory?

Kohlberg's theory has been criticized for possibly measuring only moral reasoning and not moral behavior, and for possible culture and gender bias.

Personality Development

Objective 10.4: Describe Thomas and Chess's temperament theory.

Thomas and Chess emphasized the innate, biological components of traits (such as sociability) and observed that babies often exhibit differences in **temperament** shortly after birth. They found three categories of temperament (*easy*, *difficult*, and *slow-to-warm-up* children) that appear to be consistent throughout childhood and adulthood.

Objective 10.5: Describe Erikson's eight psychosocial stages.

Erikson's eight **psychosocial** stages of development cover the entire life span, and each stage is marked by a "psychosocial" crisis or conflict related to a specific developmental task. Four stages that occur during childhood are: *trust versus mistrust, autonomy versus shame and doubt, initiative versus guilt,* and *industry versus inferiority*. The major psychosocial identity crisis of adolescence is the search for *identity versus role confusion*. During young adulthood, the individual's task is to establish *intimacy versus isolation*. During middle adulthood, the person must deal with *generativity versus stagnation*. At the end of life, the older adult must establish *ego integrity versus despair* at the realization of lost opportunities.

Objective 10.6: What are the major criticisms of Erikson's stages?

Erikson's eight stages are difficult to test scientifically, and they may not apply cross-culturally.

Meeting the Challenges of Adulthood

Objective 10.7: Discuss the major problems with long-term relationships.

A good marriage is one of the most difficult and important tasks of adulthood. Researchers have found six major traits and factors in happy marriages: *established "love maps," shared power and mutual support, conflict management, similarity*, a *supportive social environment*, and a *positive emphasis*. Family violence, teenage pregnancy, and divorce all have significant effects on development. However, **resilient** children who survive abusive and stress-filled childhoods usually have good intellectual functioning, a relationship with a caring adult, and the ability to regulate their attention, emotions, and behavior.

Objective 10.8: Describe how work and retirement affect development.

The kind of work we do can affect our health, friendships, where we live, and even our leisure activities. Life satisfaction after retirement appears to be most strongly related to good health, control over one's life, social support, and participation in community services and social activities.

Objective 10.9: What are the three major theories of aging?

One theory of successful aging, **activity theory**, says people should remain active and involved throughout the entire life span. Another major theory, **disengagement theory**, says the elderly naturally and gracefully withdraw from life because they welcome the relief from roles they can no longer fulfill. Although the disengagement theory is no longer in favor, the **socioemotional selectivity theory** does find that the elderly tend to decrease their total number of social contacts as they become more selective with their time.

Grief and Death

Objective 10.10: Describe grief and list its four stages.

Grief is a natural and painful reaction to a loss. For most people, grief consists of four major stages—*numbness, yearning, disorganization/despair*, and *resolution*.

Objective 10.11: Discuss cultural and age variations in attitudes toward death and dying.

Attitudes toward death and dying vary greatly across cultures and among age groups. Some cultures regard death as a time for celebration, whereas others see it as a time for serious grief. Although adults understand the *permanence, universality*, and *nonfunctionality* of death, children often don't master these concepts until around age 7.

Objective 10.12: What are Kübler-Ross's five stages of death and dying, are they a myth, and what is thanatology?

Kübler-Ross's theory of the five-stage psychological process when facing death (*denial, anger, bargaining, depression*, and *acceptance*) has been widely criticized and is now generally considered a myth. However, the study of death and dying, **thanatology**, has become an important topic in human development.

Objective 10.13: How do individualistic versus collectivistic cultures affect personality development?

In **individualistic cultures**, the needs and goals of the individual are emphasized over the needs and goals of the group. However, the reverse is true in **collectivistic cultures**.

Objective 10.14: Discuss the major cultural differences in ageism.

One of the greatest challenges for the elderly, at least in the United States, is the *ageism* they encounter. However, in societies that value older people as wise elders or keepers of valued traditions, the stress of aging is much less than in societies that view them as mentally slow and socially useless. There also is considerable difference in the status and treatment of different elderly subgroups, and ethnic minority elderly, especially African Americans and Latinos, face problems of both racism and ageism.

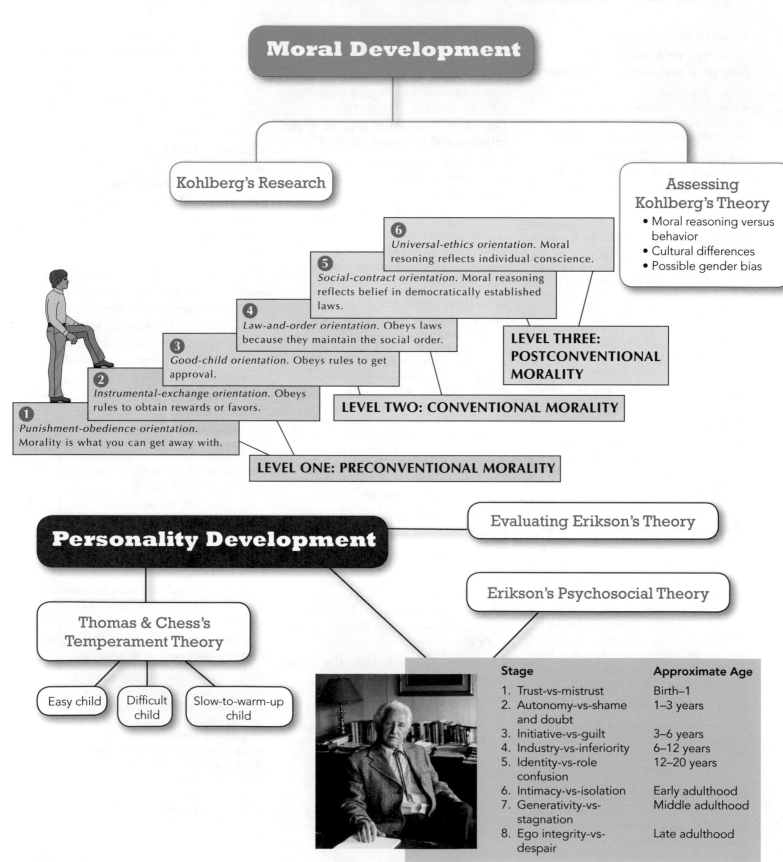

Moral Development

Kohlberg's Research

Assessing Kohlberg's Theory
- Moral reasoning versus behavior
- Cultural differences
- Possible gender bias

6 *Universal-ethics orientation.* Moral resoning reflects individual conscience.

5 *Social-contract orientation.* Moral reasoning reflects belief in democratically established laws.

4 *Law-and-order orientation.* Obeys laws because they maintain the social order.

3 *Good-child orientation.* Obeys rules to get approval.

2 *Instrumental-exchange orientation.* Obeys rules to obtain rewards or favors.

1 *Punishment-obedience orientation.* Morality is what you can get away with.

LEVEL THREE: POSTCONVENTIONAL MORALITY

LEVEL TWO: CONVENTIONAL MORALITY

LEVEL ONE: PRECONVENTIONAL MORALITY

Personality Development

Evaluating Erikson's Theory

Erikson's Psychosocial Theory

Thomas & Chess's Temperament Theory

Easy child

Difficult child

Slow-to-warm-up child

Stage	Approximate Age
1. Trust-vs-mistrust	Birth–1
2. Autonomy-vs-shame and doubt	1–3 years
3. Initiative-vs-guilt	3–6 years
4. Industry-vs-inferiority	6–12 years
5. Identity-vs-role confusion	12–20 years
6. Intimacy-vs-isolation	Early adulthood
7. Generativity-vs-stagnation	Middle adulthood
8. Ego integrity-vs-despair	Late adulthood

Meeting the Challenges of Adulthoold

Committed Relationships
Overcoming unrealistic expectations

Families
- Family violence
- Teen pregnancy and parenthood
- Resilience

Work and Retirement
- Positive careers
- Enjoying retirement
- Theories of aging

Activity

Disengagement

Socioemotional Selectivity

Grief and Death

Grief
Four stages:
- Numbness
- Yearning
- Disorganization and despair
- Resolution

Attitudes toward Death & Dying
(Culture and age variations)

The Death Experience
Kübler-Ross's 5 stages:
- Denial
- Anger
- Bargaining
- Depression
- Acceptance

Myth Buster
Kübler-Ross's theory lacks scientific support

Psychology Engages

Research Challenge
Critical Thinking
Gender & Cultural Diverstiy

ChapterEleven

Gender and Human Sexuality

We allow our ignorance to prevail upon us and make us think we can survive alone, alone in patches, alone in groups, alone in races, even alone in genders.

MAYA ANGELOU

I laugh, I love, I hope, I try, I hurt, I need, I fear, I cry. And I know you do the same things too, So we're really not that different, me and you.

COLLIN RAYE

Men and women, women and men, It will never work.

ERICA JONG

What do you think? Are men and women from different planets (Mars and Venus)? Or are they both from planet Earth? Is it possible that our sense of ourselves as men or women develops primarily from how our parents or others treat us? Or is biology the best predictor? You will learn more about your own gender development and sexuality in the first section of this chapter. Then we will discuss important findings from sex research and cultural differences in sexual practices and attitudes. The third section describes sexual arousal, response, and orientation. And the chapter concludes with discussions of sexual dysfunction and sexually transmitted infections, including AIDS (acquired immunodeficiency syndrome).

387

MYTH BUSTERS

True or False?

1. The breakfast cereal Kellogg's Corn Flakes was originally developed to discourage masturbation.

2. Nocturnal emissions and masturbation are signs of abnormal sexual adjustment.

3. Sex and gender are essentially the same.

4. Androgyny is a type of homosexuality.

5. A transsexual is just another word for a transvestite.

6. Men and women are more alike than different in their sexual responses.

7. Sexual skill and satisfaction are learned behaviors that can be increased through education and training.

8. The American Psychiatric Association and the American Psychological Association (APA) consider homosexuality a type of mental illness.

9. Sex education should begin as early as possible.

10. If you're HIV-positive (have the human immunodeficiency virus), you cannot infect someone else. You must have AIDS (acquired immunodeficiency syndrome) to spread the disease.

11. Women cannot be raped against their will.

12. A man cannot be raped by a woman.

Answers: 1. T 2. F 3. F 4. F 5. F 6. T 7. T 8. F 9. T 10. F 11. F 12. F

Studying Human Sexuality

Objective 11.1: Describe early studies of sexuality and the contributions of Ellis, Kinsey, and Masters and Johnson.

Sex is used and abused in many ways. It is a major theme in literature, movies, and music, as well as a way to satisfy sexual desires. We also use and abuse sex to gain love and acceptance from partners and peer groups, to express love or commitment in a relationship, to end relationships through affairs with others, to dominate or hurt others, and, perhaps most conspicuously, to sell products.

Early Studies: From Victorian Times to Havelock Ellis

People have probably always been interested in understanding their sexuality. But cultural forces have often suppressed and controlled this interest. During the nineteenth century, for example, polite society avoided mention of all parts of the body covered by clothing. The breast of chickens became known as "white meat," male doctors examined female patients in totally dark rooms, and some people even covered piano legs for the sake of propriety (Clark, 2011; Marcus 2008; Money, 1985a).

During this same Victorian period, medical experts warned that masturbation led to blindness, impotence, acne, and insanity (Allen, 2000; Michael et al., 1994). Believing a bland diet helped suppress sexual desire, Dr. John Harvey Kellogg and Sylvester Graham developed the original Kellogg's Corn Flakes and Graham crackers and marketed them as foods that would discourage masturbation (Markel, 2011; Money, Prakasam, & Joshi, 1991). One of the most serious concerns of many doctors was nocturnal emissions (wet dreams), which were believed to cause brain damage and death. Special devices were even marketed for men to wear at night to prevent sexual arousal (Figure 11.1).

In light of modern knowledge, it seems hard to understand these strange Victorian practices and outrageous myths about masturbation and nocturnal emissions. One of the first physicians to explore and question these beliefs was Havelock Ellis (1858–1939). When he first heard of the dangers of nocturnal emissions, Ellis was frightened—he had had personal experience with the problem. His fear led him to frantically search the medical literature. But instead of a cure, he found predictions of gruesome illness and eventual death. He was so upset he contemplated suicide.

Ellis eventually decided he could give meaning to his life by keeping a detailed diary of his deterioration. He planned to dedicate the book to science when he died. However, after several months of careful observation, he realized the books were wrong. He wasn't dying. He wasn't even sick. Angry that he had been so misinformed by the "experts," he spent the rest of his life developing reliable and accurate sex information. Today, Havelock Ellis is acknowledged as one of the most important early pioneers in the field of sex research.

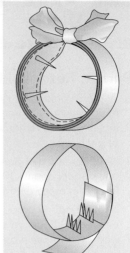

TEST YOURSELF

Figure 11.1 Victorian sexual practice During the nineteenth century, men were encouraged to wear spiked rings around their penises at night. Can you explain why?

Answer: The Victorians believed nighttime erections and emissions ("wet dreams") were dangerous. If the man had an erection, the spikes would cause pain and awaken him.

Modern Research: From Kinsey to Masters and Johnson

One of the earliest forms of modern sex research came from Alfred Kinsey and his colleagues (1948, 1953). Kinsey and his coworkers personally interviewed over 18,000 participants, asking detailed questions about their sexual activities and preferences. Their results shocked the nation. For example, they reported that 37 percent of men and 13 percent of women had engaged in adult same-sex behavior to the point of orgasm. Although Kinsey's interviewing techniques were excellent, his data has been heavily criticized for serious sampling bias (see Chapter 1, p. 26).

In recent years, hundreds of similar sex surveys and interviews have been conducted on such topics as contraception, abortion, premarital sex, sexual orientation, and sexual behavior (e.g., Buss, 1989, 2007, 2008; Ellis et al., 2008; Laumann et al., 1994). By comparing Kinsey's data to the responses found in later surveys, we can see how sexual practices have changed over the years (Goldstein, 2010).

In addition to surveys, interviews, and case studies, some researchers have employed direct laboratory experimentation and observational methods. To experimentally document the physiological changes involved in sexual arousal and response, William Masters and Virginia Johnson (1961, 1966, 1970) and their research colleagues enlisted several hundred male and female volunteers. Using intricate physiological measuring devices, the researchers carefully monitored participants' bodily responses as they masturbated or engaged in sexual intercourse. Masters and Johnson's research findings have been hailed as a major contribution to our knowledge of sexual physiology. Some of their results are discussed in later sections of this chapter.

CHECK & REVIEW

STOP *Before going on, be sure to complete this Check & Review. It is an invaluable study tool!*

Studying Human Sexuality

Part A: Retrieval Practice

1. Without looking at the book, spend 10 minutes writing a free-form essay recalling all you can remember from the previous section.

2. Now, reread the previous section, and once again spend 10 minutes writing a free-form essay on the SAME material.

   (Although time consuming, this exercise has been shown to be the single best way to improve your test scores! For more information, check out http://www.sciencemag.org/content/early/2011/01/19/science.1199327.abstract)

Part B: Practice Quiz

1. During earlier times, it was believed that _____ led to blindness, impotence, acne, and insanity, whereas _____ caused brain damage and death.
   (a) female orgasms, male orgasms;
   (b) masturbation, nocturnal emissions;
   (c) menstruation, menopause;
   (d) oral sex, sodomy

2. _____ based his/their groundbreaking research into human sexuality on personal diaries.

3. _____ popularized the use of the survey method in studying human sexuality.

4. _____ pioneered the use of direct observation and physiological measurement of bodily responses during sexual activities.

Check your answers in Appendix B.

Sex and Gender

Objective 11.2: Compare and contrast sex and gender.

Why is it that the first question most people ask after a baby is born is "Is it a girl or a boy?" What would life be like if there were no divisions according to maleness or femaleness? Would your career plans or friendship patterns change? These questions reflect the importance of *sex* and *gender* in our lives. This section begins with a look at the various ways sex and gender can be defined, followed by a discussion of gender-role development, gender-identity formation, and sex and gender differences.

What Is "Maleness" and "Femaleness"? Defining Sex and Gender

Sex Biological maleness and femaleness, including chromosomal sex; also, sexual behaviors, such as masturbation and intercourse

Gender Psychological and sociocultural meanings added to biological maleness or femaleness

In recent years, researchers have come to use the term **sex** to refer to biological elements (such as having a penis or vagina) or physical activities (such as masturbation and intercourse). **Gender**, on the other hand, encompasses the psychological and sociocultural meanings added to biology (such as "Men should be aggressive" and "Women should be nurturing"). There are at least seven dimensions or elements of *sex* and two of *gender* (Table 11.1).

Gender-Role Development: Two Major Theories

Objective 11.3: Define gender role, and describe the two major theories of gender-role development.

Gender Role Societal expectations for "appropriate" male and female behavior

Sexual orientation and gender identity also should not be confused with **gender roles**—societal expectations for "appropriate" female and male behavior. Gender roles influence our lives from the moment of birth (when we are wrapped in either a pink or blue blanket) until the moment of death (when we are buried in either a dress or a dark suit). By age 2, children are well aware of gender roles. They recognize that boys should be strong, independent, aggressive, dominant, and achieving. Conversely, girls should be soft, dependent, passive, emotional, and "naturally" interested in children

Table 11.1 DIMENSIONS OF SEX AND GENDER

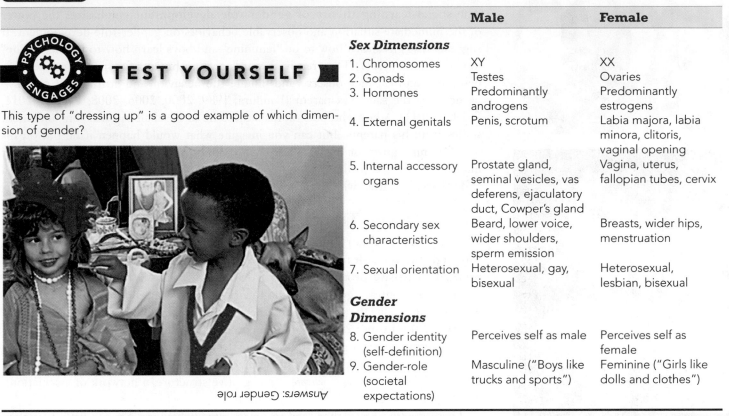

TEST YOURSELF

This type of "dressing up" is a good example of which dimension of gender?

Answers: Gender role

	Male	Female
Sex Dimensions		
1. Chromosomes	XY	XX
2. Gonads	Testes	Ovaries
3. Hormones	Predominantly androgens	Predominantly estrogens
4. External genitals	Penis, scrotum	Labia majora, labia minora, clitoris, vaginal opening
5. Internal accessory organs	Prostate gland, seminal vesicles, vas deferens, ejaculatory duct, Cowper's gland	Vagina, uterus, fallopian tubes, cervix
6. Secondary sex characteristics	Beard, lower voice, wider shoulders, sperm emission	Breasts, wider hips, menstruation
7. Sexual orientation	Heterosexual, gay, bisexual	Heterosexual, lesbian, bisexual
Gender Dimensions		
8. Gender identity (self-definition)	Perceives self as male	Perceives self as female
9. Gender-role (societal expectations)	Masculine ("Boys like trucks and sports")	Feminine ("Girls like dolls and clothes")

(Collins, 2011; King, 2012; Matlin, 2012; Renzetti et al., 2006). The gender-role expectations learned in childhood apparently influence us throughout our life (Cotter, Hermsen, & Vannerman, 2011; Guadagno et al., 2011; Leaper, 2011).

How do we develop our gender roles? The existence of similar gender roles in many cultures suggests that evolution and biology may play a role. However, most research emphasizes two major theories of gender-role development: *social learning* and *gender schema* (Figure 11.2).

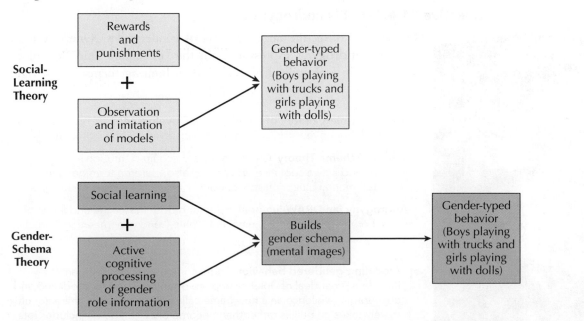

Figure 11.2 Gender-role development

▲ **Early gender-role conditioning**
What are the possible long-term effects of this type of gender-role training on young boys and girls?

Social-Learning Theory

The **social-learning theory of gender-role development** emphasizes the power of the immediate situation and observable behaviors on gender-role development. It suggests that girls learn how to be "feminine" and boys learn how to be "masculine" in two major ways: (1) They receive rewards or punishments for specific gender-role behaviors, and (2) they observe and imitate the behavior and attitudes of others—particularly the same-sex parent (Bandura, 1989, 2000, 2006, 2008; Collins, 2011; Fulcher, 2011). A boy who puts on his father's tie or baseball cap wins big, indulgent smiles from his parents. But can you imagine what would happen if he put on his mother's nightgown or lipstick? Parents, teachers, and friends generally reward or punish behaviors according to traditional boy/girl gender-role expectations. Thus, a child "socially learns" what it means to be male or female.

Gender-Schema Theory

Gender-schema theory incorporates social learning with cognition (or thinking). Although the social-learning model also involves thinking, gender development is primarily a passive process resulting from rewards, punishments, observation, and imitation. In contrast, gender-schema theory suggests that children actively observe, interpret, and judge the world around them (Bem, 1981, 1993; Hollander, Renfrow, & Howard, 2011; Leaper, 2011). As children process this information, they create internal rules governing correct gender roles for boys versus girls. Using these rules, they form *gender schemas* (mental images) of how they should act. (Recall from the discussion of Piaget in Chapter 9 that a *schema* is a cognitive structure, a network of associations, which guides perception.)

These *gender schemas* then lead to *gender-typed* behaviors. Thus, a little boy plays with fire trucks and building blocks because his parents smiled approvingly in the past. It is also because he has seen more boys than girls playing with these toys (*social-learning theory*). But his internal thought processes (*gender-schema theory*) also contribute to his choice of "masculine" toys. The child realizes he is a boy, and he has learned that boys "should" prefer fire trucks to dishes and dolls.

Androgyny
Objective 11.4: What is androgyny?

How can we offset the negative parts of gender roles? One way is to encourage **androgyny**, expressing both the "masculine" and "feminine" traits found in each individual. Rather than limiting themselves to rigid

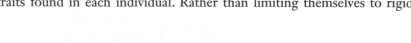

Social-Learning Theory of Gender-Role Development Gender roles are acquired though rewards, punishments, observation, and imitation

Gender-Schema Theory Gender roles are acquired through social learning and active cognitive processing; also, children form gender schemas (mental blueprints) of "correct" behaviors for boys versus girls

Androgyny [an-DRAW-juh-nee] Exhibiting both masculine and feminine traits; from the Greek andro, meaning "male," and gyn, meaning "female"

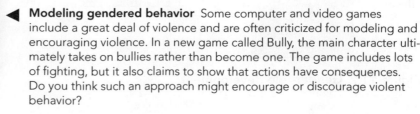

◀ **Modeling gendered behavior** Some computer and video games include a great deal of violence and are often criticized for modeling and encouraging violence. In a new game called Bully, the main character ultimately takes on bullies rather than become one. The game includes lots of fighting, but it also claims to show that actions have consequences. Do you think such an approach might encourage or discourage violent behavior?

gender-appropriate behaviors, androgynous men and women can be assertive and aggressive when necessary, but also gentle and nurturing.

Some people mistakenly believe *androgyny* is a new term for asexuality or transsexualism. However, the idea of androgyny has a long history referring to positive combinations of gender roles, like the *yin* and *yang* of traditional Chinese religions. Carl Jung (1946, 1959), an early psychoanalyst, described a woman's natural masculine traits and impulses as her "animus" and feminine traits and impulses in a man as his "anima." Jung believed we must draw on both our masculine and feminine natures to become fully functioning adults.

Using personality tests and other similar measures, modern researchers have found that *masculine* and *androgynous* individuals generally have higher self-esteem, academic scores, and creativity. They are also more socially competent and motivated to achieve, and exhibit better overall mental health (Choi, 2004; Stoltzfus et al., 2011; Wall, 2007; Woo & Oie, 2006). It seems that androgyny and masculinity, but *not* femininity, are adaptive for both sexes.

How do researchers explain this? It seems that traditional masculine characteristics (analytical, independent) are more highly valued than traditional feminine traits (affectionate, cheerful). For example, in business a good manager is generally perceived as having predominantly masculine traits (Johnson et al., 2008; Stoltzfus et al., 2011). Also, when college students in 14 different countries were asked to describe their "current self" and their "ideal self," the ideal self-descriptions for both men and women contained more masculine than feminine qualities (Williams & Best, 1990).

This shared preference for male traits helps explain why extensive observations of children on school playgrounds have found that boys who engage in feminine activities (like skipping rope or playing jacks) lose status. The reverse of this is not true for girls (Leaper, 2000). Even as adults, it is generally more difficult for men to express so-called female traits like nurturance and sensitivity than for women to adopt traditionally male traits of assertiveness and independence. In short, most societies prefer "tomboys" to "sissies."

Recent studies show that gender roles in our society are becoming less rigidly defined (Cotter, Hermsen & Vanneman, 2011; Hollander, Renfrow, & Howard, 2011). Asian American and Mexican American groups show some of the largest changes toward androgyny. And African Americans remain among the most androgynous of all ethnic groups (Denmark, Rabinowitz, & Sechzer, 2005; Duval, 2006; Renzetti et al., 2006).

) TRY THIS YOURSELF)

Are You Androgynous?

Androgyny in action Combining the traits of both genders helps many couples meet the demands of modern life.

Social psychologist Sandra Bem (1974, 1993) developed a personality measure that has been widely used in research. You can take this version of Bem's test by rating yourself on the following items. Give yourself a number between 1 (never or almost never true) and 7 (always or almost always true):

1. _____ Analytical
2. _____ Affectionate
3. _____ Competitive
4. _____ Compassionate
5. _____ Aggressive
6. _____ Cheerful
7. _____ Independent
8. _____ Gentle
9. _____ Athletic
10. _____ Sensitive

Now add up your points for all the odd-numbered items; then add up your points for the even-numbered items. If you have a higher total on the odd-numbered items, you are "masculine." If you scored higher on the even-numbered items, you are "feminine." If your score is fairly even, you may be androgynous.

Gender-Identity Formation: "Who Am I—Boy or Girl?"

Objective 11.5: Differentiate between gender identity, transsexualism, transvestism, and sexual orientation.

Now that we understand how children develop their gender roles, we need to examine an even more fundamental question: Why and how do children personally decide "I am a boy" or "I am a girl"? Let's begin with one of the most famous studies of **gender-identity** formation.

Gender Identity Self-identification as being either a man or a woman

It was an unusual circumcision. The identical twin boys, Bruce and Brian, were already 8 months old when their parents took them to the doctor to be circumcised. For many years in the United States, most male babies have had the foreskin of their penis removed during their first week of life. This is done for religious and presumed hygienic reasons. It is also assumed that newborns will experience less pain. The most common procedure is cutting or pinching off the foreskin tissue. In this case, however, the doctor used an electrocautery device, which is typically used to burn off moles or small skin growths. The electrical current used for the first twin was too high, and the entire penis was accidentally removed. (The parents canceled the circumcision of the other twin.)

In anguish over the tragic accident, the parents sought advice from medical experts. Following discussions with John Money and other specialists at Johns Hopkins University, the parents and doctors made an unusual decision—they would turn the infant with the destroyed penis into a girl. (Reconstructive surgery was too primitive at the time to restore the child's penis.)

The first step in the reassignment process occurred at age 17 months, when the child's name was changed—Bruce became "Brenda" (Colapinto, 2000). Brenda was dressed in pink pants and frilly blouses, and "her" hair was allowed to grow long. At 22 months, surgery was performed. The child's testes were removed, and external female genitals and an internal, "preliminary" vagina were created. Further surgery to complete the vagina was planned for the beginning of adolescence, when the child's physical growth would be nearly complete. At this time she would also begin to take female hormones to complete the boy-to-girl transformation.

If you apply the dimensions of sex and gender that are presented in Table 11.1 (p. 391) to the case of the reassigned twin, you can see why this is a classic in the field of human sexuality. Although born a chromosomal male, the child's genital sex was first altered by the doctor who accidentally removed the penis and later by surgeons who removed his testes and created a "preliminary" vagina. The question was whether surgery, along with female hormones and "appropriate" gender-role expectations of the parents, would be enough to create a stable female gender identity. Would the child accept the sex reassignment and identify herself as a girl?

As you will discover in the upcoming case study, David ultimately rejected his assigned female gender despite strong pressure from his family and doctors. This indicates that biology may be the most important factor in gender identity formation. A recent longitudinal study offers additional evidence of a biological link. Researchers at Johns Hopkins Hospital tracked the development of 16 otherwise normal boys who had been born without a penis, a rare defect known as *cloacal exstrophy*. Fourteen of these boys had their testes removed and were raised as girls. Despite this radical treatment, researchers observed many signs of masculine behavior, including lots of "typical" male "rough-and-tumble" play. Eight of the 14 children, ranging in age from 5 to 16, later rejected their female reassignment and declared themselves to be boys (Reiner & Gearhart, 2004).

In addition to the gender difficulties involved in David's case and the cases of the boys born without a penis, other gender identity problems may develop when a person feels he or she is trapped in a body of the wrong sex. This is known as *transsexualism* (having a gender identity opposite to biological sex). Although some may see the case of Brenda/Bruce/David as a form of transsexualism, "true" transsexuals are born chromosomally and anatomically one sex. But they have a deep and lasting discomfort with their sexual anatomy. They report feeling as if they are victims of a "birth defect," and they often seek corrective reassignment surgery. At one time, the number of men seeking reassignment was much higher than the number of women who wished to be men. But the ratio has narrowed considerably in recent years.

Is a transsexual the same as a transvestite? *Transvestism* involves individuals (almost exclusively men) who adopt the dress (cross-dressing), and often the behavior, typical of the opposite sex. Some homosexual men and women dress up as the other sex, and some entertainers cross-dress as part of their job. But for true transvestites, the cross-dressing is primarily for emotional and sexual gratification (Crooks & Bauer, 2011; King, 2012; Gherovici, 2011). In contrast, transsexuals feel that they are really members of the opposite sex imprisoned in the wrong body. Their gender identity does not match their gonads, genitals, or internal accessory organs. Transsexuals may also cross-dress. But their motivation is to look like the "right" sex rather than to obtain sexual arousal. Transvestites should also be distinguished from female impersonators (who cross-dress to entertain) and from gay men who occasionally "go in drag" (cross-dress).

Are transvestites and transsexuals also homosexual? When a person is described as *homosexual*, it is because of a **sexual orientation** toward the same sex. (The preferred terms today are *gay* and *lesbian* rather than *homosexual*.) Transvestites are usually heterosexual. Transsexuality, on the other hand, has nothing to do with sexual orientation, only with gender identity. In fact, a transsexual can be heterosexual, gay, lesbian, or *bisexual* (being sexually attracted to both males and females).

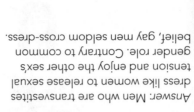

TEST YOURSELF

Why do some men cross-dress?

Answer: Men who are transvestites dress like women to release sexual tension and enjoy the other sex's gender role. Contrary to common belief, gay men seldom cross-dress.

Sexual Orientation Primary erotic attraction toward members of the same sex (homosexual, gay, lesbian), both sexes (bisexual), or the other sex (heterosexual)

Sex and Gender Differences: Nature Versus Nurture

Objective 11.6: Describe the major sex and gender differences between men and women.

Now that we have looked at the different dimensions of sex and gender and examined gender-role development, let's turn our attention to sex and gender differences between men and women.

Sex Differences

Physical anatomy is the most obvious biological difference between men and women (Figure 11.3). The average man is taller, heavier, and stronger than the average woman. He is also more likely to be bald and color blind. In addition, men and women differ in their *secondary sex characteristics* (facial hair, breasts, and so on), their signs of reproductive capability (the menarche for girls and the ejaculation of sperm for boys), and their physical reactions to middle age or the end of reproduction (the female menopause and male climacteric).

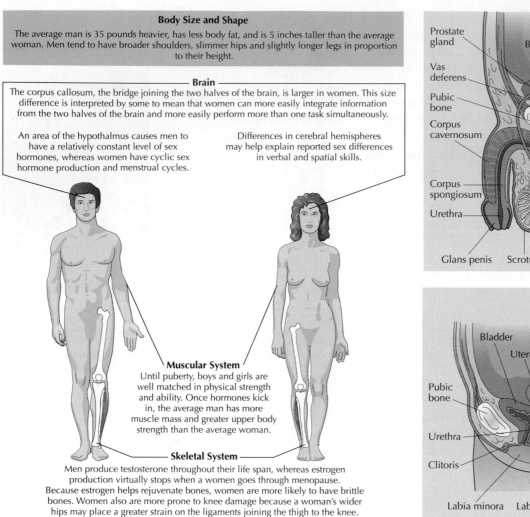

Body Size and Shape
The average man is 35 pounds heavier, has less body fat, and is 5 inches taller than the average woman. Men tend to have broader shoulders, slimmer hips and slightly longer legs in proportion to their height.

Brain
The corpus callosum, the bridge joining the two halves of the brain, is larger in women. This size difference is interpreted by some to mean that women can more easily integrate information from the two halves of the brain and more easily perform more than one task simultaneously.

An area of the hypothalamus causes men to have a relatively constant level of sex hormones, whereas women have cyclic sex hormone production and menstrual cycles.

Differences in cerebral hemispheres may help explain reported sex differences in verbal and spatial skills.

Muscular System
Until puberty, boys and girls are well matched in physical strength and ability. Once hormones kick in, the average man has more muscle mass and greater upper body strength than the average woman.

Skeletal System
Men produce testosterone throughout their life span, whereas estrogen production virtually stops when a women goes through menopause. Because estrogen helps rejuvenate bones, women are more likely to have brittle bones. Women also are more prone to knee damage because a woman's wider hips may place a greater strain on the ligaments joining the thigh to the knee.

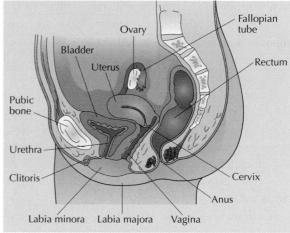

Figure 11.3 Major physical differences between the sexes *Source:* Adapted from Miracle, Tina S., Miracle, Andrew, W., and Baumeister, R. F., *Study Guide: Human sexuality: Meeting your basic needs,* 2nd edition. © 2006. Reprinted by permission of Pearson Education, Inc., Upper Saddle River, NJ.

There also are certain functional and structural differences in the brains of men and women, which result, at least in part, from the influence of prenatal sex hormones on the developing fetal brain. The differences are most apparent in the *hypothalamus, corpus callosum, cerebral hemispheres,* and *gray* versus *white matter* (Allen et al., 2007; Hyde & DeLamater, 2011; Matlin, 2012; Valla & Ceci, 2011). For example, during puberty, the female's hypothalamus directs her pituitary gland to release hormones in a cyclic fashion (the menstrual cycle). In contrast, the male's hypothalamus directs a relatively steady production of sex hormones. The corpus callosum, the web of nerve fibers connecting the cerebral hemispheres, is larger in adult women and shaped differently in women than in men. Research suggests this difference may explain why men tend to rely on one hemisphere or the other in performing tasks, whereas women tend to use both hemispheres at once. Researchers also have documented differences in the cerebral hemispheres of men and women that may account for reported differences in verbal and spatial skills, which are discussed in the next section.

Gender Differences

Do you think there are inborn psychological differences between women and men? Do you believe that women are more emotional and more concerned with aesthetics?

Table 11.2 RESEARCH-SUPPORTED SEX AND GENDER DIFFERENCES

Behavior	More Often Shown by Men	More Often Shown by Women
Sexual	• Begin masturbating sooner in life cycle and higher overall occurrence rates • Start sexual life earlier and have first orgasm through masturbation • More likely to recognize their own sexual arousal • More orgasm consistency with sexual partner	• Begin masturbating later in life cycle and lower overall occurrence rates • Start sexual life later and have first orgasm from partner stimulation • Less likely to recognize their own sexual arousal • Less orgasm consistency with sexual partner
Touching	• Touched, kissed, and cuddled less by parents • Less physical contact with other men and respond more negatively to being touched • More likely to initiate both casual and intimate touch with sexual partner	• Touched, kissed, and cuddled more by parents • More physical contact with other women and respond more positively to being touched • Less likely to initiate either casual or intimate touch with sexual partner
Friendship	• Larger number of friends and express friendship by shared activities	• Smaller number of friends and express friendship by shared communication about self
Personality	• More aggressive from a very early age • More self-confident of future success • Attribute success to internal factors and failures to external factors • Achievement more task oriented; motives are mastery and competition • More self-validating • Higher self-esteem	• Less aggressive from a very early age • Less self-confident of future success • Attribute success to external factors and failures to internal factors • Achievement more socially directed with emphasis on self-improvement; higher work motives • More dependent on others for validation • Lower self-esteem
Cognitive Abilities	• Slightly superior in math and visuospatial skills	• Slightly superior in verbal skills

Sources: Crooks & Baur, 2011; Hunt, 2011; Hyde & DeLamater, 2011; King, 2012; Masters & Johnson, 1961, 1966, 1970; Matlin, 2012.

Or that men are naturally more aggressive and competitive? Scientists have identified several gender differences, which are summarized in Table 11.2. In this section, we will focus on two of the most researched differences—cognitive abilities and aggression.

1. **Cognitive abilities** For many years, researchers have noted that women tend to score slightly higher than men on tests of verbal skills. Conversely, men score slightly higher than women on math and visuospatial tests (Castelli, Corazzini, & Geminiani, 2008; Hunt, 2011; Olszewski-Kubilius & Lee, 2011). As mentioned earlier, some researchers suggest that these differences may reflect evolution and biology—that is, evolutionary adaptations and structural differences in the cerebral hemispheres, hormones, or the degree of hemispheric specialization.

   However, some critics suggest that evolution progresses much too slowly to account for this type of behavioral adaptation. Furthermore, there are wide variations across cultures in gender differences, and biological/evolutionary explanations are difficult to test experimentally. Virtually all studies of human gender differences are *correlational* (Denmark, Rabinowitz, & Sechzer, 2005; Hardies, 2011; Matlin, 2012; Petersen & Hyde, 2011; Rydell, Rydell, & Boucher, 2010). Once again, it is extremely difficult to separate the effects of biological, psychological, and social forces—the *biopsychosocial model.*

2. **Aggression** One of the clearest and most consistent findings in gender studies is greater physical aggressiveness in males. From an early age, boys are more likely to engage in mock fighting and rough-and-tumble play. As adolescents and adults, men are more likely to commit aggressive crimes (Campbell & Muncer, 2008; Giancola & Parrott, 2008; Hay et al., 2011; King, 2012). But gender differences are clearer for physical aggression (like hitting) than for other forms of aggression. Early research also suggested that females were more likely to engage in more indirect and relational forms of aggression, such as spreading rumors and ignoring or excluding someone (Fisher, 2011; Radcliff & Joseph, 2011; Willer & Cupach, 2011). But other studies have not found clear differences (Marsee, Weems, & Taylor 2008; Shahim, 2008).

How do we explain these gender differences in aggression? Those who take a nature perspective generally cite biological factors. For example, several studies have linked the male gonadal hormone testosterone to aggressive behavior (Carré, McCormick, & Hariri, 2011; Hermans, Ramsey, & van Honk, 2008; Popma et al., 2007; Victoroff et al., 2011). In addition, studies on identical twins find that genetic factors account for about 50 percent of aggressive behavior (Burt, 2011; Cadoret, Leve, & Devor, 1997; Segal & Bouchard, 2000).

Nurturists suggest that we should be examining gender-role training and the context in which aggressive behaviors take place (Bosson & Vandello, 2011; Richardson & Hammock, 2007; Wallis, 2011). For example, children's picture books, video games, and TV programs and commercials frequently present women and men in stereotypical gender roles—with men in more aggressive roles.

Before going on, it's important to recognize that differences in aggression, like almost all gender differences, are statistically small and represent few meaningful differences. In addition, like most areas of psychology there is considerable debate over whether nature or nurture best explains gender differences.

(handwritten margin note: testosterone)

CHECK & REVIEW

STOP *Before going on, be sure to complete this Check & Review. It is an invaluable study tool!*

Sex and Gender

Part A: Retrieval Practice

1. Without looking at the book, spend 10 minutes writing a free-form essay recalling all you can remember from the previous section.

2. Now, reread the previous section, and once again spend 10 minutes writing a free-form essay on the SAME material.

Part B: Practice Quiz

1. Match the following dimensions of gender with their appropriate meaning:

___ Chromosomal sex   a. Ovaries and testes

___ Gender identity   b. XX and XY

___ Gonadal sex   c. Estrogens and androgens

___ Gender role   d. Self-perception as male or female

___ Hormonal sex   e. Breasts, beard, menstruation

___ Secondary sex characteristics   f. Uterus, vagina, prostate gland, vas deferens

___ External genitals   g. Labia majora, clitoris, penis, scrotum

___ Sexual orientation   h. Homosexual, bisexual, heterosexual

___ Internal accessory organs   i. Differing societal expectations for appropriate male and female behavior

2. Briefly summarize the two major theories of gender-role development.

3. A combination of both male and female personality traits is called _____.

4. Individuals who have the genitals and secondary sex characteristics of one sex but feel as if they belong to the other sex are known as _____. (a) transvestites; (b) heterosexuals; (c) gays or lesbians; (d) transsexuals

Check your answers in Appendix B.

Sexual Behavior

Are women and men fundamentally alike in their sexual responses? Or are they unalterably different? What causes a gay or lesbian sexual orientation? What is sexual prejudice? These are some of the questions we will explore in this section.

Sexual Arousal and Response: Gender Differences and Similarities

Objective 11.7: What are the four stages in Masters and Johnson's sexual response cycle?

Men and women have obvious differences in their sexual arousal and response. But like waffles and pancakes, they have the same basic ingredients, and overall they are much more alike than different. How do we know this? How do researchers scientifically test what happens to the human body when an individual or a couple engage in sexual activities? As you can imagine, this is a highly controversial topic for research. William Masters and Virginia Johnson (1966) were the first to conduct actual laboratory studies. With the help of 694 female and male volunteers, they attached recording devices to the volunteers' bodies and monitored or filmed their physical responses as they moved from nonarousal to orgasm and back to nonarousal. They labeled the bodily changes during this series of events a **sexual response cycle** that included four stages: *excitement*, *plateau*, *orgasm*, and *resolution* (Step-by-Step Diagram 11.1).

Sexual Orientation: Contrasting Theories and Myths

Objective 11.8: Discuss the latest research on sexual orientation.

What causes homosexuality? What causes heterosexuality? Many have asked the first question, but few have asked the second. As a result, the roots of sexual orientation are poorly understood. However, research has identified several widespread myths and misconceptions about homosexuality (Bergstrom-Lynch, 2008; Boysen & Vogel, 2007; Drucker, 2010; LeVay, 2003, 2011). (See Myth Busters Box below).

The precise cause or causes of sexual orientation are still unknown. However, most scientists believe genetics and biology play the dominant role (Bailey, Dunne, & Martin, 2000; Bao & Swaab, 2011; Ellis et al., 2008; Hines, 2011; Jannini et al., 2010; LeVay, 2011). Studies on identical and fraternal twins and adopted siblings found that if one

Sexual Response Cycle Masters and Johnson's description of the four-stage bodily response to sexual arousal, which consists of excitement, plateau, orgasm, and resolution

Gay marriage Debate, legislation, and judicial action surrounding gay marriage have brought attitudes about homosexuality into full public view.

MYTH BUSTERS

True or False?

- **Seduction theory** Gays and lesbians were seduced as children by adults of their own sex.

- **"By default" theory** Gays and lesbians were unable to attract partners of the other sex or have experienced unhappy heterosexual experiences.

- **Poor parenting theory** Sons become gay because of domineering mothers and weak fathers. Daughters become lesbians because of weak or absent mothers and having only fathers as their primary role model.

- **Modeling theory** Children raised by gay and lesbian parents usually end up adopting their parents' sexual orientation.

Answer: All four "theories" are false.

Step-by-StepDiagram11.1

Masters and Johnson's Sexual Response Cycle

Note: Sexual expression is extremely diverse, and this simplified description does not account for individual variation. It should not be used to judge what's "normal."

Step 2 During the **plateau phase**, biological and sexual arousal continue at heightened levels. In men, the penis becomes more engorged and erect while the testes swell and pull up closer to the body. In the woman, the clitoris pulls up under the clitoral hood and the entrance to the vagina contracts while the uterus rises slightly. This movement of the uterus causes the upper two-thirds of the vagina to balloon, or expand. As arousal reaches its peak, both sexes may experience a feeling that orgasm is imminent and inevitable.

Step 3 The **orgasm phase** involves a highly intense and pleasurable release of tension. In women, muscles around the vagina squeeze the vaginal walls in and out and the uterus pulsates. Muscles at the base of the penis contract in the man, causing ejaculation, the discharge of semen or seminal fluid.

Step 1 The **excitement phase** can last for minutes or hours. Arousal is initiated through touching, fantasy, or erotic stimuli. Heart rate and respiration increase and increased blood flow to the region causes penile or clitoral erection, and vaginal lubrication in women. In both men and women, the nipples may become erect, and both may experience a sex flush (reddening of the upper torso and face).

engorgemt

Step 4 Biological responses gradually return to normal during the **resolution phase**. After one orgasm, most men enter a **refractory period**, during which further excitement to orgasm is considered impossible. Many women (and some men), however, are capable of multiple orgasms in fairly rapid succession.

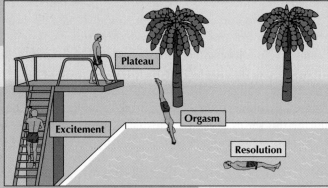

Plateau

Orgasm

Excitement

Resolution

▼ Immediately after orgasm, men generally enter a refractory period, which lasts from several minutes up to as much as a day. As men age, their refractory periods increase.

▼ Sexual response in women is a little more variable, and tends to follow one or more of three basic patterns.

This response is similar to the male pattern, but allows the possibility of multiple orgasm without falling below the plateau level of arousal.

This response occurs when a woman is aroused, but does not achieve orgasm, and resolution takes longer.

In this response, there is a rapid rise to orgasm, no definitive plateau, and a quick resolution.

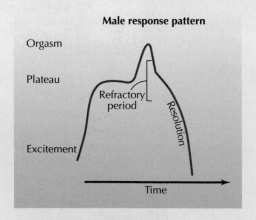

Male response pattern

Orgasm

Plateau

Refractory period

Resolution

Excitement

Time

Female response pattern

Orgasm

Plateau

Resolution

Resolution

Resolution

Excitement

Time

✗ **Excitement Phase** First stage of the sexual response cycle, characterized by increasing levels of arousal and increased engorgement of the genitals

Plateau Phase Second stage of the sexual response cycle; period of sexual excitement prior to orgasm

Orgasm Phase Third stage of the sexual response cycle, when pleasurable sensations peak and orgasm occurs

Resolution Phase Final stage of the sexual response cycle, when the body returns to its unaroused state

Refractory Period Phase following orgasm, during which further orgasm is considered physiologically impossible for men

identical twin was gay, about 48 to 65 percent of the time so was the second twin (Hyde, 2005; Långstrom et al., 2010; Moutinho, Pereira, & Jorge, 2011). (Note that if the cause were totally genetic, the percentage would be 100.) The rate for fraternal twins was 26 to 30 percent and 6 to 11 percent for adopted brothers or sisters. Estimates of homosexuality in the general population run between 2 and 10 percent.

— nature + nurture

Some researchers have also hypothesized that prenatal hormone levels affect fetal brain development and sexual orientation. Animal experiments have found that administering male hormones prenatally can cause female offspring of sheep and rats to engage in the mounting behavior associated with male sheep and rats (Bagermihl, 1999; Roselli, Reddy, & Kaufman, 2011). It is obviously unethical to experiment with human fetuses. Therefore, we cannot come to any meaningful conclusions about the effect of hormones on fetal development, and no well-controlled study has ever found a difference in adult hormone levels between heterosexuals and gays and lesbians (Hall & Schaeff, 2008; Hines, 2011; LeVay, 2003, 2011).

The origin of sexual orientation remains a mystery. However, we do know that gays and lesbians are often victimized by society's prejudice against them. Research shows that many suffer verbal and physical attacks; disrupted family and peer relationships; and high rates of anxiety, depression, substance use disorders, and suicide (Espelage et al., 2008; Hyde & DeLamater, 2011; Newcomb & Mustanski, 2010; Rivers, 2011).

Some of this prejudice supposedly stems from an irrational fear of homosexuality in oneself or others, which Martin Weinberg labeled *homophobia* in the late 1960s. Today, some researchers believe this term is too limited and scientifically unacceptable. It implies that antigay attitudes are limited to individual irrationality and pathology. Therefore, psychologist Gregory Herek (2000) prefers the term **sexual prejudice**, which emphasizes multiple causes and allows scientists to draw on the rich scientific research on prejudice.

Sexual Prejudice Negative attitudes toward an individual because of her or his sexual orientation

In 1973 both the American Psychiatric Association and the American Psychological Association officially acknowledged that homosexuality is not a mental illness. However, it continues to be a divisive societal issue in the United States. Seeing *sexual prejudice* as a socially reinforced phenomenon rather than an individual pathology, coupled with political action by gays and lesbians, may help fight discrimination and hate crimes.

CHECK & REVIEW

STOP *Before going on, be sure to complete this Check & Review. It is an invaluable study tool!*

Sexual Behavior

Part A: Retrieval Practice

1. Without looking at the book, spend 10 minutes writing a free-form essay recalling all you can remember from the previous section.

2. Now, reread the previous section, and once again spend 10 minutes writing a free-form essay on the SAME material.

Part B: Practice Quiz

1. Label the CORRECT sequence of events in Masters and Johnson's sexual response cycle on the figure below.

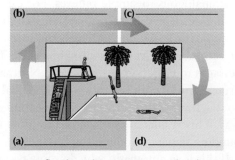

2. Briefly describe Masters and Johnson's sexual response cycle.

3. The genetic influence on sexual orientation has been supported by research reporting that _____. (a) between identical twins, if one brother is gay, the other brother has a 48 to 65 percent chance of also being gay; (b) gay men have fewer chromosomal pairs than straight men, whereas lesbians have larger areas of the hypothalamus than straight women; (c) between adoptive pairs of brothers, if the younger brother is gay, the older brother has an increased chance of also being gay; (d) parenting style influences adult sexual orientation for men but not for women

4. A homosexual orientation appears to be the result of _____. (a) seduction during childhood or adolescence by an older homosexual; (b) a family background that includes a dominant mother and a passive, detached; father; (c) a hormonal imbalance; (d) unknown factors

Check your answers in Appendix B.

Sex Problems

Objective 11.9: Describe how biological, psychological, and social forces influence sexual dysfunction.

When we are functioning well sexually, we tend to take this part of our lives for granted. But what happens when things don't go smoothly? Why does normal sexual functioning stop for some people and never begin for others? What are the major diseases that can be spread through sexual behavior? We will explore these questions in the following section.

Sexual Dysfunction: The Biopsychosocial Model

Sexual Dysfunction Impairment of the normal physiological processes of arousal and orgasm

There are many forms of **sexual dysfunction**, or difficulty in sexual functioning. And their causes are complex (Concept Organizer 11.1). In this section, we will discuss how biology, psychology, and social forces (the *biopsychosocial model*) all contribute to sexual difficulties.

Biological Factors

Although many people may consider it unromantic, a large part of sexual arousal and behavior is clearly the result of biological processes (Coolen et al., 2004; Hayes, 2011; Hyde & DeLamater, 2011; King, 2012). *Erectile dysfunction* (the inability to get or maintain an erection firm enough for intercourse) and *orgasmic dysfunction* (the inability to respond to sexual stimulation to the point of orgasm) often reflect lifestyle factors like cigarette smoking. They also involve medical conditions such as diabetes, alcoholism, hormonal deficiencies, circulatory problems, and reactions to certain prescription and nonprescription drugs. In addition, hormones (especially testosterone) have a clear effect on sexual desire in both men and women. But otherwise, the precise role of hormones in human sexual behavior is not well understood.

In addition to problems resulting from medical conditions and hormones, sexual responsiveness is also affected by the spinal cord and sympathetic nervous system. The human brain is certainly involved in all parts of the sexual response cycle. However, certain key sexual behaviors do not require an intact cerebral cortex to operate. In fact, some patients in comas still experience orgasms.

How is this possible? Recall from Chapter 2 that some aspects of human behavior are reflexive. They are unlearned, automatic, and occur without conscious effort or motivation. Sexual arousal for both men and women is partially reflexive and somewhat analogous to simple reflexes. For example, a puff of air produces an automatic closing of the eye. Similarly, certain stimuli, such as stroking of the genitals, can lead to automatic arousal in both men and women. In both situations, nerve impulses from the receptor site travel to the spinal cord. The spinal cord then responds by sending messages to target organs or glands. Normally, the blood flow into organs and tissues through the arteries is balanced by an equal outflow through the veins. During sexual arousal, however, the arteries dilate beyond the capacity of the veins to carry the blood away. This results in erection of the penis in men and an engorged clitoris and surrounding tissue in women.

If this is so automatic, why do some people have difficulty getting aroused? Unlike simple reflexes such as the eye blink, negative thoughts or high emotional states may block sexual arousal. Recall from Chapter 2 that the autonomic nervous system (ANS) is intricately involved in emotional (and sexual) responses. The ANS is composed of two subsystems: the sympathetic, which prepares the body for "fight or flight," and the parasympathetic, which maintains bodily processes at a steady, even balance. The parasympathetic branch is dominant during initial sexual excitement and throughout

ConceptOrganizer11.1

Major Male and Female Sexual Dysfunctions

Although sex therapists typically divide sexual dysfunctions into "male," "female," or "both," problems should never be considered "his" or "hers." Couples are almost always encouraged to work together to find solutions.

Male ♂		Female ♀		Both Male ♂ and Female ♀	
Disorder	**Causes**	**Disorder**	**Causes**	**Disorder**	**Causes**
Erectile dysfunction (impotence) *Inability to have or maintain an erection firm enough for intercourse* • **Primary erectile dysfunction** *lifetime erectile problems* • **Secondary erectile dysfunction** *erectile problems in at least 25% of sexual encounters*	**Physical:** Chronic illness, diabetes, circulatory conditions, heart disease, drugs, fatigue, alcohol, hormones, inappropriate or inadequate stimulation **Psychological:** Performance anxiety, difficulty expressing desires, antisexual education or upbringing	**Orgasmic dysfunction** (anorgasmia, frigidity) *Inability or difficulty in achieving orgasm* • **Primary orgasmic dysfunction** *lifetime lack of orgasm* • **Secondary orgasmic dysfunction** *was regularly orgasmic, but no longer* • **Situational orgasmic dysfunction** *orgasm occurs only under specific conditions*	**Physical:** Chronic illness, diabetes, drugs, fatigue, alcohol, hormones, pelvic disorders, inappropriate or inadequate stimulation **Psychological:** Guilt, fear of discovery, hurried experiences, difficulty expressing desires, antisexual education or upbringing	**Inhibited sexual desire** (sexual apathy) *Avoids sexual relations due to disinterest* **Sexual aversion** *Avoids sex due to overwhelming fear or anxiety*	**Physical:** Hormones, drugs, alcohol, chronic illness **Psychological:** Antisexual education or upbringing, depression, anxiety, sexual trauma, relationship problems **Psychological:** Antisexual education or upbringing, sex trauma, partner pressure, gender identity confusion
Premature ejaculation *Rapid ejaculation beyond control; partner is non-orgasmic 50% of their intercourse episodes*	**Primarily psychological:** Guilt, fear of discovery, hurried experiences, man learns to ejaculate as quickly as possible	**Vaginismus** *Involuntary vaginal spasms making penile insertion impossible or difficult and painful*	**Primarily psychological:** Inadequate lubrication, learned association of pain or fear with intercourse, antisexual education or upbringing	**Dyspareunia** *Painful intercourse*	**Primarily physical:** Inadequate lubrication, irritations, infections, genitalia disorders **Psychological:** Antisexual education or upbringing

For more information, check www.goaskalice.columbia.edu/Cat6.html. *Sources:* Adapted from Crooks & Baur, 2011; King, 2012.

the plateau phase. The sympathetic branch dominates during ejaculation and orgasm. Can you see why the parasympathetic branch *must* be in control during arousal? The body needs to be relaxed enough to allow blood to flow to the genital area.

Psychological Influences

Our bodies may be biologically prepared to become aroused and respond to erotic stimulation. But psychological forces also play a role. For example, anxieties associated with many sexual experiences, such as fear of pregnancy and sexually transmitted infections, may cause sympathetic dominance, which in turn blocks sexual arousal. Many women

"Now, that's product placement!"

Performance Anxiety Fear of being judged in connection with sexual activity

Double Standard Beliefs, values, and norms that subtly encourage male sexuality and discourage female sexuality

discover that they need locked doors, committed relationships, and reliable birth control to fully enjoy sexual relations.

What about men? Most men also prefer privacy, commitment, and freedom from pregnancy concerns. But generally, relationship status has less of an effect on male orgasms than it does on female orgasms. Apparently, women relax more under these conditions, which allows them to stay in arousal and parasympathetic dominance long enough for orgasm to occur.

Most couples also recognize that both sexes have difficulty with arousal if they drink too much alcohol or when they are stressed, ill, or fatigued. But one of the least recognized blocks of sexual arousal is **performance anxiety**, the fear of being judged in connection with sexual activity. Men commonly experience problems with erections (especially after drinking alcohol) and wonder if their "performance" will satisfy their partner. At the same time, women frequently worry about their attractiveness and their ability to orgasm. Can you see how these performance fears can lead to sexual problems? Once again, increased anxiety causes the sympathetic nervous system to dominate, which blocks blood flow to the genitals.

Like fears of negative consequences from sex and performance anxiety, *gender roles* and the *double standard* are two additional psychological factors that contribute to both male and female sexual dysfunction.

Gender-role training begins at birth and continually impacts all aspects of our life, as the story of "Brenda/David" from the beginning of this chapter shows. Can you imagine how traditional male gender roles—being dominant, aggressive, independent—could lead to different kinds of sexual thoughts and behaviors than traditional female gender roles—being submissive, passive, and dependent? Can you also imagine how this type of gender-role training may lead to a **double standard**? Men are encouraged to explore their sexuality and bring a certain level of sexual knowledge into the relationship. Conversely, women are expected to stop male advances and refrain from sexual activity until marriage.

Although overt examples of this *double standard* are less evident in modern times, covert or hidden traces of this belief still exist. Examining the gender differences in Figure 11.4, can you see how items like men wanting women to "initiate sex more often" or women wanting men "to talk more lovingly" might be remnants of the double standard?

Dating Couples

Men Wish Their Partners Would:
Be more experimental
Initiate sex more often
Try more oral-genital sex
Give more instructions
Be warmer and more involved

Women Wish Their Partners Would:
Talk more lovingly
Be more seductive
Be warmer and more involved
Give more instructions
Be more complimentary

Married Couples

Men Wish Their Partners Would:
Be more seductive
Initiate sex more often
Be more experimental
Be wilder and sexier
Give more instructions

Women Wish Their Partners Would:
Talk more lovingly
Be more seductive
Be more complimentary
Give more instructions
Be warmer and more involved

Figure 11.4 What do men and women want? When asked what they wish they had more of in their sexual relationships, men tended to emphasize activities, whereas women focused more on emotions and the relationship. *Source*: Based on Hatfield & Rapson, 1996, p. 142.

(a) Television and movies in the 1950s and 1960s allowed only married couples to be shown in a bedroom setting (and only in long pajamas and separate twin-size beds).

(b) Contrast this with modern times, where very young, unmarried couples are commonly portrayed in one bed, scantily dressed or nude, and engaging in various stages of intercourse.

(c) Note the change in body postures and clothing in these beach scenes from the 1960s and today.

Figure 11.5 Changing sexual scripts

Social Factors

In addition to biological and psychological influences on sexuality, we also learn explicit **sexual scripts** from society that teach us "what to do, when, where, how, and with whom" (Gagnon, 1990; McCormick, 2010; Ross & Coleman, 2011). For example, during the 1950s, societal messages said the "best" sex was at night, in a darkened room, with a man on top and a woman on the bottom. Today, the messages are more bold and varied, partly because of media portrayals. Compare, for example, the sexual scripts portrayed in Figure 11.5.

Sexual scripts, gender roles, and the double standard may all be less rigid today, but a major difficulty remains. Many people and sexual behaviors do not fit society's scripts and expectations. Furthermore, we often "unconsciously" internalize societal messages. But we seldom realize how they affect our values and behaviors. For example, modern men and women generally say they want equality. Yet both sexes may feel more comfortable if the woman is a virgin and the man has had many partners. Sex therapy encourages partners to examine and sometimes modify inappropriate sexual scripts, gender roles, and beliefs in the double standard.

Sexual Scripts Socially dictated descriptions of "appropriate" behaviors for sexual interactions

Sex Therapy
Objective 11.10: Discuss how sex therapists treat sexual dysfunction, and list the four major principles of Masters and Johnson's approach.

How do therapists work with sex problems? Clinicians usually begin with interviews and examinations to determine whether the problem is organic, psychological,

Table 11.3 SEXUAL EFFECTS OF LEGAL AND ILLEGAL DRUGS

Drugs	Effects
Alcohol	Moderate to high doses inhibit arousal. Chronic abuse causes damage to testes, ovaries, and the circulatory and nervous systems.
Tobacco	Decreases blood flow to the genitals, thereby reducing the frequency and duration of erections and vaginal lubrication.
Cocaine and amphetamines	Moderate to high doses and chronic use result in inhibition of orgasm and decrease in erection and lubrication.
Barbiturates	Moderate to high doses lead to decreased desire, erectile disorders, and delayed orgasm.

Source: Crooks & Baur, 2011; Hyde & Dehamater, 2011; King, 2012.

or, more likely, a combination of both (Althof, 2010; Atwood & Klucinec, 2011; Cacchioni & Wolkowitz, 2011; Gambescia & Weeks, 2007; Janssen, 2011). Organic causes of sexual dysfunction include medical conditions (such as diabetes mellitus and heart disease), medications (such as antidepressants), and drugs (such as alcohol and tobacco—see Table 11.3). Erectile disorders are the problems most likely to have an organic component. In 1998, a medical treatment for erectile problems, *Viagra*, quickly became the fastest-selling prescription drug in U.S. history. Other medications for both men and women are currently being tested—but they are not the answer to all sexual problems.

Years ago, the major psychological treatment for sexual dysfunction was long-term psychoanalysis. This treatment was based on the assumption that sexual problems resulted from *deep-seated conflicts* that originated in childhood. During the 1950s and 1960s, behavior therapy was introduced. It was based on the idea that sexual dysfunction was *learned*. (See Chapter 15 for a more complete description of both psychoanalysis and behavior therapy.) It wasn't until the early 1970s and the publication of Masters and Johnson's *Human Sexual Inadequacy* that sex therapy gained national recognition. Because the model that Masters and Johnson developed is still popular and used by many sex therapists, we will use it as our example of how sex therapy is conducted.

Masters and Johnson's Sex Therapy Program

Masters and Johnson's approach is founded on four major principles:

1. **Relationship focus** Unlike forms of therapy that focus on the individual, Masters and Johnson's sex therapy focuses on the relationship between two people. To counteract any blaming tendencies, each partner is considered fully involved and affected by sexual problems. Both partners are taught positive communication and conflict resolution skills.

2. **Investigation of both biological and psychosocial factors** Medication and many physical disorders can cause or aggravate sexual dysfunctions. Therefore, Masters and Johnson emphasize the importance of medical histories and exams. They also explore psychosocial factors, such as how the couple first learned about sex and their current attitudes, gender-role training, and sexual scripts.

3. **Emphasis on cognitive factors** Recognizing that many problems result from fears of performance and *spectatoring* (mentally watching and evaluating responses during sexual activities), couples are discouraged from setting goals and judging sex in terms of success or failure.

▲ **Experiments in sex?** William Masters and Virginia Johnson were the first researchers to use direct laboratory experimentation and observation to study human sexuality.

If you would like to improve your own, or your children's, sexual attitudes and sexual functioning, sex therapists would recommend:

- **Beginning sex education as early as possible.** Children should be given positive feelings about their bodies and an opportunity to discuss sexuality in an open, honest fashion.

- **Avoiding goal- or performance-oriented approaches.** Therapists often remind clients that there really is no "right" way to have sex. When couples or individuals attempt to judge or

evaluate their sexual lives or to live up to others' expectations, they risk making sex a job rather than a pleasure.

- **Communicating openly with your partner.** Mind reading belongs onstage, not in the bedroom. Partners need to tell each other what feels good and what doesn't. Sexual problems should be openly discussed without blame, anger, or defensiveness. If the problem does not improve within a reasonable time, consider professional help.

---

4. **Specific behavioral techniques** Couples are seen in an intensive two-week counseling program. They explore their sexual values and misconceptions and practice specific behavioral exercises. "Homework assignments" usually begin with a *sensate focus* exercise in which each partner takes turns gently caressing the other and communicating what is pleasurable. There are no goals or performance demands. Later exercises and assignments are tailored to the couple's particular sex problem.

Sexually Transmitted Infections (STIs): The Special Problem of AIDS

Objective 11.11: Discuss the major issues related to STIs and the special problem of AIDS.

Early sex education and open communication between partners are vitally important for full sexual functioning. They are also key to avoiding and controlling sexually transmitted infections (STIs), formerly called sexually transmitted diseases (STDs), venereal disease (VD), or social diseases. *STI* is the term used to describe the disorders caused by more than 25 infectious organisms transmitted through sexual activity.

Each year, of the millions of North Americans who contract one or more STIs, a substantial majority are under age 35. Also, as Figure 11.6 shows, women are at much greater risk than men of contracting major STIs. It is extremely important for sexually active people to get medical diagnosis and treatment for any suspicious symptoms and to inform their partners. If left untreated, many STIs can cause severe problems, including infertility, ectopic pregnancy, cancer, and even death.

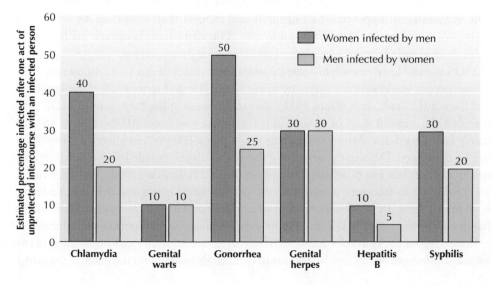

Figure 11.6 Male–female differences in susceptibility to sexually transmitted infections (STIs) These percentages represent the chances of infection for men and women after a single act of intercourse with an infected partner. Note that women are at much greater risk than men for four of these six STIs, due in part to the internal and less visible parts of female genitalia.

Figure 11.7 Common sexually transmitted infections (STIs) Note that you may have an STI without any of the danger signs listed here. If you have symptoms or concerns, see your doctor and follow all medical recommendations. This may include returning for a checkup to make sure that you are no longer infected. If you would like more information, check www.niaid.nih.gov/factsheets/stdinfo.htm. For information on protection from STIs, try www.safesex.org. *Sources:* Adapted from Crooks & Baur, 2011; King 2012.

Male Symptoms ♂	Possible STIs
• Unusual discharge from penis • Soreness inside penis	• Chlamydia • Gonorrhea • Nongonococcal urethritis (NGU)

Female Symptoms ♀	Female Possible STIs
• Unusual vaginal discharge • Out-of-cycle abdominal pain • Unusual vaginal bleeding	• Chlamydia • Gonorrhea • Monilia (yeast) • Trichomoniasis • Vaginitis

Symptoms for Both Men and Women ♂ ♀	Possible STIs
• Painful intercourse or urination • Diarrhea • Painful sore or blisters on or around genital area • Rash on hands and feet or entire body • Small, pink cauliflower growths on or around sex organs • Intense itching • Flulike feeling, sore throat • Swollen glands in groin	• Acquired immunodeficiency syndrome (AIDS) • Crabs • Genital warts • Hepatitis • Herpes • Scabies • Syphilis

The good news is that most STIs are readily cured in their early stages. See Figure 11.7 for an overview of the signs and symptoms of the most common STIs. As you read through this table, remember that many infected people are *asymptomatic*, meaning they lack obvious symptoms. You can have one or more of the diseases without knowing it. And it is often impossible to tell if a sexual partner is infectious.

STIs such as genital warts and chlamydial infections have reached epidemic proportions. Yet, **AIDS (acquired immunodeficiency syndrome)** has received the largest share of public attention. AIDS results from infection with the *human immunodeficiency virus* (*HIV*). A standard blood test can determine if someone is **HIV positive**, which means the individual has been infected by one or more of the HIV viruses. Being infected with the HIV virus, however, is not the same as having AIDS. AIDS is the final stage of the HIV infection process.

In the beginning of the infection process, the HIV virus multiplies rapidly. It is important to know that newly infected individuals are 100 to 1000 times more infectious than they are throughout the remainder of the disease. This is especially troubling because most infected people are likely to remain symptom free for months or even years. Unfortunately, during this time, they can spread the disease to others—primarily through sexual contact.

As the initial HIV infection advances to AIDS, the virus progressively destroys the body's natural defenses against disease and infection. The victim's body becomes increasingly vulnerable to opportunistic infections and cancers that would not be a threat if the immune system were functioning normally. The virus may also attack the brain and spinal cord, creating severe neurological and cognitive deterioration.

AIDS is considered one of the most catastrophic diseases of our time. An estimated 33 million people worldwide are currently living with AIDs and more than 25 million have died from it (Diffenbach & Fauci, 2011). Recent advances in the treatment of AIDS have increased the survival time of victims. But for almost everyone, AIDS remains an ultimately fatal disorder, and some researchers doubt that a 100 percent effective vaccine will ever be developed. Despite the severity of this disease, some people still engage in unsafe and/or condomless sex (Carballo-Diéguez et al., 2011; LaBrie, 2008; Teti & Bowleg, 2011), which calls for more attention to the psychological needs and drives in sexuality. In addition, there are troublesome signs of public complacency due to the false notion that drugs can now cure AIDS and to a reduced emphasis on prevention and education.

Reflecting cutbacks in sex education, AIDS myths are widespread. For instance, many people still believe AIDS can be transmitted through casual contact, such as sneezing,

AIDS (Acquired Immunodeficiency Syndrome) Human immunodeficiency viruses (HIVs) destroy the immune system's ability to fight disease, leaving the body vulnerable to a variety of opportunistic infections and cancers

HIV Positive Being infected by the human immunodeficiency virus (HIV)

shaking hands, sharing drinking glasses or towels, social kissing, sweat, or tears. Some also think it is dangerous to donate blood. Sadly, others are paranoid about gays, because male homosexuals were the first highly visible victims. All of these are false beliefs.

Infection by HIV spreads only by direct contact with bodily fluids—primarily blood, semen, and vaginal secretions. Blood *donors* are at *no* risk whatsoever. Furthermore, AIDS is not limited to the homosexual community. In fact, the AIDS epidemic is now spreading most quickly among heterosexuals, women, African Americans, Hispanics, and children (Adih et al., 2010; Swenson et al., 2010; Towe et al., 2010).

Psychology at Work

Protecting Yourself and Others from STIs

The best hope for curtailing the HIV/AIDS epidemic is through education and behavioral change. The following "safer sex" suggestions are not intended to be moralistic—but only to help reduce your chances of contracting both HIV/AIDS and other STIs.

1. *Remain abstinent or have sex with one mutually faithful, uninfected partner.* Be selective about sexual partners and postpone physical intimacy until laboratory tests verify that you are both free of STIs.

2. *Do not use intravenous illicit drugs or have sex with someone who does.* If you use intravenous drugs, do not share needles or syringes. If you must share, use bleach to clean and sterilize your needles and syringes.

3. *Avoid contact with blood, vaginal secretions, or semen.* Using latex condoms is the best way to avoid contact. (Until recently, scientists believed condoms and spermicides with nonoxynol-9 would help prevent spread of STIs. Unfortunately, recent research shows nonoxynol-9 may increase the risk, and the World Health Organization no longer recommends its use.)

4. *Avoid anal intercourse, with or without a condom.* This is the riskiest of all sexual-behaviors.

5. *Do not have sex if you or your partner are impaired by alcohol or other drugs.* The same is true for your friends. "Friends don't let friends drive (or have sex) drunk."

MYTH BUSTERS

Rape Myths and Rape Prevention

Sexuality can be a source of vitality and tender bonding. But it can also be traumatizing if it becomes a forcible act against the wishes of the other. Rape can be defined as oral, anal, or vaginal penetration forced on an unwilling, underage, or unconscious victim. As clear-cut as this definition seems, many people misunderstand what constitutes rape. To test your own knowledge, answer true or false to the following:

_____1. Women cannot be raped against their will.

_____2. A man cannot be raped by a woman.

_____3. If you are going to be raped, you might as well relax and enjoy it.

_____4. All women secretly want to be raped.

_____5. Male sexuality is biologically overpowering and beyond a man's control.

As you might have expected, all of these statements are false. Tragically, however, rape myths are believed by a large number of men and women (Carr & Van Deusen, 2004; Crooks & Baur, 2011;

Hyde & DeLameter, 2011; King, 2012; Suarez & Gadalla, 2011). Using your critical thinking skills, can you explain how each of the following factors might contribute to rape myths?

- Gender-role conditioning
- The double standard
- Media portrayals
- Lack of information

If you would like to compare your answers to ours, or would like specific information regarding rape prevention, see Appendix B.

Psychology Engages

GENDER AND CULTURAL DIVERSITY

Sexuality Across Cultures

Objective 11.12: Why are cross-cultural studies of sexuality important?

Circumcision and religion Although circumcision is an important part of some religions, it is relatively rare in most parts of the world.

Sex researchers interested in both similarities and variations in human sexual behavior conduct cross-cultural studies of sexual practices, techniques, and attitudes (Barber, 2008; Beach, 1977; Buss, 1989, 2007, 2008, 2011; Crooks & Bauer, 2011; King, 2012). Their studies of different societies put sex in a broader perspective.

Cross-cultural studies of sex also help counteract *ethnocentrism*, judging our own cultural practices as "normal" and preferable to those of other groups. For example, do you know that kissing is unpopular in Japan and unknown among some cultures in Africa and South America? Do you find it strange that Apinaye women in Brazil often bite off pieces of their mate's eyebrows as a natural part of sexual foreplay? Does it surprise you that members of Tiwi society, off the northern coast of Australia, believe that young girls will not develop breasts or menstruate unless they first experience intercourse? Do you know that the men and women of the Amazonian Yanomamo routinely wear nothing but a thin cord around their waists? Interestingly, if you were to ask a Yanomamo woman to remove the cord, she would respond in much the same way an American woman would if you asked her to remove her blouse (Hyde & DeLamater, 2011; Frayser, 1985; Gregersen, 1996). In addition, the Sambia of New Guinea believe that young boys must swallow semen to achieve manhood (Herdt, 1981). Adolescent boys in Mangaia, a small island in the South Pacific, routinely undergo superincision, a painful initiation rite in which the foreskin of the penis is slit and folded back (Marshall, 1971). Figure 11.8 gives other examples of surprising cultural variation in sexuality.

Although other cultures' practices may seem unnatural and strange to us, we forget that our own sexual rituals may appear equally curious to others. If the description of the Mangaian practice of superincision bothered you, how do you feel about our own culture's routine circumcision of infant boys? Before you object that infant circumcision in the United States is "entirely different" and "medically safe and necessary," you might want to consider the position now taken by the American Academy of Pediatrics (AAP). In 1999, they decided the previously reported medical benefits of circumcision were so statistically small that the procedure should *not* be routinely performed and this policy was reaffirmed in 2005 (American Academy of Pediatrics, 1999, 2005). However, the AAP does consider it legitimate for parents to take into account cultural, religious, and ethnic traditions in deciding whether to circumcise their sons.

If the controversy over infant male circumcision surprises you, so, too, may information about female genital mutilation. Throughout history and even today—in parts of Africa, the Middle East, Indonesia, and Malaysia—young girls undergo several types of *female genital mutilation* (FGM). FGM includes circumcision (removal of the clitoral hood), *clitoridectomy* (removal of the clitoris), and *genital infibulation* (removal of the clitoris and labia and stitching together of the remaining tissue to allow only a small opening for urine and menstrual flow). In most countries, the surgeries are performed on girls between ages 4 and 10 and often without anesthesia or antiseptic conditions. The young girls suffer numerous health problems because of these practices—the most serious from genital infibulation. Risks include severe pain, bleeding, chronic infection, and menstrual difficulties. As adults, these women frequently experience serious sexual problems, as well as dangerous childbirth complications or infertility.

What is the purpose of these procedures? The main objective is to ensure virginity (Dave, Sethi, & Morrone, 2011; Matthews, 2011; Orubuloye, Caldwell, & Caldwell, 1997; Wadesango, Rembe, & Chabaya, 2011). Without these procedures, young girls are considered unmarriageable and without status. As you might imagine, these practices create serious culture clashes. For example, physicians in Western societies are currently being asked by immigrant parents to perform these operations on their daughters. What should the doctor do? Should this practice be forbidden? Or would this be another example of ethnocentrism?

As you can see, it is a complex issue. However, in this case, the United Nations has suspended its regular policy of nonintervention in the cultural practices of nations. The World Health Organization (WHO) and the United Nations International Children's Emergency Fund (UNICEF) have both issued statements opposing female genital mutilation. They also have developed programs to combat this and other harmful practices affecting the health and well-being of women and children.

Mangaia (Polynesian Island)	Yolngu (Island near Australia)	Inis Beag (Irish Island)
Childhood sexuality: • Children readily exposed to sex. • Adolescents are given direct instruction in techniques for pleasuring their sexual partners. • Both boys and girls are encouraged to have many partners.	**Childhood sexuality:** • Permissive attitude toward childhood sexuality. • Parents soothe infants by stroking their genitals. • Nudity accepted from infancy through old age.	**Childhood sexuality:** • Sexual expression is strongly discouraged. • Children learn to abhor nudity and are given no information about sex. • Young girls are often shocked by their first menstruation.
Adult sexuality: • After marriage, three orgasms per night are not uncommon for men. • Men are encouraged to "give" three orgasms to their female partner for every one of their own. • Adults practice a wide range of sexual behaviors.	**Adult sexuality:** • Men can have many wives and are generally happy with their sex life. • Women are given no choice in marital partner and little power in the home. • Women are apathetic about sex, seldom orgasmic, and generally unhappy.	**Adult sexuality:** • Little sex play before intercourse. • Female orgasm is unknown or considered deviant. • Numerous misconceptions about sex (e.g., intercourse can be debilitating, menopause causes insanity).

▲ **Figure 11.8 Cross-cultural differences in sexual behavior**
Note: "Inis Beag" is a pseudonym used to protect the privacy of residents of this Irish island. *Sources:* Crooks & Baur, 2011; Hyde & DeLamater, 2011; Marshall, 1971; Money et al., 1991.

CASE STUDY / PERSONAL STORY

The Tragic Tale of "John/Joan"

What do you think happened to the baby boy who suffered the botched circumcision? According to John Money (Money & Ehrhardt, 1972), after his "gender reassignment" as a girl, Bruce/Brenda easily moved into her new identity. By age 3, Brenda wore nightgowns and dresses almost exclusively and liked bracelets and hair ribbons. She also reportedly preferred playing with "girl-type" toys and asked for a doll and carriage for Christmas. In contrast, her brother, Brian, asked for a garage with cars, gas pumps, and tools. By age 6, Brian was accustomed to defending his sister if he thought someone was threatening her. The daughter copied the mother in tidying and cleaning up the kitchen, whereas the boy did not. The mother agreed that she encouraged her daughter when she helped with the housework and expected the boy to be uninterested.

During their childhood, both Brenda/Bruce and her brother Brian were brought to Johns Hopkins each year for physical and psychological evaluation. The case was heralded as a complete success. It also became the model for treating infants born with ambiguous genitalia. The story of "John/Joan," (the name used by Johns Hopkins) was heralded as proof that gender is made—not born.

What first looked like a success was, in fact, a dismal failure. Follow-up studies report that Brenda never really adjusted to her assigned gender (Colapinto, 2004). Despite

David (aka "Brenda") as an adult ▼

being raised from infancy as a girl, she did not feel like a girl and avoided most female activities and interests. As she entered adolescence, her appearance and masculine way of walking led classmates to tease her and call her "cave woman." At this age, she also expressed thoughts of becoming a mechanic, and her fantasies reflected discomfort with her female role. She even tried urinating in a standing position and insisted she wanted to live as a boy (Diamond & Sigmundson, 1997).

By age 14, she was so unhappy that she contemplated suicide. The father tearfully explained what had happened earlier, and for Brenda, "All of a sudden everything clicked. For the first time, things made sense and I understood who and what I was" (Thompson, 1997, p. 83).

After the truth came out, "Brenda" reclaimed his male gender identity and renamed himself David. Following a double mastectomy (removal of both breasts) and construction of an artificial penis, he married a woman and adopted her children. David, his parents, and twin brother, Brian, all suffered enormously from the tragic accident and the no less tragic solution. He said, "I don't blame my parents." But they still felt extremely guilty about their participation in the reassignment. The family members later reconciled. But David remained angry with the doctors who "interfered with nature" and ruined his childhood.

Sadly, there's even more tragedy to tell. On May 4, 2004, 38-year-old David committed suicide. Why? No one knows what went through his mind when he decided to end his life. But he had just lost his job, a big investment had failed, he was separated from his wife, and his twin brother had committed suicide shortly before. "Most suicides, experts say, have multiple motives, which come together in a perfect storm of misery" (Colapinto, 2004).

CRITICAL THINKING

The Scarlet Letter: Paying the Price for an Easy A

By Thomas Frangicetto (Northampton Community College, Bethlehem, PA)

The Scarlet Letter A classic novel by Nathaniel Hawthorne, is the gripping story of Hester Prynne, condemned as an adulteress in puritanical Boston in the 1640s, and one of the first important female protagonists in American literature.

Easy A Based loosely on *The Scarlet Letter*, *Easy A* follows the troubles of Olive Penderghast (Emma Stone), the witty and brilliant 17-year-old high school student who tells a "little white lie" about losing her virginity and is suddenly the center of attention and rebuke. She wears the scarlet A as an act of defiance and as an homage to Hester Prynne. Both women must deal with gender-role stereotypes and society's double standard for men and women regarding their sexuality.

"I wonder if existence as a woman is worthwhile at all."

Hester Prynne, *The Scarlet Letter*

"Jeez, if I'd known that losing my virginity would create such a new persona for myself, I'd have lied about it back in eighth grade."

Olive Penderghast, *Easy A*

Did you see the critically acclaimed 2010 movie *Easy A*? If so, were you aware that it is based loosely on a classic of literature, *The Scarlet Letter*? Why is this important? In your career and personal life, you'll have conversations with people from all walks of life and all levels of education, and the more widely you read in the great classics, the more likely you will get common literary references, such as: "Reminds me of Hester's red letter" (*Scarlet Letter*)," "You're tilting at windmills" (*Don Quixote*), "She's obsessed, it's become her white whale" (*Moby Dick*), "Feels like another rabbit hole" (*Alice in Wonderland*), or "That's a real Catch 22" (*Catch 22*).

Why is this important to critical thinking? Familiarity with the classics helps you as a critical thinker to better *empathize, welcome divergent views, tolerate ambiguity, gather data,* and *apply knowledge to new situations.* The two films, *Scarlet Letter* and *Easy A*, also offer rich psychological applications and important tie-ins to this chapter's central topics—gender and sexuality.

Part I Using the following examples from *The Scarlet Letter* and *Easy A*, put a check mark by the ones you recognize and/or find helpful for mastering this chapter's key concepts.

_____*Gender role* (p. 390): Both Hester and Olive are painfully aware of their respective *societal expectations for "appropriate" male and female behavior.* Wearing the scarlet letter A becomes a metaphor for violating these expectations, though it is done for dramatic effect in *The Scarlet Letter* and for more comedic payoffs in *Easy A*.

_____*Gender identity* (p. 394): Did you understand the importance of this exercise's opening quote, which featured Hester

questioning her very existence as a woman? According to literature professor Evan Carton (cited in Seabrook, 2008), Hester's question provides a revealing insight into a patriarchal society's need to repress female sexuality, especially a woman like Hester who represents a glaring radical challenge to the social order. Similar societal limitations placed on Olive as a modern female cause her to unwittingly start rumors that balloon out of control.

_____*Androgyny* (p. 392): Hester is easily seen as a victim, but she also displays remarkable personal strength and independence—raising her daughter alone and supporting them both with embroidery work, while fighting repeated attempts from authorities to take her child away (Seabrook, 2008). Olive's feminine side is fully functional; she is sensitive and compassionate, almost to a fault. But she is also assertive, combative, and on occasion dominating in her relationships.

_____*Sex behaviors* (pp. 399–401): This is the central issue of both works, with Hester having "crossed the line" of propriety and Olive, ironically, only pretending that she has.

_____*Double standard* (p. 404): The first women's rights convention was held at Seneca Falls, New York, in 1848, two years before *The Scarlet Letter* was published. Hester Prynne can be viewed as Hawthorne's artistic contemplation of what happens when women cross cultural boundaries and gain personal power (Seabrook, 2008). The double standard Olive faces is the well-known "stud" versus "slut" dichotomy for male and female sexual behavior that is as durable as it is unfair.

_____*Sexual scripts* (p. 405): Both Hester and Olive are acutely aware of the scripts that society has written for them. Olive observes the similarity in their shared plight: "Ironically, we were studying 'The Scarlet Letter,' but isn't that always the way with these teenage tales? The literature you read in class always seems to have a strong connection with whatever angsty adolescent drama is being recounted."

Part II Critical Thinking Questions.

1. Review the topic areas under Part 1. Apply at least one CTC (see Prologue at front of book) to each. Then add a personal example to each topic based on your own gender experiences. Which of these topics is the most difficult for you to accept or apply to yourself?

2. Read the book *The Scarlet Letter*, rent the movie, or if truly pressed for time, go to: www.npr.org/templates/story/story.php?storyId=87805369, and click on "Listen to the Story" for a 12-minute synopsis of *The Scarlet Letter*. Then identity five CTCs (see Prologue) violated by any of the characters, as well as Hester's key strengths and weaknesses as a critical thinker.

3. Rent the movie *Easy A*, review the CTCs in the Prologue, and then identify at least five CTCs Olive demonstrates or violates. What grade would you give her as a critical thinker? An "easy A" or something lower?

4. According to historians, Nathaniel Hawthorne was well aware of the growing feminist insurgence at the time he was writing *The Scarlet Letter*. What does it mean to be a feminist in today's world? What CTCs do you think are needed to be a feminist, for both women and men? Go to: http://plato.stanford.edu/entries/feminism-topics, and review at least three of the topics discussed there. Now assess your own thinking on feminism. How does critical thinking affect your opinion on these topics? Be specific.

5. Going to college requires a great deal of reading and writing, but try to make time on the weekends or summer to read some of the literary classics, like *The Scarlet Letter*. One of the many values of these classics, and a college education, is that they are part and parcel of what our society considers an "educated person." Once you leave college, you'll discover for yourself how they offer numerous unforeseen advantages in all parts of your life.

RESEARCH CHALLENGE

Sex Addiction and Cybersex: Real Problems or Handy Excuses?

What do you think about the perpetual sex scandals surrounding movie stars like Charlie Sheen, athletes like Tiger Woods, or politicians and world leaders like Italy's prime minister, Silvio Berlusconi? Did you approve of golf star Tiger Woods seeking sex addiction treatment in 2010 after admitting to several affairs? Do these people suffer from a true illness that can be successfully treated, or is it just a lousy excuse for moral failings and uncontrolled lust?

At the time of this writing, the American Psychiatric Association (APA) is considering including sex addiction as a "hypersexual disorder" to the latest edition of the *Diagnostic and Statistical Manual of Mental Disorders* (see Chapter 14, pp. 496–499). According to the proposed new diagnosis, repetitively engaging in sexual behaviors when you are anxious, depressed, or stressed would be considered a warning sign for the disorder. Is sex addiction the same as alcoholism, which was once considered a moral weakness, and is now seen by most as a legitimate illness with strong genetic links? If so, how do we treat it? Total abstinence from sex is possible, but perhaps more unrealistic than it is for alcohol (Cloud, 2011). Given our hypersexual world—especially the Internet's immediate

availability—how do we restrict access to available partners and the pornography that may elicit this "addiction"?

The Internet is a great technological innovation. At school, work, and home, our computers help us work or study online, gather valuable information, or even recreationally "surf the Net." But for some—even those who are not "sex addicts"—the Internet can be harmful (Davidson & Gottschalk, 2011; Elliott & Ashfield, 2011).

A survey among 18- to 64-year-old self-identified cybersex participants found several problems associated with their online sexual activities (Schneider, 2000). For example, two women with no prior history of interest in sadomasochistic sex discovered this type of behavior online and came to prefer it. Others in the survey reported increased problems with depression, social isolation, career loss or decreased job performance, financial consequences, and, in some cases, legal difficulties.

Some Internet users also use cyberspace chat rooms and e-mail as a way to secretly communicate with an intimate other or as outlets for sexual desires they're unwilling to expose or discuss with their partners. Although these secret liaisons may be exciting, sex therapists are finding that this behavior often leads to a worsening of the participants' relationships with spouses or partners and serious harm to their marriages or primary relationships. "Cybercheating," like traditional infidelity or adultery, erodes trust and connection with the spouse or partner. The ongoing

secrecy, lying, and fantasies also increase attraction to the "virtual" relationship.

What do you think? Does sex require physical contact to count as an "affair"? If you only exchange sexual fantasies with someone on the Internet, are you unfaithful to a partner, or is it nothing more than an X-rated movie? Would you stay with someone who admitted to being a sex addict? The answers to cybersex may be as "simple" as openly discussing your respective ideas and values with your sexual partners—what each of you considers unacceptable in your relationship, both online and in everyday interactions. The issues surrounding possible sex addiction are much more complicated. Although there are a number of comprehensive and respected sex addiction programs in the United States, the prognosis, treatment, and long-term outlook are yet to be determined.

Student Engagement Exercise

Given the admittedly limited information in the Schneider (2000) study described above, what is the most likely:

1. *Research method* (experimental, descriptive, correlational, or biological)?

2. If you chose the:
   - *Experimental method*—label the IV, DV, experimental group, and control group.
   - *Descriptive method*—is this a naturalistic observation, survey, or case study?
   - *Correlational method*—is this a positive, negative, or zero correlation?
   - *Biological method*—identify the specific research tool (e.g., brain dissection, CT scan, etc.)

(Answers appear in Appendix B.)

CHECK & REVIEW

STOP *Before going on, be sure to complete this Check & Review. It is an invaluable study tool!*

Sex Problems and Psychology Engages

Part A: Retrieval Practice

1. Without looking at the book, spend 10 minutes writing a free-form essay recalling all you can remember from the previous section.

2. Now, reread the previous section, and once again spend 10 minutes writing a free-form essay on the SAME material.

Part B: Practice Quiz

1. Briefly explain the roles of the sympathetic and parasympathetic nervous systems in sexual response.

2. Sexual learning that includes "what to do, when, where, how, and with whom" is known as _____. (a) appropriate sexual behavior; (b) sexual norms; (c) sexual scripts; (d) sexual gender roles

3. What are the four principles of Masters and Johnson's sex therapy program?

4. What are five "safer sex" ways to reduce the chances of AIDS and other STIs?

5. What are the advantages of cultural studies in sex research?

6. Viewing one's own ethnic group (or culture) as central and "correct" and then judging the rest of the world according to this standard is known as _____. (a) standardization; (b) stereotyping; (c) discrimination; (d) ethnocentrism

7. Explain why the life stories of the infant twins who suffered from a botched circumcision is an example of gender identity and NOT gender role, transvestism, or sexual orientation.

8. Do you agree with the findings on sexual addiction? Why or why not?

Check your answers in Appendix B.

www.wileyplus.com

WileyPLUS presents an on-line version of this textbook along with a wealth of study resources including quizzes, practice tests, flash cards, videos, animations and other activities designed to improve your mastery of the content. Working in conjunction with these study tools, the *Psychology in Action* WileyPLUS course features Professor Karen Huffman, author of this textbook, explaining and expanding upon some of the most challenging concepts in psychology. Here is a sample of the tutorial videos available for this chapter:

- Clearing up the confusion: Gender vs. sex; androgyny; transsexual vs. transvestite vs. sexual orientation

- An animated demonstration and discussion of Masters and Johnson's sexual response cycle

- Professor Huffman leads a discussion of healthy sexuality

- Ideas for improving sexual communication, featuring a classroom demonstration with Professor Huffman

- Virtual Field Trip to Planned Parenthood, where individuals can receive information, reproductive health care, and sex education

Key Terms

To assess your understanding of the **Key Terms** in Chapter 11, write a definition for each (in your own words), and then compare your definitions with those in the text.

Sex and Gender
sex (p. 390)
gender (p. 390)
gender role (p. 390)
social-learning theory of gender-role development (p. 392)
gender-schema theory (p. 392)
androgyny [an-DRAW-jah-nee] (p. 392)
gender identity (p. 394)
sexual orientation (p. 395)

Sexual Behavior
sexual response cycle (p. 399)
excitement phase (p. 400)
plateau phase (p. 400)
orgasm phase (p. 400)
resolution phase (p. 400)
refractory period (p. 400)
sexual prejudice (p. 401)

Sex Problems
sexual dysfunction (p. 402)
performance anxiety (p. 404)
double standard (p. 404)
sexual scripts (p. 405)
AIDS (acquired immunodeficiency syndrome) (p. 408)
HIV positive (p. 408)

TRY THIS YOURSELF

Differences in Language and Communication

Are men from Mars and women really from Venus? What does scientific research say about gender differences in communication? In this video lab exercise, available to WileyPLUS subscribers, you'll become a communications expert, observing a range of encounters and communications, judging their effectiveness, accounting for the weakness and strengths of each, and then working to improve the communications. You'll be observing two people texting messages, a parent talking to a child, animals vocalizing to each other, a trainer communicating with an animal, and a man and woman having a heart-to-heart.

While participating in this on-line exercise, consider the following:

- What does this lab exercise suggest about how language and communication develop?

- Do men and women listen differently and/or speak different languages?

- How does language affect thinking, decision making, perception, and behavior?

- What's going on in the brain while all this communication is happening?

 Chapter Summary

Studying Human Sexuality

Objective 11.1: Describe early studies of sexuality and the contributions of Ellis, Kinsey, and Masters and Johnson.
Although sex has always been an important part of human interest, motivation, and behavior, it received little scientific attention before the twentieth century. Havelock Ellis was among the first to study human sexuality despite the repression and secrecy of nineteenth-century Victorian times. Alfred Kinsey and his colleagues were the first to conduct large-scale, systematic surveys and interviews of the sexual practices and preferences of Americans during the 1940s and 1950s. In the 1960s, the research team of William Masters and Virginia Johnson pioneered the use of actual laboratory measurement and observation of human physiological response during sexual activity.

Sex and Gender

Objective 11.2: Compare and contrast sex and gender.
Sex refers to biological elements (such as having a penis or vagina) or physical activities (such as masturbation and intercourse). **Gender**, on the other hand, encompasses the psychological and sociocultural meanings added to biology (such as "Men should be aggressive" and "Women should be nurturing").

Objective 11.3: Define gender role, and describe the two major theories of gender-role development.
Gender roles are the societal expectations for normal and "appropriate" female and male behavior. **Social-learning theory of gender-role development**

emphasizes rewards, punishments, observation, and imitation, whereas **gender-schema theory** combines social-learning theory with active cognitive processing.

Objective 11.4: What is androgyny?
Androgyny is a combination of traits generally considered male (assertive, athletic) with typically female characteristics (nurturant, yielding).

Objective 11.5: Differentiate between gender identity, transsexualism, transvestism, and sexual orientation.
Gender identity refers to an individual's self-identification as being either a man or a woman. *Transsexualism* is a problem with gender identity, whereas *transvestism* is cross-dressing for emotional and sexual gratification. **Sexual orientation** (being gay, lesbian, bisexual, or heterosexual)

is unrelated to either transsexualism or transvestism.

Objective 11.6: Describe the major sex and gender differences between men and women.
Studies of male and female sex differences find several obvious physical differences, such as height, body build, and reproductive organs. There also are certain functional and structural sex differences in the brain, as well as some gender differences (such as in aggression and verbal skills). But the cause of these differences (either nature or nurture) is controversial.

Sexual Behavior

Objective 11.7: What are the four stages in Masters and Johnson's sexual response cycle?
William Masters and Virginia Johnson identified a four-stage **sexual response cycle** during sexual activity—the **excitement, plateau, orgasm**, and **resolution** phases.

Objective 11.8: Discuss the latest research on sexual orientation.
Although researchers have identified several myths concerning the causes of homosexuality, the origins of sexual orientation remain a puzzle. In recent studies, the genetic and biological explanation for homosexuality has gained the strongest support. Despite increased understanding, sexual orientation remains a divisive issue in the United States.

Sex Problems

Objective 11.9: Describe how biological, psychological, and social forces contribute to sexual dysfunction.
Biology plays a key role in both sexual arousal and response. Ejaculation and orgasm are partially reflexive, and the parasympathetic nervous system must be dominant for sexual arousal. The sympathetic nervous system must dominate for orgasm to occur.

Psychological factors like negative early sexual experiences, fears of negative consequences from sex, and **performance anxiety** contribute to **sexual dysfunction**.

In addition, sexual arousal and response are also related to social forces, such as early gender-role training, the **double standard**, and **sexual scripts**, which teach us what to consider the "best" sex.

Objective 11.10: Discuss how sex therapists treat sexual dysfunction, and list the four major principles of Masters and Johnson's approach.
Clinicians generally begin with tests and interviews to determine the cause(s) of the **sexual dysfunction**. William Masters and Virginia Johnson emphasize the couple's relationship, biological and psychosocial factors, cognitions, and specific behavioral techniques. Professional sex therapists offer important guidelines for everyone: Sex education should be early and positive, a goal or performance orientation should be avoided, and communication should be kept open.

Objective 11.11: Discuss the major issues related to STIs and the special problem of AIDS.
Although the dangers and rate of STIs are high, and higher for women than men, most STIs can be cured in their early stages. The most publicized sexually transmitted infection (STI) is **AIDS (acquired immunodeficiency syndrome)**. Although AIDS is transmitted only through sexual contact or exposure to infected bodily fluids, many people have irrational fears of contagion. At the same time, an increasing number of North Americans are **HIV-positive** and therefore carriers.

Objective 11.12: Why are cross-cultural studies of sexuality important?
Cross-cultural studies provide important information on the similarities and variations in human sexuality. They also help counteract *ethnocentrism*—judging one's own culture as "normal" and preferable to others.

ChapterEleven VISUAL SUMMARY

Studying Human Sexuality

Early Studies
- Sexuality suppressed during Victorian times
- Havelock Ellis conducted early sex research

Modern Research
- Alfred Kinsey used surveys in sex research
- Masters & Johnson introduced laboratory and observational sex research

Sex & Gender

What is Maleness & Femaleness?
- Sex = biological
- Gender = psychological & sociocultural added to biology

Gender-Role Development

Two major theories:

Gender-Identity Formation

Gender identity = self identification

Key terms = transsexual, transvestite, sexual orientation

Sex & Gender Differences
- Sex differences = biological
- Gender differences = psychological.
- Androgyny = combination of traits

Social-Learning Theory

Rewards and punishments

+

Observation and imitation of models

→ Gender-typed behavior (Boys playing with trucks and girls playing with dolls)

Gender-Schema Theory

Social learning

+

Active cognitive processing of gender role information

→ Builds gender schema (mental images) → Gender-typed behavior (Boys playing with trucks and girls playing with dolls)

Sexual Behavior

Sexual Arousal & Response

Plateau

Orgasm

Excitement

Resolution

Sexual Orientation

Supported theories: Genetic/biological contributors (genetic predisposition, prenatal biasing of the brain).

MYTH BUSTERS

- **Seduction theory** Gays and lesbians were seduced as children by adults of their own sex.

- **"By default" theory** Gays and lesbians were unable to attract partners of the other sex or have experienced unhappy heterosexual experiences.

- **Poor parenting theory** Sons become gay because of domineering mothers and weak fathers. Daughters become lesbians because of weak or absent mothers and having only fathers as their primary role model.

- **Modeling theory** Children raised by gay and lesbian parents usually end up adopting their parents' sexual orientation.

Sex Problems

Sexual Dysfunctions
Possible causes:

Biological:
- Lifestyle factors and medical conditions
- Parasympathetic vs. sympathetic dominance

Psychological:
- Anxieties and fears
- Gender role training
- **Double standard**
- **Performance anxiety**

Social:
Sexual scripts
(place restrictive boundaries)

Treatment: Masters and Johnson emhasize couple's relationship, biological and psychological factors, cognitions, and behavioral techniques

Sexually Transmitted Insfections (STIs)
Most publicized STI is **AIDS**, which is transmitted only through sexual contact or exposure to infected bodily fluids, but irrational fears of contagion persist. Over one million people in the United States are **HIV-positive** and therefore are carriers.

Psychology Engages

Gender & Cultural Diversity
Case Study/Personal Story
Critical Thinking
Research Challenge

ChapterTwelve

Motivation and Emotion

No pessimist ever discovered the secret of the stars, or sailed to an uncharted land, or opened a new doorway for the human spirit. Knowledge is love and light and vision. . . . Life is an exciting business, and most exciting when it is lived for others.

    Helen Keller (1880–1968), world-famous author, activist, suffragist, speaker, and winner of many awards, including being listed in Gallup's most widely admired people of the twentieth century. She happened to be both blind and deaf.

I have a dream that my four little children will one day live in a nation where they will not be judged by the color of their skin, but by the content of their character. . . . Our lives begin to end the day we become silent about things that matter.

    Martin Luther King (1929–1968), world famous civil rights leader, author, clergyman, and winner of many awards and honors, including the Nobel Peace prize, Time Person of the Year, and being listed second on Gallup's most widely admired people of the twentieth century. He happened to be black.

All of my friends, all of, most of my clients, the individual clients, are not net losers. I made a lot of money for them. I was making 20 percent returns for them . . . What do I do with my life now?

    Bernard "Bernie" Madoff (b. 1937), former stock broker, investment adviser, and admitted operator of a massive Ponzi scheme, which defrauded thousands of investors of billions of dollars. He is now serving the maximum allowed prison sentence of 150 years. He happened to be white.

What motivated Helen Keller and Dr. Martin Luther King to pursue their dreams, in spite of illness and setbacks? Why did Bernie Madoff milk so many people of their life savings, in spite of having vast wealth of his own? What emotions did they experience when facing their varying life struggles and choices? Why do we do what we do? Where do emotions come from? How do they affect us? Read on to find some of the answers.

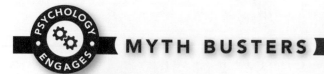

MYTH BUSTERS

True or False?

- People with high emotional intelligence (EI), like Abraham Lincoln, are often more successful than people with a high intelligence quotient (IQ)?

- Being either too excited or too relaxed can interfere with test performance?

- Getting paid for your hobbies may reduce your overall creativity and enjoyment?

- Smiling can make you feel happy and frowning can create negative feelings?

- Polygraph tests are reliable lie detectors?

- Lie detector tests may be fooled by biting your tongue?

Answers: All but one are true. Check the text for details before checking Appendix B for the answer.

Motivation Set of factors that activate, direct, and maintain behavior, usually toward some goal

Emotion Subjective feeling that includes arousal (heart pounding), cognitions (thoughts, values, and expectations), and expressive behaviors (smiles, frowns, and running)

Helen Keller, Dr. Martin Luther King, and Bernie Madoff are world-famous (or infamous) individuals, who pursued vastly different goals. But what motivates the rest of us? What drives you to fight and overcome obstacles to your personal lifetime dreams? How do you cope with the chronic anxieties and frustrations of college life? Why are you in college?

Objective 12.1: Define motivation and emotion, and explain why they're studied together.

Research in *motivation* and *emotion* attempts to answer such "what," "how," and "why" questions. **Motivation** refers to the set of factors that activate, direct, and maintain behavior, usually toward some goal. **Emotion**, on the other hand, refers to a subjective feeling that includes arousal (heart pounding), cognitions (thoughts, values, and expectations), and expressive behaviors (smiles, frowns, and running). In other words, motivation energizes and directs behavior. Emotion is the "feeling" response. (Both *motivation* and *emotion* come from the Latin *movere*, meaning "to move.")

Why cover both *motivation* and *emotion* in one chapter? Think about the joy, pride, and satisfaction that accompany your own Helen Keller or Martin Luther King type of achievements. Or the sadness, frustration, and even anger you feel when you receive a bad grade on a college exam. Motivation and emotion are inseparable.

In this chapter, we begin with the major theories and concepts of motivation, followed by three important sources of motivation—hunger, eating, and achievement. Then we turn to the basic theories and concepts related to emotion. We conclude with a look at intrinsic versus extrinsic motivation, the polygraph as a lie detector, and emotional intelligence (EI).

Theories of Motivation

Objective 12.2: Describe the six major theories of motivation.

There are six major theories of motivation that fall into three general categories—biological, psychological, and biopsychosocial (Table 12.1). As we discuss each theory, see if you can identify the one that best explains your own behaviors, such as going to college, buying a home, or changing jobs.

Table 12.1   SIX MAJOR THEORIES OF MOTIVATION

Name that theory Curiosity is an important aspect of the human experience. Which of the six theories of motivation best explains this behavior?

	Theory	Description
Biological		
	1. **Instinct**	Motivation results from innate, biological instincts, which are unlearned responses found in almost all members of a species.
	2. **Drive Reduction**	Motivation begins with biological need (a lack or deficiency) that elicits a *drive* toward behavior that will satisfy the original need and restore homeostasis.
	3. **Optimal Arousal**	Organisms are motivated to achieve and maintain an optimal level of arousal.
Psychological		
	4. **Incentive**	Motivation results from external stimuli that "pull" the organism in certain directions.
	5. **Cognitive**	Motivation is affected by expectations and attributions, or how we interpret or think about our own or others' actions.
Biopsychosocial		
	6. **Maslow's Hierarchy of Needs**	Lower biological motives (such as hunger and thirst) must be satisfied before advancing to higher needs (such as belonging and self-actualization).

Biological: Looking for Internal "Whys" of Behavior

Many theories of motivation are biologically based. They focus on inborn, genetically determined processes that control and direct behavior. Among these biologically oriented theories are *instinct*, *drive reduction*, and *optimal arousal* theories.

Instinct

Instinct theory suggests that we are motivated by inborn, genetic factors. In the earliest days of psychology, researchers like William McDougall (1908) proposed that humans had numerous "instincts," such as repulsion, curiosity, and self-assertiveness. Other researchers later added their favorite "instincts." By the 1920s, the list of recognized instincts had become so long it was virtually meaningless. One early researcher found listings for over 10,000 human instincts (Bernard, 1924).

In addition, the label *instinct* led to unscientific, circular explanations—"men are aggressive because they act aggressively" or "women are maternal because they act maternally." However, in recent years, a branch of biology called *sociobiology* has revived the case for **instincts** when defined as fixed response patterns that are unlearned and found in almost all members of a species (Figure 12.1).

Drive Reduction

In the 1930s, the concepts of drive and drive reduction began to replace the theory of instincts. According to **drive-reduction theory** (Hull, 1952), all living organisms have certain biological *needs* (such as food, water, and oxygen) that must be met if they are to survive. When these needs are unmet, a state of tension (known as a *drive*) is created, and the organism is motivated to reduce it.

Instinct theory Emphasizes inborn, genetic factors in motivation

Instinct Fixed response pattern that is unlearned and found in almost all members of a species

Drive-Reduction Theory Motivation begins with a physiological need (a lack or deficiency) that elicits a drive toward behavior that will satisfy the original need; once the need is met, a state of balance (homeostasis) is restored and motivation decreases

▲ Instinctual behaviors are obvious in many animals. Salmon swim upstream to spawn, bears hibernate, and birds build nests.

Figure 12.1 Instincts

▲ Sociobiologists such as Edward O. Wilson (1975, 1978) believe that humans also have instincts, like competition or aggression, that are genetically transmitted from one generation to the next.

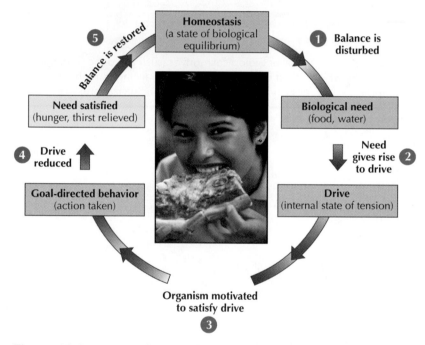

⑤ Balance is restored
Homeostasis (a state of biological equilibrium)
① Balance is disturbed
Need satisfied (hunger, thirst relieved)
Biological need (food, water)
Need gives rise to drive ②
④ **Drive reduced**
Goal-directed behavior (action taken)
Drive (internal state of tension)
Organism motivated to satisfy drive ③

Figure 12.2 Drive-reduction theory Homeostasis, the body's natural tendency to maintain a state of internal balance, is the foundation of drive reduction theory. When we are hungry or thirsty, the imbalance creates a *drive* that motivates us to search for food or water. Once action is taken and the need is satisfied, homeostasis (balance) is restored and our motivation (to seek food or water) is also decreased.

Homeostasis Body's tendency to maintain a relatively balanced and stable internal state, such as a constant internal temperature

Optimal-Arousal Theory Organisms are motivated to achieve and maintain an optimal level of arousal

Drive-reduction theory is based largely on the biological concept of **homeostasis**—a state of balance or stability in the body's internal environment, a term that literally means "standing still" (Figure 12.2).

Optimal Arousal

In addition to our obvious biological need for food and water, humans and other animals also are innately curious and require a certain amount of novelty and complexity from the environment. According to **optimal-arousal theory**, organisms are motivated to achieve and maintain an optimal level of arousal that maximizes their performance. Either too little or too much arousal diminishes performance (Figure 12.3).

Overcoming Test Anxiety Do you become overly aroused on exam day? If so, you may want to take a class in study skills or test anxiety. You also can try these basic study tips:

Step 1: *Prepare in advance.* The single most important cure for test anxiety is advance preparation and *hard work.* If you are well prepared, you will feel calmer and more in control.

- Read your textbook using the SQ4R (Survey, Question, Read, Recite, Review, and wRite) method (see Chapter 1).

- Practice good time management and distribute your study time; don't cram the night before.

- Actively listen during lectures and take detailed, summarizing notes.

- Follow the general strategies for test taking in the "Tools for Student Success" (Chapter 1) and the tips for memory improvement (Chapter 7).

(a) Monkeys and other animals will risk their own safety for the pleasure of satisfying their curiosity.

(b) The arousal motive is also apparent in the innate curiosity and exploration of the human animal.

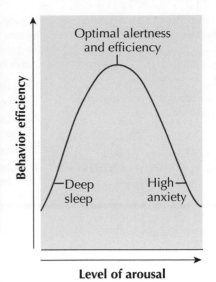

(c) Because of our need for stimulation (the *arousal motive*), our behavior efficiency increases as we move from deep sleep to increased alertness. However, once we pass the maximum level of arousal, our performance declines.

Figure 12.3 Arousal-seeking behaviors

Step 2: *Learn to cope with the anxiety*. Performance is best at a moderate level of arousal, so a few butterflies before and during exams are okay and to be expected. However, too much anxiety can interfere with concentration and cripple your performance. To achieve the right amount of arousal:

- Replace anxiety with relaxed feelings. Practice deep breathing (which activates the parasympathetic nervous system) and the relaxation response described in Chapter 3, on page 112.

- Desensitize yourself to the test situation. See Chapter 15, page 545.

- Exercise regularly. This is a great stress reliever, while also promoting deeper and more restful sleep.

TRY THIS YOURSELF

Sensation Seeking

What motivates people to bungee jump over deep canyons or white-water raft down dangerous rivers? According to research, these "high-sensation seekers" may be biologically "prewired" to need a higher than usual level of stimulation (Zuckerman, 1979, 1994, 2004).

To sample the kinds of questions that are asked on tests for sensation seeking, circle the choice (**A** or **B**) that BEST describes you:

1. **A** I would like a job that requires a lot of traveling.

   B I would prefer a job in one location.
2. **A** I get bored seeing the same old faces.

   B I like the comfortable familiarity of everyday friends.
3. **A** The most important goal of life is to live it to the fullest and experience as much as possible.

   B The most important goal of life is to find peace and happiness.
4. **A** I would like to try parachute jumping.

B I would never want to try jumping out of a plane, with or without a parachute.

5. A I prefer people who are emotionally expressive even if they are a bit unstable.

B I prefer people who are calm and even-tempered.

Source: Zuckerman, M. (1978, February). The search for high sensation, *Psychology Today*, pp. 38–46. Copyright © 1978 by the American Psychological Association. Reprinted by permission.

Research suggests that four distinct factors characterize sensation seeking (Legrand et al., 2007; Wallerstein, 2008; Zuckerman, 2004, 2008).

1. Thrill and adventure seeking (skydiving, driving fast, or trying to beat a train)
2. Experience seeking (travel, unusual friends, drug experimentation)
3. Disinhibition ("letting loose")
4. Susceptibility to boredom (lower tolerance for repetition and sameness)

Being very high or very low in sensation seeking might cause problems in relationships with individuals who score toward the other extreme. This is true not just between partners or spouses but also between parent and child and therapist and patient. There might also be job difficulties for high-sensation seekers in routine clerical or assembly-line jobs or for low-sensation seekers in highly challenging and variable occupations.

Psychological: Incentives and Cognitions

Instinct and drive-reduction theories explain some biological motivations, but why do we continue to eat even after our biological need is completely satisfied? Or why do we sometimes volunteer to work overtime when our salaries are sufficient to meet all our basic biological needs? And why do some students go to parties versus studying for exams? These questions are better answered by psychosocial theories that emphasize *incentives* and *cognition*.

Incentive—Environmental "Pulls"

Incentive Theory Motivation results from external stimuli that "pull" the organism in certain directions

Unlike the previous drive reduction theory, which states that internal factors *push* people in certain directions, **incentive theory** maintains that external stimuli *pull* people toward desirable goals or away from undesirable ones. Most of us initially eat because our hunger "pushes" us (drive reduction theory). But the sight of apple pie or ice cream too often "pulls" us toward continued eating (incentive theory).

Cognitive—Explaining Things to Ourselves

According to *cognitive theories*, motivation is directly affected by *attributions*, or how we interpret or think about our own and others' actions. If you receive a high grade in your psychology course, you can interpret that grade in several ways. You earned it because you really studied. You "lucked out." Or the textbook was exceptionally interesting and helpful (my preferred interpretation!). Interestingly, researchers have found that people who attribute their success to personal ability and effort tend to work harder toward their goals than people who attribute it to luck (Beacham et al., 2011; Houtz et al., 2007; Martinko, Harvey, & Dasborough, 2011; Weiner, 1972, 1982).

Expectancies, or what we anticipate or assume will happen, are also important to cognitive theories of motivation (Reinhard & Dickhäuser, 2011; Schunk, 2008). Your anticipated grade on a test affects your willingness to study—"If I can get an A in the course, then I will study very hard." Similarly, your expectancies regarding future salary increases or promotions at work affect your willingness to work overtime for no pay.

Biopsychosocial: Interactionism Once Again

As we've seen throughout this text, research in psychology generally emphasizes either biological or psychosocial factors (nature or nurture). But in the final analysis, the *biopsychosocial model* (an inseparable interaction between biological,

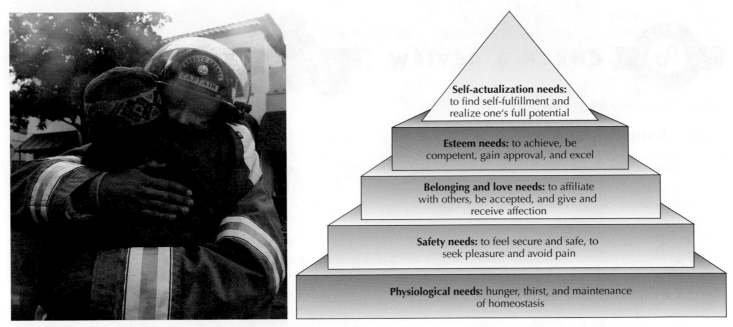

Figure 12.4 Maslow's hierarchy of needs Abraham Maslow believed that we all share a compelling need to "move up"—to grow, improve ourselves, and ultimately become "self-actualized." What higher-level needs do these people seem to be trying to fulfill? Does it appear that their lower-level needs have been met?

psychological, and social forces) almost always provides the best explanation. Theories of motivation are no exception. One researcher who recognized this three-way interaction was Abraham Maslow. Maslow believed that we all have numerous needs that compete for fulfillment, but that some needs are more important than others (Maslow, 1954, 1970, 1999). For example, your need for food and shelter is generally more important than your college grades. Maslow's **hierarchy of needs** *prioritizes* needs, with survival needs at the bottom and self-actualization needs at the top (Figure 12.4).

Maslow's hierarchy of needs seems intuitively correct. A starving person would first look for food, then seek love and friendship, then self-esteem, and finally self-actualization. This prioritizing and the concept of *self-actualization* are important contributions to the study of motivation.

On the other hand, critics argue that parts of Maslow's theory are poorly researched and biased toward Western individualism. Furthermore, his theory presupposes a homogeneous life experience, and people also sometimes seek to satisfy higher-level needs even when lower-level needs have not been met (Cullen & Gotell, 2002; Kress et al., 2011; Neher, 1991). In some nonindustrialized societies, people may be living in a war zone, subsisting on very little food, and suffering from injury and disease. Although they have not fulfilled Maslow's two lowest and most basic needs, they still seek the higher needs of strong social ties and self-esteem. In addition, during the famine and war in Somalia, many parents sacrificed their own lives to carry starving children hundreds of miles to food distribution centers. And parents at the centers often banded together to share the limited supplies. Because Maslow argued that each individual's own lower needs must be at least partially met before higher needs can influence behavior, these examples "stand Maslow's need hierarchy on its head" (Neher, 1991, p. 97). In sum, we're normally motivated to fulfill basic needs first. However, in certain circumstances we can bypass these lower stages and pursue higher-level needs.

Hierarchy of Needs Maslow's theory that lower motives (such as physiological and safety needs) must be met before advancing to higher needs (such as belonging and self-actualization)

CHECK & REVIEW

STOP *Before going on, be sure to complete this Check & Review. It is an invaluable study tool!*

Theories of Motivation

Part A: Retrieval Practice

1. Without looking at the book, spend 10 minutes writing a free-form essay recalling all you can remember from the previous section.

2. Now, reread the previous section, and once again spend 10 minutes writing a free-form essay on the SAME material.

   (Although time consuming, this exercise has been shown to be the single best way to improve your test scores! For more information, check out www.sciencemag.org/content/early/2011/01/19/science.1199327.abstract)

Part B: Practice Quiz

1. Define instinct and homeostasis.

2. The figure below illustrates the _____ theory, in which motivation decreases once homeostasis occurs.

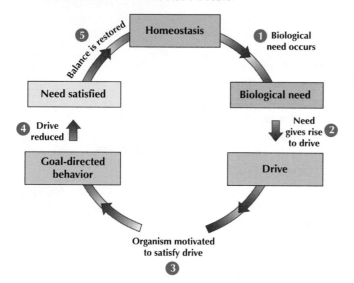

3. Match the following examples with their appropriate theory of motivation: (a) instinct; (b) drive reduction; (c) optimal arousal; (d) incentive; (e) cognitive; (f) Maslow's hierarchy of needs

____i. Joining a club because you want to be accepted by others

____ii. Two animals fighting because of their inherited, evolutionary desire for survival

____iii. Eating to reduce hunger

____iv. Studying hard for an exam because you expect that studying will result in a good grade

____v. Skydiving because you love the excitement

4. _____ theory suggests we need a certain amount of novelty and complexity from our environment.

5. _____ theories emphasize the importance of attributions and expectancies in motivating behaviors. (a) Attribution; (b) Motivational; (c) Achievement; (d) Cognitive

6. Maslow's _____ theory, illustrated in the figure below, suggests that some motives have to be satisfied before a person can advance to higher levels.

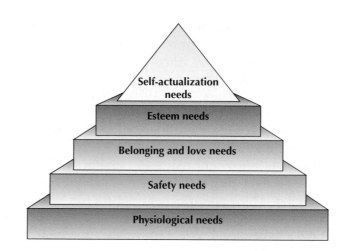

Check your answers in Appendix B.

Motivation and Behavior

Objective 12.3: Discuss the major biopsychosocial factors that influence hunger and eating.

Why do you spend hours playing a new computer game instead of studying for a major exam? Why do salmon swim upstream to spawn? Behavior results from many motives. For example, the sleep motive was covered in Chapter 5, the sex drive was explored in Chapter 11, and aggression, altruism, and interpersonal attraction will be discussed in Chapter 16. Here, we will focus on the motives behind hunger and eating and achievement.

Hunger and Eating: Multiple Biopsychosocial Factors

What motivates hunger? Is it your growling stomach? Or is it the sight of a juicy hamburger or the smell of a freshly baked cinnamon roll? Hunger is one of our strongest motivational drives. Numerous biological factors (stomach, biochemistry, brain) and many psychosocial forces (visual cues and cultural conditioning) affect our eating behaviors.

Stomach

Walter B. Cannon and A. L. Washburn (1912) conducted one of the earliest experiments exploring the internal factors in hunger (Figure 12.5). In this study, Washburn swallowed a balloon and then inflated it in his stomach. His stomach contractions and subjective reports of hunger feelings were then simultaneously recorded. Because each time Washburn reported having stomach pangs (or "growling") the balloon also contracted, the researchers concluded that stomach movement *caused* the sensation of hunger.

Can you identify what's wrong with this study? As you learned in Chapter 1, correlation does not mean causation. Furthermore, researchers must always control for the possibility of *extraneous variables*, factors that contribute irrelevant data and confuse the results. In this case, it was later found that an empty stomach is relatively inactive. The stomach contractions experienced by Washburn were an experimental artifact—something resulting from the presence of the balloon. Washburn's stomach had been tricked into thinking it was full and was responding by trying to digest the balloon!

In sum, sensory input from the stomach is not essential for feeling hungry. Dieters learn this the hard way when they try to "trick" their stomachs into feeling full by eating large quantities of carrots and celery and drinking lots of water. Also, humans and nonhuman animals without stomachs continue to experience hunger.

However, this doesn't mean there is no connection between the stomach and feeling hungry. Receptors in the stomach and intestines do detect levels of nutrients, and specialized pressure receptors in the stomach walls signal feelings of emptiness or *satiety* (fullness or satiation). The stomach and other parts of the gastrointestinal tract also release chemicals that play a role in hunger (Moran & Dailey, 2011; Näslund & Hellström, 2007; Nogueiras & Tschöp, 2005; Steinert & Beglinger, 2011). These (and other) chemical signals are the topic of our next section.

Biochemistry

Like the stomach, the brain and other parts of the body produce, and are affected by, numerous neurotransmitters, hormones, enzymes, and other chemicals that affect hunger and satiety (e.g., Arumugam et al., 2008; Cooper et al., 2011; Cummings, 2006; Wardlaw & Hampl, 2007). Research in this area is complex because of the large number of known (and unknown) bodily chemicals and the interactions among them. It's unlikely that any one chemical controls our hunger and eating. Other internal factors, such as *thermogenesis* (the heat generated in response to food ingestion), also play a role (Acheson et al., 2011; Ping-Delfos & Soares, 2011; Subramanian & Vollmer, 2002).

Brain

In addition to its chemical signals, particular brain structures also influence hunger and eating. Let's look at the *hypothalamus*, which helps regulate eating, drinking, and body temperature.

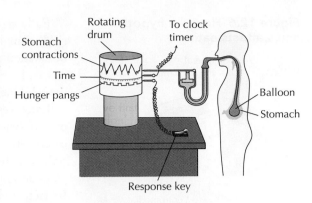

Figure 12.5 Cannon and Washburn's technique for measuring internal factors in hunger As a participant in his own study, Washburn swallowed a special balloon designed to detect stomach movement. His stomach movements were automatically recorded on graph paper attached to a rotating drum. At the same time, whenever Washburn experienced "hunger pangs," he would press a key that made a recording on the same graph paper. The two recordings (stomach movements and hunger sensations) were then compared. Finding that Washburn's stomach contractions occurred at the same time as his feelings of hunger led these early researchers to conclude that stomach movements caused hunger. Later research altered this conclusion.

Figure 12.6 How the hypothalamus affects eating

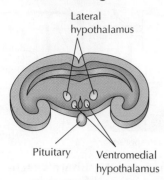

Lateral
hypothalamus

Pituitary   Ventromedial
hypothalamus

▲ This diagram shows a section of a rat's brain, including the ventromedial hypothalamus (VMH) and the lateral hypothalamus (LH).

▲ The rat on the right is of normal weight. In contrast, the ventromedial area of the hypothalamus of the rat on the left was destroyed, which led to the tripling of its body weight.

Can the environment affect body weight? Obesity is relatively common among modern Pima Indians living in the United States. However, their close relatives living nearby in Mexico who eat traditional foods are generally slim. ▼

Early research suggested that one area of the hypothalamus, the *lateral hypothalamus* (LH), stimulated eating. In contrast, the *ventromedial hypothalamus* (VMH), created feelings of satiation and signaled the animal to stop eating. When the LH area was destroyed in rats, early researchers found the animals starved to death if they were not force-fed. When the VMH area was destroyed, they overate to the point of extreme obesity (Figure 12.6).

Later research, however, showed that the LH and VMH areas are not simple on–off switches for eating. For example, lesions to the VMH make animals picky eaters—they reject food that doesn't taste good. Lesions also increase insulin secretion, which may cause overeating. Today, researchers know that the hypothalamus plays an important role in hunger and eating, but it is not the brain's "eating center." In fact, hunger and eating, like virtually all behavior, are influenced by numerous neural circuits that run throughout the brain (Berthoud & Morrison, 2008; Malik, McGlone & Dagher, 2011; van der Laan et al., 2011).

Psychosocial Factors

The internal motivations for hunger we've discussed (stomach, biochemistry, brain) are powerful. But psychosocial factors—like watching a pizza commercial on TV—can be equally important *stimulus cues* for hunger and eating (Herman & Polivy, 2008; Hou et al., 2011; Petrovich, 2011). Another important environmental influence on when, what, where, and why we eat is *cultural conditioning*. North Americans, for example, tend to eat their evening meal around 6:00 P.M. People in Spain and South America tend to eat around 10:00 P.M. When it comes to *what* we eat, have you ever eaten rat, dog, or horse meat? If you are a typical North American, this might sound repulsive to you, yet most Hindus would feel a similar revulsion at the thought of eating meat from cows.

In sum, the biological and psychosocial factors involved in the regulation of hunger and eating are complex and depend on numerous interactions. (The key mechanisms are visually summarized in Concept Organizer 12.1.) Modern researchers are still struggling to discover and explain how all these processes work together.

Eating Disorders: Obesity, Anorexia, and Bulimia

Objective 12.4: Describe the three key eating disorders—obesity, anorexia, and bulimia.

As you can see, hunger and eating are complex phenomena controlled by numerous biological, psychological, and social factors. These same biopsychosocial forces also play a role in three of our most serious eating disorders—obesity, anorexia nervosa, and bulimia nervosa.

Obesity

Obesity has reached epidemic proportions in the United States and many other developed nations. Well over half of all adults in the United States meet the current criterion for clinical *obesity* (having a body weight 15 percent or more above the ideal for one's height and age). Each year, billions of dollars are spent treating serious and life-threatening medical problems related to obesity, and consumers spend billions more on largely ineffective weight-loss products and services.

Why are so many people overweight? The simple answer is our environment, overeating, and not enough exercise (Figure 12.7). However, we all know some people who seemingly can eat anything they want and still not add pounds. This may be a result of their ability to burn calories more effectively (thermogenesis), a higher metabolic rate, or other factors. Adoption and twin studies indicate that genes also play a role. Heritability for obesity is estimated to range between 30 and 70 percent (Andersson & Walley, 2011; Johnson, 2011; Lee et al., 2008). Unfortunately, identifying the genes for obesity is difficult. Researchers have isolated over 2,000 genes that contribute to normal and abnormal weight.

ConceptOrganizer12.1

Key Mechanisms in Hunger Regulation

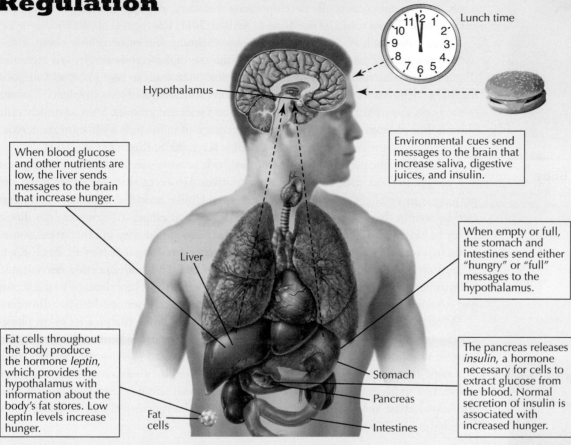

Lunch time

Hypothalamus

Environmental cues send messages to the brain that increase saliva, digestive juices, and insulin.

When blood glucose and other nutrients are low, the liver sends messages to the brain that increase hunger.

When empty or full, the stomach and intestines send either "hungry" or "full" messages to the hypothalamus.

Liver

Fat cells throughout the body produce the hormone *leptin*, which provides the hypothalamus with information about the body's fat stores. Low leptin levels increase hunger.

Fat cells

Stomach

Pancreas

Intestines

The pancreas releases *insulin*, a hormone necessary for cells to extract glucose from the blood. Normal secretion of insulin is associated with increased hunger.

Anorexia Nervosa and Bulimia Nervosa

Interestingly, as obesity has reached epidemic proportions, we've seen a similar rise in two other eating disorders—**anorexia nervosa** (self-starvation and extreme weight loss) and **bulimia nervosa** (intense, recurring episodes of binge eating followed by purging through

Anorexia Nervosa Eating disorder characterized by a severe loss of weight resulting from self-imposed starvation and an obsessive fear of obesity

Bulimia Nervosa Eating disorder involving the consumption of large quantities of food (bingeing), followed by vomiting, extreme exercise, and/or laxative use (purging)

Figure 12.7 A fattening environment For Americans, controlling weight is a particularly difficult task. We are among the most sedentary people of all nations, and we've become accustomed to "supersized" cheeseburgers, "Big Gulp" drinks, and huge servings of dessert (Carels et al., 2008; Fisher & Kral, 2008; Herman & Polivy, 2008). We've also learned that we should eat three meals a day (whether we're hungry or not); that "tasty" food requires lots of salt, sugar, and fat; and that food is an essential part of all social gatherings. To successfully lose (and maintain) weight, we must make permanent lifestyle changes regarding the amount and types of foods we eat and when we eat them. Can you see how our everyday environments, such as in the workplace scene here, might prevent a person from making healthy lifestyle changes?

Figure 12.8 Distorted body image In anorexia nervosa, body image is so distorted that even a skeletal, emaciated body is perceived as fat. Many people with anorexia nervosa not only refuse to eat but also take up extreme exercise regimens—hours of cycling or running or constant walking.

Figure 12.9 Culture and body image Does the extreme thinness of some popular movie and television stars unintentionally contribute to eating disorders?

vomiting or taking laxatives). Both disorders are serious and chronic conditions that require treatment. More than 50 percent of women in Western industrialized countries show some signs of an eating disorder, and approximately 2 percent meet the official criteria for anorexia nervosa or bulimia nervosa (Porzelius et al., 2001; Wade, Keski-Rahknonen, & Hudson, 2011; Welch et al., 2011). These disorders also are found in all socioeconomic levels. A few men occasionally develop eating disorders, although the incidence is rarer among them (Jacobi et al., 2004; Mond & Arrighi, 2011; Raevuori et al., 2008).

Anorexia nervosa is characterized by an overwhelming fear of becoming obese, a distorted body image, the need for control, and the use of dangerous weight-loss measures (Figure 12.8). The resulting extreme malnutrition often leads to osteo-porosis and bone fractures. Menstruation in women frequently stops, and computed tomography (CT) scans of the brain show enlarged ventricles (cavities) and widened grooves. Such signs generally indicate loss of brain tissue. A significant percentage of individuals with anorexia nervosa ultimately die of the disorder (Huas et al., 2011; Kaye, 2008; Rosling et al., 2011).

Occasionally, the person suffering from anorexia nervosa succumbs to the desire to eat and gorges on food, then vomits or takes laxatives. However, this type of bingeing and purging is more characteristic of *bulimia nervosa*. Unlike anorexia, bulimia is characterized by weight fluctuations within or above the normal range, which makes the illness easier to hide. Individuals with this disorder also show impulsivity in other areas, sometimes by excessive shopping, alcohol abuse, or petty shoplifting (Claes et al., 2011; Kaye, 2008; Vaz-Leal et al., 2011). The vomiting associated with both anorexia nervosa and bulimia nervosa causes eroded tooth enamel and tooth loss, severe damage to the throat and stomach, cardiac arrhythmias, metabolic deficiencies, and serious digestive disorders.

What causes anorexia nervosa and bulimia nervosa? Some theories focus on physical causes such as hypothalamic disorders, low levels of various neurotransmitters, and genetic or hormonal disorders. Other theories emphasize psychosocial factors, such as a need for perfection, being teased about body weight, a perceived loss of control, destructive thought patterns, depression, dysfunctional families, distorted body image, and sexual abuse (e.g., Caqueo-Urizar et al., 2011; Fairburn et al., 2008; Kaye, 2008; Sachdev et al., 2008).

Culture and Eating Disorders

Cultural factors also play important roles in eating disorders (Eddy et al., 2007; George & Franko, 2010; Herman & Polivy, 2008). For instance, Asian and African Americans report fewer eating and dieting disorders and greater body satisfaction than do European Americans (Taylor et al., 2007; Wang et al., 2011; Whaley, Smith, & Hancock, 2011).

Although social pressures for thinness certainly contribute to the development of eating disorders (Figure 12.9), anorexia nervosa also has been found in nonindustrialized areas like the Caribbean island of Curaçao (Ferguson, Winegard, & Winegard, 2011; Hoek et al., 2005). On that island, being overweight is socially acceptable, and the average woman is considerably heavier than the average woman in North America. However, some women there still suffer from anorexia nervosa. This research suggests that both culture and biology help explain eating disorders. Regardless of the causes, it is important to recognize the symptoms of anorexia and bulimia (Table 12.2) and seek therapy if the symptoms apply to you.

Achievement Motivation: The Need for Success

Objective 12.5: Define achievement motivation, and list the characteristics of high achievers.

Do you wonder what motivates Olympic athletes to work so hard for so many years for the remote possibility of a gold medal? Or what about someone like Thomas Edison, who patented over 1,000 inventions? What drives some people to high achievement?

Table 12.2 DSM-IV-TRª SYMPTOMS OF ANOREXIA NERVOSA AND BULIMIA NERVOSA

Symptoms of Anorexia Nervosa	Symptoms of Bulimia Nervosa
• Body weight below 85% of normal for one's height and age • Intense fear of becoming fat or gaining weight, even though underweight • Disturbance in one's body image or perceived weight • Self-evaluation unduly influenced by body weight • Denial of seriousness of abnormally low body weight • Absence of menstrual period • Purging behavior (vomiting or misuse of laxatives or diuretics)	• Normal or above-normal weight • Recurring binge eating • Eating an amount of food that is much larger than most people would consume • Feeling a lack of control over eating • Purging behavior (vomiting or misuse of laxatives or duiuretics) • Excessive exercise to prevent weight gain • Fasting to prevent weight gain • Self-evaluation unduly influenced by body weight

ªDSM-IV-TR = *Diagnostic and Statistical Manual of Mental Disorders*, fourth edition, revised.

TRY THIS YOURSELF

Figure 12.10 Measuring achievement This card is a sample from the *Thematic Apperception Test* (TAT). The strength of an individual's need for achievement is reportedly measured by stories he or she tells about the TAT drawings. If you want an informal test using this method, look closely at the two women in the photo, and then write a short story answering the following questions:

1. What is happening in this picture, and what led up to it?
2. Who are the people in this picture, and how do they feel?
3. What is going to happen in the next few moments, and in a few weeks?

Scoring Give yourself 1 point each time any of the following is mentioned: (1) defining a problem, (2) solving a problem, (3) obstructions to solving a problem, (4) techniques that can help overcome the problem, (5) anticipation of success or resolution of the problem. The higher your score on this test, the higher your overall need for achievement.

The key to understanding what motivates high-achieving individuals lies in what psychologist Henry Murray (1938) identified as a *high need for achievement* (nAch). **Achievement motivation** can be broadly defined as the desire to excel, especially in competition with others. One of the earliest tests for achievement motivation was devised by Christiana Morgan and Henry Murray (1935). Using a series of ambiguous pictures called the *Thematic Apperception Test* (TAT) (Figure 12.10), these researchers asked participants to make up a story about each picture. Their responses were scored for different motivational themes, including achievement. Since that time, other researchers have developed several questionnaire measures of achievement.

Before you read on, complete the following "Try This Yourself!" activity, on the next page, which provides insights into your own need for achievement.

What causes some people to be more achievement oriented than others? Achievement orientation appears to be largely learned in early childhood, primarily through interactions with parents. Highly motivated children tend to have parents who encourage independence and frequently reward success (e.g., Katz, Kaplan, & Buzukashvily, 2011; Maehr & Urdan, 2000). The culture that we are born and raised in also affects achievement needs (Hofer et al., 2010; Vitoroulis et al., 2011; Xu & Barnes, 2011). Events and themes in children's literature, for example, often contain subtle messages about what the culture values. In North American and western European cultures, many children's stories are about persistence and the value of hard work (Figure 12.11).

Achievement Motivation Desire to excel, especially in competition with others

Figure 12.11 Future achiever A study by Richard de Charms and Gerald Moeller (1962) found a significant correlation between the achievement themes in children's literature and the industrial accomplishments of various countries.

Characteristics of High Achievers

By Thomas Frangicetto (Northampton Community College, Bethlehem, PA)

Do you have a high need for achievement (nAch)? People with a high achievement orientation generally have more success in life and report more satisfaction with what they've accomplished in their lives. Here is a chance for you to:

- Review the six characteristics of high achievers.
- Rate yourself on those characteristics.
- Apply critical thinking components to improve your achievement motivation scores.

Part I: Researchers have identified several personality traits that distinguish people with a high nAch from those with a low nAch (McClelland, 1958, 1987, 1993; Senko, Durik, & Harackiewicz, 2008; Quintanilla, 2007). To determine your own personal need for achievement, read the six characteristics below and rate yourself according to how accurately each one describes you.

RATING:
(Not like   (Describes
me   0 1 2 3 4 5 6 7 8 9 10   me
at all)   accurately)

1. *Preference for moderately difficult tasks.* I tend to avoid tasks that are too easy because they offer little challenge and avoid extremely difficult tasks because the chance of success is too low.

2. *Preference for clear goals with competent feedback.* I prefer tasks with a clear outcome and situations in which you can receive performance feedback. I also prefer criticism from a harsh but competent evaluator to one who is friendlier but less competent.

3. *Competitive.* I am more attracted to careers and tasks that involve competition and an opportunity to excel. I enjoy the challenge of having to prove myself.

4. *Responsible.* I prefer being personally responsible for a project, and when I am directly responsible I feel more satisfaction when the task is well done.

5. *Persistent.* I am highly likely to persist at a task even when it becomes difficult, and I gain satisfaction in seeing a task through to completion.

6. *More accomplished.* In comparison to others, I generally achieve more (e.g., I typically do better on exams and earn higher grades and/or receive top honors in sports, clubs, and other activities).

Add up your total need for achievement (nAch) points. 55–60 = Very high; 49–54 = High; 43–48 = Moderately high; 37–42 = Average; 31–36 = Below average; below 30 = Low.

Part II: Review your ratings and identify one critical thinking component (CTC) (see Prologue at front of book), that you believe could help increase your score on each trait. This is an important exercise. The closer your need for achievement reflects the characteristics of high achievers, the more likely you are to accomplish your goals. Here is an example for item #1:

Preference for moderately difficult tasks. High achievers know that succeeding at an easy task results in low satisfaction. On the other hand, overly difficult tasks lead to unnecessary frustration. Therefore, the CTC "Recognizing Personal Biases" is very important. Honestly facing the facts about our knowledge and abilities helps us recognize our limitations. It can also help prevent wasteful rationalizing and blaming others for our failures. Being realistic about our abilities without being overly self-critical achieves a healthy balance.

 **CHECK & REVIEW**  **STOP** *Before going on, be sure to complete this Check & Review. It is an invaluable study tool!*

Motivation and Behavior

Part A: Retrieval Practice

1. Without looking at the book, spend 10 minutes writing a free-form essay recalling all you can remember from the previous section.

2. Now, reread the previous section, and once again spend 10 minutes writing a free-form essay on the SAME material.

Part B: Practice Quiz

1. Motivation for eating is found _____. (a) in the stomach; (b) in the ventromedial section of the hypothalamus; (c) throughout the brain; (d) throughout the body

2. Severe weight loss resulting from self-imposed starvation and an obsessive fear of obesity is called _____.

3. Maria has a need for success and prefers moderately difficult tasks, especially in competition with others. Maria probably has a high _____.

   (a) need for approval
   (b) testographic personality
   (c) power drive
   (d) need for achievement

4. What are the chief identifying characteristics of high achievers?

Check your answers in Appendix B.

Components and Theories of Emotion

We have reviewed the major theoretical explanations for motivation and specific motives such as hunger and achievement. But as we mentioned at the beginning of this chapter, motivation is inextricably linked to emotion. In this section, we begin with an exploration of the three basic components of emotion (*biological*, *cognitive*, and *behavioral*). Then we examine the four major theories that help us understand emotion (*James–Lange*, *Cannon–Bard*, *facial-feedback*, and *Schachter's two-factor*).

Three Components of Emotion: Biological, Cognitive, and Behavioral

Objective 12.6: Describe the three key components of emotions.

Emotions play an important role in our lives. They color our dreams, memories, and perceptions (Kalat & Shiota, 2012). When they are disordered, they contribute significantly to psychological problems. But what do we mean by the term *emotion*? In everyday usage, we describe emotions in terms of feeling states—we feel "thrilled" when our political candidate wins an election, "defeated" when our candidate loses, and "miserable" when our loved ones reject us. Obviously, what you and I mean by these terms, or what we individually experience with various emotions, can vary greatly among individuals. In an attempt to make the study of emotions more reliable and scientific, psychologists define and study emotions according to their three basic components (*biological*, *cognitive*, and *behavioral*).

Biological (Arousal) Component

Internal physical changes occur in our bodies whenever we experience an emotion. Imagine walking alone on a dark street in a dangerous part of town. You suddenly see someone jump from behind a stack of boxes and start running toward you. How do you respond? Like most of us, you would undoubtedly interpret the situation as threatening and would prepare to defend yourself or run. Your predominant emotion, fear, would involve several physiological reactions, including increased heart rate and blood pressure, dilated pupils, perspiration, dry mouth, rapid or irregular breathing, increased blood sugar, trembling, decreased gastrointestinal motility, and piloerection (goose bumps). These biological reactions are controlled by many parts of your body. But certain brain regions and the autonomic nervous system (ANS) play especially significant roles.

Brain

Our emotional experiences appear to result from important interactions among several areas of our brain. The cerebral cortex, the outermost layer of the brain, serves as our body's ultimate control and information-processing center, including our ability to recognize and regulate our emotions. (Recall from Chapter 1 that when a 13-pound tamping iron accidentally slammed through Phineas Gage's cortex, he could no longer monitor or control his emotions.)

In addition to the cortex, the limbic system is also essential to our emotions (Figure 12.12). Electrical stimulation of specific parts of the limbic system can produce an automatic "sham rage" that turns a docile cat into a hissing, slashing animal (Morris et al., 1996). Stimulating adjacent areas can cause the same animal to purr and lick your fingers. (The rage is called "sham" because it occurs in the absence of provocation and disappears immediately when the stimulus is removed.) Several studies have also shown that one area of the limbic system, the **amygdala**, plays a key role in emotion—especially the emotional response of fear. It sends signals to other areas of the brain, causing increased heart rate and all the other physiological reactions related to fear.

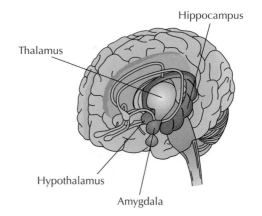

Figure 12.12 The limbic system and emotion In addition to drive regulation, memory, and other functions, the limbic system is very important to emotions. It consists of several subcortical structures that form a border (or limbus) around the brain stem.

Amygdala Limbic system structure linked to the production and regulation of emotions.

Interestingly, some forms of emotional arousal can occur without conscious awareness. Have you ever been hiking and suddenly jumped back because you thought you saw a snake on the trail, only to realize a moment later that it was just a stick? How does this happen? According to psychologist Joseph LeDoux (1996, 2002, 2007), and his colleagues (LeDoux & Doyére, 2011; Yang et al., 2011), when sensory inputs capable of eliciting emotions (the sight of the stick) arrive in the thalamus (our brain's sensory switchboard), it sends messages along two independent pathways—one going up to the cortex and the other going directly to the nearby amygdala. If the amygdala senses a threat, it immediately activates the body's alarm system, long before the cortex has had a chance to really "think" about the stimulus.

Although this dual pathway occasionally leads to "false alarms," such as mistaking a stick for a snake, LeDoux believes it is a highly adaptive warning system essential to our survival. He states that "the time saved by the amygdala in acting on the thalamic interpretation, rather than waiting for the cortical input, may be the difference between life and death."

Autonomic Nervous System (ANS)

The brain clearly plays a vital role in emotion. However, it is the autonomic nervous system (ANS) that produces the most obvious signs of emotional arousal (increased heart rate, fast and shallow breathing, trembling, and so on) (Kalat & Shiota, 2012). These largely automatic responses result from interconnections between the ANS and various glands and muscles (Figure 12.13).

Recall from Chapter 2 that the ANS has two major subdivisions: the *sympathetic nervous system* and the *parasympathetic nervous system*. When you are emotionally aroused, the sympathetic branch increases heart rate, respiration, and so on (the fight-or-flight response). When you are relaxed and resting, the parasympathetic branch works to calm the body and maintain *homeostasis*. The combined action of both the sympathetic and parasympathetic systems allows you to respond to emotional arousal and then return to a more relaxed state.

Cognitive (Thinking) Component

There is nothing either good or bad, but thinking makes it so.
SHAKESPEARE, *HAMLET*

Our thoughts, values, and expectations also help determine the type and intensity of our emotional responses. Consequently, emotional reactions are very individual. What you experience as intensely pleasurable may be boring or aversive for another.

Figure 12.13 Emotion and the autonomic nervous system During emotional arousal, the sympathetic branch of the autonomic nervous system (in connection with the brain) prepares the body for fight or flight. The hormones epinephrine and nor-epinephrine keep the system under sympathetic control until the emergency is over. The parasympathetic system returns the body to a more relaxed state (homeostasis).

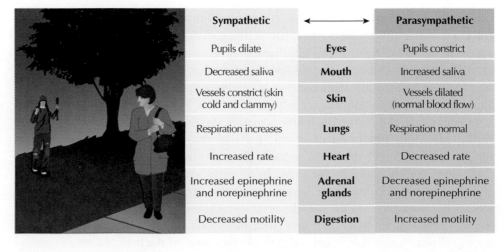

Sympathetic		Parasympathetic
Pupils dilate	**Eyes**	Pupils constrict
Decreased saliva	**Mouth**	Increased saliva
Vessels constrict (skin cold and clammy)	**Skin**	Vessels dilated (normal blood flow)
Respiration increases	**Lungs**	Respiration normal
Increased rate	**Heart**	Decreased rate
Increased epinephrine and norepinephrine	**Adrenal glands**	Decreased epinephrine and norepinephrine
Decreased motility	**Digestion**	Increased motility

To study the cognitive component of emotions, psychologists typically use self-report techniques such as paper-and-pencil tests, surveys, and interviews. But our cognitions (or thoughts) about our own and others' emotions are typically difficult to describe and measure scientifically. Individuals differ in their ability to monitor and report on their emotional states. In addition, some people may lie or hide their feelings because of social expectations or as an attempt to please the experimenter.

Furthermore, it is often impractical or unethical to artificially create emotions in a laboratory. How can we ethically create strong emotions like anger in a research participant just to study his or her emotional reactions? Finally, memories of emotions are not foolproof. You may remember that trip to Yellowstone as the "happiest camping trip ever." Your brother or sister may remember the same trip as the "worst." Our individual needs, experiences, and personal interpretations all affect the accuracy of our memories (Chapter 7).

Behavioral (Expressive) Component

Emotional expression is a powerful form of communication. An infant's smile can create instant bonding, a cry of "fire" can cause crowds to panic, and a sobbing friend can elicit heartbreaking empathy. Though we can talk about our emotions, we more often express them nonverbally through facial expressions; gestures; body position; and the use of touch, eye gaze, and tone of voice.

Facial expressions may be our most important form of emotional communication, and researchers have developed very sensitive measurement techniques allowing them to detect subtleties of feeling and differentiate honest expressions from fake ones. Perhaps most interesting is the difference between the "social smile" and the "Duchenne smile." The latter is named after French anatomist Duchenne de Boulogne, who first described it in 1862 (Figure 12.14).

Four Major Theories of Emotion: James–Lange, Cannon–Bard, Facial-Feedback, and Schachter's Two-Factor

Objective 12.7: Compare and contrast the four major theories of emotion.

Researchers generally agree on the three components of emotion (physiological, cognitive, and behavioral). There is less agreement on *how* we become emotional (Kalat & Shiota, 2012). The four major theories are the James–Lange, Cannon–Bard,

TEST YOURSELF

(a)   (b)

Figure 12.14 Duchenne smile To most people, the smile on the left looks more sincere than the one on the right. Do you know why?

Answer: (a) In a false, social smile, our voluntary cheek muscles are pulled back, but our eyes are unsmiling. (b) Smiles of real pleasure, on the other hand, use the muscles not only around the cheeks but also around the eyes. According to Duchenne de Boulogne, the eye muscle "does not obey the will" and "is put in play only by the sweet emotions of the soul" (cited in Goode, Schrof, & Burke, 1991, p. 56). Studies find that people who show a Duchenne, or real, smile and laughter elicit more positive responses from strangers and enjoy better interpersonal relationships and personal adjustment (Keltner, Kring, & Bonanno, 1999; Prkachin & Silverman, 2002).

facial-feedback, and Schachter's two-factor. Each of these theories emphasizes different sequences or aspects of the three elements (cognitions, arousal, and expression) (Step-by-Step Diagram 12.1).

James–Lange

James–Lange Theory Subjective experience of emotion results from physiological changes, rather than being their cause ("I feel sad because I'm crying"); in this view, each emotion is physiologically distinct

According to ideas originated by psychologist William James and later expanded by physiologist Carl Lange, our subjective experience of emotion results from physiological changes, rather than being their cause. Contrary to popular opinion, which says we cry because we're sad, James wrote: "We feel sorry because we cry, angry because we strike, afraid because we tremble" (James, 1890).

Why would we tremble unless we first felt afraid? According to the **James–Lange theory**, our bodily response of trembling is a reaction to a specific stimulus such as seeing a large bear in the wilderness. In other words, we perceive an event, our bodies react, and then we interpret the bodily changes as a specific emotion (Step-by-Step Diagram 12.1a). It is our awareness of our autonomic nervous system (ANS) arousal (palpitating heart, sinking stomach, flushed cheeks), our actions (running, yelling), and changes in our facial expression (crying, smiling, frowning) that produce our subjective experience of emotion. In short, arousal and expression cause emotion. According to the James–Lange theory, if there is no arousal or expression, there is no emotion.

Cannon–Bard

Cannon–Bard Theory Emotions and physiological changes occur simultaneously ("I'm crying and feeling sad at the same time"); in this view, all emotions are physiologically similar

As you've just seen, the James–Lange theory suggests emotions result from physiological changes and that each emotion is distinct. In contrast, the **Cannon–Bard theory** hold that emotions and physiological changes occur simultaneously and all emotions are physiologically similar.

Walter Cannon (1927) and Philip Bard (1934) proposed that after perception of the emotion-provoking stimulus (seeing a bear), a small part of the brain, called the thalamus, sends messages to the cortex and ANS. These messages then lead to sympathetic arousal, behavioral reactions, and *simultaneous* emotions (Step-by-Step Diagram 12.1b). The major point of the Cannon–Bard theory is that arousal and emotions occur at the *same* time—one does not cause the other.

Because all emotions are physiologically similar, arousal is not a necessary or even a major factor in emotion. Cannon supported this position with several experiments in which nonhuman animals were surgically prevented from experiencing physiological arousal. Yet these surgically altered animals still showed observable behaviors (like growling and defensive postures) that might be labeled emotional reactions (Cannon, Lewis, & Britton, 1927). Similarly, people with upper and lower spinal cord injuries differ in the amount of autonomic arousal they experience below the injury, yet they experience no difference in emotional awareness or emotional intensity (Chwalisz et al., 1988; Deady et al., 2010).

Facial-Feedback

Facial-Feedback Hypothesis Movements of the facial muscles produce and/or intensify our subjective experience of emotion

The third major explanation of emotion—the **facial-feedback hypothesis**—suggests that movements of the facial muscles produce and/or intensify our subjective experience of emotion. More specifically, sensory input (seeing a bear) is first routed to subcortical areas of the brain that activate facial movements. These facial changes then initiate and intensify emotions (Adelmann & Zajonc, 1989; Ceschi & Scherer, 2001; Dimberg & Söderkvist, 2011; Neal & Chartrand, 2011). In short, our facial expressions produce or intensify our emotions.

How do we know if we're happy, sad, or angry? Contractions of our various facial muscles send differing messages to our brain, which we then interpret as specific emotions. Like James, these researchers suggest that we don't smile because we are happy. We feel happy because we smile (Step-by-Step Diagram 12.1c).

Step-by-StepDiagram12.1

STOP This Step by Step diagram contains essential information NOT found elsewhere in the text, which is likely to appear on quizzes and exams. Be sure to study it CAREFULLY!

Four Theories of Emotion

TEST YOURSELF

Can you identify which of the four major theories of emotion best explains this bird's behavior?

"I don't sing because I am happy. I am happy because I sing."

Answer: The James–Lange theory

Emotional Stiumlus

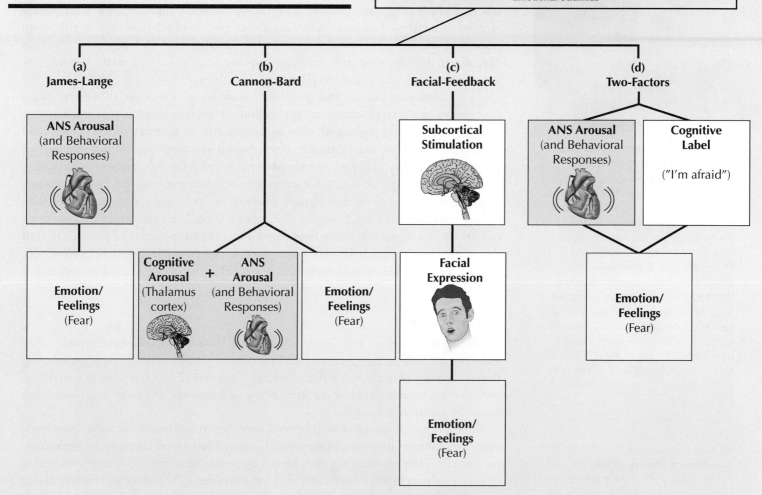

(a) James-Lange

ANS Arousal (and Behavioral Responses)

Emotion/ Feelings (Fear)

(b) Cannon-Bard

Cognitive Arousal (Thalamus cortex) **+** **ANS Arousal** (and Behavioral Responses)

Emotion/ Feelings (Fear)

(c) Facial-Feedback

Subcortical Stimulation

Facial Expression

Emotion/ Feelings (Fear)

(d) Two-Factors

ANS Arousal (and Behavioral Responses)

Cognitive Label ("I'm afraid")

Emotion/ Feelings (Fear)

TEST YOURSELF

Testing the Facial-Feedback Hypothesis

Hold a pen or pencil between your teeth with your mouth closed, as shown in the left photo. Spend about 15 to 30 seconds in this position. How do you feel? Now hold the pencil between your teeth with your mouth open and your teeth showing, as in the right photo. During the next 15 to 30 seconds, pay attention to your feelings. According to research, pleasant feelings are more likely when teeth are showing. Can you explain why?

Source: Adapted from Strack, Martin, & Stepper, 1988.

▲ **Figure 12.15 Botox and the facial-feedback hypothesis**
Botox injections are a popular cosmetic procedure, which reduces frown lines by temporarily paralyzing muscles in the forehead. Although these injections do make people look younger, they're expensive—financially and maybe emotionally. Researchers have discovered that blocking the "frown" muscles appears to short-circuit our ability to feel and interpret certain emotions—particularly negative ones (Davis et al., 2010; Havas et al., 2010). Can you see how this research with Botox supports the facial-feedback hypothesis?

Two-Factor Theory Schachter and Singer's theory that emotion depends on two factors—physiological arousal and cognitive labeling of that arousal

As you can see in Figure 12.15, research on reactions to Botox injections lends interesting credence to the *facial-feedback hypothesis*. Support also comes from Darwin's (1872) evolutionary theory, which proposed that freely expressing an emotion intensifies it.

Interestingly, research suggests that even watching another's facial expressions causes an automatic, *reciprocal* change in our own facial muscles (Dimberg & Thunberg, 1998). When people are exposed to pictures of angry faces, for example, the eyebrow muscles involved in frowning are activated. In contrast, the smile muscles show a significant increase in activity when participants are shown photos of a happy face. In follow-up research using the *subliminal perception* techniques discussed in Chapter 4, scientists have shown that this automatic, matching response occurs even *without* the participant's attention or conscious awareness (Dimberg, Thunberg, & Elmehed, 2000).

This automatic, innate, and generally unconscious imitation of others' facial expressions has several important applications. Have you ever felt depressed after listening to a friend's problems? Your unconscious facial mimicry of the person's sad expression may have led to similar physiological reactions and similar feelings of sadness. This theory may also provide personal insights for therapists who constantly work with depressed clients and for actors who simulate emotions for their livelihood. In addition, studies show that "happy workers are generally more productive than unhappy workers" (Hosie, Sevastos, & Cooper, 2006). Does this mean that unhappy coworkers or a constantly angry boss might affect the happiness (and productivity) of the general workforce? If Darwin was right that expressing an emotion intensifies it, and if watching others' emotions produces a matching response, should we reconsider traditional advice encouraging us to "express our anger"?

Two-Factors

According to Schachter and Singer's **two-factor theory**, our subjective experience of emotion depends on two factors: (1) physiological arousal and (2) cognitive labeling (interpretation) of that arousal (Step-by-Step Diagram 12.1d). If we cry at a wedding, for example, we interpret our emotion as joy or happiness. If we cry at a funeral, we label our emotion as sadness.

Schachter and Singer agree with James–Lange that arousal causes our subjective experience of an emotion. But they also agree with Cannon–Bard that all emotions are physiologically similar. They reconcile the two theories by proposing that we look to *external* rather than *internal* cues to differentiate and label our emotions. In Schachter and Singer's classic study (1962), participants were given shots of epinephrine and told it was a type of vitamin. Their subsequent arousal and labeling were then investigated (Step-by-Step Diagram 12.2).

Step-by-StepDiagram12.2

Schachter and Singer's Two-Factor Theory

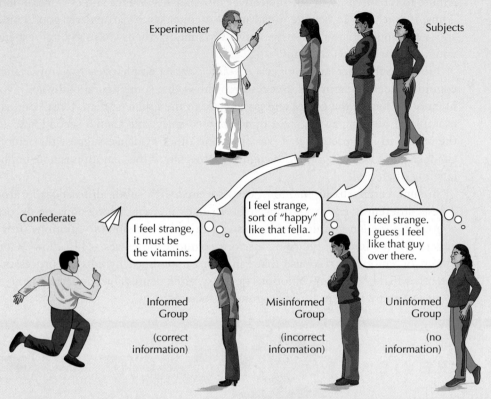

Experimenter   Subjects

Confederate

I feel strange, it must be the vitamins.

I feel strange, sort of "happy" like that fella.

I feel strange. I guess I feel like that guy over there.

Informed Group

(correct information)

Misinformed Group

(incorrect information)

Uninformed Group

(no information)

Step 1
In Schachter and Singer's classic study (1962), participants were given shots of epinephrine and told it was a type of vitamin. One group of participants was correctly informed about the expected effects (hand tremors, excitement, and heart palpitations). A second group was misinformed and told to expect itching, numbness, and a headache. A third group was told nothing about the possible effects.

Step 2
Following the injection, each participant was placed in a room with a confederate (a "stooge" who was part of the experiment but who pretended to be a fellow volunteer) who acted either happy or unhappy.

Step 3
The results showed that participants who lacked an appropriate cognitive label for their emotional arousal (the misinformed and uninformed groups) tended to look to the situation for an explanation. Thus, those placed with a happy confederate became happy, whereas those with an unhappy confederate became unhappy. Participants in the correctly informed group knew their physiological arousal was the result of the shot, so their emotions were generally unaffected by the confederate.

Evaluating Theories of Emotion

Which theory is correct? As you may imagine, each theory has its limits. For example, the *James–Lange theory* fails to acknowledge that physiological arousal can occur without emotional experience (e.g., when we exercise). This theory also requires a distinctly different pattern of arousal for each emotion. Otherwise, how do we know whether we are sad, happy, or mad? Positron emission tomography (PET) scans of the brain do show subtle differences and overall physical arousal with basic emotions, such as happiness, fear, and anger (Levenson, 1992, 2007; Werner et al., 2007). But most people are not aware of these slight variations. Thus, there must be other explanations for how we experience emotion.

The *Cannon–Bard theory* (that arousal and emotions occur simultaneously and that all emotions are physiologically similar) has received some experimental support. Recall from our earlier discussion that victims of spinal cord damage still experience emotions—often more intensely than before their injuries. Instead of the thalamus, however, other research shows that it is the limbic system, hypothalamus,

441

and prefrontal cortex that are activated in emotional experience (Boll et al., 2011; LeDoux, 2007; Sato, Kochiyama, & Yoshikawa, 2011; Somerville, Fani, & McClure-Tone, 2011).

As mentioned earlier, research on the *facial-feedback hypothesis* has found a distinctive physiological response for basic emotions such as fear, sadness, and anger—thus partially confirming James–Lange's initial position. Facial feedback does seem to contribute to the intensity of our subjective emotional experience and our overall moods. Thus, if you want to change a bad mood or intensify a particularly good emotion, adopt the appropriate facial expression. Try smiling when you're sad and expanding your smiles when you're happy.

Finally, Schachter and Singer's *two-factor theory* emphasizes the importance of cognitive labels in emotions. But research shows that some neural pathways involved in emotion bypass the cortex and go directly to the limbic system. Recall our earlier example of jumping at the sight of a supposed snake and then a second later using the cortex to interpret what it was. This and other evidence suggest that emotions can take place without conscious cognitive processes. Thus, emotion is not simply the labeling of arousal.

In sum, certain basic emotions are associated with subtle differences in arousal. These differences can be produced by changes in facial expressions or by organs controlling the autonomic nervous system. In addition, "simple" emotions (fear and anger) do not initially require conscious cognitive processes. This allows a quick, automatic emotional response that can later be modified by cortical processes. On the other hand, "complex" emotions (jealousy, grief, depression, embarrassment, love) seem to require more extensive cognitive processes.

 **CHECK & REVIEW**  **STOP** *Before going on, be sure to complete this Check & Review. It is an invaluable study tool!*

Components and Theories of Emotion

Part A: Retrieval Practice

1. Without looking at the book, spend 10 minutes writing a free-form essay recalling all you can remember from the previous section.

2. Now, reread the previous section, and once again spend 10 minutes writing a free-form essay on the SAME material.

Part B: Practice Quiz

1. Identify the following examples with the appropriate emotional component: (a) biological; (b) cognitive; (c) behavioral
   ___i.   Increased heart rate
   ___ii. Crying during a sad movie
   ___iii. Believing crying is inappropriate for men
   ___iv. Shouting during a soccer match

2. When people are emotionally aroused, the _____ branch of the _____ nervous system works to increase heart rate and blood pressure and to activate other crisis responses.

3. In a _____, as shown in this photo, the cheek muscles are pulled back and the muscles around the eyes contract.

4. We see a bear in the woods, our hearts race as we begin to run, and then we experience fear. This is best explained by _____.
   (a) the James–Lange theory;
   (b) the Cannon–Bard theory;
   (c) the facial-feedback hypothesis;
   (d) the two-factor theory

5. According to the _____, physiological arousal must be labeled or interpreted for an emotional experience to occur.
   (a) Cannon–Bard theory
   (b) James–Lange theory
   (c) facial-feedback hypothesis
   (d) two-factor theory

6. The Cannon–Bard theory of emotion suggests that physiological changes and our subjective experience of emotions occur _____.

7. According to the _____, we look to external rather than internal cues to understand emotions.
   a. Cannon–Bard theory
   b. James–Lange theory
   c. facial feedback hypothesis
   d. two-factor theory

Check your answers in Appendix B.

Critical Thinking about Motivation and Emotion

As you recall from Chapter 1, critical thinking is a core part of psychological science and a major goal of this text. In this section, we will use our critical thinking skills to explore four special (and sometimes controversial) topics in motivation and emotion—*extrinsic versus intrinsic motivation, the polygraph and lie detection, emotional intelligence, culture, evolution,* and *emotion.*

Vincent van Gogh only sold one painting during his entire lifetime, yet he was one of the most prolific nineteenth-century artists. How would you explain his motivation?

Answer: Van Gogh obviously painted for personal satisfaction or intrinsic motivation.

Extrinsic versus Intrinsic Motivation: What's Best?

Objective 12.8: Define extrinsic and intrinsic motivation, and describe how they affect motivation

Should parents reward children for getting good grades? If someone paid you to play video games, would your enjoyment decrease? Many psychologists are concerned about the widespread practice of giving external, *extrinsic* rewards to motivate behavior (e.g., Anderman & Dawson, 2011; Deci & Moller, 2005; Gunderman & Kamer, 2011). They're worried that providing extrinsic rewards will seriously affect the individual's personal, *intrinsic* motivation. **Extrinsic motivation** stems from external rewards or avoidance of punishment and is learned through interaction with the environment. In contrast, **intrinsic motivation** comes from within the individual. The person engages in an activity for its own sake or for internal satisfaction, with no ulterior purpose or need for an external reward (Concept Organizer 12.2).

Extrinsic Motivation Motivation based on external rewards or threats of punishment

Intrinsic Motivation Motivation resulting from internal, personal satisfaction from a task or activity

Polygraph and Lie Detection: Does It Work?

Objective 12.9: Discuss polygraph testing and its effectiveness in lie detection

If you suspected your friend of lying or your significant other of having an affair, would it help convince you if they took a polygraph test? Many people believe the **polygraph** can accurately detect when someone is lying. But can it? The polygraph is based on the theory that when people lie, they feel guilty and anxious. These feelings are then supposedly detected by the polygraph machine (Concept Organizer 12.3).

Polygraph Instrument that measures sympathetic arousal (heart rate, respiration rate, blood pressure, and skin conductivity) to detect emotional arousal, which in turn supposedly reflects lying versus truthfulness

Emotional Intelligence (EI): Are You "Emotionally Smart"?

Objective 12.10: What is emotional intelligence (EI), and why is it controversial?

You've heard of IQ, the intelligence quotient, but what do you know about EI—emotional intelligence? According to Daniel Goleman (1995, 2000, 2008), **emotional intelligence (EI)** involves knowing and managing one's emotions, empathizing with others, and maintaining satisfying relationships. In other words, an emotionally intelligent person successfully combines the three components of emotions (cognitive, physiological, and behavioral).

Emotional Intelligence (EI) Goleman's term for the ability to know and manage one's emotions, empathize with others, and maintain satisfying relationships

ConceptOrganizer 12.2

Extrinsic versus Intrinsic Rewards

Have you ever noticed that for all the money and glory they receive, professional athletes often don't look like they're enjoying themselves very much? What's the problem? Why don't they appreciate how lucky they are to be able to make a living by playing games?

When we perform a task for no ulterior purpose, we use internal, personal reasons ("I like it"; "It's fun"). But when extrinsic rewards are added, the explanation shifts to external, impersonal reasons ("I did it for the money"; "I did it to please my parents"). This shift generally decreases enjoyment and hampers performance. This is as true for professional athletes as it is for anyone else.

One of the earliest experiments to demonstrate this effect was conducted with pre-school children who liked to draw (Lepper, Greene, & Nisbett, 1973). As shown in the figure below, the researchers found that children who were given paper and markers and promised a reward for their drawings were subsequently less interested in drawing than children who were not given a reward or who were given an unexpected reward when they were done. Likewise, for professional athletes, what is a fun diversion for most people can easily become "just a job."

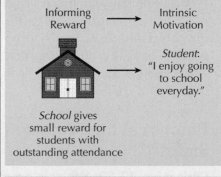

Percentage of free time spent drawing

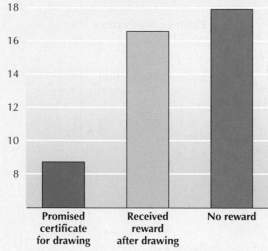

| Promised certificate for drawing | Received reward after drawing | No reward |

Not all extrinsic motivation is bad, however (Banko, 2008; Konheim-Kalkstein & van den Broek, 2008; Moneta & Siu, 2002). Extrinsic rewards are motivating if they are used to inform a person of superior performance or as a special "no strings attached" treat (Deci, 1995). In fact, they may intensify the desire to do well again. Thus, getting a raise or a gold medal can inform us and provide valuable feedback about our performance, which may increase enjoyment. But if rewards are used to control—for example, when parents give children money or privileges for achieving good grades—they inhibit intrinsic motivation (Eisenberger & Armeli, 1997; Eisenberger & Rhoades, 2002; Houlfort, 2006).

Extrinsic Motivation

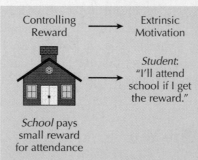

Controlling Reward → Extrinsic Motivation

Student: "I'll attend school if I get the reward."

School pays small reward for attendance

External Pressure → Extrinsic Motivation

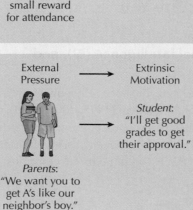

Student: "I'll get good grades to get their approval."

Parents: "We want you to get A's like our neighbor's boy."

Intrinsic Motivation

Informing Reward → Intrinsic Motivation

Student: "I enjoy going to school everyday."

School gives small reward for students with outstanding attendance

"No Strings" Treat → Intrinsic Motivation

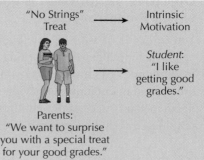

Student: "I like getting good grades."

Parents: "We want to surprise you with a special treat for your good grades."

ConceptOrganizer 12.3

Polygraph Testing

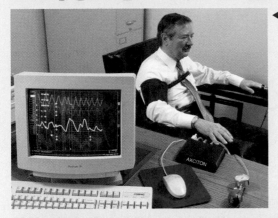

(a) During a standard polygraph test, a band around the person's chest measures breathing rate, a cuff monitors blood preasure, and finger electrodes measure sweating, or galvanic skin response (GSR).

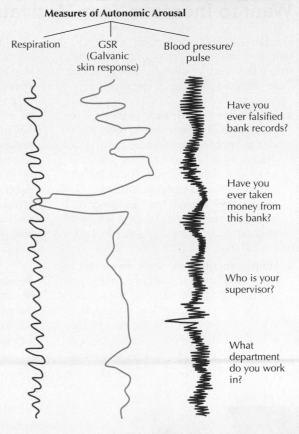

Measures of Autonomic Arousal

Respiration | GSR (Galvanic skin response) | Blood pressure/ pulse

Have you ever falsified bank records?

Have you ever taken money from this bank?

Who is your supervisor?

What department do you work in?

(b) Note how the GSR rises sharply in response to the question, "Have you ever taken money from this bank?"

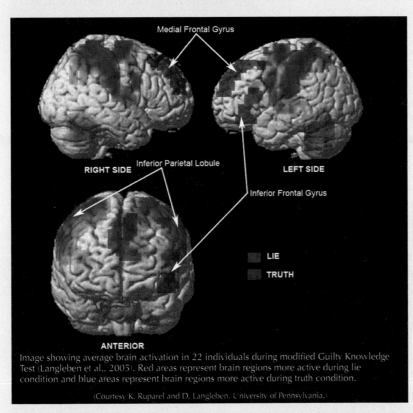

Medial Frontal Gyrus

RIGHT SIDE

Inferior Parietal Lobule

LEFT SIDE

Inferior Frontal Gyrus

LIE

TRUTH

ANTERIOR

Image showing average brain activation in 22 individuals during modified Guilty Knowledge Test (Langleben et al., 2005). Red areas represent brain regions more active during lie condition and blue areas represent brain regions more active during truth condition.

(Courtesy K. Ruparel and D. Langleben, University of Pennsylvania.)

(c) Three fMRI images highlighting areas of the cortex supposedly most involved in lying versus truth telling.

Some people say the innocent have nothing to fear from a polygraph test. However, research suggests otherwise (DeClue, 2003; Handler et al., 2009; Iacono, 2008). In fact, although proponents claim that polygraph tests are 90 percent accurate or better, actual tests show error rates ranging between 25 and 75 percent.

Traditional polygraph tests measure sympathetic and parasympathetic nervous system responses (a and b) (Grubin, 2010). The problem is that lying is only loosely related to anxiety and guilt. Some people become nervous even when telling the truth, whereas others remain calm when deliberately lying. A polygraph cannot tell which emotion is being felt (nervousness, excitement, sexual arousal etc.) or whether a response is due to emotional arousal or something else. One study found that people could affect the outcome of a polygraph by about 50 percent simply by pressing their toes against the floor or biting their tongues (Honts & Kircher, 1994).

For these reasons, most judges and scientists have serious reservations about using polygraphs as lie detectors. Scientific controversy and public concern led the U.S. Congress to pass a bill that severely restricts the use of polygraphs in the courts, in government, and in private industry. In our post–9/11 world, you can see why tens of millions to hundreds of millions of dollars have been spent on new and improved lie-detection techniques. Perhaps the most promising new technique is the use of brain scans like the functional magnetic resonance imaging (fMRI) (c).

Unfortunately, each of these new lie-detection techniques has serious shortcomings and unique problems. Researchers have questioned their reliability and validity, while civil libertarians and judicial scholars question their ethics and legalities.

▶ TRY THIS YOURSELF ▶

Want to Increase Your Motivation?

Intrinsic–extrinsic motivation has important implications for raising children, running a business, or even studying this text. Consider the following guidelines:

1. **Emphasize intrinsic reasons for behaviors.** Rather than thinking about all the people you'll impress with good grades or all the great jobs you'll get when you finish college, focus instead on personally satisfying, intrinsic reasons. Think about how exciting it is to learn new things or the value of becoming an educated person and a critical thinker.

2. **Limit concrete extrinsic rewards.** In general, it is almost always better to use the least possible extrinsic reward and for the shortest possible time period. When children are first learning to play a musical instrument, it may help to provide small rewards until they gain a certain level of mastery. But once a child is working happily or practicing for the sheer joy of it, it is best to leave him or her alone. Similarly, if you're trying to increase your study time, begin by rewarding yourself for every significant improvement. But don't reward yourself when you're handling a difficult assignment easily. Save rewards for when you need them. Keep in mind, that we're speaking primarily of concrete extrinsic rewards. Praise and positive feedback are generally safe to use and often increase intrinsic motivation (Carton, 1996; Henderlong & Lepper, 2002).

3. **Reward competency.** Use extrinsic rewards to provide feedback for competency or outstanding performance—not for simply engaging in the behavior. Schools can enhance intrinsic motivation by giving medals or privileges to students with no absences, rather than giving money for simple attendance. Similarly, you should reward yourself with a movie or a call to a friend *after* you've studied hard for your scheduled time period or done particularly well on an exam. Don't reward yourself for half-hearted attempts.

4. **Just do it!** We've mentioned many times the value of distributed practice. You really can't "cram" when it comes to workouts, brushing your teeth, losing and maintaining weight, or keeping up with employer demands. You "simply" have to get up and get started. Don't think! Just do! The first few minutes of exercise are always the hardest, and the same is true for almost every aspect of life. Getup, get started, power through! You'll thank yourself later.

Developing emotional intelligence Adults can help children identify and understand their own emotions as well as how to change them.

Goleman suggests that having a high EI explains why people of modest IQ are often more successful than people with much higher IQ scores. He believes that traditional measures of human intelligence ignore a crucial range of abilities that characterize people who excel in real life: self-awareness, impulse control, persistence, zeal and self-motivation, empathy, and social deftness.

Goleman also proposes that many societal problems, such as domestic abuse and youth violence, can be attributed to a low EI. Therefore, EI should be fostered in everyone. Proponents have suggested that law schools and other professional training programs should make EI training a curriculum staple. In addition, advocates suggest parents and educators can help children develop EI by encouraging them to identify their emotions and understand how these feelings can be changed and how they are connected to their actions (Alegre, 2011; Brackett, Rivers, & Salovey, 2011; Di Fabio & Kenny, 2011; van Heck & den Oudsten, 2008). Schools that have instituted Goleman's ideas say students show not just "more positive attitudes about ways to get along with people. They also show improvements in critical thinking skills" (Mitchell, Sachs, & Tu, 1997, p. 62).

Critics argue that the components of EI are difficult to identify and measure (Fiori & Antonakis, 2011; Mayer, Roberts, & Barsade, 2008; Walter, Cole, & Humphrey, 2011). Others fear that a handy term like EI invites misuse. Paul McHugh, director of psychiatry at Johns Hopkins University, suggests that Goleman is "presuming that someone has the key to the right emotions to be taught to children. We don't even know the right emotions to be taught to adults" (cited in Gibbs, 1995, p. 68).

EI is a controversial concept, but most researchers are pleased that the subject of emotion is being taken seriously. Further research will increase our understanding of emotion and perhaps even reveal the ultimate value of Goleman's theory.

Psychology Engages

CASE STUDY / PERSONAL STORY

Abraham Lincoln's Emotional Intelligence
(Adapted from Goodwin, 2005)

Objective 12.11: List the five key traits of emotional intelligence (EI) shown by Abraham Lincoln.

How does a self-taught farm boy of humble origins grow up to become president of the United States? General William T. Sherman provided one answer: "Of all the men I ever met, he seemed to possess more of the elements of greatness, combined with goodness, than any other" ("Life behind the legend," 2005, p. 44).

Modern psychologists might call these same elements of greatness and goodness high emotional intelligence. Consider the following:

Empathy Known for his great ability to empathize and put himself in the place of others, Lincoln refused to criticize and castigate the Southern slaveowners like other antislavery orators did. Instead, he argued: "They are just what we would be in their situation. If slavery did not now exist amongst them, they would not introduce it. If it did now exist amongst us, we should not instantly give it up" (Goodwin, 2005, p. 49).

Magnanimity Possessing a high-minded, generous spirit, Lincoln refused to bear grudges. Opponent Edwin Stanton called him a "long-armed ape" and deliberately shunned and humiliated him. However, when Lincoln needed a new War Secretary, he noble-mindedly appointed Stanton because he was the best man for this very important position.

Generosity of Spirit Lincoln often took the blame for others, shared credit for successes, and quickly conceded his errors. After General Grant's great battle at Vicksburg, Lincoln wrote, "I now wish to make the personal acknowledgment that you were right, and I was wrong" (Goodwin, 2005, p. 53).

Self-Control Rather than lashing out at others during moments of anger, Lincoln waited until his emotions settled down. He would often write hot letters to others, but would put them aside and seldom send them.

Humor Noted for his dark, depressive moods, Lincoln also possessed a wonderful self-effacing sense of humor and a gift for storytelling. His jokes and stories not only entertained, but they also contained invaluable insights and wisdom. At the end of the Civil War, many debated the fate of the Southern Rebel leaders. Lincoln wished they could "escape the country," but could not say this publicly. Instead, he told General Sherman a story: "A man once had taken the total abstinence pledge. When visiting a friend, he was invited to take a drink, but declined, on the score of his pledge. . . . His friend suggested lemonade . . . and said the lemonade would be more palatable if he were to pour in a little brandy. . . . [The] guest said, if he could do so 'unbeknown' to him, he would not object." Sherman immediately grasped the point. "Mr. Lincoln wanted [Jefferson] Davis to escape, 'unbeknown' to him" (Goodwin, 2005, p. 50).

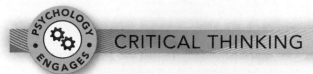

CRITICAL THINKING

The New Psychology of Success

By Thomas Frangicetto (Northampton Community College, Bethlehem, PA)

Michael Jordan—*Growth-minded* athlete par excellence; though often described as having so-called natural talent, Dweck calls him "Perhaps the *hardest working athlete* in the history of sport." To prove the point, recall that Jordan was cut from his high school varsity team. Today, his bio on the NBA website states: "By acclamation, Michael Jordan is the greatest basketball player of all time."

John McEnroe—The poster guy for the *Fixed Mindset*; inflexible and intolerant of failure, the living embodiment of the "winning is everything" attitude." Where did his attitude come from? "My dad pushed me mainly. He seemed to live for my . . . career." Dweck adds: "McEnroe brought his father the success he craved, but McEnroe didn't enjoy a moment of it."

When covering the term **prototype** (p. 285), I always ask students to name the professional athlete who *represents the best example* of the *category* "excellence in professional sports." Nine out of 10 times, Michael Jordan is the first name mentioned, even now, nearly a decade since his retirement.

What is it that launched Jordan above the rest? How was he able to maintain a sense of **hardiness** (p. 108), and take the threat of failure and convert it into a challenge, an opportunity for personal betterment? Researcher Carol Dweck, author of the widely praised, *Mindset: The New Psychology of Success* (2007), believes Jordan reflects the convergence of a *growth mindset* and optimal performance. "I can accept failure," Jordan says, "but I cannot accept not trying." Individuals with a growth mindset believe that potential is more than a promise; it's an opportunity for expanding your abilities. "If anyone has reason to think of himself as special, it's he," Dweck writes. "But . . . Jordan knew how hard he had worked to develop his abilities. He was a person who had struggled and grown, not a person who was inherently better than others." Through

hard work and determination, Michael Jordan just "stretched" himself beyond the competition.

John McEnroe, on the other hand, displays a *fixed mindset*—rigid, arrogant, argumentative, emotionally allergic to failure, uninterested in learning, challenge-avoidant, and locked into a belief system "gifted" to him by parents that demanded perfection in return for their love. But McEnroe's *talent* was so prodigious he was the top tennis player in the world for years. Despite his great gift, McEnroe was sadly unable to enjoy the one thing he could do best. "Many athletes seem to truly love to play their sports," he says, "I don't think I ever felt that way about tennis."

Part A So which mindset do you possess? Rate yourself on how well each of the following items describes you (0 = not at all, 10 = perfect match).

___1. I believe that I can improve my intelligence through studying and education.

___2. I think it is essential for people to let their intrinsic motivation guide what they do with their lives.

___3. I am confident in my ability to learn new things, and I accept setbacks as only temporary, and proof that I am trying, not reflections of my true potential.

___4. I accept that a test or an exam represents an opportunity to find out what I still need to learn, rather than a way to prove how much I don't know.

___5. I am convinced that hard work, persistence, and a strong belief in your ability to change for the better are the most important qualities of successful people.

This is a small sample of an informal survey, but it does highlight the qualities of people with a *growth mindset*. Each item you rated as 7 or higher is a reflection of your own mindset on that topic. Why is that a positive sign? Dweck's 20 years of research provides convincing evidence that the mindsets we adopt can affect the way we lead our lives and help determine whether or not we reach our full potential. Dweck's "take away message" is both simple and profound: *Believe in your ability* to better yourself in ways that matter, *take on challenges* with a fearless willingness to fail, and embrace *the value of hard work and persistence* as the keys to achievement. The quality of your life depends on it.

Part B Critical Thinking Questions

1. Review your answers to the quiz in Part A, and for each item you rated yourself as below 10 select a CTC (see Prologue at front of book), which will help move you closer to a *growth mindset* on that topic.

2. Go to www.youtube.com and enter "Carol Dweck Mindset" in the search box. Watch two or three of the short clips there and assess Dweck's critical thinking ability. Which CTCs does she demonstrate? Does she violate any?

RESEARCH CHALLENGE

Love at First Fright?

Objective 12.12: Why do we sometimes mislabel our emotions?

Suppose you are watching a scary movie with a very attractive date. You notice that your heart is pounding, your palms are sweating, and you are short of breath. Is it love? Or is it fear? As you discovered in this chapter, a wide variety of emotions are accompanied by the same physiological states. Because of this similarity, we frequently misidentify our emotions. How can we experimentally prove this?

To answer this question, Donald Dutton and Arthur Aron (1974) asked an attractive female or male experimenter (confederates) to approach 85 male passersby either on a fear-arousing or on a non-fear-arousing bridge. The female or male experimenter then asked the passerby participants to fill out questionnaires and then gave them a phone number to call if they wanted more information.

Imagine yourself as one of the participants in this experiment. You arrive at the Capilano Canyon suspension bridge in North Vancouver, British Columbia. It is a 5-foot-wide, 450-foot-long wooden bridge attached by cables spanning the Capilano

Canyon. When you walk across the bridge, it tends to tilt, sway, and wobble, and you have to stoop down to hold on to the low railings. If you happen to look down, you see nothing but rapids and exposed rocks in the river 230 feet below.

While standing at the middle of this swaying bridge, the experimenter approaches and asks you to fill out a questionnaire. Would you be attracted to this person? What if this person instead approached you on a firm wooden bridge with only a 10-foot drop to a shallow rivulet? Compared to men on the low, non-fear-arousing bridge, Dutton and Aron found that a large proportion of the men on the fear-arousing bridge not only called the phone number provided by the attractive female researcher, but also revealed a much higher level of sexual imagery in their questionnaires.

At first glance, this may sound strange. Why would men who are in a state of fear be more attracted to a woman than men who are relaxed? According to what is now called **misattribution of arousal**, the men mistakenly attributed some of their arousal to their attraction to the female experimenter.

Although Dutton and Aron conducted this experiment in 1974, dozens of follow-up studies have generally confirmed their original findings. For example, Cindy Meston and Penny Frohlich (2003) conducted a similar experiment with individuals at amusement parks who were either waiting to begin or had just gotten off a roller-coaster ride. Participants were shown a photograph of an averagely attractive person of the opposite sex. They were then asked to rate the individual on attractiveness and dating desirability.

Consistent with Dutton and Aron's earlier findings, ratings were higher among those who were exiting rather than entering

the ride. Interestingly, this effect was only found with participants riding with a non-romantic partner. When romantic couples were riding together, there were no significant differences in ratings of attractiveness or dating desirability.

Can you see how Meston and Frohlich's research illustrates steps 5 and 6 in the scientific method? As mentioned in Chapter 1 (p. 17), experimenters often replicate or extend the work of previous researchers. And, in this case, the differing results between romantic and nonromantic partners help fine-tune the original theory, which may in turn lead to new and better future theories. Both experiments also demonstrate how basic research can sometimes be applied to our everyday lives. In this case, the take-home message is: Be careful of "Love at first fright!"

Student Engagement Exercise

Given the admittedly limited information in the Dutton and Aron (1974) study described above, what is the most likely:

1. *Research method* (experimental, descriptive, correlational, or biological)?

2. If you chose the:
   - *Experimental method*—label the IV, DV, experimental group, and control group.
   - *Descriptive method*—is this a naturalistic observation, survey, or case study?
   - *Correlational method*—is this a positive, negative, or zero correlation?
   - *Biological method*—identify the specific research tool (e.g., brain dissection, CT scan, etc.)

(Answers appear in Appendix B.)

Misattribution of Arousal Physiologically aroused individuals make mistaken inferences about what is causing the arousal

GENDER AND CULTURAL DIVERSITY

Culture, Evolution, and Emotion

Objective 12.13: Discuss culturally universal emotions and differing display rules.

Where do our emotions come from? Are they a product of our evolutionary past? Do they differ from one culture to the next, or are they the same? As you might suspect, researchers have found several answers.

Cultural Similarities All people of all cultures have feelings and emotions, and all must learn to deal with them. But are these emotions the same across all cultures? Given the seemingly vast array of emotions within our own culture, it may surprise you to learn that some researchers believe all our feelings can be condensed into 7 to 10 *culturally universal* emotions. Note the strong similarities among the four lists in Table 12.3.

In addition to all cultures sharing the same basic emotions, some researchers believe that each of these emotions is expressed and recognized in essentially the same way in all cultures. They point to research that finds people from very different cultures displaying remarkably similar facial expressions when experiencing particular emotions (Biehl et al., 1997; Ekman, 1993, 2004; Matsumoto & Juang, 2008). Moreover, whether respondents are from Western or non-Western societies, they can reliably identify at least six basic emotions: happiness, surprise, anger, sadness, fear, and disgust (Berry et al., 2011; Buck, 1984; Matsumoto, 1992, 2000, 2010; Said, Haxby, & Todorov, 2011). In other words, across cultures, a frown is recognized as a sign of displeasure and a smile as a sign of pleasure (Figure 12.16).

The Role of Evolution Charles Darwin first advanced the evolutionary theory of emotion in 1872. In his classic book *The Expression of the Emotions in Man and Animals*, Darwin proposed that expression of emotions evolved in different species as a part of survival and natural selection. For example, fear helps human and nonhuman animals avoid danger, and expressions of anger and aggression are useful when fighting for mates and necessary resources. Modern evolutionary theory further suggests that basic emotions (such as fear and anger) originate in the limbic system. Given that higher brain areas (the cortex) developed later than the subcortical limbic system, evolutionary theory proposes that basic emotions evolved before thought.

Cultural differences in emotional expression Some Middle Eastern men commonly greet one another with a kiss. Can you imagine this same behavior among men in North America, who generally shake hands or pat one another's shoulders?

▲ **Plutchik's wheel of emotions** How do we explain emotions not on this list? Robert Plutchik (1984, 1994, 2000) suggested that primary emotions (inside the circle) combine to form secondary emotions (located outside the circle). Plutchik also found that emotions that lie next to each other are more alike than those that are farther apart.

Table 12.3 THE BASIC HUMAN EMOTIONS

Carroll Izard	Paul Ekman and Wallace Friesen	Silvan Tomkins	Robert Plutchik
Fear	Fear	Fear	Fear
Anger	Anger	Anger	Anger
Disgust	Disgust	Disgust	Disgust
Surprise	Surprise	Surprise	Surprise
Joy	Happiness	Enjoyment	Joy
Shame	—	Shame	—
Contempt	Contempt	Contempt	—
Sadness	Sadness	—	Sadness
Interest	—	Interest	Anticipation
Guilt	—	—	—
—	—	—	Acceptance
—	—	Distress	—

Cross-cultural studies of emotional expression tend to support the innate, evolutionary perspective. The idea of universal facial expressions makes adaptive sense because they signal others about our current emotional state (Ekman & Keltner, 1997). Studies with infants also point to an evolutionary basis for emotions. For example, did you know that infants only a few hours old show distinct expressions of emotions that closely match adult facial expressions? Or that all infants, even those born deaf and blind, show similar facial expressions in similar situations (Field et al., 1982; Gelder et al., 2006). This collective evidence points to a strong biological, evolutionary basis for emotional expression and decoding.

Cultural Differences How do we explain cultural *differences* in emotions? Although we all seem to share reasonably similar facial expressions for some emotions, each culture has its own *display rules* governing how, when, and where to express emotions (Ekman, 1993, 2004; Fok et al., 2008; Koopmann-Holm & Matsumoto, 2011; Matsumoto & Hwang, 2011). For instance, parents pass along their culture's specific display rules by responding angrily to some emotions in their children, by being sympathetic to others, and, on occasion, by simply ignoring them. In this way, children learn which emotions they may freely express and those they are expected to control. In Asian cultures, for instance, children learn to conceal negative emotions with a stoic expression or polite smile (Cheung & Park, 2010; Dresser, 1996). Young males in the Masai culture are similarly expected to conceal their emotions in public, but by appearing stern and stony-faced (Keating, 1994).

Public physical contact is also governed by display rules. North Americans and Asians are generally not touch-oriented. Only the closest family and friends might hug in greeting or farewell. In contrast, Latin Americans and Middle Easterners often embrace and hold hands as a sign of casual friendship (Axtell, 2007).

Figure 12.16 Can you identify these emotions? Most people can reliably identify at least six basic emotions—happiness, surprise, anger, sadness, fear, and disgust. On occasion, our facial expressions don't seem to match our presumed emotions, as is the case in the photo on the right. This woman has just won an important award, yet she looks sad rather than happy.

 **CHECK & REVIEW**  STOP *Before going on, be sure to complete this Check & Review. It is an invaluable study tool!*

Critical Thinking about Motivation and Emotion and Psychology Engages

Part A: Retrieval Practice

1. Without looking at the book, spend 10 minutes writing a free-form essay recalling all you can remember from the previous section.

2. Now, reread the previous section, and once again spend 10 minutes writing a free-form essay on the SAME material.

Part B: Practice Quiz

1. Which of the following would be an example of extrinsic motivation? (a) money; (b) praise; (c) threats of being fired; (d) all of these options

2. An elementary school began paying students $5 for each day they attend school. Overall rates of attendance increased in the first few weeks and then fell below the original starting point. This is because _____. (a) the students felt going to school wasn't worth $5; (b) money is a secondary versus a primary reinforcer; (c) extrinsic rewards decreased the intrinsic value of attending school; (d) the student expectancies changed to fit the situation

3. The polygraph, or lie detector, measures primarily the _____ component of emotions. (a) physiological; (b) articulatory; (c) cognitive; (d) subjective

4. Knowing and managing one's emotions, empathizing with others, and maintaining satisfying relationships are the key factors in _____. (a) self-actualization; (b) emotional intelligence; (c) emotion metacognition; (d) empathic IQ

Check your answers in Appendix B.

WileyPLUS presents an on-line version of this textbook along with a wealth of study resources including quizzes, practice tests, flash cards, videos, animations and other activities designed to improve your mastery of the content. Working in conjunction with these study tools, *the Psychology in Action* WileyPLUS course features Professor Karen Huffman, author of this textbook, explaining and expanding upon some of the most challenging concepts in psychology. Here is a sample of the tutorial videos available for this chapter:

- Understanding the role of hormones in hunger
- Virtual Field Trip to a weight loss center to learn about the benefits and risks of surgical interventions for obesity.
- How to find and keep your motivation
- What is emotional intelligence and how can we improve our EI?
- An animated, interactive exploration of how the polygraph works

Key Terms

To assess your understanding of the **Key Terms** in Chapter 12, write a definition for each (in your own words), and then compare your definitions with those in the text.

motivation (p. 422)
emotion (p. 422)

Theories of Motivation
instinct theory (p. 423)
instinct (p. 423)
drive-reduction theory (p. 423)
homeostasis (p. 424)
optimal-arousal theory
　(p. 424)
incentive theory (p. 426)
hierarchy of needs (p. 427)

Motivation and Behavior
anorexia nervosa (p. 431)
bulimia nervosa (p. 431)
achievement motivation (p. 433)

Components and Theories of Emotion
amygdala (p. 435)
James–Lange theory (p. 438)
Cannon–Bard theory (p. 438)
facial-feedback hypothesis (p. 438)
two-factor theory (p. 440)

Critical Thinking about Motivation and Emotion
extrinsic motivation (p. 443)
intrinsic motivation (p. 443)
polygraph (p. 443)
emotional intelligence (EI) (p. 443)

Psychology Engages
misattribution of arousal (p. 449)

Chapter Summary

Theories of Motivation

Objective 12.1: Define motivation and emotion, and explain why they're studied together.
Motivation refers to the set of factors that activate, direct, and maintain behavior, usually toward some goal. **Emotion**, on the other hand, refers to a subjective feeling that includes arousal (heart pounding), cognitions (thoughts, values, expectations), and expressive behaviors (smiles, frowns, running). We

study them together because they are inseparable.

Objective 12.2: Describe the six major theories of motivation.
The six theories of motivation can be grouped into three general categories: *biological, psychological,* and *biopsychosocial*. Among the biological approaches, **instinct theories** emphasize inborn, genetic components in motivation. **Drive-reduction theory** suggests that

internal tensions (produced by the body's demand for **homeostasis**) "push" the organism toward satisfying basic needs. And the **optimal-arousal theory** proposes that organisms seek an optimal level of arousal that maximizes their performance.

According to the two psychological approaches, **incentive theory** emphasizes the "pull" of external environmental stimuli, whereas *cognitive theory* focuses on the importance of attributions and expectations.

One example of the biopsychosocial approach is Maslow's **hierarchy of needs** (or motives). This theory suggests that basic survival needs must be satisfied before a person can attempt to satisfy higher needs and eventually become self-actualized.

Motivation and Behavior

Objective 12.3: Discuss the major biopsychosocial factors that influence hunger and eating.
Several biological, internal factors, including structures in the brain, numerous chemicals, and messages from the stomach and intestines, all seem to play important roles in hunger and eating. But psychosocial factors, such as stimulus cues, cultural conditioning, and willpower also play a role.

Objective 12.4: Describe the three key eating disorders—obesity, anorexia, and bulimia.
Obesity (being 15 percent or more above the ideal for one's height and age) seems to result from biological factors, such as the individual's genetic inheritance, lifestyle factors, and numerous psychological factors. **Anorexia nervosa** (extreme weight loss due to self-imposed starvation) and **bulimia nervosa** (excessive consumption of food followed by purging) are both related to an intense fear of obesity.

Objective 12.5: Define achievement motivation, and list the characteristics of high achievers.
Achievement motivation refers to the desire to excel, especially in competition with others. People with high achievement needs prefer moderately difficult tasks and clear goals with competent feedback. They also tend to be more competitive, responsible, persistent, and accomplished.

Components and Theories of Emotion

Objective 12.6: Describe the three key components of emotions.
All emotions have three basic components: *biological arousal* (e.g., heart pounding), *cognitive* (thoughts, values, and expectations), and *behavioral expressions* (e.g., smiles, frowns, running). Studies of the biological component find that most emotions involve a general, nonspecific arousal of the nervous system. The cognitive component explains how thoughts, values, and expectations help determine the type and intensity of emotional responses. The behavioral component focuses on how we express our emotions, including facial expressions.

Objective 12.7: Compare and contrast the four major theories of emotion.
Four major theories explain what causes emotion. According to the **James–Lange theory**, emotions follow from physiological changes. The **Cannon–Bard theory** suggests that emotions and physiological changes occur simultaneously. According to the **facial-feedback hypothesis**, facial movements produce and/or intensify emotions. **The two-factor theory** suggests that emotions depend on two factors—physiological arousal and a cognitive labeling of that arousal.

Critical Thinking About Motivation and Emotion

Objective 12.8: Define extrinsic and intrinsic motivation, and describe how they affect motivation.
Extrinsic motivation stems from external rewards or threats of punishment. **Intrinsic motivation** comes from personal enjoyment of a task or activity. Research shows that extrinsic rewards can lower interest and motivation if they are not based on competency.

Objective 12.9: Discuss polygraph testing and its effectiveness in lie detection.
The **polygraph** machine measures changes in sympathetic arousal (increased heart rate, blood pressure, and so on). But research shows it is a poor "lie detector" because it cannot reliably identify whether a response is due to emotional arousal or something else, such as physical exercise, drugs, tense muscles, or even previous experience with polygraph tests.

Objective 12.10: What is emotional intelligence (EI), and why is it controversial?
Emotional intelligence (EI) involves knowing and managing one's emotions, empathizing with others, and maintaining satisfying relationships. Critics argue that the components of EI are difficult to identify and measure, and fear that a handy term like EI invites misuse.

Psychology Engages

Objective 12.11: List the five key traits of emotional intelligence (EI) shown by Abraham Lincoln.
As president, Lincoln demonstrated empathy, magnanimity, generosity of spirit, self-control, and humor.

Objective 12.12: Why do we sometimes mislabel our emotions?
Different emotions produce similar feelings of arousal, which leads to mistaken inferences about these emotions and the source of their arousal.

Objective 12.13: Discuss culturally universal emotions and differing display rules.
Studies have identified 7 to 10 basic emotions that may be universal—experienced and expressed in similar ways across almost all cultures. Display rules for emotional expression differ across cultures. Most psychologists believe that emotions result from a complex interplay between evolution and culture.

Chapter Twelve VISUAL SUMMARY

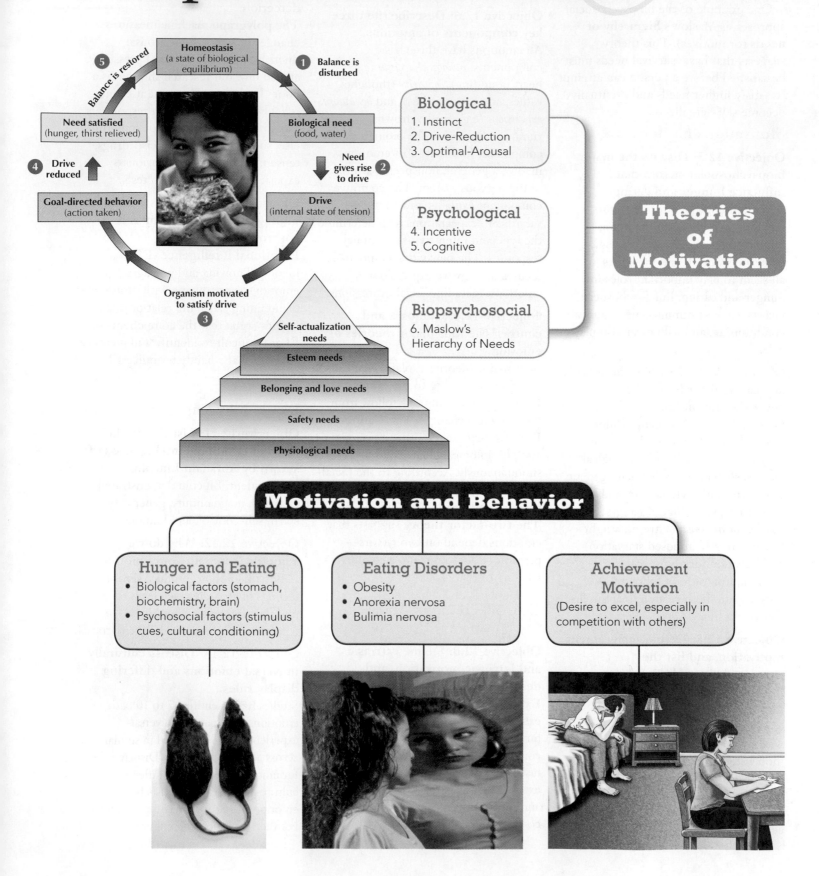

Components and Theories of Emotion

Three Components
- *Biological* (arousal—increased heart rate)
- *Cognitive* (thoughts—expectations)
- *Behavioral* (expressions—smiles, running)

Four Major Theories

James–Lange
Subjective emotion follows physiological changes

Cannon–Bard
Emotions and physiological changes occur simultaneously

Facial-Feedback
Movement of facial muscles produce and/or intensify emotions

Two-Factor
Emotions depend on two factors—physical arousal and cognitive labeling

Critical Thinking about Motivation and Emotion

Extrinsic vs. Intrinsic Motivation
- Extrinsic = external rewards &/or punishments
- Intrinsic = internal, personal satisfaction

Polygraph and Lie Detection
(Polygraph machine measures sympathetic arousal to detect emotional arousal, which in turn supposedly reflects lying)

Emotional Intelligence (EI)
(Knowing & managing emotions, empathizing, & maintaining satisfying relationships)

Psychology Engages

Case Study/Personal Story
Critical Thinking
Research Challenge
Gender & Cultural Diversity

ChapterThirteen

Personality

Consider the following personality description. How well does it describe you?

You have a strong need for other people to like and admire you. You tend to be critical of yourself. Although you have some personality weaknesses, you are generally able to compensate for them. At times, you have serious doubts about whether you have made the right decision or done the right thing.

—ADAPTED FROM ULRICH, STACHNIK, & STAINTON, 1963

Does this sound like you? A high percentage of research participants who read a similar personality description reported that the description was "very accurate"— even after they were informed that it was a phony horoscope (Hyman, 1981). Other research shows that about three-quarters of adults read newspaper horoscopes and that many of them believe that astrological horoscopes were written especially for them (Sugarman et al., 2011; Wyman & Vyse, 2008).

Why are such spurious personality assessments so popular? In part, it's because they seem to tap into our unique selves. However, the traits they supposedly reveal are characteristics that almost everyone shares. Do you know anyone who doesn't "have a strong need for other people to like and admire [them]"? The traits in horoscopes are also generally flattering, or at least neutral.

Unlike the pseudopsychologies offered in newspaper horoscopes and Chinese fortune cookies, the descriptions presented by personality researchers are based on empirical studies. In this chapter, we examine the five most prominent theories and findings in personality research and discuss the techniques that psychologists use to assess personality.

ChapterOutline

WHY STUDY PSYCHOLOGY?

Did you know...

- Early personality theorists identified over 4,500 traits to describe personality?

- Sigmund Freud believed that between the ages of 3 and 6, little boys develop a sexual longing for their mother and jealousy and hatred for their father?

- Carl Rogers believed that children raised with conditional positive regard might later have poorer mental health as adults?

- In the 1800s phrenologists believed personality could be measured by reading the bumps on your skull?

- Some measures of personality require respondents to interpret inkblots?

- We tend to notice and remember events that confirm our expectations and ignore those that are nonconforming?

Objective 13.1: Differentiate personality versus traits, and discuss early trait theories and the five-factor model.

Personality Unique and relatively stable pattern of thoughts, feelings, and actions

What is **personality**? It describes you as a person—how you are different from other people and what patterns of behavior are typical of you. You might qualify as an "extrovert," for example, if you are talkative and outgoing most of the time. Or you may be described as "conscientious" if you are responsible and self-disciplined most of the time. (Keep in mind that personality is not the same as *character*, which refers to your ethics, morals, values, and integrity.)

Trait Theories

Trait Relatively stable personal characteristic that can be used to describe someone

The terms you use to describe other people (and yourself) are called **traits**, relatively stable personal characteristics. Trait theorists are interested in first discovering how people differ (which key traits best describe them). They then want to measure how people differ (the degree of variation in traits within the individual and among individuals).

Identifying and measuring the essential traits that distinguish individual personalities sounds much easier than it actually is. Every individual differs from others in a great number of ways.

Early Trait Theorists: Allport, Cattell, and Eysenck

Much of our lives is spent in trying to understand others and in wishing others understood us better than they do.

GORDON ALLPORT

An early study of dictionary terms found almost 18,000 words that could be used to describe personality. Of these, about 4500 were considered to fit the researchers' definition of personality *traits* (Allport & Odbert, 1936).

Faced with this enormous list of potential traits, Gordon Allport (1937) believed the best way to understand personality was to study an individual and then arrange his or her unique personality traits into a hierarchy. The most important and pervasive traits were listed at the top and the least important at the bottom.

Factor Analysis Statistical procedure for determining the most basic units or factors in a large array of data

Later psychologists reduced the wide array of possible personality traits with a statistical technique called **factor analysis**. Raymond Cattell (1950, 1965, 1990)

(TRY THIS YOURSELF)

Are you a good judge of character and personality?

Which of these three individuals is a vicious serial killer, a murderer who died by lethal injection, or the author of this text?

Answer: Photo 1: Ken Bianchi, rapist and serial killer; photo 2: Karla Faye Tucker, an executed murderer; photo 3: Karen Huffman, author of this text.

condensed the list of traits to 16 source traits (see the Try This Yourself to the right). Hans Eysenck (1967, 1982, 1990) reduced the list even further. He described personality as a relationship among three basic types of traits—*extroversion–introversion*, *neuroticism* (tendency toward insecurity, anxiety, guilt, and moodiness), and *psychoticism* (exhibiting some qualities commonly found among psychotics).

Five-Factor Model (FFM): Five Basic Personality Traits

Factor analysis also was used to develop the most talked about (and most promising) modern trait theory—the **five-factor model (FFM)** (Chamorro-Premuzic, 2011; Costa & McCrae, 2011; Soto et al., 2011). Combining all the previous research findings and the long list of possible personality traits, researchers discovered that several traits came up repeatedly, even when different tests were used. These five major dimensions of personality, often dubbed the "Big Five," are shown in Table 13.1.

Five-Factor Model (FFM) Trait theory of personality that includes openness, conscientiousness, extroversion, agreeableness, and neuroticism

(TRY THIS YOURSELF)

Constructing Your Own Personality Profile

Note how Cattell's 16 source traits exist on a continuum. There are extremes at either end, such as reserved and less intelligent at the far left and outgoing and more intelligent at the far right. Average falls somewhere in the middle.

Take a pen and make a dot on the line (from 1 to 10) that represents your own degree of reservation versus outgoingness. Then make a dot for yourself on the other 15 traits. Now connect the dots. How does your personality profile compare with the profiles of creative artists, airline pilots, and writers?

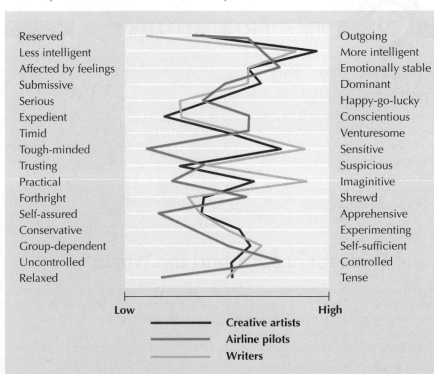

Reserved	Outgoing
Less intelligent	More intelligent
Affected by feelings	Emotionally stable
Submissive	Dominant
Serious	Happy-go-lucky
Expedient	Conscientious
Timid	Venturesome
Tough-minded	Sensitive
Trusting	Suspicious
Practical	Imaginitive
Forthright	Shrewd
Self-assured	Apprehensive
Conservative	Experimenting
Group-dependent	Self-sufficient
Uncontrolled	Controlled
Relaxed	Tense

Low   **High**

—— **Creative artists**
—— **Airline pilots**
—— **Writers**

Table 13.1   FIVE-FACTOR MODEL (FFM)

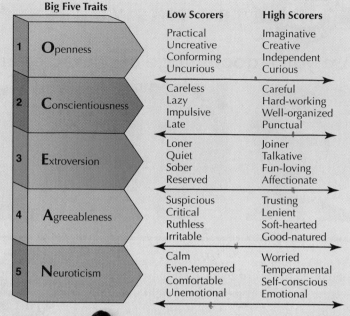

	Big Five Traits	Low Scorers	High Scorers
1	**O**penness	Practical Uncreative Conforming Uncurious	Imaginative Creative Independent Curious
2	**C**onscientiousness	Careless Lazy Impulsive Late	Careful Hard-working Well-organized Punctual
3	**E**xtroversion	Loner Quiet Sober Reserved	Joiner Talkative Fun-loving Affectionate
4	**A**greeableness	Suspicious Critical Ruthless Irritable	Trusting Lenient Soft-hearted Good-natured
5	**N**euroticism	Calm Even-tempered Comfortable Unemotional	Worried Temperamental Self-conscious Emotional

(O) Openness People who rate high in this factor are original, imaginative, curious, open to new ideas, artistic, and interested in cultural pursuits. Low scorers tend to be conventional, down to earth, narrower in their interests, and not artistic. [Interestingly, critical thinkers tend to score higher than others on this factor (Clifford, Boufal, & Kurtz, 2004).

(C) Conscientiousness This factor ranges from responsible, self-disciplined, organized, and achieving at the high end to irresponsible, careless, impulsive, lazy, and undependable at the other. Recent research finds that conscientiousness is the best predictor of longevity (Friedman & Martin, 2011).

(E) Extroversion This factor contrasts people who are sociable, outgoing, talkative, fun loving, and affectionate at the high end with introverted individuals who tend to be withdrawn, quiet, passive, and reserved.

(A) Agreeableness Individuals who score high on this factor are good-natured, warm, gentle, cooperative, trusting, and helpful. Low scorers are irritable, argumentative, ruthless, suspicious, uncooperative, and vindictive.

(N) Neuroticism (or emotional stability) People high on neuroticism are emotionally unstable and prone to insecurity, anxiety, guilt, worry, and moodiness. People at the other end are emotionally stable, calm, even-tempered, easygoing, and relaxed.

 StudyTip

You can easily remember the five factors by noting that the first letters of each of the five-factor dimensions spell the word "ocean."

 TRY THIS YOURSELF

Love and the "Big Five"

Using the figure of the five-factor model on the right of Table 13.1, above, plot your personality profile by placing a dot on each line to indicate your degree of openness, conscientiousness, and so on. Do the same for a current, previous, or prospective love partner. How do your scores compare?

♀ What Women Want in a Mate	♂ What Men Want in a Mate
1. Mutual attraction—love	1. Mutual attraction—love
2. Dependable character	2. Dependable character
3. Emotional stability and maturity	3. Emotional stability and maturity
4. Pleasing disposition	4. Pleasing disposition
5. Education and intelligence	5. Good health
6. Sociability	6. Education and intelligence
7. Good health	7. Sociability
8. Desire for home and children	8. Desire for home and children
9. Ambition and industriousness	9. Refinement, neatness
10. Refinement, neatness	10. Good looks

Mate Preferences Around the World

Now look at the mate preferences listed above. David Buss and his colleagues (1989, 1990, 2003a, 2003b) surveyed more than 10,000 men and women from 37 countries and found a surprising level of agreement in the characteristics that men and women value in a mate. Moreover, most of the Big Five personality traits are found at the top of the list. Both men and women prefer dependability (conscientiousness), emotional stability (low neuroticism), pleasing disposition (agreeableness), and sociability (extroversion) to the alternatives. These findings may reflect an evolutionary advantage for people who are conscientious, extroverted, agreeable, and free of neuroses.

Source: Buss et al., "International Preferences in Selecting Mates." *Journal of Cross-Cultural Psychology,* 21, pp. 5–47, 1990. Sage Publications, Inc.

Evaluating Trait Theories: The Pros and Cons

Objective 13.2: What are the key research findings and criticisms of trait theories?

Early trait theories led to an unmanageably long list of potential personality traits, but as you saw in the "Try This Yourself" exercise on the previous page, David Buss and his colleagues (1989, 1990, 2003) found strong support for the five-factor model (FFM). This may reflect an evolutionary advantage to people who are more conscientious, extroverted, and agreeable—and less neurotic. The evolutionary perspective also is confirmed by cross-cultural studies (Figueredo et al., 2011; McCrae, 2011; Ortiz et al., 2007; Rushton & Irwing, 2011) and comparative studies with dogs, chimpanzees, and other species (Adams, 2011; Gosling, 2008; Mehta & Gosling, 2006; Wahlgren & Lester, 2003).

Taken together, these studies suggest that the five-factor model may be a biologically based human universal, and this model is the first to achieve the major goal of trait theory—to describe and organize personality characteristics using the fewest number of traits. Critics argue, however, that the great variation seen in personalities cannot be accounted for by only five traits.

Trait theories, in general, are subject to three major criticisms:

1. **Lack of explanation** Trait theories are good at *describing* personality. But they all fail to offer *causal* explanations for why people develop specific traits or why personality traits differ across cultures (Chamorro-Premuzic, 2011; Cheung, van de Vivjer, & Leong, 2011; Funder, 2000; Furguson et al., 2011). For example, cross-cultural research has found that people of almost all cultures can be reliably grouped into the FFM. However, trait theories fail to *explain* why people in cultures that are geographically close tend to have similar personalities or why Europeans and Americans tend to be higher in extroversion and openness to experience and lower in agreeableness than people in Asian and African cultures (Allik & McCrae, 2004).

2. **Stability versus change** Trait theorists have documented a high level of personality stability after age 30. But they haven't identified which characteristics last a lifetime and which are most likely to change (Figure 13.1).

3. **Ignoring situational effects** Trait theorists have been criticized for ignoring the importance of situational and environmental effects. One sad example of how the environment influences personality comes from a longitudinal study of the FFM with a group of young children. Psychologists Fred Rogosch and Dante Cicchetti (2004) found that 6-year-old children who were victims of abuse and neglect scored significantly lower on the traits of openness to experience, conscientiousness, and

Figure 13.1 Can personality change? Michael Vick, a famous NFL quarterback with a long history of trouble both on and off the field, pled guilty to felony dog fighting charges in August of 2007, and was sentenced to state prison. Behind the scenes, Vick also had serious financial troubles due to the loss of his NFL salary, endorsement deals, and prior financial mismanagement, which forced him to file for bankruptcy. In 2010, the Philadelphia Eagles gave Vick a second chance. Everyone knew he had the athletic ability to be a good quarterback, but could he be an entirely different player and person? Prior to his jail time, Vick mainly relied almost exclusively on his natural athletic ability. Out of jail, he became a great teammate—the first to the field and the last to leave, and in 2010, he was named NFL's "Comeback Player of the Year" (Wilner, 2011). What do you think? Can people really change their personalities?

agreeableness and higher on the trait of neuroticism than did children who were not maltreated. The children were then reassessed at ages 7, 8, and 9. Unfortunately, the traits persisted. And these maladaptive personality traits create significant liabilities that may trouble these children throughout their lifetime. More research is obviously needed to identify ways to help maltreated children—and prevent the abuse itself.

As these examples show, the situation or environment can sometimes have a powerful effect on personality. For years, a heated debate—known as "trait versus situationism" or the "person–situation controversy"—existed in psychology. After two decades of continuing debate and research, both sides seem to have won (Costa et al., 2007; Figueredo et al., 2011; Mastroinni, 2011). We will return to this *interactionist* position later in this and other chapters.

CHECK & REVIEW

Before going on, be sure to complete this Check & Review. It is an invaluable study tool!

Trait Theories

Part A: Retrieval Practice

1. Without looking at the book, spend 10 minutes writing a free-form essay recalling all you can remember from the previous section.

2. Now, reread the previous section, and once again spend 10 minutes writing a free-form essay on the SAME material.

   (Although time consuming, this exercise has been shown to be the single best way to improve your test scores! For more information, check out http://www.sciencemag.org/content/early/2011/01/19/science.1199327.abstract)

Part B: Practice Quiz

1. A relatively stable and consistent characteristic that can be used to describe someone is known as _____.

2. Match the following personality descriptions with their corresponding factor from the five-factor model (FFM): (a) openness; (b) conscientiousness; (c) introversion; (d) agreeableness; (e) neuroticism
   ___i. Tending toward insecurity, anxiety, guilt, worry, and moodiness
   ___ii. Being imaginative, curious, open to new ideas, and interested in cultural pursuits

___iii. Being responsible, self-disciplined, organized, and high achieving
___iv. Tending to be withdrawn, quiet, passive, and reserved
___v. Being good-natured, warm, gentle, cooperative, trusting, and helpful

3. Trait theories of personality have been criticized for _____. (a) failing to explain why people develop their traits; (b) not including a large number of central traits; (c) failing to identify which traits last and which are transient; (d) not considering situational determinants of personality; (e) all but one of these options.

Check your answers in Appendix B.

Psychoanalytic/Psychodynamic Theories

In contrast to trait theories that *describe* personality as it exists, *psychoanalytic* (or *psychodynamic*) theories of personality attempt to *explain* individual differences by examining how *unconscious* mental forces interplay with thoughts, feelings, and actions. The founding father of psychoanalytic theory is Sigmund Freud. We will examine Freud's theories in some detail and then briefly discuss three of his most influential followers—Alfred Adler, Carl Jung, and Karen Horney.

Freud's Psychoanalytic Theory: Four Key Concepts

Objective 13.3: Describe Freud's psychoanalytic approach to personality.

Who is the best-known figure in all of psychology? Most people immediately name Sigmund Freud. Even before you studied psychology, you probably came across his name in other courses. Freud's theories have been applied in the fields of anthropology,

Conscious In Freudian terms, thoughts or motives that a person is currently aware of or is remembering

Preconscious Freud's term for thoughts, motives, or memories that exist just beneath the surface of awareness and can be easily retrieved

Unconscious Freud's term for thoughts, motives, and memories blocked from normal awareness, which still exert great influence

sociology, religion, medicine, art, and literature. Working from about 1890 until he died in 1939, Freud developed a theory of personality that has been one of the most influential—and, at the same time, most controversial—in all of science (Burger, 2011; Cautin, 2011; Cordoń, 2012; Dufresne, 2007).

In discussing Freud's theory, we will focus on four of his key concepts: *levels of awareness, personality structure, defense mechanisms*, and *psychosexual stages of development*.

Levels of Awareness

Freud called the mind the *psyche* [sie-KEY] and believed that it functioned on three levels of awareness or consciousness—**conscious, preconscious**, and **unconscious** (Figure 13.2). According to Freud, the all-important *unconscious* stores

Figure 13.2 Freud's three levels of consciousness ▼

Although Freud never used the analogy himself, his levels of awareness are often compared to an iceberg:

- The tip of the iceberg would be analogous to the *conscious* mind, which is above the water and open to easy inspection.

- The *preconscious* mind (the area only shallowly submerged) contains information that can be viewed with a little extra effort.

- The large base of the iceberg is somewhat like the *unconscious*, completely hidden from personal inspection.

Using the Freudian idea of "levels of consciousness", we might say that at this moment your conscious mind is focusing on this text. However, your preconscious may include feelings of hunger and thoughts of friends you need to contact. Any repressed sexual desires, aggressive impulses, or irrational thoughts and feelings are reportedly stored in your unconscious.

our primitive, instinctual motives, plus anxiety-laden thoughts and memories blocked from normal awareness. Freud believed the unconscious is hidden from our personal awareness (Figure 13.3). But it still has an enormous impact on our behavior—and reveals itself despite our intentions. Just as the enormous mass of iceberg below the surface destroyed the ocean liner *Titanic*, the unconscious may similarly damage our psychological lives. Freud believed that most psychological disorders originate from repressed (hidden) memories and instincts (sexual and aggressive) stored in the unconscious. To treat these disorders, Freud developed *psychoanalysis* (Chapter 15).

Personality Structure

In addition to proposing that the mind functions at three levels of awareness, Freud believed personality was composed of three interacting mental components or structures: *id, ego*, and *superego*. Each of these structures resides,

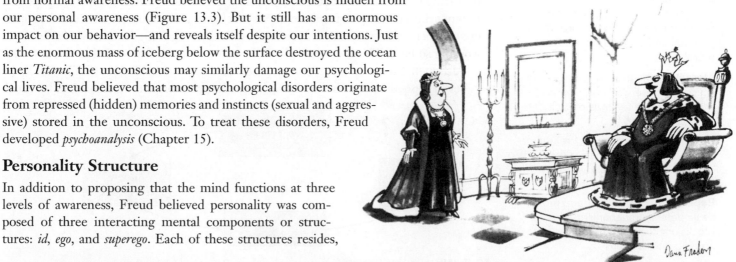

Figure 13.3 Freudian slips Freud believed that a small slip of the tongue (known as a "Freudian slip") can reflect unconscious feelings that we normally keep hidden.

▶ *"Good morning, beheaded—uh, I mean beloved."*

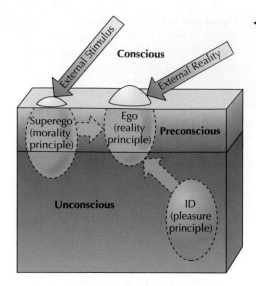

Conscious

External Stimulus
External Reality

Superego (morality principle)

Ego (reality principle)

Preconscious

Unconscious

ID (pleasure principle)

◀ **Figure 13.4 Freud's personality structure** According to Freud, personality is composed of three structures—the *id, ego,* and *superego.* The id operates on the *pleasure principle*, the ego operates on the *reality principle*, and the superego is guided by the *morality principle.* Note how the ego is primarily conscious and preconscious, whereas the id is entirely unconscious.

fully or partially, in the unconscious mind (Figure 13.4). (Keep in mind that the id, ego, and superego are mental concepts—or hypothetical constructs. They are not physical structures you could see if you dissected a human brain.)

The Id According to Freud, the **id** is made up of innate, biological instincts and urges. It is immature, impulsive, irrational, and totally unconscious. When its primitive drives build up, the id seeks immediate gratification to relieve the tension. Thus, the id operates on the **pleasure principle**, the immediate and uninhibited seeking of pleasure and the avoidance of discomfort. In other words, the ID is like a newborn baby. It wants what it wants when it wants it!

The Ego As the child grows older, the second part of the psyche, the **ego**, supposedly develops. The ego is responsible for planning, problem solving, reasoning, and controlling the id. Unlike the id, which lies entirely in the unconscious, the ego resides primarily in the conscious and preconscious. In Freud's system, the ego corresponds to the self—our conscious identity of ourselves as persons.

One of the ego's tasks is to channel and release the id's energy in ways that are compatible with the external environment. Contrary to the id's *pleasure principle*, the ego operates on the **reality principle**. This means the ego is responsible for delaying gratification until it is practical or appropriate.

The Superego The final part of the psyche to develop is the **superego**. This inner voice, sometimes known as your "conscience," is supposedly made up of a set of ethical standards or rules for behavior that resides primarily in the preconscious and unconscious. The superego develops from internalized parental and societal standards. Some Freudian followers have suggested that it operates on the **morality principle** because violating its rules results in feelings of guilt.

Id According to Freud, the primitive, instinctive component of personality, which works on the pleasure principle

Pleasure Principle In Freud's theory, the principle on which the id operates—seeking immediate gratification

Ego In Freud's theory, the rational, decision-making component of personality that operates according to the reality principle; from the Latin term *ego*, meaning "I"

Reality Principle According to Freud, the principle on which the conscious ego operates as it seeks to delay gratification of the id's impulses until appropriate outlets and situations can be found

Superego In Freud's theory, the "conscience" or moral component of the personality that incorporates parental and societal standards for morality

Morality Principle The principle on which the superego may operate, which results in feelings of guilt if its rules are violated

Defense Mechanisms In Freudian theory, the ego's protective method of reducing anxiety by distorting reality and self-deception

Repression Freud's first and most basic defense mechanism, which blocks unacceptable impulses from coming into awareness

Defense Mechanisms

What happens when the ego fails to satisfy both the id and the superego? Anxiety and/or guilt slip into conscious awareness. Because these emotions are uncomfortable, people avoid them through **defense mechanisms,** which satisfy the id and superego by distorting reality and self-deception (Figure 13.5). An alcoholic who uses his paycheck to buy drinks (a message from the id) may feel very guilty (a response from the superego). His ego then works to reduce this conflict by suggesting he deserves to drink for working so hard. This is an example of the defense mechanism called *rationalization.*

Although Freud described many kinds of defense mechanisms (Table 13.2), he believed repression was the most important. **Repression** is the mechanism by which

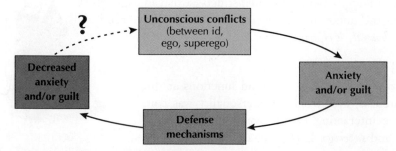

?

Unconscious conflicts (between id, ego, superego)

Decreased anxiety and/or guilt

Anxiety and/or guilt

Defense mechanisms

Figure 13.5 Why do we use defense mechanisms? Freud believed that unconscious conflicts between the Id, ego, and superego may elicit uncomfortable levels of anxiety and/or guilt. The use of defense mechanisms helps relieve the discomfort by distorting reality and self-deception. The question is, does the relief increase the chances that we'll resort to defense mechanisms whenever we experience conflicts?

Table 13.2 SAMPLE PSYCHOLOGICAL DEFENSE MECHANISMS

Defense Mechanism	Description	Example
Repression	Preventing painful or unacceptable thoughts from entering consciousness	Forgetting the details of a tragic accident
Sublimation	Redirecting socially unacceptable impulses into acceptable activities	Redirecting aggressive impulses by becoming a professional fighter
Denial	Refusing to recognize an unpleasant reality	Alcoholics refusing to admit their addiction
Rationalization	Creating a socially acceptable excuse to justify unacceptable behavior	Justifying cheating on an exam by saying "everyone else does it"
Intellectualization	Ignoring troubling emotional aspects by focusing on abstract thoughts or ideas	Emotionless discussion of your divorce while ignoring underlying pain
Projection	Transferring unacceptable thoughts, motives, or impulses to others	Becoming unreasonably jealous of your mate while denying your own attraction to others
Reaction formation	Not acknowledging unacceptable impulses and overemphasizing their opposite	Promoting a petition against adult bookstores even though you are secretly fascinated by pornography
Regression	Reverting to immature ways of responding	Throwing a temper tantrum when frustrated
Displacement	Redirecting impulses from original source toward a less threatening person or object	Yelling at a coworker after being criticized by your boss

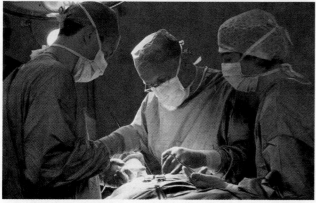

▲ **Is it bad to use defense mechanisms?** Although defense mechanisms do distort reality, some misrepresentation seems to be necessary for our psychological well-being (Cordoń, 2012; Marshall & Brown, 2008; Wenger & Fowers, 2008). During a gruesome surgery, for example, physicians and nurses may "intellectualize" the procedure as an unconscious way of dealing with their personal anxieties. Can you see how focusing on highly objective technical aspects of the situation might help these people avoid becoming emotionally overwhelmed by the potentially tragic circumstances they often encounter?

 **TEST YOURSELF**

◀ **Applying Defense Mechanisms**

Imagine that these two people (Karla and Ken) are friends who work with you, and that you can hear them talking in the parking lot. Thanks to one of your superpowers, you also can read their private thoughts. Knowing that both of them are in serious, committed relationships with other people, fill-in-the blank below each [Thought] or [Statement] with the most likely defense mechanism being exhibited. (Check your answers in Appendix B.)

Karla: [Thought] *"He's cute. I bet my boyfriend is having an affair with that woman at his office."*

1. _____

Karla: [Statement] *"Would you like to come to my house? We really need to discuss the details on our work project?"*

2. _____

Ken: [Thought] *"WOW! She's hot, but I have to go straight to the gym to work out."*

3. _____

Ken: [Statement] *"I'm sorry. My wife is waiting for me at home, and she's always upset if I'm late."*

4. _____

Karla: [Thought] *"He's such a jerk. I'm never going to talk to him again."*

5. _____

The oral stage? Is this an example of Freud's earliest stage of psychosexual development, or just a part of all infants' normal sucking behaviors?

Psychosexual Stages In Freudian theory, five developmental periods (oral, anal, phallic, latency, and genital) during which particular kinds of pleasures must be gratified if personality development is to proceed normally

Inferiority Complex Adler's idea that feelings of inferiority develop from early childhood experiences of helplessness and incompetence

the ego prevents the most anxiety-provoking or unacceptable thoughts and feelings from entering consciousness. It is the first and most basic form of anxiety reduction.

Psychosexual Stages of Development

The concept of defense mechanisms has generally withstood the test of time. And they are an accepted part of modern psychology (e.g., Chapter 3). This is not the case for Freud's theory of psychosexual stages of development.

According to Freud, strong biological urges residing within the id supposedly push all children through five universal **psychosexual stages** during the first 12 or so years of life—oral, anal, phallic, latency, and genital (Step-by-Step Diagram 13.1). The term *psychosexual* reflects Freud's emphasis on *infantile sexuality*—his belief that children experience sexual feelings from birth (although in different forms from those of adolescents or adults).

At each psychosexual stage, the id's impulses and social demands come into conflict. Therefore, if a child's needs are not met, or are overindulged, at one particular stage, the child supposedly may *fixate* and a part of the personality will remain stuck at that stage. Freud believed most individuals successfully pass through each of the five stages. But during stressful times, they may return (or *regress*) to an earlier stage in which earlier needs were badly frustrated or overgratified.

Neo-Freudian/Psychodynamic Theories: Revising Freud's Ideas

Objective 13.5: Compare Freud's versus the neo-Freudian's approaches to personality.

Some initial followers of Freud later rebelled and proposed theories of their own. Three of the most influential of these *neo-Freudians* were Alfred Adler, Carl Jung, and Karen Horney.

Adler's Individual Psychology

Alfred Adler (1870–1937) was the first to leave Freud's inner circle. Instead of seeing behavior as motivated by unconscious forces, he believed that it is purposeful and goal-directed. According to Adler's *individual psychology*, we are motivated by our goals in life—especially our goals of obtaining security and overcoming feelings of inferiority.

Adler believed that almost everyone suffers from an **inferiority complex**, or deep feelings of inadequacy and incompetence that arise from our feelings of helplessness as infants. According to Adler, these early feelings result in a "will-to-power" that can take one of two paths. It can either cause children to strive to develop superiority over others through dominance, aggression, or expressions of envy, or—more positively—it can cause children to develop their full potential and creativity and to gain mastery and control in their lives (Adler, 1964, 1998) (Figure 13.6).

◀ **Figure 13.6 Adler's upside to feelings of inferiority?** Adler suggested that the will-to-power could be positively expressed through social interest—identifying with others and cooperating with them for the social good. Can you explain how these volunteers might be fulfilling their will-to-power interest?

Step-by-StepDiagram13.1

STOP This Step by Step diagram contains essential information NOT found elsewhere in the text, which is likely to appear on quizzes and exams. Be sure to study it CAREFULLY!

Freud's Five Psychosexual Stages of Development

Objective 13.4: Summarize Freud's five psychosexual stages.

Name of Stage (Approximate age)	Erogenous Zone (Key Conflict or Developmental Task)		Supposed Symptoms of Fixation and/ or Regression
1 **Oral** (0–18 months)	**Mouth** (Weaning from breast or bottle)		Overindulgence reportedly contributes to gullibility ("swallowing" anything), dependence, and passivity. Underindulgence supposedly leads to aggressiveness, sadism, and a tendency to exploit others. Freud also believed orally fixated adults may orient their lives around their mouths—overeating, becoming alcoholic, smoking, or talking a great deal.
2 **Anal** (18 months– 3 years)	**Anus** (Toilet training)		Fixation or regression supposedly leads to highly controlled and compulsively neat (anal-retentive) personality, or messy, disorderly, rebellious, and destructive (anal-explosive) personality.
3 **Phallic** (3–6 years)	**Genitals** (Attraction to same-sex parent)		According to Freud, unresolved, sexual longing for the opposite-sex parent can lead to long-term resentment and hostility toward the same-sex parent. Freud also believed that boys develop an **Oedipus complex,** or attraction to their mothers and desire to replace their fathers. The girls' analogous experience is to develop an attachment to their fathers and harbor hostile feelings toward their mothers, whom they blame for their lack of a penis. According to Freud most girls never overcome *penis envy* or give up their rivalry with their mothers, which reportedly leads to enduring moral inferiority.
4 **Latency** (6 years–puberty)	**None** (Repression of sexual impulses, identification with same-sex parent)		The latency stage is reportedly a time of sexual "dormancy." Children do not have particular psychosexual conflicts that must be resolved during this period.
5 **Genital** (puberty–adult)	**Genitals** (Establishing intimate relationships with the opposite sex)		Unsuccessful outcomes at this stage, supposedly may lead to sexual relationships based only on lustful desires, not on respect and commitment.

(left vertical label: Psychosexual Development)

Oedipus [ED-uh-puss] Complex Period of conflict during the phallic stage when young boys are supposedly attracted to their mothers and desire to replace their fathers

Jung's Analytical Psychology

Another early Freud follower turned dissenter, Carl Jung (pronounced "YOONG"), developed *analytical psychology*. Like Freud, Jung (1875–1961) emphasized unconscious processes, but he believed that the unconscious contains positive and spiritual motives as well as sexual and aggressive forces.

Jung also thought that we have two forms of unconscious mind: the personal unconscious and the collective unconscious. The *personal unconscious* is created from our individual experiences, whereas the **collective unconscious** is identical in each person and is inherited (Jung, 1946, 1959, 1969). The collective unconscious consists of primitive images and patterns of thought, feeling, and behavior that Jung called **archetypes** (Figure 13.7).

Because of archetypal patterns in the collective unconscious, we perceive and react in certain predictable ways. One set of archetypes refers to gender roles (Chapter 11). Jung claimed that both males and females have patterns for feminine aspects of personality (anima) and masculine aspects of personality (animus), which allow us to express both masculine and feminine personality traits and to understand the opposite sex.

Horney's "Blended" Psychology

Like Adler and Jung, psychoanalyst Karen Horney (pronounced "HORN-eye") was an influential follower of Freud, who later came to reject major aspects of Freudian theory. She is remembered mostly for having developed a creative blend of Freudian, Adlerian, and Jungian theory, with added concepts of her own (Horney, 1939, 1945).

Horney is also known for her theories of personality development. She believed that adult personality was shaped by the child's relationship to the parents—not by fixation at some stage of psychosexual development, as Freud argued. Horney believed

▲ **Karen Horney (1885–1952)**
Horney argued that most of Freud's ideas about female personality reflected male biases and misunderstanding. She contended, for example, that Freud's concept of penis envy reflected women's feelings of cultural inferiority, not biological inferiority—*power envy*, not penis envy.

▲ **Figure 13.7 Jung's Archetypes in the collective unconscious**
According to Jung, the collective unconscious is the ancestral memory of the human race, which supposedly explains the similarities in religion, art, symbolism, and dream imagery across cultures, such as the repeated symbol of the snake in ancient Egyptian tomb painting and early Australian aboriginal bark painting. Can you think of other explanations?

Collective Unconscious Jung's concept of a reservoir of inherited, universal experiences that all humans share

Archetypes [AR-KEH-types] According to Jung, the images and patterns of thoughts, feelings, and behavior that reside in the collective unconscious

that a child whose needs were not met by nurturing parents would experience extreme feelings of helplessness and insecurity. How people respond to this **basic anxiety** greatly determines emotional health.

According to Horney, everyone searches for security in one of three ways: We can move toward people (by seeking affection and acceptance from others); we can move away from people (by striving for independence, privacy, and self-reliance); or we can move against people (by trying to gain control and power over others). Emotional health requires a balance among these three styles.

Basic Anxiety According to Horney, the feelings of helplessness and insecurity that adults experience because as children they felt alone and isolated in a hostile environment

Evaluating Psychoanalytic/Psychodynamic Theories: Criticisms and Enduring Influence

Objective 13.6: Discuss the major criticisms of psychoanalytic theories of personality.

Before going on, it's important to consider the major criticisms of Freud's psychoanalytic theories, as well as why Freud has had such an enduring influence on the field of psychology (Table 13.3). Today there are few Freudian purists. Instead, modern psychodynamic theorists and psychoanalysts use empirical methods and research findings to reformulate and refine traditional Freudian thinking (Cautin, 2011; Cordón, 2012;

Table 13.3 EVALUATING PSYCHOANALYTIC THEORIES

Criticisms	
• **Difficult to test** Most psychoanalytic concepts—such as the id or unconscious conflicts—cannot be empirically tested (Domhoff, 2004; Esterson, 2002; Friedman & Schustack, 2006).	a small and selective sample of humanity: upper-class women in Vienna (Freud's home) who had serious adjustment problems.
• **Overemphasizes biology and unconscious forces** Modern physhologists believe Freud underestimated the role of learning and culture in shaping personality.	• **Sexism** Many psychologists (beginning with Karen Horney) reject Freud's theories as derogatory toward women.
• **Inadequate empirical support** Freud based his theories almost exclusively on subjective case histories of adult patients. Moreover, his patients represented	• **Lack of cross-cultural support** Freudian concepts that ought to be most easily supported empirically—the biological determinants of personality—are generally not borne out by cross-cultural studies.

Enduring influences	
• Emphasis on the unconscious and its influence on behavior	• Encouraged open talk about sex in Victorian times
• Conflict among the id, ego, and superego and the resulting defense mechanisms	• Development of psychoanalysis, an influential form of therapy.
	• Sheer magnitude of Freudian theory.

Diem-Wille, 2011; Knekt et al., 2008; Tryon, 2008; Westen, 1998; Young-Bruehl & Schwartz, 2011).

But, wrong as he was on many counts, Freud still ranks as one of the giants of psychology (Burger, 2011; Celes, 2010; De Sousa, 2011; Schülein, 2007; Siegel, 2010). Furthermore, Freud's impact on Western intellectual history cannot be overstated. He attempted to explain dreams, religion, social groupings, family dynamics, neurosis, psychosis, humor, the arts, and literature.

It's easy to criticize Freud if you don't remember that he began his work at the start of the twentieth century and lacked the benefit of modern research findings and technology. We can only imagine how our current theories will look 100 years from now. Right or wrong, Freud has a lasting place among the pioneers in psychology.

CHECK & REVIEW

STOP *Before going on, be sure to complete this Check & Review. It is an invaluable study tool!*

Psychoanalytic/Psychodynamic Theories

Part A: Retrieval Practice

1. Without looking at the book, spend 10 minutes writing a free-form essay recalling all you can remember from the previous section.

2. Now, reread the previous section, and once again spend 10 minutes writing a free-form essay on the SAME material.

Part B: Practice Quiz

1. Using the analogy of an iceberg, explain Freud's three levels of consciousness.

2. The _____ operates on the pleasure principle, seeking immediate gratification. The _____ operates on the reality principle, and the _____ contains the conscience and operates on the morality principle. (a) psyche, ego, id; (b) id, ego, superego; (c) conscious, preconscious, unconscious; (d) oral stage; anal stage; phallic stage

3. Briefly describe Freud's five psychosexual stages.

4. Match the following concepts with the appropriate theorist: Adler, Jung, or Horney:

   a. inferiority complex: _____

   b. power envy: _____

   c. collective unconscious: _____

   d. basic anxiety: _____

Check your answers in Appendix B.

Humanistic Theories

Objective 13.7: Discuss humanistic theories of personality, comparing the approaches of Rogers and Maslow.

Humanistic theories of personality emphasize internal experiences—feelings and thoughts—and the individual's own feelings of basic worth. In contrast to Freud's generally negative view of human nature, humanists believe people are naturally good (or, at worst, neutral). And that they possess a positive, natural tendency toward **self-actualization**, the inborn drive to develop all one's talents and capabilities.

Self-Actualization Humanistic term for the inborn drive to develop all one's talents and capabilities

According to this view, our personality and behavior depend on how we perceive and interpret the world, not on traits, unconscious impulses, or rewards and punishments. To fully understand another human being, you must know how he or she perceives the world. Humanistic psychology was developed largely by Carl Rogers and Abraham Maslow.

Rogers's Theory: The Importance of the Self

To psychologist Carl Rogers (1902–1987), the most important component of personality is the *self*—what a person comes to identify as "I" or "me." Today, Rogerians (followers of Rogers) use the term **self-concept** to refer to all the information and beliefs you have regarding your own nature, unique qualities, and typical behaviors. Rogers believed poor mental health and maladjustment developed from a mismatch, or incongruence, between the self-concept and actual life experiences (Figure 13.8).

According to Rogers, mental health, congruence, and our self-concept are all part of our innate biological capacities. Like plants that grow in cracks in the cement, we are born into the world with an innate need to survive, grow, and enhance ourselves. Therefore, Rogers believed we can—and should—trust our own internal feelings to guide us toward mental health and happiness.

Conditional versus Unconditional Positive Regard

If everyone has an inborn, positive drive toward self-fulfillment, why do some people have low self-concepts and poor mental health? Rogers believed these outcomes generally result from early childhood experiences with parents and other adults who make their love and acceptance *conditional* and contingent on behaving in certain ways and expressing only certain feelings. If the child learns that his negative feelings and behaviors (which we all have) are totally unacceptable and unlovable, his self-concept may become distorted. He may always doubt the love and approval of others because they don't know "the real person hiding inside" (Figure 13.9).

To help children develop their fullest personality and life potential, adults need to create an atmosphere of **unconditional positive regard**—that is, a setting in which children realize that they are loved and accepted with no conditions or strings attached.

Some people mistakenly believe that, unconditional positive regard means we should allow people to do whatever they please. But humanists separate the value of the person from his or her behaviors. They accept the person's positive nature and basic worth, while discouraging destructive or hostile behaviors. Humanistic psychologists stress that children and adults should control their behavior so they can develop a healthy self-concept and healthy relationships with others.

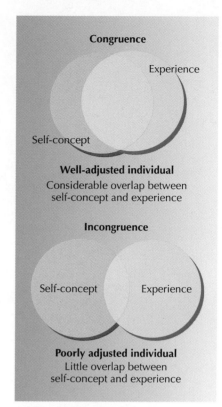

Congruence

Experience

Self-concept

Well-adjusted individual
Considerable overlap between
self-concept and experience

Incongruence

Self-concept   Experience

Poorly adjusted individual
Little overlap between
self-concept and experience

Figure 13.8 Congruence and Mental Health According to Carl Rogers, mental health and adjustment are related to the degree of congruence between a person's self-concept and life experiences. Can you see how an artistic child would likely have a higher self-concept if her family valued art than if they did not?

Self-Concept Rogers's term for all the information and beliefs individuals have about their own nature, qualities, and behavior

Unconditional Positive Regard Rogers's term for love and acceptance with no contingencies attached

◀ **Figure 13.9 Conditional love?** If a child is angry and hits his younger sister, some parents might say, "Nice children don't hit their sisters, they love them!" To gain parental approval, the child has to deny his true feelings of anger, while secretly suspecting he is not a "nice boy" because he did hit his sister and (at that moment) did not love her! A more appropriate response to the child's behavior that acknowledges that it is the behavior that is unacceptable, and not the child, might be: "I know you're angry with your sister, but we don't hit. And you won't be able to play with her for a while unless you control your anger."

Maslow's Theory: The Search for Self-Actualization

Like Rogers, Abraham Maslow (1908–1970) believed there is a basic goodness to human nature and a natural tendency toward *self-actualization*, which for him involves understanding one's own potential, accepting oneself and others as unique individuals, and taking a problem-centered approach to life situations (Maslow, 1970).

Maslow saw personality development and the quest for self-actualization as a natural progression from lower to higher levels—a basic *hierarchy of needs* (Figure 13.10). As newborns, we reportedly focus on physiological needs (hunger, thirst), and then as we grow and develop, we move on up through four higher levels. Maslow acknowledged that only a few, rare individuals, such as Albert Einstein, Mohandas Gandhi, and Eleanor Roosevelt, become fully self-actualized. For most of us, self-actualization is an ongoing *process* of growth rather than an end *product* or accomplishment—more a road to travel than a final destination. (See Chapter 12, p. 427, for more information on Maslow's theory.)

Evaluating Humanistic Theories: Three Major Criticisms

Objective 13.8: What are the major criticisms of humanistic theories of personality?

Humanistic psychology was extremely popular during the 1960s and 1970s. It was a refreshing new perspective on personality after the negative determinism of the psychoanalytic approach and the mechanical nature of learning theories. Although this early popularity has declined, many humanistic ideas have been incorporated into the field of positive psychology (see Chapter 1) and approaches for psychotherapy (Bozarth & Brodley, 2008; De Robertis, 2011; Friedman, 2011; Schneider, 2011).

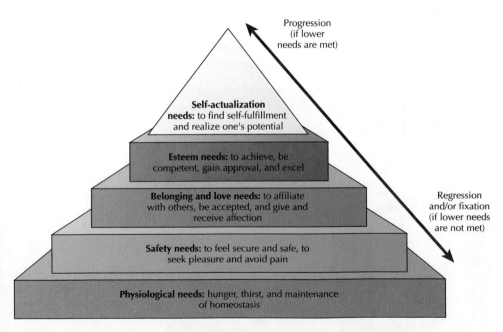

Figure 13.10 Maslow's hierarchy of needs Although our natural movement is upward from physical needs toward the highest level, *self-actualization*, Maslow also believed we sometimes "regress" toward a lower level—especially under stressful conditions. For example, during national disasters, people first rush to stockpile food and water (*physiological needs*), and then often clamor for a strong leader to take over and make things right (*safety needs*). If the disruption is extreme, we may fixate on a particular level for the rest of our lives. Similarly, if your parents divorced when you were young, your *belonging and love needs* may never be fully satisfied—leaving you in constant worry that your spouse will leave you too (Boeree, 2006).

Ironically, the strength of the humanists, their focus on positivism and subjective self experiences, is also why humanistic theories have been sharply criticized (e.g., Funder, 2000). Three of the most important criticisms are these:

1. *Naïve assumptions* Critics suggest that the humanistic perspective is unrealistic, romantic, and even naïve about human nature. For example, some believe the emphasis on the self-concept and self-esteem has led to an increase in *narcissism*, or inappropriate self-love and egocentrism. See the *Critical Thinking* exercise on p. 427 for a more information on this issue.

2. *Poor testability and inadequate evidence* Like many psychoanalytic terms and concepts, humanistic concepts (such as unconditional positive regard and self-actualization) are difficult to define operationally and test scientifically.

3. *Narrowness* Like trait theories, humanistic theories have been criticized for merely describing personality, rather than explaining it. For example, where does the motivation for self-actualization come from? To say that it is an "inborn drive" doesn't satisfy those who favor experimental research and hard data as the way to learn about personality.

CHECK & REVIEW

STOP — Before going on, be sure to complete this Check & Review. It is an invaluable study tool!

Humanistic Theories

Part A: Retrieval Practice

1. Without looking at the book, spend 10 minutes writing a free-form essay recalling all you can remember from the previous section.

2. Now, reread the previous section, and once again spend 10 minutes writing a free-form essay on the SAME material.

Part B: Practice Quiz

1. If you took the _____ approach to personality, you would emphasize internal experiences, like feelings and thoughts, and the basic worth of the individual. (a) humanistic; (b) psychodynamic; (c) personalistic; (d) motivational

2. Rogers thought that _____ is necessary for a child's uniqueness and positive self-concept to unfold naturally. (a) authoritative parenting; (b) a challenging environment; (c) unconditional positive regard; (d) a friendly neighborhood

3. Abraham Maslow's belief that all people are motivated toward personal growth and development is known as _____.

4. What are three major criticisms of humanistic theories?

Check your answers in Appendix B.

Social-Cognitive Theories

Objective 13.9: Discuss the social-cognitive perspective on personality, comparing Bandura and Rotter's approaches.

According to the social-cognitive perspective, each of us has a unique personality because of our individual history of interactions with the environment and because we *think* about the world and interpret what happens to us. Two of the most influential social-cognitive theorists are Albert Bandura and Julian Rotter.

Bandura's and Rotter's Approaches: Social Learning Plus Cognitive Processes

Bandura's Self-Efficacy and Reciprocal Determinism

Although Albert Bandura is perhaps best known for his work on observational learning or social learning (Chapter 6), he has also played a major role in reintroducing

Self-Efficacy Bandura's term for a person's learned expectation of success

Reciprocal Determinism Bandura's belief that cognitions, behaviors, and the environment interact to produce personality

▲ **Figure 13.11 Self-efficacy in action** Research shows that self-defense training has significant effects on improving women's belief that they could escape from or disable a potential assailant or rapist (Weitlauf et al., 2001). But Bandura stresses that self-efficacy is always specific to the situation. For example, women who took this course reported greater self-defense efficacy, but this increased efficacy did not transfer over to other areas of their lives.

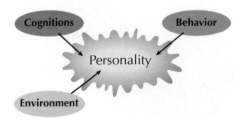

▲ **Figure 13.12 Albert Bandura's theory of reciprocal determinism** According to Bandura, thoughts (or cognitions), behavior, and the environment all interact to produce personality.

thought processes into personality theory. Cognition is central to his concept of **self-efficacy**, which refers to a person's learned expectation of success (Bandura, 1997, 2000, 2006, 2008, 2011) (Figure 13.11).

How do you generally perceive your ability to select, influence, and control the circumstances of your life? According to Bandura, if you have a strong sense of self-efficacy, you believe you can generally succeed, regardless of past failures and current obstacles. Your self-efficacy will in turn affect the challenges you accept and the effort you expend in reaching goals.

Can you see that how others respond to you also affects your chances for success? This type of mutual interaction and influence is a core part of another major concept of Bandura's—**reciprocal determinism**. According to Bandura, our cognitions (or thoughts), behaviors, and the environment are interdependent and interactive (Figure 13.12). Thus, a cognition ("I can succeed") will affect behaviors ("I will work hard and ask for a promotion"), which in turn will affect the environment ("My employer recognized my efforts and promoted me.").

Rotter's Locus of Control

Julian Rotter's theory is similar to Bandura's. He believes that prior learning experiences create *cognitive expectancies* that guide behavior and influence the environment (Rotter, 1954, 1990). According to Rotter, your behavior or personality is determined by (1) what you *expect* to happen following a specific action and (2) the *reinforcement value* attached to specific outcomes—that is, the degree to which you prefer one reinforcer to another.

To understand your personality and behavior, for instance, Rotter would use personality tests that measure your internal versus external *locus of control* (Chapter 3). These tests ask people to respond "true" or "false" to a series of statements, such as "People get ahead in this world primarily by luck and connections rather than by hard work and perseverance" or "When someone doesn't like you, there is little you can do about it."

As you may suspect, people with an *external locus of control* think environment and external forces have primary control over their lives. Conversely, *internals* think they can control events in their lives through their own efforts (Figure 13.13).

"We're encouraging people to become involved in their own rescue."

▲

Figure 13.13 Locus of control Despite the sarcasm of this cartoon, research links possession of an internal locus of control with higher achievement and better mental health (Burns, 2008; Jones, 2008; Ruthig et al., 2007).

Evaluating Social-Cognitive Theories: The Pluses and Minuses

Objective 13.10: What are the major strengths and weaknesses of the social-cognitive theories?

The social-cognitive perspective holds several attractions. First, it emphasizes how the environment affects, and is affected by, individuals. Second, it meets most standards for scientific research. It offers testable, objective hypotheses and operationally defined terms and relies on empirical data for its basic principles. Critics, however, believe social-cognitive theory is too narrow. It also has been criticized for ignoring unconscious, environmental, and emotional aspects of personality (Burger, 2011; Chamorro-Premuzic, 2011; Westen, 1998). For example, certain early experiences might have prompted a person to develop an external locus of control.

Both Bandura's and Rotter's theories emphasize cognition and social learning, but they are a long way from a strict behaviorist theory, which suggests that only environmental forces control behavior. They are also a long way from the biological theories that say inborn, innate qualities determine behavior and personality. Biological theories are the topic of our next section.

Biological Theories

Objective 13.11: How does biology contribute to personality?

As you were growing up, you probably heard comments such as "You're just like your father" or "You're so much like your mother." Does this mean that biological factors you inherited from your parents were the major contributors to your personality? This is the question we first explore in this section. We conclude with a discussion of how all theories of personality ultimately interact within the *biopsychosocial* model.

Three Major Contributors: Brain, Neurochemistry, and Genetics

Biological theories of personality focus on the brain, neurochemistry, and genetics. We begin our study with the brain.

Brain

> *To expect a personality to survive the disintegration of the brain is like expecting a cricket club to survive when all of its members are dead.*
>
> BERTRAND RUSSELL

Do you remember the case study of Phineas Gage from Chapter 2? He was the railroad supervisor who survived a horrific accident that sent a 13-pound metal rod through his frontal lobe. As shown by Gage's case, and later research, brain damage can dramatically affect personality (Blais & Boisvert, 2007; Rao et al., 2008; Reeves & Panguluri, 2011; Silver, McAllister, & Yudofsky, 2011). If you, or someone you know, has suffered brain damage from accidents, or diseases like Parkinson's or Alzheimer's, you're probably well aware of the resultant changes in behavior and personality.

Modern biological research also suggests that activity in certain brain areas may contribute to some personality traits. Tellegen (1985), for example, proposes that extroversion and introversion are associated with particular areas of the brain, and research seems to support him. For instance, fMRI brain scans of shy adults tend to show greater amygdala activation when presented with faces of strangers (Beaton et al., 2008; Casey et al., 2011; Quadflieg & MacRae, 2011).

Figure 13.14 Multiple influences on personality What gives a person certain personality characteristics, such as shyness, or conscientiousness, or aggressiveness? As shown in the figure here, research indicates that four major factors influence personality. These include *genetic (inherited) factors; nonshared environmenal factors*, or how each individual's genetic factors react and adjust to his or her particular environment; *shared environmental factors*, involving parental patterns and shared family experiences; and *error*, or unidentified factors or problems with testing.

For example, Hans Eysenck (1990) believed that certain traits (like introversion and extroversion) may reflect inherited patterns of cortical arousal, as well as social learning, cognitive processes, and the environment. Can you see how someone with an introverted personality (and therefore a higher level of cortical arousal) might try to avoid excessive stimulation by seeking friends and jobs with low stimulation levels? Eysenck's work exemplifies how trait, biological, and social-cognitive theories can be combined to provide better insight into personality—the *biopsychosocial model.* ▼

A major limitation on measurements of brain damage and brain activity is the difficulty of identifying which structures are uniquely connected with particular personality traits. Damage to one structure tends to have wide-ranging effects. Neurochemistry (our next topic) seems to offer more precise data on biological bases of personality.

Neurochemistry

Do you enjoy skydiving and taking risks in general? Neurochemistry may explain why. Research has found a consistent relationship between sensation seeking and neurochemicals like monoamine oxidase (MAO), an enzyme that regulates levels of neurotransmitters such as dopamine (Lee, 2011; Zuckerman, 1994, 2004). Dopamine also seems to be correlated with novelty seeking, impulsivity, and drug abuse (Dalley et al., 2007; Linnet et al., 2011; Marusich et al., 2011; Nemoda, Szekely, & Sasvari-Szekely, 2011).

How can traits like sensation seeking be related to neurochemistry? Studies suggest that high sensation seekers and extroverts tend to have lower levels of physiological arousal than introverts (Figueredo et al., 2011; Munoz & Anastassiou-Hadjicharalambous, 2011). Their lower arousal apparently motivates them to seek out situations that will elevate their arousal. Moreover, it is believed that a lower threshold is inherited. In other words, personality traits like sensation seeking and extroversion may be inherited. (Also see Chapter 12 on arousal and sensation seeking.)

Genetics

Heredity is what sets the parents of a teenager wondering about each other.

LAURENCE J. PETER

Psychologists also emphasize the importance and influence of genetic factors in personality. This relatively new area, called *behavioral genetics* (pp. 79–82), attempts to determine the extent to which behavioral differences among people are due to genetics as opposed to environment. For example, researchers often study similarities between identical twins, fraternal twins, and twins reared apart or together. And they frequently compare the personalities of parents with their biological and/or adopted children.

Findings from behavioral genetics generally report a relatively high correlation on certain personality traits, whereas research on parents' personalities have found moderate correlations with their biological children and very little with those of their adopted children. In sum, genetic factors contribute about 40 to 50 percent of personality (Figure 13.14) (Bouchard, 1997, 2004; Eysenck, 1967, 1990; Hopwood, 2011; McCrae et al., 2004; Plomin, 1990; Schermer, 2011; Veselka, Schermer, & Vernon, 2011). Although studies do show a strong inherited basis for personality, researchers are careful not to overemphasize genetics (Beauchamp et al., 2011; Burger, 2011; Chadwick, 2011). Some believe the importance of the unshared environment (aspects of the environment that differ from one individual to another, even within a family) has been overlooked. Others fear that research on "genetic determinism" could be misused to "prove" that an ethnic or a racial group is inferior, that male dominance is natural, or that social progress is impossible. There is no doubt that genetics studies have produced controversial results. However, it is also clear that more research is necessary before we have a cohesive biological theory of personality.

Biopsychosocial Model: Integrating the Perspectives

Objective 13.12: Describe how the biopsychosocial model blends various approaches to personality.

No one personality theory explains everything we want to know about personality. Each theory provides a different perspective into how an individual develops the distinctive set of characteristics we call "personality." Instead of adhering to any one theory, many psychologists believe in the *biopsychosocial* approach—the idea that several factors overlap in their contributions to personality (Chamorro-Premuzic, 2011; Gatchel & Kishino, 2011).

Checking Your Understanding

Fill in the term from column A that correctly matches the descriptions in Column B, and then check your answers in Appendix B.

Column A

a. Bandura
b. Horney
c. Jung
d. Superego
e. Rotter
f. Maslow
g. Rogers
h. Biological Theories
i. Psychoanalytic Theory
j. Five-Factor Model

Column B

1.____ OCEAN
2.____ Morality principle
3.____ Hierarchy of needs
4.____ Focuses on unconscious forces
5.____ Brain, neurochemistry, genetics
6.____ Self-concept and unconditional positive regard
7.____ Cognitive expectancies and locus of control
8.____ Collective unconscious and archetypes
9.____ Self-efficacy and reciprocal determinism
10.____ Basic anxiety

Before going on, be sure to complete this Check & Review. It is an invaluable study tool!

Social-Cognitive and Biological Theories

Part A: Retrieval Practice

1. Without looking at the book, spend 10 minutes writing a free-form essay recalling all you can remember from the previous section.

2. Now, reread the previous section, and once again spend 10 minutes writing a free-form essay on the SAME material.

Part B: Practice Quiz

1. Bandura's theory of _____ suggests cognitions, behavior, and the environment all interact to produce personality.

2. According to Bandura, _____ involves a person's belief about whether he or she can successfully engage in behaviors related to personal goals. (a) self-actualization; (b) self-esteem; (c) self-efficacy; (d) self-congruence

3. People with an _____ believe the environment and external forces control events, whereas those with an _____ believe in personal control.

4. _____ theories emphasize the importance of genetics in the development of personality.

5. What factor appears to have the greatest influence (40 to 50 percent) on personality? (a) the environment; (b) genetics; (c) learning; (d) unknown factors

6. The _____ approach represents a blending of several theories of personality.

7. Which theory of personality do you find most useful in understanding yourself and others? Why?

Check your answers in Appendix B.

MYTH BUSTER

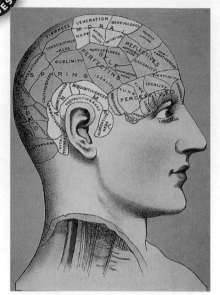

▲ **Figure 13.15 Bumps, lumps, and personality?** In the 1800s, if you wanted to have your personality assessed, you would go to a phrenologist, who would determine your personality by measuring the bumps on your skull and comparing the measurements with a chart that associated different areas of the skull with particular traits, such as *sublimity* (ability to squelch natural impulses, especially sexual) and *ideality* (ability to live by high ideals).

The assumption that personality relates to bumps on your skull is a myth and clearly wrong! However, the idea that some brain functions are localized is true (see Chapter 2).

Personality Assessment

Throughout history, people have sought information about their personality and that of others (Figure 13.15). Today, some people consult fortune-tellers, horoscope columns in the newspaper, tarot cards, and even fortune cookies in Chinese restaurants. But scientific research has provided much more reliable and valid methods for measuring personality. Clinical and counseling psychologists, psychiatrists, and other helping professionals use these modern methods to help with the diagnosis of patients and to assess their progress in therapy. Personality assessment is also used for educational and vocational counseling and by businesses to aid in employment decisions.

Measuring Personality: Do You See What I See?

Objective 13.13: How do psychologists measure personality?

Like a detective solving a mystery, modern psychologists typically use numerous methods and a complete *battery* (or series) of tests to fully *assess* personality. This assortment of measures can be grouped into a few broad categories: *interviews, observations, objective tests,* and *projective techniques.*

Interviews

We all use informal "interviews" to get to know other people. When first meeting people, we ask about their job, college major, family, and hobbies or interests. Psychologists use a more formal type of interview—both *structured* and *unstructured.* Unstructured interviews are often used for job and college selection and for diagnosing psychological problems. In an unstructured format, interviewers get impressions and pursue hunches. They also let the interviewee expand on information that promises to disclose unique personality characteristics. In structured interviews, the interviewer asks specific questions and follows a set of preestablished procedures so that the interviewee can be evaluated more objectively. The results of a structured interview are often charted on a rating scale that makes comparisons with others easier.

Observations

In addition to structured and unstructured interviews, psychologists also use direct behavioral observation to assess personality. The psychologist looks for examples of specific behaviors and follows a careful set of evaluation guidelines. For instance, a psychologist might arrange to observe a troubled client's interactions with his or her family. Does the client become agitated by the presence of certain family members and not others? Does he or she become passive and withdrawn when asked a direct question? Through careful observation, the psychologist gains valuable insights into the client's personality, as well as family dynamics (Figure 13.16).

Objective Tests

Objective self-report personality tests, or *inventories*, are standardized questionnaires that require written responses. Answers to the typically multiple-choice or true–false questions help people to describe themselves—to

◄ **Figure 13.16 Behavioral observation** Can you see how careful, scientific observation of a troubled client's real-life interactions could provide valuable personality insights?

"self-report." The tests are considered "objective" because they have a limited number of possible responses to items. They also follow empirical standards for test construction and scoring. Another important advantage is that objective tests can be administered to a large number of people in a relatively short period of time and evaluated in a standardized fashion. These advantages help explain why objective tests are by far the most widely used method for assessing personality.

You have been introduced to several objective self-report personality tests in this textbook. We describe the sensation-seeking scale in Chapter 12, and earlier in this chapter we discussed Rotter's locus-of-control scale. The complete versions of these tests measure one specific personality trait and are used primarily in research. Often, however, psychologists in clinical, counseling, and business settings are interested in assessing a range of personality traits all at once. To do this, they generally use *multitrait* (or *multiphasic*) inventories.

The most widely studied and clinically used objective, multitrait test is the **Minnesota Multiphasic Personality Inventory (MMPI)**—or its revision, the MMPI-2 (Butcher, 2000, 2011; Butcher & Perry, 2008). The test consists of over 500 statements that participants respond to with *True, False,* or *Cannot say*. The following are examples of the kinds of statements found on the MMPI:

My stomach frequently bothers me.

I have enemies who really wish to harm me.

I sometimes hear things that other people can't hear.

I would like to be a mechanic.

I have never indulged in any unusual sex practices.

Did you notice that some of these questions are about very unusual, abnormal behavior? Although the full MMPI includes many "normal" questions, the test is designed primarily to help clinical and counseling psychologists diagnose psychological disorders.

MMPI test items are grouped into 10 clinical scales, each measuring a different disorder (Table 13.4). There also are a number of validity scales designed to reflect how respondents: (1) may misunderstand the items, (2) are being uncooperative, or (3)

Minnesota Multiphasic Personality Inventory (MMPI) The most widely researched and clinically used self-report personality test (MMPI-2 is the revised version)

Table 13.4 SUBSCALES OF THE MMPI-2

Clinical Scales	Typical Interpretations of High Scores
1. Hypochondriasis	Numerous physical complaints
2. Depression	Seriously depressed and pessimistic
3. Hysteria	Suggestible, immature, self-centered, demanding
4. Psychopathic deviate	Rebellious, nonfonformist
5. Masculinity–femininity	Interests like those of other sex
6. Paranoia	Suspicious and resentful of others
7. Psychasthenia	Fearful, agitated, brooding
8. Schizophrenia	Withdrawn, reclusive, bizarre thinking
9. Hypomania	Distractible, impulsive, dramatic
10. Social introversion	Shy, introverted, self-effacing

Validity Scales	Typical Interpretations of High Scores
1. L (lie)	Denies common problems, projects a "saintly" or false picture
2. F (confusion)	Answers are contradictory
3. K (defensiveness)	Minimizes social and emotional complaints
4. ? (cannot say)	Many items left unanswered

are deliberately distorting their answers in order to fake psychological disturbances or to appear more psychologically healthy than they really are (Lange, Sullivan, & Scott, 2010; Wygant et al., 2011).

There are other objective personality measures that are less focused on psychological disorders. A good example is the *NEO Personality Inventory-Revised* (Costa & McRae, 1992), which assesses the dimensions comprising the five-factor model (discussed earlier in this chapter).

Another example with which you may be more familiar is the *Myers-Briggs Type Indicator (MBTI)*. This measure assesses four dimensions derived from Carl Jung's theory of personality: extroversion-introversion (EI), sensing-intuition (SI), thinking-feeling (TF), and judging-perceiving (JP). The MBTI has gained huge popularity among the general public, and has been used in assessments as varied as career counseling, hiring executives, and even how U.S. Presidents make foreign policy decisions (Anastasi, 2001; Bayne, 2004; Passmore, Holloway, & Rawle-Cope, 2010). Despite its popular use, questions have been raised about the MBTI's validity and test-retest reliability (i.e., whether an individual will obtain the same pattern of scores when taking the test a second time) (Hunsley & Lee, 2010; Miller, McIntire, & Lovler, 2011; Pittenger, 2005).

Objective personality tests also are often confused with *career inventories* or *vocational interest* tests. For example, the *Strong Vocational Interest Inventory* asks whether you would rather write, illustrate, print, or sell a book or whether you'd prefer the work of a salesperson or teacher. Your answers to these types of questions help identify occupations that match your unique traits, values, and interests.

Given your vocational interest test profile, along with your scores on *aptitude tests* (which measure potential abilities) and *achievement tests* (which measure what you have already learned), a counselor can help you identify the types of jobs that best suit you. Most colleges have career counseling centers where you can take vocational interest tests to guide you in your career decisions.

Projective Techniques

Unlike objective tests, **projective tests** use ambiguous, unstructured stimuli, such as inkblots, which can be perceived in many ways. As the name implies, *projective* tests reportedly allow each person to *project* his or her own unconscious conflicts, psychological defenses, motives, and personality traits onto the test materials. Because respondents are unable (or unwilling) to express their true feelings if asked directly, the ambiguous stimuli are said to provide an indirect, "psychological X-ray" of their hidden, unconscious processes. Two of the most widely used projective tests are the **Rorschach Inkblot Test** and the **Thematic Apperception Test (TAT)** (Concept Organizer 13.1).

Evaluating Personality Assessment: Are the Measurements Accurate?

Objective 13.14: Describe the key advantages and disadvantages of personality measurement.

Let's evaluate each of the four major methods of personality assessment: *interviews*, *observation*, *objective tests*, and *projective tests*.

Interviews and observations

Both interviews and observations can provide valuable insights into personality. But they are time consuming and therefore expensive. Furthermore, just as football fans can disagree over the relative merits of the same quarterback, raters of personality tests frequently disagree in their evaluations of the same individual. Interviews and observations also involve unnatural settings. And, as we saw in Chapter 1, the very presence of an observer can alter the behavior that is being studied.

Projective Tests Psychological tests using ambiguous stimuli, such as inkblots or drawings, which allow the test taker to project his or her unconscious onto the test material

Rorschach [ROAR-shock] Inkblot Test A projective test that presents a set of 10 cards with symmetrical abstract patterns, known as inkblots, and asks respondents to describe what they "see" in the image; their response is thought to be a projection of unconscious processes

Thematic Apperception Test (TAT) A projective test that shows a series of ambiguous black-and-white pictures and asks the test taker to create a story related to each; the responses presumably reflect a projection of unconscious processes

ConceptOrganizer13.1

Projective Tests

Responses to projective tests reportedly reflect unconscious parts of the personality that "project" onto the stimuli.

(a) The Rorschach Inkblot Test was introduced in 1921 by Swiss psychiatrist Hermann Rorschach. With this technique, individuals are shown 10 inkblots like this, one at a time, and are asked to report what figures or objects they see in each of them.

(b) Created by personality researcher Henry Murray in 1938, the Thematic Apperception Test (TAT) consists of a series of ambiguous black-and-white pictures that are shown to the test taker, who is asked to create a story related to each. Can you think of two different stories that a person might create for the picture of two women here? How might a psychologist interpret each story?

Reproduced with permission. This inkblot is not part of the Rorschach test.

Objective tests

Tests like the MMPI-2 provide specific, objective information about a broad range of personality traits in a relatively short period of time. However, they are also the subject of at least three major criticisms:

1. **Deliberate deception and social desirability bias** Some items on self-report inventories are easy to "see through." Thus, respondents may intentionally, or unintentionally, fake particular personality traits. In addition, some respondents want to look good and will answer questions in ways that they perceive as *socially desirable*. (The validity scales of the MMPI-2 are designed to help prevent these problems.)

2. **Diagnostic difficulties** When self-report inventories are used for diagnosis, overlapping items sometimes make it difficult to pinpoint a diagnosis. In addition, clients with severe disorders sometimes score within the normal range, and normal clients may score within the elevated range (Borghans et al., 2011; Weiner, 2008).

3. **Possible cultural bias and inappropriate use** Some critics think that the standards for "normalcy" on objective self-report tests fail to recognize the impact of culture. For example, Latinos—such as Mexicans, Puerto Ricans, and Argentineans—generally score higher than respondents from North American and western European cultures on the masculinity–femininity scale of the MMPI-2 (Dana, 2005; Ketterer, 2011; Mundia, 2011). The fact that these groups score higher may reflect their greater adherence to traditional gender roles and cultural training more than any individual personality traits.

Projective tests

Although projective tests are widely used (Chagnon, 2011; Gacono et al., 2008; Gregory, 2007; Jkiz, 2011), they are extremely time consuming to administer and

Reliability Measure of the consistency and reproducibility of test scores when the test is readministered

Validity Ability of a test to measure what it was designed to measure

interpret. However, their proponents suggest that because they have no right or wrong answers, respondents are less able to deliberately fake their responses. In addition, because these tests are unstructured, respondents may be more willing to talk about sensitive, anxiety-laden topics.

Projective tests are highly controversial (Cautin, 2011; Gacono et al., 2008, Garb et al., 2005, Harwood, Beutler, & Groth-Marnat, 2011). As you recall from Chapter 8's discussion of intelligence tests, the two most important measures of a good test are **reliability** (Are the results consistent?) and **validity** (Does the test measure what it's designed to measure?). One problem with the Rorschach, in particular, is that interpreting clients' responses depends in large part on the subjective judgment of the examiner. And some examiners are simply more experienced or skilled than others. Also, there are problems with *interrater reliability*: Two examiners may interpret the same response in very different ways.

In sum, each of these four methods has its limits. However, psychologists typically combine results from various methods to create a more complete understanding of an individual personality.

Critical Thinking and Pseudo Personality Tests: Why Are They So Popular?

Objective 13.15: List the three major fallacies associated with pseudo-personality tests.

Throughout this text, we have emphasized the value of critical thinking. By carefully evaluating the evidence and credibility of the source, critical thinkers recognize faulty logic and appeals to emotion. Applying these standards to pseudo-personality evaluations like the one in our introductory incident, we can identify at least three important logical fallacies: the *Barnum effect*, *fallacy of positive instances*, and *self-serving bias*.

Barnum Effect

Pseudo-personality descriptions and horoscope predictions are often accepted because we think they are accurate. We tend to believe these tests have somehow tapped into our unique selves. In fact, they are ambiguous, broad statements that fit just about anyone. Being so readily disposed to accept such generalizations is known as the *Barnum effect*. This name is based on P. T. Barnum, the legendary circus promoter who said, "Always have a little something for everyone" (Wyman & Vyse, 2008).

Reread the bogus personality profile in the chapter opening (p. 457). Can you see how the description, "You have a strong need for other people to like and admire you," fits almost everyone? Or do you know anyone who doesn't "at times have serious doubts whether [they've] made the right decision or done the right thing"? P. T. Barnum also said, "There's a sucker born every minute."

Fallacy of Positive Instances

Look again at the introductory personality profile and count the number of times both sides of a personality trait are given. ("You have a strong need for other people to like you" and "You pride yourself on being an independent thinker.") According to the *fallacy of positive instances*, we tend to notice and remember events that confirm our expectations and ignore those that are nonconfirming. If we see ourselves as independent thinkers, for example, we ignore the "needing to be liked by others" part. Similarly, horoscope readers easily find "Sagittarius characteristics" in a Sagittarius horoscope. However, these same readers generally overlook Sagittarius predictions that miss or when the same traits appear for Scorpios or Leos.

Self-Serving Bias

Now check the overall tone of the personality description. Can you see how the traits are generally positive and flattering—or at least neutral? According to the *self-serving bias*, we tend to prefer information that maintains our positive self-image (Krusemark et al., 2008; Shepperd, Malone, & Sweeny, 2008). In fact, research shows that the more favorable a personality description is, the more people believe it, and the more likely they are to believe it is unique to themselves (Guastello, Guastello, & Craft, 1989). (The self-serving bias also may explain why people prefer pseudo-personality tests to bona fide tests—they're generally more flattering!)

Taken together, these three logical fallacies help explain the belief in "pop psych" personality tests and newspaper horoscopes. They offer "something for everyone" (*Barnum effect*). We pay attention only to what confirms our expectations (*fallacy of positive instances*). And we like flattering descriptions (*self-serving bias*).

TEST YOURSELF

Using the information in the previous section, can you identify the two fallacies in this cartoon?

Answer: The self-serving bias and the Barnum effect.

Psychology Engages

RESEARCH CHALLENGE

Self-Esteem: Healthy Versus Fragile?

By Thomas Frangicetto (Northampton Community College, Bethlehem, PA)

In April 2008, six teenage girls viciously attacked their "friend" 16-year-old Victoria Lindsay, and videotaped it to share with others on MySpace. Ignoring Victoria's screams and pleas, one of the attackers repeatedly struck her in the face, and eventually slammed her head into a wall, knocking her unconscious.

Why? What motivated the assault? According to the arresting sheriff, this was supposedly some form of retaliation for a "dissing" of the attackers by the victim on her MySpace. Asked if the girls showed any remorse, a detective said: "None at all. . .when we had them in detention, they were joking, 'Guess we're not going to go to the beach on this spring break.'" The girls were also quoted as saying that they "weren't sorry" and that Victoria "deserved what she got."

One of psychology's most spirited, ongoing debates is over the issue of *self esteem*, generally defined as some variation of "a person's overall evaluation of his or her worth." Although research has found numerous benefits associated with high self-esteem (Baumeister, 2001; Baumeister et al., 2005; Diener & Diener, 1995), when it's defined as just having feelings of self worth even Lindsay's attackers could be seen as having "high" self-esteem!

It's important to note that research also shows a link between high self-esteem and increased aggression (Baumeister, Bushman, & Campbell, 2000; Hughes, Cavell, & Grossman, 1997; Lau et al., 2010; Salmivalli, 2001). Apparently, many assaults, physical altercations, and murders are perpetrated in response to "blows to self-esteem such as insults and humiliation" (Baumeister, 2001). High self-esteem and narcissism (self-conceit)—think egocentrism on steroids—is an especially potent mixture that sometimes leads to elevated levels of aggression.

For example, Lau and his colleagues (2010) recently tested the prediction that narcissism is positively associated with delinquency and aggression. The researchers used five separate self-report scales, for delinquency, peer conflict, anxiety and depression, self-esteem, and narcissistic personality traits, and then statistically measured the levels of interaction between all variables. The results not only confirmed the original prediction, but also found significant interaction among youth with high self-esteem *and* high narcissism with overt aggression. However, other researchers (Ostrowsky, 2010; Walker & Bright, 2009)

believe it is "inflated" or *fragile* high self-esteem, not *healthy* high self-esteem, that is the problem. That is, high "fragile" self-esteem is "in reality covering low self-esteem, and that the fragile, inflated self-esteem is part of the 'macho' cover-up of embarrassment." Why, they ask, would someone take serious offense and become violent "if they were secure in themselves?" (Walker & Bright, 2009).

In response to the difficulties and contradictions with existing definitions and categories of **self-esteem**, the California Task Force (1990) developed a definition, which we're also using in this text: *Appreciating one's own worth and importance and having the character to be accountable for oneself and to act responsibly toward others.*

Using this Task Force definition, it's easy to see that the girls who attacked Victoria Lindsay lacked both accountability and responsibility to others. They also displayed a narcissistic, *fragile* self-esteem, believing they were entitled to the admiration of others due to *how special they need to believe themselves to be.* In contrast, those with *healthy*, high self-esteem understand that they have to work hard to earn the high opinion of other people (Morf & Rhodewalt, 2001). The Task Force itself warned against using definitions that included what they regard "as its polar opposite, namely, a false, vain, and narcissistic preoccupation . . . a self-glorification . . . that prevents a healthy self-esteem" (California Task Force, 1990).

Ellen Schrier (2011), a family therapist and mother of three, applauded the Task Force efforts and framed the issue well: "The problem began when people decided that in order to build self-esteem, they must protect children from ever seeing themselves as failures. And they forgot about the *having the character to be accountable for oneself and to act responsibly toward others part,* too. It was a one-two punch definition "that got watered down to an 'all-about-me' definition instead."

In sum, the controversy over self-esteem is still unresolved. Many have blamed the so-called "self-esteem movement" for creating a generation of overly-entitled, unrealistic, narcissistic people ill-suited for today's economy (Twenge, 2006, 2010), yet it remains a staple of the "self-help industry." With the public and researchers divided over the precise definition and pros and cons of self-esteem, what's a parent, educator, or concerned citizen to do? We believe the emphasis on *accountability* and *responsibility* offered by the task force's definition, along with a clarification of *healthy* versus *fragile* self-esteem, provides much-needed public guidance. It also offers scientists a more adaptable, prosocial baseline to use as a unifying starting point for future research.

Finally, we'd like to take a bit of creative license and suggest a greater focus on environmental and social forces that also contribute to narcissistic, fragile self-esteem, which, in turn, may result in aggression. A case in point—less than a year after Lindsay was beaten, the mother of the lead attacker was "arrested on domestic violence charges after allegedly battering her daughter twice in one afternoon" (Vice, 2009). Some may too-easily suggest, "The fruit *doesn't* fall far from the tree." But what else are we to say if the fruit that falls to the ground has already been bruised and battered?

Student Engagement Exercise

Given the information in the Lau et al. (2009) study described above, what is the most likely:

1. *Research method* (experimental, descriptive, correlational, or biological)?

2. If you chose the:
   - *Experimental method*—label the IV, DV, experimental group, and control group.
   - *Descriptive method*—identify whether this is a naturalistic observation, survey, or case study.
   - *Correlational method*—label whether this is a positive, negative, or zero correlation.
   - *Biological method*—identify the specific research tool (e.g., brain dissection, CT scan, etc.)

(Answers appear in Appendix B.)

Dear diary,
Sorry to
bother you again.

LOW SELF-ESTEEM

Self-Esteem Appreciating one's own worth and importance and having the character to be accountable for oneself and to act responsibly toward others

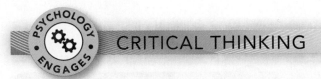

Maslow Revisited: Linking Critical Thinking and Self-Actualization

By Thomas Frangicetto (Northampton Community College, Bethlehem, PA)

Having explored Abraham Maslow's hierarchy of needs and the advantages of becoming self-actualized, would you like a few tips on how to achieve this highest level? Maslow carefully studied many individuals of extraordinarily high achievement, such as Abraham Lincoln, Thomas Jefferson, Albert Einstein, and Eleanor Roosevelt, and identified 15 common characteristics (Maslow, 1954). The following exercise will help you explore and apply 6 of the 15 characteristics to your own life.

Part 1. On the table below, enter a numerical rating (from 0 to 10), for each of the six characteristics of self-actualizers and parallel six critical thinking components.

Your Score	Self-Actualizing Characteristic	Your Score	Critical Thinking Component
_____	**1. Perceives reality clearly and is comfortable with uncertainty** *Self-actualizers* are more likely to detect the fake and dishonest in others, to judge people accurately, and are less threatened by the unknown. They are not only at ease with the ambiguous and unstructured, *they like it*! Maslow quoted Einstein saying: "The most beautiful thing we can experience is the mysterious. It is the source of all art and science."	_____	**Tolerates ambiguity** *Critical thinkers* recognize that many questions and issues are frustratingly complex, with multiple and often competing opinions and answers.
_____	**2. Affectionately identifies with other people, not selectively, but with all humanity** *Self-actualizers* sometimes feel impatient with others, but they have affection for *all* and have a genuine desire to help the human race. They often feel the *pain of the world*, and their empathy frequently leads to altruistic behavior.	_____	**Empathizes** *Critical thinkers* appreciate and try to understand others' thoughts, feelings, and behaviors. Taking the perspective of others (empathy) is the most effective antidote to egocentric thinking.
_____	**3. Establishes deep, satisfying interpersonal relationships with a few, rather than many, people** *Self-actualizers* have deeper and more profound interpersonal relationships. They are capable of more fusion, greater love, more perfect identification. But those they love profoundly are few in number, due to the time involved in the cultivation and maintenance of a truly intimate relationship.	_____	**Encourages critical dialogue** *Critical thinkers* know that the best relationships thrive on honest communication and use both intrapersonal and interpersonal intelligence to connect with others.
_____	**4. Discriminates between means and ends** *Self-actualizers* are strongly ethical in behavior as well as beliefs. They are capable of separating means from ends—if they want to do well on an exam, they will study hard, not cheat, as it would violate their personal integrity. They have high *character* and generally operate at Kohlberg's 6th stage, reflecting high *individual conscience*.	_____	**Values truth above self-interest** *Critical thinkers* do not cater to their own needs and desires at the expense of the rights of others. They know that even when it appears otherwise, the truth is always in our self-interest.
_____	**5. Possesses a democratic character structure** *Self-actualizers* believe all people are equal and can enjoy relationships with anyone, "regardless of class, education, political belief, race, and color." They believe in the dignity of all and are willing to learn from others. If they detect bias in themselves, they try to eradicate it.	_____	**Recognizes personal bias/welcomes divergent views** *Critical thinkers* attempt to face their biases head on and are willing to hear others' views in order to challenge their own ideas.
_____	**6. Resists enculturation (conformity to the culture)** *Self-actualizers* resist being pressured to conform by the culture they live in. Although they seldom actively "rebel" against tradition, they speak out when they feel it is warranted (e.g., showing bursts of indignation with injustice).	_____	**Thinks independently** *Critical thinkers* don't passively accept beliefs of others, and they resist manipulation. While maintaining a healthy skepticism, they differentiate between being skeptical and being stubborn.

Part 2. On a separate sheet of paper, briefly explain your rating for each section above and for all ratings below 10. Brainstorm with another person for ways to improve on your lowest ratings.

Want more information? You can review all 15 of Maslow's characteristics at the link below. While visiting the site, try to identify additional links between characteristics of self-actualizers and critical thinking components from the Prologue. http://brainmeta.com/index.php?p=self-actualization.

STOP *Before going on, be sure to complete this Check & Review. It is an invaluable study tool!*

Personality Assessment and Psychology Engages

Part A: Retrieval Practice

1. Without looking at the book, spend 10 minutes writing a free-form essay recalling all you can remember from the previous section.

2. Now, reread the previous section, and once again spend 10 minutes writing a free-form essay on the SAME material.

Part B: Practice Quiz

1. Match each personality test with its description:

   a. a projective test using inkblots

   b. an objective, self-report personality test

   c. a projective test using ambiguous drawings of ambiguous human situations

   ___i. MMPI-2

   ___ii. Rorschach

   ___iii. TAT

2. The *Rorschach Inkblot Test* is an example of a(n) _____ test.

3. Two important criteria for evaluating the usefulness of tests used to assess personality are _____. (a) concurrence and prediction; (b) reliability and validity; (c) consistency and correlation; (d) diagnosis and prognosis

4. Describe the three logical fallacies that encourage acceptance of pseudo-personality tests and horoscopes.

Check your answers in Appendix B.

www.wileyplus.com

WileyPLUS presents an on-line version of this textbook along with a wealth of study resources including quizzes, practice tests, flash cards, videos, animations and other activities designed to improve your mastery of the content. Working in conjunction with these study tools, the *Psychology in Action* WileyPLUS course features Professor Karen Huffman, author of this textbook, explaining and expanding upon some of the most challenging concepts in psychology. Here is a sample of the tutorial videos available for this chapter:

- An animated look at Freud's defense mechanisms
- How do psychologists measure personality?
- Professor Huffman's classroom exercise to explore student's individual personality traits
- Applying Roger's theory to our relationships
- Virtual Field Trip to a personality research lab for a glimpse into the latest findings on personality

→ Key Terms

To assess your understanding of the **Key Terms** in Chapter 13, write a definition for each (in your own words), and then compare your definitions with those in the text.

Personaliy (p. 458)

Trait Theories
trait (p. 458)
factor analysis (p. 458)
five-factor model (FFM) (p. 459)

Psychoanalytic/Psychodynamic Theories
conscious (p. 463)
preconscious (p. 463)
unconscious (p. 463)
id (p. 464)
pleasure principle (p. 464)
ego (p. 464)
reality principle (p. 464)
superego (p. 464)
morality principle (p. 464)

defense mechanisms (p. 464)
repression (p. 464)
psychosexual stages (p. 466)
inferiority complex (p. 466)
Oedipus [ED-uh-puss] complex (p. 467)
collective unconscious (p. 468)
archetypes [AR-KEH-types] (p. 468)
basic anxiety (p. 469)

Humanistic Theories
self-actualization (p. 470)
self-concept (p. 471)
unconditional positive regard (p. 471)

Social-Cognitive Theories
self-efficacy (p. 474)
reciprocal determinism (p. 474)

Personality Assessment
Minnesota Multiphasic Personality Inventory (MMPI) (p. 479)
projective tests (p. 480)
Rorschach [ROAR-shock] Inkblot Test (p. 480)
Thematic Apperception Test (TAT) (p. 480)
reliability (p. 482)
validity (p. 482)

Psychology Engages
self-esteem (p. 484)

Chapter Summary

Trait Theories

Objective 13.1: Differentiate personality versus traits, and discuss early trait theories and the five-factor model.
Personality consists of unique and relatively stable patterns of thoughts, feelings, and actions, whereas **traits** are personal characteristics we use to describe someone. Gordon Allport described individuals by their trait hierarchy. Raymond Cattell and Hans Eysenck used **factor analysis** to identify the smallest possible number of traits. More recently, researchers identified a **five-factor model (FFM)** that can be used to describe most individuals. The five traits are *openness*, *conscientiousness*, *extroversion*, *agreeableness*, and *neuroticism*.

Objective 13.2: What are the key research findings and criticisms of trait theories?
Evolutionary research and cross-cultural studies support the five-factor model. But trait theories are subject to three major criticisms: *lack of explanation* (no explanation for why people develop certain traits and why traits sometimes change), *stability versus change* (no specifics provided about which early characteristics endure and which are transient), and *ignoring situational effects*.

Psychoanalytic/Psychodynamic Theories

Objective 13.3: Describe Freud's psychoanalytic approach to personality.
Sigmund Freud founded the psychoanalytic approach to personality, which emphasizes the power of the unconscious. The mind (or psyche) reportedly functions on three levels of awareness (**conscious, preconscious,** and **unconscious**). Similarly, the personality has three distinct structures (**id, ego,** and **superego**). The ego struggles to meet the demands of both the id and superego. When these demands conflict, the ego may resort to **defense mechanisms** to relieve anxiety.

Objective 13.4: Summarize Freud's five psychosexual stages.
According to Freud, all human beings pass through five **psychosexual stages**: oral, anal, phallic, latency, and genital. How specific conflicts at each of these stages are resolved is important to personality development.

Objective 13.5: Compare Freud's versus the neo-Freudians' approaches to personality.
Three influential followers of Freud who later broke from him were Alfred Adler, Carl Jung, and Karen Horney. Known as neo-Freudians, they emphasized different issues. Adler emphasized the **inferiority complex** and the compensating will-to-power. Jung introduced the **collective unconscious** and **archetypes**. Horney stressed the importance of **basic anxiety** and refuted Freud's idea of penis envy, replacing it with power envy.

Objective 13.6: Discuss the major criticisms of psychoanalytic theories of personality.
Critics of the psychoanalytic approach, especially Freud's theories, argue that the approach is difficult to test, overemphasizes biology and unconscious forces, has inadequate empirical support, is sexist, and lacks cross-cultural support. Despite these criticisms, Freud remains a notable pioneer in psychology.

Humanistic Theories

Objective 13.7: Discuss humanistic theories of personality, comparing the approaches of Rogers and Maslow.
Humanistic theories focus on internal experiences (thoughts and feelings) and the individual's **self-concept**. Carl Rogers emphasized mental health, congruence, self-esteem, and **unconditional positive regard**. Abraham Maslow emphasized the potential for **self-actualization**.

Objective 13.8: What are the major criticisms of humanistic theories of personality?
Critics of the humanistic approach argue that these theories are based on naive assumptions and are not scientifically testable or well supported by empirical evidence. In addition, their focus on description, rather than explanation, makes them narrow.

Social-Cognitive Theories

Objective 13.9: Discuss the social-cognitive perspective on personality, comparing Bandura and Rotter's approaches.
Social-cognitive theorists emphasize the importance of our interactions with the environment and how we interpret and respond to these external events. Albert Bandura's social-cognitive approach focuses on **self-efficacy** and **reciprocal determinism**. Julian Rotter emphasizes cognitive expectancies and an internal or external locus of control.

Objective 13.10: What are the major strengths and weaknesses of the social-cognitive theories?
Social-cognitive theories are credited for their attention to environmental influences and their scientific standards. However, they have been criticized for their narrow focus and lack of attention to the unconscious, environmental, and emotional components of personality.

Biological Theories

Objective 13.11: How does biology contribute to personality?
Biological theories emphasize brain structures, neurochemistry, and inherited genetic components of personality. Research on specific traits, such as extroversion and sensation seeking, support the biological approach.

Objective 13.12: Describe how the biopsychosocial model blends various approaches to personality.
The biopsychosocial approach suggests that the major theories overlap and that each contributes to our understanding of personality.

Personality Assessment

Objective 13.13: How do psychologists measure personality?
Psychologists use four basic methods to measure or assess personality: interviews, observations, objective tests, and projective techniques.

Interviews and observations can provide insights into a wide variety of behaviors and personality traits. Interviews can be either structured or unstructured. During observations, the rater looks for examples of specific behaviors and follows a careful set of evaluation guidelines.

Objective tests, such as the **Minnesota Multiphasic Personality Inventory (MMPI-2)**, use self-report questionnaires or inventories. These tests provide objective standardized information about a large number of personality traits.

Projective tests, such as the **Rorschach Inkblot Test** and the **Thematic Apperception Test (TAT)**, ask test takers to respond to ambiguous stimuli, which reportedly provide insight into unconscious elements of personality.

Objective 13.14: Describe the key advantages and disadvantages of personality measurement.
Both *interviews* and *observations* can provide valuable insights into personality, but they are time consuming and expensive, raters frequently disagree, and they often involve unnatural settings.

Objective tests provide specific, objective information, but they are limited because of deliberate deception and social desirability bias, diagnostic difficulties, cultural bias, and inappropriate use.

Projective tests are time consuming and have questionable reliability and validity. However, because they are unstructured, respondents may be more willing to talk honestly about sensitive topics, and projective tests are harder to fake.

Objective 13.15: List the three major fallacies associated with pseudo-personality tests.
The *Barnum effect, fallacy of positive instances,* and *self-serving bias* are the three most important fallacies of pseudo-personality tests.

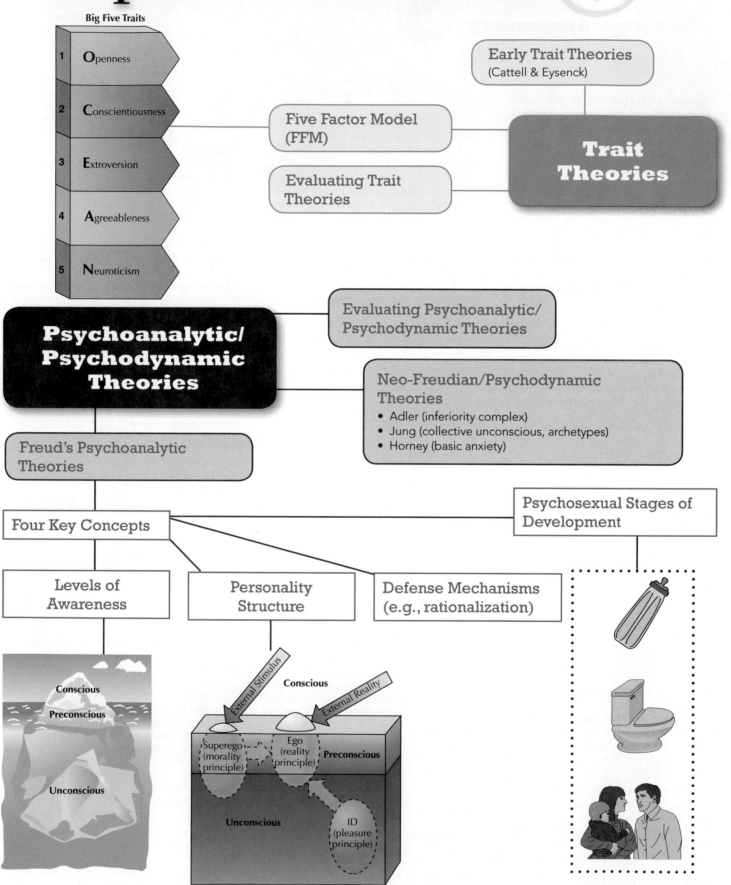

Big Five Traits

1 **O**penness
2 **C**onscientiousness
3 **E**xtroversion
4 **A**greeableness
5 **N**euroticism

Early Trait Theories
(Cattell & Eysenck)

Five Factor Model
(FFM)

Evaluating Trait
Theories

**Trait
Theories**

**Psychoanalytic/
Psychodynamic
Theories**

Evaluating Psychoanalytic/
Psychodynamic Theories

Neo-Freudian/Psychodynamic
Theories
• Adler (inferiority complex)
• Jung (collective unconscious, archetypes)
• Horney (basic anxiety)

Freud's Psychoanalytic
Theories

Psychosexual Stages of
Development

Four Key Concepts

Levels of
Awareness

Personality
Structure

Defense Mechanisms
(e.g., rationalization)

Conscious
Preconscious
Unconscious

External Stimulus
Conscious
External Reality
Superego
(morality
principle)
Ego
(reality
principle)
Preconscious
Unconscious
ID
(pleasure
principle)

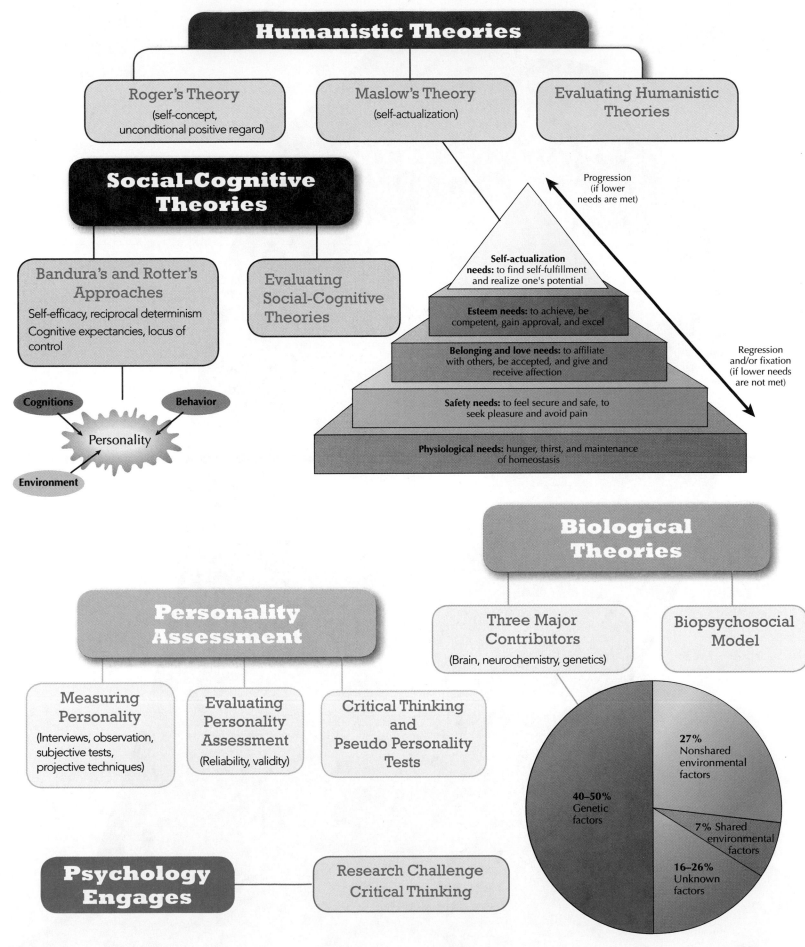

Humanistic Theories

Roger's Theory
(self-concept, unconditional positive regard)

Maslow's Theory
(self-actualization)

Evaluating Humanistic Theories

Social-Cognitive Theories

Bandura's and Rotter's Approaches

Self-efficacy, reciprocal determinism
Cognitive expectancies, locus of control

Evaluating Social-Cognitive Theories

Cognitions

Behavior

Personality

Environment

Progression
(if lower needs are met)

Self-actualization needs: to find self-fulfillment and realize one's potential

Esteem needs: to achieve, be competent, gain approval, and excel

Belonging and love needs: to affiliate with others, be accepted, and give and receive affection

Safety needs: to feel secure and safe, to seek pleasure and avoid pain

Physiological needs: hunger, thirst, and maintenance of homeostasis

Regression and/or fixation (if lower needs are not met)

Biological Theories

Three Major Contributors
(Brain, neurochemistry, genetics)

Biopsychosocial Model

Personality Assessment

Measuring Personality
(Interviews, observation, subjective tests, projective techniques)

Evaluating Personality Assessment
(Reliability, validity)

Critical Thinking and Pseudo Personality Tests

40–50% Genetic factors

27% Nonshared environmental factors

7% Shared environmental factors

16–26% Unknown factors

Psychology Engages

Research Challenge Critical Thinking

ChapterFourteen

Psychological Disorders

Have you heard of the "giraffe women" of the Kayan tribe in Thailand who wear heavy copper coils around their necks to push their faces up and make their necks look longer? At the age of 5 or 6, the first coil is normally added, but some little girls are "coiled" at the age of 2. Year after year, new coils are added. Once fastened, the rings are worn for life because the neck muscles weaken and deteriorate to the point they can no longer support the weight of the head. These coils weigh up to 12 pounds and depress the clavicle and ribs about 45 degrees from their normal position. Would you consider this behavior abnormal? Consider the following cases taken from our own Western culture:

Mary's troubles first began in adolescence. She began to miss curfew, was frequently truant, and her grades declined sharply. Mary later became promiscuous and prostituted herself several times to get drug money. . . . She also quickly fell in love and overly idealized new friends. But when they quickly (and inevitably) disappointed her, she would angrily cast them aside. . . . Mary's problems, coupled with a preoccupation with inflicting pain on herself (by cutting and burning) and persistent thoughts of suicide, eventually led to her admittance to a psychiatric hospital at age 26.

(KRING ET AL., 2010, PP. 354–355)

Rain or shine, day in and day out, 43-year-old Joshua occupies his "post" on a busy street corner wearing his standard outfit—a Red Sox baseball cap, yellow T-shirt, worn-out hiking shorts, and orange sneakers. Sometimes he can be seen "conversing" with imaginary people. Without apparent cause, he also frequently explodes into shrieks of laughter or breaks down into miserable sobs. Police and social workers keep taking him to shelters for the homeless, but Joshua manages to get back on the street before he can be treated. He has repeatedly insisted that these people have no right to keep bothering him.

(HALGIN & WHITBOURNE, 2008, P. 283)

ChapterOutline

491

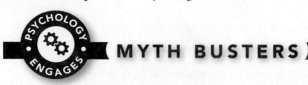

MYTH BUSTERS

Objective 14.1: Identify five common myths about mental illness.

Do you recognize these myths?

- *Myth #1: People with psychological disorders act in bizarre ways and are very different from normal people.*

  Fact: This is true for only a small minority of individuals and during a relatively small portion of their lives. In fact, sometimes even mental health professionals find it difficult to distinguish normal from abnormal individuals without formal screening.

- *Myth #2: Mental disorders are a sign of personal weakness.*

  Fact: Psychological disorders are a function of many factors, such as exposure to stress, genetic disposition, family background, and so on. Mentally disturbed individuals can't be blamed for their illness any more than we blame people who develop Alzheimer's or other physical illnesses.

- *Myth #3: Mentally ill people are often dangerous and unpredictable.*

  Fact: Only a few disorders, such as some psychotic and antisocial personality disorders are associated with violence. The stereotype that connects mental illness and violence persists because of prejudice and selective media attention.

- *Myth #4: A person who has been mentally ill never fully recovers.*

  Fact: With therapy, the vast majority of people who are diagnosed as mentally ill eventually improve and lead normal, productive lives. Moreover, mental disorders are generally only temporary.

- *Myth #5: Most mentally ill individuals can work at only low-level jobs.*

  Fact: Like all illnesses, mental disorders are complex and their symptoms, severity, and prognoses differ for each individual. Although some people are seriously disabled by their disorder, others are very productive and high functioning.

Is this behavior abnormal? Eccentric? Yes. Mentally disordered? Probably not.

For example, U.S. President Abraham Lincoln, British Prime Minister Winston Churchill, scientist Issac Newton, painter Vincent Van Gogh, and author Charles Dickens are all famous achievers who suffered from serious mental disorders at various times throughout their careers.

(*Sources:* Barlow & Durand, 2012; *Famous People with Schizophrenia,* 2011; *Famous People with Mental Illness,* 2011; Kring et al., 2010; Lilienfeld et al., 2010).

Studying Psychological Disorders

Both Mary and Joshua have severe psychological problems, and both of their stories raise interesting questions. What caused their difficulties? Was there something in their early backgrounds to explain their later behaviors? Is there something medically wrong with them? What about the "giraffe women"? What is the difference between being culturally different and being mentally disordered?

In this chapter, we will discover that abnormal behavior is subject to different interpretations over time and across cultures. We begin with a discussion of how psychological disorders are identified, explained, and classified. We then explore six major categories of psychological disorders: anxiety disorders, mood disorders, schizophrenia, substance-related disorders, dissociative disorders, and personality disorders. Finally, we look at gender and cultural factors related to mental disorders.

As the introductory cases show, mental disorders vary in type and severity from person to person. The behaviors of both Mary and Joshua are clearly abnormal. But the "giraffe women's" voluntary placement of life-threatening coils around their necks shows us that many cases of abnormal behavior are not so clear-cut. Rather than being two discrete categories, "normal" and "abnormal," abnormal behavior, like intelligence or creativity, lies along a continuum. And at the end points, people can be unusually healthy or extremely disturbed.

Step-by-StepDiagram14.1

STOP This Step by Step diagram contains essential information NOT found elsewhere in the text, which is likely to appear on quizzes and exams. Be sure to study it CAREFULLY!

Four Criteria and a Continuum of Abnormal Behavior

Note: Rather than being fixed categories, both "abnormal" and "normal" behaviors exist along a continuum, and no single criterion is adequate for Identifying all forms of abnormal behavior (Hansell & Damour, 2008).

Normal	Abnormal

Deviance
(e.g., believing others are plotting against you)

Behaviors, thoughts, or emotions may be considered deviant and abnormal when they differ from a society or culture's norms or values. A major problem with this criterion is that judgments of deviance and abnormality vary from society to society, and values change over time. For example, women attending college, participating in athletics, or having a full-time job outside the home were once considered abnormal.

Normal	Abnormal

Dysfunction
(e.g., being unable to go to work due to alcohol abuse)

Behaviors, thoughts, or emotions that seriously interfere with daily functioning may be considered abnormal. People suffering from mental illness may not be able to take proper care of themselves, work effectively, or get along well with others. Their ability to think clearly and make rational decisions also may be significantly impaired.

Normal	Abnormal

Distress
(e.g., having thoughts of suicide)

Behaviors, thoughts, or emotions that cause significant personal distress may qualify as abnormal. As we saw in the opening case, Mary's promiscuity, relationship problems, cutting and burning of herself, and suicidal thoughts all indicate serious personal distress and unhappiness.

Normal	Abnormal

Danger
(e.g., fighting with strangers)

Some people with psychological disorders exhibit behaviors, thoughts, or emotions that indicate potential danger to themselves or others. Again, Mary's persistent thoughts of suicide clearly suggest that she needs professional help. However, as you discovered in the "Myth Buster" section (page 492), people generally overestimate the danger of mental illness—thanks to exaggerated film portrayals and intense media coverage. Although danger is one of the four categories, keep in mind that research indicates that it is actually the *exception rather than the rule*.

Identifying Abnormal Behavior: Four Basic Criteria

Objective 14.2: Define abnormal behavior, and list four standards for identifying it.

Recognizing this continuum, mental health professionals often agree on at least four criteria for identifying **abnormal behavior** often called the "four D's"): *deviance, dysfunction, distress, and danger* (Step-by-Step Diagram 14.1).

Abnormal Behavior Patterns of behaviors, thoughts, or emotions considered pathological (diseased or disordered) for one or more of four reasons: deviance, dysfunction, distress, or danger

Figure 14.1 An early "treatment" for abnormal behavior? During the Stone Age, the recommended "therapy" for mental disorders was to bore holes in the skull to allow evil spirits to escape—a process known as "trephining."

Medical Model Perspective that assumes diseases (including mental illness) have physical causes that can be diagnosed, treated, and possibly cured

Psychiatry Branch of medicine dealing with the diagnosis, treatment, and prevention of mental disorders

Diagnostic and Statistical Manual of Mental Disorders (DSM-IV-TR) Classification system developed by the American Psychiatric Association used to describe abnormal behaviors; the "IV-TR" indicates it is the text revision (TR) of the fourth major revision (IV)

Neurosis Outmoded term for disorders characterized by unrealistic anxiety and other associated problems; less severe disruptions than in psychosis

Psychosis Serious mental disorders characterized by extreme mental disruption and defective or lost contact with reality

Explaining Abnormality: From Superstition to Science

Objective 14.3: Briefly describe the historical understanding of abnormal behavior.

Having explored the criteria for defining abnormal behavior, the next logical question is, "How do we explain it?" Historically, evil spirits and witchcraft have been the primary suspects (Goodwin 2009; Millon, 2004; Petry, 2011; Riva et al., 2011). Stone Age people, for example, believed that abnormal behavior stemmed from demonic possession; the "therapy" was to bore a hole in the skull so that the evil spirit could escape (Figure 14.1). During the European Middle Ages, troubled people were sometimes treated with *exorcism* in an effort to drive the Devil out through prayer, fasting, noise-making, beating, and drinking terrible-tasting brews. During the fifteenth century, many believed that some individuals chose to consort with the Devil and these supposed witches were often tortured, imprisoned for life, or executed.

As the Middle Ages ended, special mental hospitals called *asylums* began to appear in Europe. Initially designed to provide quiet retreats from the world and to protect society (Barlow & Durand, 2012; Coleborned Mackinnon, 2011; Freckelton, 2011; Millon, 2004), the asylums unfortunately became overcrowded, inhumane prisons.

Improvement came in 1792 when Philippe Pinel, a French physician in charge of a Parisian asylum, insisted that asylum inmates—whose behavior he believed to be caused by underlying physical illness—be unshackled and removed from their unlighted, unheated cells. Many inmates improved so dramatically that they could be released. Pinel's **medical model** eventually gave rise to the modern specialty of **psychiatry**.

Unfortunately, when we label people "mentally ill," we may create new problems. One of the most outspoken critics of the medical model is psychiatrist Thomas Szasz (1960, 2000, 2004). Szasz believes that the medical model encourages people to believe that they have no responsibility for their actions. He contends that mental illness is a myth used to label individuals who are peculiar or offensive to others (Adams, 2011; Breeding, 2011; Cresswell, 2008). Furthermore, labels can become self-perpetuating—that is, the person can begin to behave according to the diagnosed disorder.

Despite these potential dangers, the medical model—and the concept of mental illness—remains a founding principle of psychiatry. In contrast, psychology offers a multifaceted approach to explaining abnormal behavior (Concept Organizer 14.1).

Classifying Abnormal Behavior: Diagnostic and Statistical Manual IV-TR

Objective 14.4: Describe the purpose and criticisms of the DSM-IV-TR, and differentiate between neurosis, psychosis, and insanity.

Without a clear and reliable system for classifying and describing the wide range of psychological disorders, scientific research on them would be almost impossible, and communication among mental health professionals would be seriously impaired. Fortunately, mental health specialists share a uniform classification system: the text revision of the fourth edition of the **Diagnostic and Statistical Manual of Mental Disorders (DSM-IV-TR)** (American Psychiatric Association, 2000). A more substantial revision, the *DSMV*, is scheduled for publication in 2013.

Each revision of the *DSM* has expanded the list of disorders and changed the descriptions and categories to reflect both the latest in scientific research and changes in the way abnormal behaviors are viewed within our social context (Blashfield, Flanagan, & Raley, 2010; Sass, 2011). For example, take the terms **neurosis** and **psychosis**. In previous editions, *neurosis* reflected Freud's belief that all neurotic

ConceptOrganizer14.1

STOP This Concept Organizer contains essential information NOT found elsewhere in the text, which is likely to appear on quizzes and exams. Be sure to study it CAREFULLY!

Seven Psychological Perspectives on Abnormal Behavior

Each of the seven major perspectives in psychology emphasizes different factors believed to contribute to abnormal behavior, but in practice they overlap. Consider the phenomenon of compulsive hoarding. Everyone sometimes makes an impulse purchase, and most people are reluctant to discard some possessions that are of questionable value. But when the acquisition of and inability to discard worthless items becomes extreme, it can interfere with basic aspects of living, such as cleaning, cooking, sleeping on a bed, and moving around one's home. This abnormal behavior is associated with several psychological disorders, but it is most commonly found in people who have obsessive compulsive disorder, or OCD (an anxiety disorder discussed later in this chapter). Can you see how each of the seven major perspectives might explain compulsive hoarding?

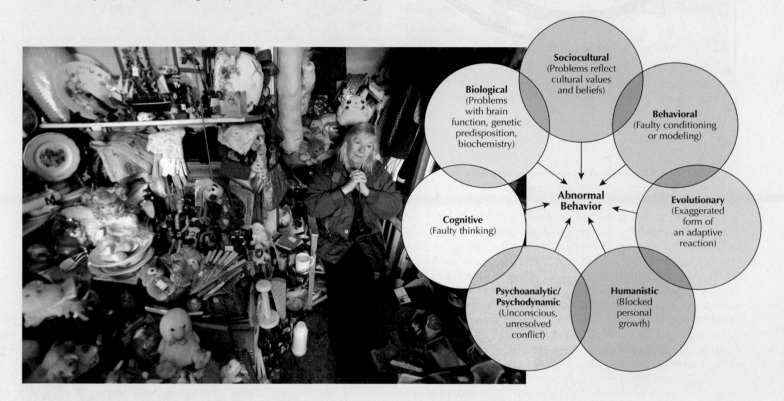

conditions arise from unconscious conflicts (Chapter 13). Now conditions that were previously grouped under the heading *neurosis* have been formally redistributed as anxiety disorders, somatoform disorders, and dissociative disorders.

Unlike neurosis, the term *psychosis* is still listed in the *DSM-IV-TR* because it remains useful for distinguishing the most severe mental disorders, such as schizophrenia and some mood disorders.

What about the term *insanity*? Where does it fit in? **Insanity** is a legal term indicating that a person cannot be held responsible for his or her actions, or is judged incompetent to manage his or her own affairs, because of mental illness. In the law, the definition of mental illness rests primarily on a person's inability to tell right from wrong. For psychologists, insanity is not the same as abnormal behavior. The case of Andrea Yates, the mother who killed her five small children, helps clarify the difference (Figure 14.2).

Insanity Legal term applied when people cannot be held responsible for their actions, or are judged incompetent to manage their own affairs, because of mental illness

▲ **Witchcraft or mental illness?** During the fifteenth century, some people who may have been suffering from mental disorders were accused of witchcraft and tortured or hung.

▲ **An early catch-22.** In the Middle Ages, "dunking tests" were used to determine whether people who behaved abnormally were possessed by demons. Individuals who did not drown while being dunked were believed to be guilty of possession and then punished (usually by hanging). Those who did drown were judged to be innocent. This was the ultimate catch-22, or no-win situation.

Figure 14.2 The insanity plea—guilty of a crime or mentally ill? On the morning of June 20, 2001, Texas mother Andrea Yates drowned her five children in the bathtub, then calmly called her husband to tell him he should come home. At Yates's trial, both the defense and prosecution agreed that Yates was mentally ill at the time of the murders, yet the jury still found her guilty and sentenced her to life in prison. (An appellate court later overturned this conviction. In 2006, Yates was found not guilty by reason of insanity and committed to a state mental hospital in which she will be held until she is no longer deemed a threat.) How could two courts come to such opposite conclusions? *Insanity* is a complicated legal term. In most states it refers to a person who cannot be held responsible for his or her actions, or is judged incompetent to manage his or her own affairs, because of mental illness. Despite high-profile cases like that of Andrea Yates, it's important to keep in mind that the insanity plea is used in less than 1 percent of all cases that reach trial, and when used, it is rarely successful (Kirschner, Litwack, & Galperin, 2004; Slobogin, 2006; West & Lichtenstein, 2006).

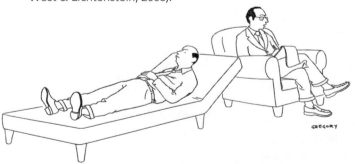

"In the mental health profession, we try to avoid negative labels, like 'a hundred and fifty bucks an hour—that's crazy!' or 'three fifty-minute sessions a week—that's insane!'"

Understanding and Evaluating the DSM

To understand a disorder, we must first name and describe it. The DSM-IV-TR identifies and describes the symptoms of approximately 400 disorders, which are grouped into 17 categories (Table 14.1). In addition to naming and describing disorders, the DSM also organizes diagnostic information into five dimensions, or axes, which allow both the person and his or her life situation to be taken into account (Figure 14.3).

Classification and diagnosis of mental disorders are essential to scientific study. Without such a system, we could not effectively identify and diagnose the wide variety of disorders, predict their future courses, or suggest appropriate treatment. The DSM also

Table 14.1 MAIN CATEGORIES OF MENTAL DISORDERS AND THEIR DESCRIPTIONS IN DSM-IV-TR
(THE FIRST SIX DISORDERS ARE DISCUSSED IN THIS CHAPTER)

Anxiety disorders

Mood disorders

Substance-related disorders

1. **Anxiety Disorders:** Problems associated with severe anxiety, such as *phobias, obsessive-compulsive disorder*, and *posttraumatic stress disorder*.

2. **Mood Disorders:** Problems associated with severe disturbances of mood, such as *depression, mania*, or alternating episodes of the two *(bipolar disorder)*.

3. **Schizophrenia and other Psychotic Disorders:** A group of disorders characterized by major disturbances in perception, language and thought, emotion, and behavior.

4. **Dissociative Disorders:** Disorders in which the normal integration of consciousness, memory, or identity is suddenly and temporarily altered, such as *amnesia* and *dissociative identity disorder*.

5. **Personality Disorders:** Problems related to lifelong maladaptive personality traits, including *antisocial personality disorders*. (violation of others' rights with no sense of guilt) or *borderline personality disorders* (impulsivity and instability in mood and relationships).

6. **Substance-related Disorders:** Problems caused by alcohol, cocaine, tobacco, and other drugs.

7. **Somatoform Disorders:** Problems related to unusual preoccupation with physical health or physical symptoms with no physical cause.

8. **Factitious Disorders:** Conditions in which physical or psychological symptoms are intentionally produced in order to assume a patient's role.

9. **Sexual and Gender Identity Disorders:** Problems related to unsatisfactory sexual activity, finding unusual objects or situations arousing; gender identity problems.

10. **Eating Disorders:** Problems related to food, such as *anorexia nervosa* and *bulimia*.

11. **Sleep Disorders:** Serious disturbances of sleep, such as *insomnia* (too little sleep), *sleep terrors*, or *hypersomnia* (too much sleep).

12. **Impulse Control Disorders (not elsewhere classified):** Problems related to *kleptomania* (impulsive stealing), *pyromania* (setting of fires), and *pathological gambling*.

13. **Adjustment Disorders:** Problems involving excessive emotional reaction to specific stressors such as divorce, family discord, or economic concerns.

15. **Delirium, Dementia, Amnestic, and Other Cognitive Disorders:** Problems caused by known damage to the brain, including Alzheimer's disease, strokes, and physical trauma to the brain.

16. **Mental Disorders due to a general medical condition (not elsewhere classified):** Problems caused by physical deterioration of the brain due to disease, drugs, and so on.

17. **Other conditions that may be a focus of clinical attention:** Problems related to physical or sexual abuse, relational problems, occupational problems, and so forth.

Most Common *DSM-IV-TR* Diagnoses

(12-month prevalence rates expressed in percentages)

Country	Anxiety Disorders	Mood Disorders	Substance-related Disorders	Any Other Psychological Disorder
United States	18.2	9.6	3.8	26.4
Japan	5.3	3.1	1.7	8.8
Mexico	6.8	4.8	2.5	12.2
France	12.0	8.5	0.7	9.1
Lebanon	11.2	6.6	1.3	16.9

Sources: Diagnostic Manual of Mental Disorders (DSM-IV-TR); World Health Survey Consortium (WHO) (2004). Reprinted with permission from the Diagnostic and Statistical Manual of Mental Disorders, copyright 2000, American Psychiatric Association.

Figure 14.3 Five axes of DSM-IV-TR Axis I describes *clinical disorders* that reflect the patient's current condition. Depression and anxiety disorders are examples of Axis I disorders. Axis II describes *trait disorders*, which are long-running personality disturbances (like antisocial personality disorder).

The other three axes are used to record important supplemental information. Axis III lists general medical conditions that may be important to the person's psychopathology (such as diabetes or hypothyroidism, which can affect mood). Axis IV is reserved for psychosocial and environmental stressors that could be contributing to emotional problems (such as job or housing troubles or the death of a family member). Axis V evaluates a person's overall level of functioning, on a scale from 1 (serious attempt at suicide or complete inability to take care of oneself) to 100 (happy, productive, with many interests). (Source: Reprinted with permission from the *Diagnostic and Statistical Manual of Mental Disorders*, copyright 2000, American Psychiatric Association.)

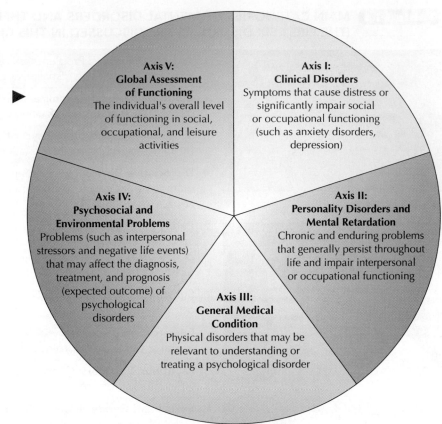

facilitates communication among professionals and patients, and it serves as a valuable educational tool. Virtually all textbooks, including this one, base their coverage of mental disorders on the DSM.

Unfortunately, the DSM does have its limitations and potential problems. For example, critics suggest that it may be casting too wide a net and *overdiagnosing*. Given that physicians and psychologists can only be compensated for treatment by insurance companies if each client is assigned a specific DSM code number, can you see how compilers of the DSM may be encouraged to add more diagnoses?

In addition, the DSM has been criticized for a potential *cultural bias*. It does provide a culture-specific section and a glossary of culture-bound syndromes, such as *amok* (Indonesia), *genital retraction syndrome* (Asia), and *windigo psychosis* (First Nations cultures), which we discuss later in this chapter (p. 523). However, the overall classification still reflects a western European and American perspective (Eap et al., 2010; Flaskerud, 2010; Gellerman & Lu, 2011; Nabar, 2011).

Perhaps the most troubling criticism about the DSM is the *problem of labels*. Consider the classic study conducted by David Rosenhan (1973) when he and his colleagues presented themselves to several hospital admissions offices with complaints of hearing voices (a classic symptom of schizophrenia). Aside from this single false complaint and providing alternate names and occupations, they answered all questions truthfully. Not surprisingly (given their reports of hearing strange voices), Rosenhan and his colleagues were all diagnosed with mental disorders and admitted to the hospital. Once admitted, however, the "patients" acted completely normal for the duration of their stays, yet none of these individuals were ever recognized by hospital staff as phony.

Can you see how once a person has been diagnosed, it becomes all too easy to overlook an individual's actual behavior in favor of the prior mental illness label? As we discussed in chapter 7, p. 260, we're more likely to notice and remember material when we've been *primed* with previous exposure in this case the label of mental illness. To hopefully reduce some of the dangers of labeling, the American Psychiatric Association (2000) recommends that diagnostic labels be applied only to people's disorders—not to people themselves. Following this suggestion, throughout this text, we refer to individuals as "a person with schizophrenia," not as "a schizophrenic." Just as someone with cancer is not "a cancer," someone with schizophrenia, depression, or anxiety are not their labeled disorders. As you know from personal experience (e.g., being called a "jock" or "nerd"), words do matter!

CHECK & REVIEW

STOP *Before going on, be sure to complete this Check & Review. It is an invaluable study tool!*

Studying Psychological Disorders

Part A: Retrieval Practice

1. Without looking at the book, spend 10 minutes writing a free-form essay recalling all you can remember from the previous section.

2. Now, reread the previous section, and once again spend 10 minutes writing a free-form essay on the SAME material.

   (Although time consuming, this exercise has been shown to be the single best way to improve your test scores! For more information, check out http://www.sciencemag.org/content/early/2011/01/19/science.1199327.abstract)

Part B: Practice Quiz

1. What are the four major standards for identifying abnormal behavior?

2. In early treatment of abnormal behavior, _____ was used to allow evil spirits to escape, whereas _____ was designed to make the body so uncomfortable it would be uninhabitable for the devil. (a) purging, fasting; (b) trephining, exorcism; (c) demonology, hydrotherapy; (d) the medical model, the dunking test

3. Briefly define neurosis, psychosis, and insanity.

4. Label the five axes of the *Diagnostic and Statistical Manual of Mental Disorders (DSM-IV-TR)* on the figure below.

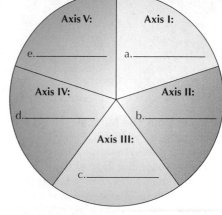

5. What are the chief advantages and disadvantages of the DSM system of classifying mental disorders?

Check your answers in Appendix B.

Anxiety Disorders

Objective 14.5: Define anxiety disorders and the five major subtypes.

I was 9 years old and sitting alone in the back of a cab as it rumbled over New York City's 59th Street bridge. I noticed the driver was watching me curiously. My feet began tapping and then shaking, and slowly my chest grew tight and I couldn't get enough air in my lungs. I tried to disguise the little screams I made as throat clearings, but the noises began to rattle the driver. I knew a panic attack was coming on, but I had to hold on, get to the studio, and get through the audition. Still, if I kept riding in that car I was certain I was going to die. The black water was just a few hundred feet below. "Stop!" I screamed at the driver. "Stop right here, please! I have to get out." "Young miss, I can't stop here." "Stop!" I must have looked like I meant it, because we squealed to a halt in the middle of traffic. I got out and began to run. I ran the entire length of the bridge and kept going. Death would never catch me as long as my small legs kept propelling me forward.

ADAPTED FROM PEARCE & SCANLON, 2002, P. 69

These are the words of actress Patty Duke describing an episode around the time she was starring as Helen Keller, the deaf and blind child in *The Miracle Worker*. Patty

Anxiety Disorder Overwhelming apprehension and fear accompanied by autonomic nervous system (ANS) arousal

▲ **A scene from The Miracle Worker** As a young girl, Patty Duke won an Academy Award for her role as Helen Keller. But even at this early age the young actress suffered from symptoms of a serious anxiety disorder.

Generalized Anxiety Disorder (GAD) Persistent, uncontrollable, and free-floating nonspecified anxiety

Duke's flight from the cab and other cases of **anxiety disorder** share one central defining characteristic—unreasonable, often paralyzing, anxiety or fear. The person feels threatened, unable to cope, unhappy, and insecure in a world that seems dangerous and hostile. Anxiety disorders—which are diagnosed twice as often in women as in men—are the most frequently occurring category of mental disorders in the general population (National Institute of Mental Health, 2011; Zerr, Holly, & Pina, 2011). Fortunately, they also are among the easiest disorders to treat and have one of the best chances for recovery (see Chapter 15).

Five Major Anxiety Disorders: The Problem of Fear

Symptoms of anxiety, such as rapid breathing and increased heart rate, plague most of us during final exams and important job interviews. But some people experience unreasonable anxiety that is so intense and chronic it seriously disrupts their lives. We will consider four major types of these anxiety disorders: *generalized anxiety disorder, panic disorder, phobia,* and *obsessive-compulsive disorder* (Figure 14.4). (Note that the fifth anxiety disorder, PTSD, was discussed in Chapter 3). Although we discuss these disorders separately, it is important to remember that people with one anxiety disorder often have others (Corr, 2011; Ibiloglu & Caykoylu, 2011).

Generalized Anxiety Disorder

This disorder affects twice as many women as it does men (Horwath & Gould, 2011). **Generalized anxiety disorder (GAD)** is characterized by chronic, uncontrollable, and excessive fear and worry that lasts at least 6 months and that is not focused on any particular object or situation. As the name implies, the anxiety is *generalized* and *nonspecific* or *free-floating*. Victims feel afraid of something, but are unable to identify and articulate the specific fear. Because of persistent muscle tension and autonomic fear reactions, people with this disorder may develop headaches, heart palpitations, dizziness, and insomnia, making it even harder to cope with normal daily activities.

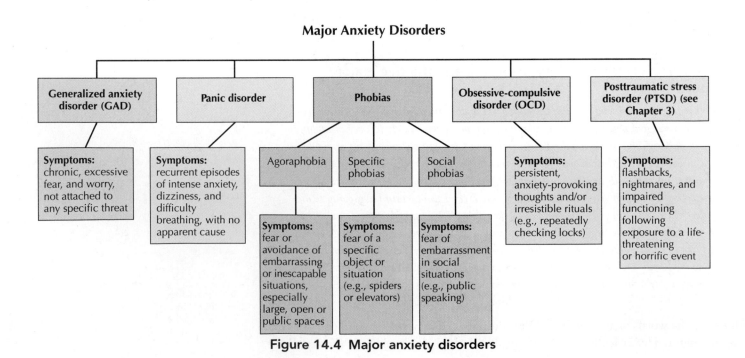

Major Anxiety Disorders

Generalized anxiety disorder (GAD)	Panic disorder	Phobias	Obsessive-compulsive disorder (OCD)	Posttraumatic stress disorder (PTSD) (see Chapter 3)

| **Symptoms:** chronic, excessive fear, and worry, not attached to any specific threat | **Symptoms:** recurrent episodes of intense anxiety, dizziness, and difficulty breathing, with no apparent cause | Agoraphobia / Specific phobias / Social phobias | **Symptoms:** persistent, anxiety-provoking thoughts and/or irresistible rituals (e.g., repeatedly checking locks) | **Symptoms:** flashbacks, nightmares, and impaired functioning following exposure to a life-threatening or horrific event |

Phobias sub-box:

Symptoms: fear or avoidance of embarrassing or inescapable situations, especially large, open or public spaces

Symptoms: fear of a specific object or situation (e.g., spiders or elevators)

Symptoms: fear of embarrassment in social situations (e.g., public speaking)

Figure 14.4 Major anxiety disorders

Panic Disorder

As we've just seen, generalized anxiety disorder involves free-floating anxiety. In contrast, **panic disorder** is marked by sudden, but brief, *attacks* of intense apprehension that cause trembling, dizziness, and difficulty breathing. The earlier discussion of Patty Duke's feeling of suffocation and certainty that she would die if she didn't immediately get out of the car are characteristic of panic attacks. These attacks generally happen after frightening experiences or prolonged stress (and sometimes even after exercise). Panic disorder is diagnosed when several apparently spontaneous panic attacks lead to a persistent concern about future attacks. In the *DSM-IV-TR*, panic disorder can be classified with or without *agoraphobia*, which is discussed below (Cully & Stanley, 2008; Horwath & Gould, 2011).

Panic Disorder Sudden and inexplicable panic attacks; symptoms include difficulty breathing, heart palpitations, dizziness, trembling, terror, and feelings of impending doom

Phobias

Phobias involve a strong, irrational fear and avoidance of objects or situations that are usually considered harmless (fear of elevators or fear of going to the dentist, for example). Although the person recognizes that the fear is irrational, the experience is still one of overwhelming anxiety, and a full-blown panic attack may follow. The *DSM-IV-TR* divides phobic disorders into three broad categories: agoraphobia, specific phobias, and social phobias.

Phobia Intense, irrational fear and avoidance of a specific object or situation

Agoraphobia People with *agoraphobia* restrict their normal activities because they fear having a panic attack in crowded, enclosed, or wide-open places where they would be unable to receive help in an emergency. In severe cases, people with agoraphobia may refuse to leave the safety of their homes.

Specific Phobias A specific phobia is a fear of a specific object or situation, such as needles, rats, spiders, or heights. Claustrophobia (fear of closed spaces) and acrophobia (fear of heights) are the specific phobias most often treated by therapists. People with specific phobias generally recognize that their fears are excessive and unreasonable, but they are unable to control their anxiety and will go to great lengths to avoid the feared stimulus.

Obsessive-Compulsive Disorder (OCD) Persistent, anxiety-provoking thoughts that will not go away (obsessions), and/or irresistible urges to perform repetitive behaviors (compulsions) to relieve the anxiety

Social Phobias People with social phobias are irrationally fearful of embarrassing themselves in social situations. Fear of public speaking and of eating in public are the most common social phobias. The fear of public scrutiny and potential humiliation may become so pervasive that normal life is severely restricted (Acarturk et al., 2008; Alden & Regambal, 2011; Moitra et al., 2011).

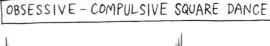

Obsessive-Compulsive Disorder (OCD)

Obsessive-compulsive disorder (OCD) is an anxiety disorder that involves persistent, anxiety-provoking thoughts that will not go away (obsessions), and/or irresistible urges to perform repetitive, ritualistic behaviors (compulsions), which help relieve the anxiety created by the obsession. In adults, this disorder is equally common in men and women, but it is more prevalent among boys when the onset is in childhood (American Psychiatric Association, 2000).

"Spin your partner round and round, then spin your partner round again, spin her round six more times, now touch the light switch near the door."

Common examples of obsessions are fear of germs, of being hurt or of hurting others, and troubling religious or sexual thoughts. Examples of compulsions are repeatedly checking, counting, cleaning, washing the body or parts of it, or putting things in a certain order. While everyone worries and sometimes double-checks, people with OCD have these thoughts and do these rituals for at least an hour or more each day, often longer (NIMH, 2011).

Imagine what it would be like to worry so obsessively about germs that you compulsively washed your hands hundreds of times a day until they were raw and bleeding. Most sufferers of OCD realize that their actions are senseless. But when they try to stop the behavior, they experience mounting anxiety, which is relieved only by giving in to the urges.

Explaining Anxiety Disorders: Multiple Roots

Objective 14.6: Identify the major contributors to anxiety disorders.

Why do people develop anxiety disorders? Research emphasizes *psychological*, *biological*, and *sociocultural* processes (the *biopsychosocial model*) (Figure 14.5).

Psychological

Psychological contributions to anxiety disorders are primarily in the form of faulty cognitions and maladaptive learning.

Faulty Cognitions People with anxiety disorders have certain thinking, or cognitive, habits that make them vulnerable or prone to fear. They tend to be *hyper-vigilant*. They constantly scan their environment for signs of danger and seem to ignore signs of safety. They also tend to magnify ordinary threats and failures. For example, most people are anxious in a public speaking situation. But those who suffer from a social phobia are excessively concerned about others' evaluation, hypersensitive to any criticism, and obsessively worried about potential mistakes. This intense self-preoccupation intensifies the social anxiety. It also leads these people to think they have failed—even when they have been successful. As you will see in Chapter 15, changing the thinking patterns of anxious people can greatly lessen their fears (Brosan et al., 2011; Lester, et al., 2011; Maric et al., 2011).

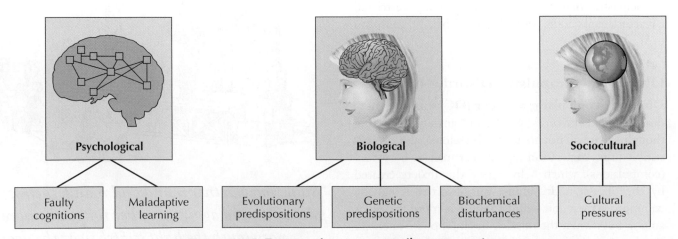

Figure 14.5 Factors that may contribute to anxiety

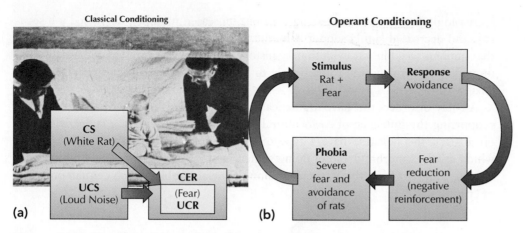

Classical Conditioning   Operant Conditioning

(a)   **(b)**

Figure 14.6 Conditioning and phobias (a) Do you recall Little Albert's classically conditioned fear of rats (Chapter 6, 209), and how classical conditioning combined with operant conditioning can lead to potential phobias? (b) Can you also see how this creates a vicious self-perpetuating vicious cycle? By avoiding the feared stimulus (the rat), the fear is "successfully" reduced and the phobia is "rewarded."

Maladaptive Learning According to learning theorists, anxiety disorders generally result from maladaptive conditioning and social learning (Chapter 6) (Cully & Stanley, 2008; Hollander & Simeon, 2011; Lovibond, 2011).

During classical conditioning, for example, a stimulus that is originally neutral (e.g., a harmless spider) becomes paired with a frightening event (a sudden panic attack) so that it becomes a conditioned stimulus that elicits anxiety. The person then begins to avoid spiders in order to reduce anxiety (an operant conditioning process known as negative reinforcement) (Figure 14.6).

Most people with phobias cannot remember a specific instance that led to their fear. Moreover, such frightening experiences do not always trigger phobias. In other words, conditioning may not be the only explanation. Social learning theorists propose that some phobias are the result of modeling and imitation. Phobias also may be learned vicariously (indirectly) (Figure 14.7).

Biological Factors

The fact that the monkey in Figure 14.7 only developed fears of the toy snake and toy crocodile, but not of the rabbit or flowers, suggests that phobias may develop from a genetic and evolutionary predisposition to fear of that which was dangerous to our ancestors (Boyer & Bergstrom, 2011; Glover, 2011; Mineka & Oehlberg, 2008; Walker et al., 2008). In addition to a possible evolutionary predisposition, studies also show that anxiety disorders may be due to disrupted biochemistry, or unusual brain activity (Anisman, Merali, & Stead, 2008; Casey, et al,. 2011; Fawcett, 2011; Westlye et al., 2011). Some people with panic disorder seem to be genetically predisposed toward an overreaction of the autonomic nervous system, further supporting the argument for a biological component. In addition, stress and arousal seem to play a role in panic attacks, and drugs such as caffeine or nicotine and even hyperventilation can trigger an attack, all suggesting a biochemical disturbance.

Sociocultural Factors

In addition to psychological and biological components, sociocultural factors can contribute to anxiety. There has been a sharp rise in anxiety disorders in the past 50 years, particularly in Western industrialized countries. Can you see how our

Figure 14.7 Vicarious (indirect) phobias Monkeys who watch artificially created videotapes of other monkeys being afraid of a toy snake, toy rabbit, toy crocodile, or flowers will develop their own set of phobias (Cook & Mineka, 1989). The fact that the "viewing" monkeys only develop fears of snakes and crocodiles, but not of flowers or toy rabbits, demonstrates that phobias are both learned and biological.

increasingly fast-paced lives—along with our increased mobility, decreased job security, and decreased family support—might contribute to anxiety? Unlike the dangers that humans faced in our evolutionary history, today's threats are less identifiable and immediate. This may lead some people to become hypervigilant and predisposed to anxiety disorders.

Anxiety disorders can have dramatically different forms in other cultures, further supporting the influence of sociocultural factors. For example, in a collectivist twist on anxiety, the Japanese have a type of social phobia called *taijin kyofusho (TKS)*, which involves morbid dread of doing something to embarrass others. This disorder is quite different from the Western version of social phobia, which centers on a fear of criticism.

 **CHECK & REVIEW**  **STOP** *Before going on, be sure to complete this Check & Review. It is an invaluable study tool!*

Anxiety Disorders

Part A: Retrieval Practice

1. Without looking at the book, spend 10 minutes writing a free-form essay recalling all you can remember from the previous section.

2. Now, reread the previous section, and once again spend 10 minutes writing a free-form essay on the SAME material.

Part B: Practice Quiz

1. Label the five major anxiety disorders on the figure below.

2. Match the descriptions below with the following specific forms of anxiety disorder: (a) generalized anxiety disorder; (b) panic disorder; (c) phobia; (d) obsessive-compulsive disorder (OCD):

___i. Severe attacks of extreme anxiety

___ii. Long-term anxiety that is not focused on any particular object or situation

___iii. Irrational fear of an object or situation

___iv. Intrusive thoughts and urges to perform repetitive, ritualistic behaviors

3. Researchers believe that anxiety disorders are probably due to some combination of _____.

4. How do learning theorists and social learning theorists explain anxiety disorders?

Check your answers in Appendix B.

Major Anxiety Disorders

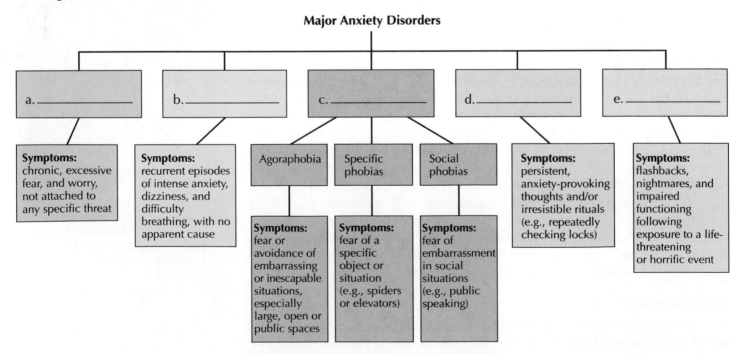

Mood Disorders

Ann had been divorced for eight months when she called a psychologist for an emergency appointment. Although her husband had verbally and physically abused her for years, she had had mixed feelings about staying in the marriage. She had anticipated feeling good after the divorce, but she became increasingly depressed. She had trouble sleeping, had little appetite, felt very fatigued, and showed no interest in her usual activities. She stayed home from work for two days because she "just didn't feel like going in." Late one afternoon, she went straight to bed, leaving her two small children to fend for themselves. Then, the night before calling for an emergency therapy appointment, she took five sleeping tablets and a couple of stiff drinks. As she said, "I don't think I wanted to kill myself; I just wanted to forget everything for awhile."

(MEYER & SALMON, 1988, p. 312)

THE DAWN OF PSYCHIATRY

Ann's case is a good example of a *mood disorder* (also known as an *affective disorder*). This category encompasses not only excessive sadness, like Ann's, but also unreasonable elation and hyperactivity.

Understanding Mood Disorders: Major Depressive Disorder and Bipolar Disorder

Objective 14.7: Compare and contrast the two major mood disorders.

As the name implies, **mood disorders** are characterized by extreme disturbances in emotional states that may include psychotic distortions of reality. There are two main types of mood disorders—*major depressive disorder* and *bipolar disorder* (Figure 14.8).

Major Depressive Disorder

Depression has been recorded as far back as ancient Egypt, when the condition was called melancholia and was treated by priests. We all feel "blue" sometimes, especially following the loss of a job, end of a relationship, or death of a loved one. People suffering from **major depressive disorder**, however, may experience a lasting and continuously depressed mood without a clear trigger or precipitating event. In addition, their sadness is far more intense, interfering with their basic ability to function, feel pleasure, or maintain interest in life (Alloy et al., 2011; Feliciano, Segal, & Vair, 2011).

People with clinical depression are so deeply sad and discouraged that they often have trouble sleeping, are likely to lose (or gain) weight, and may feel so fatigued that they cannot go to work or school or even comb their hair and brush their teeth. They may sleep both day and night, have problems concentrating, and feel so profoundly sad and guilty that they consider suicide. These feelings have no apparent cause and may be so severe that the individual loses contact with reality. As in the case of Ann, depressed individuals have a hard time thinking clearly or recognizing their own problems. Family or friends are often the ones who recognize the symptoms and encourage them to seek professional help.

Bipolar Disorder

When depression is *unipolar*, the depressive episode eventually ends and people return to a "normal" emotional level. People with **bipolar disorder** however, rebound to the opposite state, known as *mania*.

Mood Disorder Extreme disturbances in emotional states

Major Depressive Disorder Long-lasting depressed mood that interferes with the ability to function, feel pleasure, or maintain interest in life

Bipolar Disorder Repeated episodes of mania (unreasonable elation, often with hyperactivity) alternating with depression

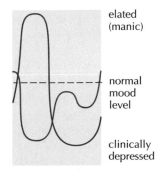

— Bipolar Disorder
— Major Depressive Disorder

Figure 14.8 Mood disorder If major depressive disorders and bipolar disorders were depicted on a graph, they might look something like this.

During a manic episode, the person is overly excited, extremely active, and easily distracted. The person exhibits unrealistically high self-esteem and an inflated sense of importance or even delusions of grandeur. He or she often makes elaborate plans for becoming rich and famous. The individual is hyperactive and may not sleep for days at a time, yet does not become fatigued. Thinking is speeded up and can change abruptly to new topics, showing "rapid flight of ideas." Speech is also rapid ("pressured speech"), and it is difficult for others to get a word in edgewise. Poor judgment is also common: A person may give away valuable possessions or go on wild spending sprees.

Manic episodes may last a few days to a few months and generally end abruptly. The following depressive episode generally lasts three times as long as the manic episode. The lifetime risk for developing bipolar disorder is low—somewhere between 0.5 and 1.6 percent, but it can be one of the most debilitating and lethal disorders with a high suicide rate (Bender & Alloy, 2011; Gutiérrez-Rojas, Jurado, & Gurpegui, 2011; Klimes-Dougan et al., 2008; Merikangas & Tohen, 2011).

MYTH BUSTERS

Objective 14.8: What do we need to know about suicide and its prevention?

Suicide and Its Prevention

Suicide is a serious danger associated with severe depression and bipolar disorders. Because of the shame and secrecy surrounding the suicidal person, there are many misconceptions and stereotypes. Can you correctly identify which of the following is true or false?

1. People who talk about suicide are not likely to commit suicide.
2. Suicide usually takes place with little or no warning.
3. Suicidal people are fully intent on dying.
4. Children of parents who attempt suicide are at greater risk of committing suicide.
5. Suicidal people remain so forever.
6. Men are more likely than women to actually kill themselves by suicide.
7. When a suicidal person has been severely depressed and seems to be "snapping out of it," the danger of suicide decreases substantially.
8. Only depressed people commit suicide.
9. Thinking about suicide is rare.
10. Asking a depressed person about suicide will push him or her over the edge and cause a suicidal act that would not otherwise have occurred.

Compare your responses to the experts' answers and explanations (Baldessarini & Tondo, 2008; Barlow & Durand, 2012; Brent & Melhem, 2008; Dutra et al., 2008; Kring et al., 2010; Lilienfeld et al., 2010; Murray, 2009).

1. and 2. **False**. About 90 percent of people who are suicidal talk about their intentions. They may say, "If something happens to me, I want you to. . ." or "Life just isn't worth living." They also provide behavioral clues, such as giving away valued possessions, withdrawing from family and friends, and losing interest in favorite activities.

3. **False**. Only about 3 to 5 percent of suicidal people truly intend to die. Most are just unsure about how to go on living. They cannot see their problems objectively enough to realize that they have alternative courses of action. They often gamble with death, arranging it so that fate or others will save them. Moreover, once the suicidal crisis passes, they are generally grateful to be alive.

4. **True**. Children of parents who attempt or commit suicide are at much greater risk of following in their footsteps. As Schneidman (1969) puts it, "The person who commits suicide puts his psychological skeleton in the survivor's emotional closet" (p. 225).

5. **False**. People who want to kill themselves are usually suicidal only for a limited period.

6. **True**. Although women are much more likely to attempt suicide, men are more likely to actually commit suicide. Men are also more likely to use stronger methods, such as guns versus pills.

7. **False**. When people are first coming out of a depression, they are actually at

greater risk! This is because they now have the energy to actually commit suicide.

8. **False**. Suicide rates are highest for people with major depressive disorders. However, suicide is also the leading cause of premature death in people who suffer from schizophrenia. In addition, suicide is a major cause of death in people with anxiety disorders and alcohol and other substance-related disorders. Furthermore, suicide is not limited to people with depression. Poor physical health, serious illness, substance abuse (particularly alcohol), loneliness, unemployment, and even natural disasters may push many over the edge.

9. **False**. Estimates from various studies are that 40 to 80 percent of the general public have thought about committing suicide at least once in their lives.

10. **False**. Because society often considers suicide a terrible, shameful act, asking directly about it can give the person permission to talk. In fact, *not asking* might lead to further isolation and depression.

How can you tell if someone is suicidal? If you believe someone is contemplating suicide, act on your beliefs. Stay with the person if there is any immediate danger. Encourage him or her to talk to you rather than withdraw. Show the person that you care, but do not give false reassurances that "everything will be okay." This type of response makes the suicidal person feel **more** alienated. Instead, openly ask if the person is feeling hopeless and suicidal. Do not be afraid to discuss suicide with people who feel depressed or hopeless, fearing that you will just put ideas into their heads. The reality is that people who are left alone or who are told they can't be serious about suicide often attempt it.

If you suspect someone is suicidal, it is vitally important that you help the person obtain counseling. Most cities have suicide prevention centers with 24-hour hotlines or walk-in centers that provide emergency counseling. Also, share your suspicions with parents, friends, or others who can help in a suicidal crisis. To save a life, you may have to betray a secret when someone confides in you.

TRY THIS YOURSELF

Non-Professional Therapy—Talking to the Depressed

I know that everyone here knows that feeling when people say to you, "Hey, shape up! Stop thinking only about your troubles. What's to be depressed about? Go swimming or play tennis and you'll feel a lot better. Pull up your socks!" And how you, hearing this, would like nothing more than to remove one of these socks and choke them to death with it. (Laughter mixed with some minor cheering).

(Cavett, 2008)

These are the words of famous columnist and commentator, Dick Cavett, speaking about his personal bouts with deep depression to a large audience currently in the throes of the same disease. If you have a friend or loved one with serious depression, it may feel like you're walking through a minefield when you're attempting to comfort and help them. What do the experts suggest that you say (or NOT say)? Here are a few general tips:

1. **Don't trivialize the disease.** Depression, like cancer or heart disease, is a critical, life-threatening illness. Asking someone "What do you have to be depressed about?" or encouraging him to "pull up his socks" is akin to asking the cancer patient why she has cancer, why she doesn't just smile and exercise more?

2. **Don't be a cheerleader or a Mr. or Ms. fix-it.** You can't pep-talk someone out of deep depression, and offering cheap advice or solutions is the best way to ensure that you'll be the last person he or she will turn to for help. According to Dick Cavett, "When you're downed by this affliction, if there were a curative magic wand on the table eight feet away, it would be too much trouble to go over and pick it up."

3. **Don't equate normal, everyday "down times" with clinical depression.** Virtually everyone has experienced down moods and times of loss and deep sadness. Unless you have experienced true, clinical depression, comments like, "I know just how you feel," only makes it clear that you don't understand what clinical depression is all about. As they say, "If you don't got it, you don't get it!"

What can you do?

Educate yourself. Your psychology instructor, college library, book stores, and the Internet all provide a wealth of information. You also can check out the resources available on our text website at www.wiley.com/college/huffman.

Be Rogerian Carl Rogers' four important qualities of communication (*empathy, unconditional positive regard, genuineness,* and *active listening*) are probably the best, and safest, approach for any situation—including talking with a depressed person.

Get help! The most dangerous problem associated with depression is the high risk of suicide. If a friend or loved one mentions suicide, or if you believe he is considering it, get professional help fast! Consider calling the police for emergency intervention, and/or the person's therapist, or the toll-free 7/24 hotline 1-800-SUICIDE.

Explaining Mood Disorders: Biological Versus Psychosocial Factors

Objective 14.9: Describe the key biological and psychosocial factors that contribute to mood disorders.

Mood disorders differ in their *severity* (how often they occur and how much they disrupt normal functioning). They also differ in their *duration* (how long they last). In this section, we will examine the latest thinking on biological and psychosocial factors that attempts to explain mood disorders.

Biological Factors

Biological factors appear to play a significant role in both major depression and bipolar disorder. Recent research shows that some patients with bipolar and depressive disorders show decreased gray matter and decreased overall functioning in the frontal lobes. This suggests that structural brain changes may contribute to (or cause) these mood disorders. Other research, however, points to imbalances of several neurotransmitters, including serotonin, norepinephrine, and dopamine (Barton et al., 2008; Lopez-Munoz & Alamo, 2011; Pu et al., 2011; Wiste et al., 2008).

This makes sense because these same neurotransmitters are involved in the capacity to be aroused or energized and in the control of other functions affected by depression such as sleep cycles and hunger. Moreover, drugs that alter the activity of these neurotransmitters also decrease the symptoms of depression (and hence are called *antidepressants*). Similarly, the drug *lithium* reduces or prevents manic episodes by preventing norepinephrine- and serotonin-sensitive neurons from being overstimulated.

Evidence also suggests that major depressive disorders, as well as bipolar disorders, may be inherited. For example, when one identical twin has a mood disorder, there is about a 50 percent chance that the other twin will also develop the illness (Boardman, Alexander, & Stallings, 2011; Elder & Mosack, 2011; Faraone, 2008). It is important to remember, however, that relatives generally have similar environments as well as similar genes.

Finally, the evolutionary perspective suggests that moderate depression may be a normal and healthy adaptive response to a very real loss (such as the death of a loved one). The depression helps us step back and reassess our goals (Nettle, 2011; Panksepp & Wyatt, 2011; Surbey, 2011; Varga, 2011). Consistent with this theory is the observation that primates also show signs of depression when they suffer a significant loss (Hennessy et al., 2011; Krishnan & Nestler, 2011; Panksepp, 2011). Clinical, severe depression may just be an extreme version of this generally adaptive response.

Psychosocial Theories

Psychosocial theories of depression and bipolar disorder focus on environmental stressors and disturbances in the person's interpersonal relationships, thought processes, self-concept, and learning history. The psychoanalytic explanation sees depression as anger turned inward against oneself when an important relationship or attachment is lost. Anger is assumed to come from feelings of rejection or withdrawal of affection, especially when a loved one dies. The humanistic school says depression results when a person's self-concept is overly demanding or when positive growth is blocked (Keen, 2011; O'Connell, 2008; Weinstock, 2008).

The **learned helplessness** theory of depression, developed by Martin Seligman (1975, 1994, 2007), maintains that when human or nonhuman animals are repeatedly

Learned Helplessness Seligman's term for a state of helplessness or resignation, in which human or nonhuman animals learn that escape from something painful is impossible, and depression results

subjected to pain that they cannot escape, they develop such a strong sense of help-lessness or resignation that they do not attempt to escape future painful experiences. In other words, when people (or nonhuman animals) learn they are unable to change things for the better, they're more likely to give up. Can you see how this might help explain citizens who accept brutally repressive governments, or people who stay in abusive relationships? Seligman also suggests that our general societal emphasis on individualism and less involvement with others make us particularly vulnerable to depression.

The learned helplessness theory may also involve a cognitive element, known as *attribution*, or the explanations people assign to their own and others' behavior. Once someone perceives that his or her behaviors are unrelated to outcomes (learned helplessness), depression is likely to occur. This is particularly true if the person attributes failure to causes that are *internal* ("my own weakness"), *stable* ("this weakness is long-standing and unchanging"), and *global* ("this weakness is a problem in lots of settings") (Alloy et al., 2011; Ball, McGuffin, & Farmer, 2008; Newby & Moulds, 2011; Wise & Rosqvist, 2006). (See the Critical Thinking exercise on pp. 522–523).

no control over future

CHECK & REVIEW

STOP *Before going on, be sure to complete this Check & Review. It is an invaluable study tool!*

Mood Disorders

Part A: Retrieval Practice

1. Without looking at the book, spend 10 minutes writing a free-form essay recalling all you can remember from the previous section.

2. Now, reread the previous section, and once again spend 10 minutes writing a free-form essay on the SAME material.

Part B: Practice Quiz

1. The two main types of mood disorders are _____.

2. A major difference between major depressive disorder and bipolar disorder is that only in bipolar disorders do people have _____. (a) hallucinations or delusions; (b) depression; (c) manic episodes; (d) a biochemical imbalance

3. List the ten major myths about suicide.

4. What is Martin Seligman's learned helplessness theory of depression?

5. According to attributional theories, depression is more likely to occur when someone attributes his or her failure to _____.

Check your answers in Appendix B.

Schizophrenia

Objective 14.10: Define schizophrenia, and describe its five major symptoms.

Imagine for the moment that your daughter has just left for college and you hear voices inside your head shouting, "You'll never see her again! You have been a bad mother! She'll die." Or what if you saw dinosaurs on the street and live animals in your refrigerator? These are actual experiences that have plagued Mrs. T for almost three decades (Gershon & Rieder, 1993).

Mrs. T suffers from **schizophrenia**, a disorder characterized by major disturbances in perception, language, thought, emotion, and behavior. As we discussed at

Schizophrenia [skit-so-FREE-nee-uh]
Group of severe disorders involving major disturbances in perception, language, thought, emotion, and behavior

the beginning of this chapter, mental disorders exist on a continuum, and many people suffering from schizophrenia can still function in daily life. For some individuals, however, schizophrenia is so severe that it is considered a *psychosis*, meaning that the person is out of touch with reality. People with schizophrenia sometimes have serious problems caring for themselves, relating to others, and holding a job. In extreme cases, the individual may withdraw from others and from reality, often into a fantasy life of delusions and hallucinations. At this point, they may require institutional or custodial care.

Researchers are divided on whether schizophrenia is a distinct disorder itself or a combination of disorders (schizophrenias). However, there is general agreement that it is one of the most widespread and devastating of all mental disorders. Approximately 1 of every 100 persons will develop schizophrenia in his or her lifetime. And approximately half of all people admitted to mental hospitals are diagnosed with this disorder. Schizophrenia usually emerges between the late teens and the mid-thirties and only rarely prior to adolescence or after age 45. It seems to be equally prevalent in men and women. For unknown reasons it is generally more severe and strikes earlier in men than in women (Chang et al., 2011; Combs et al., 2008; Faraone, 2008; Gottesman, 1991; Lee et al., 2011).

 **MYTH BUSTERS**

Objective 14.11: Explain how schizophrenia is NOT the same as dissociative-identity disorder (DID) (previously called multiple personalities).

Do people with schizophrenia have multiple personalities?

As shown in the cartoon to the right, and in popular movies, such as *Me, Myself, and Irene*, schizophrenia is commonly confused with *multiple personality disorder* (now known as *dissociative identity disorder*, p. 518). This widespread myth persists in part from confusing terminology. Literally translated, schizophrenia means "split mind," referring to a split from reality that shows itself in disturbed perceptions, language, thought, emotions, and/or behavior.

In contrast, dissociative identity disorder (DID) refers to the condition in which two or more distinct personalities exist within the same person at different times. People with schizophrenia have only one personality.

Why does this matter? Confusing schizophrenia with multiple personalities is not only technically incorrect, it also trivializes the devastating effects of schizophrenia, which may include severe anxiety, social isolation, unemployment, homelessness, substance abuse, clinical depression, and even suicide (Lilienfeld et al., 2010; Preventing Suicide, 2009; Smith et al., 2011).

"THANKS FOR CURING MY SCHIZOPHRENIA— WE'RE BOTH FINE NOW!"

Symptoms of Schizophrenia: Five Areas of Disturbance

Schizophrenia is a group or class of disorders characterized by disturbance in one or more of the following areas: *perception, language, thought, emotion* (affect), and *behavior*.

Perception

The senses of people with schizophrenia may be either enhanced (as in the case of Mrs. T) or blunted. That is, the filtering and selection processes that allow most people to concentrate on whatever they choose are impaired. Thus, sensory stimulation is jumbled and distorted. One patient reported:

> *When people are talking, I just get scraps of it. If it is just one person who is speaking, that's not so bad, but if others join in then I can't pick it up at all. I just can't get in tune with the conversation. It makes me feel all open—as if things are closing in on me and I have lost control.*

(McGhie & Chapman, 1961, p. 106)

These disruptions in sensation may explain why people with schizophrenia experience **hallucinations**—false, imaginary sensory perceptions that occur without external stimuli. Hallucinations can occur in all of the senses (visual, tactile, olfactory). But auditory hallucinations (hearing voices and sounds) are most common in schizophrenia. As with Mrs. T, people with schizophrenia often hear voices speaking their thoughts aloud, commenting on their behavior, or telling them what to do. The voices seem to come from inside their own heads or from an external source such as an animal, telephone wires, or a TV set.

Hallucinations False, Imaginary sensory perceptions that occur without external stimuli

On rare occasions, people with schizophrenia will hurt others in response to their distorted internal experiences or the voices they hear. Unfortunately, these cases receive undue media attention and create exaggerated fears of "mental patients." In reality, these people are more likely to be self-destructive and suicidal than violent toward others.

Language and Thought

Have you heard the proverb "People who live in glass houses shouldn't throw stones?" When asked to explain its meaning, a patient with schizophrenia said,

> "People who live in glass houses shouldn't forget people who live in stone houses and shouldn't throw glass."

From this brief example, can you see how for people with schizophrenia their logic is sometimes impaired and their thoughts are disorganized and bizarre? When language and thought disturbances are mild, an individual with schizophrenia jumps from topic to topic. In more severe disturbances, phrases and words are jumbled together (referred to as *word salad*). Or the person creates artificial words *(neologisms)*. The person might say "splisters" for *splinters* and *blisters* or "smever" for *smart* and *clever*.

Delusions Mistaken beliefs based on misrepresentations of reality

In addition to disturbances in language, a common thought disturbance of schizophrenia is that of **delusions**, mistaken beliefs based on misrepresentations of reality. We all experience mistaken thoughts from time to time, such as thinking a friend is trying to avoid us or that our parents' divorce was our fault. But the delusions of schizophrenia are much more extreme. For example, people suffering from schizophrenia sometimes believe others are stalking them or trying to kill them (a *delusion of persecution*). In *delusions of grandeur*, people believe they are someone very important, perhaps Jesus Christ or the queen of England. In *delusions of reference*, unrelated events are given special significance, as when a person believes a radio program or newspaper article is giving him or her a special message.

"That's the doctor who is treating me for paranoia. I don't trust him."

The most common and frightening thought disturbance experienced by people with schizophrenia is the lack of contact with reality *(psychosis)*. Imagine yourself as Mrs. T seeing dinosaurs on the street and hearing voices saying your daughter will die. Think how terrifying it would be if you lost contact with reality and could no longer separate hallucinations and delusions from reality.

Emotion

It must look queer to people when I laugh about something that has got nothing to do with what I am talking about, but they don't know what's going on inside and how much of it is running around in my head. You see, I might be talking about something quite serious to you and other things come into my head at the same time that are funny and this makes me laugh. If I could only concentrate on one thing at the same time, I wouldn't look half so silly.

(MCGHIE & CHAPMAN, 1961, p. 104)

As you can see from this quote, the emotions of people suffering from schizophrenia are sometimes exaggerated and fluctuate rapidly in inappropriate ways. In other cases, emotions may become blunted or decreased in intensity. Some people with schizophrenia have *flattened affect*—meaning almost no emotional response of any kind.

Behavior

Disturbances in behavior may take the form of social withdrawal and/or unusual actions that have special meaning. One patient shook his head rhythmically from side to side to try to shake the excess thoughts out of his mind. Another massaged his head repeatedly "to help clear it" of unwanted thoughts. In other cases, the affected person may grimace and display unusual mannerisms. These movements, however, may also be side effects of the medication used to treat the disorder (Chapter 15).

People with schizophrenia also may become *cataleptic* and assume an uncomfortable, nearly immobile stance for an extended period. A few people with schizophrenia have a symptom called *waxy flexibility*, a tendency to maintain whatever posture is imposed on them.

These abnormal behaviors are often related to disturbances in perceptions, thoughts, and feelings. For example, experiencing a flood of sensory stimuli or overwhelming confusion, a person with schizophrenia may hallucinate, experience delusions, and/or withdraw from social contacts and refuse to communicate.

Types of Schizophrenia: Recent Methods of Classification

Objective 14.12: Describe the key methods for classifying schizophrenia.

For many years, researchers divided schizophrenia into *paranoid, catatonic, disorganized, undifferentiated,* and *residual* subtypes (Table 14.2). These terms are still included in the *DSM-IV-TR* and are sometimes used by the public. But critics suggest that they have little value in clinical practice and research. They contend that this classification by subtype does not differentiate in terms of prognosis (prediction for recovery), etiology (cause), or response to treatment. Furthermore, the undifferentiated type may be a catchall for cases that are difficult to diagnose (American Psychiatric Association, 2000).

StudyTip

If you're having difficulty understanding the distinction between positive and negative symptoms of schizophrenia, think back to what you learned in Chapter 6 regarding positive and negative reinforcement and punishment. Positive can be seen as "the addition of," whereas negative refers to the "removal or loss of."

Table 14.2 SUBTYPES OF SCHIZOPHRENIA

Paranoid	Delusions (persecution and grandeur) and hallucinations (hearing voices)
Catatonic	Motor disturbances (immobility or agitated, purposeless activity) and echo speech (repeating the speech of others)
Disorganized	Incoherent speech, flat or exaggerated emotions, and social withdrawal
Undifferentiated	Varied symptoms that meet the criteria for schizophrenia but do not fall into any of the other subtypes
Residual	No longer meets the full criteria for schizophrenia but still shows some symptoms

For these reasons, researchers have proposed an alternative classification system of two groups of symptoms:

1. *Positive symptoms* involve *additions* to or exaggerations of normal thought processes and behaviors, such as delusions and hallucinations. Positive symptoms are more common when schizophrenia develops rapidly (called *acute*, or *reactive*, schizophrenia), and positive symptoms are associated with better adjustment before the onset and a better prognosis for recovery.

2. *Negative symptoms* involve the *loss* or absence of normal thought processes and behaviors. Examples include impaired attention, limited or toneless speech, flat or blunted affect (or emotions), and social withdrawal. Negative symptoms are more often found in slow-developing schizophrenia (*chronic*, or *process*, schizophrenia).

In addition to these two groups of positive or negative symptoms, the latest *DSM-IV-TR* suggests adding another dimension to reflect *disorganization of behavior*. Symptoms in this group would include rambling speech, erratic behavior, and inappropriate affect (or feelings). One advantage of either a two- or three-dimension model is the acknowledgment that schizophrenia is more than one disorder and that it has multiple causes.

Explaining Schizophrenia: Biopsychosocial Model

Objective 14.13: What are the major biological and psychosocial factors that influence schizophrenia?

Why do some people develop schizophrenia? Because the disorder comes in so many different forms, most researchers believe it results from multiple biological and psychosocial factors—the *biopsychosocial model*.

Biological Theories

An enormous amount of scientific research exists concerning possible biological factors in schizophrenia. Some research suggests that prenatal stress and viral infections, birth complications, immune responses, maternal malnutrition, and advanced paternal

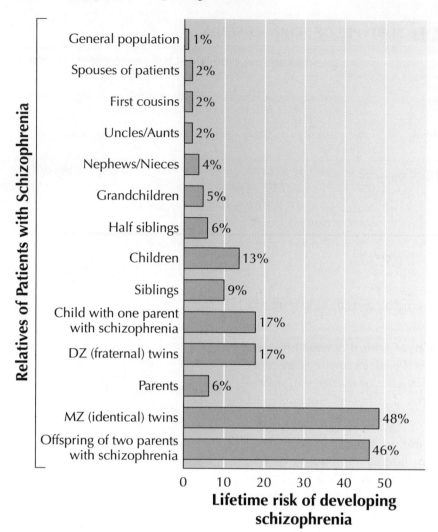

Relatives of Patients with Schizophrenia

Relative	Risk
General population	1%
Spouses of patients	2%
First cousins	2%
Uncles/Aunts	2%
Nephews/Nieces	4%
Grandchildren	5%
Half siblings	6%
Children	13%
Siblings	9%
Child with one parent with schizophrenia	17%
DZ (fraternal) twins	17%
Parents	6%
MZ (identical) twins	48%
Offspring of two parents with schizophrenia	46%

0 10 20 30 40 50

Lifetime risk of developing schizophrenia

▲ **Figure 14.9 Genetics and schizophrenia** Your lifetime risk of developing schizophrenia depends, in part, on how closely you are genetically related to someone with schizophrenia. As you evaluate the statistics, bear in mind that the risk in the general population is a little less than 1 percent (the top line on the graph). Risk increases with the degree of genetic relatedness. *Source:* Gottesman, "Schizophrenia Genesis," 1991, W. H. Freeman and Company/Worth Publishers.

age all contribute to the development of schizophrenia (Ellman & Cannon, 2008; Markham & Koenig, 2011; Weinberger & Harrison, 2011). However, most biological theories of schizophrenia focus on three main factors: *genetics, neurotransmitters,* and *brain abnormalities.*

- **Genetics** Although researchers are beginning to identify specific genes related to schizophrenia, most genetic studies have focused on twins and adoptions (Drew et al., 2011; Faraone, 2008; Owens et al., 2011; Riley & Kendler, 2011). This research indicates that the risk for schizophrenia increases with genetic similarity; that is, people who share more genes with a person who has schizophrenia are more likely to develop the disorder (Figure 14.9).

- **Neurotransmitters** Precisely how neurotransmitters contribute to schizophrenia is unclear. According to the **dopamine hypothesis**, overactivity of certain dopamine neurons in the brain may contribute to some forms of schizophrenia (Lodge & Grace, 2011; Miyake et al., 2011; Nord & Farde, 2011; Seeman, 2011). This hypothesis is based on two important observations. First, administering amphetamines increases the amount of dopamine and can produce (or worsen) some symptoms of schizophrenia, especially in people with a genetic predisposition to the disorder. Second, drugs that reduce dopamine activity in the brain reduce or eliminate some symptoms of schizophrenia. Although researchers have found that the dopamine hypothesis is more complicated than orginally thought, it is still widely believed that dopamine plays a role in schizophrenia.

- **Brain abnormalities** The third major biological theory for schizophrenia involves abnormalities in brain function and structure. Researchers have found larger cerebral ventricles (fluid-filled spaces in the brain) in some people with schizophrenia (Agartz et al., 2011; Fusar-Poli et al., 2011; Galderisi et al., 2008).

Also, some people with chronic schizophrenia have a lower level of activity in their frontal and temporal lobes—areas that are involved in language, attention, and memory (Figure 14.10). Damage in these regions might explain the thought and language disturbances that characterize schizophrenia. This lower level of brain activity, and schizophrenia itself, may also result from an overall loss of gray matter (neurons in the cerebral cortex) (Crespo-Facorro et al., 2007; Salgado-Pineda et al., 2011; White & Hilgetag, 2011).

Dopamine Hypothesis Theory that overactivity of dopamine neurons may contribute to some forms of schizophrenia

Psychosocial Theories

Clearly, biological factors play a key role in schizophrenia. But the fact that even in identical twins—who share identical genes—the heritability of schizophrenia is only 48 percent tells us that nongenetic factors must contribute the remaining percentage. Most psychologists believe that there are at least two possible psychosocial contributors.

According to the **diathesis-stress model** of schizophrenia, stress plays an essential role in triggering schizophrenic episodes in people with an inherited predisposition (or *diathesis*) toward the disease (Arnsten, 2011; Beaton & Simon, 2011; McGrath, 2011).

Some investigators suggest that communication disorders in family members may also be a predisposing factor for schizophrenia. Such disorders include unintelligible speech, fragmented communication, and parents' frequently sending severely contradictory messages to children. Several studies have also shown greater rates of relapse and worsening of symptoms among hospitalized patients who went home to families that were critical and hostile toward them or overly involved in their lives emotionally (McFarlane, 2011; Roisko et al., 2011). Finally, as you recall from Chapter 5, those at genetic risk for schizophrenia are more likely to develop it if they use marijuana heavily.

Evaluating the Theories

How should we evaluate the different theories about the causes of schizophrenia? Critics of the dopamine hypothesis and the brain damage theory argue that those theories fit only some cases of schizophrenia. Moreover, with both theories, it is difficult to determine cause and effect. The disturbed-communication theories are also hotly debated, and research is inconclusive. Schizophrenia is probably the result of a combination of known and unknown interacting factors—the *biopsychosocial model* (Step-by-Step Diagram 14.2).

Diathesis-Stress Model Suggests that people inherit a predisposition (or "diathesis") that increases their risk for mental disorders if exposed to certain extremely stressful life experiences

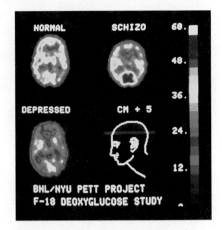

Figure 14.10 Brain activity in schizophrenia These positron emission tomography (PET) scans show variations in the brain activity of normal individuals, people with major depressive disorder, and individuals with schizophrenia. Warmer colors (red, yellow) indicate increased activity.

 **CHECK & REVIEW**  STOP *Before going on, be sure to complete this Check & Review. It is an invaluable study tool!*

Schizophrenia

Part A: Retrieval Practice

1. Without looking at the book, spend 10 minutes writing a free-form essay recalling all you can remember from the previous section.

2. Now, reread the previous section, and once again spend 10 minutes writing a free-form essay on the SAME material.

Part B: Practice Quiz

1. Schizophrenia is also a form of _____, a term describing general lack of contact with reality.

2. _____ refers to "split mind," whereas _____ refers to "split personality." (a) Psychosis, neurosis; (b) Insanity, multiple personalities; (c) Schizophrenia, dissociative identity disorder (DID); (d) Paranoia, borderline

3. Perceptions for which there are no appropriate external stimuli are called _____, and the most common type among people suffering from schizophrenia is _____. (a) hallucinations, auditory; (b) hallucinations, visual; (c) delusions, auditory; (d) delusions, visual

4. List three biological and two psychosocial factors that may contribute to schizophrenia.

Check your answers in Appendix B.

Step-by-StepDiagram14.2

STOP This Step by Step diagram contains essential information NOT found elsewhere in the text, which is likely to appear on quizzes and exams. Be sure to study it CAREFULLY!

The Biopsychosocial Model and Schizophrenia

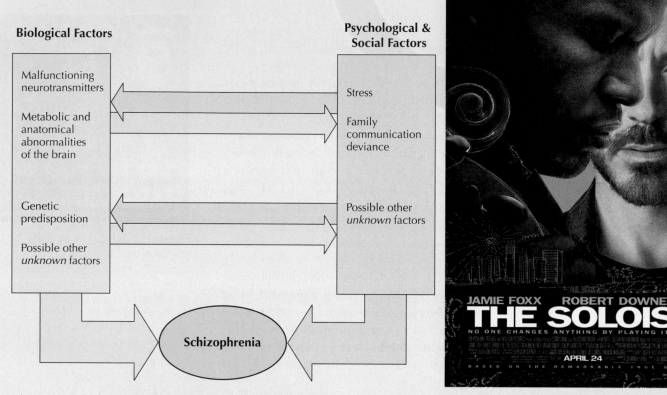

Biological Factors

- Malfunctioning neurotransmitters
- Metabolic and anatomical abnormalities of the brain
- Genetic predisposition
- Possible other *unknown* factors

Psychological & Social Factors

- Stress
- Family communication deviance
- Possible other *unknown* factors

Schizophrenia

JAMIE FOXX   ROBERT DOWNEY JR.
THE SOLOIST
NO ONE CHANGES ANYTHING BY PLAYING IT SAFE
APRIL 24
BASED ON THE REMARKABLE TRUE STORY

In his portrayal of the homeless musical prodigy, Nathaniel Ayers, actor Jamie Foxx demonstrated several classic symptoms of schizophrenia, including disturbances in perception, language, thought, behavior, and emotion. For Ayers, as with others with schizophrenia, no single factor led to his illness.

Like most physical illnesses and other mental disorders, there is strong evidence linking schizophrenia to biological, psychological, and social factors—the *biopsychosocial model*.

Other Disorders

Objective 14.14: Identify substance-related disorders and comorbidity.

We have now discussed anxiety disorders, mood disorders, and schizophrenia. In this section, we will briefly describe three additional disorders—*substance-related*, *dissociative*, and *personality disorders*.

Substance-Related Disorders: When Drug Use Becomes Abnormal

Do you consider having wine with dinner or a few beers at a party to be an acceptable way to alter mood and behavior? In the *DSM-IV-TR*, drug use becomes a disorder when the person becomes physically or psychologically dependent. As you can see in Table 14.3, **substance-related disorders** are subdivided into two general groups—*substance*

Substance-Related Disorders
Abuse of, or dependence on, a mood- or behavior-altering drug

Table 14.3 *DSM-IV-TR* SUBSTANCE ABUSE AND SUBSTANCE DEPENDENCE

Criteria for Substance Abuse	Criteria for Substance Dependence
Maladaptive use of a substance shown by one of the following:	*Three or more of the following:*
• Failure to meet obligations	• Tolerance
• Repeated use in situations where it is physically dangerous	• Withdrawal
• Continued use despite problems caused by the substance	• Substance taken for a longer time or greater amount than intended
• Repeated substance-related legal problems	• Lack of desire or efforts to reduce or control use
	• Social, recreational, or occupational activities given up or reduced
	• Much time spent in activities to obtain the substance
	• Use continued despite knowing that psychological or physical problems are worsened by it

▲ **Comorbidity and substance-related disorders**
Can you see how comorbidity can cause serious problems? How can the appropriate cause, course, or treatment be identified for someone dealing with a combination of disorders

abuse and *substance dependence*—each with specific symptoms. When alcohol or other drug use interferes with a person's social or occupational functioning, it is called *substance abuse*. Drug use becomes *substance dependence* when it also causes physical reactions, including *tolerance* (requiring more of the drug to get the desired effect) and *withdrawal* (negative physical effects when the drug is removed) (see Chapter 5).

Can people use drugs and not develop a substance-related disorder? Of course. Most people drink alcohol without creating problems in their social relationships or occupations. Unfortunately, researchers have not been able to identify ahead of time those who can safely use drugs versus those who might become abusers (Abadinsky, 2011; Koob & LeMoal, 2008; Teesson et al., 2011).

Complicating diagnosis and treatment is the fact that substance-related disorders commonly coexist with other mental disorders, including anxiety disorders, mood disorders, schizophrenia, and personality disorders (Cosci & Fava, 2011; Petrakis, Rosenheck, & Desai, 2011; Thomas et al., 2008). This co-occurrence of disorders is called **comorbidity**, and it creates serious problems.

What causes comorbidity? Perhaps the most influential hypothesis is that of *self-medication*—people drink or use other drugs to reduce their painful and frightening symptoms (Bailey & Covell, 2011; Strahan et al., 2011). One of the most common comorbid disorders is alcohol use disorder (AUD). Research shows a high correlation between alcohol use disorders and other conditions, such as depression and personality disorders (Boden & Fergusson, 2011). On the other hand, several environmental variables also predict substance abuse disorders and comorbid conditions in adolescence. These variables include reduced parental monitoring, distance from teachers, selective socialization with deviant peers, and disaffiliation with peers (Branstetter, Low, & Furman, 2011; Burk et al., 2011; Kaminer, Ford, & Clark, 2011; Young-Wolff et al., 2011).

Although it may seem contradictory to have both genetic and environmental explanations, we see once again that nature and nurture interact. Researchers suggest that the interaction might result from the fact that an alcohol-abusing youth might tend to seek out deviant peers. In addition, the same genes that contribute to a parent's lax monitoring might also contribute to his or her child's early experimentation with alcohol.

Comorbidity Co-occurrence of two or more disorders in the same person at the same time, as when a person suffers from both depression and alcoholism

The high cost of alcohol abuse
Children of alcoholic parents are at much greater risk of also abusing alcohol and developing related disorders. Is this because of a genetic predisposition, modeling by the parents, or the emotional devastation of growing up with an alcoholic parent? ▼

Regardless of the causes or correlates of alcohol abuse disorders and comorbid conditions, it is critical that patients, family members, and clinicians recognize and deal with comorbidity if treatment is to be effective. Alcohol abuse disorders often accompany serious depression, and simply stopping drinking is not a total solution (though certainly an important first step). Similarly, people suffering from schizophrenia are far more likely to relapse into psychosis, require hospitalization, neglect their medications, commit acts of violence, or kill themselves when they also suffer from AUD (Cornelius & Clark, 2008; Smith et al., 2011). Recognizing this pattern and potential danger, many individual and group programs that treat schizophrenia now also include methods used in drug abuse treatment.

Dissociative Disorders: When the Personality Splits Apart

Objective 14.15: Describe dissociative disorders and dissociative identity disorders (DID).

The most dramatic and controversial psychological disorders are **dissociative disorders** which involve a splitting apart (a *dis*-association) of significant aspects of experience from memory or consciousness. Individuals dissociate from the core of their personality by failing to recall or identify past experience *(dissociative amnesia)* (Figure 14.11), by leaving home and wandering off *(dissociative fugue)*, by losing the sense of reality and feeling estranged from the self *(depersonalization disorder)*, or by developing completely separate personalities *(dissociative identity disorder)*.

The major problem underlying all dissociative disorders is the need to escape from anxiety. By developing amnesia, running away, or creating separate personalities, the individual avoids the anxiety and stress that threaten to overwhelm him or her. Unlike most other psychological disorders, environmental variables, such as trauma and sexual abuse, are reported to be the primary cause with little or no genetic influence (Hulette, Freyd, & Fisher, 2011; Sinason, 2011; Waller & Ross, 1997).

Dissociative Identity Disorder

The most severe dissociative disorder is **dissociative identity disorder (DID)**, previously known as *multiple personality disorder* (MPD). In this disorder, two or more distinct personalities reportedly exist within the same person at different times. Each personality has unique memories, behaviors, and social relationships. Transition from one personality to another occurs suddenly and is often triggered by psychological stress. Usually, the original personality has no knowledge or awareness of the existence of the alternate subpersonalities. But all of the different personalities may be aware of lost periods of time. Often, the alternate personalities are very different from the original personality. They may be of the other sex, a different race, another age, or even another species (such as a dog or lion). The disorder is diagnosed more among women than among men. Women also tend to have more identities, averaging 15 or more, compared with men, who average 8 (American Psychiatric Association, 2000).

DID is a controversial diagnosis. Some researchers and mental health professionals suggest that many cases are faked or result from false memories and an unconscious need to please the therapist (Kihlstrom, 2005; Lawrence, 2008; Pope et al., 2007; Stafford & Lynn, 2002). These skeptics also believe that therapists may be unintentionally encouraging, and thereby overreporting, the

Dissociative Disorder Amnesia, fugue, or multiple personalities resulting from a splitting apart of experience from memory or consciousness

Dissociative Identity Disorder (DID) Presence of two or more distinct personality systems in the same individual at different times; previously known as multiple personality disorder

Figure 14.11 Dissociation as an escape The major force behind all dissociative disorders is the need to escape from anxiety. Imagine witnessing a loved one's death in a horrible car accident. Can you see how your mind might cope by blocking out all memory of the event? ▼

incidence of DID. On the other side of the debate are psychologists who accept the validity of DID and provide treatment guidelines (Brown, 2011; Chu, 2011; Dalenberg et al., 2007; Lipsanen et al., 2004; Spiegel & Maldonado, 1999).

Personality Disorders: Antisocial and Borderline

Objective 14.16: Define personality disorders, and differentiate between antisocial and borderline personality disorders.

In Chapter 13, *personality* was defined as a unique and relatively stable pattern of thoughts, feelings, and actions. What would happen if these stable patterns, called personality, were so inflexible and maladaptive that they created significant impairment of someone's ability to function socially and occupationally? This is what happens with **personality disorders**. Several types of personality disorders are included in this category in *DSM-IV-TR*, but here we'll focus on *antisocial personality disorder* and *borderline personality disorder*.

Antisocial Personality Disorder

The term **antisocial personality disorder** often is used interchangeably with the terms *sociopath* and *psychopath*. These labels describe behavior so far outside the ethical and legal standards of society that many consider it the most serious of all mental disorders. Unlike people with anxiety, mood disorders, and schizophrenia, those with this diagnosis feel little personal distress (and may not be motivated to change). Yet their maladaptive traits generally bring considerable harm and suffering to others. Although serial killers are often seen as classic examples of antisocial personality disorder, many sociopaths harm people in less dramatic ways—for example, as ruthless business people and crooked politicians.

The four hallmarks of antisocial personality disorder are *egocentrism* (preoccupation with oneself and insensitivity to the needs of others), *lack of conscience*, *impulsive behavior*, and *superficial charm* (American Psychiatric Association, 2000).

Unlike most adults, individuals with antisocial personality disorder act impulsively, without giving thought to the consequences. They are usually poised when confronted with their destructive behavior and feel contempt for anyone they are able to manipulate. They also change jobs and relationships suddenly, and they often have a history of truancy from school and of being expelled for destructive behavior. People with antisocial personalities can be charming and persuasive, and they have remarkably good insight into the needs and weaknesses of other people.

Twin and adoption studies suggest a possible genetic predisposition to antisocial personality disorder. Biological contributions are also suggested by studies that have found abnormally low autonomic activity during stress, right hemisphere abnormalities, reduced gray matter in the frontal lobes, and biochemical disturbances (Anderson et al., 2011; De Oliveira-Souza et al., 2008; Huesmann & Kirwil, 2007; Schiffer et al., 2011; Sundram et al., 2011).

Evidence also exists for environmental causes. Antisocial personality disorder is highly correlated with neglectful and/or abusive parenting styles and inappropriate modeling (Barnow et al., 2007; De Oliveira-Souza et al., 2008; Grover et al., 2007; Lyons-Ruth et al., 2007). People with antisocial personality disorder often come from homes characterized by emotional deprivation, harsh and inconsistent disciplinary practices, and antisocial parental behavior. Still other studies show a strong interaction between both heredity and environment (Douglas et al., 2011; Gabbard, 2006; Hudziak, 2008; Philibert et al., 2011).

Personality Disorder Inflexible, maladaptive personality traits that cause significant impairment of social and occupational functioning

Antisocial Personality Disorder Extreme disregard for and violation of the rights of others; guiltless, exploitive, irresponsible, intrusive, and self-indulgent and violation of the rights

Public trials and mental illness
In the summer of 2011, the world watched as Casey Anthony was tried and found innocent of allegedly murdering her two-year-old daughter. Many professionals agreed that she showed symptoms of several possible personality disorders, including antisocial and borderline. What do you think? Should professionals offer an opinion based on limited, media provided information? Do televised trials and hotly debated verdicts like this one increase myths and stereotypes about mental illness?

Borderline personality disorder (BPD) Severe instability in emotion and self-concept, along with impulsive and self-destructive behavior

Borderline Personality Disorder

Borderline personality disorder (BPD) is among the most commonly diagnosed personality disorders (Ansell & Grilo, 2007; Gunderson, 2011). The core features of this disorder are severe instability in emotion and self-concept, along with impulsive and self-destructive behavior. Originally, the term implied that the person was on the borderline between neurosis and schizophrenia (Kring et al., 2010). Today, therapists believe the term helps describe how people with BPD live on a narrow "borderline" between love and hate. Those with BPD tend to see themselves and everyone else in black and white, absolute terms—perfect or worthless (Mondimore & Kelly, 2011; Scott et al., 2011). They constantly seek reassurance from others and may quickly erupt in anger at the slightest sign of disapproval. The disorder is also typically marked by a long history of broken friendships, divorces, and lost jobs.

Mary's story of chronic, lifelong dysfunction, described in the chapter opener, illustrates the serious problems associated with this disorder. People with borderline personality disorder experience extreme difficulties in relationships. Subject to chronic feelings of depression, emptiness, and intense fear of abandonment, they also engage in destructive, impulsive behaviors, such as sexual promiscuity, drinking, gambling, and eating sprees. In addition, they may attempt suicide and sometimes engage in self-mutilating behavior (Chapman, Leung, & Lynch, 2008; Crowell et al., 2008; Lynam et al., 2011; Muehlenkamp et al., 2011).

BPD typically involves a childhood history of neglect; emotional deprivation; and physical, sexual, or emotional abuse (Christopher et al., 2007; Distel et al., 2011; Gratz et al., 2011). This disorder also tends to run in families, and some data suggest it is a result of impaired functioning of the brain's frontal lobes and limbic system, areas that control impulsive behaviors (Leichsenring et al., 2011; Schulze et al., 2011).

Some therapists have had success treating BPD (Fleischhaker et al., 2011; Leichsenring et al., 2011; Mondimore & Kelly, 2011), but people with BPD appear to have a deep well of intense loneliness and a chronic fear of abandonment. Sadly, given their troublesome personality traits, friends, lovers, and even family and therapists often do "adandon" them—thus creating a tragic self-fulfilling prophecy.

 **TEST YOURSELF**

Checking Your Knowledge of Abnormal Behavior

Test your understanding of the six major diagnostic categories of psychological disorders by matching the disorders with the possible diagnosis. Check your answers in Appendix B.

Description of Disorder

1. Julie mistakenly believes she has lots of money and is making plans to take all her friends on a trip around the world. She has not slept for days. Last month, she could not get out of bed and talked of suicide.

2. Steve is exceptionally charming and impulsive and apparently feels no remorse or guilt when he causes great harm to others.
3. Chris believes he is president of the United States and hears voices saying the world is ending.
4. Each day, Kelly repeatedly checks and rechecks all stove burners and locks throughout her house and washes her hands hundreds of times.
5. Lee has repeated bouts of uncontrollable drinking, frequently misses his Monday morning college classes, and

was recently fired for drinking on the job.
6. Susan wandered off and was later found living under a new name, with no memory of her previous life.

Possible Diagnosis

a. Anxiety disorder
b. Schizophrenia
c. Mood disorder
d. Dissociative disorder
e. Personality disorder
f. Substance-related disorder

Psychology Engages

RESEARCH CHALLENGE

Black Swan on the Couch: In search of the perfect ending

By Thomas Frangicetto (Northampton Community College, Bethlehem, PA)

In the film, *Black Swan*, ballerina Nina Sayers (Natalie Portman) was ecstatic over being selected as the "Swan Queen," until a web of stressors began to unravel her hold on reality.

"I want to be perfect," says Nina Sayers. Not just highly skilled, extraordinarily talented, or head-of-the-class brilliant . . . but *perfect*. She is a world-class ballerina and mistakes are not just unwelcome in her world—they are *forbidden*. The desperate need to be *perfect*—free of error, defect, or even a hint of a fault or blemish—can by itself cause overwhelming levels of stress and anxiety (Flora 2010; Libby, 2011; Mitalk, 2009). Studies also have linked perfectionism to many of the disorders covered in this text—*depression, anorexia nervosa, bulimia, obsessive-compulsive disorder, Type A coronary-prone behavior, panic disorder, psychosomatic disorders, migraine,* and *suicide* (Codd, 2010; Hewitt et al., 1997; Kersting, 2004).

Note that perfectionism researchers have consistently differentiated between *adaptive* perfectionism, which reflects a positive pursuit toward achievement,

and *maladaptive* perfectionism, with three key characteristics—fear of failure, hypersensitivity to criticism, and unrealistically high self-expectations (Bell, 2010; Frost et al., 1993; Hamacheck, 1978; Kersting, 2004; O'Conner, 2007).

A recent investigation in the United Kingdom performed a "psychological autopsy" on three completed student suicides: Sam, 14, Ryan, 18, and Dan, 22. All three were described as gifted and talented students who shared several characteristics of maladaptive perfectonism. Perfectionism of this type was identified as contributing to the suicides of half (10) of the total sample of 20 from which these three individual studies were drawn (Bell, 2010).

Nina's brand of maladaptive perfectionism is artfully revealed in the pointed looks, comments, and insinuations (both real *and* imagined) of others, which Nina painfully incorporates into her perfect inner storm of fear of failure. The combination of self-inflicted internal pressures and the unrealistic expectations of others—a narcissistic mother, a sexually aggressive director, and the intense cutthroat competition from the other dancers—drive her straight into madness.

Several psychologists have and other social science professionals weighed in on what was wrong with Nina. Here's a sampling:

- ***Psychosis***, a loss of contact with reality, including *false beliefs*, delusions, and *hallucinations* (James, 2010; Lamberti; 2010). Several risk factors may have made Nina prone to psychosis if she had a genetic vulnerability (see *diathesis-stress model*, p. 515). For example, a highly stressful compeition, conflicted relationships with her mother and understudy, being sexually harassed by her director, plus the abuse of *ecstasy*, a powerful *halucinogen*, can cause a

psychotic episode. In addition, her frequent vomiting and weight loss could trigger an electrolyte disturbance that could have contributed to the psychosis (James, 2010; Lamberti, 2010).

- ***Anorexia nervosa/Bulimia nervosa*** (Chapter 12). It isn't stated, but there are scenes of Nina barely nibbling at food and purging as well. As Zipkin and Dunn (2011) note: "The film highlights the dangerous trend in the dancing world towards taking extreme measures to achieve a thin physique." Flora (2010) adds: "It's not just the pressure to be thin per se that makes ballerinas susceptible, it's the interaction between that pressure and their personalities, which tend toward perfectionism and neuroticism—hallmarks of anorexia."

- ***Disturbed parent–child relationship*** Nina's story is also that of "a child identified by a powerful parent to live out that parent's unrealized dream." Nina's domineering mother lives vicariously through her daughter and emotionally "seduces the child into a one-way relationship that gratifies only the parent" (Libby, 2011).

In addition, Natalie Portman herself, a psychology major at Harvard, diagnosed Nina as suffering from OCD, or *obsessive-compulsive disorder* (p. 501), with its emphasis on fearful thoughts and repetitive, ritualistic behaviors. It's also possible to make a strong case for *borderline personality disorder* (p. 520), with symptoms of impulsive behaviors, drug use, drinking, sexual promiscuity, self-mutilation, and suicide attempts on display.

Clearly not all of the above apply. The one core problem that has wide agreement is Nina's maladaptive need for perfection.

Overall, this is Hollywood sensationalizing a descent into a complex psychological disorder, with liberties freely taken. Kaufman (2011) says it well: "The movie's brilliance does not lie in its portrayal of reality . . . (but rather) in taking us on an exhilarating and terrifying tour to the edge of madness."

After an "exhilarating and terrifying" final performance of *Swan Lake*, Nina is dying from an apparent suicide attempt and utters her last words: "I was perfect." And she was. A perfect ending at last.

Student Engagement Exercise

Given the information in the perfectionism research (Bell, 2010) described above, what is the most likely:

1. *Research method* (experimental, descriptive, correlational, or biological)?

2. If you choose the:
   • *Experimental method*—label the IV, DV, experimental group, and control group.

• *Descriptive method*—identify whether this is a naturalistic observation, survey, or case study.

• *Correlational method*—label whether this is a positive, negative, or zero correlation.

• *Biological method*—identify the specific research tool (e.g., brain dissection, CT scan, etc.)

(Answers appear in Appendix B.)

 **CRITICAL THINKING**

Objective 14.17: Briefly explain how faulty thinking may contribute to depression.

How Your Thoughts Can Make You Depressed

Respond to the following questions by circling the number that most closely describes how you would feel in the same situation. Answering carefully and truthfully will improve your metacognitive critical thinking skills and insight into how your thoughts may contribute to depression.

Situation 1

You are introduced to a new person at a party and are left alone to talk. After a few minutes, the person appears bored.

1. Is this outcome caused by you? Or is it something about the other person or the circumstances?

       1   2   3   4   5   6   7
   Other person   Me
   or circumstances

2. Will the cause of this outcome also be present in the future?

       1   2   3   4   5   6   7
       No   Yes

3. Is the cause of this outcome unique to this situation, or does it also affect other areas of your life?

       1   2   3   4   5   6   7
   Affects just this   Affects all
   situation   situations
                                   in my life

Situation 2

You receive an award for a project that is highly praised.

4. Is this outcome caused by you or something about the circumstances?

       1   2   3   4   5   6   7
   Circumstances   Me

5. Will the cause of this outcome also be present in the future?

       1   2   3   4   5   6   7
       No   Yes

6. Is the cause of this outcome unique to this situation, or does it also affect other areas of your life?

       1   2   3   4   5   6   7
   Affects just this   Affects all
   situation   situations
                                   in my life

This modified version of the *Attributional Style Questionnaire* measures people's explanations for the causes of good and bad events. People with a *depressive explanatory style* tend to explain *bad* events in terms of *internal* factors ("It's my fault"), a *stable* cause ("It will always be this way"), and a *global* cause ("It's this way in many situations"). Sadly, this pattern of negative thinking reverses when good things happen. They attribute good events to external factors and unstable, specific causes. ("I just got lucky, it'll never happen again, and it's only this one event.")

In sharp contrast, people with an *optimistic explanatory style* tend to explain bad events in terms of external factors ("It's just a bad economy"), and unstable, specific causes. ("It seldom happens to me, and it's only this one event."). When good things happen, they attribute them to internal factors ("I deserve this"), and stable, global causes ("I usually win out in most situations.").

	Depressive Explanatory Style	**Optimistic Explanatory Style**
Bad events	Internal, stable, global	External, unstable, specific
Good events	External, unstable, specific	Internal, stable, global

How did you score? High scores (5–7) on questions 1, 2, and 3 and low scores (1–3) on questions 4, 5, and 6 may mean you have a *depressive explanatory style*. In contrast, low scores on the first three questions and high scores on the last three suggest you have an *optimistic explanatory style*.

Unfortunately, if you have a bad experience and then blame it on your personal (internal) inadequacies, interpret it as unchangeable (stable), and draw far-reaching (global) conclusions, you are obviously more likely to feel depressed. This self-blaming, pessimistic, and overgeneralizing explanatory style results in a sense of hopelessness (Ball, McGuffin, & Farmer, 2008).

Critics have asked: Does a depressive explanatory style cause depression? Or does depression cause a depressive explanatory style? Could another variable, such as neurotransmitters or other biological factors, cause both? Evidence suggests that both thought patterns and biology interact and influence depression. Professional help is clearly needed for serious depression, while changing your explanatory style may help dispel mild or moderate depression.

GENDER AND CULTURAL DIVERSITY

How Gender and Culture Affect Abnormal Behavior

Objective 14.18: Identify the biological, psychological, and social factors that might explain gender differences in depression.

Among the Chippewa, Cree, and Montagnais-Naskapi Indians in Canada, there is a disorder called *windigo*—or *wiitiko*—*psychosis*, which is characterized by delusions and cannibalistic impulses. Believing that they have been possessed by the spirit of a windigo, a cannibal giant with a heart and entrails of ice, victims become severely depressed (Faddiman, 1997). As the malady begins, the individual typically experiences loss of appetite, diarrhea, vomiting, and insomnia, and he or she may see people turning into beavers and other edible animals.

In later stages, the victim becomes obsessed with cannibalistic thoughts and may even attack and kill loved ones in order to devour their flesh (Berreman, 1971).

If you were a therapist, how would you treat this disorder? Does it fit neatly into any of the categories of psychological disorders that you have learned about? We began this chapter discussing the complexities and problems with defining, identifying, and classifying abnormal behavior. Before we close, we need to add two additional confounding factors: gender and culture. In this section, we explore a few of the many ways in which men and women differ in how they experience abnormal behavior. We also look at cultural variations in abnormal behavior.

Why are Women More Depressed

In the United States, Canada, and other countries, the rate of severe depression for women is two to three times the rate for men (Barry et al., 2008; Nicholson et al., 2008; World Health Organization, 2011).

Why is there such a disparity between men and women? Research explanations can be grouped under biological influences (hormones, biochemistry, and genetic predisposition), psychological processes (ruminative thought processes), and social factors (greater poverty, work–life conflicts, unhappy marriages, and sexual or physical abuse) (Cooper et al., 2008; Jackson & Williams, 2006; Shear et al., 2007).

According to the *biopsychosocial model*, some women inherit a genetic or hormonal predisposition toward depression. This biological predisposition combines with society's socialization processes to help reinforce behaviors—such as greater emotional expression, passivity, and dependence—that increase the chances for depression (Alloy et al., 1999; Nolen-Hoeksema, Larson, & Grayson, 2000). At the same time, focusing only on classical symptoms of depression (sadness, low energy, and feelings of helplessness) may cause large numbers of depressed men to be overlooked (Fields & Cochran, 2011) (Figure 14.12).

Schizophrenia Around The World

Peoples of different cultures experience mental disorders in a variety of ways. For example, the reported incidence of schizophrenia varies within different cultures

▲ **Figure 14.12 Depression in disguise?** In our society, men are typically socialized to suppress their emotions and to show their distress by acting out (showing aggression), acting impulsively (driving recklessly and committing petty crimes), and engaging in substance abuse. How might such cultural pressures lead us to underestimate male depression?

around the world. It is unclear whether these differences result from actual differences in prevalence of the disorder or from differences in definition, diagnosis, or reporting (Berry et al., 2011; Butler, Sati, & Abas, 2011; Papageorgiou et al., 2011).

The symptoms of schizophrenia also vary across cultures (Stompe et al., 2003), as do the particular stresses that may trigger its onset.

Finally, despite the advanced treatment facilities and methods in industrialized nations, the prognosis for people with schizophrenia is actually better in nonindustrialized societies. This may be because the core symptoms of schizophrenia (poor rapport with others, incoherent speech, etc.) make it more difficult to survive in highly industrialized countries. In addition, in most industrialized nations, families and other support groups are less likely to feel responsible for relatives and friends with schizophrenia (Brislin, 2000; Eaton, Chen, & Bromet, 2011).

Avoiding Ethnocentrism

Objective 14.18: Explain why recognizing the difference between culture-general and culture-bound disorders and symptoms can help prevent ethnocentrism in the diagnosis and treatment of psychological disorders

Most research on psychological disorders originates and is conducted primarily in Western cultures. Such a restricted sampling can limit our understanding of disorders in general and lead to an ethnocentric view of mental disorders (Figure 14.13). Fortunately, cross-cultural researchers have devised ways to overcome these difficulties. For example, Robert Nishimoto (1988) has found several **culture-general symptoms** that are useful in diagnosing disorders across cultures (Table 14.4).

In addition, Nishimoto found several **culture-bound symptoms**. For example, the Vietnamese Chinese reported "fullness in head," the Mexican respondents had "problems with [their] memory," and the Anglo-Americans reported "shortness of breath" and "headaches." Apparently, people learn to express their problems in ways that are acceptable to others in the same culture (Brislin, 1997, 2000; Butler, Sati, & Abas, 2011; Dhikav et al., 2008; Iwata et al., 2011; Kanayama & Pope, 2011; Marques et al., 2011).

This division between culture-general and culture-bound symptoms also helps us understand depression. Certain symptoms of depression (such as intense sadness, poor concentration, and low

Figure 14.13 Avoiding ethnocentrism ▼

▲ (a) Some disorders are culturally specific. Thus, clinicians must consider cultural background before diagnosing someone as "psychotic" because they believe in possession by spirits or being the victim of witchcraft.

▲ (b) Other problems are shared by many cultures, such as the unexpected death of a spouse or loss of a job.

Table 14.4 TWELVE CULTURE-GENERAL SYMPTOMS OF MENTAL HEALTH DIFFICULTIES

Nervous	Trouble sleeping	Low spirits
Weak all over	Personal worries	Restless
Feel apart, alone	Can't get along	Hot all over
Worry all the time	Can't do anything worthwhile	Nothing turns out right

Source: From *Understanding Culture's Influence on Behavior,* 2nd edition by Brislin. © 2000. Reprinted with permission of Wadsworth, a division of Thomson Learning. www.thomsonrights.com.

energy) seem to exist across all cultures (World Health Organization, 2011). But there is also evidence of some culture-bound symptoms. For example, feelings of guilt are found more often in North America and Europe. And in China, *somatization* (the conversion of depression into bodily complaints (occurs more frequently than it does in other parts of the world (Helms & Cook, 1999; Lawrence et al., 2011; Lim et al., 2011).

Just as there are culture-bound and culture-general symptoms, researchers have found that mental disorders are themselves sometimes culturally bound (Figure 14.14). The earlier example of windigo psychosis, a disorder limited to a small group of Canadian Indians, illustrates just such a case.

As you can see, culture has a strong effect on mental disorders. Studying the similarities and differences across cultures can lead to better diagnosis and understanding. It also helps mental health professionals who work with culturally diverse populations understand both culturally general and culturally bound symptoms.

Figure 14.14 Culture-bound disorders Some disorders are fading as remote areas become more Westernized, whereas other disorders (such as anorexia nervosa) are spreading as other countries adopt Western values. *Source:* Barlow & Durand, 2012; Dhikav et al., 2008; Gaw, 2001; Kring et al., 2010; Laungani, 2007; Tolin et al., 2007. ▼

Puerto Rican and other Latin cultures *Ataque de nervios* ("attack of nerves")	Southeast Asian, Malaysian, Indonesian, Thai Running amok	West African Brain fog	Ethiopia Possession by the "Zar"	South Chinese and Vietnamese *Koro*	Western Nations *Anorexia nervosa* (as other countries become Westernized they're showing some rare cases of anorexia)
Symptoms: trembling, heart palpitations, and seizure-like episodes often associated with the death of a loved one, accidents, or family conflict	**Symptoms:** wild, out-of-control, aggressive behaviors and attempts to injure or kill others	**Symptoms:** "brain tiredness," a mental and physical response to the challenges of schooling	**Symptoms:** involuntary movements, mutism, and incomprehensible language	**Symptoms:** belief that the penis is retracting into the abdomen and that when it is fully retracted, death will result; attempts to prevent the supposed retraction may lead to severe physical damage	**Symptoms:** occurs primarily among young women; preoccupied with thinness, they exercise excessively and refuse to eat; death can result

CHECK & REVIEW

STOP *Before going on, be sure to complete this Check & Review. It is an invaluable study tool!*

Other Disorders and Psychology Engages

Part A: Retrieval Practice

1. Without looking at the book, spend 10 minutes writing a free-form essay recalling all you can remember from the previous section.

2. Now, reread the previous section, and once again spend 10 minutes writing a free-form essay on the SAME material.

Part B: Practice Quiz

1. The major underlying problem for all dissociative disorders is the psychological need to escape from _____.

2. What is DID?

3. A serial killer would likely be diagnosed as a(n) _____ personality in the *Diagnostic and Statistical Manual of Mental Disorders*, fourth edition, text revision.

4. One possible biological contributor to BPD is _____. (a) childhood history of neglect; (b) emotional deprivation; (c) impaired functioning of the frontal lobes; (d) all these options.

5. In the movie Black Swan, the core problem for the lead character, Nina, was her obsessive need for _____.

6. The Critical Thinking exercise on p. 522 is based on research linking depression with how we explain the causes of good and bad events in our lives. Do you agree that having a depressive explanatory style increases the odds for depression? Have you observed this in your own life or in the lives of others?

7. Some research suggests depression in men is often overlooked because they are socialized to suppress their emotions and encouraged to express their distress by acting out, being impulsive, or engaging in substance abuse. Does this ring true from your own experiences and/or observations of others? If so, how might we change this situation?

Check your answers in Appendix B.

WileyPLUS presents an on-line version of this textbook along with a wealth of study resources including quizzes, practice tests, flash cards, videos, animations and other activities designed to improve your mastery of the content. Working in conjunction with these study tools, the *Psychology in Action* WileyPLUS course features Professor Karen Huffman, author of this textbook, explaining and expanding upon some of the most challenging concepts in psychology. Here is a sample of the tutorial videos available for this chapter:

- Debunking myths about mental illness
- Mood disorders and recognizing the signs of suicide
- An animated exploration of schizophrenia
- Virtual Field Trip to meet individuals living with Bipolar Disorder
- Virtual Field Trip to meet individuals living with Obsessive-Compulsive Disorder

Key Terms

To assess your understanding of the **Key Terms** in Chapter 14, write a definition for each (in your own words), and then compare your definitions with those in the text.

Studying Psychological Disorders
abnormal behavior (p. 493)
medical model (p. 494)
psychiatry (p. 494)
Diagnostic and Statistical Manual of Mental Disorders (DSM-IV-TR) (p. 494)
neurosis (p. 494)
psychosis (p. 494)
insanity (p. 495)

Anxiety Disorders
anxiety disorder (p. 500)
generalized anxiety disorder (GAD) (p. 500)

panic disorder (p. 501)
phobia (p. 501)
obsessive-compulsive disorder (OCD) (p. 501)

Mood Disorders
mood disorder (p. 505)
major depressive disorder (p. 505)
bipolar disorder (p. 505)
learned helplessness (p. 508)

Schizophrenia
schizophrenia [skit-so-Free-nee-uh], (p. 509)
hallucinations (p. 511)
delusions (p. 511)

dopamine hypothesis (p. 514)
diathesis-stress model (p. 515)

Other Disorders
substance-related disorders (p. 516)
comorbidity (p. 517)
dissociative disorder (p. 518)
dissociative identity disorder (DID) (p. 518)
personality disorder (p. 519)
antisocial personality disorder (p. 519)
borderline personality disorder (BPD) (p. 520)

Chapter Summary

Studying Psychological Disorders

Objective 14.1: Identify five common myths about mental illness.

The five common myths are: People with psychological disorders act in bizarre ways and are very different from normal people; mental disorders are a sign of personal weakness; mentally ill people are often dangerous and unpredictable; the mentally ill never fully recover; and most can work only at low-level jobs.

Objective 14.2: Define abnormal behavior, and list four standards for identifying it.

Abnormal behavior refers to patterns of emotions, thoughts, or behaviors considered pathological for one or more of these reasons: deviance, dysfunction, distress, or danger.

Objective 14.3: Briefly describe the history of understanding abnormal behavior.

In ancient times, people commonly believed that demons were the cause of abnormal behavior. The **medical model**, which emphasizes disease, later replaced this demonological model.

Objective 14.4: Describe the purpose and criticisms of the DSM-IV-TR, and differentiate between neurosis, psychosis, and insanity.

The *Diagnostic and Statistical Manual of Mental Disorders (DSM-IV-TR)* classification system provides detailed descriptions of symptoms. It also allows standardized diagnosis and improved communication among professionals and between professionals and patients.

The *DSM* has been criticized for over-reliance on the medical model, unfairly labeling people, possible cultural bias, and for not providing dimensions and degrees of disorder.

Neurosis is an outmoded term for a disorder characterized by unrealistic anxiety and other associated problems, whereas **psychosis** is a current term for a disorder characterized by defective or lost contact with reality. **Insanity** is a legal term applied when people cannot be held responsible for their actions, or are judged incompetent to manage their own affairs, due to mental illness.

Anxiety Disorders

Objective 14.5: Define anxiety disorders and the five major subtypes.

People with **anxiety disorders** experience unreasonable, often paralyzing, anxiety or fear. In **generalized anxiety disorder (*GAD*)**, there is a persistent, uncontrollable, and free-floating anxiety. In **panic disorder**, anxiety is concentrated into sudden and inexplicable panic attacks. **Phobias** are intense, irrational fears and avoidance of specific objects or situations. **Obsessive-compulsive disorder (*OCD*)** involves persistent anxiety-arousing thoughts (obsessions) and/or ritualistic actions (compulsions). (The fifth major anxiety disorder, PTSD, was discussed in Chapter 3.)

Objective 14.6: Identify the major contributors to anxiety disorders.

Anxiety disorders are influenced by psychological, biological, and sociocultural factors (the biopsychosocial model). Psychological theories focus on faulty cognitions (hypervigilance) and maladaptive learning from classical conditioning and social learning. Biological approaches emphasize evolutionary and genetic predispositions, brain differences, and biochemistry. The sociocultural perspective focuses on environmental stressors that increase anxiety and cultural socialization that produces distinct culture-bound disorders like *taijin kyofusho* (*TKS*).

Mood Disorders

Objective 14.7: Compare and contrast the two major mood disorders.

Mood disorders are extreme disturbances of affect (emotion). In **major depressive disorder**, individuals experience a long-lasting depressed mood that interferes with their ability to function, feel pleasure or maintain interest in life. The feelings have no apparent cause, and the individual may lose contact with reality (psychosis). In **bipolar disorder**, episodes of mania and depression alternate with normal periods. During the manic episode, the person is overly excited, his or her speech and thinking are rapid, and poor judgment is common. The person also may experience delusions of grandeur and act impulsively.

Objective 14.8: What do we need to know about suicide and its prevention?

Suicide is a serious problem associated with depression. If you are having suicidal thoughts, seek help immediately. You also can help others who may be contemplating suicide by becoming involved and showing concern.

Objective 14.9: Describe the key biological and psychosocial factors that contribute to mood disorders.

Biological theories of mood disorders emphasize brain function abnormalities and disruptions in neurotransmitters (especially serotonin, norepinephrine, and dopamine). Genetic predisposition also plays a role in both major depression and bipolar disorder.

Psychosocial theories of mood disorders emphasize disturbed interpersonal relationships, faulty thinking, poor self-concept, and maladaptive learning. According to **learned helplessness** theory, depression results from repeatedly failing to escape from a punishing situation.

Schizophrenia

Objective 14.10: Define schizophrenia, and describe its five major symptoms.

Schizophrenia is a serious psychotic mental disorder that afflicts approximately 1 of every 100 people. The five major symptoms are disturbances in perception (**hallucinations**), language (word salad and neologisms), thought (impaired logic and **delusions**), emotion (exaggerated, changeable, or blunted), and behavior (social withdrawal, bizarre mannerisms, catalepsy, waxy flexibility).

Objective 14.11: Explain how schizophrenia is NOT the same as dissociative identity disorder (DID) (previously called multiple personalities).

People with DID reportedly have two or more distinct personalities within them at different times. People with schizophrenia suffer a serious loss of contact with reality, but have only one personality.

Objective 14.12: Describe the key methods for classifying schizophrenia.

There are five major subtypes of schizophrenia—*paranoid, catatonic, disorganized, undifferentiated,* and *residual*. There are also two groups of symptoms—*positive* and *negative*.

Objective 14.13: What are the major biological and psychosocial factors that influence schizophrenia?

Biological theories of schizophrenia emphasize the role of genetics (people inherit a predisposition), disruptions in neurotransmitters (the **dopamine hypothesis**), and abnormal brain structure and function (such as enlarged ventricles and lower levels of activity in the frontal and temporal lobes). Psychosocial theories of schizophrenia focus on the **diathesis-stress model** and disturbed communication.

Other Disorders

Objective 14.14: Identify substance-related disorders and comorbidity.

Substance-related disorders involve abuse of, or dependence on, a mood- or behavior-altering drug. People with substance-related disorders also commonly suffer from other psychological disorders, a condition known as **comorbidity**.

Objective 14.15: Describe dissociative disorders and dissociative identity disorder (DID).

In **dissociative disorders**, critical elements of personality split apart. This split is manifested in a disassociation of significant aspects of experience from memory or consciousness. Developing completely separate personalities [**dissociative identity disorder (DID)**] is the most severe dissociative disorder.

Objective 14.16: Define personality disorders, and differentiate between antisocial and borderline personality disorders.

Personality disorders involve inflexible, maladaptive personality traits. The best-known type is the **antisocial personality**, characterized by a profound disregard for, and violation of, the rights of others. Research suggests this disorder may be related to genetic inheritance, defects in brain activity, or disturbed family relationships. **Borderline personality disorder (BPD)** is the most commonly diagnosed personality disorder. It is characterized by impulsivity and instability in mood, relationships, and self-image.

Objective 14.17: Briefly explain how faulty thinking may contribute to depression.

People with a depressive explanatory style tend to attribute bad events to internal factors and stable, global causes, and good events to external factors and unstable, specific causes. This pattern of negative thinking increases the chances for depression.

Objective 14.18: Identify the biological, psychological, and social factors that might explain gender differences in depression.

Men and women differ in how they experiencee and express abnormal behavior. For example, in North America severe depression in much more common in women than in men. Biological, psychological, and social factors probably combine to explain this phenomenon.

Objective 14.19: Explain why recognizing the difference between culture-general and culture-bound disorders and symptoms can prevent ethnocentrism in the diagnosis and treatment of psychological disorders.

Culture-general symptoms (nervousness, or trouble sleeping) are similarly expressed and identified in most cultures, whereas culture-bound symptoms ("fullness in the head") are unique to certain cultures. Similarly, culture-general disorders (schizophrenia) are similar across cultures, whereas culture-bound disorders (Koro) are unique. Recognizing these differences helps us expand our understanding of disorders and can thereby reduce our ethnocentrism.

ChapterFourteen VISUAL SUMMARY

Studying Psychological Disorders

Identifying Abnormal Behavior
Four Criteria on a Continuum:
1. Deviance
2. Dysfunction
3. Distress
4. Danger

Explaining Abnormality

- Sociocultural (Problems reflect cultural values and beliefs)
- Biological (Problems with brain function, genetic predisposition, biochemistry)
- Behavioral (Faulty conditioning or modeling)
- Cognitive (Faulty thinking)
- Evolutionary (Exaggerated form of an adaptive reaction)
- Psychoanalytic/Psychodynamic (Unconscious, unresolved conflict)
- Humanistic (Blocked personal growth)

→ Abnormal Behavior

Classifying Abnormal Behavior

Anxiety Disorders

Explaining Anxiety Disorders

Five Major Anxiety Disorders

| Generalized anxiety disorder (GAD) | Panic disorder | Phobias | Obsessive-compulsive disorder (OCD) | Posttraumatic stress disorder (PTSD) (see Chapter 3) |

Generalized anxiety disorder (GAD)

Symptoms: chronic, excessive fear, and worry, not attached to any specific threat

Panic disorder

Symptoms: recurrent episodes of intense anxiety, dizziness, and difficulty breathing, with no apparent cause

Phobias

- Agoraphobia
  - **Symptoms:** fear or avoidance of embarrassing or inescapable situations, especially large, open or public spaces
- Specific phobias
  - **Symptoms:** fear of a specific object or situation (e.g., spiders or elevators)
- Social phobias
  - **Symptoms:** fear of embarrassment in social situations (e.g., public speaking)

Obsessive-compulsive disorder (OCD)

Symptoms: persistent, anxiety-provoking thoughts and/or thoughts and/or irresistible rituals (e.g., repeatedly checking locks)

Posttraumatic stress disorder (PTSD)

Symptoms: flashbacks, nightmares, and impaired functioning following exposure to a life-threatening or horrific event

Psychological
- Faulty cognitions
- Maladaptive learning

Biological
- Evolutionary predispositions
- Genetic predispositions
- Biochemical disturbances

Sociocultural
- Cultural pressures

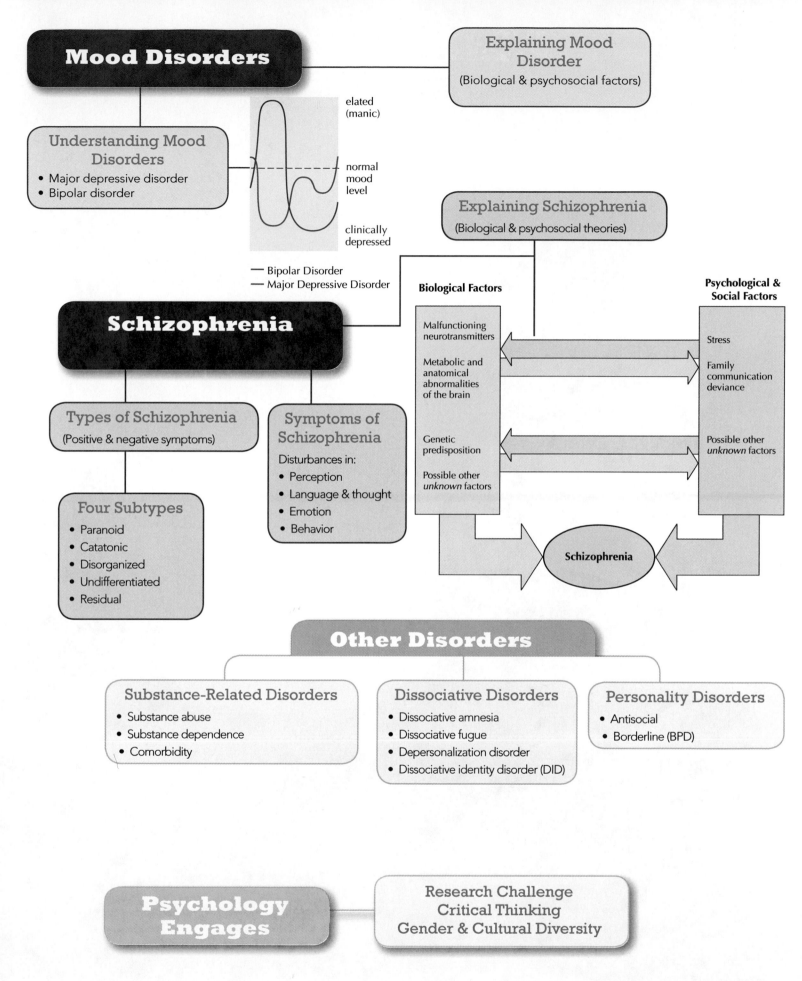

Mood Disorders

Explaining Mood Disorder
(Biological & psychosocial factors)

Understanding Mood Disorders
- Major depressive disorder
- Bipolar disorder

elated (manic)

normal mood level

clinically depressed

— Bipolar Disorder
— Major Depressive Disorder

Explaining Schizophrenia
(Biological & psychosocial theories)

Schizophrenia

Biological Factors

Malfunctioning neurotransmitters

Metabolic and anatomical abnormalities of the brain

Genetic predisposition

Possible other *unknown* factors

Psychological & Social Factors

Stress

Family communication deviance

Possible other *unknown* factors

Types of Schizophrenia
(Positive & negative symptoms)

Symptoms of Schizophrenia

Disturbances in:
- Perception
- Language & thought
- Emotion
- Behavior

Four Subtypes
- Paranoid
- Catatonic
- Disorganized
- Undifferentiated
- Residual

Schizophrenia

Other Disorders

Substance-Related Disorders
- Substance abuse
- Substance dependence
- Comorbidity

Dissociative Disorders
- Dissociative amnesia
- Dissociative fugue
- Depersonalization disorder
- Dissociative identity disorder (DID)

Personality Disorders
- Antisocial
- Borderline (BPD)

Psychology Engages

Research Challenge
Critical Thinking
Gender & Cultural Diversity

ChapterFifteen

Therapy

Mentally ill people and their treatment have been the subject of some of Hollywood's most popular and influential films. Sadly, in addition to the false or exaggerated portrayals of mental health treatment facilities, people with mental illness are generally depicted as either cruel, sociopathic criminals (Anthony Hopkins in *Silence of the Lambs*) or helpless, overwhelmed victims (Jack Nicholson in *One Flew Over the Cuckoo's Nest* and Natalie Portman in *Black Swan*). Although these portrayals may boost movie ticket sales, they also perpetuate harmful stereotypes (Kondo, 2008).

Like many people, your impressions of therapy may be unfairly guided by these Hollywood depictions. Although some are able to recognize and resist faulty stereotypes and unfair stigmas about mental illness and therapy, the negative portrayals and harmful myths persist (Lilienfeld et al., 2010; Rüsch et al., 2011; Thoits, 2011). To offset these misconceptions, we will present a balanced, factual overview of the latest research on psychotherapy and mental illness. As you'll see, modern psychotherapy can be very effective and prevent much needless suffering, not only for people with psychological disorders but also for those seeking help with everyday problems in living.

Voices from two clients and two therapists:

I yearned to get better; I told myself I was getting better. In fact, the depression was still there, like a powerful undertow. Sometimes it grabbed me, yanked me under; other times, I swam free.

TRACY THOMPSON

The most miraculous moments of my life were not when my daughter and son were born, but when the Prozac pills shot down my throat and catapulted me into a world called sane.

LAUREN SLATER

In my early professionals years I was asking the question: How can I treat, or cure, or change this person? Now I would phrase the question in this way: How can I provide a relationship which this person may use for his own personal growth?

CARL ROGERS

The best years of your life are the ones in which you decide your problems are your own. You do not blame them on your mother, the ecology, or the president. You realize that you control your own destiny.

ALBERT ELLIS

MYTH BUSTERS

Do you recognize these myths?

- *Myth: There is one best therapy.*

  Fact: Many problems can be treated equally well with many different forms of therapy.

- *Myth: Therapists can read your mind.*

  Fact: Good therapists often seem to have an uncanny ability to understand how their clients are feeling and to know when someone is trying to avoid certain topics. This is not due to any special mind-reading ability. It reflects their specialized training and daily experience working with troubled people.

- *Myth: People who go to therapists are crazy or weak.*

  Fact: Most people seek counseling because of stress in their lives or because they realize that therapy can improve their level of functioning. It is difficult to be objective about our own problems. Seeking therapy is a sign not only of wisdom but also of personal strength.

- *Myth: Only the rich can afford therapy.*

  Fact: Therapy can be expensive. But many clinics and therapists charge on a sliding scale based on the client's income. Some insurance plans also cover psychological services.

- *Myth: If I am taking meds, I don't need therapy.*

  Fact:

  Medications, such as antidepressants, are only one form of therapy. They can change brain chemistry, but they can't teach us to think or behave differently. Research suggests a combination of drugs and psychotherapy may be best for some situations, whereas in other cases, psychotherapy alone is most effective.

Objective 15.1: Identify four common myths about therapy, and its three general approaches.

Throughout this text, we've focused on the scientific study of behavior and mental processes, with an emphasis on "normal" functioning. In the previous chapter, we observed what happens when functioning goes awry, and now we'll examine how mental health workers try to help those whose behaviors, thoughts, or emotions are dysfunctional.

According to one expert (Kazdin, 1994), there may be over 400 approaches to professional psychotherapy. To organize our discussion, we have grouped treatments into three categories: *insight therapies*, *behavior therapies*, and *biomedical therapies* (Figure 15.1). After exploring these approaches, we conclude with a discussion of issues that are common to all major forms of psychotherapy.

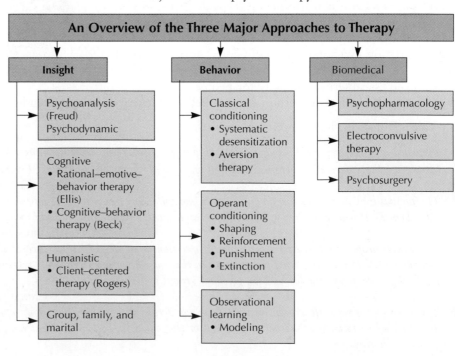

Figure 15.1 An Overview of the Three Major Approaches to Therapy

Insight Therapies

Objective 15.2: Define psychotherapy and insight therapy.

We begin our discussion of professional **psychotherapy** with traditional *psychoanalysis* and its modern counterpart, *psychodynamic* therapy. Then we explore *cognitive, humanistic, group,* and *family therapies.* Although these therapies differ significantly, they're often grouped together as **insight therapies** because they seek to improve psychological functioning by increasing *insight* (or awareness) into underlying motives and improvement in the client's thoughts feelings, and/or behaviors.

Psychoanalysis/Psychodynamic Therapies: Unlocking the Secrets of the Unconscious

Objective 15.3: Define psychoanalysis and list its five major methods.

As the name implies, in **psychoanalysis**, a person's *psyche* (or mind) is *analyzed.* Traditional psychoanalysis is based on Sigmund Freud's central belief that abnormal behavior is caused by unconscious conflicts among the three parts of the psyche—the *id, ego,* and *superego* (Chapter 13).

During psychoanalysis, these unconscious conflicts are brought to consciousness. The patient discovers the underlying reasons for his or her behavior and comes to realize that the childhood conditions under which the conflicts developed no longer exist. Once this realization (or insight) occurs, the conflicts can be resolved and the patient can develop more adaptive behavior patterns (Cordón 2012; Johnson, 2011).

Unfortunately, according to Freud, the ego has strong *defense mechanisms* that block unconscious thoughts from coming to light. Thus, to gain insight into the unconscious, the ego must be "tricked" into relaxing its guard. With that goal, psychoanalysts employ five major methods: *free association, dream analysis, analysis of resistance, analysis of transference,* and *interpretation* (Figure 15.2).

Psychotherapy Techniques employed to improve psychological functioning and promote adjustment to life

Insight Therapies Variety of therapies seeking to improve psychological functioning by increasing awareness into underlying motives and improvement in thoughts, feelings, and/or behaviors

Psychoanalysis Freudian therapy designed to bring unconscious conflicts into conscious awareness; also Freud's theoretical school of thought

▲ **Sigmund Freud (1856–1939)** Freud believed that during psychoanalysis the therapist's (or psychoanalyst's) major goal was to bring unconscious conflicts into consciousness.

Figure 15.2 Freud's psychoanalysis

"**The way this works is that you say the first thing that comes to your mind...**"

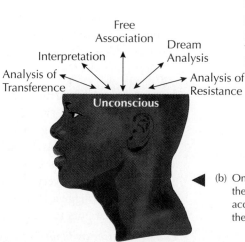

(b) Once the patient is fully relaxed, the psychoanalyst attempts to access the unconscious through these five methods.

(a) As shown in this cartoon, the technique called "free association" and a patient lying on a couch are common portrayals of traditional psychoanalysis. Why do they use a couch? Freud believed that this arrangement—with the therapist out of the patient's view and the patient relaxed—makes the unconscious more accessible and helps patients relax their defenses.

Free Association In psychoanalysis, reporting whatever comes to mind without monitoring its contents

Dream Analysis In psychoanalysis, interpreting the underlying true meaning of dreams to reveal unconscious processes

Resistance In psychoanalysis, the person's inability or unwillingness to discuss or reveal certain memories, thoughts, motives, or experiences

Transference In psychoanalysis, the patient may displace (or transfer) unconscious feelings about a significant person in his or her life onto the therapist

Interpretation A psychoanalyst's explanation of a patient's free associations, dreams, resistance, and transference; more generally, any statement by a therapist that presents a patient's problem in a new way

1. *Free association* According to Freud, when you let your mind wander and remove conscious censorship over thoughts—a process called **free association**—interesting and even bizarre connections seem to spring into awareness. Freud believed that the first thing to come to a patient's mind is often an important clue to what the person's unconscious wants to conceal. Having the patient recline on a coach, with only the ceiling to look at, is believed to encourage free association.

2. *Dream analysis* Recall from Chapter 5 that, according to Freud, defenses are lowered during sleep, and forbidden desires and unconscious conflicts can be freely expressed during dreams. Even while dreaming, however, these feelings and conflicts are recognized as being unacceptable and must be disguised as images that have deeper symbolic meaning. Thus, during Freudian **dream analysis**, a therapist might interpret a dream of riding a horse or driving a car (the surface description or *manifest content*) as a desire for, or concern about, sexual intercourse (the hidden, underlying meaning or *latent content*).

3. *Analysis of resistance* During free association or dream analysis, Freud believed patients often show **resistance**—the inability or unwillingness to discuss or reveal certain memories, thoughts, motives, or experiences. For example, suddenly "forgetting" what they were saying, changing the subject, not talking, and/or arriving late or missing appointments. It is the therapist's job to confront this resistance and to help patients face their problems.

4. *Analysis of transference* During psychoanalysis, patients supposedly disclose intimate feelings and memories, and patients often apply (or *transfer*) some of their unresolved emotions and attitudes from past relationships onto the therapist. The therapist uses this process of **transference** to help the patient "relive" painful past relationships in a safe, therapeutic setting so that he or she can move on to healthier relationships.

5. *Interpretation* The core of all psychoanalytic therapy is **interpretation**. During free association, dream analysis, resistance, and transference, the analyst listens closely and tries to find patterns and hidden conflicts. At the right time, the therapist explains (or *interprets*) the underlying meanings to the client.

Evaluation

Objective 15.4: What are the two major criticisms of psychoanalysis?

As you can see, most of psychoanalysis rests on the assumption that repressed memories and unconscious conflicts actually exist. But, as noted in Chapters 7 and 13, this assumption is the subject of a heated, ongoing debate. Critics also point to two other problems with psychoanalysis (Messer & Gurman, 2011; Miltenberger, 2011; Siegel, 2010):

- *Limited applicability* Critics argue that psychoanalysis seems to suit only a select group of highly motivated, articulate patients with less severe disorders. Psychoanalysis also is time consuming (often lasting several years with four to five sessions a week) and expensive. And it seldom works well with severe mental disorders, such as schizophrenia. This is logical because psychoanalysis is based on verbalization and rationality—the very abilities most significantly disrupted by serious disorders. Finally, critics suggest that spending years chasing unconscious conflicts from the past allows patients to escape from the responsibilities and problems of adult life.

- *Lack of scientific credibility* The goals of psychoanalysis are explicitly stated—to bring unconscious conflicts to conscious awareness. But how do you know when this goal has been achieved? A serious problem with psychoanalysis is that its "insights" (and therefore its success) cannot be proven or disproven.

Psychoanalysts acknowledge that it is impossible to scientifically document certain aspects of their therapy. However, there is evidence that psychoanalysis can be effective with some chronic disorders, and that most patients benefit (Braaten, 2011; Herbert & Forman, 2010; Spurling, 2011).

Modern Psychodynamic Therapy

Objective 15.5: Differentiate between psychoanalysis and psychodynamic therapy.

Partly in response to criticisms of traditional psychoanalysis, more streamlined forms of psychoanalysis have been developed. In modern **psychodynamic therapy**, treatment is briefer, the patient is treated face to face (rather than reclining on a couch), and the therapist takes a more directive approach (rather than waiting for unconscious memories and desires to slowly be uncovered).

Also, contemporary psychodynamic therapists focus less on unconscious, early childhood roots of problems, and more on conscious processes and current problems (Hunsley & Lee, 2010; Zuckerman, 2011). Such refinements have helped make psychoanalysis shorter, more available, and more effective for an increasing number of people (Figure 15.3).

Psychodynamic Therapy A briefer, more directive, and more modern form of psychoanalysis focusing more on conscious processes and current problems

Figure 15.3 Interpersonal therapy (IPT) As the name implies, *interpersonal* therapy (IPT) focuses almost exclusively on the client's current relationships. Its goal is to relieve immediate symptoms and help the client learn better ways to solve future interpersonal problems. Originally designed for acute depression, IPT is similarly effective for a variety of disorders, including depression, marital conflict, eating disorders, parenting problems, and drug addiction (Aldenhoff, 2011; Cuijpers et al., 2011; Hardy, 2011).

 TEST YOURSELF

PT: Sometimes it doesn't seem worth the effort to continue.
TH: Have you had any thoughts of wanting to kill yourself?
PT: No, not really.
TH: What have you thought of doing?
PT: Nothing that's worth mentioning.
TH: Have you ever thought of taking an overdose of pills?
PT: No, I haven't.
TH: What about cutting yourself or jumping off a bridge?
PT: No, those options aren't very good. You might not die.
TH: Have you thought of a way you think might be more certain, perhaps like using a gun?
PT: (long pause) I have thought of shooting myself.

No small segment of therapy can truly convey an actual full-length therapy session. However, this brief excerpt of an exchange between a patient (PT) and therapist (TH) using a *psychodynamic* approach does demonstrate several psychoanalytic/psychodynamic techniques. Try to identify examples of free association, dream analysis, resistance, or transference in this discussion.

Answer: The clearest example is resistance. When the therapist asks her about thoughts of suicide, she initially resists and then admits she has thought of shooting herself. Keep in mind that all therapists in this situation would probe beyond this point in the discussion to follow up on the patient's suicide risk.

CHECK & REVIEW

STOP *Before going on, be sure to complete this Check & Review. It is an invaluable study tool!*

Psychoanalysis/Psychodynamic Therapies

Part A: Retrieval Practice

1. Without looking at the book, spend 10 minutes writing a free-form essay recalling all you can remember from the previous section.

2. Now, reread the previous section, and once again spend 10 minutes writing a free-form essay on the SAME material.

   (Although time consuming, this exercise has been shown to be the single best way to improve your test scores! For more information, check out www

.sciencemag.org/content/early/ 2011/01/19/science.1199327.abstract)

Part B: Practice Quiz

1. The system of psychotherapy developed by Freud that seeks to bring unconscious conflicts into conscious awareness is known as _____. (a) transference; (b) cognitive restructuring; (c) psychoanalysis; (d) the "hot seat" technique

2. Which psychoanalytic concept best explains the following situations?

a. Mary is extremely angry with her therapist, who seems unresponsive and uncaring about her personal needs.

b. Although John is normally very punctual in his daily activities, he is frequently late for his therapy session.

3. What are the two major criticisms of psychoanalysis?

4. How does modern psychodynamic therapy differ from psychoanalysis?

Check your answers in Appendix B.

The mind is its own place, and in itself can make a Heavn' of Hell, a Hell of Heav'n

JOHN MILTON,
PARADISE LOST, LINE 247

Cognitive therapy Therapy that treats problem behaviors and mental processes by focusing on faulty thought processes and beliefs

Self-Talk Internal dialogue; the things people say to themselves when they interpret events

Cognitive Restructuring Process in cognitive therapy to change destructive thoughts or inappropriate interpretations

Cognitive-Behavior Therapy Combines cognitive therapy (changing faulty thinking) with behavior therapy (changing faulty behaviors)

Rational-Emotive Behavior Therapy (REBT) Ellis's cognitive therapy to eliminate emotional problems through rational examination of irrational beliefs

Cognitive Therapies: Focusing on Faulty Thoughts and Beliefs

Objective 15.6: Discuss cognitive therapy, self-talk, cognitive restructuring, and cognitive-behavior therapy.

Cognitive therapy assumes that faulty thought processes—beliefs that are irrational, overly demanding, or that fail to match reality—create problem behaviors and emotions (Friedberg & Belsford, 2011; Miltenberger, 2011; Wright, Thase, & Beck, 2011).

Like psychoanalysts, cognitive therapists believe that exploring unexamined beliefs can produce insight into the reasons for disturbed behaviors. However, instead of believing that therapeutic change occurs because of insight into unconscious processes, cognitive therapists believe that insight into negative **self-talk** (the unrealistic things a person tells himself or herself) is most important. Through a process called **cognitive restructuring**, this insight allows clients to challenge their thoughts, change how they interpret events, and modify maladaptive behaviors (Figure 15.4).

This last point of changing maladaptive behavior is the central goal of a closely aligned type of cognitive therapy, called **cognitive-behavior therapy**. As you'll see in the upcoming section, the aptly named behavior therapists focus on changing behavior, and cognitive-behavior therapists work to reduce both self-destructive thoughts *and* self-destructive behaviors.

Albert Ellis and Rational-Emotive Behavior Therapy (REBT)

Objective 15.7: What is the general goal of Ellis's rational–emotive behavior therapy (REBT)?

One of the best-known cognitive therapists, Albert Ellis, suggested irrational beliefs are the primary culprit in problem emotions and behaviors. According to Ellis, outside events do not cause us to have feelings. We feel as we do because of our irrational beliefs. Therefore, his **rational-emotive behavior therapy (REBT)** is directed toward challenging and changing these irrational beliefs (Ellis, 2007; Ellis & Ellis,

Figure 15.4 Using cognitive restructuring to improve sales

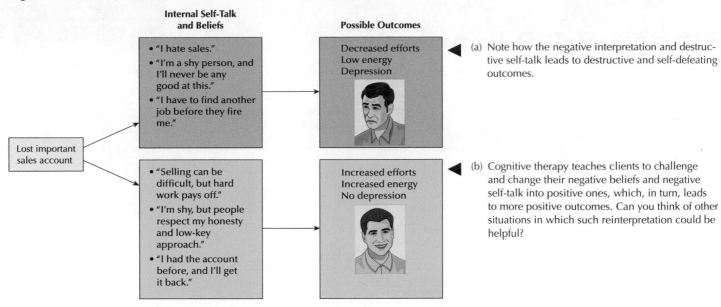

Internal Self-Talk and Beliefs

Lost important sales account

- "I hate sales."
- "I'm a shy person, and I'll never be any good at this."
- "I have to find another job before they fire me."

- "Selling can be difficult, but hard work pays off."
- "I'm shy, but people respect my honesty and low-key approach."
- "I had the account before, and I'll get it back."

Possible Outcomes

Decreased efforts
Low energy
Depression

Increased efforts
Increased energy
No depression

(a) Note how the negative interpretation and destructive self-talk leads to destructive and self-defeating outcomes.

(b) Cognitive therapy teaches clients to challenge and change their negative beliefs and negative self-talk into positive ones, which, in turn, leads to more positive outcomes. Can you think of other situations in which such reinterpretation could be helpful?

2011; Vernon, 2011). Ellis called REBT an A–B–C–D approach: **A** stands for *activating event*, **B** the person's *belief system*, **C** the emotional and behavioral *consequences*, and **D** *disputing* erroneous beliefs. (See Step-by-Step Diagram 15.1.)

Ellis also suggested that when we demand certain "musts" ("I must get into graduate school") and "shoulds" ("He should love me") from ourselves and others, we create emotional distress and behavioral dysfunctions (Ellis & Ellis, 2011). Unfortunately, these unrealistic, irrational beliefs, generally go unexamined until they are confronted directly. In therapy, Ellis actively argued with clients, cajoling and teasing them, sometimes in very blunt language. Once clients recognized their self-defeating thoughts, he worked with them on how to *behave* differently—to test out new beliefs and to learn better coping skills.

With or without professional therapy, many of us would benefit from examining and overcoming our irrational beliefs. If you'd like to apply Ellis's approach to your own life, complete the following *Try This Yourself* activity.

[In therapy,] I had a great many sex and love cases where people were absolutely devastated with somebody with whom they were compulsively in love who didn't love them back. They were killing themselves with anxiety and depression.
ALBERT ELLIS

TRY THIS YOURSELF

Overcoming Irrational Misconceptions

Albert Ellis believed that people often require the help of a therapist to see through their defenses and to challenge their self-defeating thoughts. However, you may be able to improve your own irrational beliefs and responses with the following suggestions:

1. **Identify and confront your belief system.** Identify your irrational beliefs by asking yourself why you feel the particular emotions you do. By confronting your thoughts and feelings, you can discover the irrational assumptions that are creating the problem consequences.

2. **Evaluate consequences.** Rather than perpetuating negative emotions by assuming they must be experienced, focus on whether your reactions make you more effective and enable you to solve your problems. For example, it is gratifying when people you cherish love you in return, but if they do not, continuing to pursue them or insisting that they must love you will only be self-defeating.

3. **Practice effective ways of thinking and behaving.** Imagine and rehearse thoughts and behaviors that are more effective and outcomes that are more successful.

Albert Ellis (1913–2007)

Step-by-StepDiagram15.1

STOP This Step by Step diagram contains essential information NOT found elsewhere in the text, which is likely to appear on quizzes and exams. Be sure to study it CAREFULLY!

Ellis's A-B-C-D Approach

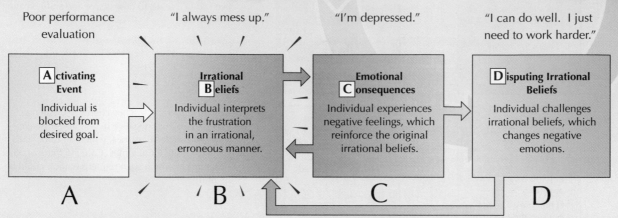

Poor performance evaluation

Activating Event

Individual is blocked from desired goal.

"I always mess up."

Irrational **B**eliefs

Individual interprets the frustration in an irrational, erroneous manner.

"I'm depressed."

Emotional **C**onsequences

Individual experiences negative feelings, which reinforce the original irrational beliefs.

"I can do well. I just need to work harder."

Disputing Irrational Beliefs

Individual challenges irrational beliefs, which changes negative emotions.

A   B   C   D

According to Albert Ellis, our emotional reactions are produced by our interpretation of an (A) *activating event*, not by the event itself. For example, if you receive a poor performance evaluation at work, you might directly attribute your bad mood to the negative feedback. Ellis would argue that your irrational (B) belief ("I always mess up") between the event and the *emotional* (C) *consequences* is what upset you. Furthermore, ruminating on all the other bad things in your life maintains your negative emotional state. Ellis's therapy emphasizes (D) *disputing*, or challenging, these irrational beliefs, which, in turn, causes changes in maladaptive emotions—it breaks the vicious cycle.

Aaron Beck

Aaron Beck's Cognitive Therapy

Objective 15.8: Describe Beck's cognitive therapy.

Like Ellis, Aaron Beck believes that psychological problems result from illogical thinking and from destructive self-talk, but Beck developed a somewhat different form of *cognitive-behavior therapy* to treat psychological problems, especially depression (Beck, 1976, 2000, Hollon, 2011; Rosner, 2011; Wright, Thase, & Beck, 2011). Beck has identified several distorted thinking patterns that he believes are associated with depression-prone people:

1. *Selective perception* Focusing selectively on negative events while ignoring positive events. ("Why am I the only person alone at this party?")

2. *Overgeneralization* Overgeneralizing and drawing negative conclusions about one's self-worth. ("I'm worthless because I failed that exam.")

3. *Magnification* Exaggerating the importance of undesirable events or personal shortcomings, and seeing them as catastrophic and unchangeable. ("She left me, and I'll never find someone like her again!")

4. *All-or-nothing thinking* Seeing things in black-or-white categories—everything is either totally good or bad, right or wrong, a success or a failure. ("If I don't get straight A's, I'll never get a good job.")

In Beck's cognitive-behavior therapy, clients are first taught to recognize and keep track of their thoughts. Then, the therapist trains the client to develop ways to test these automatic thoughts against reality. If the client believes that straight A's are necessary for a certain job, the therapist needs to find only one instance of this not being the case to refute the belief. Obviously, the therapist chooses the tests carefully so that they do not confirm the client's negative beliefs but lead instead to positive outcomes.

This approach—identifying dysfunctional thoughts followed by active testing— helps depressed people discover that negative attitudes are largely a product of unrealistic or faulty thought processes.

At this point, Beck introduces the *behavior* phase of therapy, persuading the client to actively pursue pleasurable activities. Depressed individuals often lose motivation, even for experiences they used to find enjoyable. Simultaneously taking an active rather than a passive role and reconnecting with enjoyable experiences help in recovering from depression.

Evaluating Cognitive Therapies

Objective 15.9: What are the chief successes and criticisms of cognitive therapy?

Cognitive therapies are highly effective treatments for depression, anxiety disorders, bulimia nervosa, anger management, addiction, procrastination, and even some symptoms of schizophrenia and insomnia (Hofman, 2011; Kalodner, 2011; Mehta et al., 2011; Thomas et al., 2011; Young, Connor, & Feeney, 2011).

However, both Beck and Ellis have been criticized for ignoring or denying the client's unconscious dynamics, overemphasizing rationality, and minimizing the importance of the client's past (Hammack, 2003). Other critics suggest that cognitive therapies are successful because they employ *behavior techniques*, not because they change the underlying cognitive structure (Bandura, 1969, 1997, 2006, 2008; Messer & Gurman, 2011; Miltenberger, 2011). Imagine that you sought treatment for depression and learned to construe events more positively and to curb your *all-or-nothing* thinking. Further imagine that your therapist also helped you identify activities and behaviors that would promote greater fulfillment. If you found your depression lessening, would you attribute the improvement to your changing thought patterns or to changes in your overt behavior?

Humanistic Therapies: Blocked Personal Growth

Objective 15.10: Define humanistic therapy and describe Rogers's client-centered therapy.

Humanistic therapy assumes that people with problems are suffering from a disruption of their normal growth potential, and, hence, their self-concept (Chapter 13). When obstacles are removed, the individual is free to become the self-accepting, genuine person everyone is capable of being.

Carl Rogers and Client-Centered Therapy

One of the best-known humanistic therapists, Carl Rogers, developed an approach that encourages people to actualize their potential and relate to others in genuine ways. His approach is referred to as **client-centered therapy**. Using the term *client* instead of *patient* was very significant to Rogers. He believed the label "patient" implied being sick or mentally ill rather than responsible and competent. Treating people as clients demonstrates *they* are the ones in charge of the therapy (Rogers, 1961, 1980). It also emphasizes the equality of the therapist–client relationship.

Humanistic Therapy Therapy that focuses on removing obstacles that block personal growth and potential

The only person who is educated is the one who has learned how to learn and change.

CARL ROGERS

Client-Centered Therapy Rogers's therapy emphasizing the client's natural tendency to become healthy and productive; techniques include empathy, unconditional positive regard, genuineness, and active listening

P. BYRNES.

"Just remember, son, it doesn't matter whether you win or lose—unless you want Daddy's love."

Empathy In Rogerian terms, an insightful awareness and ability to share another's inner experience

Unconditional Positive Regard Rogers's term for love and acceptance with no contingencies attached

Genuineness In Rogerian terms, authenticity or congruence; the awareness of one's true inner thoughts and feelings and being able to share them honestly with others

Active Listening Listening with total attention to what another is saying; involves reflecting, paraphrasing, and clarifying what the person says and means

Client-centered therapy, like other insight therapies, explores thoughts and feelings to obtain insight into the causes for behaviors. For Rogerian therapists, however, the focus is on providing an accepting atmosphere and encouraging healthy emotional experiences. Clients are responsible for discovering their own maladaptive patterns.

Rogerian therapists create a therapeutic relationship by focusing on four important qualities of communication: *empathy, unconditional positive regard, genuineness,* and *active listening.*

1. **Empathy** is a sensitive understanding and sharing of another person's inner experience. When we put ourselves in other people's shoes, we enter their inner world. Therapists pay attention to body language and listen for subtle cues to help them understand the emotional experiences of clients. To help clients explore their feelings, the therapist uses open-ended statements such as "You found that upsetting" or "You haven't been able to decide what to do about this" rather than asking questions or offering explanations.

2. **Unconditional positive regard** is genuine caring for people based on their innate value as individuals. Because humanists believe human nature is positive and each person is unique, clients can be respected and cherished without their having to prove themselves worthy of the therapist's esteem. Unconditional positive regard allows the therapist to trust that clients have the best answers for their own lives.

   To maintain a climate of unconditional positive regard, the therapist avoids making evaluative statements such as "That's good" and "You did the right thing." Such comments give the idea that the therapist is judging them and that clients need to receive approval. Humanists believe that when people receive unconditional caring from others, they become better able to value themselves in a similar way.

3. **Genuineness**, or *authenticity*, is being aware of one's true inner thoughts and feelings and being able to share them honestly with others. When people are genuine, they are not artificial, defensive, or playing a role. In turn, when therapists are genuine with their clients, they believe their clients will, in turn, develop self-trust and honest self-expression.

4. **Active listening** involves reflecting, paraphrasing, and clarifying what the client says and means. To *reflect* is to hold a mirror in front of the person, enabling that person to see him- or herself. To *paraphrase* is to summarize in different words what the client is saying. To *clarify* is to check that both the speaker and listener are on the same wavelength. By being an *active listener*, the clinician communicates that he or she is genuinely interested in what the client is saying (Figure 15.5).

Evaluating Humanistic Therapies

Objective 15.11: What are the key criticisms of humanistic therapy?

Supporters say there is empirical evidence for the efficacy of client-centered therapy (Benjamin, 2011; Hardcastle et al., 2008; Hazler, 2011; Messer & Gurman, 2011). But

◀ **Figure 15.5 Active listening** Noticing a client's brow furrowing and hands clenching while he is discussing his marital problems, a clinician might respond, "It sounds like you're angry with your wife and feeling pretty miserable right now." Can you see how this statement *reflects* the client's anger, *paraphrases* his complaint, and gives *feedback* to clarify the communication?

critics argue that the basic tenets of humanistic therapy, such as self–actualization and self-awareness, are difficult to test scientifically. Most of the research on the outcomes of humanistic therapy relies on client self-reports. However, people undergoing any type of therapy are motivated to justify their time and expense. In addition, research on specific therapeutic techniques, such as Rogerian "empathy" and "active listening," has had mixed results (Clark, 2007; Hodges & Biswas-Diener, 2007; Norcross & Wampold, 2011).

 TEST YOURSELF

Client-Centered Therapy in Action

Carl Rogers (1902–1987)

To check your understanding of *empathy*, *unconditional positive regard*, *genuineness*, and *active listening*, identify the techniques being used in the following excerpt (Shea, 1988, pp. 32–33). Then, compare your responses with those in Appendix B.

THERAPIST (TH): What has it been like coming down to the emergency room today?

CLIENT (CL): Unsettling, to say the least. I feel very awkward here, sort of like I'm vulnerable. To be honest, I've had some horrible experiences with doctors. I don't like them.

TH: I see. Well, they scare the hell out of me, too (smiles, indicating the humor in his comment).

CL: (Chuckles) I thought you were a doctor.

TH: I am (pauses, smiles)—that's what's so scary.

CL: (Smiles and laughs)

TH: Tell me a little more about some of your unpleasant experiences with doctors, because I want to make sure I'm not doing anything that is upsetting to you. I don't want that to happen.

CL: Well, that's very nice to hear. My last doctor didn't give a hoot about what I said, and he only spoke in huge words.

In case you're wondering, this is an excerpt from an actual session—humor and informality can be an important part of the therapeutic process.

 **CHECK & REVIEW**  **STOP** *Before going on, be sure to complete this Check & Review. It is an invaluable study tool!*

Cognitive and Humanistic Therapies

Part A: Retrieval Practice

1. Without looking at the book, spend 10 minutes writing a free-form essay recalling all you can remember from the previous section.

2. Now, reread the previous section, and once again spend 10 minutes writing a free-form essay on the SAME material.

Part B: Practice Quiz

1. Cognitive therapists assume that problem behaviors and emotions are caused by _____.

2. The figure to the right illustrates the process by which the therapist and client work to change destructive ways of thinking called _____.

3. What are the four steps (the A–B–C–D) of Ellis's REBT?

4. Using Beck's four destructive thought patterns associated with depression, label the following thoughts:

_____ a. Mary left me, and I'll never fall in love again. I'll always be alone.

_____ b. My ex-spouse is an evil monster, and our entire marriage was a sham.

"I can't do this perfectly. I'm worthless!" "I may not be perfect, but I'm learning."

5. List the four major Rogerian therapy techniques.

Check your answers in Appendix B.

Group, Family, and Marital Therapies: Healing Interpersonal Relationships

Objective 15.12: Discuss group, self-help, family, and marital therapies.

The therapies described thus far all consider the individual as the unit of analysis and treatment. In contrast, group, family, and marital therapies treat multiple individuals simultaneously.

Group Therapy

Group Therapy A number of people meet together to work toward therapeutic goals

Self-Help Group Leaderless or nonprofessionally guided groups in which members assist each other with a specific problem, as in Alcoholics Anonymous

In **group therapy**, multiple people meet together to work toward therapeutic goals. Typically, 8 to 10 people meet with a therapist on a regular basis, usually once a week for two hours. The therapist can work from any of the psychotherapeutic orientations discussed in this chapter. And, as in individual therapy, members of the group talk about problems in their own lives.

A variation on group therapy is the **self-help group**. Unlike other group therapy approaches, a professional does not guide these groups. They are simply groups of people who share a common problem (such as alcoholism, single parenthood, or breast cancer) and who meet to give and receive support. Faith-based 12-step programs such as *Alcoholics Anonymous*, *Narcotics Anonymous*, and *Spenders Anonymous* are examples of self-help groups.

Although group members don't get the same level of individual attention found in one-on-one therapies, group and self-help therapies provide their own unique advantages (Corey, 2011; Jaffe & Kelly, 2011; Messer & Gurman, 2011; Qualls, 2008):

1. *Less expense* In a typical group of eight or more, the cost of traditional one-on-one therapy can be divided among all members of the group. Self-help groups, which typically operate without a professional therapist, are even more cost-saving.

2. *Group support* During times of stress and emotional trouble, it is easy to imagine that we are alone and that our problems are unique. Knowing that others have similar problems can be very reassuring. In addition, seeing others improve can be a source of hope and motivation.

3. *Insight and information* Because group members typically have comparable problems, they can learn from each other's mistakes and share insights. Furthermore, when a group member receives similar comments about his or her behavior from several members of the group, the message may be more convincing than if it comes from a single therapist.

4. *Behavior rehearsal* Group members can role play one another's employer, spouse, parents, children, or prospective dates. By role playing and observing different roles in relationships, people gain practice with new social skills. They also gain valuable feedback and insight into their problem behaviors.

Therapists often refer their patients to group therapy and self-help groups to supplement individual therapy. Someone who has a problem with alcohol, for example, can find comfort and help with others who have "been there." They exchange useful information, share their coping strategies, and gain hope by seeing others overcome or successfully manage their shared problems. Research on self-help groups for alcoholism, obesity, and other disorders suggests they can be effective—either alone or in addition to individual psychotherapy (Aderka et al., 2011; Jaffe & Kelly, 2011; McEvoy, 2007; Oei & Dingle, 2008; Silverman et al., 2008).

Family and Marital Therapies

Mental health problems do not affect three or four out of five persons but one out of one.

Dr. William Menninger

Because a family or marriage is a particularly close and intimate system of interdependent parts, the problem of any one individual unavoidably affects all the others, and therapy can help everyone involved (Dattilio & Nichols, 2011; Friedlander et al., 2011; Stratton et al., 2011). A teen's delinquency or a spouse's drug problem affects both members of the couple and each individual within the family.

Sometimes the problems parents have with a child arise from conflicts in the marriage. Other times a child's behavior creates distress in an otherwise well-functioning couple. The line between *marital* (or *couples*) therapy and *family therapy* is often blurred. Given that most married couples have children, our discussion will focus on family therapy, in which the primary aim is to change maladaptive family interaction patterns (Figure 15.6). All members of the family attend therapy sessions. At times the therapist may also see family members individually or in twos or threes. (The therapist, incidentally, may take any orientation—cognitive, behavioral, etc.)

Family therapy is useful in treating a number of disorders and clinical problems. As we discussed in Chapter 14, patients with schizophrenia are more likely to relapse if their family members express emotions, attitudes, and behaviors that involve criticism, hostility, or emotional overinvolvement, and family therapy can help family members modify their behavior toward the patient. It also seems to be the most favorable setting for the treatment of marital infidelity, anger management, and adolescent drug abuse (Dakof, Godley, & Smith, 2011; Mead, 2012; Minuchin, 2011; O'Farrell, 2011).

▲ **Figure 15.6 Family therapy**
Many families initially come into therapy believing that one member is *the* cause of all their problems ("Johnny's delinquency" or "Mom's drinking"). However, family therapists often find that this "identified patient" is the scapegoat (a person blamed for someone else's problems) for deeper disturbances. For example, instead of confronting their own problems with intimacy, the parents may focus all their attention and frustration on the delinquent child. It is usually necessary to change ways of interacting within the family system to promote the health of individual family members and the family as a whole.

TRY THIS YOURSELF

Improving Your Informal "Counseling" skills

Having concluded our discussion of insight therapies, you may be wondering how to distill the various techniques into something useful (and safe) to use when comforting a troubled friend or relative. If so, try the "Three A's":

• **Active listening** People with problems need to be heard—not interrupted.

Show them you're sincerely interested by using appropriate eye contact, posture, tone of voice, and supportive replies.

• **Acceptance** Troubled people need acceptance—not judgment. Try to understand their problems from *their* perspective, not yours. Use empathy

to practice acceptance and gain perspective.

• **Avoid advice** People with problems know more about their situations and troubles than you do. Provide understanding and support—not advice.

CHECK & REVIEW

STOP Before going on, be sure to complete this Check & Review. It is an invaluable study tool!

Group, Family, and Marital Therapies

Part A: Retrieval Practice

1. Without looking at the book, spend 10 minutes writing a free-form essay recalling all you can remember from the previous section.

2. Now, reread the previous section, and once again spend 10 minutes writing a free-form essay on the SAME material.

Part B: Practice Quiz

1. In _____, multiple people meet together to work toward therapeutic goals.

2. What are the four major advantages of group therapy?

3. Why do therapists often refer their patients to self-help groups?

4. _____ treats the family as a unit, and members work together to solve problems. (a) Aversion therapy; (b) An encounter group; (c) A self-help group; (d) Family therapy

Check your answers in Appendix B.

Behavior Therapies

Objective 15.13: What is behavior therapy?

Have you ever understood why you were doing something that you would rather not do, but continued to do it anyway? Sometimes having insight into a problem does not automatically solve it. **Behavior therapy** focuses on the problem behavior itself, rather than on any underlying causes (Miltenberger, 2011; Powell & Newgent, 2011). That is not to say that the person's feelings and interpretations are disregarded; they are just not emphasized. The therapist diagnoses the problem by listing the maladaptive behaviors that occur and the adaptive behaviors that are absent. The therapist then attempts to shift the balance of the two, drawing on principles of classical conditioning, operant conditioning, and observational learning (Chapter 6).

Behavior Therapy Group of techniques based on learning principles used to change maladaptive behaviors

Classical Conditioning: The Power of Association

Objective 15.14: Describe how classical conditioning, operant conditioning, and observational learning are used in behavior therapy.

Behavior therapists use the principles of classical conditioning to decrease maladaptive behavior by creating new stimulus associations and behavioral responses to replace the faulty ones. Two techniques based on these principles are *systematic desensitization* and *aversion therapy*.

1. **Systematic desensitization** begins with relaxation training, followed by imagining or directly experiencing various versions of a feared object or situation while remaining deeply relaxed (Wolpe & Plaud, 1977).

The goal is to replace an anxiety response with a relaxation response when confronting the feared stimulus. Recall from Chapter 2 that the parasympathetic nerves control autonomic functions when we are relaxed. Because the opposing sympathetic nerves are dominant when we are anxious, it is physiologically impossible to be both relaxed and anxious at the same time.

Desensitization is a three-step process. First, a client is taught how to maintain a state of deep relaxation that is physiologically incompatible with an anxiety response. Next, the therapist and client construct a *hierarchy*, or ranked listing of 10 or so anxiety-arousing images (Step-by-Step Diagram 15.2a). In the final step, the relaxed client mentally visualizes or physically experiences items at the bottom of the hierarchy. The client then works his or her way upward to the most anxiety-producing images at the top of the hierarchy. If at any time an image or a situation begins to create anxiety, the client stops momentarily and returns to a state of complete relaxation. Eventually, the fear response is extinguished.

Systematic Desensitization Gradual process of extinguishing a learned fear (or phobia) by working through a hierarchy of fear-evoking stimuli while staying deeply relaxed

Aversion Therapy Pairing an aversive (unpleasant) stimulus with a maladaptive behavior

2. **Aversion therapy** uses principles of classical conditioning to create anxiety rather than extinguish it (Figure 15.7). People who engage in excessive drinking, for example, build up a number of pleasurable associations. These pleasurable associations cannot always be prevented. However, aversion therapy provides *negative associations* to compete with the pleasurable ones. Someone who wants to stop drinking, for example, could take a drug called Antabuse that causes vomiting whenever alcohol enters the system. When the new connection between alcohol and nausea has been classically conditioned, engaging in the once desirable habit will cause an immediate negative response (Step-by-Step Diagram 15.2b).

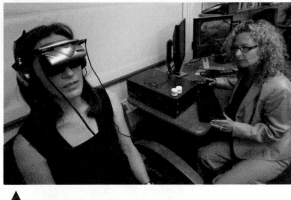

Figure 15.7 Virtual reality therapy Rather than mental imaging or actual physical experiences of a fearful situation, modern therapy can use the latest in computer technology—virtual reality headsets and data gloves. A client with a fear of heights, for example, can have experiences ranging from climbing a stepladder all the way to standing on the edge of a tall building, while never leaving the therapist's office.

TRY THIS YOURSELF

Do You Have Test Anxiety?

Nearly everyone is somewhat anxious before an important exam. If you find this anxiety helpful and invigorating, skip ahead to the next section. However, if the days and evenings before a major exam are ruined by your anxiety and you sometimes "freeze up" while taking the test, you can benefit from an informal type of systematic desensitization.

Step 1: Review and practice the relaxation technique taught in Chapter 3.

Step 2: Create a 10-step "test-taking" hierarchy—starting with the least anxiety-arousing image (perhaps the day your instructor first mentions an upcoming

exam) and ending with actually taking the exam.

Step 3: Beginning with the least arousing image—hearing about the exam—picture yourself at each stage. While maintaining a calm, relaxed state, work your way through all 10 steps. If you become anxious at any stage, stay there, repeating your relaxation technique until the anxiety diminishes.

Step 4: If you start to feel anxious the night before the exam, or even during the exam itself, remind yourself to relax. Take a few moments to shut your eyes and review how you worked through your hierarchy.

Step-by-StepDiagram15.2

Overcoming Maladaptive Behaviors—Phobias and Alcoholism

(a) Systematic Desensitization To treat phobias, the client begins with relaxation training and the construction of a hierarchy, or ranked listing, of anxiety-arousing images or situations. Starting first with an image that produces very little anxiety and escalating to those that arouse extreme anxiety. To extinguish a driving phobia, the patient begins with images of actually sitting behind the wheel of a nonmoving car and ends with driving on a busy expressway.

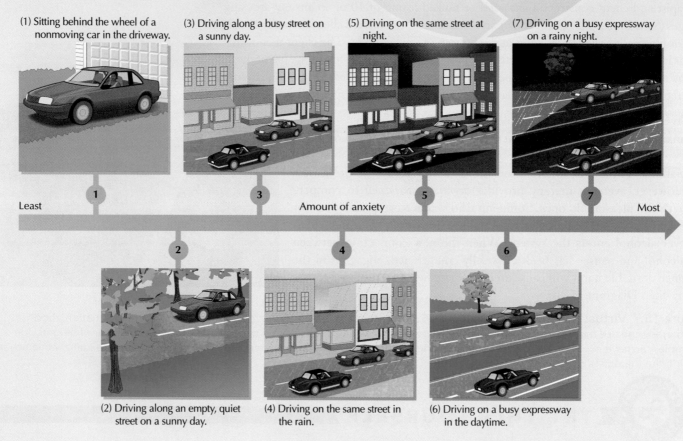

(1) Sitting behind the wheel of a nonmoving car in the driveway.

(3) Driving along a busy street on a sunny day.

(5) Driving on the same street at night.

(7) Driving on a busy expressway on a rainy night.

Least   1   3   Amount of anxiety   5   7   Most

(2) Driving along an empty, quiet street on a sunny day.

(4) Driving on the same street in the rain.

(6) Driving on a busy expressway in the daytime.

(b) Aversion therapy To treat alcoholism, a nausea-producing drug (Antabuse) is paired with alcohol to create an aversion (dislike) for drinking.

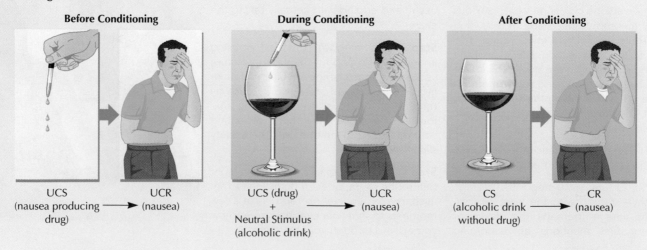

Before Conditioning

UCS (nausea producing drug) → UCR (nausea)

During Conditioning

UCS (drug) + Neutral Stimulus (alcoholic drink) → UCR (nausea)

After Conditioning

CS (alcoholic drink without drug) → CR (nausea)

546

Aversion therapy has had some limited success, but it has always been controversial. Is it ethical to hurt someone (even when the person has given permission)? It also has been criticized because it does not provide lasting relief. Do you recall the taste aversion studies in Chapter 6? It was discovered that when sheep meat was tainted with a nausea-producing drug, coyotes quickly learned to avoid sheep. Why doesn't it work with people? Interestingly, humans understand that the nausea is produced by the Antabuse and do not generalize their learning to the alcohol itself. Once they leave treatment, most alcoholics go back to drinking (and do not continue taking the Antabuse).

Operant Conditioning: Increasing the "Good" and Decreasing the "Bad"

Behavior therapists commonly use operant conditioning techniques like reinforcement and *shaping*—providing rewards for successive approximations of the target behavior—to increase desired behaviors. To decrease undesirable behaviors, they may use limited punishment and extinction (Figure 15.8).

One of the most successful applications of shaping and reinforcement has been with developing language skills in children with autism. First, the child is rewarded for any sounds, and later, only for words and sentences.

Shaping also can help people acquire social skills. If you are painfully shy, for example, a behavior therapist might first ask you to role-play simply saying hello to someone you find attractive. Then, you might practice behaviors that gradually lead you to suggest a get-together or date. During such *role playing*, or *behavior rehearsal*, the clinician would give you feedback and reinforcement.

Adaptive behaviors can also be taught or increased with techniques that provide immediate reinforcement in the form of *tokens* (Miltenberger, 2011; Reed & Martens, 2011). For example, patients in an inpatient treatment facility might at first be given tokens (to be exchanged for primary rewards, such as food, treats, TV time, a private room, or outings) for merely attending group therapy sessions. Later they will be rewarded only for actually participating in the sessions. Eventually, the tokens can be discontinued when the patient receives the reinforcement of being helped by participation in the therapy sessions.

▲ **Figure 15.8 The "Nanny"—psychology at work** Have you noticed how the lead character in the popular TV program *The Nanny* uses informal operant conditioning techniques, like shaping and reinforcement, to encourage adaptive behaviors? To decrease maladaptive behaviors, she also uses behavior therapy techniques, such as withdrawing attention (extinction) or time-out procedures (punishment).

Modeling Therapy Watching and imitating models that demonstrate desirable behaviors

Observational Learning: Modeling and Imitation

We all learn many things by observing others. Therapists use this principle in **modeling therapy**, in which clients are asked to observe and imitate appropriate *models* as they perform desired behaviors. For example, Albert Bandura and his colleagues (1969) asked clients with snake phobias to watch other (non-phobic) people handle snakes. After only two hours of exposure, over 92 percent of the phobic observers allowed a snake to crawl over their hands, arms, and necks. When the therapy combines live modeling with direct and gradual practice, it is called *participant modeling*. Modeling also is involved in social skills training and assertiveness training (Figure 15.9).

Figure 15.9 Psychology in action During modeling therapy, clients learn how to interview for a job by first watching the therapist role-play the part of the interviewee. The therapist models the appropriate language (assertively asking for a job), body posture, and so forth. ▶

The client then imitates the therapist's behavior and plays the same role. Over the course of several sessions, the client becomes gradually desensitized to the anxiety of interviews and learns valuable interview skills.

Evaluating Behavior Therapies: How Well Do They Work?

Objective 15.15: What are the key successes and criticisms of behavior therapies?

Behavior therapy has been effective with various problems, including phobias, obsessive-compulsive disorder, eating disorders, autism, intellectual disabilities, and delinquency (Antony & Roemer, 2011; Haynes, O'Brien, & Kaholokula, 2011; Miltenberger, 2011; Truscott, 2010). Some patients have even returned to their homes and communities after years of institutionalization. However, critics of behavior therapy raise important questions that fall into two major categories:

1. *Generalizability* Critics argue that in the "real world" patients are not consistently reinforced, and their newly acquired behaviors may disappear. To deal with this possibility, behavior therapists work to gradually shape clients toward rewards that are typical of life outside the clinical setting.

2. *Ethics* Critics contend that it can be unethical for one person to control another's behavior. Behaviorists reply that rewards and punishments already control our behaviors, and that behavior therapy actually increases a person's freedom by making these controls *overt* and by teaching people to change their own behavior.

 **CHECK & REVIEW**  **STOP** *Before going on, be sure to complete this Check & Review. It is an invaluable study tool!*

Behavior Therapies

Part A: Retrieval Practice

1. Without looking at the book, spend 10 minutes writing a free-form essay recalling all you can remember from the previous section.

2. Now, reread the previous section, and once again spend 10 minutes writing a free-form essay on the SAME material.

Part B: Practice Quiz

1. A group of techniques used to change maladaptive behaviors is known as _____.

2. In behavior therapy, _____ techniques use shaping and reinforcement to increase adaptive behaviors. (a) classical conditioning; (b) modeling; (c) operant conditioning; (d) social learning

3. Describe how shaping can be used to develop desired behaviors.

4. What are the two key criticisms of behavior therapy?

Check your answers in Appendix B.

Biomedical Therapies

Objective 15.16: Define biomedical therapy.

Biomedical Therapy Using biological interventions (drugs, electroconvulsive therapy, and psychosurgery) to treat psychological disorders

Biomedical therapies are based on the premise that mental health problems are caused, at least in part, by chemical imbalances or disturbed nervous system functioning. In most cases, a physician or psychiatrist, rather than a psychologist, must prescribe biomedical therapies. But psychologists commonly work with patients receiving biomedical therapies, and are involved in research programs to evaluate the therapy's effectiveness. In this section, we will discuss three forms of biomedical therapies: *psychopharmacology*, *electroconvulsive therapy* (*ECT*), and *psychosurgery*.

Psychopharmacology: Treating Psychological Disorders with Drugs

Objective 15.17: Discuss psychopharmacology, electroconvulsive therapy (ECT), and psychosurgery.

Since the 1950s, drug companies have developed an amazing variety of chemicals to treat abnormal behaviors. In some cases discoveries from **psychopharmacology** (the study of drug effects on mind and behavior) have helped correct a chemical imbalance (Gaylord, 2011; Noggle, et al., 2012). In these instances, using a drug is similar to administering insulin to people with diabetes, whose own bodies fail to manufacture enough. In other cases, drugs are used to relieve or suppress the symptoms of psychological disturbances even when the underlying cause is not thought to be biological. Psychiatric drugs are classified into four major categories: antianxiety, antipsychotic, mood stabilizer, and antidepressant (Concept Organizer 15.1).

Electroconvulsive Therapy and Psychosurgery: Promising or Perilous?

In **electroconvulsive therapy (ECT)**, also known as *electroshock therapy* (EST), a moderate electrical current is passed through the brain between two electrodes placed on the outside of the head (Figure 15.10). The current triggers a widespread firing of neurons, or convulsions. The convulsions produce many changes in the central and peripheral nervous systems, including activation of the autonomic nervous system, increased secretion of various hormones and neurotransmitters, and changes in the blood–brain barrier.

During the early years of ECT, some patients received hundreds of treatments. Today most receive 12 or fewer treatments. Sometimes the electrical current is applied only to the right hemisphere, which causes less interference with verbal memories and left-hemispheric functioning.

Modern ECT is used primarily in cases of severe depression that do not respond to antidepressant drugs or psychotherapy and with suicidal patients, because it works faster than antidepressant drugs (Kobeissi et al., 2011; Loo et al., 2011; Pfeiffer et al., 2011).

Although clinical studies of ECT conclude that it is effective for very severe depression, its use remains controversial because it creates massive functional (and perhaps structural) changes in the brain. ECT is also controversial because we simply don't know why it works. Most likely it helps reestablish levels of neurotransmitters that control moods.

The most extreme, and least used, biomedical therapy is **psychosurgery**—brain surgery to reduce serious, debilitating psychological problems. (It is important to note

Psychosurgery Surgical alteration of the brain to bring about desirable behavioral, cognitive, or emotional changes; generally used when patients have not responded to other forms of treatment

What about herbal remedies? Some recent research suggests that the herbal supplement St. John's Wort may be an effective treatment for mild to moderate depression, with fewer side effects than traditional medications (Howland, 2010; Kasper et al., 2011; Solomon et al., 2011). However, other studies have found the drug to be ineffective for people with major depression (Hypericum Depression Trial Study, 2002). Herbal supplements, like kava, valerian, and gingko biloba, also have been used in the treatment of anxiety, insomnia, and memory problems (e.g., Dante & Facchinetti, 2011; Sarris & Byrne, 2011). Although many people assume that these products are safe because they are "natural," they can produce a number of potentially serious side effects. For this reason and also because the U.S. Food and Drug Administration does not regulate herbal supplements, researchers advise caution, more research, and a wait-and-see approach (Camfield, Sarris, & Berk, 2011; Dante & Facchinetti, 2011).

Psychopharmacology The study of drug effects on brain and behavior

Electroconvulsive Therapy (ECT) Biomedical therapy based on passing electrical current through the brain; used almost exclusively to treat serious depression when drug therapy fails

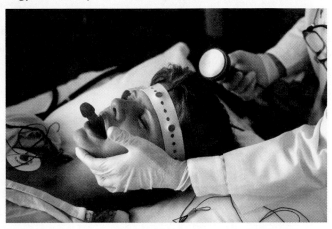

▲ **Figure 15.10 Electroconvulsive therapy (ECT)** Electroconvulsive therapy may seem barbaric, but for some severely depressed people it is their only hope for lifting the depression. Unlike portrayals of ECT in movies like *One Flew Over the Cuckoo's Nest* and *The Snake Pit*, patients show few, if any, visible reactions to the treatment owing to modern muscle-relaxant drugs that dramatically reduce muscle contractions during the seizure. Most ECT patients are also given an anesthetic to block their memories of the treatment, but some patients still find the treatment extremely uncomfortable. However, many others find it lifesaving (Jain et al., 2008; Khalid et al., 2008).

ConceptOrganizer 15.1

STOP This Concept Organizer contains essential information NOT found elsewhere in the text, which is likely to appear on quizzes and exams. Be sure to study it CAREFULLY!

Drug Treatments for Psychological Disorders

"Before Prozac, she *loathed* company."

How Prozac and other SSRI antidepressants work

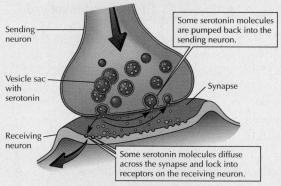

Some serotonin molecules are pumped back into the sending neuron.

Sending neuron

Vesicle sac with serotonin

Synapse

Receiving neuron

Some serotonin molecules diffuse across the synapse and lock into receptors on the receiving neuron.

(a)

▲ Under normal conditions, a nerve impulse (or action potential) travels down the axon to the terminal buttons of a sending neuron. If the vesicle sac of this particular neuron contains the neurotransmitter serotonin, the action potential will trigger its release. Some of the serotonin will travel across the synapse and lock into the receptors on the receiving neuron. Excess serotonin within the synapse will be pumped back up into the sending neuron for storage (the "serotonin reuptake").

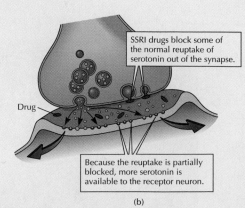

SSRI drugs block some of the normal reuptake of serotonin out of the synapse.

Drug

Because the reuptake is partially blocked, more serotonin is available to the receptor neuron.

(b)

◄ When selective serotonin reuptake inhibitors (SSRIs), like Prozac, are taken to treat depression and other disorders, they block the normal reuptake of excess serotonin that lingers in the synaptic gap after being released from the sending neuron. This leaves more serotonin molecules free to stimulate receptors on the receiving neuron, which enhances its mood-lifting effects.

Description	Examples (Trade Names)
• **Antianxiety drugs** (also known as *anxiolytics* and "minor tranquilizers") lower the sympathetic activity of the brain—the crisis mode of operation—so that anxious responses are diminished or prevented and are replaced by feelings of tranquility and calmness.	Ativan Halcion Librium Restoril Valium Xanax
• **Antipsychotic drugs**, or *neuroleptics*, are used to treat schizophrenia and other acute psychotic states. Unfortunately, these drugs are often referred to as "major tranquilizers," creating the mistaken impression that they invariably have a strong sedating effect. The main effect of antipsychotic drugs is to diminish or eliminate psychotic symptoms, including hallucinations, delusions, withdrawal, and apathy. Traditional antipsychotics work by decreasing activity at the dopamine receptors in the brain. A large majority of patients show marked improvement when treated with antipsychotic drugs.	Clozaril Haldol Mellaril Navane Prolixin Risperdal Seroquel Thorazine
• **Mood-stabilizer drugs**, such as *lithium*, can help relieve manic episodes and depression for people suffering from bipolar disorder. Because lithium acts relatively slowly—it can take 3 or 4 weeks before it takes effect—its primary use is in preventing future episodes and helping to break the manic-depressive cycle.	Eskalith CR Lithobid Tegretol
• **Antidepressant drugs** are used primarily to treat people with depression. There are five types of antidepressant drugs: *tricyclics, monoamine oxidase inhibitors (MAOIs), selective serotonin reuptake inhibitors (SSRIs)*, serotonin and noepinephrine reuptake inhibitors (SNRIs), and *atypical antidepressants*. Each class of drugs affects neurochemical pathways in the brain in slightly different ways, increasing or decreasing the availability of certain chemicals. SSRIs (such as *Paxil* and *Prozac*) are by far the most commonly prescribed antidepressants. The atypical antidepressants are a miscellaneous group of drugs used for patients who fail to respond to the other drugs or for people who experience side effects common to other antidepressants.	Anafranil Celexa Cymbalta Effexor Elavil Nardil Norpramin Parnate Paxil Prozac Tofranil Wellbutrin Zoloft

Antianxiety Drugs Medications used to produce relaxation, reduce anxiety, and decrease overarousal in the brain

Antipsychotic Drugs Medications used to diminish or eliminate hallucinations, delusions, withdrawal, and other symptoms of psychosis; also known as neuroleptics or major tranquilizers

Mood-Stabilizer Drugs Medications used to treat the combination of manic episodes and depression characteristic of bipolar disorders

Antidepressant Drugs Medications used to treat depression, some anxiety disorders, and certain eating disorders (such as bulimia)

that psychosurgery is *not* the same as brain surgery used to remove physical problems, such as a tumor or blood clot.) Attempts to change disturbed thoughts, feelings, and behavior by altering the brain have a long history. In Roman times, for example, it was believed that a sword wound to the head could relieve insanity. In 1936, a Portuguese neurologist, Egaz Moniz, treated uncontrollable psychoses by cutting the nerve fibers between the frontal lobes (where association areas for monitoring and planning behavior are found) and lower brain centers (Gross & Schäfer, 2011; Hergenhahn 2009; Valenstein, 1998). Thousands of patients underwent this procedure, called a **lobotomy**, before it was eliminated because of serious complications. Today lobotomies are almost never used. Psychiatric drugs offer a less risky and more effective treatment.

Evaluating Biomedical Therapies: Are They Effective?

Objective 15.18: What are the major contributions and criticisms of biomedical therapies?

Like all forms of therapy, the biomedical therapies have both proponents and critics.

Pitfalls of Psychopharmacology

Drug therapy provides enormous benefits, but it also poses several potential problems. First, although drugs may provide relief of symptoms, they seldom provide "cures." In addition, many patients stop taking their medications once they feel better, which generally results in the return of symptoms. Also, some patients become physically dependent on the drugs, and researchers are still learning about the long-term effects and potential interactions of drug treatments. Furthermore, psychiatric medications can cause a variety of side effects, ranging from mild fatigue to severe impairments in memory and movement (Figure 15.11).

One of the most serious side effects of long-term use of antipsychotic drugs is a movement disorder called **tardive dyskinesia**, which develops in 15 to 20 percent of patients. The symptoms generally appear after the drugs have been taken for long periods of time (hence the term *tardive*, from the Latin root for "slow"). They include involuntary movements of the tongue, facial muscles, and limbs (*dyskinesia*, meaning "disorder of movement") that can be severely disabling. When my students see films depicting schizophrenia, they often confuse the patient's sucking and smacking of the lips or lateral jaw movements as signs of the disorder rather than signs of the motor disturbances of *tardive dyskinesia*.

A final potential problem with drug treatment is that its relative inexpensiveness, and its generally faster results than traditional talk therapy, have led to its overuse in some cases.

Despite the problems associated with psychotherapeutic drugs, they have led to revolutionary changes in mental health (Gaylord, 2011; Noggle et al., 2012). Before the use of drugs, some patients were destined to spend a lifetime in psychiatric institutions. Today, most patients improve enough to return to their homes and live successful lives if they continue to take their medications to prevent relapse.

Challenges to ECT and Psychosurgery

As mentioned earlier, ECT remains controversial, but it may soon become obsolete thanks to advances in treatment, such as **repetitive transcranial magnetic stimulation (rTMS)**, in which a pulsed magnetic coil is held close to a person's head (Figure 15.12). When used to treat depression, the coil is normally placed over the prefrontal cortex, a region linked to deeper parts of the brain that regulate mood. Currently, the cost effectiveness and long-term benefits of rTMS over ECT remain uncertain,

Lobotomy Outmoded medical procedure for mental disorders, which involved cutting nerve pathways between the frontal lobes and the thalamus and hypothalamus

Tardive Dyskinesia Movement disorder involving facial muscles, tongue, and limbs; a possible side effect of long-term use of antipsychotic medications

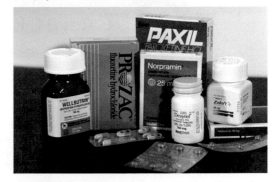

▲ **Figure 15.11 Pros and cons of drug therapy** Psychotherapeutic drugs like Paxil or Prozac often help relieve suffering and symptoms associated with psychological disorders. However, they also have major and minor side effects. Physicians and patients must carefully weigh both the costs and the benefits especially for young children.

▲ **Figure 15.12 Repetitive transcranial magnetic stimulation (rTMS)** Using powerful magnets, the coil generates currents in specific areas of the brain to treat depression.

Repetitive Transcranial Magnetic Stimulation (rTMS) Biomedical treatment involving repeated pulses of magnetic energy being passed through the brain

but studies have shown marked improvement in depression, and, unlike with ECT, patients experience no seizures or memory loss (Hadley et al., 2011; Husain & Lisanby, 2011; Polley et al., 2011).

Like ECT, psychosurgery is highly controversial, and because of its potentially serious or fatal side effects and complications, some critics suggest it should be banned altogether.

CHECK & REVIEW

STOP *Before going on, be sure to complete this Check & Review. It is an invaluable study tool!*

Biomedical Therapies

Part A: Retrieval Practice

1. Without looking at the book, spend 10 minutes writing a free-form essay recalling all you can remember from the previous section.

2. Now, reread the previous section, and once again spend 10 minutes writing a free-form essay on the SAME material.

Part B: Practice Quiz

1. The dramatic reduction in the number of hospitalized patients today compared to past decades is primarily attributable to

_____. (a) biomedical therapy; (b) psychoanalysis; (c) psychosurgery; (d) drug therapy.

2. What are the four major categories of psychiatric drugs?

3. The effectiveness of antipsychotic drugs is thought to result primarily from blockage of _____ receptors. (a) serotonin; (b) dopamine; (c) epinephrine (d) all of these options

4. In electroconvulsive therapy (ECT), _____.

   a. current is never applied to the left hemisphere

   b. convulsions activate the central and peripheral nervous systems, stimulate hormone and neurotransmitter release, and change the blood-brain barrier

   c. convulsions are extremely painful and long lasting

   d. most patients today receive hundreds of treatments because it is safer than in the past

5. ECT is used primarily to treat _____. (a) phobias; (b) conduct disorders; (c) severe depression; (d) schizophrenia

Check your answers in Appendix B.

Therapy Essentials

We mentioned at the start of this chapter that there are over 400 forms of therapy. How are you going to choose one of these for yourself or someone you know? In the first part of this section, we discuss the five goals that are common to all psychotherapies. Then we explore issues with institutionalization, and how to judge the effectiveness of therapy. We conclude with specific tips for finding a therapist.

Five Common Goals: Similarities and Eclecticism

Objective 15.19: Identify the five most common goals of therapy, and discuss the eclectic approach.

All major forms of therapy are designed to help the client in five specific areas (Concept Organizer 15.2). Depending on the individual therapist's training and the client's needs, one or more of these five areas may be emphasized more than the others.

Although most therapists work with clients in several of these areas, the emphasis varies according to the therapist's training. As you learned earlier in this chapter, psychoanalysts and psychodynamic therapists generally emphasize unconscious thoughts and emotions. Cognitive therapists focus on their client's faulty thinking and belief patterns. And humanistic therapists attempt to alter the client's negative emotional responses. Behavior therapists, as the name implies, focus on changing maladaptive behaviors, and therapists who use biomedical techniques attempt to change biological disorders.

ConceptOrganizer15.2

Five Common Goals of Therapy

Most therapies focus on one or more of these five goals. Can you identify which would be of most interest to a psychoanalyst, a cognitive therapist, a behaviorist, and a psychiatrist?

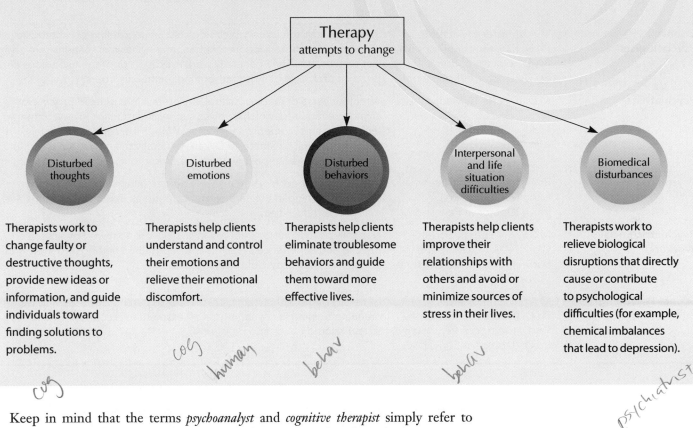

Therapy attempts to change

Disturbed thoughts

Therapists work to change faulty or destructive thoughts, provide new ideas or information, and guide individuals toward finding solutions to problems.

cog

Disturbed emotions

Therapists help clients understand and control their emotions and relieve their emotional discomfort.

cog
human

Disturbed behaviors

Therapists help clients eliminate troublesome behaviors and guide them toward more effective lives.

behav

Interpersonal and life situation difficulties

Therapists help clients improve their relationships with others and avoid or minimize sources of stress in their lives.

behav

Biomedical disturbances

Therapists work to relieve biological disruptions that directly cause or contribute to psychological difficulties (for example, chemical imbalances that lead to depression).

psychiatrist

Keep in mind that the terms *psychoanalyst* and *cognitive therapist* simply refer to the theoretical background and framework that guide a clinician's thinking. Just as Democrats and Republicans approach political matters in different ways, behavior and cognitive therapists approach therapy differently. And just as Democrats and Republicans borrow ideas from one another, clinicians from different perspectives also share ideas and techniques. Clinicians who regularly borrow freely from various theories are said to take an **eclectic approach**.

Eclectic Approach Combining techniques from various theories to find the most appropriate treatment

Psychology at Work

Careers in Mental Health

Objective 15.20: Identify the six key types of mental health professionals.

Do you enjoy helping people and think you would like a career as a therapist? Have you wondered how long you will have to go to college or the type of training that is required to be a therapist? Most colleges have counseling or career centers with numerous resources and trained staff who can help you answer these (and other) questions. To get you started, I have included a brief summary in Table 15.1 of the major types of mental health professionals, their degrees, years of required education beyond the bachelor's degree, and type of training.

Table 15.1 MAJOR TYPES OF MENTAL HEALTH PROFESSIONALS

Occupational Title	Degree	Nature of Training
Clinical Psychologists	Ph.D. (Doctor of Philosophy), Psy.D. (Doctor of Psychology)	Most often have a doctoral degree with training in research and clinical practice, and a supervised one-year internship in a psychiatric hospital or mental health facility. As clinicians, they work with patients suffering from mental disorders, but many also work in colleges and universities as teachers and researchers in addition to having their own private practice.
Counseling Psychologists	M.A. (Master of Arts), Ph.D. (Doctor of Philosophy), Psy.D. (Doctor of Psychology), Ed.D. (Doctor of Education)	Similar training to clinical psychologists, but counseling psychologists usually have a master's degree with more emphasis on patient care and less on research. They generally work in schools or other institutions and focus on problems of living rather than mental disorders.
Psychiatrists	M.D. (Doctor of Medicine)	After four years of medical school, an internship and residency in psychiatry are required, which involves supervised practice in psychotherapy techniques and biomedical therapies. With the exception of certain states in the United States, M.D.s are generally the only mental health specialists who can regularly prescribe drugs.
Psychiatric Nurses	R.N. (Registered Nurse), M.A. (Master of Arts), Ph.D. (Doctor of Philosophy)	Usually have a bachelor's or master's degree in nursing, followed by advanced training in the care of mental patients in hospital settings and mental health facilities.
Psychiatric Social Workers	M.S.W. (Master in Social Work), D.S.W. (Doctorate in Social Work), Ph.D. (Doctor of Philosophy)	Normally have a master's degree in social work, followed by advanced training and experience in hospitals or outpatient settings working with people who have psychological problems.
School Psychologists	M.A. (Master of Arts), Ph.D. (Doctor of Philosophy), Psy.D. (Doctor of Psychology), Ed.D. (Doctor of Education)	Generally begin with a bachelor's degree in psychology, followed by graduate training in psychological assessment and counseling involving school-related issues and problems.

Institutionalization: Treating Chronic and Serious Mental Disorders

Objective 15.21: Discuss involuntary commitment and deinstitutionalization.

We all believe in the right to freedom. But what about people who threaten suicide or are potentially violent? Should some people be involuntarily committed to protect them from their own mental disorders? Despite Hollywood film portrayals, forced institutionalization of the mentally ill poses serious ethical problems, and it is generally reserved for only the most serious and life-threatening situations.

Involuntary Commitment

The legal grounds for involuntary commitment vary from state to state. But, generally, people can be sent to psychiatric hospitals if they are believed to be:

• of danger to themselves (usually suicidal) or dangerous to others (potentially violent);

• in serious need of treatment (indicated by bizarre behavior and loss of contact with reality); and/or

• there is no reasonable, less restrictive alternative.

In emergencies, psychologists and other professionals can authorize temporary commitment for 24 to 72 hours. During this observation period, laboratory tests can be performed to rule out medical illnesses that could be causing the symptoms. The patient also can receive psychological testing, medication, and short-term therapy.

Deinstitutionalization

Although the courts have established stringent requirements for involuntary commitment, abuses do occur. There are also problems with long-term chronic institutionalization. And properly housing and caring for the mentally ill is very expensive. In response to these problems, many states have a policy of *deinstitutionalization*, discharging patients from mental hospitals as soon as possible and discouraging admissions.

Deinstitutionalization has been a humane and positive step for many. But some patients are discharged without continuing provision for their protection. Many of these people end up living in rundown hotels or understaffed nursing homes, in jails, or on the street with no shelter or means of support. It is important to note that a sizable percentage of homeless people do have mental disorders. The rise in homelessness is also due to such economic factors as increased unemployment, underemployment, and a shortage of low-income housing.

What else can be done? Rather than returning patients to state hospitals, most clinicians suggest expanding and improving community care (Figure 15.13). They also recommend that general hospitals be equipped with special psychiatric units where acutely ill patients receive inpatient care. For less disturbed individuals and chronically ill patients, they recommend walk-in clinics, crisis intervention services, improved residential treatment facilities, and psychosocial and vocational rehabilitation. State hospitals can then be reserved for the most unmanageable patients.

Evaluating and Finding Therapy: Does It Work? How to Choose?

Does therapy work? In this section, we will discuss questions about the effectiveness of therapy and how to find a therapist.

Judging Effectiveness

Objective 15.22: Is therapy effective, and how can we find a good therapist?

Scientifically evaluating the effectiveness of therapy can be tricky. How can you trust the perception and self-report of clients or clinicians? Both have biases and a need to justify the time, effort, and expense of therapy.

To avoid these problems, psychologists use controlled research studies. Clients are randomly assigned to different forms of therapy or to control groups who receive no treatment. After therapy, clients are independently evaluated, and reports from friends and family members are collected. Until recently, these studies were simply compared. But with a new statistical technique called *meta-analysis*, which combines and analyzes data from many studies, years of such studies and similar research can be brought together to produce a comprehensive report.

The good news, for both consumers and therapists, is that after years of controlled research and meta-analysis we have fairly clear evidence that therapy does work! Forty to 80 percent of people who receive treatment are better off than people who do not. Furthermore, short-term treatments can be as effective as long-term

▲ **Figure 15.13 Outpatient support** Community mental health (CMH) centers are a prime example of alternative treatment to institutionalization. CMH centers provide outpatient services, such as individual and group therapy and prevention programs. They also coordinate short-term inpatient care and programs for discharged mental patients, such as halfway houses and aftercare services. The downside of CMH centers and their support programs is that they are expensive. Investing in primary prevention programs (such as more intervention programs for people at high risk for mental illness) could substantially reduce these costs.

treatments (Dewan, Steenbarger, & Greenberg, 2011; Knekt et al., 2008; Lazar, 2010; Loewental & Winter, 2006; Wachtel, 2011). In addition, it has been found that some therapies are more effective than others for specific problems. For example, phobias seem to respond best to systematic desensitization, and obsessive-compulsive disorders can be significantly relieved with cognitive-behavior therapy accompanied by medication. Most studies that have compared medication alone versus medication plus therapy have found the combination to be more effective (e.g., Doyle & Pollack, 2004).

Finding a Therapist

How do we find a good therapist for our specific needs? If you have the time (and the money) to explore options, take the time to "shop around" for a therapist best suited to your specific goals. Consulting your psychology instructor or college counseling system for referrals can be an important first step. However, if you are in a crisis—you have suicidal thoughts, you have failing grades, or you are the victim of abuse—get help fast. Most communities have medical hospital emergency services and telephone hotlines that provide counseling services on a 24-hour basis. And most colleges and universities have counseling centers that provide immediate, short-term therapy to students free of charge.

If you are encouraging someone else to get therapy, you might offer to help locate a therapist and go with him for his first visit. If he refuses help and the problem affects you, it is often a good idea to seek therapy yourself. You will gain insights and skills that will help you deal with the situation more effectively.

Psychology Engages

RESEARCH CHALLENGE

Pill-Popping Preschoolers?

By Rita Jeffries (School Psychologist, San Diego, CA)

In August 2004, 28-month-old Rebecca Riley was diagnosed with ADHD (attention-deficit hyperactivity disorder) and then bipolar disorder a few months later. Over the next two years, both the number of medications and their dosages increased. Rebecca was eventually taking a daily regime of two antipsychotics, a mood stabilizer, and a drug commonly used to treat high blood pressure in adults. On December 14th, 2006, at the age of 4, Rebecca died from an overdose (Lambert, 2010).

What do you think of when someone mentions the word "preschooler"? Do you imagine children playing on a jungle gym or finger-painting? Perhaps you remember learning the alphabet or your numbers? No matter what thoughts pass through your mind, death from antidepressants, antipsychotics, or blood pressure medication is not likely to be among the first.

Are you surprised that children so young would be taking prescription medication for psychological disorders? This appears to be a growing trend over the past 20 years. Between 1991 and 1995, prescriptions for stimulants tripled, while those for antidepressants doubled (Zito et al., 2000). Spending on medication to treat ADHD for 2- to 4-year olds increased 369 percent from 2000 to 2003, and prescriptions for antipsychotic medications for children under 5 doubled from 2001 to 2007 (Medco Health Solutions, 2004; Olfson et al., 2010).

One of the most cited concerns is the lack of pharmaceutical research for young children. Side effects, long-term consequences, and the safety of drugs are usually studied on adults (Olfson et al., 2010), even though the brains and bodies of preschoolers, young children, and adolescents are clearly much different and more vulnerable than those of adults. Of all the human organs, our brains take the longest to mature. Because of this, drugs given at an early age may affect the brain in unpredictable ways. In addition, two organs that help us process drugs, the liver and kidneys, handle medication much differently in young children. Ironically, preschoolers may require higher doses of medication to achieve the same results as an adult—and with higher medication comes the higher risk of side effects (Harvard Family Health Guide, 2008).

If so much is unknown about psychotropic prescription drugs for children, why is there such a dramatic increase in prescriptions for this age group? Proponents argue that health care providers and parents are simply better informed about psychological disorders than their grandparents were. And because of this, they are better able to intervene and treat their children at an earlier age. They also contend that medication can help children manage attention deficits and social anxiety disorders that can adversely affect early schooling and socialization. Furthermore, medication is often the last resort. Doctors and parents often exhaust countless interventions before turning to medication. Instead of seeing psychotropic drugs as unethical, many parents see them as a godsend—helping their children when nothing else would (Dotinga, 2004).

Opponents to psychotropic medications for preschoolers often point to sophisticated advertising and big business's drive for profit. In 1997, the FDA relaxed requirements for pharmaceutical companies, which allowed them to advertise directly to consumers on television, and within 7 years spending on advertising had increased by 400 percent, with an estimated $1 in advertising resulting in $4.2 worth of increased sales (Henry J. Kaiser Family Foundation, 2003). Pharmaceutical companies now spend far more on advertising than they do on research, and critics say that marketing techniques have lured doctors and parents into administering powerful drugs without fully knowing the risks (Diller, 2000; Gagnon & Lexchin, 2008).

Although the argument rages on, both sides agree that more research is needed. Learning more about young children's reactions to psychotropic medication can help parents and health professionals recognize danger signs. Furthermore, if families and doctors know the long-term effects of a drug on a child's developing brain and body, they can weigh the potential risks and benefits with more confidence and better accuracy (Gleason et al., 2007).

What if you had a preschooler with a severe anxiety disorder or another serious psychological disorder? Would you consider medication? Why or why not?

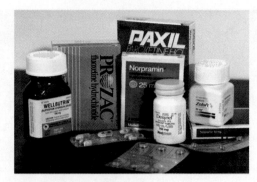

Student Engagement Exercise

Given the admittedly limited information in the studies cited in the third paragraph above, what is the most likely:

1. *Research method* (experimental, descriptive, correlational, or biological)?

2. If you chose the:
   - *Experimental method*—label the IV, DV, experimental group, and control group.
   - *Descriptive method*—identify whe-ther this is a naturalistic observation, survey, or case study.
   - *Correlational method*—label whether this is a positive, negative, or zero correlation.
   - *Biological method*—identify the specific research tool (e.g., brain dissection, CT scan, etc.)

(Answers appear in Appendix B.)

GENDER AND CULTURAL DIVERSITY

Cultural Similarities and Differences in Therapy

Objective 15.23: Describe the major similarities and differences in therapy across cultures.

The therapies described in this chapter are based on western European and North American culture. Does this mean they are unique? Or do our psychotherapists share some of the same techniques and approaches that, say, a native healer or shaman does? Or are there fundamental cultural differences between therapies? What about women? Do they have different issues in therapy? As mentioned earlier, looking at each of these questions requires critical thinking. Let's carefully consider these issues one at a time.

Cultural Similarities When we look at therapies in all cultures, we find that they have certain key features in common (Berry et al., 2011; Brislin, 2000; Buss 2011; Markus & Kitayama, 2010; Sue, Sue, & Sue, 2010):

- *Naming the problem* People often feel better just by knowing that others experience the same problem and that the therapist has had experience with their particular problem.

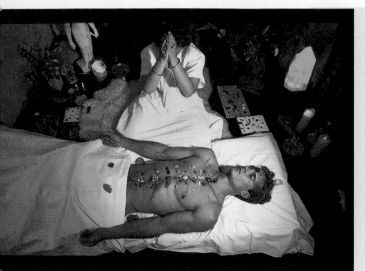

▲ **Alternative therapies** In all cultures, therapy involves specific actions or treatments. In this photo, the therapist is using crystals, laying on of stones, and meditation.

- *Qualities of the therapist* Clients must feel that the therapist is caring, competent, approachable, and concerned with finding solutions to their problem.

- *Therapist credibility* Among native healers, credibility may be established by having served as an apprentice to a revered healer. In Western cultures, word-of-mouth testimonials and status symbols (such as diplomas on the wall) establish the therapist's credibility.

- *Familiar framework* If the client believes that evil spirits cause psychological disorders, the therapist will direct treatment toward eliminating these spirits. Similarly, if the client believes in the importance of talking through their problems, insight therapy will be the likely treatment of choice.

- *Techniques that bring relief* In all cultures, therapy involves action. Either the client or the therapist must do something. Moreover, what therapists do must fit the client's expectations—whether it is performing a ceremony to expel demons or talking with the client about his or her thoughts and feelings.

- *Special time and place* The fact that therapy occurs outside the client's everyday experiences seems to be an important feature of all therapies.

Cultural Differences Although there are basic similarities in therapies across cultures, there are also important differences. In the traditional western European and North American model, the emphasis is on the "self" and on independence and control over one's life—qualities that are highly valued in individualistic cultures. In collectivist cultures, however, the focus of therapy is on interdependence and accepting the realities of one's life (Figure 15.14).

Not only does culture affect the types of therapy that are developed, but it also influences the perceptions of the therapist. What one culture considers abnormal behavior may be quite common—and even considered healthy—in others. For this reason, recognizing cultural differences is very important for both therapists and clients and for effecting behavioral change (Frew & Spiegler, 2012; Moodley, 2012; Smith, Rodriquez, & Bernal, 2011).

Figure 15.14 Emphasizing interdependence In Japanese *Naikan therapy*, the patient sits quietly from 5:30 A.M. to 9:00 P.M. for seven days and is visited by an interviewer every 90 minutes. During this time, the patient is instructed to reflect on his or her relationships with others, with the goals of discovering personal guilt for having been ungrateful and troublesome to others and developing gratitude toward those who have helped the patient (Moodley & Sutherland, 2010; Nakamura, 2006; Ozawa-de Silva, 2007; Shinfuku & Kitanishi, 2010). The reasoning is that when these goals are attained, the patient will have a better self-image and interpersonal attitude. In what ways do the goals and methods of Naikan therapy differ from the therapies we have described in this chapter? Would this approach work with Westerners? Why or why not?

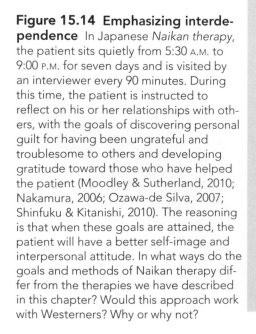

Objective 15.24: What are the unique concerns of women in therapy?

Gender and Therapy Within our individualistic Western culture, men and women present different therapy needs and problems. For example, women are generally more comfortable and familiar with their emotions, have fewer negative attitudes toward therapy, and are more likely than men to seek psychological help. In contrast, as discussed in Chapter 14, men are more likely to suppress their emotions and show their distress through being aggressive, acting impulsively, and/or engaging in substance abuse.

Research has identified five unique concerns related to gender and psychotherapy (Bruns & Kaschak, 2011; Jordan, 2011; Russo & Tartaro, 2008).

1. *Rates of diagnosis and treatment of mental disorders* Women are diagnosed and treated for mental illness at a much higher rate than men. Is this because women are "sicker" than men as a group? Or are they just more willing to admit their problems? Or perhaps the categories for illness may be biased against women. More research is needed to answer this question.

2. *Stresses of poverty* Poverty is an important contributor to many psychological disorders. Therefore, women bring special challenges to the therapy situation because of their overrepresentation in the lowest economic groups.

3. *Stresses of aging* Aging brings special concerns for women. They live longer than men, tend to be poorer, to be less educated, and to have more serious health problems. Elderly women, primarily those with age-related dementia, account for over 70 percent of the chronically mentally ill who live in nursing homes in the United States.

4. *Violence against women* Rape, violent assault, incest, and sexual harassment all take a harsh toll on women's mental health. With the exception of violent assault, these forms of violence are much more likely to happen to women than to men, and may lead to depression, insomnia, posttraumatic stress disorder, eating disorders, and other problems.

5. *Stresses of multiple roles* Women today are mothers, wives, homemakers, wage earners, students, and so on. The conflicting demands of their multiple roles often create special stresses (Figure 15.15).

◀ **Figure 15.15 Meeting women's unique needs** Therapists must be sensitive to possible connections between clients' problems and their gender. Rather than prescribing drugs to relieve depression in women, for example, it may be more appropriate for therapists to explore ways to relieve the stresses of multiple roles or poverty. Can you see how helping a single mother identify parenting resources such as play groups, parent support groups, and high-quality child care might be just as effective at relieving depression as prescribing drugs? In the case of men, how might relieving loneliness or depression help decrease their greater problems with substance abuse and aggression?

CRITICAL THINKING

Hunting for Good Therapy Films

By Thomas Frangicetto (Northampton Community College, Bethlehem, PA)

This chapter opened with Hollywood's generally negative and unrealistic portrayals of therapy. There are notable exceptions, like *Good Will Hunting*. But even this film has a few overly dramatic and unprofessional scenes. For example, during the first therapy session between Will Hunting (played by Matt Damon) and his therapist Sean (played by Robin Williams), Sean grabs Will by the throat and threatens him for insulting his deceased wife.

Despite its limits, *Good Will Hunting* provides a reasonably accurate portrayal of several therapy techniques. It also provides an opportunity to review important terms related to insight therapy and improve your critical thinking skills. If you haven't seen the film, here's a brief summary:

Will Hunting, a janitor at MIT, is an intellectual genius. But he is low in emotional intelligence (EI) (Chapter 12). Will's need

for revenge gets him into a fight, and he is court-ordered to go into therapy. A number of therapists attempt to work with Will and fail. Sean proves to be up to the task because he "speaks his language"—the language of the streets.

Key Term Review

Identify which insight therapy term is being illustrated in the following:

1. From the moment Will first walks into Sean's office, he engages in a highly creative and relentless avoidance of the therapist's attempts to get him to talk about himself. This is an example of _____.

2. Despite Will's insults and verbal attacks, Sean continues working with him while expressing a nonjudgmental attitude and genuine caring for Will. Sean is displaying _____.

3. During the therapy sessions, Sean often shares his true inner thoughts and feelings with Will. This type of honest communication is called _____.

4. Will's troublesome relationships and antisocial behaviors appear to result from his hidden belief that he is unlovable, and because he blames himself for the abuse he received as a child. How would Ellis's rational-emotive-behavior therapy explain this

in terms of the A–B–C–D approach? The *activating event* (A) is _____. The *irrational belief* (B) is _____. And the *emotional consequence* (C) is _____. Can you create a *disputing irrational belief* (D) statement that Will could use to challenge this irrational belief?

5. After listening to Will focusing solely on the negative aspects of his life and ignoring all the positives, Sean says, "All you see is every negative thing 10 miles down the road." With this statement, Sean wants Will to recognize that he is using _____, one of Beck's thinking patterns associated with depression.

Check your answers in Appendix B.

Critical Thinking Application

Sean is a therapist in need of therapy himself—he is still grieving the death of his wife. A competent therapist would never behave the way Sean does in certain scenes. However, he does effectively portray several characteristics of good professional therapy. In addition, he displays several critical thinking components (CTCs) found in the Prologue at the front of this text. *Empathy* and *active listening* are two of the most obvious components that Sean—and all therapists—employ. Can you identify other CTCs that you think a good therapist might use?

CHECK & REVIEW

STOP *Before going on, be sure to complete this Check & Review. It is an invaluable study tool!*

Therapy Essentials and Psychology Engages

Part A: Retrieval Practice

1. Without looking at the book, spend 10 minutes writing a free-form essay

recalling all you can remember from the previous section.

2. Now, reread the previous section, and once again spend 10 minutes writing a free-form essay on the SAME material.

Part B: Practice Quiz

1. Label the five most common goals of therapy on the figure below.

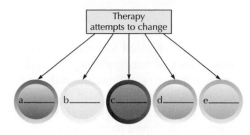

2. Match the following therapists with their primary emphasis:

___ psychoanalysts
___ humanistic therapists
___ biomedical therapists
___ cognitive therapists
___ behavior therapists

(a) faulty thinking and belief patterns
(b) unconscious thoughts
(c) biological disorders
(d) negative emotions
(e) maladaptive behaviors

3. Name the six features of therapy that are culturally universal.

4. A Japanese therapy designed to help clients discover personal guilt for having been ungrateful and troublesome to others and to develop gratitude toward those who have helped them is known as _____. (a) Kyoto therapy; (b) Okado therapy; (c) Naikan therapy; (d) Nissan therapy

5. What are the five major concerns about women in therapy?

Check your answers in Appendix B.

www.wileyplus.com

WileyPLUS presents an on-line version of this textbook along with a wealth of study resources including quizzes, practice tests, flash cards, videos, animations and other activities designed to improve your mastery of the content. Working in conjunction with these study tools, the Psychology in Action WileyPLUS course features Professor Karen Huffman, author of this textbook, explaining and expanding upon some of the most challenging concepts in psychology. Here is a sample of the tutorial videos available for this chapter:

• Debunking myths about therapy
• An animated look at cognitive behavior therapy
• A guide to treatment–where to start and how to choose the therapy that is right for you
• Professor Huffman's classroom discussion of how traditional therapy techniques can improve everyday relationships
• Virtual Field Trip to an ECT treatment center to learn more about this often misunderstood but effective treatment for severe depression

→ Key Terms

To assess your understanding of the **Key Terms** in Chapter 15, write a definition for each (in your own words), and then compare your definitions with those in the text.

Insight Therapies
psychotherapy (p. 533)
insight therapies (p. 533)
psychoanalysis (p. 533)
free association (p. 534)
dream analysis (p. 534)
resistance (p. 534)
transference (p. 534)
interpretation (p. 534)
psychodynamic therapy (p. 535)
cognitive therapy (p. 536)
self-talk (p. 536)
cognitive restructuring (p. 536)
cognitive-behavior therapy (p. 536)
rational-emotive behavior therapy (REBT) (p. 536)

humanistic therapy (p. 539)
client-centered therapy (p. 539)
empathy (p. 540)
unconditional positive regard (p. 540)
genuineness (p. 540)
active listening (p. 540)
group therapy (p. 542)
self-help group (p. 542)

Behavior Therapies
behavior therapy (p. 544)
systematic desensitization (p. 545)
aversion therapy (p. 545)
modeling therapy (p. 547)

Biomedical Therapies
biomedical therapy (p. 548)

psychopharmacology (p. 549)
electroconvulsive therapy (ECT) (p. 549)
psychosurgery (p. 549)
antianxiety drugs (p. 550)
antipsychotic drugs (p. 550)
mood-stabilizer drugs (p. 550)
antidepressant drugs (p. 550)
lobotomy (p. 551)
tardive dyskinesia (p. 551)
repetitive transcranial magnetic stimulation (rTMS) (p. 551)

Therapy Essentials
eclectic approach (p. 553)

Chapter Summary

Objective 15.1: Identify four common myths about therapy, and its three general approaches.
There are four common myths about therapy: There is one best therapy, therapists can read your mind, people who go to therapists are crazy or weak, and only the rich can afford therapy. There also are three general approaches to therapy—*insight*, *behavior*, and *biomedical*.

Objective 15.2: Define psychotherapy and insight therapy.
Psychotherapy refers to techniques employed to improve psychological functioning and promote adjustment to life. **Insight therapy** seeks to improve psychological functioning by increasing awareness into underlying motives and improvement in thoughts, feelings, and/or behaviors.

Psychoanalysis/Psychodynamic Therapies

Objective 15.3: Define psychoanalysis and list its five major methods.
Freudian **psychoanalysis** works to bring unconscious conflicts into consciousness. The five major techniques of psychoanalysis are **free association, dream analysis, analysis of resistance, analysis of transference,** and **interpretation.**

Objective 15.4: What are the two major criticisms of psychoanalysis?
It has limited applicability because it is time consuming, expensive, and suits only a small group of people. It also *lacks scientific credibility.*

Objective 15.5: Differentiate between psychoanalysis and psychodynamic therapy.
Compared to traditional psychoanalysis, modern **psychodynamic therapy** is briefer, the patient is treated face to face (rather than reclining on a couch), the therapist takes a more directive approach (rather than waiting for unconscious memories and desires to slowly be uncovered), and the focus is on conscious processes and current problems (rather than unconscious problems of the past).

Cognitive and Humanistic Therapies

Objective 15.6: Discuss cognitive therapy, self-talk, cognitive restructuring, and cognitive-behavior therapy.
Cognitive therapy focuses on faulty thought processes and beliefs to treat problem behaviors. Through insight into negative **self-talk** (the unrealistic things people say to themselves), the therapist can use **cognitive restructuring** to challenge and change destructive thoughts or inappropriate behaviors. **Cognitive-behavior therapy** focuses on changing both self-destructive thoughts and self-defeating behaviors.

Objective 15.7: What is the general goal of Ellis's rational-emotive behavior therapy (REBT)?
The general goal of **rational-emotive behavior therapy (REBT)** is to eliminate emotional problems through rational examination of irrational and self-defeating beliefs.

Objective 15.8: Describe Beck's cognitive therapy.
Beck developed a form of cognitive therapy that is particularly effective for depression. He helps clients identify their distorted thinking patterns, followed by active testing of these thoughts and encouragement toward pleasurable activities.

Objective 15.9: What are the chief successes and criticisms of cognitive therapy?
Cognitive therapies have been successful in treating a wide variety of psychological problems (e.g., Beck's success with depression). They have been criticized for ignoring the importance of unconscious processes, overemphasizing rationality, and minimizing the client's past. Some critics also attribute any success with cognitive therapies to the use of behavioral techniques.

Objective 15.10: Define humanistic therapy and describe Rogers's client-centered therapy.
Humanistic therapy assumes problems develop from blocked personal growth, and therapists work alongside clients to remove these obstacles. Rogers **client-centered therapy** emphasizes **empathy, unconditional positive regard, genuineness,** and **active listening**.

Objective 15.11: What are the key criticisms of humanistic therapy?
The basic tenets are difficult to evaluate scientifically, most outcome studies rely on self-reports, and research on their specific techniques has had mixed results.

Group, Family, and Marital Therapies

Objective 15.12: Discuss group, self-help, family, and marital therapies.
In **group therapy**, a number of people (usually 8 to 10) come together to work toward therapeutic goals. A variation on group therapy is the **self-help group** (like Alcoholics Anonymous), which is not guided by a professional. Although group members do not get the same level of attention as in individual therapy, group therapy has important advantages. First, it is less expensive. It also provides group support, insight and information, and opportunities for behavior rehearsal.

The primary aim of family and marital therapy is to change maladaptive interaction patterns. Because a family is a system of interdependent parts, the problem of any one member unavoidably affects all the others.

Behavior Therapies

Objective 15.13: What is behavior therapy?
Behavior therapies use learning principles to change maladaptive behaviors.

Objective 15.14: Describe how classical conditioning, operant conditioning, and observational learning are used in behavior therapy.
Classical conditioning principles are used to change faulty associations. In **systematic desensitization**, the client replaces anxiety with relaxation, and in **aversion therapy**, an aversive stimulus is paired with a maladaptive behavior. Shaping, reinforcement, punishment, and extinction are behavior therapy techniques based on operant conditioning principles. Observational learning techniques often include **modeling therapy**, which is based on acquisition of skills or behaviors through observation.

Objective 15.15: What are the key successes and criticisms of behavior therapies?
Behavior therapies have been successful with a number of psychological disorders. But they are criticized for possible lack of generalizability and the questionable ethics of attempting to control behavior.

Biomedical Therapies

Objective 15.16: Define biomedical therapy.
Biomedical therapies use biological techniques to relieve psychological disorders.

Objective 15.17: Discuss psychopharmacology, electroconvulsive therapy (ECT) and psychosurgery.
Psychopharmacology, or treatment with drugs, is the most common biomedical therapy. **Antianxiety drugs** (Valium, Ativan) generally are used to treat anxiety disorders, **antipsychotic drugs** (Thorazine, Haldol) treat the symptoms of schizophrenia, **antidepressant drugs** (Prozac, Effexor) treat depression, and **mood-stabilizer drugs** (lithium) can help patients with bipolar disorder. Drug therapy has been responsible for major improvements in many disorders. However, there are also problems with dosage levels, side effects, and patient cooperation.
Electroconvulsive therapy (ECT) is used primarily to relieve serious depression when medication has not worked. But it is risky and considered a treatment of last resort. **Psychosurgeries**, such as a **lobotomy**, have been used in the past but are rarely used today.

Objective 15.18: What are the major contributions and criticisms of biomedical therapies?
Drug therapy is enormously beneficial, but it also has several problems. For example, it offers symptom relief, but few "cures," patients often stop medications once symptoms are relieved, patients may become dependent, and little is known about the long-term effects and drug interactions. In addition, there are potentially dangerous side effects, and possible overuse. ECT and psychosurgery are both controversial and are generally used as a last resort.

Therapy Essentials

Objective 15.19: Identify the five most common goals of therapy, and discuss the eclectic approach.
There are numerous forms of therapy. But they all focus treatment on five basic areas of disturbance—thoughts, emotions, behaviors, interpersonal and life situations, and biomedical problems. Many therapists take an **eclectic approach** and combine techniques from various theories.

Objective 15.20: Identify the six key types of mental health professionals.
Clinical psychologists, counseling psychologists, psychiatrists, psychiatric nurses, psychiatric social workers, and school psychologists are the six most common types of mental health professionals.

Objective 15.21: Discuss involuntary commitment and deinstitutionalization.
People believed to be mentally ill and dangerous to themselves or others can be involuntarily committed to mental hospitals for diagnosis and treatment. Abuses of involuntary commitments and other problems associated with state mental hospitals have led many states to practice *deinstitutionalization*—discharging as many patients as possible and discouraging admissions. Community services such as community mental health (CMH) centers try to cope with the problems of deinstitutionalization.

Objective 15.22: Is therapy effective, and how can we find a good therapist?
Research on the effectiveness of psychotherapy has found that 40 to 80 percent of those who receive treatment are better off than those who do not receive treatment. When searching for a good therapist, it's good to "shop around," and to consult your psychology instructor or college counselors for referrals. If you're in a crisis, get immediate help through hospital emergency rooms or telephone hotlines.

Psychology Engages

Objective 15.23: Describe the major similarities and differences in therapy across cultures.
Therapies in all cultures share six culturally universal features: naming a problem, qualities of the therapist, therapist credibility, familiar framework, techniques that bring relief, and a special time and place. Important cultural differences in therapies also exist. For example, therapies in individualistic cultures emphasize the self and control over one's life, whereas therapies in collectivist cultures emphasize interdependence. Japan's Naikan therapy is a good example of a collectivist culture's therapy.

Objective 15.24: What are the unique concerns of women in therapy?
Therapists must take five considerations into account when treating women clients: higher rate of diagnosis and treatment of mental disorders, stresses of poverty, stresses of multiple roles, stresses of aging, and violence against women.

Insight Therapies

Psychoanalysis/ Psychodynamic

Five major methods designed to gain insight into the unconscious

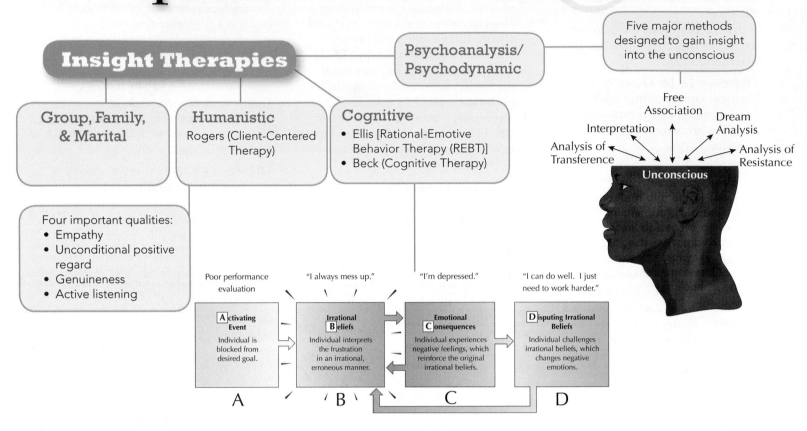

Free Association
Dream Analysis
Interpretation
Analysis of Transference
Analysis of Resistance
Unconscious

Group, Family, & Marital

Humanistic
Rogers (Client-Centered Therapy)

Four important qualities:
• Empathy
• Unconditional positive regard
• Genuineness
• Active listening

Cognitive
• Ellis [Rational-Emotive Behavior Therapy (REBT)]
• Beck (Cognitive Therapy)

Poor performance evaluation

"I always mess up."

"I'm depressed."

"I can do well. I just need to work harder."

A ctivating Event
Individual is blocked from desired goal.

B Irrational Beliefs
Individual interprets the frustration in an irrational, erroneous manner.

C Emotional Consequences
Individual experiences negative feelings, which reinforce the original irrational beliefs.

D isputing Irrational Beliefs
Individual challenges irrational beliefs, which changes negative emotions.

A   B   C   D

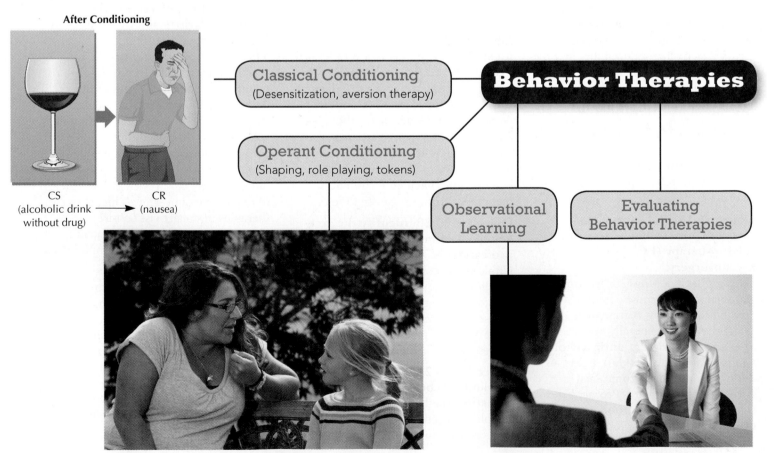

After Conditioning

CS (alcoholic drink without drug) → CR (nausea)

Classical Conditioning
(Desensitization, aversion therapy)

Behavior Therapies

Operant Conditioning
(Shaping, role playing, tokens)

Observational Learning

Evaluating Behavior Therapies

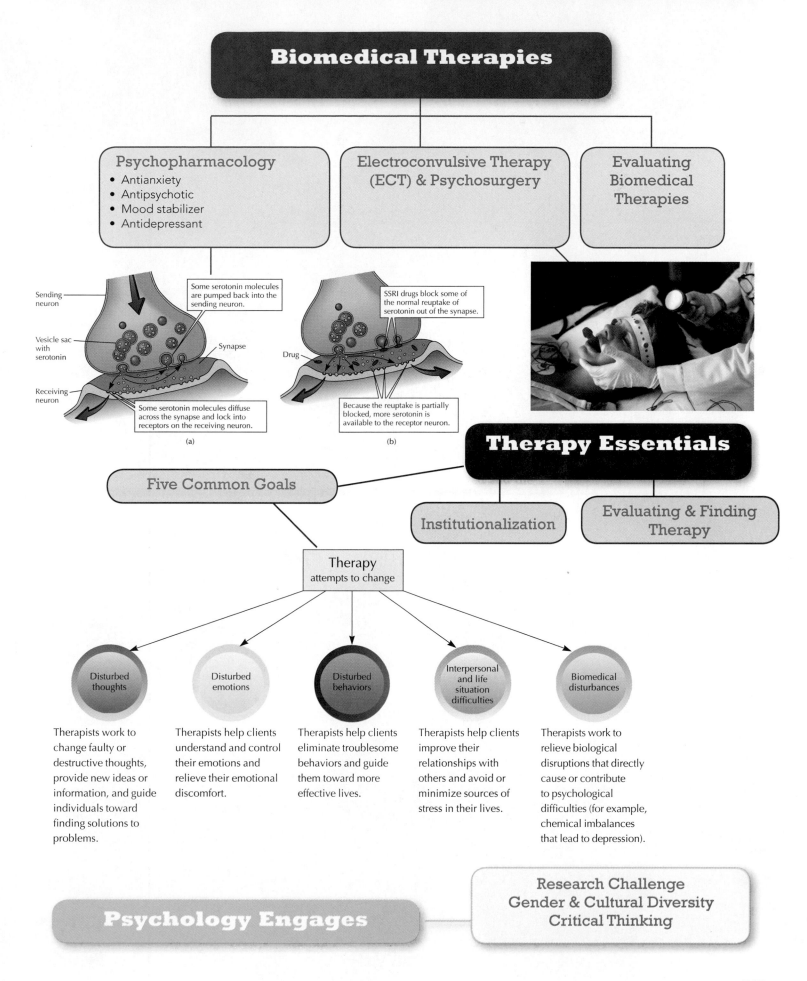

Biomedical Therapies

Psychopharmacology
- Antianxiety
- Antipsychotic
- Mood stabilizer
- Antidepressant

Electroconvulsive Therapy (ECT) & Psychosurgery

Evaluating Biomedical Therapies

Sending neuron

Some serotonin molecules are pumped back into the sending neuron.

Vesicle sac with serotonin

Synapse

Receiving neuron

Some serotonin molecules diffuse across the synapse and lock into receptors on the receiving neuron.

(a)

Drug

SSRI drugs block some of the normal reuptake of serotonin out of the synapse.

Because the reuptake is partially blocked, more serotonin is available to the receptor neuron.

(b)

Therapy Essentials

Five Common Goals

Institutionalization

Evaluating & Finding Therapy

Therapy
attempts to change

Disturbed thoughts

Therapists work to change faulty or destructive thoughts, provide new ideas or information, and guide individuals toward finding solutions to problems.

Disturbed emotions

Therapists help clients understand and control their emotions and relieve their emotional discomfort.

Disturbed behaviors

Therapists help clients eliminate troublesome behaviors and guide them toward more effective lives.

Interpersonal and life situation difficulties

Therapists help clients improve their relationships with others and avoid or minimize sources of stress in their lives.

Biomedical disturbances

Therapists work to relieve biological disruptions that directly cause or contribute to psychological difficulties (for example, chemical imbalances that lead to depression).

Psychology Engages

Research Challenge
Gender & Cultural Diversity
Critical Thinking

ChapterSixteen

Social Psychology

Could we but draw back the curtain, That surrounds each others lives,

See the naked heart and spirit; Know what spur the action gives;

Often we would find it better, Purer than we think we would.

We would love each other better, If we only understood.

ANONYMOUS

Objective 16.1: What is social psychology?

What do you think? If we could "draw back the curtain," would we find human nature pure and loveable, or are we at heart just "savage beasts"? Do you recall from page one of this text that I promised to take you on an exciting and unforgettable trip filled with invaluable discoveries about yourself and the world around you? After a brief introductory survey of psychology's history and research methods (Chapter 1), our tour officially began at the micro level of human behavior and mental processes—the neuron, brain, and other parts of the nervous system (Chapter 2). Now, at the end of our journey (Chapter 16), we come to the largest macro level of study, **social psychology**, which studies how other people influence our individual thoughts, feelings, and actions.

When social psychologists scientifically draw back the curtain that surrounds our lives, we discover theories and principles that help explain why ordinary people around the world commit acts of astounding bravery and kindness, as well as acts of unspeakable evil and cruelty.

Social Psychology Study of how others influence our thoughts, feelings, and actions

MYTH BUSTERS

True or False?

1. Most people judge others more harshly than they judge themselves?

2. Inducing cognitive dissonance is a great way to change attitudes?

3. There are positive as well as negative forms of prejudice?

4. Looks are the primary factor in our initial feelings of attraction, liking, and romantic love?

5. Opposites attract?

6. Romantic love rarely lasts longer than 1 or 2 years?

7. People wearing masks are more likely to engage in aggressive acts.

8. Groups generally make riskier or more conservative decisions than a single individual does?

9. Watching a violent sports match or punching a pillow is a not a good way to let off steam and reduce aggression?

10. When people are alone, they are more likely to help another individual than when they are in a group?

Answers: Only one of these statements is false. See if you can find the answer before checking Appendix B.

For many students and psychologists, myself included, social psychology is the most exciting of all fields because it is about you and me, and because almost everything we do is *social*. Unlike earlier chapters that focused on individual processes, like the brain and other parts of the nervous system, memory, and personality, social psychology studies how large social forces, such as groups, social roles, and norms, bring out the best and worst in all of us. This chapter begins with a look at components of social psychology and concludes with a discussion of how social psychology can help reduce prejudice, discrimination, and other destructive behaviors.

Our Thoughts About Others

Why would someone run into a burning building to rescue a stranger? Why do we fall in love with some people and not others? Trying to understand the social world often means trying to understand other people's behavior. We look for reasons and explanations for others' behavior (the process of attribution). We also develop thoughts and beliefs (attitudes) about others. Let's explore both *attributions* and *attitudes*.

Attributions: Explaining Others' Behavior

Objective 16.2: Describe the process of attribution and its two key errors.

Attribution How we explain our own and others' actions

Why are we all so interested in understanding and explaining why people do what they do? Many social psychologists believe that developing logical explanations, or **attributions**, for behavior makes us feel safer and more in control (Baumeister & Vohs, 2011; Chiou, 2007; Ferrucci et al., 2011; Heider, 1958; Krueger, 2007). To do so, we generally begin with the basic question of whether a given action stems mainly from a person's internal disposition or from the external situation.

Mistaken Attributions

Making the correct choice between disposition and situation is central to accurate attributions. Unfortunately, our judgments are frequently marred by two major errors: the *fundamental attribution error* and the *self-serving bias*.

Fundamental Attribution Error (FAE)—Judging Others

Our attributions as to the reasons for people's actions are generally accurate when we take into account *situational* influences on behavior. However, given that people have enduring personality traits (Chapter 13) and a tendency to take cognitive shortcuts (Chapter 8), we more often choose *dispositional* (personality) attributions—that is, we blame or credit people, not situations.

For example, suppose a new student joins your class and seems distant, cold, and uninterested in interaction. It's easy to conclude that she's unfriendly, and maybe even "stuck-up"—a dispositional (personality) attribution. You might be surprised to find that in one-to-one interactions with familiar, close friends, she's very warm and friendly. In other words, her behavior depends on the situation.

This bias toward personal, dispositional factors rather than situational factors in our explanations for others' behavior is so common that it is called the **fundamental attribution error (FAE)**, also known as the *actor-observer bias* (Arkes & Kajdasz, 2011; Gebauer, Krempl, & Fleisch, 2008; Kennedy, 2010; Lennon et al., 2011) (Figure 16.1).

Why do we so often jump to internal, *personal* explanations? Social psychologists suggest that one reason is that human personalities and behaviors are more *salient* (or noticeable) than situational factors, the **saliency bias**. We also tend to focus on people and "blame the victim" because of our need to believe that the world is just and fair. This **just-world phenomenon** suggests that people generally deserve what they get, while allowing us to feel safer in an uncontrollable world.

Self-serving Bias—Judging Ourselves As we've just seen, when judging others we often blame people versus the situation—the FAE. However, when judging ourselves, we tend to take personal credit for our successes and externalize our failures. This **self-serving bias** is motivated by a desire to maintain positive self-esteem and a good public image (Alloy et al., 2011; Krusemark, Campbell, & Clementz, 2008; Mc Clure et al., 2011). For example, students often credit themselves for high scores on an exam and blame the instructor, textbook, or "tricky" questions for low scores. Studies also find some people tend to "blame the victim" in cases of rape; young children tend to blame their siblings for conflicts; and both partners in a divorce are more likely to see themselves as the victim, as less responsible for the breakup, and as being more willing to reconcile (Earnshaw et al., 2011; Gray & Silver, 1990; Miller, Amacker, & King, 2011; Suarez & Gadalla, 2010; Wilson et al., 2004). Even in the business world, professional money managers generally take credit for good investments and blame others or external forces for failures (Gebauer et al., 2008; Hilary & Hsu, 2011).

Fundamental Attribution Error (FAE) Attributing people's behavior to internal (dispositional) causes rather than external (situational) factors

Saliency Bias Focusing on the most noticeable (salient) factors when explaining the causes of behavior

Just-World Phenomenon Tendency to believe that people generally get what they deserve

Self-Serving Bias Taking credit for our successes and externalizing our failures

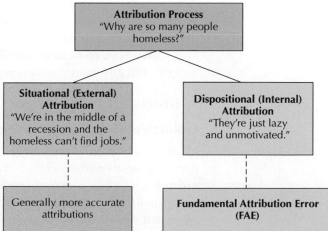

Figure 16.1 How dispositional attributions sometimes lead to the fundamental attribution error (FAE)

Can you identify the attributional error that best explains this cartoon?

"It's not my fault. It's the voters' fault for electing me!"

Answer: The jailed politician's criticism of the voters may be the result of the fundamental attribution error. His overlooking of his own faults may reflect the self-serving bias.

Culture and Attributional Biases

Objective 16.3: Describe how culture affects attributional biases.

Both the fundamental attribution error and the self-serving bias may depend in part on cultural factors. In highly *individualistic cultures*, like the United States, people are defined and understood as individual selves—largely responsible for their own successes and failures. But in *collectivistic cultures*, like that in Japan, people are defined and understood as members of their social network—responsible for doing as others expect. Accordingly, they tend to be more aware of situational constraints on behavior, making the FAE less likely (Bozkurt & Aydin, 2004; Han et al., 2011; Imada & Ellsworth, 2011; Mason & Morris, 2011).

The self-serving bias is also much less common in Eastern nations. In Japan, for instance, the ideal person is someone who is aware of his or her shortcomings and continually works to overcome them. It is not someone who thinks highly of himself or herself (Heine & Renshaw, 2002). In the East, where people do not define themselves as much in terms of their individual accomplishments, self-esteem is not related to doing better than others. Rather, fitting in and not standing out from the group is stressed. As the Japanese proverb says, "The nail that sticks up gets pounded down."

This emphasis on group relations in Asian cultures is also true of many Native Americans. For example, when the Wintun Native Americans originally described being with a close relation or intimate friend, they would not say, for example, "Linda and I," but rather, "Linda we" (Lee, 1950). This attachment to community relations instead of individual *selfhood* often seems strange to people in contemporary Western, individualist societies. But it remains common in collectivist cultures (Berry et al., 2011; Smith, 2011).

Attitudes: Our Learned Predispositions Toward Others

Objective 16.4: Define attitude and identify its three key components.

When we observe and respond to the world around us, we are seldom neutral. Rather, our responses toward subjects as diverse as pizza, people, AIDS, and abortion reflect our **attitudes**, which are learned predispositions to respond cognitively, affectively, and behaviorally to a particular object in a particular way. Social psychologists generally agree that most attitudes have three components: *cognitive (thoughts and beliefs)*, *affective (feelings)*, and *behavioral* (Figure 16.2).

Attitude Learned predisposition to respond cognitively, affectively, and behaviorally to a particular object

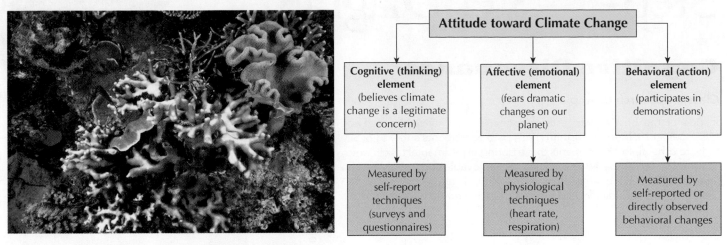

Figure 16.2 Three components of attitudes When social psychologists study attitudes, they measure each of the three components: cognitive, affective, and behavioral. Note the "bleached" coral in this photo, which many point to as a direct result of climate change.

Attitude Change through Cognitive Dissonance

Objective 16.5: What is cognitive dissonance, how does it change attitudes, and how does culture affect it?

We are not born with our attitudes—they are learned. From earliest childhood, we form them through direct experience (we eat pizza and like the taste), and through indirect learning or observation (we listen to testimonials or watch others happily eating pizza). Although attitudes begin in early childhood, they are not permanent—a fact that advertisers and politicians know and exploit.

One way to change attitudes is to make direct, persuasive appeals (such as TV ads like "Friends Don't Let Friends Drive Drunk"). An even more efficient method is to create **cognitive dissonance** (Baumeister & Bushman, 2011; Cooper & Hogg, 2007; Gringart, Helmes, & Speelman, 2008; Stone & Focella, 2011). Contradictions between our attitudes and behaviors can motivate us to change our attitudes to agree with our behaviors (Step-by-Step Diagram 16.1)

Cognitive Dissonance Unpleasant tension and anxiety caused by a discrepancy between an attitude and a behavior

TEST YOURSELF

Cognitive Dissonance and Home Buying

This family has just purchased this new home. Using cognitive dissonance theory, can you predict whether they will like the house more or less after they move in?

Answer: Moving to a new home involves a great deal of effort and money. Therefore, the family will need to justify their decision. By focusing only on the positives, they will reduce any cognitive dissonance (and increase their liking of their new home).

Step-by-StepDiagram 16.1

STOP This Step by Step diagram contains essential information NOT found elsewhere in the text, which is likely to appear on quizzes and exams. Be sure to study it CAREFULLY!

Cognitive Dissonance

Classic Research Example

In one of the best-known tests of cognitive dissonance theory, Leon Festinger and J. Merrill Carlsmith (1959) paid participants either $1 or $20 to lie to other fellow participants that a boring experimental task in which they had just participated was actually very enjoyable and fun. Those who were paid $1 subsequently changed their minds and actually reported more positive attitudes toward the task than those who were paid $20.

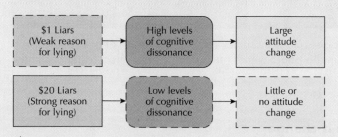

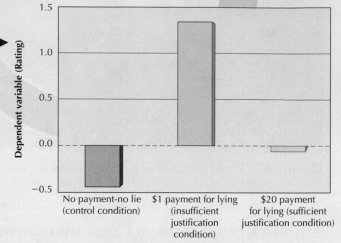

▲ Why was there more attitude change among those who were only paid $1? All participants who lied to other participants presumably recognized the discrepancy between their initial attitude (the task was boring) and their behavior (lying to others that it was enjoyable and fun). However, the participants who were given insufficient monetary justification for lying (the $1 liars) apparently experienced greather cognitive dissonance. Therefore, they expressed more liking for the dull task than those who received sufficient monetary justification (the $20 liars). This second group had little or no motivation to change their attitude—they lied for the money! (Note that $20 in 1959 would be worth about $200 today.)

Modern Example

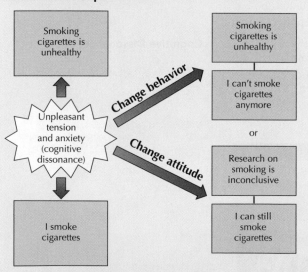

Given all the public health warnings about the dangers of smoking, why do so many people (especially health professionals) continue to smoke? They obviously could quit smoking, but like most people, they probably take the easier route. They *change one or more of their attidudes!*

Overall Summary

Cognitive Dissonance Theory*

Step 1 People are motivated to maintain consistency in their thoughts, feelings, and actions. → **Step 2** When inconsistencies or conflicts exist between our thoughts, feelings, and actions, they can lead to ... → **Step 3** Strong tension and discomfort (cognitive dissonance). → **Step 4** To reduce this cognitive dissonance, we are motivated to change our attitude or behavior.

*It's important to note that the experience of cognitive dissonance may depend on a distinctly Western way of thinking about and evaluating the self. As mentioned earlier, people in Eastern cultures tend to define themselves in collectivist, group terms—not individual behavior and accomplishments. For this reason, making a bad choice may not pose the same threat to self-esteem that it would in more individualistic cultures, such as those in the United States (Berry et al., 2011; Choi & Nisbett, 2000; Dessalles, 2011; Imada & Kitayama, 2010).

CHECK & REVIEW

STOP *Before going on, be sure to complete this Check & Review. It is an invaluable study tool!*

Our Thoughts About Others

Part A: Retrieval Practice

1. Without looking at the book, spend 10 minutes writing a free-form essay recalling all you can remember from the previous section.

2. Now, reread the previous section, and once again spend 10 minutes writing a free-form essay on the SAME material.

(Although time consuming, this exercise has been shown to be the single best way to improve your test scores! For more information, check out www.sciencemag. org/content/early/2011/01/19/science. 1199327.abstract)

Part B: Practice Quiz

1. The principles people follow in making judgments about the causes of events, others' behavior, and their own behavior are known as ___. (a) impression management; (b) stereotaxic determination; (c) attributions; (d) person perception

2. What is the fundamental attribution error?

3. Label the three components of attitudes on the following figure.

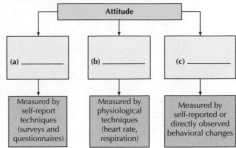

4. According to _____ theory, people are motivated to change their attitudes because of tension created by a mismatch between two or more competing attitudes or between their attitudes and behavior.

Check your answers in Appendix B.

Our Feelings About Others

Having explored our thoughts about others (attribution and attitudes), we now focus on our feelings about others. We begin by examining the negative feelings (and thoughts and actions) associated with *prejudice* and *discrimination*. Then we'll explore the generally positive feelings of *interpersonal attraction*.

Prejudice and Discrimination: It's the Feeling That Counts

Objective 16.6: Define prejudice, identify its three key components, and differentiate between prejudice and discrimination.

Prejudice, which literally means "prejudgment," is a learned, generally *negative* attitude directed toward specific people solely because of their membership in an identified group. Prejudice is not innate. It is learned. It also creates enormous problems for its victims and limits the perpetrator's ability to accurately judge others and process information.

Positive forms of prejudice do exist, such as "all women love babies" or "African Americans are natural athletes." However, most research and definitions of prejudice focus on the negative forms. It's also interesting to note that even positive forms of prejudice can be harmful. For example, women might think there must be something wrong with them if they don't like being around babies. Similarly, African Americans might see athletics or entertainment as their major routes to success.

Like all attitudes, prejudice is composed of three elements: *cognitive* (**stereotypes** about people strictly because of their membership in a group), *affective* (emotions associated with objects of prejudice), and *behavioral* (predispositions to **discriminate against** members of the group).

Although the terms *prejudice* and *discrimination* are often used interchangeably, they are not the same. *Prejudice* refers to an *attitude*. **Discrimination** refers to *action*. The two often coincide, but not always (Figure 16.3).

THE FAMILY CIRCUS

"That's the DOLL aisle, Daddy. Somebody might see us!"

Prejudice A learned, generally negative, attitude toward members of a group; includes thoughts (stereotypes), feelings, and behavioral tendencies (possible discrimination)

Stereotype A set of beliefs about the characteristics of people in a group that is generalized to all group members; also, the cognitive component of prejudice

Discrimination Negative behaviors directed at members of a group

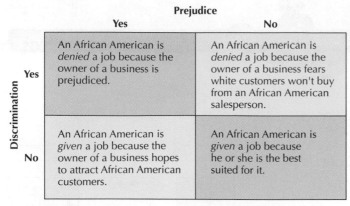

	Prejudice	
	Yes	**No**
Discrimination Yes	An African American is *denied* a job because the owner of a business is prejudiced.	An African American is *denied* a job because the owner of a business fears white customers won't buy from an African American salesperson.
No	An African American is *given* a job because the owner of a business hopes to attract African American customers.	An African American is *given* a job because he or she is the best suited for it.

Figure 16.3 Prejudice and discrimination Note how prejudice and discrimination are closely related, but either condition can exist without the other. The only situation in this example without prejudice or discrimination is when someone is given a job simply because he or she is the best candidate.

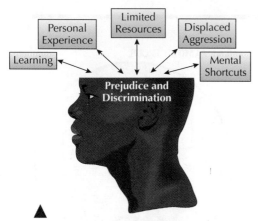

Figure 16.4 Common sources of prejudice and discrimination

Major Sources of Prejudice and Discrimination

Objective 16.7: Discuss the five major sources of prejudice and discrimination.

How do prejudice and discrimination originate? Why do they persist? Five commonly cited sources of prejudice and discrimination are: *learning, personal experience, limited resources, displaced aggression*, and *mental shortcuts* (Figure 16.4).

Learning People learn prejudice the same way they learn all attitudes—primarily through *classical* and *operant conditioning* and *social learning* (Chapter 6). For example, repeated exposure to stereotypical portrayals of minorities and women on tv, movies and magazines teach children that such images are correct. Similarly, hearing parents, friends, and teachers express their prejudices also reinforces prejudice (Jackson, 2011; Kassin, Fein, & Markus, 2008; Levitan, 2008; Livingston & Drwecki, 2007; Tropp & Mallett, 2011). *Ethnocentrism*, believing one's own culture represents the norm or is superior to all others, is also a form of learned prejudice.

Personal Experience People also develop prejudice through direct experience. For example, when people make prejudicial remarks or "jokes," they often gain attention and even approval from others. Sadly, derogating others also seems to boost one's self-esteem (Fein & Spencer, 1997; Hodson, Rush, & MacInnis, 2010; Plummer, 2001). Also, once someone has one or more negative interactions or experiences with members of a specific group, they may generalize their bad feelings and prejudice to all members of that group.

Limited Resources Most people understand that prejudice and discrimination exact a high price on their victims, but few acknowledge the significant economic and political advantages they offer to the dominant group (Costello & Hodson, 2011; Kteily, Sidanius, & Levin, 2011; Perry & Sibley, 2011; Schaefer, 2008). For example, the stereotype that blacks and Mexicans are inferior to whites helps justify and perpetuate a social order in the United States, in which whites hold disproportionate power and resources.

Displaced Aggression As we discuss in the next section, frustration sometimes leads people to attack the source of frustration. But, as history has shown, when the cause of frustration is ambiguous, or too powerful and capable of retaliation, people often redirect their aggression toward an alternative, innocent target, known as a *scapegoat*. There is strong historical evidence for the dangers of scapegoating. Jewish people were blamed for economic troubles in Germany prior to World War II. In America, beginning in the 1980s, gay men were blamed for the AIDs epidemic, and since the 9/11 terrorist attacks certain immigrant groups are being blamed for the recent economic troubles (Figure 16.5).

Figure 16.5 Prejudice and immigration Can you identify which of the five sources of prejudice best explains this behavior?

The price of prejudice If pictures truly are "worth a thousand words," these photos speak volumes about the atrocities associated with prejudice: (a) the Holocaust, when millions of Jews, and other minorities, were exterminated by the Nazis, (b) slavery in the United States, where Africans were bought and sold as slaves, and (c) recent acts of genocide in Sudan, where thousands have been slaughtered.

Mental Shortcuts Prejudice may stem from normal attempts to simplify a complex social world (Ambady & Adams, 2011; Dotsch, Wigboldus, & van Knippenberg, 2011; Kulik, 2005; Sternberg, 2007, 2009). Stereotypes allow people to make quick judgments about others, thereby freeing up their mental resources for other activities. In fact, stereotypes and prejudice can occur even without a person's conscious awareness or control. This process is known as "automatic" or "implicit" bias (Cattaneo et al., 2011; Columb & Plant, 2011; Dovidio, Pagotto, & Hebl, 2011).

People use stereotypes to classify others in terms of their membership in a group. Given that people generally classify themselves as part of the preferred group, they also create ingroups and outgroups. An *ingroup* is any category that people see themselves as belonging to; an *outgroup* is any other category.

Compared with how they judge members of the outgroup, people tend to judge ingroup members as being more attractive, having better personalities, and so on—a phenomenon known as **ingroup favoritism** (Ahmed, 2007; DiDonato, Ullrich, & Krueger, 2011; Harth, Kessler, & Leach, 2008). People also tend to recognize greater diversity among members of their ingroup than they do among members of outgroups (Bendle, 2011; Cehajic, Brown, & Castano, 2008; Ryan, Casas, & Thompson, 2010; Wilson & Hugenberg, 2010). A danger of this **outgroup homogeneity effect** is that when members of minority groups are not recognized as varied and complex individuals, it is easier to treat them in discriminatory ways.

A good example is war. Viewing people on the other side as simply faceless enemies makes it easier to kill large numbers of soldiers and civilians. This dehumanization and facelessness also helps perpetuate our current high levels of fear and anxiety associated with terrorism (Dunham, 2011; Haslam et al., 2007; Hutchinson & Rosenthal, 2011).

Understanding the many causes of prejudice is just a first step toward overcoming it, and later in this chapter, we consider several methods psychologists recommend to reduce prejudice.

Ingroup Favoritism Viewing members of the ingroup more positively than members of an outgroup

Outgroup Homogeneity Effect Judging members of an outgroup as more alike and less diverse than members of the ingroup

Interpersonal Attraction: Why We Like and Love Others

What causes us to feel admiration, liking, friendship, intimacy, lust, or love? All of these social experiences reflect **interpersonal attraction,** or positive feelings toward another.

Interpersonal Attraction Positive feelings toward another

Three Key Factors in Attraction—Physical Attractiveness, Proximity, and Similarity

Objective 16.8: What are the three key factors in attraction?

Social psychologists have identified three compelling factors in interpersonal attraction—*physical attractiveness*, *proximity*, and *similarity*. Physical attractiveness and proximity are most influential in the beginning stages of relationships. However, similarity is more important in maintaining long-term relationships.

Physical Attractiveness *Physical attractiveness* (size, shape, facial characteristics, and manner of dress) is one of the most important factors in our initial liking or loving of others (Back et al., 2011; Bryan, Webster, & Mahaffey, 2011; Buss, 2003, 2005, 2007, 2008, 2011; Cunningham, Fink, & Kenix, 2008; Lippa, 2007; Regan, 2011).

Like it or not, attractive individuals are seen as more poised, interesting, cooperative, achieving, sociable, independent, intelligent, healthy, and sexually warm than unattractive people (Jaeger, 2011; Moore, Filippou, & Perrett, 2011; Tsukiura & Cabeza, 2011; Willis, Esqueda, & Schacht, 2008). Human infants just a few days old prefer attractive human faces, and 3-to-4-month olds prefer attractive over unattractive domestic and wild cat faces (Quinn et al., 2008). Perhaps even more distressing, premature infants who are rated as physically more attractive by nurses caring for them thrive better during their hospital stay. They gain more weight and are released earlier than infants perceived as less attractive, presumably because they receive more nurturing (Badr & Abdallah, 2001). Attractive defendents in a simulated vehicular homicide case were also given shorter sentences than unattractive defendants (Staley, 2008).

How do those of us who are not "superstar beautiful" manage to find mates? The good news is that perceived attractiveness for *known* people, in contrast to *unknown* people, is strongly influenced by nonphysical traits. This means that factors like respect, positive interactions, similarity, and familiarity increase our judgments of beauty in friends and family (Barelds et al., 2011; Kniffin & Wilson, 2004; Lewandowski, Aron, & Gee, 2007; Morry Kito, & Ortiz, 2011; Reis et al., 2011). Also, what people judge as "ideally attractive" may be quite different from what they eventually choose for a mate. According to the *matching hypothesis*, men and women of approximately equal physical attractiveness tend to select each other as partners (Regan, 1998; Sprecher & Regan, 2002; Taylor et al., 2011). Further good news, as you will see in the following application section, is that *flirting* offers a "simple" way to increase attractiveness.

Psychology at Work

The Art and Science of Flirting

Objective 16.9: Discuss scientific research on flirting.

Picture yourself watching a man (Tom) and woman (Kaleesha) at a singles' bar.

As Tom approaches the table, Kaleesha sits up straighter, smiles, and touches her hair. Tom asks her to dance. Kaleesha quickly nods and stands up while smoothing her skirt. During the dance, she smiles and sometimes glances at him from under her lashes. When the dance finishes, Kaleesha waits for Tom to escort her back to her chair. She motions him to sit in the adjacent chair, and they engage in a lively conversation. Kaleesha allows her leg to briefly graze his. When Tom reaches for popcorn from the basket in front of Kaleesha, she playfully pulls it away. This surprises Tom, and he frowns at Kaleesha. She quickly turns away and starts talking to her friends. Despite his repeated attempts to talk to her, Kaleesha ignores him.

What happened? Did you recognize Kaleesha's sexual signals? Did you understand why she turned away at the end? If so, you are skilled in the art and science of flirting. If not, you may be very interested in the work of Monica Moore at the University of Missouri (1998). Moore is a scientist interested in describing and understanding flirting and the role it plays in human courtship. She has observed and recorded many scenes—in singles' bars and shopping malls—like the one with Tom and Kaleesha. Although she prefers the term *nonverbal courtship signaling*, what Moore and her colleagues have spent thousands of hours secretly observing is *flirting*.

From these naturalistic observations, we know a great deal more about what works, and doesn't work, in courtship. First of all, both men and women flirt. But women generally initiate a courtship. The woman signals her interest with glances that may be brief and darting, or direct and sustained. Interested women often smile at the same time they gesture with their hands—often with an open or extended palm. Primping (adjusting clothing or patting hair) is also common. A flirting woman will also make herself more noticeable by sitting straighter, with stomach pulled in and breasts pushed out.

Once contact is made and the couple is dancing or sitting at a table, Moore noticed the woman increases the level of flirting. She orients her body toward his, whispers in his ear, and frequently nods and smiles in response to his conversation. Most significant, she touches the man or allows the man to touch her. Like Kaleesha with Tom, allowing her leg to graze his is a powerful indication of her interest.

Women also use play behaviors to flirt. They tease, mock-hit, and tell jokes. They do this to inject humor, while also testing the man's receptivity to humor. As in the case of Tom's reaction to the popcorn tease, when a man doesn't appreciate the playfulness, a woman often uses rejection signals to cool or end the relationship. Other studies confirm Moore's description of women's nonverbal sexual signaling (Lott, 2000).

Now that you know what to look for, watch for flirting behavior in others—or perhaps in your own life. According to Moore and other researchers, flirting may be the single most important thing a woman can do to increase her attractiveness. Because the burden of making the first approach is usually the man's, men are understandably cautious and uncomfortable. They generally welcome a woman clearly signaling her interest.

Two cautions are in order. First, signaling interest does not mean that the woman is ready to have sex with the man. She flirts because she wants to get to know the man better. She'll later decide whether she wants to develop a relationship. Second, Moore reminds women to "use their enhanced flirting skills only when genuinely interested" (1997, p. 69). Flirting should be reserved for times when you genuinely want to attract and keep the attention of a particular partner.

Proximity Attraction also depends on people being in the same place at the same time. Thus, **proximity**, or geographic nearness, is another major factor in attraction. A study of friendship in college dormitories found that the person next door was more often liked than the person two doors away, the person two doors away was liked more than someone three doors away, and so on (Priest & Sawyer, 1967).

Proximity Attraction based on geographic closeness

Why is proximity so important? It's largely because of *mere exposure*. Just as familiar people become more physically attractive over time, repeated exposure also increases overall liking (Monin, 2003; Rhodes, Halberstadt, & Brajkovich, 2001). This makes sense from an evolutionary point of view. Things we have seen before are less likely to pose a threat than novel stimuli. It also explains why modern advertisers tend to run highly redundant ad campaigns with familiar faces and jingles. In short, repeated exposure increases liking! (See Figure 16.6 for another example.)

One caution: Repeated exposure to a *negative* stimulus can *decrease* attraction, as evidenced by the high number of negative political ads. Politicians have learned that repeatedly running an attack ad associating an opposing candidate with negative cues (like increased taxes) decreases the viewers' liking of the opponent.

Figure 16.6 The face in the mirror Why do we so often dislike photos of ourselves? According to the *mere exposure effect*, people, like the model in these photos, generally prefer a *reversed* image (the one on the left) because it is the *familiar* one we are accustomed to seeing in the mirror. However, when presented with reversed and nonreversed (normal camera angle) photos, close friends prefer the nonreversed images (Mita, Dermer, & Knight, 1977).

Need Complementarity Attraction toward those with qualities we admire but personally lack

Need Compatibility Attraction based on sharing similar needs

On the other hand, running ads showing themselves in a positive light (kissing babies, helping flood victims) helps build positive associations and increased liking.

Similarity Once we've had repeated opportunity to get to know someone through simple physical proximity, and assuming we find him or her attractive, we then need something to hold the relationship together over time. The major cementing factor for long-term relationships, whether liking or loving, is *similarity*. We tend to prefer, and stay with, people (and organizations) who are most like us, those who share our ethnic background, social class, interests, and attitudes (Böhm et al., 2010; Caprara et al., 2007; Morry, Kito, & Ortiz, 2011; Sanbonmatsu, Uchino, & Birmingham, 2011). In other words, "Birds of a feather flock together."

What about the old saying "opposites attract"? It does seem that this bit of common folklore is contradictory. But the term *opposites* here probably refers to personality traits rather than to social background or values. An attraction to a seemingly opposite person is more often based on the recognition that in one or two important areas that person offers something we lack. If you are a talkative and outgoing person, for example, your friendship with a quiet and reserved individual may endure because each of you provides important resources for the other. Psychologists refer to this as **need complementarity**, as compared with the **need compatibility** represented by similarity. In sum, lovers can enjoy some differences, but the more alike people are, the more their liking endures.

Loving Others

Objective 16.10: Differentiate between Sternberg's theory and romantic and companionate love.

We can think of interpersonal attraction as a fundamental building block of how we feel about others. But how do we make sense of love? Many people find the subject to be alternately mysterious, exhilarating, comforting—and even maddening. In this

TEST YOURSELF

Based on your reading of this section, can you explain what is wrong with Kvack's love for the wooden dummy?

Answers: Research shows that similarity is the best predictor of long-term relationships. As shown here, however, many people ignore dissimilarities and hope that their chosen partner will change over time.

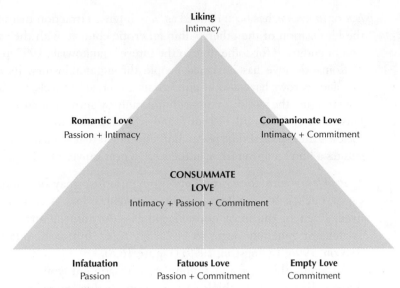

Figure 16.7 The triangle of love According to Sternberg, love is based on three central, inner components (intimacy, passion, and commitment), with "lesser" feelings located outside.

section, we explore three perspectives on love—*Sternberg's theory, romantic love*, and *companionate love*.

Sternberg's Triangular Theory of Love Are you lucky in love? Eminent psychologist Robert J. Sternberg was not! So he did what any dyed-in-the-wool researcher might do—he studied it. Sternberg, a well-known researcher on creativity, wisdom, critical thinking, and intelligence (recall his *Triarchic Theory of Intelligence*, Chapter 8), researched his own love problems and produced another triarchic (triangular) theory—this time for love (Sternberg, 1986, 1988, 2006) (Figure 16.7). His three key components are based on feelings of:

- *Intimacy*—emotional closeness and connectedness, mutual trust, friendship, warmth, private sharing of self-disclosure, and forming of "love maps."

- *Passion*—sexual attraction and desirability, physical excitement, "a state of intense longing to be with the other."

- *Commitment*—permanence and stability, the decision to stay in the relationship for the long haul, and the feelings of security that go with this intention.

For Sternberg, a healthy degree of all three components in both partners characterizes the fullest form of love, *consummate love*, and other research agrees that these three components are all "positively correlated with successful relationships" (Martin, 2008). Trouble occurs when one of the partners has higher or lower need for one or more of the components. For example, if one partner has a much higher need for intimacy and the other partner has a stronger interest in passion, this lack of compatibility can be fatal to the relationship—unless the partners are willing to compromise and strike a mutually satisfying balance (Sternberg, 1988).

Would you like to see how your relationship measures up on Sternberg's "triangle of love"? Take this "love test": http:webhome.idirect.com/%7Ekehamilt/ipsylovetest.html

Try this second link for even more information on Sternberg's research and theory. The love you save might be your own! www.psychologytoday.com/articles/200007/whats-your-love-story

Romantic Love When you think of romantic love, do you think of falling in love, a magical experience that puts you on cloud nine? **Romantic love**, also called *passionate*

Sternberg's Triangular Theory of Love The fullest form of love, consummate love, depends on a healthy degree of three components—*intimacy, passion*, and *commitment*

Romantic Love Intense feeling of attraction to another within an erotic context and with future expectations

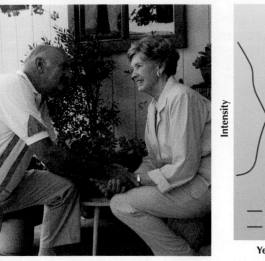

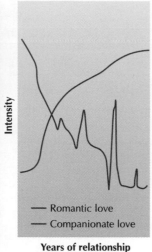

Figure 16.8 Love over the life span Romantic love is high in the beginning of a relationship but tends to diminish over time, with periodic resurgences or "spikes." Companionate love usually increases over time (e.g., this couple just celebrated their 60th wedding anniversary).

Companionate Love Strong and lasting attraction characterized by trust, caring, tolerance, and friendship

love or *limerence*, has been defined as "any intense attraction that involves the idealization of the other, within an erotic context, with the expectation of enduring for some time in the future" (Jankowiak, 1997, p. 8).

Romantic love has intrigued people throughout history. Its intense joys and sorrows have also inspired countless poems, novels, movies, and songs around the world. A cross-cultural study by anthropologists William Jankowiak and Edward Fischer found romantic love in 147 of the 166 societies they studied. The researchers concluded that "romantic love constitutes a human universal or, at the least, a near universal" (1992, p. 154).

Problems with Romantic Love Romantic love may be almost universal, but it's not problem free. First, romantic love is typically short lived. Even in the most devoted couples, the intense attraction and excitement generally begin to fade after 6 to 30 months (Hatfield & Rapson, 1996; Livingston, 1999) (Figure 16.8).

Although this research finding may disappoint you, as a critical thinker do you really think any emotion of this intensity could last forever? What would happen if other intense emotions, such as anger or joy, were eternal? Moreover, given the time-consuming nature of romantic love, what would happen to other parts of our lives, such as school, career, and family?

Another major problem with romantic love is that it is largely based on mystery and fantasy. People fall in love with others not necessarily as they are but as they want them to be (Fincham & Cui, 2011; Fletcher & Kerr, 2010; Fletcher & Simpson, 2000; Levine, 2001). What happens to these illusions when we are faced with everyday interactions and long-term exposure? Our "beautiful princess" isn't supposed to snore. And our "knight in shining armor" doesn't look very knightly flossing his teeth. And, of course, no princess or knight would ever notice our shortcomings, let alone comment on them.

How can we keep romantic love alive? One of the best ways to fan the flames is through some form of frustration that keeps you from fulfilling your desire for the presence of your love. Researchers have found that this type of interference (for example, the parents in Shakespeare's *Romeo and Juliet*) often increases the feelings of love (Driscoll, Davis, & Lipetz, 1972).

Because romantic love depends on uncertainty and fantasy, it can also be kept alive by situations in which we never really get to know the other person. This may explain why computer chat room romances or old high school sweethearts have such a tug on our emotions. Because we never really get to test these relationships, we can always fantasize about what might have been.

One of the most constructive ways of keeping romantic love alive is to recognize its fragile nature and nurture it with carefully planned surprises, flirting, flattery, and special dinners and celebrations. In the long run, however, romantic love's most important function might be to keep us attached long enough to move on to companionate love.

Companionate Love **Companionate love** is based on admiration and respect, combined with deep feelings of caring for the person and commitment to the relationship. Studies of close friendships show that satisfaction grows with time as we come to recognize the value of companionship and of having an intimate confidante (Gottman, 2011; Kim & Hatfield, 2004; Regan, 2011). Unlike romantic love, which is very short lived, companionate love seems to grow stronger with time and often lasts a lifetime (Figure 16.8).

Companionate love is what we feel for our best friends. It also is the best bet for a strong and lasting marriage. But finding and keeping a long-term companionate love is no easy task. Many of our expectations for love are based on romantic fantasies and unconscious programming from fairy tales and TV shows in which everyone lives happily ever after. Therefore, we are often ill equipped to deal with the hassles and boredom that come with any long-term relationship.

One tip for maintaining companionate love is to *overlook each other's faults.* Studies of both dating and married couples find that people report greater satisfaction with—and stay longer in—relationships where they have a somewhat idealized or unrealistically positive perception of their partner (Barelds & Dijkstra, 2011; Campbell et al., 2001; Fletcher & Simpson, 2000; Regan, 2011). This makes sense in light of research on cognitive dissonance (discussed earlier). Idealizing our mates allows us to believe we have a good deal—and hence avoids the cognitive dissonance that might naturally arise every time we saw an attractive alternative. As Benjamin Franklin wisely put it, "Keep your eyes wide open before marriage, half shut afterwards."

CHECK & REVIEW

STOP *Before going on, be sure to complete this Check & Review. It is an invaluable study tool!*

Our Feelings About Others

Part A: Retrieval Practice

1. Without looking at the book, spend 10 minutes writing a free-form essay recalling all you can remember from the previous section.

2. Now, reread the previous section, and once again spend 10 minutes writing a free-form essay on the SAME material.

Part B: Practice Quiz

1. Explain how prejudice differs from discrimination.

2. Saying that members of another ethnic group "all look alike to me" may be an example of _____. (a) ingroup favoritism; (b) the outgroup homogeneity (c) outgroup negativism; (d) ingroup bias

3. Which of the three key factors in attraction is most important in your own life?

4. Compare the dangers associated with romantic love with the benefits of companionate love.

Check your answers in Appendix B.

Our Actions Toward Others

Having just completed our whirlwind examination of how our thoughts and emotions influence others—and vice versa—we turn to topics associated with actions toward others. We begin with a look at social influence (conformity and obedience) and then continue with group processes (membership and decision making). We conclude by exploring two opposite kinds of behavior—aggression and altruism.

Social Influence: Conformity and Obedience

Our culture teaches us to believe certain things, feel certain ways, and act in accordance with these beliefs and feelings. These influences are so strong and so much a part of who we are that we rarely recognize them. Just as a fish doesn't know it's in water, we are largely unaware of the strong impact cultural and social factors have on all our behaviors. In this section, we will discuss two kinds of *social influence*: conformity and obedience.

Conformity—Going Along with Others

Objective 16.11: Define conformity, and explain the three factors that contribute to this behavior.

Imagine that you have volunteered for a psychology experiment on perception. You are seated around a table with six other students. You are all shown a card with three lines labeled A,

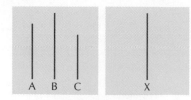

Figure 16.9 Solomon Asch's study of conformity Participants were shown four lines such as these and then asked which line (A, B, or C) was most similar to the one on the right (X).

Figure 16.10 Norms for personal space Culture and socialization have a lot to do with shaping norms for personal space. If someone invades the invisible "personal bubble" around our bodies, we generally feel very uncomfortable. People from Mediterranean, Muslim, and Latin American countries tend to maintain smaller interpersonal distances than do North Americans and Northern Europeans (Axtell, 2007; Steinhart, 1986). Children also tend to stand very close to others until they are socialized to recognize and maintain a greater personal distance. Furthermore, friends stand closer than strangers, women tend to stand closer than men, and violent prisoners prefer approximately three times the personal space of nonviolent prisoners (Axtell, 2007; Gilmour & Walkey, 1981; Lawrence & Andrews, 2004).

B, and C, as in Figure 16.9. *You are then asked to select the line that is closest in length to a fourth line, X.*

At first, everyone agrees on the correct line. On the third trial, however, the first participant selects line A, obviously a wrong answer. When the second, third, fourth, and fifth participants also say line A, you really start to wonder: "What's going on here? Are they blind? Or am I?"

What do you think you would do at this point in the experiment? Would you stick with your convictions and say line B, regardless of what the others have answered? Or would you go along with the group?

In the original version of this experiment, conducted by Solomon Asch (1951), six of the seven participants were actually confederates of the experimenter (that is, they were working with the experimenter and purposely gave wrong answers). Their incorrect responses were actually designed to test the participant's degree of **conformity**.

More than one-third of Asch's participants conformed—they agreed with the group's obviously incorrect choice. In contrast, participants in a control group experienced no group pressure and almost always chose correctly. Surprisingly, Asch's study has been conducted dozens of times, in at least 17 countries, and always with similar results (Baumeister & Vohs, 2011; Mori & Arai, 2010; Takano & Sogon, 2008).

Why would so many people conform? To the onlooker, conformity is often difficult to understand. Even the conformer sometimes has a hard time explaining his or her behavior. Let's look at three factors that drive conformity:

- *Normative social influence* Have you ever asked what others are wearing to a party, or watched your dining companion to decide what fork to use at an expensive dinner party? Such inquiries reflect our shared need for approval and acceptance by the group, a process called **normative social influence**. **Norms** are unwritten rules for behavior that are adhered to by members of a group. Most norms are quite subtle and implicit, like the one for personal space (Figure 16.10).

- *Informational social influence* Like most of us, you've probably asked for advice and even bought a specific product simply because of friends' recommendations. We conform in this case not to gain their approval (the previous *normative social influence*). We conform because we assume they have more information than we do. Participants in Asch's experiment observed all the other participants giving unanimous decisions on the length of the lines, so they logically may have conformed because they believed the others had more information.

- *Reference groups* The third major factor in conformity is the power of **reference groups**—people we most admire, like, and want to resemble. Attractive actors and popular sports stars are paid millions of dollars to endorse products because advertisers know that we want to be as cool as Wesley Snipes or as beautiful as Jennifer Lopez. Of course, we also have more important reference groups in our lives—parents, friends, family members, teachers, religious leaders, and so on.

Conformity Changing behavior because of real or imagined group pressure

Normative Social Influence Conforming to group pressure out of a need for approval and acceptance

Norm Cultural rule of behavior prescribing what is acceptable in a given situation

Informational Social Influence Conforming because of a need for information and direction

Reference Groups People we conform to, or go along with, because we like and admire them and want to be like them

TRY THIS YOURSELF

A Personal Test of Personal Space

Approach a fellow student on campus and ask for directions to the bookstore, library, or some other landmark. As you are talking, move toward the person until you invade his or her personal space. You should be close enough to almost touch toes. How does the person respond? How do you feel? Now repeat the process with another student. This time try standing 5 to 6 feet away while asking directions. Which procedure was most difficult for you? Most people think this will be a fun assignment. However, they often find it extremely difficult to willingly break our culture's unwritten norms for personal space.

Obedience—Going Along with a Command

Objective 16.12: Define obedience and describe Milgram's classic study.

As we've seen, conformity involves going along with the group. A second form of social influence, **obedience,** involves going along with a direct command, usually from someone in a position of authority.

Conformity and obedience aren't always bad. In fact, most people conform and obey most of the time because it is in their own best interest (and everyone else's) to do so (Figure 16.11). Like most North Americans, you stand in line at the movie theater instead of pushing ahead of others. This allows an orderly purchasing of tickets. Conformity and obedience allow social life to proceed with safety, order, and predictability.

On some occasions, however, it is important not to conform or obey. We don't want teenagers (or adults) engaging in risky sex or drug use just to be part of the crowd. And we don't want soldiers (or anyone else) mindlessly following orders just because they were told to do so by an authority figure. Because recognizing and resisting destructive forms of obedience are particularly important to our society, we'll explore this material in greater depth at the end of this chapter. For the moment, imagine yourself as a volunteer in the following situation: (The setup for the experiment is illustrated in Concept Organizer 16.1.)

Obedience Following direct commands, usually from an authority figure

You have responded to a newspaper ad seeking participants for a study at Yale University. When you show up at the laboratory, an experimenter explains to you and another participant that he is studying the effects of punishment on learning and memory. You are selected to play the role of the "teacher." The experimenter leads you into a room where he straps the other participant—the "learner"—into a chair. He applies electrode paste to the learner's wrist "to avoid blisters and burns" and attaches an electrode that is connected to a shock generator.

You are led into an adjacent room and told to sit in front of this same shock generator, which is wired through the wall to the chair of the learner. The shock machine consists of 30 switches representing successively higher levels of shock, from 15 volts to 450 volts. Written labels appear below each group of switches, ranging from "Slight Shock" to "Danger: Severe Shock," all the way to "XXX." The experimenter explains that it is your job to teach the learner a list of word pairs and to punish any errors by administering a shock. With each wrong answer, you are to increase the shock by one level.

You begin teaching the word pairs, but the learner's responses are often wrong. Before long, you are inflicting shocks that you can only assume must be extremely painful because the learner is moaning and protesting. In fact, after you administer 150 volts, the learner begins to shout; "Get me out of here. . . . I refuse to go on."

Figure 16.11 Advantages of conformity and obedience These people willingly obey the firefighters who order them to evacuate a building, and many lives are saved. What would happen to our everyday functioning if most people refused to go along with the crowd or obey orders?

ConceptOrganizer16.1

What Influences Obedience?

Objective 16.13: Identify the four key factors in obedience.

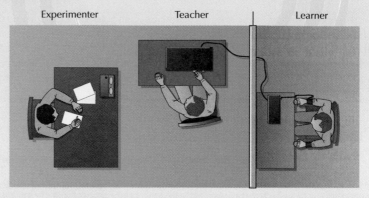

Experimenter   Teacher   Learner

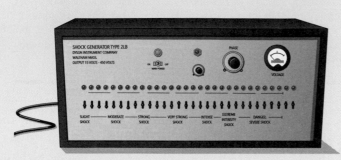

Milgram's Shock Generator

Under orders from an experimenter, would you shock a man with a known heart condition who is screaming and begging to be released? Few people believe they would. But research shows otherwise. As you can see in the first bar on the graph below, 65 percent of the participants in Milgram's original study gave the learner the full 450-volt level of shocks.

Milgram conducted a series of studies to discover the specific conditions that either increased or decreased obedience to authority:

Four Factors in Obedience

1) Legitimacy and closeness of the authority figure

When orders came from an ordinary person, and when the experimenter left the room and gave orders by phone, the participants' obedience dropped to 20 percent. (Bar B on graph.)

2) Remoteness of the victim

When the "learner" was only 1 1/2 feet away from the teacher, obedience dropped to 40 percent. When the teacher had to actually hold the learner's hand on the shock plate, obedience was only 30 percent. (Bars C and D on graph.)

3) Assignment of responsibility

When the teacher was responsible for choosing the level of shock, only 3 percent obeyed. (Bars E and F on graph.)

4) Modeling or imitating others

When teachers watched two other teachers disobey, their own obedience was only 10 percent. But after watching other teachers obey, their own obedience jumped to over 70 percent (Milgram, 1963, 1974). (Bars G and H on graph.)

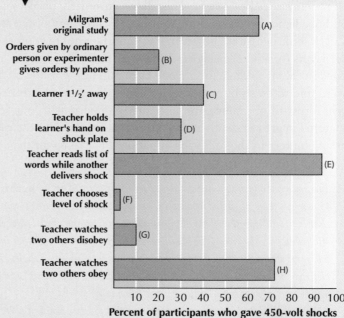

Milgram's original study (A)
Orders given by ordinary person or experimenter gives orders by phone (B)
Learner 1¹/₂' away (C)
Teacher holds learner's hand on shock plate (D)
Teacher reads list of words while another delivers shock (E)
Teacher chooses level of shock (F)
Teacher watches two others disobey (G)
Teacher watches two others obey (H)

10 20 30 40 50 60 70 80 90 100
Percent of participants who gave 450-volt shocks

You hesitate, but the experimenter tells you to continue. He insists that even if the learner refuses to answer, you must keep increasing the shock levels. But the other person is obviously in pain. What should you do?

Actual participants in this research—the "teachers"—suffered real conflict and distress when confronted with this problem. They sweated, trembled, stuttered, laughed nervously, and repeatedly protested that they did not want to hurt the learner. But still they obeyed.

The psychologist who designed this study, Stanley Milgram, was actually investigating not punishment and learning but obedience to authority. What do you think happened? Would participants obey the experimenter's prompts and commands to shock another human being?

In Milgram's public survey, fewer than 25 percent thought they would go beyond 150 volts. And no respondents predicted they would go past the 300-volt level. Yet 65 percent of the teacher-participants in this series of studies obeyed completely—going all the way to the end of the scale. They even went beyond the point when the "learner" (Milgram's confederate, who actually received no shocks at all) stopped responding altogether.

Even Milgram was surprised by his results. Before the study began, he polled a group of psychiatrists, and they predicted that most people would refuse to go beyond 150 volts and that less than 1 percent of those tested would "go all the way." The psychiatrists generally agreed that only someone who was "disturbed and sadistic" would obey to the fullest extent. But, as Milgram discovered, most of his participants—men and women, of all ages, and from all walks of life—administered the highest voltage. The study was replicated many times and in many other countries, with similarly high levels of obedience.

Being the psychological scientist that he was, Milgram wanted to follow up on his original experiment to find out exactly what conditions would increase or decrease obedience. As you can see in Concept Organizer 16.1, he identified four major factors: (1) *legitimacy and closeness of the authority figure*, (2) *remoteness of the victim*, (3) *assignment of responsibility*, and (4) *modeling or imitating others* (Blass, 1991, 2000; De Vos, 2010; Meeus & Raaijmakers, 1989; Pina e Cunha, Rego, & Clegg, 2010; Snyder, 2003).

Important Reminders Many people remain upset by Milgram's findings and seriously question the treatment of his research participants. Deception is a necessary part of some research, but the degree of deception and discomfort of participants in Milgram's research is now viewed as highly unethical. Although there have been several recent *partial* replications of Milgram's study (e.g., Burger, 2009), Milgram's original setup would never be allowed given today's research standards. Keep in mind, however, that Milgram carefully debriefed every subject after the study and followed up with the participants for several months. Furthermore, most of his "teachers" reported the experience as being personally informative and valuable.

There's another very important reminder: *The "learner" was an accomplice of the experimenter and only pretended to be shocked.* Milgram provided specific scripts that they followed at every stage of the experiment. In contrast, the "teachers" were true volunteers who believed they were administering real shocks. Although they suffered and protested, in the final analysis, they still obeyed.

 **CHECK & REVIEW**  **STOP** *Before going on, be sure to complete this Check & Review. It is an invaluable study tool!*

Social Influence

Part A: Retrieval Practice

1. Without looking at the book, spend 10 minutes writing a free-form essay recalling all you can remember from the previous section.

2. Now, reread the previous section, and once again spend 10 minutes writing a free-form essay on the SAME material.

Part B: Practice Quiz

1. Explain how conformity differs from obedience.

2. The classic study showing the power of conformity on people's behavior was conducted by _____.

3. Milgram's participants thought they were participating in an experiment designed to study the effect of _____.

4. What percentage of people in Milgram's study were willing to give the highest level of shock (450 volts)?

   (a) 45 percent;   (b) 90 percent;
   (c) 65 percent;   (d) 10 percent

Check your answers in Appendix B.

Group Processes: Membership and Decision Making

Although we seldom recognize the power of group membership, social psychologists have identified several important ways that groups affect us.

Group Membership

In simple groups, such as couples or families, as well as complex groups, like classes or sports teams, each person generally plays one or more roles. These *roles* (or sets of behavioral patterns connected with particular social positions) are specifically spelled out and regulated in some groups (e.g., the different roles of teachers and students). Other roles, like being a parent, are assumed through informal learning and inference.

Objective 16.14: Discuss the importance of roles and deindividuation in Zimbardo's Stanford prison study.

Roles How do the roles that we play within groups affect our behavior? This question fascinated social psychologist Philip Zimbardo. In his famous study at Stanford University, 24 carefully screened, well-adjusted young college men were paid $15 a day for participating in a two-week simulation of prison life (Haney, Banks, & Zimbardo, 1978; Zimbardo, 1993).

The students were randomly assigned to the role of either prisoner or guard. Prisoners were "arrested," frisked, photographed, fingerprinted, and booked at the police station. They were then blindfolded and driven to the "Stanford Prison." There, they were given ID numbers, deloused, issued prison clothing (tight nylon caps, shapeless gowns, and no underwear), and locked in cells. Participants assigned to be guards were outfitted with official-looking uniforms, billy clubs, and whistles, and they were given complete control.

Not even Zimbardo foresaw how his study would turn out. Although some guards were nicer to the prisoners than others, they all engaged in some abuse of power. The slightest disobedience was often punished with degrading tasks or the loss of "privileges" (such as eating, sleeping, and washing).

As demands increased and abuses began, the prisoners became passive and depressed. Only one prisoner fought back with a hunger strike, which ended with a forced feeding by the guards. Four prisoners had to be released within the first 4 days because of severe psychological reactions. And the entire study was stopped after only 6 days because of the alarming psychological changes in all participants. (It was originally planned to last 2 weeks.)

Although this was not a true experiment in that it lacked control groups and clear measurements of the dependent variable (Chapter 1), it offers insights into the potential effects of roles on individual behavior. According to interviews conducted after the study, the students became so absorbed in their roles that they forgot they were *volunteers* in a university study (Zimbardo, Ebbeson, & Maslach, 1977). For them the simulated *roles* of prisoner or guard became real—too real (Figure 16.12).

Many have criticized the ethics of Zimbardo's study, and it could never be replicated today. It does, however, alert us to potentially serious dangers inherent in roles and group membership. Consider the following: If this type of personality disintegration and abuse of power could be generated in a mere 6 days in a mock prison with fully informed volunteers, what happens during life imprisonment, 6-year sentences, or even overnight jail stays? Similarly, what might happen when military personnel, who are under tremendous pressure, are put in charge of guarding deadly enemies (Figure 16.13)?

What should we learn from this study? According to Stanford Magazine editor, Kevin Cool (2011), "the primal intensity of power combined with a lack of governing authority can twist anyone into a monster, momentarily. Hard though it is to admit it, we should never forget who we really are" (p. 4).

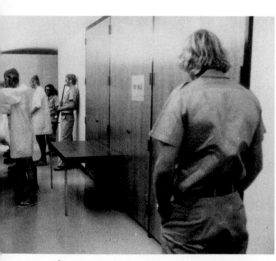

▲ **Figure 16.12 Power corrupts**
Zimbardo's prison study showed how the demands of roles and situations could produce dramatic changes in behavior in just a few days.

TEST YOURSELF

Figure 16.13 Zimbardo's study and the real world Do you remember the prisoner abuse scandal at the Iraqi Abu Ghraib prison in 2004? When these degrading photos surfaced of U.S. military guards smiling as they posed next to naked prisoners at Abu Ghraib, people around the world were shocked and outraged. Politicians and military officials claimed that the abuses were the "vile acts of a few bad soldiers" and a "gross aberration for U.S. soldiers" (Cool, 2011; De Vos, 2010; Miller, 2011; Ratnesar, 2011; Ripley, 2004; Warner, 2004; Zimbardo, 2007). Can you use information from Zimbardo's Stanford prison study to offer other explanations for the guards' behaviors?

Deindividuation Zimbardo's prison study also demonstrates an interesting phenomenon called **deindividuation**. To be deindividuated means that you feel less self-conscious, less inhibited, and less personally responsible as a member of a group than when you're alone. This is particularly likely under conditions of anonymity. To increase allegiance and conformity, groups sometimes actively encourage deindividuation, such as by requiring uniforms or masks. Unfortunately, deindividuation sometimes leads to abuses of power, angry mobs, rioters, and tragic consequences like gang rapes, lynchings, and hate crimes (Haines & Mann, 2011; Lammers & Stapel, 2011; Rodriques, Assmar, & Jablonski, 2005; Spears, 2011; Zimbardo, 2007) (Figure 16.14).

There are also positive forms of deindividuation. We all enjoy being swept along with a crowd's joyous celebration on New Year's Eve and the raucous cheering and shouting during an exciting sports competition. Deindividuation also encourages increased helping behaviors and even heroism, as we will see later in this chapter. What causes deindividuation? See Figure 16.15.

Deindividuation Reduced self-consciousness, inhibition, and personal responsibility that sometimes occurs in a group, particularly when the members feel anonymous

▲ **Figure 16.14 Deindividuation** In the classic movie *To Kill a Mockingbird*, a young girl (named Scout) asked one of the angry lynch mob members about his son. Her simple question destroyed the mob's feeling of anonymity and deindividuation. Once this happened, their anger subsided and they slowly (and harmlessly) dispersed.

▲ **Figure 16.15 Lost in the crowd** One of the most compelling explanations for deindividuation is the fact that the presence of others tends to increase arousal and feelings of anonymity. Anonymity is a powerful disinhibitor, helping to explain why vandalism seems to increase on Halloween (when people commonly wear masks) and why most crimes and riots occur at night—under the cover of darkness.

Group Decision Making

Objective 16.15: How do group polarization and groupthink affect group decision making?

We have seen that the groups we belong to and the roles that we play within them influence how we think about ourselves. But how do groups affect our decisions? Are two heads truly better than one?

Group Polarization People generally assume that group decisions are better because they're more conservative, cautious, and middle-of-the-road than individual decisions. Is this true? Initial investigations indicated that after discussing an issue, groups actually support *riskier* decisions than ones they made as individuals before the discussion (Stoner, 1961).

Subsequent research on this so-called *risky-shift phenomenon* found mixed results. Some groups did support riskier decisions, but others actually became more conservative (Liu & Latané, 1998). Interestingly, researchers discovered that the final decision (risky or conservative) depends primarily on the dominant *preexisting tendencies* of the group. If the dominant initial position is risky, the final decision will be even riskier, and the reverse is true if the initial position is conservative—a process called **group polarization**. Why? It appears that as individuals interact and share their opinions, they pick up new and more persuasive information that supports their original opinions (Baumeister & Bushman, 2011; Tindale & Posavec, 2011; Yaniv, 2011).

How is this important to your everyday life? Most of our daily interactions are with family, friends, and work buddies who share our basic values and beliefs. The danger is that when most of our information comes only from these like-minded people, we're more likely to make extreme, polarized decisions. Thus, when making important decisions, like what career to pursue, or when to buy or sell a home or stocks, we need to seek out more objective information outside our likeminded groups.

Groupthink A related phenomenon is **groupthink** (Step-by-Step Diagram 16.2). When a group is highly cohesive (a family, a panel of military advisers, an athletic team), the members' desire for agreement may lead them to ignore important information or points of view held by outsiders—especially when it is contradictory.

Many presidential errors—from Franklin Roosevelt's failure to anticipate the attack on Pearl Harbor to the losses of the space shuttles *Challenger* and *Columbia*, the terrorist attack of September 11, and the war in Iraq—have been blamed on groupthink (Barlow, 2008; Burnette, Pollack, & Forsyth, 2011; Ehrenreich, 2004; Janis, 1972, 1989; Landay & Kuhnehenn, 2004; Post, 2011; Strozier, 2011). Because most informal, political, or business groups consist of likeminded individuals, discussion generally only reinforces the group's original opinion. Thus, the group's preexisting tendencies are strengthened by the group discussion (Figure 16.16).

Group Polarization Group's movement toward either riskier or more conservative behavior, depending on the members' initial dominant tendency

Groupthink Faulty decision making that occurs when a highly cohesive group strives for agreement and avoids inconsistent information

Figure 16.16 Juries and group polarization Is group polarization a desirable part of jury deliberation? Yes and no. In an ideal world, attorneys from both sides present the facts of the case. Then, after careful deliberation, the jury moves from its initially neutral position toward the defendant to a more extreme position—either conviction or acquittal. In a not-so-ideal world, the quality of legal arguments from opposing sides may not be equal, the individual members of the jury may not be neutral at the start, and some jurors may unduly influence other jurors.

Step-by-StepDiagram16.2

STOP This Step by Step diagram contains essential information NOT found elsewhere in the text, which is likely to appear on quizzes and exams. Be sure to study it CAREFULLY!

Groupthink

Antecedent Conditions

1 A highly cohesive group of decision makers
2 Insulation of the group from outside influences
3 A directive leader
4 Lack of procedures to ensure careful consideration of the pros and cons of alternative actions
5 High stress from external threats with little hope of finding a better solution than that favored by the leader

↓

Strong desire for group consensus—the groupthink tendency

↓

Symptoms of Groupthink

1 Illusion of invulnerability
2 Belief in the morality of the group
3 Collective rationalizations
4 Stereotypes of outgroups
5 Self-censorship of doubts and dissenting opinions
6 Illusion of unanimity
7 Direct pressure on dissenters

↓

Symptoms of Poor Decision Making

1 An incomplete survey of alternative courses of action
2 An incomplete survey of group objectives
3 Failure to examine risks of the preferred choice
4 Failure to reappraise rejected alternatives
5 Poor search for relevant information
6 Selective bias in processing information
7 Failure to develop contingency plans

↓

Low probability of successful outcome

◄ (a) The process of groupthink begins when group members feel a strong sense of cohesiveness and isolation from the judgments of qualified outsiders. Add a directive leader and little chance of debate, and you have the recipe for a potentially dangerous decision.

▲

(b) Few people realize that the decision to marry can be a form of groupthink. (Remember that a "group" can have as few as two members.) When planning for marriage, a couple may show symptoms of groupthink such as an illusion of invulnerability ("We're different—we won't ever get divorced"), collective rationalizations ("Two can live more cheaply than one"), shared stereotypes of the outgroup ("Couples with problems just don't know how to communicate"), and pressure on dissenters ("If you don't support our decision to marry, we don't want you at the wedding!").

CHECK & REVIEW

STOP Before going on, be sure to complete this Check & Review. It is an invaluable study tool!

Group Processes

Part A: Retrieval Practice

1. Without looking at the book, spend 10 minutes writing a free-form essay recalling all you can remember from the previous section.
2. Now, reread the previous section, and once again spend 10 minutes writing a free-form essay on the SAME material.

Part B: Practice Quiz

1. Zimbardo stopped his prison study before the end of the scheduled 2 weeks because _____.

2. During _____, a person who feels anonymous within a group or crowd experiences an increase in arousal and a decrease in self-consciousness, inhibitions, and personal responsibility.

3. The critical factor in deindividuation is _____. (a) loss of self-esteem; (b)

anonymity; (c) identity diffusion; (d) group cohesiveness

4. What are the major symptoms of groupthink?

5. Overlooking serious problems in their relationship, a couple decides to marry because they believe they're very different from couples who divorce. This may be an example of _____. (a) mind

guarding; (b) stereotypes of the out group; (c) illusion of invulnerability; (d) none of these options

Check your answers in Appendix B.

Aggression: Explaining and Controlling It

Objective 16.16: Define aggression, and identify the biological and psychosocial factors that contribute to its expression.

Aggression is any form of behavior intended to harm or injure another living being. Why do people act aggressively? We will explore a number of possible explanations for aggression—both *biological* and *psychosocial*. Then we will look at how aggression can be controlled or reduced.

Aggression Any behavior intended to harm someone

Biological Factors

Instincts Because aggression has such a long history and is found in all cultures, many theorists believe that humans are instinctively aggressive. Evolutionary psychologists and ethologists (scientists who study animal behavior) believe that aggression evolved because it prevents overcrowding and allows the strongest animals to win mates and reproduce (Buss, 2008, 2011; Durrant & Ward, 2011; Glenn, Kurzban, & Raine, 2011; Kardong, 2008). Most social psychologists, however, reject the view that instincts drive aggression.

Genes Twin studies suggest that some individuals are genetically predisposed to have hostile, irritable temperaments and to engage in aggressive acts (Haberstick et al., 2006; Hartwell, 2008; Rhee & Waldman, 2011; Weyandt, Verdi, & Swentosky, 2011). Remember, though, that biology interacts with social experience to shape behavior.

Brain and Nervous System Electrical stimulation and the severing of specific parts of an animal's brain have direct effects on aggression. Research with brain injuries and organic disorders has also identified possible aggression circuits in the brain (Denson, 2011; Hammond & Hall, 2011; Pardini et al., 2011; Siever, 2008).

Substance Abuse and Other Mental Disorders Substance abuse (particularly alcohol) is a major factor in most forms of aggression (Tremblay, Graham, & Wells, 2008; Levinthal, 2011). Homicide rates also are higher among people with schizophrenia and antisocial disorders, particularly if they abuse alcohol (Fazel et al., 2010; Garno, Gunawardane, & Goldberg, 2008; Haddock & Shaw, 2008; Lynne-Landsmann et al., 2011; Mauri et al., 2011; Payer, Lieberman, & London, 2011).

Hormones and Neurotransmitters Studies have linked the male hormone testosterone with aggressive behavior (Geniole, Carré, & McCormick, 2011; Hermans, Ramsey, & van Honk, 2008; Juntii, Coats, & Shah, 2008; Popma et al., 2007; Sanchez-Martin et al., 2011). Violent behavior has also been correlated with lowered levels of the neurotransmitters serotonin and GABA (gamma-aminobutyric acid) (Kovacic et al., 2008; Siever, 2008; Takahashi et al., 2011).

Psychosocial Factors

Aversive Stimuli Noise, heat, pain, bullying, insults, and foul odors all can increase aggression (Anderson, 2001; Anderson, Buckley, & Carnegy, 2008; Barash & Lipton, 2011; Monks, Ortega-Ruiz, & Rodriguez-Hildalgo, 2008). According to the

Nature or nurture? From a very early age, Andrew Golden was taught to fire hunting rifles. At the age of 11, he and his friend Mitchell Johnson killed four classmates and a teacher at an elementary school in Jonesboro, Arkansas. Was this tragedy the result more of nature or nurture?

frustration–aggression hypothesis, developed by John Dollard and colleagues (1939), another aversive stimulus—frustration—creates anger, which for some leads to aggression.

Culture and Learning Social-learning theory (Chapter 6) suggests that people raised in a culture with aggressive models will learn aggressive responses (Cohen & Leung, 2011; Matsumoto & Juang, 2008; Rhee & Waldman, 2011). For example, the United States has a high rate of violent crimes, and American children grow up with numerous models for aggression, which they tend to imitate.

Violent Media The media may contribute to aggression in both children and adults. However, the research is controversial (e.g., Ferguson, 2011) and the link between violent media and aggression appears to be at least a two-way street. Laboratory studies, correlational research, and cross-cultural studies have found that exposure to TV violence increases aggressiveness and that aggressive children tend to seek out violent programs (Barlett, Harris, & Bruey, 2008; Carnagey, Anderson, & Bartholow, 2007; Giumetti & Markey, 2007; Kalnin et al., 2011; Krahné et al., 2011).

Reducing Aggression

Objective 16.17: Describe three approaches to reducing aggression.

Some therapists advise people to release aggressive impulses by engaging in harmless forms of aggression, such as exercising vigorously, punching a pillow, or watching competitive sports. But studies suggest that this type of *catharsis*, or "draining the aggression reservoir," doesn't really help (Bushman, 2002; Kuperstok, 2008). In fact, as we pointed out in Chapter 12, expressing an emotion, anger or otherwise, tends to intensify the feeling rather than reduce it.

A second approach, which does seem to effectively reduce or control aggression and stress, is to introduce *incompatible responses*. Certain emotional responses, such as empathy and humor, are incompatible with aggression. Thus, purposely making a joke or showing some sympathy for the other person's point of view can reduce anger and frustration (Garrick, 2006; Kassin, Fein, & Markus, 2008; Kaukiainen et al., 1999; Oshima, 2000; Weiner, 2006).

A third approach to controlling aggression is to improve social and communication skills. Studies show that poor communication accounts for a disproportionate share of the violence in society (Babcock et al., 2011; Gordis, Margolin, & Vickerman, 2005; Hettrich & O'Leary, 2007; Kassinove, 2007). Unfortunately, little effort is made in our schools or families to teach basic communication skills or techniques for conflict resolution.

Altruism: Why We Help (and Don't Help) Others

Objective 16.18: Define altruism, and describe the three models that attempt to explain it.

After reading about prejudice, discrimination, and aggression, you will no doubt be relieved to discover that human beings also behave in positive ways. People help and support one another by donating blood, giving time and money to charities, helping stranded motorists, and so on. There are also times when people do not help. Lets consider both responses.

Why Do We Help?

Altruism (or prosocial behavior) refers to actions designed to help others with no obvious benefit to the helper. There are three key approaches to explaining why we help—*evolutionary*, *egoistic*, and *empathy–altruism* (Concept Organizer 16.2).

Frustration–Aggression Hypothesis Blocking of a desired goal (frustration) creates anger that may lead to aggression

Altruism Actions designed to help others with no obvious benefit to the helper

ConceptOrganizer16.2

Helping

(a) **Three Models for Helping**

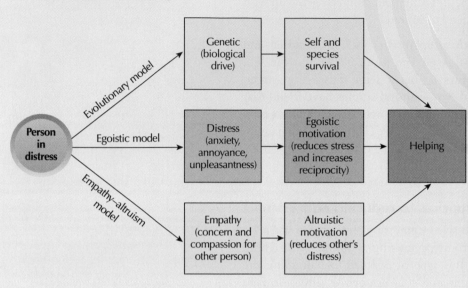

(b) **When and Why Do We Help?** According to Latané and Darley's five-step decision process, if the answer at each step is yes, help is given. If the answer is no at any point, the helping process ends.

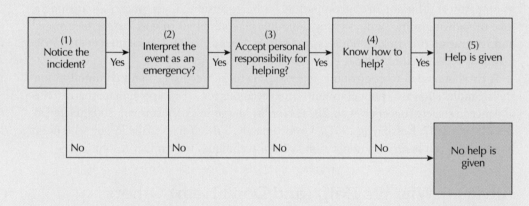

Evolutionary theory suggests that altruism is an instinctual behavior that has evolved because it favors survival of one's genes (Boyd, Richerson, & Henrich, 2011; Marshall, 2011; McNamara et al., 2008; Swami, 2011). As evidence, these theorists cite altruistic acts among lower species (e.g., worker bees cooperatively working and living only for their mother, the queen). They also point out that altruism in humans is strongest toward one's own children and other relatives. Altruism protects not the individual but the individual's genes. By helping, or even dying for, your child or sibling, you increase the odds that the genes you share will be passed on to future generations.

Other research suggests that helping may actually be a form of egoism or disguised self-interest. According to this **egoistic model**, helping is always motivated by some degree of anticipated gain. We help others because we hope for later reciprocation,

Egoistic Model Helping that's motivated by anticipated gain—later reciprocation, increased self-esteem, or avoidance of distress and guilt

592

because it makes us feel good about ourselves, or because it helps us avoid feelings of distress and guilt that loom if we don't help (Cialdini, 2009; Williams et al., 1998).

Opposing the egoistic model is the **empathy–altruism hypothesis** proposed by C. D. Batson and his colleagues (Batson, 1991, 1998, 2006, 2011; Park, Troisi, & Maner, 2011). Batson thinks some altruism is motivated by simple, selfish concerns (Concept Organizer 16.2a). In other situations, however, helping is truly selfless and motivated by concern for others (Concept Organizer 16.2b).

According to the empathy–altruism hypothesis, simply seeing another person's suffering or hearing of his or her need can create *empathy*, a subjective grasp of that person's feelings or experiences. When we feel empathic toward another, we focus on that person's distress, not our own. We're also more likely to help the person for his or her own sake. In concert with the evolutionary model, the ability to empathize may even be innate. Perceiving the emotional state of others appears to automatically activate a matching state of our own, which, in turn, increases our helping of others and our own long-term survival (Breithaupt, 2011; de Waal, 2008; Molnar-Szakacs, 2011).

Why Don't We Help?

Objective 16.19: Describe Latané and Darley's decision-making model, and other factors that help explain why we don't help.

Many theories have been proposed to explain why people help, but few explain why we do not. One of the most comprehensive explanations for helping or not helping comes from the research of Bibb Latané and John Darley (1970) (Concept Organizer 16.2b). They found that whether or not someone helps depends on a series of interconnected events and decisions. The potential helper must first *notice* what is happening, must clarify and *interpret* the event as an emergency, must accept *personal responsibility* for helping, and then must *decide how to help* and actually initiate the helping behavior.

How does this sequence explain television news reports and "caught on tape" situations in which people are robbed or attacked and no one comes to their aid? The breakdown generally comes at the third stage—*taking personal responsibility for helping*. In follow-up interviews, most onlookers report that they failed to intervene because they were certain that someone must already have called the police. Latané and Darley called this the **diffusion of responsibility** phenomenon—the dilution (or diffusion) of personal responsibility for acting by spreading it among all other group members. If you see someone drowning at the beach and you are the only person around, then responsibility falls squarely on you. But if others are present, there may be a diffusion of responsibility.

How Can We Promote Helping?

The most obvious way to increase altruistic behavior is to clarify when help is needed and then assign responsibility. For example, if you notice a situation in which it seems unclear whether someone needs help, simply ask. On the other hand, if you are the one in need of help, look directly at anyone who may be watching and give specific directions, such as "Call the police. I am being attacked!"

Helping behaviors could also be encouraged through societal rewards. Some researchers suggest that states need to enact more laws that protect the helper from potential suits. Certain existing police programs, such as Crime Stoppers, actively recruit public compliance in reporting crime, give monetary rewards, and ensure anonymity. Such programs have apparently been highly effective in reducing crime.

Empathy–Altruism Hypothesis Helping because of empathy for someone in need

Diffusion of Responsibility The dilution (or diffusion) of personal responsibility for acting by spreading it among all other group members

Aggression and Altruism

Part A: Retrieval Practice

1. Without looking at the book, spend 10 minutes writing a free-form essay recalling all you can remember from the previous section.

2. Now, reread the previous section, and once again spend 10 minutes writing a free-form essay on the SAME material.

Part B: Practice Quiz

1. What are the major biological and psychosocial factors that contribute to aggression?

2. According to research, what are the best ways to reduce aggression?

3. How do evolutionary theorists, the egoistic model, and the empathy–altruism hypothesis explain altruism?

4. Onlookers to crimes sometimes fail to respond to cries for help because of the _____ phenomenon.
   (a) empathy–altruism
   (b) egoistic model
   (c) inhumanity of large cities
   (d) diffusion of responsibility

Check your answers in Appendix B.

Psychology Engages

Applying Social Psychology to Social Problems: Reducing Prejudice, Discrimination, and Destructive Obedience

Each and every day of your life you're confronted with social problems. Driving or riding to work, you note how the freeways get busier each year. Camping in the wilderness, you find your favorite remote site occupied by other campers and cluttered with trash. Watching television, you check to see if the terror level is elevated and wonder if and when terrorists will attack. Reading the newspaper, you ask yourself what makes someone a suicide bomber.

Unfortunately, social psychology has been more successful in describing, explaining, and predicting social problems than in solving them. However, researchers have found several helpful techniques. In this section, we'll first explore what scientists have discovered about reducing prejudice. We'll then discuss effective ways to cope with destructive forms of obedience.

Reducing Prejudice and Discrimination

Objective 16.20: List four major approaches useful for reducing prejudice and discrimination.

Let's go hand in hand, not one before another.

WILLIAM SHAKESPEARE

What can be done to combat prejudice? Four major approaches can be used: *cooperation and common goals, intergroup contact, cognitive retraining,* and *cognitive dissonance.*

1. *Cooperation and common goals* Research shows that one of the best ways to combat prejudice is to encourage *cooperation* rather than *competition* (Cunningham, 2002; Jackson, 2011; Sassenberg et al., 2007). Muzafer Sherif and his colleagues (1966, 1998) conducted an ingenious study to show the role of competition in promoting prejudice. The researchers artificially created strong feelings of ingroup and outgroup identification in a group of 11- and 12-year-old boys at a summer camp. They did this by physically separating the boys in different cabins and assigning

different projects to each group, such as building a diving board or cooking out in the woods.

Once each group developed strong feelings of group identity and allegiance, the researchers set up a series of competitive games, including tug-of-war and touch football. They awarded desirable prizes to the winning teams. Because of this treatment, the groups began to pick fights, call each other names, and raid each other's camps. Researchers pointed to these behaviors as evidence of the experimentally produced prejudice.

After using competition to create prejudice between the two groups, the researchers demonstrated how cooperation could be successfully used to eliminate it. They created "mini-crises" and tasks that required expertise, labor, and cooperation from both groups. This time prizes were awarded to all. The hostilities and prejudice between the groups slowly began to dissipate. At the end of the camp experience, the boys voted to return home in the same bus. And the self-chosen seating did not reflect the earlier camp divisions. Sherif's study showed not only the importance of cooperation as opposed to competition but also the importance of *common goals* (resolving the minicrises) (Figure 16.17).

2. *Intergroup contact* Another approach to reducing prejudice is increasing contact between groups (Butz & Plant, 2011; Cameron, Rutland, & Brown, 2007; Dovidio, Eller, & Hewstone, 2011; Gómez & Huici, 2008; Migacheva, Tropp, & Crocker, 2011; Wagner, Christ, & Pettigrew, 2008). But as you just discovered with Sherif's study of the boys at the summer camp, contact can sometimes increase prejudice. Increasing contact only works under certain conditions: (1) *close interaction* (if minority students are "tracked" into vocational education courses and white students are primarily in college prep courses, they seldom interact and prejudice is increased), (2) *interdependence* (both groups must be involved in superordinate goals that require cooperation), and (3) *equal status* (everyone must be at the same level). Once people have positive experiences with a group, they tend to generalize their experiences to other groups.

3. *Cognitive retraining* One of the most recent strategies in prejudice reduction requires taking another's perspective or undoing associations of negative stereotypical traits (Buswell, 2006; Müller et al., 2011; Todd et al., 2011). For example, in a computer training session, North American participants were asked to *try not* to think of cultural associations when they saw a photograph of an elderly person. They were also asked to press a *no* button when they saw a photograph of an elderly person with a trait stereotypically associated with elderly people (e.g., slow, weak). Conversely, they were instructed to press a *yes* button when they saw a photograph of an elderly person with a trait not normally associated with the elderly. After a number of trials, their response times became faster and faster, indicating they were undoing negative associations and learning positive ones. Following the training, participants were less likely to activate any negative stereotype of elderly people in another activity than were others who did not participate in the training exercise (Kawakami et al., 2000).

People can also learn to be nonprejudiced if they are taught to selectively pay attention to *similarities* rather than *differences* (Motyl et al., 2011; Phillips & Ziller, 1997). When we focus on how "black voters feel about affirmative action" or how Jewish people feel about "a Jewish candidate for vice president of the United States," we are indirectly encouraging stereotypes and ingroups versus outgroups. Can you see how this might also apply to gender? By emphasizing gender differences (*Men Are from Mars, Women Are from Venus*), we may be perpetuating gender stereotypes.

4. *Cognitive dissonance* As mentioned earlier, prejudice is a type of attitude that has three basic components—affective (feelings), behavioral tendencies, and cognitive

Figure 16.17 Reducing prejudice and discrimination Tension and conflict between groups often decrease when groups cooperate and work together for a common goal. Here people of mixed ages and ethnicities work with Habitat for Humanity to build new homes for needy families.

Only equals can be friends.
ETHIOPIAN PROVERB

You cannot judge another person until you have walked a mile in his moccasins.

AMERICAN INDIAN PROVERB

(thoughts). And one of the most efficient methods to change an attitude uses the principle of *cognitive dissonance*, a perceived discrepancy between an attitude and a behavior or between an attitude and a new piece of information. Each time we meet someone who does not conform to our prejudiced views, we experience dissonance—"I thought all gay men were effeminate. This guy is a deep-voiced professional athlete. I'm confused." To resolve the dissonance, we can maintain our stereotypes by saying, "This gay man is an exception to the rule." However, if we continue our contact with a large variety of gay men, this "exception to the rule" defense eventually breaks down and attitude change occurs.

As a critical thinker, can you see how social changes, such as school busing, integrated housing, and increased civil rights legislation, might initially create cognitive dissonance that would lead to an eventual reduction in prejudice? Moreover, do you recognize how the four methods of reducing prejudice we just described also involve cognitive dissonance? Cooperation, superordinate goals, increased contact, and cognitive retraining all create cognitive dissonance for the prejudiced person. And this uncomfortable dissonance motivates the individual to eventually change his or her attitudes, thereby reducing their prejudice.

Overcoming Destructive Obedience

Objective 16.21: Identify six ways to reduce destructive obedience.

Obedience to authority is an important part of our lives. If people routinely refused to obey police officers, firefighters, and other official personnel, our individual safety and social order would collapse. However, there are also many times when obedience may be unnecessary and destructive—and should be reduced.

For example, do you remember the story of Jim Jones? In 1978, over 900 members of the People's Temple in Guyana committed mass suicide because he ordered them to do so. People who resisted were murdered. But the vast majority gave up their lives willingly by drinking cyanide-laced Kool-Aid. A less depressing example of mass obedience occurred in 1983 when 2,075 identically dressed couples were married by the Reverend Sun Myung Moon in Madison Square Garden. Although most partners were complete strangers to one another, they married because the Reverend Moon ordered them to do so.

How do we explain (and hopefully reduce) destructive obedience? In addition to all the factors associated with Milgram's study discussed earlier, social psychologists have developed other helpful theories and concepts on the general topic of obedience.

▲ **Overcoming destructive obedience** New military recruits understand that effective military action requires quick and immediate obedience. However, social psychological principles, such as socialization, the power of the situation, and groupthink, also encourage these individuals to willingly do push-ups in response to their officer's orders. Can you explain why?

- *Socialization* As mentioned before, our society and culture have a tremendous influence on all our thoughts, feelings, and actions. Obedience is no exception. From very early childhood, we're taught to respect and obey our parents, teachers, and other authority figures. Without this obedience we would have social chaos. Unfortunately, this early (and lifelong) socialization often becomes so deeply ingrained that we no longer consciously recognize it. This helps explain many instances of mindless obedience to immoral requests from people in positions of authority. For example, participants in Milgram's study came into the research lab with a lifetime of socialization toward the value of scientific research and respect for the experimenter's authority. They couldn't suddenly step outside themselves and question the morality of this particular experimenter and his orders. American soldiers accused of atrocities in Iraq or in the Abu Ghraib prison shared this general socialization toward respect for authority combined with military training requiring immediate, unquestioning obedience. Unfortunately, history is replete with instances of atrocities committed because people were "just following orders."

- ***Power of the situation*** Situational influences also have a strong impact on obedience. For example, the roles of police officer or public citizen, teacher or student, and parent or child all have built-in guidelines for appropriate behavior. One person is ultimately "in charge." The other person is supposed to follow along. Because these roles are so well socialized, we mindlessly play them and find it difficult to recognize the point where they become maladaptive. As we discovered earlier with the Zimbardo prison study, well-adjusted and well-screened college students became so absorbed in their roles of prisoners and guards that their behaviors clearly passed the point of moral behaviors. The "simple" role of being a research participant in Milgram's study—or a soldier in Vietnam, Iraq, or Afghanistan—helps explain many instances of destructive obedience.

- ***Groupthink*** When discussing Milgram's study and other instances of destructive obedience, most people believe that they and their friends would never do such a thing. Can you see how this might be a form of *groupthink*, a type of faulty thinking that occurs when group members strive for agreement and avoid inconsistent information? When we smugly proclaim that Americans would never follow orders like some German people did during World War II, we're demonstrating several symptoms of groupthink—stereotypes of the outgroup, the illusion of unanimity, belief in the morality of the group, and so on.

- ***Foot-in-the-door*** The gradual nature of many obedience situations may also help explain why so many people were willing to give the maximum shocks in Milgram's study. The initial mild level of shocks may have worked as a **foot-in-the-door technique**, in which a first, small request is used as a setup for later, larger requests (Figure 16.18). Once Milgram's participants complied with the initial request, they might have felt obligated to continue.

- ***Relaxed moral guard*** One common intellectual illusion that hinders critical thinking about obedience is the belief that only evil people do evil things or that evil announces itself. For example, the experimenter in Milgram's study looked and acted like a reasonable person who was simply carrying out a research project. Because he was not seen as personally corrupt and evil, the participants' normal moral guard was down and obedience was maximized. This relaxed moral guard might similarly explain why so many people followed Hitler's commands to torture and kill millions of Jews during World War II. Although most believe only "monsters" would obey such an order, Milgram's research suggests otherwise. He revealed the conditions that breed obedience as well as the extent to which ordinary, everyday people will mindlessly obey an authority. As philosopher Hannah Arendt has suggested, the horrifying thing about the Nazis was not that they were so deviant but that they were so "terrifyingly normal."

- ***Disobedient models*** In addition to recognizing and understanding the power of these forces, it's equally important to remember that each of us must be personally alert to immoral forms of obedience. On occasion, we also need the courage to stand up and say "No!" One of the most beautiful and historically important examples of just this type of bravery occurred in Alabama in 1955. Rosa Parks boarded a bus and, as expected in those times, she obediently sat in the back section marked "Negroes." When the bus became crowded, the driver told her to give up her seat to a white man. Surprisingly for those days, Parks refused and was eventually forced off the bus by police and arrested. This single act of disobedience was an important catalyst for the small, but growing, civil rights movement and the later repeal of Jim Crow laws in the South. Her courageous stand also inspires the rest of us to think about when it is good to obey authorities and when to disobey unethical demands from authorities (Figure 16.19).

Foot-in-the-Door Technique A first, small request is used as a setup for a later, larger request

▲ **Figure 16.18 Foot-in-the-door technique** *If this homeowner allows the salesperson to give him a small gift (a "foot-in-the-door" technique), he's more likely to agree to buy something. Can you explain why?*

▲ **Figure 16.19 The power of one!** In late October 2005, Americans mourned the passing of Rosa Parks—the "mother of the civil rights movement." History books typically emphasize her 1955 arrest and jailing for refusing to give up her bus seat to a white man. They fail to mention that this "simple" refusal threatened her job and possibly her life. (Both her mother and husband warned her that she might be lynched for her actions.) They also overlook that long before this one defiant bus ride, Parks fought hard and courageously against segregated seating on buses and for voting rights for blacks.

RESEARCH CHALLENGE

Understanding Implicit Biases

By Siri Carpenter (Science Writer, Madison, WI)

For making anti-Semitic remarks during a drunk-driving arrest, actor Mel Gibson pleaded with the public: "Please know from my heart that I am not an anti-Semite. I am not a bigot. Hatred of any kind goes against my faith." And backing away from intimations that black people are not as intelligent as whites, biologist and Nobel laureate James Watson expressed bewilderment and contrition: "I cannot understand how I could have said what I am quoted as having said. There is no scientific basis for such a belief."

Because most people have no conception of the hidden, automatic, **implicit bias** in all of us, they react with shock and alarm when prejudiced remarks surface from those they admire. The offenders are sometimes similarly perplexed. The unsettling truth is that just about any of us could have made them. Using a variety of sophisticated methods, psychologists have established that people unwittingly hold an astounding assortment of stereotypical beliefs and attitudes about social groups: black and white, female and male, elderly and young, gay and straight, fat and thin, and so on (Agerstrom & Rooth, 2011, Greenwald et al., 2009; Price, 2011; Stanley et al., 2011).

Where do such hidden biases come from? As you recall from Chapter 8, to make sense of the world around us, we naturally put things into groups and remember relations between objects and actions or adjectives. Unfortunately, many of our implicit associations about social groups form before we are old enough to consider them rationally. In a 2006 study, researchers showed that full-fledged implicit racial bias emerges by age six—and never retreats (Baron & Banaji, 2006).

Some implicit biases also appear to be rooted in strong emotions. For example, scientists have measured white people's brain activity as they viewed a series of white and black faces and found that black faces triggered greater activity in the amygdala (a brain area associated with vigilance and sometimes fear). The effect

was most pronounced among participants who demonstrated strong implicit racial bias. Provocatively, the same study revealed that when faces were shown for half a second—enough time for participants to consciously process them—black faces instead elicited heightened activity in prefrontal brain areas associated with detecting internal conflicts and controlling responses, hinting that individuals were consciously trying to suppress their implicit associations (Cunningham et al., 2004).

Overcoming Implicit Bias

Researchers long believed that because implicit associations develop early in our lives, and because we are often unaware of their influence, they may be virtually impervious to change. But recent work suggests that we can reshape our implicit attitudes and beliefs—or at least curb their effects on our behavior.

Seeing targeted groups in more favorable social contexts can help thwart biased attitudes. In laboratory studies, seeing a black face with a church as a background, instead of a dilapidated street corner, considering familiar examples of admired blacks such as President Barack Obama, actor Denzel Washington, or athlete Michael Jordan all weaken people's implicit racial and ethnic biases. Some evidence suggests that confronting implicit biases head-on with conscious effort can also work. People who report a strong personal motivation to be nonprejudiced tend to harbor less implicit bias. And some studies indicate that people who are good at using logic and willpower to control their more primitive urges, such as trained mediators, exhibit less implicit bias.

If we accept that implicit bias is an inescapable part of the human condition, then we have a choice about how to respond. We can respond with sadness or, worse, with apathy. Or we can react with a determination to overcome bias. "The capacity for change is deep and great in us," says Harvard University psychologist Mahzarin Banaji.

Detecting Implicit Bias

How do we measure these hidden, implicit attitudes? Psychologists rely on indirect tests that do not depend on people's ability or willingness to reflect on their feelings and thoughts. The most prominent method for measuring implicit bias, the *Implicit Association Test (IAT)*, measures how quickly people sort stimuli into particular categories. Do the results of the IAT translate into the real world? A recent meta-analysis found significant links between scores on the test and daily behavior (Greenwald et al., 2009). To take the IAT and "Try This Yourself," visit https://implicit.harvard.edu/implicit.

Student Engagement Exercise

Given the information in the Cunningham et al. (2004) study described above, what is the most likely:

1. *Research method* (experimental, descriptive, correlational, or biological)?

2. If you chose the:
   - *Experimental method*—label the IV, DV, experimental group, and control group.
   - *Descriptive method*—identify whether this is a naturalistic observation, survey, or case study.
   - *Correlational method*—label whether this is a positive, negative, or zero correlation.
   - *Biological method*—identify the specific research tool (e.g., brain dissection, CT scan, etc.)

(Answers appear in Appendix B.)

(*Source:* Originally published in *Scientific American Mind*, April/May, 2008, pp. 32–39. Adapted and reprinted with permission of author, Siri Carpenter.)

Implicit Bias Hidden, automatic attitude, which may serve as a guide to behaviors independent of a person's awareness or control

GENDER AND CULTURAL DIVERSITY

Is Beauty in the Eye of the Beholder?

Objective 16.22: Describe cultural and historical similarities and differences in judgments of attractiveness.

If you found the earlier discussions (pp. 576, 598) of advantages for attractiveness unnerving, you'll be even more surprised to know that some research also shows that judgments of attractiveness appear consistent across cultures. For example, in numerous cultures around the world, women are valued more for looks and youth, whereas men are valued more for maturity, ambitiousness, and financial resources (Bryan, Webster, & Mahaffey, 2011; Buss, 1989, 1990, 1994, 2005, 2008, 2011; Chang et al., 2011; Li, Valentine, & Patel, 2011; Swami, 2011).

How can this be so universally true? Evolutionary psychologists would suggest that both men and women prefer attractive people because good looks generally indicate good health, sound genes, and high fertility. For example, facial and body symmetry appear to be key elements in attractiveness (Fink et al., 2004; Little, Jones, & DeBruine, 2011; Moore et al., 2011), and symmetry seems to be correlated with genetic health. The fact that across cultures men prefer youthful appearing women is reportedly because this is a sign of their future fertility. Similarly, women prefer men with maturity and financial resources because the responsibility of rearing and nurturing children more often falls on women's shoulders. Therefore, they prefer mature men "who will stick around" and men with greater resources to invest in children.

In contrast to this seeming universal agreement on standards of attractiveness, evidence also exists that beauty is in "the eye of the beholder." What we judge as beautiful varies somewhat from era to era and culture to culture (Figure 16.20). For example, the Chinese once practiced foot binding because small feet were considered beautiful in women. All the toes except the big one were bent under a young girl's foot and into the sole. The physical distortion made it almost impossible for her to walk. And she suffered excruciating pain, chronic bleeding, and frequent infections throughout her life (Dworkin, 1974). Even in modern times, cultural demands for attractiveness encourage an increasing number of women (and men) to undergo expensive and often painful surgery to *increase* the size of their eyes, breasts, lips, chest, and penis. They also undergo surgery to *decrease* the size of their nose, ears, chin, stomach, hips, and thighs.

Figure 16.20 Culture and attraction Which of these women do you find most attractive? Can you see how your cultural background might train you to prefer one look to the others?

CRITICAL THINKING

To Kill a Mockingbird: Is Atticus Finch a Good Critical Thinker?

By Thomas Frangicetto (Northampton Community College, Bethlehem, PA)

To Kill a Mockingbird, both the 1962 movie and the classic book by Harper Lee, presents an eloquent, persuasive argument for empathy and against prejudice and bigotry.

The story is set in Alabama, 1932. Atticus, a country lawyer, has agreed to defend Tom Robinson, a black man who has been falsely accused of raping a white woman. Atticus understands the prejudice that lurks in human nature and is also well

◀ **Atticus Finch's lesson for Scout**
"If you can learn a simple trick, Scout, you'll get along better with all kinds of folks . . . you never really know a person until you see things from his point of view. . .climb into his skin and walk around in it."

aware that a Black man at that time in Alabama might be too easily used as a scapegoat. He is a man motivated purely by a need to uphold justice.

Atticus also is emphasizing the danger of putting our *self-interest ahead of the truth*—a violation of a key critical thinking component (CTC) (see the Prologue at the front of this text). Are there other valuable critical thinking lessons from this book and movie that we should learn? Let's give it a try.

Part 1 Match the following critical thinking components (CTCs), with the corresponding six excerpts of dialogue and plot descriptions that either demonstrate or violate these CTCs.

Critical Thinking Components (CTCs)

a) *Distinguishing fact from opinion*

b) *Employing precise terms*

c) *Modifying judgment in light of new information*

d) *Recognizing personal bias*

e) *Resisting overgeneralization*

f) *Valuing truth above self-interest*

Dialogue and Plot Descriptions from *To Kill a Mockingbird*

_____**1.** After a bad first day at school, Atticus asks Scout if she knows what a compromise is. "Bendin' the law?" she asks. Atticus: "Uh, no. It's an agreement reached by mutual consent. Now, here's the way it works. You concede the necessity of goin' to school, we'll keep right on readin' the same every night, just as we always have. Is that a bargain?"

_____**2.** Atticus: "... this case should never have come to trial. The state has not produced one iota of medical evidence that the crime Tom Robinson is charged with ever took place ... It has relied instead upon the testimony of two witnesses, whose evidence has not only been called into serious question on cross-examination, but has been flatly contradicted by the defendant."

_____**3.** Atticus (closing statement to jury): "... they were confident that you gentlemen would go along with them on the assumption ... the *evil* assumption that all Negroes lie, all Negroes are basically immoral beings, all Negro men are not to be trusted around our women. An assumption that one associates with minds of their caliber, and which is, in itself, gentlemen, a lie, which I do not need to point out to you."

_____**4.** Scout's brother Jim becomes angry at her when she lets her imagination get the best of her: "There you go imagining things. Just like a girl. That's why people hate girls. So if you're going to act like a girl, you go play by yourself."

_____**5.** Throughout the movie, Atticus's son and daughter are fearful of a neighbor named Boo. Although they've never seen him they describe him as a "dangerous maniac" who "eats raw squirrels and cats and drools all the time." When "Boo" saves their lives, they learn to respect him and call him by his real name, Arthur.

_____**6.** Asked why he agreed to defend Tom Robinson, Atticus says: "If I didn't, I couldn't hold up my head in town ... I'm going to defend him to the best of my ability. He may go to the chair ... but he's not going until the truth is told."

Part 2 Read *To Kill a Mockingbird*, watch the movie, and/or read the screenplay: http://www.screenplaydb.com/film/scripts/tokillamockingbird19620208/

Critical Thinking Questions

1. Which CTCs do the jury violate in finding Tom Robinson guilty? Does Atticus violate any CTCs? Try to identify six additional CTCs.

2. Reread the opening quote to this exercise. How good are you at using the "simple trick" of empathy? Has your use of empathy ever made a situation better? Worse? Explain.

(Check your answers to Part 1 in Appendix B.)

FINAL CRITICAL THINKING TAKE HOME MESSAGE

Empathy: The Core of Our Humanity

Co-authored with Thomas Frangicetto (Northampton Community College, Bethlehem, PA)

▲ **Presence of Empathy** President Obama, addressing the Japanese people following the worst earthquake in Japan's history in 2011, promised that America would help in any way possible. "Our hearts go out to our friends in Japan ... this reminds us that despite our differences in culture or religion, our humanity is one."

Does our very humanity depend on empathy? Many who study the topic believe it does (Szalavitz & Perry, 2010; Trout, 2010). Recall from Chapter 15 that *empathy is an insightful awareness and ability to share another's inner experience*—in short, to stand in another's shoes. It involves both an *emotional* reaction and an *intellectual* appraisal. Trout (2010) contends that *emotional* empathy without rational *thought* is not only blind, but also often contradicts our best intentions. Giving money to a homeless person may make us feel good about ourselves, but if that individual is an alcoholic and uses the money to feed his addiction, the noble intention is lost. Giving the money to an agency that provides food and shelter for the homeless might be a better option.

Part I: Empathy and Your Text

Empathy may well be the most important psychological force in human experience. It is not by chance that we chose it as the topic of this exercise—and as your final "take home message."

To demonstrate just how influential and all-embracing empathy is, here is a small sampling of how it ties in to several topics throughout this text:

- **Chapter 3**—Empathizing with others helps build social skills and maintain supportive relationships, which are invaluable during difficult times or stressful circumstances.

- **Chapter 6**—*Prejudice largely results from a lack of empathy. The good news is that bigotry is learned—not innate. Therefore, empathy can change it!*

- **Chapter 8**—Knowing ourselves and being able to empathize with others primes the pump of successful interpersonal interaction.
- **Chapter 9**—The inability to consider or care about another's point of view is limiting at any age. In addition, *authoritative parents* are highly involved, tender, and *emotionally supportive*, which means they are capable of *empathically* connecting with their children.
- **Chapter 10**—*Erikson's psychosocial stages and committed relationships require* being able to *empathize* with another's feelings and thoughts. *Relationship expectations* and the development of "love maps" between couples involve sharing each other's "emotional life" and also "creation of shared meaning." In addition, *family violence* studies find that perpetrators of domestic violence, child abuse, and elder abuse lack the ability to empathize with their victims.
- **Chapter 11**—Empathy can help couples share their insecurities with honesty and sensitivity, and diminish *performance anxiety*. *Rape myths* may reflect pressures from the double standard and sexual scripts, which can be lessened through empathy and a renegotiation of "appropriate" gender roles and sexual scripts.

- **Chapter 14**—*Identifying myths about mental illness and avoiding ethnocentrism* largely depend on our ability to "stand in another's shoes."
- **Chapter 15**—*Empathy* is a key component of communication and therapy.
- **Chapter 16**—*Empathy is the core of social psychology.* It's often the deciding factor in whether or not we help others, if one country comes to the aid of another or not, and, to put it bluntly, whether or not one person is capable of abusing another, especially a "loved one."

Part 2: Critical Thinking Questions

1. Identify five additional sections from this text (and/or your personal life) that you believe are directly influenced by empathy. If you prefer, choose another topic from this text that you consider most important (e.g., metacognition, active listening, unconditional positive regard), and then provide examples of how this value affects five sections from this text and/or your personal life.

2. In the Academy Award-winning documentary *Inside Job*, it is said of the Wall Street traders whose immoral behavior brought millions of innocent people to financial ruin: "There's just a blatant disregard for how their actions impact society and families." Use the Critical Thinking Prologue at the front of this text to identify three CTCs, in addition

to *empathizing*, that the U.S. financial industry violated.

3. Empathy has been called "the cornerstone of compassion." Do you agree? What is your level of empathy on disasters like the 2011 tragedy in Japan? Why is it harder to "put yourself in the shoes of other folks" when they're on the other side of the world versus next door?

4. Identify three ways that empathizing affects your life. Are there times when it is lacking? Do you want to improve your empathy skills? Check out this video: www.youtube.com/watch?v=LfeXxkbgCVE For more personal tips, click on this link: www.chacocanyon.com/pointlookout/060830.shtml

5. Do you agree that empathizing is the "core of our humanity"? We'd like to hear from you—both pro and con. This is our last best shot at offering advice from our over 120 combined years on the planet. We strongly believe that our ability to truly engage with other human beings starts and ends with empathy. Remember to take time to actively listen, to respond with authenticity and care, and to take emotional risks guided by your intellect. We wish you many years of empathetic encounters with the people you love and who love you in return. Best Wishes, Tom Frangicetto (tfrangicetto@northampton.edu) and Karen Huffman (Khuffman@palomar.edu).

CHECK & REVIEW

STOP *Before going on, be sure to complete this Check & Review. It is an invaluable study tool!*

Psychology Engages

Part A: Retrieval Practice

1. Without looking at the book, spend 10 minutes writing a free-form essay recalling all you can remember from the previous section.

2. Now, reread the previous section, and once again spend 10 minutes writing a free-form essay on the SAME material.

Part B: Practice Quiz

1. If your college or hometown were suddenly threatened by a raging wildfire, prejudice might decrease because groups would come together to fight the fire and help rebuild the community.

This is an example of how _____ is (are) important in reducing prejudice and discrimination.

2. A social influence technique in which a first, small request is used as a setup for later requests is known as _____.

3. Explain why Rosa Parks is a good example of the power of disobedient models in reducing obedience.

4. Cross-cultural research on physical attractiveness has found all but one of the following.
   (a) The Chinese once practiced foot binding because small feet were considered attractive in women.

(b) Across most cultures, men prefer youthful-appearing women.

(c) In most Eastern cultures, men prefer women with power and financial status over beauty.

(d) For men, maturity and financial resources are more important than appearance in their ability to attract a mate.

5. What was the "simple trick" Atticus Finch taught his daughter for getting along with others?

Check your answers in Appendix B.

WileyPLUS presents an on-line version of this textbook along with a wealth of study resources including quizzes, practice tests, flash cards, videos, animations and other activities designed to improve your mastery of the content. Working in conjunction with these study tools, the *Psychology in Action* WileyPLUS course features Professor Karen Huffman, author of this textbook, explaining and expanding upon some of the most challenging concepts in psychology. Here is a sample of the tutorial videos available for this chapter:

www.wileyplus.com

- An interactive, animated exploration of cognitive dissonance
- Implicit attitudes: How what we don't know can still influence us
- Professor Huffman's classroom discussion of the power of norms and norm violations
- How to reduce ambiguity and increase your safety, featuring Professor Huffman's role playing demonstration for self-defense
- Virtual Field Trip to explore the world of internet dating services, where many people are finding love online

→Key Terms

To assess your understanding of the **Key Terms** in Chapter 16, write a definition for each (in your own words), and then compare your definitions with those in the text.

social psychology (p. 567)

Our Thoughts about Others
attribution (p. 568)
fundamental attribution error (FAE) (p. 569)
saliency bias (p. 569)
just-world phenomenon (p. 569)
self-serving bias (p. 569)
attitude (p. 570)
cognitive dissonance (p. 571)

Our Feelings about Others
prejudice (p. 573)
stereotype (p. 573)
discrimination (p. 573)

ingroup favoritism (p. 575)
outgroup homogeneity effect (p. 575)
interpersonal attraction (p. 575)
proximity (p. 577)
need complementarity (p. 578)
need compatibility (p. 578)
Sternberg's triangular theory of love (p. 579)
romantic love (p. 579)
companionate love (p. 580)

Our Actions toward Others
conformity (p. 582)
normative social influence (p. 582)
norm (p. 582)
informational social influence (p. 582)

reference groups (p. 582)
obedience (p. 583)
deindividuation (p. 587)
group polarization (p. 588)
groupthink (p. 588)
aggression (p. 590)
frustration–aggression hypothesis (p. 591)
altruism (p. 591)
egoistic model (p. 592)
empathy–altruism hypothesis (p. 593)
diffusion of responsibility (p. 593)

Psychology Engages
foot-in-the-door technique (p. 597)
implicit bias (p. 598)

→Chapter Summary

Objective 16.1: What is social psychology?
Social psychology is the study of how others influence our thoughts, feelings, and actions.

Our Thoughts About Others

Objective 16.2: Describe the process of attribution and its two key errors.
Attribution is the process of explaining the causes of behaviors or events. We do this by determining whether actions resulted from internal, *dispositional* factors or external, *situational* factors. The two key errors are: (1) the **fundamental attribution error (FAE)**, which overestimates internal, dispositional factors and underestimates external, situational factors when

judging others; and (2) the **self-serving bias**, which involves taking credit for successes and externalizing failures when judging ourselves.

Objective 16.3: Describe how culture affects attributional biases.
Collectivistic cultures, like China, are less likely to make the fundamental attribution error (FAE) and the self-serving bias because they focus on interdependence and collective responsibility. In contrast, individualistic cultures, like the United States, emphasize independence and personal responsibility.

Objective 16.4: Define attitude and identify its three key components.

An **attitude** is a learned predisposition to respond cognitively, affectively, and behaviorally toward a particular object. Its three components are: (1) cognitive (thoughts and beliefs), (2) affective (feelings), and (3) behavioral (predispositions to actions).

Objective 16.5: What is cognitive dissonance, how does it change attitudes, and how does culture affect it?
Cognitive dissonance is a feeling of discomfort caused by a discrepancy between an attitude and a behavior or between two competing attitudes. This mismatch and resulting tension motivate us to change our attitude or behavior to reduce the tension and restore balance. Individualistic

cultures experience more cognitive dissonance than collectivistic cultures because our emphasis on independence and personal responsibility creates more tension when our attitudes are in conflict.

Our Feelings About Others

Objective 16.6: Define prejudice, identify its three key components, and differentiate between prejudice and discrimination.
Prejudice is a learned, generally negative, attitude directed toward members of a group. It contains all three components of attitudes—*cognitive*, *affective*, and *behavioral*. (The cognitive component involves **stereotypes**, and the behavioral component is called **discrimination**.) Prejudice refers to an attitude, whereas discrimination refers to action. The two often coincide, but not always.

Objective 16.7: Discuss the five major sources of prejudice and discrimination.
The five major sources of prejudice are *learning* (classical and operant conditioning and social learning), *personal experience*, *limited resources displaced aggression* (scapegoating), and *mental shortcuts* (categorization). Mental shortcuts involve viewing members of the ingroup more positively than members of the outgroup (**ingroup favoritism**) and seeing less diversity in the outgroup (**outgroup homogeneity effect**).

Objective 16.8: What are the three key factors in attraction?
Physical attractiveness, **proximity**, and **similarity** are the three major factors in **interpersonal attraction**. Although people commonly believe that "opposites attract" (**need complementarity**), research shows that similarity (**need compatibility**) is more important in long-term relationships.

Objective 16.9: Discuss scientific research on flirting.
People use nonverbal flirting behaviors to increase their attractiveness and signal interest. In heterosexual couples, women are more likely to use flirting to initiate courtship.

Objective 16.10: Differentiate between Sternberg's theory, and romantic and companionate love.
Sternberg's theory of love emphasizes three key components: *intimacy, passion*, and *commitment*. A healthy degree of all three leads to the fullest form of love, called *consummate love*. **Romantic love** is intense, passionate, and highly valued in our society. However, because it is based on mystery and fantasy, it is hard to sustain. **Companionate love** relies on mutual trust, respect, and friendship and seems to grow stronger with time.

Social Influence

Objective 16.11: Define conformity, and explain the three factors that contribute to this behavior.

Conformity involves changes in behavior in response to real or imagined group pressure. People conform for approval and acceptance (**normative social influence**), out of a need for more information and direction (**informational social influence**), and to match the behavior of those they admire and want to be like (**reference group**).

Objective 16.12: Define obedience and describe Milgram's classic study.
Obedience refers to following direct commands, usually from an authority figure. Milgram's study showed that a surprisingly large number of people obey orders even when they believe another human being is physically threatened.

Objective 16.13: Identify the four key factors in obedience.
Legitimacy and closeness of the authority figure, remoteness of the victim, assignment of responsibility, and modeling or imitation of others are the four major factors in obedience.

Group Processes

Objective 16.14: Discuss the importance of roles and deindividuation in Zimbardo's Stanford prison study.
Zimbardo conducted a simulated prison study assigning college students to be either prisoners or guards. The study showed that both the roles we play in groups and **deindividuation** (reduced self-consciousness, inhibition, and personal responsibility) dramatically affect behavior.

Objective 16.15: How do group polarization and groupthink affect group decision making?
Group polarization is the process of most group members initially tending toward an extreme idea, followed by the rest of the group moving (polarizing) in that extreme direction. This phenomenon occurs because discussions with likeminded members reinforce the preexisting tendencies. **Groupthink** is a faulty type of decision making that occurs when a highly cohesive group strives for agreement and avoids inconsistent information.

Aggression and Altruism

Objective 16.16: Define aggression, and identify the biological and psychosocial factors that contribute to its expression.
Aggression is any behavior intended to harm someone. Some researchers believe it is caused by biological factors, such as instincts, genes, the brain and nervous system, substance abuse and other mental disorders, and hormones and neurotransmitters. Other researchers emphasize psychosocial factors,

such as aversive stimuli, culture and learning, and violent media.

Objective 16.17: Describe three approaches to reducing aggression.
Releasing aggressive feelings through violent acts or watching violence (catharsis) is not an effective way to reduce aggression. Introducing incompatible responses (such as humor) and teaching social and communication skills are more efficient.

Objective 16.18: Define altruism, and describe the three models that attempt to explain it.
Altruism refers to actions designed to help others with no obvious benefit to the helper. The *evolutionary model* suggests altruism is innate and has survival value, the **egoistic model** proposes that helping is motivated by anticipated gain, and the **empathy–altruism hypothesis** suggests helping increases when the helper feels empathy for the victim.

Objective 16.19: Describe Latané and Darley's decision-making model, and other factors that help explain why we don't help.
According to Latané and Darley, whether or not someone helps depends on a series of interconnected events, starting with noticing the problem and ending with a decision to help. Some people don't help because of the ambiguity of many emergencies or because of **diffusion of responsibility** (assuming someone else will respond).

Psychology Engages

Objective 16.20: List four major approaches useful for reducing prejudice and discrimination.
The four key approaches are *cooperation and common goals*, *intergroup contact*, *cognitive retraining*, and cognitive dissonance.

Objective 16.21: Identify six ways to reduce destructive obedience.
To decrease destructive obedience, we need to reexamine *socialization*, the *power of the situation*, *groupthink*, the *foot-in-the-door* technique, a *relaxed moral guard*, and *disobedient models*.

Objective 16.22: Describe cultural and historical similarities and differences in judgments of attractiveness.
Many cultures share similar standards of attractiveness (e.g., youthful appearance and facial and body symmetry are important for women, whereas maturity and financial resources are more important for men). Historically, what is judged as beautiful varies from era to era.

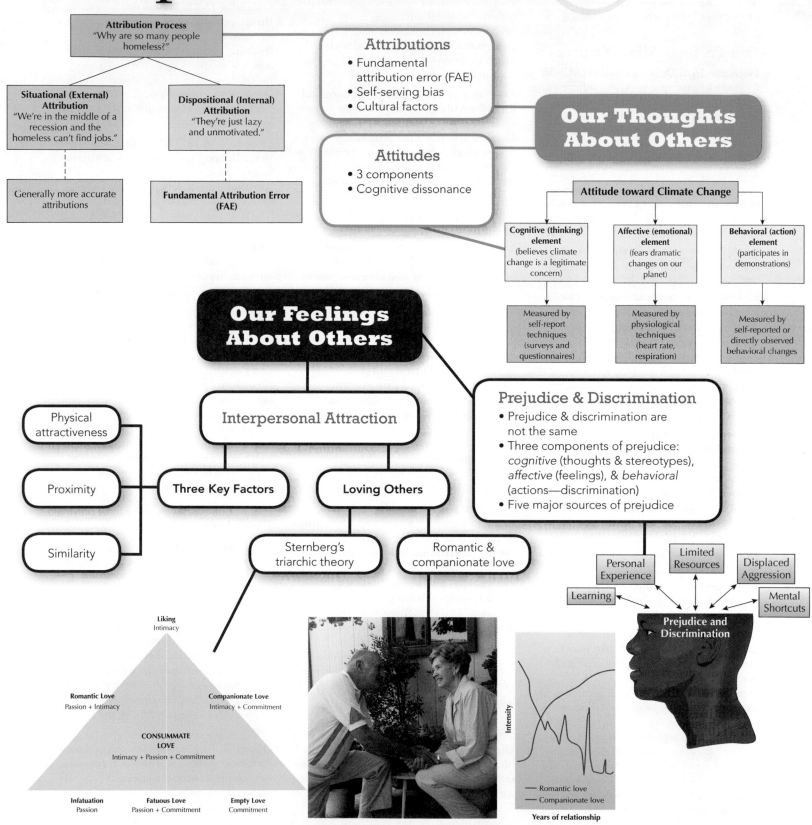

Attribution Process
"Why are so many people homeless?"

Situational (External) Attribution
"We're in the middle of a recession and the homeless can't find jobs."

Dispositional (Internal) Attribution
"They're just lazy and unmotivated."

Generally more accurate attributions

Fundamental Attribution Error (FAE)

Attributions
- Fundamental attribution error (FAE)
- Self-serving bias
- Cultural factors

Our Thoughts About Others

Attitudes
- 3 components
- Cognitive dissonance

Attitude toward Climate Change

Cognitive (thinking) element
(believes climate change is a legitimate concern)

Affective (emotional) element
(fears dramatic changes on our planet)

Behavioral (action) element
(participates in demonstrations)

Measured by self-report techniques (surveys and questionnaires)

Measured by physiological techniques (heart rate, respiration)

Measured by self-reported or directly observed behavioral changes

Our Feelings About Others

Physical attractiveness

Proximity

Similarity

Interpersonal Attraction

Three Key Factors

Loving Others

Sternberg's triarchic theory

Romantic & companionate love

Prejudice & Discrimination
- Prejudice & discrimination are not the same
- Three components of prejudice: *cognitive* (thoughts & stereotypes), *affective* (feelings), & *behavioral* (actions—discrimination)
- Five major sources of prejudice

Personal Experience

Limited Resources

Displaced Aggression

Learning

Mental Shortcuts

Prejudice and Discrimination

Liking
Intimacy

Romantic Love
Passion + Intimacy

Companionate Love
Intimacy + Commitment

CONSUMMATE LOVE
Intimacy + Passion + Commitment

Infatuation
Passion

Fatuous Love
Passion + Commitment

Empty Love
Commitment

Intensity

— Romantic love
— Companionate love

Years of relationship

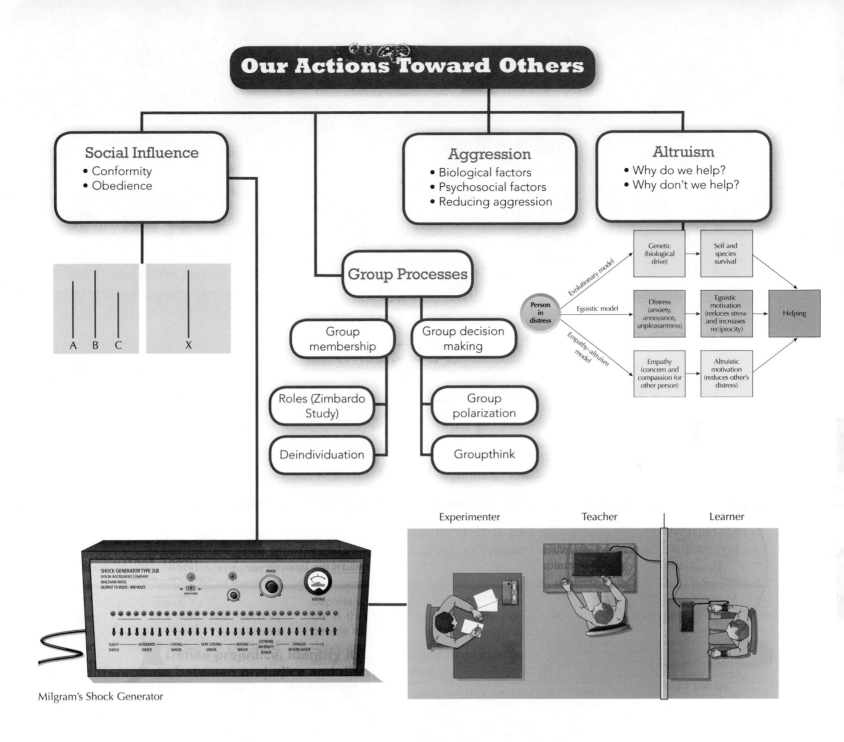

Our Actions Toward Others

Social Influence
- Conformity
- Obedience

A B C   X

Milgram's Shock Generator

SHOCK GENERATOR TYPE 2LB
DYSON INSTRUMENT COMPANY
WALTHAM MASS.
OUTPUT 15 VOLTS - 450 VOLTS

PHASE

VOLTAGE

SLIGHT   MODERATE   STRONG   VERY STRONG   INTENSE   EXTREME   DANGER
SHOCK   SHOCK   SHOCK   SHOCK   SHOCK   INTENSITY   SEVERE SHOCK
                                                       SHOCK

Aggression
- Biological factors
- Psychosocial factors
- Reducing aggression

Group Processes

Group membership

Group decision making

Roles (Zimbardo Study)

Group polarization

Deindividuation

Groupthink

Altruism
- Why do we help?
- Why don't we help?

Person in distress

Evolutionary model → Genetic (biological drive) → Self and species survival

Egoistic model → Distress (anxiety, annoyance, unpleasantness) → Egoistic motivation (reduces stress and increases reciprocity) → Helping

Empathy–altruism model → Empathy (concern and compassion for other person) → Altruistic motivation (reduces other's distress)

Experimenter   Teacher   Learner

Psychology Engages

Applying Social Psychology to Social Problems
Research Challenge
Gender & Cultural Diversity
Critical Thinking
Final Critical Thinking Take Home Message

Appendix A

Statistics and Psychology

We are constantly bombarded by numbers: "On sale for 30 percent off," "70 percent chance of rain," "9 out of 10 doctors recommend . . ." The president uses numbers to try to convince us that the economy is healthy. Advertisers use numbers to convince us of the effectiveness of their products. Psychologists use statistics to support or refute psychological theories and demonstrate that certain behaviors are indeed results of specific causal factors.

When people use numbers in these ways, they are using statistics. **Statistics** is a branch of applied mathematics that uses numbers to describe and analyze information on a subject.

Statistics make it possible for psychologists to quantify the information they obtain in their studies. They can then critically analyze and evaluate this information. Statistical analysis is imperative for researchers to describe, predict, or explain behavior. For instance, Albert Bandura (1973) proposed that watching violence on television causes aggressive behavior in children. In carefully controlled experiments, he gathered numerical information and analyzed it according to specific statistical methods. The statistical analysis helped him substantiate that the aggression of his subjects and the aggressive acts they had seen on television were related, and that the relationship was not mere coincidence.

Although statistics is a branch of applied mathematics, you don't have to be a math whiz to use statistics. Simple arithmetic is all you need to do most of the calculations. For more complex statistics involving more complicated mathematics, computer programs are available for virtually every type of computer. What is more important than learning the mathematical computations, however, is developing an understanding of when and why each type of statistic is used. The purpose of this appendix is to help you understand the significance of the statistics most commonly used.

Gathering and Organizing Data

Psychologists design their studies to facilitate gathering information about the factors they want to study. The information they obtain is known as **data** (**data** is plural; its singular is **datum**). When the data are gathered, they are generally in the form of numbers; if they aren't, they are converted to numbers. After they are gathered, the data must be organized in such a way that statistical analysis is possible. In the following section, we will examine the methods used to gather and organize information.

Variables

When studying a behavior, psychologists normally focus on one particular factor to determine whether it has an effect on the behavior. This factor is known as a **variable**, which is in effect anything that can assume more than one value (see Chapter 1). Height, weight, sex, eye color, and scores on an IQ test or a video game are all factors that can assume more than one value and are therefore variables. Some will vary between people, such as sex (you are either male *or* female but not both at the same time). Some may even vary within one person, such as scores on a video game (the same person might get 10,000 points on one try and only 800 on another). Opposed to a variable, anything that remains the same and does not vary is called a **constant**. If researchers use only females in their research, then sex is a constant, not a variable.

In nonexperimental studies, variables can be factors that are merely observed through naturalistic observation or case studies, or they can be factors about which people are questioned in a test or survey. In experimental studies, the two major types of variables are independent and dependent variables.

Independent variables are those that are manipulated by the experimenter. For example, suppose we were to conduct a study to determine whether the sex of the debater influences the outcome of a debate. In this study, one group of subjects watches a video-tape of a debate between a male arguing the "pro" side and a female arguing the "con"; another group watches the same debate, but with the pro and con roles reversed. In such a study, the form of the presentation viewed by each group (whether "pro" is argued by a male or a female) is the independent variable because the experimenter manipulates the form of presentation seen by each group. Another example might be a study to determine whether a particular drug has any effect on a manual dexterity task. To study this question, we would administer the drug to one group and no drug to another. The independent variable would be the amount of drug given (some or none). The independent variable is particularly important when using **inferential statistics**, which we will discuss later.

The **dependent variable** is a factor that results from, or depends on, the independent variable. It is a measure of some outcome or, most commonly, a measure of the subjects' behavior. In the debate example, each subject's choice of the winner of the debate would be the dependent variable. In the drug experiment, the dependent variable would be each subject's score on the manual dexterity task.

Frequency Distributions

After conducting a study and obtaining measures of the variable(s) being studied, psychologists need to organize the data in a meaningful way. Table A.1 presents test scores from a statistics aptitude test collected from 50 college students. This information is called **raw data** because there is no order to the numbers. They are presented as they were collected and are therefore "raw."

The lack of order in raw data makes them difficult to study. Thus, the first step in understanding the results of an experiment is to impose some order on the raw data. There are several ways to do this. One of the simplest is to create a **frequency distribution**, which shows the number of times a score or event occurs. Although frequency distributions are helpful in several ways, the major advantages are that they allow us to see the data in an organized manner and they make it easier to represent the data on a graph.

The simplest way to make a frequency distribution is to list all the possible test scores, then tally the number of people (N) who received those scores. Table A.2 presents a frequency distribution using the raw data from Table A.1. As you can see, the data are now easier to read. From looking at the frequency distribution, you can see that most of the test scores lie in the middle with only a few at the very high or very low end. This was not at all evident from looking at the raw data.

This type of frequency distribution is practical when the number of possible scores is 20 or fewer. However, when there are more than 20 possible scores it can be even harder to make

Table A.1 STATISTICS APTITUDE TEST SCORES FOR 50 COLLEGE STUDENTS

73	57	63	59	50
72	66	50	67	51
63	59	65	62	65
62	72	64	73	66
61	68	62	68	63
59	61	72	63	52
59	58	57	68	57
64	56	65	59	60
50	62	68	54	63
52	62	70	60	68

sense out of the frequency distribution than the raw data. This can be seen in Table A.3, which presents the Scholastic Aptitude Test scores for 50 students. Even though there are only 50 actual scores in this table, the number of possible scores ranges from a high of 1390 to a low of 400. If we included zero frequencies there would be 100 entries in a frequency distribution of this data, making the frequency distribution much more difficult to understand than the raw data. If there are more than 20 possible scores, therefore, a **group** frequency distribution is normally used.

In a **group frequency distribution**, individual scores are represented as members of a group of scores or as a range of scores (see Table A.4). These groups are called **class intervals**. Grouping these scores makes it much easier to make sense out of the distribution, as you can see from the relative ease in understanding Table A.4 as compared to Table A.3. Group frequency distributions are easier to represent on a graph.

When graphing data from frequency distributions, the class intervals are represented along the **abscissa** (the horizontal or *x* axis). The frequency is represented along the **ordinate** (the vertical or *y* axis). Information can be graphed in the form of a bar graph, called a **histogram**, or in the form of a point or line graph, called a **polygon**. Figure A.1 shows a histogram presenting the data from Table A.4. Note that the class intervals are represented along the bottom line of the graph (the *x* axis) and the height of the bars indicates the frequency in each class interval. Now look at Figure A.2. The information presented here is exactly the same as that in Figure A.1 but is represented in the form of a polygon rather than a histogram. Can you see how both graphs illustrate the same information? Even though reading information from a graph is simple, we have found that many students have never learned to read graphs. In the next section we will explain how to read a graph.

Table A.2 FREQUENCY DISTRIBUTION OF 50 STUDENTS ON STATISTICS APTITUDE TEST

Score	Frequency
73	2
72	3
71	0
70	1
69	0
68	5
67	1
66	2
65	3
64	2
63	5
62	5
61	2
60	2
59	5
58	1
57	3
56	1
55	0
54	1
53	0
52	2
51	1
50	3
Total	50

Table A.3 SCHOLASTIC APTITUDE TEST SCORES FOR 50 COLLEGE STUDENTS

1350	750	530	540	750
1120	410	780	1020	430
720	1080	1110	770	610
1130	620	510	1160	630
640	1220	920	650	870
930	660	480	940	670
1070	950	680	450	990
690	1010	800	660	500
860	520	540	880	1090
580	730	570	560	740

Table A.4 GROUP FREQUENCY DISTRIBUTION OF SCHOLASTIC APTITUDE TEST SCORES FOR 50 COLLEGE STUDENTS

Class Interval	Frequency
1300–1390	1
1200–1290	1
1100–1190	4
1000–1090	5
900–990	5
800–890	4
700–790	7
600–690	10
500–590	9
400–490	4
Total	50

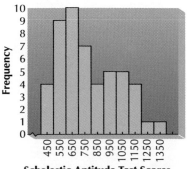

Figure A.1 A histogram illustrating the information found in Table A.4.

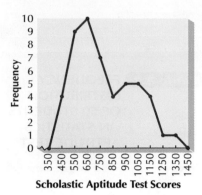

Figure A.2 A polygon illustrating the information found in Table A.4.

How to Read a Graph

Every graph has several major parts. The most important are the labels, the axes (the vertical and horizontal lines), and the points, lines, or bars. Find these parts in Figure A.1.

The first thing you should notice when reading a graph are the labels because they tell what data are portrayed. Usually the data consist of the descriptive statistics, or the numbers used to measure the dependent variables. For example, in Figure A.1 the horizontal axis is labeled "Scholastic Aptitude Test Scores," which is the dependent variable measure; the vertical axis is labeled "Frequency," which means the number of occurrences. If a graph is not labeled, as we sometimes see in TV commercials or magazine ads, it is useless and should be ignored. Even when a graph *is* labeled, the labels can be misleading. For example, if graph designers want to distort the information, they can elongate one of the axes. Thus, it is important to pay careful attention to the numbers as well as the words in graph labels.

Next, you should focus your attention on the bars, points, or lines on the graph. In the case of histograms like the one in Figure A.1, each bar represents the class interval. The width of the bar stands for the width of the class interval, whereas the height of the bar stands for the frequency in that interval. Look at the third bar from the left in Figure A.1. This bar represents the interval "600 to 690 SAT Scores," which has a frequency of 10. You can see that this directly corresponds to the same class interval in Table A.4, since graphs and tables are both merely alternate ways of illustrating information.

Reading point or line graphs is the same as reading a histogram. In a point graph, each point represents two numbers, one found along the horizontal axis and the other found along the vertical axis. A polygon is identical to a point graph except that it has lines connecting the points. Figure A.2 is an example of a polygon, where each point represents a class interval and is placed at the center of the interval and at the height corresponding to the frequency of that interval. To make the graph easier to read, the points are connected by straight lines.

Displaying the data in a frequency distribution or in a graph is much more useful than merely presenting raw data and can be especially helpful when researchers are trying to find relations between certain factors. However, as we explained earlier, if psychologists want to make predictions or explanations about behavior, they need to perform mathematical computations on the data.

Uses of the Various Statistics

The statistics psychologists use in a study depend on whether they are trying to describe and predict behavior or explain it. When they use statistics to describe behavior, as in reporting the average score on the Scholastic Aptitude Test, they are using **descriptive statistics**. When they use them to explain behavior, as Bandura did in his study of children modeling aggressive behavior seen on TV, they are using **inferential statistics**.

Descriptive Statistics

Descriptive statistics are the numbers used to describe the dependent variable. They can be used to describe characteristics of a **population** (an entire group, such as all people living in the United States) or a **sample** (a part of a group, such as a randomly selected group of 25 students from Cornell University). The major descriptive statistics include measures of central tendency (mean, median, and mode), measures of variation (variance and standard deviation), and correlation.

Measures of Central Tendency

Statistics indicating the center of the distribution are called **measures of central tendency** and include the mean, median, and mode. They are all scores that are typical of the center of the distribution. The **mean** is what most of us think of when we hear the word "average." The **median** is the middle score. The **mode** is the score that occurs most often.

Mean What is your average golf score? What is the average yearly rainfall in your part of the country? What is the average reading test score in your city? When these questions ask for the average, they are really asking for the "mean." The arithmetic **mean** is the weighted average of all the raw scores, which is computed by totaling all the raw scores and then dividing that total by the number of scores added together. In statistical computation, the mean is represented by an "X" with a bar above it ($\overline{X}$, pronounced "X bar"), each individual raw score by an "**X**," and the total number of scores by an "**N**." For example, if we wanted to compute the $\overline{X}$ of the raw statistics test scores in Table A.1, we would sum all the X's (**?X**, with ? meaning sum) and divide by N (number of scores). In Table A.1, the sum of all the scores is equal to 3100 and there are 50 scores. Therefore, the mean of these scores is

$$\overline{X} = \frac{3100}{50} = 62$$

Table A.5 illustrates how to calculate the mean for 10 IQ scores.

Median The **median** is the middle score in the distribution once all the scores have been arranged in rank order. If N (the number of scores) is odd, then there actually is a middle score and that middle score is the median. When N is even, there are two middle scores and the median is the mean of those two scores. Table A.6 shows the computation of the median for two different sets of scores, one set with 15 scores and one with 10.

Mode Of all the measures of central tendency, the easiest to compute is the **mode**, which is merely the most frequent score. It is computed by finding the score that occurs most often. Whereas there is always only one mean and only one median for each distribution, there can be more than one mode. Table A.7 shows how to find the mode in a distribution with one mode (unimodal) and in a distribution with two modes (bimodal).

There are several advantages to each of these measures of central tendency, but in psychological research the mean is used most often. A book solely covering psychological statistics will provide a more thorough discussion of the relative values of these measures.

Measures of Variation

When describing a distribution, it is not sufficient merely to give the central tendency; it is also necessary to give a **measure of variation**, which is a measure of the spread of the scores. By examining the spread, we can determine whether the scores are bunched around the middle or tend

Table A.5 COMPUTATION OF THE MEAN FOR 10 IQ SCORES

IQ Scores X
143
127
116
98
85
107
106
98
104
116
$\Sigma X = 1100$
Mean $= \overline{X} = \dfrac{\Sigma X}{N} = \dfrac{1{,}100}{10} = 110$

Table A.6 COMPUTATION OF MEDIAN FOR ODD AND EVEN NUMBERS OF IQ SCORES

IQ	IQ
139	137
130	135
121	121
116	116
107	108 ← middle score
101	106 ← middle score
98	105
96 ← middle score	101
84	98
83	97
82	N = 10
75	N is even
75	
68	
65	Median $= \dfrac{106 + 108}{2} = 107$
N = 15	
N is odd	

Table A.7 FINDING THE MODE FOR TWO DIFFERENT DISTRIBUTIONS

IQ	IQ
139	139
138	138
125	125
116 ←	116 ←
116 ←	116 ←
116 ←	116 ←
107	107
100	98 ←
98	98 ←
98	98 ←
Mode = most frequent score	Mode = 116 and 98
Mode = 116	

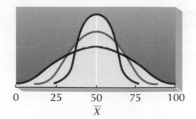

Figure A.3 Three distributions having the same mean but a different variability.

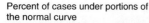

Percent of cases under portions of the normal curve

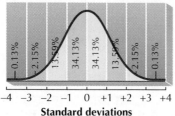

0.13% 2.15% 13.59% 34.13% 34.13% 13.59% 2.15% 0.13%

−4 −3 −2 −1   0 +1 +2 +3 +4
Standard deviations

Figure A.4 The normal distribution forms a bell-shaped curve. In a normal distribution, two-thirds of the scores lie between one standard deviation above and one standard deviation below the mean.

to extend away from the middle. Figure A.3 shows three different distributions, all with the same mean but with different spreads of scores. You can see from this figure that, in order to describe these different distributions accurately, there must be some measures of the variation in their spread. The most widely used measure of variation is the standard deviation, which is represented by a lowercase s. The standard deviation is a standard measurement of how much the scores in a distribution deviate from the mean. The formula for the standard deviation is

$$s = \sqrt{\frac{\Sigma(X - \overline{X})^2}{N}}$$

Table A.8 illustrates how to compute the standard deviation.

Most distributions of psychological data are bell-shaped. That is, most of the scores are grouped around the mean, and the farther the scores are from the mean in either direction, the fewer the scores. Notice the bell shape of the distribution in Figure A.4. Distributions such as this are called **normal** distributions. In normal distributions, as shown in Figure A.4, approximately two-thirds of the scores fall within a range that is one standard deviation below the mean to one standard deviation above the mean. For example, the Wechsler IQ tests (see Chapter 7) have a mean of 100 and a standard deviation of 15. This means that approximately two-thirds of the people taking these tests will have scores between 85 and 115.

Correlation

Suppose for a moment that you are sitting in the student union with a friend. To pass the time, you and your friend decide to play a game in which you try to guess the height of the next male who enters the union. The winner, the one whose guess is closest to the person's actual height, gets a piece of pie paid for by the loser. When it is your turn, what do you guess? If you are like most people, you will probably try to estimate the mean of all the males in the union and use that as your guess. The mean is always your best guess if you have no other information.

Now let's change the game a little and add a friend who stands outside the union and weighs the next male to enter the union. Before the male enters the union, your friend says "125 pounds." Given this new information, will you still guess the mean height? Probably not—you will probably predict *below* the mean. Why? Because you intuitively understand that there is a **correlation**, a relationship, between height and weight, with tall people usually weighing more than short people. Given that 125 pounds is less than the average weight for males, you will probably guess a less-than-average height. The statistic used to measure this type of relationship between two variables is called a correlation coefficient.

Correlation Coefficient A **correlation coefficient** measures the relationship between two variables, such as height and weight or IQ and SAT scores. Given any two variables, there are three possible relationships between them: **positive**, **negative**, and **zero** (no relationship). A positive relationship exists when the two variables vary in the same direction (e.g., as height increases, weight normally also increases). A negative relationship occurs when the two variables vary in opposite directions (e.g., as temperatures go up, hot chocolate sales go down). There is no relationship when the two variables vary totally independently of one another (e.g., there is no relationship between peoples' height and the color of their toothbrushes). Figure A.5 illustrates these three types of correlations.

The computation and the formula for a correlation coefficient (correlation coefficient is delineated by the letter "*r*") are shown in Table A.9. The correlation coefficient (*r*) always has a value between +1 and −1 (it is never greater than +1 and it is never smaller than −1). When *r* is close to +1, it signifies a high positive relationship between the two variables (as one variable

Table A.8 COMPUTATION OF THE STANDARD DEVIATION FOR 10 IQ SCORES

IQ Scores X	$X - \overline{X}$	$(X - \overline{X})^2$
143	33	1089
127	17	289
116	6	36
98	−12	144
85	−25	625
107	−3	9
106	−4	16
98	−12	144
104	−6	36
116	6	36
$\Sigma X = 1100$		$\Sigma(X - \overline{X})^2 = 2424$

Standard Deviation = s

$$= \sqrt{\frac{\Sigma(X - \overline{X})^2}{N}} = \sqrt{\frac{2424}{10}}$$

$$= \sqrt{242.4} = 15.569$$

Figure A.5 Three types of correlation. Positive correlation (top): As the number of days of class attendance increases, so does the number of correct exam items. Negative correlation (middle): As the number of days of class attendance increases, the number of incorrect exam items decreases. Zero correlation (bottom): The day of the month on which one is born has no relationship to the number of exam items correct.

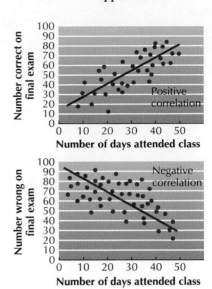

goes up, the other variable also goes up). When r is close to -1, it signifies a high negative relationship between the two variables (as one variable goes up, the other variable goes down). When r is 0, there is no linear relationship between the two variables being measured.

    Correlation coefficients can be quite helpful in making predictions. Bear in mind, however, that predictions are just that: *predictions*. They will have some error as long as the correlation coefficients on which they are based are not perfect ($+1$ or -1). Also, correlations cannot reveal any information regarding causation. Merely because two factors are correlated, it does not mean that one factor causes the other. Consider, for example, ice cream consumption and swimming pool use. These two variables are positively correlated with one another, in that as ice cream consumption increases, so does swimming pool use. But nobody would suggest that eating ice cream *causes* swimming, or vice versa. Similarly, just because Michael Jordan eats Wheaties and can do a slam dunk it does not mean that you will be able to do one if you eat the same breakfast. The only way to determine the cause of behavior is to conduct an experiment and analyze the results by using inferential statistics.

Inferential Statistics

Knowing the descriptive statistics associated with different distributions, such as the mean and standard deviation, can enable us to make comparisons between various distributions. By making these comparisons, we may be able to observe whether one variable is related to another or whether one variable has a causal effect on another. When we design an experiment specifically to measure causal effects between two or more variables, we use **inferential** statistics to analyze the data collected. Although there are many inferential statistics, the one we will discuss is the t-test, since it is the simplest.

t-Test Suppose we believe that drinking alcohol causes a person's reaction time to slow down. To test this hypothesis, we recruit 20 participants and separate them into two groups. We ask the participants in one group to drink a large glass of orange juice with one ounce of alcohol for every 100 pounds of body weight (e.g., a person weighing 150 pounds would get 1.5 ounces of alcohol). We ask the control group to drink an equivalent amount of orange juice with no alcohol added. Fifteen minutes after the drinks, we have each participant perform a reaction time test that consists of pushing a button as soon as a light is flashed. (The reaction time is the time between the onset of the light and the pressing of the button.) Table A.10 shows the data from this hypothetical experiment. It is clear from the data that there is definitely a difference in the reaction times of the two groups: There is an obvious difference between the means. However, it is possible that this difference is due merely to chance. To determine whether the difference is real or due to chance, we can conduct a *t*-test. We have run a sample *t*-test in Table A.10.

    The logic behind a *t*-test is relatively simple. In our experiment we have two samples. If each of these samples is from the *same* population (e.g., the population of all people, whether drunk or sober), then any difference between the samples will be due to chance. On the other hand, if the two samples are

Table A.9 COMPUTATION OF CORRELATION COEFFICIENT BETWEEN HEIGHT AND WEIGHT FOR 10 MALES

Height (inches) X	X²	Weight (pounds) Y	Y²	XY
73	5,329	210	44,100	15,330
64	4,096	133	17,689	8,512
65	4,225	128	16,384	8,320
70	4,900	156	24,336	10,920
74	5,476	189	35,721	13,986
68	4,624	145	21,025	9,860
67	4,489	145	21,025	9,715
72	5,184	166	27,556	11,952
76	5,776	199	37,601	15,124
71	5,041	159	25,281	11,289
700	49,140	1,630	272,718	115,008

$$r = \frac{N \cdot \Sigma XY - \Sigma X \cdot \Sigma Y}{\sqrt{[N \cdot \Sigma X^2 - (\Sigma X)^2}\sqrt{[N \cdot \Sigma Y^2 - (\Sigma Y)^2]}}$$

$$r = \frac{10 \cdot 115,008 - 700 \cdot 1,630}{\sqrt{[10 \cdot 49,140 - 700^2]}\sqrt{[10 \cdot 272,718 - 1,630^2]}}$$

$$r = 0.92$$

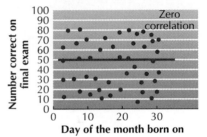

Table A.10 REACTION TIMES IN MILLISECONDS (MSEC) FOR SUBJECTS IN ALCOHOL AND NO ALCOHOL CONDITIONS AND COMPUTATION OF t

RT (msec) Alcohol X_1	RT (msec) No Alcohol X_2
200	143
210	137
140	179
160	184
180	156
187	132
196	176
198	148
140	125
159	120

$$SX_1 = 1{,}770 \qquad\qquad SX_2 = 1{,}500$$
$$N_1 = 10 \qquad\qquad N_2 = 10$$
$$\overline{X}_1 = 177 \qquad\qquad \overline{X}_2 = 150$$
$$s_1 = 24.25 \qquad\qquad s_2 = 21.86$$

$$\Sigma_{\overline{X}1} = \frac{s}{\sqrt{N_1 - 1}} = 8.08 \qquad\qquad \Sigma_{\overline{X}2} = \frac{s}{\sqrt{N_2 - 1}} = 7.29$$

$$S_{\overline{X}_1 - \overline{X}_2} = \sqrt{S_{\overline{X}_1}^2 + S_{\overline{X}_2}^2} = \sqrt{8.08^2 + 7.29^2} = 10.88$$

$$t = \frac{\overline{X}_1 - \overline{X}_2}{S_{\overline{X}1-\overline{X}2}} = \frac{177 - 150}{10.88} = 2.48$$

$$t = 2.48, p < .05$$

from *different* populations (e.g., the population of drunk people *and* the population of sober people), then the difference is a significant difference and not due to chance.

If there is a significant difference between the two samples, then the independent variable must have caused that difference. In our example, there is a significant difference between the alcohol and the no alcohol groups. We can tell this because p (the probability that this t value will occur by chance) is less than .05. To obtain the p, we need only look up the t value in a statistical table, which is found in any statistics book. In our example, because there is a significant difference between the groups, we can reasonably conclude that the alcohol did cause a slower reaction time.

Appendix B

Answers to Review Questions and Other Activities

Chapter 1 Check & Review—*Introducing Psychology (p. 9) Part B.* 1. scientific, behavior, mental processes. **2.** The process of objectively evaluating, comparing, analyzing, and synthesizing information. **3.** a. **4.** *Description* tells "what" occurred. An *explanation* tells "why" a behavior occurred. *Prediction* specifies the conditions under which a behavior or event is likely to occur. *Change* means applying psychological knowledge to prevent unwanted outcomes or bring about desired goals. **5.** explaining. **6.** b. **7.** Answers will vary by individual. **Check & Review—*Origins of Psychology (p. 16) Part B.* 1.** structuralist. **2.** Functionalists. **3.** Freudian slips supposedly reveal a person's true unconscious desires and conflicts. **4.** a. **5.** A unifying theme of modern psychology that incorporates biological, psychological, and social processes. **Check & Review–*Science of Psychology (p. 21) Part B.* 1.** c. **2.** **hypothesis**. **3.** d. **4.** **informed consent**. **5.** Obtaining informed consent from research participants and **debriefing** them after the research is conducted helps ensure the well-being of the participant and helps maintain high ethical standards. Deception is sometimes necessary in psychological research because if participants know the true purpose of the study, their response will be unnatural. **6.** Step 1=Observation and literature review, Step 2=Testable hypothesis, Step 3=Research design, Step 4=Data collection and analysis, Step 5=Publication, Step 6=**Theory** development. **Check & Review—*Experimental Research (p. 27) Part B.* 1.** Only in an experiment can experimenters manipulate, isolate, and control variables, which allows them to determine causation. **2.** d. **3.** c. **4.** The two primary problems for researchers are **experimenter bias** and **ethnocentrism**. The two problems for participants are sample bias and participant bias. To guard against experimenter bias, researchers employ blind observers, **single-blind** and **double-blind studies,** and **placebos.** To control for ethnocentrism, they use cross-cultural sampling. To offset participant problems with **sample bias,** researchers use random/representative sampling and **random assignment.** To control for **participant bias,** they rely on many of the same controls in place to prevent experimenter bias, such as double-blind studies. They also attempt to assure anonymity, confidentiality, and sometimes use deception. **Check & Review—*Descriptive, Correlational, and Biological Research (p. 35) Part B.* 1.** Descriptive. **2.** d. **3.** c. **4.** CT, PET, MRI, fMRI. **Research Challenge (p. 36) 1.** Experimental, **2.** IV=Multitasking on each of the three tests (attention to detail, memory, ability to task switch). DV=Performance scores on each of the three tests. Experimental Group=Regular/heavy multitaskers, Control Group=Nonmultitaskers. **Check & Review—*Psychology Engages (p. 45) Part B.* 1.** Answers will vary. **2.** emotions and facial recognition of emotions. **3.** Survey, Question, Read, Recite, Review, and wRite. **4.** distributed practice.

Chapter 2 Check & Review—*Neural Bases of Behavior (p. 58) Part B.* 1. Check your diagram with Figure 2.1. 2. c. 3. b. 4. **Neurotransmitters** are manufactured and released at the **synapse**, where the messages are picked up and relayed by neighboring **neurons**. **Check & Review—***The Nervous and Endocrine Systems (p. 66) Part B.* 1. **central, peripheral**. 2. d. 3. sympathetic. 4. The **sympathetic nervous system** arouses the body and mobilizes energy stores to deal with emergencies. The **parasympathetic nervous system** calms the body and conserves the energy stores. 5. Compare your answers with Figure 2.2. 6. **Hormones** are released from glands in the **endocrine system** directly into the bloodstream. **Check & Review—***Lower-Level Brain Structures (p. 70) Part B.* 1. **medulla, pons,** and **cerebellum**. 2. **cerebellum**. 3. **b**. 4. The **amygdala** is important because of its role in the production and regulation of emotions, particularly aggression and fear. 5. Compare your answers with Figure 2.11. **Check & Review—***Cerebral Cortex and Two Brains in One? (p. 78) Part B.* 1. **cerebral cortex**. 2. **occipital, temporal, frontal, parietal**. 3. a. 4. Compare your answers with Figure 2.16. 5. **corpus callosum**. **Critical Thinking (pp. 83–84) Part 1** 1. k. 2. i. 3. n. 4. l. 5. g. 6. b. 7. f. 8. d. 9. h. 10. j. 11. m. 12. c. 13. a. 14. e. **Part II** 1. Modifying judgment in light of new information/Left hemisphere and frontal lobes. 2. Listening actively/Temporal lobes. 3. Tolerating ambiguity/Sympathetic and parasympathetic nervous systems. **Research Challenge (p. 84)** 1. Experimental method. 2. IV=Action video games or non-action video games, DV= Scores on spatial-attention task and mental-rotation task. Experimental Groups=Men or women playing action video games. Control Groups=Men or women playing non-action video games. **Check & Review—***Our Genetic Inheritance and Psychology Engages (p. 87) Part B.* 1. d. 2. **Behavioral geneticists** use twin studies, adoption studies, family studies, and genetic abnormalities. 3. Simply having both men and women play action-packed video games for a few short weeks almost completely removes the previously reported gender differences in some spatial tasks. 4. c. 5. Because **natural selection** favors animals whose concern for kin is proportional to their degree of biological relatedness, most people will devote more resources, protection, love, and concern to close relatives, which helps ensure their genetic survival.

Chapter 3 Myth Busters (p. 94) Items 4, 5, and 8 are false. **Check & Review—***Understanding Stress and Sources of Stress (p. 99) Part B.* 1. a. 2. life changes 3. a blocked goal, **conflict**. 4. A forced choice between apple or pumpkin pie is an example of an **approach-approach conflict**. Having to choose between attending a desirable college versus avoiding going to that college because it's too far from home would be an **approach-avoidance conflict**. Taking an exam when you're not prepared or not taking the exam and receiving an automatic "F" is an example of an **avoidance-avoidance conflict**. 5. Answers will vary by individual. **Test Yourself (p. 102) SAM System**=fight-or-flight, adrenal medulla, catecholamines, norepinephrine, epinephrine. **HPA Axis**= endocrine system, pituitary, adrenal cortex, corticosteroids. **Check & Review–***Effects of Stress (p. 105) Part B.* 1. alarm, resistance, exhaustion. 2. b. 3. The SAM system provides an initial, rapid-acting stress response thanks to the sympathetic branch of the autonomic nervous system, which activates the adrenal medulla and the release of catecholamines that in turn increases heart rate, blood pressure, etc. 4. The HPA axis activates the pituitary gland, which alerts the adrenal cortex and the release of corticosteroids that increase blood sugar levels and metabolism. 5. Check your answers with the figure in the Step-by-Step Diagram 3.2, p. 102. **Research Challenge (p. 111)** 1. Correlational method. 2. Positive correlation–as stress increases incidence of ulcers also increases. **Check & Review—***Stress and Illness (p. 111) Part B.* 1. epinephrine, cortisol. 2. b. 3. **Hardiness** is based on three qualities: a commitment to personal goals, control over life, and viewing change as a challenge rather than a threat. People with these qualities are more successful at dealing with stress because they take a more active, positive approach and assume responsibility for their stress. 4. Severe anxiety. 5. Answers will vary by individual. *Test Yourself (p. 116)*. 1. b. 2. d. 3. g. 4. h. 5. f. 6. c. 7. e. 8. a. **Check & Review–***Health Psychology, Stress Management, and Psychology Engages (p. 119) Part B.* 1. Answers will vary by individual. 2. a. **emotion-focused**, b. **problem-focused**. 3. **internal**. 4. The eight resources are health and exercise, positive beliefs, social skills, social support, control, material resources, sense of humor, and relaxation. Individual responses will vary depending on personality and individual life style.

Chapter 4 Check & Review—*Understanding Sensation (p. 132)* **Part B.** 1. detection and interpretation. 2. **absolute threshold.** 3. a. 4. Your sensory receptors for smell adapt and send fewer messages to your brain. 5. b. **Check & Review**—*How We See (p. 138)* **Part B.** 1. Compare your diagram to Step-by-Step Diagram 4. 1. 2. After light waves enter the eye through the cornea and pupil, the lens focuses the incoming light into an image onto the **retina**, the eye's light-sensitive back surface. Special receptor cells in the retina, the **rods** and **cones**, then convert light energy into neural signals that send messages to the brain via the auditory nerve. 3. Color is processed in a **trichromatic** fashion in the retina, and in an **opponent-process** fashion in the brain. 4. b. **Check & Review**—*How We Hear (p. 141)* **Part B.** 1. Compare your answers to the Step-by-Step Diagram 4.2 2. The **outer ear** (pinna, auditory canal, eardrum) funnels sound waves to the **middle ear.** Bones in the middle ear (hammer, anvil, stirrup) amplify and send along the eardrum's vibrations to the **cochlea's** oval window, which is part of the **inner ear.** Vibrations from the oval window cause ripples in the fluid, which, in turn, cause bending of the hair cells in the cochlea's basilar membrane. 3. **Place theory** explains pitch perception according to the place where the cochlea's basilar membrane is most stimulated. **Frequency theory** says pitch perception occurs when nerve impulses sent to the brain match the frequency of the sound wave. 4. nerve. **Check & Review**—*Other Important Senses (p. 145)* **Part B.** 1. **pheromones.** 2. d. 3. d. 4. **kinesthetic. Check & Review**–*Selection and Organization (p. 155)* **Part B.** 1. **Illusions** are false or misleading perceptions of the physical world produced by actual physical distortions. Delusions are false beliefs. Hallucinations are imaginary sensory perceptions that occur without an external stimulus. 2. **feature detectors.** 3. "Horizontal cats" reared in a horizontal world fail to develop potential feature detectors for vertical lines or objects. 4. proximity, similarity, closure. 5. size constancy. 6. c. 7. **binocular cues. Research Challenge (p. 157)** 1. Experimental, 2. IV=The variety of specific tests of **extrasensory perception (ESP)** ability. DV=ESP/PSI scores on tests. Experimental Group=Subjects in all nine experiments. Control Group=According to Bem: "No control group was needed to test the psi hypothesis in this experiment," in other words, the subjects either had it or didn't. Nevertheless he did run computer control sessions mentioned in this research challenge to determine if "practice sessions retroactively" increased recall. To read Bem's report for yourself, go to this link: http://dl.dropbox.com/u/8290411/FeelingFuture.pdf In the spirit of fairness, to read a rebuttal to Bem's article, go to: http://www.ruudwetzels.com/articles/Wagenmakersetal_subm.pdf **Check & Review**–*Interpretation and Psychology Engages (p. 160)* **Part B.** 1. perceptual adaptation. 2. **perceptual set.** 3. telepathy, clairvoyance, precognition, psychokinesis. 4. usually cannot be replicated.

Chapter 5 Check & Review—*Understanding Consciousness (p. 170)* **Part B.** 1. b. 2. Mental states, other than ordinary waking consciousness, found during sleep, dreaming, **psychoactive drug** use, **hypnosis**, **meditation**, and so on. 3. focused, minimal. 4. d. **Check & Review**—*Circadian Rhythms and Stages of Sleep (p. 177)* **Part B.** 1. circadian. 2. Compare your answers with Figure 5.1. 3. b. 4. an electroencephalograph (EEG). 5. a. 6. Answers will vary by individual. **Check & Review**–*Why Do We Sleep and Dream and Sleep Disorders (p. 183)* **Part B.** 1. **Repair/restoration theory** suggests we sleep to physically restore our mind and body. **Evolutionary/circadian theory** says that sleep evolved because it helped conserve energy and provided protection from predators. 2. d. 3. c. 4. **REM.** 5. (a) **insomnia.** (b) **sleep apnea.** (c) **narcolepsy.** (d) **night terrors. Check & Review**—*Psychoactive Drugs (p. 192)* **Part B.** 1. Psychoactive. 2. **Antagonistic, agonistic.** 3. d. 4. **Physical dependence** refers to changes in the bodily processes that make a drug necessary for minimal functioning. **Psychological dependence** refers to the desire or craving to achieve a drug's effect. 5. **depressants, stimulants, opiates, hallucinogens.** *Critical Thinking (pp. 197–198)* **Clue:** *In real life Sarah's parents were arguing constantly at the time of the dream and she feared they were going to get a divorce, which they soon did.* **Possible Analysis:**

1. *Psychoanalytic/psychodynamic View:* Clearly fear and terror are the key emotions in the dream, stemming from not only the destruction of her house, but also a young adolescent's uncertainty during the dream, being unable to *tolerate the ambiguity* of not knowing why it was happening. The **manifest content,** or story line of the dream, was that something was causing Sarah's home to be destroyed. The **latent content,** or supposedly true meaning, involved the main symbol in the dream, the house, which could clearly represent her family, the people screaming in the dream.

The underlying meaning of the dream was revealed to Sarah with the help of her counselor. Sarah's parents were constantly fighting and she feared they were going to get a divorce. Sarah also believed that her futile attempt to "put the pieces back" reflected her unconscious conflict and guilty feelings. Like many other children and adolescents of divorce, Sarah felt largely responsible for the break-up of the family. Wish fulfillment, which Freud believed was at the core of most dreams doesn't seem to fit here. Except that a 14 year old caught in the middle of constantly brawling parents may secretly wish they would separate to end the hostility.

2. *Biological View*: Sarah likely had several specific thoughts that could have stimulated this dream, including "my parents hate each other," "my parents are fighting because of me," and "my family is falling apart."

3. *Cognitive View*: Sarah's dream from this view might be that it offered her a "heads-up" on what was going on with her parents and that a divorce was the inevitable solution to her parents' relentless bickering. This dream also helped in problem solving by inspiring Sarah to ask for assistance from a counselor who helped her find its meaning.

Summary: Some psychologists suggest taking an eclectic view in analyzing dreams, that is, employing the CTC of *welcoming divergent views* from several theories and *synthesizing* or using whatever works best from each theory in interpreting the dream. By applying all three theories to a dream, you enhance the possible meanings as well as increase the number of feasible solutions. ***Research Challenge (pp. 198–199)*** 1. Biological. 2. Surgical manipulation of mice genes that inhibit the receptors for nicotine. (For information on the use of animal models, see http://www.genome.gov/12514551). **Check & Review—*Healthier Ways to Alter Consciousness and Psychology Engages (p. 199)* Part B.** 1. d. 2. narrowed, highly focused attention, increased use of imagination and hallucinations, a passive and receptive attitude, decreased responsiveness to pain, and heightened suggestibility. 3. Hypnosis requires the subject to make a conscious decision to relinquish some personal control of his or her consciousness. 4. forced hypnosis, unethical behavior, faking, superhuman strength, exceptional memory. 5. Answers will vary by individual.

Chapter 6 Check & Review—*Pavlov and Watson's Contributions (p. 209)* Part B. 1. b. 2. grandma. 3. **conditioned stimulus, conditioned response**. 4. d. 5. c. 6. Answers will vary by individual. **Check & Review–*Basic Principles (p. 214)* Part B.** 1. **acquisition, stimulus generalization, stimulus discrimination, extinction, spontaneous recovery,** and **higher order-conditioning**. 2. d. 3. higher-order conditioning. 4. c. 5. You no longer respond to the sound of the fire alarm because your response has been extinquished, which occurs when the **UCS** is repeatedly withheld, and the association between the **CS** and the UCS is broken. 6. Stimulus generalization. **Check & Review—*Operant Conditioning (p. 226)* Part B.** 1. **Operant conditioning** is learning through voluntary behavior and its subsequent consequences. 2. d. 3. decreases, increases. 4. resistant. 5. Answers vary and may include: passive aggressiveness, avoidance, inappropriate modeling, temporary suppression versus elimination, learned helplessness, and increased aggression. 6. Operant conditioning occurs when organisms learn by the consequences of their responses, whereas in **classical conditioning** organisms learn by pairing up associations. Operant conditioning is voluntary, whereas classical conditioning is involuntary. The fastest and most efficient learning during classical conditioning occurs when the neutral stimulus (NS) comes *before* the unconditioned stimulus (UCS). In contrast, during operant conditioning the consequences (reinforcement or punishment) should come *after* the behavior. **Check & Review—*Cognitive-Social Learning (p. 230)* Part B.** 1. Köhler and Tolman. 2. c. 3. **latent learning**. 4. **cognitive maps**. 5. b. **Research Challenge (p. 231)** 1. Biological method. 2. Intrabrain electrical recordings. **Check & Review—*Biology of Learning (p. 233)* Part B.** 1. Mirror. 2. evolutionary. 3. Garcia and his colleagues laced freshly killed sheep with a chemical that caused nausea and vomiting in coyotes. After the coyotes ate the tainted meat and became ill, they avoided all sheep. 4. **Biological preparedness** refers to the fact that organisms are innately predisposed to form associations between certain stimuli and responses. 5. **Instinctive drift. Gender & Cultural Diversity (p. 240)**

Table 6.8 ANSWERS TO APPLYING AVATAR TO KEY LEARNING PRINCIPLES

Example	Learning Principle	Explanation
Jake is a paraplegic. The head of security, asks Avatar-Jake to cooperate and get information from the Na'vi, which will help defeat them. He tells Jake: "Get me what I need and I'll get you your legs back."	Positive Reinforcement	*Stimulus* (offer of new legs) is *added. Response* (Jake's cooperation) is *strengthened,* and thus more likely to recur.
When Jake is chased by a ferocious Thanator, he runs away and escapes by jumping from a high cliff into a waterfall.	Negative Reinforcement	*Stimulus* (being eaten alive) is *removed. Response* (Jake's running from Thanator) is *strengthened, and Jake is more likely to run in the future.*
Jake innocently thanks Neytiri for killing the viperwolves who attacked him. She smacks her bow across his face, and yells: "Don't thank! You don't thank for this! This is sad."	Positive Punishment	*Stimuli* (Neytiri's hitting and yelling) are *added. Response* (Jake saying "Thanks") is *weakened,* and thus less likely to recur.
After Jake reveals his real purpose for wanting to learn the ways of the Na'vi, he is immediately shunned by Neytiri and her people.	Negative Punishment	*Stimulus* (group acceptance) is taken away. Response (Jake telling the truth) is weakened, and thus less likely to recur.
After Neytiri strikes Jake with her bow, he winces in anticipation whenever he sees her holding it.	Classical Conditioning	Previous NS (bow) became a CS when Jake paired it with the UCS (pain). Previous UCR (fear) became a CR (fear). [The CR is also a CER (fear) because it involved an emotion.]
Jake watches Neytiri mount and ride her flying banshee. He then copies her behavior, clumsily at first, but soon gets the hang of it.	Observational Learning	Jake learns new behavior and information (how to ride flying banshees) by watching and imitating others.

Check & Review–*Psychology Engages (p. 241)* Part B. 1. d. 2. c. 3. c. 4. Answers will vary by individual.

Chapter 7 Check & Review—*Nature of Memory (p. 259)* Part B 1. a **constructive process**. 2. (a) **encoding**, (b) **retrieval**, (c) **storage**. 3. The **levels of processing model** suggests memory depends on the degree or depth of mental processing occurring when material is initially encountered. According to the **parallel distributed processing (PDP)**, or *connectionist*, model, memory resembles a vast number of interconnected units and modules distributed throughout a huge network, all operating in parallel—simultaneously. 4. (a) **sensory memory,** (b) **short-term memory (STM),** (c) **long-term memory (LTM)**. 5. **recognition, recall**. 6. Answers will vary by individual. *Research Challenge (p. 260)* 1. Experimental (note that because Ebbinghaus has only one subject, himself, this would not qualify as a true, scientific experiment). 2. IV=list of nonsense syllables, DV=percentage of items correctly recalled one hour, one day, and one week later. Experimental group=only one subject, Control group=no control group. (Again, because there was only one subject and no control group this would not qualify as a true experiment.) **Check & Review—*Forgetting, Memory, and the Criminal Justice System (p. 267)* Part B** 1. (a) retrieval failure theory, (b) decay theory, (c) motivated forgetting theory. 2. Individual answers will vary. 3. Using **distributed practice**, you would space your study time into many learning periods with rest periods in between. Using massed practice, you would "cram" all your learning into long, unbroken periods. 4. d. 5. d. 6. easy. 7. False memories are imagined events constructed in the mind, whereas repressed memories are painful memories that are supposedly "forgotten" in an effort to avoid the pain of their retrieval. **Check & Review—*Biological Bases of Memory (p. 271)* Part B** 1. Repeated stimulation of a synapse can strengthen the synapse by stimulating the dendrites to grow more spines, and the ability of a particular neuron to release its neurotransmitters can be increased or decreased. 2. d. 3. amnesia. 4. d. 5. (a) **retrograde**, (b) **anterograde**. **Check & Review**—*Psychology Engages (p. 276)* **Part B** 1. Given that the duration of short-term memory is about 30 seconds, to lengthen this time use **maintenance rehearsal**, which involves continuously repeating the material. To effectively encode memory into long-term memory, use **elaborative rehearsal**, which involves thinking about the material and relating it to other information that has already been stored. 2. Because we tend to remember information that falls at the beginning or end of a sequence, you should spend extra time studying information in the middle of the chapter. 3. organization. 4. (a) peg-word system, (b) method of loci, (c) acronyms.

Chapter 8 *Try This Yourself (p. 285)* To solve this problem, mentally rotate one of the objects and then compare the rotated image with the other object to see whether they matched or not. The figures in b are more difficult to solve because they require a greater degree of mental rotation. This also is true of real objects in physical space. It takes more time and energy to turn a cup 150 degrees to the right, than to turn it 20 degrees. **Check & Review**—*Cognitive Building Blocks and Problem Solving (p. 290)* **Part B** 1. **Mental images** are mental representations of a previously stored sensory experience, whereas **concepts** are mental representations of a group or category that shares similar characteristics. 2. c. 3. There are at least three methods—artificial concepts, natural concepts, and hierarchies. 4. **prototype**. 5. b. 6. *Preparation*, in which we identify the facts, determine which ones are relevant, and define the goal, *production*, in which we propose possible solutions, or hypotheses, and *evaluation*, in which we determine whether the solutions meet the goal. 7. b. 8. preparation. **Check & Review**—*Creativity (p. 292)* **Part B** 1. c. 2. (a) divergent, (b) convergent, (c) divergent. 3. intellectual ability, knowledge, thinking style, personality, motivation, and environment. 4. Answers will vary. **Check & Review**—*Language (p. 299)* **Part B** 1. (a) **phonemes**, (b) **morphemes**, (c) **grammar**. 2. phonemes, morphemes. 3. **overgeneralization**. 4. b. 5. a. **Check & Review**—*Intelligence (p. 305)* **Part B** 1. general intelligence. 2. **Fluid intelligence** refers to reasoning abilities, memory, and speed of information processing. **Crystallized intelligence** refers to knowledge and skills gained through experience and education. 3. d. 4. Sternberg proposed that intelligence is composed of three aspects—analytic, creative, and practical. 5. The Stanford–Binet is a single test consisting of several sets of various age-level items. The Wechsler consists of three separate tests. 6. 90. 7. WISCIV 8. (a) **reliability**, (b) **validity**, (c) **standardization**. *Research Challenge (p. 314)* 1. Descriptive method. 2. Survey. **Check & Review**—*Intelligence Controversy and Psychology Engages (p. 316)* **Part B** 1. d. 2. d. 3. (d) energy resources. 4. Answers will vary. 5. Answers will vary.

Chapter 9 **Check & Review**—*Studying Development (p. 327)* **Part B** 1. nature versus nurture, continuity versus stages, stability versus change. 2. (a) **cross-sectional**, (b) **longitudinal**. 3. d. 4. Cross-sectional, longitudinal. **Check & Review**—*Physical Development (p. 338)* **Part B** 1. The three major stages are the **germinal period, embryonic period,** and **fetal period**. 2. environmental agents. 3. brain and other parts of the nervous system 4. c. 5. primary aging. **Check & Review**—*Cognitive development (p. 345)* **Part B** 1. Piaget. 2. 1b, 2a, 3d, 4c, 5d. 3. animism. 4. Piaget has been criticized for underestimating abilities, genetic, and cultural influences, but his contributions to the understanding of a child's cognitive development offset these criticisms. **Research Challenge (p. 351)** 1. Experimental. 2. IV(Level 1)=complex vs. simple patterns, IV(Level 2)=pictures of faces vs. nonfaces. DV=how long infants stared at the various stimuli. Experimental group=infants who stared at complex patterns and pictures of faces, Comparison group=infants who stared at simple patterns and nonfaces. (Note: Sophisticated research often has more than one level (or treatment) for the independent variable. Also, in this experiment there is no control group. Instead, many experiments legitimately employ comparison groups, which still allow us to legitimately state that the IV was the cause of the effect.) **Check & Review**—*Social-Emotional Development and Psychology Engages (p. 353)* **Part B** 1. contact comfort. 2. Securely attached, anxious/avoidant, anxious/ambivalent, disorganized/disoriented. 3. Mary shows an avoidant style. Bob demonstrates an anxious/ambivalent style. Rashelle shows a secure attachment style. 4. Permissive parents either set few limits and provide little attention (the permissive-indifferent), or they're highly involved but place few demands (the permissive-indulgent). Authoritarian parents value unquestioning obedience and mature responsibility from their children. Authoritative parents are caring and sensitive, but also set firm limits and enforce them.

Chapter 10 Check & Review—*Moral Development (p. 363)* **Part B 1. Preconventional, postconventional, conventional**. 2. c. 3. preconventional. 4. Kohlberg's theory may reflect moral reasoning and not moral behavior, it also may be culturally and/or gender biased. **Check & Review—***Personality Development (p. 366)* **Part B** 1. c. 2. Thomas and Chess describe three categories of **temperament**—easy, difficult, and slow-to-warm-up—that seem to correlate with stable personality differences. 3. (a) Marcos=trust versus mistrust, (b) Ann=identity versus role confusion, (c) Teresa=initiative versus guilt, (d) George=ego integrity versus despair. 4. Stage 2=autonomy vs. shame and doubt, Stage 8=ego integrity vs. despair. **Check & Review—***Meeting the Challenges of Adulthood (p. 374)* **Part B** 1. Answers will vary. 2. good intellectual functioning, relationships with caring adults, and the ability to regulate their attention, emotions, and behavior. 3. **activity, disengagement**. 4. The **socioemotional selectivity theory** suggests that successful aging is characterized by mutual withdrawal between the elderly and society. 5. The so-called *midlife crisis* is a myth that proposes that almost everyone experiences a predictable crisis in middle age that leads to drastic changes in personality and behavior. The *empty-nest syndrome*, which suggests that most parents experience a painful separation and depression when the last child leaves home, is also a myth that is not supported by research. *Research Challenge (p. 379)* 1. Experimental. 2. IV (Level 1)=ethical behavior (not lying) vs. unethical behavior (lying), IV (Level 2)=mode of communication by mouth vs. mode of communication by email. DV=rating of consumer products (hand sanitizer or mouthwash). (Note: Sophisticated research often has more than one level (or treatment) for the IV. In this experiment, the researchers use multiple levels to examine both the simple effect of each IV, as well as interactions between the IVs. Also note that in this particular experiment there is no control group. Instead, many experiments legitimately employ comparison groups, which still allow us to legitimately state that the IV was the cause of the effect.) **Check & Review—***Grief and Death and Psychology Engages (p. 382)* **Part B** 1. numbness, yearning, disorganization/despair, resolution/reorganization. 2. Preschool children only understand the permanence of death, they do not yet comprehend the nonfunctionality or universality of death. 3. (a) bargaining, (b) denial, (c) acceptance, (d) anger, (e) depression. 4. Critics of the five stages of dying suggest that this model has not been scientifically validated, each person's bereavement or death is unique, and popularizing this stage theory may cause further avoidance and stereotyping of those who are grieving or dying. 5. **thanatology**. 6. Research shows that the greater group social support among some ethnicities may help reduce the losses that accompany aging.

Chapter 11 Check & Review—Studying *Human Sexuality (p. 390)* **Part B** 1. b. 2. Havelock Ellis. 3. Alfred Kinsey. 4. Masters and Johnson. **Check & Review—***Sex and Gender (p. 398)* **Part B** 1. (b) chromosomal sex, (d) **gender identity**, (a) gonadal sex, (i) **gender role**, (c) hormonal sex, (e) secondary sex characteristics, (g) external genitals, (h) sexual orientation, (f) internal accessory organs. 2. **Social-learning theory** emphasizes learning through rewards, punishments, and imitation. **Gender-schema theory** focuses on the active, thinking processes of the child. 3. **androgyny**. 4. d. **Check & Review—***Sexual Behavior (p. 401)* **Part B** 1. (a) **excitement**, (b) **plateau**, (c) **orgasm**, (d) **resolution**. 2. Masters and Johnson identified a four-stage **sexual response cycle** (excitement, plateau, orgasm, and resolution) that acknowledged both similarities and differences between the sexes. However differences are the focus of most research. 3. c. 4. d. **Myth Busters** *Exercise (p. 409)* **Part B.**

- *Gender role conditioning:* A main part of traditional gender conditioning is the belief that women should be the "gatekeepers" for sexuality and men should be the "pursuers." This belief contributes to the myth that male sexuality is overpowering and women are responsible for controlling the situation.
- *Double standard:* Female gender role also encourages passivity, and women are not taught how to aggressively defend themselves. People who believe the myth that women cannot be raped against their will generally overlook the fact that the female gender role encourages passivity and women are not taught how to aggressively defend themselves.

- *Media portrayals*: Novels and films typically portray a woman resisting her attacker and then melting into passionate responsiveness. This helps perpetuate the myth that women secretly want to be raped and the myth that she might as well "relax and enjoy it."
- *Lack of information*: The myth that women cannot be raped against their will overlooks the fact that most men are much stronger and much faster than most women, and a woman's clothing and shoes further hinder her ability to escape. The myth that women cannot rape men ignores the fact that men can have erections despite negative emotions while being raped. Furthermore, an erection is unnecessary, since many rapists (either male or female) often use foreign objects to rape their victims. The myth that all women secretly want to be raped overlooks the fact that if a woman fantasizes about being raped she remains in complete control, whereas in an actual rape she is completely powerless. Also, fantasies contain no threat of physical harm, while rape does.
- **Tips for Rape Prevention** Sex educators and researchers suggest the following techniques for reducing stranger rape (the rape of a person by an unknown assailant) and acquaintance (or date) rape (committed by someone who is known to the victim) (Allgeier & Allgeier, 2005, Crooks & Baur, 2005). To avoid stranger rape: 1. Follow commonsense advice for avoiding all forms of crime: lock your car, park in lighted areas, install dead-bolt locks on your doors, don't open your door to strangers, don't hitchhike, etc. 2. Make yourself as strong as possible. Take a self-defense course, carry a loud whistle with you, and demonstrate self-confidence with your body language. Research shows that rapists tend to select women who appear passive and weak (Richards et al., 1991). 3. During an attack, run away if you can, talk to the rapist as a way to stall, and/or attempt to alert others by screaming ("Help, rape, call the police") (Shotland & Stebbins, 1980). When all else fails, women should actively resist an attack, according to current research (Fischhoff, 1992, Furby & Fischhoff, 1992). Loud shouting, fighting back, and causing a scene may deter an attack. To prevent acquaintance rape: 1. Be careful on first dates—date in groups and in public places, avoid alcohol and other drugs (Gross & Billingham, 1998). 2. Be assertive and clear in your communication—say what you want and what you don't want. Accept a partner's refusal. If sexual coercion escalates, match the assailant's behavior with your own form of escalation—begin with firm refusals, get louder, threaten to call the police, begin shouting and use strong physical resistance. Don't be afraid to make a scene!

Research Challenge (p. 414) 1. Descriptive. 2. Survey. **Check & Review—*Sex Problems and Psychology Engages (p. 415)* Part B** 1. The parasympathetic branch of the autonomic nervous system dominates during sexual arousal, whereas the sympathetic branch dominates during ejaculation and orgasm. 2. c. 3. Relationship focus, integration of physiological and psychosocial factors, emphasis on cognitive factors, emphasis on specific behavioral techniques. 4. Remain abstinent or have sex with one mutually faithful, uninfected partner. Do not use IV drugs or have sex with someone who does. If you do use IV drugs, sterilize or don't share equipment. Avoid contact with blood, vaginal secretions, and semen. Avoid anal intercourse. Don't have sex if either you or your partner is impaired by drugs. 5. Cultural comparisons put sex in a broader perspective and help counteract ethnocentrism. 6. d. 7. David, the twin who suffered the botched circumcision, always had a male gender identity–despite being raised and dressed as a girl, which defies the gender role and transvestism labels. As an adult, he also married a woman, which suggests a heterosexual orientation. 8. Answers will vary.

Chapter 12 Myth Busters (p. 422) The one false answer is that polygraph tests are reliable. **Check & Review—*Theories of Motivation (p. 428)* Part B** 1. An **instinct** is an unlearned, behavioral pattern that is uniform in expression and universal in a species. **Homeostasis** is the state of balance or stability in the body's internal environment. 2. **drive-reduction theory**. 3. (a) ii, (b) iii, (c) v, (d) iv, (e) i. 4. **optimal arousal**. 5. d. 6. **hierarchy of needs. Check & Review—*Motivation and Behavior (p. 434)* Part B** 1. d. 2. **anorexia nervosa**. 3. d. 4. preference for moderately difficult tasks, competitiveness, preference for clear goals with competent feedback, responsibility, persistence, more accomplishments. **Check & Review—*Components and Theories of Emotion (p. 442)* Part B** 1. (a) i, (b) iii, (c) ii and iv. 2. sympathetic, autonomic. 3. Duchenne smile. 4. a. 5. d. 6. simultaneously. 7. d. **Research Challenge (p. 449)** 1. Experimental method. 2. IV(Level 1)=fear-arousing bridge vs. non-fear-arousing bridge. IV(Level 2)=

male or female interviewer. DV(Measure 1)=sexual content of stories DV(Measure 2)= number of calls to the male or female interviewers. Experimental group=male passersby contacted on fear-arousing bridge. Control group=male passersby contacted on non-fear-arousing bridge. (Note: Once again, sophisticated research often has more than one level (or treatment) for the independent variable, and that in this experiment there also are two measures for the dependent variable.) **Check & Review—*Critical Thinking About Motivation and Behavior and Psychology Engages (p. 451)* Part B** 1. d. 2. c. 3. a. 4. b.

Chapter 13 Check & Review—*Trait Theories (p. 462)* Part B 1. a trait. 2. (a) ii, (b) iii, (c) iv, (d) v, (e) i. 3. e. ***Applying Defense Mechanisms (p. 465)*** 1. projection. 2. rationalization. 3. sublimation. 4. displacement. 5. regression. **Check & Review–*Psychoanalytic/ Psychodynamic Theories (p. 470)* Part B** 1. The **conscious** is the tip of the iceberg and the highest level of awareness, the **preconscious** is just below the surface but can readily be brought to awareness, the **unconscious** is the large base of the iceberg and operates below the level of awareness. 2. b. 3. Freud believed an individual's adult **personality** reflected his or her resolution of the specific crisis presented in each **psychosexual stage** (oral, anal, phallic, latency, and genital). 4. (a) Adler, (b) Horney, (c) Jung, (d) Horney. **Check & Review—*Humanistic Theories (p. 473)* Part B** 1. a. 2. c. 3. self-actualization. 4. Humanistic theories are criticized for their naive assumptions, poor testability and inadequate evidence, and narrowness in merely describing, not explaining, behavior. ***Test Yourself (p. 477)*** 1. j. 2. d. 3. f. 4. i. 5. h. 6. g. 7. e. 8. c. 9. a. 10. b. **Check & Review–*Social-Cognitive and Biological Theories (p. 477)* Part B** 1. **reciprocal determinism**. 2. c. 3. external locus of control, internal locus of control. 4. Biological. 5. b. 6. biopsychosocial. 7. Answers will vary. **Research Challenge (p. 484)** 1. Correlational. 2. Positive correlation. **Check & Review—*Personality Assessment and Psychology Engages (p. 486)* Part B** 1. (a) ii, (b) i, (c) iii. 2. **projective**. 3. b. 4. People accept pseudo personality tests because they offer generalized statements that apply to almost everyone (*Barnum effect*), they notice and remember events that confirm predictions and ignore the misses (*fallacy of positive instances*), and they prefer information that maintains a positive self-image (*self-serving bias*).

Chapter 14 Check & Review—*Studying Psychological Disorders (p. 499)* Part B 1. Deviance, dysfunction, distress, or danger. 2. b. 3. Early versions of the DSM used **neurosis** to refer to mental disorders related to anxiety. In contrast, **psychosis** is currently used to describe disorders characterized by loss of contact with reality and extreme mental disruption. **Insanity** is a legal term for people with a mental disorder that implies a lack of responsibility for behavior and an inability to manage their own affairs. 4. Compare your answers with Figure 14.3 p. 498. 5. The chief advantages of the **Diagnostic and Statistical Manual (DSM)** is that it provides detailed descriptions of symptoms, which in turn allows standardized diagnosis and improved communication among professionals and between professionals and patients. The major disadvantages are that it might encourage overdiagnosing, it may be culturally biased, and the label "mental illness" may lead to social and economic discrimination. **Check & Review—*Anxiety Disorders (p. 504)* Part B** 1. Compare your answers with Figure 14.4 p. 500. 2. (a) ii, (b) i, (c) iii, (d) iv. 3. psychological, biological, and sociocultural factors. 4. Learning theorists most often believe anxiety disorders result from classical and operant conditioning. Social learning theorists argue that imitation and modeling are the cause. **Check & Review—*Mood Disorders (p. 509)* Part B** 1. **major depressive disorder** and **bipolar disorder**. 2. c. 3. Compare your answers with the Myth Busters pp. 506 and 507. 4. Seligman believes the individual becomes resigned to pain and sadness and feels unable to change, which leads to depression. 5. causes that are internal, stable, and global. **Check & Review—*Schizophrenia (p. 515)* Part B** 1. psychosis. 2. c. 3. a. 4. Three biological causes include genetics, neurotransmitters, and brain abnormalities. Two possible psychosocial causes of **schizophrenia** may be the **diathesis-stress model** and family communication problems. ***Test Yourself (p. 520)*** 1. c. 2. e. 3. b. 4. a. 5. f. 6. d. **Research Challenge (p. 522)** 1. Descriptive method. 2. Case study. **Check & Review—*Other Disorders and Psychology Engages (p. 525)* Part B** 1. anxiety. 2. **Dissociative identity disorder (DID)** refers to a dissociative disorder characterized by the presence of two or more distinct personality systems within the same individual. 3. **Antisocial**. 4. d. 5. perfection. 6. Answers will vary. 7. Answers will vary.

Chapter 15 Check & Review—*Psychoanalysis/Psychodynamic Therapies (p. 536)* Part B 1. c. 2. Mary may be exhibiting **transference**, reacting to her therapist as she apparently did to someone earlier in her life. John is most likely exhibiting **resistance,** arriving late because he fears what his unconscious might reveal. 3. Limited applicability, lack of scientific credibility. 4. Modern **psychodynamic therapy** is briefer, face-to-face, more directive, and emphasizes current problems and conscious processes. *Test Yourself (p. 541)* All four techniques are shown in this example: **empathy** ("they scare the hell out of me too"), **unconditional positive regard** (therapist's acceptance and nonjudgmental attitude and caring about not wanting to do "anything that is upsetting" to the client), **genuineness** (the therapist's ability to laugh and make a joke at his or her own expense), and **active listening** (therapist demonstrated genuine interest in what the client was saying). **Check & Review—*Cognitive and Humanistic Therapies (p. 541)* Part B** 1. faulty thought processes and beliefs. 2. **cognitive restructuring.** 3. The activating event, the belief system, the emotional consequence, and disputing irrational thoughts. 4. a) magnification, b) all-or-nothing thinking. 4. a) empathy, b) unconditional positive regard, (c) genuineness, (d) active listening. **Check & Review—*Group, Family, and Marital Therapies (p. 544)* Part B** 1. **group therapy.** 2. less expense, group support, insight and information, behavior rehearsal. 3. **Self-help groups** are recommended as a supplement to individual therapy. 4. d. **Check & Review—*Behavior Therapies (p. 548)* Part B** 1. **behavior therapy.** 2. c. 3. By rewarding successive approximations of a target behavior, the patient is *shaped* toward more adaptive behaviors. 4. Behavior therapy is criticized for possible lack of generalizability and questionable ethics. **Check & Review—*Biomedical Therapies (p. 552)* Part B** 1. d. 2. **antianxiety, antipsychotic, mood stabilizer, antidepressant.** 3. b. 4. b. 5. c. **Research Challenge (p. 557)** 1. Descriptive method. 2. Survey. **Critical Thinking (p. 560)** 1. resistance; 2. unconditional positive regard; 3. genuineness; 4. A=troublesome relationships and antisocial behavior, B=being unlovable and blaming himself for his childhood abuse, C=feeling unloved, D=children are never responsible for their own abuse; 5. selective perception. **Check & Review—*Therapy Essentials and Psychology Engages (p. 561)* Part B** 1. Compare your answers to Concept Organizer 15.2 p. 553. 2. (a) cognitive therapists, (b) psychoanalysts, (c) biomedical therapists, (d) humanistic therapists, (e) behavior therapists. 3. Naming the problem, qualities of the therapist, therapist credibility, placing the problem in a familiar framework, applying techniques that bring relief, a special time and place. 4. c. 5. Rates of diagnosis and treatment of mental disorders, stresses of poverty, stresses of aging, violence against women, stresses of multiple roles.

Chapter 16 Myth Busters (p. 568) Number 5 is false. **Check & Review—*Our Thoughts About Others (p. 573)* Part B** 1. c. 2. When judging the causes of others' behaviors, we tend to overestimate internal personality factors and underestimate external situational factors. 3. (a) cognitive, (b) affective, (c) behavioral. 4. cognitive dissonance. **Check & Review—*Our Feelings About Others (p. 581)* Part B** 1. **Prejudice** is an attitude with behavioral tendencies that may or may not be activated. **Discrimination** is actual negative behavior directed at members of an outgroup. 2. b. 3. Answers will vary. 4. Romantic love is short lived (6 to 30 months) and largely based on mystery and fantasy, which leads to inevitable disappointment. Companionate love is long lasting and grows stronger with time. **Check & Review—*Social Influence (p. 585)* Part B** 1. **Conformity** involves changing behavior in response to real or imagined pressure from others. **Obedience** involves giving in to a command from others. 2. Solomon Asch. 3. the effects of punishment on learning and memory. 4. c. **Check & Review—*Group Processes (pp. 589–590)* Part B** 1. Guards were abusing their power and prisoners were becoming dehumanized and depressed. 2. **deindividuation.** 3. b. 4. illusion of invulnerability, belief in the morality of the group, collective rationalizations, stereotypes of the outgroup, self-censorship of doubts and dissenting opinions, illusion of unanimity, and direct pressure on dissenters. 5. b. **Check & Review—*Aggression and Altruism (p. 594)* Part B** 1. The major biological factors are instincts, genes, brain and nervous system, substance abuse and other mental disorders, hormones and neurotransmitters. The key psychosocial factors are aversive stimuli, culture and learning, and violent media. 2. Introduce incompatible responses and improve social and communication skills. 3. According to evolutionary theorists, **altruism** evolved because it favored overall genetic survival. The **egoistic model** says helping is motivated by anticipated gain for the helper. The **empathy—altruism hypothesis** suggests helping is activated when the helper feels empathy for the victim. 4. d. **Research Challenge (p. 598)** 1. Descriptive method. 2. Survey. **Check & Review—*Psychology Engages (p. 601)* Part B** 1. cooperation and common goals. 2. the **foot-in-the-door technique.** 3. Rosa Parks' act of disobedience was an important role model for others and a catalyst for the small but growing civil rights movement, which led to the later repeal of Jim Crow laws in the South. 4. c. 5. empathizing.

Glossary

Abnormal Behavior Patterns of behaviors, thoughts, or emotions considered pathological (diseased or disordered) for one or more of four reasons: deviance, dysfunction, distress, or danger *Page 493*

Absolute Threshold Minimum amount of a stimulus that an observer can reliably detect *Page 129*

Accommodation Automatic adjustment of the eye, which occurs when muscles change the shape of the lens so that it focuses light on the retina from objects at different distances *Page 134*

Accommodation In Piaget's theory, adjusting existing mental patterns (schemas), or developing new ones, to better fit with new information; mental schemas are changed to accommodate new information *Page 339*

Achievement Motivation Desire to excel, especially in competition with others *Page 433*

Acquisition Basic classical conditioning when a neutral stimulus (NS) is consistently paired with an unconditioned stimulus (UCS) so that the NS comes to elicit a conditioned response (CR) *Page 211*

Action Potential Neural impulse, or brief electrical charge, that carries information along the axon of a neuron. The action potential is generated when positively charged ions move in and out through channels in the axon's membrane *Page 54*

Activation–Synthesis Hypothesis Hobson's theory that dreams are by-products of random stimulation of brain cells; the brain attempts to combine (or synthesize) this spontaneous activity into coherent patterns, known as dreams *Page 179*

Active Listening Listening with total attention to what another is saying; involves reflecting, paraphrasing, and clarifying what the person says and means *Page 540*

Activity Theory of Aging Successful aging is fostered by a full and active commitment to life *Page 373*

Addiction Broad term describing a compulsion to use a specific drug or engage in a certain activity *Page 185*

Ageism Prejudice or discrimination based on physical age *Page 336*

Aggression Any behavior intended to harm someone *Page 590*

Agonist Drug Mimics and enhances a neurotransmitter's effect *Page 183*

AIDS (Acquired Immunodeficiency Syndrome) Human immunodeficiency viruses (HIVs) destroy the immune system's ability to fight disease, leaving the body vulnerable to a variety of opportunistic infections and cancers *Page 408*

Algorithm Logical, step-by-step procedure that, if followed correctly, will eventually solve the problem *Page 287*

Alternate States of Consciousness (ASCs) Mental states, other than ordinary waking consciousness, found during sleep, dreaming, psychoactive drug use, hypnosis, and so on *Page 168*

Altruism Actions designed to help others with no obvious benefit to the helper *Page 591*

Alzheimer's [ALTS-high-merz] Disease (AD) Progressive mental deterioration characterized by severe memory loss *Page 270*

Amygdala Limbic system structure linked to the production and regulation of emotions (e.g., aggression and fear) *Page 69*

Amygdala Limbic system structure linked to the production and regulation of emotions *Page 435*

Androgyny [an-DRAW-juh-nee] Exhibiting both masculine and feminine traits; from the Greek andro, meaning "male," and gyn, meaning "female" *Page 392*

Anorexia Nervosa Eating disorder characterized by a severe loss of weight resulting from self-imposed starvation and an obsessive fear of obesity *Page 431*

Antagonist Drug Blocks normal neurotransmitter functioning *Page 183*

Anterograde Amnesia Inability to form new memories after a brain injury; forward-acting amnesia *Page 270*

Antianxiety Drugs Medications used to produce relaxation, reduce anxiety, and decrease overarousal in the brain *Page 550*

Antidepressant Drugs Medications used to treat depression, some anxiety disorders, and certain eating disorders (such as bulimia) *Page 550*

Antipsychotic Drugs Medications used to diminish or eliminate hallucinations, delusions, withdrawal, and other symptoms of psychosis; also known as neuroleptics or major tranquilizers *Page 550*

Antisocial Personality Disorder Extreme disregard for, and violation of the rights of others; guiltless, exploitive, irresponsible, intrusive, and self-indulgent *Page 519*

Anxiety Disorder Overwhelming apprehension and fear accompanied by autonomic nervous system (ANS) arousal *Page 500*

Applied Research Research designed to solve practical problems *Page 16*

Approach–Approach Conflict Forced choice between two options which have equally desirable charac-teristics *Page 98*

Approach–Avoidance Conflict Forced choice within one option, which has desirable and undesirable characteristics *Page 98*

Archetypes [AR-KEH-types] According to Jung, the images and patterns of thoughts, feelings, and behavior that reside in the collective unconscious *Page 468*

Assertiveness Standing up for your rights without infringing on those of others *Page 670*

Assimilation In Piaget's theory, applying existing mental patterns (schemas) to new information; new information is incorporated (assimilated) into existing schemas *Page 339*

Association Areas So-called quiet areas in the cerebral cortex involved in interpreting, integrating, and acting on information processed by other parts of the brain *Page 73*

Attachment Strong emotional bond with special others that endures over time *Page 346*

Attitude Learned predisposition to respond cognitively, affectively, and behaviorally to a particular object *Page 570*

Attribution How we explain our own and others' actions *Page 568*

Audition Sense or act of hearing *Page 138*

Autocratic (Authoritarian) Leader Emerges during times of crisis to make all major decisions, assign tasks to members of the group, and demand full obedience *Page 620*

Automatic Processes Mental activities requiring minimal attention and having little impact on other activities *Page 170*

Autonomic Nervous System (ANS) Subdivision of the peripheral nervous system (PNS) that controls involuntary functions, such as heart rate and digestion. It is further subdivided into the sympathetic nervous system, which arouses, and the parasympathetic nervous system, which calms *Page 62*

Availability Heuristic Judging the likelihood or probability of an event based on how readily available other instances of the event are in memory *Page 289*

Aversion Therapy Pairing an aversive (unpleasant) stimulus with a maladaptive behavior *Page 545*

Avoidance–Avoidance Conflict Forced choice between two options both of which have undesirable characteristics *Page 98*

Axon Long, tubelike structure that conveys impulses away from the neuron's cell body toward other neurons or to muscles or glands *Page 53*

Babbling Vowel/consonant combinations that infants begin to produce at about 4 to 6 months of age *Page 296*

Bait-and-Switch Technique Offering an attractive proposal, then making it unavailable or unappealing and offering a more costly alternative *Page 654*

Basic Anxiety According to Horney, the feelings of helplessness and insecurity that adults experience because as children they felt alone and isolated in a hostile environment *Page 469*

Basic Research Research conducted to advance scientific knowledge *Page 16*

Behavior Therapy Group of techniques based on learning principles used to change maladaptive behaviors *Page 544*

Behavioral Genetics Study of the relative effects of heredity and the environment on behavior and mental processes *Page 79*

Behavioral Perspective Emphasizes objective, observable environmental influences on overt behavior *Page 12*

Binocular Cues Visual input from two eyes that allows perception of depth or distance *Page 151*

Biofeedback Involuntary bodily process (such as blood pressure or heart rate) is recorded, and the information is fed back to an organism to increase voluntary control over that bodily function *Page 236*

Biological Perspective Emphasizes genetics and biological processes in the brain and other parts of the nervous system *Page 14*

Biological Preparedness Built-in (innate) readiness to form associations between certain stimuli and responses *Page 232*

Biological Research Scientific studies of the brain and other parts of the nervous system *Page 31*

Biomedical Therapy Using biological interventions (drugs, electroconvulsive therapy, and psychosurgery) to treat psychological disorders *Page 548*

Biopsychosocial Model Unifying theme of modern psychology that incorporates biological, psychological, and social processes *Page 15*

Bipolar Disorder Repeated episodes of mania (unreasonable elation, often with hyperactivity) alternating with depression *Page 505*

Blind Spot Point at which the optic nerve leaves the eye; contains no receptor cells for vision—thus creating a "blind spot" *Page 134*

Borderline Personality Disorder (BPD) Severe instability in emotion and self-concept, along with impulsive and self-destructive behavior *Page 520*

Bottom-Up Processing Information processing beginning "at the bottom," with raw sensory data that are sent "up" to the brain for higher-level analysis; data-driven processing that moves from the parts to the whole *Page 126*

Brainstem Area of the brain that houses parts of the hindbrain, midbrain, and forebrain, and helps regulate reflex activities critical for survival (such as heartbeat and respiration) *Page 66*

Bulimia Nervosa Eating disorder involving the consumption of large quantities of food (bingeing), followed by vomiting, extreme exercise, and/or laxative use (purging) *Page 431*

Burnout State of psychological and physical exhaustion resulting from chronic exposure to high levels of stress and little personal control *Page 96*

Cannon–Bard Theory Emotions and physiological changes occur simultaneously ("I'm crying and feeling sad at the same time"); in this view, all emotions are physiologically similar *Page 438*

Case Study In-depth study of a single research participant *Page 28*

Cataclysmic Event Stressful occurrences that occur suddenly and generally affect many people simultaneously *Page 99*

Cell Body Part of the neuron containing the cell nucleus, as well as other structures that help the neuron carry out its functions; also known as the soma *Page 53*

Central Nervous System (CNS) Brain and spinal cord *Page 58*

Central Route to Persuasion Method of persuasion in which a highly involved, motivated, and attentive audience is convinced on the basis of logic and careful analysis of the arguments *Page 655*

Cerebellum [sehr-uh-BELL-um] Hindbrain structure responsible for coordinating fine muscle movement, balance, and some perception and cognition *Page 67*

Cerebral Cortex Thin surface layer on the cerebral hemispheres that regulates most complex behavior, including sensations, motor control, and higher mental processes *Page 70*

Charismatic Leader Possesses a compelling vision that transforms follower's beliefs, values, and goals *Page 618*

Chromosome Threadlike molecule of DNA (deoxyribonucleic acid) that carries genetic information *Page 79*

Chronic Stressors State of ongoing arousal in which the parasympathetic system cannot activate the relaxation response *Page 96*

Chunking Grouping separate pieces of information into a single unit (or chunk) *Page 253*

Circadian [sir-KADE-ee-un] **Rhythms** Biological changes that occur on a *24-hour cycle* (circa = "about" and dies = "day") *Page 171*

Classical Conditioning Learning through involuntarily paired associations; it occurs when a previously neutral stimulus (NS) is paired (associated) with an unconditioned stimulus (UCS) to elicit a conditioned response (CR) *Page 208*

Client-Centered Therapy Rogers's therapy emphasizing the client's natural tendency to become healthy and productive; techniques include empathy, unconditional positive regard, genuineness, and active listening *Page 539*

Cochlea [KOK-lee-uh] Three-chambered, snail-shaped structure in the inner ear containing the receptors for hearing *Page 138*

Coercive Power Based on the ability to use punishment, or the, threat of it, for failure to comply with desired behavior *Page 623*

Cognition Mental activities involved in acquiring, storing, retrieving, and using knowledge *Page 283*

Cognitive Dissonance Unpleasant tension and anxiety caused by a discrepancy between an attitude and a behavior *Page 571*

Cognitive Map Mental image of a three-dimensional space that an organism has navigated *Page 227*

Cognitive Perspective Focuses on thinking, perceiving, and information processing *Page 13*

Cognitive Restructuring Process in cognitive therapy to change destructive thoughts or inappropriate interpretations *Page 536*

Cognitive Therapy Therapy that treats problem behaviors and mental processes by focusing on faulty thought processes and beliefs *Page 536*

Cognitive-Behavior Therapy combines cognitive therapy (changing faulty thinking) with behavior therapy (changing faulty behaviors) *Page 536*

Cognitive-Social Theory Emphasizes the roles of thinking and social learning in behavior *Page 227*

Collective Unconscious Jung's concept of a reservoir of inherited, universal experiences that all humans share *Page 468*

Collectivistic Cultures Needs and goals of the group are emphasized over the needs and goals of the individual *Page 380*

Communication Interdependent process of sending, receiving, and understanding messages *Page 638*

Comorbidity Co-occurrence of two or more disorders in the same person at the same time, as when a person suffers from both depression and alcoholism *Page 517*

Companionate Love Strong and lasting attraction characterized by trust, caring, tolerance, and friendship *Page 580*

Concept Mental representation of a group or category that shares similar characteristics (e.g., the concept of a river groups together the Nile, the Amazon, and the Mississippi because they share the common characteristic of being a large stream of water that empties into an ocean or lake) *Page 285*

Concrete Operational Stage Piaget's third stage of cognitive development (roughly age 7 to *11*); child can perform mental operations on concrete objects and understand reversibility and conservation, but thinking is tied to concrete, tangible objects and events *Page 342*

Conditioned Emotional Response (CER) Classically conditioned emotional response to a previously neutral stimulus (NS) *Page 208*

Conditioned Response (CR) Learned reaction to a conditioned stimulus (CS) that occurs because of previous repeated pairings with an unconditioned stimulus (UCS) *Page 208*

Conditioned Stimulus (CS) Previously neutral stimulus that, through repeated pairings with an unconditioned stimulus (UCS), now elicits a conditioned response (CR) *Page 208*

Conditioning Process of learning associations between stimuli and behavioral responses *Page 206*

Conduction Deafness Middle-ear deafness resulting from problems with transferring sound waves to the inner ear *Page 140*

Cones Visual receptor cells, concentrated near the center of the retina, responsible for color vision and fine detail; most sensitive in brightly lit conditions *Page 134*

Confirmation Bias Preferring information that confirms preexisting positions or beliefs, while ignoring or discounting contradictory evidence *Page 289*

Conflict Forced choice between two or more incompatible goals or impulses *Pages 97, 659*

Conformity Changing behavior because of real or imagined group pressure *Page 582*

Confounding Variables Nuisance variables that may affect the outcome of the study and lead to erroneous conclusions *Page 23*

Conscious In Freudian terms, thoughts or motives that a person is currently aware of or is remembering *Page 463*

Consciousness Organism's awareness of its own self and surroundings (Damasio, 1999) *Page 168*

Conservation Understanding that certain physical characteristics (such as volume) remain unchanged, even when their outward appearance changes *Page 342*

Consolidation Process by which neural changes associated with recent learning become durable and stable *Page 270*

Constructive Process Organizing and shaping of information during processing, storage, and retrieval of memories *Page 248*

Continuous Reinforcement Every correct response is reinforced *Page 219*

Control Group Group that receives no treatment in an experiment *Page 23*

Controlled Processes Mental activities requiring focused attention that generally interfere with other ongoing activities *Page 170*

Conventional Level Kohlberg's second level of moral development, in which moral judgments are based on compliance with the rules and values of society *Page 362*

Convergence Binocular depth cue in which the closer the object, the more the eyes converge, or turn inward *Page 154*

Convergent Thinking Narrowing down alternatives to converge on a single correct answer (e.g., standard academic tests generally require convergent thinking) *Page 292*

Cooing Vowel-like sounds infants produce beginning around 2 to 3 months of age *Page 296*

Corpus Callosum [CORE-pus] [cah-LOH-suhm] Bundle of nerve fibers connecting the brain's left and right hemispheres *Page 75*

Correlation Coefficient Number indicating strength and direction of the relationship between two variables (from −1.00 to +1.00) *Page 30*

Correlational Research Research method in which variables are observed or measured (without directly manipulating) to identify relationships between them *Page 29*

Creativity Ability to produce valued outcomes in a novel way *Page 291*

Critical Period A time of special sensitivity to specific types of learning, which shapes the capacity for future development *Page 325*

Critical Thinking Process of objectively evaluating, comparing, analyzing, and synthesizing information *Page 5*

Cross-Sectional Method Measures individuals of various ages at one point in time and gives information about age differences *Page 326*

Crystallized Intelligence Knowledge and skills gained through experience and education that tend to increase over the life span *Page 300*

Debriefing Upon completion of the research, participants are informed of the study's design and purpose, and explanations are provided for any possible deception *Page 19*

Defense Mechanisms In Freudian theory, the ego's protective method of reducing anxiety by distorting reality and self-deception *Page 464*

Deindividuation Reduced self-consciousness, inhibition, and personal responsibility that sometimes occurs in a group, particularly when the members feel anonymous *Page 587*

Delusions Mistaken beliefs based on misrepresentations of reality *Page 511*

Democratic (Participative) Leader Encourages group discussion and decision making through consensus building *Page 620*

Dendrites Branching neuron structures that receive neural impulses from other neurons and convey impulses toward the cell body *Page 52*

Dependent Variable (DV) Variable that is measured; it is affected by (or dependent on) the independent variable *Page 23*

Depressants Drugs that act on the brain and other parts of the nervous system to decrease bodily processes and overall responsiveness *Page 188*

Depth Perception The ability to perceive three-dimensional space and to accurately judge distance *Page 151*

Descriptive Research Research methods that observe and record behavior and mental processes without producing causal explanations *Page 27*

Developmental Psychology Study of age-related changes in behavior and mental processes from conception to death *Page 324*

Diagnostic and Statistical Manual of Mental Disorders (DSM-IV-TR) Classification system developed by the American Psychiatric Association used to describe abnormal behaviors; the "IV-TR" indicates it is the text revision (TR) of the fourth major revision (IV) *Page 494*

Diathesis-Stress Model Suggests that people inherit a predisposition (or "diathesis") that increases their risk for mental disorders if exposed to certain extremely stressful life experiences *Page 515*

Difference Threshold Minimal difference needed to notice a stimulus change; also called the "just noticeable difference" (JND) *Page 129*

Diffusion of Responsibility The dilution (or diffusion) of personal responsibility for acting by spreading it among all other group members *Page 593*

Discrimination Negative behaviors directed at members of a group *Page 573*

Discriminative Stimulus Cue signaling when a specific response will lead to the expected reinforcement *Page 226*

Disengagement Theory of Aging Successful aging is characterized by mutual withdrawal between the elderly and society *Page 373*

Dissociative Disorder Amnesia, fugue, or multiple personalities resulting from a splitting apart of experience from memory or consciousness *Page 518*

Dissociative Identity Disorder (DID) Presence of two or more distinct personality systems in the same individual at different times; previously known as multiple personality disorder *Page 518*

Distress Unpleasant, threatening stress *Page 94*

Distributed Practice Practice (or study) sessions are interspersed with rest periods *Page 264*

Divergent Thinking Thinking that produces many alternatives from a single starting point; a major element of creativity (e.g., finding as many uses as possible for a paper clip) *Page 291*

Door-in-the-Face Technique Beginning with a very large, intrusive request followed by a smaller request *Page 653*

Dopamine Hypothesis Theory that overactivity of dopamine neurons may contribute to some forms of schizophrenia *Page 514*

Double Standard Beliefs, values, and norms that subtly encourage male sexuality and discourage female sexuality *Page 404*

Double-Blind Study Both the researcher and the participants are unaware (blind) of who is in the experimental or control group *Page 25*

Dream Analysis In psychoanalysis, interpreting the underlying true meaning of dreams to reveal unconscious processes *Page 534*

Drive-Reduction Theory Motivation begins with a physiological need (a lack or deficiency) that elicits a drive toward behavior that will satisfy the original need; once the need is met, a state of balance (homeostasis) is restored and motivation decreases *Page 423*

Drug Abuse Drug taking that causes emotional or physical harm to the drug user or others *Page 185*

Eclectic Approach Combining techniques from various theories to find the most appropriate treatment *Page 553*

Ego In Freud's theory, the rational, decision-making component of personality that operates according to the reality principle; from the Latin term *ego*, meaning "I" *Page 464*

Egocentrism Inability to consider another's point of view, which Piaget considered a hallmark of the preoperational stage *Page 341*

Egoistic Model Helping that's motivated by anticipated gain—later reciprocation, increased self-esteem, or avoidance of distress and guilt *Page 592*

Elaborative Rehearsal Linking new information to previously stored material (also known as deeper levels of processing) *Page 250*

Electroconvulsive Therapy (ECT) Biomedical therapy based on passing electrical current through the brain; used almost exclusively to treat serious depression when drug therapy fails *Page 549*

Embodied Cognition A cognitive science research program emphasizing the environment's formative role in the development of cognitive processes; cognitions (thoughts, perceptions, attitudes, beliefs) are shaped ("grounded") by interactions with the environment *Page 378*

Embryonic Period Second stage of prenatal development, which begins after uterine implantation and lasts through the eighth week *Page 329*

Emotion Subjective feeling that includes arousal (heart pounding), cognitions (thoughts, values, and expectations), and expressive behaviors (smiles, frowns, and running) *Page 422*

Emotional Conflict Difficulties between individuals or organizations that arise over feelings of anger, mistrust, dislike, fear, and the like *Page 661*

Emotional Intelligence (EI) Goleman's term for the ability to know and manage one's emotions, empathize with others, and maintain satisfying relationships *Page 443*

Emotion-Focused Coping Managing one's emotional reactions to a stressful situation *Page 112*

Empathy In Rogerian terms, an insightful awareness and ability to share another's inner experience *Page 540*

Empathy–Altruism Hypothesis Helping because of empathy for someone in need *Page 593*

Encoding Specificity Principle Retrieval of information is improved when conditions of recovery are similar to the conditions when information was encoded *Page 258*

Encoding Processing information into the memory system *Page 249*

Encoding, Storage, Retrieval (ESR) Model Memory is formed through three processess: *encoding* (getting information in), *storage* (retaining information for future use), and *retrieval* (recovering information) *Page 249*

Endocrine [EN-doh-krin] System Collection of glands located throughout the body that manufacture and secrete hormones into the bloodstream *Page 64*

Endorphins [en-DOR-fins] Chemical substances in the nervous system that are similar in structure and action to opiates; involved in pain control, pleasure, and memory *Page 57*

Episodic Memory Subsystem of explicit/declarative memory that stores memories of personally experienced events; a mental diary of a person's life *Page 255*

Equity Theory Individuals need a sense of balance in which output is equal to input *Page 625*

Ethnocentrism Believing one's culture is typical of all cultures; also, viewing one's own ethnic group (or culture) as central and "correct" and judging others according to this standard *Page 26*

Eustress Pleasant, desirable stress *Page 94*

Evolutionary Perspective Focuses on natural selection, adaptation, and evolution of behavior and mental processes *Page 14*

Evolutionary Psychology Branch of psychology that studies how evolutionary processes, like natural selection and genetic mutations, affect behavior and mental processes *Page 79*

Evolutionary/Circadian Theory Sleep evolved to conserve energy and as protection from predators; also serves as part of the circadian cycle *Page 178*

Excitement Phase First stage of the sexual response cycle, characterized by increasing levels of arousal and increased engorgement of the genitals *Page 400*

Expectancy Theory Expectancy of outcomes, their desirability, and the effort needed to achieve them all affect worker motivation *Page 626*

Experimental Group Group that receives a treatment in an experiment *Page 23*

Experimental Research Carefully controlled scientific procedure that involves manipulation of variables to determine cause and effect *Page 21*

Experimenter Bias Occurs when researcher influences research results in the expected direction *Page 25*

Expert Power Based on experience and expertise (physician, lawyer) *Page 623*

Explicit (Declarative) Memory Subsystem within long-term memory that consciously stores facts, information, and personal life experiences *Page 254*

External Locus of Control Believing that chance or outside forces beyond one's control determine one's fate *Page 114*

Extinction Gradual disappearance of a conditioned response (CR); occurs when unconditioned stimulus (UCS) is withheld whenever the conditioned stimulus (CS) is presented *Page 212*

Extrasensory Perception (ESP) Perceptual, or "psychic," abilities that supposedly go beyond the known senses (e.g., telepathy, clairvoyance, precognition, and psychokinesis) *Page 157*

Extrinsic Motivation Motivation based on external rewards or threats of punishment *Page 443*

Facial-Feedback Hypothesis Movements of the facial muscles produce and/or intensify our subjective experience of emotion *Page 438*

Factor Analysis Statistical procedure for determining the most basic units or factors in a large array of data *Page 458*

Feature Detectors Specialized neurons that respond only to certain sensory information *Page 146*

Fetal Alcohol Syndrome (FAS) Combination of birth defects, including organ deformities and mental, motor, and/or growth retardation, that results from maternal alcohol abuse *Page 330*

Fetal Period Third, and final, stage of prenatal development (eight weeks to birth), which is characterized by rapid weight gain in the fetus and the fine detailing of bodily organs and systems *Page 329*

Five-Factor Model (FFM) Trait theory of personality that includes openness, conscientiousness, extroversion, agreeableness, and neuroticism *Page 459*

Fixed Interval (FI) Schedule Reinforcement occurs after a predetermined time has elapsed; the interval (time) is fixed *Page 219*

Fixed Ratio (FR) Schedule Reinforcement occurs after a predetermined set of responses; the ratio (number or amount) is fixed *Page 219*

Fluid Intelligence Aspects of innate intelligence, including reasoning abilities, memory, and speed of information processing, that are relatively independent of education and tend to decline as people age *Page 300*

Foot-in-the-Door Technique A first, small request is used as a setup for a later, larger request *Pages 597, 653*

Forebrain Collection of upper level brain structures including the thalamus, hypothalamus, limbic system, and cerebral cortex *Page 68*

Formal Operational Stage Piaget's fourth stage of cognitive development (around age 11 and beyond), characterized by abstract and hypothetical thinking *Page 342*

Fovea Tiny pit in the center of the retina filled with cones; responsible for sharp vision *Page 134*

Free Association In psychoanalysis, reporting whatever comes to mind without monitoring its contents *Page 534*

Frequency Theory Explains that pitch perception occurs when nerve impulses sent to the brain match the frequency of the sound wave *Page 140*

Frontal Lobes Two lobes at the front of the brain governing motor control, speech production, and higher functions, such as thinking, personality, emotion, and memory *Page 71*

Frustration Unpleasant tension, anxiety, and heightened sympathetic activity resulting from a blocked goal *Page 97*

Frustration–Aggression Hypothesis Blocking of a desired goal (frustration) creates anger that may lead to aggression *Page 591*

Functional Fixedness Tendency to think of an object functioning only in its usual or customary way *Page 289*

Fundamental Attribution Error (FAE) Attributing people's behavior to internal (dispositional) causes rather than external (situational) factors *Page 569*

Gate-Control Theory Theory that pain sensations are processed and altered by mechanisms within the spinal cord *Page 131*

Gender Identity Self-identification as being either a man or a woman *Page 394*

Gender Role Societal expectations for "appropriate" male and female behavior *Page 390*

Gender Psychological and sociocultural meanings added to biological maleness or femaleness *Page 390*

Gender-Schema Theory Gender roles are acquired through social learning and active cognitive processing; also, children form gender schemas (mental blueprints) of "correct" behaviors for boys versus girls *Page 392*

Gene Segment of DNA (deoxyribonucleic acid) that occupies a specific place on a particular chromosome and carries the code for hereditary transmission *Page 79*

General Adaptation Syndrome (GAS) Selye's three-stage (alarm, resistance, exhaustion) reaction to chronic stress *Page 100*

Generalized Anxiety Disorder (GAD) Persistent, uncontrollable, and free-floating nonspecified anxiety *Page 500*

Genuineness In Rogerian terms, authenticity or congruence; the awareness of one's true inner thoughts and feelings and being able to share them honestly with others *Page 540*

Germinal Period First stage of prenatal development, which begins with ovulation, conception, and implantation in the uterus (the first two weeks) *Page 329*

Glial Cells Cells that provide structural, nutritional, and other support for the neurons, as well as communication within the nervous system; also called glia or neuroglia *Page 52*

Goal-Setting Theory Having specific and difficult, but attainable, goals leads to higher performance *Page 625*

Grammar System of rules (syntax and semantics) used to create language and communication *Page 294*

Great-Person Theory Leadership results from specific inherited personality traits *Page 618*

Group Polarization Group's movement toward either riskier or more conservative behavior, depending on the members' initial dominant tendency *Page 588*

Group Therapy A number of people meet together to work toward therapeutic goals *Page 542*

Groupthink Faulty decision making that occurs when a highly cohesive group strives for agreement and avoids inconsistent information *Page 588*

Gustation Sense of taste *Page 143*

Habituation The brain's reduced responsiveness to unchanging stimuli *Page 148*

Hallucinations False, imaginary sensory perceptions that occur without external stimuli *Page 511*

Hallucinogens [hal-LOO-sin-oh-jenz] Drugs that produce sensory or perceptual distortions called hall-ucinations *Page 190*

Halo Error Tendency to rate individuals either too high or too low based on one outstanding trait *Page 615*

Hardiness Resilient personality with a strong commitment to personal goals, control over life, and viewing change as a challenge rather than a threat *Page 108*

Hassles Small problems of daily living that accumulate and sometimes become a major source of stress *Page 96*

Hawthorne Effect People change their behavior because of the novelty of the research situation or because they know they are being observed *Page 610*

Health Psychology Studies how biological, psychological, and social factors interact in health and illness *Page 111*

Heritability Measure of the degree to which a characteristic is related to genetic, inherited factors versus the environment *Page 80*

Heuristic Simple rule or shortcut for problem solving that does not guarantee a solution but does narrow the alternatives *Page 287*

Hierarchy of Needs Maslow's theory that lower motives (such as physiological and safety needs) must be met before advancing to higher needs (such as belonging and self-actualization) *Page 427*

Higher-Order Conditioning Neutral stimulus (NS) becomes a conditioned stimulus (CS) through repeated pairings with a previously conditioned stimulus (CS) *Page 213*

Hindbrain Collection of brain structures including the medulla, pons, and cerebellum *Page 67*

Hippocampus Part of the limbic system involved in forming and retrieving memories *Page 69*

HIV Positive Being infected by the human immunodeficiency virus (HIV) *Page 408*

Homeostasis Body's tendency to maintain a relatively balanced and stable internal state, such as a constant internal temperature *Pages 103, 424*

Hormones Chemicals manufactured by endocrine glands and circulated in the bloodstream to produce bodily changes or maintain normal bodily functions *Page 64*

HPA Axis Body's delayed stress response, involving the hypothalamus, pituitary, and adrenal cortex; also called the hypothalamic-pituitary-adrenocortical (HPA) system *Page 100*

Humanistic Perspective Emphasizes free will, self-actualization, and human nature as naturally positive and growth-seeking *Page 13*

Humanistic Therapy Therapy that focuses on removing obstacles that block personal growth and potential *Page 539*

Hypnosis Trancelike state of heightened suggestibility, deep relaxation, and intense focus *Page 195*

Hypothalamus [hi-poh-THAL-uh-muss] Small brain structure beneath the thalamus that helps govern drives (hunger, thirst, sex, and aggression) and hormones *Page 69*

Hypothesis Specific, testable prediction about how one factor, or variable, is related to another *Page 18*

Id According to Freud, the primitive, instinctive component of personality, which works on the pleasure principle *Page 464*

Illusion False or misleading perception *Page 146*

Implicit Bias Hidden, automatic attitude, which may serve as a guide to behaviors independent of a person's awareness or control *Page 598*

Implicit (Nondeclarative) Memory Subsystem within long-term memory consisting of unconscious procedural skills and simple classically conditioned responses *Page 255*

Imprinting Innate form of learning within a critical period that involves attachment to the first large moving object seen *Page 346*

Incentive Theory Motivation results from external stimuli that "pull" the organism in certain directions *Page 426*

Independent Variable (IV) Variable that is manipulated to determine its causal effect on the dependent variable *Page 23*

Individualistic Cultures Needs and goals of the individual are emphasized over the needs and goals of the group *Page 380*

Industrial/Organizational (I/O) Psychology Applied field of psychology concerned with the development and application of scientific principles to the workplace *Page 608*

Inferiority Complex Adler's idea that feelings of inferiority develop from early childhood experiences of helplessness and incompetence *Page 466*

Informational Social Influence Conforming because of a need for information and direction *Page 582*

Informed Consent Participant's agreement to take part in a study after being told what to expect *Page 19*

Ingroup Favoritism Viewing members of the ingroup more positively than members of an outgroup *Page 575*

Inner Ear Cochlea, semicircular canals, and vestibular sacs, which generate neural signals sent to the brain *Page 138*

Insanity Legal term applied when people cannot be held responsible for their actions, or are judged incompetent to manage their own affairs, because of mental illness *Page 495*

Insight Therapies Variety of therapies seeking to improve psychological functioning by increasing awareness into underlying motives and improvement in thoughts, feelings, and/or behaviors *Page 533*

Insight Sudden understanding of a problem that implies the solution *Page 227*

Insomnia Persistent problems in falling asleep, staying asleep, or awakening too early *Page 181*

Instinct Theory Emphasizes inborn, genetic factors in motivation *Page 423*

Instinct Fixed response pattern that is unlearned and found in almost all members of a species *Page 423*

Instinctive Drift Conditioned responses shift (or drift) back toward innate response patterns *Page 233*

Intelligence Global capacity to think rationally, act purposefully, and deal effectively with the environment *Page 300*

Internal Locus of Control Believing that one controls one's own fate *Page 114*

Interpersonal Attraction Positive feelings toward another *Page 575*

Interpretation A psychoanalyst's explanation of a patient's free associations, dreams, resistance, and transference; more generally, any statement by a therapist that presents a patient's problem in a new way *Page 534*

Intrinsic Motivation Motivation resulting from internal, personal satisfaction from a task or activity *Page 443*

James–Lange Theory Subjective experience of emotion results from physiological changes, rather than being their cause ("I feel sad because I'm crying"); in this view, each emotion is physiologically distinct *Page 438*

Job Analysis Details description of the tasks involved in a job, as well as the knowledge, skills, abilities, and other personal characteristics (KSAOs) an employee must possess to be successful on the job *Page 612*

Job Stressors Work-related stress, including unemployment, role conflict, and burnout *Page 96*

Just-World Phenomenon Tendency to believe that people generally get what they deserve *Page 569*

Kinesics A form of nonverbal communication using gestures and body language *Page 643*

Kinesthesis Sensory system for detecting body posture, orientation, and movement of individual body parts *Page 145*

Laissez-Faire Leader Minimally involved in decision making and encourages workers to make their own decisions and manage themselves *Page 621*

Language Acquisition Device (LAD) According to Chomsky, an innate mechanism that enables a child to analyze language and extract the basic rules of grammar *Page 295*

Language Form of communication using sounds and symbols combined according to specified rules *Page 293*

Latent Content According to Freud, a dream's unconscious, hidden meaning, which is transformed into symbols within the story line or manifest content of the dream *Page 179*

Latent Learning Hidden learning that exists without behavioral signs *Page 228*

Law of Effect Thorndike's rule that the probability of an action being repeated is strengthened when it is followed by a pleasant or satisfying consequence *Page 216*

Leadership Using interpersonal influence to inspire or persuade others to support the goals and perform the tasks desired by the leader *Page 617*

Learned Helplessness Seligman's term for a state of helplessness or resignation, in which human or nonhuman animals learn that escape from something painful is impossible, and depression results *Page 508*

Learning Relatively permanent change in behavior or mental processes due to experience *Page 205*

Legitimate Power Based on a job title or position (president, police officer) *Page 623*

Levels of Processing Model Degree or depth of mental processing occurring when material is initially encountered; determines how well material is later remembered *Page 249*

Limbic System Interconnected group of forebrain structures involved with emotions, drives, and memory *Page 69*

Lobotomy Outmoded medical procedure for mental disorders, which involved cutting nerve pathways between the frontal lobes and the thalamus and hypothalamus *Page 551*

Longitudinal Method Measures a single individual or group of individuals over an extended period and gives information about age changes *Page 326*

Long-Term Memory (LTM) Third stage of memory that stores information for long periods of time; its capacity is virtually limitless, and its duration is relatively permanent *Page 254*

Long-Term Potentiation (LTP) Long-lasting increase in neural excitability, which may be a biological mechanism for learning and memory *Page 267*

Lowball Technique Getting someone to commit to an attractive proposal before revealing the hidden costs *Page 654*

Maintenance Rehearsal Repeating information over and over to maintain it in short-term memory (STM) *Page 250*

Major Depressive Disorder Long-lasting depressed mood that interferes with the ability to function, feel pleasure, or maintain interest in life *Page 505*

Manifest Content According to Freud, a dream's "surface" remembered story line, which contains dream symbols that disguise the hidden, latent content of the dream *Page 179*

Massed Practice Time spent learning is grouped (or massed) into long, unbroken intervals (also known as cramming) *Page 264*

Maturation Development governed by automatic, genetically predetermined signals *Page 325*

Medical Model Perspective that assumes diseases (including mental illness) have physical causes that can be diagnosed, treated, and possibly cured *Page 494*

Meditation Group of techniques designed to focus attention, block out all distractions, and produce an alternate state of consciousness (ASC) *Page 193*

Medulla [muh-DUL-uh] Hindbrain structure responsible for vital, automatic functions, such as respiration and heartbeat *Page 67*

Memory Internal record or representation of some prior event or experience *Page 248*

Mental Image Mental representation of a previously stored sensory experience, including visual, auditory, olfactory, tactile, motor, or gustatory imagery (e.g., visualizing a train and hearing its horn) *Page 284*

Mental Set Persisting in using problem-solving strategies that have worked in the past rather than trying new ones *Page 288*

Meta-Analysis Statistical procedure for combining and analyzing data from many studies *Page 17*

Midbrain Collection of brain structures in the middle of the brain responsible for coordinating movement patterns, sleep, and arousal *Page 68*

Middle Ear Hammer, anvil, and stirrup, which concentrate eardrum vibrations onto the cochlea's oval window *Page 138*

Minnesota Multiphasic Personality Inventory (MMPI) The most widely researched and clinically used self-report personality test (MMPI-*2* is the revised version) *Page 479*

Mirror Neurons Brain cells that fire both when performing specific actions and when observing specific actions or emotions of another. This "mirroring" may explain empathy, imitation, language, and the emotional deficits of some mental disorders *Page 231*

Misattribution of Arousal Physiologically aroused individuals make mistaken inferences about what is causing the arousal *Page 449*

Misinformation Effect Memory distortion resulting from misleading post-event information *Page 263*

Mixed Messages Communication problem occurring when a person's words simultaneously convey two conflicting messages, or the words communicate the opposite message of the body language or behavior *Page 647*

Mnemonic [nih-MON-ik] Device Memory-improvement technique based on encoding items in a special way *Page 273*

Modeling Therapy Watching and imitating models that demonstrate desirable behaviors *Page 547*

Monocular Cues Visual input from a single eye alone that contributes to perception of depth or distance *Page 151*

Mood Disorder Extreme disturbances in emotional states *Page 505*

Mood-Stabilizer Drugs Medications used to treat the combination of manic episodes and depression characteristic of bipolar disorders *Page 550*

Morality Principle The principle on which the superego may operate, which results in feelings of guilt if its rules are violated *Page 464*

Morpheme [MOR-feem] Smallest meaningful unit of language, formed from a combination of phonemes *Page 294*

Motivation Set of factors that activate, direct, and maintain behavior, usually toward some goal *Page 422*

Myelin [My-uh-lin] Sheath Layer of fatty insulation wrapped around the axon of some neurons, which increases the rate at which nerve impulses travel along the axon *Page 53*

Narcolepsy [NAR-co-lep-see] Sudden and irresistible onsets of sleep during normal waking hours. (narco = "numbness" and lepsy = "seizure") *Page 181*

Natural Selection Driving mechanism behind evolution that allows individuals with genetically influenced traits that are adaptive in a particular environment to stay alive and produce offspring *Page 83*

Naturalistic Observation Observation and recording behavior and mental processes in the participant's natural state or habitat *Page 28*

Nature–Nurture Controversy Ongoing dispute over the relative contributions of nature (heredity) and nurture (environment) *Page 6*

Need Compatibility Attraction based on sharing similar needs *Page 578*

Need Complementarity Attraction toward those with qualities we admire but personally lack *Page 578*

Need for Cognition Personality trait reflecting the extent to which people engage in and enjoy effortful cognitive activities *Page 656*

Negative Punishment Taking away (or removing) a stimulus, thereby weakening a response and making it less likely to recur *Page 221*

Negative Reinforcement Taking away (or removing) a stimulus, thereby strengthening a response and making it more likely to recur *Page 218*

Nerve Deafness Inner-ear deafness resulting from damage to the cochlea, hair cells, or auditory nerve *Page 140*

Neurogenesis [nue-roe-JEN-uh-sis] Process by which new neurons are generated *Page 60*

Neuron Nerve cell that processes and transmits information; basic building block of the nervous system responsible for receiving and transmitting electro-chemical information *Page 52*

Neuroplasticity Brain's ability to reorganize and change its structure and function throughout the life span *Page 59*

Neuroscience Interdisciplinary field studying how biological processes relate to behavior and mental processes *Page 51*

Neurosis Outmoded term for disorders characterized by unrealistic anxiety and other associated problems; less severe disruptions than in psychosis *Page 494*

Neurotransmitters Chemicals released by neurons that travel across the synaptic gap and allow neurons to communicate with one another *Page 55*

Neutral Stimulus (NS) Stimulus that, before conditioning, does not naturally bring about the response of interest *Page 208*

Night Terrors Abrupt awakenings from NREM (non–rapid-eye-movement) sleep accompanied by intense physiological arousal and feelings of panic *Page 182*

Nightmares Anxiety-arousing dreams generally occurring near the end of the sleep cycle, during REM sleep *Page 182*

Non–Rapid-Eye-Movement (NREM) Sleep Stages 1 to 4 of sleep with Stage 1 as the lightest level and Stage 4 as the deepest level *Page 176*

Nonverbal Communication Process of sending and receiving messages through means other than words *Page 642*

Norm Cultural rule of behavior prescribing what is acceptable in a given situation *Page 582*

Normative Social Influence Conforming to group pressure out of a need for approval and acceptance *Page 582*

Obedience Following direct commands, usually from an authority figure *Page 583*

Object Permanence Piagetian term for an infant's understanding that objects (or people) continue to exist even when they cannot be seen, heard, or touched directly *Page 341*

Observational Learning Learning new behaviors or information by watching and imitating others (also known as social learning or modeling) *Page 228*

Obsessive-Compulsive Disorder (OCD) Persistent, anxiety-provoking thoughts that will not go away (obsessions), and/or irresistible urges to perform repetitive behaviors (compulsions) to relieve the anxiety *Page 501*

Occipital [ahk-SIP-ih-tul] Lobes Two lobes at the back of the brain responsible for vision and visual perception *Page 73*

Oedipus [ED-uh-puss] Complex Period of conflict during the phallic stage when young boys are supposedly attracted to their mothers and desire to replace their fathers *Page 467*

Olfaction Sense of smell *Page 141*

Operant Conditioning Learning through voluntary behavior and its subsequent consequences; reinforcement increases behavioral tendencies, whereas punishment decreases them *Page 215*

Operational Definition Precise description of how the variables in a study will be observed and measured (For example, drug abuse might be operationally defined as "the number of missed work days due to excessive use of an addictive substance.") *Page 18*

Opiates Drugs derived from opium that numb the senses and relieve pain (The word *opium* comes from the Greek word meaning "juice.") *Page 189*

Opponent-Process Theory Hering's theory that color perception is based on three systems of color opposites—blue–yellow, red–green, and black–white *Page 136*

Optimal-Arousal Theory Organisms are motivated to achieve and maintain an optimal level of arousal *Page 424*

Organizational Citizenship Behavior (OCB) Behavior that goes beyond formal job requirements and is beneficial to the organization *Page 629*

Organizational Culture Group's shared pattern of thought and action; a common perception held by the organization's members *Page 614*

Organizational Psychology Branch of I/O psychology that focuses on the individual employee within the social context of the workplace *Page 617*

Orgasm Phase Third stage of the sexual response cycle, when pleasurable sensations peak and orgasm occurs *Page 400*

Outer Ear Pinna, auditory canal, and eardrum, which funnel sound waves to the middle ear *Page 138*

Outgroup Homogeneity Effect Judging members of an outgroup as more alike and less diverse than members of the ingroup *Page 575*

Overextension Overly broad use of a word to include objects that do not fit the word's meaning (e.g., calling all men "Daddy") *Page 296*

Overgeneralization Applying the basic rules of grammar even to cases that are exceptions to the rule (e.g., saying "mans" instead of "men") *Page 296*

Panic Disorder Sudden and inexplicable panic attacks; symptoms include difficulty breathing, heart palpitations, dizziness, trembling, terror, and feelings of impending doom *Page 501*

Paralanguage Form of nonverbal communication, which includes the pace, pitch, and volume at which words are spoken, and the tone of voice and inflections used by the speaker *Page 645*

Parallel Distributed Processing (PDP) Model Memory results from weblike connections among interacting processing units operating simultaneously, rather than sequentially (also known as the connectionist model) *Page 251*

Parasympathetic Nervous System Subdivision of the autonomic nervous system (ANS) responsible for calming the body and conserving energy *Page 62*

Parietal [puh-RYE-uh-tul] Lobes Two lobes at the top of the brain where bodily sensations are received and interpreted *Page 73*

Partial (Intermittent) Reinforcement Some, but not all, correct responses are reinforced *Page 219*

Participant Bias Occurs when experimental conditions influence the participant's behavior or mental processes *Page 26*

Perception Process of selecting, organizing, and interpreting sensory information into meaningful patterns *Page 126*

Perceptual Constancy Tendency for the environment to be perceived as remaining the same even with changes in sensory input *Page 150*

Perceptual Set Readiness to perceive in a particular manner based on expectations *Page 153*

Performance Anxiety Fear of being judged in connection with sexual activity *Page 404*

Performance Evaluation Formal procedure used to assess an employee's success at his or her job *Page 615*

Peripheral Nervous System (PNS) All nerves and neurons connecting the central nervous system to the rest of the body *Page 58*

Peripheral Route to Persuasion Method of persuasion in which an uninvolved, unmotivated, and inattentive audience is convinced on the basis of irrelevant or extraneous factors, such as attractiveness *Page 655*

Personality Disorder Inflexible, maladaptive personality traits that cause significant impairment of social and occupational functioning *Page 519*

Personality Unique and relatively stable pattern of thoughts, feelings, and actions *Page 458*

Personality–Job Fit Theory Identifies six personality types and proposes that a "good fit" between personality type and occupation determines job satisfaction *Page 629*

Persuasion Communication intended to change attitudes *Page 650*

Pheromones [FARE-oh-mones] Airborne chemicals that affect behavior, including recognition of family members, aggression, territorial marking, and sexual mating *Page 142*

Phobia Intense, irrational fear and avoidance of a specific object or situation *Page 501*

Phoneme [FOE-neem] Smallest basic unit of speech or sound *Page 294*

Physical Dependence Changes in bodily processes that make a drug necessary for minimal functioning *Page 185*

Place Theory Explains that pitch perception is linked to the particular spot on the cochlea's basilar membrane that is most stimulated *Page 139*

Placebo (pluh-SEE-boh) Inactive substance or fake treatment used as a control technique, usually in drug research, or given by a medical practitioner to a patient *Page 26*

Plateau Phase Second stage of the sexual response cycle; period of sexual excitement prior to orgasm *Page 400*

Pleasure Principle In Freud's theory, the principle on which the id operates— seeking immediate gratification *Page 464*

Polygraph Instrument that measures sympathetic arousal (heart rate, respiration rate, blood pressure, and skin conductivity) to detect emotional arousal, which in turn supposedly reflects lying versus truthfulness *Page 443*

Pons Hindbrain structure involved in respiration, movement, waking, sleep, and dreaming *Page 67*

Positive Psychology Scientific study of optimal human functioning, emphasizing positive emotions, positive traits, and positive institutions *Page 13*

Positive Punishment Adding (or presenting) a stimulus, thereby weakening a response and making it less likely to recur *Page 221*

Positive Reinforcement Adding (or presenting) a stimulus, thereby strengthening a response and making it more likely to recur *Page 218*

Postconventional Level Kohlberg's highest level of moral development, in which individuals develop personal standards for right and wrong and define morality in terms of abstract principles and values that apply to all situations and societies *Page 362*

Posttraumatic Stress Disorder (PTSD) Anxiety disorder following exposure to a life-threatening or other extreme event that evoked great horror or helplessness; characterized by flashbacks, nightmares, and impaired functioning *Page 109*

Preconscious Freud's term for thoughts, motives, or memories that exist just beneath the surface of awareness and can be easily retrieved *Page 463*

Preconventional Level Kohlberg's first level of moral development, in which morality is based on rewards, punishment, and exchange of favors *Page 362*

Prejudice A learned, generally negative, attitude toward members of a group; it includes thoughts (stereotypes), feelings, and behavioral tendencies (possible discrimination) *Page 573*

Premack Principle Using a naturally occurring high-frequency response to reinforce and increase low-frequency responses *Page 218*

Preoperational Stage Piaget's second stage of cognitive development (roughly age 2 to 7), characterized by the ability to employ significant language and to think symbolically, but the child lacks operations (reversible mental processes), and thinking is egocentric and animistic *Page 341*

Primary Appraisal Deciding if a situation is harmful, threatening, or challenging *Page 112*

Primary Reinforcers Stimuli that increase the probability of a response because they satisfy an unlearned, biological need (e.g., food, water, and sex) *Page 217*

Priming Prior exposure to a stimulus (or prime) facilitates or inhibits the processing of new information, even when one has no conscious memory of the initial learning and storage *Page 258*

Proactive Interference Old information interferes with remembering new information; forward-acting interference *Page 262*

Problem-Solving Coping Dealing directly with a stressor to decrease or eliminate it *Page 113*

Projective Tests Psychological tests using ambiguous stimuli, such as inkblots or drawings, which allow the test taker to project his or her unconscious onto the test material *Page 480*

Prototype Representation of the "best" or most typical example of a category (e.g., baseball is a prototype of the concept of sports) *Page 285*

Proxemics A form of nonverbal communication involving physical and personal space *Page 644*

Proximity Attraction based on geographic closeness *Page 577*

Psychiatry Branch of medicine dealing with the diagnosis, treatment, and prevention of mental disorders *Page 494*

Psychoactive Drugs Chemicals that change conscious awareness, mood, and/ or perception *Page 183*

Psychoanalysis Freudian therapy designed to bring unconscious conflicts into conscious awareness; also Freud's theoretical school of thought *Page 533*

Psychoanalytic Approach Focuses on unconscious processes and unresolved conflicts *Page 11*

Psychodynamic Perspective Focuses on unconscious dynamics, internal motives, conflicts, and childhood experiences *Page 11*

Psychodynamic Therapy A briefer, more directive, and more modern form of psychoanalysis focusing more on conscious processes and current problems *Page 535*

Psychological Dependence Desire or craving to achieve a drug's effect *Page 185*

Psychology Scientific study of behavior and mental processes *Page 4*

Psychoneuroimmunology [sye-koh-NEW-roh-IM-you-NOLL-oh-gee] Interdisciplinary field that studies the effects of psychological and other factors on the immune system *Page 103*

Psychopharmacology The study of drug effects on brain and behavior *Page 549*

Psychophysics Studies the link between the physical characteristics of stimuli and the sensory experience of them *Page 128*

Psychosexual Stages In Freudian theory, five developmental periods (oral, anal, phallic, latency, and genital) during which particular kinds of pleasures must be gratified if personality development is to proceed normally *Page 466*

Psychosis Serious mental disorders characterized by extreme mental disruption and defective or lost contact with reality *Page 494*

Psychosocial Stages Erikson's theory that individuals pass through eight developmental stages, each involving a crisis that must be successfully resolved *Page 364*

Psychosurgery Surgical alteration of the brain to bring about desirable behavioral, cognitive, or emotional changes; generally used when patients have not responded to other forms of treatment *Page 549*

Psychotherapy Techniques employed to improve psychological functioning and promote adjustment to life *Page 533*

Puberty Biological changes during adolescence that lead to an adult-sized body and sexual maturity *Page 334*

Punishment Weakens a response and makes it less likely to recur *Page 215*

Random Assignment Using chance methods to assign participants to experimental or control conditions, thus minimizing the possibility of biases or preexisting differences in the groups *Page 26*

Rapid-Eye-Movement (REM) Sleep Stage of sleep marked by rapid eye movements, high-frequency brain waves, paralysis of large muscles, and dreaming *Page 175*

Rational-Emotive Behavior Therapy (REBT) Ellis's cognitive therapy to eliminate emotional problems through rational examination of irrational beliefs *Page 536*

Reality Principle According to Freud, the principle on which the conscious ego

operates as it seeks to delay gratification of the id's impulses until appropriate outlets and situations can be found *Page 464*

Recall Retrieving a memory using a general cue *Page 257*

Reciprocal Determinism Bandura's belief that cognitions, behaviors, and the environment interact to produce personality *Page 474*

Recognition Retrieving a memory using a specific cue *Page 258*

Reference Groups People we conform to, or go along with, because we like and admire them and want to be like them *Page 582*

Referent Power Derived from one's feelings of identification with another (movie stars, athletes, friends) *Page 623*

Reflex Innate, automatic response to a stimulus (e.g., knee-jerk reflex) *Page 60*

Refractory Period Phase following orgasm, during which further orgasm is considered physiologically impossible for men *Page 400*

Reinforcement Strengthens a response and makes it more likely to recur *Page 215*

Relationship-Oriented Leader Helps maintain group morale, satisfaction, and motivation *Page 622*

Relearning Learning material a second time, which usually takes less time than original learning (also called the savings method) *Page 260*

Reliability Measure of the consistency and reproducibility of test scores when the test is readministered *Pages 305, 482*

Repair/Restoration Theory Sleep serves a recuperative function, allowing organisms to repair or replenish key factors *Page 178*

Repetitive Transcranial Magnetic Stimulation (rTMS) Biomedical treatment involving repeated pulses of magnetic energy being passed through the brain *Page 551*

Replication Repeating a research study, using different procedures or participants in varied settings, to check the confidence in prior findings *Page 17*

Representativeness Heuristic Estimating the probability of something

based on how well the circumstances match (or represent) our previous prototype *Page 289*

Repression Freud's first and most basic defense mechanism, which blocks unacceptable impulses from coming into awareness *Page 464*

Resiliency Ability to adapt effectively in the face of threats *Page 370*

Resistance In psychoanalysis, the person's inability or unwillingness to discuss or reveal certain memories, thoughts, motives, or experiences *Page 534*

Resolution Phase Final stage of the sexual response cycle, when the body returns to its unaroused state *Page 400*

Reticular Formation (RF) Diffuse set of neurons that helps screen incoming information and controls arousal *Page 68*

Retina Light-sensitive inner surface of the back of the eye, which contains the receptor cells for vision (rods and cones) *Page 134*

Retinal Disparity Binocular cue to distance in which the separation of the eyes causes different images to fall on each retina *Page 154*

Retrieval Cue Clue or prompt that helps stimulate recall or retrieval of a stored piece of information from long-term memory *Page 257*

Retrieval Recovering information from memory storage *Page 249*

Retroactive Interference New information interferes with remembering old information; backward-acting interference *Page 262*

Retrograde Amnesia Loss of memory for events before a brain injury; backward-acting amnesia *Page 269*

Reward Power Based on the ability to give rewards for complying with desired behavior *Page 623*

Rods Visual receptor cells in the retina that detect shades of gray and are responsible for peripheral vision; most important in dim light and at night *Page 134*

Role Conflict Forced choice between two or more different and incompatible role demands *Page 96*

Romantic Love Intense feeling of attraction to another within an erotic context and with future expectations *Page 579*

Rorschach [ROAR-shock] Inkblot Test A projective test that presents a set of 10 cards with symmetrical abstract patterns, known as inkblots, and asks respondents to describe what they "see" in the image; their response is thought to be a projection of unconscious processes *Page 480*

Saliency Bias Focusing on the most noticeable (salient) factors when explaining the causes of behavior *Page 569*

SAM System Body's initial, rapid-acting stress response, involving the sympathetic nervous system and the adrenal medulla; also called the sympatho-adreno-medullary (SAM) system *Page 100*

Sample Bias Occurs when research participants are not representative of the larger population *Page 26*

Savant Syndrome Condition in which a person with limited mental abilities exhibits exceptional skill or brilliance in some limited field *Page 306*

Schema Cognitive structures or "blueprints" of organized ideas that grow and differentiate with experience *Page 339*

Schizophrenia [skit-so-FREE-nee-uh] Group of severe disorders involving major disturbances in perception, language, thought, emotion, and behavior *Page 509*

Secondary Appraisal Assessing one's resources and choosing a coping method *Page 112*

Secondary Reinforcers Stimuli that increase the probability of a response because of their learned value (e.g., money and material possessions) *Page 218*

Selective Attention Filtering out and attending only to important sensory messages *Page 146*

Self-Actualization Humanistic term for the inborn drive to develop all one's talents and capabilities *Page 470*

Self-Concept Rogers's term for all the information and beliefs individuals have about their own nature, qualities, and behavior *Page 471*

Self-Efficacy Bandura's term for a person's learned expectation of success *Page 474*

Self-Esteem Appreciating one's own worth and importance and having the character to be accountable for oneself and to act responsibly toward others *Page 484*

Self-Help Group Leaderless or nonprofessionally guided groups in which members assist each other with a specific problem, as in Alcoholics Anonymous *Page 542*

Self-Serving Bias Taking credit for our successes and externalizing our failures *Page 569*

Self-Talk Internal dialogue; the things people say to themselves when they interpret events *Page 536*

Semantic Memory Subsystem of explicit/declarative memory that stores general knowledge; a mental encyclopedia or dictionary *Page 255*

Semantics Set of rules for using words to create meaning; or the study of meaning *Page 294*

Sensation Process of detecting, converting, and transmitting raw sensory information from the external and internal environments to the brain *Page 126*

Sensorimotor Stage Piaget's first stage of cognitive development (birth to approximately age 2), in which schemas are developed through sensory and motor activities *Page 339*

Sensory Adaptation Sensory system's reduced responsiveness to unchanging stimuli *Page 131*

Sensory Memory First memory stage that holds sensory information; relatively large capacity, but duration is only a few seconds *Page 252*

Serial-Position Effect Information at the beginning and end of a list is remembered better than material in the middle *Page 257*

Sex Biological maleness and femaleness, including chromosomal sex; also, sexual behaviors, such as masturbation and intercourse *Page 390*

Sexual Dysfunction Impairment of the normal physiological processes of arousal and orgasm *Page 402*

Sexual Orientation Primary erotic attraction toward members of the same sex (homosexual, gay, lesbian), both sexes (bisexual), or the other sex (heterosexual) *Page 395*

Sexual Prejudice Negative attitudes toward an individual because of her or his sexual orientation *Page 401*

Sexual Response Cycle Masters and Johnson's description of the four-stage bodily response to sexual arousal, which consists of excitement, plateau, orgasm, and resolution *Page 399*

Sexual Scripts Socially dictated descriptions of "appropriate" behaviors for sexual interactions *Page 405*

Shaping Reinforcement delivered for successive approximations of the desired response *Page 220*

Short-Term Memory (STM) Second memory stage that temporarily stores sensory information and decides whether to send it on to long-term memory (LTM); capacity is limited to five to nine items and duration is about 30 seconds *Page 252*

Single-Blind Study Only the researcher, and not the participants, knows who is in either the experimental or control group *Page 25*

Sleep Apnea Repeated interruption of breathing while asleep because air passages to the lungs are physically blocked or the brain stops activating the diaphragm *Page 181*

Sleeper Effect Information from an unreliable source, which was initially discounted, later gains credibility because the source is forgotten *Page 264*

Social Psychology Study of how others influence our thoughts, feelings, and actions *Page 567*

Social-Learning Theory of Gender-Role Development Gender roles are acquired though rewards, punishments, observation, and imitation *Page 392*

Sociocultural Perspective Emphasizes social interaction and cultural determinants of behavior and mental processes *Page 14*

Socioemotional Selectivity Theory of Aging A natural decline in social contact occurs as older adults become more selective with their time *Page 373*

Somatic Nervous System (SNS) Subdivision of the peripheral nervous system (PNS) that connects to sensory receptors and controls skeletal muscles *Page 62*

Source Amnesia Forgetting the true source of a memory (also called source confusion or source misattribution) *Page 264*

Split-Brain Surgery Cutting of the corpus callosum to separate the brain's two hemispheres. When used medically to treat severe epilepsy, split-brain patients provide data on the functions of the two hemispheres *Page 75*

Spontaneous Recovery Sudden, temporary reappearance of a previously extinguished conditioned response (CR) *Page 212*

Standardization Establishment of the norms and uniform procedures for giving and scoring a test *Page 304*

Statistical Significance Statistical statement of how likely it is that a study's result occurred merely by chance *Page 18*

Stem Cell Immature (uncommitted) cells that have the potential to develop into almost any type of cell depending on the chemical signals they receive *Page 60*

Stereotype Threat Negative stereotypes about minority groups cause some members to doubt their abilities *Page 312*

Stereotype A set of beliefs about the characteristics of people in a group that is generalized to all group members; also, the cognitive component of prejudice *Page 573*

Sternberg's Triangular Theory of Love The fullest form of love, consummate love, depends on a healthy degree of three components—*intimacy, passion,* and *commitment* *Page 579*

Stimulants Drugs that act on the brain and other parts of the nervous system to increase overall activity and general responsiveness *Page 188*

Stimulus Discrimination Only the conditioned stimulus (CS) elicits the conditioned response (CR) *Page 212*

Stimulus Generalization Stimuli similar to the original conditioned

stimulus (CS) elicit a conditioned response (CR) *Page 211*

Storage Retaining information for future use *Page 249*

Stress Nonspecific response of the body to any demand made upon it; the arousal, both physical and mental, to situations or events that we perceive as threatening or challenging *Page 94*

Stressor Trigger or stimulus that prompts a stressful reaction *Page 94*

Subliminal Pertaining to stimuli presented below conscious awareness *Page 130*

Substance-Related Disorders Abuse of, or dependence on, a mood- or behavior-altering drug *Page 516*

Substantive Conflict Disagreement between individuals or organizations over the goals to be pursued or the means for their accomplishment *Page 661*

Superego In Freud's theory, the "conscience" or moral component of the personality that incorporates parental and societal standards for morality *Page 464*

Survey Research technique that questions a large sample of people to assess their behaviors and attitudes *Page 28*

Sympathetic Nervous System Subdivision of the autonomic nervous system (ANS) responsible for arousing the body and mobilizing its energy during times of stress; also called the "fight-or-flight" system *Page 62*

Synapse [SIN-aps] Gap between the axon tip of the sending neuron and the dendrite or cell body of the receiving neuron. During an action potential, chemicals called neurotransmitters are released and flow across the synaptic gap *Page 55*

Syntax Grammatical rules that specify how words and phrases should be arranged in a sentence to convey meaning *Page 294*

Systematic Desensitization Gradual process of extinguishing a learned fear (or phobia) by working through a hierarchy of fear-evoking stimuli while staying deeply relaxed *Page 545*

Tardive Dyskinesia Movement disorder involving facial muscles, tongue, and limbs; a possible side effect of long-term use of antipsychotic medications *Page 551*

Task-Oriented Leader Helps a group complete a task or reach a particular goal *Page 622*

Taste Aversion Classically conditioned negative reaction to a particular taste that has been associated with nausea or other illness *Page 232*

Telegraphic Speech Two- or three-word sentences of young children that contain only the most necessary words *Page 296*

Temperament An individual's innate disposition or behavioral style and characteristic emotional response *Page 363*

Temporal Lobes Two lobes on each side of the brain above the ears invol-ved in audition (hearing), language comprehension, memory, and some emotional control *Page 73*

Teratogen [Tuh-RAT-uh-jen] Environmental agent that causes damage during prenatal development; the term comes from the Greek word *teras,* meaning "malformation" *Page 330*

Thalamus [TAHL-uh-muss] Forebrain structure at the top of the brainstem; serves as the brain's switchboard relaying sensory messages to the cerebral cortex *Page 68*

Thanatology [than-uh-TAHL-uh-gee] The study of death and dying; the term comes from thanatus, the Greek name for a mythical personification of death, and was borrowed by Freud to represent the death instinct *Page 377*

Thematic Apperception Test (TAT) A projective test that shows a series of ambiguous black-and-white pictures and asks the test taker to create a story related to each; the responses presumably reflect a projection of unconscious processes *Page 480*

Theory Systematic, interrelated set of concepts that explain a body of data *Page 17*

Three-Stage Memory Model Memory storage requires passage of information through three stages (sensory, short-term, and long-term) *Page 251*

Tip-of-the-Tongue (TOT) Phenomenon Feeling that specific information is stored in long-term memory but being temporarily unable to retrieve it *Page 263*

Tolerance Bodily adjustment to higher and higher levels of a drug, which leads to decreased sensitivity *Page 185*

Top-Down Processing Information processing starting "at the top," with higher-level cognitive processes (such as, expectations and knowledge), and then working down; conceptually driven processing that moves from the whole to the parts *Page 126*

Trait Relatively stable personal characteristic that can be used to describe someone *Page 458*

Transference In psychoanalysis, the patient may displace (or transfer) unconscious feelings about a significant person in his or her life onto the therapist *Page 534*

Trichromatic Theory Theory stating that color perception results from three types of cones in the retina, each most sensitive to either red, green or blue. Other colors result from a mixture of these three *Page 136*

Two-Factor Theory Schachter and Singer's theory that emotion depends on two factors—physiological arousal and cognitive labeling of that arousal *Page 440*

Type A Personality Behavior characteristics including intense ambition, competition, exaggerated time urgency, and a cynical, hostile outlook *Page 107*

Type B Personality Behavior characteristics consistent with a calm, patient, relaxed attitude *Page 107*

Unconditional Positive Regard Rogers's term for love and acceptance with no contingencies attached *Pages 471, 540*

Unconditioned Response (UCR) Unlearned reaction to an unconditioned stimulus (UCS) that occurs without previous conditioning *Page 208*

Unconditioned Stimulus (UCS) Stimulus that elicits an unconditioned response (UCR) without previous conditioning *Page 208*

Unconscious Freud's term for thoughts, motives, and memories blocked from normal awareness, which still exert great influence *Page 463*

Validity Ability of a test to measure what it was designed to measure *Pages 305, 482*

Variable Interval (VI) Schedule Reinforcement occurs unpredictably; the interval (time) varies *Page 219*

Variable Ratio (VR) Schedule Reinforcement occurs unpredictably; the ratio (number or amount) varies *Page 219*

Vestibular Sense Sense of body movement and position, also called the sense of balance *Page 144*

Withdrawal Discomfort and distress, including physical pain and intense cravings, experienced after stopping the use of addictive drugs *Page 185*

Working Memory Alternate term for short-term memory (STM), which emphasizes the active processing of information *Page 254*

References

Aamodt, M. G. (2010). *Industrial/organizational psychology* (6th ed.). Belmont, CA: Cengage.

Aarts, H. (2007). Unconscious authorship ascription: The effects of success and effect-specific information priming on experienced authorship. *Journal of Experimental Social Psychology, 43,* 119–126.

Abadinsky, H. (2011). *Drug use and abuse: A comprehensive introduction* (7th ed.). Belmont, CA: Cengage.

Abbey, C., & Dallos, R. (2004). The experience of the impact of divorce on sibling relationships: A qualitative study. *Clinical Child Psychology and Psychiatry, 9(2),* 241–259.

Abbott, A. (2004). Striking back. *Nature, 429* (6990), 338–339.

Aboa-Éboulé, C. (2008). Job strain and recurrent coronary heart disease events—Reply. *Journal of the American Medical Association, 299,* 520–521.

Aboa-Éboulé, C., Brisson, C., Maunsell, E., Benoît, M., Bourbonnais, R., Vézina, M., Milot, A., Théroux, P., & Dagenais, G. R. (2007). Job strain and risk of acute recurrent coronary heart disease events. *Journal of the American Medical Association, 298,* 1652–1660.

About James Randi. (2002). *Detail biography.* Retrieved from http://www.randi.org/jr/bio .html.

Abraham, A., & Windmann, S. (2007). Creative cognition: The diverse operations and the prospect of applying a cognitive neuroscience perspective. *Methods, 42,* 38–48.

Abrams, L., White, K. K., & Eitel, S. L. (2003). Isolating phonological components that increase tip-of-the-tongue resolution. *Memory & Cognition, 31(8),* 1153–1162.

Acarturk, C., de Graaf, R., van Straten, A., ten Have, M., & Cuijpers, P. (2008). Social phobia and number of social fears, and their association with comorbidity, health-related quality of life and help seeking: A population-based study. *Social Psychiatry and Psychiatric Epidemiology, 43,* 273–279.

Acerbi, A., & Nunn, C. L. (2011). Predation and the phasing of sleep: An evolutionary individual-based model. *Animal Behaviour, 81(4),* 801–811.

Achenbaum, W. A., & Bengtson, V. L. (1994). Re-engaging the disengagement theory of aging: On the history and assessment of theory development in gerontology. *Gerontologist, 34,* 756–763.

Acheson, K., Blondel-Lubrano, A., Oguey-Araymon, S., Beaumont, M., Emady-Azar, S., Ammon-Zufferey, C., Monnard, I., Pinaud, S., Nielsen-Moennoz, C., & Bovetto, L. (2011). Protein choices targeting thermogenesis and metabolism. *The American Journal of Clinical Nutrition, 93(3),* 525–534.

Ackerman, J. M., & Kenrick, D. T. (2009). Selfishness and sex or cooperation and family values? *Behavioral and Brain Sciences, 32(1),* 21.

Adachi, P. J. C., & Willoughby, T. (2011). The effect of violent video games on aggression: Is it more than just the violence? *Aggression and Violent Behavior, 16(1),* 55–62.

Adams, M. (2011). Evolutionary genetics of personality in nonhuman primates. In M. Inoue-Murayama, S. Kawamura, & A. Weiss (Eds.), *From genes to animal behavior* (pp. 137–164). Tokyo, Japan: Springer.

Adams, R. E., & Boscarino, J. A. (2011). A structural equation model of perievent panic and posttraumatic stress disorder after a community disaster. *Journal of Traumatic Stress, 24(1),* 61–69.

Adams, W. A. (2011). Words matter: The legacy of Thomas Szasz. [Review of the book *The Myth of Mental Illness: Foundations of a Theory of Personal Conduct* (50th Anniversary Edition), by T. Szasz]. *PsycCRITIQUES, 56(10).*

Adelmann, P. K., & Zajonc, R. B. (1989). Facial efference and the experience of emotion. *Annual Review of Psychology, 40,* 249–280.

Aderka, I., Hermesh, H., Marom, S., Weizman, A., & Gilboa-Schechtman, E. (2011). Cognitive behavior therapy for social phobia in large groups. *International Journal of Cognitive therapy, 4(1),* 92–103.

Adib, W. K., Hu, X., Campsmith, M. L., & Espinoza, L. (2010). Estimated lifetime risk for diagnosis of HIV infection among Hispanics/Latinos—37 states and Puerto Rico, 2007. *Journal of the American Medical Association, 304(18),* 2012–2013.

Adinoff, B. (2004). Neurobiologic processes in drug reward and addiction. *Harvard Review of Psychiatry, 12(6),* 305–320.

Adler, A. (1964). The individual psychology of Alfred Adler. In H. L. Ansbacher & R. R. Ansbacher (Eds.), *The individual psychology of Alfred Adler.* New York, NY: Harper & Row.

Adler, A. (1998). *Understanding human nature.* Center City, MN: Hazelden Information Education.

Adolph, K. E., Karasik, L. B., & Tamis-LeMonda, C. S. (2011). Corrigendum to: "Using social information to guide action: Infants' locomotion over slippery slopes." *Neural Networks, 24(2),* 217.

Agartz, I., Brown, A., Rimol, L., Hartberg, C., Dale, A., Melle, I., Djurovic, S., & Andreassen, O. (2011). Common sequence variants in the major histocompatibility complex region associate with cerebral ventricular size in schizophrenia. *Biological Psychiatry.* Advance online publication. doi: 10.1016/j .biopsych.2011.02.034.

Agerström, J., & Rooth, D-O. (2011). The role of automatic obesity stereotypes in real hiring discrimination. *Journal of Applied Psychology, 96(4),* 790–805.

Agrillo, C. (2011). Near-death experience: Out-of-body and out-of-brain? *Review of General Psychology, 15*(1), 1–10.

Agrò, F., Liguori, A., Petti, F., Bangrazi, F., Cataldo, R., & Totonelli, A. (2005). Does acupuncture analgesia have a bihumoral mechanism? *The Pain Clinic, 17*, 243–244.

Ahlsén, E. (2008). Embodiment in communication – Aphasia, apraxia, and the possible role of mirroring and imitation. *Clinical Linguistics & Phonetics, 22*, 311–315.

Ahmadi, S., Zarrindast, M. R., Nouri, M., Haeri-Rohani, A. & Rezayof, A. (2007). N-Methyl-D-aspartate receptors in the ventral tegmental area are involved in retrieval of inhibitory avoidance memory by nicotine. *Neurobiology of Learning and Memory, 88*, 352–358.

Ahmed, A. M. (2007). Group identity, social distance, and intergroup bias. *Journal of Economic Psychology, 28*, 324–337.

Ainsworth, M. D. S. (1967). *Infancy in Uganda: Infant care and the growth of love.* Baltimore, MD: Johns Hopkins University Press.

Ainsworth, M. D. S., Blehar, M., Waters, E., & Wall, S. (1978). *Patterns of attachment: Observations in the strange situation and at home.* Hillsdale, NJ: Erlbaum.

Akers, R. M., & Denbow, D. (2008). *Anatomy and physiology of domestic animals.* Hoboken, NJ: Wiley.

Akrami, N., Ekehammar, B., & Bergh, R. (2011). Generalized prejudice: Common and specific components. *Psychological Science, 22*(1), 57–59.

Alberts, A., Elkind, D., & Ginsberg, S. (2007). The personal fable and risk-taking in early adolescence. *Journal of Youth and Adolescence, 36*, 71–76.

Alcock, J. (2011). Back from the future: Parapsychology and the Bem affair. *The Committee for Skeptical Inquiry* (CSI). Retrieved from http://www.csicop.org/specialarticles/show/back_from_the_future

Alden, L. E., & Regambal, M. J. (2011). Interpersonal processes in the anxiety disorders. In L. M. Horowitz & S. Strack (Eds.), *Handbook of interpersonal psychology: Theory, research, assessment, and therapeutic interventions* (pp. 449–469). Hoboken, NJ: John Wiley.

Aldenhoff, J. (2011). Interpersonal therapy. *European Psychiatry, 26*(1). 1782.

Alegre, A. (2011). Parenting styles and children's emotional intelligence: What do we know? *The Family Journal, 19*(1), 56–62.

Ali, M., & Ajilore, O. (2011). Can marriage reduce risky health behavior for African-Americans? *Journal of Family and Economic Issues, 32*(2), 191–203.

Allam, M. D.-E., Soussignan, R., Patris, B., Marlier, L., & Schaal, B. (2010). Long-lasting memory for an odor acquired at the mother's breast. *Developmental Science, 13*(6), 849–863.

Allan, K., & Gabbert, F. (2008). I still think it was a banana: Memorable "lies" and forgettable "truths." *Acta Psychologica, 127*, 299–308.

Allen, L. S., Hines, M., Shryne, J. E., & Gorski, R. A. (2007). Two sexually dimorphic cell groups in the human brain. In G. Einstein (Ed.), *Sex and the brain* (pp. 327–337). Cambridge, MA: MIT Press.

Allen, P. L. (2000). *The wages of sin: Sex and disease, past and present.* Chicago, IL: University of Chicago Press.

Allik, J., & McCrae, R. R. (2004). Toward a geography of personality traits: Patterns of profiles across 36 cultures. *Journal of Cross-Cultural Psychology, 35*(1), 13–28.

Alloy, L. B., & Clements, C. M. (1998). Hopelessness theory of depression. *Cognitive Therapy and Research, 22*, 303–335.

Alloy, L. B., Abramson, L. Y., Whitehouse, W. G., Hogan, M. E., Tashman, N. A., Steinberg, D. L., Rose, D. T., & Donovan, P. (1999). Depressogenic cognitive styles: Predictive validity, information processing and personality characteristics, and developmental origins. *Behavior Research and Therapy, 37*, 503–531.

Alloy, L. B., Wagner, C. A., Black, S. K., Gerstein, R. K., & Abramson, L. Y. (2011). The breakdown of self-enhancing and self-protecting cognitive biases in depression. In M. D. Alicke & C. Sedikides (Eds.), *Handbook of self-enhancement and self-protection* (pp. 358–379). New York, NY: Guilford Press.

Allport, G. W. (1937). *Personality: A psychological interpretation.* New York, NY: Holt, Rinehart and Winston.

Allport, G. W., & Odbert, H. S. (1936). Traitnames: A psycho-lexical study. *Psychological Monographs: General and Applied, 47*, 1–21.

Almela, M., Hidalgo, V., Villada, C., Espín, L., Gómez-Amor, J., & Salvador, A. (2011). The impact of cortisol reactivity to acute stress on memory: Sex differences in middle-aged people. *Stress: The International Journal on the Biology of Stress, 14*(2), 117–127.

Althof, S. (2010). Sex therapy: Advances in paradigms, nomenclature, and treatment. *Academic Psychiatry, 34*(5), 390–396.

Alvarez, D. (2011). "I had to teach hard": Traumatic conditions and teachers in post-Katrina classrooms. *The High School Journal, 94*(1), 28–39.

Amato, P. R. (2006). Marital discord, divorce, and children's well-being: Results from a 20-year longitudinal study of two generations. In A. Clarke-Stewart & J. Dunn (Eds.)., *Families count: Effects on child and adolescent development* (pp. 179–202). *The Jacobs Foundation series on adolescence.* New York, NY: Cambridge University Press.

Amato, P. R. (2007). Transformative processes in marriage: Some thoughts from a sociologist. *Journal of Marriage and Family, 69*, 305–309.

Amazing meeting. (2011). *The amazing one: James Randi.* Retrieved from http://www.amazingmeeting.com/speakers#randi

Ambady, N., & Adams, R. B., Jr. (2011). Us versus them: The social neuroscience of perceiving out-groups. In A. Todorov, S. T. Fiske, & D. A. Prentice (Eds.), *Oxford series in social cognition and social neuroscience. Social neuroscience: Toward understanding the underpinnings of the social mind* (pp. 135–143). New York, NY: Oxford University Press.

Amendments to the 2002 "Ethical principles of psychologists and code of conduct." (2010). *American Psychologist, 65*(5), 493.

American Academy of Pediatrics. (1999). Circumcision policy statement. *Pediatrics, 103*, 686–693.

American Academy of Pediatrics. (2005). Policy statement: AAP publications retired and reaffirmed. *Pediatrics, 116*, 796.

American Cancer Society (2004). *Women and smoking.* Retrieved from http://cancer.org/docroot/PED/content/PED_10_2X_Women_and_Smoking.asp?sitearea5PED.

American Heart Association. (2008). *Heart disease and stroke statistics—2008 update.* Retrieved from http://www.americanheart.org/presenter.jhtml?identifier=3054076

American Medical Association. (2008). *Alcohol and other drug abuse.* Retrieved from http://www.ama-assn.org/ama/pub/category/3337.html.

American Psychiatric Association. (2000). *Diagnostic and statistical manual of mental disorders* (4th ed. TR). Washington, DC: American Psychiatric Press.

American Psychiatric Association. (2002). *APA Let's talk facts about posttraumatic stress disorder.* Retrieved from http://www.psych.org/disasterpsych/fs/ptsd.cfm.

American Psychological Association (APA). (1984). *Behavioral research with animals.* Washington, DC: Author.

American Psychological Association (APA). (1992). Ethical principles of psychologists and code of conduct. *American Psychologist, 47*, 1597–1611.

American Psychological Association (APA). (2001). *Is multitasking more efficient? Shifting mental gears costs time, especially when shifting to less familiar tasks.* Retrieved from http://www.apa.org/news/press/releases/2001/08/multitasking.aspx

American Psychological Association (APA). (2002). *Ethical Principles of Psychologists and Code of Conduct.* Retrieved from http://www.apa.org/ethics/code2002.html

American Psychological Association (APA). (2009). *Center for workforce studies.* Washington, DC: American Psychological Association.

Amundson, J. K., & Nuttgens, S. A. (2008). Strategic eclecticism in hypnotherapy: Effectiveness research considerations. *American Journal of Clinical Hypnosis, 50,* 233–245.

Anastasi, T. E. (2001). Presidential decision-making during selected foreign policy crises from 1950–1968 analyzed through the use of the Myers-Briggs Type Indicator. Dissertation Abstracts International Section A: Humanities and Social Sciences, pp. 1576. US: ProQuest Information & Learning.

Anderman, E., & Dawson, H. (2011). Learning with motivation. In R. Mayer & P. Alexander (Eds.), *Handbook of research on learning and instruction* (pp. 219–242). New York, NY: Routledge.

Anderson, C. A. (2001). Heat and violence. *Current Directions in Psychological Science, 10(1),* 33–38.

Anderson, C. A. (2004). An update on the effects of playing violent video games. *Journal of Adolescence, 27(1),* 113–122.

Anderson, C. A., Anderson, K. B., Dorr, N., DeNeve, K. M., & Flanagan, M. (2000). Temperature and aggression. *Advances in Experimental Social Psychology, 32,* 63–133.

Anderson, C. A., Buckley, K. E., & Carnegey, N. L. (2008). Creating your own hostile environment: A laboratory examination of trait aggressiveness and the violence escalation cycle. *Personality and Social Psychology Bulletin, 34,* 462–473.

Anderson, J. R., Betts, S., Ferris, J. L., & Fincham, J. M. (2011). Cognitive and metacognitive activity in mathematical problem solving: Prefrontal and parietal patterns. *Cognitive, Affective & Behavioral Neuroscience, 11(1),* 52–67.

Anderson, M. C., Bjork, R. A. & Bjork, E. L. (1994). Remembering can cause forgetting: Retrieval dynamics in long-term memory. *Journal of Experimental Psychology: Learning, Memory, and Cognition, 20,* 1063–1087.

Anderson, N. E., Wan, L., Young, K. A., & Stanford, M. S. (2011). Psychopathic traits predict startle habituation but not modula-

tion in an emotional faces task. *Personality and Individual Differences, 50(5),* 712–716.

Anderson, V., Brown, S., Newitt, H., & Hoile, H. (2011). Long-term outcome from childhood traumatic brain injury: Intellectual ability, personality, and quality of life. *Neuropsychology, 25(2),* 176–184.

Andersson, J., & Walley, A. (2011). The contribution of heredity to clinical obesity. In R.H. Lustig (Ed.), *Obesity before birth* (pp. 25–52). New York, NY: Springer.

Andrade, T. G. C. S., & Graeff, F. G. (2001). Effect of electrolytic and neurotoxic lesions of the median raphe nucleus on anxiety and stress. *Pharmacology, Biochemistry & Behavior, 70(1),* 1–14.

Andrasik, F. (2006). Psychophysiological disorders: Headache as a case in point. In F. Andrasik (Ed.), *Comprehensive handbook of personality and psychopathology: Vol. 2: Adult Psychopathology* (pp. 409–422). Hoboken, NJ: Wiley.

Andreassi, J. K., & Thompson, C. A. (2007). Dispositional and situational sources of control: Relative impact on work-family conflict and positive spillover. *Journal of Managerial Psychology, 22(8),* 722–740.

Ang, S., Rodgers, J. L., & Wänström, L. (2010). The Flynn Effect within subgroups in the U.S.: Gender, race, income, education, and urbanization differences in the NLSY-children data. *Intelligence, 38(4),* 367–384.

Anguas-Wong, A. M., & Matsumoto, D. (2007). Reconocimiento de la expresión facial de la emoción en mexicanos universitarios. [Acknowledgement of emotional facial expression in Mexican college students.] *Revista de Psicología, 25,* 277–293.

Anisman, H., Merali, Z., & Stead, J. D. H. (2008). Experiential and genetic contributions to depressive- and anxiety-like disorders: Clinical and experimental studies. *Neuroscience & Biobehavioral Reviews, 32,* 1185–1206.

Ansell, E. B., & Grilo, C. M. (2007). Personality disorders. In M. Hersen, S. M. Turner, & D. C. Beidel (Eds.), *Adult psychopathology and diagnosis* (5th ed.) (pp. 633–678). Hoboken, NJ: Wiley.

Antony, M. M., & Roemer, L. (2011). Summary. In M. M. Antony & L. Roemer, *Theories of psychotherapy: Behavior therapy* (pp. 123–128). Washington, DC: American Psychological Association.

Aou, S., (2006). Role of medial hypothalamus on peptic ulcer and depression. In C. Kubo & T. Kuboki (Eds), *Psychosomatic medicine: Proceedings of the 18th World Congress on Psychosomatic Medicine.* New York, NY: Elsevier Science.

APA Press Release. (2001). Is multitasking more efficient? Shifting mental gears costs time, especially when shifting to less familiar tasks. *American Psychological Association.* Retrieved from http://www.apa.org/news/press/releases/2001/08/multitasking.aspx

Appel, M., & Richter, T. (2007). Persuasive effects of fictional narratives increase over time. *Media Psychology, 10,* 113–134.

Appiah, K. A. (2008). *Experiments in ethics.* Cambridge, MA: Harvard University Press.

Appiah, K. A. (2010). More experiments in ethics. *Neuroethics, 3(3),* 233–242.

Arbib, M. A., & Mundhenk, T. N. (2005). Schizophrenia and the mirror system: An essay. *Neuropsychologia, 43,* 268–280.

Archer, T. (2011). Physical exercise alleviates debilities of normal aging and Alzheimer's disease. *Acta Neurologica Scandinavica, 123(4),* 221–238.

Areepattamannil, S. (2010). Parenting practices, parenting style, and children's school achievement. *Psychological Studies, 55(4),* 283–289.

Aricò, D., Drago, V., Foster, P. S., Heilman, K. M., Williamson, J., & Ferri, R. (2010). Effects of NREM sleep instability on cognitive processing. *Sleep Medicine, 11(8),* 791–798.

Arieh, Y., & Marks, L. E. (2008). Cross-modal interaction between vision and hearing: A speed-accuracy analysis. *Perception & Psychophysics, 70,* 412–421.

Arkes, H., & Kajdasz, J. (2011). Intuitive theories of behavior. In National Research Council (Ed.), *Intelligence analysis: Behavioral and social scientific foundations* (pp. 143–168). Washington, DC: The National Academies Press.

Arnedt, J. T., Conroy, D. A., Armitage, R., & Brower, K. J. (2011). Cognitive-behavioral therapy for insomnia in alcohol dependent patients: A randomized controlled pilot trial. *Behaviour Research and Therapy, 49(4),* 227–233.

Arnsten, A. F. T. (2011). Prefrontal cortical network connections: Key site of vulnerability in stress and schizophrenia. *International Journal of Developmental Neuroscience, 29(3),* 215–223.

Arumugam, V., Lee, J-S., Nowak, J. K., Pohle, R. J., Nyrop, J. E., Leddy, J. J., & Pelkman, C. L. (2008). A high-glycemic meal pattern elicited increased subjective appetite sensations in overweight and obese women. Appetite, 50, 215–222.

Asch, S. E. (1951). Effects of group pressure upon the modification and distortion of judgment. In H. Guetzkow (Ed.), *Groups, leadership, and men*. Pittsburgh, PA: Carnegie Press.

Ashbourne, L. M., Daly, K. J., & Brown, J. L. (2011). Responsiveness in father-child relationships: The experience of fathers. *Fathering, 9(1)*, 69–86.

Atkinson, R. C., & Shiffrin, R. M. (1968). Human memory: A proposed system and its control processes. In K. W. Spence & J. T. Spence (Eds.), *The psychology of learning and motivation* (Vol. 2) (pp. 90–91). New York, NY: Academic Press.

Atwood, J. D., & Klucinec, E. (2011). Current state of sexuality theory and therapy. In J. L. Wetchler (Ed.), *Handbook of clinical issues in couple therapy* (2nd ed.) (pp. 95–112). New York, NY: Routledge/Taylor & Francis Group.

Aubert, A., & Dantzer, R. (2005). The taste of sickness: Lipopolysaccharide-induced finickiness in rats. *Physiology & Behavior, 84(3)*, 437–444.

Audet, K., & Le Mare, L. (2011). Mitigating effects of the adoptive caregiving environment on inattention/overactivity in children adopted from romanian orphanages. *International Journal of Behavioral Development, 35(2)*, 107–115.

Austin, M. (2009). Texting while driving: How dangerous is it? *Car and Driver*. Retrieved from http://www.caranddriver.com/features/09q2/texting_while_driving_how_dangerous_is_it_-feature

Aviv, A. (2011). Leukocyte telomere dynamics, human aging, and life span. In E. J. Masoro & S. N. Austad (Eds.), *The handbooks of aging consisting of three Vols. Handbook of the biology of aging* (7th ed.) (pp. 163–176). San Diego, CA: Elsevier Academic Press.

Axtell, R. E. (1998). *Gestures: The do's and taboos of body language around the world*, revised and expanded ed. New York, NY: Wiley.

Axtell, R. E. (2007). *Essential do's and taboos: The complete guide to international business and leisure travel*. Hoboken, NJ: Wiley.

Ayers, S., Baum, A., McManus, C., Newman, S., Wallston, K., Weinman, J., & West, R. (Eds.). (2007). *Cambridge handbook of psychology, health, and medicine*. New York, NY: Cambridge University Press.

Azar, B. (2010). Virtual violence: Researchers disagree about whether violent video games increase aggression. *Monitor on Psychology, 41(11)*, 38.

Azizian, A., & Polich, J. (2007). Evidence for attentional gradient in the serial position memory curve from event-related potentials. *Journal of Cognitive Neuroscience, 19*, 2071–2081.

Babcock, J., Graham, K., Canady, B., & Ross, J. (2011). A proximal change experiment testing two communication exercises with intimate partner violent men. *Behavior Therapy, 42(2)*, 336–347.

Back, M. D., Penke, L., Schmukle, S. C., Sachse, K., Borkenau, P., & Asendorpf, J. B. (2011). Why mate choices are not as reciprocal as we assume: The role of personality, flirting and physical attractiveness. *European Journal of Personality, 25(2)*, 120–132.

Baddeley, A. D. (1992). Working memory. *Science, 255*, 556–559.

Baddeley, A. D. (1998). Recent developments in working memory. *Current Opinion in Neurobiology, 8*, 234–238.

Baddeley, A. D. (2000). Short-term and working memory. In E. Tulving & F. I. M. Craik (Eds.), *The Oxford handbook of memory* (pp. 77–92). New York, NY: Oxford University Press.

Baddeley, A. D. (2007). Working memory, thought, and action. *Oxford psychology series*. New York, NY: Oxford University Press.

Badr, L. K., & Abdallah, B. (2001). Physical attractiveness of premature infants affects outcome at discharge from the NICU. *Infant Behavior & Development, 24*, 129–133.

Bagermihl, B. (1999). *Biological exuberance: Animal homosexuality and natural diversity*. New York, NY: St Martins Press.

Baggott, M. J., Coyle, J. R., Erowid, E., Erowid, F., & Robertson, L. C. (2011). Abnormal visual experiences in individuals with histories of hallucinogen use: A web-based questionnaire. *Drug and Alcohol Dependence, 114(1)*, 61-67.

Baghdaserians, E. S. (2011). Authoritarian and authoritative parenting styles: A cross-cultural study of Armenian American and European Americans' parenting styles of young children. *Dissertation Abstracts International Section A: Humanities and Social Sciences, 71(8-A)*, 2742.

Bagley, S. L., Weaver, T. L., & Buchanan, T. W. (2011). Sex differences in physiological and affective responses to stress in remitted depression. *Physiology & Behavior*. Retrieved from http://www.ncbi.nlm.nih.gov/pubmed/21396947

Bailey, J. M., Dunne, M. P., & Martin, N. G. (2000). Genetic and environmental influences on sexual orientation and its correlates in an Australian twin sample. *Journal of Personality and Social Psychology, 78(3)*, 524–536.

Bailey, K. R., & Mair, R. G. (2005). Lesions of specific and nonspecific thalamic nuclei affect prefrontal cortex-dependent spects of spatial working memory. *Behavioral Neuroscience, 119(2)*, 410–419.

Bailey, S., & Covell, K. (2011). Pathways among abuse, daily hassles, depression, and substance use in adolescents. *The New School Psychology Bulletin, 8(2)*, 4–14.

Baillargeon, R. (2000). Reply to Bogartz, Shinskey, and Schilling; Schilling; and Cashon and Cohen. *Infancy, 1*, 447–462.

Baillargeon, R. (2008). Innate ideas revisited: For a principle of persistence in infants' physical reasoning. *Perspectives on Psychological Science, 3*, 2–13.

Baird, A. D., Scheffer, I. E., & Wilson, S. J. (2011). Mirror neuron system involvement in empathy: A critical look at the evidence. *Social Neuroscience*. doi: 10.1080/17470919.2010.547085

Baizer, J. S., Paolone, N. A., & Witelson, S. F. (2011). Nonphosphorylatedneurofilament protein is expressed by scattered neurons in the human vestibular brainstem. *Brain Research, 1382*, 45–56.

Baker, D. B. (2012). *The Oxford handbook of the history of psychology: Global perspectives*. New York, NY: Oxford University Press.

Baker, D. G., Nievergelt, C. M., & O'Connor, D. T. (2011). Biomarkers of ptsd: Neuropeptides and immune signaling. *Neuropharmacology*. Retrieved from http://www.ncbi.nlm.nih.gov/pubmed/21392516

Baker, D., & Nieuwenhuijsen, M. J. (Eds.) (2008). *Environmental epidemiology: Study methods and application*. New York, NY: Oxford University Press.

Baldessarini, R. J., & Tondo, L. (2008). Lithium and suicidal risk. *Bipolar Disorders, 10*, 114–115.

Baldwin, C. L., & Ash, I. K. (2011). Impact of sensory acuity on auditory working memory span in young and older adults. *Psychology and Aging, 26(1)*, 85–91.

Baldwin, N. (2001). *Edison: Inventing the century*. Chicago, IL: University of Chicago Press.

Balfour, D. J. K. (2004). The neurobiology of tobacco dependence: A preclinical perspective on the role of the dopamine projections to the nucleus. *Nicotine & Tobacco Research, 6(6)*, 899–912.

Balk, D. E. (2008). A modest proposal about bereavement and recovery. *Death Studies, 32,* 84–93.

Balk, D., Wogrin, C., Thornton, G., & Meagher, D. (Eds.) (2007). *Handbook of thanatology: The essential body of knowledge for the study of death, dying, and bereavement.* New York, NY: Routledge/Taylor & Francis Group.

Ball, H. A., McGuffin, P., & Farmer, A. E. (2008). Attributional style and depression. *British Journal of Psychiatry, 192,* 275–278.

Bandura, A. (1969). *Principles of behavior modification.* New York, NY: Holt, Rinehart and Winston.

Bandura, A. (1986). *Social foundations of thought and action: A social cognitive theory.* Englewood Cliffs, NJ: Prentice Hall.

Bandura, A. (1989). Human agency in social cognitive theory. American Psychologist, 44(9), 1175–1184.

Bandura, A. (1991). Human agency: The rhetoric and the reality. American Psychologist, 46(2), 157–162.

Bandura, A. (1997). *Self-efficacy: The exercise of control.* New York, NY: Freeman.

Bandura, A. (2000). Exercise of human agency through collective efficacy. *Current Directions in Psychological Science, 9*(3), 75–83.

Bandura, A. (2003). On the psychosocial impact and mechanisms of spiritual modeling: Comment. *International Journal for the Psychology of Religion, 13*(3), 167–173.

Bandura, A. (2006). Going global with social cognitive theory: From prospect to paydirt. In D. E. Berger & K. Pezdek (Eds.), *The rise of applied psychology: New frontiers and rewarding careers* (pp. 53–79). Mahwah, NJ: Erlbaum.

Bandura, A. (2008). Reconstrual of "free will" from the agentic perspective of social cognitive theory. In J. Baer, J. C. Kaufman, & R. F. Baumeister (Eds.), *Are we free? Psychology and free will* (pp. 86–127). New York, NY: Oxford University Press.

Bandura, A. (2011). A social cognitive perspective on positive psychology. *Revista de Psicología Social, 26*(1), 7–20.

Bandura, A. (2011). The social and policy impact of social cognitive theory. In M. Mark, S. Donaldson, & B. Campbell (Eds.), *Social psychology and evaluation* (pp. 33–70). New York, NY: Guilford Press.

Bandura, A., Ross, D., & Ross, S. (1961). Transmission of aggression through imitation of aggressive models. *Journal of Abnormal & Social Psychology, 63,* 575–582.

Bandura, A., & Walters, R. H. (1963). *Social learning and personality development.* New York, NY: Holt, Rinehart and Winston.

Bangert, A. S., Reuter-Lorenz, P. A., & Seidler, R. D. (2011). Dissecting the clock: Understanding the mechanisms of timing across tasks and temporal intervals. *Acta Psychologica, 136(1),* 20–34.

Banich, M. T., & Compton, R. J. (2011). *Cognitive neuroscience* (3rd ed.). Belmont, CA: Cengage.

Bankó, É. M., & Vidnyánszky, Z. (2010). Retention interval affects visual short-term memory encoding. *Journal of Neurophysiology, 103(3),* 1425–1430.

Banko, K. M. (2008). Increasing intrinsic motivation using rewards: The role of the social context. *Dissertation Abstracts International: Section B: The Sciences and Engineering, 68*(10-B), 7005.

Banks, M. S., & Salapatek, P. (1983). Infant visual perception. In M. M. Haith & J. J. Campos (Eds.), *Handbook of child psychology.* New York, NY: Wiley.

Bao, A., & Swaab, D. (2011). Sexual differentiation of the human brain: Relation to gender identity, sexual orientation and neuropsychiatric disorders. *Frontiers in Neuroendocrinology, 32*(2), 214–226.

Barash, D. P., & Lipton, J. E. (2011). *Payback: Why we retaliate, redirect aggression, and take revenge.* New York, NY: Oxford University Press.

Barbeau, E.-J., Puel, M., & Pariente, J. (2010). La mémoire déclarative antérograde et ses modèles [Anterograde declarative memory and its models]. *Revue Neurologique, 166*(8–9), 661–672.

Barber, N. (2008). Explaining cross-national differences in polygyny intensity: Resource-defense, sex ratio, and infectious diseases. *Cross-Cultural Research: The Journal of Comparative Social Science, 42,* 103–117.

Barbui, C., Cipriani, A., Patel, V., & Ayuso-Mateos, J. L., & Ommeren, M. V. (2011). Efficacy of antidepressants and benzodiazepines in minor depression: Systematic review and meta-analysis. *The British Journal of Psychiatry, 198,* 11–16.

Barczak, B., Miller, T. W., Veltkamp, L. J., Barczak, S., Hall, C., & Kraus, R. (2010). Transitioning the impact of divorce on children throughout the life cycle. In T. W. Miller (Ed.), *Handbook of stressful transitions across the lifespan* (pp. 185–215). New York, NY: Springer Science + Business Media.

Barelds, D. P. H., & Dijkstra, P. (2011). Positive illusions about a partner's personality and relationship quality. *Journal of Research in Personality, 45*(1), 37–43.

Barelds, D., Dijkstra, P., Koudenburg, K., & Swami, V. (2011). An assessment of positive illusions of the physical attractiveness of romantic partners. *Journal of Social and Personal Relationships.* Advance online publication. doi: 10.1177/0265407510385492

Bargai, N., Ben-Shakar, G., & Shalev, A. Y. (2007). Posttraumatic stress disorder and depression in battered women: The mediating role of learned helplessness. *Journal of Family Violence, 22*(5), 267–275.

Bar-Haim, Y., Dan, O., Eshel, Y., & Sagi-Schwartz, A. (2007). Predicting childrens' anxiety from early attachment relationships. *Journal of Anxiety Disorders, 21,* 1061–1068.

Barlett, C. P., Harris, R. J., & Bruey, C. (2008). The effect of the amount of blood in a violent video game on aggression, hostility, and arousal. *Journal of Experimental Social Psychology, 44,* 539–546.

Barlow, D. H. (Ed.). (2008). *Clinical handbook of psychological disorders: A step-by-step treatment manual (4th ed.).* New York, NY: Guilford Press.

Barlow, D. H., & Durand, V. M. (2012). *Abnormal psychology: An integrative approach* (6th ed.). Belmont, CA: Cengage.

Barner, D, Wood, J., Hauser, M., & Carey, S. (2008). Evidence for a non-linguistic distinction between singular and plural sets in rhesus monkeys. *Cognition, 107,* 603–622.

Barnow, S., Ulrich, I., Grabe, H-J., Freyberger, H. J., & Spitzer, C. (2007). The influence of parental drinking behaviour and antisocial personality disorder on adolescent behavioural problems: Results of the Greifswalder family study. *Alcohol and Alcoholism, 42,* 623–628.

Baron, A. S., & Banaji, M. R. (2006). The development of implicit attitudes: Evidence of race evaluations from ages 6 and 10 and adulthood. *Psychological Science, 17*(1), 53–58.

Barry, L. C., Allore, H. G., Guo, Z., Bruce, M. L., & Gill, T. M. (2008). Higher burden of depression among older women: The effect of onset, persistence, and mortality over time. *Archives of General Psychiatry, 65,* 172–178.

Barsalou, L. (2008). Grounded cognition. *Annual Review of Psychology, 59,* 617–645.

Barton, D. A., Esler, M. D., Dawood, T., Lambert, E. A., Haikerwal, D. et al., (2008). Elevated brain serotonin turnover in patients with depression: Effect of genotype and therapy. *Archives of General Psychiatry, 65,* 38–46.

Barton, J. J. S. (2008). Prosopagnosia associated with a left occipitotemporal lesion. *Neuropsychologia, 46,* 2214–2224.

Bastien, C. H. (2011). Insomnia: Neurophysiological and neuropsychological approaches. *Neuropsychology Review, 21(1),* 22–40.

Batchelder, W. H. (2010). Cognitive psychometrics: Using multinomial processing tree models as measurement tools. In S. E. Embretson (Ed.), *Measuring psychological constructs: Advances in model-based approaches* (pp. 71–93). Washington, DC: American Psychological Association.

Bateman, C. R., & Valentine, S. R. (2010). Investigating the effects of gender on consumers' moral philosophies and ethical intentions. *Journal of Business Ethics, 95(3),* 393–414.

Bates, A. L. (2007). How did you get in? Attributions of preferential selection in college admissions. *Dissertation Abstracts International: Section B: The Sciences and Engineering, 68*(4-B), 2694.

Batey, M., Furnham, A., & Safiullina, X. (2010). Intelligence, general knowledge and personality as predictors of creativity. *Learning and Individual Differences, 20(5),* 532–535.

Batson, C. D. (1991). *The altruism question: Toward a social-psychological answer.* Hillsdale, NJ: Erlbaum.

Batson, C. D. (1998). Altruism and prosocial behavior. In D.T. Gilbert, S.T. Fiske, & G. Lindzey (Eds.). *The handbook of social psychology, Vol. 2* (4th ed.) (pp. 282–316). Boston, MA: McGraw-Hill.

Batson, C. D. (2006). "Not all self-interest after all": Economics of empathy-induced altruism. In D. De Cremer, M. Zeelenberg, & J. K. Murnighan (Eds.), *Social psychology and economics* (pp. 281–299). Mahwah, NJ: Erlbaum.

Batson, C. D. (2011). *Altruism in humans.* New York, NY: Oxford University Press.

Batson, C. D., & Ahmad, N. (2001). Empathy-induced altruism in a prisoner's dilemma II: What if the target of empathy has defected? *European Journal of Social Psychology, 31(1),* 25–36.

Bauer, P. J., & Lukowski, A. F. (2010). The memory is in the details: Relations between memory for the specific features of events and long-term recall during infancy. *Journal of Experimental Child Psychology, 107(1),* 1–14.

Baumeister, R. F. (2001). Violent pride: Do people turn violent because of self-hate, or self-love? *Scientific American, 284(4),* 96–101.

Baumeister, R. F., & Bushman, B. (2011). *Social psychology and human nature, comprehensive edition* (2nd ed.). Belmont, CA: Cengage.

Baumeister, R. F., Bushman, B. J., & Campbell, W. K. (2000). Self-esteem, narcissism, and aggression: Does violence result from low self-esteem or from threatened egotism? *Current Directions in Psychological Science,* 9, 26–29.

Baumeister, R. F., Campbell, J. D., Krueger, J. I., & Vohs, K. D. (2005). Exploding the self-esteem myth. *Scientific American.com.* Retrieved from http://www.papillonsartpalace.com/exSplodin.htm

Baumeister, R., & Vohs, K. (2011). *New directions in social psychology.* Thousand Oaks, CA: Sage.

Baumrind, D. (1980). New directions in socialization research. *American Psychologist, 35,* 639–652.

Baumrind, D. (1991). Effective parenting during the early adolescent transition. In P. A. Cowan & E. M. Hetherington (Eds.), *Family transition* (pp. 111–163). Hillsdale, NJ: Erlbaum.

Baumrind, D. (1995). *Child maltreatment and optimal caregiving in social contexts.* New York, NY: Garland.

Bava, S., & Tapert, S. F. (2010). Adolescent brain development and the risk for alcohol and other drug problems. *Neuropsychology Review, 20(4),* 398–413.

Bayne, R. (2004). *Psychological types at work: An MBTI perspective.* London, England: Thomson.

Beach, F. A. (1977). *Human sexuality in four perspectives.* Baltimore: The Johns Hopkins University Press.

Beacham, A., Stetson, B., Braekkan, K., Rothschild, C., Herbst, A., & Linfield, K. (2011). Causal attributions regarding personal exercise goal attainment in exerciser schematics and aschematics. *International Journal of Sport and Exercise Psychology, 9*(1), 48–63.

Beachkofsky, A. L. (2010). Marital satisfaction: Ideal versus real mate. *Dissertation Abstracts International: Section B: The Sciences and Engineering, 51,* 5891.

Beaton, E. A., & Simon, T. J. (2011). How might stress contribute to increased risk for Schizophrenia in children with Chromosome 22q11.2 deletion syndrome? *Journal of Neurodevelopmental Disorders, 3*(1), 68–75.

Beaton, E. A., Schmidt, L. A., Schulkin, J., Antony, M. M., Swinson, R. P., & Hall, G. B. (2008). Different neural responses to stranger and personally familiar faces in shy and bold adults. *Behavioral Neuroscience, 122,* 704–709.

Beauchamp, M. R., Rhodes, R. E., Kreutzer, C., & Rupert, J. L. (2011). Experiential versus genetic accounts of inactivity: Implications for inactive individuals' self-efficacy beliefs and intentions to exercise. *Behavioral Medicine, 37(1),* 8–14.

Beck, A. T. (1976). *Cognitive therapy and the emotional disorders.* New York, NY: International Universities Press.

Beck, A. T. (2000). *Prisoners of hate.* New York, NY: Harper Perennial.

Begley, S. (2009, January 31). Of Voodoo and the Brain: Patterns of neural activity and thoughts or feelings are not as tightly linked as scientists have claimed. *Newsweek.* Retrieved from http://www.newsweek.com/2009/01/30/of-voodoo-and-the-brain.html

Beilin, H. (1992). Piaget's enduring contribution to developmental psychology. *Developmental Psychology, 28,* 191–204.

Beins, B. C. (2010). Teaching measurement through historical sources. *History of Psychology, 13(1),* 89–94.

Bekris, L. M., Yu, C.-E., Bird, T. D., & Tsuang, D. W. (2010). Genetics of Alzheimer disease. *Journal of Geriatric Psychiatry and Neurology, 23(4),* 213–227.

Bell, J, Stanley, N., Mallon, S., & Manthorpe, J. (2010). The role of perfectionism in student suicide: Three case studies from the UK. *Omega, 61(3),* 251–267.

Bell, V., Oakley, D. A., Halligan, P. W., & Deeley, Q. (2011). Dissociation in hysteria and hypnosis: Evidence from cognitive neuroscience. *Journal of Neurology, Neurosurgery & Psychiatry, 82(3),* 332–339.

Bellebaum, C., & Daum, I. (2011). Mechanisms of cerebellar involvement in associative learning. *Cortex: A Journal Devoted to the Study of the Nervous System and Behavior, 47(1),* 128–136.

Belson, K. (2011, March 30). Workers give glimpse of Japan's nuclear crisis. *The New York Times,* 160 (55,361). Retrieved from http://www.nytimes.com

Bem, D. J. (2011). Feeling the future: Experimental evidence for anomalous retroactive influences on cognition and affect. *Journal of Personality and Social Psychology.* Retrieved from http://dl.dropbox.com/u/8290411/Feeling Future.pdf

Bem, S. L. (1974). The measurement of psychological androgyny. *Journal of Consulting and Clinical Psychology, 42(2),* 155–162.

Bem, S. L. (1981). Gender schema theory: A cognitive account of sex typing. *Psychological Review, 88,* 354–364.

Bem, S. L. (1993). *The lenses of gender: Transforming the debate on sexual inequality.* New Haven, CT: Yale University Press.

Bender, R. E., & Alloy, L. B. (2011). Life stress and kindling in bipolar disorder: Review of the evidence and integration with emerging biopsychosocial theories. *Clinical Psychology Review, 31*(3), 383–398.

Bendersky, M., & Sullivan, M. W. (2007). Basic methods in infant research. In A. Slater & M. Lewis (Eds.), *Introduction to infant development* (2nd ed.). New York, NY: Oxford University Press.

Bendle, N. T. (2011). Out-group homogeneity bias and strategic market entry. *Dissertation Abstracts International Section A: Humanities and Social Sciences, 71(9-A),* 3341.

Ben-Eliyahu, S., Page, G. G., & Schleifer, S. J. (2007). Stress, NK cells, and cancer: Still a promissory note. *Brain, Behavior, & Immunity, 21,* 881–887.

Benjamin, E. (2011). Humanistic psychology and the mental health worker. *Journal of Humanistic Psychology, 51(1),* 82–111.

Benjamin, L. T., Cavell, T. A., & Shallen-Berger, W. R. (1984). Staying with initial answers on objective tests: Is it a myth? *Teaching of Psychology, 11,* 133–141.

Bensafi, M. Sobel, N., & Khan, R. M. (2007). Hedonic-specific activity in piriform cortex during odor imagery mimics that during odor perception. *Journal of Neurophysiology, 98,* 3254–3262.

Benton, D. A., Esler, M. D., Dawood, T., Lambert, E. A., Haikerwal, D., Brenchley, C., Socratous, F., Hastings, J., Guo, L., Wiesner, G., Kaye, D. M., Bayles, R., Schlaich, M. P., & Lambert, G. W. (2008). Elevated brain serotonin turnover in patients with depression: Effect of genotype and therapy. *Archives of General Psychiatry, 65,* 38–46.

Benton, T. R., McDonnell, S., Ross, D. F., Thomas III, W. N., & Bradshaw, E. (2007). Has eyewitness research penetrated the American legal system? A synthesis of case history, juror knowledge, and expert testimony. In R. C. L. Lindsay, D. F. Ross, J. D. Read, & M. P. Toglia (Eds.), *The handbook of eyewitness psychology, Vol II: Memory for people* (pp. 453–500). Mahwah, NJ: Erlbaum.

Berchtold, N. C. (2008). Exercise, stress mechanisms, and cognition. In W. W. Spirduso, L. W. Poon, & W. Chodzko-Zajko (Eds), *Exercise and its mediating effects on cognition* (pp. 47–67). *Aging, exercise, and cognition series.* Champaign, IL: Human Kinetics.

Berenbaum, S., & Beltz, A. (2011). Sexual differentiation of human behavior: Effects of prenatal and pubertal organizational hormones. *Frontiers in Neuroendocrinology, 32(2),* 183–200.

Berger, M., Speckmann, E.-J., Pape, H. C., & Gorji, A. (2008). Spreading depression enhances human neocortical excitability in vitro. *Cephalalgia, 28,* 558–562.

Berges, I.-M., Seale, G., & Ostir, G. V. (2011). Positive affect and pain ratings in persons with stroke. *Rehabilitation Psychology, 56(1),* 52–57.

Bergner, R. M. (2011). What is behavior? And so what? *New Ideas in Psychology, 29(2),* 147–155.

Bergstrom-Lynch, C. A. (2008). Becoming parents, remaining childfree: How same-sex couples are creating families and confronting social inequalities. *Dissertation Abstracts International Section A: Humanities and Social Sciences, 68(8-A),* 3608.

Berk, L. (2011). *Infants, children, and adolescents* (7th ed.). Upper Saddle, NJ: Prentice Hall.

Bermeitinger, C., Goelz, R., Johr, N., Neumann, M., Ecker, U. K. H., & Doerr, R. (2009). The hidden persuaders break into the tired brain. *Journal of Experimental Social Psychology, 45(2),* 320–326.

Bernabé, D. G., Tamae, A. C., Biasoli, É. R., & Oliveira, S. H.P. (2011). Stress hormones increase cell proliferation and regulates interleukin-6 secretion in human oral squamous cell carcinoma cells. *Brain, Behavior, and Immunity, 25(3),* 574–583.

Bernard, L. L. (1924). *Instinct.* New York, NY: Holt.

Bernet, W., & Ash, D. R. (2007). *Children of divorce: A practical guide for parents, therapists, attorneys, and judges* (2nd ed.). Malabar, FL: Krieger.

Berreman, G. (1971). *Anthropology today.* Del Mar, CA: CRM Books.

Berry, J., Poortinga, Y., Breugelmans, S., Chasiotis, A., & Sam, D. (2011). *Cross-cultural psychology: Research and applications* (3rd ed.). Cambridge, UK: Cambridge University Press.

Berthoud, H-R., & Morrison, C. (2008). The brain, appetite, and obesity. *Annual Review of Psychology, 59,* 55–92.

Berti, S. (2010). Arbeitsgedächtnis: Vergangenheit, Gegenwart und Zukunft eines theoretischen Konstruktes [Working memory: The past, the present, and the future of a theoretical construct]. *Psychologische Rundschau, 61(1),* 3–9.

Berwick, R. C., Okanoya, K., Beckers, G. J. L., & Bolhuis, J. J. (2011). Songs to syntax: The linguistics of birdsong. *Trends in Cognitive Sciences, 15(3),* 113–121.

Berzoff, J. (2011). *Inside out and outside in: Psychodynamic clinical theory and psychopathology in contemporary multicultural contexts* (3rd ed.). Lanham, MD: Rowman & Littlefield.

Besnard, J., Allain, P., Aubin, G., Osiurak, F., Chauviré, V., Etcharry-Bouyx, F., & Le Gall, D. (2010). Utilization behavior: Clinical and theoretical approaches. *Journal of the International Neuropsychological Society, 16,* 453–462.

Bethmann, A., Tempelmann, C., De Bleser, R., Scheich, H., & Brechmann, A. (2007). Determining language laterality by fMRI and dichotic listening. *Brain Research, 1133,* 145–157.

Beyers, W., & Seiffge-Krenke, I. (2010). Does identity precede intimacy? Testing Erikson's theory on romantic development in emerging adults of the 21st century. *Journal of Adolescent Research, 25(3),* 387–415.

Bhanoo, S. N. (2011). Altering a mouse gene turns up aggression, Study says. *The New York Times, 160,* pp. 55,303.

Bhattacharya, S. K., & Muruganandam, A. V. (2003). Adaptogenic activity of Withania somnifera: An experimental study using a rat model of chronic stress. *Pharmacology, Biochemistry & Behavior, 75(3),* 547–555.

Bianchi, M., Franchi, S., Ferrario, P., Sotgiu, M. L., & Sacerdote, P. (2008). Effects of the bisphosphonate ibandronate on hyperalgesia, substance P, and cytokine levels in a rat model of persistent inflammatory pain. *European Journal of Pain, 12,* 284–292.

Biehl, M., Matsumoto, D., Ekman, P., Hearn, V., Heider, K., Kudoh, T., & Ton, V. (1997). Matsumoto and Ekman's Japanese and Caucasian facial expressions of emotion (JACFEE): Reliability data and cross-national differences. *Journal of Nonverbal Behavior, 21,* 3–21.

Billiard, M. (2007). Sleep disorders. In L. Candelise, R. Hughes, A. Liberati, B. M. J. Uitdehaag, & C. Warlow (Eds.), Evidence-based neurology: Management of neurological disorders (pp. 70–78). *Evidence-based medicine.* Malden, MA: Blackwell Publishing.

Bink, M. L., & Marsh, R. L. (2000). Cognitive regularities in creative activity. *Review of General Psychology, 4*(1), 59–78.

Binstock, R. H., & George, L. K. (Eds.). (2011). *The handbooks of aging consisting of three Vols. Handbook of aging and the social sciences* (7th ed.). San Diego, CA: Elsevier Academic Press.

Bjornaes, H., Stabell, K. E., Roste, G. K., & Bakke, S. J. (2005). Changes in verbal and nonverbal memory following anterior temporal lobe surgery for refractory seizures: Effects of sex and laterality. *Epilepsy & Behavior, 6(1)*, 71–84.

Bjorvatn, B., Grønli, J., & Pallesen, S. (2010). Prevalence of different parasomnias in the general population. *Sleep Medicine, 11(10)*, 1031–1034.

Blais, M. C., & Boisvert, J-M. (2007). Psychological adjustment and marital satisfaction following head injury: Which critical personal characteristics should both partners develop? *Brain injury, 21*, 357–372.

Blakemore, C., & Cooper, G. F. (1970). Development of the brain depends on the visual environment. *Nature, 228*, 477–478.

Blashfield, R. K., Flanagan, E., & Raley, K. (2010). Themes in the evolution of the 20th-century DSMs. In T. Millon, R. F. Krueger, & E. Simonsen (Eds.), *Contemporary directions in psychopathology: Scientific foundations of the DSM-V and ICD-11* (pp. 53–71). New York, NY: Guilford Press.

Blass, T. (1991). Understanding behavior in the Milgram obedience experiment: The role of personality, situations, and their interactions. *Journal of Personality and Social Psychology, 60(3)*, 398–413.

Blass, T. (2000). Stanley Milgram. In A. E. Kazdin (Ed.), *Encyclopedia of psychology* (Vol. 5) (pp. 248–250). Washington, DC: American Psychological Association.

Blonigen, D. M., Carlson, M. D., Hicks, B. M., Krueger, R. F., & Iacono, W. G. (2008). Stability and change in personality traits from late adolescence to early adulthood: A longitudinal twin study. *Journal of Personality, 76*, 229–266.

Blum, H. P. (2011). To what extent do you privilege dream interpretation in relation to other forms of mental representations? *The International Journal of Psychoanalysis, 92(2)*, 275–277.

Blume-Marcovici, A. (2010). Gender differences in dreams: Applications to dream work with male clients. *Dreaming, 20(3)*, 199–210.

Boardman, J., Alexander, K., & Stallings, M. (2011). Stressful life events and depression among adolescent twin pairs. *Biodemography and Social Biology, 57(1)*, 53–66.

Bob, P. (2008). Pain, dissociation and subliminal self-representations. *Consciousness and Cognition: An International Journal, 17*, 355–369.

Boccato, G., Capozza, D., Falvo, R., & Durante, F. (2008). Capture of the eyes by relevant and irrelevant onsets. *Social Cognition, 26*, 224–234.

Boden, J. M., & Fergusson, D. M. (2011). Alcohol and depression. *Addiction, 106(5)*, 906–914.

Bodenhausen, G. V., & Richeson, J. A. (2010). Prejudice, stereotyping, and discrimination. In R. F. Baumeister & E. J. Finkel (Eds.), *Advanced social psychology: The state of the science* (pp. 341–383). New York, NY: Oxford University Press.

Boeree, C. G. (2006). Personality theories: Abraham Maslow. *Webspace*. Retrieved from http://webspace.ship.edu/cgboer/maslow.html

Boettger, M. K., Schwier, C., & Bär, K.-J. (2011). Sad mood increases pain sensitivity upon thermal grill illusion stimulation: Implications for central pain processing. *Pain, 152(1)*, 123–130.

Bohbot, V. D., & Corkin, S. (2007). Posterior parahippocampal place learning in H. M. *Hippocampus, 17*, 863–872.

Böhm, R., Schütz, A., Rentzsch, K., Körner, A., & Funke, F. (2010). Are we looking for positivity or similarity in a partner's outlook on life? Similarity predicts perceptions of social attractiveness and relationship quality. *The Journal of Positive Psychology, 5(6)*, 431–438.

Bohm-Starke, N., Brodda-Jansen, G., Linder, J., & Danielson, I. (2007). The result of treatment on vestibular and general pain thresholds in women with provoked vestibulodynia. *Clinical Journal of Pain, 23(7)*, 598–604.

Boll, S., Gamer, M., Kalisch, R., & Büchel, C. (2011). Processing of facial expressions and their significance for the observer in subregions of the human amygdala. *NeuroImage, 56(1)*, 299–306.

Bond, F. W., & Bunce, D. (2000). Mediators of change in emotion-focused and problemfocused worksite stress management intervention. *Journal of Occupational Health Psychology, 5*, 153–163.

Bonk, W. J., & Healy, A. F. (2010). Learning and memory for sequences of pictures, words, and spatial locations: An exploration of serial position effects. *The American Journal of Psychology, 123(2)*, 137–168.

Bor, D., Billington, J., & Baron-Cohen, S. (2007). Savant memory for digits in a case of synaesthesia and Asberger Syndrome is related to hyperactivity in the lateral prefrontal cortex. *Neurocase, 13*, 311–319.

Bor, J., Brunelin, J., Sappey-Marinier, D., Ibarrola, D., d'Amato, T., Suaud-Chagny, M.-F., & Saoud, M. (2011). Thalamus abnormalities during working memory in schizophrenia. An fMRI study. *Schizophrenia Research, 125(1)*, 49–53.

Borbely, A. A. (1982). Circadian and sleep dependent processes in sleep regulation. In J. Aschoff, S. Daan, & G. A. Groos (Eds.), *Vertebrate circadian rhythms* (pp. 237–242). Berlin: Springer/Verlag.

Borchers, B. J. (2007). Workplace environment fit, commitment, and job satisfaction in a nonprofit association. *Dissertation Abstracts International: Section B: The Sciences and Engineering, 67(7-B)*, 4139.

Borghans, L, Golsteyn, B., Heckman, J., & Humphries, J. (2011). Identification problems in personality psychology. (Report No. 16917). Retrieved from National Bureau of Economic Research website: http://www.nber.org/papers/w16917

Borra, R. (2008). Working with the cultural formulation in therapy. *European Psychiatry, 23*, S43–S48.

Borrego, J., Ibanez, E. S., Spendlove, S. J., & Pemberton, J. R. (2007). Treatment acceptability among Mexican American parents. *Behavior Therapy, 38(3)*, 218–227.

Borrero, J. C., Bartels-Meints, J. A., Sy, J. R., & Francisco, M. T. (2011). Fixed-time schedule effects in combination with response-dependent schedules. *Journal of Applied Behavior Analysis, 44(1)*, 163–167.

Borst, G., Kievit, R. A., Thompson, W. L., & Kosslyn, S. M. (2011). Mental rotation is not easily cognitively penetrable. *Journal of Cognitive Psychology, 23(1)*, 60–75.

Boscarino, J. A., Adams, R. E., & Figley, C. R. (2011). Mental health service use after the World Trade Center disaster: Utilization trends and comparative effectiveness. *Journal of Nervous and Mental Disease, 199(2)*, 91–99.

Bösche, W. (2010). Violent video games prime both aggressive and positive cognitions. *Journal of Media Psychology: Theories, Methods, and Applications, 22(4)*, 139–146.

Bosson, J., & Vandello, J. (2011). Precarious manhood and its links to action and aggression. *Current Directions in Psychological Science, 20(2)*, 82–86.

Bouchard, T. J., Jr. (1994). Genes, environment, and personality. *Science, 264*, 1700–1701.

Bouchard, T. J., Jr. (1997). The genetics of personality. In K. Blum & E. P. Noble (Eds.), *Handbook of psychiatric genetics* (pp. 273–296). Boca Raton, FL: CRC Press.

Bouchard, T. J., Jr. (1999). The search for intelligence. *Science, 284*, 922–923.

Bouchard, T. J., Jr. (2004). Genetic influence on human psychological traits: A survey.

Current Directions in Psychological Science, 13(4), 148–151.

Bouchard, T. J., Jr. & McGue, M. (1981). Familial studies of intelligence: A review. *Science, 212*(4498), 1055–1059.

Bouchard, T. J., Jr., McGue, M., Hur, Y., & Horn, J. M. (1998). A genetic and environmental analysis of the California Psychological Inventory using adult twins reared apart and together. *European Journal of Personality, 12,* 307–320.

Bourke, R. S., Anderson, V., Yang, J. S. C., Jackman, A. R., Killedar, A., Nixon, G. M., Davey, M., Walker, A., Trinder, J., & Horne, R. S. C. (2011). Neurobehavioral function is impaired in children with all severities of sleep disordered breathing. *Sleep Medicine, 12(3),* 222–229.

Bourne, L. E., Dominowski, R. L., & Loftus, E. F. (1979). *Cognitive processes.* Englewood Cliffs, NJ: Prentice Hall.

Bouton, M. E. (1994). Context, ambiguity, and classical conditioning. *Current Directions in Psychological Science, 2,* 49–53.

Bouton, M. E. (2011). Learning and the persistence of appetite: Extinction and the motivation to eat and overeat. *Physiology & Behavior, 103(1),* 51–58.

Bouton, M. E., Todd, T. P., Vurbic, D., & Winterbauer, N. E. (2011). Renewal after the extinction of free operant behavior. *Learning & Behavior, 39(1),* 57–67.

Bowers, K. S., & Woody, E. Z. (1996). Hypnotic amnesia and the paradox of intentional forgetting. *Journal of Abnormal Psychology, 105,* 381–390.

Bowlby, J. (1969). *Attachment and loss: Vol. 1. Attachment.* New York, NY: Basic Books.

Bowlby, J. (1973). *Attachment and loss: Vol. 2. Separation and anxiety.* New York, NY: Basic Books.

Bowlby, J. (1982). Attachment and loss: Retrospect and prospect. *American Journal of Orthopsychiatry, 52,* 664–678.

Bowlby, J. (1989). *Secure attachment.* New York, NY: Basic Books.

Bowlby, J. (2000). *Attachment.* New York, NY: Basic Books.

Bowman, L.L., Levine, L.E., Waite, B.M., & Gendron, M. (2010). Can students really multitask? An experimental study of instant messaging while reading. *Computers & Education, 54(4),* 927–931.

Boyd, R., Richerson, P. J., & Henrich, J. (2011). Rapid cultural adaptation can facilitate the evolution of large-scale cooperation. *Behavioral Ecology and Sociobiology, 65(3),* 431–444.

Boyer, P., & Bergstrom, B. (2011). Threat-detection in child development: An evolutionary perspective. *Neuroscience and Biobehavioral Reviews, 35(4),* 1034–1041.

Boyle, S. H., Williams, R. B., Mark, D. B., Brummett, B. H., Siegler, I. C., Helms, M. J., & Barefoot, J. C. (2004). Hostility as a predictor of survival in patients with coronary artery disease. *Psychosomatic Medicine, 66(5),* 629–632.

Boysen, G. A., & Vogel, D. L. (2007). Biased assimilation and attitude polarization in response to learning about biological explanations of homosexuality. *Sex Roles, 56,* 755–762.

Bozarth, J. D., & Brodley, B. T. (2008). Actualization: A functional concept in client-centered therapy. In B. E. Levitt (Ed.), *Reflections on human potential: Bridging the person-centered approach and positive psychology* (pp. 33–45). Ross-on-Wye, England: PCCS Books.

Bozkurt, A. S., & Aydin, O. (2004). Temel yükleme hatasinin degisik yas ve iki alt kültürde incelenmesi. [A developmental investigation of fundamental attribution error in two subcultures.] *Türk Psikoloji Dergisi, 19,* 91–104.

Braaten, E. B. (2011). Psychotherapy: Interpersonal and insight-oriented approaches. In E. B. Braaten, *APA LifeTools imprint. How to find mental health care for your child* (pp. 171–183). Washington, DC: American Psychological Association.

Brackett, M., Rivers, S., & Salovey, P. (2011). Emotional Intelligence: Implications for personal, social, academic, and workplace success. *Social and Personality Psychology Compass, 5(1),* 88–103.

Bradley, R. H., & Corwyn, R. F. (2008). Infant temperament, parenting, and externalizing behavior in first grade: A test of the differential susceptibility hypothesis. *Journal of Child Psychology and Psychiatry, 49,* 124–131.

Branstetter, S., Low, S., & Furman, W. (2011). The influence of parents and friends on adolescent substance use: A multidimensional approach. *Journal of Substance Abuse, 16(2),* 150–160.

Breeding, J. (2011). Thomas Szasz: Philosopher of liberty. *Journal of Humanistic Psychology, 51(1),* 112–128.

Breithaupt, F. (2011). How is it possible to have empathy? Four models. In P. Leverage, H. Mancing, R. Schweickert, & J. M. William (Eds.), *Theory of mind and literature* (pp. 273–288). West Lafayette, IN: Purdue University Press.

Breland, K., & Breland, M. (1961). The misbehavior of organisms. *American Psychologist, 16,* 681–684.

Brent, D. A., & Melhem, N. (2008). Familial transmission of suicidal behavior. *Psychiatric Clinics of North America, 31,* 157–177.

Brislin, R. W. (1997). *Understanding culture's influence on behavior* (2nd ed.). San Diego, CA: Harcourt Brace.

Brislin, R. W. (2000). *Understanding culture's influence on behavior* (3rd ed.). Ft. Worth, TX: Harcourt.

Brock, O., & Bakker, J. (2011). Potential contribution of prenatal estrogens to the sexual differentiation of mate preferences in mice. *Hormones and Behavior, 59(1),* 83–89.

Brooks, D. (April 30, 2009). Genius: The modern view. *The New York Times.* Retrieved from http://www.nytimes.com/2009/05/01/opinion/01brooks.html

Brosan, L., Hoppitt, L., Shelfer, L., Sillence, A., & Mackintosh, B. (2011). Cognitive bias modification for attention and interpretation reduces trait and state anxiety in anxious patients referred to an out-patient service: Results from a pilot study. *Journal of Behavior Therapy and Experimental Psychiatry, 42(3),* 258–264.

Brosnan, S. F. (2011). An evolutionary perspective on morality. *Journal of Economic Behavior & Organization, 77(1),* 23–30.

Brown, A., & Whiteside, S. P. (2008). Relations among perceived parental rearing behaviors, attachment style, and worry in anxious children. *Journal of Anxiety Disorders, 22,* 263–272.

Brown, A. C., Wolchik, S. A., Tein, J-Y., & Sandler, I. N. (2007). Maternal acceptance as a moderator of the relation between threat to self appraisals and mental health problems in adolescents from divorced families. *Journal of Youth and Adolescence, 36,* 927–938.

Brown, E., Deffenbacher, K., & Sturgill, K. (1977). Memory for faces and the circumstances of encounter. *Journal of Applied Psychology, 62,* 311–318.

Brown, L. S. (2011). Guidelines for Treating Dissociative Identity Disorder in Adults, Third Revision: A tour de force for the dissociation field. *Journal of Trauma & Dissociation, 12(2),* 113–114.

Brown, R., & Kulik, J. (1977). Flashbulb memories. *Cognition, 5,* 73–99.

Brown, R., & McNeill, D. (1966). The "tip of the tongue" phenomenon. *Journal of Verbal Learning and Verbal Behavior, 5,* 325–337.

Bruns, C. M., & Kaschak, E. (2011). Feminisms: Feminist therapies in the 21st century. *Women & Therapy, 34*(1–2), 1–5.

Bryan, A. D., Webster, G. D., & Mahaffey, A. L. (2011). The big, the rich, and the powerful: Physical, financial, and social dimensions of dominance in mating and attraction. *Personality and Social Psychology Bulletin, 37(3),* 365–382.

Buchsbaum, B. R., Padmanabhan, A., & Berman, K. F. (2011). The neural substrates of recognition memory for verbal information: Spanning the divide between short- and long-term memory. *Journal of Cognitive Neuroscience, 23(4),* 978–991.

Buck, R. (1984). *The communication of emotion.* New York, NY: Guilford Press.

Buckle, J. L., & Fleming, S. J. (2011). Death, Dying, and Bereavement. Parenting after the death of a child: A practitioner's guide. New York, NY: Routledge/Taylor & Francis Group.

Bugental, D. B., & Johnston, C. (2000). Parental and child cognitions in the context of the family. *Annual Review of Psychology, 51,* 315–344.

Bühler, M., Vollstädt-Klein, S., Kobiella, A., Budde, H., Reed, L. J., Braus, D. F., Büchel, C., & Smolka, M. N. (2010). Nicotine dependence is characterized by disordered reward processing in a network driving motivation. *Biological Psychiatry, 67(8),* 745–752.

Bullock, K. (2011). The influence of culture on end-of-life decision making. *Journal of Social Work in End-Of-Life & Palliative Care, 7(1),* 83–98.

Bunde, J., & Suls, J. (2006). A quantitative analysis of the relationship between the cook-medley hostility scale and traditional coronary artery disease risk factors. *Health Psychology, 25,* 493–500.

Buontempo, G., & Brockner, J. (2008). Emotional intelligence and the ease of recall judgment bias: The mediating effect of private self-focused attention. *Journal of Applied Social Psychology, 38,* 159–172.

Burger, J. M. (2009). Replicating Milgram: Would people still obey today? *American Psychologist, 64(1),* 1–11.

Burger, J. M. (2011). *Personality* (8th ed.). Belmont, CA: Cengage.

Burk, L. R., Armstrong, J. M., Goldsmith, H. H., Klein, M. H., Strauman, T. J., Costanzo, P., & Essex, M. J. (2011). Sex, temperament, and family context: How the interaction of early factors differentially predict adolescent alcohol use and are mediated by proximal adolescent factors. *Psychology of Addictive Behaviors, 25(1),* 1–15.

Burka, J. B., & Yuen, L. M. (2008). *Procrastination: Why You Do It, What to Do About It Now (2nd ed.).* New York, NY: DaCapo Lifelong Books.

Burnette, J., Pollack, J., & Forsyth, D. (2011). Leadership in extreme contexts: A groupthink analysis of the May 1996 Mount Everest disaster. *Journal of Leadership Studies, 4(4),* 29–40.

Burns, S. M. (2008). Unique and interactive predictors of mental health quality of life among men living with prostate cancer. *Dissertation Abstracts International: Section B: The Sciences and Engineering, 68(10-B),* 6953.

Burr, A., Santo, J. B., & Pushkar, D. (2011). Affective well-being in retirement: The influence of values, money, and health across three years. *Journal of Happiness Studies, 12(1),* 17–40.

Burrows, J., & Carlisle, J. (2010). They don't want it ramming down their throats. Learning from the perspectives of current and ex-smokers with smoking-related illness to improve communication in primary care: A qualitative study. *Primary Health Care Research and Development, 11(3),* 206–214.

Burstrem, J. B. (2010). *Religion, gender, and military policies in Avatar.* Retrieved from http://www.jgcinema.com/single.php?sl=a-avatar-cameron-civilization-colonization-war

Burt, K. B., & Masten, A. S. (2010). Development in the transition to adulthood: Vulnerabilities and opportunities. In J. E. Grant & M. N. Potenza (Eds.), *Young adult mental health* (pp. 5–18). New York, NY: Oxford University Press.

Burt, S. A. (2011). The importance of the phenotype in explorations of gene-environment interplay. In A. Booth, S. M. McHale, & N. S. Landale (Eds.), *National symposium on family issues. Biosocial foundations of family processes* (pp. 85–94). New York, NY: Springer.

Bushman, B. J. (2002). Does venting anger feed or extinguish the flame? Catharsis, rumination, distraction, anger and aggressive responding. *Personality & Social Psychology Bulletin, 28(6),* 724–731.

Bushman, B. J., Baumeister, R. F., & Stack, A. D. (1999). Catharsis, aggression, and persuasive influence: Self-fulfilling or self-defeating prophecies? *Journal of Personality and Social Psychology, 76,* 367–376.

Bushman, B. J., Baumeister, R. F., Thomaes, S., Ryu, E., Begeer, S., & West, S. (2009). Looking again, and harder, for a link between low self-esteem and aggression. *Journal of Personality, 77,* 424–446.

Buss, D. M. (1989). Sex differences in human mate preferences: Evolutionary hypotheses tested in 37 cultures. *Behavioral and Brain Sciences, 12,* 1–49.

Buss, D. M. (1994). Mate preferences in 37 countries. In W. J. Lonner & R. Malpass, R. (Eds.), *Psychology and culture.* Boston, MA: Allyn and Bacon.

Buss, D. M. (2003). *The evolution of desire: Strategies of human mating.* New York, NY: Basic Books.

Buss, D. M. (2005). *The handbook of evolutionary psychology.* Hoboken, NJ: Wiley.

Buss, D. M. (2007). The evolution of human mating. *Acta Psychologica Sinica. 39,* 502–512.

Buss, D. M. (2011). *Evolutionary psychology: The new science of the mind* (4th ed.). Upper Saddle River, NJ: Prentice-Hall.

Buss, D. M. and 40 colleagues. (1990). International preferences in selecting mates: A study of 37 cultures. *Journal of Cross-Cultural Psychology, 21,* 5–47.

Buss, K. A. (2011). Which fearful toddlers should we worry about? Context, fear regulation, and anxiety risk. *Developmental Psychology, 47(3),* 804–819.

Buswell, B. N. (2006). The role of empathy, responsibility, and motivations to respond without prejudice in reducing prejudice. *Dissertation Abstracts International: Section B: The Sciences and Engineering, 66,* 6968.

Butcher, J. N. (2000). Revising psychological tests: Lessons learned from the revision of the MMPI. *Psychological Assessment, 12(3),* 263–271.

Butcher, J. N. (2005). *A beginner's guide to the MMPI-2 (2nd ed.).* Washington, DC: American Psychological Association.

Butcher, J. N. (2011). *A beginner's guide to the MMPI-2 (3rd ed.).* Washington, DC: American Psychological Association.

Butcher, J. N., & Perry, J. N. (2008). *Personality assessment in treatment planning: Use of the MMPI-2 and BTPI.* New York, NY: Oxford University Press.

Butcher, J. N., & Rouse, S. V. (1996). Personality: Individual differences and clinical assessment. *Annual Review of Psychology, 47,* 87–111.

Butler, R., Sati, S., & Abas, M. (2011). Assessing mental health in different cultures. In M. Abou-Saleh, C. Katona, & A. Kumar (Eds.), *Principle and practice of geriatric psychiatry* (3rd ed.) (pp. 711–716). Hoboken, NJ: Wiley.

Butterweck, V. (2003). Mechanism of action of St John's Wort in depression: What is known? *CNS Drugs, 17*(8), 539–562.

Butz, D. A., & Plant, E. A. (2011). Approaching versus avoiding intergroup contact: The role of expectancies and motivation. In L. R. Tropp & R. K. Mallett (Eds.), *Moving beyond prejudice reduction: Pathways to positive intergroup relations* (pp. 81–98). Washington, DC: American Psychological Association.

Buysse, D. J., Strollo, P. J., Jr., Black, J. E., Zee, P. G., & Winkelman, J. W. (2008). Sleep disorders. In R. E. Hales, S. C.Yudofsky, & G. O. Gabbard (Eds.). *The American Psychiatric Publishing textbook of psychiatry* (5th ed.) (pp. 921–969). Arlington, VA: American Psychiatric Publishing, Inc.

Buzawa, E., Buzawa, C., & Stark, E. (2012). *Responding to domestic violence: The integration of criminal justice and human services* (4ᵗʰ ed.). Thousand Oaks, CA: Sage.

Cabýoglu, M. T., Ergene, N., & Tan, U. (2006). The mechanism of acupuncture and clinical applications. *International Journal of Neuroscience, 116,* 115–125.

Cacchioni, T., & Wolkowitz, C. (2011). Treating women's sexual difficulties: The body work of sexual therapy. *Sociology of Health & Illness, 33*(2), 266–279.

Cacioppo, J. T., Berntson, G. G., Bechara, A., Tranel, D., & Hawkley, L. C. (2011). Could an aging brain contribute to subjective well being?: The value added by a social neuroscience perspective. In A. Tadorov, S. T. Fiske, & D. Prentice (Eds.), *Social Neuroscience: Toward Understanding the Underpinnings of the Social Mind* (pp. 249–262). New York, NY: Oxford University Press.

Cadoret, R. J., Leve, L. D., & Devor, E. (1997). Genetics of aggressive and violent behavior. *Psychiatric Clinics of North America, 20,* 301–322.

Caggiano, V., Fogassi, L., Rizzolatti, G., Pomper, J. K., Their, P., Giese, M. A., & Casile, A. (2011). View-based encoding of actions in mirror neurons of area F5 in macaque premotor cortex. *Current Biology, 21,* 144–148.

Cal, W-H., Blundell, J., Han, J., Greene, R. W., & Powell, C. M. (2006). Postreactivation glucocorticoids impair recall of established fear memory. *Journal of Neuroscience, 26*(37), 9560–9566.

California Task Force to Promote Self-esteem and Personal and Social Responsibility. (1990). *Toward a State of Esteem.* Sacramento, CA: California State Department of Education.

Call, J. (2011). How artificial communication affects the communication and cognition of the great apes. *Mind & Language, 26(1),* 1–20.

Cameron, L., Rutland, A. & Brown, R. (2007). Promoting children's positive intergroup attitudes towards stigmatized groups: Extended contact and multiple classification skills training. *International Journal of Behavioral Development, 31,* 454–466.

Camfield, D. A., Sarris, J. & Berk, M. (2011). Nutraceuticals in the treatment of obsessive compulsive disorder (OCD): A review of mechanistic and clinical evidence. *Progress in Neuro-Psychopharmacology & Biological Psychiatry, 35(4),* 887–895.

Camos, V., & Barrouillet, P. (2011). Developmental change in working memory strategies: From passive maintenance to active refreshing. *Developmental Psychology, 47(3),* 898–904.

Campbell, A., & Muncer, S. (2008). Intent to harm or injure? Gender and the expression of anger. *Aggressive Behavior, 34,* 282–293.

Campbell, J. R., & Feng, A. X. (2011). Comparing adult productivity of American mathematics, physics, and chemistry Olympians with Terman's longitudinal study. *Roeper Review: A Journal on Gifted Education, 33(1),* 18–25.

Campbell, L., Simpson, J. A., Kashy, D. A., & Fletcher, G. J. O. (2001). Ideal standards, the self, and flexibility of ideals in close relationships. *Personality & Social Psychology Bulletin, 27*(4), 447–462.

Campbell, L., Vasquez, M., Behnke, S., & Kinscherff, R. (2010). Therapy. In L. Campbell, M. Vasquez, S. Behnke, & R. Kinscherff (Eds.), *APA Ethics Code commentary and case illustrations* (pp. 339–372). Washington, DC: American Psychological Association.

Canals, J., Hernández-Martínez, C., & Fernández-Ballart, J. D. (2011). Relationships between early behavioural characteristics and temperament at 6 years. *Infant Behavior & Development, 34*(1), 152–160.

Cannon, W. B. (1927). The James-Lange theory of emotions: A critical examination and an alternative theory. *American Journal of Psychology, 39,* 106–124.

Cannon, W. B., Lewis, J. T., & Britton, S. W. (1927). The dispensability of the sympathetic division of the autonomic nervous system. *Boston Medical Surgery Journal, 197,* 514.

Cannon, W. B., & Washburn, A. (1912). An explanation of hunger. *American Journal of Physiology, 29,* 441–454.

Capellini, I., Preston, B. T., McNamara, P., Barton, R. A., & Nunn, C. L. (2010). Ecological constraints on mammalian sleep architecture. In P. McNamara, R. A. Barton, & C. L. Nunn (Eds.), *Evolution of sleep: Phylogenetic and functional perspectives* (pp. 12–33). New York, NY: Cambridge University

Caprara, G. V., Vecchione, M., Barbaranelli, C., & Fraley, R. C. (2007). When likeness goes with liking: The case of political preference. *Political Psychology, 28,* 609–632.

Caqueo-Urízar, A., Ferrer-García, M., Toro, J., Gutiérrez-Maldonado, J., Peñaloza, C., Cuadros-Sosa, Y., & Gálvez-Madrid, M. J. (2011). Associations between sociocultural pressures to be thin, body distress, and eating disorder symptomatology among Chilean adolescent girls. *Body Image, 8*(1), 78–81.

Carballo-Diéguez, A., Ventuneac, A., Dowsett, G. W., Balan, I., Bauermeister, J., Remien, R. H., Dolezal, C., Giguere, R., & Mabragaña, M. (2011). Sexual pleasure and intimacy among men who engage in "bareback sex." *AIDS and Behavior, 15(1),* S57–S65.

Carels, R. A., Konrad, K., Young, K. M., Darby, L. A., Coit, C., Clayton, A. M., & Oemig, C. K. (2008). Taking control of your personal eating and exercise environment: A weight maintenance program. *Eating Behaviors, 9,* 228–237.

Carey, B. (2008, December 4). H. M., an unforgettable amnesiac, dies at 82. *The New York Times.* Retrieved from http://www.nytimes.com/2008/12/05/us/05hm.html

Carey, B. (2009). A Dream Interpretation: Tune ups for the brain. *The New York Times,* p. 159.

Carey, B. (2011, March 19). Lessons for Japan's survivors: The psychology of recovery. *The New York Times.* Retrieved from http://www.nytimes.com

Carlat, D. (2008). *Brain scans as mind readers? Don't believe the hype.* Retrieved from http://www.wired.com/print/medtech/health/magazine/16–06/mf_neurohacks.

Carlson, N. (2011). *Foundations of behavioral neuroscience* (8ᵗʰ ed.). Upper Saddle River, NJ: Prentice Hall.

Carmody, J. (2009). Invited commentary: Evolving conceptions of mindfulness in clinical settings. *Journal of Cognitive Psychotherapy, 23,* 270–280.

Carnagey, N. L., Anderson, C. A., & Bartholow, B. D. (2007). Media violence and social neuroscience: New questions and new opportunities. *Current Directions in Psychological Science, 16,* 178–182.

Carpenter, S. (2011) Body of thought. *Scientific American Mind, 21,* 38–45.

Carr, J. L., & VanDeusen, K. M. (2004). Risk factors for male sexual aggression on college campuses. *Journal of Family Violence, 19*(5), 279–289.

Carr, K. D. (2011). Food scarcity, neuroadaptations, and the pathogenic potential of dieting in an unnatural ecology: Binge eating and drug abuse. *Physiology & Behavior*. doi: 10.1016/j.physbeh.2011.04.023

Carré, J., McCormick, C., & Hariri, A. (2011). The social neuroendocrinology of human aggression. *Psychoneuroendocrinology*. Retrieved from http://www.sciencedirect.com/science/article/pii/S0306453011000369

Carroll, J. B. (1993). *Human cognitive abilities: A survey of factor-analytic studies*. Cambridge, England: Cambridge University Press.

Carroll, J. E., Low, C. A., Prather, A. A., Cohen, S., Fury, J. M., Ross, D. C., & Marsland, A. L. (2011). Negative affective responses to a speech task predict changes in interleukin (IL)-6. *Brain, Behavior, and Immunity, 25*(2), 232–238.

Carstensen, L. L., Turan, B., Scheibe, S., Ram, N., Ersner-Hershfield, H., Samanez-Larkin, G. R., Brooks, K., & Nesselroade, J. R. (2011). Emotional experience improves with age: Evidence based on over 10 years of experience sampling. *Psychology and Aging, 26*(1), 21–33.

Carter, E., & Wang, X-J. (2007). Cannabinoid-mediated disinhibition and working memory: Dynamical interplay of multiple feedback mechanisms in a continuous attractor model of prefrontal cortex. *Cerebral Cortex, 17*(Suppl 1), 16–26.

Carton, J. S. (1996). The differential effects of tangible rewards and praise on intrinsic motivation: A comparison of cognitive evaluation theory and operant theory. *Behavior Analyst, 19*, 237–255.

Caruso, E. M. (2008). Use of experienced retrieval ease in self and social judgments. *Journal of Experimental Social Psychology, 44*, 148–155.

Carvalho, C., Mazzoni, G., Kirsch, I., Meo, M., & Santandrea, M. (2008). The effect of posthypnotic suggestion, hypnotic suggestibility, and goal intentions on adherence to medical instructions. *International Journal of Clinical and Experimental Hypnosis, 56*, 143–155.

Carvalho, J., & Nobre, P. (2011). Biopsychosocial determinants of men's sexual desire: Testing an integrative model. *Journal of Sexual Medicine, 8*(3), 754–763.

Casarett, D. J. (2011). Rethinking hospice eligibility criteria. *JAMA: Journal of the American Medical Association, 305*(10), 1031–1032.

Casey, B. J., Ruberry, E. J., Libby, V., Glatt, C. E., Hare, T., Soliman, F., Duhoux, S., Frielingsdorf, H., & Tottenham, N. (2011). Transitional and translational studies of risk for anxiety. *Depression and Anxiety, 28*(1), 18–28.

Castelli, L., Corazzini, L. L., & Geminiani, G. C. (2008). Spatial navigation in large-scale virtual environments: Gender differences in survey tasks. *Computers in Human Behavior, 24*, 1643–1667.

Cathers-Schiffman, T. A., & Thompson, M. S. (2007). Assessment of English-and Spanish-speaking students with the WISC-III and Leiter-R. *Journal of Psychoeducational Assessment, 25*, 41–52.

Cattaneo, Z., Mattavelli, G., Platania, E., & Papagno, C. (2011). The role of the prefrontal cortex in controlling gender-stereotypical associations: A TMS investigation. *NeuroImage, 56*(3), 1839–1846.

Cattell, R. B. (1941). Some theoretical issues in adult intelligence testing. *Psychological Bulletin, 38*, 592.

Cattell, R. B. (1950). *Personality: A systematic, theoretical, and factual study*. New York, NY: McGraw-Hill.

Cattell, R. B. (1963). Theory of fluid and crystallized intelligence: A critical experiment. *Journal of Educational Psychology, 54*, 1–22.

Cattell, R. B. (1965). *The scientific analysis of personality*. Baltimore, MD: Penguin.

Cattell, R. B. (1971). *Abilities: Their structure, growth, and action*. Boston, MA: Houghton Mifflin.

Cattell, R. B. (1990). Advances in Cattellian personality theory. In L. A. Pervin (Ed.), *Handbook of personality: Theory and research*. New York, NY: Guilford Press.

Cautin, R. L. (2011). A century of psychotherapy, 1860–1960. In J. C. Norcross, G. R. VandenBos, & D. K. Freedheim (Eds.), *History of psychotherapy: Continuity and change* (2nd ed.) (pp. 3–38).

Cautin, R. L. (2011). Invoking history to teach about the scientist-practitioner gap. *History of Psychology, 14*(2), 197–203.

Cavett, D. (2008). Smiling through. New York Times. Retrieved from http://cavett.blogs.nytimes.com/2008/06/27/smiling-through/?scp=6&sq=dick%20cavett&st=cse

Cehajic, S., Brown, R., & Castano, E. (2008). Forgive and forget? Antecedents and consequences of intergroup forgiveness in Bosnia and Herzegovina. *Political Psychology, 29*, 351–367.

Celada, T. C. (2011). Parenting styles as related to parental self-efficacy and years living in the United States among Latino immigrant mothers. *Dissertation Abstracts International: Section B: The Sciences and Engineering, 71*(9-B), 5783.

Celes, L. A. M. (2010). Clinica psicanalitica: Aproximações histórico-conceituais e contemporâneas e perspectivas futuras [Psychoanalytic practice: Historical, conceptual and contemporary approaches and future perspectives]. *Psicologia: Teoria e Pesquisa, 26* (SpecIssue), 65–80.

Centers for Disease Control and Prevention (CDC). (2008). *Fact sheets*. Retrieved from http://www.cdc.gov/hiv/resources/factsheets/index.htm#Surveillance.

Centers for Disease Control and Prevention (CDC). (2008). *Quick stats*. Retrieved from http://www.cdc.gov/alcohol/quickstats/general_info.htm.

Centers for Disease Control and Prevention (CDC). (2008). *Tobacco use*. Retrieved from http://www.cdc.gov/HealthyYouth/tobacco/index.htm.

Centers for Disease Control and Prevention (CDC). (2011). *Health effects of cigarette smoking*. Retrieved from http://www.cdc.gov/tobacco/data_statistics/fact_sheets/health_effects/effects_cig_smoking/

Cervone, D., & Pervin, L. A. (2010). *Personality theory and research* (11th ed.). Hoboken, NJ: Wiley.

Cervone, D., & Shoda, Y. (1999). Beyond traits in the study of personality coherence. *Current Directons in Psychological Science, 8*(a), 27–32.

Cesaro, P., & Ollat, H. (1997). Pain and its treatments. *European Neurology, 38*, 209–215.

Ceschi, G., & Scherer, K. R. (2001). Contrôler l'expression faciale et changer l'émotion: Une approche développementale. The role of facial expression in emotion: A developmental perspective. *Enfance, 53*(3), 257–269.

Chadwick, R. (2011). Personal genomes: No bad news? *Bioethics, 25*(2), 62–65.

Chagnon, J.Y. (2011). L'apport des épreuves projectives—Approche psychanalytique—Au bilan psychologique de l'enfant et de l'adolescent. Bilan de 30 ans de travaux [The contribution of projective tests—The psychoanalytical approach—To psychological evaluations of children and adolescents an assessment of 30 years of studies]. *Neuropsychiatrie de l'Enfance et de l'Adolescence, 59*(1), 48–53.

Chamberlin, N. L., & Saper, C. B. (2009). The agony of the ecstasy: Serotonin and obstructive sleep apnea. *Neurology, 73*(23), 1947–1948.

Chamorro-Premuzic, T. (2011). *Personality and individual differences*. Malden, MA: Blackwell.

Chan, C., & Chui, E. (2011). Association between cultural factors and caregiving burden for Chinese spousal caregivers of frail elderly in Hong Kong. *Aging and Mental Health, 15*(4), 500–509.

Chan, T., Kyere, K., Davis, B. R., Shemyakin, A., Kabitzke, P. A., Shair, H. N., Barr, G., & Wiedenmayer, C. P. (2011). The role of the medial prefrontal cortex in innate fear regulation in infants, juveniles, and adolescents. *The Journal of Neuroscience, 31(13)*, 4991–4999.

Chance, P. (2009). *Learning and behavior: Active learning edition* (6th ed.). Belmont, CA: Cengage.

Chandrashekar, J., Hoon, M. A., Ryba, N. J. P., & Zuker, C. S. (2006). The receptors and cells for mammalian taste. *Nature, 444*, 288–294.

Chang, G., Orav, J., McNamara, T. K., Tong, MY., & Antin, J. H. (2005). Psychosocial function after hematopoietic stem cell transplantation. *Psychosomatics: Journal of Consultation Liaison Psychiatry, 46*(1), 34–40.

Chang, L., Wang, Y., Shackelford, T. K., & Buss, D. M. (2011). Chinese mate preferences: Cultural evolution and continuity across a quarter of a century. *Personality and Individual Differences, 50*(5), 678–683.

Chang, R. C., Stout, S., & Miller, R. R. (2004). Comparing excitatory backward and forward conditioning. *Quarterly Journal of Experimental Psychology: Comparative & Physiological Psychology, 57B*(1), 1–23.

Chang, W., Tang, J., Hui, C., Chiu, C., Lam, M., Wong, G., Chung, D., Law, C., Tso, S., Chan, K., Hung, S., & Chen, E. (2011). Gender differences in patients presenting with first-episode psychosis in Hong Kong: A three-year follow up study. *Australian and New Zealand Journal of Psychiatry, 45*(3), 199–205.

Chapman, A. L., Leung, D. W., & Lynch, T. R. (2008). Impulsivity and emotion dysregulation in borderline personality disorder. *Journal of Personality Disorders, 22*, 148–164.

Charland, W. A. (1992, January). Nightshift narcosis. *The Rotarian, 160*, 16–19.

Charles, E. P. (2007). Object permanence, an ecological approach. *Dissertation Abstracts International: Section B: The Sciences and Engineering, 67*(8-B), 4737.

Cheever, N. A. (2010). The cultivation of social identity in single women: The role of single female characterizations and marriage and romantic relationship portrayals on television. *Dissertation Abstracts International: Section B: The Sciences and Engineering, 71*(6–B), 3979.

Chellappa, S. L., Frey, S., Knoblauch, V., & Cajochen, C. (2011). Cortical activation patterns herald successful dream recall after NREM and REM sleep. *Biological Psychology, 87*(2), 251–256.

Cheng, M. (2010, November 2). Study says booze does more harm than drugs. *The Washington Post*. Retrieved from http://www.washingtonpost.com

Cheng, S.-T., & Li, K.-K. (2010). Combining major life events and recurrent hassles in the assessment of stress in Chinese adolescents: Preliminary evidence. *Psychological Assessment, 22*(3), 532–538.

Cheung, F., van de Vijver, F., & Leong, F. (2011, January 24). Toward a new approach to the study of personality in culture. *American Psychologist*. Advance online publication. doi: 10.1037/a0022389

Cheung, R. Y. M., & Park, I. J. K. (2010). Anger suppression, interdependent self-construal, and depression among Asian American and European American college students. *Cultural Diversity and Ethnic Minority Psychology, 16*(4), 517–525.

Chiou, W-B. (2007). Customers' attributional judgments towards complaint handling in airline service: A confirmatory study based on attribution theory. *Psychological Reports, 100*, 1141–1150.

Chipongian, L. (2000). The cognitive advantages of balanced bilingualism. *Brain connection*. Retrieved from http://brainconnection.positscience.com/topics/?main=fa/cognitive-bilingualism

Cho, H., Lee, S., & Wilson, K. (2010). Magazine exposure, tanned women stereotypes, and tanning attitudes. *Body Image, 7*(4), 364–367.

Cho, S. & Lin, C. (2011). Influence of family processes, motivation, and beliefs about intelligence on creative problem solving of scientifically talented individuals. *Roeper Review, 33* (1), 46–58.

Choi, I., & Nisbett, R. E. (2000). Cultural psychology of surprise: Holistic theories and recognition of contradiction. *Journal of Personality and Social Psychology, 79*(6), 890–905.

Choi, N. (2004). Sex role group differences in specific, academic, and general self-efficacy. *Journal of Psychology: Interdisciplinary & Applied, 138*(2), 149–159.

Chomsky, N. (1968). *Language and mind*. New York, NY: Harcourt, Brace, World.

Chomsky, N. (1980). *Rules and representations*. New York, NY: Columbia University Press.

Chong, E., & Ma, X. (2010). The influence of individual factors, supervision and work environment on creative self-efficacy. *Creativity and Innovation Management, 19*(3), 233–247.

Choquet, H., & Meyre, D. (2011). The molecular basis of obesity: Current status and future prospects. *Current Genomics, 12*(3), 154–168.

Chou, Y.-C., Chiao, C., & Fu, L.-Y. (2011). Health status, social support, and quality of life among family carers of adults with profound intellectual and multiple disabilities (PIMD) in Taiwan. *Journal of Intellectual and Developmental Disability, 36*(1), 73–79.

Chrisler, J. C. (2008). The menstrual cycle in a biopsychosocial context. In F. Denmark & M. A. Paludi (Eds.), *Psychology of women: A handbook of issues and theories* (2nd ed.) (pp. 400–439). *Women's psychology*. Westport, CT: Praeger/Greenwood.

Christakou, A., Brammer, M., & Rubia, K. (2011). Maturation of limbic corticostriatal activation and connectivity associated with developmental changes in temporal discounting. *NeuroImage, 54*(2), 1344–1354.

Christandl, F., Fetchenhauer, D., & Hoelzl, E. (2011). Price perception and confirmation bias in the context of a VAT increase. *Journal of Economic Psychology, 32*(1), 131–141.

Christensen, D. (2000). Is snoring a diZ-ZZease? Nighttime noises may serve as a wake-up call for future illness. *Science News, 157*, 172–173.

Christensen, H., Anstey, K. J., Leach, L. S., & Mackinnon, A. J. (2008). Intelligence, education, and the brain reserve hypothesis. In F. I. M. Craik & T. A. Salthouse (Eds.), *The handbook of aging and cognition* (3rd ed.) (pp. 133–188). New York, NY: Psychology Press.

Christenson, K. A. (2011). PSTD symptoms expressed in direct and indirect child victims of domestic violence. *Dissertation Abstracts International: Section B: The Sciences and Engineering, 71*(8-B), 5115.

Christianson, H. F. (2010). Psychological adjustment and quality of life with late-stage cancer patients: Empirical evaluation and critique of cognitive adaptation theory. *Dissertation Abstracts International: Section B: The Sciences and Engineering*, 5154.

Christopher, K., Lutz-Zois, C. J., & Reinhardt, A. R. (2007). Female sexual-offenders: Personality pathology as a mediator of the relationship between childhood sexual abuse history and sexual abuse. *Child Abuse & Neglect, 31*, 871–883.

Chu, J. (2011). *Rebuilding shattered lives: Treating complex PTSD and Dissociative Disorders* (2nd ed.). Hoboken, NJ: Wiley.

Chu, M., & Kita, S. (2011). The nature of gestures' beneficial role in spatial problem solving. *Journal of Experimental Psychology: General, 140*(1), 102–116.

Chu, M., & Sotaro, K. (2011). The nature of gestures' beneficial role in spatial problem solving. *Journal of Experimental Psychology: General, 140*(1), 102–116.

Churchland, P. S. (2011). *Braintrust: What neuroscience tells us about morality*. Princeton, NJ: Princeton University Press.

Cialdini, R. B. (2001). *Influence: Science and practice*. Boston, MA: Allyn & Bacon.

Cialdini, R. B. (2009). *Influence: Science and practice* (5th ed.). Boston, MA: Allyn & Bacon.

Cipriani, G., Dolciotti, C., Picchi, L., & Bonuccelli, U. (2011). Alzheimer and his disease: A brief history. *Neurological Sciences, 32*(2), 275–279.

Cirelli, C., Shaw, P. J., Rechtschaffen, A., & Tononi, G. (1999). No evidence of brain cell degeneration after long-term sleep deprivation in rats. *Brain Research, 840*(1–2), 184–193.

Claes, L., Bijttebier, P., Mitchell, J. E., de Zwaan, M., & Mueller, A. (2011). The relationship between compulsive buying, eating disorder symptoms, and temperament in a sample of female students. *Comprehensive Psychiatry, 52*(1), 50–55.

Clark, A. (2011). *The history of sexuality in Europe: A sourcebook and reader*. London, UK: Routledge.

Clark, A. J. (2007). *Empathy in counseling and psychotherapy: Perspectives and practices*. Mahwah, NJ: Erlbaum.

Clark, K. B., & Clark, M. P. (1939). The development of consciousness of self and the emergence of racial identification in Negro preschool children. *Journal of Social Psychology, 10*, 591–599.

Clark, U. S., & Williams, D. (2011). Exercise and the brain. In R. A. Cohen & L. H. Sweet (Eds.), *Brain imaging in behavioral medicine and clinical neuroscience* (pp. 257–273). New York, NY: Springer.

Clarke, A., Foster-Drain, R., Sudler Milligan, C., Shah, I., Mack, D., & Lowe, B. (2011). Engaging high-risk adolescents in pregnancy prevention programming: Service delivery in low-income housing developments. *Journal of Children and Poverty, 17*(1), 7–24.

Claxton-Oldfield, S., Wasylkiw, L., Mark, M., & Claxton-Oldfield, J. (2011). The Inventory of Motivations for Hospice Palliative Care Volunteerism: A tool for recruitment and retention. *American Journal of Hospice & Palliative Medicine, 28*(1), 35–43.

Clay, R. (2003). An empty nest can promote freedom, improved relationships. *Monitor on Psychology, 34(4)*. Retrieved from http://psycnet.apa.org/psycextra/300092003-024.pdf

Clay, R.A. (2009). Mini-multitaskers. For young people, a tendency to multitask may impoverish learning, productivity and even friendships. *Monitor on Psychology, 40*(2), 38.

Cleeremans, A., & Sarrazin, J. C. (2007). Time, action, and consciousness. *Human Movement Science, 26*, 180–202.

Clifford, J. S., Boufal, M. M., & Kurtz, J. E. (2004). Personality traits and critical thinking: Skills in college students empirical tests of a two-factor theory. *Assessment, 11*(2), 169–176.

Cloud, J. (2011, February 28). The truth about sex addiction. *Time*, 44–50.

Clulow, C. (2007). John Bowlby and couple psychotherapy. *Attachment & Human Development, 9*, 343–353.

Codd, M. (2010). Perfectionism and the gifted adolescent: Recognizing and helping gifted adolescents deal with their perfectionistic tendencies. *Rhode Island Advocates for Gifted Adolescents*. Retrieved from http://www.riage.org/articles/perfectionism-and-the-gifted-adolescent/

Coelho, F. M. S., Pradella-Hallinan, M., Pedrazzoli, M., Soares, C. A. S., Fernandes, G. B. P., Gonçalves, A. L., Leite, A., Tufik, S., & Bittencourt, L. R. A. (2010). Traditional biomarkers in narcolepsy: Experience of a Brazilian sleep centre. *Arquivos de Neuro-Psiquiatria, 68*(5), 712–715.

Cohen, D., & Leung, A. K. (2011). Violence and character: A CuPS (culture × person × situation) perspective. In P. R. Shaver & M. Mikulincer (Eds.), Herzilya series on personality and social psychology. Human aggression and violence: Causes, manifestations, and consequences (pp. 187–200). Washington, DC: American Psychological Association.

Cohen, S., & Lemay, E. P. (2007). Why would social networks be linked to affect and health practices? *Health Psychology, 26*, 410–417.

Cohen, S., Hamrick, N., Rodriguez, M. S., Feldman, P. J., Rabin, B. S., & Manuck, S. B. (2002). Reactivity and vulnerability to stress associated risk for upper respiratory illness. *Psychosomatic Medicine, 64*(2), 302–310.

Coifman, K. G., Bonanno, G. A., Ray, R. D., & Gross, J. J. (2007). Does repressing coping promote resilience? Affective-autonomic response discrepancy during bereavement. *Journal of Personality and Social Psychology, 92*, 745–758.

Coila, B. (2009). What is epigenetics? *Genetics and Evolution*. Retrieved from http://www.suite101.com/content/what-is-epigenetics-a104553

Colapinto, J. (2000). *As nature made him: The boy that was raised as a girl*. New York, NY: HarperCollins.

Colapinto, J. (2004, June 3). *What were the real reasons behind David Reimer's suicide?* Retrieved from http://slate.msn.com/id/2101678/.

Cole, D. L. (1982). Psychology as a liberating art. *Teaching of Psychology, 9*, 23–26.

Cole, M., & Gajdamaschko, N. (2007). Vygotsky and culture. In H. Daniels, J. Wertsch, & M. Cole (Eds.), *The Cambridge companion to Vygotsky* (pp. 193–211). New York, NY: Cambridge University Press.

Cole, M., Gray, J., Glick, J. A., & Sharp, D. W. (1971). *The cultural context of learning and thinking*. New York, NY: Basic Books.

Coleborne, C., & MacKinnon, D. (2011). *Exhibiting madness in museums: Remembering psychiatry through collection and display*. New York, NY: Routledge.

Coles, C. D., Goldstein, F. C., Lynch, M. E., Chen, X., Kable, J. A., Johnson, K. C., & Hu, X. (2011). Memory and brain Vol. in adults prenatally exposed to alcohol. *Brain and Cognition, 75*(1), 67–77.

Coley, R. L., & Chase-Lansdale, P. L. (1998). Adolescent pregnancy and parenthood: Recent evidence and future directions. *American Psychologist, 53*(2), 152–166.

Collins, R. (2011). Content analysis of gender roles in media: Where are we now and where should we go? *Sex Roles, 64*(3–4), 290–298.

Collocan, L. K., Tuma, F. K., & Fleischman, A. R. (2004). Research with victims of disaster: Institutional review board considerations. *IRB: Ethics and Human Research, 26*, 9–11.

Colrain, I. M. (2011). Sleep and the brain. *Neuropsychology Review, 21*(1), 1–4.

Columb, C., & Plant, E. A. (2011). Revisiting the Obama Effect: Exposure to Obama reduces implicit prejudice. *Journal of Experimental Social Psychology, 47*(2), 499–501.

Colvin, G. (2008). *Talent is overrated: What really separates world-class performers from everybody else*. New York, NY: Penguin Group.

Combs, D. R., Basso, M. R., Wanner, J. L., & Ledet, S. N. (2008). Schizophrenia. In M. Hersen & J. Rosqvist (Eds.), *Handbook of psychological assessment, case conceptualization, and*

treatment, Vol 1: Adults (pp. 352–402). Hoboken, NJ: Wiley.

Compton, M. T., Broussard, B., Ramsay, C. E., & Stewart, T. (2011). Pre-illness cannabis use and the early course of nonaffective psychotic disorders: Associations with premorbid functioning, the prodrome, and mode of onset of psychosis. *Schizophrenia Research, 126(1–3),* 71–76.

Confer, J. C., Easton, J. A., Fleischman, D. S., Goetz, C. D., Lewis, D. M. G., Perilloux, C., & Buss, D. M. (2010). Evolutionary psychology: Controversies, questions, prospects, and limitations. *American Psychologist, 65(2),* 110–126.

Connor, J., Norton, R., Ameratunga, S., Robinson, E., Civil, I., Dunn, R., Bailey, J., & Jackson, R. (2002). Driver sleepiness and risk of serious injury to car occupants: Population based case control study. *BMJ: British Medical Journal, 324(7346),* 1125–1128.

Connor, K. M., & Davidson, J. R. T. (2002). A placebo-controlled study of Kava kava in generalized anxiety disorder. *International Clinical Psychopharmacology, 17(4),* 185–188.

Conrad, C. D. (2010). A critical review of chronic stress effects on spatial learning and memory. *Progress in Neuro-Psychopharmacology & Biological Psychiatry, 34(5),* 742–755.

Considering a Career. (2011). Becoming a health psychologist. *APA Division 38.* Retrieved from http://www.health-psych .org/AboutHowtoBecome.cfm

Constantino, M. J., Manber, R., Ong, J., Kuo, T. F., Huang, J. S., & Arnow, B. A. (2007). Patient expectations and therapeutic alliance as predictors of outcome in group cognitive-behavioral therapy for insomnia. *Behavioral Sleep Medicine, 5,* 210–228.

Conway, M. A., & Pleydell-Pearce, C. W. (2000). The construction of autobiographical memories in the self-memory system. *Psychological Review, 107,* 261–288.

Conzen, P. (2010). Erik H. Erikson: Pionier der psychoanalytischen identitätstheorie [Erik H. Erikson: A pioneer of the psychoanalytic identity theory]. *Forum der Psychoanalyse: Zeitschrift für klinische Theorie & Praxis, 26(4),* 389–411.

Cook, M., & Mineka, S. (1989). Observational conditioning of fear to fear-relevant versus fear-irrelevant stimuli in rhesus monkeys. *Journal of Abnormal Psychology, 98,* 448–459.

Cool, K. (2011, July/August). A shadowy reminder of an ugly truth. *Stanford,* 44–51.

Coolen, L. M., Allard, J., Truitt, W. A., & McKenna, K. E. (2004). Central regulation of ejaculation. *Physiology & Behavior, 83,* 203–215.

Cooper, C., Manela, M., Katona, C., & Livingston, G. (2008). Screening for elder abuse in dementia in the LASER-AD study: Prevalence, correlates, and validation of instruments. *International Journal of Geriatric Psychiatry, 23,* 283–288.

Cooper, J. A., Watras, A. C., Paton, C. M., Wegner, F. H., Adams, A. K., & Schoeller, D. A. (2011). Impact of exercise and dietary fatty acid composition from a high-fat diet on markers of hunger and satiety. *Appetite, 56(1),* 171–178.

Cooper, J., & Hogg, M. A. (2007). Feeling the anguish of others: A theory of vicarious dissonance. In M. P. Zanna (Ed.), *Advances in experimental social psychology* (pp. 359–403). San Diego, CA: Elsevier.

Cooper, J., Heron, T. E., & Heward, W. L. (2007). *Applied behavior analysis* (2nd ed.). Upper Saddle River, NJ: Prentice-Hall.

Cooper, W. E. Jr., Pérez-Mellado, V., Vitt, L. J., & Budzinsky, B. (2002). Behavioral responses to plant toxins in two omnivorous lizard species. *Physiology & Behavior, 76(2),* 297–303.

Cordón, L. (2012). *All things Freud: An encyclopedia of Freud's world* (Vols. 1–2). Santa Barbara, CA: Greenwood.

Coren, S. (1996). *Sleep thieves: An eye-opening exploration into the science and mysteries of sleep.* New York, NY: Freeman.

Corey, G. (2011). *Theory and practice of group counseling* (8th ed.). Belmont, CA: Cengage.

Corkin, S. (2002). What's new with the amnesic patient H.M.? *Nature Reviews Neuroscience, 3,* 153–160.

Cornelius, J. R., & Clark, D. B. (2008). Depressive disorders and adolescent substance use disorders. In Y. Kaminer & O. G. bukstein (Eds.), *Adolescent substance abuse: Psychiatric comorbidity and high-risk behaviors* (pp. 221–242). New York, NY: Routledge/Taylor & Francis Group.

Cornum, R., Matthews, M. D., & Seligman, M. E. P. (2011). Comprehensive soldier fitness: Building resilience in a challenging institutional context. *American Psychologist, 66(1),* 4–9.

Corr, C. A., & Corr, D. M. (2007). Historical and contemporary perspectives on loss, grief, and mourning. In D. Balk, C. Wogrin, G. Thornton, & D. Meagher (Eds.), *Handbook of thanatology: The essential body of knowledge for the study of death, dying, and bereavement* (pp. 131–142). New York, NY: Routledge/Taylor & Francis Group.

Corr, C. A., Nabe, C. M., & Corr, D. M. (2009). *Death and dying: Life and living* (6th ed.). Belmont, CA: Wadsworth.

Corr, P. J. (2011). Anxiety: Splitting the phenomenological atom. *Personality and Individual Differences, 50(7),* 889–897.

Cosci, F., & Fava, G. A. (2011). New clinical strategies of assessment of comorbidity associated with substance use disorders. *Clinical Psychology Review, 31(3),* 418–427.

Costa, P. T., Jr., & McCrae, R. R. (2011). The five-factor model, five-factor theory, and interpersonal psychology. In L. M. Horowitz & S. Strack (Eds.), *Handbook of interpersonal psychology: Theory, research, assessment, and therapeutic interventions* (pp. 91–104). Hoboken, NJ: John Wiley.

Costa Jr., P. T., McCrae, R. R., & Martin, T. A. (2008). Incipient adult personality: The NEO-PI-3 in middle-school-aged children. *British Journal of Developmental Psychology, 26,* 71–89.

Costa Jr., P. T., Terracciano, A., Uda, M., Vacca, L., Mameli, C., Pilia, G., Zonderman, A. B., Lakatta, E., Schlessinger, D., & McCrae, R. R. (2007). Personality traits in Sardinia: Testing founder population effects on trait means and variances. *Behavior Genetics, 37,* 376–387.

Costello, K., & Hodson, G. (2011). Social dominance-based threat reactions to immigrants in need of assistance. *European Journal of Social Psychology, 41(2),* 220–231.

Costello, M. J., Sproule, B., Victor, J. C., Leatherdale, S. T., Zawertailo, L., & Selby, P. (2011). Effectiveness of pharmacist counseling combined with nicotine replacement therapy: A pragmatic randomized trial with 6,987 smokers. *Cancer Causes & Control, 22(2),* 167–180.

Cotter, D., Hermsen, J., & Vanneman, R. (2011). The end of the gender revolution? Gender role attitudes from 1977–2008. *American Journal of Sociology, 116(4),* 1–31.

Cougle, J. R., Bonn-Miller, M. O., Vujanovic, A. A., Zvolensky, M. J., & Hawkins, K. A. (2011). Posttraumatic stress disorder and Cannabis use in a nationally representative sample. *Psychology of Addictive Behaviors.* Retrieved from http://psycnet.apa.org/index.cfm?fa=buy. optionToBuy&id=2011-07480-001.

Coulson, S., & Wu, Y. C. (2005). Right hemisphere activation of joke-related information: An event-related brain potential study. *Journal of Cognitive Neuroscience, 17(3),* 494–506.

Courage, M. L., & Adams, R. J. (1990). Visual acuity assessment from birth to three years using the acuity card procedures: Cross-sectional and longitudinal samples. *Optometry and Vision Science, 67,* 713–718.

Cox, N., Dewaele, A., van Houtte, M., & Vincke, J. (2011). Stress-related growth, coming out, and internalized homonegativity in lesbian, gay, and bisexual youth. An examination of stress-related growth within the minority stress model. *Journal of Homosexuality, 58*(1), 117–137.

Coyle, D. (2009). *The talent code.* New York, NY: Random House.

Coyne, J. C., & Tennen, H. (2010). Positive psychology in cancer care: Bad science, exaggerated claims, and unproven medicine. *Annals of Behavioral Medicine, 39*(1), 16–26.

Craik, F. I. M., & Lockhart, R. S. (1972). Levels of processing: A framework for memory research. *Journal of Verbal Learning and Verbal Behavior, 11*, 671–684.

Craik, F. I. M., & Tulving, E. (1975). Depth of processing and the retention of words in episodic memory. *Journal of Experimental Psychology. 104*, 68–294.

Craik, F. I. M., Bialystok, E., & Freedman, M. (2010). Delaying the onset of Alzheimer disease: Bilingualism as a form of cognitive reserve. *Neurology, 75*(19), 1726–1729.

Cravey, T., & Mitra, A. (2011). Demographics of the sandwich generation by race and ethnicity in the United States. *Journal of Socio-Economics, 40*(3), 306–311.

Crawford, C. S. (2008). Ghost in the machine: A genealogy of phantom-prosthetic relations (amputation, dismemberment, prosthetic). *Dissertation Abstracts International Section A: Humanities and Social Sciences, 68*(7-A), 3173.

Creer, D. J., Romberg, C., Saksida, L. M., van Praag, H., & Bussey, T. J. (2010). Running enhances spatial pattern separation in mice. *Proceedings of the National Academy of Sciences of the United States of America.* Retrieved from http://www.pnas.org/content/early/2010/01/11/0911725107.abstract

Crespo-Facorro, B., Barbadillo, L., Pelayo-Terán, J., Rodríguez-Sánchez, J. M., & Teran, J. M. (2007). Neuropsychological functioning and brain structure in schizophrenia. *International Review of Psychiatry, 19*, 325–336.

Cresswell, M. (2008). Szasz and his interlocutors: Reconsidering Thomas Szasz's "Myth of Mental Illness" thesis. *Journal for the Theory of Social Behaviour, 38*, 23–44.

Crone, C. C., & Gabriel, G. (2002). Herbal and nonherbal supplements in medical-psychiatric patient populations. *Psychiatric Clinics of North America, 25*(1), 211–230.

Crowell, S. E., Beauchaine, T. P., & Lenzenweger, M. F. (2008). The development of borderline personality disorder and self-injurious behavior. In T. P. Beauchaine & S. P. Hinshaw (Eds.), *Child and adolescent psychopathology* (pp. 510–539). Hoboken, NJ: Wiley.

Crowley, K. (2011). Sleep and sleep disorders in older adults. *Neuropsychology Review, 21*(1), 41–53.

Crown, P. L. (2010). Learning in and from the past. In D. F. Lancy, J. Bock, & S. Gaskins (Eds.), *The anthropology of learning in childhood* (pp. 397–418). Walnut Creek, CA: AltaMira Press.

Cuijpers, P., Geraedts, A., van Oppen, P., Andersson, G., Markowitz, J., & van Straten, A. (2011). Interpersonal psychotherapy for depression: A meta-analysis. *American Journal of Psychiatry, 168*, 581–592.

Cullen, D., & Gotell, L. (2002). From orgasms to organizations: Maslow, women's sexuality and the gendered foundations of the needs hierarchy. *Gender, Work & Organization, 9*(5), 537–555.

Cully, J. A., & Stanley, M. A. (2008). Assessment and treatment of anxiety in later life. In K. Laidlaw & B. Knight (Eds.), *Handbook of emotional disorders in later life: Assessment and treatment* (pp. 233–256). New York, NY: Oxford University Press.

Cummings, D. E. (2006). Ghrelin and the short-and long-term regulation of appetite and body weight. *Physiology & Behavior, 89*, 71–84.

Cummings, E., & Henry, W. E. (1961). *Growing old: The process of disengagement.* New York, NY: Basic Books.

Cunningham, G. B. (2002). Diversity and recategorization: Examining the effects of cooperation on bias and work outcomes. *Dissertation Abstracts International Section A: Humanities and Social Sciences, 63*, 1288.

Cunningham, G. B., Fink, J. S., & Kenix, L. J. (2008). Choosing an endorser for a women's sporting event: The interaction of attractiveness and expertise. *Sex Roles, 58*, 371–378.

Cunningham, W. A., Johnson, M. K., Raye, C. L., Gatenby, J. C., Gore, J. C., & Banaji, M. R. (2004). Separable neural components in the processing of black and white faces. *Psychological Science, 15*, 806–813.

Curley, J. P., Jensen, C. L., Mashoodh, R., & Champagne, F. A. (2011). Social influences on neurobiology and behavior: Epigenetic effects during development. *Psychoneuroendocrinology, 36*(3), 352–371.

Curtiss, S. (1977). *Genie: A psycholinguistic study of a modern-day "wild child."* New York, NY: Academic Press.

Cushen, P. J., & Wiley, J. (2011). Aha! Voila! Eureka! Bilingualism and insightful problem solving. *Learning and Individual Differences.* doi: 10.1016/j.lindif.2011.02.007

Cvetkovic, D., & Cosic, I. (Eds.). (2011). *States of Consciousness: Experimental Insights into Meditation, Waking, Sleep and Dreams.* New York, NY: Springer.

Daan, S. (2011). How and why? The lab versus the field. *Sleep and Biological Rhythms, 9*(1), 1–2.

Dabby, R., Sadeh, M., Gilad, R., Lampl, Y., Cohen, S., Inbar, S., & Leshinsky-Silver, E. (2011). Chronic non-paroxysmal neuropathic pain—Novel phenotype of mutation in the sodium channel SCN9A gene. *Journal of the Neurological Sciences, 301*(1–2), 90–92.

Dacher, M., & Nugent, F. S. (2011). Opiates and plasticity. *Neuropharmacology.* Retrieved from http://www.ncbi.nlm.nih.gov/pubmed/21272593

Dack, C., Reed, P., & McHugh, L. (2010). Multiple determinants of transfer of evaluative function after conditioning with free-operant schedules of reinforcement. *Learning & Behavior, 38*(4), 348–366.

Dackis, C. A., & O'Brien, C. P. (2001). Cocaine dependence: A disease of the brain's reward centers. *Journal of Substance Abuse Treatment, 21*(3), 111–117.

Daffner, K. R. (2010). Promoting successful cognitive aging: A comprehensive review. *ournal of Alzheimer's Disease, 19*(4), 1101–1122.

Dahl, A., Campos, J. J., & Witherington, D. C. (2011). Emotional action and communication in early moral development. *Emotion Review, 3*(2), 147–157.

Dailey, M. N., Joyce, C., Lyons, M. J., Kamachi, M., Ishi, H., Gyoba, J., & Cottrell, G. W. (2010). Evidence and a computational explanation of cultural differences in facial expression recognition. *Emotion, 10*(6), 874–893.

Dakof, G. A., Godley, S. H., & Smith, J. E. (2011). The adolescent community reinforcement approach and multidimensional family therapy: Addressing relapse during treatment. In Y. Kaminer & K. C. Winters (Eds.), *Clinical manual of adolescent substance abuse* treatment (pp. 239–268). Arlington, VA: American Psychiatric Publishing.

Dalenberg, C., Loewenstein, R., Spiegel, D., Brewin, C., Lanius, R., Frankel, S., Gold, S., Van der Kolk, B., Simeon, D., Vermetten, E., Butler, L., Koopman, C., Courtois, C., Dell, P., Nijenhuis, E., Chu, J., Sar, V., Palesh, O., Cuevas, C., & Paulson, K. (2007). Scientific study of the dissociative disorders. *Psychotherapy and Psychosomatics, 76*, 400–401.

D'Alessio, D., & Allen, M. (2002). Selective exposure and dissonance after decisions. *Psychological Reports, 91*(2), 527–532.

Dalley, J. W., Fryer, T. D., Brichard, L., Robinson, E. S. J, Theobald, D. E. H., Lääne, K., Peña, Y., Murphy, E. R., Shah, Y., Probst, K., Abakumova, I., Aigbirhio, F. I., Richards, H. K., Hong, Y., Baron, J.-C., Everitt, B. J., & Robbins, T. W. (2007). Nucleus accumbens D2/3 receptors predict trait impulsivity and cocaine reinforcement. *Science, 315,* 1267–1270.

Damasio, A. R. (1999). *The feeling of what happens: Body and emotion in the making of consciousness.* New York, NY: Harcourt Brace.

Dana, R. H. (1998). Cultural identity assessment of culturally diverse groups. *Journal of Personality Assessment, 70*(1), 1–16.

Dana, R. H. (2005). *Multicultural assessment: Principles, applications, and examples.* Mahwah, NJ: Erlbaum.

Dandekar, M. P., Nakhate, K. T., Kokare, D. M., & Subhedar, N. K. (2011). Effect of nicotine on feeding and body weight in rats: Involvement of cocaine- and amphetamine-regulated transcript peptide. *Behavioural Brain Research, 219(1),* 31–38.

Dante, G., & Facchinetti, F. (2011). Herbal treatments for alleviating premenstrual symptoms: A systematic review. *Journal of Psychosomatic Obstetrics & Gynecology, 32(1),* 42–51.

Dantzer, R., O'Connor, J. C., Freund, G. C., Johnson, R. W., & Kelley, K. W. (2008). From inflammation to sickness and depression: When the immune system subjugates the brain. *Nature Reviews Neuroscience, 9,* 46–57.

Darmani, N. A., & Crim, J. L. (2005) Delta-9- tetrahydrocannabinol prevents emesis more potently than enhanced locomotor activity produced by chemically diverse dopamine D2/D3 receptor agonists in the least shrew (Cryptotis parva). *Pharmacology Biochemistry and Behavior, 80,* 35–44.

Darwin, C. (1859). *On the origin of species.* London, England: Murray.

Darwin, C. (1872). *The expression of the emotions in man and animals.* London, England: Murray.

Dattilio, F. M., & Nichols, M. P. (2011). Reuniting estranged family members: A cognitive-behavioral-systemic perspective. *American Journal of Family Therapy, 39*(2), 88–99.

Dave, A., Sethi, A., & Morrone, A. (2011). Female Genital Mutilation: What Every American Dermatologist Needs to Know. *Dermatologic Clinics, 29*(1), 103–109.

Davidson, J., & Gottschalk, P. (2011). Characteristics of the Internet for criminal child sexual abuse by online groomers. *Criminal Justice Studies: A Critical Journal of Crime, Law & Society, 24(1),* 23–36.

Davies, I. (1998). A study of colour grouping in three languages: A test of the linguistic relativity hypothesis. *British Journal of Psychology, 89,* 433–452.

Davis, C. C., & Balzano, Q. (2011). Cell phone activation and brain glucose metabolism. *Journal of the American Medical Association, 305*(20), 2066.

Davis, C. L., Tomporowski, P. D., McDowell, J. E., Austin, B. P., Miller, P. H., Yanasak, N. E., Allison, J., & Naglieri, J. A. (2011). Exercise improves executive function and achievement and alters brain activation in overweight children: A randomized, controlled trial. *Health Psychology, 30(1),* 91–98.

Davis, J. I., Senghas, A., Brandt, F., & Ochsner, K. N. (2010). The effects of BOTOX injections on emotional experience. *Emotion, 10(3),* 433–440.

Dawson, D., Noy, Y. I., Härmä, M., Åkerstedt, T., & Belenky, G. (2011). Modelling fatigue and the use of fatigue models in work settings. *Accident Analysis and Prevention, 43(2),* 549–564.

de Charms, R., & Moeller, G. H. (1962). Values expressed in American children's readers: 1800–1950. *Journal of Abnormal and Social Psychology, 64*(2), 136–142.

De Coteau, T. J., Hope, D. A., & Anderson, J. (2003). Anxiety, stress, and health in northern plains Native Americans. *Behavior Therapy, 34*(3), 365–380.

De Kleine, E., & Van der Lubbe, R. H. J. (2011). Decreased load on general motor preparation and visual-working memory while preparing familiar as compared to unfamiliar movement sequences. *Brain and Cognition, 75*(2), 126–134.

De Neys, W., & Vanderputte, K. (2011). When less is not always more: Stereotype knowledge and reasoning development. *Developmental Psychology, 47*(2), 432–441.

de Oliveira-Souza, R., Moll, J., Ignácio, F. A., & Hare, R. D. (2008). Psychopathy in a civil psychiatric outpatient sample. *Criminal Justice and Behavior, 35,* 427–437.

De Sousa, A. (2011). Freudian theory and consciousness: A conceptual analysis. *Brain, Mind and Consciousness, 9*(1), 210–217.

De Vos, J. (2010). From Milgram to Zimbardo: The double birth of postwar psychology/psychologization. *History of the Human Sciences, 23*(5), 156–175.

de Waal, F. B. M. (2008). Putting the altruism back into altruism: The evolution of empathy. *Annual Review of Psychology, 59,* 279–300.

De Wall, C. N., & Anderson, C. A. (2011). The general aggression model. In P. R. Shaver & M. Mikulincer (Eds.), *Herzilya series on personality and social psychology. Human aggression and violence: Causes, manifestations, and consequences* (pp. 15–33). Washington, DC: American Psychological Association.

De Witte, L., Brouns, R., Kavadias, D., Engelborghs, S., De Deyn, P. P., & Mariën, P. (2011). Cognitive, affective and behavioural disturbances following vascular thalamic lesions: A review. *Cortex: A Journal Devoted to the Study of the Nervous System and Behavior, 47(3),* 273–319.

Deady, D. K., North, N. T., Allan, D., Smith, M. J. L., & O'Carroll, R. E. (2010). Examining the effect of spinal cord injury on emotional awareness, expressivity and memory for emotional material. *Psychology, Health & Medicine, 15*(4), 406–419.

Dean-Borenstein, M. T. (2007). The long-term psychosocial effects of trauma on survivors of human-caused extreme stress situations. *Dissertation Abstracts International: Section B: The Sciences and Engineering, 67*(11-B), 6733.

Deary, I. J., Bell, P. J., Bell, A. J., Campbell, M. L., & Fazal, N. D. (2004). Sensory discrimination and intelligence: Testing Spearman's other hypothesis. *American Journal of Psychology, 117*(1), 1–18.

Deary, I. J., Ferguson, K. J., Bastin, M. E., Barrow, G. W. S., Reid, L. M., Seckl, J. R., Wardlaw, J. M., & MacLullich, A. M. J. (2007). Skull size and intelligence, and King Robert Bruce's IQ. *Intelligence, 35,* 519–528.

Deason, R. G., & Marsolek, C. J. (2005). A critical boundary to the left-hemisphere advantage in visual-word processing. *Brain & Language, 92(3),* 251–261.

DeCasper, A. J., & Fifer, W. D. (1980). Of human bonding: Newborns prefer their mother's voices. *Science, 208,* 1174–1176.

Deci, E. L. (1995). *Why we do what we do: The dynamics of personal autonomy.* New York, NY: Putnam's Sons.

Deci, E. L., & Moller, A. C. (2005). The concept of competence: A starting place for understanding intrinsic motivation and self-determined extrinsic motivation. In A. J. Elliot & C. S. Dweck (Eds.), *Handbook of competence and motivation* (pp. 579–597). New York, NY: Guilford.

Deci, E. L., Koestner, R., & Ryan, R. M. (1999). A meta-analytic review of experiments examining the effects of extrinsic rewards on intrinsic motivation. *Psychological Bulletin, 125*(6), 627–668.

DeClue, G. (2003). The polygraph and lie detection. *Journal of Psychiatry & Law, 31*(3), 361–368.

Del Giudice, M. (2011). Alone in the dark? Modeling the conditions for visual experience in human fetuses. *Developmental Psychobiology, 53*(2), 214–219.

Delahanty, D. L., Liegey, D. A., Hayward, M., Forlenza, M., Hawk, L. W., & Baum, A. (2000). Gender differences in cardiovascular and natural killer cells reactivity to acute stress following a hassling task. *International Journal of Behavioral Medicine, 7*, 19–27.

Delgado-Gaitan, C. (1994). Socializing young children in Mexican-American families: An intergenerational perspective. In P.M. Greenfield & R.R. Cocking (Eds.), *Cross-cultural roots of minority child development* (pp. 55–86). Hillsdale, NJ: Erlbaum.

Dement, W. C. (1992, March). The sleepwatchers. *Stanford*, pp. 55–59.

Dement, W. C., & Vaughan, C. (1999). *The promise of sleep.* New York, NY: Delacorte Press.

Dement, W. C., & Wolpert, E. (1958). The relation of eye movements, bodily motility, and external stimuli to dream content. *Journal of Experimental Psychology, 53*, 543–553.

Dempster, M., McCorry, N. K., Brennan, E., Donnelly, M., Murray, L. J., & Johnston, B. T. (2011). Do changes in illness perceptions predict changes in psychological distress among oesophageal cancer survivors? *Journal of Health Psychology, 16*(3), 500–509.

den Boer, J. A. (2000). Social anxiety disorder/social phobia: Epidemiology, diagnosis, neurobiology, and treatment. *Comprehensive Psychiatry, 41*(6), 405–415.

Denmark, F. L., Rabinovitz, V. C., & Sechzer, J. A. (2005). *Engendering psychology: Women and gender revisited* (2nd ed.). Boston, MA: Allyn and Bacon.

Dennis, W., & Dennis, M. G. (1940). Cradles and cradling customs of the Pueblo Indians. *American Anthropologist, 42*, 107–115.

Denson, T. F. (2011). A social neuroscience perspective on the neurobiological bases of aggression. In P. R. Shaver & M. Mikulincer (Eds.), *Herzilya series on personality and social psychology. Human aggression and violence: Causes, manifestations, and consequences* (pp. 105–120). Washington, DC: American Psychological Association.

DeRobertis, E. M. (2011). Existential-humanistic and dynamic systems approaches to child development in mutual encounter. *The Humanistic Psychologist, 39*(1), 3–23.

DeSpelder, L. A., & Strickland, A. (2007). Culture, socialization, and death education. In D. Balk, C. Wogrin, G. Thornton, & D. Meagher (Eds.), *Handbook of thanatology: The essential body of knowledge for the study of death, dying, and bereavement* (pp. 303–314). New York, NY: Routledge/Taylor & Francis Group.

Dessalles, J. (2011). Sharing cognitive dissonance as a way to reach social harmony. *Social Science Information/ Sur Les Sciences Sociales, 50*, 116–127.

Detterman, D. K. (2010). What happened to moron, idiot, imbecile, feebleminded, and retarded? [Review of the book: What happened to moron, idiot, imbecile, feebleminded, and retarded? AIDD Ad Hoc committee on terminology and classification, intellectual disability: Definition, classification, and systems of supports, 11th Ed, American Association on Iintellectual and Developmental Disabilities]. *Intelligence, 38*(5), 540–541.

Deutscher, G. (2010). *Through the language glass: Why the world looks different in other languages.* New York, NY: Metropolitan Books/ Henry Holt and Company.

DeValois, R. L. (1965). Behavioral and electrophysiological studies of primate vision. In W. D. Neff (Ed). *Contributions to sensory physiology* (Vol. 1). New York, NY: Academic Press.

Dewan, M. J., Steenbarger, B. N., & Greenberg, R. P. (2011). Brief psychotherapies. In R. E. Hales, S. C. Yudofsky, & G. O. Gabbard (Eds.), *Essentials of psychiatry* (3rd ed.) (pp. 525–539). Arlington, VA: American Psychiatric Publishing.

Dhikav, V., Aggarwal, N., Gupta, S., Jadhavi, R., & Singh, K. (2008). Depression in Dhat syndrome. *Journal of Sexual Medicine, 5*, 841–844.

Di Fabio, A., & Kenny, M. E. (2011). Promoting emotional intelligence and career decision making among Italian high school students. *Journal of Career Assessment, 19*(1), 21–34.

Diamond, B. J., Mayes, A. R., & Meudell, P. R. (2011). Priming, recognition and autonomic discrimination in amnesia. *Neurocase, 17*(1), 76–90.

Diamond, M., & Sigmundson, H. K. (1997). Sex reassignment at birth: Long-term review and clinical implications. *Archives of Pediatrics and Adolescent Medicine, 151*, 298–304.

Diaz, M. T., Barrett, K. T., & Hogstrom, L. J. (2011). The influence of sentence novelty and figurativeness on brain activity. *Neuropsychologia, 49*(3), 320–330.

DiDonato, T. E., Ullrich, J., & Krueger, J. I. (2011). Social perception as induction and inference: An integrative model of intergroup differentiation, ingroup favoritism, and differential accuracy. *Journal of Personality and Social Psychology, 100*(1), 66–83.

Dieffenbach, C., & Fauci, A. (2011). Thirty years of HIV and AIDS: Future challenges and opportunities. *Annals of Internal Medicine, 154*(11), 1–6.

Diego, M. A., & Jones, N. A. (2007). Neonatal antecedents for empathy. In T. Farrow & P. Woodruff (Eds.), *Empathy in mental illness* (pp. 145–167). New York, NY: Cambridge University Press.

Diehm, R., & Armatas, C. (2004). Surfing: An avenue for socially acceptable risk-taking, satisfying needs for sensation seeking and experience seeking. *Personality & Individual Differences, 36*(3), 663–677.

Diekelmann, S., Wilhelm, I., Wagner, U., & Born, J. (2011). Elevated cortisol at retrieval suppresses false memories in parallel with correct memories. *Journal of Cognitive Neuroscience, 23*(4), 772–781.

Diem-Wille, G. (2011). *The early years of life: Psychoanalytical development theory according Freud, Klein, and Bion.* London, UK: Karnac Books.

Diener, E. (2008). Myths in the science of happiness, and directions for future research. In M. Eid & R. J. Larsen (Eds.), *The science of subjective well-being* (pp. 493–514). New York, NY: Guilford Press.

Diener, E., & Biswas-Diener, R. (2008). *Happiness: Unlocking the mysteries of psychological wealth.* Hoboken, NJ: Wiley-Blackwell.

Diener, E., & Diener, M. (1995). Cross-cultural correlates of life satisfaction and self-esteem. *Journal of Personality and Social Psychology, 68*, 653–663.

Diener, M. L., Isabella, R. A., Behunin, M. G., & Wong, M. S. (2008). Attachment to mothers and fathers during middle childhood: Associations with child gender, grade, and competence. *Social Development, 7*, 84–101.

Diener, M. L., Mengelsdorf, S. C., McHale, J. L., & Frosch, C. A. (2002). Infants' behavioral strategies for emotion regulation with fathers and mothers: Associations with emotional expressions and attachment quality. *Infancy, 3*(2), 153–174.

Dierdorff, E. C., Bell, S. T., & Beloblav, J. A. (2011). The power of "we": Effects of psychological collectivism on team performance over time. *Journal of Applied Psychology, 96*(2), 247–262.

Dijksterhuis, A., Aarts, H., & Smith, P. K. (2005). The power of the subliminal: On subliminal persuasion and other potential applications. In R. R. Hassin, J. S. Uleman, & J. A. Bargh (Eds.), The new unconscious (pp. 77–106). *Oxford series in social cognition and social neuroscience.* New York, NY: Oxford University Press.

Dill, K. E., & Thill, K. P. (2007). Video game characters and the socialization of gender roles: Young people's perceptions mirror sexist media depictions. *Sex Roles, 57,* 851–864.

Diller, L. (2000, March 9). Kids on drugs: A behavioral pediatrician questions the wisdom of medicating our children. *Salon.* Retrieved from http://www.salon.com/health/feature/2000/03/09/kid_drugs/index.html

Dillman, D. A., Smyth, J. D., & Christian, L. M. (2009). *Internet, mail, and mixed-mode surveys: The tailored design method.* (3rd ed.) Hoboken, NJ: Wiley.

Dillon, S. (2009, January 22). Study sees an Obama effect as lifting Black test-takers. *The New York Times.* Retrieved from http://www.nytimes.com/2009/01/23/education/23gap.html

Dimberg, U., & Söderkvist, S. (2011). The voluntary facial action technique: A method to test the facial feedback hypothesis. *Journal of Nonverbal Behavior, 35*(1), 17–33.

Dimberg, U., & Thunberg, M. (1998). Rapid facial reactions to emotion facial expressions. *Scandinavian Journal of Psychology, 39*(1), 39–46.

Dimberg, U., Thunberg, M., & Elmehed, K. (2000). Unconscious facial reactions to emotional facial expressions. *Psychological Science, 11*(1), 86–89.

Diniz, D. G., Foro, C. A. R., Rego, C. M. D., Gloria, D. A., de Oliveira, F. R. R., Paes, J. M. P., de Sousa, A., Tokuhashi, T., Trindade, L., Turiel, M., Vasconcelos, E., Torres, J., Cunnigham, C., Perry, H., da Costa Vasconcelos, P., & Diniz, C. W. P. (2010). Environmental impoverishment and aging alter object recognition, spatial learning, and dentate gyrus astrocytes. *European Journal of Neuroscience, 32*(3), 509–519.

DiPietro, J. A. (2000). Baby and the brain: Advances in child development. *Annual Review of Public Health, 21,* 455–71.

Distel, M. A., Middeldorp, C. M., Trul, T. J., Derom, C. A, Willemsen, G., & Boomsma, D. I. (2011). Life events and borderline personality features: The influence of gene-environment interaction and gene-environment

correlation. *Psychological Medicine: A Journal of Research in Psychiatry and the Allied Sciences, 41*(4), 849–860.

Doane, L. D., Kremen, W. S., Eaves, L. J., Eisen, S. A., Hauger, R., Hellhammer, D., Levine, S., Lupien, S., Lyons, M. J., Mendoza, S., Prom-Wormley, E., Xian, H., York, T.P., Franz, C., Jacobson, K. C. (2010). Associations between jet lag and cortisol diurnal rhythms after domestic travel. *Health Psychology, 29*(2), 117–123.

Doghramji, K. (2000, December). *Sleepless in America: Diagnosing and treating insomnia.* Retrieved from http://psychiatry. medscape.com/Medscape/psychiatry/ ClinicalMgmt/CM.v02/public/indexCM.v02.html.

Dohnke, B., Weiss-Gerlach, E., & Spies, C. D. (2011). Social influences on the motivation to quit smoking: Main and moderating effects of social norms. *Addictive Behaviors, 36*(4), 286–293.

Doka, K. J., & Martin, T. L. (2010). *Series in death, dying, and bereavement. Grieving beyond gender: Understanding the ways men and women mourn* (rev. ed.). New York, NY: Routledge/Taylor & Francis Group.

Domhoff, G. W. (1999). New directions in the study of dream content using the Hall and Van de Castle coding system. *Dreaming, 9,* 115–137.

Domhoff, G. W. (2003). *The scientific study of dreams: Neural networks, cognitive development, and content analysis.* Washington, DC: American Psychological Association.

Domhoff, G. W. (2004). Why did empirical dream researchers reject Freud? A critique of historical claims by Mark Solms. *Dreaming, 14*(1), 3–17.

Domhoff, G. W. (2005). A reply to Hobson. (2005). *Dreaming, 15*(1), 30–32.

Domhoff, G. W. (2007). Realistic simulation and bizarreness in dream content: Past findings and suggestions for future research. In D. Barrett & P. McNamara (Eds.), *The new science of dreaming: Volume 2. Content, recall, and personality correlates* (pp. 1–27). Praeger perspectives. Westport, CT: Praeger.

Domhoff, G. W. (2010). Dream content is continuous with waking thought, based on preoccupations, concerns, and interests. *Sleep Medicine Clinics, 5*(2), 203–215.

Domhoff, G. W., & Schneider, A. (2008). Similarities and differences in dream content at the cross-cultural, gender, and individual levels. *Consciousness and Cognition: An International Journal, 17*(4), 1257–1265.

Domjan, M. (2005). Pavlovian conditioning: A functional perspective. *Annual Review of Psychology, 56,* 179–206.

D'Onofrio, B. M., Turkheimer, E., Emery, R. E., Maes, H. H., Silberg, J., & Eaves, L. J. (2007). A children of twins study of parental divorce and offspring psychopathology. *Journal of Child Psychology and Psychiatry, 48,* 667–675.

Donohue, R. (2006). Person-environment congruence in relation to career change and career persistence. *Journal of Vocational Behavior, 68,* 504–515.

Dorrian, J., Sweeney, M., & Dawson, D. (2011). Modeling fatigue-related truck accidents: Prior sleep duration, recency and continuity. *Sleep and Biological Rhythms, 9*(1), 3–11.

Dotinga, R. (2004, February 5). Popping pills in preschool. *Wired.* Retrieved from http://www.wired.com/medtech/drugs/news/2004/02/62154

Dotsch, R., Wigboldus, D. H. J., & van Knippenberg, A. (2011). Biased allocation of faces to social categories. *Journal of Personality and Social Psychology, 100*(6), 999–1014.

Douglas, K., Chan, G., Gelernter, J., Arias, A., Anton, R., Poling, J., Farrer, L, & Kranzler, H. (2011). 5-HTTLPR as a potential moderator of the effects of adverse childhood experiences on risk of antisocial personality disorder. *Psychiatric Genetics.* Advance online publication. doi: 10.1097/YPG.0b013e3283457c15

Dovidio, J. F., Eller, A., & Hewstone, M. (2011). Improving intergroup relations through direct, extended and other forms of indirect contact. *Group Processes & Intergroup Relations, 14*(2), 147–160.

Dovidio, J. F., Pagotto, L., & Hebl, M. R. (2011). Implicit attitudes and discrimination against people with physical disabilities. In R. Wiener & S. L. Willborn (Eds.), *Disability and aging discrimination: Perspectives in law and psychology* (pp. 157–183). New York, NY: Springer Science + Business Media.

Dowman, R. (2011). The role of somatic threat feature detectors in the attentional bias toward pain: Effects of spatial attention. *Psychophysiology, 48*(3), 397–409.

Doyle, A., & Pollack, M. H. (2004). Long-term management of panic disorder. *Journal of Clinical Psychiatry. 65*(Suppl5), 24–28.

Dresser, N. (1996). *Multicultural manners: New rules of etiquette for a changing society.* New York, NY: Wiley.

Dressier, S. G., & Voracek, M. (2011). No association between two candidate markers of prenatal sex hormones: Digit ratios (2D:4D and other) and finger-ridge counts. *Developmental Psychobiology, 53*(1), 69–78.

Drew, L. J., Crabtree, G. W., Markx, S., Stark, K. L., Chaverneff, F., Xu, B., Mukai, J., Fenelon, K., Hsu, P., Gogos, J., & Karayiorgou, M. (2011). The 22q11.2 microdeletion: Fifteen years of insights into the genetic and neural complexity of psychiatric disorders. *International Journal of Developmental Neuroscience, 29(3),* 259–281.

Driscoll, A. K., Russell, S. T., & Crockett, L. J. (2008). Parenting styles and youth well-being across immigrant generations. *Journal of Family Issues, 29,* 185–209.

Driscoll, R., Davis, K. E., & Lipetz, M. E. (1972). Parental interference and romantic love: The Romeo and Juliet effect. *Journal of Personality and Social Psychology, 24,* 1–10.

Drosopoulos, S., Harrer, D., & Born, J. (2011). Sleep and awareness about presence of regularity speed the transition from implicit to explicit knowledge. *Biological Psychology, 86(3),* 168–173.

Drucker, D. J. (2010). Male sexuality and Alfred Kinsey's 0–6 Scale: Toward "a sound understanding of the realities of sex." *Journal of Homosexuality, 57(9),* 1105–1123.

Duckworth, A. L. & Seligman, M. E. P. (2005). Self-discipline outdoes IQ in predicting academic performance of adolescents. *Psychological Science, 16 (12),* 939–944.

Duckworth, K., & Borus, J. F. (1999). Population-based psychiatry in the public sector and managed care. In A. M. Nicholi (Ed.), *The Harvard guide to psychiatry* (pp. 735–823). Cambridge, MA: Harvard University Press.

Dufresne, T. (2007). *Against Freud: Critics talk back.* Palo Alto, CA: Stanford University Press.

Duijts, S. F. A., Zeegers, M. P. A., & Borne, B. V. (2003). The association between stressful life events and breast cancer risk: A meta-analysis. *International Journal of Cancer, 107,* 1023–1029.

Dumontheil, I., Houlton, R., Christoff, K., & Blakemore, S.-J. (2010). Development of relational reasoning during adolescence. *Developmental Science, 13(6),* F15–F24.

Dunham, Y. (2011). An angry = Outgroup effect. *Journal of Experimental Social Psychology, 47(3),* 668–671.

Duniec, E., & Raz, M. (2011). Vitamins for the soul: John bowlby's thesis of maternal deprivation, biomedical metaphors and the deficiency model of disease. *History of Psychiatry, 22(1),* 93–107.

Durrant, R., & Ward, T. (2011). Evolutionary explanations in the social and behavioral sciences: Introduction and overview. *Aggression and Violent Behavior.* Advance online publication. doi:10.1016/j.avb.2011.02.010

Dutra, L., Callahan, K., Forman, E., Mendelsohn, M., & Herman, J. (2008). Core schemas and suicidality in a chronically traumatized population. *Journal of Nervous and Mental Disease, 196,* 71–74.

Dutton, D. G., & Aron, A. P. (1974). Some evidence for heightened sexual attraction under conditions of high anxiety. *Journal of Personality & Social Psychology, 30,* 510–517.

Duval, D. C. (2006). The relationship between African centeredness and psychological androgyny among African American women in middle adulthood. *Dissertation Abstracts International: Section B: The Sciences and Engineering.* 67(2-B), 1146.

Dweck, C. (2007). *Mindset: The new psychology of success.* New York, NY: Ballantine Books.

Dworkin, A. (1974). *Woman hating.* New York, NY: E. P. Dutton.

Dysvik, E., Kvaløy, J. T., Stokkeland, R., & Natvig, G. K. (2010). The effectiveness of a multidisciplinary pain management program managing chronic pain on pain perceptions, health-related quality of life and stages of change—A non-randomized controlled study. *International Journal of Nursing Studies, 47(7),* 826–835.

e! Science News. (2011). *Scripps research scientists reveal key mechanism governing nicotine addiction.* Retrieved from http://esciencenews.com/articles/2011/01/30/scripps.research.scientists.reveal.key.mechanism.governing.nicotine.addiction

Eagly, A. H., & Koenig, A. M. (2006). Social role theory of sex differences and similarities: Implication for prosocial behavior. In K. Dindia & D. J. Canary (Eds.), *Sex differences and similarities in communication* (2nd ed.) (pp. 161–177). Mahwah, NJ: Erlbaum.

Eaker, E. D., Sullivan, L. M., Kelly-Hayes, M., D'Agostino, R. B., & Benajmin, E. J. (2007). Marital status, marital strain, and risk of coronary heart disease or total mortality: The Framingham offspring study. *Psychosomatic Medicine, 69,* 509–513.

Eap, S., Gobin, R. L., Ng, J., Hall, G. C., Nagayama, T. (2010). Sociocultural issues in the diagnosis and assessment of psychological disorders. In J. E. Maddux & J. P. Tangney (Eds), *Social psychological foundations of clinical psychology* (pp. 312–328). New York, NY: Guilford Press.

Earnshaw, V. A., Pitpitan, E. V., & Chaudoir, S. R. (2011). Intended responses to rape as functions of attitudes, attributions of fault, and emotions. *Sex Roles, 64(5–6),* 382–393.

Easterbrooks, M. A., Chaudhuri, J. H., Bartlett, J. D., & Copeman, A. (2011). Resilience in parenting among young mothers: Family and ecological risks and opportunities. *Children and Youth Services Review, 33(1),* 42–50.

Easterlin, N. (2010). Cognitive ecocriticism: Human wayfinding, sociality, and literary interpretation. In L. Zunshine (Ed.), *Introduction to cognitive cultural studies* (pp. 257–274). Baltimore, MD: Johns Hopkins University Press.

Eaton, W., Chen, C., & Bromet, E. (2011). Epidemiology of schizophrenia. In M. Tsuang, M. Tohen, & P. Jones (Eds.), *Textbook in Psychiatric Epidemiology,* (3rd ed., pp. 263–287). Hoboken, NJ: Wiley.

Ecker, U. K. H., Lewandowsk, Y., S., & Tang, D. T. W. (2010). Explicit warnings reduce but do not eliminate the continued influence of misinformation. *Memory & Cognition, 38(8),* 1087–1100.

Ecker, U. K. H., Lewandowsky, S., & Apai, J. (2011). Terrorists brought down the plane!—No, actually it was a technical fault: Processing corrections of emotive information. *The Quarterly Journal of Experimental Psychology, 64(2),* 283–310.

Eddy, K. T., Hennessey, M., & Thompson-Brenner, H. (2007). Eating pathology in East African women: The role of media exposure and globalization. *Journal of Nervous and Mental Disease, 195,* 196–202.

Ehrenreich, B. (2004, July 15). *All together now.* Retrieved from http://select.nytimes.com/gst/abstract.html?res=F00E16FA3C5E0C768DDDAE0894DC404482.

Eisenberger, R., & Armeli, S. (1997). Can salient reward increase creative performance without reducing intrinsic creative interest? *Journal of Personality and Social Psychology, 72,* 652–663.

Eisenberger, R., & Rhoades, L. (2002). Incremental effects of reward on creativity. *Journal of Personality and Social Psychology, 81(4),* 728–741.

Eisenberger, R., & Stinglhamber, F. (2011). *Perceived organizational support: Fostering enthusiastic and productive employees.* Washington, DC: American Psychological Association.

Ekman, P. (1980). *The face of man.* New York, NY: Garland.

Ekman, P. (1993). Facial expression and emotion. *American Psychologist, 48,* 384–392.

Ekman, P. (2003). Emotions inside out: 130 years after Darwin's "The expression of emotions in man and animal." *Annals of the New York Academy of Science, 1000,* 1–6.

Ekman, P. (2004). *Emotions revealed: Recognizing faces and feelings to improve communication and emotional life.* Thousand Oaks, CA: Owl Books.

Ekman, P., & Keltner, D. (1997). Universal facial expressions of emotion: An old controversy and new findings. In U. C. Segerstrale & P. Molnar (Eds.), *Nonverbal communication: Where nature meets culture* (pp. 27–46). Mahwah, NJ: Erlbaum.

Elder, B., & Mosack, V. (2011). Genetics of depression: An overview of the current science. *Issues in Mental Health Nursing, 32*(4), 192–202.

Elder, G. (1998). The life course as developmental theory. *Current Directions in Psychological Science, 69,* 1–12.

Elkind, D. (1967). Egocentrism in adolescence. *Child Development, 38,* 1025–1034.

Elkind, D. (1981). *The hurried child.* Reading, MA: Addison-Wesley.

Elkind, D. (2000). A quixotic approach to issues in early childhood education. *Human Development, 43*(4–5), 279–283.

Elkind, D. (2007). *The hurried child: Growing up too fast too soon* (25th anniversary ed.). Cambridge, ME: Da Capo Press.

Elliott, I. A., & Ashfield, S. (2011). The use of online technology in the modus operandi of female sex offenders. *Journal of Sexual Aggression, 17(1),* 92–104.

Ellis, A. (1961). *A guide to rational living.* Englewood Cliffs, NJ: Prentice-Hall.

Ellis, A. (1996). *Better, deeper, and more enduring brief therapy.* New York, NY: Institute for Rational Emotive Therapy.

Ellis, A. (1997). Using rational emotive behavior therapy techniques to cope with disability. *Professional Psychology: Research and Practice, 28,* 17–22.

Ellis, A. (2003a). Early theories and practices of rational emotive behavior therapy and how they have been augmented and revised during the last three decades. *Journal of Rational- Emotive & Cognitive Behavior Therapy, 21*(3–4), 219–243.

Ellis, A. (2003b). Similarities and differences between rational emotive behavior therapy and cognitive therapy. *Journal of Cognitive Psychotherapy, 17*(3), 225–240.

Ellis, A. (2004). Why rational emotive behavior therapy is the most comprehensive and effective form of behavior therapy. *Journal of Rational Emotive & Cognitive Behavior Therapy, 22*(2), 85–92.

Ellis, A., & Ellis, D. J. (2011a). *Rational emotive behavior therapy.* Washington, DC: American Psychological Association.

Ellis, A., & Ellis, D. J. (2011b). *Theories of psychotherapy. Rational emotive behavior therapy.* Washington, DC: American Psychological Association.

Ellis, L., Ficek, C., Burke, D., & Das, S. (2008). Eye color, hair color, blood type, and the rhesus factor: Exploring possible genetic links to sexual orientation. *Archives of Sexual Behavior, 37,* 145–149.

Ellman, L. M., & Cannon, T. D. (2008). Environmental pre-and perinatal influences in etiology. In K. T. Mueser & D. V. Jeste (Eds.), *Clinical handbook of schizophrenia* (pp. 65–73). New York, NY: Guilford.

Elman, I., Zubieta, J.-K., & Borsook, D. (2011). The missing P in psychiatric training: Why it is important to teach pain to psychiatrists. *Archives of General Psychiatry, 68(1),* 12–20.

Elovainio, M., Merjonen, P., Pulkki-Råback, L., Kivimäki, M., Jokela, M., Mattson, N., Koskinen, T., Viikari, J., Raitakari, O., & Keltikangas-Järvinen, L. (2011). Hostility, *metabolic syndrome,* inflammation and cardiac control in young adults: The young Finns study. *Biological Psychology, 87*(2), 234–240.

Engelhardt, C. R., Bartholow, B. D., Kerr, G. T., & Bushman, B. J. (2011). This is your brain on violent video games: Neural desensitization to violence predicts increased aggression following violent video game exposure. *Journal of Experimental Social Psychology.* doi:10.1016/j.jesp.2011.03.027

Engle, S. (2006). *More college freshmen commit to social and civic responsibility, UCLA survey reveals.* Retrieved from http://www.gseis.ucla.edu/heri/PDFs/CIRPPressRelease05.PDF.

Engvig, A., Fjell, A. M., Westlye, L. T., Moberget, T., Sundseth, Ø., Larsen, V. A., & Walhovd, K. B. (2010). Effects of memory training on cortical thickness in the elderly. *NeuroImage, 52*(4), 1667–1676.

Enoch, M.-A. (2011). The role of early life stress as a predictor for alcohol and drug dependence. *Psychopharmacology, 214(1),* 17–31.

Epley, N. (2008). Rebate psychology. *New York Times.* Retrieved from http://select.nytimes.com/mem/tnt.html?tntget=2008/01/31/opinion/31epley.html

Erdelyi, M. H. (2010). The ups and downs of memory. *American Psychologist, 65(7),* 623–633.

Erdelyi, M. H., & Applebaum, A. G. (1973). Cognitive masking: The disruptive effect of an emotional stimulus upon the perception of contiguous neutral items. *Bulletin of the Psychonomic Society, 1,* 59–61.

Ergeneli, A., Ilsev, A., & Karap?nar, P. B. (2010). Work-family conflict and job satisfaction relationship: The roles of gender and interpretive habits. *Gender, Work and Organization, 17(6),* 679–695.

Ericsson, K. A. (2006). The influence of experience and deliberate practice on the development of superior expert performance. In K. A. Ericsson, N. Charness, P. Feltovich, and R. R. Hoffman, R. R. (Eds.). *Cambridge handbook of expertise and expert performance* (pp. 685–706). Cambridge, UK: Cambridge University Press.

Ericsson, K. A., & Charness, N. (1994). Expert performance: Its structure and acquisition. *American Psychologist, 49*(8), 725–747.

Ericsson, K. A., Krampe, R., & Tesch-Roemer, C. (1993). The role of deliberate practice in the acquisition of expert performance. *Psychology Review, 100*(3), 363–406.

Erikson, E. (1950). *Childhood and society.* New York, NY: Norton.

Erlacher, D., & Schredl, M. (2004). Dreams reflecting waking sport activities: A comparison of sport and psychology students. *International Journal of Sport Psychology, 35*(4), 301–308.

Ertekin-Taner, N. (2007). Genetics of Alzheimer's disease: A centennial review. *Neurologic Clinics, 25,* 611–667.

Eschleman, K. J., Bowling, N. A., & Alarcon, G. M. (2010). A meta-analytic examination of hardiness. *International Journal of Stress Management, 17*(4), 277–307.

Eslick, A. N., Fazio, L. K., & Marsh, E. J. (2011). Ironic effects of drawing attention to story errors. *Memory, 19(2),* 184–191.

Espelage, D. L., Aragon, S. R., Birkett, M., & Koenig, B. W. (2008). Homophobic teasing, psychological outcomes, and sexual orientation among high school students: What influence do parents and schools have? *School Psychology Review, 37,* 202–216.

Espy, K. A., Fang, H., Johnson, C., Stopp, C., Wiebe, S. A., & Respass, J. (2011). Prenatal tobacco exposure: Developmental outcomes in the neonatal period. *Developmental Psychology, 47(1),* 153–169.

Esseily, R., Nadel, J., & Fagard, J. (2010). Object retrieval through observational learning in 8- to 18-month-old infants. *Infant Behavior & Development, 33(4),* 695–699.

Esterson, A. (2002). The myth of Freud's ostracism by the medical community in 1896–1905: Jeffrey Masson's assault on truth. *History of Psychology, 5(2),* 115–134.

Ethical Principles of Psychologists and Code of Conduct. (2002). Retrieved from http://www.apa.org/ethics/code2002.html.

Evans, G. W., Boxhill, L., & Pinkava, M. (2008). Poverty and maternal responsiveness: The role of maternal stress and social resources. *International Journal of Behavioral Development, 32,* 232–237.

Evans, J. S. B. T. (2003). In two minds: Dual process accounts of reasoning. *Trends in Cognitive Sciences, 7*(10), 454–459.

Everett, C., & Everett, S. V. (1994). *Healthy divorce.* San Francisco, CA: Jossey-Bass.

Eysenck, H. J. (1967). *The biological basis of personality.* Springfield, IL: Charles C Thomas.

Eysenck, H. J. (1982). *Personality, genetics, and behavior: Selected papers.* New York, NY: Prager.

Eysenck, H. J. (1990). Biological dimensions of personality. In L. A. Pervin (Ed.), *Handbook of personality: Theory and research* (pp. 244–276). New York, NY: Guilford Press.

Eysenck, H. J. (1991). *Smoking, personality, and stress: Psychosocial factors in the prevention of cancer and coronary heart disease.* New York, NY: Springer-Verlag.

Faces of the week. (2008, May 14). *BBC News.* Retrieved from http://news.bbc.co.uk/2/hi/uk_news/magazine/3712013.stm

Faddiman, A. (1997). *The spirit catches you and you fall down.* New York, NY: Straus & Giroux.

Fairburn, C. G., Cooper, Z., Shafran, R., & Wilson, G. T. (2008). Eating disorders: A transdiagnostic protocol. In D. H. Barlow (Ed.), *Clinical handbook of psychological disorders: A step-by-step treatment manual* (4th ed.) (pp. 578–614). New York, NY: Guilford Press.

Famous People with Mental Illness (2011). *NAMI.* Retrieved from http://www.nami.org/Content/ContentGroups/Policy/Updates/Updates_andamp__What_s_New___Healthcare_Reform_EEOC_Famous_People.htm

Famous People with Schizophrenia (2011). *HubPages.* Retrieved from http://hubpages.com/hub/famous-people-with-schizophrenia

Fang, X., & Corso, P. S. (2007). Child maltreatment, youth violence, and intimate partner violence: Developmental relationships. *American Journal of Preventive Medicine, 33,* 281–290.

Fantz, R. L. (1956). A method for studying early visual development. *Perceptual and Motor Skills, 6,* 13–15.

Fantz, R. L. (1963). Pattern vision in newborn infants. *Science, 140,* 296–297.

Faraone, S. V. (2008). Statistical and molecular genetic approaches to developmental psychopathology: The pathway forward. In J. J. Hudziak (Ed.), *Developmental psychopathology and wellness: Genetic and environmental influences* (pp. 245–265). Arlington, VA: American Psychiatric Publishing.

Faraut, B., Boudjeltia, K. Z., Dyzma, M., Rousseau, A., David, E., Stenuit, P., Franck, T.,

Van Antwerpen, P., Vanhaeverbeek, M., & Kerkhofs, M. (2011). Benefits of napping and an extended duration of recovery sleep on alertness and immune cells after acute sleep restriction. *Brain, Behavior, and Immunity, 25(1),* 16–24.

Fassler, O., Lynn, S. J., & Knox, J. (2008). Is hypnotic suggestibility a stable trait? *Consciousness and Cognition: An International Journal, 17,* 240–253.

Fawcett, J. (2011). Anxiety and worry: The brain as a pain machine. *Psychiatric Annals, 41(2),* 53.

Fazel, S., Buxrud, P., Ruchkin, V., & Grann, M. (2010). Homicide in discharged patients with schizophrenia and other psychoses: A national case-control study. *Schizophrenia Research, 123(2–3),* 263–269.

Feeney, J. A. (2008). Adult romantic attachment: Developments in the study of couple relationships. In J. Cassidy & P. R. Shaver (Eds.), *Handbook of attachment theory, research, and clinical applications* (2nd ed.) (pp. 456–481). New York, NY: Guilford Press.

Feigelman, W., & Gorman, B. S. (2010). Prospective predictors of premature death: Evidence from the National Longitudinal Study of Adolescent Health. *Journal of Psychoactive Drugs, 42(3),* 353–361.

Fein, S. & Spencer, S. J. (1997). Prejudice as selfimage maintenance: Affirming the self through derogating others. *Journal of Personality and Social Psychology, 73(1),* 31–44.

Feldman, D. C., & Beehr, T. A. (2011). A three-phase model of retirement decision making. *American Psychologist, 66(3),* 193–203.

Feldman, R. (2007). Maternal-infant contact and child development: Insights from the kangaroo intervention. In L. L'Abate (Ed.), *Low-cost approaches to promote physical and mental health: Theory, research, and practice* (pp. 323–351). New York, NY: Springer.

Feldman, R. S. (1982). *Development of nonverbal behavior in children.* Seacaucus, NJ: Springer-Verlag.

Feliciano, L., Segal, D. L., & Vair, C. L. (2011). Major depressive disorder. In K. H. Sorocco & S. Lauderdale (Eds.), *Cognitive behavior therapy with older adults: Innovations across care settings* (pp. 31–64). New York, NY: Springer.

Feng, J., Spence, I., & Pratt, J. (2007). Playing an action video game reduces gender differences in spatial cognition. *Psychological Science, 18,* 850–855.

Fennis, B. M., & Stroebe, W. (2010). *The psychology of advertising.* New York, NY: Psychology Press.

Ferguson, C. J. (2010). Violent crime research: An introduction. In C. J. Ferguson (Ed.), *Violent crime: Clinical and social implications* (pp. 3–18). Thousand Oaks, CA: Sage.

Ferguson, C. J. (2011). Video games and youth violence: A prospective analysis in adolescents. *Journal of Youth and Adolescence, 40(4),* 377–391.

Ferguson, C. J., Winegard, B., & Winegard, B. M. (2011). Who is the fairest one of all? How evolution guides peer and media influences on female body dissatisfaction. *Review of General Psychology, 15(1),* 11–28.

Fernández-Ballesteros, R., Zamarrón, M. D., Díez-Nicolás, J., López-Bravo, M. D., Molina, M. A., & Schettini, R. (2011). Productivity in old age. *Research on Aging, 33(2),* 205–226.

Ferrari, M., Robinson, D. K., & Yasnitsky, A. (2010). Wundt, Vygotsky and Bandura: A cultural-historical science of consciousness in three acts. *History of the Human Sciences, 23(3),* 95–118.

Ferrari, P. F., Rozzi, S., & Fogassi, L. (2005). Mirror neurons responding to observation of actions made with tools in monkey ventral premotor cortex. *Journal of Cognitive Neuroscience, 17,* 212–226.

Ferretti, P., Copp, A., Tickle, C., & Moore, G. (Eds.) (2006). *Embryos, genes, and birth defects* (2nd ed.). Hoboken, NJ: Wiley.

Ferrucci, L. M., Cartmel, B., Turkman, Y. E., Murphy, M. E., Smith, T., Stein, K. D., & McCorkle, R. (2011). Causal attribution among cancer survivors of the 10 most common cancers. *Journal of Psychosocial Oncology, 29(2),* 121–140.

Festinger, L. A. (1957). *A theory of cognitive dissonance.* Palo Alto, CA: Stanford University Press.

Festinger, L. A., & Carlsmith, L. M. (1959). Cognitive consequences of forced compliance. *Journal of Abnormal and Social Psychology, 58,* 203–210.

Ficca, G., Axelsson, J., Mollicone, D. J., Muto, V., & Vitiello, M. V. (2010). Naps, cognition and performance. *Sleep Medicine Reviews, 14(4),* 249–258.

Field, A. P. (2006). Is conditioning a useful framework for understanding the development and treatment of phobias? *Clinical Psychology Review, 26,* 857–875.

Field, K. M., Woodson, R., Greenberg, R., & Cohen, D. (1982). Discrimination and imitation of facial expressions by neonates. *Science, 218*, 179–181.

Field, T. M. (1998). Massage therapy effects. *American Psychologist, 53*, 1270–1281.

Field, T. M. (2007). *The amazing infant.* Malden, MA: Blackwell.

Field, T. M., & Hernandez-Reif, M. (2001). Sleep problems in infants decrease following massage therapy. *Early Child Development & Care, 168*, 95–104.

Field, T., Diego, M., & Hernandez-Reif, M. (2007). Massage therapy research. *Developmental Review, 27*, 75–89.

Fields, A. J. (2010). Multicultural research and practice: Theoretical issues and maximizing cultural exchange. *Professional Psychology: Research and Practice, 41(3)*, 196–201.

Fields, A., & Cochran, S. (2011). Men and depression: Current perspectives for health care professionals. *American Journal of Lifestyle Medicine, 5(1)*, 92–100.

Fife, R., & Schrager, S. (2011). *Family violence: What health care providers need to know.* Sudbury, MA: Jones & Bartlett Learning.

Figueredo, A., Jacobs, W., Burger, S., Gladden, P., & Olderbak, S. (2011). The biology of personality. In G. Terzis & R. Arp (Eds.), *Information and living systems: Philosophical and scientific perspectives* (pp. 371–406). Boston, MA: MIT Press.

Fincham, F. D., & Cui, M. (Eds.). (2011). *Advances in personal relationships. Romantic relationships in emerging adulthood.* New York, NY: Cambridge University Press.

Fine, J. (2010). *Why Avatar didn't win the Oscar: Psychologist Dr. Jeffrey Fine asserts the corporate world is bulldozing America.* Retrieved from http://www.prnewswire.com/news-releases/why-avatar-didnt-win-the-oscar-psychologist-dr-jeffrey-fine-asserts-the-corporate-world-is-bulldozing-america-87453192.html

Fink, A., Grabner, R. H., Gebauer, D., Reishofer, G., Koschutnig, K., & Ebner, F. (2010). Enhancing creativity by means of cognitive stimulation: Evidence from an fMRI study. *NeuroImage, 52(4)*, 1687–1695.

Fink, B., Manning, J. T., Neave, N., & Grammer, K. (2004). Second to fourth digit ratio and facial asymmetry. *Evolution and Human Behavior, 25(2)*, 125–132.

Fink, B., & Penton-Voak, I. (2002). Evolutionary psychology of facial attractiveness. *Current Directions in Psychological Science, 11(5)*, 154–158.

Fiori, M., & Antonakis, J. (2011). The ability model of emotional intelligence: Searching for valid measures. *Personality and Individual Differences, 50(3)*, 329–334.

Fisher, C. B., & Fried, A. L. (2008). Internet-mediated psychological services and the American Psychological Association Ethics Code. In D. N. Bersoff (Ed.), *Ethical conflicts in psychology* (4th ed.) (pp. 376–383). Washington, DC: American Psychological Association.

Fisher, G. L. (2011). Ponytails & death-ray looks: A review of research on relational aggression among adolescent girls. *Dissertation Abstracts International: Section B: The Sciences and Engineering, 71(8-B)*, 5182.

Fisher, J. O. & Kral, T. V. E. (2008). Super-size me: Portion size effects on young children's eating. *Physiology & Behavior, 94*, 39–47.

Fisk, J. E., Bury, A. S., & Holden, R. (2006). Reasoning about complex probabilistic concepts in childhood. *Scandinavian Journal of Psychology, 47*, 497–504.

Flaskerud, J. H. (2010). DSM proposed changes, part I: Criticisms and influences on changes. *Issues in Mental Health Nursing, 31(10)*, 686–688.

Flavell, J. H., Miller, P. H., & Miller, S. A. (2002). *Cognitive development* (4th ed.). Upper Saddle River, NJ: Prentice-Hall.

Fleischhaker, C., Böhme, R., Sixt, B., Brück, C., Schneider, C., & Schulz, E. (2011). Dialectical Behavioral Therapy for Adolescents (DBT-A): A clinical trial for patients with suicidal and self-injurious behavior and borderline symptoms with a one-year follow-up. *Child and Adolescent Psychiatry and Mental Health, 5*, Article ID 3.

Fleischmann, B. K., & Welz, A. (2008). Cardiovascular regeneration and stem cell therapy. *Journal of the American Medical Association, 299(6)*, 700–701.

Fletcher, G. J. O., & Kerr, P. S. G. (2010). Through the eyes of love: Reality and illusion in intimate relationships. *Psychological Bulletin, 136(4)*, 627–658.

Fletcher, G. J. O., & Simpson, J. A. (2000). Ideal standards in close relationships: Their structure and functions. *Current Directions in Psychological Science, 9*, 102–105.

Flora, C. (2010). Black Swan: Art and madness. *Psychology Today.* Retrieved from http://www.psychologytoday.com/blog/brainstorm/201012/black-swan-art-and-madness

Flores, Y. G. (2008). Race related stress of Latino elders: Implications for quality of life. *Dissertation Abstracts International: Section B: The Sciences and Engineering, 68(8-B)*, 5567.

Flynn, J. R. (1987). Massive IQ gains in 14 nations: What IQ tests really measure. *Psychological Bulletin, 101*, 171–191.

Flynn, J. R. (1991). *Asian Americans: Achievement beyond IQ.* Hillsdale, NJ: Lawrence Erlbaum Associates.

Flynn, J. R. (2000). IQ gains and fluid g. *American Psychologist, 55(5)*, 543.

Flynn, J. R. (2003). Movies about intelligence: The limitations of g. *Current Directions in Psychological Science, 12(3)*, 95–99.

Flynn, J. R. (2006). The history of the American mind in the 20th century: A scenario to explain gains over time and a case for the irrelevance of g. In P. C. Kyllonen, R. D. Roberts, & L. Stankov (Eds.), *Extending intelligence* (pp. 207–233). Mahwah, NJ: Erlbaum.

Flynn, J. R. (2007). *What is intelligence?: Beyond the Flynn Effect.* New York, NY: Cambridge University Press.

Foer, J. (2008, October 5). The unspeakable odyssey of the motionless boy. *Esquire.* Retrieved from http://www.esquire.com/features/unspeakable-odyssey-motionless-boy-1008?click=main_sr

Fogarty, A., Rawstorne, P., Prestage, G., Crawford, J., Grierson, J., & Kippax, S. (2007). Marijuana as therapy for people living with HIV/AIDS: Social and health aspects. *AIDS Care, 19*, 295–301.

Fogassi, L., Ferrari, P. F., Gesierich, B., Rozzi, S., Chersi, F., & Rizzolatti, G. (2005). Parietal lobe: From action understanding to intention understanding. *Science, 308*, 662–667.

Fogel, S. M., & Smith, C. T. (2011). The function of the sleep spindle: A physiological index of intelligence and a mechanism for sleep-dependent memory consolidation. *Neuroscience and Biobehavioral Reviews, 35(5)*, 1154–1165.

Fok, H. K., Hui, C. M., Bond, M. H., Matsumoto, D., & Yoo, S. H. (2008). Integrating personality, context, relationship, and emotion type into a model of display rules. *Journal of Research in Personality, 42*, 133–150.

Font, E., & Carazo, P. (2010). Animals in translation: Why there is meaning (but probably no message) in animal communication. *Animal Behaviour, 80(2)*, e1–e6.

Ford, D. Y. (2011). *Reversing underachievement among gifted Black students* (2nd ed.). Waco, TX: Prufrock Press.

Foulkes, D. (1993). Children's dreaming. In D. Foulkes & C. Cavallero (Eds.), *Dreaming as cognition* (pp. 114–132). New York, NY: Harvester Wheatsheaf.

Foulkes, D. (1999). *Children's dreaming and the development of consciousness.* Cambridge, MA: Harvard University Press.

Fowler, C. D., Qun, L., Johnson, P. M., Marks, M. M., & Kenny. P. J. (2011). Habenular α5 nicotinic receptor subunit signaling controls nicotine intake. *Nature.* doi:10.1038/nature09797

Fraley, R. C., & Shaver, P. R. (1997). Adult attachment and the suppression of unwanted thoughts. *Journal of Personality and Social Psychology, 73,* 1080–1091.

Frankenburg, W., Dodds, J., Archer, P., Shapiro, H., & Bresnick, B. (1992). The Denver II: A major revision and restandardization of the Denver Developmental Screening Test. *Pediatrics, 89,* 91–97.

Frayser, S. (1985). *Varieties of sexual experience: An anthropological perspective on human sexuality.* New Haven, CT: Human Relations Area Files Press.

Frazier, P., Keenan, N., Anders, S., Perera, S., Shallcross, S., & Hintz, S. (2011). Perceived past, present, and future control and adjustment to stressful life events. *Journal of Personality and Social Psychology, 100(4),* 749–765.

Freckelton, I. (2011). Review of The architecture of madness: Insane asylums in the United States. [Review of the book The architecture of madness: Insane asylums in the United States]. *Psychiatry, Psychology and Law, 18(1),* 160–162.

Frederikse, M. W., Lu, A., Aylward, E., Barta. P., & Pearlson, G. (1999). Sex differences in the inferior parietal lobule. *Cerebral Cortex, 9(8),* 896–901.

Fredricks, J. A., & Eccles, J. S. (2005). Family socialization, gender, and sport motivation and involvement. *Journal of Sport & Exercise Psychology, 27(1),* 3–31.

Freeman, J. B., & Ambady, N. (2011). A dynamic interactive theory of person construal. *Psychological Review, 118(2),* 247–279.

Freeman, W. J. (2007). Indirect biological measures of consciousness from field studies of brains as dynamical systems. *Neural Networks, 20,* 1021–1031.

Frenda, S. J., Nichols, R. M., & Loftus, E. F. (2011). Current issues and advances in misinformation research. *Current Directions in Psychological Science, 20(1),* 20–23.

Freud, S. (1900/1953). The interpretation of dreams. In J. Stratchey (Ed. and Trans.), *The standard edition of the complete psychological works of Sigmund Freud* (Vols. 4 and 5). London, England: Hogarth Press. (Original work published 1900.)

Freud, S. (1923/1961). The ego and the id. In J. Stratchey (Ed. and Trans.), *The standard edition of the complete psychological works of Sigmund Freud* (Vol. 19). London, England: Hogarth Press. (Original work published 1923.)

Freund, A. M., & Ritter, J. O. (2009). Midlife crisis: A debate. *Gerontology, 55(5),* 582–591.

Frew, J., & Spiegler, M. (Eds.). (2012). *Contemporary psychotherapies for a diverse world.* New York, NY: Routledge.

Frick, R. S., Wang, J., & Carlson, R. G. (2008). Depressive symptomatology in young adults with a history of MDMA use: a longitudinal analysis. *Journal of Psychopharmacology, 22(1),* 47–54.

Fridberg, D. J., Vollmer, J. M., O'Donnell, B. F., & Skosnik, P. D. (2011). Cannabis users differ from non-users on measures of personality and schizotypy. *Psychiatry Research, 186(1),* 46–52.

Friedberg, R. D., & Brelsford, G. M. (2011). Core principles in cognitive therapy with youth. *Child and Adolescent Psychiatric Clinics of North America, 20(2),* 369–378.

Frieden, T. (2011). The psychology of irrational health scares. *Big Think.* Retrieved from http://bigthink.com/thomasfrieden

Friedlander, M. L., Escudero, V., Heatherington, L., & Diamond, G. M. (2011). Alliance in couple and family therapy. *Psychotherapy, 48(1),* 25–33.

Friedman, H. (2011). It's premature to write the obituary for humanistic psychology: Comments on humanistic psychology for the 50th anniversary of the Journal of Humanistic Psychology. *Journal of Humanistic Psychology.* Advance online publication. doi: 10.1177/0022167811409043

Friedman, H. S., & Martin, L. R. (2011). *The longevity project.* New York, NY: Penguin Group.

Friedman, H., & Schustack, M. (2006). *Personality: Classic theories and modern research* (3rd ed.). Boston, MA: Allyn & Bacon/Longman.

Friedman, J. H. (2010). Parkinson's disease psychosis 2010: A review article. *Parkinsonism & Related Disorders, 16(9),* 553–560.

Friedman, J. H. (2011). Managing idiopathic Parkinson's disease in patients with schizophrenic disorders. *Parkinsonism & Related Disorders, 17(3),* 198–200.

Friedman, M., & Rosenman, R. H. (1959). Association of specific overt behavior patterns with blood and cardiovascular findings: Blood cholesterol level, blood clotting time, incidence of arcus senilis and clinical coronary artery disease. *Journal of the American Medical Association, 169,* 1286–1296.

Friedman, R., & James, J. W. (2008). The myth of the stages of dying, death, and grief. *Skeptic, 14(2),* 37–41.

Frost, G. (2008). Stop procrastination and take action. *Ezine articles.* Retrieved from http://ezinearticles.com/?Stop-Procrastination-and-Take-Action&id=987197

Frost, R. O., Heimberg, R. G, Holt, C. S., Mattai, J. I., & Neubauer, A. L. (1993). A comparison of two measures of perfectionism. *Personality and Individual Differences, 14,* 119–126.

Fry, C. L. (1985). Culture, behavior, and aging in the comparative perspective. In J. E. Birren, K. W. Schaie, et al. (Eds.), *Handbook of the psychology of aging* (2nd ed.) (pp, 216–244). New York, NY: Van Nostrand Reinhold Co.

Fu, M., & Zuo, Y. (2011). Experience-dependent structural plasticity in the cortex. *Trends in Neurosciences, 34(4),* 177–187.

Fujimura, J. H., Rajagopalan, R., Ossorio, P. N., & Doksum, K. A. (2010). Race and ancestry: Operationalizing populations in human genetic variation studies. In I. Whitmarsh & D. S. Jones (Eds.), *What's the use of race? Modern governance and the biology of difference* (pp. 169–183). Cambridge, MA: MIT Press.

Fukase, Y., & Okamoto, Y. (2010). Psychosocial tasks of the elderly: A reconsideration of the eighth stage of Erikson's epigenetic scheme. *Japanese Journal of Developmental Psychology, 21(3),* 266–277.

Fulcher, M. (2011). Individual differences in children's occupational aspirations as a function of parental traditionality. *Sex Roles, 64(1–2),* 117–131.

Fuller, B., & García Coll, C. (2010). Learning from Latinos: Contexts, families, and child development in motion. *Developmental Psychology, 46(3),* 559–565.

Fumagalli, M., Ferrucci, R., Mameli, F., Marceglia, S., Mrakic-Sposta, S., Zago, S., Lucchiari, C., Consonni, D., Nordio, F., Pravettoni, G., Cappa, S., & Priori, A. (2010). Gender-related differences in moral judgments. *Cognitive Processing, 11(3),* 219–226.

Funder, D. C. (2000). Personality. *Annual Review of Psychology, 52,* 197–221.

Funder, D. C. (2001). The really, really fundamental attribution error. *Psychological Inquiry, 12*(1), 21–23.

Furguson, E., Chamorro-Premuzic, T., Pickering, A., & Weiss, A. (2011). Five into one does go: A critique of the general factor of personality. In T. Chamorro-Premuzic, S. von Stumm, & A. Furnam (Eds.), *Wiley-Blackwell handbook of individual differences* (pp. 162–186). Chichester, UK: Wiley-Blackwell.

Furman, E. (1990, November). Plant a potato, learn about life (and death). *Young Children, 46*(1), 15–20.

Furukawa, T., Nakano, H., Hirayama, K., Tanabashi, T., Yoshihara, K., Sudo, N., Kubo, C., & Nishima, S. (2010). Relationship between snoring sound intensity and daytime blood pressure. *Sleep and Biological Rhythms, 8*(4), 245–253.

Fusar-Poli, P., Borgwardt, S., Crescini, A., Deste, G., Kempton, M. J., Lawrie, S., Mc Guire, P., & Sacchetti, E. (2011). Neuroanatomy of vulnerability to psychosis: A voxel-based meta-analysis. *Neuroscience and Biobehavioral Reviews, 35*(5), 1175–1185.

Gabbard, G. O. (2006). Mente, cervello e disturbi di personalita. / Mind, brain, and personality disorders. *Psicoterapia e scienze umane, 40,* 9–26.

Gabry, K. E., Chrousos, G. P., Rice, K. C., Mostafa, R. M., Sternberg, E., Negrao, A. B., Webster, E. L., McCann, S. M., & Gold, P. W. (2002). Marked suppression of gastric ulcerogenesis and intestinal responses to stress by a novel class of drugs. *Molecular Psychiatry, 7*(5), 474–483.

Gacono, C. B., Evans, F. B., & Viglione, D. J. (2008). Essential issues in the forensic use of the Rorschach. In C. B. Gacono (Ed.), F. B. Evans (Ed.), N. Kaser-Boyd (Col.), & L. A. Gacono (Col.), *The handbook of forensic Rorschach assessment* (pp. 3–20). *The LEA series in personality and clinical psychology.* New York, NY: Routledge/Taylor & Francis Group.

Gadd, D., & Dixon, B. (2011). *Losing the race: Thinking psychosocially about racially motivated crime.* London, England: Karnac Books.

Gaetz, M., Weinberg, H., Rzempoluck, E., & Jantzen, K. J. (1998). Neural network classifications and correlational analysis of EEG and MEG activity accompanying spontaneous reversals of the Necker Cube. *Cognitive Brain Research, 6,* 335–346.

Gagnepain, P., Henson, R., Chételat, G., Desgranges, B., Lebreton, K., & Eustache, F. (2011). Is neocortical–hippocampal connectivity a better predictor of subsequent recollection than local increases in hippocampal activity? New insights on the role of priming. *Journal of Cognitive Neuroscience, 23*(2), 391–403.

Gagnon, J. H. (1990). The explicit and implicit use of the scripting perspective in sex research. *Annual Review of Sex Research, 1,* 1–43.

Gagnon, M., & Lexchin, J. (2008). The cost of pushing pills: A new estimate of pharmaceutical promotion expenditures in the United States. *PLoS Medicine. 5*(1), 29–33.

Galderisi, S., Quarantelli, M., Volpe, U., Mucci, A., Cassano, G. B., Invernizzi, G., Rossi, A., Vita, A., Pini, S., Cassano, P., Daneluzzo, E., De Peri, L., Stratta, P., Brunetti, A., & Maj, M. (2008). Patterns of structural MRI abnormalities in deficit and nondeficit schizophrenia. *Schizophrenia Bulletin, 34,* 393–401.

Gallup, G. G., Jr., & Frederick, D. A. (2010).The science of sex appeal: An evolutionary perspective. *Review of General Psychology, 14*(3), 240–250.

Gambescia, N., & Weeks, G. (2007). Sexual dysfunction. In N. Kazantzis & L. L'Abate (Eds.), *Handbook of homework assignments in psychotherapy: Research, practice, prevention* (pp. 351–368). New York, NY: Springer Science + Business Media.

Gangestad, S. W. (2011). Human adaptations for mating: Frameworks for understanding patterns of family formation and fertility. In A. Booth, S. M. McHale, & N. S. Landale (Eds.), *National symposium on family issues. Biosocial foundations of family processes* (pp. 117–148). New York, NY: Springer.

Ganong, L. H., Coleman, M., Markham, M., & Rothrauff, T. (2011). Predicting postdivorce coparental communication. *Journal of Divorce & Remarriage, 52*(1), 1–18.

Gansler, D. A., Lee, A. K. W., Emerton, B. C., D'Amato, C., Bhadelia, R., Jerram, M., & Fulwiler, C. (2011). Prefrontal regional correlates of self-control in male psychiatric patients: Impulsivity facets and aggression. *Psychiatry Research: Neuroimaging, 191*(1), 16–23.

Garb, H. N., Wood, J. M., Lilienfeld, S. O., & Nezworski, M. T. (2005). Roots of the Rorschach controversy. *Clinical Psychology Review, 25,* 97–118.

García, E. E., & Náñez, J. E., Sr. (2011). Education circumstances. In E. E. García & J. E. Náñez, Sr., *Bilingualism and cognition: Informing research, pedagogy, and policy* (pp. 103–114). Washington, DC: American Psychological Association.

Garcia, G. M., & Stafford, M. E. (2000). Prediction of reading by Ga and Gc specific cognitive abilities for low-SES White and Hispanic English-speaking children. *Psychology in the Schools, 37*(3), 227–235.

Garcia, J. (2003). Psychology is not an enclave. In R. Sternberg (Ed.), *Psychologists defying the crowd: Stories of those who battled the establishment and won* (pp. 67–77). Washington, DC: American Psychological Association.

Garcia, J., & Koelling, R. S. (1966). Relation of cue to consequence in avoidance learning. *Psychonomic Science, 4,* 123–124.

Gardella, A. (2010). Hiring employees, with help or without. Retrieved from http://www.nytimes.com/2010/10/28/business/smallbusiness/28sbiz.html?_r=2&src=dayp

Gardner, H. (1998). A multiplicity of intelligences. *Scientific American Presents Exploring Intelligence, 9,* 18–23.

Gardner, H. (1999, February). Who owns intelligence? *Atlantic Monthly,* pp. 67–76.

Gardner, H. (2002). The pursuit of excellence through education. In M. Ferrari (Ed.), *Learning from extraordinary minds* (pp. 3–35). Mahwah, NJ: Erlbaum.

Gardner, H. (2008). Who owns intelligence? In M. H. Immordino-Yang (Ed.), *Jossey-Bass Education Team. The Jossey-Bass reader on the brain and learning* (pp. 120–132). San Francisco: Jossey-Bass.

Gardner, H. (2011). *Frames of mind.* New York, NY: Basic Books.

Gardner, H., & Traub, J. (2010). A debate on "multiple intelligences" In D. Gordon (Ed.), *The Dana Foundation's Cerebrum. Cerebrum 2010: Emerging ideas in brain science* (pp. 34–61). Washington, DC: Dana Press.

Gardner, M. K. (2011). Theories of intelligence. In M. A. Bray & T. J. Kehle (Eds.), *Oxford library of psychology: The Oxford handbook of school psychology* (pp. 79–100). New York, NY: Oxford University Press.

Garno, J. L., Gunawardane, N., & Goldberg, J. F. (2008). Predictors of trait aggression in bipolar disorder. *Bipolar Disorders, 10,* 285–292.

Garrick, J. (2006). The humor of trauma survivors: Its application in a therapeutic milieu. *Journal of Aggression, Maltreatment & Trauma, 12,* 169–182.

Garry, M., & Gerrie, M. P. (2005). When photographs create false memories. *Current Directions in Psychological Science, 14,* 321–324.

Gasser, L., & Malti, T. (2011). Relationale und physische Aggression in der mittleren Kindheit: Zusammenhänge mit moralischem

Wissen und moralischen Gefühlen [Relational and physical aggression in middle childhood: Relations with moral knowledge and moral emotions]. *Zeitschrift für Entwicklungspsychologie und Pädagogische Psychologie, 43(1)*, 29–38.

Gasser, S., & Raulet, D. H. (2006). Activation and self-tolerance of natural killer cells. *Immunology Review, 214*, 130–142.

Gatchel, R. J., & Kishino, N. D. (2011). The biopsychosocial perspective of pain and emotion. In G. MacDonald & L. A. Jensen-Campbell (Eds.), *Social pain: Neuropsychological and health implications of loss and exclusion* (pp. 181–191).

Gaw, A. C. (2001). *Concise guide to cross- cultural psychiatry. Concise guides.* Washington, DC: American Psychiatric Association.

Gaylord, L. (2011). *Practical clinical psychopharmacology: An evidence-based, experiential handbook.* Hackensack, NJ: World Scientific Publishing.

Gazzaniga, M. S. *(2000). The mind's past.* Berkeley, CA: University California Press.

Gazzaniga, M. S. (2009). The fictional self. Personal identity and fractured selves: Perspectives from philosophy, ethics, and neuroscience. In D. J. H. Mathews, H. Bok, & P. V. Rabins (Eds.), *Personal identity and fractured selves: Perspectives from philosophy, ethics, and neuroscience* (pp. 174–185). Baltimore, MD: Johns Hopkins University Press.

Geangu, E., Benga, O., Stahl, D., & Striano, T. (2010). Contagious crying beyond the first days of life. *Infant Behavior & Development, 33(3)*, 279–288.

Geary, D. C. (2010). *Male, female: The evolution of human sex differences.* Washington, DC: American Psychological Association.

Gebauer, H., Krempl, R., & Fleisch, E. (2008). Exploring the effect of cognitive biases on customer support services. *Creativity and Innovation Management, 17*, 58–70.

Gebele, N., Morling, K., Rösler, U., & Rau, R. (2011). Objektive Erfassung von Job Demands und Decision Latitude sowie Zusammenhänge der Tätigkeitsmerkmale mit Erholungsunfähigkeit [Objective assessment of job demands and decision latitude and the relationship of the job characteristics to relaxation ability]. *Zeitschrift für Arbeits- und Organisationspsychologie, 55(1)*, 32–45.

Gelder, B. D., Meeren, H. K., Righart, R. Stock, J. V., van de Riet, W. A., & Tamietto, M. (2006). Beyond the face: Exploring rapid influences of context on face processing. *Progress in Brain Research, 155*, 37–48.

Gellerman, D. M., & Lu, F. G. (2011). Religious and spiritual issues in the outline for cultural formulation. In J. R. Peteet, F. G. Lu, & W. E Narrow (Eds.), *Religious and spiritual issues in psychiatric diagnosis: A research agenda for DSM-V* (pp. 207–220). Washington, DC: American Psychiatric Association.

Geniole, S. N., Carré, J. M., & McCormick, C. M. (2011). State, not trait, neuroendocrine function predicts costly reactive aggression in men after social exclusion and inclusion. *Biological Psychology, 87(1)*, 137–145.

Genome.gov: National Human Genome Research Institute. (2010). *Knockout Mice.* Retrieved from http://www.genome.gov/ 12514551

George, J. B. E., & Franko, D. L. (2010). Cultural issues in eating pathology and body image among children and adolescents. *Journal of Pediatric Psychology, 35(3)*, 231–242.

Gergen, K. J. (2010). The acculturated brain. *Theory & Psychology, 20(6)*, 795–816.

Gershon, E. S., & Rieder, R. O. (1993). Major disorders of mind and brain. *Mind and brain: Readings from Scientific American Magazine* (pp. 91–100). New York, NY: Freeman.

Gherovici, P. (2011). Psychoanalysis needs a sex change. *Gay & Lesbian Issues and Psychology Review, 7(1)*, 3–18.

Giancola, P. R., & Parrott, D. J. (2008). Further evidence for the validity of the Taylor aggression paradigm. *Aggressive Behavior, 34*, 214–229.

Gibb, S., Fergusson, D., & Horwood, L. (2011). Relationship duration and mental health outcomes: findings from a 30-year longitudinal study. *The British Journal of Psychiatry, 198*, 24–30.

Gibbs, N. (1995, October 2). The EQ factor. *Time*, pp. 60–68.

Gibson, E. J., & Walk, R. D. (1960). The visual cliff. *Scientific American, 202(2)*, 67–71.

Gigerenzer, G., & Goldstein, D. G. (2011). The recognition heuristic: A decade of research. *Judgment and Decision Making, 6(1)*, 100–121.

Gignac, G. E., & Vernon, P. A. (2003). Biological approaches to the assessment of human intelligence. In Cecil R. Reynolds & Randy W. Kamphaus (Eds.), *Handbook of psychological and educational assessment of children: Intelligence, aptitude, and achievement* (2nd ed.), (pp. 325–342). New York, NY: Guilford Press.

Gilbert, F., & Daffern, M. (2011). Illuminating the relationship between personality disorder and violence: Contributions of the general aggression model. *Psychology of Violence.* Retrieved from http:// psycnet.apa.org/index.cfm?fa=search. displayRecord&id=DCAF7F48-A3DE- 5951-A7DD-D6F9E97A3C05&resultID=1 &page=1&dbTab=all

Gillham, J., Adams-Deutsch, Z., Werner, J., Reivich, K., Coulter-Heindl, V., Linkins, M., Winder, B., Peterson, C., Park, N., Abenavoli, R., Contero, A., & Seligman, M. E. P. (2011). Character strengths predict subjective well-being during adolescence. *The Journal of Positive Psychology, 6(1)*, 31–44.

Gilligan, C. (1977). In a different voice: Women's conception of morality. *Harvard Educational Review, 47(4)*, 481–517.

Gilligan, C. (1990). Teaching Shakespeare's sister. In C. Gilligan, N. Lyons, & T. Hanmer (Eds.), *Mapping the moral domain* (pp. 73–86). Cambridge, MA: Harvard University Press.

Gilligan, C. (1993). Adolescent development reconsidered. In A. Garrod (Ed.), *Approaches to moral development: New research and emerging themes.* New York, NY: Teachers College Press.

Gilmour, D. R., & Walkey, F. H. (1981). Identifying violent offenders using a video measure of interpersonal distance. *Journal of Consulting and Clinical Psychology, 49*, 287–291.

Gimbel, S. I., & Brewer, J. B. (2011). Reaction time, memory strength, and fMRI activity during memory retrieval: Hippocampus and default network are differentially responsive during recollection and familiarity judgments. *Cognitive Neuroscience, 2(1)*, 19–26.

Gini, G., Pozzoli, T., & Hauser, M. (2011). Bullies have enhanced moral competence to judge relative to victims, but lack moral compassion. *Personality and Individual Differences, 50(5)*, 603–608.

Gini, M., Oppenheim, D., & Sagi-Schwartz, A. (2007). Negotiation styles in mother-child narrative co-construction in middle childhood: Associations with early attachment. *International Journal of Behavioral Development, 31*, 149–160.

Ginzburg, H. M., & Bateman, D. J. (2008). New Orleans medical students post-Katrina—An assessment of psychopathology and anticipatory transference of resilience. *Psychiatric Annals, 38*, 145–156.

Girardi, P., Monaco, E., Prestigiacomo, C., Talamo, A., Ruberto, A., & Tatarelli, R. (2007). Personality and psychopathological profiles in individuals exposed to mobbing. *Violence & Victims, 22*, 172–188.

Giumetti, G. W., & Markey, P. M. (2007). Violent video games and anger as predictors of aggression. *Journal of Research in Personality, 41*, 1234–1243.

Gleason, M., Egger, H., Emslie, G., Greenhill, L., Kowatch, R., Lieberman, A., Luby,

J., Owens, J., Scahill, L., Scheeringa, M., Stafford, B., Wise, B., & Zeanan, C. (2007). Pharmacological treatment for very young children: Contexts and guidelines. *Journal of the American Academy of Child & Adolescent Psychiatry*. 46(12), 1532–1572.

Glenberg, A. (2010). Embodiment as a unifying perspective for psychology. *Wiley Interdisciplinary Reviews: Cognitive Science, 1,* 586–596.

Glenn, A. L., Kurzban, R., & Raine, A. (2011). Evolutionary theory and psychopathy. *Aggression and Violent Behavior.* Advance online publication. doi: 10.1016/j.avb.2011.03.009

Glicksohn, A., & Cohen, A. (2011). The role of Gestalt grouping principles in visual statistical learning. *Attention, Perception, & Psychophysics, 73(3),* 708–713.

Glover, V. (2011). Annual research review: Prenatal stress and the origins of psychopathology: An evolutionary perspective. *Journal of Child Psychology and Psychiatry, 52(4),* 356–367.

Godden, D. R., & Baddeley, A. D. (1975). Context-dependent memory in two natural environments: On land and underwater. *British Journal of Psychology, 66,* 325–331.

Goldberg, B., Frank, V., Bekenstein, S., Garrity, P., & Ruiz, J. (2011). Successful community engagement: Laying the foundation for effective teen pregnancy prevention. *Journal of Children and Poverty, 17(1),* 65–86.

Goldberg, M. (2009). *Avatar review.* Retrieved from http://collider.com/avatar-review/12806/

Golden, W. L. (2006). Hypnotherapy for anxiety, phobias and psychophysiological disorders. In R. A. Chapman (Ed.), *The clinical use of hypnosis in cognitive behavior therapy: A practitioner's casebook* (pp. 101–137). New York, NY: Springer.

Goldschmidt, L., Richardson, G. A., Willford, J., & Day, N. L. (2008). Prenatal marijuana exposure and intelligence test performance at age 6. *Journal of the American Academy of Child & Adolescent Psychiatry, 47,* 254–263.

Goldstein, E. G. (2011). *Cognitive psychology: Connecting mind, research, and everyday experience* (3rd ed.). Belmont, CA: Cengage.

Goldstein, I. (2010). Looking at sexual behavior 60 years after Kinsey. *Journal of Sexual Medicine, 7(Suppl 5),* 246–247.

Goldstein, M., (2011). Adolescent Pregnancy. In M. Golstein (Ed.), *The MassGeneral Hospital for Children Adolescent Handbook* (pp. 111–133). New York, NY: Springer.

Goleman, D. (1980, February). 1,528 little geniuses and how they grew. *Psychology Today,* 28–53.

Goleman, D. (1995). *Emotional intelligence: Why it can matter more than IQ.* New York, NY: Bantam.

Goleman, D. (2000). *Working with emotional intelligence.* New York, NY: Bantam Doubleday.

Goleman, D. (2008). Leading resonant teams. In F. Hesselbein & A. Shrader (Eds.), *Leader to leader 2: Enduring insights on leadership from the Leader to Leader Institute's award-winning journal* (pp. 186–195). Leader to Leader Institute. San Francisco, CA: Jossey-Bass.

Gollan, T. H., & Acenas, L. R. (2004). What Is a TOT? Cognate and translation effects on tip-of-the-tongue states in Spanish-English and Tagalog-English bilinguals. *Journal of Experimental Psychology: Learning, Memory, & Cognition, 30(1),* 246–269.

Gómez, Á., & Huici, C. (2008). Vicarious intergroup contact and role of authorities in prejudice reduction. *The Spanish Journal of Psychology, 11,* 103–114.

Gómez-Laplaza, L. M., & Gerlai, R. (2010). Latent learning in zebrafish (Danio rerio). *Behavioural Brain Research, 208(2),* 509–515.

Gonzaga, G. C., Carter, S., & Buckwalter, J. (2010). Assortative mating, convergence, and satisfaction in married couples. *Personal Relationships, 17(4),* 634–644.

Goodall, C. E., & Slater, M. D. (2010). Automatically activated attitudes as mechanisms for message effects: The case of alcohol advertisements. *Communication Research, 37(5),* 620–643.

Goodall, J. (1990). *Through a window: My thirty years with the chimpanzees of Gombe.* Boston, MA: Houghton-Mifflin.

Goodman, G. S., Ghetti, S., Quas, J. A., Edelstein, R. S., Alexander, K. W., Redlich, A. D., Cordon, I. M., & Jones, D. P. H. (2003). A prospective study of memory for child sexual abuse: New findings relevant to the repressedmemory controversy. *Psychological Science, 14(2),* 113–118.

Goodman, M., & Yehuda, R. (2002). The relationship between psychological trauma and borderline personality disorder. *Psychiatric Annals, 32(6),* 337–345.

Goodwin, C. J. (2011). *A history of modern psychology* (4th ed.). Hoboken, NJ: Wiley.

Gordis, E. B., Margolin, G., & Vickerman, K. (2005). Communication and frightening behavior among couples with past and recent histories of physical marital aggression. *American Journal of Community Psychology, 36,* 177–191.

Gorelik, G., Shackelford, T. K., & Salmon, C. A. (2010). New horizons in the evolutionary science of the human family. *Review of General Psychology, 14(4),* 330–339.

Gorlick, A. (2009). Study finds people who multitask often bad at it. *PhysOrg.com.* Retrieved from http://www.physorg.com/news170349575.html

Gosch, E. A., Findiesen, A. G., & DiTomasso, R. A. (2010). Behavioral strategies. In R. A. DiTomasso, B. A. Golden, & H. Morris (Eds.), *Handbook of cognitive behavioral approaches in primary care* (pp. 247–264). New York, NY: Springer.

Gosling, S. D. (2008). Personality in nonhuman animals. *Social and Personality Compass, 2,* 985–1001.

Gosling, S. D., & John, O. P. (1999). Personality dimensions in nonhuman animals: A cross-species review. *Current Directions in Psychological Science, 8,* 69–75.

Gosling, S. D., Kwan, V. S. Y., & John, O. P. (2004). A dog's got personality: A cross-species comparative approach to personality judgments in dogs and humans. *Journal of Personality and Social Psychology, 85,* 1161–1169.

Gottesman, I. I. (1991). *Schizophrenia genesis: The origins of madness.* New York, NY: Freeman.

Gottesman, I. I., & Hanson, D. R. (2005). Human development: Biological and genetic processes. *Annual Review of Psychology, 56,* 263–286.

Gottfredson, G. D., & Duffy, R. D. (2008). Using a theory of vocational personalities and work environments to explore subjective well-being. *Journal of Career Assessment, 16,* 44–59.

Gottman, J. M. (2011). *The science of trust: Emotional attunement for couples.* New York, NY: W W Norton & Co.

Gottman, J. M., & Levenson, R. W. (2002). A two-factor model for predicting when a couple will divorce: Exploratory analyses using 14-year longitudinal data. *Family Process, 41(1),* 83–96.

Gottman, J. M., & Notarius, C. I. (2000). Decade review: Observing marital interaction. *Journal of Marriage & the Family, 62(4),* 927–947.

Gottman, J. M., Coan, J., Carrere, S., & Swanson, C. (1998). Predicting happiness and stability from newlywed interactions. *Journal of Marriage and the Family, 60,* 42–48.

Gracely, E. J. (1998). Why extraordinary claims demand extraordinary proof. *Quackwatch*. Retrieved from http://www.quackwatch.org/01QuackeryRelatedTopics/extraproof.html

Gracely, R. H., Farrell, M. J., & Grant, M. A. (2002). Temperature and pain perception. In H. Pashler & S. Yantis (Eds.), *Steven's handbook of experimental psychology: Vol. 1. Sensation and perception* (3rd ed.) (pp. 619–651). Hoboken, NJ: Wiley.

Gradinger, F., Cieza, A., Stucki, A., Michel, F., Bentley, A., Oksenberg, A., Rogers, A., Stucki, G., & Partinen, M. (2011). Part 1. International Classification of Functioning, Disability and Health (ICF) Core Sets for persons with sleep disorders: Results of the consensus process integrating evidence from preparatory studies. *Sleep Medicine, 12(1),* 92–96.

Graham-Bermann, S. A., & Levendosky, A. A. (2011). *How intimate partner violence affects children: Developmental research, case studies, and evidence-based intervention.* Washington, DC: American Psychological Association.

Grant, A. M., & Berry, J. W. (2011). The necessity of others is the mother of invention: Intrinsic and prosocial motivations, perspective taking, and creativity. *Academy of Management Journal, 54(1),* 73–96.

Grant, J. A., Courtemanche, J., & Rainville, P. (2011). A non-elaborative mental stance and decoupling of executive and pain-related cortices predicts low pain sensitivity in Zen meditators. *Pain, 152(1),* 150–156.

Grant, S., et al. (1996). Activation of memory circuits during the cue-elicited cocaine craving. *Proceedings of the National Academy of Sciences, 93,* 12–40.

Gratz, K. L., Latzman, R. D., Tull, M. T., Reynolds, E. K., & Lejuez, C.W. (2011). Exploring the association between emotional abuse and childhood borderline personality features: The moderating role of personality traits. *Behavior Therapy.* Advance online publication. doi:10.1016/j.beth.2010.11.003

Gray, J. D., & Silver, R. C. (1990). Opposite sides of the same coin: Former spouses' divergent perspectives in coping with their divorce. *Journal of Personality & Social Psychology, 59,* 1180–1191.

Gray-Stanley, J. A., & Muramatsu, N. (2011). Work stress, burnout, and social and personal resources among direct care workers. *Research in Developmental Disabilities, 32(3),* 1065–1074.

Green, A. J., & De-Vries, K. (2010). Cannabis use in palliative care—An examination of the evidence and the implications for nurses. *Journal of Clinical Nursing, 19(17–18),* 2454–2462.

Green, C. D. (2009). Darwinian theory, functionalism, and the first American psychological revolution. *American Psychologist, 64(2),* 75–83.

Green, J. P., & Lynn, S. J. (2011). Hypnotic responsiveness: Expectancy, attitudes, fantasy proneness, absorption, and gender. *International Journal of Clinical and Experimental Hypnosis, 59(1),* 103–121.

Greenberg, D. L. (2004). President Bush's false "flashbulb" memory of 9/11/01. *Applied Cognitive Psychology, 18(3),* 363–370.

Greenberg, J. (2002). Who stole the money, and when? Individual and situational determinants of employee theft. *Organizational Behavior and Human Decision Processes, 89(1),* 985–1003.

Greenberg, J., Pyszczynski, T., Solomon, S., Pinel, E., Simon, L., & Jordon, K. (1993). Effects of self-esteem on vulnerability- denying defensive distortions: Further evidence of an anxiety-buffering function of self-esteem. *Journal of Experimental Social Psychology, 29(3),* 229–251.

Greene, E., & Ellis, L. (2008). *Decision making in criminal justice.* In D. Carson, R. Milne, F. Pakes, K. Shalev, & A. Shawyer (Eds.), *Applying psychology to criminal justice* (pp. 183–200). New York, NY: Wiley.

Greenfield, P. M. (1994). *Cross-cultural roots of minority child development.* Hillsdale, NJ: Erlbaum.

Greenfield, P. M. (1997). You can't take it with you: Why ability assessments don't cross cultures. *American Psychologist, 52,* 1115–1124.

Greenfield, P. M. (2004). *Weaving generations together: Evolving creativity in the Maya of Chiapas.* Santa Fe, NM: School of American Research Press.

Greenlees, M. J., Phillips, B. L., & Shine, R. (2010). Adjusting to a toxic invader: Native Australian frogs learn not to prey on cane toads. *Behavioral Ecology, 21(5),* 966–971.

Greenwald, A. G., Banaji, M. R., Rudman, L. A., Farnham, S. D., Nosek, B. A., & Mellott, D. S. (2002). A unified theory of implicit attitudes, stereotypes, self-esteem, and self-concept. *Psychological Review, 109,* 3–25.

Greenwald, A. G., McGhee, D. E., & Schwartz, J. L. K. (1998). Measuring individual differences in implicit cognition: The implicit association test. *Journal of Personality and Social Psychology, 74,* 1464–1480.

Greenwald, A. G., Poehlman, T. A., Uhlmann, E., Banaji, M. R. (2009). Understanding and using the Implicit Association Test III: Meta-analysis of predictive validity. *Journal of Personality and Social Psychology, 97(1),* 17–41.

Gregersen, E. (1996). *The world of human sexuality: Behaviors, customs, and beliefs.* New York, NY: Irvington.

Gregory, R. J. (2007). *Psychological testing: History, principles, and applications (5th ed.).* Needham Heights, MA: Allyn and Bacon.

Gregory, R. J. (2011). *Psychological testing: History, principles, and applications* (6th ed.). Boston, MA: Allyn & Bacon.

Griffin, A. S., & Galef, Jr., B. G. (2005). Social learning about predators: Does timing matter? *Animal Behavior, 69,* 669–678.

Grigorenko, E. L., Jarvin, L., & Sternberg, R. J. (2002). School-based tests of the triarchic theory of intelligence: Three settings, three samples, three syllabi. *Contemporary Educational Psychology, 27(2),* 167–208.

Gringart, E., Helmes, E., & Speelman, C. (2008). Harnessing cognitive dissonance to promote positive attitudes toward older workers in Australia. *Journal of Applied Social Psychology, 38,* 751–778.

Grondin, S., Ouellet, B., & Roussel, M. (2004). Benefits and limits of explicit counting for discriminating temporal intervals. *Canadian Journal of Experimental Psychology, 58(1),* 1–12.

Gross, D., & Schäfer, G. (2011). Egas Moniz (1874–1955) and the "invention" of modern psychosurgery: A historical and ethical reanalysis under special consideration of Portuguese original sources. *Journal of Neurosurgery, 30(2),* 1–7.

Grossman, P., Niemann, L., Schmidt, S., & Walach, H. (2004). Mindfulness-based stress reduction and health benefits. A meta-analysis. *Journal of Psychosomatic Research, 57,* 35–43.

Grossmann, K., Grossmann, K. E., Fremmer- Bombik, E., Kindler, H., Scheuerer-Englisch, H., & Zimmermann, P. (2002). The uniqueness of the child-father attachment relationship: Fathers' sensitive and challenging play as a pivotal variable in a 16-year longitudinal study. *Social Development, 11(3),* 307–331.

Grover, K. E., Carpenter, L. L., Price, L. H., Gagne, G. G., Mello, A. F., Mello, M. F., & Tyra, A. R. (2007). The relationship between childhood abuse and adult personality disorder symptoms. *Journal of Personality Disorders, 21,* 442–447.

Gruber, S. A., Silveri, M. M., Dahlgren, M. K., & Yurgelun-Todd, D. (2011). Why so impulsive? White matter alterations are associated with impulsivity in chronic marijuana smokers. *Experimental and Clinical Psychopharmacology.* Retrieved from http://www.ncbi.nlm.nih.gov/pubmed/21480730

Grubin, D. (2010). The polygraph and forensic psychiatry. *Journal of the American Academy of Psychiatry and the Law, 38(4),* 446–451.

Guadagno, R. E., Muscanell, N. L., Okdie, B. M., Burk, N. M., & Ward, T. B. (2011). Even in virtual environments women shop and men build: A social role perspective on Second Life. *Computers in Human Behavior, 27(1),* 304–308.

Guastello, S. J., Guastello, D. D., & Craft, L. L. (1989). Assessment of the Barnum effect in computer-based test interpretations. *Journal of Psychology, 123,* 477–484.

Gudelsky, G. A., & Yamamoto, B. K. (2008). Actions of 3,4-methylenedioxymethamphetamine (MDMA) on cerebral dopaminergic, serotonergic and cholinergic neurons. *Pharmacology, Biochemistry and Behavior, 90,* 198–207.

Guidelines for Ethical Conduct in the Care and Use of Animals. (2008). Retrieved from http://www.apa.org/science/anguide.html. Guidelines for the treatment of animals in behavioural research and teaching. (2005). *Animal Behaviour, 69(1),* i–vi.

Guilford, J. P. (1967). *The nature of human intelligence.* New York, NY: McGraw-Hill.

Guillery, R. W., & Sherman, S. M. (2011). Branched thalamic afferents: What are the messages that they relay to the cortex? *Brain Research Reviews, 66(1–2),* 205–219.

Gunderman, R., & Kamer, A. (2011). Rewards. *Journal of the American College of Radiology, 8(5),* 341–344.

Gunderson, J. G. (2011). Borderline personality disorder. *The New England Journal of Medicine, 364(21),* 2037–2042.

Gunnar, M. R. (2010). A commentary on deprivation-specific psychological patterns: Effects of institutional deprivation. *Monographs of the Society for Research in Child Development, 75(1),* 232–247.

Gurman, A. S., & Snyder, D. K. (2011). Couple therapy. In J. C. Norcross, G. R. VandenBos, & D. K. Freedheim (Eds.), *History of psychotherapy: Continuity and change* (2nd ed.) (pp. 485–496). Washington, DC: American Psychological Association.

Gurung, R. A. R. (2010). *Health psychology: A cultural approach* (2nd ed.). Belmont, CA: Wadsworth/Cengage Learning.

Gustafsson, P. E., Anckarsäter, H., Lichtenstein, P., Nelson, N., & Gustafsson, P. A. (2010). Does quantity have a quality all its own? Cumulative adversity and up- and down-regulation of circadian salivary cortisol levels in healthy children. *Psychoneuroendocrinology, 35(9),* 1410–1415.

Gustavson, C. R., & Garcia, J. (1974, August). Pulling a gag on the wily coyote. *Psychology Today,* 68–72.

Gutiérrez-Rojas, L., Jurado, D., & Gurpegui, M. (2011). Factors associated with work, social life and family life disability in bipolar disorder patients. *Psychiatry Research, 186(2–3),* 254–260.

Guzzetta, A., Baldini, S., Bancale, A., Baroncelli, L., Ciucci, F., Ghirri, P., Putignano, E., Sale, A., Viegi, A., Berardi, N., Boldrini, A., Cioni, G., & Maffei, L. (2009). Massage accelerates brain development and the maturation of visual function. *The Journal of Neuroscience, 29(18),* 6042–6051.

Haab, L., Trenado, C., Mariam, M., & Strauss, D. J. (2011). Neurofunctional model of large-scale correlates of selective attention governed by stimulus-novelty. *Cognitive Neurodynamics, 5(1),* 103–111.

Haberstick, B. C., Schmitz, S. Young, S. E., & Hewitt, J. K. (2006). Genes and developmental stability of aggressive behavior problems at home and school in a community sample of twins aged 7–12. *Behavior Genetics, 36,* 809–819.

Haddock, G., & Shaw, J. J. (2008). Understanding and working with aggression, violence, and psychosis. In K. T. Mueser & D. V. Jeste (Eds.), *Clinical handbook of schizophrenia* (pp. 398–410). New York, NY: Guilford Press.

Hadley, D., Anderson, B. S., Borckardt, J. J., Arana, A., Li, X., Nahas, Z., & George, M. S. (2011). Safety, tolerability, and effectiveness of high doses of adjunctive daily left prefrontal repetitive transcranial magnetic stimulation for treatment-resistant depression in a clinical setting. *The Journal of ECT, 27(1),* 18–25.

Haeffel, G. J., & Vargas, I. (2011). Resilience to depressive symptoms: The buffering effects of enhancing cognitive style and positive life events. *Journal of Behavior Therapy and Experimental Psychiatry, 42(1),* 13–18.

Haier, R. J., Chueh, D., Touchette, P., Lott, I., Buchsbaum, M. S., MacMillan, D., Sandman, C., LaCasse, L., & Sosa, E. (1995). Brain size and cerebral glucose metabolic rate in nonspecific mental retardation and Down Syndrome. *Intelligence, 20,* 191–210.

Haig, D. (2011). Sympathy with Adam Smith and reflexions on self. *Journal of Economic Behavior & Organization, 77(1),* 4–13.

Haines, R., & Mann, J. (2011). A new perspective on de-individuation via computer-mediated communication. *European Journal of Information Systems, 20,* 156–167.

Hakvoort, E. M., Bos, H. M. W., Van Balen, F., & Hermanns, J. M. A. (2011). Postdivorce relationships in families and children's psychosocial adjustment. *Journal of Divorce & Remarriage, 52(2),* 125–146.

Halgin, R. P., & Whitbourne, S. K. (2008). *Abnormal psychology: Clinical perspectives on psychological disorders.* New York, NY: McGraw-Hill.

Hall, C. (1953). *The meaning of dreams.* New York, NY: Harper and Brothers.

Hall, C. S., & Van de Castle, R. L. (1996). *The content analysis of dreams.* New York, NY: Appleton-Century-Crofts.

Hall, P. A., Schaeff, C. M. (2008). Sexual orientation and fluctuating asymmetry in men and women. *Archives of Sexual Behavior, 37,* 158–165.

Hall, S., & Adams, R. (2011). Newlyweds' unexpected adjustments to marriage. *Family and Consumer Sciences Research Journal, 39(4),* 375–387.

Hall, W., & Degenhardt, L. (2010). "Adverse health effects of non-medical cannabis use"—Authors' reply. *The Lancet, 375(9710),* 197.

Hamacheck, D. (1978). Psychodynamics of normal and neurotic perfectionism. *Psychology: A Journal of Human Behavior, 15,* 27–33.

Hamaideh, S. H. (2011). Burnout, social support, and job satisfaction among Jordanian mental health nurses. *Issues in Mental Health Nursing, 32(4),* 234–242.

Hamilton, J. P., & Gotlib, I. H. (2008). Neural substrates of increased memory sensitivity for negative stimui in major depression. *Biological Psychiatry, 63,* 1155–1162.

Hammack, P. L. (2003). The question of cognitive therapy in a postmodern world. *Ethical Human Sciences & Services, 5(3),* 209–224.

Hammond, D. C. (2005). Neurofeedback with anxiety and affective disorders. *Child & Adolescent Psychiatric Clinics of North America, 14(1),* 105–123.

Hammond, D. C. (2007). What is neurofeedback? *Journal of Neurotherapy, 10,* 25–36.

Hammond, J. L., & Hall, S. S. (2011). Functional analysis and treatment of aggressive behavior following resection of a craniopharyngioma. *Developmental Medicine & Child Neurology, 53*(4), 369–374.

Hampton, T. (2006). Stem cells probed as diabetes treatment. *Journal of American Medical Association, 296*, 2785–2786.

Hampton, T. (2007). Stem cells ease Parkinson symptoms in monkeys. *Journal of American Medical Association, 298*, 165.

Han, S., Mao, L., Qin, J., Friederici, A. D., & Ge, J. (2011). Functional roles and cultural modulations of the medial prefrontal and parietal activity associated with causal attribution. *Neuropsychologia, 49*(1), 83–91.

Handler, M., Honts, C. R., Krapohl, D. J., Nelson, R., & Griffin, S. (2009). Integration of pre-employment polygraph screening into the police selection process. *Journal of Police and Criminal Psychology, 24*(2), 69–86

Haney, C., Banks, C., & Zimbardo, P. (1978). Interpersonal dynamics in a simulated prison. *International Journal of Criminology and Penology, 1*, 69–97.

Hanley, S. J., & Abell, S. C. (2002). Maslow and relatedness: Creating an interpersonal model of self-actualization. *Journal of Humanistic Psychology, 42*(4), 37–56.

Hannan, J. L., Blaser, M. C., Pang, J. J., Adams, S. M., Pang, S. C., & Adams, M. A. (2011). Impact of hypertension, aging, and antihypertensive treatment on the morphology of the pudendal artery. *Journal of Sexual Medicine, 8*(4), 1027–1038.

Hansell, J. H., & Damour, L. K. (2008). *Abnormal psychology* (2nd ed.). Hoboken, NJ: Wiley.

Harasty, J., Double, K. L., Halliday, G. M., Kril, J. J., & McRitchie, D. A. (1997). Language-associated cortical regions are proportionally larger in the female brain. *Archives in Neurology, 54 (2)*, 171–176.

Harati, H., Majchrzak, M., Cosquer, B., Galani, R., Kelche, C., Cassel, J.-C., & Barbelivien, A. (2011). Attention and memory in aged rats: Impact of lifelong environmental enrichment. *Neurobiology of Aging, 32*(4), 718–736.

Hardcastle, S., Taylor, A., Bailey, M., & Castle, R. (2008). A randomized controlled trial on the effectiveness of a primary health care based counseling intervention on physical activity, diet and CHD risk. *Patient Education and Counseling, 70*, 31–39.

Hardies, K. (2011). The never-ending story of "hardwired" gender differences. *Sex Roles.* Retrieved from http://www.springerlink.com/content/tp7402v74375k3m3/

Hardy, G., Barkham, M., Shapiro, D., Guthrie, E., & Margison, F. (Eds.). (2011).

Psychodynamic-interpersonal therapy. Thousand Oaks, CA: Sage.

Hardy, J. B., & Zabin, L. S. (1991). *Adolescent pregnancy in an urban environment: Issues, programs, and evaluation.* Baltimore: Urban and Schwarzenberg.

Harkness, S., Super, C. M., Sutherland, M. A., Blom, M. J. M., Moscardino, U., Mavbdis, C. J., & Axia, G. (2007). Culture and the construction of habits in daily life: Implications for the successful development of children with disabilities. *OTJR: Occupation, Participation and Health, 27*, 33S-40S.

Harlow, H. F., & Harlow, M. K. (1966). Learning to love. *American Scientist, 54*, 244–272.

Harlow, H. F., & Zimmerman, R. R. (1959). Affectional responses in the infant monkey. Science, 130, 421–432.

Harlow, H. F., Harlow, M. K., & Meyer, D. R. (1950). Learning motivated by a manipulation drive. *Journal of Experimental Psychology, 40*, 228–234.

Harlow, J. (1868). Recovery from the passage of an iron bar through the head. *Publications of the Massachusetts Medical Society, 2*, 237–246.

Harris, J. A. (2011). The acquisition of conditioned responding. *Journal of Experimental Psychology: Animal Behavior Processes, 37*(2), 151–164.

Harrison, E. (2005). *How meditation heals: Scientific evidence and practical applications* (2nd ed.). Berkeley, CA: Ulysses Press.

Harth, N. S., Kessler, T., & Leach, C. W. (2008). Advantaged group's emotional reactions to intergroup inequality. The dynamics of pride, guilt, and sympathy. *Personality and Social Psychology Bulletin, 34*, 115–129.

Hartwell, L. (2008). *Genetics* (3ed ed.). New York, NY: McGraw-Hill.

Harvard Family Health Guide. (2008, May). *Treating preschoolers with psychiatric disorders.* Cambridge, MA. Retrieved from http://www.health.harvard.edu/fhg/updates/Treating-preschoolers-with-psychiatric-disorders.shtml

Harwood, T., Beutler, L, & Groth-Marnat, G. (2011). *Integrative assessment of adult personality* (3rd ed.). New York, NY: Guilford Press.

Haslam, N., Loughnan, S., Reynolds, C., & Wilson, S. (2007). Dehumanization: A new perspective. *Social and Personality Psychology Compass, 1*, 409–422.

Hatfield, E., & Rapson, R. L. (1996). *Love and Sex: Cross-cultural perspectives.* Needham Heights, MA: Allyn & Bacon.

Hatfield, E. & Rapson, R. L. (2005). *Love and sex: Cross-cultural perspectives.* Lanham, MA: University Press of America.

Hatsukami, D. K. (2008). Nicotine addiction: Past, present and future. *Drug and Alcohol Dependence, 92*, 312–316.

Havas, D. A., Glenberg, A. M., Gutowski, K. A., Lucarelli, M. J., & Davidson, R. J. (2010). Cosmetic use of botulinum toxin-A affects processing of emotional language. *Psychological Science, 21*(7), 895–900.

Hawes, D. R. (2010). Not so fast with psychic-phenomena research! *Psychology Today Blogs.* Retrieved from http://www.psychologytoday.com/blog/evolved-primate/201010/not-so-fast-psychic-phenomena-research

Hay, D. F. (1994). Prosocial development. *Journal of Child Psychology and Psychiatry, 35*, 29–71.

Hay, D., Nash, A., Caplan, M., Swartzentruber, J., Ishikawa, F., & Vespo, J. (2011). The emergence of gender differences in physical aggression in the context of conflict between young peers. *British Journal of Developmental Psychology, 29*(2), 158–175.

Hayes, R. D. (2011). Circular and linear modeling of female sexual desire and arousal. *Journal of Sex Research, 48(2–3)*, 130–141.

Hayflick, L. (1977). The cellular basis for biological aging. In C. E. Finch & L. Hayflick (Eds.), *Handbook of the biology of aging* (pp. 159–186). New York, NY: Van Nostrand Reinhold.

Hayflick, L. (1996). *How and why we age.* New York, NY: Ballantine Books.

Haynes Stewart, T., Clifton, R., Daniels, L., Perry, R., Chipperfield, J., & Ruthing, J. (2011). Attribution retrainings: Reducing the likelihood of failure. *Social Psychology of Education, 14*, 75–92.

Haynes, S., O'Brien, W., & Kaholokula, J. (2011). *Behavioral assessment and case formulation.* Hoboken, NJ: Wiley.

Hazan, C., & Shaver, P. (1987). Romantic love conceptualized as an attachment process. *Journal of Personality and Social Psychology, 52*, 511–524.

Hazan, C., & Shaver, P. R. (1994). Attachment as an organizational framework for research on close relationships. *Psychological Inquiry, 5*, 1–22.

Hazler, R. J. (2011). Person-centered theory. In D. Capuzzi & D. R. Gross (Eds.), *Counseling and psychotherapy* (5th ed.) (pp. 143–166). Alexandria, VA: American Counseling Association.

Healy, A. F., & McNamara, D. S. (1996). Verbal learning and memory: Does the modal model still work? *Annual Review of Psychology, 47,* 143–172.

Healy, A. F., Shea, K. M., Kole, J. A., & Cunningham, T. F. (2008). Position distinctiveness, item familiarity, and presentation frequency affect reconstruction of order in immediate episodic memory. *Journal of Memory and Language, 58,* 746–764.

Heffner, J. L., Mingione, C., Blom, T. J., & Anthenelli, R. M. (2011). Smoking history, nicotine dependence, and changes in craving and mood during short-term smoking abstinence in alcohol dependent vs. control smokers. *Addictive Behaviors, 36(3),* 244–247.

Heider, F. (1958). *The psychology of interpersonal relations.* New York, NY: Wiley.

Heimann, M., & Meltzoff, A. N. (1996). Deferred imitation in 9–and 14-month-old infants. *British Journal of Developmental Psychology, 14,* 55–64.

Heine, S. J., & Renshaw, K. (2002). Interjudge agreement, self-enhancement, and liking: Cross-cultural divergences. *Personality & Social Psychology Bulletin, 28(5),* 578–587.

Heinrich, A., & Schneider, B. A. (2011). Elucidating the effects of ageing on remembering perceptually distorted word pairs. *The Quarterly Journal of Experimental Psychology, 64(1),* 186–205.

Heller, S. (2005). *Freud A to Z.* Hoboken, NJ: Wiley.

Helms, J. E., & Cook, D. A. (1999). *Using race and culture in counseling and psychotherapy: Theory and process.* Boston, MA: Allyn & Bacon.

Henderlong, J., & Lepper, M. R. (2002). The effects of praise on children's intrinsic motivation: A review and synthesis. *Psychological Bulletin, 128,* 774–795.

Henderson, J. A., & Anglin, J. M. (2003). Facial attractiveness predicts longevity. *Evolution and Human Behavior, 24,* 351–356.

Hennessy, M. B., Paik, K. D., Caraway, J. D., Schiml, P. A., & Deak, T. (2011). Proinflammatory activity and the sensitization of depressive-like behavior during maternal separation. *Behavioral Neuroscience, 125(3),* 426–433.

Henry J. Kaiser Family Foundation. (2003, June 10). *Impact of direct-to-consumer advertising on prescription drug spending.* Menlo Park, CA. Retrieved from http://www.kff.org/rxdrugs/6084-index.cfm

Herbert, J. D., & Forman, E. M. (2010). *Acceptance and mindfulness in cognitive behavior therapy: Understanding and applying the new therapies.* Hoboken, NJ: Wiley-Blackwell.

Herdt, G. H. (1981). *Guardians of the flutes: Idioms of masculinity.* New York, NY: McGraw-Hill.

Herek, G. (2000). The psychology of prejudice. *Current Directions in Psychological Science, 9,* 19–22.

Hergenhahn, B. R. (2009). *An introduction to the history of psychology* (6th ed.). Belmont, CA: Cengage.

Herman, B. H., & O'Brien, C. P. (1997). Clinical medications development for opiate addiction: Focus on nonopiods and opiod antagonists for the amelioration of opiate withdrawal symptoms and relapse prevention. *Seminars in Neuroscience, 9,* 158.

Herman, C. P., & Polivy, J. (2008). External cues in the control of food intake in humans: The sensory-normative distinction. *Physiology & Behavior, 94,* 722–728.

Herman, L. M., Richards, D. G., & Woltz, J. P. (1984). Comprehension of sentences by bottlenosed dolphins. *Cognition, 16,* 129–139.

Hermans, E. J., Ramsey, N. F., & van Honk, J. (2008). Exogenous testosterone enhances responsiveness to social threat in the neural circuitry of social aggression in humans. *Biological Psychiatry, 63(3),* 263–270.

Hernandez-Reif, M., Diego, M., & Field, T. (2007). Preterm infants show reduced stress behaviors and activity after 5 days of massage therapy. *Infant Behavior & Development, 30,* 557–561.

Hertzog, C., & Jopp, D. S. (2010). Resilience in the face of cognitive aging: Experience, adaptation, and compensation. In P. S. Fry & C. L. M. Keyes (Eds.), *New frontiers in resilient aging: Life-strengths and well-being in late life* (pp. 130–161). New York, NY: Cambridge University Press

Hetherington, E. M. (2006). The influence of conflict, marital problem solving, and parenting on children's adjustment in nondivorced, divorced, and remarried families. In A. Clarke-Stewart & J. Dunn (Eds), *Families count.* New York, NY: Cambridge University Press.

Hettich, E. L., & O'Leary, K. D. (2007). Females' reasons for their physical aggression in dating relationships. *Journal of Interpersonal Violence, 22,* 1131–1143.

Heutink, M., Post, M. W. M., Wollaars, M. M., & van Asbeck, F. W. A. (2011). Chronic spinal cord injury pain: Pharmacological and non-pharmacological treatments and treatment effectiveness. *Disability and Rehabilitation: An International, Multidisciplinary Journal, 33(5),* 433–440.

Hewitt, J. K. (1997). The genetics of obesity: What have genetic studies told us about the environment? *Behavior Genetics, 27,* 353–358.

Hewitt, P. L., Newton, J., Flett, G. L., & Callander, L. (1997). Perfectionism and suicide ideation in adolescent psychiatric patients. *Journal of Abnormal Child Psychology, 25(2),* 95–107.

Heyder, K. Suchan, B., & Daum, I. (2004). Cortico-subcortical contributions to executive control. *Acta Psychologica, 115(2–3),* 271–289.

High cost of smoking. (2008). Retrieved from http://articles.moneycentral.msn.com/Insurance/InsureYourHealth/HighCostOfSmoking.aspx

Higham, P. A., Luna, K., & Bloomfield, J. (2011). Trace-strength and source-monitoring accounts of accuracy and metacognitive resolution in the misinformation paradigm. *Applied Cognitive Psychology, 25(2),* 324–335.

Higley, E. R. (2008). Nighttime interactions and mother-infant attachment at one year. *Dissertation Abstracts International: Section B: The Sciences and Engineering,. 68,* 2008, 5575.

Hilary, G., & Hsu, C. (2011). Endogenous overconfidence in managerial forecasts. *Journal of Accounting and Economics, 51(3),* 300–313.

Hilgard, E. R. (1978). Hypnosis and consciousness. *Human Nature, 1,* 42–51.

Hilgard, E. R. (1986). *Divided consciousness: Multiple controls in human thought and action* (expanded ed.). New York, NY: Wiley-Interscience.

Hilgard, E. R. (1992). Divided consciousness and dissociation. *Consciousness and Cognition, 1,* 16–31.

Hill, P. L., & Lapsley, D. K. (2011). Adaptive and maladaptive narcissism in adolescent development. In C. T. Barry, P. K. Kerig, K. K. Stellwagen, & T. D. Barry (Eds.), *Narcissism and Machiavellianism in youth: Implications for the development of adaptive and maladaptive behavior* (pp. 89–105). Washington, DC: American Psychological Association.

Hillier, S. M., & Barrow, G. M. (2011). *Aging, the individual, and society* (9th ed.). Belmont, CA: Cengage.

Hines, M. (2011). Gender development and the human brain. *Annual Review of Neuroscience, 34,* 69–88.

Hirshkowitz, M., Moore, C. A., & Minhoto, G. (1997). The basics of sleep. In M. R. Pressman & W. C. Orr (Eds.), *Understanding sleep: The evaluation and treatment of sleep disorders: Application and practice in health psychology* (pp. 11-34). Washington, DC: American Psychological Association.

Hobson, J. A. (1988). *The dreaming brain.* New York, NY: Basic Books.

Hobson, J. A. (1999). *Dreaming as delirium: How the brain goes out of its mind.* Cambridge, MA: MIT Press.

Hobson, J. A. (2002). *Dreaming: An introduction to the science of sleep*. New York, NY: Oxford University Press.

Hobson, J. A. (2005). In bed with Mark Solms? What a nightmare! A reply to Domhoff. *Dreaming, 15*(1), 21–29.

Hobson, J. A., & McCarley, R. W. (1977). The brain as a dream state generator: An activation-synthesis hypothesis of the dream process. *American Journal of Psychiatry, 134*, 1335–1348.

Hobson, J. A., & Silvestri, L. (1999). Parasomnias. *The Harvard Mental Health Letter, 15*(8), 3–5.

Hobson, J. A., Sangsanguan, S., Arantes, H., & Kahn, D. (2011). Dream logic—The inferential reasoning paradigm. *Dreaming, 21(1)*, 1–15.

Hocking, M. C., Barnes, M., Shaw, C., Lochman, J. E., Madan-Swain, A., & Saeed, S. (2011). Executive function and attention regulation as predictors of coping success in youth with functional abdominal pain. *Journal of Pediatric Psychology, 36(1)*, 64–73.

Hodges, S. D., & Biswas-Diener, R. (2007). Balancing the empathy expense account: Strategies for regulating empathic response. In T. Farrow & P. Woodruff (Eds.), *Empathy in mental illness* (pp. 389–407). New York: Cambridge University Press.

Hodson, G., & Costello, K. (2007). Interpersonal disgust, ideological orientations, and dehumanization as predictors of intergroup attitudes. *Psychological Science, 18*, 691–698.

Hodson, G., Rush, J., & MacInnis, C. C. (2010). A joke is just a joke (except when it isn't): Cavalier humor beliefs facilitate the expression of group dominance motives. *Journal of Personality and Social Psychology, 99*(4), 660–682.

Hoek, H. W., van Harten, P. N., Hermans, K. M. E., Katzman, M. A., Matroos, G. E., & Susser, E. S. (2005). The incidence of anorexia nervosa on Curacao. *American Journal of Psychiatry, 162*, 748–752.

Hofer, A., Siedentopf, C. M., Ischebeck, A., Rettenbacher, M. A., Verius, M., Golaszewski, S. M., Felber, S., & Fleischhacker, W. W. (2007). Neural substrates for episodic encoding and recognition of unfamiliar faces. *Brain and Cognition, 63*, 174–181.

Hofer, J., Busch, H., Bender, M., Ming, L., & Hagemeyer, B. (2010). Arousal of achievement motivation among student samples in three different cultural contexts: Self and social standards of evaluation. *Journal of Cross-Cultural Psychology, 41*(5–6), 758–775.

Hoff, E. (2009). *Language development* (4th ed.). Belmont, CA: Wadsworth.

Hoffman, M. L. (1993). Empathy, social cognition, and moral education. In A. Garrod (Ed.), *Approaches to moral development: New research and emerging themes*. New York, NY: Teachers College Press.

Hoffman, M. L. (2000). *Empathy and moral development: Implications for caring and justice*. New York, NY: Cambridge University Press.

Hoffman, M. L. (2007). The origins of empathic morality in toddlerhood. In C. A. Brownell & C. B. Kopp (Eds.), *Socioemotional development in the toddler years: Transitions and transformations* (pp. 132–145). New York, NY: Guilford Press.

Hofmann, S. (2011). *An introduction to modern CBT: Psychological solutions to mental health problems*. Hoboken, NJ: Wiley-Blackwell.

Hofmann, W., De Houwer, J., Perugini, M., Baeyens, F., & Crombez, G. (2010). Evaluative conditioning in humans: A meta-analysis. *Psychological Bulletin, 136(3)*, 390–421.

Holden, C. (1980). Identical twins reared apart. *Science, 207*, 1323–1325.

Holland, J. L. (1985). *Making vocational choices: A theory of vocational personalites and work environments* (2nd ed). Englewood Cliffs, NJ: Prentice Hall.

Holland, J. L. (1994). *Self-directed search form R*. Lutz, Fl: Psychological Assessment Resources.

Hollander, E., & Simeon, D. (2011). Anxiety disorders. In R. E. Hales, S. C. Yudofsky, & G. O. Gabbard (Eds.), *Essentials of psychiatry* (3rd ed.) (pp. 185–228). Arlington, VA: American Psychiatric Publishing.

Hollander, J., Renfrow, D., & Howard, J. (2011). *Gendered situations, gendered selves: A gender lens on social psychology* (2ⁿᵈ ed.). Lanham, MD: Rowman and Littlefield.

Hollon, S. D. (2011). Cognitive and behavior therapy in the treatment and prevention of depression. *Depression and Anxiety, 28*(4), 263–266.

Holt, N. L., & Dunn, J. G. H. (2004). Longitudinal idiographic analyses of appraisal and coping responses in sport. *Psychology of Sport & Exercise, 5*(2), 213–222.

Hölzel, B. K., Carmody, J., Vangel, M., Congleton, C., Yerramsetti, S. M., Gard, T., & Lazar, S. W. (2009). Mindfulness practice leads to increases in regional brain gray matter density. *Psychiatry Research: Neuroimaging, 191*(1), 36–43.

Honts, C. R., & Kircher, J. C. (1994). Mental and physical countermeasures reduce the accuracy of polygraph tests. *Journal of Applied Psychology, 79*(2), 252–259.

Hopfer, C. (2011). Club drug, prescription drug, and over-the-counter medication abuse: Description, diagnosis, and intervention. In Y. Kaminer & K. C. Winters (Eds.), *Clinical manual of adolescent substance abuse treatment* (pp. 187–212). Arlington, VA: American Psychiatric Publishing.

Hoppe, A. (2011). Psychosocial working conditions and well-being among immigrant and German low-wage workers. *Journal of Occupational Health Psychology, 16(2)*, 187–201.

Hopper, L. M., Flynn, E. G., Wood, L. A. N., & Whiten, A. (2010). Observational learning of tool use in children: Investigating cultural spread through diffusion chains and learning mechanisms through ghost displays. *Journal of Experimental Child Psychology, 106(1)*, 82–97.

Hopwood, C. J., Donnellan, M. B., Blonigen, D. M., Krueger, R. F., McGue, M., Iacono, W. G., & Burt, S. A. (2011). Genetic and environmental influences on personality trait stability and growth during the transition to adulthood: A three-wave longitudinal study. *Journal of Personality and Social Psychology, 100*(3), 545–556.

Horn, E., & Hoskins, W. (2011). Death education: An internationally relevant approach to grief counseling. *Journal for International Counselor Education, 3*(1), 25–38.

Horn, J. L. (1965). Fluid and crystallized intelligence: A factor analytic and developmental study of the structure among primary mental abilities. (*Unpublished doctoral dissertation*). University of Illinois, Champain, Illinois.

Horney, K. (1939). *New ways in psychoanalysis*. New York, NY: International Universities Press.

Horney, K. (1945). *Our inner conflicts: A constructive theory of neurosis*. New York, NY: Norton.

Horwath, E., & Gould, F. (2011). Epidemiology of anxiety disorders. In M. Tsuang, M. Tohen, & P. Jones (Eds.), *Textbook in Psychiatric Epidemiology*, (3rd ed.) (pp. 311–328). Hoboken, NJ: Wiley.

Hosie, P. J., Sevastos, P. P., & Cooper, Cary L. (2006). Happy-performing managers: The impact of affective wellbeing and intrinsic job satisfaction in the workplace. *New horizons in management*. Northampton, MA: Edward Elgar Publishing.

Hou, R., Mogg, K., Bradley, B. P., Moss-Morris, R., Peveler, R., & Roefs, A. (2011). External eating, impulsivity and attentional bias to food cues. *Appetite, 56*(2), 424–427.

Houck, J. A. (2007). A comparison on grief reactions in cancer, HIV/AIDS, and suicide bereavement. *Journal of HIV/AIDS & Social Services, 6*(3), 97–112.

Houlfort, N. (2006). The impact of performance-contingent rewards on perceived autonomy and intrinsic motivation. *Dissertation Abstracts International Section A: Humanities and Social Sciences, 67*(2–A), 460.

Houtz, J. C., Matos, H., Park, M-K. S., Scheinholtz, J., & Selby, E. (2007). Problem-solving style and motivational attributions. *Psychological Reports, 101,* 823–830.

Howarth, R. (2011). Concepts and controversies in grief and loss. *Journal of Mental Health Counseling, 33*(1), 4–10.

Howell, K. K., Coles, C. D., & Kable, J. A. (2008). The medical and developmental consequences of prenatal drug exposure. In J. Brick (Ed.), *Handbook of the medical consequences of alcohol and drug abuse* (2nd ed.) (pp. 219–249). *The Haworth Press series in neuropharmacology.* New York, NY: Haworth Press/Taylor and Francis Group.

Howland, J., Rohsenow, D. J., Calise, T. V., MacKillop, J., & Metrik, J. (2011). Caffeinated alcoholic beverages: An emerging public health problem. *American Journal of Preventive Medicine, 40*(2), 268–271.

Howland, R. H. (2010). Update on St. John's wort. *Journal of Psychosocial Nursing and Mental Health Services, 48*(11), 20–24.

Hsiu-Hui, C. (2007). *Work stress and death from overwork.* Retrieved from http://www.ceps.com.tw/ec/ecjnlarticleView.aspx.

Huang, L. N., & Ying, Y. (1989). Japanese children and adolescents. In J. T. Gibbs & Ln N. Huang (Eds.), *Children of color.* San Francisco: Jossey-Bass.

Huang, M., & Hauser, R. M. (1998). Trends in Black–White test-score differentials: II. The WORDSUM Vocabulary Test. In U. Neisser (Ed.), *The rising curve: Long-term gains in IQ and related measures* (pp. 303–334). Washington, DC: American Psychological Association.

Huas, C., Caille, A., Godart, N., Foulon, C., Pham, S. A., Divac, S., Dechartres, A., Lavoisy, G., Guelfi, J. D., Rouillon, F., & Falissard, B. (2011). Factors predictive of ten-year mortality in severe anorexia nervosa patients. *Acta Psychiatrica Scandinavica, 123*(1), 62–70.

Hubel, D. H., & Wiesel, T. N. (1965). Receptive fields and the functional architecture in two nonstriate visual areas (18 and 19) of the cat. *Journal of Neurophysiology, 28,* 229–289.

Hubel, D. H., & Wiesel, T. N. (1979). Brain mechanisms of vision. *Scientific American, 241,* 150–162.

Hudziak, J. J. (Ed.). (2008). *Developmental psychopathology and wellness: Genetic and environmental influences.* Arlington, VA: American Psychiatric Publishing.

Huesmann, L. R., & Kirwil, L. (2007). Why observing violence increases the risk of violent behavior by the observer. In D. J. Flannery, A. T. Vazsonyi, & I. D. Waldman (Eds.), *The Cambridge handbook of violent behavior and aggression* (pp. 545–570), New York, NY: Cambridge University Press.

Huesmann, L. R., Dubow, E. F., & Boxer, P. (2011). The transmission of aggressiveness across generations: Biological, contextual, and social learning processes. In P. R. Shaver & M. Mikulincer (Eds.), *Herzilya series on personality and social psychology. Human aggression and violence: Causes, manifestations, and consequences* (pp. 123–142). Washington, DC: American Psychological Association.

Huffman, A. H., Youngcourt, S. S., Payne, S. C., & Castro, C. A. (2008). The importance of construct breadth when examining interrole conflict. *Educational and Psychological Measurement, 68*(3), 515–530.

Huffman, C. J., Matthews, T. D., & Gagne, P. E. (2001). The role of part-set cuing in the recall of chess positions: Influence of chunking in memory. *North American Journal of Psychology, 3*(3), 535–542.

Hughes, B. M., Howard, S., James, J. E., & Higgins, N. M. (2011). Individual differences in adaptation of cardiovascular responses to stress. *Biological Psychology, 86*(2), 129–136.

Hughes, J. N., Cavell, T. A., & Grossman, P. B. (1997). A positive view of self: Risk or protection for aggressive children? *Development and Psychopathology, 9,* 75–94.

Huizinga, M., Burack, J. A., & Van der Molen, M. W. (2010). Age-related change in shifting attention between global and local levels of hierarchical Stimuli. *Journal of Cognition and Development, 11*(4), 408–436.

Hulette, A., Freyd, J., & Fisher, P. (2011). Dissociation in middle childhood among foster children with early maltreatment experiences. *Child Abuse & Neglect, 35,* 123–126.

Hull, C. (1952). *A behavior system.* New Haven, CT: Yale University Press.

Hull, E. M. (2011). Sex, drugs and gluttony: How the brain controls motivated behaviors. *Physiology & Behavior.* doi: 10.1016/j.physbeh.2011.04.057

Hunsley, J., & Lee, E. M. (2010). *Introduction to clinical psychology* (2nd ed.). Toronto, ON: Wiley.

Hunt, E. (2011). *Human intelligence.* New York, NY: Cambridge University Press.

Hurlemann, R., Matusch, A., Hawellek, B., Klingmuller, D., Kolsch, H., Maier, W., & Dolan, R. J. (2007). Emotion-induced retrograde amnesia varies as a function of noradrenergic-glucocorticord activity. *Psychopharmacology, 194,* 261–269.

Hurley, S. (2008). The shared circuits model (SCM): How control, mirroring, and simulation can enable imitation, and deliberation, and mindreading. *Behavioral and Brain Sciences, 31,* 1–22.

Hurt, H. (2008, February 9). Sending an SOS for a PC exorcist. *New York Times.* Retrieved from http://www.nytimes.com/2008/02/09/business/smallbusiness/09pursuits.html

Husain, M. M., & Lisanby, S. H. (2011). Repetitive transcranial magnetic stimulation (rTMS): A noninvasive neuromodulation probe and intervention. *The Journal of ECT, 27*(1), 2.

Hutchinson-Phillips, S., Gow, K., & Jamieson, G. A. (2007). Hypnotizability, eating behaviors, attitudes, and concerns: A literature survey. *International Journal of Clinical and Experimental Hypnosis, 55,* 84–113.

Hutchison, P., & Rosenthal, H. E. S. (2011). Prejudice against Muslims: Anxiety as a mediator between intergroup contact and attitudes, perceived group variability and behavioural intentions. *Ethnic and Racial Studies, 34*(1), 40–61.

Hutson, M. (2007). Neurorealism. *New York Times.* Retrieved from http://www.nytimes.com/2007/12/09/magazine/09neurorealism.html?_r=1&scp=1&sq=neurorealism%20hutson&st=cse&oref=slogin

Huurre, T., Junkkari, H., & Aro, H. (2006). Long-term psychosocial effects of parental divorce: A follow-up study from adolescence to adulthood. *European Archives of Psychiatry and Clinical Neuroscience, 256,* 256–263.

Hvas, L. (2001). Positive aspects of menopause: A qualitative study. *Maturitas, 39*(1), 11–17.

Hyde, J. S. (2005). The genetics of sexual orientation. In J. S. Hyde (Ed.), *Biological substrates of human sexuality* (pp. 9–20). Washington, DC: American Psychological Association.

Hyde, J. S. (2007). *Half the human experience: The psychology of women* (7th ed.). Boston, MA: Houghton Mifflin.

Hyde, J. S., & DeLamater, J. D. (2011). *Understanding human sexuality* (11th ed.). New York, NY: McGraw-Hill.

Hyman, R. (1981). Cold reading: How to convince strangers that you know all about them. In K. Fraizer (Ed.), *Paranormal borderlands of science* (pp. 232–244). Buffalo, NY: Prometheus.

Hyman, R. (1996). The evidence for psychic functioning: Claims vs. reality. *Skeptical Inquirer, 20,* 24–26.

Hyman, R. (2010). Meta-analysis that conceals more than it reveals: Comment on Storm et al. *Psychological Bulletin, 136(4)*, 486–490.

Hypericum Depression Trial Study Group. (2002). Effect of Hypericum performatum (St John's wort) in major depressive disorder: A randomized controlled trial. *JAMA: Journal of the American Medical Association, 287*(14), 1807–1814.

Iacono, W. G. (2008). Accuracy of polygraph techniques: Problems using confessions to determine ground truth. *Physiology & Behavior, 95(1–2)*, 24–26.

Iacono, W. G., & Lykken, D. T. (1997). The validity of the lie detector: Two surveys of scientific opinion. *Journal of Applied Psychology, 82*(3), 426–433.

Iaria, G., Fox, C. J., Scheel, M., Stowe, R. M., & Barton, J. J. S. (2010). A case of persistent visual hallucinations of faces following LSD abuse: A functional magnetic resonance imaging study. *Neurocase, 16(2)*, 106–118.

Iavarone, A., Patruno, M., Galeone, F., Chieffi, S., & Carlomagno, S. (2007). Brief report: Error pattern in an autistic savant calendar calculator. *Journal of Autism and Developmental Disorders, 37*, 775–779.

Ibiloglu, A. O., & Caykoylu, A. (2011). The comorbidity of anxiety disorders in bipolar I and bipolar II patients among Turkish population. *Journal of Anxiety Disorders, 25*(5), 661–667.

Ilg, R., Wohlschlager, A. M., Gaser, C., Liebau, Y., Dauner, R., Woller, A., Zimmer, C., Zihl, J., & Muhlau, M. (2008). Gray matter increase induced by practice correlates with task-specific activation: a combined functional and morphometric magnetic resonance Imaging study. *Journal of Neuroscience, 28*, 4210–4215.

Imada, T., & Ellsworth, P. C. (2011). Proud Americans and lucky Japanese: Cultural differences in appraisal and corresponding emotion. *Emotion, 11(2)*, 329–345.

Imada, T., & Kitayama, S. (2010). Social eyes and choice justification: Culture and dissonance revisited. *Social Cognition, 28*(5), 589–608.

Institute for Laboratory Animal Research (ILAR). (2009). *Home Page.* Retrieved from http://dels.nas.edu/ilar_n/ilarhome/

Inui, K., Urakawa, T., Yamashiro, K., Otsuru, N., Takeshima, Y., Nishihara, M., Motomura, E., Kida, T., & Kakigi, R. (2010). Echoic memory of a single pure tone indexed by change-related brain activity. *BMC Neuroscience, 11*, Article ID 135.

Irish, M., Lawlor, B. A., O'Mara, S. M., & Coen, R. F. (2011). Impaired capacity for autonoetic reliving during autobiographical event recall in mild Alzheimer's disease. *Cortex: A Journal Devoted to the Study of the Nervous System and Behavior, 47(2)*, 236–249.

Irwin, M. (2008). There's no good proof the real *Medium*, Allison DuBois, has ever cracked a case, but her fans don't care. *Phoenix New Times.* Retrieved from http://www.phoenixnewtimes.com/2008-06-12/news/there-s-no-good-proof-the-real-medium-allison-dubois-has-ever-cracked-a-case-but-her-fans-don-t-care/

Irwin, M., Mascovich, A., Gillin, J. C., Willoughby, R., Pike, J., & Smith, T. L. (1994). Partial sleep deprivation reduced natural killer cell activity in humans. *Psychosomatic Medicine, 56(6)*, 493–498.

Ivanovic, D. M., Leiva, B. P., Pérez, H. T., Olivares, M. G., Díaz, N. S., Urrutia, M. S. C., Almagià, A. F., Toro, T. D., Miller, P. T., Bosch, E. O., & Larraín, C. G. (2004). Head size and intelligence, learning, nutritional status and brain development: Head, IQ, learning, nutrition and brain. *Neuropsychologia, 42(8)*, 1118–1131.

Iversen, L. (2003). Cannabis and the brain. *Brain, 126(6)*, 1252–1270.

Iwata, Y., Suzuki, K., Takei, N., Toulopoulou, T., Tsuchiya, K. J., Matsumoto, K., Takagai, S., Oshiro, M., Nakamura, K., & Mori, N. (2011). Jiko-shisen-kyofu (fear of one's own glance), but not taijin-kyofusho (fear of interpersonal relations), is an east Asian culture-related specific syndrome. *Australian and New Zealand Journal of Psychiatry, 45(2)*, 148–152.

Jackendoff, R. (2003). Foundations of language, brain, meaning, grammar, evolution. *Applied Cognitive Psychology, 17(1)*, 121–122.

Jackson, L. M. (2011). Development of prejudice in children. In L. M. Jackson, *The psychology of prejudice: From attitudes to social action* (pp. 81–101). Washington, DC: American Psychological Association.

Jackson, L. M. (2011). *The psychology of prejudice: From attitudes to social action.* Washington, DC: American Psychological Association.

Jackson, M. & McKibben, B. (2009). *Distracted: The erosion of attention and the coming dark age.* Amherst, NY: Prometheus Books.

Jackson, P. B., & Williams, D. R. (2006). Culture, race/ethnicity, and depression. In C. L. M. Keyes & S. H. Goodman (Eds), *Women and depression: A handbook for the social, behavioral, and biomedical sciences* (pp. 328–359). New York, NY: Cambridge University Press.

Jacob, P. (2008). What do mirror neurons contribute to human social cognition? *Mind & Language, 23*, 190–223.

Jacobi, C., Hayward, C., de Zwaan, M., Kraemer, H. C., & Agras, W. S. (2004). Coming to terms with risk factors for eating disorders: Application of risk terminology and suggestions for a general taxonomy. *Psychological Bulletin, 130*(1), 19–65.

Jacquette, D. (Ed.). (2010). *Philosophy for everyone. Cannabis: What were we just talking about?* Hoboken, NJ: Wiley-Blackwell.

Jaeger, M. (2011). "A thing of beauty is a joy forever"? Returns to physical attractiveness over the life course. *Social Forces, 89(3)*, 983–1003.

Jaehne, E. J., Majumder, I., Salem, A., & Irvine, R. J. (2011). Increased effects of 3, 4-methylenedioxymethamphetamine (ecstasy) in a rat model of depression. *Addiction Biology, 16(1)*, 7–19.

Jaffe, S. L., & Kelly, J. F. (2011). Twelve-step mutual-help programs for adolescents. In Y. Kaminer & K. C. Winters (Eds.), *Clinical manual of adolescent substance abuse treatment* (pp. 269–282). Arlington, VA: American Psychiatric Publishing.

Jaffee, S., & Hyde, J. S. (2000). Gender differences in moral orientation: A meta-analysis. *Psychological Bulletin, 126*(5), 703–726.

Jain, G., Kumar, V., Chakrabarti, S., & Grover, S. (2008). The use of electroconvulsive therapy in the elderly: A study from the psychiatric unit of a North Indian teaching hospital. *Journal of ECT, 24*, 122–127.

James, S. D. (2008, May 7). Wild child speechless after tortured life. *ABC News.* Retrieved from http://abcnews.go.com/Health/story?id=4804490&page=1

James, S. D. (2010). Black Swan: Psychiatrists diagnose ballerina's descent. *Whas11. com.* Retrieved from http://www.whas11.com/home/BLACK-SWAN-Psychiatrists-Diagnose-Ballerinas-Descent-112189774.html

James, W. (1890). *The principles of psychology* (Vol. 2). New York, NY: Holt.

James, W. H. (2005). Biological and psychosocial determinants of male and female human sexual orientation. *Journal of Biosocial Science, 37,* 555–567.

Jamieson, G. A., & Hasegawa, H. (2007). *New paradigms of hypnosis research.* In G. A. Jamieson (Ed.), *Hypnosis and conscious states: The cognitive neuroscience perspective* (pp. 133–144). New York, NY: Oxford University Press.

Janis, I. L. (1972). *Victims of groupthink: A psychological study of foreign-policy decisions and fiascoes.* Boston, MA: Houghton Mifflin.

Janis, I. L. (1989). *Crucial decisions: Leadership in policymaking and crisis management.* New York, NY: Free Press.

Jankowiak, W. (1997). *Romantic passion: A universal experience.* New York, NY: Columbia University Press.

Jankowiak, W., & Fischer, E. (1992). Cross-cultural perspective on romantic love. *Ethnology, 31,* 149–155.

Jannini, E. A., Blanchard, R., Camperio-Ciani, A., & Bancroft, J. (2010). Male homosexuality: Nature or culture? *Journal of Sexual Medicine, 7*(10), 3245–3253.

Janssen, E. (2011). Sexual arousal in men: A review and conceptual analysis. *Hormones and Behavior, 59*(5), 708–716.

Jarvis, S. (2011). Conceptual transfer: Crosslinguistic effects in categorization and construal. *Bilingualism: Language and Cognition, 14*(1), 1–8.

Jeltsch, A., & Fischle, W. (2011). Editorial: Molecular epigenetics: Connecting human biology and disease with little marks. *ChemBioChem, 12*(2), 183–184.

Jensen, L. A. (2011). The cultural-developmental theory of moral psychology: A new synthesis. In L. A. Jensen (Ed.), *Bridging cultural and developmental approaches to psychology: New syntheses in theory, research, and policy* (pp. 3–25). New York, NY: Oxford University Press.

Jensen, M. P., Ehde, D. M., Gertz, K. J., Stoelb, B. L., Dillworth, T. M., Hirsh, A. T., Molton, I., & Kraft, G. H. (2011). Effects of self-hypnosis training and cognitive restructuring on daily pain intensity and catastrophizing in individuals with multiple sclerosis and chronic pain. *International Journal of Clinical and Experimental Hypnosis, 59*(1), 45–63.

Jensen, M. P., Hakimian, S., Sherlin, L. H., & Fregni, F. (2008). New insights into neuromodulatory approaches for the treatment of pain. *The Journal of Pain, 9,* 193–199.

Jinap, S., & Hajeb, P. (2010).Glutamate. Its applications in food and contribution to health. *Appetite, 55(1),* 1–10.

Jkiz, T. (2011). The history and development of the Rorschach test in Turkey. *Rorschachiana, 32*(1), 72–90.

Johnson, A. L. (2011). Psychoanalytic theory. In D. Capuzzi & D. R. Gross (Eds.), *Counseling and psychotherapy* (5th ed.) (pp. 59–76). Alexandria, VA: American Counseling Association.

Johnson, D. M., Delahanty, D. L., & Pinna, K. (2008). The cortisol awakening response as a function of PTSD severity and abuse chronicity in sheltered battered women. *Journal of Anxiety Disorders, 22,* 793–800.

Johnson, L. (2011). The genetic epidemiology of obesity: A case study. In M. Teare (Ed.), *Genetic Epidemiology: Methods in molecular biology* (pp. 227–237). New York, NY: Springer.

Johnson, N. J. (2008). Leadership styles and passive-aggressive behavior in organizations. *Dissertation Abstracts International: Section B: The Sciences and Engineering, 68*(7-B), 4828.

Johnson, S. C., Dweck, C. S., & Chen, F. S. (2007). Evidence for infants' internal working methods of attachment. *Psychological Science, 18,* 501–502.

Johnson, S. K., Murphy, S. E., Zewdie, S., & Reichard, R. J. (2008). The strong, sensitive type: Effects of gender stereotypes and leadership prototypes on the evaluation of male and female leaders. *Organizational Behavior and Human Decision Processes, 106,* 39–60.

Johnson, V. I. (2011). Adult children of divorce and relationship education: Implications for counselors and counselor educators. *The Family Journal, 19*(1), 22–29.

Johnson, W. B., & Murray, K. (2007). *Crazy love: Dealing with your partner's problem personality.* Atascadero, CA: Impact Publishers.

Johnson, W., & Bouchard Jr., T. J. (2007). Sex differences in mental ability: A proposed means to link them to brain structure and function. *Intelligence, 35,* 197–209.

Johnson, W., Bouchard Jr., T. J., McGue, M., Segal, N. L., Tellegen, A., Keyes, M., & Gottesman, I. I. (2007). Genetic and environmental influences on the Verbal- Perceptual-Image Rotation (VPR) model of the structure of mental abilities in the Minnesota study of twins reared apart. *Intelligence, 35,* 542–562.

Johnson, W., Bouchard, T. J. Jr., Krueger, R. F., McGue, M., & Gottesman, I. I. (2004). Just one g: Consistent results from three test batteries. *Intelligence, 32*(1), 95–107.

Johnson, W., Brett, C. E., & Deary, I. J. (2010). The pivotal role of education in the association between ability and social class attainment: A look across three generations. *Intelligence, 38(1),* 55–65.

Johnson, W., McGue, M., Krueger, R. F., & Bouchard, T. J. Jr. (2004). Marriage and personality: A genetic analysis. *Journal of Personality and Social Psychology. 86*(2), 285–294.

Johnstone, L. (1999). Adverse psychological effects of ECT. *Journal of Mental Health, 8*(1), 69–85.

Jolliffe, C. D., & Nicholas, M. K. (2004). Verbally reinforcing pain reports: An experimental test of the operant conditioning of chronic pain. *Pain, 107,* 167–175.

Jones, B. C., DeBruine, L. M., & Little, A. C. (2007). The role of symmetry in attraction to average faces. *Perception & Psychophysics, 69,* 1273–1277.

Jones, D. G., Anderson, E. R., & Galvin, K. A. (2003). Spinal cord regeneration: Moving tentatively towards new perspectives. *NeuroRehabilitation, 18*(4), 339–351.

Jones, E. (2008). Predicting performance in first-semester college basic writers: Revisiting the role of self-beliefs. *Contemporary Educational Psychology, 33,* 209–238.

Jones, E. G. (2006). *The thalamus.* New York, NY: Cambridge University Press.

Jopp, D. S., & Schmitt, M. (2010). Dealing with negative life events: Differential effects of personal resources, coping strategies, and control beliefs. *European Journal of Ageing, 7(3),* 167–180.

Jordan, J. V. (2011). The Stone Center and relational–cultural theory. In J. C. Norcross, G. R. VandenBos, & D. K. Freedheim (Eds.), *History of psychotherapy: Continuity and change* (2nd ed.) (pp. 357–362). Washington, DC: American Psychological Association.

Jost, K., Bryck, R. L., Vogel, E. K., & Mayr, U. (2011) Are old adults just like low working memory young adults? Filtering efficiency and age differences in visual working memory. *Cerebral Cortex, 21*(5), 1147–1154.

Jung, C. G. (1946). *Psychological types.* New York, NY: Harcourt Brace.

Jung, C. G. (1959). The archetypes and the collective unconscious. In H. Read,

M. Fordham, & G. Adler (Eds.), *The collected works of C. G. Jung, Vol. 9*. New York, NY: Pantheon.

Jung, C. G. (1969). The concept of collective unconscious. In *Collected Works* (Vol. 9, Part 1). Princeton, NJ: Princeton University Press (Original work published 1936).

Jung, H. (2006). Assessing the influence of cultural values on consumer susceptibility to social pressure for conformity: Self-image enhancing motivations vs. information searching motivation. In L. R. Kahle & C-H. Kim (Eds.), *Creating images and the psychology of marketing communication (pp. 309–329). Advertising and Consumer Psychology*. Mahwah, NJ: Erlbaum.

Jung, R. E., & Haier, R. J. (2007). The Parieto-Frontal Integration Theory (P-FIT) of intelligence: Converging neuroimaging evidence. *Behavioral and Brain Sciences, 30*, 135–154.

Juntii, S. A., Coats, J. K., & Shah, N. M. (2008). A genetic approach to dissect sexually dimorphic behaviors. *Hormones and Behavior, 53*, 627–637.

Jurado-Berbel, P., Costa-Miserachs, D., Torras-Garcia, M., Coll-Andreu, M., & Portell-Cortés, I. (2010). Standard object recognition memory and "what" and "where" components: Improvement by post-training epinephrine in highly habituated rats. *Behavioural Brain Research, 207(1)*, 44–50.

Kagan, J. (1998). Biology and the child. In W. Damon & R. M. Lerner (Eds.), *Handbook of child psychology (Vol. 1)* (pp. 177–235). New York, NY: Wiley.

Kagan, J. (2005). Personality and temperament: Historical perspectives. In M. Rosenbluth, S. H. Kennedy, & R. M. Bagby (Eds), *Depression and personality: Conceptual and clinical challenges* (pp. 3–18). Washington, DC: American Psychiatric Publishing.

Kahneman, D. (2003). Experiences of collaborative research. *American Psychologist, 58(9)*, 723–730.

Kakihara, F., Tilton-Weaver, L., Kerr, M., & Stattin, H. (2010). The relationship of parental control to youth adjustment: Do youths' feelings about their parents play a role? *Journal of Youth and Adolescence, 39(12)*, 1442–1456.

Kalat, J. W., & Shiota, M. N. (2012). *Emotion* (2nd ed.). Belmont, CA: Cengage.

Kalnin, A. J., Edwards, C. R., Wang, Y., Kronenberger, W. G., Hummer, T. A., Mosier, K. M., Dunn, D., & Mathews, V. P. (2011). The interacting role of media violence exposure and aggressive–disruptive behavior in adolescent brain activation during an emotional Stroop task. *Psychiatry Research: Neuroimaging, 192(1)*, 12–19.

Kalodner, C. R. (2011). Cognitive-behavioral theories. In D. Capuzzi & D. R. Gross (Eds.), *Counseling and psychotherapy* (5th ed.) (pp. 193–213). Alexandria, VA: American Counseling Association.

Kaminer, Y., Ford, J. D., & Clark, D. (2011). Assessment and treatment of internalizing disorders: Depression, anxiety disorders, and posttraumatic stress disorder. In Y. Kaminer & K. C. Winters (Eds.), *Clinical manual of adolescent substance abuse treatment* (pp. 307–347). Arlington, VA: American Psychiatric Publishing.

Kana, R. K., Wadsworth, H. M., & Travers, B. G. (2011). A systems level analysis of the mirror neuron hypothesis and imitation impairments in autism spectrum disorders. *Neuroscience and Biobehavioral Reviews, 35(3)*, 894–902.

Kanai, A. (2009). "Karoshi (work to death)" in Japan. *Journal of Business Ethics, 84(Suppl2)*, 209–216.

Kanayama, G., & Pope, H. G., Jr. (2011). Gods, men, and muscle dysmorphia. *Harvard Review of Psychiatry, 19(2)*, 95–98.

Kapitza, K. P., Passie, T., Bernateck, M., & Karst, M. (2010). First non-contingent respiratory biofeedback placebo versus contingent biofeedback in patients with chronic low back pain: A randomized, controlled, double-blind trial. *Applied Psychophysiology and Biofeedback, 35(3)*, 207–217.

Kaplan, L. E. (2006). Moral reasoning of MSW social workers and the influence of education. *Journal of Social Work Education, 42*, 507–522.

Karatsoreos, I. N., Bhagat, S., Bloss, E. B., Morrison, J. H., & McEwen, B. S. (2011). Disruption of circadian clocks has ramifications for metabolism, brain, and behavior. *PNAS Proceedings of the National Academy of Sciences of the United States of America, 108(4)*, 1657–1662.

Kardong, K. (2008). *Introduction to biological evolution* (2nd ed.). New York, NY: McGraw-Hill.

Kareev, Y. (2000). Seven (indeed, plus or minus two) and the detection of correlations. *Psychological Review, 107(2)*:397–402.

Karremans, J. C., Stroebe, W., & Claus, J. (2006). Beyond Vicary's fantasies: The impact of subliminal priming and brand choice. *Journal of Experimental Social Psychology, 42*, 792–798.

Kasper, S., Caraci, F., Forti, B., Drago, F. & Aguglia, E. (2010). Efficacy and tolerability of Hypericum extract for the treatment of mild to moderate depression. *European Neuropsychopharmacology, 20(11)*, 747–765.

Kassin, S., Fein, S., & Markus, H. R. (2008). *Social psychology* (7th ed.). Belmont, CA: Cengage.

Kassinove, H. (2007). Finding a useful model for the treatment of aggression. In T. A. Cavell & K. T. Malcolm (Eds.), *Anger, aggression and interventions for interpersonal violence* (pp. 77–96). Mahwah, NJ: Erlbaum.

Kastenbaum, R. (1999). Dying and bereavement. In J. C. Cavanaugh & S. K. Whitbourne (Eds.), *Gerontology: An interdisciplinary perspective* (pp. 155–185). New York, NY: Oxford University Press.

Kastenbaum, R. J. (2007). *Death, society, and human experience* (9th ed.). Upper Saddle River, NJ: Prentice Hall.

Katz, I., Kaplan, A., & Buzukashvily, T. (2011). The role of parents' motivation in students' autonomous motivation for doing homework. *Learning and Individual Differences*. Retrieved from http://psycnet.apa.org/index.cfm?fa=search.displayRecord&id=DCA17C60-C727-2106-4411-ECA5ABDE6885&resultID=1&page=1&dbTab=all

Kauffman, J. (2008). What is "no recovery?" *Death Studies, 32*, 74–83.

Kaufman, J. A., Tszka, J. M., Patterson, F. P., Erwin, J. M., Hof, P. R. & Allman, J. M. (2010). Structural Diffusion MRI of a Gorilla Brain Performed Ex Vivo at 9.4 Tesla. In D. Broadfield, M. Yuan, K. Schick, & N. Toth (Eds.), The human brain evolved, Paleoneurological studies in honor of Ralph L. Holloway (pp. 171–181). Bloomington, IN: Stone Age Institute Press.

Kaufman, J. C. (2002). Dissecting the golden goose: Components of studying creative writers. *Creativity Research Journal, 14(1)*, 27–40.

Kaufman, S. B. (2011). Black Swan, creativity, and artistic expression at the edge of madness. *Psychology Today Blog*. Retrieved from http://www.psychologytoday.com/blog/beautiful-minds/201101/black-swan-creativity-and-artistic-expression-the-edge-madness?page=2

Kaukiainen, A., Björkqvist, K., Lagerspetz, K., Österman, K., Salmivalli, C., Rothberg, S., et al. (1999). The relationships between social intelligence, empathy, and three types of aggression. *Aggressive Behavior, 25(2)*, 81–89.

Kawakami, K., Dovidio, J. F., & Dijksterhuis, A. (2003). Effect of social category priming on personal attitudes. *Psychological Science, 14*, 315–319.

Kawakami, K., Dovidio, J. F., Moll, J., Hermsen, S., & Russin, A. (2000). Just say no (to stereotyping): Effects of training in the negation of stereotypic associations on stereotype activation. *Journal of Personality & Social Psychology, 78,* 871–888.

Kaye, W. (2008). Neurobiology of anorexia and bulimia nervosa. *Physiology & Behavior, 94,* 121–135.

Kaysen, D., Pantalone, D. W., Chawla, N., Lindgrren, K. P., Clum, G. A., Lee, C., & Resick, P. A. (2008). Posttraumatic stress disorder, alcohol use, and physical health concerns. *Journal of Behavioral Medicine, 31,* 115–125.

Kazdin, A. E. (1994). Methodology, design, and evaluation in psychotherapy research. In A.E. Bergin & S.L. Garfield (Eds.), *Handbook of psycho and behavior change* (4th ed.) (pp. 19–71). New York, NY: Wiley.

Kazdin, A. E. (2008). *Behavior modification in applied settings (6th ed.).* Long Grove, IL: Waveland Press.

Kazdin, A. E. (2011). *Single-case research designs: Methods for clinical and applied settings* (2nd ed.). New York, NY: Oxford University Press.

Keating, C. R. (1994). World without words: Messages from face and body. In W. J. Lonner & R. Malpass (Eds.), *Psychology and culture* (pp. 175–182). Boston, MA: Allyn & Bacon.

Keefe, F. J., Shelby, R. A., & Somers, T. J. (2010). Catastrophizing and pain coping: Moving forward. *Pain, 149(2),* 165–166.

Keen, E. (2011). Emotional narratives: Depression as sadness—Anxiety as fear. *The Humanistic Psychologist, 39(1),* 66–70.

Keen, S. (1991). *Faces of the enemy: Reflections of the hostile imagination.* New York, NY: Harper- Collins.

Keith, T. Z., & Reynolds, M. R. (2010). Cattell-Horn-Carroll abilities and cognitive tests: What we've learned from 20 years of research. *Psychology in the Schools, 47(7),* 635–650.

Keller, H. (1962). Quoted in R. Harrity & R. G. Martin, *The three lives of Helen Keller* (p. 23). Garden City, NY: Doubleday.

Keller, J., & Bless, H. (2008). *The interplay of stereotype threat and regulatory focus.* In Y. **Kashima, K. Fiedler, & P. Freytag (Eds.),** *Stereotype dynamics: Language-based approaches to the formation, maintenance, and transformation of stereotypes* (pp. 367–389). Mahwah, NJ: Erlbaum.

Kellogg, R. (2011). *Fundamentals of Cognitive Psychology* (2ⁿᵈ ed.). Thousand Oaks, CA: Sage.

Kelly, G., Brown, S., Todd, J., & Kremer, P. (2008). Challenging behaviour profiles of people with acquired brain injury living in community settings. *Brain Injury, 22,* 457–470.

Keltner, D., Kring, A. M., & Bonanno, G. A. (1999). Fleeting signs of the course of life: Facial expression and personal adjustment. *Current Directions in Psychological Science, 8(1),* 18–22.

Kemeny, M. E. (2007). Psychoneuroimmunology. In H. S. Friedman & R. C. Silver (Eds.), *Foundations of health psychology* (pp. 92–116). New York, NY: Oxford University Press.

Kendler, K. S., & Prescott, C. A. (2006). *Genes, environment, and psychopathology: Understanding the causes of psychiatric and substance use disorders.* New York, NY: Guilford Press.

Kendler, K. S., Gallagher, T. J., Abelson, J. M., & Kessler, R. C. (1996). Lifetime prevalence, demographic risk factors, and diagnostic validity of nonaffective psychosis as assessed in a U. S. community sample. *Archives of General Psychiatry, 53,* 1022–1031.

Kenealy, P. M. (1997). Mood-state-dependent retrieval: The effects of induced mood on memory reconsidered. *Quarterly Journal of Experimental Psychology: Human Experimental Psychology, 50A,* 290–317.

Kennedy, M. M. (2010). Attribution error and the quest for teacher quality. *Educational Researcher, 39(8),* 591–598.

Kerschreiter, R., Schulz-Hardt, S., Mojzisch, A., & Frey, D. (2008). Biased information search in homogeneous groups: Confidence as a moderator for the effect of anticipated task requirements. *Personality & Social Psychology Bulletin, 34,* 679–691.

Kersting, K. (2004). Cons of perfectionism include self-criticism. *Monitor on Psychology, 35(5),* 20.

Kesebir, P. (2011). Existential functions of culture: The monumental immortality project. In A. K.-y. Leung, C.-y. Chiu, & Y.-y. Hong (Eds.), *Culture and psychology. Cultural processes: A social psychological perspective* (pp. 96–110). Cambridge, UK: Cambridge University Press.

Ketterer, H. L. (2011). Examining the measurement invariance of the MMPI-2 Restructured Clinical (RC) scales across Korean and American normative samples. *Dissertation Abstracts International: Section B: The Sciences and Engineering, 71(7-B),* 4532.

Khalid, N., Atkins, M., Tredget, J., Giles, M., Champney-Smith, K., & Kirov, G. (2008). The effectiveness of electroconvulsive therapy in treatment-resistant depression. *Journal of ECT, 24,* 141–145.

Kieffer, K. M., Schinka, J. A., & Curtiss, G. (2004). Person-environment congruence and personality domains in the prediction of job performance and work quality. *Journal of Counseling.Psychology, 51(2),* 168–177.

Kiester, E. (1984, July). The playing fields of the mind. *Psychology Today,* 18–24.

Kihlstrom, J. F. (2004). An unbalanced balancing act: Blocked, recovered, and false memories in the laboratory and clinic. *Clinical Psychology: Science & Practice, 11(1),* 34–41.

Kihlstrom, J. F. (2005). Dissociative disorders. *Annual Review of Clinical Psychology, 1,* 227–253.

Kiley, D. (2011). Chrysler splits with new media strategies over f-bomb tweet. *Ad Age Digital.* Retrieved from http://adage.com/article/digital/chrysler-splits-media-strategies-f-bomb-tweet/149335/

Killen, M., & Hart, D. (1999). *Morality in everyday life: Developmental perspectives.* New York, NY: Cambridge University Press.

Kilpatrick, L. A., Suyenobu, B. Y., Smith, S. R., Bueller, J. A., Goodman, T., Creswell, J. D., Tillisch, K., Mayer, E., & Naliboff, B. D. (2011). Impact of mindfulness-based stress reduction training on intrinsic brain connectivity. *NeuroImage, 56(1),* 290–298.

Kim, D-H., Moon, Y-S., Kim, H-S., Jung, J-S, Park, H-M., Suh, H-W., Kim, Y-H., & Song, DK. (2005). Effect of Zen meditation on serum nitric oxide activity and lipid peroxidation. *Progress in Neuropsychopharmacology & Biological Psychiatry, 29(2),* 327–331.

Kim, H. (2011). Consequences of parental divorce for child development. *American Sociological Review, 76(3),* 487–512.

Kim, J., & Hatfield, E. (2004). Love types and subjective well-being: A cross cultural study. *Social Behavior & Personality, 32(2),* 173–182.

Kim, J-H., Auerbach, J. M., Rodriquez-Gomez, J. A., Velasco, I., Gavin, D., Lumelsky, N., Lee, SH., Nguyen, J., Sanchez-Pernaute, R., Bankiewicz, K., & McKay, R. (2002). Dopamine neurons derived from embryonic stem cells function in an animal model of Parkinson's disease. *Nature, 418,* 50–56.

Kim, S. U. (2004). Human neural stem cells genetically modified for brain repair in neurological disorders. *Neuropathology, 24(3),* 159–171.

Kim, U., & Choi, S. (1995). Individualism, collectivism, and child development: A Korean perspective. In P. M. Greenfield & R. R. Cocking (Eds.), *Cross-cultural roots* of minority child development (pp. 227–257). Hillsdale, NJ: Erlbaum.

Kim, Y. H. (2008). Rebounding from learned helplessness: A measure of academic resilience using anagrams. Dissertation Abstracts International: Section B: The Sciences and Engineering. 68(10-B), 6947.

King, B. M. (2012). Human sexuality today (7th ed.). Boston, MA: Allyn & Bacon.

King, N. J., Clowes-Hollins, V., & Ollendick, T. H. (1997). The etiology of childhood dog phobia. Behaviour Research and Therapy, 35, 77.

King, S. A., & Moreggi, D. (2007). Internet self-help and support groups: The pros and cons of text-based mutual aid. In J. Gackenbach (Ed.), Psychology and the Internet: Intrapersonal, interpersonal, and transpersonal implications (2nd ed.) (pp. 221–244). San Diego, CA: Academic Press.

King, S. L. (2008). A prospective study of physiological hyperarousal and coping as correlates of symptoms of acute stress disorder and posttraumatic stress disorder in motor vehicle crash survivors. Dissertation Abstracts International: Section B: The Sciences and Engineering, 68(10-B), 6587.

Kinsbourne, M. (1972). Behavioral analysis of the repetition deficit in conduction aphasia. Neurology, 22(11), 1126–1132.

Kirk, K. M., Bailey, J. M., Dunne, M. P., & Martin, N. G. (2000). Measurement models for sexual orientation in a community twin sample. Behavior Genetics, 30(4), 345–356.

Kirsch, I., & Braffman, W. (2001). Imaginative suggestibility and hypnotizability. Current Directions in Psychological Science, 10(2), 57–61.

Kirsch, I., & Lynn, S. J. (1995). The altered state of hypnosis. American Psychologist, 50, 846–858.

Kirsch, I., Mazzoni, G., & Montgomery, G. H. (2006). Remembrance of hypnosis past. American Journal of Clinical Hypnosis, 49, 171–178.

Kirschner, S. M., Litwack, T. R., & Galperin, G. J. (2004). The defense of extreme emotional disturbance: A qualitative analysis of cases in New York county. Psychology, Public Policy, & Law, 10(1–2), 102–133.

Kisilevsky, B. S., Hains, S. M. J., Lee, K., Xie, X., Huang, H., Ye, H., Zhang, K., & Wang, Z. (2003). Effects of experience on fetal voice recognition. Psychological Science, 14(3), 220–224.

Kistner, J., Counts-Allan, C., Dunkel, S., Drew, C. H., David-Ferdon, C., & Lopez, C. (2010). Sex differences in relational and overt aggression in the late elementary school years. Aggressive Behavior, 36(5), 282–291.

Kitayama, S., & Cohen, D. (Eds.). (2007). Handbook of cultural psychology. New York, NY: Guilford Press.

Kleider, H. M., Pezdek, K., Goldinger, S. D., & Kirk, A. (2008). Schema-driven source misattribution errors: Remembering the expected from a witnessed event. Applied Cognitive Psychology, 22, 1–20.

Kliger, D., & Kudryavtsev, A. (2010). The availability heuristic and investors' reaction to company-specific events. Journal of Behavioral Finance, 11(1), 50–65.

Klimes-Dougan, B., Lee, C-Y. S., Ronsaville, D., & Martinez, P. (2008). Suicidal risk in young adult offspring of mothers with bipolar or major depressive disorder: A longitudinal family risk study. Journal of Clinical Psychology, 64, 531–540.

Knack, J. M., Gomez, H. L., & Jensen-Campbell, L. A. (2011). Bullying and its long-term health implications. In G. MacDonald & L. A. Jensen-Campbell (Eds.), Social pain: Neuropsychological and health implications of loss and exclusion (pp. 215–236). Washington, DC: American Psychological Association.

Knaus, B. (2010) Ditch the "I'm a Procrastinator" label. Psychology Today Blogs. Retrieved from http://www.psychologytoday.com/blog/science-and-sensibility/201009/ditch-the-i-m-procrastinator-label

Knekt, P., Lindfors, O., Laaksonen, M. A., Raitasalo, R., Haaramo, P., Järvikoski, A., & The Helsinki Psychotherapy Study Group, Helsinki, Finlan. (2008). Effectiveness of short-term and long-term psychotherapy on work ability and functional capacity—A randomized clinical trial on depressive and anxiety disorders. Journal of Affective Disorders, 107, 95–106.

Kniffin, K. M., & Wilson, D. S. (2004). The effect of nonphysical traits on the perception of physical attractiveness: Three naturalistic studies. Evolution & Human Behavior, 25, 88–101.

Knoblauch, K., Vital-Durand, F., & Barbur, J. L. (2000). Variation of chromatic sensitivity across the life span. Vision Research, 41(1), 23–36.

Ko, S.-G., Lee, T.-H., Yoon, H.-Y., Kwon, J.-H., & Mather, M. (2011). How does context affect assessments of facial emotion? The role of culture and age. Psychology and Aging, 26(1), 48–59.

Kobasa, S. (1979). Stressful life events, personality, and health: An inquiry into hardiness. Journal of Personality and Social Psychology, 37, 1–11.

Kobeissi, J., Aloysi, A., Tobias, K., Popeo, D., & Kellner, C. H. (2011). Resolution of severe suicidality with a single electroconvulsive therapy. The Journal of ECT, 27(1), 86–88.

Köfalvi, A. (Ed.). (2008). Cannabinoids and the brain. New York, NY: Springer Science + Business Media.

Kohlberg, L. (1964). Development of moral character and moral behavior. In L. W. Hoffman & M. L. Hoffman (Eds.), Review of child development research (Vol. 1). New York, NY: Sage.

Kohlberg, L. (1969). Stage and sequence: The cognitive-developmental approach to socialization. In D. A. Goslin (Ed.), Handbook of socialization theory and research. Chicago, IL: Rand McNally.

Kohlberg, L. (1981). The meaning and measurement of moral development. Worcester, MA: Clark University Press.

Kohlberg, L. (1984). The psychology of moral development: Essays on moral development (Vol. 2). San Francisco: Harper & Row.

Köhler, W. (1925). The mentality of apes. New York, NY: Harcourt, Brace.

Koike, T., Kan, S., Misaki, M., & Miyauchi, S. (2011). Connectivity pattern changes in default-mode network with deep non-REM and REM sleep. Neuroscience Research, 69(4), 322–330.

Kondo, N. (2008). Mental illness in film. Psychiatric Rehabilitation Journal, 31, 250–252.

Kondo, N., & Oh, J. (2010). Suicide and karoshi (death from overwork) during the recent economic crises in Japan: The impacts, mechanisms and political responses. Journal of Epidemiology and Community Health, 64(8), 649–650.

Konheim-Kalkstein, Y. L., & van den Broek, P. (2008). The effect of incentives on cognitive processing of text. Discourse Processes, 45, 180–194.

Konigsberg, R. D. (2011). The truth about grief: The myth of its five stages and the new science of loss. New York, NY: Simon & Schuster.

Koob, G. F., & Le Moal, M. L. (2008). Addiction and the brain antireward system. Annual Review of Psychology, 59, 29–53.

Koopmann-Holm, B., & Matsumoto, D. (2011). Values and display rules for specific emotions. Journal of Cross-Cultural Psychology, 42(3), 355–371.

Koppel, J. (2000). Good/Grief. New York, NY: Harperperennial.

Koropeckyj-Cox, T., & Call, V. R. A. (2007). Characteristics of older childless persons and parents: Cross-national comparisons. *Journal of Family Issues, 28*, 1362–1414.

Koss, M. P., White, J. W., & Kazdin, A. E. (2011). Violence against women and children: Perspectives and next steps. In M. P. Koss, J. W. White, & A. E. Kazdin (Eds.), *Violence against women and children, Vol. 2. Navigating solutions* (pp. 261–305). Washington, DC: American Psychological Association.

Kovacic, Z., Henigsberg, N., Pivac, N., Nedic, G., & Borovecki, A. (2008). Platelet serotonin concentration and suicidal behavior in combat related posttraumatic stress disorder. *Progress in Neuro-Psychopharmacology & Biological Psychiatry, 32*, 544–551.

Kracher, B., & Marble, R. P. (2008). The significance of gender in predicting the cognitive moral development of business practitioners using the Socioemotional Reflection Objective Measure. *Journal of Business Ethics, 78*, 503–526.

Kracke, W. H. (2010). Kagwahiv mourning I: Dreams of a bereaved father. In R. A. LeVine (Ed.), *Blackwell anthologies in social and cultural anthropology. Psychological anthropology: A reader on self in culture* (pp. 154–164). Hoboken, NJ: Wiley-Blackwell.

Krahé, B., Möller, I., Huesmann, L. R., Kirwil, L., Felber, J., & Berger, A. (2011). Desensitization to media violence: Links with habitual media violence exposure, aggressive cognitions, and aggressive behavior. *Journal of Personality and Social Psychology, 100(4)*, 630–646.

Krauss, L. M. (2011). When science goes psychic: No sacred mantle. *The New York Times.* Retrieved from http://www.nytimes.com/roomfordebate/2011/01/06/the-esp-study-when-science-goes-psychic/publication-is-not-a-sacred-mantle

Krebs, D. (2007). Understanding evolutionary approaches to human behavior. *Human Development, 50*, 286–291.

Krebs, D. L. (2007). Deciphering the structure of the moral sense: A review of moral minds: How nature designed our universal sense of right and wrong. *Evolution and Human Behavior, 28*, 294–296.

Krebs, D. L., & Hemingway, A. (2008). The explanatory power of evolutionary approaches to human behavior: The case of morality. *Psychological Inquiry, 19*, 35–38.

Kress, T., Aviles, C., Taylor, C., & Winchell, M. (2011). Individual/collective human needs: (Re) theorizing Maslow using critical, sociocultural, feminist, and indigenous lenses. In C. Malott & B. Porfilio (Eds.), *Critical pedagogy in the twenty-first century: A new generation of scholars* (pp. 135–157). Charlotte, NC: Information Age Publishing.

Kreuger, J. I. (2011). Bem, Bayes, and the limits of statistical inference: Is there psi? Don't look to stats. *Psychology Today Blogs.* Retrieved from http://www.psychologytoday.com/blog/one-among-many/201101/bem-bayes-and-the-limits-statistical-inference

Kring, A. M., Johnson, S. L., Davison, G. C., Neale, J. M. (2010). *Abnormal psychology (11th ed.).* Hoboken, NJ: Wiley.

Krishna, G. (1999). *The dawn of a new science.* Los Angeles, CA: Institute for Consciousness Research.

Krishnan, V., & Nestler, E. (2011). Animal models of depression: Molecular perspectives. *Molecular and Functional Models in Neuropsychiatry, 7*, 121–147.

Krueger, J. I. (2007). From social projection to social behaviour. *European Review of Social Psychology, 18*, 1–35.

Kruglanski, A. W., & Gigerenzer, G. (2011). Intuitive and deliberate judgments are based on common principles. *Psychological Review, 118(1)*, 97–109.

Krukowski, K., Eddy, J., Kosik, K. L., Konley, T., Janusek, L. W., & Mathews, H. L. (2011). Glucocorticoid dysregulation of natural killer cell function through epigenetic modification. *Brain, Behavior, and Immunity, 25(2)*, 239–249.

Krusemark, E. A., Campbell, W. K., & Clementz, B. A. (2008). Attributions, deception, and event related potentials: An investigation of the self-serving bias. *Psychophysiology, 45*, 511–515.

Krypel, M. N., & Henderson-King, D. (2010). Stress, coping styles, and optimism: Are they related to meaning of education in students' lives? *Social Psychology of Education, 13(3)*, 409–424.

Ksir, C. J., Hart, C. I., & Ray, O. S. (2008). *Drugs, society, and human behavior.* New York, NY: McGraw-Hill.

Kteily, N. S., Sidanius, J., & Levin, S. (2011). Social dominance orientation: Cause or 'mere effect'?: Evidence for SDO as a causal predictor of prejudice and discrimination against ethnic and racial outgroups. *Journal of Experimental Social Psychology, 47(1)*, 208–214.

Kubiak, T., Vögele, C., Siering, M., Schiel, R., & Weber, H. (2008). Daily hassles and emotional eating in obese adolescents under restricted dietary conditions—The role of ruminative thinking. *Appetite, 51*, 206–209.

Kubicek, B., Korunka, C., Raymo, J. M., & Hoonakker, P. (2011). Psychological well-being in retirement: The effects of personal and gendered contextual resources. *Journal of Occupational Health Psychology, 16(2)*, 230–246.

Kübler-Ross, E. (1975). *Questions and answers on death and dying.* Oxford, England: Macmillan.

Kübler-Ross, E. (1983). *On children and death.* New York, NY: Macmillan.

Kübler-Ross, E. (1997). *Death: The final stage of growth.* New York, NY: Simon & Schuster.

Kübler-Ross, E. (1999). *On death and dying.* New York, NY: Simon & Schuster.

Kühn, S., & Gallinat, J. (2011). Common biology of craving across legal and illegal drugs—A quantitative meta-analysis of cue-reactivity brain response. *European Journal of Neuroscience, 33(7)*, 1318–1326.

Kulich, C., Ryan, M. K., & Haslam, S. A. (2007). Where is the romance for women leaders? The effects of gender on leadership attributions and performance-based pay. *Applied Psychology: An International Review, 56*, 582–601.

Kulik, L. (2005). Intrafamiliar congruence in gender role attitudes and ethnic stereotypes: The Israeli case. *Journal of Comparative Family Studies, 36(2)*, 289–303.

Kullmann, D. M., & Lamsa, K. P. (2011). LTP and LTD in cortical GABAergic interneurons: Emerging rules and roles. *Neuropharmacology, 60(5)*, 712–719.

Kumar, G., Markert, R. J., & Patel, R. (2011). Assessment of hospice patients' goals of care at the end of life. *American Journal of Hospice & Palliative Medicine, 28(1)*, 31–34.

Kuperstok, N. (2008). Effects of exposure to differentiated aggressive films, equated for levels of interest and excitation, and the vicarious hostility catharsis hypothesis. *Dissertation Abstracts International: Section B: The Sciences and Engineering 68(7-B)*, 4806.

Kvavilashvili, L., Mirani, J., Schlagman, S., Erskine, J. A. K., & Kornbrot, D. E. (2010). Effects of age on phenomenology and consistency of flashbulb memories of September 11 and a staged control event. *Psychology and Aging, 25(2)*, 391–404.

Kyriacou, C. P., & Hastings, M. H. (2010). Circadian clocks: Genes, sleep, and cognition. *Trends in Cognitive Sciences, 14(6)*, 259–267.

LaBrie, J. W., Pedersen, E. R., Thompson, A. D., & Earleywine, M. (2008). A brief decisional balance intervention increases motivation and behavior regarding condom use in high-risk heterosexual college men. *Archives of Sexual Behavior, 37(2),* 330–339.

Lachman, M. E. (2004). Development in midlife. *Annual Review of Psychology, 55,* 305–331.

Lackner, J. R., & DiZio, P. (2005). Vestibular, proprioceptive, and haptic contributions to spatial orientation. *Annual Review of Psychology, 56,* 115–147.

Lacroix, C. C. (2011). High stakes stereotypes: The emergence of the "Casino Indian" trope in television depictions of contemporary Native Americans. *Howard Journal of Communications, 22(1),* 1–23.

Lader, M. (2007). Limitations of current medical treatments for depression: Disturbed circadian rhythms as a possible therapeutic target. *European Neuropsychopharacology, 17,* 743–755.

Lader, M., Cardinali, D. P., & Pandi- Perumal, S. R. (Eds.). (2006). *Sleep and sleep disorders: A neuropsychopharmacological approach.* New York, NY: Springer-Verlag.

Lahav. O., & Mioduser, D. (2008). Haptic-feedback support for cognitive mapping of unknown spaces by people who are blind. *International Journal of Human-Computer Studies, 66,* 23–35.

Lamberg, L. (1998). Gay is okay with APA—Forum honors landmark 1973 events. *Journal of the American Medical Association, 280,* 497–499.

Lambert, L. (2010, April 10). Rebecca Riley's doctor is on the defense. *Patriot Ledger.* Retrieved from http://www.patriotledger .com

Lamberti, S. (2010). Cited in S. D. James, Black Swan: Psychiatrists diagnose ballerina's descent. *Whas11.com.* Retrieved from http://www.whas11.com/home/BLACK-SWAN-Psychiatrists-Diagnose-Ballerinas-Descent-112189774.html

Lammers, J., & Stapel, D. (2011). Power increases dehumanization. *Group Processes & Intergroup Relations, 14*(1), 113–126.

Lancaster, R. S. (2007). *Stop Sylvia Browne: Sylvia Browne's best evidence.* Retrieved from http://www.stopsylvia.com/articles/ac360_brownesbestevidence.shtml

Lanciano, T., Curci, A., & Semin, G. R. (2010). The emotional and reconstructive determinants of emotional memories: An experimental approach to flashbulb memory investigation. *Memory, 18(5),* 473–485.

Landay, J. S., & Kuhnehenn, J. (2004, July 10). Probe blasts CIA on Iraq data. *The Philadelphia Inquirer,* p. AO1.

Lande, F. J., & Conte, J. M. (2010). *Work in the 21ˢᵗ Century* (3ʳᵈ ed.). Hoboken, NJ: Wiley.

Landeira-Fernandez, J. (2004). Analysis of the cold-water restraint procedure in gastric ulceration and body temperature. *Physiology & Behavior, 82*(5), 827–833.

Landsbergis, P. A., Schnall, P. L., Belkic, K. L., Baker, D., Schwartz, J. E., & Pickering, T. G. (2011). Workplace and cardiovascular disease: Relevance and potential role for occupational health psychology. In J. C. Quick & L. E. Tetrick (Eds.), *Handbook of occupational health psychology* (2nd ed.) (pp. 243–264). Washington, DC: American Psychological Association.

Lanfranchi, A. (2010). Was brauchen kinder um in unserer Gesellschaft FIT zu sein?: Transkription des Vortrages: Yvonne Traber [What children need—the goodness of FIT (the FIT-concept)]. *Psychotherapie Forum, 18*(2), 74–79.

Langballe, E. M., Innstrand, S. T., Aasland, O. G., & Falkum, E. (2011). The predictive value of individual factors, work-related factors, and work-home interaction on burnout in female and male physicians: A longitudinal study. *Stress and Health: Journal of the International Society for the Investigation of Stress, 27(1),* 73–85.

Langdon, P. E., Clare, I. C. H., & Murphy, G. H. (2011). Moral reasoning theory and illegal behaviour by adults with intellectual disabilities. *Psychology, Crime & Law, 17(2),* 101–115.

Lange, R. T., Sullivan, K. A., & Scott, C. (2010). Comparison of MMPI-2 and PAI validity indicators to detect feigned depression and PTSD symptom reporting. *Psychiatry Research, 176*(2–3), 229–235.

Langlois, J. H., Kalakanis, L., Rubenstein, A. J., Larson, A., Hallam, M., & Smoot, M. (2000). Maxims or myths of beauty? A meta-analytic and theoretical review. *Psychological Bulletin, 126*(3), 390–423.

Långström, N., Rahman, Q., Carlström, E., & Lichtenstein, P. (2010). Genetic and environmental effects on same-sex sexual behavior: A population study of twins in Sweden. *Archives of Sexual Behavior, 39*(1), 75–80.

LaPointe, L. L. (Ed.. (2005). Feral children. *Journal of Medical Speech-Language Pathology, 13,* vii–ix.

Lapsley, D. K. (2006). Moral stage theory. In M. Killen & J. Smetana (Eds.), *Handbook of moral development* (pp. 37–66). Mahwah, NJ: Erlbaum.

Larkby, C. A., Goldschmidt, L.., Hanusa, B. H., & Day, N. L. (2011). Prenatal alcohol exposure is associated with conduct disorder in adolescence: Findings from a birth cohort. *Journal of the American Academy of Child & Adolescent Psychiatry, 50*(3), 262–271.

Latane, B., & Darley, J. M. (1970). *The unresponsive bystander: Why doesn't he help?* New York, NY: Appleton-Century-Crofts.

Latinus, M., VanRullen, R., & Taylor, M. J. (2010). Top-down and bottom-up modulation in processing bimodal face/voice stimuli. *BMC Neuroscience, 11,* Article ID 36.

Lau, A. S. (2010). Physical discipline in Chinese American immigrant families: An adaptive culture perspective. *Cultural Diversity and Ethnic Minority Psychology, 16*(3), 313–322.

Lau, K. S. L., Marsee, M. A., Kunimatsu, M. M., & Fassnacht, G. M. (2010). Examining associations between narcissism, behavior problems, and anxiety in non-referred adolescents. *Child Youth Care Forum, 40(3),* 163–176.

Laumann, E., Gagnon, J., Michael, R., & Michaels, S. (1994). *The social organization of sexuality, IL: Sexual practices in the United States.* Chicago, IL: University of Chicago Press.

Laungani, P. D. (2007). *Understanding cross-cultural psychology.* Thousand Oaks, CA: Sage.

Lavazza, A., & De Caro, M. (2010). Not so fast. On some bold neuroscientific claims concerning human agency. *Neuroethics, 3(1),* 23–41.

Lawrence, C., & Andrews, K. (2004). The influence of perceived prison crowding on male inmates' perception of aggressive events. *Aggressive Behavior, 30,* 273–283.

Lawrence, M. (2008). Review of the bifurcation of the self: The history and theory of dissociation and its disorders. *American Journal of Clinical Hypnosis, 50,* 281–282.

Lawrence, V., Murray, J., Klugman, A., & Banerjee, S. (2011). Cross-cultural variation in the experience of depression in older people in the UK. In M. Abou-Saleh, C. Katona, & A. Kumar (Eds.), *Principle and practice of geriatric psychiatry* (3rd ed.) (pp. 711–716). Hoboken, NJ: Wiley.

Lazar, S. (2010). *Psychotherapy is worth it: A comprehensive review of its cost-effectiveness.* Arlington, VA: American Psychiatric Publishing.

Lazar, S. W., Kerr, C. E., Wasserman, R. H., Gray, J. R., Greve, D. N., Treadway, M.

T., McGarvey, M., Quinn, B. T., Dusek, J. A., Benson, H., Rauch, S. L., Moore, C. I., Fischl, B. (2005). Meditation experience is associated with increased cortical thickness. *Neuroreport, 16*(17), 1893–1897.

Lazarus, R. S. (1993). Coping theory and research: Past, present, and future. *Psychosomatic Medicine, 55,* 234–247.

Lazarus, R. S. (1999). *Stress and emotion: A new synthesis.* New York, NY: Springer.

Lazarus, R. S. (2000). Toward better research on stress and coping. *American Psychologist, 55,* 665–673.

Leaming, M. R., & Dickinson, G. E. (2011). *Understanding dying, death, and bereavement* (7th ed.). Belmont, CA: Cengage

Leaper, C. (2000). Gender, affiliation, assertion, and the interactive context of parent-child play. *Developmental Psychology, 36*(3), 381–393.

Leaper, C. (2011). Research in developmental psychology on gender and relationships: Reflections on the past and looking into the future. *British Journal of Developmental Psychology, 29*(2), 347–356.

Leary, C. E., Kelley, M. L., Morrow, J., & Mikulka, P. J. (2008). Parental use of physical punishment as related to family environment, psychological well-being, and personality in undergraduates. *Journal of Family Violence, 23*(1), 1–7.

Lecrubier, Y., Clerc, G., Didi, R., & Kieser, M. (2002). Efficacy of St. John's wort extract WS 5570 in major depression: A double-blind, placebo-controlled trial. *American Journal of Psychiatry, 159*(8), 1361–1366.

LeDoux, J. E. (1996a). *The emotional brain: The mysterious underpinnings of emotional life.* New York, NY: Simon & Schuster.

LeDoux, J. E. (1996b). Sensory systems and emotion: A model of affective processing. *Integrative Psychiatry, 4,* 237–243.

LeDoux, J. E. (1998). *The emotional brain.* New York, NY: Simon & Schuster.

LeDoux, J. E. (2002). *Synaptic self: How our brains become who we are.* New York, NY: Viking.

LeDoux, J. E. (2007). Emotional memory. *Scholarpedia, 2,* 180.

LeDoux, J. E., & Doyère, V. (2011). Emotional memory processing: Synaptic connectivity. In S. Nalbantian, P. M. Matthews, & J. L. McClelland (Eds.), *The memory process: Neuroscientific and humanistic perspectives* (pp. 153–171). Cambridge, MA: MIT Press.

Lee, D. (1950). The conception of the self among the Wintu Indians. *In D. Lee (Ed.),* *Freedom and culture.* Englewood Cliffs, NJ: Prentice-Hall.

Lee, J. J. (2007). A g beyond Homo sapiens? Some hints and suggestions. *Intelligence, 35,* 253–265.

Lee, J., Jiang, J., Sim, K., Tay, J., Subramaniam, M., & Chong, S. (2011). Gender differences in Singaporean Chinese patients with schizophrenia. *Asian Journal of Psychiatry, 4*(1), 60–64.

Lee, J.-H., Chung, W.-H., Kang, E.-H., Chung, D.-J., Choi, C.-B., Chang, H.-S., Lee, J.-H., Hwang, S.-H., Han, H., Choe, B.Y., & Kim, H.-Y. (2011). Schwann cell-like remyelination following transplantation of human umbilical cord blood (hUCB)-derived mesenchymal stem cells in dogs with acute spinal cord injury. *Journal of the Neurological Sciences, 300*(1–2), 86–96.

Lee, J-H., Kwon, Y-D., Hong, S-H., Jeong, H-J., Kim, H-M., & Um, J-Y. (2008). Interleukin-1 beta gene polymorphism and traditional constitution in obese women. *International Journal of Neuroscience, 118,* 793–805.

Lee, R., Chong, B., & Coccaro, E. (2011). Growth hormone responses to GABAB receptor challenge with baclofen and impulsivity in healthy control and personality disorder subjects. *Psychopharmacology, 215*(1), 41–48.

Lee, S. S. (2011). Deviant peer affiliation and antisocial behavior: Interaction with monoamine oxidase A (MAOA) genotype. *Journal of Abnormal Child Psychology: An official publication of the International Society for Research in Child and Adolescent Psychopathology, 39*(3), 321–332.

Lee, S. W. S., & Schwarz, N. (2010). Dirty hands and dirty mouths: Embodiment of the moral-purity metaphor is specific to the motor modality involved in moral transgression. *Psychological Science, 21*(10), 1423–1425.

Lefrancois, G. R. (2012). *Theories of human learning: What the professor said* (6th ed.). Belmont, CA: Wadsworth/Cengage.

Leglise, A. (2008). *Progress in circadian rhythm research.* Hauppauge, NY: Nova Science.

Legrand, F. D., Gomà-i-freixanet, M., Kaltenbach, M. L., & Joly, P. M. (2007). Association between sensation seeking and alcohol consumption in French college students: Some ecological data collected in "open bar" parties. *Personality and Individual Differences, 43,* 1950–1959.

Lebavot, K., & Simoni, J. M. (2011). The impact of minority stress on mental health and substance use among sexual minority women. *Journal of Consulting and Clinical Psychology, 79*(2), 159–170.

Leichsenring, F., Leibing, E., Kruse, J., New, A., & Leweke, F. (2011). Borderline personality disorder. *The Lancet, 377*(9759), 74–84.

Leichtman, M. D. (2006). Cultural and maturational influences on long-term event memory. In L. Balter & C. S. Tamis-LeMonda (Eds.), *Child psychology: A handbook of contemporary issues* (2nd ed.) (pp. 565–589). New York, NY: Psychology Press.

Leichtman, M. D. (2011). A global window on memory development. In L. A. Jensen (Ed.), *Bridging cultural and developmental approaches to psychology: New syntheses in theory, research, and policy* (pp. 49–70). New York, NY: Oxford University Press.

Leichtman, M. D., & Ceci, S. J. (1995). The effects of stereotypes and suggestions on preschoolers' reports. *Developmental Psychology, 31,* 568–578.

Leidy, M. S., Schofield, T. J., Miller, M. A., Parke, R. D., Coltrane, S., Braver, S., Cookston, J., Fabricius, W., Saenz, D., & Adams, M. (2011). Fathering and adolescent adjustment: Variations by family structure and ethnic background. *Fathering, 9*(1), 44–68.

Lele, D. U. (2008). The influence of individual personality and attachment styles on romantic relationships (partner choice and couples' satisfaction). *Dissertation Abstracts International: Section B: The Sciences and Engineering, 68,* 6316.

Lennon, A., Watson, B., Arlidge, C., & Fraine, G. (2011). 'You're a bad driver but I just made a mistake': Attribution differences between the 'victims' and 'perpetrators' of scenario-based aggressive driving incidents. *Transportation Research Part F: Traffic Psychology and Behaviour, 14*(3), 209–221.

Lenz, K. M., & McCarthy, M. M. (2010). Organized for sex—Steroid hormones and the developing hypothalamus. *European Journal of Neuroscience, 32*(12), 2096–2104.

León, T. C., Nouwen, A., Sheffield, D., Jaumdally, R., & Lip, G. Y. H. (2010). Anger rumination, social support, and cardiac symptoms in patients undergoing angiography. *British Journal of Health Psychology, 15*(4), 841–857.

LePage, P., Akar, H., Temli, Y., Sen, D., Hasser, N., & Ivins, I. (2011). Comparing teachers' views on morality and moral education, a comparative study in Turkey and the United States. *Teaching and Teacher Education, 27*(2), 366–375.

Lepistö, S., Luukkaala, T., & Paavilainen, E. (2011). Witnessing and experiencing domestic violence: A descriptive study of adolescents. *Scandinavian Journal of Caring Sciences, 25*(1), 70–80.

Leppänen, J. M. (2011). Neural and developmental bases of the ability to recognize social signals of emotions. *Emotion Review, 3*(2), 179–188.

Lepper, M. R., Greene, D., & Nisbett, R. E. (1973). Undermining children's intrinsic interest with extrinsic rewards: A test of the overjustification hypothesis. *Journal of Personality and Social Psychology, 28,* 129–137.

Leri, A., Anversa, P., & Frishman, W. H. (Eds.) (2007). *Cardiovascular regeneration and stem cell therapy.* Hoboken, NJ: Wiley-Blackwell.

Lerner, J. S., Gonzalez, R. M., Small, D. A., & Fischhoff, B. (2003). Effects of fear and anger on perceived risks of terrorism: A national field experiment. *Psychological Science, 14,* 144–150.

Leslie, M. (2000, July/August). The Vexing Legacy of Lewis Terman. *Stanford Magazine.* Retrieved from http://www.stanfordalumni.org/news/magazine/2000/julaug/articles/terman.html.

Lester, K. J., Mathews, A., Davison, P. S., Burgess, J. L., & Yiend, J. (2011). Modifying cognitive errors promotes cognitive well being: A new approach to bias modification. *Journal of Behavior Therapy and Experimental Psychiatry, 42*(3), 298–308.

Lettvin, J. Y., Maturana, H. R., McCulloch, W. S., & Pitts, W. H. (1959). What the frog's eye tells the frog's brain. *Proceedings of the Institute of Radio Engineers, 47,* 1940–1951.

LeVay, S. (2003). Queer science: The use and abuse of research into homosexuality. *Archives of Sexual Behavior, 32*(2),187–189.

LeVay, S. (2011). *Gay, straight, and the reason why: The science of sexual orientation.* New York, NY: Oxford University Press.

Levenson, R. W. (1992). Autonomic nervous system differences among emotions. *Psychological Science, 3,* 23–27.

Levenson, R. W. (2007). Emotion elicitation with neurological patients. In J. A. Coan & J. J. B. Allen (Eds.), *Handbook of emotion elicitation and assessment. Series in affective science.* (pp. 158–168). New York, NY: Oxford University Press.

Lever, J. P. (2008). Poverty, stressful life events, and coping strategies. *The Spanish Journal of Psychology, 11,* 228–249.

Levine, J. R. (2001). *Why do fools fall in love: Experiencing the magic, mystery, and meaning of successful relationships.* New York, NY: Jossey-Bass.

Levinson, C. A., Giancola, P. R., & Parrott, D. J. (2011). Beliefs about aggression moderate alcohol's effects on aggression. *Experimental and Clinical Psychopharmacology, 19*(1), 64–74.

Levinthal, C. (2011). *Drugs, behavior, and modern society (7th ed.).* Boston, MA: Prentice Hall.

Levitan, L. C. (2008). Giving prejudice an attitude adjustment: The implications of attitude strength and social network attitudinal composition for prejudice and prejudice reduction. *Dissertation Abstracts International: Section B: The Sciences and Engineering, 68* (8-B), 5634.

Levy, B., Wegman, D., Baron, S., & Sokas, R. (2011). *Occupational and environmental health: Recognizing and preventing disease and injury* (6th ed.). New York, NY: Oxford University Press.

Levy, F., & Krebs, P. R. (2006). Cortical-subcortical re-entrant circuits and recurrent behavior. *Australian and New Zealand Journal of Psychiatry, 40,* 752–758.

Levy, K. N., Ellison, W. D., Scott, L. N., & Bernecker, S. L. (2011). Attachment style. *Journal of Clinical Psychology, 67*(2), 193–201.

Lew, A. R. (2011). Looking beyond the boundaries: Time to put landmarks back on the cognitive map? *Psychological Bulletin, 137*(3), 484–507.

Lewandowski Jr., G. W., Aron, A., & Gee, J. (2007). Personality goes a long way: The malleability of opposite-sex physical attractiveness. *Personal Relationships, 14,* 571–585.

Lewin, D., & Herron, H. (2007). Signs, symptoms, and risk factors: Health visitors' perspectives of child neglect. *Child Abuse Review, 16,* 93–107.

Lewis, M. B. (2011). Who is the fairest of them all? Race, attractiveness and skin color sexual dimorphism. *Personality and Individual Differences, 50*(2), 159–162.

Lewis, S. (1963). *Dear Shari.* New York, NY: Stein & Day.

Li, J-C. A. (2008). Rethinking the case against divorce. *Dissertation Abstracts International Section A: Humanities and Social Sciences, 68,* 4093.

Li, N. P., Bailey, J. M., Kenrick, D. T., & Linsenmeier, J. A. W. (2002). The necessities and luxuries of mate preferences: Testing the tradeoffs. *Journal of Personality and Social Psychology, 82*(6), 947–955.

Li, N. P., Valentine, K. A., & Patel, L. (2011). Mate preferences in the US and Singapore: A cross-cultural test of the mate preference priority model. *Personality and Individual Differences, 50*(2), 291–294.

Li, S., Lindenberger, U., Hommel, B., Aschersleben, G., Prinz, W., & Baltes, P. B. (2004). Transformations in the couplings among intellectual abilities and constituent cognitive processes across the life span. *Psychological Science, 15*(3), 155–163.

Li, Y., Kong, H., Song, Q., & Cai, J.-X. (2010). Chronic stress impairs learning and memory and changes frontal and hippocampal synaptosomal membrane fluidity in rats. *Acta Psychologica Sinica, 42*(2), 235–240.

Libby, E. W. (2011). The Black Swan: A lesson in parent/child relationships. *Psychology Today.* Retrieved from http://www.psychologytoday.com/blog/the-favorite-child/201102/the-black-swan-lesson-in-parentchild-relationships-0

Libon, D. J., Xie, S. X., Moore, P., Farmer, J., Antani, S., McCawley, G., Cross, K., & Grossman, M. (2007). Patterns of neuropsychological impairment in frontotemporal dementia. *Neurology, 68,* 369–375.

Lieberman, P. (1998). *Eve spoke: Human language and human evolution.* New York, NY: Norton.

Liew, S.-L., Ma, Y., Han, S., & Aziz-Zadeh, L. (2011). Who's afraid of the boss: Cultural differences in social hierarchies modulate self-face recognition in Chinese and Americans. *PLoS ONE, 6*(2). Retrieved from http://www.psy.pku.edu.cn/~hanshihui/2011/2011%20Liew%20and%20Han%20PLoS%20ONE%20reprint.pdf

Lilienfeld, S. O., Lynn, S. J., Ruscio, J., & Beyerstein, B. L. (2010). *50 great myths of popular psychology: Shattering widespread misconceptions about human behavior.* New York, NY: Wiley-Blackwell.

Lim, L., Chang, W., Yu, X., Chiu, H., Chong, M., & Kua, E. (2011). Depression in Chinese elderly populations. *Asia-Pacific Psychiatry, 3*(2), 46–53.

Lin, J., Kroenke, C. H., Epel, E., Kenna, H. A., Wolkowitz, O. M., Blackburn, E., & Rasgon, N. L. (2011). Greater endogenous estrogen exposure is associated with longer telomeres in postmenopausal women at risk for cognitive decline. *Brain Research, 1379,* 224–231.

Líndal, E., & Stefánsson, J. G. (2011). The long-term psychological effect of fatal accidents at sea on survivors: A cross-sectional study of North-Atlantic seamen. *Social Psychiatry and Psychiatric Epidemiology, 46*(3), 239–246.

Lindberg, B., Axelsson, K., & Öhrling, K. (2008). Adjusting to being a father to an infant born prematurely: Experiences from Swedish fathers. *Scandinavian Journal of Caring Sciences, 22,* 79–85.

Linden, E. (1993). Can animals think? *Time,* pp. 54–61.

Lindwall, M., Rennemark, M., & Berggren, T. (2008). Movement in mind: The relationship of exercise with cognitive status for older adults in the Swedish National Study on Aging and Care (SNAC). *Aging & Mental Health, 12,* 212–220.

Linnet, J., Møller, A., Peterson, E., Gjedde, A., & Doudet, D. (2011). Dopamine release in ventral striatum during Iowa Gambling Task performance is associated with increased excitement levels in pathological gambling. *Addiction, 106*(2), 383–390.

Lipowski, Z. J. (1986). Psychosomatic medicine: Past and present: I. Historical background. *Canadian Journal of Psychiatry, 31,* 2–7.

Lippa, R. A. (2007). The preferred traits of mates in a cross-national study of heterosexual and homosexual men and women: An examination of biological and cultural influences. *Archives of Sexual Behavior, 36,* 193–208.

Lipsanen, T., Korkeila, J., Peltola, P., Järvinen, J., Langen, K., & Lauerma, H. (2004). Dissociative disorders among psychiatric patients: Comparison with a nonclinical sample. *European Psychiatry, 19*(1), 53–55.

Little, A., Jones, B., & DeBruine, L. (2011). Facial attractiveness: Evolutionary based research. *Philosophical Transactions of the Royal Society B, 366*(1571), 1638–1659.

Liu, J. H., & Latané, B. (1998). Extremitization of attitudes: Does thought- and discussion-induced polarization cumulate? *Basic and Applied Social Psychology, 20,* 103–110.

Livingston, M. (2011). A longitudinal analysis of alcohol outlet density and domestic violence. *Addiction, 106*(5), 919–925.

Livingston, R. W., & Drwecki, B. B. (2007). Why are some individuals not racially biased? Susceptibility to affective conditioning predicts nonprejudice toward Blacks. *Psychological Science, 18,* 816–823.

Lodge, D. J., & Grace, A. A. (2011). Developmental pathology, dopamine, stress and schizophrenia. *International Journal of Developmental Neuroscience, 29*(3), 207–213.

Loewenthal, D., & Winter, D. (Eds.. (2006). *What is psychotherapeutic research?* London, England: Karnac Books.

Loftus, E. (1982). Memory and its distortions. In A. G. Kraut (Ed.), *The G. Stanley Hall Lecture Series Vol. 2,* (pp. 123–154). Washington, DC: American Psychological Association.

Loftus, E. (2002, May/June). My story: Dear Mother. *Psychology Today,* 67–70.

Loftus, E. F. (1993). Psychologists in the eyewitness world. *American Psychologist, 48,* 550–552.

Loftus, E. F. (1997). Memory for a past that never was. *Current Directions in Psychological Science, 6*(3), 60–65.

Loftus, E. F. (2000). Remembering what never happened. In E. Tulving, et al. (Eds.), *Memory, consciousness, and the brain: The Tallinn Conference* (pp. 106–118). Philadelphia, PA: Psychology Press/Taylor & Francis.

Loftus, E. F. (2001). Imagining the past. *Psychologist, 14*(11), 584–587.

Loftus, E. F. (2007). Memory distortions: Problems solved and unsolved. In M. Garry, & H. Hayne (Eds.), *Do justice and let the skies fall* (pp. 1–14). Mahwah, NJ: Erlbaum.

Loftus, E. F. (2010). Afterword: Why parapsychology is not yet ready for prime time. Debating psychic experience: Human potential or human illusion? In S. Krippner & H. L. Friedman (Eds.), *Debating psychic experience: Human potential or human illusion?* (pp. 211–214). Santa Barbara, CA: Praeger/ABC-CLIO.

Loftus, E. F. (2011). How I got started: From semantic memory to expert testimony. *Applied Cognitive Psychology, 25*(2), 347–348.

Loftus, E. F., & Cahill, L. (2007). Memory distortion from misattribution to rich false memory. In J. S. Nairne (Ed.), *The foundations of remembering: Essays in honor of Henry L. Roediger, III* (pp. 413–425). New York, NY: Psychology Press.

Loftus, E., & Ketcham, K. (1994). *The myth of repressed memories: False memories and allegations of sexual abuse.* New York, NY: St. Martin's Press.

Loftus, E., & Polage, D. C. (1999). Repressed memories: When are they real? When are they false? *Psychiatric Clinics of North America, 22,* 61–70.

Loftus, G. R. (2007). Elizabeth F. Loftus: The early years. In M. Garry & H. Hayne (Eds.), *Do justice and let the sky fall: Elizabeth Loftus and her contributions to science, law, and academic freedom* (pp. 27–31). Mahwah, NJ: Erlbaum.

Logan, R. W., Arjona, A., & Sarkar, D. K. (2011). Role of sympathetic nervous system in the entrainment of circadian natural-killer cell function. *Brain, Behavior, and Immunity, 25*(1), 101–109.

Logothetis, N. K. (2008). What we can do and what we cannot do with fMRI. *Nature, 453,* 869–878. Retrieved from http://www.nature.com/nature/journal/v453/n7197/abs/nature06976.html

London, L. H., Tierney, G., Buhin, L., Greco, D. M., & Cooper, C. J. (2002). Kids' college: Enhancing children's appreciation and acceptance of cultural diversity. *Journal of Prevention & Intervention in the Community, 24*(2), 63–78.

Loo, C. K., Mahon, M., Katalinic, N., Lyndon, B., & Hadzi-Pavlovic, D. (2011). Predictors of response to ultrabrief right unilateral electroconvulsive therapy. *Journal of Affective Disorders, 130*(1–2), 192–197.

Lopez, F., & Hsu, P-C. (2002). Further validation of a measure of parent-adult attachment style. *Measurement & Evaluation in Counseling & Development, 34,* 223–237.

Lopez, J. C. (2002). Brain repair: A spinal scaffold. *Nature Reviews Neuroscience, 3,* 256.

Lopez-Larson, M. P., Bogorodzki, P., Rogowska, J., McGlade, E., King, J. B., Terry, J., & Yurgelun-Todd, D. (2011). Altered prefrontal and insular cortical thickness in adolescent marijuana users. *Behavioural Brain Research, 220*(1), 164–172.

Lopez-Munoz, F., & Alamo, C. (2011). *Neurobiology of depression.* Boca Raton, FL: CRC Press.

Lorenz, K. Z. (1937). The companion in the bird's world. *Auk, 54,* 245–273.

Lorenz, K. Z. (1981). *The foundations of ethology.* New York, NY: Springer-Verlag.

Lores-Arnaiz, S., Bustamante, J., Czernizyniec, A., Galeano, P., Gervasoni, M. G., Martinez, A. R., Paglia, N., Cores, V., & Lores-Arnaiz, M. R. (2007). Exposure to enriched environments increases brain nitric oxide synthase and improves cognitive performance in prepubertal but not in young rats. *Behavioural Brain Research, 184,* 117–123.

Lott, D. A. (2000). *The new flirting game.* London, England: Sage.

Lovibond, P. (2011). Learning and anxiety: A cognitive perspective. In T. Schachtman & S. Reilly (Eds.), *Associative learning and conditioning theory: Human and non-human applications* (pp. 104–120). Oxford, UK: Oxford University Press.

Loxton, N. J., Nguyen, D., Casey, L., & Dawe, S. (2008). Reward drive, rash impulsivity and punishment sensitivity in problem gamblers. *Personality & Individual Differences, 45,* 167–173.

Lozano, A. M. (2011). Harnessing plasticity to reset dysfunctional neurons. *The New England Journal of Medicine, 364*(14), 1367–1368.

Lu, Z. L., Williamson, S. J., & Kaufman, L. (1992). Behavioral lifetime of human auditory sensory memory predicted by physiological measures. *Science, 258,* 1668–1670.

Luijten, M., Veltman, D. J., van den Brink, W., Hester, R., Field, M., Smits, M., &

Franken, I. H. A. (2011). Neurobiological substrate of smoking-related attentional bias. *NeuroImage, 54(3),* 2374–2381

Lundberg, U. (2011). Neuroendocrine measures. In R. J. Contrada & A. Baum (Eds.), *The handbook of stress science: Biology, psychology, and health* (pp. 531–542). New York, NY: Springer.

Lundy, B. L., & Skeel, M. M. (2010). Decreased empathic sensitivity for distressed infants in neurotic adults: The mediating role of remembered parental rejection. *Motivation and Emotion, 34(4),* 407–417.

Luria, A. R. (1968). *The mind of a mnemonist: A little book about a vast memory.* New York, NY: Basic Books.

Luria, A. R. (1976). *Cognitive development: Its cultural and social foundations.* Cambridge, MA: Harvard University Press.

Luxton, D. D., Skopp, N. A., & Maguen, S. (2010). Gender differences in depression and PTSD symptoms following combat exposure. *Depression and Anxiety, 27(11),* 1027–1033.

Lyn, H., Greenfield, P. M., Savage-Rumbaugh, S., Gillespie-Lynch, K., & Hopkins, W. D. (2011). Nonhuman primates do declare! A comparison of declarative symbol and gesture use in two children, two bonobos, and a chimpanzee. *Language & Communication, 31(1),* 63–74.

Lynam, D. R., Miller, J. D., Miller, D. J., Bornovalova, M. A., & Lejuez, C. W. (2011). Testing the relations between impulsivity-related traits, suicidality, and nonsuicidal self-injury: A test of the incremental validity of the UPPS model. *Personality Disorders: Theory, Research, and Treatment, 2(2),* 151–160.

Lynn, R., & Harvey, J. (2008). The decline of the world's IQ. *Intelligence, 36,* 112–120.

Lynn, S. J. (2007). Hypnosis reconsidered. *American Journal of Clinical Hypnosis, 49,* 195–197.

Lynn, S. J., Rhue, J. W. & Kirsch, I. (Eds.). (2010). *Handbook of clinical hypnosis* (2ⁿᵈ ed.). Washington, DC: American Psychological Association.

Lynn, S. J., Vanderhoff, H., Shindler, K., & Stafford, J. (2002). Defining hypnosis as a trance vs. cooperation: Hypnotic inductions, suggestibility, and performance standards. *American Journal of Clinical Hypnosis, 44(3–4),* 231–240.

Lynne-Landsman, S. D., Graber, J. A., Nichols, T. R., & Botvin, G. J. (2011). Trajectories of aggression, delinquency, and substance use across middle school among urban, minority adolescents. *Aggressive Behavior, 37(2),* 161–176.

Lyons-Ruth, K., Holmes, B. M., Sasvari-Szekely, M., Ronai, Z., Nemoda, Z., & Pauls, D. (2007). Serotonin transporter polymorphism and borderline or antisocial traits among low-income young adults. *Psychiatric Genetics, 17,* 339–343.

Lyubimov, N.N. (1992). *Electrophysiological characteristics of sensory processing and mobilization of hidden brain reserves. 2nd Russian-Swedish Symposium New Research in Neurobiology,* Moscow, Russia: Russian Academy of Science Institute of Human Brain.

Maas, J. B. (1999). *Power sleep.* New York, NY: HarperPerennial.

Maas, J., B., Wherry, M. L., Axelrod, D. J., Hogan, B. R., & Bloomin, J. (1999). *Power sleep: The revolutionary program that prepares your mind for peak performance.* New York, NY: HarperPerennial.

Macmillan, M. B. (2000). *An odd kind of fame: Stories of Phineas Gage.* Cambridge, MA: MIT Press.

Madole, K. L., Oakes, L. M., & Rakison, D. H. (2011). Information-processing approaches to infants' developing representation of dynamic features. In L. M. Oakes, C. H. Cashon, M. Casasola, & D. H. Rakison (Eds.), *Infant perception and cognition: Recent advances, emerging theories, and future directions* (pp. 153–177). New York, NY: Oxford University Press.

Maehr, M. L., & Urdan, T. C. (2000). *Advances in motivation and achievement: The role of context.* Greewich, CT: JAI Press.

Mahoney, A. (2011). Goodness of fit: The challenge of parenting gifted children. In J. L. Jolly, D. J. Treffinger, T. F. Inman, & J. F. Smutny (Eds.), *Parenting gifted children: The authoritative guide from the National Association for Gifted Children* (pp. 539–545). Waco, TX: Prufrock Press.

Mahoney, C. R., Castellani, J., Kramer, F. M., Young, A., & Lieberman, H. R. (2007). Tyrosine supplementation mitigates working memory decrements during cold exposure. *Physiology & Behavior, 92,* 575–582.

Maillard, L., Barbeau, E. J., Baumann, C., Koessler, L., Bénar, C., Chauvel, P., & Liégeois-Chauvel, C. (2011). From perception to recognition memory: Time course and lateralization of neural substrates of word and abstract picture processing. *Journal of Cognitive Neuroscience, 23(4),* 782–800.

Main, M. & Solomon, J. (1986). Discovery of an insecure-disorganized attachment pattern. In T. Brazelton & M. W. Yogman (Eds.), *Affective development in infancy* (pp. 95–124). Westport, CT: Ablex Publishing.

Main, M. & Solomon, J. (1990). Procedures for identifying infants as disorganized/disoriented during the Ainsworth Strange Situation. In M. T. Greenberg, D. Cicchetti, & E. M. Cummings (Eds.), *Attachment in the preschool years: Theory, research, and intervention, The John D and Catherine T. MacArthur Foundation series on mental health and development* (pp. 121–160). Chicago, IL: University of Chicago Press.

Maisto, S. A., Galizio, M., & Connors, G. J. (2011). *Drug use and abuse* (6ᵗʰ ed.). Belmont, CA: Cengage.

Majid, H., & Hirshkowitz, M. (2010). Therapeutics of narcolepsy. *Sleep Medicine Clinics, 5(4),* 659–673.

Major, B., & O'Brien, L. T. (2005). The social psychology of stigma. *Annual Review of Psychology, 56,* 393–421.

Major, B., Spencer, S., Schmader, T., Wolfe, C., & Crocker, J. (1998). Coping with negative stereotypes about intellectual performance: The role of psychological disengagement. *Personality & Social Psychology Bulletin, 24(1),* 34–50.

Malik, S., McGlone, F., & Dagher, A. (2011). State of expectancy modulates the neural response to visual food stimuli in humans. *Appetite, 56(2),* 302–309.

Malt, B. C., & Wolff, P. (Eds.). (2010). *Words and the mind: How words capture human experience.* New York, NY: Oxford University Press.

Malti, T. (2007). Moral emotions and aggressive behavior in childhood. In G. Steffgen & M. Gollwitzer (Eds.), *Emotions and aggressive behavior* (pp. 185–200). Ashland, OH: Hogrefe & Huber.

Manago, A. M., & Greenfield, P. M. (2011). The construction of independent values among Maya women at the forefront of social change: Four case studies. *Ethos, 39(1),* 1–29.

Maner, J. K., DeWall, C. N., & Gailliot, M. T. (2008). Selective attention to signs of success: Social dominance and early stage interpersonal perception. *Personality and Social Psychology Bulletin, 34,* 488–501.

Manly, J. J., Byrd, D., Touradji, P., Sanchez, D., & Stern, Y. (2004). Literacy and cognitive change among ethnically diverse elders. *International Journal of Psychology, 39(1),* 47–60.

Manning, B. (2007). Sex and perceptions of mate value in women: An evolutionary perspective. *Dissertation Abstracts International: Section B: The Sciences and Engineering, 68(6–B),* 4177.

Maran, M. (2010). *My lie: A true story of false memory.* New York, NY: Jossey-Bass.

Marano, H. E. (2003). Procrastination: Ten things to know. *Psychology Today.* Retrieved from http://www.psychologytoday.com/articles/200308/procrastination-ten-things-know

Marano, H. E. (2010). Why we procrastinate. *Psychology Today.* Retrieved from http://www.psychologytoday.com/articles/200507/why-we-procrastinate

Marazziti, D., Masala, I., Baroni, S., Polini, M., Massimetti, G., Giannaccini, G., Betti, L., Italiani, P., Fabbrini, L., Caglieresi, C., Moschini, C., Canale, D., Lucacchini, A., & Mauri, M. (2010). Male axillary extracts modify the affinity of the platelet serotonin transporter and impulsiveness in women. *Physiology & Behavior, 100(4),* 364–368.

Marcus, S. (2008). *The other Victorians: A study of sexuality and pornography in mid-nineteenth-century England.* Piscataway, NJ: Transaction Publishers.

Maric, M., Heyne, D. A., van Widenfelt, B. M., & Westenberg, P. M. (2011). Distorted cognitive processing in youth: The structure of negative cognitive errors and their associations with anxiety. *Cognitive Therapy and Research, 35(1),* 11–20.

Marin, M.-F., Lord, C., Andrews, J., Juster, R.-P., Sindi, S., Arsenault-Lapierre, G., Fiocco, A., & Lupien, S. J. (2011). Chronic stress, cognitive functioning and mental health. *Neurobiology of Learning and Memory.* Retrieved from http://www.ncbi.nlm.nih.gov/pubmed/21376129

Mark, G. P., Shabani, S., Dobbs, L. K., & Hansen, S. T. (2011). Cholinergic modulation of mesolimbic dopamine function and reward. *Physiology & Behavior.* doi: 10.1016/j.physbeh.2011.04.052

Markel, H. (2011). John Harvey Kellogg and the pursuit of wellness. *Journal of the American Medical Association, 305(17),* 1814–1815.

Market Opinion Research International (MORI) (1999, May 20). Animal experimentation: Special report tipsheet from New Scientist. *New Scientist.* Retrieved from http://www.newswise.com/articles/animal-experimentation-special-report-tipsheet-from-new-scientist

Market Opinion Research International (MORI) (2005, January). *Use of animals in medical research for coalition for medical progress.* London, England: Author.

Markey, P. M., & Markey, C. N. (2010). Vulnerability to violent video games: A review and integration of personality research. *Review of General Psychology, 14(2),* 82–91.

Markham, J. A., & Koenig, J. I. (2011). Prenatal stress: Role in psychotic and depressive diseases. *Psychopharmacology, 214(1),* 89–106.

Marks, D. F. (1990). Comprehensive commentary, insightful criticism. *Skeptical Inquirer, 14,* 413–418.

Marks, D. F., Murray, M. D., Evans, B., & Estacio, E. V., (2011). *Health psychology: Theory, research and practice* (3rd ed.). London, UK: Sage.

Marks, L. D., Hopkins, K. C., Monroe, P. A., Nesteruk, O., & Sasser, D. D. (2008). "Together, we are strong": A qualitative study of happy, enduring African American marriages. *Family Relations, 57,* 172–185.

Markstrom, C. A., & Marshall, S. K. (2007). The psychosocial inventory of ego strengths: Examination of theory and psychometric properties. *Journal of Adolescence, 30,* 63–79.

Markus, H. R., & Kitayama, S. (1998). The cultural psychology of personality. *Journal of Cross-Cultural Psychology, 29,* 63–87.

Markus, H. R., & Kitayama, S. (2003). Culture, self, and the reality of the social. *Psychological Inquiry, 14(3–4),* 277–283.

Markus, H. R., & Kitayama, S. (2010). Cultures and selves: A cycle of mutual constitution. *Perspectives on Psychological Science, 5(4),* 420–430.

Marques, L., Robinaugh, D., LeBlanc, N., & Hinton, D. (2011). Cross-cultural variations in the prevalence and presentation of anxiety disorders. *Expert Review of Neurotherapeutics, 11(2),* 313–322.

Marsee, M. A., Weems, C. F., Taylor, L. K. (2008). Exploring the association between aggression and anxiety in youth: A look at aggressive subtypes, gender, and social cognition. *Journal of Child and Family Studies, 17,* 154–168.

Marsh, A.A., Elfenbein, H.A., Ambady, N. (2007). Separated by a common language: Nonverbal accents and cultural stereotypes about Americans and Australians. *Journal of Cross-Cultural Psychology, 38,* 284–301.

Marshall, D. S. (1971). Sexual behavior in Mangaia. In D. S. Marshall & R. C. Suggs (Eds.), *Human sexual behavior* (pp. 103–162). Englewood Cliffs, NJ: Prentice Hall.

Marshall, J. A. R. (2011). Ultimate causes and the evolution of altruism. *Behavioral Ecology and Sociobiology, 65(3),* 503–512.

Marshall, M., & Brown, J. D. (2008). On the psychological benefits of self-enhancement. In E. C. Chang (Ed.). *Self-criticism and self-enhancement: Theory, research, and clinical implications* (pp. 19–35). Washington, DC: American Psychological Association.

Marshall, V., & Bengston, V. (2011). Theoretical perspectives on the sociology of aging. In R. Settersten & J. Angel (Eds.), *Handbook of Sociology of Aging* (pp. 17–33). New York, NY: Springer.

Martella, D., Casagrande, M., & Lupiáñez, J. (2011). Alerting, orienting and executive control: The effects of sleep deprivation on attentional networks. *Experimental Brain Research, 210(1),* 81–89.

Martens, U., Ansorge, U., & Kiefer, M. (2011).Controlling the unconscious: Attentional task sets modulate subliminal semantic and visuomotor processes differentially. *Psychological Science, 22(2),* 282–291.

Martin, C. L., & Fabes, R. (2009). *Discovering child development* (2nd ed.). Belmont, CA: Cengage.

Martin, L. A., Doster, J. A., Critelli, J. W., Purdum, M., Powers, C., Lambert, P. L., & Miranda, V. (2011). The 'distressed' personality, coping, and cardiovascular risk. *Stress and Health: Journal of the International Society for the Investigation of Stress, 27(1),* 64–72.

Martin, S. (2008). How psychology helps you every day. *Psychology Today Monitor.* Retrieved from http://www.apa.org/monitor/2008/10/sternberg.aspx

Martinelli, E. A. (2006). Paternal role development and acquisition in fathers of pre-term infants: A qualitative study. *Dissertation Abstracts International: Section B: The Sciences and Engineering, 66(9-B),* 5125.

Martinko, M. J., Harvey, P., & Dasborough, M. T. (2011). Attribution theory in the organizational sciences: A case of unrealized potential. *Journal of Organizational Behavior, 32(1),* 144–149.

Marusich, J. A., Darna, M., Charnigo, R. J., Dwoskin, L. P., & Bardo, M. T. (2011). A multivariate assessment of individual differences in sensation seeking and impulsivity as predictors of amphetamine self-administration and prefrontal dopamine function in rats. *Experimental and Clinical Psychopharmacology.* Advance online publication. doi:10.1037/a0023897

Maslow, A. H. (1954). *Motivation and personality.* New York, NY: Harper & Row.

Maslow, A. H. (1970). *Motivation and personality (2nd ed.).* New York, NY: Harper & Row.

Maslow, A. H. (1999). *Toward a psychology of being* (3rd ed.). New York, NY: Wiley.

Mason, M. F., & Morris, M. W. (2010). Culture, attribution and automaticity: A social cognitive neuroscience view. *Social Cognitive and Affective Neuroscience, 5(2–3),* 292–306.

Masten A. S., & Coatsworth, J. D. (1998). The development of competence in favorable and unfavorable environments. *American Psychologist, 53*, 205–220.

Masten, A. S., Wright, M. O. (2010). Resilience over the lifespan: Developmental perspectives on resistance, recovery, and transformation. In J. W. Reich, J. Alex, & J. S. Stuart (Eds.), *Handbook of adult resilience* (pp. 213–237). New York, NY: Guilford Press.

Masters, W. H., & Johnson, V. E. (1961). Orgasm, anatomy of the female. In A. Ellis & A. Abarbonel (Eds.), *Encyclopedia of Sexual Behavior,* Vol. 2. New York, NY: Hawthorn.

Masters, W. H., & Johnson, V. E. (1966). *Human sexual response.* Boston, MA: Little, Brown.

Masters, W. H., & Johnson, V. E. (1970). *Human sexual inadequacy.* Boston, MA: Little, Brown.

Mastroinni, G. (2011). The person-situation debate: Implications for military leadership and civilian-military relations. *Journal of Military Ethics, 10*(1), 2–16.

Matlin, M. W. (2003). From menarche to menopause: Misconceptions about women's reproductive lives. *Psychology Science, 45*(Suppl2), 106–122.

Matlin, M. W. (2012). *The psychology of women* (7th ed.). Belmont, CA: Cengage.

Matlin, M. W., & Foley, H. J. (1997). *Sensation and perception* (4th ed.). Boston, MA: Allyn and Bacon.

Matsumoto, D. (1992). More evidence for the universality of a contempt expression. *Motivation and Emotion, 16*, 363–368.

Matsumoto, D. (2000). *Culture and psychology: People around the world.* Belmont, CA: Wadsworth.

Matsumoto, D. (2010). *APA handbook of interpersonal communication.* Washington, DC: American Psychological Association.

Matsumoto, D., & Hwang, H. S. (2011). Culture, emotion, and expression. In M. J. Gelfand, C.-y. Chiu, & Y.-y. Hong (Eds.), *Advances in culture and psychology. Advances in culture and psychology* (Vol. 1) (pp. 53–98). New York, NY: Oxford University Press.

Matsumoto, D., & Juang, L. (2008). *Culture and psychology* (4th ed.). Belmont, CA: Cengage.

Matsumoto, D., & Kupperbusch, C. (2001). Idiocentric and allocentric differences in emotional expression, experience, and the coherence between expression and experience. *Asian Journal of Social Psychology, 4*(2), 113–131.

Matthews, B. (2011). Female genital mutilation: Australian law, policy and practical challenges for doctors. *Medical Journal of Australia, 194*(3), 139–141.

Matthews, J. (2011). *Starting from scratch: The origin and development of expression, representation and symbolism in human and non-human primates.* New York, NY: Psychology Press.

Mauri, M.C., Rovera, C., Paletta, S., De Gaspari, I.F., Maffini, M., & Altamura, A.C. (2011). Aggression and psychopharmacological treatments in major psychosis and personality disorders during hospitalisation. *Progress in Neuro-Psychopharmacology & Biological Psychiatry.* Advance online publication. doi:10.1016/j.pnpbp.2011.05.008

May, A., Hajak, G., Gaenssbauer, S., Steffens, T., Langguth, B., Kleinjung, T., & Eichhammer, P. (2007). Structural brain alterations following 5 days of intervention: Dynamic aspects of neuroplasticity. *Cerebral Cortex, 17*, 205–210.

May-Collado, L. J. (2010). Changes in whistle structure of two dolphin species during interspecific associations. *Ethology, 116*(11), 1065–1074.

Mayer, J. D., Roberts, R. D., & Barsade, S. G. (2008). Human abilities: Emotional intelligence. *Annual Review of Psychology, 59*, 507–536.

Mayers, A. G., Baldwin, D. S., Dyson, R., Middleton, R. W., & Mustapha, A. (2003). Use of St John's wort (Hypericum perforatum L) in members of a depression self-help organization: A 12-week open prospective pilot study using the HADS scale. *Primary Care Psychiatry, 9*(1), 15–20.

Mays, V. M., Cochran, S. D., & Barnes, N. W. (2007). Race, race-based discrimination, and health outcomes among African Americans. *Annual Review of Psychology, 58*, 201–225.

Mazzoni, G., & Memon, A. (2003). Imagination can create false autobiographical memories. *Psychological Science, 14*, 186–188.

Mazzoni, G., & Vannucci, M. (2007). Hindsight bias, the misinformation effect, and false autobiographical memories. *Social Cognition, 25*, 203–220.

McCabe, C., & Rolls, E. T. (2007). Umami: A delicious flavor formed by convergence of taste and olfactory pathways in the human brain. *European Journal of Neuroscience, 25*, 1855–1864.

McCart, M. R., Zajac, K., Danielson, C. K., Strachan, M., Ruggiero, K. J., Smith, D. W., Saunders, B., Kilpatrick, D. G. (2011). Interpersonal victimization, posttraumatic stress disorder, and change in adolescent substance use prevalence over a ten-year period. *Journal of Clinical Child and Adolescent Psychology, 40*(1), 136–143.

McCarthy, M. J., Zhang, H., Neff, N. H., & Hadjiconstantinou, M. (2011). Desensitization of δ-opioid receptors in nucleus accumbens during nicotine withdrawal. *Psychopharmacology, 213*(4), 735–744.

McClelland, D. C. (1958). Risk-taking in children with high and low need for achievement. In J. W. Atkinson (Ed.), *Motives in fantasy, action, and society.* Princeton, NJ: Van Nostrand.

McClelland, D. C. (1987). Characteristics of successful entrepreneurs. *Journal of Creative Behavior, 3*, 219–233.

McClelland, D. C. (1993). Intelligence is not the best predictor of job performance. *Current Directions in Psychological Science, 2*, 5–6.

McClelland, J. L. (1995). Constructive memory and memory distortions: A parallel-distributed processing approach. In D. L. Schachter (Ed.), *Memory distortions: How minds, brains, and societies reconstruct the past* (pp. 69–90). Cambridge. MA: Harvard University Press.

McClelland, J. L. (2011). Memory as a constructive process: The parallel distributed processing approach. In S. Nalbantian, P. M. Matthews, & J. L. McClelland (Eds.), *The memory process: Neuroscientific and humanistic perspectives* (pp. 129–155). Cambridge, MA: MIT Press.

McClure, J., Meyer, L. H., Garisch, J., Fischer, R., Weir, K. F., & Walkey, F. H. (2011). Students' attributions for their best and worst marks: Do they relate to achievement? *Contemporary Educational Psychology, 36*(2), 71–81.

McCormick, N. B. (2010). Sexual scripts: Social and therapeutic implications. *Sexual and Relationship Therapy, 25*(1), 96–120.

McCrae, R. (2011). Cross-Cultural Research on the Five-Factor Model of Personality. *Online Readings in Psychology and Culture, Unit 4.* Retrieved from *http://scholarworks.gvsu.edu/orpc/vol4/iss4/1*

McCrae, R. R. (2004). Human nature and culture: A trait perspective. *Journal of Research in Personality, 38*(1), 3–14.

McCrae, R. R., & Costa, P. T. Jr. (1990). *Personality in adulthood.* New York, NY: Guilford Press.

McCrae, R. R., & Costa, P. T. Jr. (1999). A five factor theory of personality. In L. A.

Pervin, & O. P. John (Eds.), *Handbook of personality: Theory and research* (pp. 139–153). New York, NY: Guilford Press.

McCrae, R. R., & Sutin, A. R. (2007). New frontiers for the Five-Factor Model: A preview of the literature. *Social and Personality Psychology Compass, 1*, 423–440.

McCrae, R. R., Costa, P. T. Jr., Hrebíčková, M., Urbánek, T., Martin, T. A., Oryol, V. E., Rukavishnikov, A. A., & Senin, I. G. (2004). Age differences in personality traits across cultures: Self-report and observer perspectives. *European Journal of Personality, 18*(2), 143–157.

McCrae, R. R., Costa, P. T. Jr., Martin, T. A., Oryol, V. E., Rukavishnikov, A. A., Senin, I. G., Hrebíčková, M., & Urbánek, T. (2004). Consensual validation of personality traits across cultures. *Journal of Research in Personality, 38*(2), 179–201.

McCrae, R. R., Costa, P. T., Jr., Ostendorf, F., Angleitner, A., Hrebickova, M., Avia, M. D., Sanz, J., Sanchez-Bernardos, M. L., Kusdil, M. E., Woodfield, R., Saunders, P. R., & Smith, P. B. (2000). Nature over nurture: Temperament, personality, and life span development. *Journal of Personality and Social Psychology, 78*(1), 173–186.

McDougall, W. (1908). *Social psychology.* New York, NY: Putnam's Sons.

McEvoy, P. M. (2007). Effectiveness of cognitive behavioural group therapy for social phobia in a community clinic: A benchmarking study. *Behaviour Research and Therapy, 45*, 3030–3040.

McFarlane, W. R. (2006). Family expressed emotion prior to onset of psychosis. In S. R. H. Beach, M. Z. Wamboldt, N. J. Kaslow, R. E. Heyman, M. B. First, et al., (Eds), *Relational processes and DSM-V: Neuroscience, assessment, prevention, and treatment* (pp. 77–87). Washington, DC: American Psychiatric Association.

McFarlane, W. R. (2011). Integrating the family in the treatment of psychotic disorders. In R. Hagen, D. Turkington, T. Berge, & R. W. Gråwe (Eds.), *International Society for the Psychological Treatments of the Schizophrenias and Other Psychoses. CBT for psychosis: A symptom-based approach* (pp. 193–209). New York, NY: Routledge/Taylor & Francis Group.

McGhie, A., & Chapman, H. (1961). Disorders of attention and perception in early schizophrenia. *British Journal of Medical Psychology, 34*, 103–116.

McGrath, J. (2011). Environmental risk factors for schizophrenia. In D. Weinberger, & P. Harrison (Eds.), *Schizophrenia* (3rd ed.) (pp. 226–244). Hoboken, NJ: Wiley.

McGrath, J. M. (2009). Touch and massage in the newborn period: Effects on biomarkers and brain development. *The Journal of Perinatal & Neonatal Nursing, 23*(4), 304–306.

McGrath, J., Welham, J., Scott, J., Varghese, D., Degenhardt, L., Hayatbakhsh, M. R., Alati, R., Williams, G., Bor, W., & Najman, J. M. (2010). Association between cannabis use and psychosis-related outcomes using sibling pair analysis in a cohort of young adults. *Archives of General Psychiatry, 67*(5), 440–447.

McGrath, P. (2002). Qualitative findings on the experience of end-of-life care for hematological malignancies. *American Journal of Hospice & Palliative Care, 19*(2), 103–111.

McGrew, K., & Flanagan, D. (1998). *The Intelligence Test Desk Reference: Gf-Gc cross-battery assessment.* Boston, MA: Allyn and Bacon.

McGue, M., Bouchard, T. J., Iacono, W. G., & Lykken, D. T. (1993). Behavioral genetics of cognitive ability: A life-span perspective. In R. Plomin & G. McClearn (Eds.), *Nature, nurture, and psychology* (pp. 59–76). Washington, DC: American Psychological Association.

McGuinness, T. M., & Schneider, K. (2007). Poverty, child mistreatment, and foster care. *Journal of the American Psychiatric Nurses Association,13*, 296–303.

McHenry, R. (2010). Multitasking to death. *Encyclopedia Britannica Blog.* Retrieved from http://www.britannica.com/blogs/2010/05/multitasking-to-death/

McKinney, C., Donnelly, R., & Renk, K. (2008). Perceived parenting, positive and negative perceptions of parents, and late adolescent emotional adjustment. *Child and Adolescent Mental Health, 13*, 66–73.

McLoyd, V. C. (2011). How money matters for children's socioemotional adjustment: Family processes and parental investment. In G. Carlo, L. J. Crockett, & M. A. Carranza (Eds.), *Nebraska symposium on motivation. Health disparities in youth and families: Research and applications* (pp. 33–72). New York, NY: Springer.

McNamara, J. M. (2007). Long-term disadvantage among elderly women: The effects of work history. *Social Service Review, 81*, 423–452.

McNamara, J. M., Barta, Z., Fromhage, L., & Houston, A. I. (2008). The coevolution of choosiness and cooperation. *Nature, 451*, 189–201.

McNamara, P., McLaren, D., & Durso, K. (2007). Representation of the self in REM and NREM dreams. *Dreaming, 17*, 113–126.

McNeill, E. H. (2011). Hope as a strategy for improving student achievement and dissuading repeat pregnancy in pregnant and parenting adolescents. *Dissertation Abstracts International Section A: Humanities and Social Sciences, 71*(8-A), 2769.

Mead, E. (2012). *Family therapy education and supervision.* Hoboken, NJ: Wiley.

Meaney, M. J. (2010). Epigenetics and the biological definition of gene x environment interactions. *Child Development, 81*(1), 41–79.

Medco Health Solutions. (2004, May 17). *Medco Study Reveals Pediatric Spending Spike on Drugs to Treat Behavioral Problems.* Franklin Lakes, NJ. Retrieved from http://phx.corporate-ir.net/phoenix.zhtml?c=131268&p=irol-newsArticle&ID=571791&highlight

Medina, J. J. (1996). *The clock of ages: Why we age.* Cambridge, MA: Cambridge University Press.

Medina, J. L., Vujanovic, A. A., Smits, J. A. J., Irons, J. G., Zvolensky, M. J., & Bonn-Miller, M. O. (2011). Exercise and coping-oriented alcohol use among a trauma-exposed sample. *Addictive Behaviors, 36*(3), 274–277.

Meeus, W., & Raaijmakers, Q. (1989). Autoritätsgehorsam in Experimenten des Milgram-Typs: Eine Forschungsübersicht [Obedience to authority in Milgram-type studies: A research review]. *Zeitschrift für Sozialpsychologie, 20*(2), 70–85.

Meghan, O. (2010). Good grief: Is there a better way to be bereaved? *The New Yorker,* 66–72.

Mehta, P. H., Gosling, S. D. (2006). How can animal studies contribute to research on the biological bases of personality? In T. Canli (Ed.), *Biology of personality and individual differences* (pp. 427–448). New York, NY: Guilford.

Mehta, S., Orenczuk, S., Hansen, K. T., Aubut, J.-A. L., Hitzig, S. L., Legassic, M., & Teasell, R. (2011). An evidence-based review of the effectiveness of cognitive behavioral therapy for psychosocial issues post-spinal cord injury. *Rehabilitation Psychology, 56*(1), 15–25.

Meltzer, G. (2000). Genetics and etiology of schizophrenia and bipolar disorder. *Biological Psychiatry, 47*(3), 171–178.

Meltzer, L. (2004). Resilience and learning disabilities: Research on internal and external protective dynamics. *Learning Disabilities Research & Practice,19*(1), 1–2.

Meltzoff, A. N., & Moore, M. K. (1977). Imitation of facial and manual gestures by human neonates. *Science, 198*, 75–78.

Meltzoff, A. N., & Moore, M. K. (1985). Cognitive foundations and social functions of imitation and intermodal representation in infancy. In J. Mehler & R. Fox (Eds.), *Neonate cognition: Beyond the blooming buzzing confusion*. Hillsdale, NJ: Erlbaum.

Meltzoff, A. N., & Moore, M. K. (1994). Imitation, memory, and the representation of persons. *Infant Behavior and Development, 17*, 83–99.

Melzack, R. (1999). Pain and stress: A new perspective. In R. J. Gatchel & D. C. Turk (Eds.), *Psychosocial factors in pain: Critical perspectives* (pp. 89–106). New York, NY: Guilford Press.

Melzack, R., & Wall, P. D. (1965). Pain mechanisms: A new theory. *Science, 150*, 971–979.

Mercadillo, R. E., Díaz, J. L., Pasaye, E. H., & Barrios, F. A. (2011). Perception of suffering and compassion experience: Brain gender disparities. *Brain and Cognition, 76(1)*, 5–14.

Merikangas, K., & Tohen, M. (2011). Epidemiology of biopolar disorder in adults and children. In M. Tsuang, M. Tohen, & P. Jones (Eds.), *Textbook in psychiatric epidemiology*, (3rd ed.) (pp. 329–342). Hoboken, NJ: Wiley.

Mermelstein, R., & Wahl, S. K. (2009). Prevention of tobacco use. In S. M. Miller, D. J. Bowen, R. T. Croyle, & J. H. Rowland (Eds.), *Handbook of cancer control and behavioral science: A resource for researchers, practitioners, and policymakers* (pp. 151–165). Washington, DC: American Psychological Association.

Merrill, D. A., & Small, G. W. (2011). Prevention in psychiatry: Effects of healthy lifestyle on cognition. *Psychiatric Clinics of North America, 34(1)*, 249–261.

Messer, S., & Gurman, A. (2011). *Essential psychotherapies: Theory and practice* (3rd ed.). New York, NY: Guilford Press.

Meston, C. M., & Frohlich, P. F. (2003). Love at first fright: Partner salience moderates roller-coaster-induced excitation transfer. *Archives of Sexual Behavior, 32(6)*, 537–544.

Metcalf, P., & Huntington, R. (1991). *Celebrations of death: The anthropology of mortuary ritual* (2nd ed.). Cambridge, England: Cambridge University Press.

Meyer, D. E., & Kieras, D. E. (1999, September.). Executive-process interactive control (EPIC): A cognitive architecture for comprehensive precise computational modeling of human multiple-task performance in laboratory and real-world contexts. *Invited address presented at the meeting of the European Society for Cognitive Psychology*. Ghent, Belgium.

Meyer, D. E., & Kieras, D. E. (2004). Computational modeling of human multiple-task performance and mental workload. *US DOD Report*. Retrieved from http://www.storming-media.us/98/9890/A989024.html

Meyer, L. H. (2011). Making sense of differently able minds. *PsyCRITIQUES*. Retrieved from http://psycnet.apa.org/critiques/56/9/6.html

Meyer, R. G., & Salmon, P. (1988). *Abnormal psychology* (2nd ed.). Boston, MA: Allyn & Bacon.

Meyer, U., Nyffleler, M., Schwendener, S., Knuesel, I., Yee, B. K., & Feldon, J. (2008). Relative prenatal and postnatal maternal contributions to schizophrenia-related neurochemical dysfunction after in utero immune challenge. *Neuropsychopharmacology, 33*, 441–456.

Michael, R., Gagnon, J., Laumann, E., & Kolata, G. (1994). *Sex in America*. Boston, MA: Little, Brown.

Mieg, H. A. (2011). Focused cognition: Information integration and complex problem solving by top inventors. In K. L. Mosier & U. M. Fischer (Eds.), *Expertise: Research and applications. Informed by knowledge: Expert performance in complex situations* (pp. 41–54). New York, NY: Psychology Press.

Migacheva, K., & Tropp, L. R. (Ed.), & Crocker, J. (2011). Focusing beyond the self: Goal orientations in intergroup relations. In L. R. Tropp & R. K. Mallett (Eds.), *Moving beyond prejudice reduction: Pathways to positive intergroup relations* (pp. 99–115). Washington, DC: American Psychological Association.

Mihic, L., Wells, S., Graham, K., Tremblay, P. F., & Demers, A. (2009). Situational and respondent-level motives for drinking and alcohol-related aggression: A multilevel analysis of drinking events in a sample of Canadian university students. *Addictive Behaviors, 34(3)*, 264–269.

Mikulincer, M., & Goodman, G. S. (Eds.). (2006). *Dynamics of romantic love: Attachment, caregiving, and sex*. New York, NY: Guilford Press.

Milgram, S. (1963). Behavioral study of obedience. *Journal of Abnormal and Social Psychology, 67*, 371–378.

Milgram, S. (1974). *Obedience to authority: An experimental view*. New York, NY: Harper & Row.

Miller, A. K., Amacker, A. M., & King, A. R. (2011). Sexual victimization history and perceived similarity to a sexual assault victim: A path model of perceiver variables predicting victim culpability attributions. *Sex Roles, 64(5–6)*, 372–381.

Miller, B., Wood, B., Balkansky, A., Mercader, J., & Panger, M. (2006). *Anthropology*. Boston, MA: Allyn & Bacon/Longman.

Miller, G. (2004). Brain cells may pay the price for a bad night's sleep. *Science, 306(5699)*, 1126.

Miller, G. (2011). Using the psychology of evil to do good. *Science, 332(6029)*, 530–532.

Miller, G. A. (1956). The magical number seven, plus or minus two: Some limits on our capacity for processing information. *Psychological Review, 63*, 81–97.

Miller, J. G., & Bersoff, D. M. (1998). The role of liking in perceptions of the moral responsibility to help: A cultural perspective. *Journal of Experimental Social Psychology, 34*, 443–469.

Miller, L. (2008). *From difficult to disturbed: Understanding and managing dysfunctional employees*. New York, NY: AMACOM.

Miller, L. A., McIntire, S. A., & Lovler, R. L. (2011). *Foundations of psychological testing: A practical problem* (3rd ed.). Thousand Oaks, CA: Sage.

Miller, L. K. (2005). What the savant syndrome can tell us about the nature and nurture of talent. *Journal for the Education of the Gifted, 28*, 361–373.

Miller, M., & Kantrowitz, B. (1999, January 25). Unmasking Sybil: A reexamination of the most famous psychiatric patient in history. *Newsweek*, pp. 11–16.

Miller, S. R., Tserakhava, V., & Miller, C. J. (2011). "My child is shy and has no friends: What does parenting have to do with it"? *Journal of Youth and Adolescence, 40(4)*, 442–452.

Millet, J. (2010). Twice as many job seekers for every job. *Criteria Corp*. Retrieved from http://blog.criteriacorp.com/2010/11/05/twice-as-many-job-seekers-for-every-job/

Millon, T. (2004). *Masters of the mind: Exploring the story of mental illness from ancient times to the new millennium*. Hoboken, NJ: Wiley.

Miltenberger, R. G. (2008). *Behavior modification: Principles and procedures* (4th ed.). Belmont, CA: Cengage.

Miltenberger, R. G. (2011). *Behavior modification: Principles and procedures.* (5th ed.). Beverly, MA: Wadsworth.

Milton, J., & Wiseman, R. (1999). Does psi exist? Lack of replication of an anomalous process of information transfer. *Psychological Bulletin, 125*, 387–391.

Mineka, S., & Oehlberg, K. (2008). The relevance of recent developments in classical conditioning to understanding the etiology and maintenance of anxiety disorders. *Acta Psychologica, 127*, 567–580.

Mineka, S., & Oehman, A. (2002). Phobias and preparedness: The selective, automatic, and encapsulated nature of fear. *Biological Psychiatry, 51(9)*, 927–937.

Mingroni, M. A. (2004). The secular rise in IQ. *Intelligence, 32*, 65–83.

Minuchin, S. (2011). *Families and family therapy* (2nd ed.). New York, NY: Routledge.

Minuchin, S., Lee, W-Y., & Simon, G. M. (2007). *Mastering family therapy: Journeys of growth and transformation* (2nd ed.). Hoboken, NJ: Wiley.

Miracle, T. S., Miracle, A. W., & Baumeister, R. F. (2006). *Human sexuality: Meeting your basic needs* (2nd ed.). Upper Saddle River, NJ: Pearson Education.

Mischel, W, Shoda, Y., & Ayduk, O. (2008). *Introduction to personality: Toward an integrative science of the person* (8th ed.). Hoboken, NJ: Wiley.

Misteli, M., Duschek, S., Richter, A., Grimm, S., Rezk, M., Kraehenmann, R., Boeker, H., Seifritz, E., & Schuepbach, D. (2011). Gender characteristics of cerebral hemodynamics during complex cognitive functioning. *Brain and Cognition, 76(1)*, 123–130.

Mita, T. H., Dermer, M., & Knight, J. (1977). Reversed facial images and the mere-exposure hypothesis. *Journal of Personality and Social Psychology, 35(8)*, 597–601.

Mitalk Perfectionism. (2009). Perfectionism: Did you know? *MiTalk: University of Michigan.* Retrieved from http://mitalk.umich.edu/perfectionism.php#whatson03

Mitchell, B. A., & Lovegreen, L. D. (2009). The empty nest syndrome in midlife families: A multimethod exploration of parental gender differences and cultural dynamics. *Journal of Family Issues, 30(12)*, 1651–1670.

Mitchell, E., Sachs, A., & Tu, J. I-Chin (1997, September 29). Teaching feelings 101. *Time*, p. 62.

Mitchell, S. J., Lewin, A., Rasmussen, A., Horn, I. B., & Joseph, J. G. (2011). Maternal distress explains the relationship of young African American mothers' violence exposure with their preschoolers' behavior. *Journal of Interpersonal Violence, 26(3)*, 580–603.

Mitrani, J. (2010). Minding the gap between neuroscientific and psychoanalytic understanding of autism. *Journal of Child Psychotherapy, 36(3)*, 240–258.

Mittag, O., & Maurischat, C. (2004). Die Cook-Medley Hostility Scale (Ho-Skala) im Vergleich zu den Inhaltsskalen "Zynismus", "Ärger" sowie "Typ A" aus dem MMPI-2: Zur zukünftigen Operationalisierung von Feindseligkeit [A comparison of the Cook-Medley Hostility Scale (Ho-scale) and the content scales "cynicism," "anger," and "type A" out of the MMPI-2: On the future assess-

ment of hostility]. *Zeitschrift für Medizinische Psychologie, 13(1)*, 7–12.

Miyake, N., Thompson, J., Skinbjerg, M., & Abi-Dargham, A. (2011). Presynaptic dopamine in schizophrenia. *CNS Neuroscience & Therapeutics, 17(2)*, 104–109.

Mograss, M. A., Guillem, F., & Godbout, R. (2008). Event-related potentials differentiates the processes involved in the effects of sleep on recognition memory. *Psychophysiology, 45*, 420–434.

Möbler, H., Rudolph, U., Boison, D., Singer, P., Feldon, J., & Yee, B. K. (2008). Regulation of cognition and symptoms of psychosis: Focus on GABA-sub(A) receptors and glycine transporter 1. *Pharmacology, Biochemistry & Behavior, 90*, 58–64.

Moilanen, J., Aalto, A.-M., Hemminki, E., Aro, A. R., Raitanen, J., & Luoto, R. (2010). Prevalence of menopause symptoms and their association with lifestyle among Finnish middle-aged women. *Maturitas, 67(4)*, 368–374.

Moitra, E., Beard, C., Weisberg, R. B., & Keller, M. B. (2011). Occupational impairment and social anxiety disorder in a sample of primary care patients. *Journal of Affective Disorders, 130(1–2)*, 209–212.

Mollborn, S., & Lovegrove, P. J. (2011). How teenage fathers matter for children: Evidence from the ECLS-B. *Journal of Family Issues, 32(1)*, 3–30.

Molnar-Szakacs, I. (2011). From actions to empathy and morality—A neural perspective. *Journal of Economic Behavior & Organization, 77(1)*, 76–85.

Monastra, V. J. (2008). Electroencephalographic biofeedback in the treatment of ADHD. In V. J. Monastra (Ed.), *Unlocking the potential of patients with ADHD: A model for clinical practice* (pp. 147–159). Washington, DC: APA.

Mond, J., & Arrighi, A. (2011). Gender differences in perceptions of the severity and prevalence of eating disorders. *Early Intervention in Psychiatry, 5(1)*, 41–49.

Mondimore, F., & Kelly, P. (2011). *Borderline personality disorder: New reasons for hope.* Baltimore, MD: Johns Hopkins University Press.

Moneta, G. B., & Siu, C. M. Y. (2002). Trait intrinsic and extrinsic motivations, academic performance, and creativity in Hong Kong college students. *Journal of College Student Development, 43(5)*, 664–683.

Money, J. (1985). Sexual reformation and counter-reformation in law and medicine. *Medicine and Law, 4*, 479–488.

Money, J., & Ehrhardt, A. A. (1972). *Man and woman, boy and girl.* Baltimore, MD: The Johns Hopkins University Press.

Money, J., Prakasam, K. S., & Joshi, V. N. (1991). Semen-conservation doctrine from ancient Ayurvedic to modern sexological theory. *American Journal of Psychotherapy, 45*, 9–13.

Monin, B. (2003). The warm glow heuristic: When liking leads to familiarity. *Journal of Personality and Social Psychology, 85(6)*, 1035–1048.

Monks, C. P., Ortega-Ruiz, R., & Rodríguez-Hidalgo, A. J. (2008). Peer victimization in multicultural schools in Spain and England. *European Journal of Developmental Psychology, 5*, 507–535.

Montoro-García, S., Shantsila, E., & Lip, G. Y. H. (2011). Platelet reactivity in prolonged stress disorders—A link with cardiovascular disease? *Psychoneuroendocrinology, 36(2)*, 159–160.

Moodley, R. (2012). *Handbook of counseling and psychotherapy in an international context.* New York, NY: Routledge.

Moodley, R., & Sutherland, P. (2010). Psychic retreats in other places: Clients who seek healing with traditional healers and psychotherapists. *Counselling Psychology Quarterly, 23(3)*, 267–282.

Moore, F. R., Smith, M. J. L., Taylor, V., & Perrett, D. I. (2011). Sexual dimorphism in the female face is a cue to health and social status but not age. *Personality and Individual Differences, 50(7)*, 1068–1073.

Moore, F., Filippou, D., & Perrett, D. (2011). Intelligence and attractiveness in the face: Beyond the attractiveness halo effect. *Journal of Evolutionary Psychology.* Advance online publication. doi: 10.1556/JEP.9.2011.3.2

Moore, M. M. (1998). The science of sexual signaling. In G. C. Brannigan, E. R. Allgeier, & A. R. Allgeier (Eds.), *The sex scientists* (pp. 61–75). New York, NY: Longman.

Moran, T., & Dailey, M. (2011) Intestinal feedback signaling and satiety. *Physiology & Behavior.* doi: 10.1016/j.physbeh.2011.02.005

Morewedge, C. K., & Norton, M. J. (2009). When dreaming is believing: The (motivated) interpretation of dreams. *Journal of Personality and Social Psychology, 96*, 249–264.

Morf, C. C., & Rhodewalt, F. (2001). Unraveling the paradoxes of narcissism: A dynamic self-regulatory processing model. *Psychological Inquiry, 12(4)*, 177–196.

Morgan, C. D., & Murphy, C. (2010). Differential effects of active attention and age on event-related potentials to visual and olfactory stimuli. *International Journal of Psychophysiology, 78(2)*, 190–199.

Morgan, C. D., & Murray, H. A. (1935). A method of investigating fantasies. The Thematic Apperception Test. *Archives of Neurology and Psychiatry, 34*, 289–306.

Mori, K., & Arai, M. (2010). No need to fake it: Reproduction of the Asch experiment without confederates. *International Journal of Psychology, 45*(5), 390–397.

Morris, J. S., Frith, C. D., Perrett, D. L., Rowland, D., Young, A. W., Calder, A. J., & Dolan, R. J. (1996). A differential neural response in the human amygdala to fearful and happy expressions. *Nature, 383,* 812–815.

Morris, S. G. (2007). Influences on childrens' narrative coherence: Age, memory breadth, and verbal comprehension. *Dissertation Abstracts International: Section B: The Sciences and Engineering, 68*(6–B), 4157.

Morrison, C., & Westman, A. S. (2001). Women report being more likely than men to model their relationships after what they have seen on TV. *Psychological Reports, 89*(2), 252–254.

Morry, M. M. (2005). Relationship satisfaction as a predictor of similarity ratings: A test of the attraction-similarity hypothesis. *Journal of Social and Personal Relationships, 22,* 561–584.

Morry, M. M., Kito, M., & Ortiz, L. (2011). The attraction–similarity model and dating couples: Projection, perceived similarity, and psychological benefits. *Personal Relationships, 18*(1), 125–143.

Moshman, D. (2011). *Adolescent rationality and development: Cognition, morality, and identity* (3rd ed.). New York, NY: Psychology Press.

Moss, D. (2004). Biofeedback. *Applied Psychophysiology & Biofeedback, 29*(1), 75–78.

Motyl, M., Hart, J., Pyszczynski, T., Weise, D., Maxfield, M., & Siedel, A. (2011). Subtle priming of shared human experiences eliminates threat-induced negativity toward arabs, immigrants, and peace-making. *Journal of Experimental Social Psychology.* Advance online publication. doi:10.1016/j.jesp.2011.04.010

Moulin, C. (Ed.). (2011). *Human memory* (Vols. 1–4). Thousand Oaks, CA: Sage.

Moulton, S. T., & Kosslyn, S. M. (2011). Imagining predictions: Mental imagery as mental emulation. In M. Bar (Ed.), *Predictions in the brain: Using our past to generate a future* (pp. 95–106). New York, NY: Oxford University Press.

Moutinho, A., Pereira, A., & Jorge, G., (2011). Biology of homosexuality. *European Psychiatry, 26,* 1741–1753.

Muehlenkamp, J. J., Ertelt, T. W., Miller, A. L., & Claes, L. (2011). Borderline personality symptoms differentiate non-suicidal and suicidal self-injury in ethnically diverse adolescent outpatients. *Journal of Child Psychology and Psychiatry, 52*(2), 148–155.

Mui, A. C. (1992). Caregiver strain among Black and White daughter caregivers: A role theory perspective. *The Gerontologist, 32,* 203–212.

Mulckhuyse, M., van Zoest, W., & Theeuwes, J. (2008). Capture of the eyes by relevant and irrelevant onsets. *Experimental Brain Research, 186,* 225–235.

Müller,, B., Kühn,S., van Baaren, R., Dotsch, R., Brass, M., & Dijksterhuis, A. (2011). Perspective taking eliminates differences in co-representation of out-group members' actions. *Experimental Brain Research, 211* (3–4), 423–428.

Mundia, L. (2011). Social desirability, non-response bias and reliability in a long self-report measure: Illustrations from the MMPI-2 administered to Brunei student teachers. *Educational Psychology, 31*(2), 207–224.

Munoz, L., & Anastassiou-Hadjicharalambous, X. (2011). Disinhibited behaviors in young children: Relations with impulsivity and autonomic psychophysiology, *Biological Psychology, 86*(3), 349–359.

Murray, A. (2009). *Suicide in the Middle Ages: The violent against themselves* (Vol. 1). New York, NY: Oxford University Press.

Murray, A. D., Staff, R. T., McNeil, C. J., Salarirad, S., Starr, J. M., Deary, I. J., & Whalley, L. J. (2011). Brain lesions, hypertension and cognitive ageing in the 1921 and 1936 Aberdeen birth cohorts. *Age.* doi:10.1007/s11357-011-9233-5

Murray, H. A. (1938). *Explorations in personality.* New York, NY: Oxford University Press.

Murty, V. P., Ritchey, M., Adcock, R. A., & LaBar, K. S. (2011). Reprint of: fMRI studies of successful emotional memory encoding: A quantitative meta-analysis. *Neuropsychologia, 49*(4), 695–705.

Music, G. (2011). *Nurturing natures: Attachment and children's emotional, sociocultural and brain development.* New York, NY: Psychology Press.

Myerson, J., Rank, M. R., Raines, F. Q., & Schnitzler, M. A. (1998). Race and general cognitive ability: The myth of diminishing returns to education. *Psychological Science, 9,* 139–142.

Nabar, K. K. (2011). Individualistic ideology as contained in the "Diagnostic & Statistical Manual of Mental Disorders-Fourth Edition-Text Revision" personality disorders: A relational-cultural critique. *Dissertation Abstracts International: Section B: The Sciences and Engineering, 71*(9-B), 5800.

Nabi, R.L., Moyer-Gusé, E., & Byrne, S. (2007). All joking aside: A serious investigation into the persuasive effect of funny social issue messages. *Communication Monographs, 74,* 29–54.

Naglieri, J. A., & Ronning, M. E. (2000). Comparison of White, African American, Hispanic, and Asian children on the Naglieri Nonverbal Ability Test. *Psychological Assessment, 12*(3), 328–334.

Naish, P. L. N. (2006). Time to explain the nature of hypnosis? *Contemporary Hypnosis, 23,* 33–46.

Nakajima, S., & Masaki, T. (2004). Taste aversion learning induced forced swimming in rats. *Physiology & Behavior, 80*(5), 623–628.

Nakamura, K. (2006). The history of psychotherapy in Japan. *International Medical Journal, 13,* 13–18.

Nakao, M. (2010). Work-related stress and psychosomatic medicine. *BioPsychoSocial Medicine, 4,* Article ID 4.

Nakashima, M., Morikawa, Y., Sakurai, M., Nakamura, K., Miura, K., Ishizaki, M., Kido, T, Naruse, U., Suwazono, Y., & Nakagawa, H. (2011). Association between long working hours and sleep problems in white-collar workers. *Journal of Sleep Research, 20*(1, Pt1), 110–116.

Nasehi, M., Piri, M., Jamali-Raeufy, N., & Zarrindast, M. R. (2010). Influence of intracerebral administration of NO agents in dorsal hippocampus (CA1) on cannabinoid state-dependent memory in the step-down passive avoidance test. *Physiology & Behavior, 100*(4), 297–304.

Nash, M., & Barnier, A. (Eds.). (2008). *The Oxford handbook of hypnosis.* New York, NY: Oxford University Press.

Näslund, E., & Hellström, P. M. (2007). Appetite signaling: From gut peptides and enteric nerves to brain. *Physiology & Behavior, 92,* 256–262.

Nathan, R., Rollinson, L., Harvey, K., & Hill, J. (2003). The Liverpool violence assessment: An investigator-based measure of serious violence. *Criminal Behaviour & Mental Health, 13*(2), 106–120.

National Center for Health Statistics. (2004). *New report examines Americans' health behaviors.* Retrieved from http://gov/nchs/pressroom/04facts/healthbehaviors.htm.

National Institute of Mental Health (NIMH). (2001). *Facts about anxiety disorders.* Retrieved from http://www.nimh.nih.gov/publicat/ adfacts.cfm.

National Institute of Mental Health (NIMH). (2008). *Anxiety disorders.* Retrieved from http://www.nimh.nih.gov/ health/publications/anxiety-disorders/ summary.shtml

National Institute of Mental Health (NIMH). (2008). *When unwanted thoughts take over: Obsessive-compulsive disorder.* Retrieved from http://www.nimh.nih.gov/ health/publications/when-unwanted-thoughts-take-over-obsessive-compulsive-disorder/complete-publication.shtml

National Institute of Mental Health (NIMH). (2011, June 20). Obsessive-compulsive disorder, OCD. Retrieved from http://www.nimh.nih.gov/health/topics/obsessive-compulsive-disorder-ocd/index.shtml

National Institute of Mental Health (NIMH). (2011, May 3). Anxiety disorders. Retrieved from http://www.nimh.nih.gov/health/topics/anxiety-disorders/index.shtml

National Institute on Alcohol Abuse and Alcoholism (NIAAA). (2007). *Binge drinking.* Retrieved from http://pubs.niaaa.nih.gov/publications/AA73/AA73.htm

National Institute on Drug Abuse (NIDA). (2005). *NIDA infofacts: Club drugs.* Retrieved from http://www.nida.nih.gov/infofacts/club drugs.html.

National Institute on Drug Abuse (NIDA). (2010). NIDA InfoFacts: Club Drugs (GHB, Ketamine, and Rohypnol). Retrieved from http://www.drugabuse.gov/Infofacts/club-drugs.html

National Institute on Drug Abuse (NIDA). (2010). Research report series: Cocaine abuse and addiction. Retrieved from http://www.nida.nih.gov/PDF/RRCocaine.pdf

National Institute on Drug Abuse (NIDA). (2011). *Tobacco/Nicotine.* Retrieved from http://www.nida.nih.gov/drugpages/nicotine.html

National Organization on Fetal Alcohol Syndrome. (2006). *What are the statistics and facts about FAS and FASD?* (November 3, 2006). Retrieved from http://www.nofas.org/faqs.aspx?id512.

National Organization on Fetal Alcohol Syndrome. (2008). *Facts about FAS and FASD.* Retrieved from http://www.nofas.org/family/facts.aspx

National Research Council (NRC). (2003). *The polygraph and lie detection.* Retrieved from http://fermat.nap.edu/catalog/10420.html.

National Sleep Foundation. (2007). *Myths and facts about sleep.* Retrieved from http://www.sleepfoundation.org/site/c.huIXKjM0IxF/b.2419251/k.2773/Myths__and_Facts__About_Sleep.

Navarro, M. (2008). Who are we? New dialogue on mixed race. *New York Times.* Retrieved from http://www.nytimes.com/2008/03/31/us/politics/31race.html.

Neal, D., & Chartrand, T. (2011). Embodied emotion perception: Amplifying and dampening facial feedback modulates emotion perception accuracy. *Social Psychological and Personality Science.* Retrieved from http://spp.sagepub.com/content/early/2011/04/21/1948550611406138

Neale, J. M., Oltmanns, T. F., & Winters, K. C. (1983). Recent developments in the assessment and conceptualization of schizophrenia. *Behavioral Assessment, 5,* 33–54.

Neenan, M. (2008). Tackling procrastination: An REBT perspective for coaches. *Journal of Rational-Emotive & Cognitive Behavior Therapy, 26,* 53–62.

Neher, A. (1991). Maslow's theory of motivation: A critique. *Journal of Humanistic Psychology, 31,* 89–112.

Neisser, U. (1967). *Cognitive psychology.* New York, NY: Appleton-Century-Crofts.

Neisser, U. (1998). Introduction: Rising test scores and what they mean. In U. Neisser (Ed.), *The rising curve: Long-term gains in IQ and related measures* (pp. 3–22). Washington, DC: American Psychological Association.

Nelis, D., Kotsou, I., Quoidbach, J., Hansenne, M., Weytens, F., Dupuis, P., & Mikolajczak, M. (2011). Increasing emotional competence improves psychological and physical well-being, social relationships, and employability. *Emotion, 11(2),* 354–366.

Nemoda, Z., Szekely, A., & Sasvari-Szekely, M. (2011). Psychopathological aspects of dopaminergic gene polymorphisms in adolescence and young adulthood. *Neuroscience and Biobehavioral Reviews.* Advance online publication. doi:10.1016/j.neubiorev.2011.04.002

Neto, F., & Furnham, A. (2005). Gender-role portrayals in children's television advertisements. *International Journal of Adolescence & Youth, 12(1–2),* 69–90.

Nettle, D. (2011). Normality, disorder, and evolved function: The case of depression. In P. Adriaens & A. de Block (Eds.), *Maladapting minds: Philosophy, psychiatry, and evolutionary theory* (pp.198–215). New York, NY: Oxford University Press.

Neubauer, A. C., Grabner, R. H., Freudenthaler, H. H., Beckmann, J. F., & Guthke, J. (2004). Intelligence and individual differences in becoming neurally efficient. *Acta Psychologica, 116(1),* 55–74.

Neugarten, B. L., Havighurst, R. J., & Tobin, S. S. (1968). The measurement of life satisfaction. *Journal of Gerontology, 16,* 134–143.

Newby, J. M., & Moulds, M. L. (2011). Intrusive memories of negative events in depression: Is the centrality of the event important? *Journal of Behavior Therapy and Experimental Psychiatry, 42(3),* 277–283.

Newcomb, M. E., & Mustanski, B. (2010). Internalized homophobia and internalizing mental health problems: A meta-analytic review. *Clinical Psychology Review, 30(8),* 1019–1029.

Newcombe, N. S. (2010). On tending to our scientific knitting: Thinking about gender in the context of evolution. In J. C. Chrisler & **D. R. McCreary (Eds.),** *Handbook of gender research in psychology, Vol. 1. Gender research in general and experimental psychology* (pp. 259–274). New York, NY: Springer Science + Business Media.

Newell, K. M., Mayer-Kress, G., Hong, S. L., & Liu, Y.-T. (2010). Decomposing the performance dynamics of learning through time scales. In P. C. M. Molenaar & K. M. Newell (Eds.), *Individual pathways of change: Statistical models for analyzing learning and development* (pp. 71–86). Washington, DC: American Psychological Association.

Newton, J., Flett, G. L., & Callander, L. (1997). Perfectionism and suicide ideation in adolescent psychiatric patients. *Journal of Abnormal Child Psychology, 25(2),* 95–107.

Ng, S. M., Li, A. M., Lou, V. W. Q., Tso, I. F., Wan, P. Y. P., & Chan, D. F. Y. (2008). Incorporating family therapy into asthma group intervention: A randomized waitlist-controlled trial. *Family Process, 47,* 115–130.

Ngo, H-Y., Lau, C-M, & Foley, S. (2008). Strategic human resource management, firm performance, and employee relations climate in China. *Human Resource Management, 47,* 73–90.

Niaura, R., Todaro, J.F., Stroud, L., Spiro, A., Ward, K.D., & Weiss, S. (2002). Hostility, the metabolic syndrome, and incident cornary heart disease. *Health Psychology, 21* (6), 598–593.

Nicholson, A., Pikhart, H., Pajak, A., Malyutina, S., Kubinova, R., Peasey, A., Topor-Madry, R., Nikitin, Y., Capkova, N., Marmot, M., & Bobak, M. (2008). Socioeconomic status over the life-course and depressive symptoms in men and women in Eastern Europe. *Journal of Affective Disorders, 105,* 125–136.

Nickell, J. (2001). John Edward: Hustling the bereaved. *Skeptical Inquirer, 25,* 6.

Nickerson, R. (1998). Confirmation bias: A ubiquitous phenomenon in many guises. *Review of General Psychology, 2,* 175–220.

Nickerson, R. S., & Adams, M. J. (1979). Longterm memory for a common object. *Cognitive Psychology, 11*, 287–307.

Niedenthal, P. (2007). Embodying emotion. *Science, 316*, 1002–1005.

Nikolaou, A., Schiza, S. E., Chatzi, L., Koudas, V., Fokos, S., Solidaki, E., & Bitsios, P. (2011). Evidence of dysregulated affect indicated by high alexithymia in obstructive sleep apnea. *Journal of Sleep Research, 20*(1, *Pt1*), 92–100.

Nisbet, M. (2000). The best case for ESP? Generation sXeptic. *Skeptical Inquirer.* Retrieved from http://www.csicop.org/specialarticles/show/best_case_for_esp/

Nisbett, R. E. (2009). *Intelligence and how to get it: Why schools and cultures count.* New York, NY: W.W. Norton & Co.

Nishimoto, R. (1988). A cross-cultural analysis of psychiatric symptom expression using Langer's twenty-two item index. *Journal of Sociology and Social Welfare, 15*, 45–62.

Noggle, C., Dean, R., Crowe, S., Soltys, S., & Robinson, S. (Eds.). (2012). *The neuropsychology of psychopharmacology.* New York, NY: Springer.

Nogueiras, R., & Tschöp, M. (2005). Separation of conjoined hormones yields appetite rivals. *Science, 310*, 985–986.

Nolen-Hoeksema, S., Larson, J., & Grayson, C. (2000). Explaining the gender difference in depressive symptoms. *Journal of Personality and Social Psychology, 77*, 1061–1072.

Norambuena, X. A., Quintana, G. R., Ponce, F. P., & Vogel, E. H. (2010). Asociaciones excitatorias entre el contexto y la consecuencia en la reinstalación de respuestas extinguidas en el aprendizaje causal humano [Excitatory context-consequence associations in the reinstatement of extinguished responses in human causal learning]. *Terapia Psicológica, 28*(1), 55–67.

Norcross, J. C., & Wampold, B. E. (2011). Evidence-based therapy relationships: Research conclusions and clinical practices. *Psychotherapy, 48*(1), 98–102.

Nord, M., & Farde, L. (2011). Antipsychotic occupancy of dopamine receptors in schizophrenia. *CNS Neuroscience & Therapeutics, 17*(2), 97–103.

Novotney, A. (2010). Procrastination or 'intentional delay'? *gradPSYCH, 8*(1), 14. Retrieved from http://www.apa.org/gradpsych/2010/01/procrastination.aspx

Nusbaum, F., Redouté, J., Le Bars, D., Volckmann, P., Simon, F., Hannoun, S., Ribes, G., Gaucher, J., Laurent, B., & Sappey-Marinier, D. (2011). Chronic low-back pain modulation is enhanced by hypnotic analgesic suggestion by recruiting an emotional network: A PET imaging study. *International Journal of Clinical and Experimental Hypnosis, 59*(1), 27–44.

O'Brien, C. W., & Moorey, S. (2010). Outlook and adaptation in advanced cancer: A systematic review. *Psycho-oncology, 19*(1), 1239–1249.

O'Connell, K. L. (2008). What can we learn? Adult outcomes in children of seriously mentally ill mothers. *Journal of Child and Adolescent Psychiatric Nursing, 21*, 89–104.

O'Connor, D. B., Archer, J., Hair, W. M., Wu, F. C. W. (2002). Exogenous testosterone, aggression, and mood in eugonadal and hypogonadal men. *Physiology & Behavior, 75*(4), 557–566.

O'Connor, R. (2007). The relations between perfectionism and suicidality: A systematic review. *Suicide and Life-Threatening Behavior, 37*(6), 698–714.

Oei, T. P. S., & Dingle, G. (2008). The effectiveness of group cognitive behaviour therapy for unipolar depressive disorders. *Journal of Affective Disorders, 107*, 5–21.

O'Farrell, T. J. (2011). Family therapy. In M. Galanter & H. D. Kleber (Eds.), *Psychotherapy for the treatment of substance abuse* (pp. 329–350). Arlington, VA: American Psychiatric Publishing.

Ogilvie, R. D., Wilkinson, R. T., & Allison, S. (1989). The detection of sleep onset: Behavioral, physiological, and subjective convergence. *Sleep, 12*(5), 458–474.

Ohio State University Department of Linguistics. (2011). *Language files: Materials for an introduction to language and linguistics* (11ᵗʰ ed.). Columbus, OH: Ohio State University Press.

Olfson, M., Crystal, S., Huang, C., & Gerhard, T. (2010). Very young, privately insured children. *Journal of the American Academy of Child & Adolescent Psychiatry, 49*(1), 13–23.

Olson, I. R., Berryhill, M. E., Drowos, D. B., Brown, L., & Chatterjee, A. (2010). A calendar savant with episodic memory impairments. *Neurocase, 16*(3), 208–218.

Olszewski-Kubilius, P., & Lee, S.-Y. (2011). Gender and other group differences in performance on off-level tests: Changes in the 21st century. *Gifted Child Quarterly, 55*(1), 54–73.

O'Neill, J. W., & Davis, K. (2011). Work stress and well-being in the hotel industry. *International Journal of Hospitality Management, 30*(2), 385–390.

Ophir, E, Nass, C., & Wagner, A.D. (2009). Cognitive control in media multitaskers. *Proceedings of the National Academy of Sciences (PNSA).* Retrieved from http://www.scribd.com/doc/19081547/Cognitive-control-in-media-multitaskers.

Oppenheimer, D. M. (2004). Spontaneous discounting of availability in frequency judgment tasks. *Psychological Science, 15*(2), 100–105.

Orne, M. T. (2006). The nature of hypnosis. artifact and essence: An experimental study. *Dissertation Abstracts International: Section B: The Sciences and Engineering, 67*(2-B), 1207.

O'Rourke, M. (2010, February 1). Good grief: Is there a better way to be bereaved? *New Yorker.* Retrieved from http://www.newyorker.com/arts/critics/atlarge/2010/02/01/100201crat_atlarge_orourke

Ortiz, F. A., Church, A. T., Vargas-Flores, J. D. J., Ibáñez-Reyes, J., Flores-Galaz, M., Luit-Briceño, J. I., &Escamilla, J. M. (2007). Are indigenous personality dimensions culture-specific? Mexican inventories and the Five-Factor Model. *Journal of Research in Personality, 41*, 618–649.

Orubuloye, I., Caldwell, J., & Caldwell, P. (1997). Perceived male sexual needs and male sexual behavior in southwest Nigeria. *Social Science and Medicine, 44*, 1195–1207.

Orzel-Gryglewska, J. (2010). Consequences of sleep deprivation. *International Journal of Occupational Medicine and Environmental Health, 23*(1), 95–114.

Oshima, K. (2000). Ethnic jokes and social function in Hawaii. *Humor: International Journal of Humor Research, 13*(1), 41–57.

Osler, M., McGue, M., Lund, R., & Christensen, K. (2008). Marital status and twins' health and behavior: An analysis of middle-aged Danish twins. *Psychosomatic Medicine, 70*, 482–487.

Ostreicher, M. L., Moses, S. N., Rosenbaum, R. S., & Ryan, J. D. (2010). Prior experience supports new learning of relations in aging. *The Journals of Gerontology: Series B: Psychological Sciences and Social Sciences, 65B*(1), 32–41.

Ostrov, J. M., & Keating, C. F. (2004). Gender differences in preschool aggression during free play and structured interactions: An observational study. *Social Development, 13*(2), 255–277.

Ostrowsky, M. K. (2010). Are violent people more likely to have low self-esteem or high self-esteem? *Aggression and Violent Behavior, 15*, 69–75.

Overstreet, M. F., & Healy, A. F. (2011). Item and order information in semantic memory: Students' retention of the "CU fight song" lyrics. *Memory & Cognition, 39(2),* 251–259.

Owens, J., & Massey, D. S. (2011). Stereotype threat and college academic performance: A latent variables approach. *Social Science Research, 40(1),* 150–166.

Owens, R. (2011). *Language development: An introduction* (8th ed.). Boston, MA: Allyn & Bacon.

Owens, S., Rijsdijk, F., Picchioni, M., Stahl, D., Nenadic, I., Murray, R., & Toulopoulou, T. (2011). Genetic overlap between schizophrenia and selective components of executive function. *Schizophrenia Research, 127(1),* 181–187.

Oz, M. (2011). "Bath salts:" Evil lurking at your corner store. *Time.* Retrieved from http://www.time.com/time/magazine/article/0,9171,2065249,00.html

Pace, T. W. W., & Heim, C. M. (2011). A short review on the psychoneuroimmunology of posttraumatic stress disorder: From risk factors to medical comorbidities. *Brain, Behavior, and Immunity, 25(1),* 6–13.

Padwa, H., & Cunningham, J. (2010). *Addiction: A reference encyclopedia.* Santa Barbara, CA: ABC-CLIO.

Palermo, R., Willis, M. L., Rivolta, D., McKone, E., Wilson, C. E., & Calder, A. J. (2011). Impaired holistic coding of facial expression and facial identity in congenital prosopagnosia. *Neuropsychologia, 49(5), 1225–1235.*

Palermo, T. M., Eccleston, C., Lewandowski, A. S., de C. Williams, A. C., & Morley, S. (2010). Randomized controlled trials of psychological therapies for management of chronic pain in children and adolescents: An updated meta-analytic review. *Pain, 148(3),* 387–397.

Palmer, S., & Ellis, A. (1995). Stress counseling and stress management: The rational emotive behavior approach. Dr. Stephen Palmer interviews Dr. Albert Ellis. *The Rational Emotive Behaviour Therapist, 3,* 82–86.

Palmer, S., & Gyllensten, K. (2008). How cognitive behavioural, rational emotive behavioural or multimodal coaching could prevent mental health problems, enhance performance, and reduce work related stress. *Journal of Rational-Emotive & Cognitive Behavior Therapy, 26,* 38–52.

Panksepp, J. (2005). Affective consciousness: Core emotional feelings in animals and humans. *Consciousness & Cognition: An International Journal, 14(1),* 30–80.

Panksepp, J. (2011). The neurobiology of social loss in animals: Some keys to the puzzle of psychic pain in humans. In G. MacDonald & L. A. Jensen-Campbell (Eds.), *Social pain: Neuropsychological and health implications of loss and exclusion* (pp. 11–51). Washington, DC: American Psychological.

Panksepp, J., & Watt, D. (2011). Why does depression hurt? Ancestral primary-process separation-distress (PANIC/GRIEF) and diminished brain reward (SEEKING) processes in the genesis of depressive affect. *Psychiatry: Interpersonal and Biological Processes, 74(1),* 5–13.

Pannese, A., & Hirsch, J. (2011). Self-face enhances processing of immediately preceding invisible faces. *Neuropsychologia, 49(3),* 564–573.

Papageorgiou, G., Cañas, F., Zink, M., & Rossi, A. (2011). Country differences in patient characteristics and treatment in schizophrenia: Data from a physician-based survey in Europe. *European Psychiatry, 26(1, Suppl 1),* 17–28.

Papathanassoglou, E. D. E., Giannakopoulou, M., Mpouzika, M., Bozas, E., & Karabinis, A. (2010). Potential effects of stress in critical illness through the role of stress neuropeptides. *Nursing in Critical Care, 15(4),* 204–216.

Pardini, M., Krueger, F., Hodgkinson, C., Raymont, V., Ferrier, C., Goldman, D., Strenziok, M., Guida, S., & Grafman, J. (2011). Prefrontal cortex lesions and MAO-A modulate aggression in penetrating traumatic brain injury. *Neurology, 76(12),* 1038–1045.

Parihar, V. K., Hattiangad, B., Kuruba, R., Shuai, B., & Shetty, A. K. (2011). Predictable chronic mild stress improves mood, hippocampal neurogenesis and memory. *Molecular Psychiatry, 16(2),* 171–183.

Paris, J. (2010). Biopsychosocial models and psychiatric diagnosis. In T. Millon, R. F. Krueger, & E. Simonsen (Eds.), *Contemporary directions in psychopathology: Scientific foundations of the DSM-V and ICD-11* (pp. 473–482). New York, NY: Guilford Press.

Park, A. (2011, February 22). Study: Cell phones cause changes in brain activity. *Time Healthland.* Retrieved from http://healthland.time.com/2011/02/22/study-cell-phones-cause-changes-in-brain-activity/

Park, D. C., & Bischof, G. N. (2011). Neuroplasticity, aging, and cognitive function. In K. W. Schaie & S. L. Willis (Eds.), *The handbooks of aging consisting of three Vols. Handbook of the psychology of aging* (7th ed.) (pp. 109–119). San Diego, CA: Elsevier Academic Press.

Park, L., Troisi, J., & Maner, J. (2011). Egoistic versus altruistic concerns in communal relationships. *Journal of Social and Personal Relationships, 28(3),* 315–335.

Parker, J. G., Zweifel, L. S., Clark, J. J., Evans, S. B., Phillips, P. E. M., & Palmiter, R. D. (2010). Absence of NMDA receptors in dopamine neurons attenuates dopamine release but not conditioned approach during Pavlovian conditioning. *PNAS Proceedings of the National Academy of Sciences of the United States of America, 107(30),* 13491–13496.

Parkes, C. M. (1972). *Bereavement: Studies of grief in adult life.* New York, NY: International Universities Press.

Parkes, C. M. (1991). Attachment, bonding, and psychiatric problems after bereavement in adult life. In C. M. Parkes, J. Stevenson-Hinde, & P. Marris (Eds.), *Attachment across the life cycle* (pp. 268–292). London, England: Tavistock/Routledge.

Parmar, P., Ibrahim, M., & Rohner, R. P. (2008). Relations among perceived spouse acceptance, remembered parental acceptance in childhood, and psychological adjustment among married adults in Kuwait. *Cross-Cultural Research: The Journal of Comparative Social Science, 42,* 67–76.

Parrott, A., Morinan, A., Moss, M., & Scholey, A. (2004). *Understanding drugs and behavior.* Hoboken, NJ: Wiley.

Passmore, J., Holloway, M., & Rawle-Cope, M. (2010). Using MBTI type to explore differences and the implications for practice for therapists and coaches: Are executive coaches really like counselors? *Counseling Psychology Quarterly, 23(1),* 1–16.

Paterson, H. M., Kemp, R. I., & Ng, J. R. (2011). Combating co-witness contamination: Attempting to decrease the negative effects of discussion on eyewitness memory. *Applied Cognitive Psychology, 25(1),* 43–52.

Patterson, F., & Linden, E. (1981). *The education of Koko.* New York, NY: Holt, Rinehart and Winston.

Patterson, P. (2002). *Penny's journal: Koko wants to have a baby.* Retrieved from http://www.koko.org/world/journal.phtml?offset58

Patti, C. L., Zanin, K. A., Sanday, L., Kameda, S. R., Fernandes-Santos, L., Fernandes, H. A., Anderson, M., Tufik, S., & Frussa-Filho, R. (2010). Effects of sleep deprivation on memory in mice: Role of state-dependent learning. *Sleep: Journal of Sleep and Sleep Disorders Research, 33(12),* 1669–1679.

Paul, M. A., Gray, G. W., Lieberman, H. R., Love, R. J., Miller, J. C., Trouborst, M., & Arendt, J. (2011). Phase advance with separate and combined melatonin and light treatment. *Psychopharmacology, 214(2),* 515–523.

Payer, D. E., Lieberman, M. D., & London, E. D. (2011). Neural correlates of affect processing and aggression in methamphetamine dependence. *Archives of General Psychiatry, 68(3)*, 271–282.

PCI, Population Communications International. (2005). *What is PCI?* Retrieved from http://population.org/index.shtml

Pearce, A., & Scanlon, M. (2002, July/August). Through a lens darkly. *Psychology Today*, 69.

Pechtel, P., & Pizzagalli, D. A. (2011). Effects of early life stress on cognitive and affective function: An integrated review of human literature. *Psychopharmacology, 214(1)*, 55–70.

Pedrazzoli, M., Pontes, J. C., Peirano, P., & Tufik, S. (2007). HLA-DQB1 genotyping in a family with narcolepsy-cataplexy. *Brain Research, 1165*, 1–4.

Peele, S. (2010). Robert Downey Jr. Relapses! *Psychology Today*. Retrieved from http://www.psychologytoday.com/blog/addiction-in-society/201010/robert-downey-jr-relapses

Pekun, R., Goetz, T, Frenzel, A. & Barchfeld, P. (2011). Measuring emotions in students' learning and performance: The achievement emotions questionnaire (AEQ). *Contemporary Educational Psychology, 36*, 36–48.

Pellegrino, J. E., & Pellegrino, L. (2008). Fetal alcohol syndrome and related disorders. In P. J. Accardo (Ed.), *Capute and Accardo's neurodevelopmental disabilities in infancy and childhood: Vol 1: Neurodevelopmental diagnosis and treatment* (3rd ed.) (pp. 269–284). Baltimore, MD: Paul H Brookes.

Penfield, W. (1947). Some observations in the cerebral cortex of man. *Proceedings of the Royal Society, 134*, 349.

Perea, G., & Araque, A. (2010). GLIA modulates synaptic transmission. *Brain Research Reviews, 63(1–2)*, 93–102.

Pérez-Mata, N., & Diges, M. (2007). False recollections and the congruence of suggested information. *Memory, 15*, 701–717.

Perlman, A., Pothos, E. M., Edwards, D. J., & Tzelgov, J. (2010). Task-relevant chunking in sequence learning. *Journal of Experimental Psychology: Human Perception and Performance, 36(3)*, 649–661.

Perry, R., & Sibley, C. G. (2011). Social dominance orientation: Mapping a baseline individual difference component across self-categorizations. *Journal of Individual Differences, 32(2)*, 110–116.

Persson, J., Lind, J., Larsson, A., Ingvar, M., Sleegers, K., Van Broeckhoven, C., Adolfsson, R., Nilsson, L-G., & Nyberg, L. (2008). Altered deactivation in individuals with genetic risk for Alzheimer's disease. *Neuropsychologia, 46*, 1679–1687.

Pessoa, L. (2010). Emotion and cognition and the amygdala: From "what is it?" to "what's to be done?" *Neuropsychologia, 48(12)*, 3416–3429.

Petersen, J. L., & Hyde, J. S. (2011) Gender differences in sexual attitudes and behaviors: A review of meta-analytic results and large datasets. *Journal of Sex Research, 48(2–3)*, 149–165.

Peterson, Z. D., & Muehlenhard, C. L. (2004). Was it rape? The Function of women's rape myth acceptance and definitions of sex in labeling their own experiences. *Sex Roles, 51*, 129–144.

Petrakis, I. L., Rosenheck, R., & Desai, R. (2011). Substance use comorbidity among veterans with posttraumatic stress disorder and other psychiatric illness. *The American Journal on Addictions, 20(3)*, 185–189.

Petrov, A. A. (2011). Category rating is based on prototypes and not instances: Evidence from feedback-dependent context effects. *Journal of Experimental Psychology: Human Perception and Performance, 37(2)*, 336–356.

Petrovich, G. D. (2011). Learning and the motivation to eat: Forebrain circuitry. *Physiology & Behavior*. doi: 10.1016/j.physbeh.2011.04.059

Petry, Y. (2011). 'Many things surpass our knowledge': An early modern surgeon on magic, witchcraft and demonic possession. *Social History of Medicine*. Advance online publication. doi:10.1093/shm/hkr047

Pettigrew, T. F. (1998). Reactions towards the new minorities of Western Europe. *Annual Review of Sociology, 24*, 77–103.

Pettit, J. W., Lewinsohn, P. M., Seeley, J. R., Roberts, R. E., & Yaroslavsky, I. (2010). Developmental relations between depressive symptoms, minor hassles, and major events from adolescence through age 30 years. *Journal of Abnormal Psychology, 119(4)*, 811–824.

Pfeiffer, P. N., Valenstein, M., Hoggatt, K. J., Ganoczy, D., Maixner, D., Miller, E. M., & Zivin, K. (2011). Electroconvulsive therapy for major depression within the Veterans Health Administration. *Journal of Affective Disorders, 130(1–2)*, 21–25.

Pham, T.M., Winblad, B., Granholm, A-C., & Mohammed, A. H. (2002). Environmental influences on brain neurotrophins in rats. *Pharmacology, Biochemistry & Behavior, 73(1)*, 167–175.

Philibert, R., Wernett, P., Plume, J., Packer, H., Brody, G., & Beach, S. (2011). Gene environment interactions with a novel variable Monoamine Oxidase A transcriptional enhancer are associated with antisocial personality disorder. *Biological Psychology*. Advance online publication. doi:10.1016/j.biopsycho.2011.04.007

Phillips, A. C., & Hughes, B. M. (2011). Introductory paper: Cardiovascular reactivity at a crossroads: Where are we now? *Biological Psychology, 86(2)*, 95–97.

Phillips, S. T., & Ziller, R. C. (1997). Toward a theory and measure of the nature of nonprejudice. *Journal of Personality and Social Psychology, 72*, 420–434.

Piaget, J. (1962). *Play, dreams and imitation in Childhood*. New York, NY: Norton.

Pietschnig, J., Voracek, M., & Formann, A. K. (2011). Female Flynn effects: No sex differences in generational IQ gains. *Personality and Individual Differences, 50(5)*, 759–762.

Pihlajamäki, M., O'Keefe, K., O'Brien, J., Blacker, D., & Sperling, R. A. (2011). Failure of repetition suppression and memory encoding in aging and Alzheimer's disease. *Brain Imaging and Behavior, 5(1)*, 36–44.

Pina e Cunha, M., Rego, A., & Clegg, S. R. (2010). Obedience and evil: From Milgram and Kampuchea to normal organizations. *Journal of Business Ethics, 97(2)*, 291–309.

Pinel, P, & Dehaene, S. (2010). Beyond hemispheric dominance: Brain regions underlying the joint lateralization of language and arithmetic to the left hemisphere. *Journal of Cognitive Neuroscience, 22(1)*, 48–66.

Ping-Delfos, W., & Soares, M. (2011). Diet induced thermogenesis, fat oxidation and food intake following sequential meals: Influence of calcium and vitamin D. *Clinical Nutrition, 30(3)*, 376–383.

Pittenger, D. J. (2005). Cautionary comments regarding the Myers-Briggs Type Indicator. *Consulting Psychology Journal: Practice and Research, 57*, 210–221.

Pixner, S., Moeller, K., Hermanova, V., Nuerk, H.-C., & Kaufmann, L. (2011). Whorf reloaded: Language effects on nonverbal number processing in first grade—A trilingual study. *Journal of Experimental Child Psychology, 108(2)*, 371–382.

Plassmann, H., O'Doherty, J., Shiv, B., & Rangel, A. (2008). Marketing actions can modulate neural representations of experienced pleasantness. *Proceedings of the National Academy of Sciences, 105*, 1050–1054.

Plaufcan, M. R.(2010). Avatar. *Journal of Feminist Family Therapy, 22(4)*, 313–317.

Plomin, R. (1990). The role of inheritance in behavior. *Science, 248*, 183–188.

Plomin, R. (1997, May). Cited in B. Azar, Nature, nurture: Not mutually exclusive. *APA Monitor*, p. 32.

Plomin, R. (1999). Genetics and general cognitive ability. *Nature, 402*, C25–C29.

Plomin, R., & Crabbe, J. (2000). DNA. *Psychological Bulletin, 126*, 806–828.

Plomin, R., DeFries, J. C., & Fulker, D. W. (2007). *Nature and nurture during infancy and early childhood.* New York, NY: Cambridge University Press.

Plummer, D. C. (2001). The quest for modern manhood: Masculine stereotypes, peer culture and the social significance of homophobia. *Journal of Adolescence, 24(1)*, 15–23.

Plutchik, R. (1984). Emotions: A general psychoevolutionary theory. In K. R. Scherer, & P. Ekman (Eds.), *Approaches to emotion.* Hillsdale, NJ: Erlbaum.

Plutchik, R. (1994). *The psychology and biology of emotion.* New York, NY: HarperCollins.

Plutchik, R. (2000). *Emotions in the practice of psychotherapy: Clinical implications of affect theories.* Washington, DC: American Psychological Association.

Poling, A. (2010). Progressive-ratio schedules and applied behavior analysis. *Journal of Applied Behavior Analysis, 43(2)*, 347–349.

Polley, K. H., Navarro, R., Avery, D. H., George, M. S., & Holtzheimer, P. E. (2011). 2010 updated Avery-George-Holtzheimer Database of rTMS depression studies. *Brain Stimulation, 4(2)*, 115–116.

Pomponio, A. T. (2002). *Psychological consequences of terror.* New York, NY: Wiley.

Pope Jr., H. G., Barry, S., Bodkin, J. A., & Hudson, J. (2007). "Scientific study of the dissociative disorders": Reply. *Psychotherapy and Psychosomatics, 76*, 401–403.

Popma, A., Vermeiren, R., Geluk, C. A. M. L., Rinne, T., van den Brink, W., Knol, D. L., Jansen, L. M. C., van Engeland, H., & Doreleijers, T. A. H. (2007). Cortisol moderates the relationship between testosterone and aggression in delinquent male adolescents. *Biological Psychiatry, 61*, 405–411.

Popova, S., Stade, B., Johnston, M., MacKay, H., Lange, S., Bekmuradov, D., & Rehm, J. (2011). Evaluating the cost of fetal alcohol spectrum disorder. *Journal of Studies on Alcohol and Drugs, 72(1)*, 163–164.

Porzelius, L. K., Dinsmore, B. D., & Staffelbach, D. (2001). Eating disorders. In M. Hersen & V. B. Van Hasselt (Eds.), *Advanced abnormal psychology* (2nd ed.) (pp. 261–281). Dordrecht, Netherlands: Kluwer Academic Publishers.

Post, J. M. (2011). Crimes of obedience: "Groupthink" at Abu Ghraib. *International Journal of Group Psychotherapy, 61(1)*, 49–66

Posthuma, D., de Geus, E. J. C., & Boomsma, D. I. (2001). Perceptual speed and IQ are associated through common genetic factors. *Behavior Genetics, 31(6)*, 593–602.

Posthuma, D., de Geus, E. J. C., Baare, W. E. C., Hulshoff Pol, H. E., Kahn, R. S., & Boomsma, D. I. (2002). The association between brain volume and intelligence is of genetic origin. *Nature Neuroscience, 5(2)*, 83–84.

Posthuma, D., Neale, M. C., Boomsma, D. I., & de Geus, E. J. C. (2001). Are smarter brains running faster? Heritability of alpha peak frequency, IQ, and their interrelation. *Behavior Genetics, 31(6)*, 567–579.

Potter, M. (2012). Grieving and suffering. In Perrin, K., Sheehan, C., Potter, M., & Kazanowski, M (Eds.), *In Palliative Care Nursing: Caring for Suffering* Patients (pp. 53–76). Sudbury, MA: Jones & Bartlett Learning.

Potter, N. (2011). ESP study gets published in scientific journal. *ABC World News.* Retrieved from http://abcnews.go.com/Technology/extrasensory-perception-scientific-journal-esp-paper-published-cornell/story?id=12556754

Pournaghash-Tehrani, S. (2011). Domestic violence in Iran: A literature review. *Aggression and Violent Behavior, 16(1)*, 1–5.

Powell, M., & Newgent, R. (2011). Assertiveness and mental health professionals: Differences between insight-oriented and action-oriented clinicians. *The Professional Counselor, 1(2)*, 92–98.

Powell-Hopson, D., & Hopson, D. S. (1988). Implications of doll color preferences among Black preschool children and White preschool children. *Journal of Black Psychology, 14*, 57–63.

Prado, J., Carp, J., & Weissman, D. H. (2011). Variations of response time in a selective attention task are linked to variations of functional connectivity in the attentional network. *NeuroImage, 54(1)*, 541–549.

Pratt, M. W., Skoe, E. E., & Arnold, M. (2004). Care reasoning development and family socialisation patterns in later adolescence: A longitudinal analysis. *International Journal of Behavioral Development, 28(2)*, 139–147.

Preuss, U. W., Zetzsche, T., Jäger, M., Groll, C., Frodl, T., Bottlender, R., Leisinger, G., Hegerl, U., Hahn, K., Möller, H. J., & Meisenzahl, E. M. (2005). Thalamic volume in first-episode and chronic schizophrenic subjects: A volumetric MRI study. *Schizophrenia Research, 73(1)*, 91–101.

Preventing suicide. (2009). *Preventing suicide in people who have schizophrenia.* Retrieved from http://www.schizophrenia.com/suicide.html

Price, D. D., Finniss, D. G., & Benedetti, F. (2008). A comprehensive review of the placebo effect: Recent advances and current thought. *Annual Review of Psychology, 59*, 565–590.

Price, M. (2011, June). Implicit bias could derail business deals. *Monitor on Psychology, 42(6)*. Retrieved from http://psycnet.apa.org/psycextra/569102011-005.pdf

Priest, R. F., & Sawyer, J. (1967). Proximity and peership: Bases of balance in interpersonal attraction. *American Journal of Sociology, 72*, 633–649.

Prigatano, G. P., & Gray, J. A. (2008). Predictors of performance on three developmentally sensitive neuropsychological tests in children with and without traumatic brain injury. *Brain Injury, 22*, 491–500.

Pring, L., & Hermelin, B. (2002). Numbers and letters: Exploring an autistic savant's unpractised ability. *Neurocase, 8(4)*, 330–337.

Pring, L., Woolf, K., & Tadic, V. (2008). Melody and pitch processing in five musical savants with congenital blindness. *Perception, 37*, 290–307.

Prior, A., & MacWhinney, B. (2010). A bilingual advantage in task switching. *Bilingualism: Language and Cognition, 13(2)*, 253–262.

Procianoy, R., S., Mendes, E. W., & Silveira, R. C. (2010). Massage therapy improves neurodevelopment outcome at two years corrected age for very low birth weight infants. *Early Human Development, 86(1)*, 7–11.

Prouix, M. J. (2007). Bottom-up guidance in visual search for conjunctions. *Journal of Experimental Psychology, 33*, 48–56.

Pruchnicki, S. A., Wu, L. J., & Belenky, G. (2011). An exploration of the utility of mathematical modeling predicting fatigue from sleep/wake history and circadian phase applied in accident analysis and prevention: The crash of Comair Fight 5191. *Accident Analysis and Prevention, 43(3)*, 1056–1061.

Psychology Matters. (2006, June 30). *Pushing buttons.* Retrieved from http://www.psychologymatters.org/pushbutton.

Pu, S., Yamada, T., Yokoyama, K., Matsumura, H., Kobayashi, H., Sasaki, N., Mitani, H., Adachi, A., Kaneko, K., Nakagome, K. (2011). A multi-channel near-infrared spectroscopy study of prefrontal cortex activation during working memory task in major depressive disorder. *Neuroscience Research, 70(1)*, 91–97.

Pullum, G. K. (1991). *The great Eskimo vocabulary hoax and other irreverent essays on the study of language.* Chicago, IL: University of Chicago Press.

Putting the power of television to good use. (2005). *APA online: Psychology matters.* Retrieved from http://www.psychologymatters.org/ Bandura.html

Pychyl, T. (2010). *The procrastinator's digest.* Retrieved from http://www.procrastinatorsdigest.com/pages/introduction.html

Quadflieg, S. & MacRae, C. (2011). Neuroimaging methods in social cognition. In K. Klauer, A. Voss, & C. Stahl (Eds.), *Cognitive methods in social psychology* (pp. 340–366). New York, NY: Guilford Press.

Qualls, S. H. (2008). Caregiver family therapy. In K. Laidlaw & B. Knight (Eds.), *Handbook of emotional disorders in later life: Assessment and treatment* (pp. 183–209). New York, NY: Oxford University Press.

Quartana, P. J., & Burns, J. W. (2010). Emotion suppression affects cardiovascular responses to initial and subsequent laboratory stressors. *British Journal of Health Psychology, 15(3),* 511–528.

Quinn, P. C., Kelly, D. J., Lee, K., Pascalis, O., & Slater, A. M. (2008). Preference for attractive faces in human infants extends beyond conspecifics. *Developmental Science, 11,* 76–83.

Quintanilla, Y. T. (2007). Achievement motivation strategies: An integrative achievement motivation program with first year seminar students. *Dissertation Abstracts International Section A: Humanities and Social Sciences, 68* (6-A), 2339.

Radcliff, K., & Joseph, L. (2011) Girls just being girls: Mediating relational aggression and victimization. *Preventing School Failure: Alternative Education for Children and Youth, 55(3),* 171–179.

Radvansky, G. A. (2011). *Human memory* (2nd ed.). Upper Saddle River, NJ: Pearson.

Raevuori, A., Keski-Rahkonen, A., Hoek, H. W., Sihvola, E., Rissanen, A., & Kaprio, J. (2008). Lifetime anorexia nervosa in young men in the community: Five cases and their co-twins. *International Journal of Eating Disorders, 41,* 458–463.

Raggi, A., Plazzi, G., Pennisi, G., Tasca, D., & Ferri, R. (2011). Cognitive evoked potentials in narcolepsy: A review of the literature. *Neuroscience and Biobehavioral Reviews, 35(5),* 1144–1153.

Rahardjo, H. E., Brauer, A., Mägert, H.-J., Meyer, M., Kauffels, W., Taher, A., Rahardjo, D., Jonas, U., Kuczyk, M., & Ückert, S. (2011). Endogenous vasoactive peptides and the human vagina—A molecular biology and functional study. *Journal of Sexual Medicine, 8(1),* 35–43.

Rai, T. S., & Fiske, A. P. (2011). Moral psychology is relationship regulation: Moral motives for unity, hierarchy, equality, and proportionality. *Psychological Review, 118(1),* 57–75.

Raine, A., Lencz, T., Bihrle, S., LaCasse, L., & Colletti, P. (2000). Reduced prefrontal gray matter volume and reduced autonomic activity in antisocial personality disorder. *Archives of General Psychiatry, 57,* 119–127.

Raine, A., Meloy, J.R., Bihrle, S., Stoddard, J., LaCasse, L., & Buchsbaum, M.S. (1998). Reduced prefrontal and increased subcortical brain functioning assessed using positron emission tomography in predatory and effective murderers. *Behavioral Sciences & the Law, 16(3),* 319–332.

Raine, A., & Yang, Y. (2006). The neuroanatomical bases of psychopathy: A review of brain imaging findings. In C. J. Patrick (Ed.), *Handbook of the psychopathy* (pp. 278–295). New York, NY: Guilford Press.

Randi, J. (1997). *An encyclopedia of claims, frauds, and hoaxes of the occult and supernatural: James Randi's decidedly skeptical definitions of alternate realities.* New York, NY: St Martin's Press.

Randi, J. (2006). John Edwards revisited. *James Randi's Swift.* Retrieved from http://www.randi.org/jr/2006-04/042106edward.html

Rantanen, M., Mauno, S., Kinnunen, U., & Rantanen, J. (2011). Do individual coping strategies help or harm in the work–family conflict situation? Examining coping as a moderator between work–family conflict and well-being. *International Journal of Stress Management, 18(1),* 24–48.

Rao, V., Spiro, J. R., Handel, S., & Onyike, C. U. (2008). Clinical correlates of personality changes associated with traumatic brain injury. *Journal of Neuropsychiatry & Clinical Neurosciences, 20,* 118–119.

Raphel, S. (2008). Kinship care and the situation for grandparents. *Journal of Child and Adolescent Psychiatric Nursing, 21,* 118–120.

Rapp, B., & Lipka, K. (2011). The literate brain: The relationship between spelling and reading. *Journal of Cognitive Neuroscience, 23(5),* 1180–1197.

Ratner, C. (2011). *Macro cultural psychology: A political philosophy of mind.* New York, NY: Oxford University Press.

Ratnesar, R. (2011, July/August). The menace within. *Stanford, 44*–51.

Rattat, A.-C., & Droit-Volet, S. (2010). The effects of interference and retention delay on temporal generalization performance. *Attention, Perception, & Psychophysics, 72(7),* 1903–1912.

Rattaz, C., Goubet, N., & Bullinger, A. (2005). The calming effect of a familiar odor on full-term newborns. *Journal of Developmental & Behavioral Pediatrics, 26,* 86–92.

Rauch, S. A. M., Defever, E., Oetting, S., Graham-Bermann, S. A., & Seng, J. S. (2011). Optimism, coping, and posttraumatic stress severity in women in the childbearing year. *Psychological Trauma: Theory, Research, Practice, and Policy.* Retrieved from http://psycnet.apa.org/index.cfm?fa=buy.optionToBuy&id=2011-06454–001

Rauer, A. J. (2007). Identifying happy, healthy marriages for men, women, and children. *Dissertation Abstracts International: Section B: The Sciences and Engineering, 67(10-B),* 6098.

Read, D., & Grushka-Cockayne, Y. (2011). The similarity heuristic. *Journal of Behavioral Decision Making, 24(1),* 23–46.

Rechtschaffen, A., & Siegel, J.M. (2000). Sleep and Dreaming. In E. R. Kandel, J. H. Schwartz, & T. M. Jessel (Eds.), *Principles of Neuroscience* (4th ed.) (pp. 936–947). New York, NY: McGraw-Hill.

Reddy, L., Remy, F., Vayssiere, N., & VanRullen, R. (2011). Neural correlates of the continuous wagon wheel illusion: A functional MRI study. *Human Brain Mapping, 32(2),* 163–170.

Reed, D. D., & Martens, B. K. (2011). Temporal discounting predicts student responsiveness to exchange delays in a classroom token system. *Journal of Applied Behavior Analysis, 44(1),* 1–18.

Reeves, R. R., & Panguluri, R. L. (2011). Neuropsychiatric complications of traumatic brain injury. *Journal of Psychosocial Nursing and Mental Health Services, 49(3),* 42–50.

Regan, P. (1998). What if you can't get what you want? Willingness to compromise ideal mate selection standards as a function of sex, mate value, and relationship context. *Personality and Social Psychology Bulletin, 24,* 1294–1303.

Regan, P. (2011). *Close relationships.* New York, NY: Routledge/Taylor & Francis Group.

Reifman, A. (2000). Revisiting the Bell Curve. *Psychology, 11,* 21–29.

Reiner, W. G., & Gearbart, J. P. (2004). Discordant sexual identity in some genetic males with cloacal exstrophy assigned to female sex at birth. *New England Journal of Medicine, 350,* 333–341.

Reinhard, M.-A., & Dickhäuser, O. (2011). How affective states, task difficulty, and self-concepts influence the formation and consequences of performance expectancies. *Cognition and Emotion, 25(2),* 220–228.

Reinhard, M-A., Messner, M., & Sporer, S. L. (2006). Explicit persuasive intent and its impact on success at persuasion: The determining roles of attractiveness and likeableness. *Journal of Consumer Psychology, 16,* 249–259.

Reis, H. T., Maniaci, M. R., Caprariello, P. A., Eastwick, P. W., & Finkel, E. J. (2011). Familiarity does indeed promote attraction in live interaction. *Journal of Personality and Social Psychology.* Advance online publication. doi:10.1037/a0022885

Reisfield, G. M. (2010). Medical cannabis and chronic opioid therapy. *Journal of Pain & Palliative Care Pharmacotherapy, 24(4),* 356–361.

Reivich, K. J., Seligman, M. E. P., & McBride, S. (2011). Master resilience training in the U.S. Army. *American Psychologist, 66(1),* 25–34.

Rendell, M., Weden, M., Favreault, M., & Waldron, H. (2011). The protective effect of marriage for survival: A review and update. *Demography, 48(2),* 481–506.

Renvoize, E., Hanson, M., & Dale, M. (2011). Prevalence and causes of young onset dementia in an English health district. *International Journal of Geriatric Psychiatry, 26(1),* 106–107.

Renzetti, C., Curran, D., & Kennedy- Bergen, R. (2006). *Understanding diversity.* Boston, MA: Allyn & Bacon/Longman.

Rest, J., Narvaez, D., Bebeau, M., & Thoma, S. (1999). A neo-Kohlbergian approach: The DIT and schema theory. *Educational Psychology Review, 11(4),* 291–324.

Reynolds, M. R., Keith, T. Z., Ridley, K. P., & Patel, P. G. (2008). Sex differences in latent general and broad cognitive abilities for children and youth: Evidence from higher-order MG-MACS and MIMIC models. *Intelligence, 36,* 236–260.

Rezayat, M., Niasari, H., Ahmadi, S., Parsaei, L., & Zarrindast, M. R. (2010). N-methyl-D-aspartate receptors are involved in lithium-induced state-dependent learning in mice. *Journal of Psychopharmacology, 24(6),* 915–921.

Rezayof, A., Alijanpour, S., Zarrindast, M-R., & Rassouli, Y. (2008). Ethanol state-dependent memory: Involvement of dorsal hippocampal muscarinic and nicotinic receptors. *Neurobiology of Learning and Memory, 89,* 441–447.

Rhee, S. H., & Waldman, I. D. (2011). Genetic and environmental influences on aggression. In P. R. Shaver & M. Mikulincer (Eds.), *Herzilya series on personality and social psychology. Human aggression and violence: Causes, manifestations, and consequences* (pp. 143–163). Washington, DC: American Psychological Association.

Rhoades, K. A., Leve, L. D., Harold, G. T., Neiderhiser, J. M., Shaw, D. S., & Reiss, D. (2011). Longitudinal pathways from marital hostility to child anger during toddlerhood: Genetic susceptibility and indirect effects via harsh parenting. *Journal of Family Psychology, 25(2),* 282–291.

Rhodes, G., Halberstadt, J., & Brajkovich, G. (2001). Generalization of mere exposure effects to averaged composite faces. *Social Cognition, 19(1),* 57–70.

Rial, R. V., Akaârir, M., Gamundí, A., Nicolau, C., Garau, C., Aparicio, S., Tejada, S., Gené, L., González, J., De Vera, L. M., Coenen, Anton M., Barceló, P., & Esteban, S. (2010). Evolution of wakefulness, sleep and hibernation: From reptiles to mammals. *Neuroscience and Biobehavioral Reviews, 34(8),* 1144–1160.

Richardson, D. S., & Hammock, G. S. (2007). Social context of human aggression: Are we paying too much attention to gender? *Aggression and Violent Behavior, 12,* 417–426.

Ridley, R. M., Baker, H. F., Cummings, R. M., Green, M. E., & Leow-Dyke, A. (2005). Mild topographical memory impairment following crossed unilateral lesions of the mediodorsal thalamic nucleus and the inferotemporal cortex. *Behavioral Neuroscience, 119(2),* 518–525.

Rieber, R. (2012). *Encyclopedia of the history of psychological theories.* New York, NY: Springer.

Riebschleger, J., & Cross, S., (2011). Loss and grief experiences of mentors in social work education. *Mentoring & Tutoring: Partnership in Learning, 19(1),* 65–82.

Riley, B., & Kendler, K., (2011). Classical genetic studies of schizophrenia. In D. Weinberger, & P. Harrison (Eds.), *Schizophrenia* (3rd ed.) (pp. 245–268). Hoboken, NJ: Wiley.

Ripley, A. (2004, June 31). Redefining torture. *Time, 163,* p. 29.

Ritchey, M., LaBar, K. S., & Cabeza, R. (2011). Level of processing modulates the neural correlates of emotional memory formation. *Journal of Cognitive Neuroscience, 23(4),* 757–771.

Riva, M. A., Tremolizzo, L., Spicci, M., Ferrarese, C., De Vito, G., Cesana, G. C., & Sironi, V. A. (2011). The disease of the moon: The linguistic and pathological evolution of the English term "lunatic". *Journal of the History of the Neurosciences, 20(1),* 65–73.

Rivera-Ramos, Z. A., & Buki, L. P. (2011). I will no longer be a man! Manliness and prostate cancer screenings among Latino men. *Psychology of Men & Masculinity, 12(1),* 13–25.

Rivers, I. (2011). *Homophobic bullying: Research and theoretical perspectives.* New York, NY: Oxford University Press.

Rizolatti, G., Fadiga, L., Fogassi, L. & Gallese, V. (2002). From mirror neurons to imitation: Facts and speculations. In A. N. Meltzoff & W. Prinz (Eds.), *The imitative mind: Development, evolution, and brain bases.* Cambridge, MA: Cambridge University Press.

Rizolatti, G., Fogassi, L. & Gallese, V. (2006, November). In the mind. *Scientific American,* 54–61.

Roach, G. D., Darwent, D., Sletten, T. L., & Dawson, D. (2011). Long-haul pilots use in-flight napping as a countermeasure to fatigue. *Applied Ergonomics, 42(2),* 214–218.

Robbins, S. P. (1996). *Organizational behavior: Concepts, controversies, and applications.* Englewood Cliffs, NJ: Prentice Hall.

Roberson, D., & Hanley, J. R. (2010). Relatively speaking: An account of the relationship between language and thought in the color domain. In B. C. Malt & P. Wolff (Eds.), *Words and the mind: How words capture human experience* (pp. 183–198). New York, NY: Oxford University Press.

Robinson, F. P. (1946). *Effective study.* New York, NY: Harper & Row.

Robinson, F. P. (1970). *Effective study* (4th ed.). New York, NY: Harper & Row.

Robinson, S. J., & Rollings, L. J. L. (2011). The effect of mood-context on visual recognition and recall memory. *Journal of General Psychology, 138(1),* 66–79.

Rodrigues, A., Assmar, E. M., & Jablonski, B. (2005). Social-psychology and the invasion of Iraq. *Revista de Psicología Social, 20,* 387–398.

Rodrigues, J., Sauzéon, H., Langevin, S., Raboutet, C., & N'Kaoua, B. (2010). Memory performance depending on task characteristics and cognitive aids: A-levels of processing approach in young adults. *European Review of Applied Psychology/Revue*

Européenne de Psychologie Appliquée, 60(1), 55–64.

Rodsiri, R., Spicer, C., Green, A. R., Marsden, C. A., & Fone, K. C. F. (2011). Acute concomitant effects of MDMA binge dosing on extracellular 5-HT, locomotion and body temperature and the long-term effect on novel object discrimination in rats. *Psychopharmacology, 213(2–3)*, 365–376.

Rogalsky, C., Love, T., Driscoll, D., Anderson, S. W., & Hickok, G. (2011). Are mirror neurons the basis of speech perception? Evidence from five cases with damage to the purported human mirror system. *Neurocase: The Neural Basis of Cognition, 17(2)*, 178–187.

Rogers, C. R. (1961). *On becoming a person.* Boston, MA: Houghton Mifflin.

Rogers, C. R. (1980). *A way of being.* Boston, MA: Houghton Mifflin.

Rogosch, F. A., & Cicchetti, D. (2004). Child maltreatment and emergent personality organization: Perspectives from the five-factor model. *Journal of Abnormal Child Psychology, 32(2)*, 123–145.

Rohner, R. (1986). *The warmth dimension.* Newbury Park, CA: Sage.

Rohner, R. P. (2008). Parental acceptance-rejection theory studies of intimate adult relationships. (2008). *Cross-Cultural Research: The Journal of Comparative Social Science, 42*, 5–12.

Rohner, R. P., & Britner, P. A. (2002). World-wide mental health correlates of parental acceptance-rejection: Review of cross-cultural and intracultural evidence. *Cross-Cultural Research: The Journal of Comparative Social Science, 36*, 15–47.

Rohrer, D., & Pashler, H. (2010). Recent research on human learning challenges conventional instructional strategies. *Educational Researcher, 39(5)*, 406–412.

Roisko, R., Wahlberg, K.-E., Hakko, H., Wynne, L., & Tienari, P. (2011). Communication deviance in parents of families with adoptees at a high or low risk of schizophrenia-spectrum disorders and its associations with attributes of the adoptee and the adoptive parents. *Psychiatry Research, 185(1–2)*, 66–71.

Romero, S. G., McFarland, D. J., Faust, R., Farrell, L., & Cacace, A. T. (2008). Electrophysiological markers of skill-related neuroplasticity. *Biological Psychology, 78*, 221–230.

Rosch, E. (1978). Principles of organization. In E. Rosch & H. L. Lloyd (Eds.), *Cognition and categorization.* Hillsdale, NJ: Erlbaum.

Rosch, E. H. (1973). Natural categories. *Cognitive Psychology, 4*, 328–350.

Rose, C. (Executive Producer). (1994, October 14). An interview with Quentin Tarantino.

[*Charlie Rose*]. New York, NY: Public Broadcasting Service.

Rose, C. R., & Konnerth, A. (2002). Exciting glial oscillations. *Nature Neuroscience, 4*, 773–774.

Rose, S. A., Feldman, J. F., Jankowski, J. J., & Van Rossem, R. (2011). The structure of memory in infants and toddlers: An SEM study with full-terms and preterms. *Developmental Science, 14(1)*, 83–91.

Roselli, C., Reddy, R., & Kaufman, K. (2011). The development of male-oriented behavior in rams. *Frontiers in Neuroendocrinology, 32(2)*, 164–169.

Rosenström, T., Hintsanen, M., Kivimäki, M., Jokela, M., Juonala, M., Viikari, J. S., Raitakari, O., & Keltikangas-Järvinen, L. (2011). "Change in job strain and progression of atherosclerosis: The Cardiovascular Risk in Young Finns study": Correction to Rosenström et al. (2011). *Journal of Occupational Health Psychology, 16(2)*, 201.

Rosenzweig, E. S., Barnes, C. A., & McNaughton, B. L. (2002). Making room for new memories. *Nature Neuroscience, 5(1)*, 6–8.

Rosenzweig, M. R., & Bennett, E. L. (1996). Psychobiology of plasticity: Effects of training and experience on brain and behavior. *Behavioural Brain Research, 78(1)*, 57–65.

Rosenzweig, M. R., Bennett, E. L., & Diamond, M. C. (1972). Brain changes in response to experience. *Scientific American, 226*, 22–29.

Rosenzweig, S., Greeson, J. M., Reibel, D. K., Green, J. S., Jasser, S. A., & Beasley, D. (2010). Mindfulness-based stress reduction for chronic pain conditions: Variations in treatment outcomes and role of home meditation practice. *Journal of Psychosomatic Research, 68(1)*, 29–36.

Rosling, A., Sparén, P., Norring, C., & von Knorring, A. (2011). Mortality of eating disorders: A follow-up study of treatment in a specialist unit 1974–2000. *International Journal of Eating Disorder, 44(4)*, 304–310.

Rosner, R. I. (2011). Aaron T. Beck's drawings and the psychoanalytic origin story of cognitive therapy. *History of Psychology.* Advance online publication. doi:10.1037/a0023892

Rosnow, R. L., & Rosenthal, R. (2008). *Beginning behavioral research* (6th ed.). Upper Saddle River, NJ: Prentice-Hall.

Ross, B. M., & Millson, C. (1970). Repeated memory of oral prose in Ghana and New York. *International Journal of Psychology, 5*, 173–181.

Ross, D., Kincaid, H., Spurrett, D., & Collins, P. (Eds.). (2010). *What is addiction?* Cambridge, MA: MIT Press.

Ross, J. N., & Coleman, N. M. (2011). Gold Digger or Video Girl: The salience of an emerging hip-hop sexual script. *Culture, Health & Sexuality, 13(2)*, 157–171.

Rossignol, S., Barrière, G., Frigon, A., Barthélemy, D., Bouyer, L., Provencher, J., Leblond, H., & Bernard, G. (2008). Plasticity of locomotor sensorimotor interactions after peripheral and/or spinal lesions. *Brain Research Reviews, 57*, 228–240.

Roth, M. L., Tripp, D. A. Harrison, M. H., Sullivan, M., & Carson, P. (2007). Demographic and psychosocial predictors of acute perioperative pain for total knee arthroplasty. *Pain Research & Management, 12*, 185–194.

Rothstein, J. B., Jensen, G., & Neuringer, A. (2008). Human choice among five alternatives when reinforcers decay. *Behavioural Processes, 78*, 231–239.

Rotten Tomatoes. (2011). *Avatar* (2009). Retrieved from http://www.rottentomatoes.com/m/avatar/

Rotter, J. B. (1954). *Social learning and clinical psychology.* Englewood Cliffs, NJ: Prentice Hall.

Rotter, J. B. (1990). Internal versus external control of reinforcement: A case history of a variable. *American Psychologist, 45*, 489–493.

Rowe, B., & Levine, D. (2011). *Concise introduction to linguistics* (3rd ed.). Upper Saddle River, NJ: Prentice Hall.

Rozencwajg, P., Cherfi, M., Ferrandez, A. M., Lautrey, J., Lemoine, C., & Loarer, E. (2005). Age related differences in the strategies used by middle aged adults to solve a block design task. *International Journal of Aging & Human Development, 60(2)*, 159–182.

Rubinstein, E. (2008). Judicial perceptions of eyewitness testimony. *Dissertation Abstracts International: Section B: The Sciences and Engineering, 68(8-B)*, 5592.

Rubinstein, J. S., Meyer, D. E., & Evans, J. E. (2001). Executive Control of Cognitive Processes in Task Switching. *Journal of Experimental Psychology, Human Perception and Performance, 27(4)*, 763–797.

Rumbaugh, D. M., von Glasersfeld, E. C., Warner, H., Pisani, P., & Gill, T. V. (1974). Lana (chimpanzee) learning language: A progress report. *Brain & Language, 1(2)*, 205–212.

Rüsch, N., Corrigan, P. W., Todd, A. R., & Bodenhausen, G. V. (2011). Automatic stereotyping against people with schizophrenia, schizoaffective and affective disorders. *Psychiatry Research*, *186*(1), 34–39.

Rushton, J. P., & Jensen, A. R. (2010). The rise and fall of the Flynn effect as a reason to expect a narrowing of the Black–White IQ gap. *Intelligence*, *38(2)*, 213–219.

Rushton, P., & Irwing, P. (2011). The general factor of personality: Normal and abnormal. In T. Chamorro-Premuzic, S. von Stumm, & A. Furnam (Eds.), *Wiley-Blackwell handbook of individual differences* (pp. 132–161). Chichester, UK: Wiley-Blackwell.

Russell, J. A. (Ed.). (2007). Stress milestones. *Stress: The International Journal on the Biology of Stress*, *10(1)*, 1–2.

Russo, N. F., & Tartaro, J. (2008). Women and mental health. In F. L. Denmark & M. A. Paludi (Eds.), *Psychology of women: A handbook of issues and theories* (2nd ed.) (pp. 440–483). *Women's psychology*. Westport, CT: Praeger/Greenwood.

Ruthig, J. C., Chipperfield, J. G., Perry, R. P. Newall, N. E., & Swift, A. (2007). Comparative risk and perceived control: Implications for psychological and physical well-being among older adults. *Journal of Social Psychology*, *147*, 345–369.

Rutter, M. (2007). Gene-environment interdependence. *Developmental Science*, *10*, 12–18.

Rutter, V. E. (2005). The case for divorce: Under what conditions is divorce beneficial and for whom? *Dissertation Abstracts International Section A: Humanities and Social Sciences*, *65*(7-A), 2784.

Ruzek, J. I., Schnurr, P. P., Vasterling, J. J., & Friedman, M. J. (2011). *Caring for veterans with deployment-related stress disorders: Iraq, Afghanistan, and beyond.* Washington, DC: American Psychological Association.

Ryan, C. S., Casas, J. F., & Thompson, B. K. (2010). Interethnic ideology, intergroup perceptions, and cultural orientation. *Journal of Social Issues*, *66*(1), 29–44.

Ryan, J. P., Sheu, L. K., & Gianaros, P. J. (2011). Resting state functional connectivity within the cingulate cortex jointly predicts agreeableness and stressor-evoked cardiovascular reactivity. *NeuroImage*, *55(1)*, 363–370.

Ryan, M. K., Haslam, S. A., Hersby, M. D., & Bongiorno, R. (2011). Think crisis–think female: The glass cliff and contextual variation in the think manager–think male stereotype. *Journal of Applied Psychology*, *96*(3), 470–484.

Ryback, D., Ikemi, A., & Miki, Y. (2001). Japanese psychology in crisis: Thinking inside the (empty) box. *Journal of Humanistic Psychology*, *41*(4), 124–136.

Rydell, R. J., Rydell, M. T., & Boucher, K. L. (2010). The effect of negative performance stereotypes on learning. *Journal of Personality and Social Psychology*, *99*(6), 883–896.

Rymer, R. (1993). *Genie: An abused child's first flight from silence.* New York, NY: HarperCollins.

Sabet, K. A. (2007). The (often unheard) case against marijuana leniency. In M. Earleywine (Ed), *Pot politics: Marijuana and the costs of prohibition* (pp. 325–352). New York, NY: Oxford University Press.

Sacchetti, B., Sacco, T., & Strata, P. (2007). Reversible inactivation of amygdala and cerebellum but not perirhinal cortex impairs reactivated fear memories. *European Journal of Neuroscience*, *25*(9), 2875–2884.

Sachdev, P., Mondraty, N., Wen, W., & Gulliford, K. (2008). Brains of anorexia nervosa patients process self-images differently from non-self-images: An fMRI study. *Neuropsychologia*, *46*, 2161–2168.

Sack, R. L. (2010). Jet lag. *The New England Journal of Medicine*, *362*(5), 440–447.

Sack, R. L., Auckley, D., Auger, R. R., Carskadon, M. A., Wright, Jr., K. P., Vitiello, M. V., & Zhdanova, I. V. (2007). Circadian rhythm sleep disorders: Part I, basic principles, shift work and jet lag disorders: An American academy of sleep medicine review. *Sleep: Journal of Sleep and Sleep Disorders Research*, *30*, 1460–1483.

Sacks, O. (1995) *An anthropologist on Mars.* New York, NY: Vintage books.

Sacks, O. (2006, June 19). Stereo Sue. *New Yorker*, 64–73.

Sagan, C. (1980). "Encyclopaedia Galactica" *Cosmos*. PBS. No. 12. 01:24

Said, C., Haxby, J., and Todorov, A. (2011). Brain systems for assessing the affective value of faces. *Philosophical Transactions of the Royal Society B*, *366*, 1660–1670.

Salas, E., DeRouin, & Gade, P.A. (2007). The military's contribution to our science and practice: People, places, and findings. In L. L. Koppes (Ed.), *Historical perspectives in industrial and organizational psychology* (pp.169–189). Mahwah, NJ: Erlbaum.

Salekin, R. T., & Averett, C. A. (2008). Personality in childhood and adolescence. In M. Hersen & A. M. Gross (Eds.), *Handbook of clinical psychology, vol 2: Children and adolescents* (pp. 351–385). Hoboken, NJ: Wiley.

Salgado-Pineda, P., Fakra, E., Delaveau, P., McKenna, P. J., Pomarol-Clotet, E., & Blin, O. (2011). Correlated structural and functional brain abnormalities in the default mode network in schizophrenia

patients. *Schizophrenia Research*, *125*(2–3), 101–109.

Salihu, H. M., Kornosky, J. L., Lynch, O'N., Alio, A. P., August, E. M., & Marty, P. J. (2011). Impact of prenatal alcohol consumption on placenta-associated syndromes. *Alcohol*, *45*(1), 73–79.

Salmivalli, C. (2001). Feeling good about oneself, being bad to others? Remarks on self-esteem, hostility, and aggressive behavior. *Aggression and Violent Behavior*, *6*, 375–393.

Salmivalli, C., & Kaukiainen, A. (2004). "Female aggression" revisited: Variable-and personcentered approaches to studying gender differences in different types of aggression. *Aggressive Behavior*, *30*(2),158–163.

Salovey, P., & Mayer, J. D. (1990). Emotional intelligence. *Imagination,Cognition, and Personality*, *9*, 185–211.

Salovey, P., Bedell, B. T., Detweiler, J. B., & Mayer, J. D. (2000). Current directions in emotional intelligence research. In M. Lewis & J.M. Haviland (Eds.), *Handbook of emotions* (2nd ed.) (pp. 504–520). New York, NY: Guilford Press.

Salthouse, T. A. (2011). Cognitive correlates of cross-sectional differences and longitudinal changes in trail making performance. *Journal of Clinical and Experimental Neuropsychology*, *33*(2), 242–248.

Saltus, R. (2000, June 22). Brain cells are coaxed into repair duty. *Boston Globe*, A18.

Salvatore, P., Ghidini, S., Zita, G., De Panfilis, C., Lambertino, S., Maggini, C., & Baldessarini, R. J. (2008). Circadian activity rhythm abnormalities in ill and recovered bipolar I disorder patients. *Bipolar Disorders,10*, 256–265.

Samson, R. D., Frank, M. J., & Fellous, J.-M. (2010). Computational models of reinforcement learning: The role of dopamine as a reward signal. *Cognitive Neurodynamics*, *4(2)*, 91–105.

Samuels-Dennis, J. A., Ford-Gilboe, M., & Ray, S. (2011). Single mother's adverse and traumatic experiences and post-traumatic stress symptoms. *Journal of Family Violence*, *26(1)*, 9–20.

Sanbonmatsu, D. M., Uchino, B. N., & Birmingham, W. (2011). On the importance of knowing your partner's views: Attitude familiarity is associated with better interpersonal functioning and lower ambulatory blood pressure in daily life. *Annals of Behavioral Medicine*, *41*(1), 131–137.

Sanchez Jr., J. (2006). Life satisfaction factors impacting the older Cuban-American population. *Dissertation Abstracts International*

Section A: Humanities and Social Sciences, 67 (5–A), 1864.

Sánchez-Martín, J. R., Azurmendi, A., Pascual-Sagastizabal, E., Cardas, J., Braza, F., Braza, P., Carreras, M., & Muñoz, J. M. (2011). Androgen levels and anger and impulsivity measures as predictors of physical, verbal and indirect aggression in boys and girls. *Psychoneuroendocrinology, 36(5),* 750–760.

Sandi, C. (2011). Glucocorticoids act on glutamatergic pathways to affect memory processes. *Trends in Neurosciences, 34(4),* 165–176.

Sandoval, A. M. R., & Acuña, L. (2008). La Escala de Reajuste Social para niños de primaria en México [The Social Readjustment Rating Scale for elementary school children in Mexico]. *Revista Latinoamericana de Psicología, 40(2),* 335–344.

Saniotis, A. (2010). Evolutionary and anthropological approaches towards understanding human need for psychotropic and mood altering substances. *Journal of Psychoactive Drugs, 42(4),* 477–484.

Sapolsky, R. (2003). Taming stress. *Scientific American,* pp. 87–95.

Sapolsky, R. M. (1992). *Stress, the aging brain, and the mechanisms of neuron death.* Cambridge, MA: MIT Press.

Sara, S. J. (2010). Reactivation, retrieval, replay and reconsolidation in and out of sleep: Connecting the dots. *Frontiers in Behavioral Neuroscience, 4,* Article ID 185.

Sarris, J., & Byrne, G. J. (2011). A systematic review of insomnia and complementary medicine. *Sleep Medicine Reviews, 15(2),* 99–106.

Sass, H. (2011). Conceptual history of classification. *European Psychiatry, 26(1),* 1778.

Sassenberg, K., Moskowitz, G. B., Jacoby, J., & Hansen, N. (2007). The carry-over effect of competition: The impact of competition on prejudice towards uninvolved outgroups. *Journal of Experimental Social Psychology, 43,* 529–538.

Satcher, N. D. (2007). Social and moral reasoning of high school athletes and non-athletes. *Dissertation Abstracts International Section A: Humanities and Social Sciences, 68*(3–A), 928.

Sathyaprabha, T. N., Satishchandra, P., Pradhan, C., Sinha, S., Kaveri, B., Thennarasu, K., Murthy, B. T. C., & Raju, T. R. (2008). Modulation of cardiac autonomic balance with adjuvant yoga therapy in patients with refractory epilepsy. *Epilepsy & Behavior, 12,* 245–252.

Satler, C., Garrido, L. M., Sarmiento, E. P., Leme, S., Conde, C., & Tomaz, C. (2007). Emotional arousal enhances declarative memory in patients with Alzheimer's disease. *Acta Neurologica Scandinavica, 116,* 355–360.

Sato, S. M., Schulz, K. M., Sisk, C. L., & Wood, R. I. (2008). Adolescents and androgens, receptors and rewards. *Hormones and Behavior, 53,* 647–658.

Sato, W., Kochiyama, T., & Yoshikawa, S. (2011). The inversion effect for neutral and emotional facial expressions on amygdala activity. *Brain Research, 1378,* 84–90.

Savic, I., Berglund, H., & Lindström, P. (2007). Brain response to putative pheromones in homosexual men. In G. Einstein (Ed.), *Sex and the brain* (pp. 731–738). Cambridge, MA: MIT Press.

Saxton, M. (2010). *Child language: Acquisition and development.* Thousand Oaks, CA: Sage.

Schachter, S., & Singer, J. E. (1962). Cognitive, social, and physiological determinants of emotional state. *Psychological Review, 69,* 379–399.

Schachtman, T., & Reilly, S. (2011). *Associative learning and conditioning theory: Human and non-human applications.* Oxford, UK: Oxford University Press.

Schaefer, R. T. (2008). Power and power elite. In V. Parillo (Ed.), *Encyclopedia of social problems.* Thousand Oaks, CA: Sage.

Schaie, K. W. (1994). The life course of adult intellectual development. *American Psychologist, 49,* 304–313.

Schaie, K. W. (2008). A lifespan developmental perspective of psychological ageing. In K. Laidlaw & B. Knight (Eds.), *Handbook of emotional disorders in later life: Assessment and treatment* (pp. 3–32). New York, NY: Oxford University Press.

Scheel, M. H. (2010). Resource depletion promotes automatic processing: Implications for distribution of practice. *Psychological Reports, 107(3),* 860–872.

Schenck, C. H., & Mahowald, M. W. (2010). Therapeutics for parasomnias in adults. *Sleep Medicine Clinics, 5(4),* 689–700.

Schepers, R. J., & Ringkamp, M. (2010). Thermoreceptors and thermosensitive afferents. *Neuroscience and Biobehavioral Reviews, 34(2),* 177–184.

Scherer, K. R., & Wallbott, H. G. (1994). Evidence for universal and cultural variation of differential emotion response patterning. *Journal of Personality and Social Psychology, 66(2),* 310–328.

Schermer, J., Vernon, P., Maio, G., & Jang, K. (2011). A behavior genetic study of the connection between social values and personality. *Twin Research and Human Genetics, 14(3),* 233–239.

Schiffer, B., Muller, B., Scherbaum, N., Hodgins, S., Forsting, M., Wiltfang, J., Gizewski, E., & Leygraf, N. (2011). Disentangling structural brain alterations associated with violent behavior from those associated with substance use disorders. *Archives of General Psychiatry.* Advance online publication. doi:10.1001/archgenpsychiatry.2011.61

Schifferstein, H. N. J. (2010). From salad to bowl: The role of sensory analysis in product experience research. *Food Quality and Preference, 21(8),* 1059–1067.

Schifferstein, H. N. J., & Hilscher, M. C. (2010). Multisensory images for everyday products: How modality importance, stimulus congruence and emotional context affect image descriptions and modality vividness ratings. *Journal of Mental Imagery, 34(3–4),* 63–98.

Schim, S. M., Briller, S. H., Thurston, C. S., & Meert, K. L. (2007). Life as death scholars: Passion, personality, and professional perspectives. *Death Studies, 31,* 165–172.

Schlaepfer, T. E., Harris, G. J., Tien, A.Y., Peng, L., Lee, S., & Pearlson, G. D. (1995). Structural differences in the cerebral cortex of healthy female and male subjects: A magnetic resonance imaging study. *Psychiatry Research, 61,* 129–35.

Schmitt-Rodermund, E., & Silbereisen, R. K. (2008). Well-adapted adolescent ethnic German immigrants in spite of adversity: The protective effects of human, social, and financial capital. *European Journal of Developmental Psychology, 5,* 186–209.

Schmitter-Edgecombe, M., & Seelye, A. M. (2011). Predictions of verbal episodic memory in persons with Alzheimer's disease. *Journal of Clinical and Experimental Neuropsychology, 33(2),* 218–225.

Schneider, D. M., & Sharp, L. (1969). *The dream life of a primitive people: The dreams of the Yir Yoront of Australia.* Ann Arbor, MI: University of Michigan.

Schneider, J. P. (2000). A qualitative study of cybersex participants: Gender differences, recovery issues, and implications for therapists. *Sexual Addiction & Compulsivity, 7,* 249–278.

Schneider, K. (2011). Toward a humanistic positive psychology: Why can't we just get along? *Existential Analysis, 22(1),* 32–38.

Schneidman, E. S. (1969). Suicide, lethality and the psychological autopsy. *International Psychiatry Clinics, 6,* 225–250

Schnider, A. (2008). *The confabulating mind: How the brain creates reality.* New York, NY: Oxford University Press.

Schredl, M., Paul, F., Lahl, O., & Göritz, A. S. (2010). Gender differences in dream content: Related to biological sex or sex role orientation? *Imagination, Cognition and Personality, 30(2)*, 171–183.

Schrier, D. (2011). *Think your kid's smart? Don't tell him!* Retrieved from http://mamasoncall.com/2011/02/think-your-kids-smart-dont-tell-him/

Schubert, T., & Semin, G. (2009). Embodiment as a unifying perspective for psychology. *European Journal of Social Psychology, 39*, 1135–1141.

Schuett, S., Heywood, C. A., Kentridge, R. W., & Zihl, J. (2008). The significance of visual information processing in reading: Insights from hemianopic dyslexia. *Neuropsychologia, 46*, 2445–2462.

Schülein, J. A. (2007). Science and psychoanalysis. *Scandinavian Psychoanalytic Review, 30*, 13–21.

Schultz, D. P., & Schultz, S. E. (2012). *A history of modern psychology* (10th ed.). Belmont, CA: Wadsworth/Cengage Learning

Schultz, K. (2008). Constructing failure, narrating success: Rethinking the "problem" of teen pregnancy. In D. L. Browning (Ed.), Adolescent identities: A collection of readings (pp. 113–137). *Relational perspectives book series.* New York, NY: The Analytic Press/Taylor & Francis Group.

Schulze, L., Domes, G., Krüger, A., Berger, C., Fleischer, M., Prehn, K., Schmahl, C., Grossmann, A., Hauenstein, K., & Herpertz, S. C. (2011). Neuronal correlates of cognitive reappraisal in borderline patients with affective instability. *Biological Psychiatry, 69(6)*, 564–573.

Schunk, D. H. (2008). Attributions as motivators of self-regulated learning. In D. H. Schunk & B. J. Zimmerman (Eds.), *Motivation and self-regulated learning: Theory, research, and applications* (pp. 245–266). Mahwah, NJ: Lawrence Erlbaum.

Schwartz, C., Chabanet, C., Lange, C., Issanchou, S., & Nicklaus, S. (2011). The role of taste in food acceptance at the beginning of complementary feeding. *Physiology & Behavior.* doi: 10.1016/j.physbeh.2011.04.061

Schwartz, M. W., & Morton, G. J. (2002). Obesity: Keeping hunger at bay. *Nature, 418*, 595–597.

Schweckendiek, J., Klucken, T., Merz, C. J., Tabbert, K., Walter, B., Ambach, W., Vaitl, D., & Stark, R. (2011). Weaving the (neuronal) web: Fear learning in spider phobia. *NeuroImage, 54(1)*, 681–688.

Science Daily. (2011, January 31). Key mechanism governing nicotine addiction discovered. *Science Daily.* Retrieved from http://www.sciencedaily.com/releases/2011/01/110130194139.htm

Scott, L. N., Levy, K. N., Adams, R. B., Jr., & Stevenson, M. T. (2011). Mental state decoding abilities in young adults with borderline personality disorder traits. *Personality Disorders: Theory, Research, and Treatment, 2(2)*, 98–112.

Scott, T. R. (2011). Taste as a basis for body wisdom. *Physiology & Behavior.* Retrieved from http://www.sciencedirect.com/science/article/pii/S0031938411001752

Scribner, S. (1977). Modes of thinking and ways of speaking: Culture and logic reconsidered. In P. N. Johnson-Laird & P. C. Wason (Eds.), *Thinking: Readings in cognitive science* (pp. 324–339). New York, NY: Cambridge University Press.

Seabrook, A. (2008). Hester Prynne: Sinner, victim, object, winner. *National Public Radio.* Retrieved from http://www.npr.org/templates/story/story.php?storyId=87805369

Seeman, P. (2011). All roads to schizophrenia lead to dopamine supersensitivity and elevated dopamine D2High receptors. *CNS Neuroscience & Therapeutics, 17(2)*, 118–132.

Seery, M. D. (2011). Challenge or threat? Cardiovascular indexes of resilience and vulnerability to potential stress in humans. *Neuroscience and Biobehavioral Reviews.* Retrieved from http://www.sciencedirect.com/science/article/pii/S0149763411000467

Segal, N. L., & Bouchard, T. J. (2000). *Entwined lives: Twins and what they tell us about human behavior.* New York, NY: Plumsock.

Segall, M. H., Dasen, P. R., Berry, J. W., & Portinga, Y. H. (1990). *Human behavior in global perspective: An introduction to cross-cultural psychology.* Elmsford, NY: Pergamon Press.

Segerstrom, S., C., & Miller, G. E. (2004). Psychological stress and the human immune system: A meta-analytic study of 30 years of inquiry. *Psychological Bulletin, 130(4)*, 601–630.

Seligman, M. E. P. (1975) *Helplessness: On depression, development, and death.* San Francisco, CA: Freeman.

Seligman, M. E. P. (1994). *What you can change and what you can't.* New York, NY: Alfred A. Knopf.

Seligman, M. E. P. (2003). The past and future of positive psychology. In C. L. M. Keyes & J. Daidt (Eds.), *Flourishing: Positive psychology and the life well-lived.* Washington, DC: American Psychological Association.

Seligman, M. E. P. (2007). Coaching and positive psychology. *Australian Psychologist, 42*, 266–267.

Selye, H. (1936). A syndrome produced by diverse nocuous agents. *Nature, 138*, 32.

Selye, H. (1974). *Stress without distress.* New York, NY: Harper & Row.

Senko, C., Durik, A. M., & Harackiewicz, J. M. (2008). Historical perspectives and new directions in achievement goal theory: Understanding the effects of mastery and performance-approach goals. In J. Y. Shah & W. L. Gardner (Eds.), *Handbook of motivation science* (pp. 100–113). New York, NY: Guilford Press.

Sentse, M., Ormel, J., Veenstra, R., Verhulst, F. C., & Oldehinkel, A. J. (2011). Child temperament moderates the impact of parental separation on adolescent mental health: The trails study. *Journal of Family Psychology, 25(1)*, 97–106.

Shaffer, R. & Jadwiszczok, A. (2010). Psychic defective: Sylvia Browne' history of failure. *Skeptical Inquirer, 34.* 2. Retrieved from http://www.csicop.org/si/show/psychic_defective_sylvia_brownes_history_of_failure/

Shahim, S. (2008). Sex differences in relational aggression in preschool children in Iran. *Psychological Reports, 102*, 235–238.

Shamay-Tsoory, S. G., Adler, N., Aharon-Peretz, J., Perry, D., & Mayseless, N. (2011). The origins of originality: The neural bases of creative thinking and originality. *Neuropsychologia, 49(2)*, 178–185.

Shapiro, J. R. (2011). Different groups, different threats: A multi-threat approach to the experience of stereotype threats. *Personality and Social Psychology Bulletin, 37(4)*, 464–480.

Sharps, M. J., Hess, A. B., Casner, H., Ranes, B., & Jones, J. (2007). Eyewitness memory in context: Toward a systematic understanding of eyewitness evidence. *The Forensic Examiner, 16*, 20–27.

Shaver, P. R., & Mikulincer, M. (2005). Attachment theory and research: Resurrection of the psychodynamic approach to personality. *Journal of Research in Personality, 39(1)*, 22–45.

Shea, S.C. (1988). *Psychiatric interviewing: The art of understanding.* Philadelphia, PA: Saunders.

Shear, K., Halmi, K. A., Widiger, T. A., & Boyce, C. (2007). Sociocultural factors and gender. In W. E. Narrow, M. B. First, P. J. Sirovatka, & D. A. Regier (Eds.), *Age and gender considerations in psychiatric diagnosis: A research agenda for DSM-V* (pp. 65–79). Arlington, VA: American Psychiatric Publishing.

Sheppard, L. D., & Vernon, P. A. (2008). Intelligence and speed of information-processing: A review of 50 years of research. *Personality & Individual Differences, 44*, 535–551.

Shepperd, J., Malone, W., & Sweeny, K. (2008). Exploring causes of the self-serving bias. *Social and Personality Psychology Compass, 2,* 895–908.

Sherif, M. (1966). *In common predicament: Social psychology of intergroup conflict and cooperation.* Boston, MA: Houghton Mifflin.

Sherif, M. (1998). Experiments in group conflict. In J. M. Jenkins, K. Oatley, & N. L. Stein (Eds.), *Human emotions: A reader* (pp. 245–252). Malden, MA: Blackwell.

Shermer, M. (2003). Psychic Drift: Why most scientists do not believe in ESP and psi phenomena. *Scientific American.* Retrieved from http://www.scientificamerican.com/article.cfm?id=psychic-drift

Shettleworth, S. J. (2010). Clever animals and killjoy explanations in comparative psychology. *Trends in Cognitive Sciences, 14(11),* 477–481.

Shin, R.-M., Tully, K., Li, Y., Cho, J.-H., Higuchi, M., Suhara, T., & Bolshakov, V. Y. (2010). Hierarchical order of coexisting pre- and postsynaptic forms of long-term potentiation at synapses in amygdala. *PNAS Proceedings of the National Academy of Sciences of the United States of America, 107(44),* 19073–19078.

Shinfuku, N., & Kitanishi, K. (2010). Buddhism and psychotherapy in Japan. Religion and psychiatry: Beyond boundaries. In P. J. Verhagen, H. M. van Praag, J. J. López-Ibor, J. L. Cox, & D. Moussaoui (Eds.), *Religion and psychiatry: Beyond boundaries* (pp. 181–191). Wiley-Blackwell.

Shirom, A. (2011). Job-related burnout: A review of major research foci and challenges. In J. C. Quick & L. E. Tetrick (Eds.), *Handbook of occupational health psychology* (2nd ed.) (pp. 223–241). Washington, DC: American Psychological Association.

Shoji, H., & Mizoguchi, K. (2011). Aging-related changes in the effects of social isolation on social behavior in rats. *Physiology & Behavior, 102(1),* 58–62.

Shultz, T. R. (2011). Computational modeling of infant concept learning: The developmental shift from features to correlations. In L. M. Oakes, C. H. Cashon, M. Casasola, & D. H. Rakison (Eds.), *Infant perception and cognition: Recent advances, emerging theories, and future directions* (pp. 125–152). New York, NY: Oxford University Press.

Shweder, R. A. (2011). Commentary: Ontogenetic cultural psychology. In L. A. Jensen (Ed.), *Bridging cultural and developmental approaches to psychology: New syntheses in theory, research, and policy* (pp. 303–310). New York, NY: Oxford University Press.

Sidhu, M., Malhi, P., & Jerath, J. (2010). Intelligence of children from economically disadvantaged families: Role of parental education. *Psychological Studies, 55(4),* 358–364

Sieber-Blum, M. (2010). Epidermal neural crest stem cells and their use in mouse models of spinal cord injury. *Brain Research Bulletin, 83,* 189–193.

Siegala, M., & Varley, R. (2008). If we could talk to the animals. *Behavioral & Brain Sciences, 31,* 146–147.

Siegel, A. B. (2010). Dream interpretation in clinical practice: A century after Freud. *Sleep Medicine Clinics, 5(2),* 299–313.

Siegel, J. M. (2000, January). Narcolepsy. *Scientific American,* pp. 76–81.

Siegel, J. M. (2008). Do all animals sleep? *Trends in Neurosciences, 31,* 208–213.

Siegel, P. H., Schraeder, M., & Morrison, R. (2008). A taxonomy of equity factors. *Journal of Applied Social Psychology, 38,* 61–75.

Siever, L. J. (2008). Neurobiology of aggression and violence. *American Journal of Psychiatry, 165,* 429–442.

Sieving, R., Resnick, M., Garwick, A., Bearinger, L., Beckman, K., Oliphant, J., Plowman, S., & Rush, K. (2011). A clinic-based, youth development approach to teen pregnancy prevention. *American Journal of Health Behavior, 35(3),* 346–358.

Sillén, A., Lilius, L., Forsell, C., Kimura, T., Winblad, B., & Graff, C. (2011). Linkage to the 8p21.1 region including the CLU gene in age at onset stratified Alzheimer's disease families. *Journal of Alzheimer's Disease, 23(1),* 13–20.

Sills, R. C., & Garman, R. H. (2011). Gene expression, biomarkers, and glial cells in nervous system diseases. *Toxicologic Pathology, 39,* 97–98.

Silver, J., McAllister, T., & Yudofsky, S. (Eds.). (2011). *Textbook of traumatic brain injury* (2nd ed.). Arlington, VA: American Psychiatric Publishing.

Silverman, W. K., Pina, A. A., & Viswesvaran, C. (2008). Evidence-based psychosocial treatments for phobic and anxiety disorders in children and adolescents. *Journal of Clinical Child and Adolescent Psychology, 37,* 105–130.

Silvestri, A. J., & Root, D. H. (2008). Effects of REM deprivation and an NMDA agonist on the extinction of conditioned fear. *Physiology & Behavior, 93,* 274–281.

Simon, C. (2007). *Neurology.* New York, NY: Oxford University Press.

Simpson, A., & Riggs, K. J. (2011). Three- and 4-year-olds encode modeled actions in two ways leading to immediate imitation and delayed emulation. *Developmental Psychology, 47(3),* 834–840.

Sinason, V. (Ed.). (2011). *Attachment, trauma, and multiplicity: Working with Dissociative Identity Disorder* (2nd ed.). New York, NY: Routledge.

Sinclair, L. (2011). Designer drug's rapid spread causes alarm on several fronts. *Psychiatric News, 46(8),* 8.

Singer, L. T., & Richardson, G. A. (2011). Introduction to "understanding developmental consequences of prenatal drug exposure: Biological and environmental effects and their interactions." *Neurotoxicology and Teratology, 33(1),* 5–8.

Sirois, F. (2003). Procrastination and intentions to perform health behaviors: The role of self-efficacy and consideration of future consequences. *Presented at the American Psychological Association Conference.* Toronto, Ontario, Canada.

Skelhorn, J., Griksaitis, D., & Rowe, C. (2008). Colour biases are more than a question of taste. *Animal Behaviour, 75,* 827–835.

Skewes, J. C., Roepstorff, A., & Frith, C. D. (2011). How do illusions constrain goal-directed movement: Perceptual and visuomotor influences on speed/accuracy trade-off. *Experimental Brain Research, 209(2),* 247–255.

Skinner, B. F. (1948). Superstition in the pigeon. *Journal of Experimental Psychology, 38,* 168–172.

Skinner, B. F. (1953). *Science and human behavior.* New York, NY: Macmillan.

Skinner, B. F. (1961). Diagramming schedules of reinforcement. *Journal of the Experimental Analysis of Behavior, 1,* 67–68.

Skinner, B. F. (1992). "Superstition" in the pigeon. *Journal of Experimental Psychology: General, 121(3),* 273–274.

Skinner, E. I., & Fernandes, M. A. (2008). Interfering with remembering and knowing: Effects of divided attention at retrieval. *Acta Psychologica, 127,* 211–221.

Skinner, R., Conlon, L., Gibbons, D., & McDonald, C. (2011). Cannabis use and non-clinical dimensions of psychosis in university students presenting to primary care. *Acta Psychiatrica Scandinavica, 123(1),* 21–27.

Skinta, M. D. (2008). The effects of bullying and internalized homophobia on psychopathological symptom severity in a community sample of gay men. *Dissertation Abstracts International: Section B: The Sciences and Engineering, 68(7-B),* 4847.

Sleep Education Blog. (2010, July 19). Bowler scores another sleep-deprived guinness world record. Retrieved from http://sleepeducation.blogspot.com/2010/07/bowler-scores-another-sleep-deprived.html

Slobogin, C. (2006). *Minding justice: Laws that deprive people with mental disability of life and liberty.* Cambridge, MA: Harvard University Press.

Slobounov, S. M. (2008). *Injuries in athletics: Causes and consequences.* New York, NY: Springer.

Slováčková, B., & Slováček, L. (2007). Moral judgement competence and moral attitudes of medical students. *Nursing Ethics, 14,* 320–328.

Smeets, T. (2011). Acute stress impairs memory retrieval independent of time of day. *Psychoneuroendocrinology, 36(4),* 495–501.

Smith, B. (2011). Hypnosis today. *Monitor on Psychology, 42(1),* 6.

Smith, C. A., & Kirby, L. D. (2011). The role of appraisal and emotion in coping and adaptation. In R. J. Contrada & A. Baum (Eds.), *The handbook of stress science: Biology, psychology, and health* (pp. 195–208). New York, NY: Springer.

Smith, C., & Smith, D. (2003). Ingestion of ethanol just prior to sleep onset impairs memory for procedural but not declarative tasks. *Sleep, 26(2),* 185–191.

Smith, D. (2002). The theory heard 'round the world. *Monitor on Psychology,* p. 30–32.

Smith, E. E. (1995). Concepts and categorization. In E. E. Smith & D. N. Osherson (Eds.), *Thinking: An invitation to cognitive science* (2nd ed.) (pp. 3–33). Cambridge, MA: MIT Press.

Smith, J. C. (2010). *Pseudoscience and extraordinary claims of the paranormal: A critical thinker's toolkit.* Hoboken, NJ: Wiley-Blackwell.

Smith, K. D. (2007). Spinning straw into gold: Dynamics of Rumpelstiltskin style of leadership. *Dissertation Abstracts International Section A: Humanities and Social Sciences, 68(5–A),* 1760.

Smith, M. T., Huang, M. I., & Manber, R. (2005). Cognitive behavior therapy for chronic insomnia occurring within the context of medical and psychiatric disorders. *Clinical Psychology Review, 25,* 559–592.

Smith, M., Wang, L., Cronenwett, W., Goldman, M., Mamah, D., Barch, D., & Csernansky, J. (2011). Alcohol use disorders contribute to hippocampal and subcortical shape differences in schizophrenia. *Schizophrenia Research.* Advance online publication. doi:10.1016/j.schres.2011.05.014

Smith, P. (2011). Cross-cultural perspectives on identity. In S. Schwartz, K. Luyckx, & V. Vignoles (Eds.), *Handbook of identity theory and research* (Vols. 1–2) (pp. 249–265). New York, NY: Springer.

Smith, P. B. (2010). Cross-cultural psychology: Some accomplishments and challenges. *Psychological Studies, 55(2),* 89–95.

Smith, P., Frank, J., Bondy, S., & Mustard, C. (2008). Do changes in job control predict differences in health status? Results from a longitudinal national survey of Canadians. *Psychosomatic Medicine, 70,* 85–91.

Smith, T. W., Orleans, C. T., & Jenkins, C. D. (2004). Prevention and health promotion: Decades of progress, new challenges, and an emerging agenda. *Health Psychology, 23(2),* 126–131.

Smith, T., Rodriguez, M., & Bernal, G. (2011). Culture. *Journal of Clinical Psychology, 67(2),* 166–175.

Smith, V. W. (2006). The development and field testing of a school psychology employment interview instrument. *Dissertation Abstracts International Section A: Humanities and Social Sciences, 67(2-A),* 418.

Smith, V., Reddy, J., Foster, K., Asbury, E., & Brooks, J. (2011). Public perceptions, knowledge and stigma towards people with schizophrenia. *Journal of Public Mental Health, 10(1),* 45–56.

SmithBattle, L., & Leonard, V. W. (2006). Teen mothers and their teenaged children: The reciprocity of developmental trajectories. *Advances in Nursing Science, 29,* 351–365.

Snarey, J. R. (1985). Cross-cultural universality of social-moral development: A critical review of Kohlbergian research. *Psychological Bulletin, 97,* 202–233.

Snarey, J. R. (1995). In communitarian voice: The sociological expansion of Kohlbergian theory, research, and practice. In W. M. Kurtines & J. L. Gerwirtz (Eds.), *Moral development: An introduction* (pp. 109–134). Boston, MA: Allyn & Bacon.

Snijders, T. J., Ramsey, N. F., Koerselman, F., & van Gijn, J. (2010). Attentional modulation fails to attenuate the subjective pain experience in chronic, unexplained pain. *European Journal of Pain, 14(3),* e1–e10.

Snyder, C. R. (2003). "Me conform? No way": Classroom demonstrations for sensitizing students to their conformity. *Teaching of Psychology, 30(1),* 59–61.

Snyder, J. S., & Alain, C. (2007). Sequential auditory sense analysis is preserved in normal aging adults. *Cerebral Cortex, 17,* 501–512.

Soler, C., Nunez, M., Gutierrez, R., Nunez, J., Medina, P., Sancho, M., Alvarez, J. & Nunez, A. (2003). Facial attractiveness in men provides clues to semen quality. *Evolution and Human Behavior, 24,* 199–207.

Solms, M. (1997). *The neuropsychology of dreams.* Mahwah, NJ: Lawrence Erlbaum.

Solomon, D., Ford, E., Adams, J., & Graves, N. (2011). Potential of St. John's wort for the treatment of depression: The economic perspective. *Australian and New Zealand Journal of Psychiatry, 45(2),* 123–130.

Somers, T. J., Moseley, G. L., Keefe, F. J., & Kothadia, S. M. (2011). Neuroimaging of pain: A psychosocial perspective. In R. A. Cohen & L. H. Sweet (Eds.), *Brain imaging in behavioral medicine and clinical neuroscience* (pp. 275–292). New York, NY: Springer.

Somerville, L. H., Fani, N., & McClure-Tone, E. B. (2011). Behavioral and neural representation of emotional facial expressions across the lifespan. *Developmental Neuropsychology, 36(4),* 408–428.

Son, L. K., & Metcalfe, J. (2000). Metacognitive and control strategies in study-time allocation. *Journal of Experimental Psychology: Learning, Memory, & Cognition, 26,* 204–221.

Soto, C. J., John, O. P., Gosling, S. D., & Potter, J. (2011). Age differences in personality traits from 10 to 65: Big Five domains and facets in a large cross-sectional sample. *Journal of Personality and Social Psychology, 100(2),* 330–348.

Sowell, E. R., Mattson, S. N., Kan, E., Thompson, P. M., Riley, E. P., Edward, P., & Toga, A. W. (2008). Abnormal cortical thickness and brain-behavior correlation patterns in individuals with heavy prenatal alcohol exposure. *Cerebral Cortex, 18,* 136–144.

Spano, R., Koenig, T. L., Hudson, J. W., & Leiste, M. R. (2010). East meets west: A nonlinear model for understanding human growth and development. *Smith College Studies in Social Work, 80(2–3),* 198–214.

Spearman, C. (1923). *The nature of "intelligence" and the principles of cognition.* London, England: Macmillan.

Spears, R. (2011). Group identities: The social identity perspective. In S. Schwartz, K. Luyckx, & V. Vignoles (Eds.), *Handbook of identity theory and research* (Vols. 1–2) (pp. 201–224). New York, NY: Springer.

Sperry, L. (2011). *Assessment of couples and families: Contemporary and cutting-edge strategies* (2nd ed.). New York, NY: Routledge.

Spiegel, D. (1999). An altered state. *Mind/Body Health Newsletter, 8(1),* 3–5.

Spiegel, D., & Maldonado, J. R. (1999). Dissociative disorders. In R. E. Hales, S. C. Yudofsky, & J. C. Talbott (Eds.), *American psychiatric press textbook of psychiatry* (pp. 665–710). Washington, DC: American Psychiatric Press.

Spinweber, C. L. (1993). Randy Gardner. In M. A. Carskadon (Ed.), *Encyclopedia of sleep and dreaming*. New York, NY: Macmillan.

Spitz, R. A., & Wolf, K. M. (1946). The smiling response: A contribution to the ontogenesis of social relations. *Genetic Psychology Monographs, 34,* 57–123.

Sprecher, S., & Regan, P. C. (2002). Liking some things (in some people) more than others: Partner preferences in romantic relationships and friendships. *Journal of Social & Personal Relationships, 19*(4), 463–481.

Spurling, L. (2011). Review of Off the couch: Contemporary psychoanalytic approaches. [Review of the book Off the couch: Contemporary psychoanalytic approaches]. *Psychodynamic Practice: Individuals, Groups and Organisations, 17*(1), 99–100.

Stafford, C. A. (2011). Bilingualism and enhanced attention in early adulthood. *International Journal of Bilingual Education and Bilingualism, 14*(1), 1–22.

Stafford, J., & Lynn, S. J. (2002). Cultural scripts, memories of childhood abuse, and multiple identities: A study of role-played enactments. *International Journal of Clinical & Experimental Hypnosis, 50*(1), 67–85.

Stalder, T., Kirschbaum, C., Heinze, K., Steudte, S., Foley, P., Tietze, A., & Dettenborn, L. (2010). Use of hair cortisol analysis to detect hypercortisolism during active drinking phases in alcohol-dependent individuals. *Biological Psychology, 85*(3), 357–360.

Stanley, D. A., Sokol-Hessner, P., Banaji, M. R., & Phelps, E. A. (2011). Implicit race attitudes predict trustworthiness judgments and economic trust decisions. *PNAS Proceedings of the National Academy of Sciences of the United States of America, 108*(19), 7710–7775.

Steel, P. (2010). The procrastination equation: Everything you wanted to know about procrastination but put off finding out. *Psychology Today Blogs.* Retrieved from http://www.psychologytoday.com/blog/the-procrastination-equation

Steele, C. M., & Aronson, J. (1995). Stereotype threat and the intellectual test performance of African Americans. *Journal of Personality and Social Psychology, 69,* 797–811.

Steiner, L. M., Suarez, E. C., Sells, J. N., & Wykes, S. D. (2011). Effect of age, initiator status, and infidelity on Women's divorce adjustment. *Journal of Divorce & Remarriage, 52*(1), 33–47.

Steinert, R., & Beglinger, C. (2011). Nutrient sensing in the gut: Interactions between chemosensory cells, visceral afferents and the secretion of satiation peptides. *Physiology & Behavior.* Retrieved from http://www.ncbi.nlm.nih.gov/pubmed/21376067

Steinmayr, R., & Spinath, B. (2009). The importance of motivation as a predictor of school achievement. *Learning and Individual Differences, 19,* 80–90.

Stella, N., Schweitzer, P., & Piomelli, D. (1997). A second endogenous cannabinoid that modulates long-term potentiation. *Nature, 382,* 677–678.

Stelmack, R. M., Knott, V., & Beauchamp, C. M. (2003). Intelligence and neural transmission time: A brain stem auditory evoked potential analysis. *Personality & Individual Differences, 34*(1), 97–107.

Sternberg, R. J. (1985). *Beyond IQ: A triarchic theory of human intelligence.* New York, NY: Cambridge University Press.

Sternberg, R. J. (1986). A triangular theory of love. *Psychological Review, 93*(2), 119–135.

Sternberg, R. J. (1988). *The triangle of love.* New York, NY: Basic Books.

Sternberg, R. J. (1998). Principles of teaching for successful intelligence. *Educational Psychologist, 33,* 65–72.

Sternberg, R. J. (1999). The theory of successful intelligence. *Review of General Psychology, 3,* 292–316.

Sternberg, R. J. (2005). The importance of converging operations in the study of human intelligence. *Cortex. 41*(2), 243–244.

Sternberg, R. J. (2006). A duplex theory of love. In R. J. Sternberg & K. Weis (Eds.). *The new psychology of love* (pp. 184–199). New Haven, CT: Yale University Press.

Sternberg, R. J. (2007). Developing successful intelligence in all children: A potential solution to underachievement in ethnic minority children. In M. C. Wang & R. D. Taylor (Eds.), *Closing the achievement gap.* Philadelphia, PA: Laboratory for Student Success at Temple University.

Sternberg, R. J. (2008). The triarchic theory of human intelligence. In N. Salkind (Ed.), *Handbook of multicultural assessment* (3rd ed.). New York, NY: Jossey-Bass.

Sternberg, R. J. (2009). *Cognitive psychology* (5th ed.). Belmont, CA: Wadsworth.

Sternberg, R. J. (2010). Teaching for creativity. In R. A. Beghetto & J. C. Kaufman (Eds.), *Nurturing creativity in the classroom* (pp. 394–414). New York, NY: Cambridge University Press.

Sternberg, R. J. (2012). *Cognitive psychology* (6th ed.). Belmont, CA: Cengage.

Sternberg, R. J. (Ed.). (2004). *Definitions and conceptions of giftedness.* Thousand Oaks, CA: Corwin Press.

Sternberg, R. J., & Grigorenko, E. L. (2008). Ability testing across cultures. In L. Suzuki (Ed.), *Handbook of multicultural assessment* (3rd ed.) (pp. 449–470). New York, NY: Jossey-Bass.

Sternberg, R. J., & Hedlund, J. (2002). Practical intelligence, g, and work psychology. *Human Performance, 15*(1–2), 143–160.

Sternberg, R. J., & Kaufman, S. (Eds.). (2012). *The Cambridge handbook of intelligence.* Cambridge, UK: Cambridge University Press.

Sternberg, R. J., & Lubart, T. I. (1992). Buy low and sell high: An investment approach to creativity. *Current Directions in Psychological Science, 1*(1), 1–5.

Sternberg, R. J., & Lubart, T. I. (1996). Investing in creativity. *American Psychologist, 51*(7), 677–688.

Sternberg, R. J., Jarvin, L., & Grigorenko, E. L. (2011). *Explorations in giftedness.* New York, NY: Cambridge University Press.

Stewart, J. C., Fitzgerald, G. J., & Kamarck, T. W. (2010). Hostility now, depression later? Longitudinal associations among emotional risk factors for coronary artery disease. *Annals of Behavioral Medicine, 39*(3), 258–266.

Stoessl, A. J. (2011). Neuroimaging in Parkinson's disease. *Neurotherapeutics, 8*(1), 72–81.

Stokes, D., & Lappin, M. (2010). Neurofeedback and biofeedback with 37 migraineurs: A clinical outcome study. *Behavioral and Brain Functions, 6,* Article ID 9.

Stollhoff, R., Jost, J., Elze, T., & Kennerknecht, I. (2011). Deficits in long-term recognition memory reveal dissociated subtypes in congenital prosopagnosia. *PLoS ONE, 6*(1). Article ID e15702.

Stoltzfus, G., Nibbelink, B., Vredenburg, D., & Hyrum, E. (2011). Gender, gender role, and creativity. *Social Behavior and Personality: An International Journal, 39*(3), 425–432.

Stompe, T. G., Ortwein-Swoboda, K., Ritter, K., & Schanda, H. (2003). Old wine in new bottles? Stability and plasticity of the contents of schizophrenic delusions. *Psychopathology, 36*(1), 6–12.

Stone, E., Shackelford, T. & Goetz, A. (2011). Sexual arousal and the pursuit of attractive mating opportunities. *Personality and Individual Differences.* Retrieved from http://www.sciencedirect.com/science/article/pii/S0191886911002510

Stone, J., & Focella, E. (2011). Postdecisional self-enhancement and self-protection: The role of the self in cognitive dissonance processes. In M. D. Alicke & C. Sedikides (Eds.), *Handbook of self-enhancement and self-protection* (pp. 192–210). New York, NY: Guilford Press.

Stone, K. L., & Redline, S. (2006). Sleep-related breathing disorders in the elderly. *Sleep Medicine Clinics, 1*(2), 247–262.

Stoner, J. A. (1961). *A comparison of individual and group decisions involving risk.* Unpublished master's thesis, School of Industrial Management, MIT, Cambridge, MA.

Strack, F., Martin, L. L., & Stepper, S. (1988). Inhibiting and facilitating conditions of the human smile: A nonobstrusive test of the facial feedback hypothesis. *Journal of Personality and Social Psychology, 54*, 768–777.

Strada, E. A. (2011). Professional self-care. In S. H. Qualls & J. E. Kasl-Godley (Eds.), *Wiley series in clinical geropsychology. End-of-life issues, grief, and bereavement: What clinicians need to know* (pp. 294–309). Hoboken, NJ: John Wiley.

Strahan, E., Panayiotou, G., Clements, R., & Scott, J. (2011). Beer, wine, and social anxiety: Testing the "self-medication hypothesis" in the US and Cyprus. *Addiction Research & Theory, 19*(4), 302–311.

Strange, D., Garry, M., Bernstein, D. M., & Lindsay, D. S. (2011). Photographs cause false memories for the news. *Acta Psychologica, 136*(1), 90–94.

Stratton, P., Reibstein, J., Lask, J., Singh, R., & Asen, E. (2011). Competences and occupational standards for systemic family and couples therapy. *Journal of Family Therapy, 33*(2), 123–143.

Straub, R. O. (2011). *Health psychology: A biopsychosocial approach* (3rd ed.). New York, NY: Worth.

Strauss, J. R. (2010). The baby boomers meet menopause: Attitudes and roles. *Dissertation Abstracts International Section A: Humanities and Social Sciences, 70*(8-A), 3196.

Strozier, C. B. (2011). Torture, war, and the culture of fear after 9/11. *International Journal of Group Psychotherapy, 61*(1), 67–72.

Study finds 21st birthday binge. (2008, May 19). *APA Press Release.* Retrieved from http://www.apa.org/releases/21birthday0508.html.

Suarez, E., & Gadalla, T. M. (2010). Stop blaming the victim: A meta-analysis on rape myths. *Journal of Interpersonal Violence, 25*(11), 2010–2035.

Subramanian, S., & Vollmer, R. R. (2002). Sympathetic activation fenfluramine depletes brown adipose tissue norepinephrine content in rats. *Pharmacology, Biochemistry & Behavior, 73*(3), 639–646.

Sue, D., Sue, D. W., & Sue, S. (2010). *Understanding abnormal behavior* (9th ed.). Belmont, CA: Cengage.

Sue, D.W., & Sue, D. (2008). *Counseling the culturally diverse: Theory and practice* (5th ed.). Hoboken, NJ: Wiley.

Süer, C., Dolu, N., Artis, A. S., Sahin, L., Yilmaz, A., & Cetin, A. (2011). The effects of long-term sleep deprivation on the long-term potentiation in the dentate gyrus and brain oxidation status in rats. *Neuroscience Research, 70*(1), 71–77.

Sugarman, H., Impey, C., Buxner, S., & Antonellis, J. (2011). Astrology beliefs among undergraduate students. *Astronomy Education Review, 10*(1). doi:10.3847/AER2010040

Sullivan, M. J. L. (2008). Toward a biopsychomotor conceptualization of pain: Implications for research and intervention. *Clinical Journal of Pain, 24*, 281–290.

Sullivan, M. J. L., Tripp, D. A., & Santor, D. (1998). *Gender differences in pain and pain behavior: The role of catastrophizing.* Paper presented at the annual meeting of the American Psychological Association, San Francisco.

Sullivan, P. F., Kendler, K. S., & Neale, M. C. (2003). Schizophrenia as a complex trait: Evidence from a meta-analysis of twin studies. *Archives of General Psychiatry, 60*(12), 1187–1192.

Sullivan, T. P., & Holt, L. J. (2008). PTSD symptom clusters are differentially related to substance use among community women exposed to intimate partner violence. *Journal of Traumatic Stress, 21*, 173–180.

Suls, J., Davidson, K., & Kaplan, R. (Eds.). (2010). *Handbook of health psychology and behavioral medicine* (pp. 370–380). New York, NY: Guilford Press.

Sundie, J. M., Kenrick, D. T., Griskevicius, V., Tybur, J. M., Vohs, K. D., & Beal, D. J. (2011). Peacocks, Porsches, and Thorstein Veblen: Conspicuous consumption as a sexual signaling system. *Journal of Personality and Social Psychology, 100*(4), 664–680.

Sundram, F., Deeley, Q., Sarkar, S., Daly, E., Latham, R., Barker, G., & Murphy, D. (2011). White matter microstructural abnormalities in antisocial personality disorder: A pilot diffusion tensor imaging study. *European Psychiatry, 26*(1), 957.

Superville, D. (2011, February, 9). Obama has kicked smoking habit, first lady says. *CNSNews.* Retrieved from http://www.cnsnews.com/news/article/president-obama-has-stopped-smoking-wife

Surbey, M. K. (2011). Adaptive significance of low levels of self-deception and cooperation in depression. *Evolution and Human Behavior, 32*(1), 29–40.

Surtees, P. G., Wainwright, N. W. J., Luben, R. N., Khaw, K-T, & Bingham, S. A. (2009). No evidence that social stress is associated with breast cancer incidence. *Breast Cancer Research and Treatment, 120*(1), 169–174.

Swami, V. (2011). *Evolutionary psychology: A critical introduction.* Chichester, West Sussex, UK: Wiley-Blackwell.

Swami, V., & Furnham, A. (2008). *The psychology of physical attraction.* New York, NY: Routledge/Taylor & Francis Group.

Sweldens, S., Van Osselaer, S. M. J., & Janiszewski, C. (2010). Evaluative conditioning procedures and the resilience of conditioned brand attitudes. *Journal of Consumer Research, 37*(3), 473–489.

Swenson, R. R., Rizzo, C. J., Brown, L. K., Vanable, P. A., Carey, M. P., Valois, R. F., DiClemente, R., & Romer, D. (2010). HIV knowledge and its contribution to sexual health behaviors of low-income African American adolescents. *Journal of the National Medical Association, 102*(12), 1173–1182.

Szalavitz, M., & Perry, B.D. (2010). *Born to love: Why empathy is essential—and endangered.* New York, NY: Harper Collins Publishers.

Szasz, T. (1960). The myth of mental illness. *American Psychologist, 15*, 113–118.

Szasz, T. (2000). Second commentary on "Aristotle's function argument." *Philosophy, Psychiatry, & Psychology, 7*, 3–16.

Szasz, T. (2004). The psychiatric protection order for the "battered mental patient." *British Medical Journal, 327*(7429), 1449–1451.

Tafarodi, R. W., Wild, N., & Ho, C. (2010). Parental authority, nurturance, and two-dimensional self-esteem. *Scandinavian Journal of Psychology, 51*(4), 294–303.

Takahashi, A., Quadros, I. M., de Almeida, R. M. M., & Miczek, K. A. (2011). Brain serotonin receptors and transporters: Initiation vs. termination of escalated aggression. *Psychopharmacology, 213*(2–3), 183–212.

Takano, Y., & Sogon, S. (2008). Are Japanese more collectivistic than Americans? Examining conformity in in-groups and the reference-group effect. *Journal of Cross-Cultural Psychology, 39*, 237–250.

Talarico, J. M., & Rubin, D. C. (2007). Flashbulb memories are special after all; in phenomenology, not accuracy. *Applied Cognitive Psychology, 21,* 557–578.

Talitwala, E. M. (2007). Fathers' parenting strategies: Their influence on young people's social relationships. *Dissertation Abstracts International Section A: Humanities and Social Sciences, 68*(5-A), 2191.

Tal-Or, N., & Papirman, Y. (2007). The fundamental attribution error in attributing fictional figures' characteristics to the actors. *Media Psychology, 9,* 331–345.

Talwar, V., Harris, P., & Schleifer, M. (Eds.). (2011). *Children's understanding of death: From biological to religious conceptions.* Cambridge, UK: Cambridge University Press.

Tanaka, T., Yoshida, M., Yokoo, H., Tomita, M., & Tanaka, M. (1998). Expression of aggression attenuates both stress-induced gastric ulcer formation and increases in noradrenaline release in the rat amygdala assessed intracerebral microdialysis. *Pharmacology, Biochemistry & Behavior, 59*(1), 27–31.

Tang, Y.-P., Wang, H., Feng, R., Kyin, M., & Tsien, J. Z. (2001). Differential effects of enrichment on learning and memory function in NR2B transgenic mice. *Neuropharmacology, 41*(6), 779–790.

Tarter, R. E., Vanyukov, M., Kirisci, L., Reynolds, M., & Clark, D. B. (2006). Predictors of marijuana use in adolescents before and after licit drug use: Examination of the gateway hypothesis. *American Journal of Psychiatry, 163,* 2134–2140.

Task Force of the National Advisory Council on Alcohol Abuse and Alcoholism, National Institute on Alcohol Abuse and Alcoholism (2002). *A call to action: Changing the culture of drinking at U.S. colleges.* Washington, DC: National Institutes of Health. Retrieved from http://www.collegedrinkingprevention. gov/.NIAAACollegeMaterials/TaskForce/ TaskForce_TOC.aspx.

Taub, E., Gitendra, U., & Thomas, E. (2002). New treatments in neurorehabilitation founded on basic research. *Nature Reviews Neuroscience, 3,* 228–236.

Taylor, D. J., Lichstein, K. L., & Durrence, H. H. (2003). Insomnia as a risk factor. *Behavioral Sleep Medicine, 1,* 227–247.

Taylor, L., Fiore, A., Mendelsohn, G., & Cheshire, C. (2011). "Out of my league": A real-world test of the matching hypothesis. *Personality and Social Psychology Bulletin, 37*(7), 942–954.

Taylor, S., & Jang, K. L. (2011). Biopsychosocial etiology of obsessions and compulsions: An integrated behavioral–genetic and cognitive–behavioral analysis. *Journal of Abnormal Psychology, 120*(1), 174–186.

Taylor, S. E., & Armor, D. A. (1996). Positive illusions and coping with adversity. *Journal of Personality, 64,* 873–898.

Taylor, S. E., & Sherman, D. K. (2008). Self-enhancement and self-affirmation: The consequences of positive self-thoughts for motivation and health. In J. Y. Shah & W. L. Gardner (Eds.), *Handbook of motivation science* (pp. 57–70). New York, NY: Guilford Press.

Taylor, S. E., & Stanton, A. L. (2007). Coping resources, coping processes, and mental health. *Annual Review of Clinical Psychology, 3,* 377–401.

Tedlock, B. (1992). The role of dreams and visionary narratives in Mayan cultural survival. *Ethos, 20*(4), 453–376.

Teesson, M., Hall, W., Proudfoot, H., & Degenhardt, L. (2011). *Addictions* (2nd ed.). Hove, UK: Psychology Press.

Tellegen, A. (1985). Structures of mood and personality and their relevance to assessing anxiety with an emphasis on self-report. In A. H. Tuma & J. D. Maser (Eds.), *Anxiety and the anxiety disorders* (pp. 681–706). Hillsdale, NJ: Erlbaum.

Terbune, D. B., & Cardeña, E. (2010). Differential patterns of spontaneous experiential response to a hypnotic induction: A latent profile analysis. *Consciousness and Cognition: An International Journal, 19*(4), 1140–1150.

Terbune, D. B., Cardeña, E., & Lindgren, M. (2011). Dissociative tendencies and individual differences in high hypnotic suggestibility. *Cognitive Neuropsychiatry, 16*(2), 113–135.

Terman, L. M. (1916). *The measurement of intelligence.* Boston, MA: Houghton Mifflin.

Terman, L. M. (1954). Scientists and nonscientists in a group of 800 gifted men. *Psychological Monographs, 68*(7), 1–44.

Teti, M., & Bowleg, L. (2011). Shattering the myth of invulnerability: Exploring the prevention needs of sexual minority women living with HIV/AIDS. *Journal of Gay & Lesbian Social Services: The Quarterly Journal of Community & Clinical Practice, 23*(1), 69–88.

Tewarie, R. D. S. N., Hurtado, A., Bartels, R. H. M. A., Grotenhuis, J. A., & Oudega, M. (2010). A clinical perspective of spinal cord injury. *NeuroRehabilitation, 27*(2), 129–139.

Thagard, P., & Stewart, T. C. (2011). The AHA! experience: Creativity through emergent binding in neural networks. *Cognitive Science: A Multidisciplinary Journal, 35*(1), 1–33.

Thanellou, A., & Green, J. T. (2011). Spontaneous recovery but not reinstatement of the extinguished conditioned eyeblink response in the rat. *Behavioral Neuroscience.* Retrieved from http://www.ncbi.nlm.nih. gov/pubmed/21517145

Thelen, E., Schoner, G., Scheier, C., & Smith, L. B. (2001). The dynamics of embodiment: A field theory of infant perservative reaching. *Behavioral and Brain Sciences, 24,* 1–86.

Thoits, P. A. (2010). Stress and health: Major findings and policy implications. *Journal of Health and Social Behavior, 51*(1, Suppl), S41–S53.

Thoits, P. A. (2011). Resisting the stigma of mental illness. *Social Psychology Quarterly, 74*(1), 6–28.

Thomas, A., & Chess, S. (1977). *Temperament and development.* New York, NY: Brunner/Mazel.

Thomas, A., & Chess, S. (1987). Round-table: What is temperament: Four approaches. *Child Development, 58,* 505–529.

Thomas, A., & Chess, S. (1991). Temperament in adolescence and its functional significance. In R. M. Lerner, A. C. Petersen, & J. Brooks-Gunn (Eds.), *Encyclopedia of adolescence* (Vol. 2). New York, NY: Garland.

Thomas, N., Rossell, S., Farhall, J., Shawyer, F., & Castle, D. (2011). Cognitive behavioural therapy for auditory hallucinations: Effectiveness and predictors of outcome in a specialist clinic. *Behavioural and Cognitive Psychotherapy, 39*(2), 129–138.

Thomas, S. E., Randall, P. K., Book, S. W., & Randall, C. L. (2008). The complex relationship between co-occurring social anxiety and alcohol use disorders: What effect does treating social anxiety have on drinking? *Alcoholism: Clinical and Experimental Research, 32,* 77–84.

Thompson, D. (1997, March 24). A boy without a penis. *Time,* 83.

Thompson, R. F. (2005). In search of memory traces. *Annual Review of Clinical Psychology, 56,* 1–23.

Thorndike, E. L. (1898). Animal intelligence. *Psychological Review Monograph, 2*(8).

Thorndike, E. L. (1911). *Animal intelligence.* New York, NY: Macmillan.

Thornhill, R., Gangestad, S. W., Miller, R., Scheyd, G., McCollough, J. K., & Franklin, M. (2003). Major histocompatibility complex genes, symmetry, and body scent attractiveness in men and women. *Behavioral Ecology, 14*(5), 668–678.

Three stages of Alzheimer's disease. (2011). *The Lancet, 377*(9776), 1465.

Tice, D. M., & Baumeister, R. F. (1997). Longitudinal study of procrastination, performance, stress, and health: The costs and benefits of dawdling. *Psychological Science, 8,* 454–458.

Tindale, S., & Posavac, E. (2011). The social psychology of stakeholder processes: Group processes and interpersonal relations. In M. Mark, S. Donaldson, & B. Campbell (Eds.) *Social psychology and evaluation* (pp. 189–209). New York, NY: Guilford Press.

Tirodkar, M. A., & Jain, A. (2003). Food messages on African American television shows. *American Journal of Public Health, 93*(3), 439–441.

Todd, A. R., Bodenhausen, G. V., Richeson, J. A., & Galinsky, A. D. (2011). Perspective taking combats automatic expressions of racial bias. *Journal of Personality and Social Psychology, 100*(6), 1027–1042.

Todorov, A., & Bargh, J. A. (2002). Automatic sources of aggression. *Aggression & Violent Behavior, 7*(1), 53–68.

Toivanen, S., & Modin, B. (2011). Social determinants of health at different phases of life. *International Journal of Behavioral Medicine, 18*(1), 1–4.

Tolin, D. F., Robison, J. T., Gaztambide, S., Horowitz, S., & Blank, K. (2007). Ataques de nervios and psychiatric disorders in older Puerto Rican primary care patients. *Journal of Cross-Cultural Psychology, 38,* 659–669.

Tolman, E. C., & Honzik, C. H. (1930). Introduction and removal of reward and maze performance in rats. *University of California Publications in Psychology, 4,* 257–275.

Topham, G. L., Hubbs-Tait, L., Rutledge, J. M., Page, M. C., Kennedy, T. S., Shriver, L. H., & Harrist, A. W. (2011). Parenting styles, parental response to child emotion, and family emotional responsiveness are related to child emotional eating. *Appetite, 56*(2), 261–264.

Torelli, C. J., & Shavitt, S. (2011). The impact of power on information processing depends on cultural orientation. *Journal of Experimental Social Psychology.* doi: 10.1016/j.jesp.2011.04.003

Torpy, J. M., & Golub, R. M. (Ed.). (2011). Sleep apnea. *JAMA: Journal of the American Medical Association, 305*(9), 956.

Torpy, J. M., Lynm, C., & Glass, R. M. (2007). Chronic stress and the heart. *Journal of the American Medical Association, 298,* 1722.

Towe, V. L., Sifakis, F., Gindi, R. M., Sherman, S. G., Flynn, C., Hauck, H., &

Celentano, D. D. (2010). Prevalence of HIV infection and sexual risk behaviors among individuals having heterosexual sex in low income neighborhoods in Baltimore, MD: The BESURE Study. *Journal of Acquired Immune Deficiency Syndromes, 53*(4), 522–528.

Tranter, L. J., & Koutstaal, W. (2008). Age and flexible thinking: An experimental demonstration of the beneficial effects of increased cognitively stimulating activity on fluid intelligence in healthy older adults. *Aging, Neuropsychology, & Cognition, 15,* 184–207.

Trappey, C. (1996). A meta-analysis of consumer choice and subliminal advertising. *Psychology and Marketing, 13,* 517–530.

Trawick-Smith, J., & Dziurgot, T. (2011). 'Good-fit' teacher–child play interactions and the subsequent autonomous play of preschool children. *Early Childhood Research Quarterly, 26*(1), 110–123.

Tremblay, P. F., Graham, K., & Wells, S. (2008). Severity of physical aggression reported by university students: A test of the interaction between trait aggression and alcohol consumption. *Personality and Individual Differences, 45,* 3–9.

Trew, A., Searles, B., Smith, T., & Darling, E. M. (2011). Fatigue and extended work hours among cardiovascular perfusionists: 2010 survey. *Perfusion.* Retrieved from http://prf.sagepub.com/content/early/2011/05/12/0267659111409278.abstract

Triandis, H. C. (2001). Individualism-collectivism and personality. *Journal of Personality, 69*(6), 907–924.

Triandis, H. C. (2007). Culture and psychology: A history of the study of their relationship. In S. Kitayama & D. Cohen (Eds), *Handbook of cultural psychology* (pp. 59–76). New York, NY: Guilford.

Troll, L. E., Miller, S. J., & Atchley, R. C. (1979). *Families in later life.* Belmont, CA: Wadsworth.

Trombello, J. M., Schoebi, D., & Bradbury, T. N. (2011). Relationship functioning moderates the association between depressive symptoms and life stressors. *Journal of Family Psychology, 25*(1), 58–67.

Tronci, V., & Balfour, D. J. K. (2011). The effects of the mGluR5 receptor antagonist 6-methyl-2-(phenylethynyl)-pyridine (MPEP) on the stimulation of dopamine release evoked by nicotine in the rat brain. *Behavioural Brain Research, 219*(2), 354–357.

Tropp, L. R., & Mallett, R. K. (2011). *Moving beyond prejudice reduction: Pathways to positive intergroup relations.* Washington, DC: American Psychological Association.

Trout, J. D. (2010). *Why empathy matters: The science and psychology of better judgment.* New York, NY: Penguin Books.

Trull, T., Sher, K. J., Minks-Brown, C., Durbin, J., & Burr, R. (2000). Borderline personality disorder and substance use disorders: A review and integration. *Clinical Psychology Review, 20,* 235–253.

Truscott, D. (2010). Behavioral. In D. Truscott, *Becoming an effective psychotherapist: Adopting a theory of psychotherapy that's right for you and your client* (pp. 37–51). Washington, DC: American Psychological Association.

Tryon, W. W. (2008). Whatever happened to symptom substitution? *Clinical Psychology Review, 28,* 963–968.

Tsien, J. Z. (2000, April). Building a brainier mouse. *Scientific American,* pp. 62–68.

Tsukiura, T., & Cabeza, R. (2011). Shared brain activity for aesthetic and moral judgments: implications for the Beauty-is-Good stereotype. *Social Cognitive and Affective Neuroscience, 6*(3), 138–148.

Tucker, B. (2007). Perception of interannual covariation and strategies for risk reduction among Mikea of Madagascar: Individual and social learning. *Human Nature, 18,* 162–180.

Tulving, E. (2000). Concepts of memory. In E. Tulving & F. I. M. Craik (Eds.), *The Oxford handbook of memory* (pp. 33–44). New York, NY: Oxford University Press.

Tulving, E., & Thompson, D. M. (1973). Encoding specificity and retrieval processes in episodic memory. *Psychological Review, 80,* 352–373.

Tversky, A., & Kahneman, D. (1974). Judgment under uncertainty: Heuristics and biases. *Science, 185,* 1124–1131.

Tversky, A., & Kahneman, D. (1993). Probabilistic reasoning. In A. I. Goldman (Ed.), *Readings in philosophy and cognitive science* (pp. 43–68). Cambridge, MA: The MIT Press.

Twenge, J. (2006). *Generation me: Why today's young Americans are more confident, assertive, entitled—and more miserable than ever* before. New York, NY: Free Press.

Twenge, J. (2010). *The narcissism epidemic: Living in the age of entitlement.* New York, NY: Free Press.

Twenge, J. M., Baumeister, R. F., Tice, D. M., & Stucke, T. S. (2001). If you can't join them, beat them: Effects of social exclusion on aggressive behavior. *Journal of Personality and Social Psychology, 81*(6), 1058–1069.

Tyson, P. J., Jones, D., & Elcock, J. (2011). *Psychology in social context: Issues and debates.* Hoboken, NJ: Wiley-Blackwell.

Ulrich, R. E., Stachnik, T. J., & Stainton, N. R. (1963). Student acceptance of generalized personality interpretations. *Psychological Reports, 13,* 831–834.

Uswatte, G., & Taub, E. (2010). You can teach an old dog new tricks: Harnessing neuroplasticity after brain injury in older adults. In P. S. Fry & C. L. M. Keyes (Eds.), *New frontiers in resilient aging: Life-strengths and well-being in late life* (pp. 104–129). New York, NY: Cambridge University Press.

Vaish, A., Missana, M., & Tomasello, M. (2011). Three-year-old children intervene in third-party moral transgressions. *British Journal of Developmental Psychology, 29*(1), 124–130.

Valdes, A. M., Deary, I. J., Gardner, J., Kimura, M., Lu, X., Spector, T. D., Aviv, A., & Cherkas, L. F. (2010). Leukocyte telomere length is associated with cognitive performance in healthy women. *Neurobiology of Aging, 31*(6), 986–992.

Valenstein, E. S. (1998). *Blaming the brain: The truth about drugs and mental health.* New York, NY: Free Press.

Valla, J., & Ceci, S. (2011). Can sex differences in science be tied to the long reach of prenatal hormones: Brain organization theory, digit ratio (2d/4d), and sex differences in preferences and cognition. *Perspectives on Psychological Science, 6*(2), 134–146.

Van de Carr, F. R., & Lehrer, M. (1997). *While you are expecting: Your own prenatal classroom.* New York, NY: Humanics Publishing.

van der Laan, L. N., de Ridder, D. T. D., Viergever, M. A., & Smeets, P. A. M. (2011). The first taste is always with the eyes: A meta-analysis on the neural correlates of processing visual food cues. *NeuroImage, 55*(1), 296–303.

van Heck, G. L., & den Oudsten, B. L. (2008). Emotional intelligence: Relationships to stress, health, and well-being. In A. Vingerhoets & I. Nyklícek (Eds.), *Emotion regulation: Conceptual and clinical issues* (pp. 97–121). New York, NY: Springer Science + Business Media.

van Leeuwen, M., van den Berg, S. M., & Boomsma, D. I. (2008). A twin-family study

of general IQ. *Learning and Individual Differences, 18,* 76–88.

van Marle, H. J. C. (2010). Violence in the family: An integrative approach to its control. *International Journal of Offender Therapy and Comparative Criminology, 54*(4), 475–477.

Van Overwalle, F. (2011). A dissociation between social mentalizing and general reasoning. *NeuroImage, 54*(2), 1589–1599.

Van Puyvelde, M., Vanfleteren, P., Loots, G., Deschuyffeleer, S., Vinck, B., Jacquet, W., & Verhelst, W. (2010). Tonal synchrony in mother–infant interaction based on harmonic and pentatonic series. *Infant Behavior & Development, 33*(4), 387–400.

van Stegeren, A. H. (2008). The role of the noradrenergic system in emotional memory. *Acta Psychologica, 127,* 532–541.

Varga, S. (2011). Evolutionary psychiatry and depression: Testing two hypotheses. *Medicine, Health Care and Philosophy.* Advance online publication. DOI: 10.1007/s11019-010-9305-9

Vase, L., Nikolajsen, L., Christensen, B., Egsgaard, L. L., Arendt-Nielsen, L., Svensson, P., & Jensen, T. S. (2011). Cognitive-emotional sensitization contributes to wind-up-like pain in phantom limb pain patients. *Pain, 152*(1), 157–162.

Vaughan, A. (2008). *The fMRI smackdown cometh.* Retrieved from http://www.mindhacks.com/blog/2008/06/the_fmri_smackdown_c.html

Vaughan, P. (2004). Telling stories, saving lives. *Population Communications International (PCI).* Retrieved from http://popula-tion.org/entsummit/transcript04_vaughan.shtm.

Vaughn, D. (1996). *The Challenger launch decision: Risky technology, culture, and deviance at NASA.* Chicago, IL: University of Chicago Press.

Vaz-Leal, F., Rodríguez-Santos, L, García-Herráiz, A., & Ramos-Fuentes, I. (2011). Neurobiological and psychopathological variables related to emotional instability: A study of their capability to discriminate patients with bulimia nervosa from healthy controls. *Neuropsychobiology, 63*(4), 242–251.

Vega, C. (2010). Cognitive flexibility advantages in bilingual children. *Dissertation Abstracts International: Section B: The Sciences and Engineering, 61,* 7230.

Vélez, C. E., Wolchik, S. A., Tein, J.-Y., & Sandler, I. (2011). Protecting children from the consequences of divorce: A longitudinal study of the effects of parenting on children's coping processes. *Child Development, 82*(1), 244–257.

Venables, N. C., Patrick, C. J., Hall, J. R., & Bernat, E. M. (2011). Clarifying relations between dispositional aggression and brain potential response: Overlapping and distinct contributions of impulsivity and stress reactivity. *Biological Psychology, 86*(3), 279–288.

Venter, J. C., Adams, M. D., Myers, E. W., Li, P. W., Mural, R. J., et al. (2001). The sequence of the human genome. *Science, 291*(5507), 1304–1351.

Verleger, R., Ludwig, J., Kolev, V., Yordanova, J., & Wagner, U. (2011). Sleep effects on slow-brain-potential reflections of associative learning. *Biological Psychology, 86*(3), 219–229.

Vernon, A. (2011). Rational emotive behavior therapy. In D. Capuzzi & D. R. Gross (Eds.), *Counseling and psychotherapy* (5th ed.) (pp. 237–261). Alexandria, VA: American Counseling Association.

Vertosick, F. T. (2000). *Why we hurt: The natural history of pain.* New York, NY: Harcourt.

Veselka, L., Schermer, J. A., Martin, R. A., & Vernon, P. A. (2010). Laughter and resiliency: A behavioral genetic study of humor styles and mental toughness. *Twin Research and Human Genetics, 13*(5), 442–449.

Veselka, L., Schermer, J. A., & Vernon, P. (2011). Beyond the big five: The dark triad and the Supernumerary Personality Inventory. *Twin Research and Human Genetics, 14*(2), 158–168.

Vice, D. (2009). Christina Garcia, mother of brawling teen, Mercades Nichols, jailed on domestic violence charges. *The Weekly Vice.* Retrieved from http://www.theweeklyvice.com/2009/02/christina-garcia-mother-of-brawling.html

Vickers, J. C., Dickson, T. C., Adlard, P. A., Saunders, H. L., King, C. E., & McCormack, G. (2000). The cause of neuronal degeneration in Alzheimer's disease. *Progress in Neurobiology, 60*(2), 139–165.

Victoroff, J., Quota, S., Adelman, J. R., Celinska, B., Stern, N., Wilcox, R., & Sapolsky, R. M. (2011). Support for religio-political aggression among teenaged boys in Gaza: Part 2: Neuroendocrinological findings. *Aggressive Behavior, 37*(2), 121–132.

Villanti, A. C., McKay, H. S., Abrams, D. B., Holtgrave, D. R., & Bowie, J. V. (2010). Smoking-cessation interventions for U.S. young adults: A systematic review. *American Journal of Preventive Medicine, 39*(6), 564–574.

Villarreal, D. M., Do, V., Haddad, E., & Derrick, B. E. (2002). MDA receptor antagonists sustain LTP and spatial memory: Active processes mediate LTP decay. *Nature Neuroscience, 5(1),* 48–52.

Vinokur, A. D., Pierce, P. F., Lewandowski-Romps, L., Hobfoll, S. E., & Galea, S. (2011). Effects of war exposure on air force personnel's mental health, job burnout and other organizational related outcomes. *Journal of Occupational Health Psychology, 16(1),* 3–17.

Vitoroulis, I., Schneider, B., Vasquez, C., Soteras del Toro, M., & Gonzales, Y. (2011). Perceived parental and peer support in relation to Canadian, Cuban, and Spanish adolescents' valuing of academics and intrinsic academic motivation. *Journal of Cross-Cultural Psychology.* doi: 10.1177/0022022111405657

Vogt, D. S., Rizvi, S. L., Shipherd, J. C., & Resick, P. A. (2008). Longitudinal investigation of reciprocal relationship between stress reactions and hardiness. *Personality and Social Psychology Bulletin, 34,* 61–73.

Völker, S. (2007). Infants' vocal engagement oriented towards mother versus stranger at 3 months and avoidant attachment behavior at 12 months. *International Journal of Behavioral Development, 31,* 88–95.

Volkow, N. D., Tomasi, D., Gene-Jack, W., Vaska, P., Fowler, J. S., Telang, F., Alexoff, D., Logan, J., & Wong, C. (2011). Effects of cell phone radiofrequency signal exposure on brain glucose metabolism. *Journal of the American Medical Association, 305(8),* 808–813.

Vorria, P., Vairami, M., Gialaouzidis, M., Kotroni, E., Koutra, G., Markou, N., Marti, E., & Pantoleon, I. (2007). Romantic relationships, attachment syles, and experiences of childhood. *Hellenic Journal of Psychology, 4,* 281–309.

Wachtel, P. L. (2008). *Relational theory and the practice of psychotherapy.* New York, NY: Guilford.

Wachtel, P. L. (2011). *Inside the session: What really happens in psychotherapy.* Washington, DC: American Psychological Association.

Wade, T., Keski-Rahkonen, A., & Hudson, J. (2011). Epidemiology of eating disorders. In M. Tsuang, M. Tohen, and P. B. Jones (Eds.), *Textbook in psychiatric epidemiology* (3rd ed.) (pp. 343–360). Hoboken, NJ: Wiley.

Wadesango, N., Rembe, S., & Chabaya, O. (2011). Violation of women's rights by harmful traditional practices. *Anthropologist, 13(2),* 121–129.

Wagensmakers, E., Wetzels, R., Borsboom, D., & van der Maas, H. (2011). *Journal of Personality and Social Psychology.* Retrieved from http://dl.dropbox.com/u/1018886/Bem6.pdf

Wagner, D. A. (1982). Ontogeny in the study of culture and cognition. In D. A. Wagner & H. W. Stevenson (Eds.), *Cultural perspectives on child development* (pp. 105–123). San Francisco, CA: Freeman.

Wagner, U., Christ, O., & Pettigrew, T. F. (2008). Prejudice and group-related behaviors in Germany. *Journal of Social Issues, 64,* 403–416.

Wagner, U., Hallschmid, M., Verleger, R., & Born, J. (2003). Signs of REM sleep dependent enhancement of implicit face memory: A repetition priming study. *Biological Psychology, 62(3),* 197–210.

Wagstaff, G. G., Cole, J., Wheatcroft, J., Marshall, M., & Barsby, I. (2007). A componential approach to hypnotic memory facilitation: Focused meditation, context reinstatement and eye movements. *Contemporary Hypnosis, 24,* 97–108.

Wahlgren, K., & Lester, D. (2003). The big four: Personality in dogs. *Psychological Reports, 92,* 828.

Wakfield, M., Flay, B., Nichter, M., & Giovino, G. (2003). Role of the media in influencing trajectories of youth smoking. *Addiction, 98*(Suppl 1), 79–103.

Wakschlag, L. S., Henry, D. B., Blair, R. J. R., Dukic, V., Burns, J., & Pickett, K. E. (2011). Unpacking the association: Individual differences in the relation of prenatal exposure to cigarettes and disruptive behavior phenotypes. *Neurotoxicology and Teratology, 33(1),* 145–154.

Walderhaug, E., Cosgrove, K. P., Bhagwagar, Z., & Neumeister, A. (2011). The relationship between mood, stress, and tobacco smoking. In R. A. Cohen & L. H. Sweet (Eds.), *Brain imaging in behavioral medicine and clinical neuroscience* (pp. 147–161). New York, NY: Springer.

Walker, E., Kestler, L., Bollini, A., & Hochman, K. M. Schizophrenia: Etiology and course. (2004). *Annual Review of Psychology, 55,* 401–430.

Walker, F. R., Hinwood, M., Masters, L., Deilenberg, R. A., & Trevor, A. (2008). Individual differences predict susceptibility to conditioned fear arising from psychosocial trauma. *Journal of Psychiatric Research, 42,* 371–383.

Walker, I., & Crogan, M. (1998). Academic performance, prejudice, and the jigsaw classroom: New pieces to the puzzle. *Journal of Community and Applied Social Psychology, 8,* 381–393.

Walker, J. S., & Bright, J. A. (2009). False inflated self-esteem and violence: A systematic review and cognitive model. *The Journal of Forensic Psychiatry and Psychology, 20,* 1–32.

Wall, A. (2007). Review of integrating gender and culture in parenting. *The Family Journal, 15,* 196–197.

Wallace, A. F. C. (1958). Dreams and wishes of the soul: A type of psychoanalytic theory among the seventeenth century Iroquois. *American Anthropologist, 60,* 234–248.

Waller, M. R., & McLanahan, S. S. (2005). "His" and "her" marriage expectations: Determinants and consequences. *Journal of Marriage & Family, 67(1),* 53–67.

Waller, N. G., & Ross, C. A. (1997). The prevalence and biometric structure of pathological dissociation in the general population: Taxometric and behavior genetics findings. *Journal of Abnormal Psychology, 106,* 499–510.

Wallerstein, G. (2008). *The pleasure instinct: Why we crave adventure, chocolate, pheromones, and music.* New York, NY: Wiley.

Wallis, C. (2009). The multitasking generation. *TIME.com.* Retrieved from http://www.time.com/time/magazine/article/0,9171,1174696-6,00.html

Wallis, C. (2011). Performing gender: A content analysis of gender display in music videos. *Sex Roles, 64(3–4),* 160–172.

Walter, F., Cole, M., & Humphrey, R. (2011). Emotional Intelligence. *Academy of Management Perspectives, 25(1),* 45–59.

Walther, E., Langer, T., Weil, R., & Komischke, M. (2011). Preferences surf on the currents of words: Implicit verb causality influences evaluative conditioning. *European Journal of Social Psychology, 41(1),* 17–22.

Wamsley, E. J., & Stickgold, R. (2010). Dreaming and offline memory processing. *Current Biology, 20(23),* 1010–1913.

Wamsley, E. J., Hirota, Y., Tucker, M. A., Smith, M. R., Doan, T., & Antrobus, J. S. (2007). Circadian and ultradian influences on dreaming: A dual rhythm model. *Brain Research Bulletin, 71,* 347–354.

Wang, F., DesMeules, M., Luo, W., Dai, S., Lagace, C., & Morrison, H. (2011). Leisure-time physical activity and marital status in relation to depression between men and women: A prospective study. *Health Psychology, 30(2),* 204–211.

Wang, Q. (2008). Emotion knowledge and autobiographical memory across the preschool years: A cross-cultural longitudinal investigation. *Cognition, 108,* 117–135.

Wang, S., Quan, J., Kanaya, A. M., & Fernandez, A. (2011). Asian Americans and obesity in California: A protective effect of biculturalism. *Journal of Immigrant and Minority Health, 13(2),* 276–283.

Ward, L. M., Epstein, M., Caruthers, A., & Merriwether, A. (2011). Men's media use, sexual cognitions, and sexual risk behavior: Testing a mediational model. *Developmental Psychology, 47(2),* 592–602.

Ward, T. B. (2007). Creative cognition as a window on creativity. *Methods, 42,* 28–37.

Wardlaw, G. M., & Hampl, J. (2007). *Perspectives in nutrition* (7th ed.). New York, NY: McGraw-Hill.

Warner, M. (2004, May 11). Heart of darkness. *PBS Online NewsHour.* Retrieved from http://www.pbs.org/newshour/bb/middle_east/jan-june04/prisoners_5-11.html.

Wasan, A. D., Kong, J., Pham, L.-D., Kaptchuk, T. J., Edwards, R., & Gollub, R. L. (2010).The impact of placebo, psychopathology, and expectations on the response to acupuncture needling in patients with chronic low back pain. *The Journal of Pain, 11(6),* 555–563.

Wass, T. S. (2008). Neuroanatomical and neurobehavioral effects of heavy prenatal alcohol exposure. In J. Brick (Ed.), *Handbook of the medical consequences of alcohol and drug abuse* (2nd ed.) (pp. 177–217). *The Haworth Press series in neuropharmacology.* New York, NY: Haworth Press/Taylor and Francis Group.

Waters, A. J., & Gobet, F. (2008). Mental imagery and chunks: Empirical and conventional findings. *Memory & Cognition, 36,* 505–517.

Watson, D. L., & Tharp, R. G. (2007). *Self-directed behavior* (9th ed.). Belmont, CA: Wadsworth.

Watson, J. (1913). Psychology as the behaviorist views it. *Psychological Review, 20,* 158–177.

Watson, J. B., Mednick, S. A., Huttunen, M. & Wang, X. (1999). Prenatal teratogens and the development of adult mental illness. *Development & Psychopathology, 11(3),* 457–466.

Watson, J. B., & Rayner, R. (1920). Conditioned emotional reactions. *Journal of Experimental Psychology, 3,* 1–14.

Watson, J. B., & Rayner, R. (2000). Conditioned emotional reactions. *American Psychologist, 55(3),* 313–317.

Watson, J. C., Goldman, R. N., & Greenberg, L. S. (2011). Humanistic and experiential theories of psychotherapy. In J. C. Norcross, G. R. VandenBos, & D. K. Freedheim (Eds.), *History of psychotherapy: Continuity and change* (2nd ed.) (pp. 141–172). Washington, DC: American Psychological Association.

Watson, K. K., Matthews, B. J., & Allman, J. M. (2007). Brain activation during sight gags and language-dependent humor. *Cerebral Cortex, 17,* 314–324.

Watson, S., Thornton, C. G., & Engelland, B. T. (2010). Skin color shades in advertising to ethnic audiences: The case of African Americans. *Journal of Marketing Communications, 16(4),* 185–201.

Weatherhead, S., & Flaherty-Jones, G. (2011). *The pocket guide to therapy: A 'how to' of the core models.* Thousand Oaks, CA: Sage.

Weaver, M. F., & Schnoll, S. H. (2008). Hallucinogens and club drugs. In M. Galanter & H. D. Kleber (Eds.), *The American Psychiatric Publishing textbook of substance abuse treatment* (4th ed.) (pp. 191–200). Arlington, VA: American Psychiatric Publishing.

Wechsler, D. (1944). *The measurement of adult intelligence* (3rd ed.). Baltimore, MD: Williams & Wilkins.

Wechsler, D. (1977). *Manual for the Wechsler Intelligence Scale for Children* (Rev.). New York, NY: Psychological Corporation.

Wechsler, H., Lee, J. E., Kuo, M., Seibring, M., Nelson, T. F., & Lee, H. (2002). Trends in college binge drinking during a period of increased prevention efforts: Findings from 4 Harvard School of Public Health College Alcohol Study Surveys, 1993–2001. *Journal of American College Health, 50,* 203–217.

Wegener, D. T., Clarl, J. K., & Petty, R. E. (2006). Not all stereotyping is created equal: Differential consequences of thoughtful versus nonthoughtful stereotyping. *Journal of Personality and Social Psychology, 90,* 42–59.

Weidner, G., & Kendel, F. (2010). Prevention of coronary heart disease. In J. M. Suls, K. W. Davidson, & R. M. Kaplan (Eds.), *Handbook of health psychology and behavioral medicine* (pp. 354–369). New York, NY: Guilford Press.

Weil, M. M., & Rosen, L. D. (1997). *Coping with technology @ work @ home @ play.* New York, NY: Wiley.

Weinberger, D., & Harrison, P. (Eds.). (2011). *Schizophrenia* (3rd ed.). Hoboken, NJ: Wiley.

Weiner, B. (1972). *Theories of motivation.* Chicago: Rand-McNally.

Weiner, B. (1982). The emotional consequences of causal attributions. In M. S. Clark & S. T. Fiske (Eds.), *Affect and cognition.* Hillsdale, NJ: Erlbaum.

Weiner, B. (2006). *Social motivation, justice, and the moral emotions: An attributional approach.* Mahwah, NJ: Erlbaum.

Weiner, G. (2008). *Handbook of personality assessment.* Hoboken, NJ: Wiley.

Weiner, M. F. (2008). Perspective on race and ethnicity in Alzheimer's disease research. *Alzheimer's & Dementia, 4,* 233–238.

Weinstock, M. (2008). The long-term behavioural consequences of prenatal stress. *Neuroscience & Biobehavioral Reviews, 32,* 1073–1086.

Weisberg, D.S., Keil, F.C., Goodstein, J., Rawson E. & Gray, J.R. (2008). The seductive allure of neuroscience explanations. *Journal of Cognitive Neuroscience, 20,* 470–477.

Weissing, F. J., Edelaar, P., & van Doorn, G. S. (2011). Adaptive speciation theory: A conceptual review. *Behavioral Ecology and Sociobiology, 65(3),* 461–480.

Weitlauf, J. C., Cervone, D., Smith, R. E., & Wright, P. M. (2001). Assessing generalization in perceived self-efficacy: Multidomain and global assessments of the effects of self-defense training for women. *Personality & Social Psychology Bulletin, 27(12),* 1683–1691.

Welch, E., Birgegård, A., Parling, T., & Ghaderi, A. (2011). Eating Disorder Examination Questionnaire and Clinical Impairment Assessment Questionnaire: General population and clinical norms for young adult women in Sweden. *Behaviour Research and Therapy, 49(2),* 85–91.

Wenger, A., & Fowers, B. J. (2008). Positive illusions in parenting: Every child is above average. *Journal of Applied Social Psychology, 38,* 611–634.

Werner, J. S., & Wooten, B. R. (1979). Human infant color vision and color perception. *Infant Behavior and Development, 2(3),* 241–273.

Werner, K. H., Roberts, N. A., Rosen, H. J., Dean, D. L., Kramer, J. H., Weiner, M. W., Miller, B. L., & Levenson, R. W. (2007). Emotional reactivity and emotion recognition in frontotemporal lobar degeneration. *Neurology, 69,* 148–155.

West, D. A., & Lichtenstein B. (2006). Andrea Yates and the criminalization of the filicidal maternal body. *Feminist Criminology, 1,* 173–187.

Westen, D. (1998). Unconscious thought, feeling, and motivation: The end of a centurylong debate. In R. F. Bornstein & J. M. Masling (Eds.), *Empirical perspectives on the psychoanalytic unconscious* (pp. 1–43). Washington, DC: American Psychological Association.

Westlye, L. T., Bjørnebekk, A., Grydeland, H., Fjell, A. M., & Walhovd, K. B. (2011). Linking an anxiety-related personality trait to brain white matter microstructure: Diffusion tensor imaging and Harm Avoidance. *Archives of General Psychiatry, 68*(4), 369–377.

Westover, A. N., McBride, S., & Haley, R. W. (2007). Stroke in young adults who abuse amphetamines or cocaine: A population-based study of hospitalized patients. *Archives of General Psychiatry, 64,* 495–502.

Weyandt, L. L., Verdi, G., & Swentosky, A. (2011). Oppositional, Conduct, and Aggressive Disorders. In S. Goldstein & C. R. Reynolds (Eds.), *Handbook of neurodevelopmental and genetic disorders in children* (2nd ed.) (pp. 151–170). New York, NY: Guilford Press.

Whaley, A., Smith, M., & Hancock, A. (2011). Ethnic/racial differences in the self-reported physical and mental health correlates of adolescent obesity. *Journal of Health Psychology.* Retrieved from http://www.ncbi.nlm.nih.gov/pubmed/21464113

Wheat, A. L., & Larkin, K. T. (2010). Biofeedback of heart rate variability and related physiology: A critical review. *Applied Psychophysiology and Biofeedback, 35*(3), 229–242.

Whitbourne, S. K. (2011). *Adult development and aging: Biopsychosocial perspectives* (4th ed.). Hoboken, NJ: Wiley.

Whitbourne, S. K., & Mathews, M. J. (2009). Pathways in Adulthood: A counterpoint to the midlife crisis myth. *American Psychological Association Annual Convention.* Toronto, Ontario, CN.

White, J. R., & Freeman, A. S. (2000). *Cognitivebehavioral group therapy for specific problems and populations.* Washington, DC: American Psychological Association.

White, T., & Hilgetag, C. C. (2011). Gyrification and neural connectivity in schizophrenia. *Development and Psychopathology, 23*(1), 339–352.

White, T., Andreasen, N. C., & Nopoulos, P. (2002). Brain volumes and surface morphology in monozygotic twins. *Cerebral Cortex, 12*(5), 486–493.

Whited, M. C., & Larkin, K. T. (2009). Sex differences in cardiovascular reactivity: Influence of the gender role relevance of social tasks. *Journal of Psychophysiology, 23*(2), 77–84.

Whitman, D. (2011). *Cognition.* Hoboken, NJ: Wiley.

Whorf, B. L. (1956). Science and linguistics. In J. B. Carroll (Ed.), *Language, thought and reality.* Cambridge, MA: MIT Press.

Wickelgren, I. (1998). Teaching the brain to take drugs. *Science, 280,* 2045–2047.

Wickelgren, I. (2002). *Animal studies raise hopes for spinal cord repair.* Retrieved from http://www.sciencemag.org/cgi/content/full/297/5579/178.

Wickett, J. C., Vernon, P. A., & Lee, D. H. (2000). Relationships between factors of intelligence and brain volume. *Personality and Individual Differences, 29*(6), 1095–1122.

Wickramasekera II, I. (2008b). Review of hypnotizability, absorption and negative cognitions as predictors of dental anxiety: Two pilot studies. *American Journal of Clinical Hypnosis, 50,* 285–286.

WickramasekeraII, I. (2008a). Review of how can we help witnesses to remember more? It's an eyes open and shut case. *American Journal of Clinical Hypnosis, 50,* 290–291.

Widiger, T. A., & Sankis, L. M. (2000). Adult psychopathology. *Annual Review of Psychology, 51,* 377–404.

Wiegand, T., Thai, D., & Benowitz, N. (2008). Medical consequences of the use of hallucinogens: LSD, mescaline, PCP, and MDMA ("ecstasy"). In J. Brick (Ed.), *Handbook of the medical consequences of alcohol and drug abuse* (2nd ed.) (pp. 461–490). *The Haworth Press series in neuropharmacology.* New York, NY: Haworth Press/Taylor and Francis Group.

Willer, E. K., & Cupach, W. R. (2011). The meaning of girls' social aggression: Nasty or mastery? In W. R. Cupach & B. H. Spitzberg (Eds.), *The dark side of close relationships II* (pp. 297–326). New York, NY: Routledge/Taylor & Francis Group.

Williams, A. L., Haber, D., Weaver, G. D., & Freeman, J. L. (1998). Altruistic activity: Does it make a difference in the senior center? *Activities, Adaptation and Aging, 22*(4), 31–39.

Williams, G., Cai, X. J., Elliott, J. C., & Harrold, J. A. (2004). Anabolic neuropeptides. *Physiology & Behavior, 81*(2), 211–222.

Williams, J. E. (2010). Anger/hostility and cardiovascular disease. In M. Potegal, G. Stemmler, & C. Spielberger (Eds.), *International handbook of anger: Constituent and concomitant biological, psychological, and social processes* (pp. 435–447). New York, NY: Springer Science + Business Media.

Williams, J. E., & Best, D. L. (1990). *Sex and psyche: Gender and self viewed cross-culturally.* Newbury Park, CA: Sage.

Williams, L. E., & Bargh, J. A. (2008). Experiencing physical warmth promotes interpersonal warmth. *Science, 24,* 606–607.

Williams, S. S. (2001). Sexual lying among college students in close and casual relationships. *Journal of Applied Social Psychology, 31*(11), 2322–2338.

Williamson, A., Lombardi, D. A., Folkard, S., Stutts, J., Courtney, T. K., & Connor, J. L. (2011). The link between fatigue and safety. *Accident Analysis and Prevention, 43*(2), 498–515.

Willingham, D.B. (2001). *Cognition: The thinking animal.* Upper Saddle River, NJ: Prentice Hall.

Willis, M. S., Esqueda, C. W., & Schacht, R. N. (2008). Social perceptions of individuals missing upper front teeth. *Perceptual and Motor Skills, 106,* 423–435.

Wilner, B. (February 5, 2011). Vick wins Comeback Player award. *Associated Press.* Retrieved from http://news.yahoo.com/s/ap/20110206/ap_on_sp_fo_ne/fbn_comeback_player

Wilson, A. E., Smith, M. D., Ross, H. S., & Ross, M. (2004). Young children's personal accounts of their sibling disputes. *Merrill-Palmer Quarterly, 50*(1), 39–60.

Wilson, C. (1967). Existential psychology: A novelist's approach. In J. F. T. Bugental (Ed.), *Challenges of humanistic psychology.* New York, NY: McGraw-Hill.

Wilson, E. O. (1975). *Sociobiology: The new synthesis.* Cambridge, MA: Harvard University Press.

Wilson, E. O. (1978). *On human nature.* Cambridge, MA: Harvard University Press.

Wilson, J. P., & Hugenberg, K. (2010). When under threat, we all look the same: Distinctiveness threat induces ingroup homogeneity in face memory. *Journal of Experimental Social Psychology, 46*(6), 1004–1010.

Wilson, R. S., Gilley, D. W., Bennett, D. A., Beckett L. A., & Evans, D. A. (2000). Person-specific paths of cognitive decline in Alzheimer's disease and their relation to age. *Psychology & Aging, 15*(1), 18–28.

Wilson, S., & Nutt, D. (2008). *Sleep disorders.* London, England: Oxford University Press.

Wilson, T. G. (2005). Psychological treatment of eating disorders. *Annual Review of Clinical Psychology, 1,* 439–465.

Winkler, E. (2012). *Understanding language. A basic course in linguistics* (2nd ed.). New York, NY: Continuum.

Wise, D., & Rosqvist, J. (2006). Explanatory style and well-being. In J. C. Thomas, D. L. Segal, & M. Hersen (Eds.), *Comprehensive Handbook of Personality and Psychopathology, Vol. 1: Personality and Everyday Functioning* (pp. 285–305). Hoboken, NJ: Wiley.

Wise, P. M. (2006). Aging of the female reproductive system. In E. J. Masor & S. N. Austed (Eds.), *Handbook of the biology of aging* (6th ed.). San Diego, CA: Academic.

Wiste, A. K., Arango, V., Ellis, S. P., Mann, J. J., & Underwood, M. D. (2008). Norepinephrine and serotonin imbalance in the locus coeruleus in bipolar disorder. *Bipolar Disorders, 10,* 349–359.

Witelson, S. F., Kigar, D. L., & Harvey, T. (1999). The exceptional brain of Albert Einstein. *The Lancet, 353,* 2149–2153.

Witherington, D. C., Campos, J. J., Anderson, D. I., Lejeune, L., & Seah, E. (2005). Avoidance of heights on the visual cliff in newly walking infants. *Infancy, 7,* 285–298.

Wixted, J. T. (2004). The psychology and neuroscience of forgetting. *Annual Review of Psychology, 55,* 235–269.

Wixted, J. T. (2005). A theory about why we forget what we once knew. *Current Directions in Psychological Science, 14*(1), 6–9.

Wolf, G. (2008). Want to remember everything you'll ever learn? Surrender to this algorithm. *Wired Magazine.* Retrieved from http://www.wired.com/print/medtech/health/magazine/16-05/FF_Wozniak

Wolpe, J. & Plaud, J.J. (1997). Pavlov's contributions to behavior therapy. *American Psychologist, 52*(9), 966–972.

Wong, S. (2008). Diversity—Making space for everyone at NASA/Goddard Space Flight Center using dialogue to break through barriers. *Human Resource Management, 47,* 389–399.

Woo, M., & Oei, T. P. S. (2006). The MMPI-2 Gender-Masculine and Gender-Feminine scales: Gender roles as predictors of psychological health in clinical patients. *International Journal of Psychology, 41,* 413–422.

Woodruff-Pak, D. S., & Disterhoft, J. F. (2008). Where is the trace in trace conditioning? *Trends in Neurosciences, 31,* 105–112.

Woollams, A. M., Taylor, J. R., Karayanidis, F., & Henson, R. N. (2008). Event-related potentials associated with masked priming of test cues reveal multiple potential contributions to recognition memory. *Journal of Cognitive Neuroscience, 20,* 1114–1129.

Working Yourself to Death. (2003). *Facts of Life: Issue Briefings for Health Reporters, 8*(9). Retrieved from http://www.cfah.org/factsof-life/vol8no9.cfm#1.

Workman, L., & Reader, W. (2008). *Evolutionary psychology: An introduction.* New York, NY: Cambridge University Press.

World Health Organization (WHO). (1992). *ICD-10: International statistical classification of diseases and related health problems* (10th rev. ed). Arlington, VA: American Psychiatric Publishing.

World Health Organization (WHO). (2007). *Cultural diversity presents special challenges for mental health.* Retrieved from http://www.paho.org/English/DD/PIN/pr071010.htm

World Health Organization (WHO). (2008). *Mental health and substance abuse.* Retrieved from http://www.searo.who.int/en/section1174/section1199/section1567_6741.htm

World Health Organization (WHO). (2011). *Depression.* Retrieved from http://www.who.int/topics/depression/en/

Worthman, C. M. (2010). The ecology of human development: Evolving models for cultural psychology. *Journal of Cross-Cultural Psychology, 41*(4), 546–562.

Wright, J. H., & Beck, A. T. (1999). Cognitive therapies. In R. E. Hales, S. C. Yudofsky, & J. A. Talbott (Eds.), *American Psychiatric Press textbook of psychiatry.* Washington, DC: American Psychiatric Press.

Wright, J. H., Thase, M. E., & Beck, A. T. (2011). Cognitive therapy. In R. E. Hales, S. C. Yudofsky, & G. O. Gabbard (Eds.), *Essentials of psychiatry* (3rd ed.) (pp. 559–587). Arlington, VA: American Psychiatric Publishing.

Wright, K. (2003). Relationships with death: The terminally ill talk about dying. *Journal of Marital and Family Therapy, 29*(4), 439–454.

Wu, C., & Chao, R. K. (2011). Intergenerational cultural dissonance in parent–adolescent relationships among Chinese and European Americans. *Developmental Psychology, 47*(2), 493–508.

Wygant, D., Anderson, J., Sellbom, M., Rapier, J., Allgeier, L, & Granacher, R. (2011). Association of the MMPI-2 Restructured Form (MMPI-2-RF) validity scales with structured malingering criteria. *Psychological Injury and Law, 4*(1), 13–23.

Wyman, A. J., & Vyse, S. (2008). Science versus the stars: A double-blind test of the validity of the NEO Five Factor Inventory and computer-generated astrological natal charts. *Journal of General Psychology, 135,* 287–300.

Wynne, C. D. L. (2007). What the ape said. *Ethology, 113,* 411–413.

Xu, L., & Barnes, L. (2011). Measurement invariance of scores from the inventory of school motivation across Chinese and U.S. college students. *International Journal of Testing, 11*(2), 178–210.

Yacoubian, G. S. Jr., Green, M. K., & Peters, R. J. (2003). Identifying the prevalence and correlates of ecstasy and other club drug (EOCD) use among high school seniors. *Journal of Ethnicity in Substance Abuse, 2*(2), 53–66.

Yadav, V. K., Oury, F., Suda, N., Liu, Z-W., Gao, X-B., et al. (2009). A serotonin-dependent mechanism explains the leptin regulation of bone mass, appetite, and energy expenditure. *Cell, 138*(5), 976–989.

Yamada, H. (1997). *Different games, different rules: Why Americans and Japanese misunderstand each other.* London, England: Oxford University Press.

Yamagishi, T. (2011). Micro-macro dynamics of the cultural construction of reality: A niche construction approach to culture. In M. J. Gelfand, C-Y. Chiu, & Y-Y. Hong (Eds.), *Advances in culture and psychology. Advances in culture and psychology* (Vol. 1) (pp. 251–308). New York, NY: Oxford University Press.

Yang, J., Xu, X., Du, X., Shi, C., Fang, F. (2011). Effects of unconscious processing on implicit memory for fearful faces. *PLoS ONE 6*(2). Retrieved from http://www.plosone.org/article/info%3Adoi%2F10.1371%2Fjournal.pone.0014641

Yang, T.-X., Chan, R. C. K., & Shum, D. (2011). The development of prospective memory in typically developing children. *Neuropsychology, 25*(3), 342–352.

Yang, Z., & Tong, E. M. W. (2010). The effects of subliminal anger and sadness primes on agency appraisals. *Emotion, 10*(6), 915–922.

Yaniv, I. (2011). Group diversity and decision quality: Amplification and attenuation of the framing effect. *International Journal of Forecasting, 27*(1), 41–49.

Yarmey, A. D. (2004). Eyewitness recall and photo identification: A field experiment. *Psychology, Crime & Law, 10*(1), 53–68.

Yegneswaran, B., & Shapiro, C. (2007). Do sleep deprivation and alcohol have the same effects on psychomotor performance? *Journal of Psychosomatic Research, 63,* 569–572.

Yeung, D., Wong, C., & Lok, D. (2011). Emotion regulation mediates age differences in emotions. *Aging and Health. 15*(3), 414–418.

Young, J. D., & Taylor, E. (1998). Meditation as a voluntary hypometabolic state of biological estivation. *News in Physiological Science, 13,* 149–153.

Young, R. M., Connor, J. P., & Feeney, G. F. X. (2011). Alcohol expectancy changes over a 12-week cognitive–behavioral therapy program are predictive of treatment success. *Journal of Substance Abuse Treatment, 40*(1), 18–25.

Young, S. J., van Doornik, J., & Sanger, T. D. (2011). Visual feedback reduces co-contraction in children with dystonia. *Journal of Child Neurology, 26*(1), 37–43.

Young, T. (1802). Color vision. *Philosophical Transactions of the Royal Society,* 12.

Young, T., Skatrud, J., & Peppard, P. E. (2004). Risk factors for obstructive sleep apnea in adults. *JAMA: Journal of the American Medical Association, 291*(16), 2013–2016.

Young-Bruehl, E., & Schwartz, M. (2011). Warum die psychoanalyse keine geschichte hat [Why psychoanalysis has no history]. *Psyche: Zeitschrift für Psychoanalyse und ihre Anwendungen, 65*(2), 97–118.

Young-Wolff, K. C., Kendler, K. S., Ericson, M. L., & Prescott, C. A. (2011). Accounting for the association between childhood maltreatment and alcohol-use disorders in males: A twin study. *Psychological Medicine: A Journal of Research in Psychiatry and the Allied Sciences, 41*(1), 59–70.

Yu, X., Fumoto, M., Nakatani, Y., Sekiyama, T., Kikuchi, H., Seki, Y., Sato-Suzuki, I., & Arita, H. (2011). Activation of the anterior prefrontal cortex and serotonergic system is associated with improvements in mood and EEG changes induced by zen meditation practice in novices. *International Journal of Psychophysiology, 80*(2), 103–111.

Yuki, M., Maddux, W.W. & Masuda, T. (2007). Are the windows to the soul the same in the East and West? Cultural differences in using the eyes and mouth as cues to recognize emotions in Japan and the United States. *Journal of Experimental Social Psychology, 43,* 303–311.

Zanetti, L., Picciotto, M. R., & Zoli, M. (2007). Differential effects of nicotinic antagonists perfused into the nucleus accumbens or the ventral tegmental area on cocaine-induced dopamine release in the nucleus accumbens of mice. *Psychopharmacology, 190,* 189–199.

Zaragoza, M. S., Mitchell, K. J., Payment, K., & Drivdahl, S. (2011). False memories for suggestions: The impact of conceptual elaboration. *Journal of Memory and Language, 64*(1), 18–31.

Zeanah, C. H. (2000). Disturbances of attachment in young children adopted from institutions. *Journal of Developmental & Behavioral Pediatrics, 21*(3), 230–236.

Zélanti, P. S., & Droit-Volet, S. (2011). Cognitive abilities explaining age-related changes in time perception of short and long durations. *Journal of Experimental Child Psychology, 109*(2), 143–157.

Zelazo, P. D., Chandler, M., & Crone, E. (Eds.). (2010). *The Jean Piaget symposium series. Developmental social cognitive neuroscience.* New York, NY: Psychology Press.

Zerr, A. A., Holly, L. E., & Pina, A. A. (2011). Cultural influences on social anxiety in African American, Asian American, Hispanic and Latino, and Native American adolescents and young adults. In C. A. Alfano & D. C. Beidel (Eds.), *Social anxiety in adolescents and young adults: Translating developmental science into practice* (pp. 203–222). Washington, DC: American Psychological Association.

Zhan, J.-Y., Wilding, J., Cornish, K., Shao, J., Xie, C.-H., Wang, Y.-X., Lee, K., Karmiloff-Smith, A., & Zhao, Z.-Y. (2011). Charting the developmental trajectories of attention and executive function in Chinese school-aged children. *Child Neuropsychology, 17*(1), 82–95.

Zhang, L. F., & He, Y. F. (2011). Thinking styles and the Eriksonian stages. *Journal of Adult Development, 18*(1), 8–17.

Zhang, Y., Haddad, E., Torres, B., & Chen, C. (2011). The reciprocal relationships among parents' expectations, adolescents' expectations, and adolescents' achievement: A two-wave longitudinal analysis of the NELS data. *Journal of Youth and Adolescence, 40*(4), 479–489.

Zhao, Z., Huang, L., Wu, H., Li, Y., Zhang, L., Yin, Y., Xiang, Z., Zhao, Z. (2010). Neuropeptide S mitigates spatial memory impairment induced by rapid eye movement sleep deprivation in rats. *NeuroReport: For Rapid Communication of Neuroscience Research, 21*(9), 623–628.

Zhaoping, L., & Guyader, N. (2007). Interference with bottom-up feature detection by higher-level object recognition. *Current biology, 17,* 26–31.

Zhong, C-B., & Leonardelli, G. J. (2008). Cold and lonely: Does social exclusion literally feel cold? *Psychological Science, 19*(9), 838–842.

Zhong, C-B., & Liljenquist, K. (2006). Washing away your sins: Threatened morality and physical cleansing. *Science, 313,* 1451–1452.

Zillmer, E. A., Spiers, M. V., & Culbertson, W. (2011). *Principles of neuropsychology* (3rd ed.). Belmont, CA: Cengage.

Zimbardo, P. (2007). *The Lucifer effect: Understanding how good people turn evil.* New York, NY: Random House.

Zimbardo, P. G. (1993). Stanford prison experiment: A 20-year retrospective. *Invited presentation at the meeting of the Western Psychological Association,* Phoenix, AZ.

Zimbardo, P. G. (2004). A situationist perspective on the psychology of evil: Understanding how good people are transformed into perpetrators. In A. G. Miller (Ed.), *The social psychology of good and evil* (pp. 21–50). New York, NY: Guilford Press.

Zimbardo, P. G., Ebbeson, E. B., & Maslach, C. (1977). *Influencing attitudes and changing behavior.* Reading, MA: Addison-Wesley.

Zipkin, B. A., & Dunn, R. (2011). The Black Swan of ballet. *Exchanges.* Retrieved from http://uncexchanges.wordpress.com/

Zipkin, B. A. & Dunn, R. (2011). The Black Swan of ballet. *Exchanges.* Retrieved from http://uncexchanges.wordpress.com/?s= black+swan

Zito, J. M., Safer, S. J., dosReis, S., Gardner, J. F., Boles, M., & Lynch, F. (2000). Trends in the prescribing of psychotropic medications to preschoolers. *Journal of the American Medical Association, 283*(8), 1025–1030.

Zucker, K. J. (2008). Special issue: Biological research on sex-dimorphic behavior and sexual orientation. *Archives of Sexual Behavior, 37,* 1.

Zuckerman, L., &, Weiner, I. (2005). Maternal immune activation leads to behavioral and pharmacological changes in the adult offspring. *Journal of Psychiatric Research, 39*(3), 311–323.

Zuckerman, M. (1978, February). The search for high sensation. *Psychology Today*, 38–46.

Zuckerman, M. (1979). *Sensation seeking: Beyond the optimal level of arousal.* Hillsdale, NJ: Erlbaum.

Zuckerman, M. (1994). *Behavioral expressions and biosocial bases of sensation seeking.* New York, NY: Cambridge University Press.

Zuckerman, M. (2004). The shaping of personality: Genes, environments, and chance encounters. *Journal of Personality Assessment, 82*(1), 11–22.

Zuckerman, M. (2008). Rose is a rose is a rose: Content and construct validity. *Personality and Individual Differences, 45*, 110–112.

Zuckerman, M. (2011). Psychodynamic approaches. In M. Zuckerman, *Personality science: Three approaches and their applications to the causes and treatment of depression* (pp. 11–45). Washington, DC: American Psychological Association.

Zweig, J. (2007). *Your money and your brain: How the new science of neuroeconomics can help make you rich.* New York, NY: Simon & Schuster.

Photo Credits

The Kobal Collection/The Picture Desk, Page 239. © Benjamin Harris, Page 244, (top). © Library of Congress Prints and Photographs Division, Page 245, (bottom left). © Alamy, Page 245, (bottom center). © Twentieth Century-Fox Film Corporation/The Kobal Collection/ The Picture Desk, Page 245, (bottom right).

Chapter 7 © Jon Feingersh/Blend Images/ Corbis, Page 246. © Jupiterimages/Workbook Stock/Getty Images, Inc., Page 248. © Jodi Cobb/NG Image Collection, Page 252, (left). © Blue Jean Images/Getty Images, Page 252, (right). © James P. Blair/NG Image Collection, Page 253, (top). © Paul Bradbury/OJO Images/ Getty Images, Inc., Page 253, (bottom). © Antonio M. Rosario/ Photographer s Choice/ Getty Images, Page 258, (top). © Jupiter Images, Page 258, (bottom). © Nicole Duplaix/ National Geographic/Getty Images, Page 259. © Ted Tamburo/NG Image Collection, Page 250. © Danny Shanahan/cartoonbank.com. All Rights Reserved, Page 261. © cartoon by WILEY "Non Sequitur" (c) Distributed by Universal Press Syndicate/Univeral Uclick., Page 263. © Jonathan Nourok/PhotoEdit, Page 264, (top). © Bettmann/Corbis Images, Page 264, (bottom left). © Bettmann/Corbis Images, Page 264, (bottom right). © (c) The New Yorker Collection 2006 Tom Cheney from Cartoonbank.com, Page 265, (top). © AP/Wide World Photos, Page 265, (bottom). © Paul Conklin/PhotoEdit, Page 266. © Daniel L. Geiger/SNAP/Alamy, Page 267. © (c)AP/ Wide World Photos, Page 268, (top). © (c) AP/Wide World Photos, Page 268, (bottom). © Eleanor Bentall/Corbis Images, Page 270, (top right). © Science Source/Photo Researchers, Inc., Page 270, (bottom). © Nat Farbman/Time Life Pictures/Getty Images, Inc., Page 275. © AP/Wide World Photos, Page 280. © Daniel L. Geiger/SNAP/Alamy, Page 281, (top left). © (c)AP/Wide World Photos, Page 281, (top right). © Science Source/Photo Researchers, Inc., Page 281, (bottom right).

Chapter 8 © Digital Vision/Getty Images, Page 282. © Frans Lanting Studio/Alamy, Page 284, (top). © Thomas Barwick/Getty Images, Inc., Page 284, (bottom). © Stephen St. John/NG Image Collection, Page 285, (top). © Gordon Wiltsie/NG Image Collection, Page 285, (bottom). © Digital Vision/Getty Images, Page 287. © Gary Buss/Taxi/Getty Images, Page 288. © AP/Wide World Photos, Page 290. © National Archives/Taxi/Getty Images, Page 291. © Michael Travis/Corbis, Page 292. © Sidney Harris/ScienceCartoonPlus. com, Page 294. © Myrleen Ferguson Cafe/ PhotoEdit, Page 295, (top right). © image100/

Age Fotostock America, Inc., Page 295, (bottom). © iStockphoto, Page 296, (top). © iStockphoto, Page 296, (top center). © iStockphoto, Page 296, (center). © David Young-Wolff/PhotoEdit, Page 296, (bottom center). © Frans Lanting Studio/Alamy, Page 296, (bottom). © Wellcome Department of Cognitive Neurology/Photo Researchers, Page 297, (top left). © Masterfile, Page 297, (top right). © WDCN/Univ. College London/ Photo Researchers, Page 297, (bottom right). © Jeff Rotman/Photo Researchers, Page 298. © Sidney Harris/ScienceCartoonPlus.com, Page 299. © AP/Wide World Photos, Page 302, (left). © iStockphoto, Page 302, (center). © Kevin Winter/AMA2010/Getty Images, Inc., Page 302, (right). © Sonja Flemming/CBS/ Getty Images, Inc., Page 307, (top). © The New Yorker Collection 1998 Roz Chast from cartoonbank.com. All Rights Reserved., Page 307, (bottom). © Courtesy Richard J. Haier, University of California-Irvine, Page 308. © PhotoDisc, Inc./Getty Images, Page 309, (top). © T.K. Wanstal/The Image Works, Page 309, (bottom). © Sidney Harris/ScienceCartoonPlus. com, Page 310. © REUTERS/Larry Downing/ Landov, Page 312. © Hugh Sitton/Corbis, Page 315. © Popperfoto//Getty Images, Inc., Page 313. © Hill Street Studios/Getty Images, Inc., Page 317. © Thomas Barwick/Getty Images, Inc., Page 320, (top). © iStockphoto, Page 320, (bottom). © Sonja Flemming/CBS/Getty Images, Inc., Page 321.

Chapter 9 © George Diebold/Photographers Choice/Getty Images, Page 322. © David M. Phillips/Photo Researchers, Page 324, (top). © The New Yorker Collection 1991 Michael Crawford from cartoonbank.com. All Rights Reserved., Page 324, (bottom). © Karen Huffman, Page 328, (top). © Francis Leroy, Biocosmos/Photo Researchers, Inc., Page 328, (bottom center). © David M. Phillips/ Photo Researchers, Page 328, (bottom). © Biophoto Associates/Photo Researchers, Page 329, (top right). © Petit Format/ Nestle/Photo Researchers, Page 329, (left). © David H. Wells/ Corbis, Page 331. © Victor Englebert/Photo Researchers, Page 333. © Zits Partnership. Reprinted with special permission of King Features Syndicate., Page 334. © AP/Wide World Photos, Page 335. © Arnie Levin (c) The New Yorker Collection/ The Cartoon Bank, Inc., Page 336, (top). © Eyecandy Images / Alamy, Page 336, (bottom). © Everett Collection Inc / Alamy, Page 337. © amana images inc. /Alamy, Page 339. © The Copyright Group/SuperStock, Page 341. © Doug Goodman/Photo Researchers, Inc., Page 340, (top). © Reprinted with special

permission of King Features Syndicate, Page 340, (center). © Ellen B. Senisi/The Image Works, Page 340, (bottom center). © Roy Melnychuk/ Taxi/Getty Images, Page 340, (bottom). © PCN Photography/Alamy, Page 342. © A.N. Meltzoff & M.K. Moore, Imitation of facial and manual gestures by human neonates. Science, 1977, 198, 75–78, Page 343, (top). © Ellen Senisi/ The Image Works, Page 343, (bottom). © Nina Leen/Getty Images/Time Life Pictures, Page 346. © Image Source/Getty Images, Page 347, (bottom left). © Banana Stock/AgeFotostock, Page 347, (bottom right). © OMG/Brand X Pictures/Getty Images, Page 349, (top). © Karen Huffman, Page 349, (bottom). © Nina Leen/Time Life Pictures/Getty Images, Page 347, (top). © James L. Stanfield/NG Image Collection, Page 347, (center left). © Jodi Cobb /NGS Image Sales, Page 347, (center right). © Hugh Sitton/Stone/Getty Images, Page 352, (left). © Wojnarowicz/The Image Works, Page 352, (right). © Ariel Skeley/Getty Images, Inc., Page 354. © Nina Leen/Time Life Pictures/ Getty Images, Page 357.

Chapter 10 © Elisa Cicinelli/Brand X Pictures/Getty, Page 358. © Image Source/ Getty Images, Page 360. © The New Yorker Collection 2002 Alex Gregory from cartoonbank.com. All Rights Reserved., Page 361. © Jonathan Nourok/Stone/Getty Images, Page 363. © Steve Raymer/NG Image Collection, Page 365, (top far left). © Prof. Karen Huffman, Page 365, (top center left). © Dynamic Graphics, Inc./Creatas, Page 365, (top center right). © PhotoDisc/ Getty Images, Inc., Page 365, (top far right). © Randy Olson/NG Image Collection, Page 365, (bottom left). © Pablo Corral Vega/NG Image Collection, Page 365, (bottom center left). © IT Stock, Page 365, (bottom center right). © Richard Olsenius/NG Image Collection, Page 365, (bottom right). © Prof. Karen Huffman, Page 366, (left). © Steve Raymer/NG Image Collection, Page 366, (top far left). © Richard Olsenius/NG Image Collection, Page 366, (right). © Andersen Ross/Blend Images/Getty Images, Page 368. © FOX SEARCHLIGHT / THE KOBAL COLLECTION /The Picture Desk, Page 369. © Akram Saleh/Getty Images, Page 370. © Zuma/NewsCom, Page 372, (left). © Richard Nowitz/NG Image Collection, Page 372, (center). © Jennifer Mitchell/Splash News/NewsCom, Page 372, (right). © Steve Cole/Getty Images, Page 373, (top). © Michael Newman/PhotoEdit, Page 373, (bottom). © Mike Kemp/RubberBall/Getty Images, Page 375, (top). © Steven G. Smith/Corbis, Page 375, (bottom). © Associated Press, Page 376, (top). © Susan Van Etten/PhotoEdit, Page 376,

Collection, Page 524, (top). © Benelux/Zefa/Corbis, Page 524, (bottom).

Chapter 15 © Jose Luis Pelaez, Inc./Blend Images/Corbis, Page 530. © United Artists/Fantasy Films/The Kobal Collection/The Picture Desk, Page 531. © Zigy Kaluzny/Stone/Getty Images, Page 532. © CartoonStock, Page 533, (bottom left). © Hulton-Deutsch Collection/Corbis, Page 533, (right). © Zigy Kaluzny/Stone/Getty Images, Page 535. © Bettman/Corbis, Page 537. © Courtesy Aaron T. Beck, MD, Page 538. © Pat Byrnes/The Cartoon Bank, Inc., Page 540, (top). © David Young Wolff/PhotoEdit, Page 540, (bottom). © Roger Ressmeyer/Corbis, Page 541. © Tony Freeman/PhotoEdit, Page 543. © Sidney Harris/ScienceCartoonPlus.com, Page 544. © Syracuse Newspapers / D. Lassman/The Image Works, Page 545, (top). © Stockbyte/Getty Images, Page 545, (bottom). ©Max Schulte/ABC via/Getty Images, Page 547, (top). © Digital Vision/Getty Images, Page 547, (bottom). © Will McIntyre/Photo Researchers, Inc., Page 549, (top). © Cordelia Molloy/Photo Researchers, Inc., Page 549, (bottom). © The New Yorker Collection 1993 Lee Lorenz from cartoonbank.com. All Rights Reserved., Page 550. © John Neuberger/PhotoEdit, Page 551,

(top). © Richard T. Nowitz/Photo Researchers, Inc., Page 551, (bottom). © James Shaffer/PhotoEdit, Page 555. © Rita Jeffries, Page 556. © image100/Corbis, Page 557, (top). © John Neuberger/PhotoEdit, Page 557, (bottom). © Sky Bonillo/PhotoEdit, Page 558. © Zia Soleil/Iconica/Getty Images, Inc., Page 559. © Miramax/The Kobal Collection/The Picture Desk, Page 560. © CartoonStock, Page 564, (top). © Max Schulte/ABC via/Getty Images, Page 564, (left). © Digital Vision/Getty Images, Page 564, (right). © Will McIntyre/Photo Researchers, Inc., Page 565.

Chapter 16 © Digital Vision/Getty, Page 566. © Chris Fortuna/Getty Images, Inc., Page 568. © Bruce Ayers/Getty Images, Page 569. © cartoonbank.com. All Rights Reserved, Page 570. © Images & Stories/Alamy, Page 571, (top). © Jenny Acheson/Getty Images, Page 571, (bottom). © Spencer Grant/PhotoEdit, Page 572. © Bill Keane, Inc. Reprinted with special permission of King Features Syndicate., Page 573. © Librado Romero/The New York Times/Redux Pictures, Page 574. © AP/Wide World Photos, Page 575, (left). © Granger Collection, Page 575, (center). © Anthony Njuguna/Reuters/Corbis, Page 575, (right). © Image Source/Getty Images, Inc., Page

577. © Bernhard Kuhmsted/Retna, Page 578, (top). © Reprinted with special permission of King Features Syndicate., Page 578, (bottom). ©Karen Huffman, Page 580. ©AP/Wide World Photos, Page 582. © AP/Wide World Photos, Page 583.©Philip G. Zimbardo, Inc., Page 586. © AP/Wide World Photos, Page 587, (top). © The Kobal Collection/The Picture Desk, Page 587, (bottom left). © Roger Kisby/Corbis, Page 587, (bottom right). © Exactostock / SuperStock, Page 588. © Joel Satore/NGS Image Sales, Page 589. © Najlah Feanny-Hicks/Corbis, Page 590. © Bruce Ayers/Getty Images, Page 592, (top right). © Sam Sarkis/Photodisc/Getty, Page 592, (bottom left). © AP/Wide World Photos, Page 595. © Leif Skoogfors/Corbis, Page 596. © Lawrence Migdale/Photo Researchers, Page 597, (top). © William Philpott/Reuters/Corbis, Page 597, (bottom). © Courtesy of Siri Carpenter, Page 598, (right). © Nancy Brown/Photographers Choice/Getty Images, Inc.P0570-, Page 599, (top). © Philippe Bourseiller/The Image Bank/Getty Images, Inc., Page 599, (center). © The Kobal Collection/The Picture Desk, Page 599, (bottom). © Zhang Jun/XinHua/Xinhua Press/Corbis, Page 600. © Karen Huffman, Page 604.

Text and Illustration Credits

Chapter 1   Figure 1.3: *From www.payscale.com/best-colleges/salary-report.asp*

Chapter 2   Table 2.2: From Kimura, D.; *Sex Differences in the Brain*, Scientific American, Sept. 1002, pg. 120 © 1992 Jared Schneidman Designs.

Chapter 3   Table 3.1: From Holmes & Rahe, *The social readjustment rating scale*, © 1967 Journal of Psychosomatic Research, 11, pg. 213–218. Reprinted with permission from Elsevier. Test Yourself pg. 97: From Kanner, A. D., Coyne, J. C., Schaefer, C., & Lazarus, R. S. (1981). Comparison of two modes of stress measurement: Daily hassles and uplifts versus major life events. Journal of Behavioral Medicine, 4, 1–39. Figure 3.6: From "Hostility, the metabolic syndrome, and incident coronary heart disease," R. Niaura, Ph.D., published in Health Psychology, 2002.

Chapter 4   Figure 4.20: From Erdelyi, M.H. & Applebaum, A.G., *Cognitive Masking*, © 1973 Bulletin of the Psychonomic Society I, pg. 59–61. Figure 4.21: From Luria, A.R., *Cognitive development: Its cultural and social foundations*, Harvard University Press (1976). Reprinted with permission of Harvard University Press. Copyright © 1976 by the President and Fellows of Harvard College.

Chapter 5   Figure 5.2: From Carpenter, S., and Huffman, K., *Visualizing Psychology* (2e). Reprinted with permission of John Wiley & Sons, Inc. Concept Organizer 5.2: From What a Psychologist Sees, drawings of the brain (page 134). From Carpenter, S. and Huffman, K., *Visualizing Psychology* (2e). Reprinted with permission of John Wiley & Sons, Inc.

Chapter 7   Figure 7.4: Huffman, Matthews, & Gagne, 2001; Waters & Gobet, 2008. Figure 7.9 (b): From Bahrick, Bahrick, and Wittlinger; *Those Unforgettable High School Days*. Reprinted with permission from Psychology Today Magazine, © 1978 Sussex Publishers, Inc.

Chapter 8   Try This Yourself pg. 285: From Shepard and Metzler; *Mental Rotation of Three-Dimensional Objects*, © 1971 American Association for the Advancement of Science. Figure 8.10: From Gardner; *The Atlantic Monthly*, Feb. 1999 pp. 67–76, © 1999 Howard Gardner. Table 8.4: From Sternberg; *Beyond IQ*, © 1985 Cambridge University Press. Objective 8.16: From Sternberg; *The Theory of Successful Intelligence*, Review of General Psychology, 3, pg. 292–316, © 1999 American Psychological Association.

Chapter 9   Step-by-Step Diagram 9.2 (c): From Frankenburg & Dodds, Denver II Training Manual © 1991 *Denver Developmental Materials*. Figure 9.9: From Tanner, J.M., Whitehouse, R.N., and Takaislu, M., "Male/female growth sport." *Archives of Diseases in Childhood*, 41, 454–471, 1966. Reprinted with permission. Figure 9.12: From Chart of elderly achievers. In *The brain: A user's manual*. Copyright © 1982 by Diagram Visual Information.

Chapter 10   Step-by-Step Diagram 10.1: From Kohlberg, L. "Stage and Sequence: The Cognitive Development Approach to Socialization." In D.A. Goslin, *The Handbook of Socialization Theory and Research*. Chicago: Rand McNally, 1969, p. 376 (Table 6.2). Table 10.1: From Self Directed Search Form R. Copyright © 1985 by John L. Holland, Ph.D. Reprinted by permission of Psychological Assessment Resources, Inc. Figure 10.3: From Brown, Adams, and Kellam, Research in community and mental health (1981). Reprinted with permission. Figure 10.5: From Cartensen et al.; The Social Context of Emotion, Annual Review of Geriatrics & Gerontology, 17, pg. 331, © 1997 Springer Publishing Company Inc., New York 10012. Used by permission. Figure 10.6: From Mackey, R.A., & O'Brien, B.A. (1998). Marital conflict management: Gender and ethnic differences. Social Work, 43 (2), 128–141.

Chapter 11   Figure 11.3: From Miracle, Miracle, & Baumeister; *Human Sexuality: Meeting Your Basic Needs*, Study Guide. Figure 11.4: From Hatfield, Elaine and Rapson, Richard L, Love, sex, and intimacy. Copyright © 1993 by Elaine Hatfield and Richard L. Rapson. Reprinted by permission of Addison-Wesley Educational Publishers Inc. Figure 11.6: From Strong, DeVault, and Sayad, Core Concepts in human sexuality. Mountain View, California: Mayfield. Reprinted by permission.

Chapter 12   Table 12.3: From Plutchik; *Emotion: A Psychoevolutionary Synthesis*, © 1980 Published by Allyn and Bacon, Boston, MA. Copyright © 1980 by Pearson Education. Adapted by permission of the publisher.

Chapter 13   Try This Yourself pg. 459: From Cattell; "Personality Pinned Down," Psychology Today, pg. 44, Reprinted with Permission from Psychology Today Magazine, © 1974 Sussex Publishers, Inc.

Chapter 14   Table 14.1: From Diagnostic and Statistical Manual of Mental Disorders; fourth edition text revision, Washington DC, © 2000 American Psychiatric Association. Figure 14.19: From Gottesman, *Schizophrenia Genesis*, © 1991 W.H. Freeman. Figure 14.3: From Diagnostic and Statistical Manual of Mental Disorders; fourth edition text revision, Washington DC, © 2000 American Psychiatric Association. Table 14.4: From Understanding Culture's Influence on Behavior, 2nd edition by Brislin. © 2000. Reprinted with permission of Wadsworth, a division of Thomson Learning. www.thomsonrights.com.

Name Index

Subject Index

Timeline

►1879

WILHELM WUNDT
Creates the first psychology laboratory at the University of Leipzig in Germany; publishes the first psychology text, *Principles of Physiological Psychology*; considered the founder of experimental psychology.

►1890

JAMES MCKEEN CATTELL
Publishes *Mental Tests and Measurements*, which marks the beginning of psychological assessment.

WILLIAM JAMES
Writes *The Principles of Psychology*, in which he promotes his psychological ideas that are later grouped together under the term *functionalism*.

►1891

MARY WHITON CALKINS
Establishes psychology laboratory at Wellesley; later becomes the first woman president of APA.

JAMES MARK BALDWIN
Establishes first psychology laboratory at the University of Toronto.

LEY HALL
first American psychology; es what some the first American gy lab at Johns University; later e American gical Association

---

►1906

IVAN PAVLOV
Publishes his learning research on the salivation response in dogs, which later became known as classical conditioning.

►1913

JOHN WATSON
Publishes his article "Psychology as the Behaviorist Views It," in which he describes the science of behaviorism.

►1914

CARL JUNG
Splits with Freud and forms an offshoot of psychoanalysis called analytical psychology.

NET
the first intelligence nce. Lewis Terman ished the Stanford-lligence Scale, which the world's foremost e test.

►1932

JEAN PIAGET
Publishes *The Moral Judgment of the Child*; later becomes a very important figure in child development and cognitive psychology.

►1937

GORDON ALLPORT
Publishes *Personality: A Psychological Interpretation*; considered the father of modern personality theory.

►1938

B. F. SKINNER
Publishes *Behavior of Organisms*; helps found behaviorism; later becomes one of the most prominent psychologists of the 20th century.

BORING
nfluential *A Experimental*

G KOHLER
estalt Psychology, es Gestalt approach.

►1954

KENNETH B. CLARK
Research with his wife Mamie helps overturn racial discrimination in schools; later becomes the first African American president of APA.

ABRAHAM MASLOW
Helps found humanistic psychology; later develops an influential theory of motivation.

►1957

LEON FESTINGER
Develops what many consider the most important and comprehensive theory in social psychology—the theory of cognitive dissonance.

►1958

HERBERT SIMON
Presents his views on information processing theory; later receives the Nobel Prize for his research on cognition.

HARRY HARLOW
Publishes *The Nature of Love*, describing his experiments with rhesus monkeys and the importance of contact comfort on attachment.

PSYCHIATRIC N
e first *Diagnostic al Manual of rders* (DSM).

►1978

PHILIP ZIMBARDO
Publishes results of his controversial Stanford Prison Experiment; also famous for research on shyness, cults, evil, and heroism.

►1980

DAVID HUBEL & TORSTEN WIESEL
Win the Nobel Prize for their work identifying cortical cells that respond to specific events in the visual field.

►1987

ANNE ANASTASI
Author of the classic text on psychological testing, as well as numerous articles on psychological testing and assessment; later awarded the National Medal of Science.

ORTH
s the importance t in the social of children.

►187

G. STAN
Receive
Ph.D. in
establis
conside
psycho
Hopkins
founds
Psycho
(APA).

►1905

ALFRED B
Develops
test in Fr
later pub
Binet Inte
becomes
intellige

►1929

EDWIN G.
Publishes
History of
Psycholog
WOLFGAN
Publishes G
which outlin

►1952

AMERICAN
ASSOCIATIO
Publishes t
and Statisti
Mental Dis

►1970

MARY AINSW
Demonstrate
of attachme
developmen

HISTORY OF PSYCHOLOGY TIMELINE FROM 1878 TO 2000

▶1878

G. STANLEY HALL
Receives first American Ph.D. in psychology; establishes what some consider the first American psychology lab at Johns Hopkins University; later founds the American Psychological Association (APA).

▶1879

WILHELM WUNDT
Creates the first psychology laboratory at the University of Leipzig in Germany; publishes the first psychology text, *Principles of Physiological Psychology*; considered the founder of experimental psychology.

▶1890

JAMES MCKEEN CATTELL
Publishes *Mental Tests and Measurements*, which marks the beginning of psychological assessment.

WILLIAM JAMES
Writes *The Principles of Psychology*, in which he promotes his psychological ideas that are later grouped together under the term *functionalism*.

▶1891

MARY WHITON CALKINS
Establishes psychology laboratory at Wellesley; later becomes the first woman president of APA.

JAMES MARK BALDWIN
Establishes first psychology laboratory at the University of Toronto.

▶1905

ALFRED BINET
Develops the first intelligence test in France. Lewis Terman later published the Stanford-Binet Intelligence Scale, which becomes the world's foremost intelligence test.

▶1906

IVAN PAVLOV
Publishes his learning research on the salivation response in dogs, which later became known as classical conditioning.

▶1913

JOHN WATSON
Publishes his article "Psychology as the Behaviorist Views It," in which he describes the science of behaviorism.

▶1914

CARL JUNG
Splits with Freud and forms an offshoot of psychoanalysis called analytical psychology.

▶1929

EDWIN G. BORING
Publishes influential *A History of Experimental Psychology*.

WOLFGANG KOHLER
Publishes Gestalt Psychology, which outlines Gestalt approach.

▶1932

JEAN PIAGET
Publishes *The Moral Judgment of the Child*; later becomes a very important figure in child development and cognitive psychology.

▶1937

GORDON ALLPORT
Publishes *Personality: A Psychological Interpretation*; considered the father of modern personality theory.

▶1938

B. F. SKINNER
Publishes *Behavior of Organisms*; helps found behaviorism; later becomes one of the most prominent psychologists of the 20th century.

▶1952

AMERICAN PSYCHIATRIC ASSOCIATION
Publishes the first *Diagnostic and Statistical Manual of Mental Disorders* (DSM).

▶1954

KENNETH B. CLARK
Research with his wife Mamie helps overturn racial discrimination in schools; later becomes the first African American president of APA.

ABRAHAM MASLOW
Helps found humanistic psychology; later develops an influential theory of motivation.

▶1957

LEON FESTINGER
Develops what many consider the most important and comprehensive theory in social psychology—the theory of cognitive dissonance.

▶1958

HERBERT SIMON
Presents his views on information processing theory; later receives the Nobel Prize for his research on cognition.

HARRY HARLOW
Publishes *The Nature of Love*, describing his experiments with rhesus monkeys and the importance of contact comfort on attachment.

▶1970

MARY AINSWORTH
Demonstrates the importance of attachment in the social development of children.

▶1978

PHILIP ZIMBARDO
Publishes results of his controversial Stanford Prison Experiment; also famous for research on shyness, cults, evil, and heroism.

▶1980

DAVID HUBEL & TORSTEN WIESEL
Win the Nobel Prize for their work identifying cortical cells that respond to specific events in the visual field.

▶1987

ANNE ANASTASI
Author of the classic text on psychological testing, as well as numerous articles on psychological testing and assessment; later awarded the National Medal of Science.